Praise for

The American Dietetic Association's

Complete Food & Nutrition Guide

"This is a **truly comprehensive,** easy-to-read guide for the whole family. It is a wonderful resource for healthy meal planning."

—Jeanne Jones, syndicated columnist Cook It Light, author, lecturer, consultant

"Jam-packed with practical eating and food safety tips." —USA *Today*

"*The American Dietetic Association's Complete Food & Nutrition Guide* may **the ultimate healthy-eating primer.** How often can it be said of a book that it may extend your life?"

—*Fitness* magazine

"**Intelligent advice** about sensible eating."—Washington Times

"This is a wealth of information—**chock-full of practical tips** and very reader-friendly. Should be on everyone's bookshelf."

—Evelyn Tribole, RD, nutrition columnist and best-selling author

"**A must** for everyone's kitchen."—The Oregonian

"Brimming with tips—from choosing the best baby food to eating for healthy aging."

—*Shape* magazine

"Tackles most of the nutritional issues that concern Americans today... **up-to-date and helpful.**"

—Seattle Times

"Very approachable."—*Fast and Healthy* magazine

"No matter what your age or stage, you'll find useful, **easy-to-understand,** science-based answers to all your nutrition questions."

—*Fayetteville Observer* (NC)

"... anyone, even those not nutritionally inclined, can open the book and find something interesting."

—*St. Louis Journal* Publications

"...**solid all-around guide to nutrition** that's fun just to pick up and peruse."

—*Environmental Nutrition*

"Helpful tips and guidelines for good eating **for everyone in the family.**" —*Dallas Child*

"A readable and timely book for the lay reader. **Duyff gives sound advice.**"

—*Library Journal*

THE AMERICAN DIETETIC ASSOCIATION'S COMPLETE FOOD & NUTRITION GUIDE

by
Roberta Larson Duyff, MS, RD, CFCS

CHRONIMED PUBLISHING

The American Dietetic Association's Complete Food and Nutrition Guide

Library of Congress Cataloging-in-Publication Data

Duyff, Roberta, Larson

The American Dietetic Association's complete food and nutrition guide / Roberta Larson Duyff

p. cm.

Includes bibliographical references and index

ISBN 1-56561-160-8 (paperback)

1. Nutrition—Popular works I. American Dietetic Association, II. Title

RA784.D89 1996

613.2—dc20 96-36143
CIP

Technical Editor: Betsy Hornick, MS, RD
Editor: Jeff Braun
Cover Design: Terry Dugan Design
Text Design: Liana Raudys and David Enyeart
Illustrations: Neverne Covington
Art/Production Manager: Claire Lewis

Printed in the United States of America

Published by
Chronimed Publishing
P.O. Box 59032
Minneapolis, MN 55459-0032

10 9 8 7 6 5 4 3 2 1

Acknowledgments

As I completed each phase of this book, I became ever more grateful and indebted to the many professionals and colleagues—in the fields of nutrition and dietetics, health, family and consumer sciences, food science, culinary arts, education, and communications—who have shared with me their knowledge, experience, and expertise throughout the years. Although there are many, I extend my thanks to:

➢ The American Dietetic Association, for the honor of writing this book on behalf of the association's nearly 70,000 members.

➢ Betsy Hornick, MS, RD, ADA Publications, for her nutrition expertise, editorial guidance, and commitment to excellence at every phase in the development of this book. Deb McBride, ADA Publications, and literary agent Lynn Rosen supported me and Betsy at every turn.

➢ ADA members and reviewers, who volunteered countless hours to check for content accuracy, clarity, and comprehensiveness. Special thanks to Susan Borra, RD, Mary Carey, PhD, RD, Dayle Hayes, MS, RD, Marsha Hudnall, MS, RD, Nancy Schwartz, PhD, RD, and Madeleine Sigman-Grant, PhD, RD.

➢ ADA's National Center for Nutrition and Dietetics staff members for their quick, enthusiastic fact checking.

➢ Registered dietitians and other food, nutrition, and health professionals throughout the country who served as resources and experts for this project. And those who reviewed selected portions of the book, including Julie Burns, MS, RD, Suzanne Havala, MS, RD, FADA, Sue Murvich, MS, RD, and Ann Semenske, RD.

➢ The fine team of editors and designers at Chronimed Publishing, especially Jeff Braun, David Enyeart, and Claire Lewis, who have directed this project through to its completion.

➢ Sherri Hoyt, RD, for her contributions on food sensitivity, infant and child feeding, and nutrition during pregnancy and breast-feeding.

➢ Edith Syrjala Eash, EdM, MPH, RD, who encouraged my career as a registered dietitian.

➢ Anne Piatek, MS, RD, for encouraging me to write this book.

➢ My family, especially my mother, Jeane Larson, and my friends, who shared their support, understanding, and encouragement.

➢ My husband, Phil, who read every chapter for clarity and consumer friendliness... and offered the sensitivity and loving support I needed to write this book.

Roberta L. Duyff, MS, RD, CFCS

The American Dietetic Association is the largest group of food and nutrition professionals in the world. As the advocate of the profession, the ADA serves the public by promoting optimal nutrition, health, and well-being.

For more information...

For expert answers to your nutrition questions, call the ADA/National Center for Nutrition and Dietetics Hot Line at (900) 225-5267, and speak directly with a registered dietitian (RD). To listen to recorded messages or obtain a referral to an RD in your area, call (800) 366-1655.

Foreword

The American Dietetic Association (ADA), with nearly 70,000 members, is the largest society of food and nutrition professionals in the world. The ADA strives to be the source of the most sound, scientifically based food and nutrition information for the American people. The ADA believes that you can obtain all essential nutrients from an eating style that emphasizes variety, balance, moderation, and taste, but recognizes that Americans are bombarded with many confusing and contradictory messages about food and nutrition. Members of ADA include registered dietitians (RD), registered dietetic technicians (DTR), and individuals with advanced degrees related to food, nutrition, and health.

To resolve the multitude of questions and concerns you may have about eating right, The American Dietetic Association has combined the expertise of its members with the latest research to create *The American Dietetic Association's Complete Food & Nutrition Guide*. This interactive guide stands out from other nutrition books because it emphasizes individual choice and the control that each of us has over our own food, nutrition, and activity behaviors. It focuses on fitness, health, and sound nutrition as well as the importance of great tasting food. The strategies and suggestions offered can help you make choices that will lead to success in achieving optimal health and well-being.

The American Dietetic Association's Complete Food & Nutrition Guide focuses on a healthful diet for all stages of life. It describes nutrition and health concepts in clear, straightforward language, has many useful charts, graphs, and illustrations, and each chapter offers you the opportunity to assess your own food and nutrition knowledge and practices. This comprehensive guide also demonstrates through real-life examples and tips how sound nutrition habits and physical activity can be incorporated into diverse lifestyles.

Everyone deserves an opportunity to achieve good health without sacrificing the enjoyment of great tasting and safe food. To help Americans achieve this goal, *The American Dietetic Association's Guide to Food & Nutrition* is designed to translate nutrition recommendations into practical, timely advice for you and your whole family. Topics that Americans are most interested in are covered, including safe practices for losing weight; ways to lower fat intake; tips for smarter grocery shopping; making wise food choices in restaurants; maintaining food safety in the home; plus many more. You will be well-armed to distinguish between fact and fiction and make better decisions about food selection that fits your individual tastes.

This book should be part of the home library of everyone interested in health, nutrition, and fitness. Not only is it an excellent reference with reasonable answers to common questions, but it also offers real-life solutions to food and nutrition dilemmas faced by today's consumers. This guide is meant to complement, not replace, the expertise and services of a qualified nutrition professional, such as a registered dietitian.

On behalf of the members of The American Dietetic Association, may healthy choices and good eating be yours!

The American Dietetic Association

Notice:

Consult Your Health Care Professional

Readers are advised to seek the guidance of a licensed physician or health care professional before making changes in health care regimens, since each individual case or need may vary. This book is intended for informational purposes only and is not for use as an alternative to appropriate medical care. While every effort has been made to ensure that the information is the most current available, new research findings, being released with increasing frequency, may invalidate some data.

TABLE of CONTENTS

Chapter 3
Fat Facts

Chapter 4
Vitamins and Minerals: Enough, But Not Too Much

Chapter 5
Sweet Talk: Sugar and Other Sweeteners

Chapter 6
Fiber: Your Body's Broom

Chapter 7
Sodium: A Salty Subject

Chapter 8
Fluids: Often Overlooked

Chapter 9
Sensitive About Food

Chapter 10
What's On Today's Table?

Chapter 11
Planning to Eat Smart

Chapter 12
Supermarket Smarts

Chapter 13
The Safe Kitchen

Chapter 14
Kitchen Nutrition

Chapter 15
Your Food Away From Home

Chapter 16
Off to a Healthy Start

Chapter 17
Food to Grow On

Chapter 18
For Women Only

Chapter 19
Smart Eating for Healthy Adults

Chapter 20
Nutrition for Older Adults

Chapter 21
Athlete's Guide: Winning Nutrition

Chapter 22
The Vegetarian Way

Chapter 23
Well Informed?

Resources

Introduction

The American Dietetic Association's Complete Food & Nutrition Guide has been created for you as a practical, up-to-date resource for healthful eating. From cover to cover, you'll see how healthful eating—combined with physical activity—promotes fitness. And you'll learn how nutrition and taste can go hand in hand!

To help with your everyday eating dilemmas, this book is filled with practical advice—whatever your lifestyle or needs. From weight control to low-fat eating... supermarket shopping to eating out... vegetarian eating to sports nutrition, you'll find a myriad of tips for ease, convenience, and good taste. Look for the easy-to-follow charts, graphs, sidebars, and illustrations, including "Kitchen Nutrition" tips and "Label Lingo."

As your complete resource on nutrition, you can refer to this book again and again at every age and stage of life—from choosing the healthiest baby food to preventing osteoporosis. With chapters that address nutrition throughout the life cycle, this book is meant for you, and for all those you care about... perhaps a child, spouse, companion, aging parent, or friend.

For your personal nutrition "check-up," you'll find opportunities to assess your own nutrition knowledge and everyday food choices. Take the quiz, "Truth or Consequences," in chapter 1 to see what you already know about a broad range of nutrition topics. Want more information? The answers refer you to in-depth discussions throughout the book. Look closely at your own food choices, with a personal "Nutrition Check-up" in chapters 2 through 23. Then apply what you know about food, nutrition, and health to the everyday situations presented in "Real Life Nutrition" at the end of these chapters.

When nutrition makes the news, this book can help you judge the headlines and separate fad from fact. Its food and nutrition advice comes from The American Dietetic Association, the authority America turns to for food and nutrition advice, with over 80 years of nutrition expertise and research.

With their calls to the Consumer Nutrition Hot Line—a service of The American Dietetic Association's National Center for Nutrition and Dietetics—thousands of consumers have helped shape the focus and content of *The American Dietetic Association's Complete Food & Nutrition Guide*. We hope the answers to their food and nutrition questions will also answer many of yours!

Read, enjoy, be active, and eat healthy... for life!

CHAPTER ONE

FOOD CHOICES FOR FITNESS

Your life is filled with choices! Every day you make thousands of choices, many related to food. Some seem trivial. Others are important. A few may even set the course of your life. But as insignificant as a single choice may seem, made over and over, it can have a major impact on your health—and your life!

This book is about choices—those you, your family, and your friends make every day about food, nutrition, and health. Within its pages, you'll find reliable nutrition information and sound advice, based on scientific evidence. It offers you practical ways to eat healthy in almost any situation and at every phase of life. And it encourages you to enjoy the pleasures of food. After all, taste is the number one reason most people choose one food over another.

Most important, the flexible guidelines help you choose nutritious, flavorful foods to match your own needs, preferences, and lifestyle—even as your life and family situation change. You'll find that eating for health is one of the wisest decisions you'll ever make.

What Is "Fit"?

What does the term "fitness" mean to you? To many people, "fitness" relates to physical activity—perhaps a rigorous daily exercise regimen. To some, the term may mean a trim or muscular body or the ability to finish a 10K run. Others may think of fitness simply as being free of disease and other health problems.

Yet, the true definition of fitness is far broader and more personal. It refers to your own optimal health and overall well-being. Fitness is your good health—at its very best!

Fitness: Your Overall Health

Being fit translates to every aspect of your health—not only your physical health, but your emotional and mental well-being, too. In fact, all three are interconnected. And nutrition and physical activity are fundamental to each one.

When you're fit, you have:

- stamina and a positive outlook to handle the mental challenges of everyday life and the emotional ups and downs,

➢ reduced risk for many health problems, including serious diseases, such as heart disease, cancer, and diabetes,

➢ the chance to look and feel your best,

➢ physical strength and endurance to protect yourself in case of an emergency, and

➢ a better chance for a higher quality of life, and perhaps a longer one, too.

Fit at Every Age

Fitness is ageless. Fitness at every age comes from a lifestyle that includes good nutrition and regular physical activity. The sooner you start, the better your health.

Make the most of your own fitness potential at every age and stage of your life. By adapting your food choices and physical activity to match your needs, you can follow a life-long pattern of personal habits that promote health. That's what this book is all about—eating for health throughout the cycle of life, and enjoying great tasting food along the way.

Good nutrition and regular physical activity are two lifestyle habits that promote fitness—but certainly not the only ones. Other lifestyle decisions may positively affect your health, too: getting adequate sleep, not smoking, managing stress, drinking alcoholic beverages in moderation, wearing a seat belt, observing good hygiene, getting regular medical check-ups, obtaining adequate health care—to name a few.

Nutrition Fuels Fitness

You've heard the term "nutrition" all your life. The food-fitness connection is what it's all about. In a nutshell, nutrition is how food nourishes your body. And being well-nourished depends on getting enough of the nutrients your body needs—but not too much.

Today's understanding of nutrition is based on years of scientific study. Interest in food and health actually has a long history and was even recorded by the ancient Greeks. But it wasn't until the 19th century that the mysteries of nutrition began to unfold. Since then, scientists have been able to answer many nutrition questions. And research continues as scientists explore emerging questions about food, nutrients, and their role in health.

Today's nutrition advice is supported by solid scientific evidence. So unlike the ancients, you have a valid basis for choosing food for health. It's up to you to apply nutrition principles and advice for your own well-being.

To make wise food choices, you need sound nutrition information. As you read through this first chapter, check your own nutrition knowledge using "Your Nutrition Check-up: Truth—or Consequences?" later in this chapter. What you know—and don't know—just may surprise you!

Nutrition—Why So Important?

At every stage of life, healthful eating fuels fitness. Well-nourished children and teens grow, develop, and learn better. Good nutrition helps ensure a healthy pregnancy and successful breast-feeding. And healthful eating and active living help people feel their best, work productively, and lower their risks for some diseases.

Heart disease, certain cancers, diabetes, stroke, and osteoporosis are the main causes of disability and death in the United States. Your chance for developing these problems can drop dramatically by eating healthily. Good nutrition also can lower your risks for obesity, high blood pressure, and high blood cholesterol—all risk factors for serious diseases.

To protect yourself from these health problems, you're wise to know more. Know your family health history—and if any close relatives have any risk factors. And learn to manage your weight, body fat, blood pressure, and blood cholesterol levels through food choices and an active lifestyle. Throughout this book, you'll find guidance you need.

Food Is Pleasure!

Your food choices have been influenced over time by many other factors: your culture, your emotions, your surroundings, the people around you, your view of yourself, the foods available to you, and certainly what you know about food and nutrition.

Why do you choose one food over another? Along with its nutritional value, food is a source of pleasure and good taste. It's no surprise that people entertain and celebrate with food, or look forward to a special dish. Good nutrition can add pleasure to eating—especially as you eat a greater variety of food and learn how to include your food favorites in an overall healthful eating style.

Nutrients—Classified Information

Foods are complex substances. While you enjoy the sensual qualities of food—the appearance, aroma, texture, and flavor—your body relies on the life-sustaining functions that nutrients in food perform.

Because your body can't make them, many nutrients in food, and the energy some provide, are essential to your health. During digestion, food is broken down into nutrients, which are absorbed into your bloodstream and carried to every cell of your body, where the major work load of body functions occurs.

More than 40 nutrients in food are classified into six groups. Although each nutrient has a specific and unique function to perform, they work in partnership for your good health:

Carbohydrates are your body's main source of energy, or calories. They're classified in two groups: complex carbohydrates (or starches) and sugars. *Chapter 5, "Sweet Talk: Sugars and Other Sweeteners" takes a closer look at all kinds of carbohydrates.*

Fiber, another carbohydrate, aids digestion and offers protection from some diseases. *See chapter 6, "Fiber: Your Body's Broom."* However, even though fiber is important to your health, it's not a nutrient, because it is not digested and absorbed into the body.

Fats supply energy, too. But they have other functions, including transporting nutrients and being part of many body cells. Fats are made of fatty acids. Because your body can't make them, some fatty acids are essential in food. Fatty acids aren't all the same; some are more saturated, others more unsaturated. *You'll learn about their chemical structure and about cholesterol in chapter 3, "Fat Facts."*

Proteins supply amino acids. Amino acids are building blocks that build, repair, and maintain your

Be Healthy: It's All About You

Make healthy choices that fit your lifestyle so you can do the things you want to do.

Be realistic: Make small changes over time in what you eat and the level of activity you do. After all, small steps work better than giant leaps.

Be adventurous: Expand your tastes to enjoy a variety of foods.

Be flexible: Go ahead and balance what you eat and the physical activity you do over several days. There's no need to worry about just one meal or one day.

Be sensible: Enjoy all foods, just don't overdo it.

Be active: Walk the dog, don't just watch the dog walk!

Source: *The Dietary Guidelines Alliance*, 1996. ✦

body tissues. Your body makes nonessential amino acids; others are essential in your food choices. *For more about amino acids, refer to "Protein Power" on page* 561. Proteins also provide energy when carbohydrates and fat are in short supply. If they're broken down and used for energy, they can't be used to maintain body tissue.

Vitamins trigger many body processes. They work like spark plugs, setting off chemical reactions in body cells. Each vitamin regulates different body processes. Because their roles are so specific, one cannot replace another.

Minerals are "spark plugs," too. And, like vitamins, they each have a unique job description. *To learn more, refer to chapter* 4, *"Vitamins and Minerals: Enough, But Not Too Much."*

Water regulates body processes. It carries nutrients and other body chemicals to your cells and also carries waste products away. Water helps regulate your body temperature. And it makes up 55 to 75 percent of your body weight. *For more about water and health, refer to "A Fluid Asset" on page* 171.

Nutrients: How Much?

Look at the people around you. Everybody you see needs the same nutrients—just in different amounts. Age, gender, and body size are among the reasons why nutrient needs differ. Children and teenagers, for example, need more of some nutrients because they're growing. Pregnancy and breast-feeding increase the demand for most nutrients and energy. And men often need more of most nutrients because their bodies are typically larger than those of most women.

For specific nutrient advice, you can refer to the Dietary Reference Intakes (DRIs), which are daily nutrient recommendations based on age and sex. They're set at levels designed to decrease the risk of chronic disease through nutrition.

Dietary Reference Intakes, or DRIs, is a new umbrella term, first used in 1997. It includes the more familiar Recommended Dietary Allowance (RDA), as well as a new term, Adequate Intake (AI).

RDAs are recommended levels of nutrients to meet the needs of almost all healthy individuals in a specific age and gender group.

AI has a similar meaning to RDA. Except the guidelines for some nutrients are stated as AIs because there's not enough scientific evidence to set a firm RDA.

The DRIs (RDAs and AIs) apply to your average nutrient intake over several days, not just one day and certainly not one meal.

Currently, there's also an estimated recommended range of intake for six more vitamins and minerals. Until science generates more information, the advice for these can't be any more specific. Another term also fits under the DRI umbrella.

***Tolerable Upper Intake Level* (UL)** isn't a recommended amount. In fact, there's no known benefit for healthy people to consuming more than RDA levels. Instead ULs represent the maximum intake that probably won't pose risks for health problems for almost all healthy people in that age and gender group. Why set limits? With the growing use of fortified foods and dietary supplements, especially in large doses, it's helpful for consumers to recognize safe upper limits.

The DRIs are set by the Food and Nutrition Board of the National Academy of Sciences/ National Research Council. This group of scientists considers the most current research evidence before making recommendations. Periodically, these recommendations are updated as scientists learn more about the relationship between nutrients and health. In 1997, new recommendations were released for the bone-building nutrients: calcium, phosphorus, magnesium, vitamin D, and fluoride. Within a few years, guidelines for other nutrients will be updated in stages. *A complete listing of the DRIs appears on page* 607.

Food Choices: To Your Health!

Healthful eating is one of your best personal investments! Health is linked to many things. Certainly your genes, your age, your surroundings, your lifestyle, your health care, and your culture all make a difference. But good nutrition and physical activity are central players, too.

What's the secret to healthful eating? It's no secret at all—just solid advice. Enjoy an overall eating plan with most of your energy, or calories, from grain products, vegetables, fruits, reduced-fat milk products, lean meat, fish, poultry, and legumes. And consume less energy, or calories, from fats and sweets. Let's explore just what this means—and how to do it.

A Glimpse at the Dietary Guidelines

The Dietary Guidelines for Americans sum up what you need to know to eat for health. In seven statements, they describe food choices that can help you get enough, but not too much, of the nutrients and energy your body needs.

The Dietary Guidelines encourage you to choose meals and snacks that help you maintain, even improve, your health. By following their advice, you'll also reduce your risk for many common health problems.

Developed by the U.S. Department of Agriculture, these guidelines apply to all healthy Americans ages two and over. And they consider what you eat over several days, rather than for just one day, or one meal or snack.

The Dietary Guidelines reflect sound nutrition science and the most up-to-date information known about eating for health. Like the DRIs, they're periodically updated as nutrition experts learn more. Here's what they advise.

Food Variety—A Priority!

Guideline 1: Eat a variety of foods.

Variety may be the "spice of life." Variety in food choices is key to enjoying the many tastes of food. It's also basic to good nutrition and your good health. Each day your body needs the nutrients

Dietary Guidelines for Americans

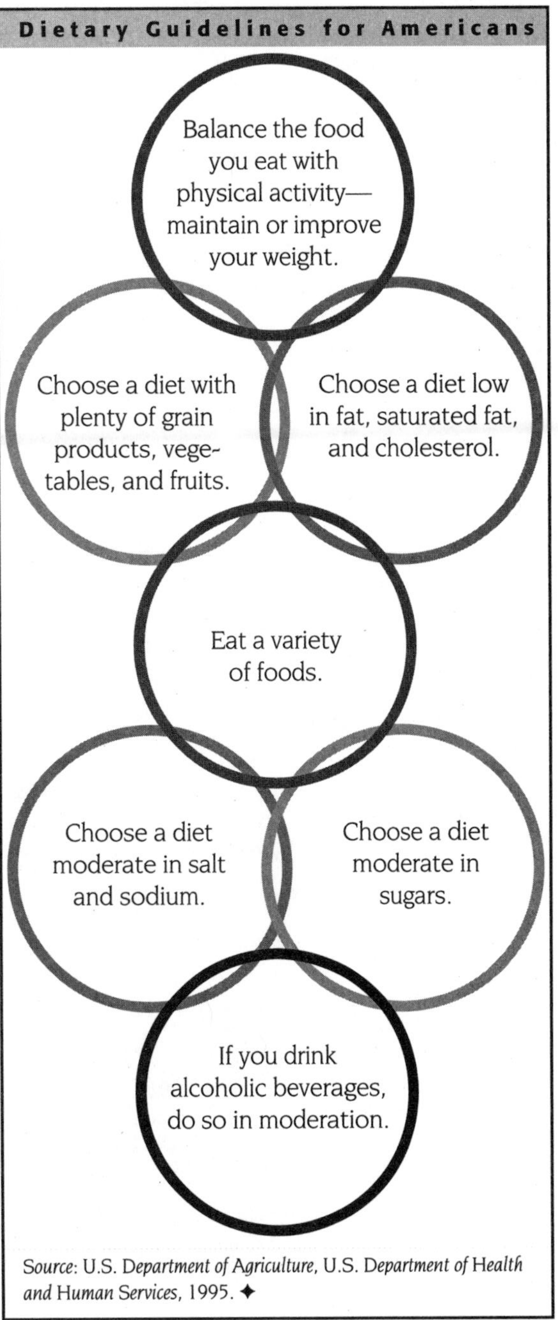

Source: U.S. *Department of Agriculture*, U.S. *Department of Health and Human Services*, 1995. ✦

and other healthful substances that a varied eating plan provides. Most foods and beverages have more than one nutrient. But none has them all.

To get the nutrients and other food substances your body needs—in ample amounts—enjoy a variety of foods from the Food Guide Pyramid. Consume the number of servings recommended for each day. Gradually include new foods in your food choices, too. *Refer to the Pyramid on page 6. Learn more about using the Pyramid to plan meals and snacks in "The Food Guide Pyramid: Your Healthful Eating Guide" on page* 243.

Follow the guidance of the Food Guide Pyramid! It translates the nutrient recommendations and the Dietary Guidelines for Americans into practical advice. The Pyramid shows the kinds and amounts of food people ages two and over are wise to eat each day.

"Weight" for Health—
The Food-Activity Connection

Guideline 2: Balance the food you eat with physical activity—maintain or improve your weight.

Are you at your healthy weight? The typical American adult gains weight with every decade. But extra pounds of body fat probably aren't in your best health interest. Added body fat increases the risk for many health problems, including high blood pressure, heart disease, stroke, diabetes, certain types of cancer, arthritis, breathing problems, and other illnesses.

Most adults are wise not to gain weight. If you're overweight, and especially if you already have one of these health problems, you're wise to trim down. At the very least, manage your weight so you don't gain more. (*Note*: Being overweight is a problem when extra pounds come from excess body fat. Strenuous workouts build muscle. Extra weight isn't a problem when it comes from more muscle.)

Food Guide Pyramid:
A Guide to Daily Food Choices

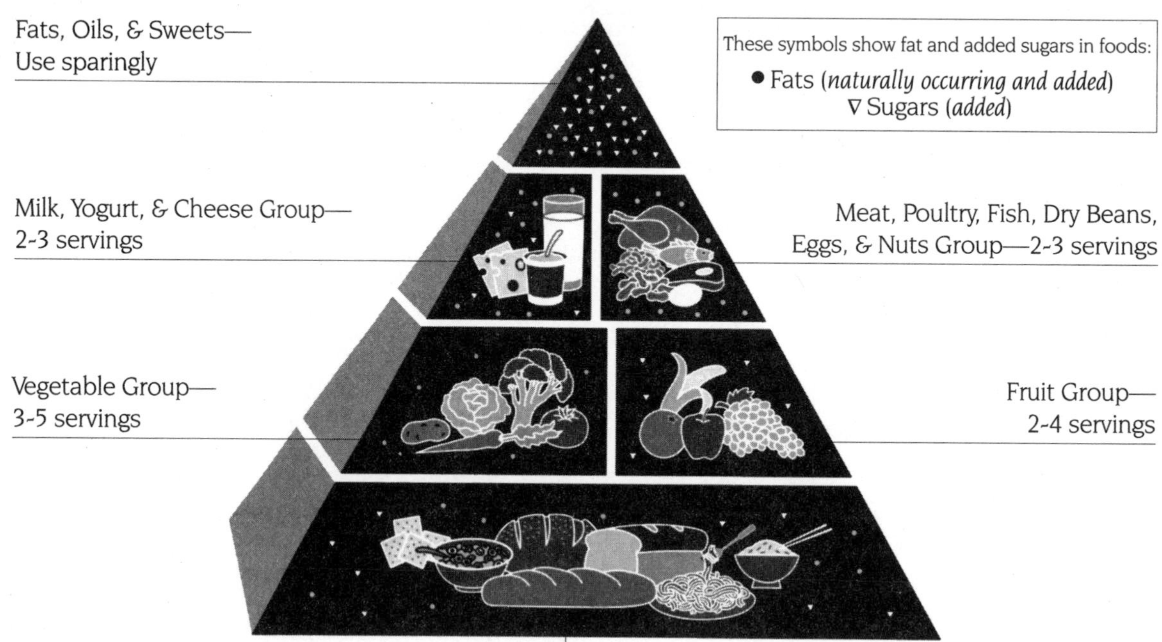

Source: U.S. *Department of Agriculture*.

Manage your weight with a combination approach—balancing the energy, or calories, in your eating plan with at least 30 minutes of moderate physical activity on most, if not all, days of the week. Start with small steps. *For examples of moderate physical activity, see page 7. For more about managing your body weight, refer to "Your Healthy Weight," chapter 2.*

Grain Products, Vegetables, and Fruits—Enjoy!

Guideline 3: *Choose a diet with plenty of grain products, vegetables, and fruits.*

Grain products, vegetables (including legumes), and fruits—you need more of these foods than others. Just check the number of servings on the Food Guide Pyramid. In spite of their health benefits, many people don't consume enough. Grain products, vegetables, and fruits are excellent sources of many nutrients, including vitamins, minerals, complex carbohydrates (starch), as well as fiber and other healthful food substances. Legumes also are high in protein. Unless you add sauces, dressings, and other high-fat ingredients, or use high-fat cooking methods such as frying, these foods are low in fat, too. For your good health, get most of your food energy from grain products, vegetables, and fruits.

These foods offer another health benefit: much lower risk for some health problems, including heart disease and certain types of cancers.

How might you go about eating more of these foods? Divide your plate into pie-shaped sections. Fill about 75 percent of the plate with grain products, vegetables, and fruits.

For more about the vitamins and minerals in grain products, vegetables, and fruits, refer to "Vitamins and Minerals: Enough, But Not Too Much," chapter 4. For more about their fiber and complex carbohydrates, refer to chapter 6, "Fiber: Your Body's Broom," and "From Complex to Simple" on page 125.

MODERATE ACTIVITY: WHAT IS IT?

If some activities use more energy than others, you may wonder...just what does "moderate physical activity" really mean?

Moderate physical activity uses about 150 calories a day, or about 1,000 calories a week. For that amount of energy expenditure, you might spend more time on less vigorous activities, such as brisk walking, or spend less time on more vigorous activities, such as running:*

Washing and waxing a car	for 45-60 min.
Washing windows or floors	for 45-60 min.
Playing volleyball	for 45 min.
Playing touch football	for 30-45 min.
Gardening	for 30-45 min.
Wheeling self in wheelchair	for 30-40 min.
Walking 1 3/4 miles	in 35 min.
Basketball (shooting baskets)	for 30 min.
Bicycling 5 miles	in 30 min.
Dancing fast (social)	for 30 min.
Pushing a stroller 1 1/2 miles	in 30 min.
Raking leaves	for 30 min.
Walking 2 miles	in 30 min.
Water aerobics	for 30 min.
Swimming laps	for 20 min.
Wheelchair basketball	for 20 min.
Basketball (playing a game)	for 15-20 min.
Bicycling 4 miles	in 15 min.
Jumping rope	for 15 min.
Running 1 1/2 miles	in 15 min.
Shoveling snow	for 15 min.
Stairwalking	for 15 min.

* Some activities can be performed at various intensities. The suggested durations correspond to the expected intensity of effort.

Source: Physical Activity and Health: A Report of the Surgeon General, *Centers for Disease Control and Prevention*, 1996. ✦

The "Low Down" on Fats, Saturated Fats, and Cholesterol

Guideline 4: *Choose a diet low in fat, saturated fat, and cholesterol.*

Fat is a nutrient that's essential for health. Besides supplying energy, it contains essential fatty acids and carries vitamins A, D, E, and K into your bloodstream. Yet too much fat, especially saturated fat, and too much cholesterol can negatively affect health.

Although many people consume less fat, saturated fat, and cholesterol than they did a decade ago, on average, Americans still consume too much. It's well known that high-fat diets are linked to many health problems, including high blood cholesterol and obesity, as well as heart disease and some cancers.

Cutting down on fat and saturated fat—but not cutting it out entirely—is a sensible way to eat for health. Learn to choose lean meat and low-fat foods. Use low-fat cooking methods. Go easy on high-fat dressings, sauces, and spreads. *For more about fat and cholesterol in moderation in a healthful eating plan, refer to "Fat Facts," chapter 3.*

Sugars—A Moderate Issue

Guideline 5: *Choose a diet moderate in sugars.*

In one form or another, sugars—a form of carbohydrate—are present in many foods you eat. Sugars in food come from two sources: (1) naturally occurring sugar, such as the sugars found in fruits and dairy foods, and (2) added sugars, used for both flavor and function in a variety of foods during processing and preparation.

Complex carbohydrates from grain products, vegetables, and fruits are broken down into sugars during digestion. To the human body, all sugars look and act alike, regardless of their source.

Carbohydrates, including sugars, are your body's main source of energy. For sugars, moderation is your guideline for consuming enough, but not overdoing, especially if your energy needs are low. Some foods with sugars supply energy, or calories, but few nutrients. And both sugars and starches promote tooth decay, too.

To help you moderate sugars in your overall diet, read the carbohydrate information on food labels. *For more about sugars in a healthful eating plan, refer to chapter 5, "Sweet Talk: Sugar and Other Sweeteners."*

Salt and Sodium—Moderation Again

Guideline 6: *Choose a diet moderate in salt and sodium.*

Sodium is a nutrient and a natural part of many foods. And salt is made of sodium and chloride. As nutrients, sodium and chloride help your body maintain fluid balance and regulate blood pressure. So why the guideline?

For many people, extra sodium passes right through the body. However, others have blood pressure that's sodium-sensitive; for these people, a high sodium intake, along with obesity, heredity, or getting older, contributes to high blood pressure. Reducing sodium and salt intake reduces the risk of high blood pressure for them. Moderation is a wise guideline because people may not know if their blood pressure is sodium-sensitive. A high sodium intake also may increase the need for calcium because more calcium is excreted in urine.

To consume moderate amounts of sodium and salt, enjoy more fresh fruits and vegetables. Use herbs and spices as your main flavor enhancers. And learn to read sodium information on food labels. *For more about salt and sodium in a healthful eating plan, refer to chapter 7, "Sodium: A Salty Subject."*

Alcoholic Beverages—Go Easy

Guideline 7: *If you drink alcoholic beverages, do so in moderation.*

On their own, alcoholic beverages offer calories, but essentially no nutrients. So they don't nourish your body. In excess, their alcohol can be harmful—and may become a substitute for nutritious foods.

If you choose to drink alcoholic beverages, keep your intake moderate. This means no more than

Eat Right America™

Eat a variety of nutrient-rich foods. You need more than 40 different nutrients for optimal health and well-being. And no single food supplies them all.

Always remember, small changes in your diet can make big differences in your overall health.

The nutrition information on labels of most packaged foods can help you make wise food choices. When shopping, use the Nutrition Facts panel on food products as your guide to healthful eating.

Remember, no matter where you eat or buy foods, your favorite foods can fit into a healthful eating style.

In case of snack attacks, today's supermarket has a wide variety of foods to choose from. Stock up, so you'll have the choices you want when you need them.

Good nutrition starts with you. Whether at home, at a cafeteria, or at work, good nutrition is part of a healthful lifestyle.

Have fun! Discover nutrition by trying new ethnic dishes, cooking methods, and restaurants.

Try a low-fat version of your favorite restaurant order—have it broiled instead of fried, or ask for the chef's recommendation for a low-fat dish.

An eating style that promotes fitness and health is varied, balanced, and moderate.

Make changes gradually. Just as there are no "superfoods" or easy answers to a healthful diet, don't expect to totally revamp your eating habits overnight.

Eat moderate portions. By keeping portion sizes reasonable, it is easier to eat the foods you want.

Remember that pasta, rice, and most bread and cereal products are low in fat and offer valuable nutrients and fiber.

Investigate lower-fat food preparation methods, such as steaming and grilling.

Choose something different for dessert such as fresh fruit, sherbet, or low-fat yogurt.

Ask a registered dietitian (RD) for reliable food and nutrition information. Call The American Dietetic Association's Consumer Nutrition Hot Line at (800) 366-1655 for answers to your nutrition questions. You also can listen to recorded nutrition messages and ask for a referral to an RD in your area.

Source: *National Center for Nutrition and Dietetics of The American Dietetic Association*, 1994. ✦

one drink a day for women and two for men. Beverages with alcohol can enhance the enjoyment of meals and for some people, moderate drinking may be linked with a lowered risk for heart disease.

However, drinking alcoholic beverages also can be risky. Alcohol may impair judgment, which can lead to accidents and injury. In time, some people become dependent on alcohol. Drinking higher amounts is linked to many health problems, including high blood pressure, stroke, heart disease, certain cancers, birth defects, and diseases of the liver and pancreas. And it's linked to social problems, too, including violence and suicide. *For more about alcoholic beverages and advice for consuming them, refer to "Alcoholic Beverages: In Moderation" on page 184.*

The Bottom Line: Variety, Balance, Moderation

Food variety—along with balance and moderation—is the cornerstone of an eating style that's both healthful and enjoyable. These same qualities apply to daily food choices that almost all healthy people need, regardless of their age, food preferences, energy needs, and lifestyle. In fact, they sum up the seven messages of the Dietary Guidelines!

have you ever *wondered*?

...what the term "calorie-dense foods" means? These foods are high in calories, or energy, but low in nutrients. Fats, oils, and sweets in the Pyramid tip are calorie dense. By contrast, nutrient-dense foods are high in nutrients compared with their calorie count. The wide variety of foods in the five food groups are nutrient dense.

...how the Dietary Guidelines for Americans compare with the American Heart Association, National Cancer Institute, and American Cancer Society guidelines? These dietary guidelines all offer sound eating advice for health. They're all based on strong scientific evidence. And they're consistent with each other. ✦

Just what do the three messages of variety, balance, and moderation mean?

Vary your food choices. Food variety provides the many nutrients your body needs for energy, health, and growth. No food—or food category—supplies all the nutrients your body needs. For good health, choose foods from all five food groups.

Think of food variety as a "nutrition coalition." In partnership, different foods provide the nutrients your body needs. Food variety has another bonus. Vary the flavors, textures, and colors of the many different foods available to get maximum enjoyment from your meals and snacks!

Balance your food choices over time. Get enough—but not too much—of each type of food and each nutrient. When you eat a food high in fat, choose others from the array of foods that are low in fat. Balance food energy from your food choices with physical activity to manage your body weight.

Moderate your portion sizes. That way, you can enjoy all the foods you like. At the same time, you can follow an eating style that promotes life-long fitness. Moderation has another meaning. Choose foods and beverages to control the energy, or calories, you consume, and the total amount of fat, saturated fat, cholesterol, sugars, and sodium. If you consume alcoholic beverages, the message of moderation applies, too.

How do you eat to get the variety, balance, and moderation that's best for your health? Just climb the Food Guide Pyramid to fitness. *Turn to page 243 to learn how the Pyramid applies to you.*

Every Food Can Fit!

In a healthful eating plan, you can enjoy all your favorite foods. As a skillful consumer, you can make every food fit into your eating plan, keeping the principles of variety, balance, and moderation in mind.

Throughout this book, you'll get plenty of guidance to do just that! You'll learn more about nutrition and fitness—and how you can eat the foods you like within a healthful overall eating plan.

Strategic Planning For Smart Nutrition

Almost any time is the perfect time to take control of your food choices, even change your eating style if needed. But the sooner you invest in your health, the greater the benefit.

This book provides a practical view of sound nutrition. And you'll learn sensible ways to eat for fitness. Some advice is meant for you; other advice may apply to family members or friends.

As you read sections of this book, use these steps to make investments in your health and the health of your family:

Audit your present lifestyle. Start by keeping track of what, when, and why you eat or drink. For example, you might snack when you feel bored. Or you might order fried foods when you need a quick meal. Use a food log to pinpoint eating behavior you want to change. *Refer to "Dear Diary..." on page 37 for tips on keeping a food log.*

Set goals. Know your intent. And be realistic. Change doesn't mean eliminating a food or food habit. It probably just means focusing more on moderation and balance.

Make a plan for change. Divide big goals, such as "I will eat better," into smaller, more specific goals, such as "I will eat more vegetables." And list concrete steps to achieve your goals. For example:

Goal: Eat less fat.

Steps: Use low-calorie salad dressing. Buy lean meat. Order a baked potato rather than fries, or share an order of fries.

Be patient. Make gradual changes. Permanent change takes time, commitment, and encouragement. Most health goals (for example, losing weight, lowering blood cholesterol) take a lifelong commitment. Stick with it even if success takes several months or longer. And remember that small steps toward reaching a goal add up over time!

Monitor your progress. If you get off track, pick up where you left off, and start again. You can do it!

Seek help from a health professional. A registered dietitian can help you on the road to change.

Reward yourself. Change is hard work that deserves recognition. Pat yourself on the back with a game of racquetball, a walk in the park, a new CD, or a new outfit. Feeling good is the best reward!

Reevaluate your plan every month or two. See how changes you've made fit with your goals. You may even set a new goal to tackle!

For more about the benefits of physical activity—and ways you can be more physically active yourself, check the pages listed below:

For most healthy people, including those managing their body weight... *"Get Physical!" on page 31 and "Ten Reasons to Make the 'Right Moves'" on page 531.*

For children... *"Get Up and Move, Turn Off the Tube!" on page 441.*

For teens... *"Move Your 'Bod'" on page 449.*

For adults... *"Inactivity: Hazardous to Your Health" on page 482.*

For older adults... *"Never Too Late for Exercise" on page 513.*

For travelers... *"Eating on the Road" on page 384.*✦

your nutrition check-up

Truth—or Consequences?

Take this quick nutrition "knowledge check-up" for a taste of the nutrition issues presented in other chapters of this book. The more you know, the better able you'll be to make wise food choices—and perhaps live a longer, healthier life.

Answer true or false, or select the best answer for each question. (H*int*: There may be more than one correct answer!) Compare your answers to the correct answers on page 14, and give yourself one point for each correct response.

1. Perhaps you've heard this guideline: consume no more than 30 percent of your calories, or energy, from fat. What food(s) does that apply to?
   a. your lunch or dinner
   b. any food you buy
   c. your snacks
   d. what you eat over several days

2. Fifty-five to 60 percent of your energy should come from carbohydrates, mostly from complex carbohydrates and the rest from sugars.
   a. true b. false

3. Fiber may promote your health by...
   a. giving you energy.
   b. aiding with digestion.
   c. protecting you from some cancers.
   d. protecting you from heart disease.

4. You can count on thirst to tell you when you need to drink more fluids.
   a. true b. false

5. Carrots are an excellent source of vitamin A. You're not a carrot eater? You might substitute...
   a. sweet potatoes c. orange juice
   b. mangoes d. spinach

6. Taking a daily nutrient supplement is your best assurance of getting enough vitamins and minerals.
   a. true b. false

7. Trying to moderate the sodium and salt in your food choices? A salty taste is the best way to tell if a food is high in sodium.
   a. true b. false

8. You've probably heard or seen this advice from nutrition experts: "Eat five a day." What does it mean?
   a. Eat a food from all five food groups daily.
   b. Eat five servings of bread, pasta, rice, or other grains daily.
   c. Eat at least five fruit and vegetable servings daily.
   d. Eat three meals plus two snacks daily.

9. Almost half of your adult bone mass was formed when you were a teenager.
   a. true b. false

10. Women of child-bearing age: You need more iron than men do. Which lunch-bag food(s) is a good source of iron? (Men, you can answer this, too.)
   a. hard-cooked egg
   b. roast beef sandwich
   c. microwave bean soup
   d. granola bar

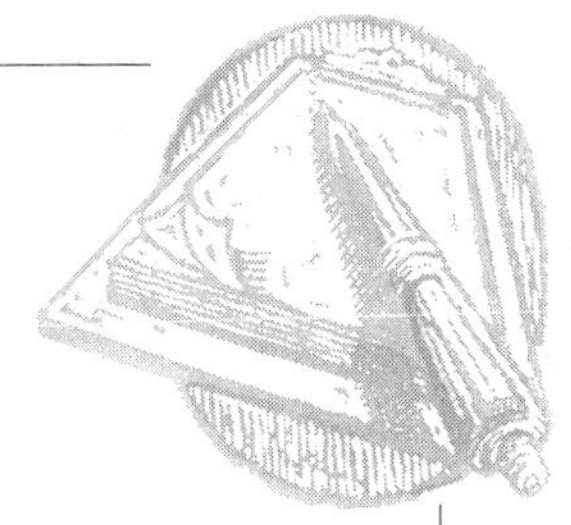

11. Breast milk and most infant formulas have iron. Once babies start eating solids, they may become iron deficient unless they consume a good source of iron. Which food would supply iron for an older baby?
   a. strained carrots   c. fortified cereal
   b. teething biscuits   d. apple juice

12. Another woman's question: Even before pregnancy, you need enough folate to protect against birth defects. What food(s) are good sources?
   a. vegetable salad   c. baked beans
   b. orange juice   d. broiled chicken

13. Overweight? If so, the risk for heart disease is higher if your excess weight is on your hips, rather than your abdomen.
   a. true   b. false

14. To eat healthy, you may need to give up some favorite foods. Some foods are "good" for you; others are "bad" for you.
   a. true   b. false

15. To lose weight, you need to go on a diet.
   a. true   b. false

16. Fasting can offer you a good jump start on weight loss.
   a. true   b. false

17. If you're a lacto-vegetarian, what can you eat with whole-grain products to increase the amount of iron your body absorbs from them?
   a. orange juice   c. enriched rice
   b. red bell pepper   d. milk

18. As a strict vegetarian, what would be your best calcium source?
   a. yogurt   c. broccoli
   b. spinach   d. fortified tofu

19. You can depend on color or smell to tell you if food is safe to eat.
   a. true   b. false

20. When you trim fat off meat, you get rid of the cholesterol.
   a. true   b. false

21. A potato has three times more fiber if you keep the peel on.
   a. true   b. false

22. Headaches often are caused by the foods you eat.
   a. true   b. false

23. Suppose you're reading the food label on a 15-ounce can of minestrone soup. What do the Nutrition Facts refer to?
   a. amount of nutrients for all the soup in the can
   b. amount of nutrients in one serving

24. Which two quickservice menus likely provide less fat and calories than the other two?
   a. meat-cheese pizza slice, side salad (low-calorie Italian dressing), unsweetened iced tea
   b. grilled chicken sandwich, BBQ baked beans, 2 percent milk
   c. fried fish fillet sandwich (tartar sauce), coleslaw, regular soft drink
   d. large taco salad with guacamole in a fried taco shell, orange juice

25. If you lose one pound during strenuous activity, you've lost two cups of fluids through sweat.
   a. true   b. false

your nutrition check-up (continued)

1. *d*. The "no more than 30 percent" guideline applies to your total eating pattern over several days, not to a single food or to a single meal.

2. *a*. Most of your energy should come from "carbs"—complex, as well as simple. Complex carbohydrates, or starches, are found in grains, legumes, and vegetables. Sugars, the most simple form of carbohydrate, are either naturally present in foods such as fruit and milk, or added. Either way, your body uses them in the same way—to fuel body processes and physical activity.

3. *b, c, and d*. Of these four choices, there's only one role that fiber doesn't play. Fiber can't be digested, so it can't produce energy. However, it may offer protection from some cancers and heart disease. Fiber also reduces the risks for diabetes, constipation, hemorrhoids, and diverticulosis. And it may help you control your weight, too!

4. *b*. Although it's one sign, you may not feel thirsty—even when your body has a fluid deficit. That's often true for older adults or for people who've been involved in strenuous physical activity. The best guideline: Drink fluids before, during, and after exercise, even when it's cold outside. Drink plenty of liquids; just quenching your thirst may not be enough.

5. *a, b, and d*. For vitamin A, eat plenty of deep yellow, orange, and some dark green leafy vegetables—and some deep yellow fruits. Try to eat at least one serving daily. *Note: Orange juice has some vitamin A. But vitamin C and potassium are among its better nutrient assets.*

6. *b*. A varied and balanced eating plan—not a nutrition supplement—is your best assurance of adequate nutrition! Supplements won't provide the full array of nutrients and other substances that food supplies for your good health. How do you make sure you eat for variety and balance? Follow the advice of the Food Guide Pyramid.

7. *b*. Actually, many foods with sodium don't have a salty flavor. The Nutrition Facts panel on the food label—not the flavor of food—is your best guide to sodium content!

8. *c*. The five-a-day advice is a way to remind you to count to five—eat at least three vegetable servings and two fruit servings daily. Why? Besides being low in fat and sodium and high in carbohydrates, fruits and vegetables can be good sources of vitamins A and C, other vitamins, some minerals, and other plant substances. *Note: Experts also advise you to eat enough from all five food groups daily.*

9. *a*. Healthy bones are the reason that teens need plenty of calcium! Even when they stop growing taller, their bones continue to grow more strong and dense. Teens—girls, for example—who don't consume enough calcium put their bones at risk for the rest of their lives.

10. *b and c*. For iron, go for the roast beef sandwich and bean soup. Meat and legumes (beans and lentils) are two good iron sources. Egg yolks have some, too, but it's not used as well as iron from meat. And the granola bar? It probably doesn't have much. But check the Nutrition Facts panel on the food label.

11. *c*. Infant cereals are typically fortified with iron. These are baby's first solid foods. Start with rice cereal, and wait until baby's first birthday for wheat cereal, since it may cause a reaction.

12. *a, b, and c*. Leafy vegetables, some fruits (including oranges), and legumes are among the good sources of folate. Chicken, meat, fish, and dairy foods aren't good sources.

13. *b*. Actually, the reverse is true. Excess body fat around the abdomen, midriff, or waistline is riskier for heart disease than fat that settles in the hips or thighs. For the least risk of all, maintain your healthy weight!

14. *b.* No single food is either "good" or "bad." Instead, your overall food choices over the course of a day or several days are the issue. Even a healthful food, such as broccoli or milk, wouldn't be healthful if that's all you ate. You need variety, balance, and moderation. The same goes for soft drinks and candy. If your food choices overall are healthful—without too many calories—you can enjoy these foods in moderation.

15. *b.* The way to lose body fat is to burn more energy, or calories, than you consume. Just being more physically active may be enough to help you lose weight—or at least keep you from gaining. Along with that, follow a healthful eating plan without excess calories.

16. *b.* When you fast, the weight you lose first is water and muscle loss—not body fat. Water weight comes right back when you begin eating again, and the muscle may be lost forever. By fasting, you deprive your body of nutrients needed for health.

17. *a and b.* Vitamin C helps your body absorb iron from foods of plant origin and from egg yolks. Both orange juice and red bell peppers (both high in vitamin C) are good choices. Note: *Enriched rice has iron, but like whole-grains, it needs a vitamin C-rich partner to aid iron absorption. A lacto-vegetarian may drink milk, but it does not supply iron or vitamin C.*

18. *c and d.* Some green vegetables, including broccoli, supply calcium. Tofu and soy milk are good sources—if they're calcium-fortified. Note: *Although spinach contains calcium, it also has oxalates, a substance that keeps your body from absorbing calcium. Yogurt is an excellent source of calcium; however, strict vegetarians don't consume dairy foods.*

19. *b.* You can't depend on the smell or appearance of food as clues to whether or not it's safe to eat. Bacteria that transfer to food can multiply in just a matter of several hours, giving no detectable signs of contamination, such as changes in flavor or color.

20. *b.* In meat, the cholesterol is in the lean meat, as well as the fat. When you trim off fat, you reduce the cholesterol and fat. But you won't eliminate the cholesterol.

21. *a.* The edible peel of vegetables and fruits is a good source of fiber. Keep it on!

22. *b.* Certain components of food—either naturally present or added—may trigger headaches. But there's no scientific proof for direct food causes. Probably headaches are caused by a combination of environmental, emotional, and physical factors.

23. *b.* The Nutrition Facts panel on any food package refers to one serving only. It doesn't necessarily refer to all the food in the container—unless there's one serving per package. If you eat more or less than one serving, you consume more or less of those nutrients.

24. *a and b.* In quickservice foods, frying, sauces, and regular salad dressings are some reasons why fat grams and calories add up.

25. *a.* Weigh yourself before and after physical activity. The weight you lose is fluid, not fat. To avoid dehydration, replace each pound you lose with two cups of water.

Now total your score and check your nutrition savvy.

If you scored...

21 *to* 25 *points*: You're nutrition savvy. But do your food choices reflect what you know? Even with a perfect 25 points, there's more to learn as science continues to reveal more about nutrition, and food, and their relation to health.

16 *to* 20 *points*: You know a lot already—but you still have more to learn. Read on!

your nutrition check-up (continued)

15 *points or less*: Since you're checking out your nutrition know-how, healthy eating is important to you. To make wise food choices for your health, you're smart to learn more. The answers to these questions—and more—are explored in the chapters that follow.

In fact, you'll likely find most of the answers to your nutrition questions as you read this book. *When you need to find other reliable sources of nutrition information, refer to chapter 23, "Well Informed?"*

CHAPTER TWO

YOUR HEALTHY WEIGHT

We often take it for granted, but good health is one of the most precious gifts of life. A healthy weight—maintained throughout life—helps you achieve good health in several ways, including reducing the risk for many ongoing diseases.

What is a healthy weight? It's the weight that's best for you—not necessarily the lowest weight you think you can be. A healthy weight actually is a range that's statistically related to good health. Being above or below that range increases the risk of health problems, or decreases the likelihood of good health.

The smart approach to your best weight is really no secret—only common sense. An active lifestyle, along with an eating pattern chosen for variety, balance, and moderation, makes all the difference. Maintaining your healthy weight permanently is best for health, not an ongoing weight cycle of ups and downs.

Body Basics: What's Your Healthy Weight?

The answer isn't as simple as stepping onto a bathroom scale, then comparing your weight to a chart. Your own healthy weight is one that's right for you. It may be quite different from someone else's weight, even if he or she is the same height, gender, and age as you are.

What makes the difference? Your genetic makeup plays a role because it determines your height and the size and shape of your body frame. A genetic link to body fat may exist, too. However, fat-gene discoveries are still preliminary findings from animal studies; scientists don't know yet if they apply to humans.

Of course, genetics isn't the only reason weight differs from person to person. Your metabolic rate, which is the rate your body burns energy, makes a difference. So does your body composition. Muscle burns more calories than body fat does. Your level of physical activity and what you eat both play a role, too.

Whether or not your own weight is healthy for you depends on several factors: where your body fat is located, how much of your weight is fat, and if you have weight-related health problems, such as diabetes or high blood pressure.

Of Apples and Pears

Stand in front of a full-length mirror, preferably nude. How do you look? Be your own judge. Are you shaped like an apple or a pear? When it comes to your health, being an "apple" can be riskier than being a "pear."

People come in many sizes and shapes: tall and short, stocky or lanky, muscular or not. These differences are a unique part of being human. For this reason, there's no such thing as a "perfect body," or an ideal body weight, shape, or size that everyone should strive for.

Likewise, losing weight, or maintaining a target weight, is easier for some than others—in spite of their commitment to healthful eating and physical activity. That, too, is part of what makes each of us unique.

Regardless of your size and shape, you can choose a healthful lifestyle—and so live a fuller, more productive life and reduce your risk for health problems. Assess your own health habits. Make choices for good health with yourself in mind. Choose a healthful eating style. Be physically active. And make your goal your healthy weight, not some unattainable goals.

Remember: Fitness goes beyond maintaining the body weight that's healthy for you. It's a total package of your physical, mental, and social health. And that feels good! ✦

Where your body stores fat is a clue to your healthy weight. Excess body fat that settles in the stomach area around the waist, giving an apple-like shape, puts a person at higher risk for early heart disease, high blood pressure, diabetes, and certain types of cancer. In contrast, excess weight carried below the waist—in the hips, buttocks, and thighs—doesn't appear to be as risky to health.

If mirror tests don't reveal whether you're an "apple" or a "pear," get out the tape measure and figure your waist-to-hip ratio. Here's how it's done:

- Stand relaxed. Measure your waist at its smallest point. Don't pull in your stomach.
- Then measure your hips at the largest part of your buttocks and hips.
- Divide your waist measurement by your hip measurement. If the number is nearly or more than 1.0, consider yourself an "apple." You're at greater risk for some health problems, such as heart disease. If your number is considerably less than 1.0, you're a "pear." For you, extra weight may be less of a health issue.

For a healthy weight, the waist-to-hip ratio for most women should fall below 0.80; for men, below 0.95 is best.

For the most part, being an "apple" or a "pear" is an inherited tendency for those who gain weight. In other words, fat distribution is partially influenced by genes. However, smoking and drinking too many alcoholic beverages also seem to increase fat carried in the stomach area; as a result, they increase the risk of weight-related health problems. Conversely, vigorous exercise helps reduce stomach fat, helping to decrease these health risks.

What's a Healthy Adult Weight?

The weight chart on page 19 is a guideline, showing a healthy weight range for adults—both men and women of all ages. It's based on height. There's no difference in weight ranges for age because the health risks appear to be the same, regardless of age.

The ranges are generous. The higher weights typically apply to people with more muscle and a larger frame, such as many men and some women. Muscle and bone weigh more than fat. The ranges don't suggest that weight gain within the range is necessarily healthful.

What if your weight falls above the range? For most people, that's less healthy. The higher your weight is above the range, the greater your risk for weight-related health problems.

What if your weight is below the range? Again, that may be healthy for you. But it also may suggest a health problem. Check with a health professional.

Remember that looking at body weight alone does not determine whether your weight is healthy. Consider the location and amount of body fat you carry as well.

Body Weight Versus Body Fat

What do you weigh? And how do you compare to the weight chart below? A weight chart can give you an idea of how your weight compares to a healthy weight.

Checking your body mass index (BMI) is another way to assess your weight and your risks for weight-related health problems at the same time. As a flexible guide, BMI allows for individual differences. *Refer to "At Risk? Check Your Body Mass Index" on page 20 to assess your* BMI *and its implications for health.*

Your body composition—how much of your weight is body fat—and not necessarily where you fit on a chart, is one of the most important factors in evaluating your weight. The location and amount of body fat are actually better predictors of health risk than body weight. For example, a person's weight may fit right within the recommended range, but he

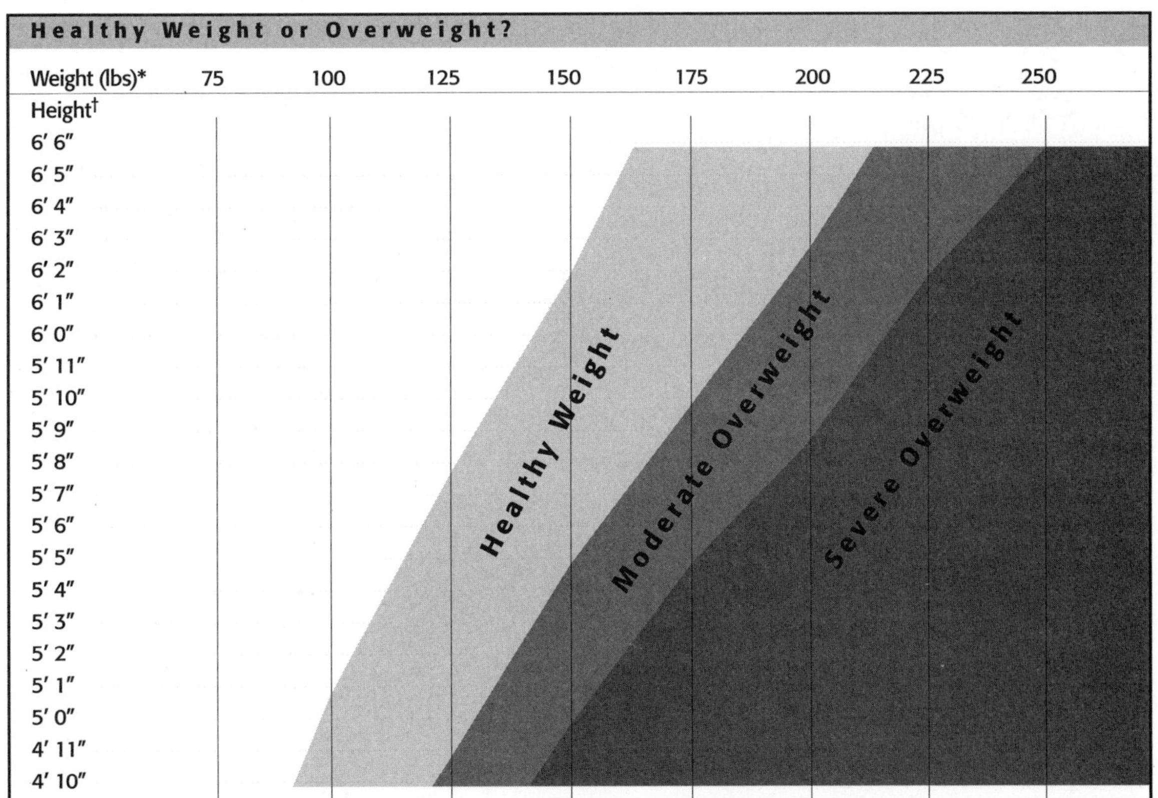

Source: Report of the Dietary Guidelines Advisory Committee on the Dietary Guidelines for Americans, 1995.
* *without clothes;* † *without shoes*

or she may still carry too much body fat. Constant dieting and inactivity can lead to an unhealthy amount of body fat. Conversely, a muscular person may seem to be overweight according to charts, but may not be overfat. This is because muscle weighs more than fat.

How can you figure how much of your weight is body fat (often referred to as percent body fat)? Short of expensive tests such as underwater weighing, it's difficult to get an exact measure. A health professional might use a skinfold caliper to measure the fat layer on several parts of your body, such as arm, midriff, and thigh. Even without the caliper, you can get an idea with a simple pinch test. *See "Can You Pinch an Inch?" to learn how.*

Remember, a scale by itself can't tell if you're carrying too much fat and how your weight is distributed. And perhaps most important, a scale shouldn't dictate how you feel about yourself.

At Risk? Check Your Body Mass Index

Body mass index (BMI) is another "tool" for helping you judge your body weight—and whether you're at risk for health problems associated with weight.

Rather than looking just at body weight, BMI factors in the amount of body fat you have. People with a higher percentage of body fat tend to have a higher BMI than those who have a greater percentage of muscle. Carrying excess body fat, not muscle, puts you at greater risk for health problems such as heart disease and diabetes.

Like other measures, use BMI only as a guideline, and consult your doctor about the weight that's healthy for you.

Here's how to figure your body mass index:

1. *Convert your body weight to kilograms*
(1 kilogram = 2.2 pounds):

body weight (pounds) ÷ 2.2 = weight (kilograms)
For example: 132 *pounds* ÷ 2.2 = 60 *kilograms*

2. *Convert your height to meters*
(1 meter = 39.37 inches):

height (inches) ÷ 39.37 = height (meters)
For example: 65 *inches* ÷ 39.37 = 1.65 *meters*

3. *Calculate your body mass index:*

your weight (kg) ÷ your height (m)^2 = BMI
For example: 60 *kg* ÷ (1.65 *m* x 1.65 *m*) = 22.03 BMI

4. *Check your* BMI *against your risk for health problems related to body weight.*

BMI	Risk for Health Problems Related to Body Weight
20 - 25	Very low risk
26 - 30	Low risk
31 - 35	Moderate risk
36 - 40	High risk
40 +	Very high risk

For example, a BMI of 22 is considered low risk for health problems related to body weight.

A BMI of 27.3 or more for women, and 27.8 or more for men is defined as overweight, according to the National Center for Health Statistics. Severe overweight is defined as 32.3 or more for women and 32.1 for men. *To find your* BMI *quickly with out calculating, refer to the chart in the appendix on page* 613.

CAN YOU PINCH AN INCH?

Using your thumb and forefinger, pinch a fold of skin on the back of your upper arm. If the fold is more than one-inch thick, you're likely overfat.

What Does the Doctor Say?

Do you need to lose weight? Probably not if your weight falls within the healthy weight range for your height, if you've gained less than 10 pounds since you reached your adult height, and if you're healthy. Your doctor may advise weight loss, however, if you're carrying excess body fat around your stomach area and you're overweight, if you have a weight-related health problem, or if you have a family history of these types of problems.

Have you ever finished a physical exam feeling that your weight was within a healthy range, only to have your doctor suggest that you trim—or perhaps gain—a few pounds? For some physical conditions, such as high blood pressure, diabetes, high blood cholesterol, or arthritis, your physician may advise some weight loss even though you appear to have a healthy weight.

A doctor may advise some weight gain for other reasons, perhaps to replace weight losses and aid recovery after a prolonged illness or surgery, or to help withstand some medical treatments.

Energy Basics: Calorie Math

You can't touch them or see them. Food supplies them, but they're not nutrients. Your body burns them to keep you alive—and moving. What are they? They're calories! To understand how to achieve and maintain your healthy weight, you need to start with the calorie basics.

A Measure of Energy

Calories actually are units of energy. Back in science class, you probably learned the technical definition: 1 calorie is the amount of energy needed to raise the temperature of 1 gram of water by 1 degree Celsius. In the world of nutrition and health, the term "calorie" refers to the amount of energy in food and the amount of energy the body uses.

In food, calories are energy locked inside three nutrients: carbohydrate, fat, and protein. These nutrients are released from food during digestion, then absorbed into the bloodstream and converted to glucose, or blood sugar.

In your body, food energy in glucose finally gets released into trillions of body cells where it's used to power all your body's work—from your heartbeat, to push-ups, to the smile that spreads across your face. Energy from food you don't need right away can be stored as body fat or perhaps as glycogen, a form of carbohydrate. Your body uses these energy stores later.

To clear up confusion in semantics—energy, or calories, that physically powers your body isn't the same as feeling energetic, or having that feeling of vitality. However, there's certainly a connection.

A sense of vitality is psychological, as well as physical. And it relates to your overall health and well-being. In other words, having the energy to run a six-minute mile comes from more than eating a healthful meal a few hours earlier.

That feeling of vitality comes from a total package: being rested, able to control stress, physically active, well-nourished, and free of disease—and feeling good about yourself!

WHERE DOES ENERGY COME FROM?

Three nutrients—carbohydrate, protein, and fat—and alcohol supply energy, or calories, in food. Gram for gram, fat and alcohol supply more than either carbohydrate or protein.

Source of Energy	Calories per Gram
Fat	9
Alcohol	7
Carbohydrate	4
Protein	4

Food Power

When you read food labels or check a calorie counter, you see that most foods supply calories, or energy—some more than others. But what accounts for the differences?

The calorie content of any food depends on its nutrient content: how much carbohydrate, fat, and protein it contains. One gram of either carbohydrate or protein supplies 4 calories, and 1 gram of fat provides 9 calories.

Although not a nutrient, alcohol also supplies calories—7 calories per gram. A glass of wine or a beer or two may add up to more calories than you think. *Refer to page 188, "Alcohol and Calories: How Much?" for the calories in these beverages.*

Three nutrient categories don't provide calories: vitamins, minerals, and water. Two other components of food—cholesterol and fiber—don't supply energy to your body either.

As a rule of thumb, foods that are watery, watery-crisp, or fibrous tend to have fewer calories than foods that are more fatty or greasy. (Remember, water is calorie free.) For example, celery, which has more water and fiber than french fries, also has fewer calories.

How Many Calories for You?

Your body's need for energy, or fuel, never stops. From the moment you were conceived to the time of death, your body needs a constant supply of energy to stay alive.

Taking a Cheeseburger Lunch Apart

How do you build your burger? And what do you eat with it? Each ingredient offers a different proportion of energy nutrients—and, as a result, a different amount of calories. Tomato and lettuce, for example, have more water, which is a calorie-free nutrient. Mayonnaise contains more fat, which is the nutrient with the most calories per gram.

When all these ingredients are eaten together in a meal—as a cheeseburger, carrot and zucchini sticks, pear, cookies, and milk—the calories from fat are balanced by calories from carbohydrate and protein.

	Calories	% Calories from carbohydrate	% Calories from fat	% Calories from protein
Cheeseburger				
Whole-wheat roll (1)	114	71	17	12
Mayonnaise (2 teaspoons)	38	24	76	0
Extra lean beef patty (3 ounces cooked)	161	0	59	41
American cheese slice (1 ounce)	93	9	67	24
Lettuce leaf (1)	3	59	12	29
Tomato slice (1)	13	74	12	14
Fresh Vegetables				
Carrot sticks (1/2 cup)	45	87	4	9
Zucchini sticks (1/2 cup)	9	66	7	27
Pear (1 medium)	97	92	5	2
Gingersnaps (2)	68	54	42	4
Skim milk (8 ounces)	86	56	5	39

Total calories—727
Total carbohydrate—48% of total calories
Total fat—32% of total calories
Total protein—20% of total calories

Note: *Remember, your goal is to consume no more than 30% of your total calories from fat over several days, not in individual foods or in one meal.*

How much? Energy needs vary from person to person. Even your own energy needs change at different ages and stages of life. Your age, basal metabolic rate, body size and composition, physical condition, and activity level all contribute to how much energy you need.

Powering your body can be compared to fueling your car. Your heart is like the fuel pump; arteries, like the gas line. Your lungs, like a carburetor, allow oxygen to mix with the fuel, so that combustion can take place in your many body cells, just as combustion occurs in the engine of your car.

To continue the analogy, both your car and your body need a source of energy just to keep idling. When you move, your body—like your car—burns more fuel, and uses even more to go faster and farther. Some bodies—and some cars—are more fuel efficient than others. That is, they use less energy to do the same amount of work. Age, size, shape, physical condition, and even the type of "fuel" affect fuel efficiency. *"How Does Your Body Use Energy?" on page 25 shows the proportion of energy used for each role in your body.*

Your Basic Energy Needs

Energy for basal metabolism is energy your body burns on "idle." In scientific terms, basal metabolic rate (BMR) is the level of energy needed to keep involuntary body processes going. That includes your heartbeat, breathing, generating body heat, perspiring to keep cool, transmitting messages to your brain, and producing thousands of body chemicals.

When we think of calories, energy burned through physical activity often comes to mind. Yet basal metabolism represents about 60 percent of your body's energy need.

"Rule of Ten." The simple "rule of ten" offers a quick estimate of how much energy your body uses for its basic needs. Figure 10 calories per pound of body weight to meet routine energy demands.

Consider a 170-pound male. He would burn about 1,700 calories (170 pounds x 10 calories per pound) per day for basal metabolism and about 2,800 calories total per day. (That's 60 percent of total calories for his basic energy needs.) Now calculate for yourself—about how much energy does your body require for its basic needs?

The "rule of ten" offers an easy estimate for basic energy needs. However, it doesn't allow for individual differences. Age, gender, genetics, and body composition and size, among other factors, aren't taken into account. While you can't do anything to change your age, gender, or genetic makeup, you can boost the rate at which your body burns energy.

The Age Factor. The "rule of ten" isn't meant for kids—especially not infants. From infancy through adolescence, energy demands for growth are high. Because they're building bone, muscle, and other tissue, young people can consume more calories

Can pasta make you fat? The Dietary Guidelines for Americans and the Food Guide Pyramid recommend an eating pattern with plenty of complex carbohydrates from foods such as breads, cereals, rice, pasta, fruits, and vegetables. Some news stories have suggested a debate over the benefits of one of these foods: pasta.

Limited research notes that high intakes of pasta and other high carbohydrate foods may cause weight gain in "insulin-resistant" people. For these individuals, it's speculated, the body reacts to sugars and starches by overproducing insulin—and so causing too much starch to be stored as fat.

However, most of us don't gain weight on a high-carbohydrate diet. Instead, high-fat diets, uncontrolled portion sizes from any source of food, including pasta, and not enough physical activity are the real factors in weight gain! ✦

per pound than adults can. Children's body proportions differ from those of adults, also affecting their basic energy needs. If you've ever watched a growing teenager eat, you know that energy needs are high during adolescence. During infancy, energy needs are higher per pound of body weight than any other time in life!

By the time people reach adulthood, their need for calories starts to decline. For each decade, energy needs drop about 2 percent. For example, a woman who needs about 2,200 calories per day for her total energy needs at age 25 might need 2 percent less, or 2,154 calories per day, at age 35. She may need another 2 percent less by age 45 and so on. But at any age, it's possible to keep energy needs up with increased physical activity.

Body composition and hormones change with age. As people become less active, muscle mass decreases. Body fat takes its place. Because body fat burns less energy than muscle, fewer calories are needed to maintain body weight, and basal metabolic rate goes down.

CALORIES: LOOKING OVER THE CHOICES

There's more to food than just calories. Some foods provide substantial amounts of vitamins and minerals, making them "nutrient dense." Others are "calorie-dense"—they supply mainly calories and relatively few nutrients. To understand nutrient density, compare the nutrients in 2⅔ slices of whole-wheat bread and one raised doughnut. The amount of calories in the bread and doughnut are the same, but the bread provides greater amounts of vitamins and minerals and far less fat.

Source: The Healthy Weigh: A Practical Food Guide. Chicago: *The American Dietetic Association*, 1991. ✦

If you continue to follow your teenage eating habits—and live a less active lifestyle—extra pounds that creep on with age should come as no surprise! Unused calories get stored as body fat.

Family Matters. Why can one person down more total calories day after day and never gain a pound, while for another person, weight control is a constant challenge? Among people with the same age, height, and activity level, some seem to convert more extra calories to body fat, while others seem to burn it off.

Genetic makeup and inherited body build account for some differences in basal metabolic rate—a difference you can't change! Families do tend to pass on food habits to one another, too. That also may account for similarities in body weight. But a fast—or slow—metabolic rate may be inherited, while food habits are not.

Body Size, Shape, and Composition. If you're the one filling the gas tank, you know that a heavy, full-size car usually burns more fuel per mile than a small, sleek sports car. Likewise, your body size affects your energy needs.

Body shape and composition make a difference, too. Your body is made of lean tissue, such as muscle and bone, as well as body fat. A lean, muscular body has a higher metabolic rate than a body type that's softly rounded with more fat tissue.

Ounce for ounce, muscle burns more energy than body fat does. So the higher your proportion of muscle to fat, the more calories you need to maintain your weight. To make up for changes that come with age, get physically active. Boost your BMR by building more muscle!

Body type affects energy needs in still other ways. A softly-rounded body type has a greater tendency to store body fat then a lean, sinewy body. A tall, thin body also has more surface area than a short body, and as a result, more heat loss; the net result—more calories burned to maintain normal body temperature.

The Gender Gap. The ratio of muscle to fat is a normal gender difference, accounting for differences in basal metabolic rate. Up to age 10 or so, energy needs for boys and girls are about the same. Puberty triggers change. When boys start developing more muscle, they need more calories; their added height and size demand more energy, too.

By adulthood, men usually have 10 to 20 percent more muscle and less body fat than women of the same age and weight. That's one reason why men's basic energy needs are higher. Muscle building among men may account for part of the difference. In contrast, women's bodies naturally keep body fat stores in reserve for pregnancy and breast-feeding.

During pregnancy and breast-feeding, a woman's energy needs go up. To meet the energy demands of a full-term pregnancy, women need about 300 extra calories a day—or about 80,000 extra calories over nine months. To breast-feed her baby, a woman needs about 500 extra calories a day during the time she's breast-feeding.

Hot—Or Cold? Outside temperature affects internal energy production. On chilly days, your BMR "burns" a little higher to keep you warm during prolonged exposure to cold. Shivering and moving to keep warm use energy, too. In hot temperatures, your body's air conditioning system burns a bit more energy.

The Diet Factor. Do you think that skipping meals or eating a very-low-calorie diet gives a weight-loss edge? Reconsider. Severe calorie restriction actually can make your body more energy efficient and cause the rate at which your body burns energy from food to slow down. You then require fewer calories to perform the same body processes. This slowdown in metabolic rate is your body's strategy for survival.

An Exercise Perk. Depending on the length and intensity of exercise, a physical workout can boost your BMR for several hours afterwards. That's a benefit added to the energy you already burned through exercise.

Activity: Energy Burner

Now, it's time to stop "idling." Shift from "neutral" to "first gear." Put your foot on the pedal, and start rolling! Energy that your body burns for physical activity compares to the fuel your car burns as it moves down the road.

Movement of any kind—a blink of your eye, a wave of your hand, or a jog around the block—uses energy. In fact, about 30 percent of your body's energy need powers physical activity. At best, that estimate is imprecise because activity levels differ so much. Very active people need more calories, using up about 40 percent of their total energy for physical activity.

Common sense says that some physical activities burn more energy than others. The amount of energy used to power physical activity actually depends on three things: the type of activity, its intensity, and how long you do it. Suppose you walk with a friend of the same age and body size. The one who pumps his or her arms and takes an extra lap around the block burns more energy. *The chart on page 26, "Burning Calories with Activity," shows how much energy—or how many calories—gets used for common, nonstop activities.*

Not surprisingly, body size makes a difference. It takes somewhat more energy to move if you weigh 170 pounds compared to 120. The more you weigh, the more calories you burn. That's one reason why men, who often weigh more, use more calories than women. *For more on energy and nutrition for physical activity, see chapter 21, "Athlete's Guide: Winning Nutrition."*

Basic energy needs (basal metabolism) 60%
Physical activity 30%
Digestion of food and
absorption of nutrients 10%

Energy use for the day 100%

The Food Connection

The act of eating actually burns calories. Digesting food and absorbing nutrients uses about 10 percent of your day's energy expenditure—about 180 calories if you consume 1,800 calories daily. But don't count on these processes to burn up all the energy in anything you eat.

Burning Calories with Activity

Activity	Body weight:	Calories burned per hour 120 lbs	170 lbs
Aerobic dance		330	460
Archery		190	270
Basketball		330	460
Bicycling (<10 mph)		220	310
Bowling		165	230
Calisthenics		250	345
Driving a car		110	155
Eating		80	115
Food preparation		135	190
Gardening		275	385
Golf (walking)		250	345
Hiking		330	460
Horseback riding		220	310
Housework		135	190
Jogging		385	540
Mowing lawn		300	425
Racquetball		385	540
Reading		70	100
Rowing, stationary		385	540
Running, 10 mph		880	1230
Sitting (watching TV)		55	75
Sitting (writing, typing)		100	140
Skating, roller		385	540
Skiing, cross-country		440	615
Skiing, downhill		385	540
Sleeping		50	70
Soccer		385	540
Swimming, leisure		330	460
Tennis		385	540
Walking, brisk		220	310
Weight training		165	230

Source: Compendium of physical activities: Classification of energy costs of human physical activities. *Medicine and Science in Sports and Exercise*. *Vol*. 25, *pp*. 71-80, 1993.

Energy in Balance

There's nothing magical about controlling weight. To maintain weight, "energy in" must balance "energy out." In other words, your calorie intake must equal the calories your body burns. To lose or gain, you need to tip the energy balance.

For weight loss, you need to consume fewer calories than you burn each day. Do that by either cutting back on calories or by exercising more. Better yet, do both.

If you need to gain weight, tip the balance in the other direction; consume more calories than your body uses.

What's the bottom line? Be aware that no matter what their source—carbohydrates, fat, or protein—your body stores most of the excess calories you consume as body fat.

Calorie Myth-Takes

Over the years, calorie myths of all kinds have passed from person to person. How many of these unfounded notions sound familiar?

Myth: Grapefruit burns calories.
Fact: Digestion of any food requires a small amount of energy. But no food—nor food component—has any special ability to "melt away" body fat.

Myth: Margarine has fewer calories than butter.
Fact: Regular stick margarine and butter contain the same number of calories—about 36 calories per teaspoon. For a spread with fewer calories, try jelly or jam with 16 calories per teaspoon.

Myth: A rich, fudgy brownie, before bedtime, is more fattening than the same brownie eaten for lunch.
Fact: The clock doesn't make a difference. No matter when they're eaten, calories seem to have the same effect in the body. Too many can add up to extra body fat. Timing has no direct effect on how your body uses the calories. Evidence does suggest that eating regular meals, especially breakfast, helps to reduce fat intake and minimize impulsive snacking, which can add up to excess calories over the course of a day.

Myth: Toasting bread reduces its calorie content.
Fact: That's nothing more than wishful thinking. Toasting doesn't "burn off" any calories—it just changes the flavor and texture a bit.

Myth: Potatoes and bread are fattening.
Fact: By themselves, they're not high in calories—88 calories for a medium (4-ounce) potato and 70 calories for an average-size slice of bread. Both potatoes and bread are great sources of complex carbohydrates. However, high-fat toppings or spreads can add up to excess calories. Consider the calories in one tablespoon: sour cream (30 calories), butter or margarine (100 calories), and regular mayonnaise (100 calories).

Weighing the Risks

According to the Centers of Disease Control and Prevention, one in three American adults is obese—up from one in four in the mid-1980s. Increases in childhood and adolescent obesity are also occurring.

According to the Institute of Medicine, obesity is defined as an excess of body fat, whereas overweight refers to an excess of body weight that includes fat, bone, and muscle. Men with more than 25 percent body fat and women with more than 30 percent body fat are considered to be obese.

The causes of obesity are more complex than energy imbalance. Because it runs in families, genetics may play a role—especially if the conditions are right. A child's surroundings and upbringing are factors, too. With one obese parent, the chances of being overweight are 40 percent; that doubles when both parents are obese. People who inherit a sluggish metabolism are more likely to gain weight. There's good evidence that today's inactive lifestyles contribute heavily to weight problems. For example, studies link excessive television viewing to the incidence of obesity. Today's technology, video games, and computers likely play a role, too! Other psychological, social, and lifestyle factors add to the complexity of individual reasons for obesity.

What about being too thin? The reasons for being underweight are as complex and unique as being overweight. Genetics may be a factor here, too. As with obesity, thinness tends to run in families. Some people may inherit a speedy metabolism. For many reasons, the appetite center of the brain may not signal hunger, so people may feel full even when they're not. Other psychological, physical, economic, social, and lifestyle factors also may get in the way of eating well. *Refer to "Too Thin—A Problem?" on page 40.*

CALORIE PUZZLE

One pound of body fat equals about 3,500 calories. Therefore, losing a pound requires a 3,500-calorie deficit. The opposite is true for weight gain. The following scenarios describe how an average person might gain or lose weight.

➢ If you added 250 calories from an extra sandwich, fruit salad, or a bag of chips to your normal eating plan every day—without boosting your activity level—how long might it take to gain 1 pound?

3,500 calories = 1 pound of body fat
3,500 calories ÷ 250 calories per day
= 14 days

➢ If you burned 100 extra calories by walking about 30 minutes during your lunch hour five days a week—without boosting your calorie intake—how much weight might you lose in 14 weeks?

100 calories per day x 5 days
= 500 calories per week
500 calories per week x 14 weeks
= 7,000 total calories burned
7,000 calories = 2 pounds of body fat

YOUR "WEIGH": FIGURING YOUR ENERGY NEEDS

How much energy does your body need in a day? For a rough guesstimate, do the following "energy math."

1. *Figure your basic energy needs* (BMR). Multiply your healthy weight (in pounds) by 10 for women and by 11 for men. If you're overweight, use the average weight within the healthy weight range given for your height on "Healthy Weight or Overweight?" on page 19.

weight x ____ = ____ calories for basic needs

2. *Figure your energy needs for physical activity.* Check the activity level that matches your lifestyle:

____ *Sedentary*: mainly sitting, driving a car, lying down, sleeping, standing, reading, typing, or other low intensity activities

____ *Light activity*: light exercise, such as walking, for no more than 2 hours daily

____ *Moderate activity*: moderate exercise, such as heavy housework, gardening, dancing, and very little sitting

____ *Very active*: active physical sports or labor-intensive job, such as construction work or ditch digging

Multiply your basic energy needs by the percent that matches your activity level: sedentary—20%; light activity—30%; moderate activity—40%; or very active—50%.

___ calories for basic needs
x ___% for activity level

= ___ calories for physical activity

continued on page 29

Obesity: A Hazard to Health

Sometime spend an hour or so carrying around a 5- or 10-pound bag of sugar or flour, or a heavy metropolitan phone book. Tiring? That's the extra burden on your body and heart when you carry extra pounds of body fat. The more excess body fat you have, the greater that burden. Every body system—including the lungs, the heart, and the skeleton—needs to work harder.

Many health problems are linked to obesity and adult weight gain, among them high blood cholesterol levels, heart disease, stroke, high blood pressure, diabetes, some forms of cancer, arthritis, breathing problems, and other illnesses. For this reason, weight gain—except during pregnancy—isn't recommended. If your weight is above recommended ranges, if you can pinch more than an inch of body fat, and if you have any of these health problems, you're wise to shed a few pounds. *"A Weighty Issue" on page 486 explores the links between obesity, a high-fat diet, and cardiovascular health.*

Obesity leads to a synergistic cycle of inactivity, too. Often extra body weight makes physical activity more tiring—even everyday activities such as walking up the stairs or walking through the mall. Inactivity can lead to more weight gain and more muscle loss. Obesity can have an emotional price tag, too, if body image leads to poor self-esteem and social isolation.

Now consider the health benefits of trimming down. Reducing 5 to 10 percent of excess body weight is enough to lower the risks for many chronic diseases. Even this small weight shift helps lower blood pressure, total and LDL blood cholesterol levels, triglyceride levels, and blood sugar. In addition, HDL cholesterol levels may go up. *To learn about total, LDL, and HDL cholesterol and triglycerides, refer to the "'Fat' Dictionary" on page 55.* Weight loss may have emotional benefits, too—boosting self-esteem and lowering the risk for depression.

Obesity and Kids: A Heavy Burden

America's youth are getting fatter! Today nearly 25 percent of children and teens are obese—and the results can last a lifetime. Inactivity is also on the rise, contributing to the prevalence of overweight.

Although obese children don't automatically become obese adults, there's reason for caution. Eating and activity patterns for life often are established during childhood. Those who are overweight as teens may have more risk for ongoing health problems as adults, according to some studies. What's more, weight problems affect self image, and as a result, self-esteem. How children feel about themselves can affect almost every aspect of their lives now—and on into their adult years.

Weight-loss regimens for adults are not meant for children or teens. Young people need enough calories and nutrients for their growth and development. Often increased exercise, rather than cutting calories, is enough to promote a healthful weight. Before devising a plan to help your child or teenager lose weight, talk to your doctor or registered dietitian (RD).

For more about healthy food choices and lifestyles for children and teens, refer to chapter 17, "Food to Grow On." There you'll also find guidelines for helping youth reach and maintain their healthy weight.

Weight Management: Strategies That Work!

Whether you need to lose, gain, or maintain, make health, not appearance, your first priority for weight control. Once you achieve your healthy weight, make it permanent—not a continuing cycle of weight loss and weight gain.

The key to managing your weight throughout your life is a positive attitude and the right kind of motivation. If you're trying to lose weight to fit into a bathing suit before vacation, or to look good for your school reunion, or because your spouse is nagging you to drop a belt size, your commitment and efforts are likely to fizzle out over time. Internal motivators—health, increased energy, self-esteem, feeling in control—increase your chances for lifelong success!

YOUR "WEIGH": FIGURING YOUR ENERGY NEEDS (CONTINUED)

3. *Figure energy for digestion and absorbing nutrients.* Add your calories for basic needs and calories for physical activity, then multiply the total by 10%.

(___ calories for basic needs + ___ calories for physical activity) x 10% =
___ calories for digestion and absorbing nutrients

4. *Add up your total energy needs by adding calories for each purpose.*

calories for basic needs
+ calories for physical activity
+ calories for digestion and absorbing nutrients =
____ calories for your total energy needs

As an example, consider this 40-year-old female, who works at a desk and walks during her lunch hour. She weighs 125 pounds, which is healthy for her height.

Basic energy needs: 125 pounds x 10
= 1250 calories

Energy for physical activity:
1250 calories x .30 = 375 calories

Energy for digestion and absorbing nutrients:
(1250 + 375 calories) x .10 = 162.5 calories

Total energy needs:
1250 calories + 375 calories + 162.5 calories
= **1787.5 calories** ✦

If you're at your healthy weight, these strategies for weight management are meant for you, too. A word of caution: If your weight problem is excessive—too much or too little—or if you have health problems, talk to your doctor before you get started. Children, pregnant women, and people over age 65 shouldn't attempt weight control without a doctor's advice.

WEIGHT CYCLING—THE "YO-YO" PROBLEM

Carrying a few extra pounds of body weight may be less harmful than "yo-yo" dieting! The cycle of repeatedly losing and regaining weight can make weight management more difficult in the long run. It may lead to a slower basal metabolic rate, eating disorders, and poor self-esteem. According to some studies, weight cycling may even increase the risk for some ongoing health problems, such as heart disease and some forms of cancer. Moreover, lost weight that repeatedly comes back may lead to feelings of frustration and failure.

Weight cycling often comes from quick-fix diets, weight-loss gimmicks, and other risky strategies. Without physical activity, each time the dieter sheds a few pounds, he or she loses lean body mass, along with body fat. Because the approach for weight loss is short-lived, pounds quickly go back on. Without exercise, those regained pounds are mostly body fat, which burns less energy than muscle. As the cycle repeats itself, the dieter needs fewer and fewer calories to maintain weight, and it gets harder and harder to lose weight. The cycle of "failure, success, failure" makes it psychologically harder to try again, too.

If repeated "ups and downs" of dieting describe your weight problem, shift your approach to management. You can break the cycle. Go for long-term approaches, rather than short-term results. Make gradual and permanent changes in the way you eat, your activity level, and your lifestyle. It's the only way to be healthy—for life. ✦

Ready? Set... Go for It!

Are you among those people who have gained and lost the same 10 pounds over and over again? A repeated cycle of weight loss and weight gain isn't the best approach to weight management. Whether your objective is weight loss, weight gain, or weight maintenance, your lifelong success may depend on some new ways of thinking.

Make health, not appearance, your weight-management priority. Strive for your best weight for health. That's not necessarily the lowest weight you could be—or what you consider your "ideal" number. Your healthy weight is a realistic goal. *Refer to page* 17, *"Body Basics: What's Your Healthy Weight?"*

Focus on a healthy lifestyle—for a lifetime—not on "dieting." For the long run, the notion of dieting is often counterproductive. Dieting alone is often a short-term tactic without long-term results. The concept of "dieting" carries a lot of negative baggage: guilt, "shoulds," and "can't haves." For most people, "dieting" results in failure.

Make behavior changes if you need to, following these tactics for weight management:

- healthful eating,
- regular physical activity, and
- acceptance of the weight you achieve through a healthy lifestyle.

Tailor your overall approach to you. A plan that works must match your schedule, your budget, your family situation, and your personal needs, to name a few. Experts have found that two out of three people who were successful at weight control personalized their efforts. That is, they made changes that fit their lifestyles. *Refer to "Check It Out!" on page* 35.

Make strategies action-oriented and specific—what you will do to achieve or maintain your healthy weight. Perhaps you'll walk for 15 minutes each day during your lunch break, or you'll drink milk rather than a milk shake with your fast-food lunch. If you're too vague—"I'll eat fewer high-fat foods" instead of "I'll switch from fried to broiled chicken"—you won't be able to judge your success.

If you need to lose or gain weight, set realistic goals—ones that can work for you! Start with your current weight or your lifestyle, not where you want to be. Make your goals attainable, short-term. For example, the challenge of trimming 5 pounds at a time seems more do-able than losing 25 or more pounds. Like any project, going little by little isn't so overwhelming, and it's healthier.

Think long-term; act gradually. It's true that fasting and starvation-type diets can peel off pounds, but as water loss! And grueling exercise regimens certainly tone the body. But for most people, these tactics aren't realistic ways to live—and they may not be healthful either. A short-term approach for lifetime concerns just doesn't work.

Instead of trying quick fixes, gradually make realistic changes in your lifestyle and eating habits. A weight shift of 1/2 to 1 pound a week is healthy. Any more than 2 pounds of weight loss a week suggests that you're exercising too much or eating too little. Remember: Your extra pounds didn't creep on overnight. They don't disappear that way either!

Be realistic with your self-talk. Skip the absolutes—"always," "never," and "must" in your tactics. I always skip dessert. I'll never eat another french fry. I must swim 20 laps every other day. Get rid of "shoulds," too. I should get up early and walk.

Cut yourself some slack. Nobody's perfect. Allow for occasional slip-ups. And don't feel guilty. Just get right back on track. Like riding a horse again after falling off, the longer you wait, the harder it is!

Plan to indulge occasionally. By doing this, you may be more successful in the long run.

Make a lifestyle change and commitment. Your weight dilemma is probably a result of a number of factors, including your genetic makeup, metabolic rate, and gender, as well as your lifestyle—how you usually eat and how much you exercise. Make a physically active lifestyle and healthful eating an everyday habit.

Expect to be successful. Reaching life's goals are often a self-fulfilling prophecy. Positive self-talk and an enthusiastic approach to weight management set you up for success!

Get Physical!

Move it to lose it! Exercise has been cited as the most powerful tool for weight management. A physically-active lifestyle offers many rewards—from heart health to strong bones to stress relief, plus many other benefits. Yet many people don't

Like sound eating habits, regular physical activity is part of a healthy lifestyle. Apply the same principles—variety, balance, and moderation—to both food choices and exercise. Always check with your physician before beginning any exercise program.

Variety: Enjoy many different activities to exercise different muscles, including your heart.

Balance: Because different activities have different benefits, balance your exercise pattern. For overall fitness, you need exercises that build cardiovascular endurance, muscular strength, bone strength, and flexibility.

Moderation: Exercise to keep fit, without overdoing. You don't need a heavy workout every day. And although exercise recommendations vary, health experts do advise 30 minutes or more of moderate exercise in your daily routine, most days of the week.

Source: The Food Guide Pyramid: Your Personal Guide to Healthful Eating. International Food Information Council, U.S. Department of Agriculture, Food Marketing Institute, 1995. ✦

Do you find it difficult to fit 30 minutes of physical activity into your life every day? Think again. Even with a busy lifestyle, you can boost your activity level. These everyday activities can count toward your day's total if they're done with moderate intensity—and most take little, if any, extra time.

1. Get up 30 minutes earlier in the morning, and take a brisk walk to start your day. Need someone to get you going? Schedule your walk with a neighbor.

2. Forget the drive-through carwash. Wash the car yourself. Bonus: You'll save money at the same time.

3. Take stairs instead of the elevator or escalator. Walking up stairs is a great heart exerciser and calorie burner!

4. Park at the far end of the parking lot for a longer walk. Get off the bus a stop ahead. Then walk the rest of the way to your destination.

5. Are you a computer user—on and off the job? Give yourself at least five minutes of exercise for every hour of computer time.

6. Walk around your building—outside or inside—during your lunch hour or coffee break. You'll burn energy rather than being tempted to nibble on a snack.

7. Get a dog, and walk together. No dog? Then walk your cat—or pet pig—on a leash.

8. Play actively with your kids, grand kids, or pets. Some dogs like to play frisbee as much as kids do!

9. Before and after dinner, walk—and talk—with your family. To burn more energy if you have an infant, use a baby carrier on your back rather than push a stroller.

continued on page 33

get enough. *Refer to "Moderate Activity: What Is It?" on page 7.*

Our technological, push-button society makes life easier and more productive. But sedentary lifestyles set us up for weight problems. One hundred years ago—even 25 years ago—many everyday activities were more physically intensive than they are today. And people could consume more calories as a result. Now, the more we sit, the less energy we need, and the more likely we are to gain weight.

Think of the impact of the personal computer. Back in the days of the manual typewriter, a typist, on average, burned 15 more calories an hour than doing the same work today on a computer. For someone who does word processing for four hours a day, that adds up to 60 calories a day, or 300 calories over a five-day work week. When you add up all the energy savings—from escalators to home appliances to electric garage door openers—you can see why inactivity has become so common and why weight control has become a challenge.

The Exercise Edge

Study after study shows that people who keep physically active are more successful at losing—and keeping off—extra pounds of body fat. In fact, physical activity appears to be the key to maintaining a healthy weight.

Consider these reasons why exercise can help you manage your weight and enhance your body image:

➢ Physical activity burns energy. The longer, more frequently, and more rigorously you exercise, the more energy you burn. When you burn more than you consume, your body uses its energy stores, and you lose weight. Consider the effect of just 30 minutes of brisk walking added to your day. You would burn about 110 calories daily if you're a 120-pound person, and about 155 calories if you weigh about 170 pounds. In just four to five weeks, that adds up to more than 3,500 calories, or one pound of body fat.

➢ Physical activity helps you keep muscle and lose body fat. Without exercise on a weight-loss diet, you lose lean body tissue along with body fat.

➢ Physically active people have more lean body mass. Even when you're not moving, lean body mass requires more energy to maintain than fat tissue. So at the same weight, you may be able to consume slightly more calories without gaining weight than someone with more body fat.

➢ Exercise speeds up your basal metabolic rate for up to 12 hours, even after you stop. You'll burn more energy even at rest.

➢ Stepping up to a moderately-active lifestyle won't necessarily give you a ravenous appetite. In fact, people who exercise regularly often eat less than those who don't. Regular and moderate exercise actually may suppress appetite a bit.

➢ Exercise can help relieve stress. Remember: Stress may lead to nibbling on more food and more calories than your body needs.

➢ Being active creates a "trimmer" mindset. As some people get more physically active, they opt for foods with less fat and fewer calories, and more complex carbohydrates. The reason? It just seems to "feel good."

➢ A firm, lean body—the result of physical activity—looks trimmer than one that's flabby with more body fat, even at the same weight. Think of your body as a "package" of lean tissue and body fat; muscle takes less space than body fat. Although looks shouldn't be the only reason for being physically active, it's a great benefit!

What role does physical activity play for people who need to gain weight? Because the benefits go beyond weight control, everyone needs exercise. There's no need to cut back on physical activity unless a person's physical activity pattern is excessive—or if a physician advises a slower pace.

Weight control is just one reason to keep physically active. *For other benefits of physical activity, refer to "Ten Reasons to Make the 'Right Moves'," on page 531.*

An Active Lifestyle

For weight control, you don't need to be an exercise fanatic with strenuous daily workouts to get the benefits. Step aerobics at a fitness club or

20 Everyday Ways to Get Moving (continued)

10. Do some backyard gardening. (Bonus: Grow fresh vegetables and herbs if you can.) In the fall, rake leaves.

11. Ride your bike to work or to a friend's home—if it's safe to do. Walk to do errands that are just a few blocks away.

12. While you watch television, do household chores or projects: mop the kitchen floor or refinish a piece of furniture. Avoid the "couch potato" syndrome.

13. Catch up with your around-the-house work: wash the windows, vacuum or shampoo the carpet, clean the garage or basement, sweep the sidewalk.

14. Use the exercise equipment you already own. Do two things at one time: ride your stationary bicycle while you read the morning paper or news magazine. Watch the morning news while you work out on your rowing machine.

15. Push your lawn mower instead of using the power-assisted drive. Skip the snow blower; shovel the snow by hand if you're fit.

16. Make homemade bread. Knead the dough by hand, not with a bread machine or food processor.

17. Use the restroom or pay phone that's at the other end of the building so you get an opportunity to walk.

18. Plan an active family vacation or weekend outing. Rather than sit on a beach, go canoeing, hiking, or snow skiing.

19. "Walk your talk!" If you like to chat on the phone, buy a portable one so you don't need to sit still.

20. Rent an exercise video, rather than a movie. And work out with the video as a leisure-time activity. ✦

30 minutes on an exercise bike every day may not be right for you. That's OK because moderate, consistent physical activity can do the job. In fact, any activity you enjoy and stay with can be the right one for you. If you make exercise enjoyable, you're more likely to stick with it.

For significant health benefits, including weight management, experts advise a total of 30 minutes or more of moderate activity on most, if not all, days of the week. Smaller increments are also OK. They just need to add up to at least 30 minutes: for example, 10 minutes of brisk walking during your lunch hour, 15 minutes of leisure-time bike riding, and 5 minutes of sweeping the sidewalk in front of your home.

If you haven't been physically active, then build up gradually. Remember: Any increase in your physical activity can make a difference. You don't need an all-or-nothing mentality!

To tip the energy balance in favor of weight loss, you may wish to burn more calories. *As you read on page 25, "Activity: Energy Burner," the energy expenditure of physical activity goes up in three ways.* The longer, the more frequent, and the more intense your activity, the more energy you burn. Regardless, choose physical activities that you enjoy and can stick with.

Keep in mind that even though some weight-loss regimens make "spot-reducing" promises, your body can't get rid of fat in just the problem places. As you exercise and burn more calories than you consume, your body draws energy from all its fat stores, including the problem spots. If you keep on moving, fat will eventually disappear in all the right places.

Refer to pages 441 and 449 for tips to keep kids and teens physically active. Adults can find some practical exercise advice on page 480 and page 513.

When You Want to Lose

Eating to control weight and eating for good health may seem like two separate goals. Actually, they're one and the same. One simple food plan—the Food Guide Pyramid—presents an eating plan that can accomplish both objectives. To tip the energy balance in one direction or the other, or to keep it level, you simply need to adjust your food choices and number of servings within each of the five major groups of the Food Guide Pyramid. *For more about following these guidelines, refer to page 243, "The Food Guide Pyramid: Your Healthful Eating Guide."*

Remember that one pound of body fat contains 3,500 calories worth of stored energy. For weight loss, you need to create a 3,500-calorie deficit for each pound you want to lose. Experts suggest striving for a 500-calorie deficit per day, so you lose weight at the safe rate of about one pound per week. You can do that by cutting back on what you eat or being more physically active—or better yet, by doing both.

To trim energy intake, should you count calories or figure fat? Counting calories to manage weight can be a tedious task. You can get a calorie counter that lists calories in many foods, or try a computer program that makes the task easier.

Keeping track of fat grams is another option and a good way learn about the fat content of food. Because fat provides more than twice the calories per gram than carbohydrate or protein, it may be easier to lose and maintain a healthy weight by keeping your fat intake within recommended guidelines: no more than 30 percent of your day's calories should come from fat. Trimming fat grams trims calories, but keep in mind that the total calories consumed and burned through activity are what determine body weight.

Not every food you eat needs to be low fat or low calorie. The idea is: Balance low-fat and high-fat, high-calorie foods over the course of a day—or even a few days—so your average fat intake hovers at 30 percent or less of your total calorie intake. *For more about fat in a healthful diet, refer to page 67, "Moderation: Key to a Healthful Diet."*

How many calories, how much fat? To get the nutrients your body needs, don't drop below 1,600 calories a day. Children and teenagers especially need adequate calories and nutrients for growth, as well as for normal body function and physical activity.

If you eat...	Allow yourself up to about...
1,600 calories	53 grams of fat
1,800 calories	60 grams of fat
2,000 calories	66 grams of fat
2,200 calories	73 grams of fat
2,400 calories	80 grams of fat

Scrupulous fat budgeting isn't the only way to bring your fat intake in line with health recommendations. These shortcuts help you reach the same goal—and trim calories at the same time:

Eat a variety of foods from the Food Guide Pyramid. To trim calories, eat the serving amount from the lower end of the range for each food group. If you do, you'll be taking in about 1,600 calories, or roughly the amount for many sedentary women and some older adults.

Cut back on fat in your food choices. Trim fat and calories in your cooking style. Buy lower-fat substitutes of your higher-fat favorites. Order foods with less fat and calories when you eat out. Sometimes switching from high- to low-fat foods is enough to make a difference. *For more on low-fat eating, refer to page* 68, *"Trim Fat in Your Eating Style."*

Fill up on fruits, vegetables, and whole-grains. Being high in fiber and low in fat, they can help satisfy you without many calories. Bonus: They may take more time to chew—so you eat less! *For tips on eating more fiber-rich foods, refer to "For Fiber—Variety!" on page* 148.

Learn how to eat what you like! Enjoy a variety of foods—including your favorites. No one food by itself can make you fat. You'll more likely stick to your eating plan if you don't deprive yourself. Just eat small amounts in moderation. *For tips on taming food cravings, refer to page* 45, *"Eat What You Crave!"*

Control your portion sizes. Even calories in low-fat foods can tip your energy balance when servings are bigger than you need. *For more on serving sizes, refer to page* 39, *"Get Portion Savvy," and page* 245, *"What Counts As One Serving?"*

Use the Nutrition Facts information on food labels— and choose the foods that match your needs. You'll find the amounts of fat and calories for one serving right on the label. Be aware that serving sizes on the food label may differ from those on the Food Guide Pyramid. Check the front of the label, too, where you'll find descriptive terms for foods with fewer calories and fat. What do the label terms mean? *To learn how to use nutrition information on a food label, refer*

Ready to start a weight control plan? To make sure the program is safe and effective, ask yourself a few questions before you begin:

- Does the plan include a variety of foods from all five major groups in the Food Guide Pyramid?
- Does the plan include appealing foods you will enjoy eating for the rest of your life, not just a few weeks or months?
- Are the foods available at the supermarket where you usually shop?
- Does the plan allow you to eat your favorite foods—in fact, any foods?
- Does the plan recommend changes in your eating habits that also fit your lifestyle and budget?
- Does the plan include an adequate amount of energy—from at least the minimum number of servings from the Food Guide Pyramid?
- Does the plan include physical activity?

If you cannot answer "yes" to all these questions, chances are this weight-loss program won't bring long-term success. Success comes only when you make healthful, permanent changes in eating and physical activity habits. ✦

to page 270, "Today's Food Labels." And check the chart on this page, "Label Lingo: Calories."

Go easy on wine, beer, and other alcoholic drinks. Alcohol supplies calories—7 calories per gram. A 12-ounce beer contains about 150 calories but few nutrients, and a 5-ounce glass of white wine has 100 calories. Besides providing a large dose of alcohol, downing a six-pack on a hot summer day can add up to a whopping 900 calories, and splitting a one-liter bottle of wine can supply 325 calories or more. Drinking alcoholic beverages can also stimulate your appetite so you may eat more. *For tips on cutting back on alcoholic drinks, see page 187, "Taking Control!"*

Calories

Nutrition Facts on the food label list the calories in a single serving. In addition, "calorie lingo" on the package can alert you to certain food products as you search supermarket displays. *Refer to "Label Lingo: Fats and Cholesterol" on page 71 to learn the label language for fat.*

LABEL TERM...	MEANS...
Calorie free	less than 5 calories
Low calorie	40 calories or less
Reduced or fewer calories	at least 25% fewer calories*
Light or lite	one-third fewer calories or 50% less fat*; if more than half the calories are from fat, fat content must be reduced by 50% or more
Low calorie meals	120 calories or less per 100 grams
Light meal	"low fat" or "low calorie" meal

* *as compared with a standard serving size of the traditional food*

Snack smart. It's easy to think about meals, yet forget about snacks when you're watching what you eat. Make sure to fit snacks into your overall eating plan for the day. Choose them wisely by the calories and nutrients they keep. And practice the art of fat balancing so you can enjoy some higher-fat snacks, such as chocolate bars, nuts, or chips. Just eat them less often and in smaller amounts. And balance them with lower-fat snacks—pretzels, bread sticks, raisins, fruit, or raw vegetables—the next time. *For more about snacking, refer to "That Snack Attack!" on page 261.*

Ask a registered dietitian for more guidance on choosing healthful foods for weight loss. *Refer to page 580, "How to Find Nutrition Help" for tips on finding a qualified nutrition expert in your area.*

Slimming Habits

Look at your eating habits. Do you snack on high-calorie foods at work because everyone else does? Do you eat fast so you can get on quickly with your day? Are you a stand-up diner?

To manage your weight effectively, you may need to rethink your old ways of eating—and identify habits that promote weight gain. Consider what, when, why, where, and how you eat. Then make some changes for a more healthful eating style.

Plan meals and snacks ahead. Haphazard eating often becomes high-calorie eating. Pack low-calorie snacks, such as raw vegetables, to eat at work when others snack on candy, doughnuts, or chips.

Shop on a full stomach. That way you won't be tempted to buy extra goodies or to nibble on free samples. Write out your shopping list, too, when you're not hungry.

Stick to a schedule. There's no hard-and-fast rule about eating three meals a day. Nevertheless, it does help to establish regular eating patterns. Studies show that missed meals can lead to impulsive snacking and overeating and may even lower the rate at which your body burns energy.

Eat from plates, not food packages. When you nibble chips or crackers from a package or snack on ice cream from the carton, you don't know how much you've eaten. It's probably more than you think.

Portion foods before bringing them to the table. You'll likely eat less when serving bowls and platters aren't placed on the table. Use smaller bowls and dinner plates so small portions look like more. *Refer to page 39, "Get Portion Savvy," for more tips on portion control.*

Eat slowly. Savor the flavor of each bite. After all, it takes about 20 minutes for your stomach to signal your brain that you're full—which curbs your urge for a second helping. Slow down by putting down your fork between bites. Eat with chopsticks, if they slow you down. Sip, rather than gulp, your beverage. Swallow before filling your fork again.

Forget the "clean plate club." You don't need to eat everything on your plate if you're satisfied already.

Sit down to eat. Focus on your food, rather than nibbling while you do other things. That way you know that you've eaten.

Just eat. Make eating the only event—and enjoy it. When you eat unconsciously while you watch television, read, or drive, you may consume more than you think.

Choose foods that take more time to eat. For example, peeling and eating an orange takes longer than drinking a glass of orange juice.

Stop eating when you leave the table. Avoid the urge to nibble on leftovers as you clear the table and clean up.

When you get the urge to nibble (especially if you're not hungry), do something else. Jog, call a friend, walk the dog, or step out into your garden.

Eating Triggers

You have all the best intentions. Then something triggers your desire to eat—even though you're not hungry. Instead of looking inside the refrigerator or diving into a bowl of snacks, get in touch with the emotions and situations that trigger your eating. Learn to differentiate between physical hunger and other "emotionally driven" hungers. It also helps to find an appropriate diversion.

Do you eat when you're bored? Find some other options. Make a list of fun activities: perhaps rent a

DEAR DIARY...

Help yourself to weight control by keeping tab on what you eat. Research shows that people who keep a food and exercise diary are often more successful at weight management than those who don't.

There's nothing complicated about keeping a record. Use any kind of notebook as your diary. If you carry your laptop computer everywhere, keep your records there. Or buy a day-to-day food and activity diary to keep with you.

For the record, write down the amounts and kinds of foods and beverages you eat every day. To get a handle on any eating "triggers," write your mood and rate your hunger level each time you eat. Put down the time and place, too. List the amount of time you spend in physical activity, along with what you do. Keep your food and activity record for at least a week or two. Then review it to get a closer look at your eating and physical activity habits.

Most people can spot problem areas easily: perhaps the high-fat snack every afternoon at 3 p.m., or the nighttime snacks eaten in front of the television. Keeping records offers one way to identify areas you might need to change. It also can help you focus on your weight goals—and think twice before indulging in a high-fat snack when you're not hungry. ✦

movie, go shopping, call a friend, surf the Internet, or play with your kids. Post your list on the refrigerator. When you're bored or upset, pick one of these activities instead of eating.

Control mood-triggered eating. Avoid the urge to eat as a way to relax, quell anger, or overcome depression or loneliness.

Learn to deal with emotions in a positive, more appropriate way. Compared with nibbling, physical activity—perhaps a brisk walk, a bike ride, or a tennis game—offers a more lasting way to resolve your moods. Sometimes some positive self-talk or a brief change of scenery does the trick!

Be aware of social situations that trigger eating—such as parties, entertaining friends, dating, and happy-hour business meetings. Then create your own ways to avoid overeating.

Remember: out of sight, out of mind. If the sight of candy, chips, and other high-calorie foods lures you, store them in an inconvenient place. Better yet, don't keep them around. Instead stock up on fruit, raw vegetables, and other foods with fewer calories.

Accomplished something special? Reward yourself, but not with food. Buy something new to wear, read, or entertain you. Go to a play, concert, or sports event. Indulge yourself by calling your friends. Don't make success your trigger for eating.

Watch out for seasonal triggers: perhaps nibbling while watching fall and winter sports on television, "cooling off" in hot weather with a six-pack of beer, or eating and entertaining during the holidays. Or eat smaller portions or different foods if only eating will do. If you're not sure what triggers your eating, keep a food diary for a week or two. *"Dear Diary" on page 37 offers some tips for doing so.*

KITCHEN NUTRITION
holiday meals go lean!

Holiday menus—or almost any meal—may be modified to lower the calories and the fat content. Often the differences go almost unnoticed. Compare this traditional menu with its leaner version. Then refer to chapter 14 for tips on trimming calories and fat in food preparation.

ORIGINAL MENU	LEANER MENU
3 oz. skinless roast duck breast	3 oz. skinless roast turkey
1/2 cup stuffing	1/2 cup wild rice pilaf
1/2 cup broccoli with 2 Tbsp. hollandaise sauce	1/2 cup broccoli with lemon juice
1/4 cup cranberry relish	1/4 cup cranberry relish
1 medium crescent roll	1 fresh whole-grain roll
1 slice pecan pie	1 slice pumpkin pie
Total calories: 1,320	Total calories: 805
Total fat: 70 grams	Total fat: 20 grams

Party "Tid-Bites"

Celebrate! Food is one of the pleasures of parties, holiday festivities, and other social gatherings. Just because you're trying to eat healthfully doesn't mean you need to avoid celebrations or accept a few extra party pounds. Any foods—even traditional holiday treats—can fit into a healthful eating plan for the calorie conscious. The secret is moderation and balance.

Whether a stand-up event or a sit-down dinner, these party tips can help you hold the line:

Be realistic. Trying to lose weight during the holidays may be a self-defeating goal. Instead strive to maintain your weight.

Balance party eating with other meals. Eat small, lower-calorie meals during the day so you can enjoy celebration foods, too—without overdoing your energy intake for the day.

Take the edge off your hunger before a party. Eat a small, low-fat snack, such as fruit or a bagel. Feeling hungry can sabotage even the strongest willpower!

When you arrive at a party, avoid rushing to the food. Greet people you know—conversation is calorie-free! Get a beverage, and settle into the festivities before eating. You may eat less.

Ask for sparkling water and a lime twist rather than wine, champagne, or a mixed drink. Sparkling water doesn't supply calories.

Move your socializing away from the buffet table. Conversations take your attention away from food. Unconscious nibbling becomes too easy.

Make just one trip to the party buffet. And be selective. Choose only the foods you really want to eat and keep portions small. Often just a taste satisfies a craving or curiosity.

Opt for lower-calorie party foods. Perhaps enjoy raw vegetables with a small dollop of dip, just enough to coat the end of the vegetable. Try boiled shrimp or scallops with cocktail sauce or lemon. Go easy on fried appetizers and cheese cubes.

If you're bringing a dish, make it healthfully delicious. That way, you'll know there's something more healthful you can munch on. Perhaps bring raw vegetables with a yogurt or cottage cheese dip, or bring a platter of juicy, fresh fruit.

Enjoying a sit-down dinner party? Make your first helping small. If your host or hostess expects you to take seconds, the total amount may be about the same as your normal-size portions.

Forget the all-or-nothing mindset. Depriving yourself of special holiday foods, or feeling guilty when you do enjoy them, isn't part of a healthy eating strategy. And deprivation and guilt certainly are not part of the holiday spirit!

When you're entertaining, make over your menus with fewer calories and fat. Your guests probably won't detect the difference. *For a holiday dinner makeover, refer to page 38, "Kitchen Nutrition: Holiday Meals Go Lean!"*

Have fun! Sharing food is part of many celebrations. Enjoying a traditional holiday meal or party foods with family and friends doesn't need to destroy healthful food habits you've nurtured all year long.

Motivation Boosters

With weight control as part of your lifestyle, food choices for a healthful diet and physical activity become second nature. But when you need a boost to stay on track, try these strategies:

Make lifestyle changes with a friend or family member! A partner increases the enjoyment factor of physical activity and healthful eating.

Enlist support. Family and friends can help you keep on track. Those who have the support of

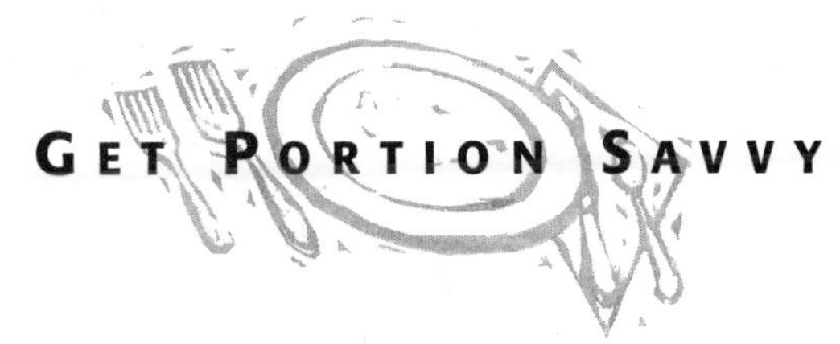

GET PORTION SAVVY

"It's not too big. It's not too small. It's just right!" As a weight management strategy, keep tabs on portion sizes. The portion, or serving size, determines the number of calories. Even low-fat foods—for example, pasta, rice, beans, or potatoes—can add up to a hefty calorie count when portions get big.

How portion savvy are you? Without using a measuring cup, try pouring one cup of dry cereal—or scooping a half-cup of ice cream—into a bowl. Now check using a measuring cup. Chances are, you've overestimated. Most people do. That's why many people quite innocently overdo their calorie intake.

The Food Guide Pyramid offers standard serving sizes as part of its guideline for healthy eating. *"Sizing Up Healthful Servings" on page 245 tells what they are.* Use measuring cups and spoons, and perhaps a kitchen scale to compare your helpings with these serving sizes or the serving sizes listed on the Nutrition Facts panel of food labels. ✦

family members, particularly a spouse, more likely manage their weight successfully. Watch out for those who attempt to sabotage your efforts. If it's right for you, join a support group.

Please yourself. Remember, the most important reason to maintain your healthy weight is you.

Track your progress—but not too often. Avoid the urge to step onto the scale every day. Once a week is often enough. Since weight fluctuates from day to day due to fluid loss and retention, you may not get a true picture if you weigh yourself too frequently.

For women, weight gain from water retention may be a normal part of a monthly menstrual cycle. Usually that passes in a few days.

Celebrate any success. Weight loss doesn't need to be an all-or-nothing venture. If you've been carrying around excess pounds, even small changes can make a difference in your health and reduce your risk for disease.

Enjoy how good your healthy weight feels. You may reward yourself with a new garment, a bouquet of flowers, a new music CD, or a special outing. Still there's no greater motivation than knowing you're in control and caring for you!

Too Thin—A Problem?

Maybe. Being too thin can be a health risk, especially if being underweight results from undereating. An eating pattern with too few calories may not supply the nutrients a person needs to keep his or her body running normally. Children who undereat may not get enough nutrients or energy for growth and development either. A lack of food energy may cause fatigue, irritability, and lack of concentration. And those with a poor diet may have trouble warding off infections.

For normal weight people, a layer of body fat just under the skin helps protect the body from cold. But very thin people have only a very thin fat layer, so lack insulation to keep them warm. That becomes an increasing problem for the thin, frail elderly, especially if they don't have adequate heating in their homes.

If you lose weight suddenly and don't know the cause, talk to your doctor. This may be an early symptom of other health problems.

When You Want to Gain

There's plenty written about weight loss; that's because it's a common problem. However, under some circumstances, people may need to gain weight. For some people weight gain is as hard as weight loss is for others!

The obvious approach for weight gain is this—consume more energy than your body burns. For every pound of body weight you gain, you need to consume 3,500 calories more than your body burns. As with weight loss, do so in a healthful way.

***Follow the guidelines of the* Food Guide Pyramid—** and eat more servings from the five major food groups. Go for the higher end of the serving ranges. Trying to gain weight by overdoing food from the Pyramid tip and other high-fat foods isn't the answer, even for someone who's thin!

Stick to the guideline: no more than 30 percent calories from fat, unless your doctor advises more. Controlling fat in your eating is good for your heart, in fact for your whole body, not just your weight.

Choose some foods with concentrated calories. That way you won't need to increase the volume of food too much. Try dried fruits or fruits canned in heavy syrup, instead of fresh fruits. Fortify soups, casseroles, and fluid milk with dry milk powder. Enjoy some higher-calorie condiments, such as a dollop of sour cream on a baked potato. Garnish salads with olives, avocados, and cheese, which have more calories.

Eat more frequently—five to six small meals a day—if your appetite is small. For example, eat breakfast at 7 a.m. and again at 10 a.m. Eating two or three large meals during the day may be too much to handle at one time.

Drink fluids 30 minutes before and after meals—not with meals. By limiting beverages at mealtime, you'll have more room for food.

Focus on nutrient-rich foods and beverages. Don't fill up on low- and no-calorie foods or drinks, such as diet sodas or hard candies. Rather than coffee, tea, and water, drink juice, milk, and milk shakes.

Enjoy a snack before bedtime.

Stimulate your appetite if you just don't feel like eating. *Refer to* "No Appetite?" *on this page for ideas.*

Use the Nutrition Facts information on the food label. The label can help you choose nutrient-rich foods which also supply the calories you need. *See page* 270, *"Today's Food Labels" for more on label reading.*

Try a commercial supplement. Or make your own shake or nog if you can't get enough calories from your regular meals and snacks. Check with your doctor or registered dietitian for guidance.

Ask a registered dietitian for more guidance on choosing healthful foods for weight gain. *Refer to page* 580, *"How to Find Nutrition Help" for tips on finding a qualified nutrition expert in your area.*

Note: The suggestions indicated here are not meant for people with eating disorders, whose weight problems are complex and often life threatening.

(*Adapted from*: Pass the Calories, Please! *by Gail Farmer, Chicago*: *The American Dietetic Association,* 1994.)

No Appetite?

People lose their appetite for all kinds of reasons: illness, pain, fatigue, depression, stress, medication, or disease, or a combination of these. The appetite control center of your brain might be affected, signaling that you're not hungry even when you should be. You may lose your appetite and tolerance for food when you're sick—even though you need nourishment to get well. Or emotional stress may affect your desire for and ability to handle food.

Cope with a loss of appetite. Eat by the clock rather than by hunger. It may be easier to consume all the calories you need. Take advantage of the "up" times. When you feel well and your appetite is good, eat and enjoy! And try these ideas for stimulating your appetite:

Add some pizzazz to your foods! Colorful foods, appealing texture, and an appetizing aroma are helpful aids to increasing food intake.

Become involved in food selection and preparation.

Drink a glass of beer or wine before meals. This often gives your appetite a jump-start. But check with your doctor first.

Eat meals with friends. The pleasure of being with others may be an appetite booster.

Fill the house with enticing food aromas, such as freshly-baked bread, cake, or cookies.

Keep favorite foods on hand for meals and snacks. You may eat more when food is readily available.

Make mealtimes pleasant. A relaxed and attractive setting with soft music or flowers on the table may perk up your appetite.

Try eating your meal away from the dining room table, such as picnic style in the living room or at a candle-lit table in front of the fireplace. Sometimes a change of pace helps.

Plan for longer meal times. Don't schedule activities close to meals.

Walk before meals. A short walk often helps stimulate appetites.

Stay away from unpleasant or unsettling topics of conversation at mealtimes—especially if stress is a problem for you .

(*Adapted from*: Pass the Calories, Please! *by Gail Farmer, Chicago*: *The American Dietetic Association,* 1994.)

Eating Disorders: Problems, Signs, and Help

An estimated one million or more Americans suffer from eating disorders. Between 5 and 20 percent will die from medical complications as a result. Eating disorders—anorexia nervosa and bulimia—are actually distorted eating habits, often related to emotional problems. Anorexia typically results in low body weight. It's linked to menstrual irregularity, osteoporosis in women, and greater risk of early death in women and men. Bulimia may or may not be linked to low body weight. Both require qualified medical care, including psychiatric and nutrition counseling.

Anorexia and Bulimia: What Are They?

Anorexia nervosa is sometimes called the "starvation sickness." Obsessed with food, weight, and thinness, people suffering from anorexia deny their hunger and refuse to eat—even after extreme weight loss. As they consume too few calories for their basic needs, their bodies slowly waste away. By starving themselves, people with anorexia don't get the nutrients they need for normal body functions.

THREE THINGS TO KNOW ABOUT EATING DISORDERS

Experts aren't certain about the exact causes of eating disorders. But they do agree on these key points:

- Food itself is not the primary problem. Instead it's a symptom of serious distress.
- Early detection is crucial. The sooner the person gets help, the better the chance for permanent recovery.
- Help is available. Team treatment, including medical and dental care, psychotherapy, nutrition education, and family counseling, provides the best results. ✦

Bulimia is marked by binge eating and purging. The person gorges, usually on high-calorie foods, and then intentionally vomits or uses laxatives or diuretics. A diuretic increases urine production. The consequences are serious: dehydration, organ damage, internal bleeding from the stress of vomiting, tooth decay from acids in vomit, and in some cases, death.

Many people with eating disorders alternate between anorexia and bulimia. Reports indicate that 60 percent of people who have dieted extensively or starved themselves resort to binging and purging to keep their weight off.

When does an eating disorder start? Generally it begins with an ordinary weight-loss diet, begun either just before or after a major life change or trauma. However, there's no clear understanding of the exact causes.

We do know, however, that eating disorders are more than food problems. The person's whole life—schoolwork or career, family life, day to day patterns, emotions, growth, overall health—gets wrapped in the eating issues.

Who's at Risk?

People of most any age and either gender may develop an eating disorder. However, some groups of people are more at risk than others.

- Females clearly are the most susceptible. In fact, approximately 95 percent of all people with anorexia are women.
- Adolescents are at particular risk. Estimates indicate that as many as one out of every 250 teenage girls will develop at least some symptoms of anorexia.
- Athletes, such as dancers and gymnasts, who must control their weight, are susceptible.
- Eating disorders are being increasingly identified in males, as well as in adults and even in children as young as 8-, 9-, and 10-years old.

Eating Disorders: The Warning Signs
Eating disorders produce warning signs. If you or someone you know shows any combination of these symptoms, be concerned!

People with anorexia may:

- Eat tiny portions, refuse to eat, and deny they are hungry.
- Show abnormal weight loss—as much as 15 percent or more of body weight—or a large weight loss in a short time span.
- Act hyperactive, depressed, moody, and insecure.
- Have an intense fear of being fat.
- See themselves as fat, wanting to lose more weight, even when they are very thin.
- Exercise excessively and compulsively.
- Suffer from constipation and irregular menstrual periods.
- Develop fine, downy hair on their arms and face.
- Complain of nausea or bloating after eating normal amounts of food.
- Binge eat, then purge, perhaps by vomiting or using laxatives or diuretics.

People with bulimia may:

- Become secret eaters.
- Disappear after eating—often to the bathroom.
- Show great fluctuations in weight, and may be normal weight or may be overweight.
- Feel out of control when eating.
- Eat enormous meals, but not gain weight.
- Feel ashamed and depressed after gorging.
- Have swollen parotid glands. The parotid glands, located near the ears, are one of the salivary glands.
- Experience irregular menstrual periods.
- Binge eat, then purge.
- Abuse alcohol or drugs.
- Become dependent on laxatives, diuretics, emetics, or diet pills to lose weight. Emetics, such as syrup of ipecac, induce vomiting.
- Develop dental problems caused by acid from vomiting. Acids eat away at tooth enamel.

What to Do
If you suspect a friend or family member has anorexia or bulimia, don't wait until a severe weight loss or a serious medical problem proves you are right. There's plenty you can do before that happens:

Act to get help. Speak to the person about your concern. Enlist assistance from family and friends. Talk to medical professionals, a social worker, or the school nurse or counselor if the person is a student. Call your local mental health association. A registered dietitian can also give you an expert perspective on eating disorders. *Refer to page* 580, "*How to Find Nutrition Help,*" *to locate a registered dietitian in your area.*

The best treatment for an eating disorder combines medical, psychological, and nutrition counseling. Participation in self-help groups for the patient, as well as group counseling for family members, is an important part of treatment.

Expect resistance. A person with anorexia usually doesn't believe that he or she needs assistance or is in any danger. Someone with bulimia may acknowledge the problem, but still refuse to seek help. But the faster he or she gets help, the greater the chances for full recovery.

Prepare for long-term treatment. Recovery may take from several months to several years. Symptoms and attitudes of eating disorders rarely disappear quickly. Family support groups are particularly effective in helping relatives of people with anorexia or bulimia survive the long ordeal.

"Diets" That Don't Work!

Every year Americans spend more than $30 billion in the weight-loss industry—often for diet plans and gimmicks that don't work! The lure of quick, easy weight loss is hard to resist, especially for those unwilling to make a commitment to lifelong behavioral change. Although the diets are ineffective, weight-loss hopefuls willingly give the next craze a chance. The result? Wasted money, weight regained, a feeling of failure, and perhaps damage to health.

For those who try one fad diet after another, weight cycling becomes a common problem. *Refer to "Weight Cycling—The 'Yo-Yo' Problem," on page* 30.

"Magical" Food Diets

The "grapefruit diet," the "all-you-can-eat fruit diet," the "rice diet," "the cabbage soup diet"! There's a weight-loss diet for almost every taste.

Single food or single food group diets don't work for several reasons, however. They lack variety. They don't provide adequate amounts of all the nutrients the body needs for health. And the dieter runs the risk of overeating the foods featured on the so-called diet plan. But because these diets don't teach new eating habits either, people usually don't stick with them anyway.

High-Protein Diets

A high-protein diet doesn't build muscle and burn fat as some people think. Only regular physical activity and training builds muscle strength. While athletes may need slightly higher levels of protein, diets that focus on protein-rich foods, such as meat, poultry, fish, eggs, and dairy foods, may be missing nutrients from fruits, vegetables, and grain products. In other words, the diet may lack certain vitamins and minerals, as well as complex carbohydrate and fiber. One obvious result of replacing carbohydrate food sources with protein-rich foods is that the body has less energy—a serious problem for athletes.

Depending on the protein sources chosen, the diet may also be high in fat and calories since fat contains twice the calories per gram as protein and carbohydrate. Cholesterol and saturated fat may be high, too. Very high protein diets also can put a strain on the liver and kidneys. For those who do lose, rapid weight loss may be water loss, not body fat. And a diet low in carbohydrates may cause a condition called ketosis with symptoms of weakness, nausea, and dehydration. This diet plan isn't a healthy eating plan for life-long health!

High-Fiber, Low-Calorie Diets

Most of us need more fiber to promote good health. Twenty-five to 30 grams of fiber daily is recommended. Too much—perhaps resulting from fiber supplements—may be too much of a good thing.

As a component of food, fiber isn't absorbed by the body; therefore, it doesn't contribute calories. That's why high-fiber foods, such as whole grains, vegetables, legumes, and fruits are included in weight-loss diets. Their high-fiber content makes these diets quite filling.

Yet, very high fiber diets also may come up short on protein foods. An excessively high fiber diet can cause constipation and dehydration if extra fluids aren't consumed.

Bulk fillers, which are high in fiber, aren't advised. They reduce hunger by first absorbing liquid, then swelling up in the stomach. These products can be harmful when they obstruct the digestive tract. *Refer to "About Fiber Pills and Powders..." on page* 151.

Moderation of dietary fiber is a more healthful approach to weight loss. Adding fiber to a healthful weight-loss plan—one that doesn't go below 1,600 calories per day—is a smart idea!

Very Low Calorie Liquid Diets

Low-calorie liquid formulas were developed for short-term use under the supervision of a physician. For some people, they serve a purpose—if nutrition education also teaches new eating habits. Used as a liquid diet without other foods, they're very low in calories—providing just 300 to 800 calories a day.

Several years ago, these formulas were changed after deaths were attributed to their use. Newer formulas have more vitamins, minerals, and high-quality protein.

What are the problems of liquid diets? Without medical supervision and nutrition education, they don't teach new ways of eating food. So people usually don't stay with them—and there's usually no long-term weight loss. They also may result in fatigue, constipation, nausea, diarrhea, or hair loss.

Fasting

Fasting has been touted as a tactic for jump-starting weight-loss. As with very low calorie diets, however, fasting deprives the body of energy and nutrients needed for normal functions. Any rapid weight loss is mostly water and muscle loss. Fasting also may cause fatigue and dizziness—with less energy for being active. And it feeds the cycle of "yo-yo" dieting.

As an aside, there's a misconception that fasting "cleans out" the system, removing toxic wastes. To the contrary, body chemicals called ketones build up in the body when carbohydrates aren't available for energy. Ketosis puts a burden on the kidneys; ketones that accumulate can be harmful to health.

Gimmicks, Gadgets, and Other "Miracles"

Promoters advertise the "great wonders of the weight-loss world"—appetite-suppressing eyeglasses, magic weight-loss earrings, diet patches, electric muscle stimulators, spirulina (a species of blue-green algae), starch and fat blockers, creams that melt fat away, and many, many others. Some sound almost amusing.

All these products really have been offered for sale and purport to promote weight loss. Yet none prove effective. Some even may be harmful. And they're all a waste of money!

For instance, the popular press often advertises massages and other therapies for getting rid of so-called "cellulite." But there's nothing unique about dimpled fat on thighs and hips. Cellulite is simply normal body fat under the skin that looks lumpy when the fat layer gets thick, allowing connective, fibrous-looking tissue that holds fat in place to show. The lumpy look can disappear with normal weight loss.

You've also probably seen weight-loss programs based on sweating off extra weight. Sweating in a sauna—or wearing a rubber belt or nylon clothes that make you perspire during exercise—may cause weight loss. However, the pounds that disappear come from water loss, not body fat. As soon as you drink or eat, weight returns to normal.

Instead of helping to achieve a healthful weight goal, "sweating off" pounds may damage health through dehydration. *Refer to chapter 8, "Fluids: Often Overlooked," for more about dehydration and the body's need for water.*

EAT WHAT YOU CRAVE!

If the sight of certain foods puts your mind into a tailspin, you may need to readjust your approach to eating. An overly-restrictive diet may "feed" a food craving—and set you up to overindulge!

The jury is still out on the true cause of food cravings. It may be physiological, psychological, or both. We don't yet know if food cravings are linked to a need to resupply the body with nutrients it lacks or if cravings are reinforced by positive emotional and social links to certain foods.

Studies do suggest that avoiding certain foods altogether often makes them irresistible. The result? Giving in to a food craving, and perhaps overeating. Then guilt creeps in, and people try to resist those foods once again, only to overindulge and feel guilty again.

What's the better approach? Eat a small portion of any food you enjoy—even if it's higher in fat or calories. Even when you're trying to shed pounds, you can enjoy high-calorie foods, as long as your eating plan is varied, balanced, and moderate. As another option, try to satisfy your palate with a low-fat, low-calorie version. ✦

When You Need Help...

If you have weight problems of any kind or more questions about controlling your own weight, it's OK to seek outside advice and help. But be wary. Not every weight-loss "professional" is qualified to give the help you need. Steer clear of weight-loss programs and products that offer claims for quick fixes. They often promise far more than they actually can deliver.

have you ever *wondered*

... if diet pills help with weight loss? Over-the-counter diet pills, or appetite suppressants, work by curbing the appetite, but usually just for a few weeks. Some have unpleasant side effects and some can be addictive, with potential damage to the heart and nervous system. They may be prescribed to help a person start a lifelong program for weight management, but they're not a substitute for adopting healthful eating habits over the long term. They should never be taken for very long—and only under a doctor's supervision.

... if obesity can be controlled with medication? Researchers are currently studying the possibilities of treating obesity with drugs. The drugs being studied may be able to control obesity by various actions, including suppressing appetite through natural hormones, increasing the body's inner thermostat to burn more calories, and reducing the absorption of dietary fat. There's still a lot to learn about the potential benefits and risks of these medications.

... if your stomach shrinks when you eat less? No, your body doesn't work that way. Although your stomach can expand to accommodate a large intake of food, it doesn't stretch out indefinitely. As food passes to your intestines, the stomach goes back to its normal size. When you cut back on calories, your stomach keeps its normal size, even if your appetite isn't as big. ✦

First and foremost, choose a program that suits your personality and lifestyle. In addition, find a program with a maintenance plan that includes physical activity and counseling that focuses on realistic behavioral changes. In the end, you supply your own motivation, but the plan must promote your good health. Above all, choose a plan you can live with. *Refer to the checklist on this page, "Questions to Ask...About Diet Programs" as a way to judge a weight management plan.*

If you need help finding a weight-control program, talk with a registered dietitian. A registered dietitian is trained to help you figure out what kind of weight-management system will fit with your lifestyle.

For more help in finding a qualified nutrition professional or reliable information about nutrition and health, refer to page 580, "How to Find Nutrition Help."

Questions to Ask... About Diet Programs

Millions of Americans participate in organized weight-loss programs each year. Many are run by qualified medical and nutrition experts and can effectively help their clients lose weight and keep it off permanently. However, others make overblown claims and tout products that are ineffective and costly, and their staff may not have appropriate credentials. Before you sign on the dotted line, ask questions like these:

What are the approach and goals of the program?

What are the health risks?

How will you assess my health status before recommending the program? Many programs recommend a medical check-up before starting.

Will the program include instruction, guidance, and skill building to help me learn to eat in a more healthful way—for the long term? How?

Will the program include guidance on physical activity—again for a lifetime? How?

What data can you show me that proves your program actually works? What has been written about the program's success besides individual testimonials?

Do customers keep off the weight after they leave the diet program? Ask for results over two to five years. The Federal Trade Commission requires weight-loss companies to back up their claims.

What are the costs for membership, weekly fees, food, supplements, maintenance, and counseling? What's the payment schedule? Are any costs covered under health insurance? Do you give refunds if I drop out?

Will you monitor my success at three- to six-month intervals, then modify the program if needed?

Do you have a maintenance program? Is it part of the package or does it cost extra?

What kind of professional support is provided? What are the credentials and experiences of these professionals? (Detailed information should be available on request.)

What are the program's requirements? Are there special menus or foods, counseling visits, or exercise plans?

For more guidance on evaluating a weight-control plan, refer to "Check It Out!" on page 35.

SPOTTING A FRAUD

Does it sound too good to be true? Then it probably is! Be wary. Over the years, promoters of fraudulent weight-loss schemes have laced their claims with words and phrases like these:

ancient	*guaranteed*
breakthrough	*magical*
discovered in Europe	*miraculous*
cure	*mysterious*
easy	*new discovery*
effortless	*quick*
exotic	*secret*

have you ever *wondered*

... *if foods described as "nonfat" are "nonfattening"*? Not necessarily. A food that is fat-free may still be high in calories. You need to read the Nutrition Facts on the food label to find out. Even then, no food by itself is fattening. What you eat over several days may tip the scale toward weight gain. *To learn how to read a food label, refer to page* 270, *"Today's Food Labels."*

... *if surgery and liposuction were options for weight loss*? No, not for most people. Gastric bypass surgery, done by shortening the small intestine or by making the stomach smaller, does promote weight loss. However, because the side effects can be harmful, doctors rarely advise surgery—and then only as a final resort in life-threatening situations when other approaches haven't worked. Liposuction, the surgical removal of fat tissue from various body areas, is often only a short-term solution. If eating and exercise habits remain the same, it's likely that the weight will be regained.

... *if every person's body has a unique setpoint, or a preset weight that it tries to return to*? That's a theory without conclusive evidence. Even if a setpoint exists, it's probably a range that can be set a little lower with more physical activity and food choices with fewer calories and fat. Or for someone who's too thin, eating a few extra calories may help adjust the setpoint a bit higher.

... *what to do when your weight seems to hit a plateau*? Be patient. Plateaus are a normal part of weight loss. Your body requires fewer calories to function as you lose weight. Allow time to readjust. Gradually adding more activity may help nudge you off the weight-loss plateau.

... *if you should join a support group to lose weight*? Perhaps, but that's an individual matter. Weight-loss organizations and support groups often educate participants as they offer psychological support. And many, but not all, are coordinated by qualified nutrition experts. *The information on page* 46, *"Questions to Ask... About Diet Programs," can help you judge*. For some people, peer support offers motivation, especially if they pay to attend the program. There's a downside, however. Without a weight maintenance program, many people gain weight again when they're no longer in the group.

... *why it seemed easy to lose weight in your teens and* 20s, *and why it's so hard now*? There could be several reasons why it seems harder as an adult—a less active lifestyle, different eating habits, or changes in your body. Although metabolism slows during each decade of your adult years, increased physical activity can boost the rate at which your body uses energy for your basic energy needs. Many past attempts at dieting may complicate the picture, too. Low-calorie diets help you shed fat and some muscle tissue. But when you regain weight, you tend to regain it as fat. Because fat tissue requires fewer calories to maintain than muscle does, you need to cut calories even more. The remedy? Exercise. It burns fat and can build muscle, making weight loss easier.

... *can you lose weight just by counting fat grams*? Maybe. High-fat foods tend to be high-calorie foods. But you'll only lose weight if you don't compensate by eating more of other foods. ✦

your nutrition check-up

Weight Loss Readiness Test

Are you ready to lose weight? Your attitude affects your ability to succeed. Take this readiness quiz to learn if you need to adjust your attitude before you begin.

Mark each statement as "true" or "false." Be honest with yourself! The answers should reflect the way you really think—not how you'd like to be!

1. ___I have thought a lot about my eating habits and physical activities. And I know what I might change.
2. ___I know that I need to make permanent, not temporary, changes in my eating and activity patterns.
3. ___I will only feel successful if I lose a lot of weight.
4. ___I know that it's best if I lose weight slowly.
5. ___I'm thinking about losing weight now because I really want to, not because someone else thinks I should.
6. ___I think losing weight would solve other problems in my life.
7. ___I am willing and able to increase my regular physical activity.
8. ___I can lose weight successfully if I have no "slipups."
9. ___I am willing to commit time and effort each week to organize and plan my food and activity choices.
10. __Once I lose a few pounds but reach a plateau (can't seem to lose more), I usually lose the motivation to keep going toward my weight goal.
11. __I want to start a weight-loss program, even though my life is unusually stressful right now.

Now Score Yourself

Look at your answers for items 1, 2, 4, 5, 7, and 9. Score "1" if you answered "true" and "0" if you answered "false." For items 3, 6, 8, 10, and 11, score "0" for each "true" answer and "1" for each false answer. Total your points.

No one score indicates if you're ready or not to start losing weight. But the higher your total score, the more likely you'll be successful.

If you scored 8 or higher, you probably have good reasons to lose weight now. And you know some of the steps that can help you succeed.

If you scored 5 to 7 points, you may need to reevaluate your reasons for losing weight and the strategies you'd follow.

If you scored 4 or less, now may not be the right time for you to lose weight. You may be successful initially. But you may not be able to sustain the effort to reach or maintain your weight goal. Reconsider your reasons and approach, then try again.

your nutrition check-up (continued)

Interpret your Score

Your answers can clue you in on some stumbling blocks to your weight loss success. Any item you scored as "0" suggests a misconception about weight loss, or a problem area for you. So let's look at each item a bit more closely.

1. You can't change what you don't understand. To learn more about your eating habits and activity pattern, keep records for a week. Record what, when, and why you eat—and any obstacles to regular physical activity, too.

2. You may be able to lose weight in the short-run with drastic or highly-restrictive changes in your eating habits or activity pattern. But they may be hard to live with permanently. Your food and activity plans should be healthful ones you can sustain and enjoy.

3. Many people fantasize about reaching a weight goal that's unrealistically low. If that sounds like you, rethink your meaning of success. A reasonable goal takes body type into consideration—and sets smaller, achievable "mile markers" along the way. Successful, realistic weight loss can be comfortably maintained through sensible eating and regular activity.

4. If you equate success with fast weight loss, you'll have problems keeping weight off. This "quick fix" attitude can backfire when you face the challenges of weight maintenance. The best and healthiest approach is to lose weight slowly while learning strategies to keep weight off permanently.

5. To be successful, the desire for and commitment to weight loss must come from you—not your best friend or a family member. People who lose weight, then keep it off, take responsibility for their weight goals and choose their own approach. Then friends and family become an important source of support.

6. Being overweight may contribute to some social problems, but it's rarely the single cause. Thinking you can solve all your problems by losing weight isn't realistic. And it may set you up for disappointment. While body image and self-esteem are strongly linked, it's most important to feel good about your body, which in turn can motivate you to maintain healthy behaviors.

7. A habit of regular, moderate physical activity is a key factor to successfully losing weight—and keeping it off. For weight control, exercise doesn't need to be strenuous to be effective. Any moderate physical activity that you enjoy and will do regularly counts. Just get moving and keep moving!

8. Most people don't expect perfection in their daily lives. Yet, they often feel they must stick to a weight-loss program perfectly. Perfection at weight loss isn't realistic. Rather than view lapses as catastrophes, see them as opportunities to find what triggers your problems and develop strategies for the future.

9. To successfully lose weight, you must take time to assess your problem areas, then develop the approach that's best for you. Success requires planning, commitment, and time.

10. First of all, a plateau in an ongoing weight-loss program is perfectly OK—and normal. So don't give up too soon! Before you lose your motivation, think about any past efforts that have failed, then identify strategies that can help you overcome those hurdles.

11. Weight loss itself can be a source of stress. So if you're already under stress, you may find a weight-loss program somewhat difficult to implement right now. Try to resolve other stressors in your life before starting your weight-loss effort.

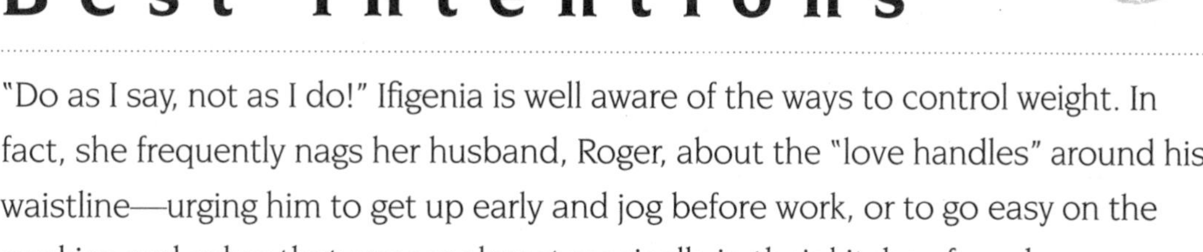

real life nutrition

Best Intentions

"Do as I say, not as I do!" Ifigenia is well aware of the ways to control weight. In fact, she frequently nags her husband, Roger, about the "love handles" around his waistline—urging him to get up early and jog before work, or to go easy on the cookies and cakes that appear almost magically in their kitchen from her mom. He promises to try harder—if she thinks he needs to.

But she groans about the flab that's beginning to appear around her own hips, too. "I never used to have this problem. Thank goodness for loose clothing. I just need to get away from my computer and get some exercise. Maybe tomorrow," she thinks, as she handles yet another rush memo that appears on her computer via E-mail—and once more eats lunch sitting at her desk.

Going through her mail at home that evening, she sees what may be her solution—an easy way to melt pounds away. It says, "No need for exercise. Just focus on fruits, vegetables, and salads, and send for this diet supplement." She puts that on her immediate "do list," before taking the fried chicken dinner she bought on the way home out of the bag.

Advice for achieving and maintaining healthy weight:

- As people get older, they often gain weight, partly from a slower metabolic rate and partly from their lifestyle. With more exercise and perhaps a shift in eating habits, Ifigenia might be able to trim a few pounds—and certainly avoid gaining more.

- Trying to please Ifigenia certainly is a good reason for Roger to keep tab on his weight. However, he may be more successful with his own internal motivation—good health for his own sake!

- Jogging or brisk walking would be good early-morning exercise for Roger and for Ifigenia, too. Getting some physical activity together might be a good inducement for sticking with an early morning plan for physical activity. Without physical activity it's hard to maintain a healthy weight!

- Ifigenia might include more physical activity in her work day—walking during her lunch hour; using the steps at the office, not the elevator; or taking a mid-afternoon break to walk to the mailbox. In any case, Ifigenia and Roger need to make physical activity a part of their everyday life—with at least 30 minutes of moderate activity almost daily.

- Eating at a desk isn't a habit that encourages good nutrition. Ifigenia would be wise to take a break for a healthful lunch. Besides, getting away from her desk would be good for her head—she'd approach work in the afternoon with a fresh perspective!

real life nutrition (continued)

➢ Ifigenia may need to rethink her food choices. If high-fat meals such as the fried chicken dinner are the norm, calories may be too high. Fat is a concentrated energy source. She needs to find easy ways to serve foods with less fat.

➢ Ifigenia shouldn't fall prey to quick weight loss plans. A diet plan that focuses on just a few foods won't teach her a new way of eating—even if they are fruits and vegetables. She'll probably abandon the plan quickly and regain any weight she loses. What's more, the plan requires buying a supplement that may not only be a waste of money, but may not promote her overall good health in the long run.

Chapter Three

Fat Facts

Fat is a hot topic! For the past decade, health issues related to fat and cholesterol have captured the attention of the general public. Dietary recommendations from health experts advise lowering the total fat, saturated fat, and cholesterol in our diets. Media stories continually report findings from new research studies on the connections between fat, cholesterol, and health. Nutrition books, cookbooks, and magazine articles tout low-fat messages. The food industry continues to launch reduced-fat and fat-free food products. Food packages themselves provide information about fat and cholesterol. Not surprisingly, many people are making a "change of plate," learning to prepare and choose foods with less fat.

While other nutrition-related concerns have emerged on the scene, attention to fat likely will be around for some time. Evidence is clear that a high-fat diet relates to many chronic health problems, among them, heart disease, some types of cancer, diabetes, and obesity. More and more aging Baby Boomers are being forced to face the "fat facts of life." And people of all ages are recognizing that a moderate fat intake will promote their good health—for the long run.

Americans already have cut down on their total fat intake. On average, people are consuming about 34 percent of their calories from total fat. While this figure reflects a downward trend in fat intake, there's still room to improve.

Fat Matters

Suppose your doctor said, "You need to get your serum cholesterol level down. Your triglycerides are borderline-high. And cut the fat, especially the saturated fat, in your diet." Just what would all those statements mean to you? And what would you do about them? To understand the role of fat in both health and chronic disease, we need to start with the basics.

Fat: A Nutrient for Health

With all the attention on fat today, you may be surprised to learn that fat isn't the evil that some purport it to be. Instead, it's a nutrient, necessary for your health. In moderate amounts, fat performs a full workload of functions in your body. You actually can't live without it! That's why you should not eat a fat-free diet. You need a moderate amount of fat for health—at least 15 to 20 percent of your overall calories, according to the Food and

Agriculture Organization/World Health Organization. The issue of concern is the total amount and types of fat you consume. So, on the positive side, just how does fat help keep you healthy?

For one, fat works as a partner in your body, supporting the work of other nutrients. Just as sugar dissolves in water, some vitamins dissolve in fat. That's how vitamins A, D, E, and K are carried in food and into your bloodstream. Without fat, these fat-soluble vitamins cannot fully nourish your body. *Read more about these vitamins in chapter* 4, *"Vitamins and Minerals: Enough, But Not Too Much."*

Certain fats are essential, specifically two fatty acids—linoleic acid and linolenic acid—which your body can't make. (Fatty acids are building blocks of fat.) In order for children to grow normally and adults to maintain healthy skin, foods must supply these fatty acids. Both linoleic acid and linolenic acid are widely available in food. If food choices are varied, getting enough of these fatty acids is easy. *For guidelines on fat intake for children, refer to "Fat Facts for Tots," page* 425.

have you ever wondered

...if there's a difference between fat and cholesterol? Yes, there is! Cholesterol is a fat-like substance, but it's not a fat. Cholesterol is only found in foods from animals, including dairy products, butter, egg yolks, meat, fish, and poultry. Cholesterol is not found in vegetable oils, margarine, egg whites, or plant foods like grains, fruits, and vegetables.

...if "low fat" means "low calorie"? No, not necessarily. Fat itself is a concentrated source of energy, or calories. So reducing the fat content may trim calories. But carbohydrate-rich ingredients may take their place and so keep the calorie content up. On packaged foods, read the Nutrition Facts on the food label to find out. Even if the calories are less, go easy on your portion size of low-fat or fat-free foods. Eating a whole box of fat-free cookies isn't a "low calorie" experience! ✦

Like carbohydrate and protein, fat supplies energy, or calories, to power your physical activity and the many body processes that keep you alive. (Remember, a calorie is defined as a unit of energy.) Fat is a concentrated energy source, supplying 9 calories for each fat gram. To compare, carbohydrate and protein provide less than half that amount—just 4 calories per gram.

Your body uses fat for energy, but saves any extra in your body's fatty tissues, mostly in fat cells. Body fat also is known as adipose tissue. When you need an extra energy supply, your body can draw on these fat stores.

A certain amount of body fat also serves other functions: to cushion your body organs and protect them from injury, and to form a fat layer under the skin. This fat layer offers insulation, helping you stay warm on a cold winter day.

Fat in food also helps satisfy hunger by making you feel full after eating. That's because fat takes longer to leave your stomach than either carbohydrate and protein do. And that's why you may feel hungry again within an hour or two of eating a very low-fat meal.

Why Foods Contain Fat

Fat offers qualities that make food taste good. As an ingredient in food, fat carries flavor. It also gives a smooth, creamy texture to foods like ice cream and peanut butter. When foods such as cake or a brownie seem to melt in your mouth, that's just what's happening; the fat is melting! And from meat to baked foods, fat makes many foods moist and tender, or brown and crispy.

But can you cut the fat in a recipe? To a certain extent, yes. The recipe still may work if you use less. But eliminating fat altogether may not give the result you expect. As a recipe ingredient, fat gives food many desirable qualities:

In baked foods. Fat tenderizes; adds moisture; holds in air so baked foods are light; and affects the shape, for example, in cookies. With too little fat, baked goods might be tough or dry, or they may not rise properly.

In sauces. Fat keeps foods from curdling and forms part of an emulsion. An emulsion is a mixture of two substances, such as fat and water, that stay together instead of separating, as they normally would.

In other cooked foods. Fat helps conduct heat as food cooks, for example, when food is sautéed (cooked quickly in a small amount of fat) or fried.

In cooked meat, poultry, and fish. Fat seals in moisture as foods are basted, or brushed with liquid during cooking. Sometimes the surface gets dry if it isn't basted.

For foods cooked in a pan. Fat lubricates the pan so food won't stick.

In all kinds of food. Fat helps carry flavor and nutrients, provides texture (mouth feel), and adds satiety value. Satiety is a feeling of satisfaction.

For tips on modifying the fat content of recipes, refer to page 331, "*Recipes: Judge for Yourself!*"

Sorting the Fats

"Lipids," "fat," "cholesterol," "fatty acids," "triglycerides," "lipoproteins," "hydrogenated," "omega-3s," "trans fatty acids"—the dictionary of fat terms seems endless, often confusing. Just what do all these terms really mean?

Actually, there's no one kind of fat. The term "lipids" refers to all kinds of fatty substances, including fats and cholesterol. A common quality among lipids is that they don't dissolve in water.

"Fat" Dictionary

Lipid: scientific term that refers to fat, cholesterol, and other fat-like substances; lipids do not dissolve in water.

Lipoproteins: protein-coated packages that carry fat in the bloodstream. They may carry cholesterol, too. Without the protein coating, lipids or fat cannot travel through the bloodstream.

Cholesterol: waxy, fat-like substance found in foods of animal origin and in every body cell.

Blood (serum) cholesterol: cholesterol that flows in the bloodstream. The body manufactures most of its blood cholesterol; some is also absorbed from foods you eat.

Have a craving for rich chocolates or desserts? Your "fat tooth," not your "sweet tooth," may account for that urge to indulge.

In this world of high-fat foods, some people may be culturally conditioned to develop a "fat tooth." Appeal for high-fat foods may come from the qualities that fat imparts: for example, a smooth, creamy milk shake; a flaky, tender pastry; and a juicy steak. There may be other reasons, too, why people prefer foods that are rich in fat—or more likely, sweetened fat like that found in many rich desserts. And, on-again-off-again dieting may amplify a fat craving, some studies say.

No matter what the reason for a so-called "fat tooth," you can overcome a preference for fat:

Fool your tastebuds. Get a smooth, creamy consistency with low-fat and fat-free ingredients: low-fat yogurt as a base for savory dips; thick puréed fruit as a dessert sauce; and creamy buttermilk as a base for milk shakes.

Indulge a "fat tooth." Share a rich dessert with someone else to cut your fat grams and calories in half.

Recondition your eating style. *Refer to the tips on page 68, "Trim Fat in Your Eating Style," and gradually shift to a lower-fat diet.* ✦

EAT YOUR OMEGA-3S

There's no doubt about it: seafood can be good for your health. Overall, it has less total fat and less saturated fat than meat and poultry. So eating fish regularly may help lower blood cholesterol levels. Moreover, seafood supplies several vitamins and minerals. Recently, there's been interest in the omega-3 fatty acid content of fish, too.

Omega-3 fatty acids—polyunsaturated fatty acids of a somewhat different structure—are found mostly in seafood, especially higher-fat, cold-water varieties, such as mackerel, albacore tuna, salmon, sardines, and lake trout. Both soybean oil and canola oil supply some omega-3s, too. Although inconclusive, some research suggests that omega-3s may help prevent blood platelets from clotting and sticking to artery walls. As a result, they may help lower the risk for blocked blood vessels and heart attacks. Omega-3s may help prevent arteries from hardening, too.

By themselves, omega-3 fatty acids aren't a magic remedy for heart disease. But combined with other nutritional benefits of eating seafood, they may have a protective effect. To enjoy the benefits, make fish a regular part of your eating style; try to include seafood two or three times a week.

Although fish oil supplements contain omega-3 fatty acids, they're not advised as a substitute for fish or as a dietary supplement. And popping a fish oil capsule won't undo the effects of an otherwise high-fat diet. The safety, effectiveness, and proper dosage for fish oil supplements hasn't been determined. Instead, enjoy fish for its nutritional benefits, flavor—and variety in your eating style. ✦

Dietary cholesterol: cholesterol in food, found only in foods of animal origin, and never in foods from plant sources, even if they contain fat.

HDL-blood cholesterol: cholesterol carried by high-density lipoproteins. So lipids can travel in your blood, they're packed in particles called lipoproteins. HDLs, also known as "good" cholesterol, carry cholesterol away from body tissue, so it can be excreted. HDLs are only in the body, not in food.

LDL-blood cholesterol: cholesterol carried by low-density lipoproteins. LDLs, also known as "bad" cholesterol, carry cholesterol to body tissues and may form deposits on the walls of arteries and other blood vessels. LDLs are only in the body, not in food.

Fat: group of compounds made of glycerol and fatty acids. Fat is one of three main nutrients in food that supply energy; the others are carbohydrate and protein. Fat can also be stored in the body.

Adipose tissue: scientific term for body fat

Dietary fat: fat in food

Triglycerides: scientific name for the common form of fat, found in both the body and in foods. Most body fat is stored in the form of triglycerides. Triglycerides are made of fatty acids.

Fatty acids: basic units of fat molecules, arranged as chains of carbon, hydrogen, and oxygen. Fats are mixtures of different fatty acids.

Monounsaturated fatty acids: fatty acids missing one hydrogen pair on their chemical chain. Foods high in monounsaturated fatty acids are liquid at room temperature. Canola, nut, and olive oils are high in monounsaturated fatty acids.

Polyunsaturated fatty acids: fatty acids missing two or more hydrogen pairs on their chemical chains. Foods high in polyunsaturated fatty acids are liquid or soft at room temperature. Corn, safflower, soybean, and sunflower oils are high in polyunsaturated fatty acids. Fat in seafood is mainly polyunsaturated, too.

Saturated fatty acids: fatty acids that have all the hydrogen they can hold on their chemical chains. They come mainly from animal foods, such as meat, poultry, butter, and whole milk and from coconut, palm, and palm kernel oils. Foods high in saturated fatty acids are firm at room temperature.

Omega-3 fatty acids: fatty acids that are highly polyunsaturated. They are mostly found in seafood, especially higher-fat fish, such as albacore tuna, mackerel, and salmon.

Trans fatty acids: one type of fatty acid, formed during the process of hydrogenation. They're also found naturally in some foods. Most trans fatty acids in the diet come from hydrogenated fats.

Hydrogenated fats: unsaturated fats that are processed to make them stable and solid at room temperature. Hydrogen is added to their chemical makeup and makes them more saturated while extending their shelf life.

Not All Are Created Equal

Whether solid or liquid, fats that we consume are made up of fatty acids and glycerol. Most fats in food are referred to as triglycerides, so named because of their chemical structure. When fats from food are digested, they're broken down into fatty acids and glycerol. In turn, the body uses them to form other lipids, which are used for a variety of functions. When fat is stored in your body, it's in the form of a triglyceride.

In scientific terms, fatty acids are chains of carbon, hydrogen, and oxygen. Fatty acids aren't all the

Fats and Oils: How Do They Compare?

Fats and oils contain a combination of all three types of fatty acids in various proportions. The following chart shows these proportions. You'll notice that coconut oil, palm kernel oil, and butter are composed mainly of saturated fatty acids, while canola, safflower, and sunflower oils are composed primarily of unsaturated fatty acids.

	Cholesterol (mg/Tbsp.)	Saturated Fatty Acid	Monounsaturated Fatty Acid	Polyunsaturated Fatty Acid
Canola oil	0	6%	62%	32%
Safflower oil	0	9%	12%	75%
Sunflower oil	0	10%	20%	66%
Corn oil	0	13%	24%	59%
Olive oil	0	14%	74%	8%
Margarine, soft tub*	0	14%	32%	31%
Margarine, stick*	0	14%	39%	24%
Soybean oil	0	15%	43%	38%
Peanut oil	0	17%	46%	32%
Vegetable shortening	0	25%	45%	26%
Cottonseed oil	0	26%	18%	52%
Chicken fat	11	30%	45%	21%
Lard	12	39%	45%	11%
Palm oil	0	49%	37%	9%
Beef fat (tallow)	14	50%	42%	4%
Cocoa butter	0	60%	33%	3%
Butter	33	62%	29%	4%
Palm kernel oil	0	81%	11%	2%
Coconut oil	0	87%	6%	2%

The sum of the saturated, monounsaturated, and polyunsaturated fatty acids may not equal 100%. This is because some fats contain other components in addition to fatty acids.

** corn and hydrogenated corn oil*

same, however. They differ depending on whether they're saturated or unsaturated. The term "saturation" refers to how many hydrogen atoms link to each carbon in the chain.

➢ When hydrogen is linked to all the carbon atoms on the chain, a fatty acid is saturated.

➢ When hydrogen atoms are missing, the fatty acid is unsaturated. A polyunsaturated fatty acid has two or more missing hydrogen pairs; a monounsaturated fatty acid is missing only one hydrogen pair on its chemical chain.

Now let's apply this bit of chemistry to real life. What, for example, makes margarine different from vegetable oil? Their fatty acid content. No matter what food they're in, all fats are mixtures of fatty acids: saturated, polyunsaturated, and monounsaturated. The proportion of each determines the characteristics of fats and their effect on human health.

➢ Fats made mostly of saturated fatty acids usually are solid at room temperature. Animal products and tropical vegetable oils (coconut, palm kernel, and palm) contain mainly saturated fatty acids. As a general guideline, harder and more stable fats are more saturated. Examples include butter, stick margarine, shortening, and the fat in cheese and meat.

➢ By contrast, fats that contain mostly polyunsaturated fatty acids usually are liquid at room temperature. Safflower, sunflower, corn, and soybean oils contain the highest amounts of polyunsaturated fats.

➢ Foods with mostly monounsaturated fatty acids also are liquid at room temperature. They're found in some vegetable oils, such as canola, olive, and peanut oils.

Coconut oil, palm kernel oil, and butter are composed mainly of saturated fatty acids, while canola, safflower, and sunflower oils are mostly unsaturated fatty acids. *The chart on page 57, "Fats and Oils: How Do They Compare?," shows the proportions of various fatty acids in fats and oils.*

Besides fats and oils, the proportion of fatty acids varies in foods that contain fat. For example, seafood and meat both have saturated and unsaturated fatty acids. However, seafood has a higher proportion of polyunsaturated fatty acids; meat, more saturated fatty acids.

As described, the differences in fatty acid account not only for the varying characteristics of food, for example, liquid oil compared with firm margarine. But their degree of saturation also has a significant role in health. To *reduce your saturated fat intake, see page 72, "For Less Saturated Fat..."*

Hydrogenated: Firmer at Room Temperature
Through processing, it's possible to change the structure of fat, making it more saturated. The

have you ever wondered

...why some margarines are firmer than others? All margarines are made from vegetable oil. In stick margarine, the fatty acids are more hydrogenated, and as a result more firm, than the fatty acids in soft margarine that's sold in tubs or as "squeeze" margarine. Tub and squeeze margarines also contain more water, and sometimes have air whipped in so they'll often be lower in fat and calories. You'll find that butter-margarine blends may be even firmer than stick margarines. This is because of the saturated fatty acids in butter, which help keep the product firm.

...if melting a fat, such as butter, stick margarine, or lard, makes it less saturated? That's an interesting question since unsaturated fats are liquid at room temperature. However, the answer is "no." Simply heating and melting doesn't change the structure of fatty acids. As soon as lard, margarine, or butter is cooled to room temperature, it's solid again.

...what shortening really is? It's simply another term that refers to fat. Although solid at room temperature, it may come from either an animal or a vegetable source. ✦

process is called hydrogenation, so named because missing hydrogen is added to fatty acid chains. As a result, oils become semi-solid and more stable at room temperature. Usually, hydrogenation is partial, making fat anywhere from 5 to 60 percent saturated.

An example is stick margarine, made by hydrogenating vegetable oil. Although they both may be 100 percent corn oil, the stick margarine is firmer than tub margarines. It's been hydrogenated and now has a higher proportion of saturated fatty acids.

As early as 1911, cottonseed oil was hydrogenated to produce vegetable shortening. Today, this process also gives desirable qualities to food. For example, because hydrogenated fats are more stable, the shelf life of some foods, such as crackers and margarine, is extended. For that reason, foods don't develop a rancid flavor and odor as quickly. Hydrogenating the oil in peanut butter gives a creamy consistency; oil stays mixed in and doesn't rise to the top. And stick margarine and vegetable shortening remain firm at room temperature when their oil is partially hydrogenated.

As fats become more saturated during hydrogenation, fatty acids with a different structure form. They're called trans fatty acids. The term "trans" simply describes the chemical makeup of a fatty acid. Although most trans fatty acids come from hydrogenated oil, they also occur naturally in beef, pork, lamb, butter, and milk. Compared with other fats, their contribution to your overall diet is probably quite small.

Lately, there's been discussion about trans fatty acids in hydrogenated fats—and their effect on blood cholesterol levels. There's little scientific evidence to suggest the necessity of cutting back on certain foods only because of trans fatty acids. Even if they do influence blood cholesterol levels, as speculated, the effect is much less than that of saturated fats. Until more is known, health experts still offer the same recommendation: Keep your total fat intake to no more than 30 percent of your overall energy intake and moderate your intake of saturated fats.

By reading food labels, you can tell if a processed food is made with hydrogenated oil, but not necessarily whether it contains trans fatty acids. Look for the term "partially hydrogenated vegetable oil" on the ingredient list for margarine and many prepared foods, cookies, and crackers. Because hydrogenated fat is considered saturated, the amount of hydrogenated fat will be included in the saturated fat total listed on the Nutrition Facts panel of a food label.

Fat: More Than Meets the Eye!

Visible or not, almost all foods contain fat in varying amounts. Some are very high in fat; others have just trace amounts.

The fat content of some foods is obvious: for example, in butter, oil, and margarine. Even in certain cuts of meat and poultry with the skin on, fat is easy to see—and easy to trim off.

In most foods, however, you'll find clues to fat content on food labels. The Nutrition Facts panel tells how much. Salad dressings, many baked foods, chips, crackers, chocolate, nuts, avocados, sauces, meat, poultry, fish, cheese, dairy products, and egg yolks, for example, all have fats in varying amounts. Obviously, fried foods contain more fat than those that are baked or steamed.

have you ever *wondered*

...if olive oil has fewer calories and less fat than butter? Because liquid oils are concentrated, and solid fats may contain other ingredients besides fat, oils generally contain slightly more fat and calories than equal amounts of solid fat. Per tablespoon, olive oil contains about 14 grams of fat and 120 calories compared to butter with about 12 grams of fat and 100 calories. The main difference is in the types of fatty acids. Olive oil has a higher proportion of monounsaturated fatty acids; butter has more saturated fatty acids. ✦

Which foods supply the most fat in the typical American diet?

➢ On average, the greatest amounts of fat in the American diet come directly from fats and oils, as well as salad dressings, candy, gravies, sauces, and other foods from the tip of the Food Guide Pyramid. *Refer to "The Food Guide Pyramid: Your Healthful Eating Guide" on page 243.*

➢ Depending on food choices, meat, poultry, fish, and eggs may account for the next largest amount of fat in an average diet, followed by milk, cheese, yogurt, and frozen desserts.

➢ Fruits, vegetables, and grains don't supply much fat. With only a few exceptions, these foods are high in fat only if fat is added during food preparation or processing, for example, in french fries or in croissants. *The chart on pages 61 to 63 lists amounts of fats and cholesterol in typical foods.*

About Fat Replacers...

You know the value of cutting back on fat, but you also enjoy the taste of your favorite high-fat snacks and other foods. If used to replace full-fat products, not as extras, foods made with fat replacers offer an option for reducing your overall fat intake. They have much of the taste, texture, and appearance of traditional higher-fat foods. Besides being lower in fat, they're usually, but not always, lower in saturated fat, cholesterol, and calories as well.

Fat itself gives unique characteristics to food. So when fat is removed from a "recipe," many characteristics of the food change, too. To give these foods a familiar texture, appearance, and taste, fat replacers often are added.

Food manufacturers use different types of fat replacers—some are carbohydrate-based, some are protein-based, and others are fat-based. Most types contribute calories, although less than if fat was used. Because no fat replacer acts exactly like fat, most reduced-fat and fat-free products contain a mixture of fat replacers.

Fat vs. Fat Replacers: How Does the Fat Content Compare?

	Traditional Food (g fat)	Made with a Fat Replacer (g fat)
margarine, 1 Tbsp.	7 - 12	0 - 6
salad dressing		
creamy, 2 Tbsp.	11 - 21	0 - 8
clear, 2 Tbsp.	5 - 20	0 - 6
mayonnaise, 1 Tbsp.	11	0 - 5
cheese		
hard, 1 ounce	8 - 11	4 - 5
processed, 1 ounce	7 - 9	0 - 4
cream cheese, 2 Tbsp.	9 - 10	0 - 5
sour cream, 1 Tbsp.	3	0 - 1
ice cream, 1/2 cup	7 - 26	0.3 - 2

Source: Pennington, J.A.T. Bowes & Church's Food Values of Portions Commonly Used, 16th Edition. Philadelphia: J.B. Lippincott Company, 1994.

Carbohydrate-based Fat Replacers
Modified starches, dextrins, cellulose, gums, and other carbohydrate ingredients work by combining with water to provide texture, appearance, and mouthfeel that are similar to fat. Fat-free salad dressings, for example, contain carbohydrate-based substitutes. The calories in carbohydrate-based replacers range from almost nothing to 4 calories per gram. The difference is that some, such as modified starches and dextrins, are digested; others, such as cellulose, are barely digestible. Most of these fat replacers can withstand heat; however, they can't be used for frying.

Puréed prunes and applesauce are sometimes used as fat replacers in baked foods. They're an easy fat substitute you can try yourself. Prunes and applesauce add bulk and flavor, too.

Protein-based Fat Replacers
Made with protein from egg whites or skim milk, these fat replacers provide a creamy sensation and improve appearance and texture when fat is removed. Low-fat cheese made with a protein-based substitute gives an appearance and texture that comes close to full-fat cheese. Most protein-based replacers aren't used in foods prepared at high temperatures. That's because the

Primer: Fat, Saturated Fat, and Cholesterol in Food

	Total fat (g)	Saturated fatty acids (g)	Cholesterol (mg)	Calories
BREADS, CEREALS, RICE, PASTA				
Bread, 1 slice				
white	1	trace	trace	70
whole-wheat	1	trace	0	65
Bagel, with egg, 1	1	trace	14	155
Biscuit, 1 medium	3	1	2	105
Roll, dinner, 1	2	trace	0	85
Croissant, 1 medium	12	7	62	230
Muffin, 1 large	6	2	44	185
Pancake, 1 medium	3	1	26	90
Waffle, 1 medium	5	2	39	205
Doughnut, yeast, 1	14	5	21	245
Danish pastry, 1 (2 oz.)	13	4	49	240
Oatmeal, cooked, 1/2 cup	1	trace	0	70
Shredded wheat, 1 large biscuit	trace	trace	0	85
Granola, 1/3 cup	10	2	0	180
Rice, white, cooked, 1/2 cup	trace	trace	0	110
Fried rice (with egg and vegetables), 1/2 cup	6	1	21	120
Cookie, 1 medium				
Oatmeal	3	1	5	60
Chocolate chip	4	1	6	70
Cake, devil's-food, frosted, 1/12 of 8-inch	16	5	32	405
MILK, YOGURT, CHEESE				
Milk, 1 cup				
Whole	8	5	33	150
2% fat	5	3	18	120
1% fat	3	2	10	105
Skim	trace	trace	4	85
Yogurt, 1 cup				
Nonfat plain	trace	trace	4	135
Low-fat plain	4	2	15	155
Low-fat fruit flavored	3	2	10	250
Cottage cheese, 1/2 cup				
Creamed	5	3	16	110
Low-fat, 1% fat	1	1	5	82
Cheese, 1 oz.				
Natural cheddar	9	6	29	115
Mozzarella, part-skim milk	5	3	16	110
Process American	9	6	27	105
Vanilla ice cream, 1/2 cup	7	4	27	135
Vanilla ice milk, 1/2 cup	3	2	9	90
Frozen yogurt, 1/2 cup	2	1	8	105

Primer: Fat, Saturated Fat, and Cholesterol in Food (continued)

	Total fat (g)	Saturated fatty acids (g)	Cholesterol (mg)	Calories
VEGETABLES				
Potatoes				
Boiled, 1/2 cup	trace	trace	0	65
Potato salad, 1/2 cup	8	1	50	135
French fries, 10 strips	8	3	0	160
Au gratin, 1/2 cup	9	4	19	175
Chips, 1 oz.	10	3	0	150
Cabbage, 1/2 cup				
Cooked	trace	trace	0	15
Creamy coleslaw	11	2	6	125
Celery and carrot sticks, 8	trace	0	0	10
Stir-fried vegetables, 1/2 cup	trace	trace	0	45
MEATS, POULTRY, FISH, BEANS, EGGS, AND NUTS				
Beef				
Lean cut (eye of round), roasted, 3 oz.				
Lean and fat	11	4	61	195
Lean only	4	2	59	145
Fattier cut (chuck blade), braised, 3 oz.				
Lean and fat	22	9	88	295
Lean only	11	4	90	215
Ground, cooked, 3 oz. patty				
Regular	17	7	76	245
Lean	16	6	73	230
Extra lean	14	5	71	215
Pork center loin, roasted, 3 oz.				
Lean and fat	11	4	68	180
Lean	8	3	67	150
Beef liver, braised, 3 oz.	4	2	331	135
Chicken, light and dark meat, roasted, 3 oz.				
With skin	12	3	74	200
Without skin	6	2	75	160
Halibut fillets, baked, 3 oz.	1	trace	49	95
Tuna, canned, 3 oz.				
In oil	7	1	25	170
In water	1	trace	25	115
Crabs, hardshell, steamed, 2 medium	2	trace	95	95
Shrimp, steamed or boiled, 8 extra large	2	trace	160	110
Frankfurters, 2 (3 oz.)	27	10	47	300
Dry beans, cooked, 1/2 cup	trace	trace	0	110
Peanut butter, 2 Tbsp.	16	3	0	190
Sunflower seeds, 2 Tbsp.	10	1	0	105
Egg, large, cooked, 1				
Yolk	5	2	213	60
White	0	0	0	15

Primer: Fat, Saturated Fat, and Cholesterol in Food (continued)

	Total fat (g)	Saturated fatty acids (g)	Cholesterol (mg)	Calories
FRUITS				
Apple, 1 medium	trace	trace	0	80
Avocado, 1/2 medium	15	2	0	160
Banana, 1 medium	1	trace	0	105
Olives, 5 large				
Green	3	trace	0	25
Ripe	3	trace	0	30
Orange, 1 medium	trace	trace	0	60
Peach, 1 medium	trace	trace	0	20
Strawberries, 5 berries	1	trace	0	20
Mixed fruit cup with cream dressing, 1/2 cup	3	2	9	80
FATS, OILS, SWEETS				
Butter, 1 Tbsp.	12	7	31	100
Butter-margarine blend, 1 Tbsp.	12	5	16	100
Margarine, 1 Tbsp.				
Soft	12	2	0	100
Stick	12	2	0	100
Liquid (squeezable)	12	2	0	100
Diet	6	1	0	50
Vegetable oil (corn), 1 Tbsp.	14	2	0	120
Hydrogenated vegetable shortening, 1 Tbsp.	13	3	0	115
Salad dressing, 1 Tbsp.				
Mayonnaise (regular)	12	2	7	100
Mayonnaise, reduced-calorie	5	1	5	50
Mayonnaise-type	7	1	4	70
Mayonnaise-type, reduced-calorie	4	1	4	45
Italian	7	1	0	70
Italian, low-calorie	1	trace	1	15
Cream, 1 Tbsp.				
Sour	3	2	6	30
Light (table)	3	2	10	30
Nondairy, frozen	1	trace	0	20
Cream cheese, 1 Tbsp.	5	3	16	50
Pie, apple, 1/8 of 9-inch	22	5	0	455
Cheesecake, 1/12 of 9-inch	25	10	86	405
Sherbet, 1/2 cup	2	1	7	135
Milk chocolate bar, 1 oz.	9	5	6	145

Source: Human Nutrition Information Service/United States Department of Agriculture, Choose a Diet Low in Fat, Saturated Fat, and Cholesterol, *Home and Garden Bulletin Number 253-4, July, 1993.*

protein coagulates, and they no longer function in ways similar to fat.

Protein-based replacers contribute 1 to 4 calories per gram, compared with 9 calories per fat gram. What accounts for the calorie range? These replacers may be blended with ingredients, such as cellulose, that can't be digested. Protein-based replacers also provide small amounts of amino acids.

Simplesse® is one example of a protein-based fat replacer being used today, primarily in frozen dairy dessert products.

Fat-based Replacers

These are made with fats that have been chemically altered. They provide few or no calories as compared to fat because the body is unable to fully absorb the fatty acids. They may be used in baked foods, some fried foods, cake mixes, frosting, and dairy foods.

Olestra is a calorie-free fat replacer made from vegetable oils and sugar. It contributes no calories because it passes through the body without being digested and absorbed. Olestra provides the characteristics of fat in cooking, especially for frying and snack foods. OLEAN® is the brand name for olestra that you'll see on food labels. Because olestra isn't digested, some vitamins carried by fat aren't fully absorbed. For this reason, fat-soluble vitamins are added to foods made with olestra. For some people, consuming foods with olestra may be linked to digestive discomfort.

Salatrim® is another fat-based replacer used in baked goods, dairy products, and confection-type products. It provides calories, but only 5 calories per gram (as compared to 9 calories per gram in fat) because it is only partially absorbed in the body.

What type of foods contain fat replacers?
Many high-fat foods have a low-fat or fat-free counterpart made by replacing some or all of the fat with fat replacers: for example, margarine, salad dressing, mayonnaise, cheese, sour cream, ice cream, cookies, baked foods, and candy. Some low-fat ice creams contain either a protein-based fat replacer or a combination of starches and gums.

Both carbohydrate- and protein-based fat replacers supply calories, so the energy contributed by fat-modified foods may or may not be less than the original food. If you're concerned about calories, check the Nutrition Facts panel on the food label.

Fat replacers are used in processed foods with varying degrees of success. But as the food industry develops new technology, consumers can expect to see more good-tasting, reduced-fat and fat-free products become available. From a food safety standpoint, both scientific studies and review by the Food and Drug Administration (FDA) indicate they are safe. *Refer to "Additives: Safe at the Plate" on page 225 to learn about the FDA review process.*

have you ever wondered

...what a label stating 98% fat free means? You might think this means that only 2% of the total calories come from fat. Actually, the percent is referring to weight and not calories. So 98% fat free means that 2% of the weight of the total serving comes from fat. By law, when manufacturers use a % fat free on a label, the amount of total fat must be below 3 grams of fat per serving. This amount is quite low, but may be more than you'd think when reading the % fat-free claim. ✦

Cholesterol: Different From Fat

To clear up a common misperception, cholesterol is a fat-like substance, but it's not a fat itself. Cholesterol has a different structure from fat and performs different functions in the human body. Some functions promote health; some don't. Because fat and cholesterol often appear together in foods of animal origin, and because their roles in health are so intertwined, they're easily mixed up.

Like fat, cholesterol often gets a "bad rap." Yet, it's part of every body cell and of some hormones, including sex hormones like estrogen. As part of a body chemical called bile, it helps the body digest and absorb fat, too. With the help of sunlight, cholesterol in your skin can change to vitamin D, a nutrient essential for bone building. However, too much cholesterol in the bloodstream is linked to heart disease.

Blood vs. Dietary Cholesterol

Confused about cholesterol? You're not alone! Actually, the term itself refers to two different types. Blood, or serum, cholesterol circulates in the bloodstream. Dietary cholesterol comes from food.

While many factors affect blood cholesterol levels, the cholesterol that circulates in your body comes from two sources:

Your body produces enough cholesterol for your needs. Your liver makes most of it, but every body cell can also make cholesterol. In fact, when the body makes too much, the risk for heart disease goes up. Your body converts the extra it makes to body fat and can leave some as buildup in your arteries. Unlike adults, infants and children's bodies don't produce enough cholesterol. So for children under age 2, it's important that their diets supply cholesterol. *Refer to "Fat Facts for Tots" on page 425.*

Cholesterol also comes from foods and beverages—but only foods of animal origin, such as eggs, meat, poultry, fish, and dairy foods. Animals produce cholesterol, but plants don't! A diet high in dietary cholesterol is one factor that elevates blood cholesterol levels for some people. That's why moderation is advised. Dietary cholesterol doesn't automatically become blood cholesterol. Your total fat, especially saturated fat, has a more significant effect on blood cholesterol levels than dietary cholesterol alone does. *Refer to "Why Do Blood Cholesterol Levels Rise?" on page 487. For the cholesterol content of many foods, refer to the chart on page 61, "Primer: Fat, Saturated Fat, and Cholesterol in Food."*

The "Good" and the "Bad"

Have you ever wondered what the terms "good" cholesterol and "bad" cholesterol really mean? They actually refer to cholesterol that's carried in your blood by two types of lipoproteins. The terms don't relate to cholesterol in food.

Because cholesterol doesn't mix with water, it can't be carried alone in your bloodstream. Instead, it's combined in "packages" with fat and protein. These packages, called lipoproteins, carry cholesterol both to and from your body cells. Your total blood

have you ever wondered

...why olive oil and canola oil receive so much attention? They're both high in monounsaturated fatty acids and low in saturated fatty acids. Monounsaturated fatty acids in foods may help lower blood cholesterol levels more than polyunsaturated fatty acids do. However, simply adding olive or canola oils to an already high-fat diet is not the point. These oils are still 100 percent fat with 120 calories per tablespoon. The goal for health is to use oils high in monounsaturated fatty acids instead of other fats and oils.

...if cholesterol supplies calories? The answer is "no." Although cholesterol is often confused with fat, it's not a source of energy, or calories. So eating too much can't make you fat. Unlike fat, carbohydrate, and protein, cholesterol isn't broken down, so the body cannot derive any energy from it.

...if eating oat bran will help lower your blood cholesterol level? No single food will lower your blood cholesterol level. However, oat bran is a soluble fiber, which can have a cholesterol-lowering effect—if your total fat intake is fairly low. For soluble fiber, enjoy a variety of foods with soluble fiber, including cooked beans, a bowl of cooked oatmeal, or an oat bran muffin. While an oat bran muffin supplies soluble fiber, it also may contain about 5 grams of fat—more if it's bigger. ✦

cholesterol consists of high-density lipoproteins and low-density lipoproteins.

High-density lipoprotein* (HDL) *cholesterol carries cholesterol from every part of the body, bringing it back to the liver for disposal. High levels of HDL-blood cholesterol, sometimes called "good" cholesterol, are associated with a decreased risk of heart disease.

Low-density lipoprotein* (LDL) *cholesterol carries cholesterol from the liver to other tissues. Along the way, it forms deposits on the walls of arteries and other blood vessels. High levels of LDL-blood cholesterol, sometimes called "bad" cholesterol, are associated with an increased risk of heart disease.

HDL- and LDL-blood cholesterol are found only in your bloodstream, not in food. Your food choices do influence LDL levels, however. If you lower the saturated fat and cholesterol in your diet, you'll likely bring down LDL-blood cholesterol levels. And if you're physically active, you'll likely keep HDL-blood cholesterol higher. *To learn more, refer to* "HDLs and LDLs: *The Ups and Downs*" *on page* 487.

Cholesterol: In What Foods?

What foods contain cholesterol? Only foods of animal origin. Egg yolks and organ meats are especially high in cholesterol. And in varying amounts, meat, poultry, seafood, dairy products, and animal fats, such as butter or lard, all supply cholesterol, too.

As mentioned before, cholesterol and saturated fatty acids often occur together in foods. That's why they sometimes get confused. Sirloin steak, butter, and cheddar cheese, for example, all contain both saturated fatty acids and cholesterol. Some foods, such as shellfish and organ meats, are high in cholesterol, yet they're low in saturated fatty acids. In foods of animal origin, both lean and fatty tissues contain cholesterol. That's why some low-fat foods, such as squid and shrimp, can be relatively high in cholesterol. The sauce or butter they're dipped in can boost their cholesterol content, too.

Even though some foods of plant origin are high in fat or saturated fat, they have no cholesterol. That means that vegetables, fruit, beans and peas, grains, and seeds are all cholesterol free. Unlike the cell membranes of animal tissue, the cell walls of plants don't contain cholesterol. Instead, they contain fiber. Nuts, for example, have no cholesterol, even though they're high in fat—deriving 80 to 89 percent of their calories from fat.

So why do some vegetable dishes and grain-based baked goods contain cholesterol? Ingredients such as egg yolk, cheese, milk, meat, poultry, butter, or lard were added. Examples include refried beans made with lard, greens cooked with bacon, and muffins made with butter and egg yolks. Depending on the recipe, the amount of cholesterol per serving will vary.

KITCHEN NUTRITION
low-fat chips

If you love chips, try these easy homemade chips using bagels, pita bread, tortillas, or potatoes. They'll taste great with yogurt cheese spread! (*See page* 70.)

Bagels: Thinly slice a whole, uncut bagel into little rounds.
Pita bread: Separate the pita into halves and slice into quarters.
Tortillas: Slice soft corn or flour tortillas into quarters.
Potatoes: Cut small potatoes with the skin on into thin slices.

Place on a baking sheet in a single layer. Spray lightly with vegetable oil cooking spray. For a flavor twist, sprinkle with garlic powder, butter-flavored granules, or your favorite herbs or spices. Bake in a 350° F oven until they're crisp, about 15 to 20 minutes. ✦

When shopping, if you spot a food that's labeled "no cholesterol" or "cholesterol free," it cannot have any more than 2 grams of saturated fat. However, you'll want to read the rest of the food label to find out about the total fat content; it may not be low in fat.

Too Much of a Good Thing?

Today, many Americans are concerned about the amount of fat in their diets. And rightly so. On average, Americans consume too much: 34 percent of their calories from fat. Although our fat intake is dropping, it's still higher than the guideline set by health experts: no more than 30 percent of total calories from fat in your total diet. *Refer to* "*The* 30% *Guideline*" *on page* 68.

High-fat diets are linked to higher blood cholesterol levels and a greater chance for heart disease. As people have cut back on fat, saturated fat, and cholesterol, fewer are dying from heart disease. Eating a high-fat diet also increases the risk for some types of cancer and obesity. For this reason, the Dietary Guidelines for Americans advise: Choose a diet low in fat, saturated fat, and cholesterol. *For more on the Dietary Guidelines for Americans, see chapter* 1.

Weight control is another good reason to watch fat grams. High-fat foods are often high in calories, too. Whether they're saturated or unsaturated, calories from fat are all alike. Every fat gram supplies 9 calories, which is more than twice the amount provided by 1 gram of carbohydrate or protein. And excess calories, whether from fat, carbohydrate, or protein, are stored in the body as fat. *Remember*: The total amount of calories eaten, not just the calories from fat, is the issue in weight management. *Check the* "*Primer: Fat, Saturated Fat, and Cholesterol in Food*" *on page* 61 *to compare the calories in several higher-fat foods. See page* 29 *for more on weight control.*

More about the effects of fat, saturated fat, and cholesterol on heart disease and cancer is found in "*Prevention: Nutrition and Health Problems*" *on page* 484.

Moderation: Key to a Healthful Diet

Eating a variety of foods in moderate amounts is the best way to control the fat, saturated fat, and cholesterol in your eating style. To help you do this, follow guidelines from the Food Guide Pyramid.

The Pyramid is a practical guide for choosing a healthful diet that's just right for you—plenty of grain foods, such as bread, rice, cereal, and pasta; fruits and vegetables; enough dairy products, lean

FAT MATH

Just how much is 30 percent of your calories from total fat, with less than 10 percent from saturated fat? The amount varies because it's based on your energy needs. Here's how you would make those calculations if you consumed 2,000 calories a day:

To figure calories from total fat per day...
30% (or 0.30) x 2,000 calories = 600 calories from total fat

To figure total fat grams per day...
600 calories from total fat ÷ 9 calories per gram of fat = 66.66 or 67 grams of total fat per day

To figure calories from saturated fat per day...
10% (or 0.10) x 2,000 calories = 200 calories from saturated fat*

To figure grams of saturated fat per day...
200 calories from unsaturated fat ÷ 9 calories = 22 grams of saturated fat (of the 67 grams total fat) per day*

*Because it's recommended to also consume no more that 10 percent of calories from monounsaturated and polyunsaturated fats, this same figure would apply for mono- and polyunsaturated fats. ✦

meat, poultry, and fish, as well as legumes and moderate amounts of eggs and nuts. The Pyramid also advises moderate amounts of fats and oils, such as margarine, butter, and salad dressings, which add flavor and texture to many foods in your diet. Enjoy them as you keep total fat under control.

Fat and Cholesterol: Know Your Limits

Unlike many other nutrients, there's no Recommended Dietary Allowance (RDA) for fat. The amount advised depends on your overall energy needs. There's no RDA for dietary cholesterol, either. No matter what your energy intake, though, the cholesterol guideline for healthy individuals remains the same: 300 milligrams or less per day.

By now, the guideline for fat intake is well known: for healthy Americans, consume no more than 30 percent of total calories from fat. That's more than enough to keep you healthy. After age 2, children should gradually adopt a diet that, by age 5, contains no more than 30 percent of calories from fat.

The "30 percent" guideline includes:

- less than 10 percent of total calories from saturated fats,
- about 10 percent from monounsaturated fats, and
- about 10 percent from polyunsaturated fats.

The 30% Guideline

If you eat this many calories a day	Your calories from fat would be no more than...	Your daily fat intake* should be no more than...
1,600	480 calories	53 grams
2,000	600 calories	67 grams**
2,200	660 calories	73 grams
2,500	750 calories	83 grams**
2,800	840 calories	93 grams
3,200	960 calories	107 grams

* *Numbers may be rounded.*

** *The Daily Values for fat on the Nutrition Facts panel are rounded to 65 grams and 80 grams for calorie levels of 2,000 and 2,500 respectively.*

Where should the other 70 or more percent of calories come from? Fifty-five to 60 percent should come from carbohydrate, mostly complex carbohydrates from foods such as bread, cereal, rice, and pasta. The remainder, from protein.

To clear up any confusion, the "30 percent" guideline applies to the total diet, not to a single food or to a single meal. It's actually the percent of calories you consume from fat—over several days—that can impact your health.

In real numbers, how much is 30 percent calories from fat? The specific amount depends on a person's energy needs. And that depends on age, gender, body size, and activity level.

To figure your own fat budget, see the example in "Fat Math" on page 67. Or use the chart below.

You can also check the bottom of the Nutrition Facts panel on many food labels. For a 2,000- and a 2,500-calorie diet, it shows how many fat grams equal the "30 percent" guideline.

To determine how many calories you need to maintain your current weight, refer to "Your 'Weigh': Figuring Your Energy Needs" on page 28.

Trim Fat in Your Eating Style

Are you like most Americans who consume about 34 percent or more of your calories from fat? From a health standpoint, you'd probably benefit by cutting back! Keep in mind that there are many ways to trim fat and it's not necessary to do them all. To start, try a few strategies listed here. Once you've mastered them, try a few more. Here's how:

For Less Total Fat...

Know where fat comes from. You can't cut back unless you know the sources. *Refer to page 61, "Primer: Fat, Saturated Fat, and Cholesterol in Food," as a resource.*

The Nutrition Facts panel on food labels tells you how much fat a single serving of each food contains. You could tally up how much fat you ate per day with the labels. But that would be tedious. So instead consider the following tips! *To learn how to best use the* Nutrition Facts *panel, refer to* "Get All the Facts!" *on page* 271.

Consider all the foods you can eat! A healthful diet—without too much fat—consists of grains, fruits, vegetables, lean meat, skinless poultry, fish, and lower-fat dairy foods. Choose a variety of these foods in moderate amounts. *Refer to page* 243, "The Food Guide Pyramid: Your Healthful Eating Guide," *to learn more about following a varied, balanced, and moderate eating plan.*

Consume lean meat (beef, pork, and lamb) and skinless poultry. Loin and round cuts of meat have less fat. Trim visible fat from meat and poultry, too. Lean meat, however, still contains fat and cholesterol. The cholesterol in meat is found in both the fat and in lean muscle tissue. So trimming the fat and buying lean cuts will reduce the cholesterol in meat, but won't make it cholesterol free. Lean meat isn't the same as fat-free; it just has less fat.

Make your meals "fishy." As a change from meat in "center plate," enjoy seafood a couple times a week, prepared a low-fat way.

Eat "five-a-day" fruits and vegetables. Besides being low in fat and delicious, fruits and veggies fill you up and help curb your appetite for higher-fat foods. Soluble fiber in some fruits and vegetables—including apples and brussels sprouts—also have a cholesterol-lowering effect. To spark your thinking of the variety of tasty fruits and vegetables available in today's supermarkets, *refer to* "Garden of Eatin': Uncommon Vegetables" *on page* 215 *and* "Fresh Ideas: Uncommon Fruit" *on page* 219.

Go for grains! Choose lower-fat grain products—pasta, rice, breakfast cereal, bagels, tortillas, pita, and other lower-fat breads. By consuming more of your energy from carbohydrate-rich foods, the percent of energy from fat goes down!

Include those with soluble fiber, such as oats. And go easy on doughnuts, sweet rolls, higher-fat muffins, cakes, and cookies. *Refer to chapter 6,* "Fiber: Your Body's Broom."

Choose low-fat or skim dairy products. You'll reduce total fat, but the bone-building nutrients in low-fat and whole milk products are otherwise about the same.

Go easy on fats and oils. That includes vegetable oils, butter, margarine, lard, cream cheese, and bacon used in cooking, as well as high-fat salad dressings, sauces, and many candies. Use herbs and seasonings rather than high-fat sauces to add refreshing flavor to food. Interestingly, while butter is an animal fat and margarine is a vegetable fat, their fat content is the same: about 12 fat grams and 100 calories per tablespoon.

Check food labels for fat facts. Almost all food labels carry a Nutrition Facts panel, which lists the amount of calories, calories from fat, total fat, saturated fat, and cholesterol. You may also find words such as "low-fat" or "lean" on food labels, which describe the amount of fat, too. When you're shopping, use this nutrition information to help guide your food purchases. *To learn more about food labels, refer to* "Today's Food Labels" *on page* 270 *and* "Label Lingo: Fats and Cholesterol" *on page* 71.

Choose low-fat food products. You'll find plenty of reduced-fat and fat-free choices on supermarket

Each spread, salad dressing, or topping below has the same amount of total fat—about 4 to 5 grams. Notice the differences in the amounts!

- 1 teaspoon stick margarine or butter
- 1 teaspoon regular mayonnaise
- 2 teaspoons Italian salad dressing
- 3 teaspoons light margarine
- 3 teaspoons reduced-fat mayonnaise
- 3 teaspoons cream cheese
- 4 teaspoons light (table) cream
- 4 teaspoons sour cream

KITCHEN NUTRITION
yogurt cheese

Create this "fat replacer" in your own kitchen. Yogurt cheese makes a thick spread for crackers or bagels; a creamy dip or salad dressing; a flavorful topper on baked potatoes and tacos; or a rich-tasting cheesecake or cream soup. Best of all, it's low in fat and high in calcium.

- Line a strainer with cheesecloth (double thickness) or a paper coffee filter. Or use a strainer specially designed for making yogurt cheese. Place the strainer over a deep bowl.
- Spoon gelatin-free yogurt into the strainer and cover. (Check the label to find out if it contains gelatin. Yogurt may be plain, vanilla, lemon, coffee, or fruit flavored; however, this doesn't work with fat-free yogurt.) Refrigerate. Allow the liquid whey to drain into the bowl for 2 to 24 hours, depending on how firm you want the "cheese" to be. Drained for 24 hours, 32 ounces of yogurt yield about 1 1/2 cups of yogurt cheese.

To flavor, blend 1 1/2 cups of plain yogurt cheese with one of these combinations:

- 2/3 cup apricot preserves and 3 tablespoons chopped almonds or walnuts
- 1/4 cup crumbled blue cheese, 1 1/2 cups grated apple or pear, and 1 teaspoon sugar
- 3 ounces salmon, 2 tablespoons chopped green onion, and 1 tablespoon chopped parsley
- 3 tablespoons herb blend, 1 teaspoon garlic, and pepper (to taste)

For more low-fat cooking tips, refer to chapter 14, "Kitchen Nutrition."

Source: St. Louis District Dairy Council ✦

shelves, for example, fat-free salad dressing and low-fat ice cream. *To go aisle-by-aisle through the grocery store, refer to "Your Shopping Guide" on page 279.* Be aware that many lower-fat processed foods have the same amount or more total calories than their traditional counterparts. You'll want to read the Nutrition Facts panel on the food label to compare.

Balance higher-fat food choices with lower-fat foods. That way, you can eat within your fat budget for the day and still enjoy moderate amounts of higher-fat foods. *For tips, refer to "Quick, Easy Trade-Offs" on page 256.*

Watch your "snack fats." Snacking itself is fine. In fact, smart snacks fill in missing nutrient gaps, help to control hunger, and can provide an energy boost between meals. But some popular snack foods are higher in fat than you may realize. *Refer to page 264, "Snacks With Less Fat," for nutritious snack options.*

De-fat your cooking style. By changing the way you prepare food, you can trim the fat content without losing flavor. For example, broil, bake, boil, steam, stir-fry, or microwave foods, rather than fry. *For more fat-cutting tips for a variety of foods, refer to page 335, "Fat and Cholesterol Trimmers."*

Add flavor with herbs and spices. Skip high-fat flavorings or sauces on vegetables, meats, poultry, and fish, and maximize flavors with herbs and spices instead. Use low-fat or fat-free marinades to tenderize and add flavor to lean cuts of meat. Rub mixtures of seasonings on tender cuts of meat before cooking for wonderful blends of flavors. *Refer to "Rub Combos" on page 351 for some easy rub recipes.*

Substitute "lean" for higher-fat cuisine. And when you can, substitute foods and ingredients high in unsaturated fatty acids for those high in saturated fatty acids. *The chart on page 340, "Easy Substitutions to Cut Fat and/or Cholesterol," offers a list of ways to trim fat and cholesterol from recipes.*

Watch your portion size. The amount of fat and cholesterol in your food choices depends on both what you eat and how much. Extra-large portions of higher-fat foods provide extra-large amounts of fat. As an example, a total of 5 to 7 ounces of meat, poultry, or fish each day is probably enough to meet your nutrient needs. *Refer to page 245, "What Counts as One Serving?" to learn more about portion control.*

Make beans the "main event" at meals occasionally. Meals with cooked dry beans as the main protein source have several cholesterol-lowering qualities. Usually they're lower in total fat, saturated fat, and cholesterol—yet higher in complex carbohydrates and fiber. Be aware that vegetarian meals aren't always low in fat. *For guidelines on planning healthful vegetarian meals, refer to "'Vegging Out' the Healthful Way!" on page 568.*

Order "lean" when you order out. Whether you choose fast-food or order off a menu in a restaurant, look for menu clues that suggest less fat. Ask questions about the menu, for example, how food is prepared, and go easy on foods that are fried, breaded, or prepared with rich sauces or gravy. *For tips to make your next restaurant meal lower in fat, refer to "May I Take Your Order?" on page 363 and "On the 'Leaner' Side" on page 361.*

Make small changes for big differences. Cutting back from 35 or 40 percent calories from fat to 30 percent doesn't need to be a huge change in your

Fats and Cholesterol

Anytime you head to the supermarket check the labels. On the front of many food labels, you'll find words that describe the fat or cholesterol content of the food inside.

LABEL TERM...	MEANS...
FOR FAT CONTENT...	
Fat free	less than 0.5 gram fat per serving
Low fat	3 grams or less of fat per serving
Reduced or less fat	at least 25% less fat* per serving
Light	one-third fewer calories or 50% less fat* per serving
___ % fat free	the food meets the definition of "low fat" or "fat free" if stated as 100% fat free
Light meal	"low fat" (at least 50% less fat per serving*) or "low calorie" meal (at least 1/3 fewer calories per serving*)
Low-fat meal	3 grams or less fat per 100 grams, and 30 percent or less calories from fat
FOR SATURATED FAT CONTENT...	
Saturated fat free	less than 0.5 gram saturated fat and less than 0.5 gram trans fatty acids per serving
Low saturated fat	1 gram or less saturated fat per serving and no more than 15% of calories from saturated fat
Reduced or less saturated fat	at least 25% less saturated fat*
FOR CHOLESTEROL CONTENT...	
Cholesterol free	less than 2 milligrams cholesterol and 2 grams or less of saturated fat per serving
Low cholesterol	20 milligrams or less cholesterol and 2 grams or less of saturated fat per serving
Reduced or less cholesterol	at least 25% less cholesterol* and 2 grams or less of saturated fat per serving
FOR FAT, SATURATED FAT, AND CHOLESTEROL CONTENT...	
Lean**	less than 10 grams total fat, 4.5 grams or less saturated fat, and 95 milligrams cholesterol per 3-ounce serving and per 100 grams
Extra lean**	less than 5 grams total fat, 2 grams saturated fat, and 95 milligrams cholesterol per 3-ounce serving and per 100 grams

** as compared with a standard serving size of the traditional food;*
*** on packaged seafood or game meat, cooked meat, or cooked poultry*

have you ever wondered

...if coconut milk is high in fat? One cup of canned coconut milk (made by combining grated coconut meat and coconut water) contains 445 calories and 48 fat grams (of which 43 fat grams are saturated). Coconut water, or liquid, drained from a fresh coconut—without any grated coconut meat—has just 46 calories and less than 1 fat gram per cup. Just 1/4-cup of dried, sweetened coconut has 87 calories and 6 fat grams.

...if salmon is lower in fat than chicken? Salmon has about 185 calories and 9 fat grams per 3-ounce cooked portion compared with 190 calories and 9 fat grams in the same portion of roasted, light-meat chicken with the skin on. Skinless, this same portion of chicken contains about 150 calories and 3 fat grams.

...if air-popped popcorn is always low in fat? No, not always. If you buy it ready made, check the Nutrition Facts for the fat and saturated fat content. Although the package may say "air popped," oil may be added after popping as a flavoring. For microwave popcorn, check the label to see if oil is added—and how much and what kind.

... if ghee is a good substitute for butter? Commonly used in the cuisine of India, ghee is clarified butter. It's been heated, then strained to remove milk solids so the fat is slightly concentrated—with more fat and calories per teaspoon. Why clarify butter? Without the milk solids, it can be heated to a higher temperature without burning.

... how the fat in feta cheese compares with other cheeses? It's somewhat lower—but not much. An ounce of feta cheese has 6 grams of fat, which includes 4 grams of saturated fat. By comparison, 1 ounce of cheddar cheese has 9 total fat grams, including 6 grams of saturated fat. With their intense pungent flavors, however, smaller amounts of stronger cheeses like feta, and others such as Parmesan and blue cheese, go a long way in delivering flavor. ✦

eating pattern. Often eating a small portion of a high-fat dessert, switching to leaner meat and to low-fat or nonfat dairy products, and eating broiled rather than fried foods is enough to make a daily difference!

As an added benefit, eating less fat may translate to enjoying more food! By cutting back on high-fat foods, there may be room in your day's eating plan for more carbohydrate-rich foods. And low-fat foods often supply fewer calories, so you may be able to have a second helping!

For Less Saturated Fat...

Use liquid vegetable oils when you can. They have less saturated fatty acids and more unsaturated fatty acids than fats that are firm at room temperature. And go easy on animal fats, too, since they're more saturated. For example, choose soft tub or squeeze (liquid) margarine in place of stick margarine or butter. And try polyunsaturated or monounsaturated oil in recipes calling for melted shortening or butter. *Check "Lean Tips...for Baked Goods" on page 341 for making substitutions with vegetable oil in baked goods.*

Cut back on total fat. You'll likely reduce saturated fats, too.

Read the food label. Use the Nutrition Facts about saturated fat to choose foods with less. Check the ingredient list, too. The food is likely higher in saturated fat if any of these ingredients is among the first several listed: butter, partially hydrogenated vegetable oil, coconut oil, palm oil, palm kernel oil, cocoa butter, meat fat, lard, egg yolk, whole milk solids, cream, or cheese.

For Less Cholesterol...

Eat no more than four egg yolks a week. That includes the eggs in prepared foods, such as bread, cakes, and pancakes. Limiting egg yolks is advised because the yolk has all the cholesterol—about 215 milligrams in the yolk from a large egg. An egg white has no cholesterol. To limit egg yolks, you might substitute two egg whites for one whole egg in baked goods. Or use an egg substitute.

Go easy on organ meats, such as liver. Even though they're nutritious, they're high in cholesterol.

Look for leaner meat, fish, poultry, and low-fat dairy foods. You won't eliminate all the cholesterol. But you'll trim away some of the cholesterol as well as fat.

Check labels to find foods that are low in cholesterol or cholesterol free. *Refer to the chart, "Label Lingo: Fats and Cholesterol" on page 71 to learn just what these terms mean.*

your nutrition check-up

Fat and Cholesterol Audit

What's the fat and cholesterol quotient of your eating style? For each section, check one box in each column that matches your usual food choices over the course of a day or several days. Choosing from every column is okay. That's part of making trade-offs! Remember, your overall fat intake over time is what counts—not each individual choice.

Column 1 (3 points)	**Column 2** (2 points)	**Column 3** (1 point)
❒ reasonable portions, totaling 5 to 7 ounces of meat, poultry, or fish per day	❒ some reasonable portions and some bigger portions, totaling somewhat more than 7 ounces of meat, poultry, or fish per day	❒ big portions of meat, poultry, and fish, totaling much more than 7 ounces per day
❒ low-fat and skim milk dairy products	❒ both low-fat and whole-milk dairy products, and some higher-fat products, such as cheese	❒ whole-milk dairy products and higher-fat products, such as cheese
❒ a variety of lean meat, skinless poultry, and fish	❒ some lean and some higher-fat meat and poultry	❒ high-fat meat, such as juicy steak or high-fat sausage, or poultry with skin on
❒ broiled, grilled, or roasted foods, such as meat, poultry, and fish, and steamed, boiled, or baked vegetables	❒ some broiled, grilled, or roasted foods, and others that are fried	❒ mostly fried or sautéed meat, poultry, fish, and vegetables
❒ little or no gravy or creamy, high-fat sauces	❒ some gravy or high-fat sauces	❒ plenty of gravy and/or high-fat sauces
❒ low-fat salad dressing or small amount (1 tablespoon per serving) of regular salad dressing	❒ some regular salad dressing	❒ liberal use of regular salad dressing
❒ fruit, frozen yogurt, and other low-fat desserts and snacks	❒ some low-fat desserts and snacks, and some with more fat, such as regular ice cream, cake, and cookies	❒ plenty of high-fat desserts and snacks

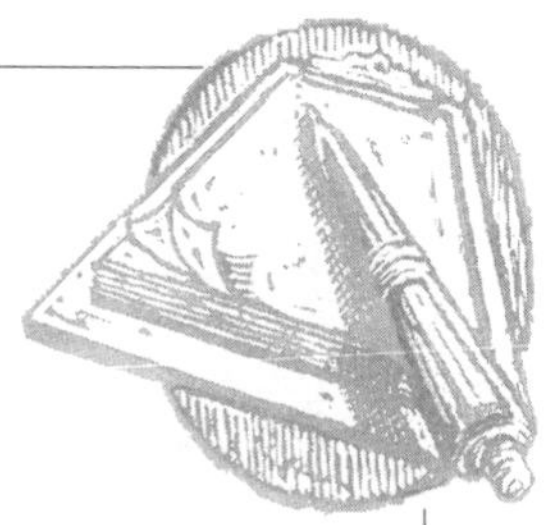

❒ small amounts of margarine, butter, or high-fat spread or toppings on breads or vegetables—or none at all	❒ mostly just small amounts of margarine, butter, or other high-fat spreads or toppings on breads or vegetables	❒ liberal amounts of margarine, butter, or other high-fat spreads or toppings on bread or vegetables
❒ bagels, bread, tortillas, and other low-fat breads	❒ some low-fat breads and some higher-fat breads, such as croissants, muffins, and doughnuts	❒ mostly higher-fat breads
❒ no more than 3 to 4 egg yolks each week	❒ usually just 3 to 4 egg yolks a week, but sometimes more	❒ more than 4 egg yolks per week
Column 1 Subtotal _____	*Column 2 Subtotal* _____	*Column 3 Subtotal* _____

Now for the totals...

Your score: _____ . Depending on which column you checked, each box is worth 3, 2, or 1 point(s).

If you scored...

20 *to* 30 *points*— You've taken a low-fat eating style to heart!

...16 *to* 19 *points*—You've got the idea of moderation. Yet you still have room to trim fat and cholesterol in your food choices a bit more.

...10 *to* 15 *points*—For your good health, you're wise to rethink your overall eating style for less fat and cholesterol.

real life nutrition

For Your Health's Sake

As part of March, National Nutrition Month®, Manuel took part in a health fair at work. Going from one exhibit to another, a computer suddenly caught his eye. It would analyze his food choices for a whole day.

With great concentration, he entered everything—even the gravy on his potatoes, his mid-morning doughnut, and the margarine on his bread—and the amounts of each. Sherri, a registered dietitian, was nearby, offering guidance as Manuel needed it.

Then, with a touch of the finger, the computer analyzed his choices and printed his personal nutrition analysis.

"Actually, it's better to analyze your choices over several days," noted Sherri. "That gives a more accurate picture. But this may offer a glimpse at how you're eating. Is this pretty typical of what you eat on a weekday?" Manuel nodded.

"Then your fat intake is high. Here it's close to 50 percent of your day's calories. To stay healthy, hitting no more than 30 percent would be better. Hmmm, the calories seem high, too." Manuel unconsciously patted his midriff and figured that this might explain his slowly expanding belly.

Among the foods they discussed were his daily eggs and bacon for breakfast; the daily doughnut for his mid-morning break; the double-burger, fries, and shake for lunch; and fried fish, potatoes and gravy, and rich dessert for dinner. Manuel came up short on vegetables and fruits—although he did eat some. And he ate toast for breakfast and a roll for dinner, with plenty of margarine.

Manuel had paid attention to other food and nutrition information at the health fair. "So, I'd be wise to cut back on fat, especially on saturated fat, and to eat more fruits and vegetables. Cutting down on fat would cut down on calories, too."

Sherri nodded with a reassuring smile. "Do you walk or run or do anything else that's active in your free time? How about at work?" He shook his head in response to both questions. She reinforced the value of physical activity. And together they took a few moments to discuss ways he could make gradual changes to moderate the fat in his food choices.

real life nutrition (continued)

Health-smart advice for gradually cutting back on fat.

➢ Manuel could choose some lower-fat foods in the cafeteria at work—perhaps a regular burger, or 2 percent milk instead of the shake, or a salad (easy on the dressing) instead of the fries.

➢ For his benefit and that of his whole family, he might go easy on fried foods, and instead eat more baked, grilled, or roasted foods.

➢ He might enjoy more fruits, vegetables, and grains in his meals and snacks. Getting more calories from carbohydrate would lower the percent of calories from fat. These foods offer vitamins, minerals, and fiber, too.

➢ Instead of a rich dessert every night, he occasionally might choose fruit or frozen yogurt with less fat.

➢ For breakfast, Manuel might eat cereal topped with fruit and low-fat milk in place of his daily eggs and bacon. He might enjoy eggs and bacon one or two times a week.

➢ He might take a look at the size of his portions. One way to eat less fat is to eat smaller amounts.

➢ Manuel might use the Nutrition Fact panel on food labels to choose foods with less fat, especially saturated fat.

➢ Since he enjoys some high-fat foods, he might fit them into his meals or snacks but cut back on fat elsewhere. That's making fat trade-offs!

➢ Manuel also needs to add physical activity to his lifestyle. That's as important to health and weight management as healthy eating!

CHAPTER FOUR

VITAMINS AND MINERALS

enough, but not too much

Nutrition history has recorded many fascinating stories, describing how vitamin-rich foods have cured diseases that confounded doctors of the past:

➢ The scourge of scurvy, which plagued seafarers several hundred years ago, was finally cured by stocking ships with lemons, oranges, and limes. Hence, British sailors were called "limeys." Scurvy is caused by a deficiency of vitamin C, a nutrient that citrus fruits provide in abundance.

➢ Night blindness, often caused by a deficiency of vitamin A, was known in ancient Egypt. The recommended cure of the day: eating ox or rooster livers. Today it's well-known that liver contains more vitamin A than many other foods.

➢ Giving children cod liver oil to prevent rickets was known in the 19th century. But not until 1922, when vitamin D was discovered, did scientists know what substance in cod liver oil gave protection.

➢ Beriberi, a deficiency of thiamin, was noted in Asia as polished, or white, rice became more popular than unrefined, or brown, rice. The cure was discovered accidentally when chickens with symptoms of beriberi ate the part of rice that was discarded after polishing. It contained the vitamin-rich germ. Today, the process of enrichment adds thiamin and other B vitamins back to polished rice.

The cure for beriberi led to the first identification of vitamins—named for *vita* meaning life and *amine* referring to any compound with nitrogen. In time, scientists learned that some vitamins don't contain nitrogen. The letter "e" was dropped, and this nutrient category became known as "vitamins."

Only in the past 100 years have we known that vitamins existed—or what they do and what foods they come from. Even within the past 25 years, we've discovered a lot about vitamins and minerals. And there's much more yet to learn!

➢ Today, science has unlocked the puzzles related to many vitamin and mineral deficiencies.

➢ Today, we've isolated more than 40 nutrients in food, and we know the functions and sources of many. Breakthroughs in nutrition now focus less on cures, and more on ways that nutrients promote health and help protect against health problems, such as cancer, heart disease, and osteoporosis, to name a few.

➢ Today, we're also learning more about the balance of vitamins and minerals—and the variety of foods—that allow the body to absorb and use them most efficiently. In other words: we're discovering what's enough, but not too much for our unique, individual needs.

Vitamins and Minerals: Team Players!

Vitamins and minerals are key to all the processes that take place in your body. But they don't work alone. Instead they work in close partnership with other nutrients to make everything happen.

Vitamins are complex chemical substances that work as regulators. Often they act as coenzymes, or partners, with enzymes, the proteins that cause reactions to take place in your body.

Minerals are part of many cells, including (but not only) the hard parts: bone, teeth, and nails. Minerals also are part of enzymes, and they may trigger your body's enzymatic reactions.

Vitamins and minerals truly are team players. From helping carbohydrates, proteins, and fat produce energy, to assisting with protein synthesis (the creation of new proteins), to making it easier for you to see in the dark, vitamins and minerals are responsible for keeping the body functioning normally.

Compared with carbohydrates, proteins, and fats, your body needs vitamins and minerals in only small amounts. So vitamins and minerals often are called micronutrients. The term "micro" refers to the small amount you need. Don't let these small amounts fool you, however. Vitamins and minerals don't supply energy directly. But they do regulate many processes that produce energy—and do a whole lot more!

Read on to explore the many vitamins and minerals we know most about: their varied, yet integrated role in health; recommended intakes (for most, but not all); and food sources.

Within this chapter, you'll learn even more about several others: vitamins A and C, calcium, and iron. These four consistently appear on the Nutrition Facts panel of food labels.

Vitamins: The Basics

Vitamins belong in two groups: water-soluble and fat-soluble. Each name describes an important quality—how they are carried in food and transported in your body.

As their name implies, water-soluble vitamins (B-complex vitamins and vitamin C) dissolve in water. They're carried in your bloodstream. For the most part, they aren't stored in your body—at least not in significant amounts. Instead, your body uses what it needs, then excretes the extra through urine. Since your body doesn't store water-soluble vitamins, regular intake of these nutrients helps avoid deficiencies.

The B-complex vitamins are a family of nutrients, with related roles in health. They include thiamin (vitamin B_1), riboflavin (vitamin B_2), niacin, vitamin B_6, folic acid, vitamin B_{12}, biotin, and pantothenic acid. Although their functions are varied and unique, most help your body produce energy within its trillions of cells.

Water-soluble vitamins are destroyed more easily by food preparation, processing, and storage than fat-soluble vitamins are. *For food handling tips, refer to "Kitchen Nutrition: Simple Ways to Keep Vitamins in Food" on page* 88.

Even though excess amounts of water-soluble vitamins pass out of your body, moderation is still the best approach. Taking large doses of vitamin C from a dietary supplement may create extra work for your kidneys, causing kidney stones and diarrhea. Likewise, too much niacin, vitamin B_6, folic acid, and pantothenic acid also may be harmful.

You've probably guessed that fat-soluble vitamins dissolve in fat. That's how they're carried into your bloodstream and throughout your body—attached to body chemicals made with lipids, or fat. That's one reason you need moderate amounts of fat in your food choices. Four vitamins—A, D, E, and K—are fat-soluble.

Your body is able to store fat-soluble vitamins in your body fat. So getting a fresh supply each day isn't essential. In fact, consuming too much fat-soluble vitamins for too long—usually from vitamin pills or other dietary supplements—can be harmful. Vitamins A and D, for example, can build up to toxic, or poisonous, levels. High intakes of vitamins E and K usually aren't linked to symptoms of toxicity.

What is a dietary supplement? The definition used to be limited to vitamins, minerals, and other essential nutrients, taken in tablet, capsule, or liquid form. But today's definition also includes a broader range of products touted as nutritional substances, including vitamins, minerals, fiber, herbs, other botanicals, amino acids, concentrates, and extracts, all used as supplements. *For more about dietary supplements, refer to "Dietary Supplements: Use and Abuse" on page 111.*

The following section describes how vitamins keep you healthy: their functions, effects of getting too little or too much, Daily Reference Intakes (including the Recommended Dietary Allowances), and sources. *The appendix on page 605 gives specific guidelines for many vitamins for people of all ages.*

Note: On the following pages, the amounts of vitamins in food have been rounded.

Fat-Soluble Vitamins

Vitamin A

Refer also to "Carotenoids: 'Color' Your Food Healthy" on page 90.

What it does:

- ➢ Helps your eyes see normally in the dark, helping adjust to the lower level of light.
- ➢ Promotes the growth and health of cells and tissues throughout your body.
- ➢ Protects you from infections by keeping skin and tissues in your mouth, stomach, intestines, and respiratory, genital, and urinary tracts healthy.

ON THE LABEL

Without looking, do you know what vitamins and minerals always appear on food labels? The ones required on the Nutrition Facts panel are four that need your special attention: vitamins A and C, calcium, and iron. Consume enough of these nutrients to reduce your risk for some common health problems. Other nutrients may appear voluntarily. *For more about food labels, refer to "Today's Food Labels" on page 270.* ✦

Nutrition Facts

Serving Size 1 cup (248g)
Servings Per Container 4

Amount Per Serving	
Calories 150	Calories from Fat 35
	% Daily Value*
Total Fat 4g	**6%**
Saturated Fat 2.5g	**12%**
Cholesterol 20mg	**7%**
Sodium 170mg	**7%**
Total Carbohydrate 17g	**6%**
Dietary Fiber 0g	**0%**
Sugars 17g	
Protein 13g	
Vitamin A 4% •	Vitamin C 6%
Calcium 40% •	Iron 0%

* Percent Daily Values are based on a 2,000 calorie diet. Your daily values may be higher or lower depending on your calorie needs:

	Calories:	2,000	2,500
Total Fat	Less than	65g	80g
Sat Fat	Less than	20g	25g
Cholesterol	Less than	300mg	300mg
Sodium	Less than	2,400mg	2,400mg
Total Carbohydrate		300g	375g
Dietary Fiber		25g	30g

Calories per gram:
Fat 9 • Carbohydrate 4 • Protein 4

➢ Works as an antioxidant in the form of carotenoids, and may reduce your risk for certain cancers and other diseases of aging.

***If you don't get enough*:** Night blindness; other eye problems; dry, scaly skin; problems with reproduction; and poor growth are symptoms of a significant deficiency.

***If you consume excess amounts*:** Because it's stored in your body, large intakes of vitamin A, taken over time, can be quite harmful. The symptoms can be headaches, dry and scaly skin, liver damage, bone and joint pain, vomiting or appetite loss, abnormal bone growth, nerve damage, and birth defects. Almost always, it's caused by high intakes from dietary supplements not from food or from beta carotene in fruits and vegetables.

***How much you need*:** From age 11 on, 1,000 retinol equivalents (RE)* of vitamin A are recommended for males, and 800 REs for females. There's no increased need during pregnancy. However, breast-feeding requires about 500 RE more. (*Both retinol and beta carotene content of food determine RE.)

Be aware that vitamin A is also measured in International Units (IU)—used for food labels and dietary supplements.

***Where it's mostly found*:** Your body actually gets vitamin A in two ways. Vitamin A, in the form of retinol, comes from foods of animal origin, such as liver, fish oil, eggs, milk fortified with vitamin A, and other vitamin A fortified foods.

From plants, it comes from carotenoids, such as beta carotene, that convert to vitamin A in your body. Carotenoids are found in red, yellow, orange, and many dark-green leafy vegetables. *Refer to "Vitamin A: Good Picks" on page 91 for a list of good sources and amounts.*

Vitamin D

See also "Vitamin D: The Sunshine Vitamin" on page 510.

***What it does*:**

➢ Promotes the absorption of two minerals—calcium and phosphorus.

➢ Helps deposit these minerals in bones and teeth, making them stronger and healthier.

***If you don't get enough*:** In your older years, you may have greater loss of bone mass (osteoporosis) and your risk of softening of the bones (osteomalacia) increases. Children with a significant vitamin D deficiency may develop rickets, or defective bone growth. Fortifying milk with vitamin D has virtually wiped out rickets in the United States.

***If you consume excess amounts*:** Because it's stored in your body, too much vitamin D can be toxic, possibly leading to kidney stones or damage, weak muscles, weak bones, excessive bleeding, and other problems. An overdose usually comes from dietary supplements, not food—and not from overexposure to sunlight. For that reason, an upper limit, or Tolerable Upper Intake Level, of 2,000 International Units (IU), or 50 micrograms, per day for people ages one and over was set as part of the Dietary Reference Intakes (DRIs). *Refer to page 4 to learn more about the Tolerable Upper Intake Levels of the* DRIs.

***How much you need*:** From birth through age 50, the recommendation for an Adequate Intake (AI) has been set at 200 International Units daily (IU), or 5 micrograms cholecalciferol, with no increased need during pregnancy or breast-feeding. To maintain healthy bones, the 1997 revised guideline for Vitamin D doubles, going up to 400 IU, or 10 micrograms, daily for adults over age 50. Over 70 years, the guideline increases to 600 IU, or 15 micrograms, per day. *Refer to page 4 for more about Adequate Intakes, as part of the* DRIs.

***Where it's mostly found*:** Vitamin D is known as the "sunshine vitamin" because your body can make it after sunlight, or ultraviolet light, hits your skin. As a precaution, especially during the winter, for people who don't get outdoors much, and for older people whose skin is less efficient with this conversion, milk is fortified with vitamin D.

Cheese, eggs, some fish (sardines and salmon), and fortified breakfast cereals and margarine also contain small amounts of vitamin D.

Food	Vitamin D (International Units)
milk, most types (1 cup)	100
cornflakes (1 cup)	40
egg, large (1)	25
margarine (1 teaspoon)	20
salmon with bones (3 ounces)	10

Vitamin E

Refer also to "Vitamin E: One Main Mission" *on page* 92.

What it does:

- Works as an antioxidant, reducing the risk of health problems, such as heart disease and cancer, that appear as you get older.

If you don't get enough: Because it's so abundant in the food supply, a deficiency of vitamin E is rare. The two exceptions are premature, very-low birthweight infants and people who don't absorb fat normally. In these cases, the nervous system can be affected.

If you consume excess amounts: People who take large doses by mouth don't appear to have major symptoms. However, taking large doses of vitamin E as a dietary supplement also doesn't appear to have any benefits—and isn't recommended.

How much you need: The RDA guideline for males age 11 and over is 10 milligrams of alpha-tocopherol equivalents each day. For females of the same age, it's less: 8 milligrams per day. Pregnancy increases the recommendation to 10 milligrams per day, and breast-feeding, to 11 milligrams daily.

Note: Vitamin E is a group of substances called tocopherals with different potencies. The amount is given in alpha-tocopherol equivalents as a standard measure.

Where it's mostly found: The best sources of vitamin E are vegetable oils: for example, soybean, corn, cottonseed, and safflower. That includes margarine, salad dressing, and other foods made from oil. Nuts, seeds, and wheat germ—all high in oil—are good sources, too. Leafy-green vegetables also provide smaller amounts.

Food	Vitamin E (mg alpha-tocopherol)
Almonds, dried (1 ounce)	6.5
Wheat germ (1/4 cup)	4
Peanut butter (2 tablespoons)	3
Corn oil (1 tablespoon)	2
Spinach, raw (1 cup)	1

Vitamin K

What it does:

- Makes proteins that cause your blood to coagulate, or clot, when you're bleeding. That way, bleeding stops.
- Helps your body make some other body proteins for your blood, bones, and kidneys.

have you ever wondered

...if hair analysis is a valid way to diagnose a vitamin or mineral deficiency? Except to detect poisonous elements, such as lead or arsenic, hair analysis isn't a valid way to check your nutritional status. The reasons are many. Among them, hair grows slowly; the condition of hair strands differs along their length. Chemicals used to clean and treat hair affect its composition. Differences in age and gender also affect the quality of hair. Too often, those who promote hair analysis for nutrition reasons are also trying to promote dietary supplements. Buyer, beware!

...if vitamin E *in skin moisturizers gets rid of wrinkles?* Vitamins, amino acids, cocoa butter, or other nutrients in skin creams and cosmetics can't remove or prevent aging skin. The only possible exception is Retin-A, sold by prescription, which may slow the process. However, there's no research on its long-term effects. Protecting your skin from damage caused by ultraviolet light (sunshine) is the most important way you can slow the process of wrinkling. And moisturizing your skin daily with skin cream, preferably one containing a sun block of SPF 15 or more will help, too. ✦

If you don't get enough: Blood doesn't coagulate normally. Except for rare health problems, a deficiency of vitamin K is very unlikely. Prolonged use of antibiotics could be a problem since they destroy some bacteria in your intestines that produce vitamin K.

If you consume excess amounts: No symptoms have been observed—but moderation is still the best approach. People taking blood-thinning drugs, or anticoagulants, need to eat foods with vitamin K in moderation. Too much can make blood clot faster.

How much you need: The RDA advises 80 micrograms daily for men age 25 and more, and 65 micrograms daily for women of the same age. Neither pregnancy nor breast-feeding increase the recommendation. To make sure infants have enough, newborns typically receive a shot of vitamin K.

Where it's mostly found: Like vitamin D, vitamin K is one your body can produce on its own—this time from certain bacteria in your intestines.

The best food sources are green-leafy vegetables, such as spinach and broccoli. However, a variety of foods provide smaller amounts: milk and other dairy foods, meat, eggs, cereal, fruits, and other vegetables.

Food	Vitamin K (mcg)
spinach, raw (1 cup)	145
broccoli, raw (1/2 cup)	60
egg, large (1)	25
wheat bran (1 ounce)	25
wheat germ (1 ounce)	10
milk (1 cup)	10
strawberries (1/2 cup)	10
orange, medium (1)	5

Water-Soluble Vitamins

Thiamin (vitamin B_1)

What it does:

➢ Helps produce energy from carbohydrates in all the cells of your body.

If you don't get enough: Because most people consume many grain products, a thiamin deficiency is rare in the United States today with one exception: chronic alcoholics. Symptoms include fatigue, weak muscles, and nerve damage. Before refined grains were enriched with thiamin, a deficiency was common, sometimes resulting in a disease called beriberi, which affects mainly the cardiovascular and nervous systems.

If you consume excess amounts: Your body excretes any excess amount you may consume. Contrary to popular claims, extra amounts have no energy-boosting effect.

How much you need: The RDA is tied to your energy needs: 1.2 milligrams daily for males, age 14 through adulthood. For females, the recommendation is 1.0 milligrams daily from age 14 through 18 and 1.1 milligrams daily from age 19 on. During pregnancy, the amount recommended goes up to 1.4 milligrams daily; during breast-feeding, 1.5 milligrams daily.

Where it's mostly found: Whole-grain and enriched grain products, such as bread, rice, pasta, tortillas, and fortified cereals provide much of the thiamin we eat. Enrichment adds back nutrients, including many B vitamins, lost when grains are refined. Pork, liver, and other organ meats provide significant amounts, too.

Food	Thiamin (mg)
Beef liver, braised (3 ounces)	9.2
Pork, lean, broiled (3 ounces)	0.9
Enriched corn tortilla	0.2
Enriched rice, cooked (1/2 cup)	0.2
Whole-grain bread (1 slice)	0.1

Riboflavin (vitamin B_2)

What it does:

➢ Helps produce energy in all cells of your body.

➢ Helps change the amino acid called tryptophan in your food into niacin. (Protein is made of many different amino acids.)

If you don't get enough: Except for people who are severely malnourished, a deficiency isn't likely. Then the symptoms include eye disorders (including cataracts), dry and flaky skin, and a sore, red tongue. Contrary to popular myth, riboflavin deficiency doesn't cause hair loss.

If you consume excess amounts: No reports suggest problems from consuming too much.

How much you need: Like thiamin, the RDA for riboflavin is tied to your energy needs. Adult men need 1.3 milligrams daily and adult women need 1.1 milligrams daily. During pregnancy, the recommendation is 1.4 milligrams; during breast-feeding the amount goes up to 1.6 milligrams daily.

Where it's mostly found: Milk and other dairy foods are major sources of riboflavin. Some organ meats—liver, kidney, and heart—are excellent sources. Enriched bread and other grain products, eggs, meat, green-leafy vegetables, and nuts supply smaller amounts. Ultraviolet light, such as sunlight, destroys riboflavin. That's why milk is packed in opaque plastic or cardboard containers, not clear glass.

Food	Riboflavin (mg)
Beef liver, braised (3 ounces)	3.5
Yogurt, skim with dry milk solids (1 cup)	1.6
Milk, skim (1 cup)	0.4
Enriched corn tortilla (1)	0.2
Egg, large (1)	0.1
Whole-grain bread (1 slice)	0.1

Niacin

What it does:

- Helps your body use sugars and fatty acids.
- Helps enzymes function normally in your body.
- Helps produce energy in all the cells of your body.

If you don't get enough: For people who consume adequate amounts of protein-rich foods, a niacin deficiency isn't likely. Pellagra is caused by a significant niacin deficiency. Symptoms include diarrhea, mental disorientation, and skin problems.

If you consume excess amounts: Consuming excessive amounts, likely from a dietary supplement, may cause flushed skin, rashes, or liver damage. The Tolerable Upper Intake Level (UL) is 35 milligrams daily for adults. Self-prescribing large doses of niacin to lower blood cholesterol may lead to adverse effects—and may not give cholesterol-lowering benefits. If your doctor prescribes niacin, be sure to take it in the recommended dosage.

How much you need: Niacin recommendations are given in NE, or niacin equivalents. That's because it comes from two sources: niacin itself and from the amino acid called tryptophan, part of which converts to niacin.

Like thiamin and riboflavin, the recommendation is tied to energy needs. The advice for adult males is 16 milligrams NE daily and for adult females, 14 milligrams NE daily. During pregnancy, 18 milligrams NE is advised; during breast-feeding, 17 milligrams NE daily.

Where it's mostly found: Foods high in protein are typically good sources of niacin: poultry, fish, beef, peanut butter, and legumes. Niacin is also added to many enriched and fortified grain products.

have you ever *wondered*

...if microwave cooking destroys vitamins? Even proper cooking can destroy some water-soluble vitamins, such as B vitamins and vitamin C. For several reasons, more vitamins are retained with microwave cooking than with most other methods: very short cooking time, covered cooking, and little or no cooking water. *Refer to "Kitchen Nutrition: Simple Ways to Keep Vitamins in Food" on page* 88. ✦

Food	Niacin (mg NE)
turkey breast, roasted, without skin (3 ounces)	4.5
peanut butter (2 tablespoons)	4
enriched spaghetti, cooked (1/2 cup)	2.5
codfish, cooked (3 ounces)	2
enriched corn tortilla (1)	1.5
black-eyed peas, frozen, cooked (1/2 cup)	0.5
lima beans, boiled (1/2 cup)	0.5
yogurt, skim with dry milk solids (1 cup)	0.5

Pyridoxine (vitamin B_6)

What it does:

➢ Helps your body make nonessential amino acids, or proteins, which are then used to make body cells.

➢ Helps turn the amino acid called tryptophan into two important body substances: niacin and serotonin (a messenger in your brain).

➢ Helps produce other body chemicals, including insulin, hemoglobin, and antibodies that fight infection.

If you don't get enough: A deficiency can cause mental convulsions among infants, depression, nausea, or greasy, flaky skin. For infants, breast milk and properly-prepared infant formulas contain enough.

If you consume excess amounts: Large doses, taken over time, can cause nerve damage. The Tolerable Upper Intake Level (UL) is 100 milligrams daily for adults.

How much you need: The RDA is 1.3 milligrams daily for adult males and females through age 50. After age 50, the RDA increases to 1.7 milligrams daily for males and 1.5 milligrams for females. The amount increases to 1.9 milligrams daily during pregnancy and 2.0 milligrams daily during breast-feeding.

Where it's mostly found: Chicken, fish, pork, liver, and kidney are the best sources. Whole grains, nuts, and legumes also supply reasonable amounts.

Food	Pyridoxine (mg)
chicken, light meat, skinless, roasted (3 ounces)	0.5
pork, loin, roasted, (3 ounces)	0.4
peanut butter (2 tablespoons)	0.1
black beans, boiled (1/2 cup)	0.1
whole-wheat spaghetti, cooked (1/2 cup)	0.1
almonds (1 ounce)	0.1

have you ever *wondered*

...about the difference between the terms "enriched" and "fortified"? Both terms indicate that nutrients—usually vitamins or minerals—were added to make a food more nutritious. Enriched means adding back nutrients that were lost during food processing. For example, B vitamins, lost when wheat is refined, are added back to white flour. Fortified means adding nutrients that weren't present originally. For example, milk is fortified with vitamin D, a nutrient that helps your body absorb the calcium and phosphorus in milk. And according to a new law, most enriched grain products are now being fortified with folic acid to reduce the incidence of certain birth defects.

Folate (folic acid or folacin)

What it does:

➢ Plays an essential role in making new body cells, by helping to produce DNA and RNA, the cell's master plan for cell reproduction.

➢ Works with vitamin B_{12} to form hemoglobin in red blood cells.

➢ May help protect against heart disease.

➢ Helps lower the risk of delivering a baby with neural tube defects, such as spina bifida.

If you don't get enough: A deficiency affects normal cell division and protein synthesis, especially impairing growth. Anemia, caused by malformed blood cells that can't carry as much oxygen, may be the result of a folate deficiency.

Pregnant women who don't get enough folate, especially during the first trimester, have a greater risk of delivering a baby with neural tube defects such as spina bifida. (The neural tube in an embryo becomes the spinal cord.) To reduce risk, all women of childbearing years should consume adequate amounts. *Refer to "Pregnancy: Before You Begin" on page* 457.

If you consume excess amounts: Consuming too much can mask a vitamin B_{12} deficiency and may interfere with certain medications. Taking excess amounts as a dietary supplement offers no known benefits. The Tolerable Upper Intake Level (UL) is 1,000 micrograms daily of folic acid, the form of folate in fortified foods and supplements.

How much you need: For folate, the RDA for males from age 14 through adulthood is 400 micrograms daily. Folate can come from foods with naturally-occuring folate, as well as from foods fortified with folic acid and from supplements.

As added protection against neural tube defects, women capable of becoming pregnant (14–50 years) should get 400 micrograms of folic acid daily from fortified foods, vitamin supplements, or a combination of the two, in addition to the folate found naturally in certain foods. Pregnancy increases the recommended amount to 600 micrograms daily; during breast-feeding, 500 micrograms is advised.

Where it's mostly found: Leafy vegetables, some fruits, legumes, liver, yeast breads, and wheat germ, and fortified cereals are among the good sources of folate. Enriched grain products—such as most breads, flour, crackers, corn grits, cornmeal, farina, rice, macaroni, and noodles—must also be fortified with folic acid. Folic acid is the form of folate used in fortified foods and supplements. Unenriched grain products, such as some imported pastas, may not be fortified with folic acid. To be sure, check the Nutrition Facts label of grain products to see if folic acid has been added.

Food	Folate (mcg)
spinach, boiled (1/2 cup)	130
navy beans, boiled (1/2 cup)	125
wheat germ (1/4 cup)	80
avocado (1/2)	55
orange, medium (1)	45
bread, fortified with folate (1 slice)	40
peanuts, dried (1 ounce)	30
butterhead lettuce (3 leaves)	15
milk, skim (1 cup)	15

Vitamin B_{12} (cobalamin)

Refer to "Vitamin B_{12}*: A Challenge for Vegans" on page* 563.

What it does:

➢ Works closely with folate to make red blood cells.

➢ Serves as a vital part of many body chemicals and so occurs in every body cell.

➢ Helps your body use fatty acids and some amino acids.

If you don't get enough: A deficiency may result in anemia, fatigue, nerve damage, a smooth tongue, or very sensitive skin. A deficiency of vitamin B_{12} can be masked—and even progress—if extra folic acid is taken to treat or prevent anemia.

Either for genetic or medical reasons, some people develop a deficiency—pernicious anemia—because they can't absorb vitamin B_{12}. They're missing a body chemical called intrinsic factor that comes from their stomach lining. This problem can be medically treated with injections of vitamin B_{12}.

Strict vegetarians, who eat no animal products, and their infants are at risk for developing a vitamin B_{12} deficiency. This could cause severe anemia and irreversible nerve damage. The elderly are also at risk. Including foods fortified with vitamin B_{12} or dietary supplements can prevent vitamin B_{12} deficiency.

If you consume excess amounts: No symptoms are known—but taking extra vitamin B_{12} to boost energy has no basis in science.

KITCHEN NUTRITION
simple ways to keep vitamins in food

➢ Leave edible skins on vegetables and fruits. And trim away as little as possible. Most vitamins and minerals are found in the outer leaves, skin, and area just below the skin—not in the center.

➢ Cook vegetables or fruits in a small amount of water—or none at all. Steam or microwave them. Avoid soaking them as you wash. Some vitamins dissolve in water.

➢ Cut vegetables that need to be cooked longer, but in larger pieces. With fewer surfaces exposed, less vitamins are lost.

➢ Cook vegetables and fruits in a covered pot. That way steam doesn't escape, and cooking time is faster.

➢ Eat vegetables and fruits raw. Or cook as quickly as possible—just until tender-crisp. Some vitamins, such as B vitamins and vitamin C, are destroyed easily by heat.

➢ Save liquid from cooking vegetables; add it to soups, stews, and sauces.

➢ Cook vegetables without adding baking soda. Although the alkali in baking soda keeps vegetables looking greener, it also destroys some vitamins.

➢ Keep milk in opaque containers—and in the refrigerator. Leaving it in a clear, glass pitcher on the table allows some riboflavin to be destroyed by sunlight. ✦

For more on handling and preparing food to maintain its vitamin content, refer to "Food 'Prep': The Nutrition-Flavor Connection" on page 328.

How much you need: The RDA is 2.4 micrograms daily for adults. The recommendation increases to 2.6 micrograms daily during pregnancy and 2.8 milligrams daily during breast-feeding.

Where it's mostly found: Vitamin B_{12} comes from animal products—meat, fish, poultry, eggs, milk, and other dairy foods. Some fortified foods may contain it, too.

Food	Vitamin B_{12} (mcg)
salmon, cooked (3 ounces)	2.6
beef tenderloin lean, broiled (3 ounces)	2.2
yogurt, skim with dry milk solids (1 cup)	1.4
shrimp, cooked (3 ounces)	1.3
milk (1 cup)	0.5
chicken, light meat, skinless, roasted (3 ounces)	0.3
egg, large (1)	0.1

Biotin

What it does:

➢ Helps your body produce energy in your cells.

➢ Helps metabolize (or use) protein, fat, and carbohydrate from food.

If you don't get enough: That's rarely a problem for healthy people who eat a healthful diet. In those rare cases, these symptoms may appear: heart abnormalities, appetite loss, fatigue, depression, or dry skin.

If you consume excess amounts: There are no reported effects of consuming excess amounts.

How much you need: The Adequate Intake (AI) for biotin is 30 micrograms daily for adult males and females, including pregnancy. The AI increases to 35 micrograms daily during breast-feeding.

Where it's mostly found: Biotin is found in a wide variety of foods. Eggs, liver, yeast breads, and cereals are among the best sources.

Food	Biotin (mcg)
egg, large (1)	10
wheat germ (1/4 cup)	6
oatmeal, cooked (1/2 cup)	5
shredded wheat cereal (1 1/2 ounces)	4
pancakes (three 4-inch)	3

Pantothenic Acid

What it does:

➢ Helps your body cells produce energy.

➢ Helps metabolize (or use) protein, fat, and carbohydrate from food.

If you don't get enough: That's rarely a problem for healthy people who eat a healthful diet.

If you consume excess amounts: The only apparent effects are occasional diarrhea and water retention.

How much you need: The Adequate Intake (AI) for pantothenic acid is 5 milligrams daily for adults. During pregnancy and breast-feeding, the AI increases to 6 and 7 milligrams, respectively.

Where it's mostly found: Pantothenic acid is widely available in food. Meat, poultry, fish, whole-grain cereals, and legumes are among the better sources. Milk, vegetables, and fruits also contain varying amounts.

Food	Pantothenic Acid (mg)
salmon, cooked (3 ounces)	1.7
chicken, light meat, skinless, roasted (3 ounces)	0.9
yogurt, whole milk (1 cup)	0.9
sweet potato, mashed, cooked (1/2 cup)	0.9
milk, skim (1 cup)	0.8
ham, lean (3 ounces)	0.8
corn, boiled (1/2 cup)	0.7
egg, large (1)	0.7
whole-wheat macaroni, cooked (1/2 cup)	0.3
kidney beans, cooked (1/2 cup)	0.2

Vitamin C (ascorbic acid)

See "Vitamin C: More Jobs Than You Think!" on page 91.

What it does:

➢ Helps produce collagen, a connective tissue that holds muscles, bones, and other tissues together.

➢ Helps keep capillary walls and blood vessels firm, and so protects you from bruising.

➢ Helps your body absorb iron from plant sources of food.

➢ Helps keep your gums healthy.

➢ Helps heal any cuts and wounds and can protect you from infection by keeping your immune system healthy.

If you don't get enough: Eventually, a severe deficiency of vitamin C leads to scurvy, a disease that causes loose teeth, excessive bleeding, and swollen gums. Wounds may not heal properly either. Because vitamin C-rich foods are widely available, scurvy is rare in the United States today.

have you ever wondered

...if bleeding gums mean you're not getting enough vitamin C? It's not likely unless you have a severe deficiency. Most cases of bleeding gums come from poor oral hygiene. Brushing and flossing regularly helps keep your gums healthy. *For more about healthy gums, refer to page* 498.

...what choline does.? Choline, a natural food component, is widely distributed in food. Milk, liver, eggs and peanuts are especially good sources. Choline appears to play a role in many body processes. However, there is much to be learned about its role in human health. In 1998, an Adequte Intake (AI) level for choline was set for the first time (*see page* 607). The Tolerable Upper Intake Level for adults is 3.5 milligrams daily. ✦

VITAMIN C: MORE THAN CITRUS

Citrus fruits—orange, grapefruit, tangerine—are well-known sources of vitamin C. Yet many other fruits and vegetables are excellent sources, too. Enjoy at least one serving of vitamin C-rich foods daily.

Food	Approximate Milligrams (mg)
Guava, medium (1)	165
Red bell pepper (1/2 cup)	95
Papaya, medium (1/2)	95
Orange juice, from frozen concentrate (3/4 cup)	75
Orange, medium (1)	60
Broccoli, boiled (1/2 cup)	60
Green bell pepper (1/2 cup)	45
Kohlrabi, boiled (1/2 cup)	45
Strawberries (1/2 cup)	45
Grapefruit, white (1/2)	40
Cantaloupe (1/2 cup)	35
Tomato juice (3/4 cup)	35
Mango, medium (1/2)	30
Tangerine, medium (1)	25
Potato, baked with skin (1)	25
Cabbage, raw (1/2 cup)	25
Tomato, medium, raw (1)	25
Collard greens, frozen, boiled (1/2 cup)	25
Spinach, raw (1 cup)	15

Some fruit drinks and other processed foods are fortified with vitamin C. Check the Nutrition Facts panel for the amount per serving. And remember, if you rely only on fortified foods as your vitamin C source, you may miss out on other nutrients and compounds present in foods with naturally-occurring vitamin C. ✦

If you consume an excess amount: Because vitamin C is water-soluble, your body excretes the excess. Very large doses may cause kidney stones and diarrhea. But effects of taking large amounts over a long period of time isn't known.

How much you need: For people age 15 and over (males and females), 60 milligrams of vitamin C (the amount in a 3/4-cup of orange juice) daily supplies enough for everyday needs. Women need somewhat more during pregnancy (70 milligrams) and breast-feeding (90 to 95 milligrams). People who smoke need about twice as much vitamin C as nonsmokers—at least 100 milligrams of vitamin C daily.

Where it's mostly found: Most vitamin C comes from plant sources of food. All citrus fruits, including oranges, grapefruits, and tangerines, are good sources. And many other fruits and vegetables, including berries, melons, peppers, many dark-green leafy vegetables, potatoes, and tomatoes supply significant amounts, too. *Refer to "Vitamin C: More Than Citrus" on this page for a list of good sources and amounts.*

Antioxidant Vitamins: A Closer Look

You've probably read the headlines: "Antioxidants Promote Health!" or "Antioxidants Prevent Aging."

A quick trip through the supermarket shows that many food manufacturers are fortifying food with antioxidant vitamins: beta carotene (which forms vitamin A), vitamin C, and vitamin E. Just what makes these three antioxidant vitamins unique? What foods supply them? How do they work in your body? And how may antioxidants promote health and reduce the risk of chronic, or ongoing, diseases? *"Rounding Up Free Radicals" on page 93 explains how antioxidants appear to work.*

Carotenoids: "Color" Your Food Healthy

Imagine a beautiful autumn day. Leaves of red, orange, and yellow rustle in the branches overhead. The colors of the season belong to carotenoids, or plant pigments that are generally red, orange, and deep yellow.

The array of colors in fruits and vegetables also come from carotenoids. The clues to their presence are obvious in the vibrant palette of produce in your supermarket. It's no surprise that apricots, cantaloupes, mangos, carrots, red and yellow peppers, and sweet potatoes, for example, all contain carotenes. Broccoli, kale, romaine lettuce, and spinach have carotene, too—even though they're dark green! The orange-yellow color of their carotene gets hidden by the chlorophyll in the leaves. *The chart "Vitamin A: Good Picks" on this page lists good food sources and amounts.*

Beta carotene is the carotenoid most familiar to us. Actually the plant world has more than 500 known carotenoids, with 50 in food that convert to vitamin A. Of those, only a few have been analyzed in fruits and vegetables: alpha carotene, beta carotene, gamma carotene, lycopene, lutein, and zeaxanthin.

By changing to vitamin A, beta carotene performs many functions in your overall health. *Refer to "Vitamins: The Basics" on page* 80. Beta carotene has another role as an antioxidant vitamin, potentially offering protection from some diseases and degenerative aspects of aging.

For foods high in beta carotene and other carotenoids, try to choose red, orange, deep-yellow, and some dark-green leafy vegetables every day. Be aware that color is a clue, not an assurance, that fruits and vegetables are good sources of beta carotene. For example, despite their color, neither corn nor snow peas have much beta carotene—but they do supply other nutrients.

Vitamin C: More Jobs Than You Think!

Also known as ascorbic acid, vitamin C is a water-soluble vitamin. As an antioxidant, vitamin C protects your body in much the same way that beta carotene and vitamin E do. The main difference is that vitamin C attacks free radicals in body fluids, not in fat tissue. Being water soluble, it may protect different parts of your body.

Vitamin C has many other responsibilities for your health, too. Among them, vitamin C helps form the connective tissue that holds the many structures of your body together. It keeps capillaries healthy so

VITAMIN A: GOOD PICKS

Either from retinol or beta carotene, many foods are good sources of vitamin A. These foods are some examples of "good picks." Enjoy at least one serving of vitamin A-rich foods daily.

Food	Approximate Retinol Equivalents (RE)*
Beef liver, cooked (3 ounces)	9,085
Sweet potato, mashed (1/2 cup)	2,800
Carrot (1 medium)	2,025
Kale, boiled (1/2 cup)	480
Mango, medium (1/2)	405
Turnip greens, cooked (1/2 cup)	395
Spinach, raw (1 cup)	375
Papaya, medium (1/2)	305
Red bell pepper, raw (1/2 cup)	285
Apricot (3)	275
Cantaloupe (1/2 cup)	260
Milk, skim (1 cup)	150
Romaine lettuce (1 cup)	145
Egg, large (1)	95
Tomato, medium, raw (1)	75
Milk, whole (1 cup)	75
Broccoli, raw (1/2 cup)	70
Green bell pepper, raw (1/2 cup)	30
Collards, frozen, boiled (1/2 cup)	30
Orange, medium (1)	30

Many fortified foods, including breakfast cereals, are sources of vitamin A, too. Read the Nutrition Facts panel on food labels to see how much they supply. ✦

* *The vitamin A content of food is measured in both Retinol Equivalents (RE) and International Units (IU). The Recommended Dietary Allowances (RDA) are expressed in REs, while the % Daily Values—used on food labels and many dietary supplements—are based in IUs.*

you don't bruise easily, and your gums healthy so they don't bleed.

Vitamin C works in partnership with iron, too, helping the body to absorb iron from plant sources of food. *Refer to "Iron in Foods: Heme vs. Non-Heme" on page* 110. In fact, an adequate daily supply of vitamin C in your food choices can increase the absorption of non-heme iron (mostly from plant sources) by as much as two to four times. As a result, for those who get most of their iron from plant sources of food, including vegetarians, vitamin C takes on special importance.

Over the years, vitamin C developed celebrity status with claims that it can prevent or cure the common cold. Although those claims have been overblown, an adequate intake of vitamin C does play an important role in fighting infection. For colds, extra vitamin C may have a mild antihistamine effect, perhaps shortening the duration of a cold and making the symptoms more mild. However, scientific evidence doesn't justify taking large doses of vitamin C on a regular basis to boost immunity.

Because vitamin C isn't stored in the body, you're wise to consume a vitamin C-rich food daily. *The chart "Vitamin C: More Than Citrus" on page 90 list several good sources.* If you habitually consume a vitamin C-rich fruit or juice with breakfast, you probably consume enough.

Vitamin E: One Main Mission

For years, vitamin E has been surrounded by pseudo-scientific myths. It's been misguidedly acclaimed as a cure for almost all that ails you: for example, improving sexual prowess, curing infertility, preventing aging, curing heart disease and cancer, improving athletic performance, to name just a few. The benefits of vitamin E don't extend this far, but it does appear to play a broad role in promoting your health.

Unlike many other vitamins, the main role of vitamin E—a fat-soluble vitamin—appears to be as an antioxidant. As such, it protects body cells from oxidation, which leads to cell damage. This cell damage can lead ultimately to health problems, such as cancer, heart disease, and cataracts, that appear as you get older. Vitamin E appears to work hand-in-hand with other antioxidants like vitamin C and selenium to offer protection from some chronic diseases.

Vitamin E is actually a group of substances called tocopherols, all with different potencies. For this reason, they're often measured as milligrams of alpha-tocopherol equivalents.

PHYTOCHEMICALS—WHAT ROLE IN HEALTH?

Besides nutrients, there's another "crop" of compounds in plant foods—legumes, vegetables, fruits, and whole grains—that may affect your body. Collectively they're called phytochemicals, meaning plant chemicals.

Phytochemicals are substances that plants naturally produce to protect themselves against viruses, bacteria, and fungi. And they include hundreds of naturally-occurring substances, including carotenoids, flavonoids, indoles, isoflavones, capsaicin, and protease inhibitors. As with vitamins and minerals, different plant foods supply different kinds and amounts of phytochemicals.

Their exact role in promoting health is still uncertain. However, certain phytochemicals may help protect against some cancers, heart disease, and other chronic health conditions. So, stay tuned!

Until scientific research learns more, the nutrition bottom line still applies: Include a wide variety of fruits, vegetables, legumes, and grains, including whole grains. And count on food, not dietary supplements, for the health qualities they provide. That way, you'll reap the potential benefits of the many phytochemicals found in all kinds of foods from plant sources. ✦

Where do you get vitamin E? Vitamin E is found most abundantly in vegetable oils, salad dressings, margarine, and other processed foods made with vegetable oils. Vitamin E also is found in wheat germ, whole-grain products, seeds, nuts, and peanut butter. It's also added to processed foods as a preservative. (*Note*: Heating vegetable oils to high temperatures, as in frying, destroys vitamin E.)

In vegetable oils, nuts, and seeds, vitamin E protects their unsaturated fats from oxidation. Typically, foods high in unsaturated fats also are good sources of vitamin E.

Rounding Up Free Radicals

Just how do antioxidant vitamins work? First, let's take a close look inside the body to learn more about oxygen. To produce energy, every cell in your body needs a constant supply of oxygen. For this reason, oxygen is basic to life.

There's another side to the oxygen story, however. When body cells burn oxygen, they form free radicals, or oxygen by-products. These free radicals can damage body cells and tissues, as well as the DNA, which is your body's master plan for reproducing cells. Environmental factors, such as cigarette smoke, burns, and ultraviolet light, also cause free radicals to form in your body.

Damage caused by oxidation is quite familiar: for example, the quick browning on a cut apple or pear, and rancidity in oils. However, if you dip your apple or pear in orange juice which has vitamin C, it stays white. And if vitamin E is added as a preservative to vegetable oil, it doesn't turn rancid as fast.

In your body, the process is similar. Free radicals cause oxidation, or cell damage that may lead to the onset of health problems, such as cancer, artery and heart disease, cataracts, arthritis, and some deterioration that goes with aging. Antioxidants in your body counteract the effects of free radicals.

Three antioxidant vitamins appear to play a very unique role by "neutralizing" free radicals: beta carotene, vitamin C, and vitamin E. Some enzymes that have trace minerals—selenium, copper, zinc, and manganese—act as antioxidants, too. As scavengers, antioxidant vitamins mop up free radicals. The result? Free radicals are converted to harmless waste products that get eliminated before they do damage. Antioxidants even may help undo some of the damage already done to body cells.

Each antioxidant has its own biological job description. Being water-soluble, vitamin C removes free radicals from fluids inside and outside of body cells. Beta carotene and vitamin E, because they're fat-soluble, are present in lipids and fat tissues in your body. Antioxidants seem to complement each other. Because they work together, an excess or deficiency of one many inhibit the benefits of other antioxidants.

A "Garden" of Antioxidants

Where should your source of antioxidant vitamins come from? An eating style with plenty of fruits and vegetables (at least five a day) is undisputed as the wisest approach to good health. Eating plenty of

Vitamins and Minerals

The lingo on the front of many food packages describes the amount of vitamins or minerals found in a single serving. For specific amounts of the nutrients described, check the Nutrition Facts on the label.

High, Rich in, Excellent source of means 20% or more of Daily Value*.

Good source, Contains, Provides means 10 to 19% of Daily Value*.

More, Enriched, Fortified, Added means 10% or more of Daily Value*. ✦

**as compared with a standard serving size of the traditional food*

whole-grain foods (at least three servings daily), as well as nuts, containing vitamin E is important, too. *Refer to "Fruits and Vegetables: Count Five a Day!" on page* 96 *and "Whole Grains: For Goodness Sake" on page* 103.

Many foods on supermarket shelves are fortified with antioxidant vitamins: C, E, and beta carotene. While they may not supply enough of these vitamins for their possible protective benefits, they do serve as sources of these essential nutrients. Fruits and vegetables are still the best sources of beta carotene and vitamin C and may contain other natural compounds that help prevent health problems, such as some cancers and heart disease.

There's debate about consuming additional amounts of antioxidants from dietary supplements. Scientists don't know exactly how much would be enough—or how many years you'd need to take them. And they don't know enough yet about side effects that might appear from taking supplemental antioxidants over long periods of time. So far, for example, taking beta carotene or vitamin A,C, or E supplements hasn't been shown to reduce cancer risk, and high doses of beta carotene from supplements may be harmful. Continuing research on antioxidant vitamins will unlock the answers. Until more is known, continue to enjoy the wide variety of fruits, vegetables, and grains with naturally-occurring antioxidants.

Minerals—Not "Heavy Metal"

The term "minerals" may conjure up thoughts of rocks. But to your body, minerals are another group of essential nutrients, needed to both regulate body processes and give your body structure.

Like vitamins, minerals help trigger, or regulate, a myriad of processes that continually take place in your body. And so they are essential to your life. For example, they regulate fluid balance, muscle contractions, and nerve impulses.

Even though they make up only a small percentage—about 4 percent—of your weight, minerals also help give your body structure. They not only give structure to bones and teeth, but muscle, blood, and other body tissue all contain minerals, too.

Unlike vitamins, minerals are inorganic. Minerals can't be destroyed by heat or other food handling processes. In fact, if you've ever completely burned food, perhaps while cooking over a fire, the little bit of ash left over is its mineral content.

You might think of minerals in two categories—major minerals and trace minerals—depending on how much you need. Regardless of amount, they're all essential.

Major minerals: Major minerals are needed in greater amounts—more than 250 milligrams recommended daily. Calcium, phosphorus, and magnesium fit in this category, along with three electrolytes—sodium, chloride, and potassium.

Electrolytes are grouped together because their work is interrelated. They regulate body fluids in and out of every cell, and they transmit nerve, or electrical, impulses. *To learn more about electrolytes, refer to "Sodium: You Need Some!" on page* 158.

Trace Minerals: Your body needs just small amounts—less than 20 milligrams daily—of the trace minerals, or trace elements: chromium, copper, fluoride, iodine, iron, manganese, molybdenum, selenium, and zinc. Recommended Dietary Allowances have only been set for a few of them: iron, zinc, iodine, and selenium. Until science learns more, others are presented either as Adequate Intake Levels or as a range of Estimated Safe and Adequate Daily Dietary Intakes.

Other trace elements have been identified, including tin, arsenic, silicon, vanadium, nickel, and boron. But we know even less about their role in human health or how much the body needs. For minerals, such as arsenic, the amount is likely very small. No RDAs nor "safe and adequate" ranges are set for them yet. A healthful diet that's varied, balanced, and moderate is the best way to consume safe, adequate amounts.

All minerals are absorbed into your intestines, and transported and stored in your body in different ways. Some pass directly into your bloodstream, where they're transported to cells; any excess passes out of the body through urine. Others attach to proteins and become part of your body structure. Because they're stored, excess amounts can be harmful if the levels consumed are too high for too long.

The following section describes how these minerals keep you healthy: their functions, effects of getting too little or too much, Dietary Reference Intakes, and sources. *Specific guidelines for many minerals appear on pages 606 and 607.*

Note: On the following pages, the amounts of minerals in foods have been rounded.

Major Minerals

Calcium

Refer to "Calcium: A Closer Look" on page 105.

What it does:

- ➢ Builds bones, both in length and strength, becoming part of bone tissue.
- ➢ Helps your bones remain strong by slowing the rate of bone loss as you age.
- ➢ Helps your muscles contract and your heart beat.
- ➢ Plays a role in normal nerve function.
- ➢ Helps your blood clot if you're bleeding.

If you don't get enough: For children, not getting enough calcium may interfere with growth; a severe deficiency may keep them from reaching their potential adult height. Even a mild deficiency over a lifetime can affect bone density and bone loss, increasing the risk for osteoporosis, or brittle bone disease. *Refer to "Bone Up on Calcium" on page 105.*

If you consume excess amounts: Unless the doses are very large (more than 2,500 milligrams daily), adverse effects for adults are unlikely. Very large doses over a prolonged period of time may cause kidney stones and poor kidney function. Your body may not absorb other minerals, such as iron, magnesium, and zinc, properly. These problems could occur from consuming too much through a calcium supplement, not from milk or other calcium-rich foods. The Tolerable Upper Intake Level (UL) from the Dietary Reference Intakes is set at 2,500 milligrams daily from age 1 on through adulthood.

How much you need: The 1997 updates increased calcium guidelines. For age 9 through 18, the Adequate Intake (AI) is 1,300 milligrams daily. As an adult through age 50, the AI is 1,000 milligrams of calcium daily. After that, the recommendation goes back up to 1,200 milligrams calcium daily for both men and women to help maintain bone mass. Calcium recommendations for women who are pregnant or breast-feeding are the same as for other women in their respective age group. *Refer to "Calcium: Enough vs. Optimal Amounts" on page 106.*

have you ever wondered

...how tortillas made with corn could have calcium? Made in the traditional Mexican way, corn tortillas can supply significant amounts of calcium, especially to people who eat them as the main bread in their diet. Corn itself doesn't have calcium. But to prepare corn for tortillas, it's first soaked in slake lime to remove the hard coating on corn kernels. This lime isn't from citrus fruit; instead it's calcium oxide, which is safe when used this way in food processing.

...how frozen yogurt compares nutritionally to regular yogurt? Regular yogurt—plain or fruit flavored—supplies considerably more calcium than frozen yogurt. The nutrient content of frozen yogurt is variable but more similar to low-fat ice cream than to regular yogurt. But because no federal standards exist for frozen yogurt, you'll want to read the label to learn the nutrient content. ✦

Fruits and Vegetables: Count Five a Day!

As a child, you probably enjoyed fruits and vegetables for their vibrant colors, crunch, and wonderful flavors. You probably also learned that fruits and vegetables were good for you. Today, science has a better understanding of the reasons why they should be part of a varied, balanced, and moderate diet. Although their nutrient content varies, fruits and vegetables are good sources of vitamins A (and beta carotene) and C. Some also supply significant amounts of folacin, vitamin B_6, potassium, calcium, magnesium, and selenium. Each of these nutrients plays a role in the normal, everyday functioning of your body and may help lower the risks of some cancers, heart disease, and other health problems. Fruits and vegetables are also good sources of complex carbohydrates and fiber and, unless added, are low in fat, saturated fat, and sodium.

The Dietary Guidelines for Americans offers this advice: Choose a diet with plenty of grain products, vegetables, and fruits. *For more, refer to "A Glimpse at the Dietary Guidelines" on page* 5.

As a daily guideline, the Food Guide Pyramid recommends three to five servings of vegetables, and two to four servings of fruit along with a variety of food. Eating at least the minimum number of servings adds up to "five a day." *For more variety, refer to "Garden of Eatin': Uncommon Vegetables" on page* 215 *and "Fresh Ideas: Uncommon Fruit" on page* 219.

Try to eat at least one vitamin A-rich choice daily. Many fruits and vegetables contain beta carotene, which forms vitamin A.

Eat at least one vitamin C-rich choice daily.

Eat at least one high-fiber choice daily. *Refer to chapter* 6, *"Fiber: Your Body's Broom."*

Eat vegetables from the cabbage family several times a week. Cruciferous vegetables, such as bok choy, broccoli, collards, cabbage, turnips, and others, may help to protect against colon and rectal cancer. *Refer to "What Are Cruciferous Vegetables...And What Do They Do?" on page* 249.

Five + Five + Five Ways to Enjoy More!

1. ***Wake up to fruit!*** Make a habit of drinking juice, or complementing cereal, yogurt, or pancakes with naturally sweet sliced or dried fruit.

2. ***Try some "grate" ways.*** Add grated, shredded, or chopped vegetables, such as zucchini, spinach, and carrots to lasagna, meatloaf, mashed potatoes, and mixed meat, poultry, pasta, and grain dishes.

3. ***Be saucy with fruit.*** Purée berries, apples, peaches, or pears, for a thick, sweet sauce on grilled or broiled seafood or poultry.

4. ***Get creative with pizza.*** Order or make it "deluxe" with vegetable toppings: broccoli florets, carrot shreds, thinly-sliced zucchini, chopped spinach, red and green bell pepper strips, chopped tomato, or any other veggie!

5. ***Drink juice as a snack beverage.*** Try a variety of juices: grapefruit, apple, cranberry, orange, grape, papaya, tomato, and mango juices, as well as apricot or pear nectar. Even mix them up!

6. ***Bake with fruits and vegetables.*** Use puréed fruit, such as applesauce, prunes, bananas, or peaches, in place of about half the fat in recipes for homemade breads, muffins, pancakes, cookies, and other baked goods. For flavor, texture, and nutrients, blend in shredded zucchini, carrots, or dried fruits.

7. *"Sandwich" in fruit and vegetables.* Add pizzazz to sandwiches by including sliced pineapple, apple, peppers, cucumbers, sprouts, and tomato as fillings.

8. *Combine it with veggies.* Make a quick stir-fry or combine pasta with just about any vegetables. Or add them to soup. These are great ways to use up fresh vegetables before they spoil. *Hint:* Add legumes, too.

9. *Take a fruit to lunch!* Make a habit of tucking an apple, tangerine, two plums or kiwis, grapes, cherries, dried fruits, or other fruit into your briefcase, tote bag, or lunch bag. Fruit is a great traveler for snacks, too.

10. *Stuff an omelette with veggies.* Turn your omelette into a hearty meal with crisp, tasty vegetables like broccoli, squash, carrots, peppers, tomatoes, or onions.

11. *Toss up a vegetable salad.* Add extra cut-up vegetables, legumes, and fruits to salads.

12. *When you eat out, order more vegetables and fruits.* Choose a vegetable appetizer or soup. Order a side dish of vegetables, legumes, or a salad with a meal, or fruit for dessert.

13. *Count your beans.* If you consume enough protein-rich foods from the Meat, Poultry, Fish, Dry Beans, Eggs, and Nuts Group, legumes can count as a serving from the Vegetable Group. Try adding cooked beans, peas, or lentils to salads, casseroles, and pasta dishes.

14. *Make dips and spreads with vegetables and fruit.* Spicy salsas can be made with tomato, bell peppers, onions, and cilantro. For a tangy twist, also look for salsas with pineapple, mango, or peaches. Try hummus, made with mashed chickpeas; or caponata; or baba ghanoush, made with eggplant.

15. Stock your 'fridge with raw vegetables and fruits—"nature's fast food"—cleaned, fresh, and ready to eat.

For more ideas on adding vegetables and fruits to your diet, refer to the "Pyramid Pointers" on pages 247 and 253.

Produce "Package"

	VITAMIN A	VITAMIN C	FOLATE	POTAS-SIUM	DIETARY FIBER
VEGETABLES					
Beans, kidney (1/2 cup)			X	X	X
Beans, lima (1/2 cup)		X		X	X
Black-eyed peas (1/2 cup)			X		X
Broccoli (1/2 cup)	X	X	X		X
Carrots (1/2 cup)	X				X
Collards (1/2 cup)	X	X			
Kale (1/2 cup)	X	X			
Lentils (1/2 cup)			X	X	X
Peas, green (1/2 cup)		X	X	X	X
Peas, split (1/2 cup)			X	X	X
Potato (1 medium)				X	
Potato, with skin (1 medium)		X		X	X
Spinach, cooked (1/2 cup)	X	X	X	X	X
Squash, winter (1/2 cup)	X	X		X	X
Sweet potato (1 medium)	X	X		X	X
Tomato (1)	X	X		X	X
Turnip greens (1/2 cup)	X	X	X		
FRUITS					
Apple, with skin (1)		X			X
Apricot, dried (3)	X	X		X	X
Banana (1)		X		X	X
Cantaloupe (1/2 cup)	X	X		X	
Grapefruit (1/2)		X			
Grapefruit juice (3/4 cup)		X		X	
Honeydew melon (1/2 cup)		X		X	
Orange (1)		X	X		X
Orange juice (3/4 cup)		X	X	X	
Pear, with skin (1)		X			X
Prunes (4)					X
Prune juice (3/4 cup)				X	
Strawberries (1/2 cup)		X			X
Watermelon (1 cup)	X	X			

Note: *A good source of a vitamin or mineral contributes at least 10 percent of its Daily Value (DV) in a selected serving size. A source of dietary fiber contributes at least 2 grams of dietary fiber in a selected serving size.*

Where it's mostly found: Milk and other dairy foods such as yogurt and most cheeses are the best sources of calcium. In addition, some dark green leafy vegetables (kale, broccoli, bok choy), fish with edible bones, calcium-fortified soy milk, and tofu made with calcium sulfate also supply significant amounts. *Refer to "Counting Up Calcium" on page 107 for a list of good sources and amounts.*

Phosphorus

What it does:

- ➢ Helps generate energy in every cell of your body.
- ➢ Acts as the main regulator of energy metabolism in your body's organs.
- ➢ Is a major component of bones and teeth, second only to calcium.
- ➢ Serves as part of DNA and RNA, which are your body's master plan for cell growth and repair.

If you don't get enough: A deficiency is quite rare, except for small premature babies who consume only breast milk, or for people who take an antacid with aluminum hydroxide for a long time. In those rare cases, the symptoms include bone loss, weakness, loss of appetite, and pain.

If you consume excess amounts: An excess amount may lower the level of calcium in the blood—a problem if calcium intake is low. As a result, bone loss may increase. Consuming too much phosphorus doesn't appear to be a problem in the United States. The Tolerable Upper Intake Level (UL) for phosphorus is 4,000 milligrams a day for people ages nine through 70; after age 70, it's 3,000 milligrams phosphorus daily. For pregnancy, the level drops slightly to 3,500 milligrams phosphorus daily.

How much you need: As updated in 1997, the RDA for phosphorus is 1,250 milligrams daily for ages 9 through 18, then decreases to 700 milligrams daily for adults of all ages. Scientific evidence shows that people need less than previously thought.

Where it's mostly found: Almost all foods contain phosphorus. Protein-rich foods—milk, meat, poultry, fish, and eggs—contain the most. Legumes and nuts are good sources as well. Even bread and other baked foods have some. You'll also find phosphorus in colas and pepper-type soft drinks.

Food	Phosphorous (mg)
milk, whole (1 cup)	230
perch, cooked (3 ounces)	220
lean ground beef, cooked (3 ounces)	60
cheddar cheese (1 ounce)	145
kidney beans, cooked (1/2 cup)	125
tofu (1/2 cup)	120
peanut butter (2 tablespoons)	105
egg, large (1)	90
cola (12 ounces)	45

Magnesium

What it does:

- ➢ Serves as an important part of more than 300 body enzymes. Enzymes are body chemicals that regulate all kinds of body functions, including producing energy, making body protein, and muscle contractions.
- ➢ Helps maintain body cells in nerves and muscles.
- ➢ Serves as a component of bones.

If you don't get enough: A deficiency is rare except in diseases where the body doesn't absorb magnesium properly. Then symptoms might include irregular heartbeat, nausea, weakness, and mental derangement.

If you consume an excess amount: Consuming too much magnesium from food probably won't do any harm—unless it can't be excreted properly due to kidney disease.

How much you need: As updated in 1997, the RDA for teenage boys is 410 milligrams magnesium daily to age 18; for teenage girls, 360 milligrams daily. The RDA for adult males is 400 milligrams daily through age 30, then 420 milligrams daily after that. For females, the recommendation is 310 milligrams daily through age 30, then 320 milligrams daily after age 30. Neither pregnancy or breast-feeding increase the need for magnesium.

Where it's mostly found: Magnesium is found in varying amounts in all kinds of foods. The best sources are legumes, nuts, and whole grains. Green vegetables are good sources, too.

Food	Magnesium (mg)
spinach, boiled (1/2 cup)	80
peanut butter (2 tablespoons)	50
black-eyed peas, boiled (1/2 cup)	45
pecans, dried (1 ounce)	35
whole-wheat bread (1 slice)	25
parsnips, boiled (1/2 cup)	25
whole-wheat spaghetti, cooked (1/2 cup)	20
lima beans, boiled (1/2 cup)	15

Major Minerals: Electrolytes

Chloride

What it does:

- Helps regulate fluids in and out of body cells.
- As a component of stomach acid, helps with the digestion of your food and the absorption of nutrients.
- Helps transmit nerve impulses, or signals.

If you don't get enough: Because salt is such a common part of the diet, a deficiency of chloride isn't likely if you're healthy. Chloride loss goes along with sodium loss; they're replenished together. Their deficiency symptoms are similar, too.

If you consume excess amounts: For people who are sensitive, there may be a link to high blood pressure. But more study is needed.

How much you need: There's no RDA for chloride. However, most healthy people can satisfy their chloride needs with a minimum of 750 milligrams daily. Higher amounts don't appear to have any extra benefits.

Where it's mostly found: Salt is made of sodium and chloride. So salt and salty foods are the main sources of chloride. As a point of reference, 1/4 teaspoon of salt contains 750 milligrams of chloride.

Potassium

Refer to "Potassium: Another Reason for 'Five a Day'" on page 159.

What it does:

- Helps regulate fluids and mineral balance in and out of body cells.
- Helps maintain your normal blood pressure.
- Helps transmit nerve impulses, or signals.
- Helps your muscles contract.

If you don't get enough: For healthy people, a potassium deficiency is rare. But when vomiting, diarrhea, and laxative use goes on for too long, the body may lose excess amounts. Kidney problems may also cause severe loss. The deficiency symptoms caused by these problems include weakness, appetite loss, nausea, and fatigue. You may need a potassium supplement if you're taking medication for high blood pressure. Talk to your doctor.

If you consume excess amounts: Harmful effects of consuming too much are rare because excess amounts usually are excreted. If an excess can't be excreted, it can cause heart problems. People with kidney problems may not be able to get rid of excess potassium and may be advised to limit potassium-containing foods and to avoid using potassium chloride as a salt substitute.

How much you need: There is no RDA for potassium. But the minimum amount suggested for adults is 2,000 milligrams a day; some experts suggest more, about 3,500 milligrams per day, to help protect against high blood pressure.

Where it's mostly found: Potassium is found in a wide range of foods, especially fruits, many vegetables, and fresh meat, poultry, and fish. Less processed foods tend to have more potassium.

Food	Potassium (mg)
banana, medium (1)	450
milk, whole (1 cup)	370
haddock, cooked (3 ounces)	340
okra, boiled (1/2 cup)	255
turkey, light and dark meat, roasted, skinless (3 ounces)	255
orange, medium (1)	250
tomato, raw	135
bell pepper (1/2 cup)	90

Sodium

Refer to chapter 7, "Sodium: A Salty Subject."

What it does:

- Helps regulate the movement of body fluids in and out of your body cells.
- Helps your muscles relax, including your heart.
- Helps transmit nerve impulses, or signals.
- Helps regulate your blood pressure.

If you don't get enough: Unless you've experienced diarrhea or vomiting for a long time, or you have kidney problems, a sodium deficiency isn't likely. But if that happens, symptoms might include nausea, dizziness, and muscle cramps.

If you consume an excess amount: For healthy people, excess sodium is excreted. But some kidney diseases interfere with sodium excretion, causing fluid retention and swelling. For people who are sodium sensitive, a diet high in sodium can promote high blood pressure.

How much you need: As with the other electrolytes, there is no RDA for sodium. However, the minimum amount considered safe and adequate is 500 milligrams daily for healthy adults, which is much less than most people consume. The Daily Value used for food labeling is 2,400 milligrams of sodium.

Where it's mostly found: Processed foods account for about 80 percent of the sodium in food. The rest comes from table salt and the small amount that occurs naturally in food. As a point of reference, 1/4 teaspoon of salt contains 500 milligrams of sodium.

Food	Sodium (mg)
beef bologna (1 ounce)	305
cheddar cheese (1 ounce)	175
whole-wheat bread (1 slice)	160
milk, whole (1 cup)	120

The Nutrition Facts panel on food labels tell how much sodium comes from a single serving of food. *Refer to "Get All the Facts!" on page 271 to learn how to read sodium information on the food label.*

Trace Minerals

Chromium

What it does:

- Works with insulin to help your body use glucose, or blood sugar. *Refer to "Sugar: What Is It?" on page 123 to learn more about glucose.*

If you don't get enough: Because chromium works closely with insulin, a deficiency can look like diabetes. *Refer to "Diabetes: A Major Health Concern" on page 499 for more about diabetes.*

If you consume excess amounts: Consuming harmful amounts from dietary sources is highly unlikely.

How much you need: There is no RDA for chromium. However, for adults, 50 to 200 micrograms daily is considered safe and adequate.

Where it's mostly found: Meat, eggs, whole-grain products, and cheese are all good sources.

Food	Chromium (mcg)
shredded wheat cereal (2 ounces)	65
peas, cooked (1 cup)	60
cheese, American (1 ounce)	48
liver, braised (3 ounces)	42
egg, cooked (1 large)	26

Copper

What it does:

➢ Helps your body make hemoglobin, needed to carry oxygen in red blood cells.

➢ Serves as a part of many body enzymes.

➢ Helps your body produce energy in the cells.

If you don't get enough: A deficiency rarely comes from a lack of copper in the diet, but instead from genetic problems or from consuming too much zinc. As another cause, excess zinc from dietary supplements can hinder copper absorption.

If you consume excess amounts: Harmful effects of copper from dietary sources are extremely rare in the United States.

How much you need: There is no RDA for copper. However, for adults, 1.5 to 3.0 milligrams daily is considered safe and adequate.

Where it's mostly found: Organ meats, especially liver, seafood, nuts, and seeds are the best sources of copper. Cooking in copper pots also increases the copper content of foods.

Food	Copper (mg)
beef liver, braised (3 ounces)	2.4
salmon, cooked (3 ounces)	0.3
sunflower seeds (1/4 cup)	0.6
peanuts (1/4 cup)	0.5
mushrooms, cooked (1/2 cup)	0.4

Fluoride

Refer to "The Fluoride Connection" on page 175.

What it does:

➢ Helps harden tooth enamel, and so helps protect your teeth from decay.

➢ May offer some protection from osteoporosis, or brittle bone disease, by helping to strengthen bones.

If you don't get enough: Tooth enamel may be weak.

If you consume excess amounts: With excessive fluoride, teeth become mottled, or marked with brown stains, although teeth are healthy in every other way. Be aware that these stains may have other causes as well. The Tolerable Upper Intake Level (UL) is 2.2 milligrams fluoride daily for children age 4 through 8; from age 9 on through adulthood, the UL is 10 milligrams fluoride daily.

How much you need: As updated in 1997, an Adequate Intake (AI) for fluoride has been set. AI levels for children are as follows: age 4 to 8, 1 milligram fluoride daily and age 9 to 13, 2 milligrams of fluoride daily. For teens the AI is set for 3 milligrams fluoride daily. For adults, the guideline is 4 milligrams fluoride daily for males and 3 milligrams daily for females. There are no increased needs during pregnancy or breast-feeding. A fluoride supplement may be prescribed during infancy. *Refer to "Vitamin & Mineral Supplements for Breast-Fed Babies" on page* 400.

Where it's mostly found: Fluoride is not widely available in food. Two significant sources are tea, especially if its made with fluoridated water, and fish with edible bones, such as canned salmon.

The primary means for obtaining fluoride is drinking and cooking with fluoridated (fluoride added) water. Many municipal water supplies are fluoridated; however, most bottled waters are not. Some types of cooking utensils, such as Teflon with its fluoride-containing polymer, also can increase the fluoride content of food. The content of fluoride in food varies widely and is affected by the environment in which the food originated.

Iodine

What it does

➢ Serves as part of a thyroid hormone called thyroxin, which regulates the rate at which your body uses energy.

If you don't get enough: With an iodine deficiency, the body can't make enough thyroxin. As a result, the rate at which the body burns energy slows down, and weight gain may become a problem. Goiter, an enlarged thyroid gland, is the deficiency disease often caused by a lack of iodine. With the use of iodized salt, goiter rarely is caused by an iodine deficiency.

If you consume excess amounts: Goiter also can be induced when people consume high levels of iodine—but not at levels consumed in the United States.

How much you need: The RDA for iodine is 150 micrograms daily for adults. During pregnancy, the recommendation goes up to 175 micrograms; during breast-feeding, 200 micrograms daily.

Where it's mostly found: Iodine is found naturally in saltwater fish. Foods grown near coastal areas also contain iodine, but many people don't have access to these foods. For this reason, salt is iodized, assuring an adequate amount of iodine in the food supply, even if you consume only modest amounts of salt. One-half teaspoon of iodized salt provides almost enough iodine to reach the RDA for a day.

Food	Iodine (mcg)
table salt, iodized (1/4 teaspoon)	100
cod, cooked (3 ounces)	87
potato, cooked (1 medium)	7
spinach, cooked (1/2 cup)	5
almonds (1 ounce)	4

Iron

Refer to "Iron: A Closer Look" on page 109.

What it does:

➢ Serves as an essential part of hemoglobin, which carries oxygen in your blood from your lungs to every body cell.

If you don't get enough: Although there may be other causes, an iron deficiency can lead to anemia, along with fatigue and infections. Among women with regular menstrual loss, iron deficiency is more common.

If you consume excess amounts: Iron can build up to dangerous levels for people with a genetic problem called hemochromatosis. Taking adult iron supplements can be harmful for children. Children should get immediate medical attention if they take an overdose of iron supplements.

How much you need: The RDA for adult men is 10 milligrams daily. For women through age 50, 15 milligrams is recommended daily. From age 51 on, women need about 10 milligrams daily, too.

During pregnancy, the recommendation goes up to 30 milligrams daily; during breast-feeding, 15 milligrams daily is enough.

Where it's mostly found: Iron comes from foods of both animal (heme iron) and plant (non-heme) sources. It's better absorbed from heme iron and when vitamin C is consumed at the same meal. *Refer to "Counting Up Iron" on page 110 for a list of good sources and amounts.*

Manganese

What it does:

➢ Serves as part of many enzymes.

If you don't get enough: The chances of not getting enough are very low since manganese is so widely distributed in the food supply.

If you consume excess amounts: Consuming harmful levels from food is very rare, too.

How much you need: There is no RDA for manganese. However, for adults, 2 to 5 milligrams daily is considered safe and adequate.

Where it's mostly found: Whole-grain products are the best sources of manganese, along with some fruits and vegetables. Tea is also a good source.

Food	Manganese (mg)
pineapple, raw (1/2 cup)	1.3
whole-wheat spaghetti, cooked (1/2 cup)	1
whole-wheat bread (1 slice)	0.6
tea, instant powder (1 teaspoon)	0.5
lentils, boiled (1/2 cup)	0.5
kale, boiled (1/2 cup)	0.3
strawberries (1/2 cup)	0.2

Molybdenum

What it does:

- ➢ Works with riboflavin to incorporate the iron stored in the body into hemoglobin for making red blood cells.
- ➢ Part of many body enzymes.

If you don't get enough: With a normal diet, there's no need to worry about a deficiency.

If you consume excess amounts: Too much may interfere with the body's ability to use copper. But harmful levels are quite uncommon.

How much you need: There is no RDA for molybdenum. However, for adults, 75 to 250 micrograms daily is considered safe and adequate.

Where it's mostly found: Molybdenum is found mostly in milk, legumes, breads, and grain products. The amount consumed in a typical eating pattern appears adequate. Little is known about the actual amounts found in foods.

Food	Molybdenum (mcg)
lima beans, cooked (1/2 cup)	300
liver, braised (3 ounces)	125
wheat germ	60

WHOLE GRAINS: FOR GOODNESS SAKE

Nutrition experts advise: Enjoy at least three servings of whole-grain foods daily. Besides being low in fat with little or no cholesterol, whole-grain foods are rich in complex carbohydrates, dietary fiber, vitamins, and minerals. They supply other plant chemicals, or phytochemicals, that seem to keep you healthy, too. *"What Is a Whole Grain?" on page 144 explains where the nutrients and fiber come from. Refer to "Fiber's 'Benefit Package': A Closer Look" on page 145.*

Whole-grain foods are important sources of antioxidant nutrients, including vitamins A and E and selenium. And they supply minerals, such as zinc, copper, and iron, and vitamin B_6—all essential for your good health.

When you're shopping, look for "whole grain" or "whole wheat" on packages. Or you might find "whole" in front of grains, such as barley, corn, oats, rice, and wheat. Then check the ingredient list; whole-grain products should be among the first listed. Brown rice is the only whole-grain rice. *For tips on buying bread, refer to "Which Bread Is Whole Grain?" on page 145.*

There are a variety of whole-grain foods: bread, breakfast cereal, waffles, pancakes, crackers, cookies, and muffins, along with other nutty, crusty, tasty, and less familiar grains. *Refer to "Today's Grains" on page 221 for descriptions of less common grains, including some whole grains.* ✦

Selenium

What it does:

- ➢ Works as an antioxidant with vitamin E, to protect cells from damage that may lead to cancer, heart disease, and other health problems.
- ➢ Aids cell growth.

If you don't get enough: The general signs of a deficiency in humans aren't clear, but it may affect the heart muscle.

If you consume excess amounts: A normal diet with a variety of foods generally provides moderate levels of selenium. Very high levels from dietary supplements can be quite harmful.

How much you need: The RDA is 70 micrograms daily for adult men. For women, it's 55 micrograms daily. During pregnancy, the recommendation increases to 65 micrograms daily; during breast-feeding, 75 micrograms daily.

Where it's mostly found: The richest sources are seafood, liver, and kidney, as well as other meats. Grain products and seeds contain selenium, but the amount depends on the selenium content of the soil in which they're grown. Fruits and vegetables generally don't have much.

Food	Selenium (mcg)
chicken, light meat, skinless (3 ounces)	26
brown rice, cooked (1/2 cup)	13
egg, large	12
whole-wheat bread (1 slice)	11
peanuts (1/4 cup)	3

Zinc

What it does:

- ➢ Promotes cell reproduction and tissue growth and repair. Adequate zinc intake is essential for growth.
- ➢ Serves as part of more than 70 enzymes.
- ➢ Helps your body use carbohydrate, protein, and fat.

If you don't get enough: A deficiency during childhood can cause retarded growth; during pregnancy, birth defects. Other symptoms include appetite loss, skin changes, and reduced resistance to infections.

If you consume excess amounts: Although uncommon in the United States, too much zinc from dietary supplements can have harmful side effects, including impaired copper absorption.

How much you need: The RDA for adult males is 15 milligrams daily; for adult females, 12 milligrams daily. During pregnancy, the recommendation increases to 15 milligrams daily; during breast-feeding, 19 milligrams daily.

Where it's mostly found: Good sources of zinc include foods of animal origin, including meat, seafood, and liver. Eggs and milk supply zinc in smaller amounts.

Whole-grain products, wheat germ, black-eyed peas, and fermented soybean paste (miso) also contain zinc, but in a form that's less available to the body.

Food	Zinc (mg)
beef, ground lean (3 ounces)	4.5
wheat germ (1/4 cup)	3.5
crab, canned (3 ounces)	3.5
wheat bran (1/2 cup)	2
tofu (1/2 cup)	2
sunflower seeds, (1 ounce)	1.5
black-eyed peas, frozen, boiled (1/2 cup)	1
almonds (1 ounce)	1
milk, whole (1 cup)	1
peanut butter (2 tablespoons)	0.8
tuna, canned, packed in water (3 ounces)	0.7
egg, large (1)	0.5
whole-wheat bread (1 slice)	0.4

Calcium: A Closer Look

The human body contains more calcium than any other mineral. For an average 130-pound adult, about 1,200 grams—almost 3 pounds—of the body is calcium. Your body composition, of course, depends on the size of your body frame, the density of your bones, and, if you're older, how much bone you've lost through aging.

Of that amount, about 99 percent of your body's calcium is in your bones. The remaining one percent is found in your other body fluids and cells.

Bone Up on Calcium

Most of us mentally connect the growing years with the need for calcium. That's true, but "boning up" is actually a life-long process—starting at the moment of conception. During the childhood and teen years, bones grow long and wide. By age 20 or so, that phase of bone building is complete. But the period of building toward peak bone-mass continues until age 30 to 35. Bones become more stronger and more dense—and more calcium becomes part of the bone matrix.

Your bones are in a constant state of change. Because bones are living tissue, calcium gets deposited and withdrawn daily from your skeleton, much like money in a bank. Small amounts are withdrawn if needed for other functions. To keep bones strong, you need to make regular calcium deposits to replace the losses—and even build up a little "nest egg" of calcium for when your food choices come up short.

Calcium doesn't work alone. It works in partnership with other nutrients, including both phosphorus and vitamin D. Vitamin D helps absorb and deposit calcium in bones and teeth, making them stronger. Phosphorus is also an important part of the structure of bone.

If you don't consume enough calcium—or if your body doesn't adequately absorb it (perhaps because you're short on vitamin D)—your body may withdraw more calcium from bones than you deposit. This process gradually depletes bone, leaving a void in places where calcium otherwise would be deposited, eventually making bones more porous and fragile. *Refer to "Which Bone Is Healthy?" on page 496 to compare healthy bone with osteoporotic bone.*

After age 30 to 35, bones slowly lose minerals that give them strength. That's a natural part of the aging process. Whatever calcium a woman has "banked" in her skeleton will be the amount in her bones when she enters menopause.

During the child-bearing years, the hormone estrogen appears to protect bones, keeping them strong. But with the onset of menopause, bone loss speeds up for women, as estrogen levels go down. If women achieve their peak bone mass as younger adults, their risk for osteoporosis, or brittle bone disease, later in life is reduced. Their bones are strong enough before menopause to offer protection.

An adequate calcium intake is one important factor in building healthy bones. Adequate exercise is another. Regular, weight-bearing physical activities, such as walking, strength-training, dancing, and tennis, stimulate bone formation. This type of activity triggers nerve impulses that, in turn, activate other body chemicals to deposit calcium in bones.

Women—and men, too: You can build bone if you're under 35, or after that, slow the bone loss that comes with aging.

- ➢ Consume adequate calcium. *Refer to "Calcium: Enough vs. Optimal Amounts" on page 106.*
- ➢ Be careful about weight loss; eating plans that severely restrict food often restrict calcium, too.
- ➢ Participate regularly in weight-bearing activities—at least three times weekly.
- ➢ Avoid smoking and excessive amounts of alcohol; both interfere with bone health.

For more about calcium during the bone-building adolescent years, refer to "Calcium: A Growing Issue" on page 447. And to review the many factors that relate to osteoporosis, refer to "Osteoporosis: Reduce the Risks" on page 496.

Beyond Bone Health

Like other nutrients, calcium has other roles besides those it's best known for: building bones and teeth. Although used in just a small amount, calcium helps your muscles contract, your heart beat, your blood clot, and your nervous system send messages. These functions are vital to your health. If your food choices don't supply enough calcium to do this work, your body withdraws calcium from your bones.

Calcium also may offer some protection from other health problems that often show up in the middle years: high blood pressure, heart disease, kidney stones, and if you're at high risk, possibly colon cancer. Research regarding the protective effect of calcium on these conditions is just emerging. But if you're already consuming enough calcium for bone health, you may get these benefits, too! *For more about how calcium may help control blood pressure, refer to* "Not Too 'Pressured'" *on page* 493.

You say you're not a milk drinker? Just whisk one or two ingredients, such as those below, with one cup of milk—cold or hot, skim or whole—and give it a refreshing, new flavor! (And enjoy added benefits of 300 milligrams of calcium from the milk.)

- 1/2 cup of fresh or frozen puréed berries: strawberries, raspberries, or blueberries
- 2 tablespoons orange juice concentrate and 1/2 teaspoon vanilla extract
- 1/4 teaspoon of vanilla, almond, amaretto, or maple extract
- 1 puréed banana with 1/2 teaspoon honey
- 1/2 cup of cranberry juice cocktail and a small scoop of low-fat vanilla ice cream
- 1 tablespoon creamy peanut butter and 2 tablespoons chocolate syrup ✦

Calcium: Enough vs. Optimal Amounts

There's no doubt that calcium is as important to you as an adult, as it was during your childhood. The reasons really aren't that different.

How much calcium do you need? That depends on your age and your stage of life. With 1997 updates, calcium recommendations increased in order to help develop and maintain optimal bone mass. For children and teens, ages 9 through 18, an Adequate Intake (AI) level of 1,300 milligrams daily is advised. For adults age 19 through 50, 1,000 milligrams calcium daily is recommended. For the age 50 plus generation, the recommended amount goes back up to 1,200 milligrams calcium daily for men and women. *For more about AIs, refer to* "Nutrients: How Much?" *on page* 4.

To reduce the risks of osteoporosis, many nutrition experts believe that even more calcium is better for your bones. So, the National Institutes of Health Consensus Panel on Osteoporosis advise an optimal calcium intake that's higher than the AI—1,500 milligrams calcium daily for post-menopausal women not on estrogen and for adults over age 65.

Calcium Supplements: A Bone Builder?

For people of every age, food choices can supply an adequate amount of calcium. However, as an extra safeguard, many doctors also recommend calcium supplements, especially for menopausal and post-menopausal women to help slow bone loss that comes with hormonal changes. Many women simply don't consume enough calcium. If you're advised to take calcium supplements, keep these pointers in mind:

- Read the label. Over-the-counter supplements are not the same. The amount of calcium differs among products.
- Avoid calcium supplements with dolomite or bone meal. They might contain very small amounts of lead and other metals.

➢ Take calcium supplements as intended—as a supplement, not as your only important source of calcium. Although calcium supplements may boost calcium intake, they don't provide other nutrients your bones need: vitamin D, magnesium, phosphorus, and boron. Milk, for example, provides vitamin D, a nutrient which helps deposit calcium in your bones.

➢ If you take both calcium and iron supplements, take them at different times of the day. They'll each be better absorbed when taken on their own.

➢ If you take two or three tablets daily, space them throughout the day. That way, they'll be absorbed better. Calcium in supplements is best absorbed in doses of 500 milligrams or less and when consumed with food.

➢ Drink plenty of fluids with calcium supplements to avoid constipation. In fact, if you take your calcium supplement with milk, the lactose and vitamin D in the milk can help to enhance absorption of the calcium.

➢ If you don't drink milk and are looking for an alternative to calcium pills, consider calcium-

Counting Up Calcium

Dairy foods supply 75 percent of all the calcium in the U.S. food supply. Besides providing calcium, they also supply protein, vitamin D, and phosphorus, which together help the body absorb and deposit calcium in bones.

Other foods also supply calcium. Some deep-green leafy vegetables and fish with edible bones provide significant amounts. Many processed foods, such as orange juice and breakfast cereal, may be fortified with calcium.

Leafy-green vegetables and grain products supply some calcium. However, some vegetables, such as spinach, contain oxalates; grains may contain phytates. Both bind with some minerals, including calcium, magnesium, and iron, partially blocking their absorption. Caffeine can interfere with calcium absorption, too.

Food	**Approximate Calcium (milligrams)**
Yogurt, plain, nonfat (1 cup)	450
Tofu, regular (processed with calcium*) (1/2 cup)	435
Yogurt, plain, low-fat (1 cup)	415
Yogurt, fruit (1 cup)	315
Milk, skim (1 cup)	300
Milk, 2% (1 cup)	295
Milk, whole (1 cup)	290
Chocolate milk, 1% (1 cup)	285
Chocolate milk, 2% (1 cup)	285
Calcium-fortified soy milk (8 ounces)	250-300
Swiss cheese (1 ounce)	270
Calcium-fortified orange juice (3/4 cup)	225
Cheese pizza** (1/8 of a 15-inch pizza)	220
Cheddar cheese (1 ounce)	205
Salmon, canned with edible bones (3 ounces)	205
Mozzarella cheese, part skim (1 ounce)	185
Macaroni and cheese ** (1/2 cup)	180
Blackstrap molasses (1 tablespoon)	170
Pudding (1/2 cup)	150
Tofu, regular (processed without calcium*) (1/2 cup)	130
Frozen yogurt (1/2 cup)	105
Turnip greens (1/2 cup)	100
Sardines with edible bones (1 ounce)	90
Ice cream (1/2 cup)	85
Dried figs (3)	80
Cottage cheese (1/2 cup)	75
Tempeh (1/2 cup)	75
Parmesan cheese (1 tablespoon)	70
Milk chocolate bar (1 ounce)	70
Mustard greens (1/2 cup)	50
Okra (1/2 cup)	50
Orange (1)	50
Kale (1/2 cup)	45
Broccoli (1/2 cup)	45
Anchovies with edible bones (5)	45
Tortillas (made from lime-processed corn*)	40
Pinto beans (1/2 cup)	40
Rutabaga (1/2 cup)	35
Chinese cabbage (1/2 cup)	30
Cream cheese (2 tablespoons)	25
Tuna, canned (3 ounces)	10
Lettuce greens (1/2 cup)	10

** Read the labels.*

*** The amount of calcium may vary, depending on the ingredients.*

fortified juice. One cup of calcium-fortified juice contains about 300 milligrams of calcium, the same amount as in one cup of milk, and provides vitamin C, folate and other nutrients.

➢ Remember: Using supplements as a substitute for food sources can give you a false sense of security. Calcium supplements can't make up for your lifestyle choices or for overall poor health habits either. Regular physical activity is important for healthy bones. For healthy bones, avoid smoking, too!

For more about osteoporosis and bone health, refer to "*Osteoporosis: Reduce the Risks*" *on page* 496.

Calci-Yumm: How to Eat More!
Need more calcium in your food choices? Give your meal and snack choices a calcium boost in these easy ways:

Make it a habit! Eat two to three servings—or more—of foods from the Milk, Yogurt, and Cheese group each day. Include fruity yogurt with breakfast and a refreshing glass of milk for lunch or dinner for two easy servings. Three cups of milk, regardless of whether it's whole or skim, supply about 900 milligrams of calcium. *To compare various types of milk, refer to* "*Milk: A Good Calcium Source*" *on page* 180.

Reach for milk—during your "coffee break." If there's no place to buy a carton of milk, bring it from home. Refrigerate milk for a day at work in a small water bottle. Some experts say: just choosing milk at snacktime could make a big impact toward reducing the risk for osteoporosis.

Give goat milk a try. One cup supplies about 325 milligrams of calcium, slightly more than 1 cup of cow milk. The fat content varies, so you need to check the Nutrition Facts panel on the label. Look for low-fat goat milk that's fortified with vitamins A and D.

For the "new taste" of milk, try flavored milk—blueberry, banana, peanut butter—or yogurt-fruit drinks. Or make your own fruity drinks by blending milk or yogurt with fruit and ice in a blender or food processor.

Enjoy calcium-rich snacks: frozen yogurt, ice milk, cheese with crackers, plain yogurt, pudding, milk, or calcium-fortified juice. *For a calcium-rich, low-fat dip or cracker spread, refer to* "*Kitchen Nutrition: Yogurt Cheese*" *on page* 70.

At a coffee bar, order latte (steamed milk with espresso coffee) or cappuccino. Hold the fat by asking for skim milk. For more flavor, sprinkle on a little cinnamon or nutmeg. While caffeine can interfere with calcium absorption, this effect is readily offset by consuming the amount of steamed milk typically added to latte or cappuccino.

Lighten up with milk. Add milk to your coffee or tea, rather than drink it black. Milk has more calcium than powdered nondairy creamer.

Choose vegetables and fruits with more calcium: Dark leafy greens, such as kale and mustard, collard, and turnip greens; broccoli, dried beans, and bok choy are good sources of calcium. Other nondairy options include dried figs, and fortified fruits and juices.

Say "cheese" when you make or order sandwiches.

have you ever *wondered*

...if spinach will make you strong, as the famous cartoon character Popeye *believed*? It's true that spinach does contain iron. But another food component in spinach, called oxalic acid, binds with iron, impairing its absorption. So it's not the best source. Only physical exercise, not iron or any other nutrient, builds muscle strength.

...if cooking in an iron skillet improves the iron content of food? Yes, it does. Before the days of aluminum and stainless steel cookware, great-great-grandma unknowingly supplemented her family's diet with iron from her iron pots and pans. If you have cast iron cookware, you can get the benefits, too. Foods with acids, such as tomato juice, citrus juice, and vinegar, help dissolve small amounts of iron from the pot into the cooking liquids—especially good for foods that simmer and stew for a while. ✦

Choose fish with edible bones: salmon, sardines, and anchovies. Mix salmon in salads, casseroles, and other mixed dishes.

Add tofu (soybean curd) made with calcium to salads, stir-fries, and other dishes.

Boost the calcium in your food preparation. Make soups, chowders, and hot cereal with milk. Top salads, soups, and stews with shredded cheese. Mix dry milk into meatloaf and casseroles. Make vegetable dips with plain yogurt or cottage cheese. Add bok choy, broccoli, and kale to soups, casseroles, and other mixed dishes. *For more ways to add calcium-rich foods in food preparation, refer to "Calcium Boosters" on page 346.*

Look for calcium-rich foods in the grocery store. Check the Nutrition Facts panel on food labels, listing the calcium in a single serving. The amount is given as the % Daily Value, which represents the percentage of your day's calcium need supplied by one serving of that food. *Refer to chapter 12, "Supermarket Smarts," to learn more about food labels and shopping for foods with more calcium.*

You'll find many calcium-rich foods in the dairy case of the supermarket: for example, milk, yogurt, and cheese. However, descriptions on food labels can help you identify other foods that are good calcium sources. Look for "calcium-rich," "good source of calcium," and "more calcium." *Refer to page 93, "Label Lingo: Vitamins and Minerals," to see what the descriptions about calcium on food labels mean.*

Note: If you frequently have gas, cramping, and bloating after consuming milk and milk products, you may be lactose intolerant. *For more on this condition and how to include calcium-rich foods in your meals and snacks, refer to "Lactose Intolerance: A Matter of Degree" on page 194.*

Iron: A Closer Look

Iron: it's a mineral that's widely available in food. You need it in small amounts to keep healthy. Yet, iron deficiency is a common nutrition problem everywhere in the world. An iron deficiency often leads to anemia and its symptoms: fatigue, weakness, and poor health, all interfering with a person's physical ability to perform at full potential.

Iron: Its Mission

Although iron has many biological functions, its main job is to carry oxygen in the hemoglobin of red blood cells. Hemoglobin takes oxygen to your body cells where it's used to produce energy. Iron in red blood cells also helps take away carbon dioxide, a byproduct of energy production. Red blood cells have a "lifespan" of about 4 months. After that, some of their iron gets recycled. Either it's stored or used immediately to make new red blood cells. This recycling action helps protect you from an iron deficiency.

To help your body absorb more iron, create partnerships like these at your meals and snacks. Meat, poultry, fish (all three with heme iron), and vitamin C-rich foods help release more non-heme iron from foods of plant origin and egg yolks.

Absorption Enhancers	Non-heme Iron Sources
Sirloin strips	with spinach salad
Barbecued beef	with refried beans and tortillas
Ground beef	with whole-grain roll
Pork	with bean soup
Chicken	with brown rice
Ham	with scrambled eggs
Grapefruit	with bran cereal
Strawberries	with oatmeal
Red bell pepper	with whole-grain pasta
Papaya	with whole-wheat toast
Orange	with peanut butter sandwich on whole-wheat bread

Adapted from "Iron in Human Nutrition," *Cattlemen's Beef Association, Chicago,* IL 1990.

Counting Up Iron

This chart shows the amount of total iron in food. But remember, iron from most animal sources (heme iron) usually is better absorbed than iron from plant sources of food (non-heme iron).

To help reduce iron-deficiency anemia, many foods on today's supermarket shelves are enriched or fortified with iron: iron-enriched flour (also used in baked goods and pasta) and iron-fortified breakfast cereals.

FOOD	APPROXIMATE IRON (MILLIGRAMS)
SOURCES OF MOSTLY HEME IRON	
Beef liver, braised (3 ounces)	5.8
Lean sirloin, broiled (3 ounces)	2.9
Lean ground beef, broiled (3 ounces)	1.8
Skinless chicken, roasted dark meat (3 ounces)	1.1
Skinless chicken, roasted white meat (3 ounces)	1.0
Pork, lean, roasted (3 ounces)	1.0
Salmon, canned with bone (3 ounces)	0.7
SOURCES OF NON-HEME IRON	
Fortified breakfast cereal (1 cup) *	4.5-18
Pumpkin seeds (1 ounce)	4.25
Bran (1/2 cup)	3.5
Blackstrap molasses (1 tablespoon)	3.5
Soybean nuts (1/2 cup)	4.0
Spinach, boiled (1/2 cup)	3.2
Red kidney beans, cooked (1/2 cup)	2.6
Lima beans, cooked (1/2 cup)	2.5
Prune juice (3/4 cup)	2.3
Pretzels (1 ounce)	1.3
Enriched rice, cooked (1/2 cup)	1.2
Whole-wheat bread (1 slice)	0.9
Egg yolk, large (1)	0.7
Raisins, seedless (1/3 cup)	1.1
Prunes, dried (5)	1.1
Green beans, cooked (1/2 cup)	0.8
Peanut butter, chunky (2 tablespoons)	0.6
Apricots, dried (3)	0.6
White bread, made with enriched flour (1 slice)	0.7
Cod, broiled (3 ounces)	0.4
Zucchini, cooked (1/2 cup)	0.3
Cranberry juice (3/4 cup)	0.3
Unenriched rice, cooked (1/2 cup)	0.2
Grapes (1/3 cup)	0.1
Egg white, large (1)	<0.1

* *The amount varies. Read the Nutrition Facts panel on food labels.*

What happens when you don't consume enough iron—or when the iron stored in your body gets too low? Red blood cells can't carry as much oxygen, likely making you feel tired, perhaps weak, and less able to perform at your peak efficiency. These are among the symptoms of anemia. Be aware, however, that anemia has several causes—not just iron deficiency. *For more, refer to "Anemia: More Than One Cause" on page* 485.

To fill out its job description, iron also helps protect you from infections as part of an enzyme in your immune system. It helps change beta carotene to vitamin A, helps produce collagen (which holds tissues of your body together), and helps make body proteins (amino acids), among its other tasks. *To learn about amino acids, refer to "Protein Power" on page* 561.

How much iron do you need to consume? Your body is highly adaptive, absorbing more iron when its iron stores are low, and less when they're higher. Regardless, the Recommended Dietary Allowances (RDA) are set to meet the needs of the broad population. *For more about the RDAs, refer to "Nutrients: How Much?" on page* 4.

Iron needs are highest during periods of rapid growth: childhood, adolescence, child-bearing years for women, and pregnancy. Prior to menopause, women need enough iron to replace losses from menstrual flow. Iron needs also go up to support increases of blood volume during pregnancy. Not surprisingly, iron-deficiency anemia is most common among people at these ages and stages of life, too.

Iron in Foods: Heme vs. Non-Heme

If iron is abundant, why don't we "pump enough iron" from food? Iron comes from a wide variety of foods—both animal and plant origin. Most of the iron from meat, poultry, and fish is heme iron. That name comes from the way it's carried in food—as part of the hemoglobin and myglobin (similar to hemoglobin in humans) in animal tissue. Foods of plant origin contain just non-heme iron. And egg yolks have mostly non-heme iron.

The deep-red color of animal muscle comes from hemoglobin. The darker the color, the higher the content of heme iron. Beef liver, for example, which is redder than roast beef, has more iron. And dark turkey meat has more heme iron than the light meat.

What makes this difference nutritionally significant? First, consider that iron in food isn't absorbed efficiently. Much of the iron you consume never gets absorbed into your bloodstream. (Fortunately, the RDAs take this fact into account.) The amount of iron your body absorbs depends on several factors: among them, how much iron you consume and in what form (heme or non-heme); other nutrients in the meal or snack that can enhance or hinder its absorption; and how much iron your body has stored already.

Heme iron is absorbed into your body more readily than non-heme iron. Depending on how much you already have stored, anywhere from 15 to 35 percent of heme iron gets absorbed. That's good news.

Non-heme iron is a different story. Only 2 to 20 percent of non-heme iron gets absorbed. Even though foods with non-heme iron often contain more iron than those with heme iron, you may get less than you think. Again, there's good news. You can enhance your body's ability to absorb non-heme iron. Vitamin C and foods such as meat with heme iron aid non-heme iron absorption.

On the reverse side, other food substances—oxalic acid in spinach and chocolate; phytic acid in wheat bran and legumes; tannins in tea; and polyphenols in coffee—seem to inhibit non-heme iron absorption. But again, consuming vitamin C and iron from meat, fish, and poultry at the same time helps overcome these "inhibitors." *For more information about iron needs at various stages in life, refer to* "Formula: What Type?" *on page* 402, "Iron: The Fatigue Connection" *on page* 447, "Minerals—Giving Body Structure" *on page* 464, *and* "The Iron-Vitamin C Connection" *on page* 510.

These quick nutrition tips can help your body better absorb iron (non-heme) from foods of plant origin and from egg yolks:

Enjoy a vitamin C-rich food—such as an orange, cantaloupe, green pepper, or broccoli—right along with it: for example, you get more iron from a peanut butter sandwich on whole-wheat bread if you eat it with a glass of orange juice. *For a list of vitamin-C rich foods, refer to* "Vitamin C: More Than Citrus" *on page* 88. This is especially important for vegetarians who get most of their iron from plant sources. *For more guidance, refer to chapter* 22, "The Vegetarian Way."

Add a little meat, poultry, or fish (with heme iron) to foods of plant origin and egg yolks: for example, include some ground beef in a pot of chili, or sliced lean ham in an egg omelette. The presence of heme iron boosts the absorption of non-heme iron.

Unlock the iron in foods such as whole grains, spinach, legumes, and grain. Eat meat or vitamin-C rich foods along with these iron-containing foods.

Drink coffee or tea between meals—not with meals.

For more combinations, refer to "Iron: The Power of Partnership" *on page* 109.

Making the most of the iron in your food choices shows the power of nutrient partnerships—and underscores the reasons for enjoying a variety of food!

Dietary Supplements: Use and Abuse

Could a pill replace dinner? For all those who enjoy the pleasure of eating, there's good news. The answer is unequivocally "no"!

Food can provide the ideal mixture of vitamins, minerals, and other nutrients. Both the quality and the variety of food available in the United States allow us to consume an adequate diet. Besides the pleasure of eating, food choices can provide the variety and balance of nutrients and other food substances needed for health—qualities that can't be duplicated with dietary supplements.

Despite this fact, it's estimated that about one-third of adults in the United States take dietary supplements, making it a $4 billion business each year. Some people are prudent. They limit the potency of their supplement to 100 percent or less of the Recommended Dietary Allowances (RDAs). And they take just the recommended dose. However, others self-prescribe high dosages of supplements, often at the advice of a friend or media—not their health care provider. This practice can actually be dangerous.

Dietary supplements include a broad range of products. Whether in tablet, capsule, or liquid form, they include vitamins, minerals, fiber, herbs, other botanicals, amino acids, concentrates, and extracts. By law, these products must be labeled as a dietary supplement.

People take dietary supplements for many reasons—sometimes medically valid, sometimes not. In low or appropriate dosages, supplements can be beneficial for some people. However, other people may take supplements as a so-called easy road to health—a way that appears easier than making wise food choices. Some search for a magical cure, perhaps for aging skin, sexual prowess, cancer, or arthritis. Many have been misguided over the years by scientifically-unfounded promises used to market many supplements. Good nutrition, however, depends on a healthful diet—not on dietary supplements. What then is an appropriate—and inappropriate—use of dietary supplements?

Multi-Vitamin/Mineral Supplements: Who Benefits?

Do you consume a varied, balanced diet? Are you healthy? If so, you probably can get the vitamins and minerals you need from carefully-selected food choices alone. According to national dietary studies, most Americans have enough healthful foods available. So supplements usually aren't necessary —not for most healthy people if they're able and willing to eat a balanced and varied diet. For some healthy people—under some circumstances—multivitamin/mineral supplements do offer benefits. For example:

Women with heavy menstrual bleeding may need an iron supplement to replace iron from blood loss. To enhance the absorption, iron supplements are best taken with water or juice on an empty stomach. Iron supplements can be taken with food if nausea or constipation are problems, but absorption may be decreased by as much as 50 percent.

Women who are pregnant or breast-feeding need more of some nutrients, especially iron, folate, and calcium. Their doctor or registered dietitian (RD) may recommend a dietary supplement to ensure they get adequate amounts.

Health authorities advise that any woman capable of becoming pregnant should consume 400 micrograms of folic acid daily from fortified foods, vitamin supplements, or a combination of the two. This is in addition to the folate found naturally in foods such as some fruits, vegetables, and legumes. This offers a safeguard against spinal cord defects in a developing fetus. Foods fortified with folic acid include enriched grains, such as flour, breads, cereals, pasta, and rice. If a supplement is used, it should provide no more than 1,000 micrograms of folic acid daily. Be aware that some dietary supplements don't have folic acid—or at least not enough for a healthy pregnancy. *Refer to "Pregnancy: Before You Begin" on page* 457.

Menopausal women might benefit from calcium supplements, in addition to a calcium-rich diet, to slow calcium loss from bones. *Refer to "Calcium Supplements: A Bone Builder?" on page* 106.

People on very-low-calorie diets may not consume enough food to meet all their nutrient needs. Their doctor or registered dietitian may recommend a multi-vitamin supplement. Caution: Unless under a doctor's supervision, very-low-calorie diets are not advised. *See "'Diets' That Don't Work!" on page* 43.

Some vegetarians may need extra calcium, iron, zinc, and vitamins B_{12} and D—if their regular eating pattern doesn't supply much, if any, meat, dairy, and other animal products. *For more about nutrition and the vegetarian style of eating, refer to chapter* 22, *"The Vegetarian Way."*

People with limited milk intake and sunlight exposure may be advised to take a vitamin D

supplement. Still, you only need a little sunlight for your body to make enough vitamin D: 10 to 15 minutes on your hands and face, two to three times a week. Most people get that much in their daily activities, so there's no need to go sunbathing to get any more. *Refer to "Vitamin D: The Sunshine Vitamin" on page 510.*

Some babies may need a fluoride supplement—and perhaps iron or vitamin D. *Refer to "Vitamin & Mineral Supplements for Breast-Fed Babies" on page 400.*

For some health conditions, doctors prescribe supplements: for example, illnesses that impair nutrient absorption, such as digestive or liver problems, or surgery or injuries that increase the body's need for some nutrients. Some medications, such as antacids, antibiotics, laxatives, and diuretics, may interfere with the way the body uses nutrients. In these cases, a supplement may be prescribed.

In addition, anyone who is unable—or unwilling—to regularly consume a healthy diet probably should take a dietary supplement. Take them with the advice of a doctor or registered dietitian. For example, pre-menopausal women who don't consume enough calcium from food likely need a calcium supplement—unless they're willing to improve their diet.

If you have any questions about your own nutrient needs—or need for a supplement—talk to a registered dietitian or your doctor. *Refer to page 580, "How to Find Nutrition Help," for help in finding a qualified nutrition expert.*

More Isn't Always Better!

A little is good, but a lot may not be healthier. As with other nutrients, such as fat, sugars, and sodium, moderation is your smart guideline for vitamins and minerals: enough, but not too much.

Most supplements are produced in dosages close to 100 percent of the Recommended Dietary Allowances (RDAs). RDAs are nutrient amounts recommended daily for healthy people. *Refer to "Nutrients: How Much?" on page 4 for more about the RDAs.*

Supplements carry nutrition labeling so you know the amounts of vitamins and minerals in a single dosage. If you're already eating a healthful diet, you probably don't need any more of the nutrients these supplements supply. But taking a multi-vitamin-mineral supplement with a low dose—no more than 100 percent of the nutrient recommendation—as a safety net is generally considered safe.

How do you know if you're eating a healthful diet? Give yourself a "check-up." *Take the self-assessment, "How Did You Build Your Pyramid?" on page 266.*

High-potency supplements—a much higher dosage than you need—also are sold over the counter in pharmacies, grocery stores, health food stores, and through mail-order outlets. Either as single nutrient supplements or vitamin-mineral combinations, high-potency supplements often contain much greater amounts than the RDAs—which can be

have you ever wondered

...why a nutrient supplement label may list the percent of vitamin A from beta carotene? The supplement may contain beta carotene, but not vitamin A itself. However, the body converts beta carotene to vitamin A.

...if ridges or white marks on your fingernails suggest a vitamin deficiency? No, but it's a common misconception. Instead, they're often caused by a slight injury to the nail. Although they may have other causes, too, a nutrient deficiency isn't one of them. Taking gelatin pills won't make your nails stronger either. Fingernails are mainly dead protein that get their strength from sulfur in amino acids. Gelatin doesn't contain these amino acids.

....what the term 'phytonutrients' on a supplement bottle means? From 'phyto,' Greek for plant, these botanical substances are extracted from vegetables and other plant foods. Without enough scientific evidence, it's too soon to know whether supplement manufacturers have picked the right active substance, since there can be thousands to choose from, or if the amount contained in the pill actually offers any benefits. ✦

harmful. Why are they sold if you don't need so much? Currently, there's no law limiting their potency, except for folacin, which is a B vitamin. It's up to you to be prudent.

Consumed in excessive amounts, some supplements may have undesirable effects, such as fatigue, diarrhea, and hair loss. For others, the side effects may be more serious: kidney stones, liver or nerve damage, birth defects, or even death.

Because fat-soluble vitamins are stored in the body, taking high levels of some for a prolonged time can be toxic, or poisonous, or lethal. For example, excess amounts of vitamin D can cause kidney damage and bone deformity. And excess amounts of vitamin A, taken over time, can cause bone and liver damage, headaches, diarrhea, and birth defects. *Refer to page 82 for more about potential risks of excessive vitamin A.*

Water-soluble vitamin and mineral supplements also can be risky if taken in excess. For example, you may have heard that taking extra vitamin B_6 helps relieve premenstrual tension. There's no scientific evidence supporting large doses of vitamin B_6 for relief to those who experience premenstrual syndrome (PMS). Being water-soluble, many women have viewed large doses of vitamin B_6 as harmless. Instead large doses may cause irreversible nerve damage.

As another example, very high doses of vitamin C can cause diarrhea, kidney damage, and bladder problems. Liver damage may be caused by high doses of niacin. Excessive amounts of folic acid can hide the symptoms of pernicious anemia, so the disease gets worse without being detected. Large doses of vitamin A can be harmful during pregnancy. Even excessive iron can be harmful, for example, to children who swallow iron supplements intended for their mother.

Low levels of dietary supplements may contribute to excess intakes or dietary imbalances for some people. For example, those at risk for hemochromatosis need to be careful of taking extra iron. High levels of calcium intake may interfere with normal iron absorption. And zinc supplements can decrease levels of "good" cholesterol (high-density lipoprotein blood cholesterol).

The way that large doses from dietary supplements affect the body depends on many factors. Body size, supplement dose (amount and frequency), and how long it's taken all influence whether or not the supplement will be toxic for you.

Except for those few people with rare medical conditions, almost no one needs more than 100 percent of the Dietary Reference Intakes (DRIs) of any nutrient. And large doses of vitamins or minerals are appropriate only for certain medically-diagnosed health problems. Even then, their use should be monitored carefully by a doctor.

Another caution about taking dietary supplements: They can give a false sense of security. With a nutrient supplement, you may feel that you're taking care of yourself. That may be a serious problem if you neglect well-proven approaches to health or delay medical attention. If you choose to take a dietary supplement, also get regular medical check-ups and seek medical attention for any health problems.

That being said, is it possible to overdose on vitamins or minerals from food? This is highly unlikely. As we mentioned, taking very high doses of dietary supplements—or taking too many, too often—can be dangerous. But the vitamin and mineral content of food is much more balanced. In amounts normally consumed, even if you enjoy extra helpings, you won't consume toxic levels of nutrients. So eat a variety of foods—and enjoy! *Refer to "About Fiber Pills and Powders..." on page 151*

have you ever wondered

...what the term "high potency" on dietary supplement labels means? According to recent government regulations, "high potency" means that a nutrient in a food product, including a dietary supplement, provides 100 percent or more of the Daily Value (DV) for that vitamin or mineral. The term also can refer to a product with several ingredients if two-thirds of its nutrients contribute more than 100 percent of the DVs. *Refer to page 272 for more about DVs.*

and "Beyond Vitamins and Minerals: What's Known About Supplements?" on page 588 to learn about the inappropriate use of dietary supplements.

Choosing a Dietary Supplement

If your doctor or registered dietitian recommends a supplement to you—either a vitamin-mineral combination or a single nutrient, such as calcium—follow their professional guidance. Choose the product recommended for you.

If you're healthy and self-prescribe a dietary supplement, first ask yourself if you really need it. Think about the foods you typically eat and what they contain. If you're eating a healthful diet—following guidelines from the Food Guide Pyramid—you're likely getting all the nutrients you need already. *Refer to "The Food Guide Pyramid: Your Healthful Eating Guide" on page 243.* After all, why pay for something you don't need?

Check the Supplement Facts

How do you know the nutrition contribution of a dietary supplement? Check the Supplement Facts panel. Its format is similar to the familiar Nutrition Facts panel on food products. *Refer to page 270 for information about the Nutrition Facts panel on food products and to the sample Supplement Facts panel at right.*

To use the Supplement Facts panel, start by looking at the serving size; that's what the nutrition information is based on. The panel must include information, including Daily Values, for any of 14 nutrients, including sodium, vitamin A, vitamin C, calcium, and iron, if the levels are significant. Other vitamins or minerals must be listed, too, if they are added or referred to with a nutrient content claim on the label. On a Supplement Facts panel, you probably won't find a nutrient if it isn't present. For example, cod liver oil lists fat on the panel, but a calcium supplement won't because it doesn't contain fat.

The Supplement Facts panel also lists dietary ingredients, such as garlic or botanicals. The amount is listed, but Daily Values are not since there are none. If the supplement contains a botanical ingredient, the label must identify what part of the plant it comes from; for example, ginseng may come from a root. Potency often differs when different parts of a plant are used. The source of the ingredient may appear near the product's name in the Supplement Facts panel or on an ingredient statement.

On a supplement label, you also may see a statement about the structure or the function of a dietary ingredient. If the ingredient isn't a nutrient, you'll also find a disclaimer. For example, there may be a claim about the function of echinacea, but a disclaimer will say that the statement has not been evaluated by the Food and Drug Administration.

Be aware: The safety or effectiveness of dietary supplements in the dosage provided isn't regulated. It's up to you to be a discriminating consumer!✦

If you take a supplement...

Choose a vitamin-mineral combination. Limit the potency to 100 percent or less of the Daily Values (DV) for your age and gender. A supplement with 100 percent of the DV is more than enough, especially if you're eating a healthful diet, too. Avoid large doses!

Choose a supplement for your unique needs. Age, gender, and medical status are factors to consider.

Supplement Facts

Serving Size 1 Tablet

	Amount Per Serving	% Daily Value
Vitamin A (as retinyl acetate and 50% as beta-carotene)	5000 IU	100%
Vitamin C (as ascorbic acid)	60 mg	100%
Vitamin D (as cholecalciferol)	400 IU	100%
Vitamin E (as dl-alpha tocopheryl acetate)	30 IU	100%
Thiamin (as thiamin mononitrate)	1.5 mg	100%
Riboflavin	1.7 mg	100%
Niacin (as niacinamide)	20 mg	100%
Vitamin B_6 (as pyridoxine hydrochloride)	2.0 mg	100%
Folate (as folic acid)	400 mcg	100%
Vitamin B_{12} (as cyanocobalamin)	6 mcg	100%
Biotin	30 mcg	10%
Pantothenic Acid (as calcium pantothenate)	10 mg	100%

Other ingredients: Gelatin, lactose, magnesium stearate, microcrystalline cellulose, FD&C Yellow No. 6, propylene glycol, propylparaben, and sodium benzoate.

Note: If you're under stress, don't count on a stress vitamin pill to help. Stress doesn't increase nutrient needs.

For economy, consider the generic brand. Paying more for the same product generally offers no additional benefits. You also may save by buying synthetic vitamins rather than natural ones. There's no difference in their chemical make-up so your body won't know the difference. But your wallet will because the "natural" products likely will cost more.

Don't be lured by extra ingredients: choline, inositol, lecithin,* PABA*, herbs, and enzymes. They add to the cost, but offer no proven nutritional benefits.

Check the expiration date on the label. Over time, nutrient supplements lose some of their potency.

Take the supplement in the recommended dosage. There's no need to double dose on days when you've missed a meal. Rather than popping a pill, make up for foods you missed with your food choices on the next day.

Keep dietary supplements in a safe place—away from places where children may reach them! Iron supplements, meant for adults, are the most common cause of poisoning deaths among children in the United States.

Remember, no dietary supplement provides the full complement of vitamins, minerals, and other important nutrients found in food that you need for health. It has only those listed on the label. If you rely on supplements, you miss out on the full variety of nutrients, as well as fiber and other substances supplied by food.

Food before pills: Stick to the intention of dietary supplements as supplements—not replacements—for nutrients in healthful meals and snacks. Make food choices with variety, balance, and moderation in mind.

In regular check-ups, advise your doctor about any dietary supplements you chose to take on your own. *Caution*: If you're taking medication, talk with your doctor before using dietary supplements. Supplements may interfere with the action of some medications. *Refer to "Food and Medicine" on page* 526.

your nutrition check-up

Supplements—Myth or Fact?

True or false? Many misconceptions surround the issue of dietary supplements. Check what you know—and don't know—about using them.

True or False?

1. Vitamin and mineral supplements can make up for poor food choices.

2. Taking a daily vitamin and mineral supplement ensures good nutrition.

3. Taking large quantities of vitamins A, C, and E prevents cancer.

4. Vitamin pills give you extra energy.

5. People under a lot of emotional stress need "stress" vitamins.

6. Taking calcium supplements is the best way to prevent osteoporosis.

7. Physically active people and competitive athletes need to take extra vitamins or minerals to meet the additional demands of strenuous exercise.

8. People who smoke or drink in excess can protect their bodies from the harmful effects by taking vitamin pills.

9. More zinc improves your sexual prowess.

Here are the facts...

Misconceptions about dietary supplements are rampant. *And every statement above is false!* These are the facts for each statement.

1. *Fact:* No dietary supplement can fix an ongoing pattern of poor food choices. Supplements may supply some vitamins and minerals, but they don't provide all the nutritional components that food supplies for optimal health. Only a varied and balanced eating pattern provides the nutrients you need for health.

2. *Fact:* Most healthy people who follow a varied, balanced, and moderate eating plan don't need vitamin or mineral supplements. Consuming more nutrients than your body needs won't provide energy, more brain power, or protection from colds and flu.

3. *Fact:* No scientific evidence in humans proves that taking a supplement with a higher dosage of vitamins or minerals prevents cancer, although some vitamins may have a protective effect. *Refer to "Antioxidant Vitamins: A Closer Look" on page 90 for more information about antioxidant vitamins.*

4. *Fact:* As a source of energy in your food choices, only three nutrients—carbohydrate, fat, and protein—supply energy or calories. Vitamins don't. Boosting the amount of vitamins you consume, perhaps with pills or liquid dietary supplements, won't cause your cells to produce extra energy. However, B vitamins do help body cells produce energy from the three energy nutrients—they just don't boost energy themselves.

5. *Fact:* Emotional stress doesn't increase nutrient needs. Any claims promoting dietary supplements for stress relief are misleading.

6. *Fact:* Many factors contribute to osteoporosis so taking a calcium supplement can't prevent

your nutrition check-up (continued)

bone disease. Inadequate calcium intake is only one nutrition factor. Gender, body size, race, smoking, exercise levels, estrogen levels, and heredity each play a role, too.

Most people get enough calcium from milk, cheese, yogurt, and canned fish with edible bones, such as salmon and sardines. Dark-green leafy vegetables, such as broccoli and collard greens, also provide calcium. *For more about calcium and osteoporosis, refer to* "Osteoporosis: Reduce the Risks" *on page* 496.

7. *Fact*: Athletes and other physically active people are less likely to need supplements than others are. The increased demands of exercise require more energy, or calories. By eating more to meet their extra energy needs, they also consume the very small amount of extra vitamins needed for high-energy metabolism. *For more on nutrition for athletes, refer to chapter* 21, "Athlete's Guide: Winning Nutrition."

8. *Fact*: Taking dietary supplements of any kind can't protect the body from the harmful effects of smoking or alcohol abuse. Smoking does increase the body's need for vitamin C. And drinking excessive amounts of alcohol can interfere with the body's use of some nutrients. In either case, the body's need for nutrients can still be met by making food choices that match guidelines from the Food Guide Pyramid. *To learn more, refer to* "Food Guide Pyramid: Your Healthful Eating Guide" *on page* 243.

9. *Fact*: Throughout history, products have been marketed under this guise. However, no nutrient supplement, including zinc, improves sexual performance or works as an aphrodisiac. Save your money and just take care of yourself. Overall fitness works best of all!

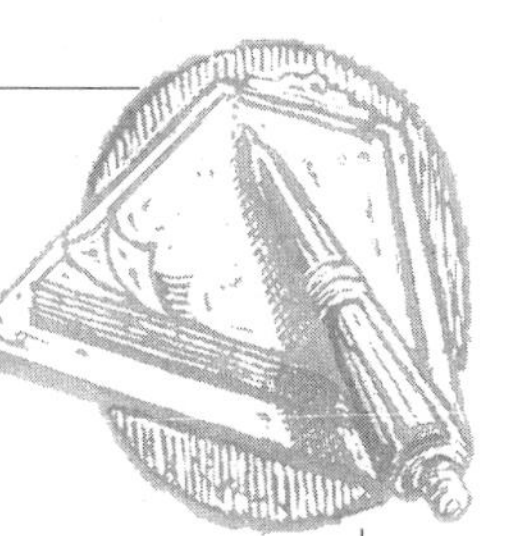

your nutrition check-up

Can You Count Up "Five a Day"?

For many reasons, fruits and vegetables are among your body's best sources of many (but not all) vitamins and minerals. That's why nutrition experts advise you to enjoy plenty of them in your daily food choices.

Take a moment to consider what you ate yesterday. How many fruits and vegetables did you consume? And were they good sources of vitamin A (beta carotene) and vitamin C? Put a letter "A" or "C" in the blank if any were.

	How Many? Vegetables	Fruits	**Write "A" or "C"**
At breakfast?	___	___	___
At lunch?	___	___	___
For snacks?	___	___	___
At dinner?	___	___	___
For dessert?	___	___	___
Subtotals	___	___	

Now repeat this exercise for two more days... and keep track. Answer "yes" or "no." Did you consume...?

	Day 1	**Day 2**	**Day 3**
At least five servings of vegetables and fruits?	___	___	___
A source of vitamin A?	___	___	___
A source of vitamin C?	___	___	___

If most of your answers are "yes," you enjoy the taste and get the nutrient benefits of plenty of fruits and vegetables.

If you mostly answered "no," *check out the ideas on page 96, "Five+Five+Five Ways to Enjoy More!"* Get your nutrients from food—not a dietary supplement.

real life nutrition

Enough... Is Enough

"A slice of toast, orange juice, coffee with milk, and a multi-vitamin pill—just in case." Mercedita quickly gulped the same breakfast she ate every morning and rushed out the door. With one hand on the car keys and other holding her portable coffee mug, she thought, "That'll hold me until afternoon. Between the coffee and the vitamin pill, I'll have enough energy to get through the morning."

Once Mercedita got to work, her day was nonstop. She often didn't take a break until early afternoon. For lunch she sipped a mug of soup. And she kept a carton of yogurt in the refrigerator for a mid-afternoon snack. She isn't on a weight-loss diet; she just didn't take time to eat.

"Tita, let's do lunch tomorrow. That new place across the street makes great salads, soups, and wonderful whole-wheat bread—and their Apple Wonderful dessert!" remarked Gertie, her coworker. "You need to take a few breaks during the day—have some fun. Plus, a sit-down meal would be good for you!"

"Thanks, but no time. I do just fine—getting plenty of nutrients, if that's what you're thinking—without spending the time for lunch. How about dinner instead?" she asked.

Gertie gave a deep sigh. "OK, then how 'bout tonight?" Mercedita agreed.

The new restaurant was great. Mercedita ordered a fabulous spinach salad, herbed chicken breast with wild rice, baby carrots, and the whole-wheat bread. "And Gertie, the Apple Wonderful is almost as good as yours!" She smiled. Then she "finished" her meal with a calcium pill and an iron pill.

Advice for making food choices that include enough—but not too much—vitamins and minerals

➢ If this is Mercedita's regular eating style, she relies too much on supplements for nourishment. As a result, she's missing out on the variety of nutrients—and other substances in food, such as fiber—that her body needs.

For good health, her daily food choices should include at least: 6 servings of grain products (including 3 whole-grain products); 3 servings of vegetables; 2 servings of fruit; 5 ounces of meat, poultry, fish, or other protein-rich food; and 2 servings of milk, yogurt, or cheese. If she follows this guideline, she probably won't need a multi-vitamin and mineral supplement.

➢ She has a misguided notion of the role of vitamins in providing energy. Neither vitamins nor coffee supply the body with energy.

real life nutrition (continued)

➢ If she chooses to take a multi-vitamin and mineral supplement, it shouldn't contain any more than 100 percent of her Recommended Daily Allowances. She needs to read the potency on the label.

➢ Mercedita doesn't get enough servings of fruits and vegetables during the day. She had only orange juice, spinach salad, baby carrots, and a partial serving of fruit in the apple dessert. As part of lunch and perhaps as a snack, she could easily enjoy fresh fruit and raw vegetables and so consume five fruits and vegetables during the day.

➢ Mercedita would be much wiser to get calcium from food, not pills. Calcium supplements don't supply other nutrients—vitamin D, phosphorus, and magnesium—that bones need to be healthy. Milk, yogurt, cheese, green leafy vegetables, and fish with edible bones all supply calcium. To her credit, she did eat yogurt as an afternoon snack at work.

➢ If she needs to take both an iron and a calcium supplement, they should not be taken together, but instead at different times of the day so they're each absorbed better.

CHAPTER FIVE

SWEET TALK

sugar and other sweeteners

Were you born with a "sweet tooth"? Probably, yes. Studies show that newborns respond to sweet tastes quicker than to other tastes: bitter, sour, or salty. Sweetness adds to the pleasure of eating!

From one source or another, sweet flavors are recorded throughout culinary history. In the earliest times, hunter-gatherer societies enjoyed the sweetness of berries and other fruit. Perhaps, say some experts, sweetness indicated that the food was safe for them to eat. As far back as the Stone Age, primitive drawings show that humans collected honey. Biblical writings and ancient Greek manuscripts tell us that honey was the main sweetener 3,000 years ago—and it remained so in the Western world until colonial times. Honey was also used by the Aztecs and Mayans, and much further north, maple syrup was used to sweeten food.

Although its origins aren't clear, sugarcane appears as early as 1200 B.C. An early epic describes a banquet of sweet things with "canes to chew" from the land of sugar, or Gur, known today as Bengal. Through trade and conquest, sugar found its way to Europe. But it remained very expensive and mainly medicinal until the 1500s. Then sugar changed population patterns, the world economy, and the course of history. With slave labor, sugar could be produced in the West Indies—and quickly took the place of honey as the Western World's primary sweetener in food and beverages.

Sugars: The Sweet Basics

Two categories of sweeteners flavor food: traditional and intense. Traditional sweeteners—sugars and sugar alcohols—are nutritive sweeteners, which nourish the body by supplying energy. Intense sweeteners, such as aspartame and saccharin, are many times sweeter than sugar. However, because they supply few, if any calories, they're considered non-nutritive. *Refer to page 136, "Intense Sweeteners: Flavor Without Calories."*

Sugar: What Is It?

Along with starch and fiber, sugars belong to a nutrient category called carbohydrates. Carbohydrates—sugars and starches—are your body's main source of fuel. Some sugars occur in foods naturally. Others are added. Regardless of the source, your body really can't tell the difference.

Carbohydrate's "Short Form"
Most often, when people hear the word "sugar," they think of table sugar. Actually there are several different sugars. Table sugar is just one of several sugars referred to as simple carbohydrates. Starches and fiber are structurally more complex. That's why they're called complex carbohydrates.

Whether simple or complex, all carbohydrates are made of the same three elements: carbon, hydrogen, and oxygen. The name "carbohydrate" actually comes from its chemical makeup. "Carbo-" means carbon; "-hydrate" means water, or H_2O. To make different types of carbohydrates, these elements first are arranged in single units. Sugars are made of just one or two units; starches and fiber have many more.

In scientific language, sugars are either monosaccharides with one sugar unit, or disaccharides with two sugar units. ("Mono-" means one, "di-" means two, and "-saccharide" means sugar.) The three types of monosaccharides are fructose, galactose, and glucose. When two join together chemically, they become disaccharides:

sucrose = glucose + fructose
lactose = glucose + galactose
maltose = glucose + glucose

Sucrose is another name for table sugar, but this same sugar is found naturally in some fruits and vegetables, too. Lactose is the naturally-occurring sugar in milk, while fructose is the sugar in fruit and in honey.

The ingredient lists on food labels show all kinds of sweeteners. Some are simply other words for sugar: for example, words ending in "-ose."

Other nutritive sweeteners you'll find on food labels may contain one or more of the sugars listed above. These sweeteners include:

- brown sugar
- confectioner's sugar
- corn syrup
- dextrin
- fruit juice concentrate
- honey
- invert sugar
- maple syrup
- raw sugar
- cane sugar
- corn sweeteners
- crystallized cane sugar
- evaporated cane juice
- high-fructose corn syrup (HFCS)
- malt
- molasses
- turbinado sugar

have you ever wondered

...if honey or brown sugar is more nutritious than table sugar? That's a common misperception. Honey is a mixture of sugars (fructose, glucose, sucrose, and other sugars), formed from nectar by bees. Ounce for ounce, the nutrient content of honey and table sugar is about the same. But because a teaspoon of honey weighs slightly more than a teaspoon of table sugar, it has somewhat more calories and carbohydrate. Honey is sweeter than table sugar, so less can be used to sweeten foods. Brown sugar is merely sugar crystals, flavored with molasses. From a nutritional standpoint, it too has 16 calories and 4 grams of carbohydrate per teaspoon—the same amounts as table sugar.

...what refined sugar is? Refined sugar is most simply described as sugar, separated either from the stalk of sugar cane or from the beet root of sugar beet. The sugar-containing juice of the plant is extracted, then processed into dried sugar crystals. It's sold as granulated or white sugar.

...what raw sugar really is? Raw sugar comes from the processing of cane sugar. It's a coarse granulated solid sugar left when clarified sugar cane juice evaporates. Because of its impurities, you can't buy 100 percent raw sugar. You can, however, buy turbinado sugar. Even though it may be referred to as raw sugar, it's more like refined sugar. Turbinado sugar is raw sugar that's been refined in a centrifuge under sanitary conditions. It has a light-tan color. Nutritionally speaking, its calorie and carbohydrate content are the same as refined, or table sugar. ✦

Made of Many Sugars
Starches and fiber have something in common. They're both polysaccharides. "Poly-" means many. If you concluded that both starches and fiber are composed of many sugar units, you're absolutely right! They're just longer chains of sugars. Starch comes from foods of plant origin, such as rice, pasta, potatoes, and beans. *For more about fiber, refer to chapter 6, "Fiber: Your Body's Broom."*

You may wonder—if starch is made of sugars, why doesn't it taste sweet? The size of the molecules makes the difference. Starch molecules are bigger. Unlike sugars, which are smaller, starch molecules don't fit on the receptors of your taste buds. But keep a starchy cracker in your mouth for a while. Once digestive enzymes in saliva break down its starch into sugar, it starts to taste sweet because the sugar molecules are small enough to be tasted.

Another polysaccharide, called glycogen, is the form of carbohydrate that's stored in your body. *For more about glycogen, refer to "Carbohydrate Power" on page 536.*

From Complex to Simple...
From complex to simple! In a nutshell, that's what happens to carbohydrates during digestion. Before they can be absorbed from your digestive tract into your bloodstream, complex carbohydrates from starches are broken down to the simplest sugars: glucose, galactose, and fructose. Then in your bloodstream, single sugars move into your body cells, where they're converted to energy. Except for fiber, all carbohydrates—sugars and starches—break down to single sugars during digestion. Your body doesn't distinguish what foods they came from.

Because they're single sugars already, monosaccharides, such as the fructose in fruits, can be absorbed just as they are. That's not the case for disaccharides: sucrose, lactose, and maltose. Digestive enzymes break them down. Some people, however, have trouble digesting the disaccharide lactose, or milk sugar. They don't produce enough of an enzyme called lactase. *To learn more about lactose sensitivity, refer to page 194.*

Only fiber, another polysaccharide, remains somewhat intact in the body. Many animals can digest fiber. However, human digestive enzymes can't break down fiber into units that are small enough for absorption. So fiber can't be an energy source. That very quality makes fiber uniquely qualified to promote your health in other ways. *To learn more, refer to chapter 6, "Fiber: Your Body's Broom."*

Carbohydrates: Your "Power" Source
Carbohydrates are your body's main energy source, powering everything from jogging, to breathing, and

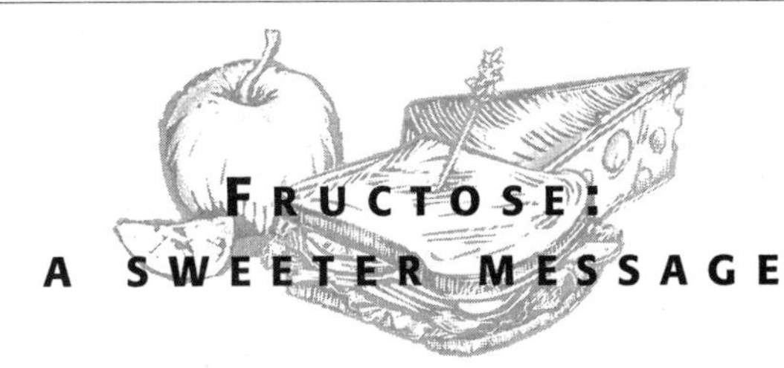

FRUCTOSE: A SWEETER MESSAGE

Is fructose any more healthful than sucrose, or table sugar? Surprisingly, the answer is no. All sugars nourish your body in the same way. Fructose and sucrose are just different sugars, and both types are simple carbohydrate. In fact, your body eventually breaks down sucrose into fructose and glucose.

Fructose is found naturally in fruit. But it's also added to certain foods, either as crystalline fructose or as high-fructose corn syrup (HFCS). Crystalline fructose is made from cornstarch, and looks and tastes much like sucrose. HFCS is a combination of fructose and dextrose, a sugar which comes from corn. Currently it's one of the most commonly consumed sweeteners in the United States.

Like any sugar, crystalline fructose and HFCS supply 4 calories per gram. They're both 1.5 times sweeter than table sugar...so a slightly smaller amount gives the same level of sweetness.

You might find crystalline fructose on the ingredient list of baked foods, frozen foods, beverages, and tabletop sweeteners. HFCS is used in soft drinks, fruit drinks, salad dressings, pickle products, ketchup, baked foods, tabletop syrups, fruits, candies, gums, and desserts. ✦

even to digesting food. Actually, glucose is the main form of carbohydrate used for energy. Because it circulates in your bloodstream, it's often called blood sugar. It's carried to every body cell, each with its own "powerhouse" for producing energy.

Your body doesn't turn all of its blood sugar into energy at the same time. As blood sugar levels rise above normal, insulin (a hormone from your pancreas) signals your liver, muscles, and other cells to store the extra. Some gets stored in the muscles and liver as glycogen, a storage form of carbohydrate. Some glucose may also be converted to body fat—if you consume more calories than your body needs.

When blood sugar levels drop below normal, another hormone called glucagon triggers the conversion of glycogen to glucose. That's how blood sugar levels stay within normal range between meals. Once glucose is back in your bloodstream, it's again ready to fuel your body cells.

Whether from sugar or starch, 1 gram of carbohydrate fuels your body with the same amount of energy: 4 calories for each gram. By comparison, protein also supplies 4 calories per gram, while fat supplies more: 9 calories per gram. *For more about carbohydrates and how they power physical activity, refer to page 536, "Carbohydrate Power."*

For health's sake, make foods with complex carbohydrates, or starch, your body's main energy source. Usually they're loaded with vitamins, minerals, and perhaps fiber, too. An added bonus: many starchy foods are low in fat.

JUST A SPOONFUL OF SUGAR...

1 teaspoon fructose	12 calories
1 teaspoon honey	21 calories
1 teaspoon jelly	16 calories
1 teaspoon brown sugar	16 calories
1 teaspoon table sugar	15 calories

Foods with complex carbohydrates form the foundation of a healthful diet. Enjoy 6 to 11 servings of bread, cereal, pasta, and rice daily. Many vegetables are good sources of complex carbohydrates, too; eat 3 to 5 servings of veggies daily. *Refer to page 243 to learn how these foods fit within an overall healthful eating style.*

Sugar Alcohol—Not a Sugar

Sugar alcohols are ingredients used to add sweet flavors to food. To clarify, the term "alcohol" refers to their chemical structure. They don't contain ethanol, as alcoholic beverages do.

Sugar alcohols—such as sorbitol, mannitol, and xylitol—are traditional sweeteners, often used instead of sugars. Many fruits and vegetables contain sugar alcohols naturally. They're also found in some sugarless chewing gum, hard candies, jams, and jellies. Besides adding sweetness, sugar alcohols also add texture, help foods stay moist, prevent browning when food is heated, and give a cooling effect to the taste of food.

Sugar alcohols supply energy, too, about 4 calories per gram. As an energy source, however, they're absorbed slowly and incompletely, and require little or no insulin for metabolism. They're not cavity-producing either because they aren't metabolized by bacteria that produce cavities.

Sorbitol and mannitol aren't as sweet as table sugar; xylitol has the same sweetness as table sugar.

For some people, sorbitol and mannitol have a laxative effect when they're consumed in large amounts. So eat foods with these sweeteners in moderation—in case your tolerance is lower.

Your Smile: Sugar and Oral Health

Imagine the wide smile that comes with those popular words: "Look, Mom, no cavities!" Today, 50 percent of America's children have cavity-free teeth. And the number is climbing. Good dental care, along with the widespread presence of fluoride toothpaste, fluoride rinses, and fluoridated water, is making smiles healthier than ever.

Just what causes cavities—and how can you and your family protect your teeth? For years, we've connected tooth decay to eating sugary foods. But whether or not you get cavities depends on many factors—and certainly not diet alone! Heredity, as well as the makeup and flow of saliva, are factors. Although part of the equation, sugar itself isn't the culprit it was once thought to be.

Plaque Attack!

The cavity-producing process starts when bacteria in your mouth mix with carbohydrates—both sugars and starches—to make acids. Bacteria is found in dental plaque, an invisible film which forms in your mouth and clings to the surfaces of your teeth and along your gum line.

Acids, produced by bacteria in the mouth, can eat away tooth enamel, causing tooth decay, also known as dental caries. Every time you eat sugars and starches, acids begin to bathe your teeth. The cavity-producing action continues for 20 to 30 minutes after you eat something starchy or sugary.

These two "equations" offer a quick summary of the action that takes place in your mouth when bacteria in plaque mix with carbohydrate in food:

plaque + carbohydrate = acid
acid + tooth enamel = potential tooth decay

As first lines of defense against tooth decay, remove the plaque by brushing and flossing. And limit the length of time that food stays in your mouth. Drinking water after a meal might be refreshing and helps to rinse away food particles and sugars, but it won't reduce the bacteria on teeth.

A Sticky Issue

Hard candy offers no more threat to your teeth than pasta does. Surprised? Any food that contains carbohydrate—pasta, bread, rice, chips, fruit, even milk, as well as cake, cookies, and candy—can "feed" the bacteria in plaque.

Table sugar, or sucrose, isn't the only sugar that plays a role in oral health. Any sugar—whether it's added or naturally-occurring—has the potential to promote cavities. Fructose in fruit, and lactose in milk, for example, also cause bacteria to produce plaque acids. So fruit juice-sweetened cookies have the same cavity potential as cookies made with table sugar.

Among young children, baby-bottle tooth decay is caused when teeth or gums are exposed to milk, breast milk, formula, fruit juice, or another sweet drink for extended periods of time. This happens most often when babies fall asleep sucking on a bottle or fall asleep frequently while breast-feeding. *For more on baby-bottle tooth decay refer to page* 407, "*Caring for Baby Teeth.*"

Do some foods promote cavities more than others? There's no definitive list that ranks the cavity-forming potential of food. However, two factors that make a difference include how often you eat (or how often carbohydrate comes in contact with your teeth) and how long it stays on your teeth.

Frequency. The more often you eat carbohydrate foods, especially between meals, the more likely acid will attack teeth. Sucking hard candy or cough drops, nibbling chips, or slowly sipping a sweetened drink all afternoon nourishes bacteria and bathes teeth with plaque acids all afternoon! The action continues for 20 to 30 minutes after you finish each candy, nibble each chip, or drink each sip of soft drink.

have you ever *wondered*

... *if presweetened cereals are more cavity-promoting than unsweetened cereals?* There's really no difference. Carbohydrates in both starches and sugars "nourish" bacteria that promote decay. Whether or not they're presweetened, their cavity factor depends on how long cereals stick between teeth or in the crevices in molars. The total content of carbohydrate really makes no difference in a food's potential to cause cavities.

Although not a dental health issue, presweetened cereals often have more calories per serving—but perhaps no more than your own spoonful of sugar sprinkled on unsweetened cereal. ✦

Form. Because some foods stick to your teeth, plaque acids continue their action long after you stop eating or drinking. The word "sticky" may conjure up thoughts of caramels. Yet caramels dissolve and leave your mouth faster than bread or chips that stick between your teeth or in the pits of your molars. It may take hours for food particles to finally leave your mouth. What a great "snack" for plaque! The faster food dissolves and leaves your mouth, the less chance it has to produce plaque acid. For example, raisins may stay on your teeth longer than a soft drink does.

Will a box of raisins or a bunch of grapes be more cavity promoting than a single raisin or single grape? Eaten at one time, portion size makes no difference. Any amount of carbohydrate gets the decay process going. It's the frequency of snacking that seems to have a bigger impact on cavity formation than size of the snack.

Brushing and flossing after eating removes the "decay duo": plaque and food particles. Swishing water around your mouth after meals and snacks may help rinse away food particles and sugars, but it won't remove plaque bacteria.

KEEP TEETH AND GUMS HEALTHY

Enjoy a balanced variety of foods from the five groups of the Food Guide Pyramid.

Go easy on between-meal snacks. When you do snack, try to eat the snack at one time rather than over a longer period.

Brush twice a day, and floss daily—unless your dentist recommends cleaning your teeth more often.

Be aware that brushing too often may be abrasive to your tooth enamel.

Brush with fluoride toothpaste that has the American Dental Association's seal of approval. The optimal amount of fluoride from toothpaste comes from brushing twice a day, not any more often.

Have regular dental check-ups, which include a thorough cleaning.

For infants, avoid the urge to pacify your baby with a bottle of juice, formula, or milk. If you choose to use a bottle as a pacifier, fill it with water only.

For children, talk to your dentist, doctor, or pediatric nurse about what amount of fluoride your child should have. If you live in a community that doesn't have an optimal amount of fluoride in the water, supplements may be recommended. ✦

"Carbs"—Not the Only Link to Oral Health
Carbohydrates aren't the only nutrition factor linked to oral health. Some nutrients make teeth stronger. And some foods are even described as "anti-cavity" foods.

For children, an overall nutritious diet promotes healthy teeth, making them stronger and more resistant to cavities. Several nutrients are especially important, including calcium, phosphorus, and vitamin D. These nutrients also build the jawbone, which helps keep teeth in place. For adults, calcium intake has little effect on keeping teeth healthy. But these same nutrients continue to be important for keeping the jawbone strong.

Tooth loss, common among the elderly, may be linked to gum, or periodontal, disease. Constant infection causes the bone structure of the jaw to gradually deteriorate. *Refer to "Keep Smiling: Prevent Gum Disease" on page 498. For more on oral health during aging, refer to "Chewing Problems?" on page 521.*

Before fluoridation of water was a common practice, tooth decay was much more prevalent. Now, adding fluoride—to drinking water, toothpaste, and mouth rinses—has become one of the most effective ways to prevent cavities. Fluoride makes the structure of teeth stronger by helping to add minerals back to microscopic cavities on the surface of tooth enamel. *To read about fluoridated water, refer to page* 175, "*The Fluoride Connection.*"

Get your juices flowing! Your body produces up to one quart of saliva a day—especially if you drink enough fluids. That's good news because saliva helps protect your teeth from decay. By clearing carbohydrates from your mouth faster, saliva helps to reduce the time that plaque acids can form. Minerals in saliva—calcium, phosphorus, and fluoride—may have a protective effect, too.

Smile, and say cheese! Some aged cheeses—for example, sharp cheddar, Monterey Jack, and Swiss—also may help protect your teeth from cavities. By increasing saliva flow, they lower acid levels. Like the milk it's made from, cheese also contains calcium and phosphorus, which may help remineralize tooth enamel.

Sugar Myths

Other than their role in tooth decay, sugars have no direct relationship to any health problem. After careful review of scientific studies, that's the conclusion of nutrition and health experts. Yet sugar myths are still widespread. Here's the real scoop on four common misconceptions about sugar.

Linked to Hyperactivity?

Following an afternoon of sweet snacks, friends, and active play, kids may be "all wired up." But don't blame the candy, cupcakes, or sweet drinks! Sugar has been wrongly accused as a cause of hyperactivity or attention deficit-hyperactive disorder (ADHD). Even though no scientific evidence supports any link between the intake of sugars and hyperactivity, many parents and other caregivers seem reluctant to put this notion aside.

The causes of nervous, aggressive, and impulsive behavior and a short attention span aren't completely understood. But experts advise adults to take stock of a child's overall environment. The excitement of a party or a special event, such as trick-or-treating or a visit to Santa—and not the sweet snacks that go with the fun—may be the reason for unruly behavior. To the contrary, some studies suggest that sugars may have a calming effect, but there's still more to be learned about that. *To clear up other misunderstandings about food and hyperactive behavior, refer to page* 200.

Causes Diabetes?

Again, the answer's "no." Sugars don't cause diabetes. Even though the scientific community debunked this myth almost 20 years ago, the misperception still persists.

In diabetes, the body can't use sugar normally. The causes are complex and still not fully known. Genetics certainly play a role, but illness, obesity, or simply getting older also may trigger diabetes.

Snack for a Healthy Smile

Keep your smile healthy! For everyone, especially children, smart snacking can lead to good oral health.

Overcome the urge to snack frequently. Bacteria in plaque produce acids that can damage teeth for 20 to 30 minutes after each exposure to carbohydrates in snacks.

Choose snacks wisely for a well-balanced eating plan. Eat fresh vegetables, fruits (such as apples), plain yogurt, cheese, milk, and popcorn.

Avoid sugary snacks that dissolve slowly in your mouth: hard candy, cough drops, and lollipops. Their sugars bathe your teeth longer. Slowly sipping a sweetened beverage or soft drink has the same effect.

Brush as soon as you can after snacking. This removes plaque and so stops the cavity-producing action of bacteria. Or at least rinse your mouth with water to get rid of food particles. ✦

While food choices don't cause diabetes, diet is part of the strategy for managing diabetes—along with physical activity and perhaps medication. To control blood sugar levels, people with diabetes manage the overall carbohydrate, protein, and fat in their diets.

In the past, people with diabetes were warned to avoid or strictly limit sugar in their food choices. But today, experts recognize that sugars and starches have similar effects on blood sugar levels. For people with diabetes, the amount of carbohydrate, not the source, is the issue. According to current advice from the American Diabetes Association, moderate amounts of sugar can be part of a well-balanced diabetic diet. For people with diabetes, a registered dietitian can help plan and monitor their diet. *For more on diabetes, refer to* "*Diabetes*: A *Major* Health *Concern" on page* 499.

Triggers Hypoglycemia?

It's highly unlikely. Yet many people explain away anxiety, headaches, and chronic fatigue as hypoglycemia caused by eating foods with sugar. Often self-diagnosed, hypoglycemic disorders are quite rare.

Hypoglycemia, or low blood sugar, is actually a condition, not a disease. Between meals, blood sugar levels naturally drop—but remain fairly constant between 60 and 110 milligrams per deciliter (mg/dL). A signal for hypoglycemia is when levels drop below about 40 mg/dL. When blood sugars fall below normal levels, there's not enough glucose immediately available for cells to produce energy. That can cause several symptoms, including sweating, rapid heartbeat, trembling, and hunger.

have you ever *wondered*

...if there's such a thing as sugar addiction? No. The term may be used loosely to explain away a so-called "sweet tooth." But addiction is defined as either an emotional or physical dependence or both, characterized by symptoms of withdrawal. That doesn't happen with sugar or any other carbohydrate. ✦

Among people with diabetes, hypoglycemia is caused by taking too much insulin, by exercising too much, or by not eating enough. In most other cases, low blood sugar is linked to other serious medical problems, such as liver disease or a tumor of the pancreas.

In rare cases, a disorder called reactive hypoglycemia occurs. As a rebound effect, the body secretes too much insulin after eating a large meal. The result is a drop in blood sugar well below normal, and symptoms such as shakiness, sweating, rapid heartbeat, and trembling may occur—but not until about two to four hours after eating. These symptoms are not to be confused with extreme hunger, which is characterized by gradually increased stomach rumbling, headache, and feelings of weakness—usually occurring six to eight hours after a meal.

If you think you're among those rare cases and that you have symptoms of reactive hypoglycemia, pay attention to how you feel two to four hours after eating. Then talk to your physician about a medical check-up and testing your blood glucose level while you're experiencing symptoms.

Also be cautious of so-called health clinics that diagnose "sugar-induced hypoglycemia" and offer treatment with costly remedies. *For more on nutrition services you can trust, refer to* "How *to* Find Nutrition *Help...*" *on page* 580.

Makes You Fat?

Another "no." Eating too many calories, not sugars, causes your body to produce extra pounds of body fat. That includes too many calories from any source—carbohydrate, fat, or protein. Just because many people like sweet tastes doesn't mean that eating sugary foods will lead to overindulgence. And eating sweets won't stimulate the appetite for more.

Do people with weight problems have a "sweeter tooth"? And do they consume more sugars than normal-weight individuals? Not necessarily, say nutrition experts. In fact, they may eat less sugar—but perhaps more fat. For those who are calorie conscious, including some sweet flavors may help to make a low-calorie diet more appealing.

To keep your healthy weight, you're wise to control all calories, including those from sugars, in your food choices. Sugary foods, for example, sweet, rich desserts and snacks, can supply more calories than you need. Those extra calories may come from fat, as well as carbohydrate. A "fat tooth," rather than a "sweet tooth," may be the reason some people overindulge. *Refer to page 55, "Your 'Fat Tooth'" to learn more.*

To manage your weight ("no gain, no loss") when you're cutting back on fat, replace lost calories with energy from carbohydrates. Choose more foods from the lower part of the Food Guide Pyramid. If you're really physically active, sugars can supply the extra energy you need. *For more on obesity and weight management, refer to chapter 2, "Your Healthy Weight."*

How Much Carbohydrate?

In the Recommended Dietary Allowances (RDAs), there's no specific advice for how much sugar—or how much carbohydrate—you need daily. *Refer to page 4 for more about the RDAs.* But experts advise consuming about 55 to 60 percent of your total daily calories from carbohydrates, mostly complex carbohydrates, and no more than 30 percent of calories from fat. In a 2,000-calorie-a-day diet, that's 1,100 calories or more from carbohydrates.

To reach this guideline, most Americans need to boost their carbohydrate intake and lower their fat intake. On average, Americans consume about 50 percent of their calories from carbohydrate and 34 percent from fat. Protein supplies about 15 percent, and alcohol, the remaining 2 percent.

If experts recommend consuming less fat and more "carbs," why do the Dietary Guidelines advise: "Choose a diet moderate in sugars"? There are two reasons.

For one, sugars contribute energy, or calories, yet no other nutrients. Some foods high in sugar supply calories and few other nutrients and, for some people, may displace more nutritious foods and the vitamins and minerals they provide. To compare, foods with complex carbohydrates usually have less fat, but more vitamins, minerals, and fiber. *For more about complex carbohydrates, refer to page 125, "From Complex to Simple..."*

Secondly, both sugars and starches in foods can promote tooth decay, especially when eaten frequently as snacks. *Refer to "Your Smile: Sugar and Oral Health" on page 126.*

When you're really active, you may need extra calories for energy. If you've eaten a varied and balanced diet, which meets the recommendations of the Food Guide Pyramid, sugars can supply some of that extra energy.

Sugars in Your Food

Natural or added, sugars are found in all kinds of food. Seventy-five years ago, homemakers baked with sugars and honey, prepared jellies and jams with sugars, and flavored homemade baked beans with molasses or sorghum molasses. In one recipe or another, about two-thirds of the sugars added to food came from domestic kitchens. Only about one-third were added during commercial food processing. Today, those numbers are reversed as more

have you ever wondered

...if a "sugar-free" food is also "calorie free"? Not necessarily, so don't let the term confuse you. A sugar-free food may not contain sugar, but may contain calories from other carbohydrates, fat, and protein. *Refer to page 133 for a label definition of "calorie free."* To find the calories and total sugars in one serving of any packaged food, read the Nutrition Facts panel on the food label.

...if sugar alcohols are listed on the food label? Total carbohydrate and sugars listed on the Nutrition Facts panel don't include sugar alcohols—mannitol, sorbitol, or xylitol. They're included only on the ingredient list. ✦

and more households depend on convenience foods, rather than home cooking.

No matter what their source, moderate amounts of sugars are part of a healthful diet, especially since they're naturally part of many foods and an essential ingredient in others.

Where Do Sugars Come From?

Fruit and vegetables, milk and bread, ketchup and salad dressing, candies and soft drinks—all kinds of foods get flavor, texture, and bulk from sugars. Some sugars occur naturally; others are added during food processing.

Sugar naturally occurs in fruits and vegetables. Through photosynthesis, plants transform the sun's energy into carbohydrates as food for growth. Plants have the unique ability to change their carbohydrates. As fruit matures, its carbohydrate shifts from starch to sugars, making fruit much sweeter and more appealing. By contrast, many vegetables—among them peas, carrots, and corn—are sweetest when they're young. As they mature, their sugars change to starches. What's the "chef's" lesson? Look for young, fresh vegetables—and serve them at their peak. In other words, don't store them too long. Serve fruits when they're ripe; you might need to allow ripening time after you buy them.

Milk, too, derives some of its pleasing flavor from lactose, its own naturally-occurring sugar. Milk isn't perceived as a sweet beverage, however. Lactose is only one-sixth as sweet as sucrose.

Through food processing, sugars—mainly sucrose and fructose—also are added to many prepared foods. Although many plants supply sugars, sugar cane and sugar beets are key sources. Sugar cane grows in the subtropics; sugar beets, in temperate climates. Sucrose comes from both. Fructose, a sugar that occurs naturally in fruit, is quickly taking a significant share of the sweetener market. *To learn a bit more about fructose, refer to page 125, "Fructose: A Sweeter Message."*

Don't forget your own kitchen. In one form or another, you're likely adding sugar to food, too: white and brown sugar, corn syrup, molasses, and honey, as well as jam, jelly, and syrup.

Although many nutritious foods contain sugars, soft drinks, candies, and other sweet snacks often contain them, too. The Food Guide Pyramid—your guide to healthful eating—shows the food groups that supply added sugars. But it doesn't show sugars that occur naturally. *Refer to page 243 to learn more about added sugars within the Food Guide Pyramid.*

There's certainly nothing wrong with adding sugars to food or choosing sweetened foods. In fact, they may add appeal to nutritious foods you otherwise avoid. The problem comes when high-sugar, low-nutrient foods crowd out more nutritious options: for example, when soft drinks, rather than milk or fruit juice, frequently accompany a meal. Following the recommendations from the Food Guide Pyramid is your first priority, then add sweets.

Sugars: More Than Sweeteners

The sweetness of sugars is the attribute that gets attention. Yet sugars contribute far more than a pleasing flavor to recipes and processed foods. From the standpoint of kitchen chemistry, sugars work as multipurpose ingredients, fulfilling functions that you may not even think about:

In yeast breads... sugars are "food" for yeast, allowing the dough to rise. Yeast doesn't consume all the sugar, however. The rest adds flavor and contributes to the aroma and delicate-brown color of the crust.

In cakes... sugars contribute to the bulk, tenderness, smooth crumb texture, and lightly-browned surface. In cakes that have air whipped in, such as angel food cake and sponge cake, sugars help hold the form.

In cookies... as sugars and shortening are creamed together, sugars help bring air into the dough. Sugars also contribute to the light-brown color, crisp texture, and even to the "cracked" surface of sugar cookies and gingersnaps.

In canned jams, jellies, and preserves... sugars help inhibit the growth of molds and yeast by tying up the water that these microorganisms need to multiply. For this reason, sugars act as preservatives.

In candy... sugar contributes to the texture, for example, the smoothness of hard candy and the creaminess of fudge. And, as it cooks, turning from white to yellow to brown, sugar develops a unique, tasty flavor.

In all kinds of food... sugar adds to the flavor, aroma, texture, color, and body of food.

What happens if you cut back on sugar in recipes? That depends. In some recipes, there's little difference—except for taste. In others, you'll notice a difference in volume, texture, color, and aroma. And in jams, jellies, and preserves, mold will grow quickly, even if they're refrigerated. *If you choose to modify the sugar in baked foods, refer to page* 347, "*Baking With Sugar.*"

Sugars: In a Healthful Diet

Sugars, in moderation, are part of a healthful diet. By adding taste, aroma, texture, color, and body to all kinds of foods, sugars—naturally-occurring or added—can make nutritious foods more appealing.

If your energy needs are low, go easy on the amount of sugars you consume, as well as the amount of fat. And consume mostly nutrient-dense foods. Those are foods that provide other nutrients, too—not just sugars or fats.

Get your "carbs" mostly from starchy foods. Pasta, rice, bread, other grain products, legumes, potatoes, and other starchy vegetables are great sources of complex carbohydrates. Because they usually supply vitamins, minerals, and perhaps fiber, they're nutrient dense.

Enjoy the sweet flavor of fruit and fruit juice—and reap the nutritional benefits! Fruit gets its sweet flavor from fructose. At the same time, it supplies vitamins A or C, or both—and folic acid, potassium, and fiber, as well as other nutrients. Some fruits aren't sweet, but are instead sour or bitter. Cranberries and limes are two examples. Sugars may be added to make these nutritious fruits or their juices more enjoyable. *Refer to "Fruit Snacks: Sweet & Nutritious" on page* 134.

Check food labels for sugar facts. To eat sugars in moderation, know their sources. Almost all food labels carry a Nutrition Facts panel, which lists the amount of calories, total carbohydrate, and sugars per serving. The sugars content is just part of the total carbohydrate. You'll find sugars in all kinds of foods, including milk, fruit, and grain products.

Check for other nutrients, too, and for foods that provide plenty of nutrients along with sugars. That way, the food may contribute as a food group serv-

Sugars

Food labels give the specific amount of all kinds of sugars in a food product. And "sugar lingo" on the label gives a quick description. Look for these terms as you walk the supermarket aisles:

LABEL TERM...	MEANS...
Calorie free	less than 5 calories
Sugar free	less than 0.5 gram sugars per serving
Reduced sugar or less sugar	at least 25% less* sugar or sugars per serving
No added sugars, without added sugar, no sugar	no sugars added during processing or packing including ingredients that contain sugar such as juice or dry fruit
Low sugar	(may not be used as a claim on food labels)

* *as compared with a standard serving size of the traditional food*

ing. *To learn how to read information on a food label, refer to "Get All the Facts!" on page 271.*

If you're curious about a food's "recipe," look for sugars on the ingredient list of a food label. Even if you don't see the word "sugar," it may be added to food and drinks. Words such as "maltose," "dextrin," "corn syrup," and "molasses" are terms for sugar. And the suffix, "-ose," refers to sugar, also. *Refer to page 124, "Carbohydrate's 'Short Form.'"*

FRUIT SNACKS: SWEET & NUTRITIOUS

Next time you have a craving for a sweet snack, reach for fruit! Besides satisfying a taste for sweets, fruit is packed with nutrients: vitamins A or C, or both—folic acid, potassium and fiber, too!

Fruit Pops. For a nutritious popsicle, freeze fruit (mango, papaya, or apricot) juice in ice cube trays or paper cups with wooden sticks.

Frozen Bananas. Push a wooden stick into half of a peeled banana. Roll in yogurt or a light coating of chocolate syrup, then in crunchy corn flakes. Wrap and freeze.

Fruit-Mix Mix. Mix up a zipper-top bag of dried fruits of your choice: apple slices, apricots, blueberries, cherries, cranberries, pear slices, and raisins, among others. (*Hint*: Brush your teeth—or rinse your mouth with water—after nibbling because dried fruit sticks to teeth!)

Frozen Chips. Slice bananas into thin rounds. Spread them flat on a baking pan; cover. Freeze and serve frozen as a fun snack. (*Hint*: The same technique works for seedless grapes or berries.)

Frugurt. Top a rainbow of cut-up fruit with low-fat yogurt. (*Hint*: It looks pretty in a clear glass or plastic cup.) ✦

If sugar appears as the first or second ingredient or if several sugars are listed, check the Nutrition Facts panel on a food label. It tells if a food or drink is high or low in sugars, total carbohydrate, and other nutrients. Sugars that occur naturally in foods, such as in fruit and milk, aren't listed on the ingredient list.

Know the meaning of label language. You may find words such as "sugar free" or "no sugar added" on flavored yogurt, canned fruit, breakfast cereal, or other foods. As you shop, read the label language, then check the Nutrition Facts panel for specific information. *For a "walk" through the supermarket, refer to "Your Shopping Guide" on page 279.*

For healthy teeth, snack smart on foods with sugars and starchy foods—but not too often. *Refer to "Snack for a Healthy Smile" on page 129.*

Watching calories? Moderate sugars in your food preparation. *For simple ideas, refer to "Kitchen Nutrition: Sweet Seasons" on page 135, or to "Sugar Savers" on page 347.*

Make sugar trade-offs. Balance sugary foods, such as cake or pastries, with those having less sugars, such as bread or crackers. That way you can enjoy them within your calorie budget for the day. *For tips, refer to "Quick, Easy Trade-Offs" on page 256.*

Go easy on foods with mostly sugars, but few other nutrients. That includes foods from the tip of the Food Guide Pyramid, such as candy, some soft drinks, jelly, jams, and syrup. Enjoy them in moderation to add flavor and pleasure to eating.

Use a light touch with the sugar spoon. Sweeten coffee or tea with just a bit of sugar. For a hint of "sweet" without the calories, try a touch of cinnamon. The same goes for sugar sprinkled on cereal or French toast. Use just a bit. Or sweeten with fresh fruit instead.

Go "50-50"—and cut calories in half. Or eat small portions. Share a sugary dessert or snack with a friend. Then eat it slowly to get the most enjoyment. Perhaps eat a miniature-size candy, not a large candy bar.

Try intense sweeteners to add flavor—yet few calories. *For tips on using these sweeteners, refer to page 138, "Cooking With Intense Sweeteners."*

Pairing Sugars and Chocolate!

A love for chocolate can be traced through the centuries. Known as a food of the gods, chocolate was highly prized in the Americas in pre-Columbian times. Native Americans from what is now Mexico served chocolate to European explorers as early as the 1500s.

By itself, chocolate has a bitter taste. But sugar, transported from plantations in the American colonies, made chocolate tasty to the European palate. By the mid-1600s, the popularity of chocolate, sweetened with sugar, had spread throughout Europe. In 1847, milk chocolate was created, and quickly became popular around the world.

As an ingredient with a distinctive flavor, chocolate can fit within a healthful eating plan. And it may add a flavor spark that makes nutritious foods, such as milk, more appealing.

Sugary, chocolate-flavored foods become a problem when they crowd out more nutritious foods—for example, if a chocolate bar replaces fruit in your lunch bag. Much of the chocolate we consume is found in confectionery and baked products that are laden with fat, too.

Melt Away Myths About Chocolate

Myth: *Chocolate causes acne.* That misconception has captured the attention of teens for years. However, hormonal changes during adolescence are the usual cause of acne, not chocolate.

Myth: *Carob bars are more healthful than chocolate bars.* Actually a carob bar has the same amount of calories and fat as a similar-size chocolate bar. Carob, a common substitute for chocolate, comes from the seeds of the carob tree, which are different from cocoa beans.

KITCHEN NUTRITION
sweet seasons

Bring out the flavors of foods with seasonings that offer the perception of sweetness: allspice, cardamom, cinnamon, ginger, mace, and nutmeg. If you add fruit, too, you'll get the benefits of their vitamins, minerals, and fiber.

➢ Add ginger to a fruit glaze. Blend frozen raspberries with a pinch of ginger and a small amount of fruit juice concentrate or sweetener. Toss the glaze with fresh berries or sliced fruit.

➢ Add a "sweet" spice of your choice to dry coffee grounds before brewing.

➢ Add zest and sweet flavor to oatmeal and other cooked breakfast cereals with allspice, mace, or nutmeg. In place of water, cook it in fruit juice (or milk for more calcium and phosphorus)! Toss with dried fruits, such as cranberries or apricots. Or top with fresh fruit.

➢ For a hint of sweet flavor in rice, cook with cardamom, cinnamon, or ginger. You might substitute juice for part of the cooking liquid. Perhaps toss in raisins, too!

➢ Add a touch of sweetness to cooked vegetables: for example, carrots with a hint of ginger, mashed sweet potatoes with cinnamon, and spinach with a sprinkle of nutmeg.

➢ Squeeze citrus juice—lemon, lime, or orange—over fresh fruit to enhance the flavor. Calorie saving tip: You save about 45 calories with a "squeeze" of juice rather than one tablespoon of sugar.

➢ Create your own "syrup" for pancakes or waffles. In a blender, purée fresh, sliced peaches, berries, or apples with a little fruit juice, honey, and a pinch of cinnamon. ✦

Myth: *Chocolate has a lot of caffeine.* While it's true that chocolate does supply caffeine, the amount is quite small. An 8-ounce carton of chocolate milk contains about 5 milligrams of caffeine, compared with 3 milligrams in 5 ounces of decaffeinated coffee. In contrast, 5 ounces of regular-brew coffee contains 115 milligrams of caffeine. *For more about caffeine in a healthful diet, refer to page 181, "Drinks: With or Without Caffeine?"*

Myth: *Some people are "chocoholics."* Not true—although some people do have a stronger preference for chocolate than others. While popping chocolate candies may become a high-calorie habit, eating chocolate itself can't become truly addictive.

Intense Sweeteners: Flavor Without Calories

"Low in calories" and "sugar free"! For many weight-conscious people and those with diabetes, these are sweet messages.

When it comes to sweetness, sugar is "top of mind." Yet intense sweeteners can deliver sweet taste with just a fraction of the calories, and they're many times sweeter than the same amount of sugar. With intense sweeteners, you only need a very small amount. *Refer to page 138, "Sweet Comparisons."*

Intense sweeteners also are known by other names: non-nutritive sweeteners, very-low-calorie sweeteners, or alternative sweeteners. They offer little if any energy, so the term "non-nutritive" is appropriate. In comparison, nutritive sweeteners, such as sugars, supply your body with energy in the form of calories.

Intense sweeteners can fit into healthful eating for just about anyone. In foods such as yogurt and pudding, they provide sweetness without adding calories or compromising nutrients. The three intense sweeteners in use today won't promote tooth decay since they aren't carbohydrates.

have you ever wondered

...if chocolate milk is OK for kids? Like regular milk, chocolate milk supplies calcium, phosphorus, protein, riboflavin and vitamin D. Chocolate milk contains more calories from added sugars, but the sugars in chocolate milk are no more cavity promoting than any other carbohydrate. ✦

Trio of Sweet Options

Perhaps no ingredient has been scrutinized by researchers as much as intense sweeteners. Before being used in food—or as a tabletop sweetener—they're first tested extensively to meet the guidelines and safety standards of the Food and Drug Administration (FDA).

Currently in the United States, three intense sweeteners have been approved: aspartame, saccharin, and acesulfame K. But watch for news about others. Approval from the FDA is being sought for sucralose, alitame, and cyclamate.

Aspartame

Aspartame is 180 to 200 times sweeter than table sugar. So a little goes a long way! Discovered in 1965, aspartame was first marketed as NutraSweet and Equal. Now it's also sold under other brand names. Aspartame isn't sugar. Instead it's a combination of mainly two amino acids—aspartic acid and phenylalanine. While amino acids are the building blocks of protein, aspartic acid and phenylalanine are joined in a way that's perceived as sweet. These same two amino acids are also found naturally in common foods such as meat, skim milk, fruit, and vegetables. When digested, your body treats them like any other amino acid in food. *For more about amino acids, refer to "Protein Power" on page 561.*

Because it contains phenylalanine, people with phenylketonuria (PKU) need to be cautious about consuming foods and beverages with aspartame. On food labels, look for "aspartame" in the ingredient list, as well as this warning: "Phenylketonurics: Contains Phenylalanine." PKU is a rare genetic disorder that doesn't allow the body to metabolize phenylalanine properly. It afflicts about one in every 15,000 people in the United States. In the U.S., all infants are screened for PKU at birth. *For more about food sensitivities, refer to chapter 9, "Sensitive About Food."*

Because it's not heat stable, aspartame is used mostly in foods that don't require cooking or baking. Among the commercial uses are puddings, gelatins, frozen desserts, yogurt, hot cocoa mix, powdered soft drinks, soft drinks, teas, breath mints, chewing gum, and tabletop sweeteners, such as Equal and SweetMate.

Cooking tip: When you prepare food with aspartame, add it after foods are cooked. Or sprinkle it on a cooked or baked product after removing it from the heat. When aspartame is heated for a long time, it may lose its sweetness.

Saccharin

Discovered in 1879, saccharin has been used as a noncaloric sweetener for about 100 years. It's produced from a substance that occurs naturally in grapes. Today, saccharin is used in soft drinks and in tabletop sweeteners, such as Sweet 'N Low and Sweet 10.

In 1977 the FDA proposed a ban on saccharin. The reason? A few studies hinted that saccharin—in very large amounts—may cause cancer in laboratory rats. However, the FDA formally withdrew its proposal for the ban in 1991. It would be very difficult to consume the large doses given to laboratory rats from food alone, and no human studies ever confirmed the findings. The warning still remains on product labels, however.

Being 300 times sweeter than table sugar, a small amount of saccharin adds a lot of flavor—without adding calories. Just 20 milligrams of saccharin gives the same sweetness as one teaspoon (4,000 milligrams, or 4 grams) of table sugar. Because the body can't break it down, saccharin doesn't provide energy. Instead it's eliminated in urine.

Cooking tip: Saccharin keeps its sweet flavor when heated. So it can be used in cooked and baked foods. Because it doesn't have the bulk that sugar has, it may not work in some recipes. *Refer to "Cooking With Intense Sweeteners" on page* 138.

Acesulfame K

Acesulfame K entered the food world quite recently. Discovered in 1967 and approved for use in the United States in 1988, acesulfame K is marketed under the brand name Sunette.

A white, odorless, crystalline sweetener, this intense sweetener provides no calories. Like saccharin, acesulfame K can't be broken down by the body and it's eliminated in the urine unchanged.

Acesulfame K is 200 times sweeter than table sugar, adding its sweet taste to candies, baked goods, desserts, soft drinks, and tabletop sweeteners, such as Sweet One and Swiss Sweet. Acesulfame K may leave a slight aftertaste when used alone at high concentrations in some foods. So it's often combined with other sweeteners, both traditional and intense.

Cooking tip: Because acesulfame K is heat stable, you can use it in cooked and baked foods. Like saccharin, it doesn't give bulk as sugar does, so it may not work in some recipes. *Refer to "Cooking with Intense Sweeteners" on page* 138.

Intense Sweeteners: For Whom?

In the 1970s the Baby Boom generation became intent on slimness; then in the 1980s, on fitness. The growing use of intense sweeteners has paralleled these interests.

From a health perspective, almost anyone can consume foods and beverages flavored with intense sweeteners. It's a matter of personal choice.

Watching your weight? Because they're usually lower in calories, foods sweetened with intense sweeteners can help you keep trim. But you need to control calories in your whole eating plan. Calorie control—from a variety of foods—is part of the weight management formula; regular physical activity is the other.

For people with diabetes, intense sweeteners can satisfy a taste for sweets without affecting blood sugar levels.

During pregnancy and breast-feeding, eating a variety of foods with enough calories and nutrients is very important. In moderation, foods with intense sweeteners can satisfy a desire for something sweet without adding excess calories. That leaves room for nutritious foods.

Foods sweetened with intense sweeteners aren't intended for infants and young children, although intense sweeteners are safe for kids to consume. They need ample calories for rapid growth. Children who are older than two years and who eat a well-balanced diet occasionally can use foods and beverages sweetened with intense sweeteners.

People with phenylketonuria (PKU) should avoid foods sweetened with aspartame. If this applies to you, check with your physician or registered dietitian for advice. *For more information on* PKU *and aspartame, refer to page* 136.

SWEET COMPARISONS

Many ingredients have a sweet flavor. Some, much more than others. For intense sweeteners, such as saccharin, a little bit goes a long way!

Sweetener	Comparing the Sweetness to Sucrose
Sorbitol	0.5
Mannitol	0.7
Sucrose	1.0
Xylitol	1.0
High-fructose corn syrup (HFCS)	1.5
Fructose (crystalline)	1.5
Cyclamate*	30
Aspartame	180
Acesulfame K	200
Saccharin	300
Sucralose*	600
Alitame*	2,000

* Not yet approved for use in food or beverages in the United States

Cooking With Intense Sweeteners

With their sugar-like flavor, intense sweeteners can be used in many recipes you already enjoy, perhaps to reduce calories. For example, sweetening an apple cobbler with saccharin rather than brown sugar might save 67 calories per serving (if a recipe to serve four calls for 1/2 cup of brown sugar).

If you use intense sweeteners, be prepared to adjust your recipe or food preparation technique. And remember, their unique cooking qualities differ from sugar.

Check the food label on sweetener packages for usage. You'll see the sugar equivalents. Since some intense sweeteners have ingredients added to give them bulk, the substitution equivalents may vary.

Know that recipes prepared with an intense sweetener may not turn out exactly like the same recipe made with sugar. That's especially true of baked foods. Sugar has many functions other than sweetness. *Refer to page* 132, "*Sugars: More Than Sweeteners.*" Check label directions for advice on using specific intense sweeteners.

If intense sweeteners are new to you, experiment a little. Add just a little sweetener until you get the sweetness level you want. Adding too much can ruin the flavor.

Use any intense sweetener in recipes that don't require heat, such as cold beverages, salads, chilled soups, frozen desserts, or fruit sauces.

Use saccharin- and acesulfame K-based sweeteners in all kinds of recipes, uncooked, cooked, and baked, according to package directions. Unlike aspartame, they both retain their sweetness when heated.

Add aspartame-based sweeteners after cooking or baking, once the food has slightly cooled. Prolonged and high heat breaks down aspartame, causing a loss of sweetness. But don't worry if it does get heated. Although you may lose flavor, aspartame is still safe to consume.

Expect a lower volume when cooking and baking with intense sweeteners instead of sugar. Sugar adds bulk as well as sweetness. Intense sweeteners with a bulking agent help bring up the volume. Or go "50-50" by substituting saccharin- or acesulfame K-based sweeteners for half the sugar, according to package directions. However, the volume still won't be as high as with 100 percent sugar.

Need more guidance? Contact the manufacturers of intense sweeteners. Usually they'll provide tips and recipes for using their products to sweeten your palate.

have you ever *wondered*

...if intense sweeteners cause tooth decay? No. Foods and drinks made with aspartame, acesulfame K, and saccharin won't promote cavities because they aren't broken down by bacteria in plaque. Since they don't "feed" bacteria, no acids form. Sugarless gum, flavored with an intense sweetener, may actually promote dental health. First, it doesn't have any carbohydrate. Secondly, gum chewing increases saliva flow, which actually helps neutralize plaque acids.

...if some people are allergic to aspartame? Scientific studies including people of all ages have not found that aspartame causes a true allergic reaction. ✦

your nutrition check-up

Sweet and Nutrient-Dense, Too?

Here's your chance to check your "sweet" choices. Are they packed with nutrients, too? Or do they provide mostly calories and few nutrients? Check the space that describes what choices you make!

Do You...?	Always	Mostly	Sometimes	Never
reach for fruit as a snack, rather than candy?	___	___	___	___
drink juice—or milk—with lunch or dinner, rather than soft drinks?	___	___	___	___
top your cereal with fruit instead of—or along with—sugar?	___	___	___	___
sweeten waffles, pancakes, or French toast with fruit, rather than just syrup?	___	___	___	___
top ice cream with fruit, not just chocolate or caramel syrup?	___	___	___	___
order juice or milk with a quickservice meal or snacks, such as a burger meal?	___	___	___	___
choose fruit for dessert, not a rich, high-calorie dessert?	___	___	___	___
go for the smaller rather than the bigger slice of pie or cake?	___	___	___	___
snack on two or three cookies with milk, rather than simply down five or six cookies?	___	___	___	___
make hot cocoa with milk, not just water?	___	___	___	___

Now rate your choices.

Total the points in each column. For each answer, give yourself:

4 points for "always"
3 points for "mostly"
2 points for "sometimes"
1 point for "never"

If you scored...

30 *and above*. Your "sweet" choices are mostly high nutrients, too. In fact, enjoy a bit of sugar now and then to add pleasure to eating.

20 *to* 29. If your overall diet is balanced and you're not overspending your calorie budget, your preference for sweets is probably okay.

10 *to* 19. Your "sweet tooth" may be crowding out nutritious foods. Check them out and consider some sweet options from the food groups, not just the Pyramid tip.

real life nutrition

Bites Between Bytes

"This job really keeps a body moving!" remarked Akim to his co-worker. "I barely have enough time for lunch or a break before our next customer needs help. Thank goodness for that canteen downstairs and those snacks we get there."

"And you know," he said, popping another hard candy into his mouth, "that bowl of candy for our customers gets me through the day, too!"

As the owner of a small computer repair business, Akim certainly does work on a time crunch—often eating at his desk when customers aren't around. He grabs a sandwich and a fruit pie from the canteen and a soft drink from a vending machine. If he gets hungry later on, there's a snack display by the coffee pot with cookies and chips.

With an impish smile, Akim jokes about the easiest strategy for eating more nutritious meals and snacks, "Get rid of our customers so I have time to go out—just kidding!" Seriously, what changes could Akim make, and why?

Tips for helping Akim control his sugar intake ... and boosting the nutrients in his meals and snacks.

➢ Akim doesn't need to avoid sugary foods entirely ... if they fit within his calorie budget. But he does need to enjoy them in moderation—and to help avoid cavities, preferably eat them with meals. Eating sugary foods between meals more likely promotes tooth decay than eating the same foods at mealtime.

➢ The "grab-and-go" sweet foods that Akim relies on at work seem to push out some more nutritious lower-calorie and low-fat foods. And his eating style makes it difficult to meet recommendations of the Food Guide Pyramid. The soft drink as his lunch beverage, fruit pie for dessert, cookies or chips for a snack, and the hard candies he frequently eats as he works all supply calories, but fewer nutrients.

➢ As other options, he might buy juice or milk from the canteen instead. If he doesn't have one already, Akim might invest in a small refrigerator for the office so he can keep juice, milk, yogurt, fruit, and other nutritious foods and drinks on hand.

➢ For more nutrients, yet a sweet taste, he might bring in an apple, peach, banana, or other fruit to enjoy as a dessert or snack.

➢ Frequent snacking on hard candies—or chips, for that matter—isn't a good dental health practice, especially since they produce damaging plaque acids for 20 to 30 minutes after he finishes each snack. He'd be better off with a more satisfying meal so he's less tempted to snack—and move the candy bowl away from his work area!

Chapter Six

Fiber

your body's broom

Your ancestors probably consumed more fiber than you do!

Before the days of advanced milling technology, gristmills ground wheat, corn, and other grains into meal or flour. Using the power of a moving river, grain was milled between two coarse stones. Then it was sifted to remove the inedible chaff, or husk, leaving all the edible parts of the grain. The bran and the germ that contain fiber and many essential nutrients remained. Whole grains were the only grains people knew. In some parts of the world, that's still true today; in fact, some people pound their grain by hand to make flour.

As technology improved, the bran and the germ were separated and removed, leaving refined white flour. With this new process came new status. White bread with its softer texture and high-class appeal became more desirable than coarser, darker bread. But it was more expensive and only available to those who could afford it. For the same reasons, white rice became more desirable than brown rice. Simply put, refined was "in"!

With this switch to refined grains, however, people became short-changed on many nutrients—including fiber—without knowing it. In the 1940s, recognizing the health consequences, manufacturers began enriching many grain products. Now, some nutrients lost during processing—thiamin, riboflavin, niacin, and iron—are added back. In some grain products, fiber is added back, too.

Only within the past 25 years have health experts realized that fiber offers more than bulk to food. It's loaded with health benefits. Today whole-grain products and other foods with fiber are "in" again!

Just what is fiber—and how does it promote your health?

Fiber: An Important Non-Nutrient

We talk about fiber as a single component of food. But it's not that simple. Actually, "fiber" is a general term, referring to complex carbohydrates that your body cannot digest or absorb into your bloodstream. Instead of being used for energy like other carbohydrates, fiber is excreted.

Because fiber can't nourish your body, it's not a nutrient. But it's still a component of food that promotes your good health in many other ways.

Fiber: Just What Is It?

Plants—and foods of plant origin—count on fiber for their shape. It's fiber that gives celery its rigid stalk and gives spinach the strong stems that hold up its leaves. That same structure "bulks up" the contents of your intestine.

WHAT IS A WHOLE GRAIN?

A whole grain is the entire edible part of any grain: wheat, corn, oats, and rice, among others. In the life cycle of plants, it's the seed from which other plants grow. Nutrients in these seeds supply the first nourishment for the plant ... before the roots are formed. The whole grain, or seed, contains three parts: endosperm, bran, and germ.

The ***bran*** makes up the outer layers of the grain. It supplies large amounts of B-vitamins, trace minerals, and dietary fiber.

The ***endosperm,*** which is the inner part of the grain, has most of the protein and carbohydrate, and just small amounts of vitamins and minerals. White flour is ground from the endosperm.

The ***germ*** is small but very important. It sprouts, generating a new plant. It has B-vitamins, trace minerals and some protein.

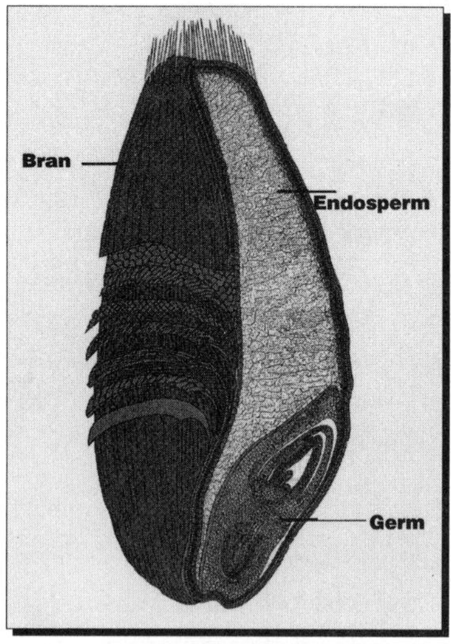

Reprinted courtesy of the Wheat Foods Council.

Like starch, most fibers are made of many sugar units, so they're actually polysaccharides. But unlike starch, fiber's chains of sugars can't be digested in the human body into simple sugars. *For more about carbohydrates—their composition and digestion—refer to page 123, "Sugar: What Is It?"*

In dairy cows, bacteria in digestive juices break down fiber in their grassy meals, providing energy they need to produce milk. However, human digestive enzymes cannot break fiber into units that are small enough for absorption. That's why fiber can't be converted into energy, or calories—at least not in your body. That very quality gives fiber its own unique roles in keeping you healthy.

(Technically, very small amounts of some fibers can be digested. But the amount is much too small to count.)

Not All Fibers Are Alike!

Soluble and insoluble: two types of fiber with two different missions! What makes them unique? Soluble fiber dissolves in water, and insoluble fiber doesn't. These differing qualities allow them to keep you healthy in different ways. *"Foods for Fiber" on page 148 lists foods that contain the two types of fiber.*

Insoluble Fiber: Aid to Digestion

Insoluble fiber: you know it as "roughage." This group of fibers—cellulose, hemicellulose, and lignin—gives structure to plant cell walls. Wheat bran, for example, is high in insoluble fiber.

Although they don't dissolve, insoluble fibers do hold on to water. And they move waste through the intestinal tract without being digested themselves, earning fiber its title as "nature's broom." By adding bulk and softness to stools, insoluble fibers promote regularity and help prevent constipation. By moving waste through the colon, insoluble fibers decrease transit time. That's the time that potentially harmful substances in food waste linger in the intestines and come in contact with the intestinal lining.

Soluble Fiber: Protective Benefits

Soft, liquid foods may have fiber, too. Surprised?

Instead of giving a coarse texture to food, soluble fibers, such as that in oat bran, dissolve to become gummy or viscous. They're often used in low-fat and nonfat food to add texture and consistency. Fibers called gums, mucilages, and pectin are all soluble.

If you've ever made jam or jelly, you're probably familiar with pectin. Pectin gives them their thick, gel-like consistency. In your body, pectin plays a different role, binding to fatty substances and promoting their excretion as waste. This quality seems to help lower blood cholesterol levels. Soluble fibers also help regulate the body's use of sugars.

Fiber's "Benefit Package": A Closer Look

Unlike many nutrients, life doesn't depend on fiber—but your overall health may! Fiber's "benefit package" not only promotes health, but also may help reduce the risk for some chronic diseases.

Fiber: Bundled With Other Nutrients

Fiber isn't a "lonely" component of food. Most foods with significant amounts of fiber, such as legumes, whole-wheat bread, strawberries, and brussels sprouts, are packed with carbohydrates (complex or simple) and other essential nutrients, too. For example, many fruits and vegetables contribute antioxidant vitamins (beta carotene and vitamin C), which may help protect against some types of cancer. Foods with more fiber often have less fat, too. *For more about antioxidant vitamins, refer to "Antioxidant Vitamins: A Closer Look" on page 90.*

As good sources of many nutrients, the health benefits of fiber-rich foods are manifold. In fact, fiber's benefits in food can't be easily separated from the contributions of other nutrients.

Avoiding the Trio: Constipation, Hemorrhoids, Diverticulosis

You already read about the benefits of insoluble fiber—the kind in wheat bran. It holds onto water, helping to soften and add bulk to waste in the intestines. This action helps stools pass through the digestive system more quickly with normal frequency and ease. As a result, fiber helps prevent constipation and the discomfort that goes with it. When soft stools easily pass out of the body, there's no need for strained bowel movements. As a result, hemorrhoids—a painful swelling of the vein near the anus—are less likely to form. With soft, regular stools, diverticulosis may be avoided, too. With diverticulosis, tiny sacs form when the intestinal wall, especially in the colon, gets weak. These sacs may become infected and quite painful.

When there's a flare-up of diverticulosis, too much fiber can irritate the intestinal tract. Even small seeds found in some berries and jams, hulls on popcorn, or fruit skins sometimes cause problems. If this is a problem for you, ask your doctor or a registered dietitian how to include fiber in your diet. *To find a registered dietitian, refer to "How to Find Nutrition Help" on page 580.*

Being "brown" doesn't make bread whole wheat! It's true that whole-grain breads are browner than breads made with refined white flour. However, in some brown bread, the rich brown color comes instead from coloring, which is listed on the label, usually as "caramel coloring."

By law, any bread labeled "whole wheat" must be made from 100 percent whole-wheat flour. "Wheat bread," however, may contain some white refined flour and some whole-wheat flour; proportions vary from product to product. With a little label reading, you can get a general idea of the amounts of each type. The flour listed first in the ingredient list is present in the greater amount.

For breads with more fiber, check the Nutrition Facts panel and the ingredient list. Look for those made with mainly whole-wheat or other whole-grain flour. ✦

Cancer Connection?

Eating plenty of fiber over the years may help prevent certain cancers, such as colon and rectal cancers. The cause of colon cancer isn't clear. But about 25 years ago scientists noted that these cancers were more common in Western countries where people ate less fiber.

A high-fiber diet may help reduce cancer risk in two ways: (1) by speeding the time it takes for waste to pass through the digestive tract, and (2) by forming a bulkier, heavier stool. Slow movement of food waste through the digestive tract allows more time for potentially harmful substances to come in contact with intestinal walls. And bulkier stools help dilute the concentration of these substances.

In contrast, a high-fat diet is associated with the risk for colon cancer. Since a high-fiber diet is usually lower in fat, it may be another reason why cancer risk seems to go down among people who eat more fiber.

"Waistline Watchers"

Fiber-rich foods may help your body keep trim! Often they're low in fat and calories. Because they take longer to chew, fiber-rich foods may help slow you down, so you eat less. With their added bulk, they help you feel full longer, making you less inclined to nibble too soon after eating. Fiber itself can't be fattening—it isn't digested!

To make a fiber-rich diet work for your waistline, remember to keep your fat intake low at the same time! (An active lifestyle is important, too!) *For more on keeping trim, refer to chapter* 2, "Your Healthy Weight."

Help for People With Diabetes

For people with diabetes, soluble fibers—especially pectin and gums—may perform another important function. By helping to control the level of blood sugar, soluble fibers may reduce the need for insulin, or medication, for some people. Incorporating at least one or two servings of beans, oats, or other sources of soluble fiber as part of a total fiber intake of 20 to 35 grams per day may help to lower fasting blood sugar levels in some people with diabetes.

The reason that soluble fibers help lower blood sugar levels isn't fully understood. Perhaps it's because fiber slows the time for emptying the stomach. As a result, glucose absorption may slow down, too. *To learn more about blood sugar and its role in diabetes, refer to page* 129, "Causes Diabetes?"

If you have diabetes and want to use more soluble fiber to help control blood sugars, talk to a registered dietitian.

Fiber—Heart Healthy, Too!

Another potential benefit: Soluble fibers may help lower the level of total blood cholesterol, mainly by lowering LDL-cholesterol, or "bad" cholesterol. Fiber seems to help bile acids, which are made of cholesterol, pass through the intestine as waste. As a result, the body absorbs less dietary cholesterol.

After more than 20 years of research with different groups of people, researchers have found that soluble fibers in beans, psyllium fiber, oats, and oat bran seem to help lower blood cholesterol levels in some people. Those same high-fiber diets were lower in fat, too. So it's not clear whether it's the higher levels of fiber, or lower levels of fat, or both factors that help lower the risk of heart disease.

have you ever wondered

. . . which one to buy: wheat germ or wheat bran? They're two different parts of the grain, so their benefits differ. The germ is the nutrient-rich inner part, and the bran is the outer coating. From a nutritional standpoint, 1 ounce (1/3 cup) of wheat bran has a lot more fiber, about 13 grams, compared with 4.4 grams of fiber in 1 ounce (1/4 cup) of wheat germ. Wheat germ has more protein, and more of some vitamins and minerals.

. . . what psyllium is? (When you pronounce it, the "p" is silent.) Psyllium—high in soluble fiber—is a grain used in some bulk-forming natural laxatives and used in some breakfast cereals. Its source is plantago, a plant that grows in India and in the Mediterranean. Although some people may be allergic to psyllium, in moderate amounts, it's safe for most people. ✦

Some scientists say that people benefit from eating fiber because it replaces fattier foods in the diet, not because of anything special about fiber itself. Until more is known about lowering blood cholesterol levels, continue to consume fiber from a variety of sources; decrease your intake of fat, especially saturated fat; maintain your healthy weight; and live an active lifestyle.

For more about lowering blood cholesterol levels, refer to page 489, *"Blood Cholesterol Countdown."*

Intestinal Gas: Part of Fiber's "Action"

Intestinal gas is a common complaint—and normal side effect—of eating a high-fiber diet. If your eating style has been typically low in fiber, minimize the discomfort that comes with "bulking up." Increase your fiber intake slowly over several months. Drink enough water, too, to help reduce the effects of intestinal gas and prevent impacted stools. *For more about water in a healthful eating pattern, refer to chapter* 8, *"Fluids: Often Overlooked."*

People especially complain—and sometimes joke—about beans and vegetables in the cabbage family: "They give me gas!" Gas forms in the intestines because humans lack the right enzymes to degrade certain carbohydrates, leaving people feeling gassy and bloated. Other foods or ingredients reported to cause gas for some include milk, wheat germ, onions, carrots, celery, bananas, raisins, dried apricots, prune juice, and sorbitol. *For more information on sorbitol, a slowly digested fruit sugar, refer to page* 126, *"Sugar Alcohol—Not a Sugar."*

There are some techniques that may help to tame the gas caused by beans.

- When preparing dry beans, soak overnight, then discard the soaking water and cook the beans in fresh water. The soaking water absorbs some of the gas-producing carbohydrates.

- Leave enough time to cook dried beans thoroughly. Then they're more easily digested.

- Take smaller helpings of bean dishes or other offending foods.

- "De-gas" canned beans by draining off the liquid and rinsing the beans well.

Several nonprescription products also offer relief from gas for some people. Products containing charcoal are taken at the end of a meal to help absorb gas in the intestines. These products can interfere with the absorption of medications, however, and are not recommended for children. Another approach is to use products containing a food enzyme called alpha-galactosidase. Sold in the form of tablets or drops used before a meal, this product helps convert gas-producing carbohydrates to more easily digestible sugars. An option that helps relieve gas symptoms rather than prevent them is products containing simethicone. This substance works by breaking large pockets of gas in the intestines into smaller bubbles.

Fiber

Although the Nutrition Facts panel on a food label gives the specific amount of fiber in foods, "fiber lingo" on the label may offer a quick description. Look for these terms as you walk the supermarket aisles:

LABEL TERM...	MEANS...
High fiber	5 grams or more per serving
Good source	2.5 to 4.9 grams per serving
More or added fiber	at least 2.5 grams more* per serving

**as compared with a standard serving size of the traditional food*

Be aware that other gas-reducing or gas-preventing products are sold—some with questionable claims. You're wise to check with your doctor before using any gas-reduction products.

Fiber: How Much Is Enough?

If you're like most Americans, your day's meals and snacks come up short on fiber, supplying only about half the amount your body needs. On average, most people consume only about 11 grams of fiber daily.

To increase the health benefits, many experts recommend eating more—20 to 35 grams of fiber daily. Unlike many vitamins and minerals, there's no Recommended Dietary Allowance (RDA) for total fiber intake—or for amounts of soluble and insoluble fiber. *For more about the RDAs, refer to page 4. For more information on fiber intake for children, refer to "How Much Fiber? Just Add Five!" on page 433.*

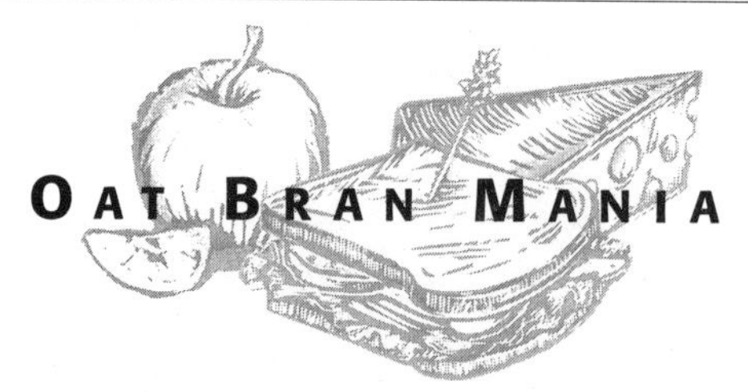

OAT BRAN MANIA

Does oat bran have any "magic" that defies heart disease? With all the media attention a few years back, some people thought so.

When research in the 1980s showed that soluble fiber in oat bran had a blood cholesterol-lowering effect, many food manufacturers rushed to position oat bran in their product line. Consumers could buy oat bran products of all kinds: breakfast cereal, muffins, and just plain oat bran to sprinkle on fruit, frozen yogurt, or any mixed dish.

As research continued, we learned that soluble fiber was just one factor linked to many others. Part of its success was due to the fact that there is less room for higher-fat foods when more high-fiber foods are part of the diet. While oat bran has its benefits, it's just part of an overall low-fat eating plan. ✦

Although fiber comes from foods of plant origin, you don't need to eat huge amounts of whole-grains, legumes, vegetables, and fruits to meet your fiber goal. Your everyday food choices can supply all you need. *Check the chart "Counting Up Fiber" on page 150 to quickly "guesstimate" your fiber intake.*

Be aware that you can overdo a good thing! Eating more than 50 to 60 grams of fiber a day may decrease the amount of vitamins and minerals your body absorbs, among them zinc, iron, magnesium, and calcium. Too much fiber can move food through the digestive tract too quickly—faster than some nutrients can be absorbed. A heavy duty amount of fiber may cause gas, diarrhea, and bloating, too. And people who fill up with too much high-fiber foods or supplements may not have an appetite for other nutrient-rich foods.

For Fiber—Variety!

As laboratory procedures have improved, consumers now know the "dietary fiber" content of food, which reflects both soluble and insoluble fiber content. Today, you'll find dietary fiber listed on the Nutrition Facts panel on labels of most packaged food products.

Foods for Fiber

Do you like to nibble on popcorn? It's a whole-grain snack—that helps boost the fiber factor in your diet. Again, fiber comes only from plant sources of food: fruits, vegetables, legumes, grains, nuts, and seeds. Milk, eggs, and meat don't supply any fiber.

Foods actually contain a "mixed bag" of fibers, having some of both types: soluble and insoluble. Good sources of soluble fiber may supply some insoluble fiber, too, and vice versa. For example, fruits and vegetables have both pectin (soluble) and cellulose (insoluble). However, fruit usually has more pectin; vegetables, more cellulose.

Here are some specific foods that provide insoluble and soluble fibers.

***Insoluble fibers*:** whole-wheat products, wheat and corn bran, and many vegetables (such as cauliflower, green beans, and potatoes), including the skins of fruits and root vegetables.

***Soluble fibers*:** dried beans and peas, oats, barley, and many fruits and vegetables (such as apples, oranges, and carrots). Psyllium seed husks also fit within this group.

Why do whole-grain products have much more fiber than grain products made with refined flour? In grains, most fiber comes from the bran (the outer layer of the grain) and the germ. When flour is milled to produce white flour, both the fibrous bran and the germ are removed—along with them, many important nutrients and fiber. Only the grain's endosperm remains. *Refer to "What Is a Whole Grain?" page 144 to see the three parts of a whole grain: bran, germ, and endosperm.*

From grain to grain, bran isn't all alike. The bran layers in different grains—wheat, rice, corn, oats, and others—have varying types and different amounts of fiber. Wheat bran, for example, has a higher concentration of fiber than most other bran. And its bran is mainly insoluble. To compare, oat bran contains mainly soluble fiber.

The fiber content of vegetables and fruits varies; some are better sources than others. A heaping bowl of fresh lettuce greens may seem loaded with fiber. However, one cup of lettuce contains just about 1 gram of fiber; instead it's mostly water. In contrast, a 1/2 cup of three-bean salad (mainly legumes) supplies more than 3 fiber grams.

Food preparation or processing may alter the fiber content of foods. Just as a sponge changes in its ability to hold water when it's chopped into very fine pieces, properties of fiber may change a bit when the structure is altered by food processing or preparation. Fiber content drops, too, when the fiber-rich part of a food is removed. *See "Which Apple for Fiber?" on this page to compare the fiber content in different forms of an apple.*

When it comes to making food choices, don't get hung up on which fiber is which—just consume enough overall. By adding a variety of fiber-rich foods to your meals and snacks, you usually get the health benefits of both soluble and insoluble fibers.

Need a Fiber Boost?

If you need a plan to follow for fiber, check the day's menu plan, "Fit Fiber In!" on page 152. Foods in italic print can supply the fiber you need. Just eat the suggested amounts of fruits and vegetables. Choose one or two whole grains every day. And consume legumes two or three times a week. You'll easily meet the 20- to 35-gram per day goal—and consume ample amounts of both soluble and insoluble dietary fibers, too.

If you need a fiber boost, gradually increase the amount you consume. The bacteria in your stomach and intestines need time to adjust to change. Adding fiber too quickly—or consuming too much on a regular basis—may result in gas, diarrhea, cramps, and bloating.

Along with extra fiber, drink plenty of water and other fluids, too. Fiber helps prevent constipation and related intestinal problems by acting like a large sponge in your colon. It holds water and keeps waste moving along. In order for fiber to do its job, you need to consume enough fluids. Aim for at least eight cups of liquids a day. *For more about fluids in a*

Apple juice, applesauce, a whole apple—which has more fiber? An apple with the peel on has more fiber than an apple without the peel. And as food changes form, its fiber content may change, too.

1 whole apple with peel	3.0 grams fiber
1 whole apple without peel	2.4 grams fiber
1/2 cup applesauce	1.8 grams fiber
3/4 cup apple juice	0.2 grams fiber

Counting Up Fiber

How much fiber do these common foods supply?

	Amount	Fiber* (grams)	Calories
Fruits			
Apple (w/skin)	1 medium	3	80
Applesauce	1/2 cup	2	55
Banana	1 medium	2	105
Blueberries	1/2 cup	2	40
Cantaloupe	1 cup	1	60
Figs, dried	2	4	95
Grapes	1/2 cup	1	30
Orange	1 medium	3	60
Orange juice	3/4 cup	<1	75
Peach (w/skin)	1 medium	1	40
Pear (w/skin)	1 medium	4	100
Prunes, dried	3	2	60
Raisins	1/4 cup	2	115
Strawberries	1 cup	4	45
Vegetables, cooked			
Broccoli	1/2 cup	2	25
Brussels sprouts	1/2 cup	3	30
Peas	1/2 cup	2	65
Potato, baked (w/skin)	1 medium	4	200
Potato, mashed	1/2 cup	1	110
Spinach	1/2 cup	2	20
Sweet potato, baked (w/skin)	1/2 medium	2	60
Zucchini	1/2 cup	1	20
Vegetables, raw			
Carrots	1 medium	2	30
Celery	1 stalk	<1	5
Cucumber, sliced	1/2 cup	<1	5
Lettuce, romaine	1 cup	1	10
Mushrooms, sliced	1/2 cup	<1	10
Spinach	1 cup	1	10
Tomato	1 medium	2	30
Legumes, cooked			
Baked beans, plain or vegetarian	1/2 cup	3	120
Kidney beans	1/2 cup	3	115
Lentils	1/2 cup	4	115
Breads, grains, and pasta			
Bagel	1 medium	1	165
Bread stick	1	<1	115
Brown rice, cooked	1/2 cup	2	110
French bread	1 slice	<1	80
Pumpernickel bread	1 slice	3	80
Spaghetti, cooked	1/2 cup	1	100
Wheat bran	1 tablespoon	2	10
Wheat germ	1 tablespoon	1	15
White bread	1 slice	<1	60
White rice, cooked	1/2 cup	1	135
Whole-wheat bread	1 slice	2	60
Breakfast cereals			
100% bran	1/3 cup	8	70
Bran flakes	3/4 cup	5	90
Corn flakes	3/4 cup	1	100
Granola w/raisins	1/4 cup	2	130
Oatmeal, cooked	3/4 cup	3	95
Raisin bran	3/4 cup	5	120
Snack foods			
Hummus dip	2 tablespoons	2	50
Peanuts, dry-roasted	1/4 cup	3	215
Popcorn, air-popped	1 cup	1	30
Sunflower seeds	1/4 cup	2	210
Walnuts	1/4 cup	1	95

**Due to the different methods used in determining fiber in foods, fiber values found on* Nutrition Facts *panels and in other sources of fiber information may vary slightly from those listed.*

Note: Nutrient values are rounded.

Sources: Bowes & Church's Food Values of Portions Commonly Used, 16th Edition, 1994; Plant Fiber in Foods, *2nd Edition,* 1990; *and manufacturer data.*

healthful diet, refer to chapter 8, *"Fluids: Often Overlooked."*

Caution: Use care when adding fiber to the diets of young children. Extra fiber may fill them up too quickly, taking away their appetite for other nutritious foods. Without the nutrients those foods supply, kids may not grow properly. Too much fiber also may interfere with their body's absorption of vitamins and minerals. *For more on feeding children, refer to chapter* 17, *"Food to Grow On."*

Elderly people and people who have had gastrointestinal surgery may feel the effects of added fiber more than others. If you're older than 65 or have had surgery on some part of your stomach, intestines, colon, or rectum, check with your doctor before adding fiber to your diet. *For more on eating in later life, refer to chapter* 20, *"Nutrition for Older Adults."*

About Fiber Pills and Powders...
Fiber-rich foods—whole grains, fruits, legumes, and vegetables—provide the added benefits associated with a high-fiber diet, including cutting down on fat. They also supply other nutrients. Fiber pills and powders don't have any added benefits.

Depending on the supplement, adding a fiber pill or powder to your food choices probably won't make much of a difference to your health—although it may help relieve constipation. So save the expense! Many fiber pills contain only small amounts of fiber, compared with the amounts found in foods. Those with more fiber may inhibit the absorption of some minerals—a problem for people whose diets are nutrient deficient. For people who do take fiber supplements for "regularity," their bodies might come to rely on them.

Most registered dietitians and doctors advise against taking fiber pills and powders as a primary source of dietary fiber.

Furthermore, no evidence proves that fiber supplements help you lose and keep weight off. You can't trick your appetite for the long run. Rather than fiber pills and powders, choose a low-fat, high-fiber diet with plenty of fruits, vegetables, whole grains, and beans. *To learn about healthful ways to manage weight, refer to "Weight Management: Strategies That Work!" on page* 29.

KITCHEN NUTRITION

cooking a pot o' beans

Back in the "olden days"—before legumes commonly were canned—dry beans and peas were stored year-round, then soaked and cooked into a hearty meal with beans.

More recently, either for lack of time or know-how, the art of bean cookery has gone through a slump. As we learn more about their health benefits, however, legumes are making a comeback. And we're learning that even dry beans and peas are easy to cook—as long as we plan ahead.

To soak the beans:

Traditional Method: Reduce cooking time by up to one half by soaking beans for at least four hours or overnight in a pot filled with room temperature water. Choose a pot that's big enough; beans expand!

Quick Method: Time short? Then bring water to a boil, and let beans soak in hot water for one to four hours, depending on the variety of beans.

To reduce the gas, rinse beans, discard the soaking water and any debris, and cook in fresh water. Not to worry, the beans, and not the soaking water, retain most of the essential nutrients.

To cook, cover beans with fresh water: about six cups of fresh water for each pound of dry beans. Add seasonings to the cooking water. Salt toughens beans by taking out the moisture, and acid foods, such as tomatoes or vinegar, slow their softening. Wait until the end of the cooking time to add these ingredients.

Cover the pot partially. To keep legumes from foaming as they cook, add a little cooking oil (1/4 teaspoon) to the water. Simmer beans until they're cooked. *See the chart on page* 154, *"Bean Bag," for simmering times.* Now, add cooked beans or peas to your favorite dish. ✦

Ten Great Ways to "Fiber Up"!

Are you ready to eat more fiber—and hit the 20- to 35-gram daily target? These 10 guidelines can put your day's food choices within range.

1. *Eat a variety of food.* With a mix of foods, you consume a mix of fibers—both soluble and insoluble. And you get the benefits of both types. *For more on eating a variety of foods, refer to page 243, "The Food Guide Pyramid: Your Healthful Eating Guide."*

2. *Read "Counting Up Fiber," on page 150 to compare fiber content.* For example, pick high-fiber snacks: popcorn, fresh fruit, raw vegetables, and nuts.

3. *Remember breakfast—a good time for fiber-rich foods.* Besides bran cereal or another fiber-rich breakfast cereal, enjoy oatmeal, whole-bran muffins, or whole-wheat waffles. In fact, check food labels for a cereal with 5 or more grams of fiber per serving. Top with fruit for a little more fiber.

4. *Switch to whole-grains—in bread, cereals, buns, bagels, and pasta,* to name a few. Besides the fiber, making sandwiches on a variety of whole-grain breads adds interest and taste. Breads with whole grain include cornbread from whole, ground cornmeal; cracked wheat bread; oatmeal bread; pumpernickel bread; rye bread; and the perennial favorite, whole-wheat bread. Eat breads made with bran, too, such as bran muffins. *Refer to "Whole Grains: For Goodness Sake" on page 103.*

Fit Fiber In!

Food Group	Suggested Number of Servings Per Day	Serving Size
Breads, cereals, rice, and pasta	6-11 (including at least 3 *whole-grain choices*)	1 slice *whole-grain, fiber-fortified, or enriched bread;* 1/2 cup of cooked white or *brown rice,* enriched or *whole-grain pasta, oatmeal,* or *bulgur;* 1/2 to 1 cup of ready-to-eat cereal, such as *bran flakes*; 1 tortilla
Vegetables	3-5	1/2 cup *cooked* or *chopped*; 1 cup *raw leafy*
Fruits	2-4	3/4 cup of juice; 1/2 cup cooked or canned fruit; 1 piece of *fresh fruit;* 1/2 cup of *berries, melon, or grapes*; 1/4 cup *dried fruit*
Milk, yogurt, and cheese	2-3	1 cup of milk or yogurt; 1 ounce of cheese
Meats, poultry, fish, *dried beans and peas*, eggs, *and nuts*	2-3	3 ounces of meat, poultry, or fish. 1/2 cup *peas or beans;* 1/4 cup *nuts;* 1 egg; or 2 tablespoons peanut butter count as 1 ounce of meat.

Note: Italicized foods are higher in fiber.

5. *Plan to eat legumes two to three times a week.* They're among the best fiber sources around and they add exciting new flavors to dishes.

6. *Eat at least five servings of fruits and vegetables daily.* Plan a cooked vegetable and a salad for dinner (that's two vegetable servings) and enjoy another for lunch. You have just two more to go!

7. *Enjoy fruits and vegetables with the edible skin on.* With the skin, a medium potato has 3.6 grams of fiber. Skinless, it has less—2.3 grams. Also enjoy the flavor and crunch of edible seeds, for example, in all kinds of berries, kiwi, and figs. They, too, supply fiber.

8. *Choose whole fruit more often than juice.* Fiber is found mainly in the peel and pulp; usually both are removed when juice is made. (Sometimes orange juice is processed with the pulp.) So juice has almost no fiber at all. *Compare the difference in "Which Apple for Fiber?" on page 149.*

9. *"Fiberize" your cooking style.* Substitute higher-fiber ingredients in recipes, such as using part whole-wheat flour in baked foods. And fortify mixed dishes with high-fiber ingredients, perhaps bran added to meatloaf. *For more cooking tips, refer to page 344, "Fiber Boosters."*

10. *Check food labels for fiber facts.* Almost all food labels carry a Nutrition Facts panel, which lists the amount of fiber per serving. Look for words such as "high in fiber" or "more fiber" on labels, too. *Refer to page 147, "Label Lingo: Fiber," to see what the descriptions about fiber on food labels mean.* Spot fiber-rich ingredients on the ingredient list. For example, look for "bran," or for "whole-grain" or "whole-wheat flour."

To learn more about food labels and shopping for foods with more fiber, refer to "Get All the Facts!" on page 271.

Legumes: A Nutritious Fiber Source

All over the world, people eat and enjoy beans, peas, and other legumes! Legumes come from plants whose seed pods split on two sides when they're ripe.

Because they're a nutritious, flavorful, and inexpensive protein source and because they're easy to grow and store, legumes have been a staple food for thousands of years. Today we recognize another benefit. Besides their versatility, legumes are among the best fiber sources! No matter what the variety, legumes are loaded with nutrients: protein, complex carbohydrates, and fiber, along with B vitamins and some other vitamins and minerals.

In the Food Guide Pyramid, legumes fit in the Meat, Poultry, Fish, Dry Beans, Eggs, and Nuts Group. Like meat, they're good sources of protein. With regard to serving sizes, one-half cup of cooked legumes (beans or lentils) counts as 1 ounce of meat; 5 to 7 ounces of meat or meat alternate is recommended daily.

Refer to "A Word About Legumes" on page 346 and to "Bean Bag" on page 154 for more on cooking with legumes.

Bean Bag

Beans of all kinds are sold as dry, canned, frozen, and fresh. Each type has a distinctive appearance and flavor, varying cooking times, and somewhat different uses. A variety bag that includes several types of beans is an easy way to taste the flavors of many types of different beans.

On average, 1 pound of dry beans equals about 2 1/4 cups of dry beans, or 5 to 6 cups of cooked beans. The yield for lentils is less; for 2 1/4 cups dry lentils, figure about 3 1/2 to 4 cups cooked. One can (15 1/2 ounces) of drained, canned beans or lentils equals about 1 2/3 cups cooked. As an aside, rinsing canned beans reduces the sodium content.

Beans and Peas	Size and Color	Flavor	Simmering Time (hours) *	Common Uses**
Adzuki or azuki bean	Small, red, shiny	Slightly sweet	½ to 1	Salads, poultry stuffing, casseroles, soups
Black bean	Small, black, shiny, kidney-shaped	Slightly sweet	1½ to 2	Stew, soup, Brazilian *feijoada,* Cuban rice and beans
Black-eyed pea or cowpea	Small, cream-colored, ovals with black spots	Vegetable-like, full-flavored	1 to 1½	Southern dishes with ham or rice, bean cakes, curries, *Hoppin' John*
Cannellini or white kidney bean	Elongated, slender, creamy white	Mild	2	Soups, stews, salads, casseroles, Italian side dishes, *pasta e fagioli*
Chickpea, or garbanzo bean	Golden, hard, pea-shaped	Nutty	2¼ to 4	Casseroles, cooked with couscous, soups, stews, *hummus, caldo gallego*
Fava or broad bean	Broad, large, oval, light brown	Nutty	1½ to 2	Stews, side dishes
Flageolet or green haricot bean	Small to medium, pale green	Nutty	1½ to 2	Mixed bean salads, vegetable side dish
Great northern	Large, white	Mild	1 to 1½	Soups, casseroles, mixed bean dishes
Lentils***	Yellow, green, or orange	Earthy	¾	Soup, *pease pudding, dhal,* curry dishes
Lima bean	Large or small, creamy white or pale green, kidney-shaped	Like chestnuts	1½	Casseroles, soups, salads, *succotash*
Mung bean	Small, olive green	Earthy	1	Soups, casseroles, purées, Asian and Indian dishes, "sprouted" for salads
Navy bean	Small, oval, white	Mild	1 to 1½	*Boston baked beans*
Pigeon pea	Small, round, slightly flat, beige, brown flecks	Mild	¾ to 1	Caribbean peas and rice
Pinto bean	Orange-pink, with rust-colored flecks, oval	Earthy, full-flavor	1 to 1½	*Mexican rice and beans, refried beans,* stew
Red kidney bean	Dark, red-brown, kidney-shaped	Full-flavored, "meaty"	1½ to 2	Stew, mixed bean salad, Cajun bean dishes, *chili con carne*
Soybean	Small, yellow or black	Full-flavored	3½ to 4	Side dish, soups, used to make tofu (bean curd), "sprouted" for salads

** Simmering time for dry beans.*

*** Traditional and ethnic dishes, italicized throughout the chart, commonly use the type of bean indicated. Refer to "Where in the World?" on page 563 for some trivia on ethnic origins of bean dishes.*

**** Lentils don't require soaking, only shorter cooking times.*

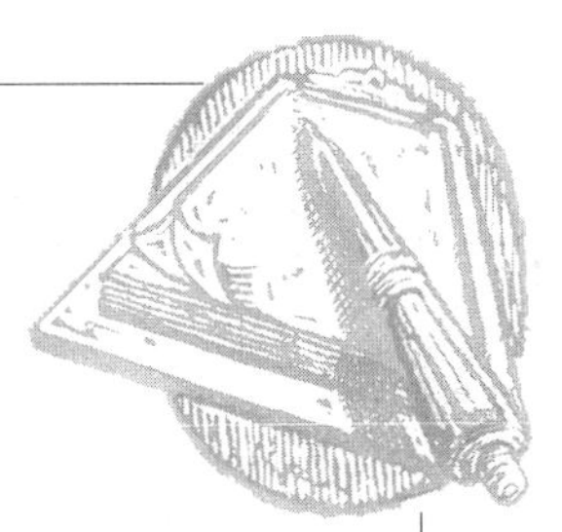

your nutrition check-up

What's Your Fiber Factor?

What's the fiber factor in your food choices? That's up to you—and what you choose to eat. In each pair, which food would add more fiber to your meals or snacks?

❒ 1 medium unpeeled apple	or	❒ 1/2 cup applesauce
❒ 1 slice whole-wheat bread	or	❒ 1 slice white bread toast
❒ 3 1/2-ounce cooked meat patty	or	❒ 1/2 cup baked beans
❒ 1/3 cup bran flakes	or	❒ 1/3 cup corn flakes
❒ 1 carrot stick	or	❒ 1 bread stick
❒ 1/2 cup white rice	or	❒ 1/2 cup brown rice
❒ 1/2 cup strawberries	or	❒ 1/2 cup grapes
❒ 1/2 cup spinach	or	❒ 1/2 cup peas
❒ 1/2 cup peanuts	or	❒ 1 ounce cheese
❒ 2 figs	or	❒ 2 prunes
❒ 2 tablespoons bean dip (hummus)	or	❒ 2 tablespoons sour cream
❒ 3/4 cup orange juice	or	❒ 1 orange
❒ 1 baked potato with skin	or	❒ 1/2 cup mashed potatoes
❒ 1 tablespoon wheat germ	or	❒ 1 tablespoon wheat bran

Now for the answers…

For each pair, these foods contain more fiber: unpeeled apple, whole-wheat bread, baked beans, bran flakes, carrot stick, brown rice, strawberries, peas, peanuts, figs, bean dip (hummus), orange, baked potato with skin, and wheat bran. *To compare the specific amounts of fiber in these pairs of foods, see the chart, "Counting Up Fiber," on page* 150.

Give yourself 5 points for each pair you got right—perfect score, 70 points. The higher the score, the more fiber in your diet—if these foods truly would be your "picks" for the day!

real life nutrition

Fiber "Optics"

"They just don't make a body like they used to," thought Alan, with a shake of his head. "Must be a few old parts in my 'plumbing' that get my digestive system out of kilter. Wonder if these fiber pills would help?" he asked himself, looking at several products on the store shelf, yet unsure whether to buy them.

Now middle-aged, Alan's been a meat-and-potatoes man most of his life. He's not big on vegetables, fruit, or whole-wheat bread. But sometimes he does pack a banana or apple with his sandwich for his brown-bag lunch. Occasionally he enjoys a bowl of baked beans or chili with beans—it sticks to his ribs, he says. But they always make him feel uncomfortable afterwards.

Lately, he's been hearing about fiber. Guys like him don't seem to get enough ... haven't been for almost a lifetime! And that may have an effect on his overall health, not just his digestive system. That's why the fiber pills on the shelf caught his eye. "So, Alan," he addressed himself, "just how do you plan to get more fiber—without the bothersome side effects?"

Suggestions for adding more fiber to Alan's meals and snacks include:

➢ Skip the fiber pills on the store shelf. Make an effort to buy—and eat—more fiber-rich foods instead: whole-grain products, vegetables, fruits, and legumes. Not only are these sources of other important nutrients, but they're also flavorful additions to his diet. Alan could use the Nutrition Facts panel and the descriptive terms on food labels to find foods with more fiber in the supermarket.

➢ Add fiber to his eating style gradually, and eat small portions of high-fiber food—at least until his body gets used to the extra fiber.

➢ Count to five as he chooses foods for the day—five servings of fruits and vegetables.

➢ Eat his potatoes with their skins on—for flavor and fiber.

➢ Choose bean dishes more frequently—perhaps try eating beans in ways new to him: perhaps three-bean salad, beans in soup or stew, and chili con carne as a potato topper.

➢ Make his sandwich with any variety of whole-grain bread, including oatmeal bread, rye bread, or cracked wheat bread.

➢ Make a habit of packing fruit with lunch, especially those with more fiber, such as an apple, peach, or pear (peels on).

➢ Drink enough water and other fluids along with boosting the fiber in his food choices.

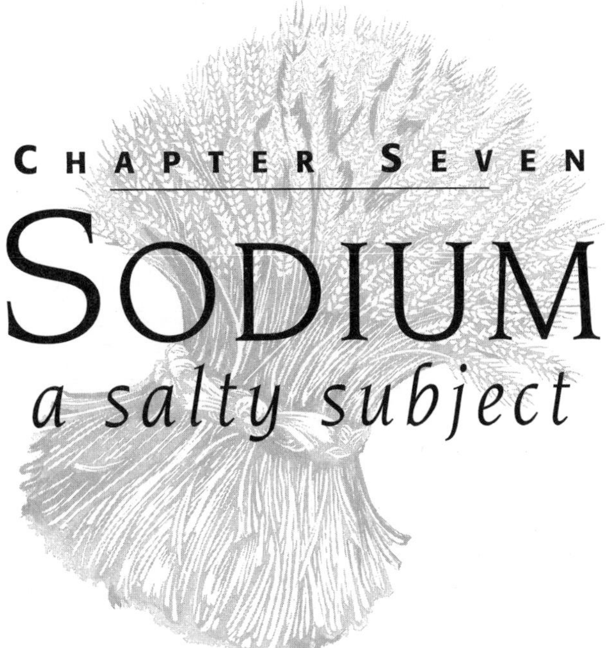

Chapter Seven

Sodium

a salty subject

Throughout recorded history, salt has played an important economic and political role—and has always been part of the world's food supply. Until the last 200 years, salt was used heavily for preserving foods: meat, fish, vegetables, and even fruit. Cheese, too, was salted more than it is today. Especially in Mediterranean regions, cooks used herbs and spices to mask strong, salty flavors. Nations that controlled the salt trade also controlled distribution and preservation of food—especially in times of shortage.

The ancient Greeks valued salt so highly that they used it for currency. Salt was even traded for slaves, hence the phrase, "He's not worth his salt." Originally Roman soldiers were given a handful of salt every day. Later they received money to buy their own salt, which was referred to as "salarium argentum"; translated, that means "salt money." The word "salary" in English is derived from this Latin term.

Because of its value, salt historically has been used symbolically, too. To the ancient Romans, salt given to a newborn symbolized the giving of wisdom. In Europe, a pinch of salt tossed three times over the left shoulder helped fend off evil. Even today, we reflect our doubts with the comment, "Take it with a grain of salt."

Until the late 1700s, the only use for salt was for food. In the 1800s, tastes began to change, and people preferred less salty foods. Also during the 19th century, other methods of food preservation, besides the use of salt, got their start: canning, freezing, and refrigeration. By the 20th century, commercially available canning, freezing, and refrigeration combined with the transportation system enabled people to have fresh foods any time of year. Today most salt is used for industrial purposes, rather than in the food supply.

In ancient times, salt's ability to preserve food helped provide a varied supply of nutrients to the population. Any other link to health or to ongoing health problems, such as high blood pressure, was unknown. As science has advanced, we've learned that the blood pressure of some people is sensitive to salt, or to the sodium it's made from. We now recognize a link between sodium and high blood pressure among some people.

Sodium and Your Health

Salt ... or sodium? Although we often refer to them in the same breath, salt and sodium aren't the same thing. Table salt is actually the common name for "sodium chloride." It's 40 percent sodium and 60 percent chloride.

Sodium: You Need Some!

The link between sodium and high blood pressure is well publicized. Yet few people know the flip side of the sodium story—why sodium is essential to health.

Sodium is a mineral that occurs naturally in food. Some of the most basic work your body does depends on sodium: maintaining proper fluid balance—controlling the movement of fluids in and out of your cells, regulating your blood pressure, transmitting nerve impulses, and helping your muscles relax, including your heart muscle.

Sodium, along with other minerals such as chloride and potassium—are collectively described by another name: electrolytes. They get their name because they transmit electrical current in your body. You can compare them to electrically-charged particles, or ions, in flashlight batteries.

If you lick your upper lip after sweating a lot, you know that body fluids have salt. You can taste it! Sodium, chloride, and potassium dissolve in body fluids. There they become separate ions. With their electrical charge, they transmit nerve impulses throughout your body. And they send messages from your brain to your muscles, causing them to relax or contract.

Have you ever sprinkled salt on a sliced eggplant or potato, then watched the liquid come to its outer surface? Salt drew fluid out of the plant cells. That same reaction happens with electrolytes in your body. They control the balance of fluids in and out of cells. Sodium and chloride mostly work outside your body cells, and potassium works mainly inside. Together they regulate the balance of fluids.

The process of fluid balance has important nutrition implications. Among them, electrolytes help move nutrients into cells and help take wastes away. Both nutrients and wastes are carried in body fluids.

For more about these minerals in health and in a variety of foods, refer to "Major Minerals: Electrolytes" on page 99.

DID YOU KNOW...?

...one teaspoon of salt contains about 2,300 milligrams of sodium?

...most of the sodium that Americans consume comes from processed or prepared food, not from the salt shaker at the kitchen table?

...a preference for salty foods is acquired?

...you can moderate the sodium in your food choices without giving up flavor? ✦

Sodium: Keeping the Balance

Your kidneys regulate the sodium level in your body. In healthy people, sodium levels don't get too concentrated—even when you consume more than you need. And excess amounts don't get stored.

Instead your body rids itself of the extra. Excess sodium passes out through urine and to a much lesser extent, through perspiration. If, for example, you eat foods high in sodium, you may urinate more to get rid of the extra. Then you probably feel thirsty because you lost fluids, too.

Is extra sodium always removed? No. When kidneys don't work properly, perhaps due to kidney disease, extra sodium isn't excreted. This causes swelling, often in the face, legs, and feet. In medical terms, this swelling is called edema.

Can you have a deficiency of sodium? Yes, but this doesn't happen under normal circumstances. However, if a person vomits or has diarrhea for a prolonged period . . . or if he or she has some type of kidney problem, sodium levels might get too low. Unless sweating is profuse and extended over a long time, sodium levels will remain normal.

Link to High Blood Pressure

High blood pressure, or hypertension, is a major risk factor for heart disease, stroke, and kidney disease. And it affects one in five Americans older than 25 years of age. High blood pressure risk is determined by various factors: family history of high blood pressure, overweight, physical inactivity, alcohol intake, and smoking.

Why is there so much attention on sodium? Most people aren't affected by excess dietary sodium. Their bodies just get rid of the extra. However, up to 30 percent of America's population is considered to have blood pressure that is sodium-sensitive. For these individuals, too much sodium in their diet contributes to high blood pressure. Likewise, if your blood pressure is sodium-sensitive, reducing sodium intake may help to lower blood pressure if it's high. There's no way yet to predict who may have blood pressure that is sodium-sensitive, however. Two possible factors are family history and aging.

Some nutrition research indicates that too little of some nutrients—potassium, calcium, and magnesium—might be an important link to high blood pressure. Adequate intake of these minerals may actually have a protective effect against high blood pressure. *For more on the calcium connection, refer to "Calcium: A Closer Look" on page 105. For more about modifying your lifestyle to control high blood pressure, refer to "High Blood Pressure: Under Control?" on page 492.*

How Much Is Enough?

To keep the body running normally, the minimum amount estimated as "safe and adequate" for healthy people is 500 milligrams of sodium a day. That's about the amount in 1/4 teaspoon of salt.

POTASSIUM: ANOTHER REASON FOR "FIVE A DAY"

Although the scientific reasons aren't fully understood, foods high in potassium may help protect against high blood pressure. Vegetables and fruits are among the best sources. Along with the other health benefits, their potassium content is another reason for consuming at least five servings of fruits and vegetables a day.

This partial list includes vegetables and fruits that are good potassium sources:

broccoli	apricot
carrot	banana
mushrooms	cantaloupe
parsnip	dates
potato	orange
spinach	prunes
sweet potato	raisins
Swiss chard	watermelon
winter squash	

Other Sources: Dry beans, lentils, peas, and peanuts are good sources of potassium, too. Milk and yogurt are good potassium sources; they also supply calcium, another mineral which may protect against high blood pressure.

Note: Potassium chloride, as a salt substitute, isn't recommended. Unless used under medical supervision, it can be harmful to health.

For more about potassium, refer to page 99.✦

Few Americans need to be concerned about getting enough. Instead, on average, most adults consume significantly more: 4,000 to 6,000 milligrams of sodium daily, or about 4 to 6 grams (1,000 milligrams = 1 gram). There's no known advantage to consuming this much sodium. To the contrary, people with sodium-sensitive blood pressure are better off with less.

You probably do not need extra salt even after strenuous physical activity. Although you lose sodium and some other minerals (electrolytes) through sweat, the amount is usually quite small.

Meals and snacks eaten after exertion normally replenish these lost minerals. You probably don't need to salt your food, take a salt tablet, or drink a sports drink with electrolytes. *For more about eating and physical performance, refer to chapter* 21, *"Athlete's Guide: Winning Nutrition."*

There's no Recommended Dietary Allowance (RDA) for sodium. *Refer to "Nutrients: How Much?" on page* 4 *for more about the* RDAs. However, 2,400 milligrams of sodium or less per day for healthy adults has been advised—and that's the amount that's used for figuring the % Daily Value for the Nutrition Facts panel of food labels. *You'll read more about Daily Values on page* 271, *"Get All the Facts!"* The American Heart Association currently recommends 3,000 milligrams or less of sodium daily.

Moderation ... Even for Healthy People

Moderation, along with variety and balance: These three qualities mark an overall healthful eating style that's good for your heart and helps control your blood pressure.

As part of the moderation message, the Dietary Guidelines for Americans advise: Choose a diet moderate in salt and sodium. For some people, eating moderate amounts of salt and sodium means cutting back. *For more about the Dietary Guidelines, refer to "A Glimpse at the Dietary Guidelines" on page* 5.

Why is that advice given to healthy people? For one, there's no way to tell if your blood pressure is sodium-sensitive. You may—or may not—develop high blood pressure from consuming too much sodium. Secondly, consuming less sodium or less salt certainly isn't harmful to healthy adults. Even if you don't have high blood pressure now, keeping your sodium intake within a moderate range is part of an overall healthful eating plan.

Note: Women who are pregnant shouldn't restrict the amount of sodium they consume in an effort to minimize water retention and swelling. Pregnancy actually increases the body's need for sodium. A normal intake provides enough for the extra need of pregnancy. *For more about eating during pregnancy, refer to "Nutrition: For You and Baby, Too!" on page* 461.

For some people, even an intake of 2,400 milligrams of sodium daily may be too much. If you have high blood pressure or some other health condition, your doctor might recommend that you reduce the amount of sodium you're consuming. Your doctor can help determine the appropriate amount of sodium for you, and a registered dietitian (RD) can help you fit this advice into your eating plan.

MEDICATIONS: SODIUM ALERT

Are you on a sodium-restricted diet? Then talk to your doctor or pharmacist about medications. Some contain sodium: including some antacids and alkalizers, headache remedies, laxatives, sedatives, and others.

If you're taking medication prescribed for high blood pressure, eating less sodium can offer some benefits. Your medication may work more effectively, and you may even be able to reduce the dosage of medication needed to keep your blood pressure within a healthful range. ✦

Sodium in Your Food Choices

Salt and sodium—to follow an eating style with moderate amounts, take a look at what they do in foods. That way, you'll have a better notion of what foods might contain sodium and salt. In turn, you'll be better able to consume a diet with moderate amounts.

Salt and Sodium: More Than Flavor

Why are salt and other sodium-containing ingredients added in food preparation and processing? Flavor probably comes to mind first. Just a few grains of salt can bring out food's natural flavors—even in sweet foods. However, sodium-containing ingredients play a broader role in the food supply.

Before the days of refrigeration, people relied on salt to preserve many foods. Salt and sodium-containing ingredients preserve food by inhibiting the growth of bacteria, yeast, and molds—and so prevent food spoilage and foodborne illness.

Even today, many foods that are cured use salt or an ingredient made with sodium (such as sodium nitrate) as a preservative. For example, ham, sausage, corned beef, and Canadian bacon are cured meats. Another way to preserve vegetables is to soak them in a brine, or a solution of water and salt. Cucumbers and okra are pickled in brine.

In many foods, salt affects the texture. For example, yeast breads with salt have a finer texture; salt-free yeast breads tend to be coarser.

In some foods, such as cheese, bread dough, and sauerkraut, salt controls the speed of fermentation. Fermentation is a process that changes the chemistry of food, and as a result its appearance and flavor.

In processed meats, including sausage, salt and sodium-containing ingredients also help hold the meat together.

Where Does Sodium Come From?

Many people think their tastebuds offer all the clues they need to the sodium content of food. However, you can't always judge the sodium content of food by its taste! Many foods with sodium don't have a salty flavor.

A shake here and a shake there—the amount of salt we sprinkle on food can add up quickly. The same is true for sodium-containing condiments, such as soy sauce, mustard, and tartar sauce. However, only about 25 percent of the sodium in the food most people eat comes from the salt shaker or sodium-containing ingredients we add to food.

Processed and prepared foods are the main sources of sodium in the average American diet. Because salt and sodium-containing ingredients serve several functions in the food supply, it's not surprising that processed foods contain varying levels of sodium.

Look for sodium-containing ingredients, then check the Nutrition Facts information for the amount of sodium in one serving of the food. If the ingredient on a food label has Na, *salt*, *soda*, or *sodium* in its name, that's a clue for sodium. ("Na" is the scientific symbol for sodium.)

have you ever wondered

...how much rinsing canned legumes reduces the sodium content? If you rinse canned legumes and other vegetables in a strainer under cool running water, you can reduce their sodium content by about 40 percent.

...if sea salt is healthier than table salt? No. Even though sea salt often may be promoted as a healthful alternative to ordinary table salt, the sodium content is comparable, and it offers no known health advantages. As with other salts, sea salt should be used judiciously. ✦

Here are just a few sodium watchwords:

Ingredients With Sodium	How They Work
baking soda (sodium bicarbonate)	leavening agent
baking powder	leavening agent
brine (salt and water)	preservative
disodium phosphate	emulsifier, stabilizer
monosodium glutamate (MSG)	flavor enhancer
NaCl (sodium chloride)	flavor enhancer, preservative
salt (sodium chloride)	flavor enhancer preservative
sodium caseinate	thickener, binder
sodium citrate	acid controller
sodium nitrate	preservative
sodium propionate	preservative, mold inhibitor
sodium sulfite	preservative for dried fruits
soy sauce	flavor enhancer
teriyaki sauce	flavor enhancer

Foods described as "broth," "cured," "corned," "pickled," and "smoked" usually contain sodium, too.

How much salt do you typically add to food? Take the "shaker test" to find out.

Cover a plate or bowl with foil or plastic wrap. Now pretend your dinner is on the plate—or that the bowl is filled with popcorn. Salt your "food" just as you would if the bowl or plate was full of food. Now measure how much salt you added. If you shook as much as 1/4 teaspoon of salt, you added almost 600 milligrams of sodium to your meal or popcorn. ✦

To learn more about reading the ingredient list on food labels, refer to "A Word About Ingredients..." on page 273. To read more about the functions of preservatives and other food additives, refer to page 225, "Additives: Safe at the Plate."

Because sodium occurs naturally, too, even unprocessed foods may contain sodium. But the amounts aren't high enough for concern.

Which food groups have the most sodium? The sodium content of foods varies—even in very similar foods. The difference comes from the way foods are prepared and processed. Foods in every group of the Food Guide Pyramid, including Fats, Oils, and Sweets, contain sodium.

Flavor...With Less Salt and Sodium

Most people eat what they like. According to consumer research, when it comes to choosing one food over another, taste ranks first. But you don't have to give up good taste. You still can have plenty of flavor with less salt and sodium.

"Salty"—An Acquired Taste

Do you like the taste of salty snacks? Does food seem to taste better after a few shakes of the salt shaker? Your preference for a strong, salty taste is acquired...probably starting in childhood. It's the saltiness that people like, not the sodium. In fact, the chloride in salt may have more to do with the flavor than the sodium does.

Except for the sensory experience, the body shifts easily to an eating pattern with less sodium. Interestingly, when people gradually cut back and learn to go with less sodium in their food choices, the desire for salty tastes declines, too. Over time, the less salt they consume, the less they want.

When it comes to taste perception, there's probably no true substitute for the taste of salt. Even salt substitutes, suggested for some people, don't give the same taste sensation. They may taste bitter or sharp.

About Salt Substitutes

Are salt substitutes a good way to moderate sodium in food choices? That depends. Salt substitutes aren't appropriate—and may not be healthful—for everyone.

Many salt substitutes contain potassium in place of sodium. For some people, potassium consumed in excess can be harmful. For example, people with kidney problems may not be able to rid their bodies of excess levels of potassium. If you're under medical care—especially for a kidney problem—check with your doctor before using salt substitutes.

Rather than salt substitutes, try herb-spice blends as a flavorful alternative to salt—or lemon or lime juice. Today's supermarkets carry a variety of salt-free seasoning blends. Remember to read the ingredient list and the Nutrition Facts panel on the label. Some herb-spice blends are neither salt- nor sodium-free. *As an alternative, make your own; see "Kitchen Nutrition: Salt-Free Herb Blends" on page* 164.

For more about the sensations of taste and flavor, refer to "On the Tip of Your Tongue...The Flavor Connection" on page 211.

Taming Your Tastebuds

To enjoy what you eat is a top priority! Fortunately, foods don't need to taste bland to be healthful. And you don't need to give up your favorite high-sodium foods—just eat them in moderation. Here's how:

Moderate your sodium intake gradually if you're accustomed to salty tastes. Because a preference for a salty taste is learned, it takes time to unlearn it, too—and to appreciate new flavor combinations.

Enjoy plenty of fresh fruits and vegetables. Most contain only small amounts of sodium and are rich in potassium. Eat them, too, as low-sodium snacks!

Choose other foods within a food group that don't have as much sodium, such as fresh meats, poultry, fish, dry and fresh legumes, eggs, milk, and yogurt. Plain rice, pasta, and oatmeal don't have much

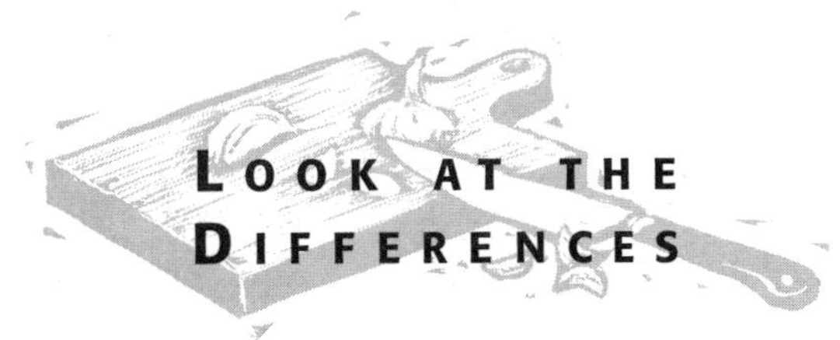

Fresh foods are an ideal choice when you're trying to reduce sodium. However, processed and prepared foods can be part of your healthful eating plan, too. Some processsed foods tend to have more sodium than others: including cured and processed meats; canned foods, such as legumes, vegetables, and fish; cheese; condiments; boxed convenience foods, such as pasta mixes or rice side dishes; and salted snack foods. Read the Nutrition Facts on food labels to find out.

You might find these differences in similar products.

	SODIUM (MG)
2 ounces canned tuna	310
2 ounces low-sodium canned tuna	135
1 medium dill pickle	835
1 medium cucumber, marinated in vinegar	5
3 ounces ham	1,030
3 ounces lean pork loin	75
3 cups regular microwave popcorn	190
3 cups air-popped popcorn	<5
3 cups salt-free microwave popcorn	0
1 cup boxed convenience rice	1,600
1 cup plain brown or white rice, seasoned with herbs	5
1 cup vegetable beef soup	840
1 cup reduced-sodium vegetable beef soup	50
1/2 cup canned green beans	170
1/2 cup frozen green beans	5
1/2 cup fresh green beans	<5
1/2 cup canned no-salt-added green beans	<5
1 cup chicken broth	1,005
1 cup low-sodium chicken broth	70

KITCHEN NUTRITION
salt-free herb blends

Enhance the flavor of food with these salt-free herb and spice combinations. To make 1/2 cup, combine the ingredients in a jar. Cover tightly, and shake. Keep in a cool, dark, dry place. Then rub or sprinkle them on food for flavor.

CHINESE FIVE-SPICE...for chicken, fish, or pork.
Blend 1/4 cup ground ginger, 2 tablespoons ground cinnamon, 1 tablespoon each of ground allspice and anise seeds, and 2 teaspoons ground cloves.

MIXED HERB BLEND...for salads, pasta salads, steamed vegetables, vegetable soup, or fish.
Blend 1/4 cup dried parsley flakes, 2 tablespoons dried tarragon, 1 tablespoon each of dried oregano, dill weed, and celery flakes.

ITALIAN BLEND...for tomato-based soups and pasta dishes, chicken, pizza, focaccia, and herbed bread.
Blend 2 tablespoons each of dried basil and dried marjoram, 1 tablespoon each of garlic powder and dried oregano, and 2 teaspoons each of thyme, crushed dried rosemary, and crushed red pepper.

CURRY BLEND...for rice, lentil, and vegetable dishes, and chicken.
Blend 2 tablespoons each of turmeric and ground coriander, 1 tablespoon ground cumin, 2 teaspoons each of ground cardamom, ground ginger, and black pepper, and 1 teaspoon each of powdered cloves, cinnamon, and ground nutmeg.

MEXICAN CHILI BLEND...for chili with beans, enchiladas, tacos, fajitas, chicken, pork, and beef.
Blend 1/4 cup chili powder, 1 tablespoon each of ground cumin and onion powder, 1 teaspoon each of dried oregano, garlic powder, and ground red pepper, and 1/2 teaspoon cinnamon.

GREEK BLEND...for seafood, poultry, and herbed bread.
Blend 3 tablespoons each of garlic powder and dried lemon peel, 2 tablespoons dried oregano, and 1 teaspoon black pepper.

EASY DIP BLEND...for mixing with cottage cheese, yogurt cheese *(see page 70)*, or low-fat sour cream...also nice on chicken and fish.
Blend 1/4 cup dried dill weed and 1 tablespoon each of dried chives, garlic powder, dried lemon peel, and dried chervil.

sodium either. Their sodium content only goes up if high-sodium ingredients are added during their preparation.

Season with herbs, spices, herbed vinegar, herb rubs, and fruit juices. *"A Pinch of Flavor: How to Cook With Herbs and Spices" on page 349 offers many ways to use herbs and spices. Or prepare the easy blends in "Kitchen Nutrition: Salt-Free Herb Blends," at left, to keep on hand.*

Learn to prepare food with less salt or high-sodium ingredients. For example, skip the urge to add salt to cooking water for pasta, rice, cereals, and vegetables. It's an easy way to cut back on sodium. In addition, salt toughens many vegetables, especially beans, as they're cooked. The salt draws water out of the plant cells. *For tips on preparing food with less salt or sodium, refer to "Salt 'Shakers'" on page 343.*

Go easy on high-sodium foods. Balance these choices with foods with less sodium. Moderating sodium intake over several days is what counts.

Read the Nutrition Facts information on the label to find the sodium content of a packaged food. You'll find the sodium content in milligrams for a single serving. The % Daily Value for sodium is given, too. That amount is based on 2,400 milligrams of sodium for the day. *To learn more about food labels, refer to "Get All the Facts!" on page 271.*

Read the nutrition descriptions on the front of food labels for a quick "read" as you walk the supermarket aisle. From soup, canned fish, vegetables, and vegetable juice...to crackers, popcorn, and snack foods...you'll find a variety of food products described as "unsalted," "no-salt-added," "reduced sodium," "sodium-free," and "low in sodium." *To learn what these words mean, refer to "Label Lingo: Salt and Sodium" on page 165.*

If you need to cut back on sodium, buy foods with less sodium. *Refer to "Your Shopping Guide" on page 279 for general shopping tips.* Try reduced-sodium products, which may offer more flavor than low-sodium products. And they're still lower in sodium than the traditional versions.

Whether you eat in a four-star or quickservice restaurant, be sodium-conscious if you eat out on a

regular basis. *Refer to "Eating Out" on this page for simple suggestions for cutting back.*

Try lightly-salted and unsalted nuts, popcorn, pretzels, and crackers if an urge for the flavor of salt strikes.

Eating Out

Unlike foods you buy at the supermarket, you usually don't know the sodium content of items on a restaurant menu. If you eat out a lot, the sodium contribution of your meals could be significant. Try these simple ways to moderate the sodium and salt in foods you order:

Move the salt shaker to another table. Or taste before you shake. Ask for a lemon wedge...or bring your own herb blend to enhance the foods' flavor if you feel the need.

Recognize menu terms that may indicate a high sodium content: pickled, smoked, au jus, soy sauce, or in broth.

Nibble on raw veggies, rather than salty snacks.

Go easy on condiments for burgers, hot dogs, and sandwiches—such as mustard, catsup, pickles, and tartar sauce. Enjoy lettuce, onion, and tomato. Remember that bacon tends to be high in sodium.

Ask the waiter, waitress, or counter person for help. Request that foods be prepared without added salt. Or ask for sauces and salad dressings on the side since they're often high in sodium. For a salad, use a twist of lemon, a splash of vinegar, or a light drizzle of dressing.

Keep your order simple. Order broiled or grilled meat—without salted seasonings—rather than entrées cooked in sauces. Often special sauces and toppings add extra sodium to food. Order plain meat-type sandwiches with fresh vegetable toppings, too, rather that salad-type fillings.

For more on healthful eating away from home, refer to chapter 15, "Your Food Away From Home."

Salt and Sodium

Do the terms "sodium" or "salt" appear on the front of the food label? If so, here's what the descriptions mean. For the specific sodium content in a serving, check the Nutrition Facts panel.

LABEL TERM	MEANS	EXAMPLES OF FOODS
Sodium free	less than 5 milligrams sodium per serving	crackers
Very low sodium	35 milligrams or less sodium per serving	chips
Low sodium	140 milligrams or less sodium per serving	soup, cereal, crackers
Reduced or less sodium	at least 25% less sodium*	soy sauce, soup, bacon, pretzels, crackers
Light in sodium	50% less sodium*; restricted to foods with more than 40 calories per serving or more than 3 grams fat per serving	crackers
Salt free	less than 5 5 milligrams sodium per serving	herb blends
Low sodium meal	140 milligrams or less sodium per 100 grams	frozen dinner
Unsalted or no added salt	no salt added during processing; does not necessarily mean sodium free	peanuts, butter, canned vegetables, microwave popcorn, crackers, breakfast cereal

**as compared with a standard serving size of the traditional food*

have you ever *wondered*

...if drinking water has much sodium? The amount of sodium in drinking water varies from place to place. Unless you're on a sodium-restricted diet, you don't need to be too concerned about the amount. If you need or wish to know the sodium content, contact your local water department.

A water softener may add significant amounts of sodium to your water—anywhere from 7 to 220 milligrams per quart. Talk to the manufacturer of the water softener to find out how much sodium is being added to your water supply.

...what iodized salt is? Iodized salt is simply table salt with iodine added. The human body needs just small amounts of iodine. By adding it to salt, people get what they need—even when they consume moderate amounts of salt and sodium. Iodine in your diet helps prevent goiter, which is a thyroid gland condition. *For more about iodine, refer to page* 102.

...how the sodium content of monosodium glutamate (MSG) *compares with salt?* MSG actually has only one-third the sodium that a comparable amount of salt has—yet it still has plenty of ability to enhance the flavor of food. *For more about* MSG, *refer to* "MSG—*Sensitive?" on page* 200.

your nutrition check-up

Sodium: A Healthful "Shake"

You know the guideline for healthful eating: Choose a diet moderate in salt and sodium. How have you addressed this "salty issue" personally? Check off the tips below that apply to you. Do you…

- ❐ shake a little salt on your food only after you taste it?
- ❐ enjoy plenty of fresh and frozen fruits and vegetables?
- ❐ keep the salt shaker in the cabinet, not on the table or kitchen counter where it's easier to use?
- ❐ skip the salt in cooking water—for pasta, rice, and vegetables?
- ❐ season food mostly with herbs, spices, or fruit juice?
- ❐ read the Nutrition Facts on food labels to check the amount of sodium in food?
- ❐ consider the sodium content of restaurant or quickservice food if you eat out regularly?
- ❐ enjoy processed meats, such as corned beef, ham, bacon, bologna, salami, hot dogs, and pastrami, in moderation?
- ❐ buy brands of prepared foods and snack foods that have less sodium or salt?
- ❐ go easy on condiments, such as mustard, ketchup, soy sauce, and tartar sauce…or use brands with less sodium?
- ❐ balance your food choices…if you enjoy some foods with more sodium, also eat others with less?

How Many Did You Check?

If you said "yes" to…

9 to 11 items: you're likely consuming moderate amounts of sodium and salt.

6 to 8 items: you're controlling the sodium and salt in your food choices but may be able to "shake the sodium habit" even more.

5 or fewer items: you may use the tips in this chapter to moderate the sodium and salt in your eating plan.

real life nutrition

Easy Does It

Shaking salt on the meal just served to her—even before tasting it—45-year-old Kim commented to her friend, "I know what you're thinking, Jan. The salt, right? As you say, 'Easy does it.'

"But my blood pressure's always been normal—Fred's, too. And I think most restaurant food doesn't taste right without it. At home I don't put much salt on food I cook—honestly. So sodium isn't really an issue for Fred and me—except maybe when we eat out."

As Kim drove home, she got to thinking. I wonder how much sodium we really do consume? We don't have high blood pressure. But my dad did…and so did Fred's mom. Maybe we should think about salt and sodium.

Back in her kitchen, the salt shaker sitting on the stove grabbed her attention. Then she started to read the food labels on foods in her cabinets and refrigerator. Some foods caught her attention. "They don't taste salty. So why would they have so much sodium?" Kim wondered. Not many fresh fruits, vegetables, meats, or poultry in our kitchen—they don't have much sodium either.

Then she did a little figuring and realized that her food choices for the day—if she ate foods from home—added up to almost 250 percent of the Daily Value for sodium…or more than 6,000 milligrams of sodium. "Hmmm. More than I expected. Maybe we should try to control the amount of sodium we consume. It certainly wouldn't hurt."

Suggestions for salt and sodium in Kim and Fred's meals and snacks include:

➢ Eat a diet moderate in salt and sodium. She probably doesn't know if her blood pressure is sodium-sensitive. But a family history of high blood pressure offers a reason to be cautious. Although their blood pressure is normal now, that may change as they get older. Fred also has a family history of high blood pressure.

➢ Taste food before salting it. Maybe it tastes great just as it is!

➢ Move the salt shaker at the restaurant to a different table. Perhaps ask for a lemon wedge to flavor food instead.

➢ Gradually cut back on the salt in their foods. If they like the salty taste, they'll gradually be satisfied with less as they cut back. Remember foods with sodium may not taste salty.

➢ Enjoy the flavors of fresh fruit, vegetables, meat, poultry, and fish. They have less

real life nutrition (continued)

sodium—unless Fred and Kim add sodium-containing ingredients as they prepare food.

➢ Read the Nutrition Facts on food labels at the store—as well as at home. Then buy foods with less sodium and salt—to match their needs.

➢ Keep the salt shaker in the kitchen cabinet, not on the stove, where it will be used as needed—not just as a habit.

➢ Learn to season foods cooked at home with herbs, spices, herbed vinegar, and fruit juice.

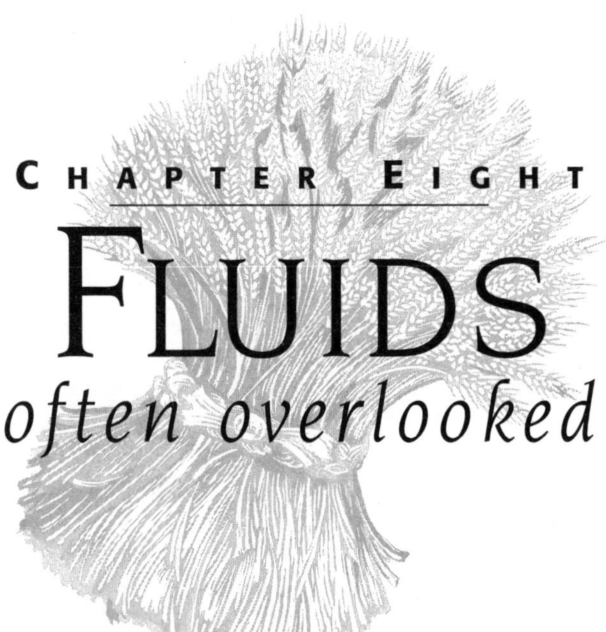

CHAPTER EIGHT

FLUIDS

often overlooked

Water? Unless your throat feels parched and sweat drips from your brow, you probably give little thought to water. Yet this clear, refreshing fluid is one of your body's most essential nutrients.

You've probably heard that water is vital to health—and to life itself. While you may survive for six weeks without food, you cannot live longer than a week or so without water. In fact, losing more than 10 percent of your body weight from dehydration, or water loss, causes extreme weakness and potential heat stroke. And a 20 percent loss is life-threatening. Water truly is the beverage of life!

A Fluid Asset

Water is the most abundant substance in the human body as well as the most common substance on earth. Like the oxygen you breathe, you can't live without it.

On average, an adult's body weight is 55 to 75 percent water—or about 10 to 12 gallons of water. The specific percentage varies from person to person, relating to body composition, age, and gender, among other factors.

Compared with body fat, lean tissue holds much more water. So the leaner you are, the higher proportion of water in your body. Males, with more muscle, carry a higher percentage of water in their bodies than females do. And younger individuals usually have more than older adults. Water accounts for about 75 percent of a newborn's weight, while the amount dwindles in the elderly to about 50 percent water weight.

Body tissue of all types contains water—some more than others. The fact that blood contains water is certainly no surprise. Your blood is about 83 percent water. Lean muscle tissue is about 73 percent water; body fat, about 25 percent water. Even though bones seem hard, they too contain water, about 22 percent by weight.

Water: An Essential Nutrient

What does water do in your body? Far more than satisfy your thirst! Thirst is actually more like a warning light that's flashing on the dashboard of your car. This physical sensation signals to you that your body needs more fluid to perform its many functions. To satisfy thirst, you drink fluids.

Water itself is a simple substance, containing just one part oxygen and two parts hydrogen. It supplies no calories. Yet every body cell, tissue, and organ, and almost every life-sustaining body process needs water to function. In fact, water is the nutrient your body needs in the greatest amount.

Whether inside or surrounding your cells, nearly every function of the human body takes place in a watery medium. Water regulates your body temperature, keeping it constant at about 98.6° F. Many body processes produce heat, including any physical activity. Through perspiration, heat escapes from your body as water evaporates on your skin.

Water transports nutrients and oxygen to your body cells and carries waste products away. It moistens body tissues, such as tissue in your mouth, eyes, and nose. Water is the main part of every body fluid, including blood, gastric (stomach) juice, saliva, amniotic fluid (for a developing fetus), and urine. By softening stools, water helps prevent constipation. And it helps cushion your joints and protects your body organs and tissues.

To keep your body functioning normally and to avoid dehydration, your body needs an ongoing water supply. During a strenuous workout, losing water weight is common, especially on a hot, humid day. Losing just one or two pounds of your body's water weight can trigger a feeling of thirst. With a little more fluid loss, the body loses strength and endurance; even mild dehydration can interfere with physical performance. With even more water loss and prolonged exposure to high temperatures, a person may suffer from heat exhaustion or risk heat stroke. A 20 percent drop in the body's water weight is defined as bare survival level.

Of all the nutrients in your diet, water is most abundant. Drinking water and other beverages are the main sources. But you "eat" quite a bit of water in solid foods, too—perhaps more than you think. Juicy fruits and vegetables, such as celery, lettuce, tomato, and watermelon, contain more than 90 percent water. Even dry foods, such as bread, supply some water. *The chart, "Food: A Water Source," on page 173 shows the percentage of water in some common foods.*

Your body has a fourth water source. About 15 percent of your body's total water supply forms in your body cells when energy is produced from carbohydrate, protein, and fat. Along with energy, water is an end product of your body's metabolism.

Dehydration: Look for Body Signals!

The effects of dehydration, or loss of body water, are progressive: thirst, then fatigue, next weakness, followed by delirium, and finally death. Although you need to pay attention to the signals of water loss, all these steps won't happen over the course of a single day.

PERCENT LOSS OF BODY WATER BY TOTAL BODY WEIGHT	PROGRESSIVE EFFECTS OF DEHYDRATION (PARTIAL LIST)
0 to 1%	thirst
2 to 5%	dry mouth, flushed skin, fatigue, headache, impaired physical performance
6%	increased body temperature, breathing rate, and pulse rate
8%	dizziness, increased weakness, labored breathing with exercise
10%	muscle spasms, swollen tongue, delirium, wakefulness
11%	poor blood circulation, failing kidney function

Fluids: How Much Is Enough?

The average adult loses about 2 1/2 quarts (about 10 cups) of water daily through perspiration (even when sitting), urination, bowel movements, and even breathing. During hot, humid weather or strenuous physical activity, fluid loss may be much higher. Unlike some other nutrients, the human body doesn't store an extra supply of water for those times when you need more. To avoid dehydration and to keep your body working normally, you must replace the fluids you lose through normal body functions.

How much water do you need each day? Your need for water actually depends on the amount of energy your body uses: for adults, 1 to 1 1/2 milliliters of water per calorie of energy expended. That's 1 to 1 1/2 liters for every 1,000 calories, or about 8 cups of water daily in a 2,000-calorie-a-day diet. (A liter is about as much as 1 quart.)

Most people need 8 to 12 cups of water daily—from drinking water, other beverages, and water in solid foods. Body weight is one factor affecting fluid need. Additional factors that may cause a need for more water include climate, level of physical activity, diet, and other physical differences. For example:

- When you're exposed to extreme temperatures—very hot or cold—your body uses more water to maintain its normal temperature.
- With strenuous work or exercise, your body loses water through perspiration, or evaporation from your skin. To figure how much water you need daily, start with 8 cups of water. Drink 1 to 3 more cups per hour as you increase the intensity and duration of your activity. *For signs that you need to drink more, refer to "Dehydration Alert" on page 535.*
- When you're exposed to heated or recirculated air for a long time, water evaporates from your skin. For example, the dry, recirculated air on planes promotes dehydration.
- Pregnancy and breast-feeding increase the amount of fluid a woman's body needs.
- Being sick makes a difference, too. Fever, diarrhea, and vomiting all cause increased water loss. Follow the advice of your health-care provider, and drink plenty of water and other fluids to prevent dehydration.
- If you eat a high-fiber diet, your body needs extra water to process the additional roughage and prevent constipation.

In healthy people, water intake and water loss balance out. If you consume more than you need, your kidneys simply eliminate the excess. You probably won't overdo on water. When you don't consume enough, your body may trigger a sensation of thirst. Thirst signals the need for fluids, but it isn't a foolproof mechanism, especially for elderly people, children, and during illness, hot weather, or strenu-

FOOD: A WATER SOURCE

It's not easy to figure just how much water you consume each day. While drinks—plain water and other beverages—supply a good portion of your water needs, solid food also provides a surprising amount.

	Percent Water by Weight
Lettuce (1/2 cup)	95
Watermelon (1/2 cup)	92
Broccoli (1/2 cup)	91
Grapefruit (1/2)	91
Milk (1 cup)	89
Orange juice (3/4 cup)	88
Carrot (1/2 cup)	87
Apple (1 medium)	84
Cottage cheese, low-fat (1/2 cup)	79
Yogurt (1 cup)	75
Potato, baked with skin (1 medium)	71
Tuna, canned, drained (3 ounces)	70
Rice, cooked (1/2 cup)	69
Kidney beans, boiled (1/2 cup)	67
Pasta, cooked (1/2 cup)	66
Chicken, roasted, no skin (3 ounces)	65
Beef, lean, roasted (3 ounces)	64
Cheddar cheese (1 ounce)	37
Whole wheat bread (1 slice)	38
Bagel (1/2)	29
Honey (1 tablespoon)	17
Butter or margarine (1 tablespoon)	16
Raisins (1/3 cup)	15
Pecans, dried (2 tablespoons)	5
Vegetable oil (1 tablespoon)	0

Calculated from Bowes & Church's Food Values of Portions Commonly Used, 16th Edition, *Jean A. T. Pennington, Philadelphia: J.B. Lippincott Company,* 1994.

ous physical activity. Waiting until you feel thirsty to drink may be too long. By then, 2 or more cups of body fluids may be gone—even when you're healthy. *For more on fluids for older adults, refer to* "Thirst-Quenchers: Drink Fluids" *on page* 512.

To see if you're drinking enough fluid, check your urine. A small volume of dark-colored urine indicates that you aren't consuming enough fluid. Besides feeling thirsty, this is your signal to drink more. Almost clear urine means you're drinking enough.

As another option, weigh yourself after strenuous physical activity. For every pound of weight you lose, replace it with 2 cups of fluid.

Caution: If you always seem thirsty or urinate too much, talk to your health-care provider. This may be a sign of diabetes. On the other hand, water retention, for reasons other than premenstrual syndrome, may suggest a kidney or a liver problem.

Drinking for Health

To keep your body well hydrated, consume enough water—8 to 12 cups—throughout the day. Because milk, juice, and some other beverages are mainly water, they can count toward your daily water intake. So does water from solid foods, although you can't really measure it.

Caffeinated beverages—coffee, tea, and some soft drinks—and alcoholic beverages aren't your body's best sources of water. Caffeine and alcohol act as diuretics, causing the body to lose water through increased urination. Decaffeinated beverages, however, don't have a diuretic effect.

If you need to increase your water intake...

- Take water breaks during the day instead of coffee breaks. If you're a subconscious "sipper," keep a cup of water on your desk.
- "Water down" your meals and snacks. Complement food with water, milk, or juice. Occasionally, start your meals with soup.
- When you walk by a water fountain, take a drink!
- Refresh yourself at snack time with juice, milk, or sparkling water.
- Alternate sparkling water for alcoholic drinks at parties and other social gatherings.
- Before, during, and after any physical activity, drink water, especially in hot weather. Consume 4 to 8 ounces of water every 15 to 20 minutes while you exercise. Don't wait until you feel thirsty! *For tips on fluids during exercise, refer to* "Thirst for Success" *on page* 532.
- Travel with a supply of bottled water. Even for day outings, pack along a bottle of water.
- Airline travel promotes dehydration. *For tips on drinking fluids in flight, refer to page* 384, "Dining at 35,000 Feet!"

Water: In Balance

As an average adult, you probably lose about 2 1/2 quarts (10 cups) of water daily. To maintain your body's fluid balance, you need to replace it each day. If you lose a little more, such as through perspiration, you'll need to drink more fluids to balance out.

YOUR BODY LOSES WATER DAILY THROUGH...	
Urine	4 to 6 cups
Perspiration	2 to 4 cups
Breath (expired air)	1 1/2 cups
Feces	2/3 cup
YOU REPLACE WATER IN YOUR BODY DAILY THROUGH...	
Water and other fluids	4 to 6 1/2 cups *
Solid food	3 to 4 1/3 cups
Water from metabolism	3/4 to 1 1/3 cups

**To be on the safe side, drink more fluids. Your body will excrete any extra.*

Hydration for the Seasons

From the bone-chilling days of winter, to the hot, sultry days of summer...throughout these dramatic temperature shifts, your body needs water to maintain its normal temperature.

In hot, humid weather your body perspires, increasing water loss. Cool, refreshing drinks may help cool your overheated body. An interesting side note: Your body has a harder time cooling down in hot, humid weather than in hot, dry weather. That's because perspiration doesn't evaporate from your skin to cool you down. Instead your skin feels sticky and hot.

Dehydration may seem like just a summer issue. But keeping your body well hydrated during winter is just as important. When the weather turns chilly, most people head indoors. There heated air evaporates the moisture on your skin. Although you may not feel thirsty, you still need to replace water loss. Even in the cold outdoors, you may perspire...perhaps from shoveling snow, skating or skiing, or being bundled up with many layers of clothing.

Refer to "Kitchen Nutrition: Super Sippers" on page 189 for easy-to-make, nonalcoholic drinks for all seasons.

What's to Drink?

Just plain water: it's the most available fluid around and often your best choice! Juice and milk make good beverage options, too, since they supply other nutrients besides water. For example, juice offers vitamins A or C, or both, and milk is calcium-rich. Other beverage choices—coffee, tea, soft drinks, and alcoholic drinks—don't offer the nutritional benefits of milk or juice.

Why drink water? For starters, water has no calories. If you're trying to avoid extra calories, that's a definite advantage. In other beverages, such as regular soft drinks and alcoholic beverages, calories really can add up. Water is also low in sodium and has no fat or cholesterol. Watching your caffeine intake? Unlike many coffees, teas, and some soft drinks, you won't find caffeine in water either.

Tap Water Versus Bottled Water

Tap water or bottled water: which should you drink? Both are regulated stringently by the government: tap water by the Environmental Protection Agency and bottled water by the Food and Drug Adminis-

Fluoride, a mineral, helps harden developing tooth enamel and so protects teeth from decay. Fluoride may also offer some protection from osteoporosis, or brittle bone disease. Many water systems contain a natural supply of fluoride. But in areas where fluoride levels are low, the water system may be fluoridated to levels recommended by the American Dental Association. The optimum fluoride level is 1 ppm—1 part fluoride per million parts water.

Fluoride is not only ingested through the water supply. In areas where water isn't fluoridated, or when bottled water without fluoride is consumed instead of tap water, dentists may prescribe fluoride supplements for children. If you're not sure about fluoride in your municipal water system, check with your local water department or public health department. If you have your own well, have it tested for fluoride.

"Topical" fluoride—applied directly to teeth with toothpaste and mouth rinse, or in the dental office by gel treatments—also helps strengthen tooth enamel. According to oral health experts, topical fluoride is more effective when fluoride is also ingested. Check the label on toothpaste and mouth rinse to see if they contain fluoride.

Be aware that consuming too much fluoride can cause the teeth to be mottled, or marked with brown spots, even though they're healthy in other ways. That most likely happens with excessive doses from a dietary supplement.

For more about healthy teeth, refer to "Your Smile: Sugar and Oral Health" on page 126 and "Caring for Baby Teeth" on page 407. ✦

tration (FDA). Especially when it comes from large municipal water systems, tap water is just as safe for drinking as bottled water.

Right from the Tap

Just turn on your faucet! Most drinking water in the United States comes right from the tap. Most of us take this for granted, but in many parts of the world, drinkable tap water is a luxury. To make our tap water safe, it's treated with chlorine to destroy bacteria that cause disease.

Chlorine, used to disinfect water, offers protection from many public health problems. In fact, chlorination is the only tried-and-true method for effectively treating water and keeping it safe from causing outbreaks of cholera, hepatitis, and other diseases. There's been some question about a by-product, called trihalomethane (THM), created when chlorine reacts with organic matter in water. If the organic material is present, the amount of THM created is very low, not enough to create a cancer risk. From a public health standpoint, protecting people from disease outbreaks far outweighs the insignificant effect of THM.

Surprisingly, water itself may not be the only nutrient in drinking water. Unless distilled, or demineralized, drinking water may contain minerals in varying amounts, such as fluoride, calcium, sodium, iron, and magnesium. The water source and how it's processed determine the actual composition of drinking water. Water from underground wells, springs, and aquifers may contain high mineral concentrations. As water from rain and snow seeps through rocks, gravel, and sand, it picks up minerals along the way. That's how some underground water becomes naturally fluoridated. *"The Fluoride Connection" on page 175 describes the link between fluoridated water and oral health.*

Water may be described as "hard" or "soft" depending on its mineral content. Hard water contains more calcium and magnesium, while soft water has more sodium. There's essentially no difference in flavor between hard and soft water. However, small amounts of iron give a metallic taste to water—but not enough to make it a significant source of dietary iron.

Because minerals in hard water interfere with the action of soap, some people prefer soft water. Hard water leaves "scum" in the tub and mineral buildup in appliances that use water; it won't lather up; and over time, hard water may leave white laundry gray.

When water is softened, sodium is added as other minerals are removed. But for most people, the amount of sodium isn't significant enough for concern. The amount added depends on the hardness of the water. For well water that must be fully softened, the amount of sodium per cup of water is about 39 milligrams. Usually it doesn't need to be fully softened. The average softened municipal water may contain about 22 milligrams of sodium per cup. Again, your own water supply may not be softened.

If you have your own water softener, you might soften only the hot water. That way, if you're sodium sensitive, you won't have extra sodium in cold drinking water.

WATER: IN CASE OF EMERGENCIES

Disaster can hit anyone, anywhere! To ensure a safe water supply for your family, disaster experts advise these precautions.

- Store a week's supply of bottled water for everyone in your family. Figure about 1 gallon of water per person per day.
- Store containers of water in a cool, dry place away from direct sunlight.
- Label bottles of water with the date. Replace them every six months to ensure freshness. ✦

What About Bottled Water?

In recent years, consumption of bottled water has soared. The industry began in the late '50s, and by the mid '90s Americans were consuming 2.5 billion gallons annually. Today about 700 brand labels of bottled water are sold in the United States. The most common types include mineral water, purified water, sparkling water, spring water, and well water.

Since both tap and bottled water are safe, why drink bottled water? According to consumer research, some people prefer the taste. Bottled water usually doesn't contain chlorine, which can give water a slight flavor. Others drink bottled water as a "chic" and healthful alternative to alcoholic or caffeinated beverages or soft drinks. As a substitute for some other beverages, consumers may drink bottled water for what it doesn't contain: calories, caffeine, or alcohol. And it's handy to carry to the office, a picnic, or a health club.

Bottled water is regulated by the Food and Drug Administration (FDA) to assure its quality, safety, and accurate labeling. Terms on labels for bottled water, such as "spring water" or "mineral water," are defined legally. If bottled water comes from a municipal water supply, the label must state that fact, unless it's been processed to be a purified water.

On bottled waters marketed for infants, you might see the term "sterile." That means the water meets FDA's standards for commercial sterilization and is technically free of bacteria. If not, the label must state that the product isn't sterile and that it should be used to prepare infant formula only as directed by a doctor or according to infant formula preparation instructions. For safety, follow that guideline.

Some people perceive that bottled water is healthier than tap water. In large municipal water systems, either bottled or tap water is safe and healthful. However, in places where the lead content of water is a concern, bottled water is a good alternative, particularly for pregnant women or families with children. Bottled water doesn't contain lead.

Some cooks prefer bottled water for cooking. It doesn't contain chlorine, which may alter slightly the flavor of soups and stews. In homes with lead pipes or lead solder, bottled water may be a good alternative in soups, stews, and other long-cooking dishes. During extended cooking times, any lead in tap water may become more concentrated.

Bottled Waters

Today's supermarket shelves offer more and more bottled waters. But what do the terms on the label mean?

Artesian water is a certain type of well water. The well must tap an aquifer that has water standing much higher than the rock, gravel, or sand. An aquifer is an underground layer of rock or sand with water.

Mineral water contains minerals at a standard level, no less than 250 parts per million (ppm) of total dissolved solids, or minerals. These minerals must be naturally present, not added. If the level is less than 500 ppm, it will be labeled "low mineral content"; if higher than 1,500 ppm, "high mineral content."

Purified water or demineralized water has been processed to remove minerals. Distilled water, which is one type of purified water, has been evaporated to steam, then recondensed to remove minerals. Minerals also may be removed by deionizing, reverse osmosis, or other processes. The name describes the process, for example, deionized drinking water.

Sparkling water is water with a "fizz." Either carbon dioxide is added, or water is naturally carbonated. If carbon dioxide is added, it can't be any more than its naturally carbonated level would be. It can only be labeled as natural sparkling water if there's no added carbonation. Seltzer and club soda are considered soft drinks, not sparkling water.

Spring water comes from a natural spring in the ground. It may or may not be carbonated. ✦

Safe Enough to Drink

For any nation, water safety is a top public health priority. In the United States, infectious disease spread by untreated water is almost nonexistent, except during natural disasters, such as floods, earthquakes, or accidental contamination of wells or municipal water. Any of these incidents can devastate a community's drinking water supply. So you're wise to know what to do in a water emergency.

When the safety of your water supply is in doubt, don't drink it! Instead take steps to make it safe from bacteria that spread infectious disease.

- Report your concern to your water company or local public health department. They may test the water or refer you to a qualified private laboratory.
- If you rely on a private well or spring, have it tested periodically. People who draw their water from a private water source are responsible for the quality of their own water supply.
- Purify contaminated drinking water by boiling tap water for at least one minute, then pouring boiled water into a sterile container.
- Use iodine or chlorine tablets to disinfect your water supply, strictly following directions on the package. These products are generally available in camping stores. Campers, hikers, and others who rely on water supplied by lakes and streams in wilderness areas might use water filtration and purification devices, as well as iodine or chlorine tablets.

In many other countries, contaminated water is an ongoing problem, spreading diarrhea and even life-threatening diseases, such as cholera and hepatitis. For globe-trotters, water is a common source of travelers' diarrhea. *Refer to page 389, "What's Safe to Drink?" for guidance on safe drinking water for travelers.* For added safety in third world areas, you might travel with a supply of iodine or chlorine tablets.

Get the Lead Out!

With the spread of infectious disease from drinking water under control, concern in the United States has shifted to certain compounds in water. Lead is a major issue.

Excessive lead in drinking and cooking water poses a serious health risk. Over time, too much lead consumed in food and beverages can build up in the body, potentially damaging the brain, nervous system, kidney, and red blood cells. Infants, children, and unborn babies are more vulnerable to lead poisoning than others.

If the water supply is monitored, where does lead come from? Often, lead can come from plumbing inside the home or from service lines. Until the mid-1980s, many houses and multi-family dwellings were constructed with water pipes and solder made of lead. Additionally, lead service lines in older communities may connect a house with the municipal water system.

If you are concerned, check your pipes and water supply. Be aware that even copper pipes might use lead solder in the joints. To have your water tested, contact your local public health department or water utility company. They may have a free testing kit, or may refer you to a government-certified laboratory that tests water safety.

If the lead problem in your water supply is severe, you might install a water filtering device or use bottled water for drinking and cooking. If less severe, follow these guidelines to help ensure the safety of your water:

have you ever wondered

...if seltzer and club soda are the same as bottled water? No. Neither is required to meet the quality standards of bottled water. Some seltzer and club soda products contain sugar and sodium, whereas bottled water, by definition, cannot.

...what flavored waters really are? Flavored waters may have just a hint of flavor, derived from a natural fruit essence. Check the label carefully though because some clear beverages also contain sugar, other sweeteners, and artificial flavors. If they do, they're soft drinks, not bottled water. Remember, being clear doesn't mean that a beverage is simply water! ✦

➢ Avoid drinking water that has been sitting in your lead plumbing for more than 6 hours.

➢ For drinking and cooking water, let the cold water faucet run for 60 seconds or more to clear water that has been sitting in the pipes and faucet. This will help flush out water with the heaviest concentration of lead.

➢ For cooking and baby formula preparation, use cold water from your tap or bottle water. Hot water dissolves lead from the pipes more quickly than cold water does.

➢ Install a water softening system only on your hot-water faucet. Hard water doesn't pick up as much lead as soft water does.

➢ As another option, use bottled water for cooking and drinking.

As a precaution: The American Academy of Pediatrics and Centers for Disease Control advise initial lead screening for all infants and toddlers (9 to 12 months). After that a follow-up schedule is generally recommended as needed. When children test above 10 micrograms per deciliter, sources of lead in the child's environment should be identified and corrected.

Juicy Story: Fruit Juice or Juice Drink?

When you're thirsty, a refreshing, fruity beverage hits the spot. Which will you reach for: fruit juice or juice drink? Either one is a good fluid replacer. Depending on the fruits they're made from, fruit juices and juice drinks supply varying amounts of vitamins A and C. Juice drinks may also be called "juice beverage" or "juice cocktail" on a product label.

You might think that 100 percent juice is nutritionally superior. Yet the percentage of juice has little bearing on the nutrient value. For example, some 100 percent fruit juices contain less than 100 percent of the Daily Value for vitamin C, while some juice drinks supply at least 100 percent in a single serving. *To learn how to read the labels on fruit juice and juice drink, refer to "Today's Food Labels" on page 270, and to learn more about vitamins A and C, refer to "Antioxidant Vitamins: A Closer Look" on page 90.*

Be aware that all juice products contain water and sugar. Fruit juice contains naturally-occurring fructose, or fruit sugar, whereas juice drinks also have added sugars, such as high-fructose corn syrup. Scientific evidence shows that your body can't distinguish naturally-occurring and added sugars. So regardless of whether a juice or juice drink is naturally sweet or sweetened, its sugars are used by your body in the same way. *Refer to chapter 5, "Sweet Talk: Sugar and Other Sweeteners."* Depending on the amount of sugars added, there may be a difference in the amount of calories per serving between fruit drinks and fruit juices.

On the label, 100 percent juices, such as orange juice, won't list sugar and water as separate ingredients. They're already present in juice. Other juices or juice drinks, such as cranberry, are made from fruits with a naturally tart taste that requires a sweetener. These juices are blended with water and sweeteners to make them palatable. A noteworthy difference between fruit juices and fruit drinks is that fruit juices often contain other important nutrients, such as folate in orange juice.

How Much Vitamin C?

Percent Daily Value of vitamin C per 3/4 cup serving

100%
Orange Juice

100%
Fortified Juice (such as cranberry)

2%
Apple Juice (unfortified)

50%

Grape Juice (unfortified)

Juicing Fruits and Vegetables

Some juice-machine promoters may lead you to believe that juicing makes fruits and vegetables healthier. Of course, fruit and vegetable juices are healthful, offering most of the vitamins and minerals found in the whole fruit or vegetable. However, juices typically have less fiber; it gets left behind in the pulp. And in spite of the "cure-all" claims, simply changing the form of food by juicing can't deliver added benefits. Enjoy juice—but don't expect miracles!

Milk, Cocoa, and Flavored Milks: Calcium-Rich Choices

Like all beverages, milk supplies that essential nutrient, water: about 89 percent by weight. And as one of the best calcium sources in the American diet, milk offers a lot more.

Milk supplies many essential nutrients, including calcium, phosphorus, riboflavin, vitamins A and D, and protein, along with water. Among the various types of milk—whole, 2 percent, 1 percent, and skim—the fat content varies, along with the calorie content.

Milk: A Good Calcium Source

MILK	CALORIES	CALCIUM (MG)	FAT (G)	CHOLESTEROL (MG)
8 OUNCES...				
buttermilk	100	285	2	10
unflavored milk				
skim	85	300	<1	5
1%	100	300	3	10
2%	120	295	5	20
whole	150	290	8	35
chocolate milk				
1%	160	285	2	–
2%	180	285	5	15
whole	210	280	8	30
4 OUNCES...				
eggnog	170	165	10	75
evaporated milk				
skim	100	370	<1	5
whole	170	330	10	35
sweetened condensed milk	490	430	13	50

Source: National Dairy Council *(Figures are rounded.)*

However, the contribution of other nutrients, including water, is about the same.

For people who otherwise might choose a less nutritious beverage, flavored milk can be a healthful option. For chocolate milk, the only difference is an additional 60 calories per 8-ounce serving from the added sweetener, and chocolate or cocoa. Whether it's flavored or unflavored, milk supplies the same amounts of vitamins and minerals, including calcium, that people of all ages need.

For a description of different types of milk, refer to "Which Milk for You?" on page 288. To compare the calories, calcium, fat, and cholesterol in various forms of milk, refer to "Milk: A Good Calcium Source" on this page. Refer to chapter 4, "Vitamins and Minerals: Enough, But Not Too Much" to learn more how minerals and vitamins contribute to your health.

The fact that many kids like chocolate milk has prompted questions among some parents:

- Does the sugar and caffeine in chocolate milk cause hyperactivity? No scientific evidence suggests a link between sugar and hyperactivity, mood swings, or academic performance. The very small amount of caffeine in the chocolate or cocoa won't make a difference either. Some soft drinks provide much more caffeine. *Refer to the chart, "Caffeine: What Sources, How Much?" on page 182.*

- What about the extra calories in chocolate milk? Eight ounces of chocolate milk has about 60 more calories than the same amount of unflavored milk, but the same amounts of calcium, phosphorus, protein, riboflavin, and vitamin D. Active children and teens can burn extra calories in regular activity or play.

On cold winter days, hot cocoa can be another good beverage choice. Made with milk, rather than water, hot cocoa supplies calcium along with the other nutrients found in milk. For hot cocoa or cocoa made from a mix, use milk for the greatest nutritional benefit.

Drinks: With or Without Caffeine?

Caffeine, a mild stimulant, has been part of the human diet for centuries. As far back as 5,000 years ago, records suggest that the Chinese were brewing tea. About 2,500 years ago, highly-valued coffee beans were used in Africa as currency. And in the Americas, the Aztecs enjoyed chocolate drinks. Today, caffeine-containing foods and beverages are a growing part of our food pattern. For many, coffee in the morning goes with their "wake up" routine.

A naturally-occurring substance in plants, caffeine is found in leaves, seeds, and fruits, among them coffee and cocoa beans, tea leaves, and kola nuts. We consume these products as coffee, chocolate, tea, and cola drinks. Caffeine is also used as an ingredient in more than 1,000 over-the-counter drugs, as well as prescription drugs, and as a subtle flavoring.

Coffee remains the chief source of caffeine in the United States. That includes drinks made with coffee, such as latte, mocha, and cappuccino. The amount of caffeine depends on the type of coffee, the amount, and whether it's caffeinated.

Soft drinks and teas can be significant sources of caffeine for children. Among soft drinks, cola isn't the only beverage with caffeine; some citrus-flavored beverages contain even more.

Caffeine acts as a mild stimulant to the central nervous system. Some people drink coffee just for that reason: to keep alert and prevent fatigue. While drinking beverages with caffeine may be a habit, they're not addictive.

Caffeine: A Health Connection?

Over the years many studies have explored the connection between caffeine and health. No scientific evidence has been found to link moderate caffeine intake to any health risks, including cancer, cardiovascular disease, fibrocystic breast disease (benign fibrous lumps), or birth defects. And no studies show that caffeine causes attention deficit disorder in children.

Caffeinated beverages aren't the best source of fluid since caffeine can have a diuretic effect, increasing water loss through urination. The diuretic effect, however, depends on the amount of caffeine. The more caffeine, the greater its potential for increasing water loss.

While caffeine can increase slightly the amount of calcium lost through urine and feces, it's the amount of calcium in about 1 teaspoon of milk that's lost for each cup of regular coffee. To help counter this effect, drink your coffee as latte or cappuccino, both made with plenty of milk. And you don't need to use whole milk to get a foam on cappuccino. A lower-fat milk (skim or 1 percent) also will do the trick.

Although many people think a cup of coffee can help "sober up" someone who drinks too much alcohol, caffeine won't counteract the effects of drinking alcoholic beverages. And neither will a cold shower or a long walk. Only time can make someone sober. A healthy liver detoxifies about one drink per hour.

In varying degrees, however, excessive caffeine intake may cause "coffee jitters," anxiety, and insomnia. Caffeine also may speed the heart rate temporarily. These physical effects of caffeine don't last long since caffeine doesn't accumulate in the body. Within three to four hours, most is excreted.

The definition of "excessive" caffeine intake is an individual matter. Caffeine sensitivity depends on many factors, including the amount and frequency of caffeine intake, body weight, physical condition,

have you ever *wondered*

...*if sports drinks are good fluid replacers?* Sports drinks are meant to replace fluids, supply calories for energy, and replace sodium and potassium lost through perspiration. Most athletes don't need a sports drink unless they've exercised vigorously for at least one hour. Even then, the body mainly needs fluids. The optimal drink for most sports activities is water! If you're more likely to drink a sports drink rather than water during physical activity, then by all means do. *For more information on fluids during athletic performance, refer to "Thirst for Success!" on page 532.* ✦

and overall anxiety level. Tolerance to caffeine develops over time. A regular coffee drinker may not notice the effects as quickly as someone who drinks just an occasional cup. For most healthy adults, moderate amounts of caffeine—200 to 300 milligrams a day, or about two cups of coffee—pose no physical problems.

Should You Cut Back?

As part of a healthful eating style, most people can enjoy caffeine-containing beverages and foods in moderation. But for those with trouble sleeping or who quickly get a case of "coffee jitters," cutting back on caffeine may be a wise decision. In addition:

➢ If you're pregnant or nursing...it's wise to go easy on caffeine. Sensitivity to caffeine may increase during pregnancy, and caffeine can pass to the baby through the placenta and through breast milk.

➢ If you have a medical problem...you should ask your physician to guide you on caffeine consumption, particularly if you suffer from high blood pressure, gastritis, or ulcers. People with stomach problems may be wise to steer clear of both caffeinated beverages and their decaffeinated counterparts. Substances in both stimulate the flow of stomach acids, potentially irritating the stomach lining.

➢ If you're older...your sensitivity to caffeine may increase with age.

Caffeine: What Sources, How Much?

The amount of caffeine in foods or beverages depends on several factors: the type of product, its preparation method, and the portion size.

	Caffeine (mg) Average	Range
Coffee* (5-ounce serving)		
Brewed, drip method	115	60-180
Brewed, percolator	80	40-170
Instant	65	30-120
Decaffeinated, brewed	3	2-5
Decaffeinated, instant	2	1-5
Espresso coffee (single, 2-ounce serving)	100	40-170
Tea (5-ounce serving)		
Brewed, major U.S. brands	40	20-90
Brewed, imported brands	60	25-110
Instant	30	25-50
Iced (12-ounce glass)	70	67-76
Decaffeinated	1	–
Some soft drinks (12 ounces)	35	30-60
Cocoa beverage (5 ounces)	5	2-20
Chocolate milk beverage (8 ounces)	5	2-7
Milk chocolate (1 ounce)	5	1-15
Dark chocolate, semi-sweet (1 ounce)	20	5-35
Baker's chocolate (1 ounce)	25	–
Chocolate-flavored syrup (1 ounce)	4	–

**A coarse grind delivers about the same amount of caffeine as a fine grind. Because caffeine is highly water soluble, it comes out in the water "first and fast."*

Source: Food and Drug Administration, National Soft Drink Association, and National Coffee Association of USA

➢ At any age...you should pay attention to the effects that caffeine may have on you, especially if coffee, tea, or soft drinks take the place of more healthful foods or beverages.

If you choose to decaffeinate your eating patterns, these are options you might consider:

Cut back gradually—if you've been ingesting a lot of caffeine—to get your body accustomed to doing with less. For some people, abruptly cutting out caffeine can result temporarily in headaches or drowsiness for a few days. A gradual cutback helps avoid this problem.

Try a mixture of half regular and half decaffeinated coffee.

Drink instant coffee or decaffeinated coffee. A cup of instant coffee usually contains less caffeine than a cup of brewed coffee. And decaffeinated coffee has almost no caffeine at all.

Brew tea for a shorter time. A one-minute brew may contain just half the caffeine that a three-minute brew contains.

Drink decaffeinated tea or caffeine-free herbal tea.

Keep a cup of water handy to sip. If you drink coffee, tea, or soft drinks mindlessly, you may be drinking more than you need.

Read soft drink labels carefully. Approximately 75 percent of soft drinks consumed in the United States contain caffeine. If you choose to drink soft drinks, look for decaffeinated drinks or those without caffeine. Color doesn't indicate the presence of caffeine; both clear and caramel-colored soft drinks may have caffeine. You may find caffeine on the ingredient list.

Read medication labels carefully. One dose of an over-the-counter pain relief capsule can contain as much caffeine as one or two cups of coffee.

For those with insomnia, avoid coffee or other caffeine sources in the evening.

Herbal Teas: Health Benefits?

Have a sip of apple-cinnamon tea, mint tea, or ginger tea. Interest in herbal teas has been rising for those seeking an alternative to caffeinated beverages—and for those hoping for other health benefits.

To clear up a misconception: Many branded herbal teas you find in the supermarket are tea leaves with herbs. The ingredient list will include "tea." And some herbal teas on the market aren't tea at all. Instead, they're infusions made with herbs, flowers, spices, or various parts of many other plants. The more correct term for them is "tisane," which means tea-like substance.

When it comes to health benefits, herbal teas haven't been studied, so not much is known. Most major branded herbal teas are considered safe to drink. Still you're wise to consume only common varieties, sold by major manufacturers.

The basis of some medicines is herbs. So it's not surprising that some herbal teas interfere with over-the-counter or prescription medications. Talk to your doctor or pharmacist before drinking them when you're on medication.

Because of their potential harmful effects, be careful about using herbs to make "teas"; comfrey, lobelia, woodruff, tonka beans, melilot, sassafras root, and many others may be harmful in large amounts. For example, comfrey may cause liver damage. Woodruff, an anticoagulant, may cause bleeding. Lobelia may cause breathing problems. Even chamomile may cause an allergic reaction.

For more on herbal teas and remedies, refer to "Herbals—Help or Harm?" *on page* 587.

CAFFEINE: HOW GROUNDED ARE YOU?

True or False

1. Decaffeinated coffee will not trigger excess acid in the stomach.

2. The caffeine in coffee cannot help sober up a person who has been drinking.

3. Noncolas are all caffeine-free.

4. Hundreds of nonprescription drugs contain caffeine.

Answers

1. *False.* Decaffeinated coffee can cause the stomach to secrete acid just the same as regular coffee.

2. *True.* Caffeine does not counteract the effects of alcohol.

3. *False.* Some citrus-flavored beverages contain the highest caffeine levels of any soft drink.

4. *True.* Caffeine is an ingredient in more than 1,000 over-the-counter drugs, as well as prescription drugs. If caffeine intake is a concern, read product labels or check with your pharmacist. ✦

Soft Drinks: OK?

Flavored, carbonated drinks have been around for about 200 years. And their popularity continues to grow—overtaking more nutritious beverages among some age groups.

The term "soft drink" originally was coined to distinguish these beverages from "hard" liquor. Yet 100 years ago, consumers asked for "pop," named for the sound made by popping open the bottle cap. Today, "soft drink"—or "soda" in some parts of the United States—refers to a beverage made with carbonated water and, usually, flavoring ingredients.

What's in a soft drink? Whether they're regular or diet varieties, soft drinks contain water: about 90 percent for regular soft drinks and about 99 percent for diet soft drinks. Carbon dioxide, added just before sealing the bottle or can, gives the fizz. Regular soft drinks are sweetened with sugar, perhaps high-fructose corn syrup and/or sugar; diet drinks with saccharin or aspartame. *Refer to chapter 5 for more information on sugar and alternative sweeteners.* The additional flavor comes from artificial and natural flavors. Acids, such as citric acid and phosphoric acid, give a tart taste and act as preservatives. Coloring may be added; however, there's a growing interest in clear drinks. Some caffeine may be added to enhance the flavor, while other ingredients may add consistency.

In moderation, soft drinks can fit within an overall healthful diet. The nutritional challenge is that too often, soft drinks take the place of more nutritious beverages, such as milk and juice. As soft drink consumption goes up, this is a growing concern. Except for water and for carbohydrate in the form of sugars, soft drinks don't supply significant amounts of nutrients. A 12-ounce can of cola, for example, supplies about 150 calories (from almost 10 teaspoons of sugar), but little else. A diet soft drink is a source of water and has almost no calories.

As your best guideline, enjoy soft drinks in moderation—as long as you consume the nutrients you need from other sources and don't overdo on calories in your overall diet.

have you ever *wondered*

...why you feel so thirsty after eating salty food? Salt is made of two minerals: sodium and chloride. When you eat a lot of salty foods, your body uses water to flush extra sodium away. With water loss, you feel thirsty, and you likely drink more. This explains why bars and cocktail lounges often serve salty snacks with drinks.

...if a few cold beers on a hot summer day are just as good as water to replace fluids? Not really. Alcohol is a diuretic, which increases urine output and so promotes dehydration—not the best fluid replacement when you're sweating already! ✦

Alcoholic Beverages: In Moderation

No one's sure who first invented beer, wine, or ale. But historians do know that societies have enjoyed these beverages throughout recorded history.

Today, moderate amounts still add pleasure to eating. For some, a single drink may be relaxing—perhaps in the company of another. For older adults and people with some chronic illnesses, a drink before a meal may be recommended to enhance appetite. And evidence suggests that moderate drinking may lower the risk for heart disease among some people.

The key to any potential benefits, however, is moderation. That's defined as no more than one drink a day for women and no more than two drinks daily for men. One drink is considered to be 12 ounces of regular beer, or 5 ounces of wine, or 1.5 ounces of 80-proof distilled spirits.

While an alcohol-containing drink or two during the day may offer no ill effects to most adults, they don't count toward a day's fluid intake. Consuming higher levels relates to an increased risk for high blood pressure and stroke. For heavy drinkers, excessive drinking can lead to many health concerns, including damage to the brain and heart, increased risk for some cancers, permanent liver damage, and an inflamed pancreas. Over many years, heavy drinking may lead to death.

Unlike nutrients, most alcohol isn't broken down through digestion. Its "pathway" to body cells moves much faster, including directly through the stomach lining and wall of the small intestine. With no food in the stomach to slow it down, absorption into the bloodstream is even faster (within about 20 minutes). From the bloodstream, it goes to every cell of the body, to some degree depressing cell activity.

Although some people drink to be the "life of the party," alcohol actually is a depressant, not a stimulant. The initial "lift" that may come with drinking is short-lived. By dulling various brain centers, alcohol may reduce concentration, coordination, and response time; cause drowsiness and interfere with normal sleep patterns; and result in slurred speech and blurred vision. Because alcohol has a diuretic effect, alcohol promotes water loss, too. That's why many people may feel thirsty after drinking a lot—perhaps the morning after.

The alcohol concentration in blood is determined by the amount of alcohol consumed over a period of time as well as body composition, body size, metabolism, and medications. A healthy liver detoxifies much of the alcohol consumed—at a rate of about 1/2 ounce per hour. The higher the blood alcohol concentration level, the longer it takes. For two regular-size drinks, consumed during a 60-minute "happy hour," the body needs two to three hours to break it down.

A single alcoholic drink affects women more than men, due in part to body size and composition. Alcohol is carried in the body's fluids, not in body fat. Because women have a smaller volume of water in their bodies than men do, the same amount of alcohol is more concentrated in the bloodstream and so potentially has a greater effect. An enzyme that helps metabolize alcohol in the body is also less active in women. As a result, women are at greater risk for problems related to alcoholism. Heavy drinking also puts women at greater risk of osteoporosis, or brittle bone disease. *Refer to* "Osteoporosis: *Reduce the Risks" on page* 496.

The advice for those who drink alcoholic beverages is: Enjoy them in moderation, with food. And don't drink if it puts you or others at risk!

No Nutrition Benefits!

Alcohol is actually a fermentation product of carbohydrates: both sugars and starches. When it's part of beverages or food, it supplies energy, or calories. Alcohol provides 7 calories for every gram, compared with 4 calories per gram of carbohydrate and protein, and 9 calories per gram of fat. A 1-ounce jigger or "shot" of vodka, for example, may be 40 to 50 percent alcohol, or up to 1/2-ounce alcohol. That equals about 14 grams and contributes about 100 calories. The additional calories come from carbohydrate.

Remember, the alcohol content of a single drink depends on the type of alcohol and the serving size. "Special" alcoholic drinks advertised on restaurant table tents usually contain more alcohol because they're bigger. The calorie content is also determined by the amount of alcohol and, for

RED WINE: HEART-HEALTHY?

Does red wine protect against heart disease? There's no conclusive answer.

Recent research suggests that a moderate amount of alcohol—red wine, as well as white wine, beer, and hard liquor—may help lower the risk for heart disease. Possibly a small amount may help increase HDL-blood cholesterol, or so-called "good" cholesterol, and it may prevent "bad" cholesterol from forming. Also speculated, alcohol may boost the body's natural clot-dissolving enzyme. However, factors other than alcohol also may play a role.

Scientists don't know enough to offer definitive advice. So, if you don't drink, protecting your heart isn't a reason to start. If you do, a drink a day may offer a benefit. But remember, other lifestyle habits—such as healthful eating, regular exercise, and not smoking—offer the most protection against heart disease! ✦

mixed drinks, the other ingredients in the drink. *Refer to the chart "Alcohol and Calories: How Much?" on page 184 for alcohol and calories in standard-size servings.*

For some people, a "beer belly" is aptly named. Calories from alcoholic beverages can add up, contributing to excess body weight. For example, a six-pack of beer, consumed on a hot summer day, supplies 900 calories. To burn off those calories, a person would need to jog without a break for about two hours. A 5-ounce glass of dry wine before dinner supplies 100 calories, or 700 calories if consumed every day of the week. Within five weeks that adds up to one pound of body fat. (A pound of body fat equals 3,500 calories.) The mixers added to drinks make the calories add up even more, yet often add few nutrients: for example, soft drink in a rum-and-cola drink; heavy cream in a Grasshopper or Brandy Alexander; and sugar in a Daiquiri or Mint Julep.

Alcoholic Beverages

You'll find this warning statement on the label of beverages containing alcohol. On wine and beer labels, you may also find information on sulfite content. *Refer to "For the Sulfite-Sensitive..." on page 199.* ✦

GOVERNMENT WARNING: (1) ACCORDING TO THE SURGEON GENERAL, WOMEN SHOULD NOT DRINK ALCOHOLIC BEVERAGES DURING PREGNANCY BECAUSE OF THE RISK OF BIRTH DEFECTS. (2) CONSUMPTION OF ALCOHOLIC BEVERAGES IMPAIRS YOUR ABILITY TO DRIVE A CAR OR OPERATE MACHINERY, AND MAY CAUSE HEALTH PROBLEMS.

CONTAINS SULFITES found in most wines to protect flavor and color.

Although it supplies calories, or energy, alcohol isn't a nutrient. To the contrary, because alcohol may interfere with nutrient absorption, heavy drinkers may not benefit from all the vitamins and minerals they consume. Unless juice or milk beverages are used as mixers, alcoholic beverages themselves supply few, if any, nutrients.

There's another nutrition issue. Poor nutrition is linked to drinking alcoholic beverages when they take the place of nutritious foods and beverages: for example, when a glass of wine with dinner takes the place of calcium-rich milk. By limiting beer, wine, and other alcoholic beverages, there's room in the diet for more nutritious foods and drinks. For the casual or moderate drinker, this may not be much of a problem; malnutrition is a significant concern for heavy drinkers.

Drinking: For Some Not Advised

The Dietary Guidelines for Americans suggest: if you drink alcoholic beverages, drink only in moderation. For adults who choose to drink, no more than one to two drinks a day are advised. Children and teenagers should avoid alcoholic beverages.

Besides the risks mentioned earlier, there are many reasons for being a nondrinker...

...if your project or work requires skill or attention. Alcohol affects productivity, which can affect your output on the job and your personal safety. Even with moderate drinking—a glass or two of wine or beer—alcohol stays with you for several hours.

...if you plan to drive or handle potentially dangerous equipment. Even low levels of blood alcohol can make you more accident prone. If you plan to drink, designate another driver from the start who won't be drinking!

...if you're pregnant or trying to get pregnant. In the United States, drinking during pregnancy is the leading cause of birth defects, or fetal alcohol syndrome. While there's not enough proof that an occasional drink is harmful, even moderate drinking may relate to low infant birthweight or a miscarriage. No safe level has been established. Too often, women drink before they even know they're pregnant, potentially compromising their baby for life. *Refer to "Pregnancy and Alcoholic Beverages Don't Mix" on page* 467 *for more on fetal alcohol syndrome.* Heavy drinking may not be wise for dad either. According to research, too much alcohol may decrease sperm count and potency and so affect fertility.

...if you're on medication, even over-the-counter kinds. Alcohol may interact with medicine, either making it less effective or more potent. The medication itself may raise blood alcohol levels or increase its adverse affects on the brain. The result, a single drink will impair judgment, coordination, and skill faster. Check warnings printed on over-the-counter medications. And talk with your doctor, pharmacist, or health care provider about your own prescribed medications. *Refer to "Food and Medicine" on page* 526.

...if you can't moderate your drinking. As part of a life-long commitment, recovering alcoholics should abstain from any alcoholic drink. Because of the genetic link to alcoholism, people with alcoholism in their family are wise to moderate their intake of alcoholic beverages, too.

...if you're a teenager or child. By drinking alcoholic beverages, teenagers and children set themselves up for the same health-related risks that adults do. Because they're still developing, the effects may be even more significant. For inexperienced teenage drivers, alcohol and driving is a very risky combination. Besides, under-age drinking is illegal.

Taking Control!
If you drink alcoholic beverages, go easy...

Don't drink on an empty stomach. Eating a little food helps slow the absorption of alcohol.

Decide ahead to limit drinks, preferably no more than one per day if you're a female or two per day if you're a male. If you choose to drink more, pace yourself. The more alcohol consumed, the longer it takes to break down. On average, the body can detoxify only one standard-size drink (about 1/2 ounce of alcohol) per hour. The rest continues to circulate until it's finally broken down.

To slow your drinking pace, put your drink down. Socialize instead.

If you have one alcoholic drink, make the next one nonalcoholic. When you do this, you consume less alcohol and give your body a chance to process the alcohol you've consumed already.

have you ever wondered

...if a little "nip" of brandy will help fight a cold? To the contrary, if you have a cold or a chronic health problem that lowers your immunity, you're wise to abstain. Alcohol can affect the body's ability to fight infectious bacteria. And it may interfere with medication.

...if an alcoholic drink will warm you up in cold weather? No. Alcohol tends to increase the body's heat loss, making people more susceptible to cold. So if you're ice fishing, cross-country skiing, or watching outside winter sports, don't expect an alcoholic drink to keep you warm.

...what the term "80 Proof" means on a bottle of liquor? The term "Proof" is an indication of the amount of alcohol. The proof is twice the alcohol content. If a label on a bottle of liquor states "80 Proof," this means that the liquor contains 40 percent alcohol. The proof will vary depending on the type of liquor.

...if the alcohol used in cooking burns off? Some alcohol does burn off or evaporate during cooking—but not all. The cooking time and the amount of alcoholic beverage in the dish determine how much alcohol is left. For example, a roast that's braised in wine for several hours has about 1 gram of alcohol in one serving. If liqueur, wine, or another alcoholic beverage is added to foods that aren't cooked or heated, the alcohol content doesn't change. ✦

Measure liquor for mixed drinks with a jigger. Use a 1-ounce jigger, not the 1 1/2-ounce size. You'll likely use less than pouring from the bottle right into the glass.

Make an alcoholic drink last longer; you'll less likely order another. Learn to sip, not gulp; perhaps use a straw for mixed drinks. Dilute drinks with water, ice, club soda, or juice to increase the volume. As a tip, frozen drinks often take longer to sip.

If you feel thirsty, drink bottled water or a soft drink, instead of another alcoholic beverage. Alcohol actually has a diuretic, or dehydrating effect.

Prefer a wine cooler? Instead of commercial drinks, mix your own using less wine.

Lighten up! Order near beer or light wine instead. Both have less alcohol.

Skip the last round before the bar closes! And, as a host, don't feel a need to refresh your guests' drinks.

Order a "virgin" cocktail...nonalcoholic mixers without the liquor. Mix in juice, carbonated water, or a soft drink instead. Remember the garnish! *Refer to "Kitchen Nutrition: Super Sippers" on page 189 for more ideas.*

Alcohol and Calories: How Much?

Although their calorie content differs, these standard-size drinks each supply about the same amount of alcohol—about 1/2 to 2/3 ounce. (Note: alcoholic drinks are not 100 percent alcohol; that's why the volume differs.)

ALCOHOLIC DRINK	CALORIES
Beer, regular, 12 ounces	150
Beer, light, 12 ounces	100
Wine, dry, 5 ounces	100
Wine cooler, 12 ounces	180
Liquor, 1 1/2 ounces*	95–110
Cordial or liqueur, 1 1/2 ounces*	160

* *An added mixer, such as a soft drink, adds more calories.*

Derived from: If You Drink Alcoholic Beverages, Do So In Moderation, *Home and Garden Bulletin Number* 253-8, *Human Nutrition Information Service*/U.S. *Department of Agriculture, July,* 1993.

Beer and Wine: What's in a Name?

Today, these products appear on supermarket shelves. But just what do the descriptions mean, and how much alcohol do they contain?

Light Beer: beer with less carbohydrate and generally about one-third fewer calories than regular beer. The alcohol content is about the same as regular beer.

Beer Cooler: beverage made of beer, flavored with citrus or orange juice, or carbonated water.

Near Beer: malt beverage that has an alcohol content below 0.5 percent by volume. It can be labeled "nonalcoholic" when there is less than 0.5 percent alcohol and "alcohol free" if there is no measurable alcohol content.

Dessert Wine (or fortified wine): wine that has brandy or distilled spirits added to it. Dessert wine has a higher alcohol content than table wine.

Light Wine: wine that contains about one-third less alcohol than table wine. The calories are less because the alcohol content is lower.

Wine Spritzer: beverage consisting of wine and club soda.

Wine Cooler: carbonated beverage containing wine, fruit juice, and added sugars. A typical 12-ounce serving contains as much alcohol and more calories than a 5-fluid-ounce glass of table wine.

Source: If You Drink Alcoholic Beverages, Do So In Moderation, Home and Garden Bulletin Number 253-8, *Human Nutrition Information Service/*U.S. *Department of Agriculture, July,* 1993.

KITCHEN NUTRITION
super sippers

Hot-Weather Thirst Quenchers

➢ For a subtle citrus flavor in ice water, add slices of lemon, lime, or orange. Or add fruited ice cubes: freeze fruit juice in your ice cube trays.

➢ Combine one 6-ounce can of grapefruit juice concentrate with two 12-ounce bottles of chilled club soda. Serve with a sprig of fresh mint. Serves four.

➢ Make a fruity slush. In a blender, purée berries, pineapple chunks, and frozen limeade concentrate. Perhaps add a little fresh mint. Once puréed, it makes a delicious, refreshing beverage.

➢ Create your own shakes. In a blender, purée melon chunks or peach slices with buttermilk, crushed ice, and a touch of ginger or cinnamon until smooth.

Cold-Weather Belly Warmers

➢ Simmer cranberry juice with cinnamon, cloves, allspice, and orange peel for about 20 minutes. Strain. Stir in skim milk, dry milk powder, and vanilla extract. Heat through.

➢ Add anise seeds, ground cinnamon, and ground cloves to ground coffee. Prepare hot coffee using the spiced ground coffee. Lighten with warm milk.

➢ Scoop praline or chocolate-swirl frozen yogurt into a mug. Pour hot cocoa or coffee over the top. Stir with a cinnamon stick. ✦

your nutrition check-up

"Wet" Your Appetite?

Now that you've read about the value of water to your health, just how much fluid do you drink during a typical day?

If yesterday was typical for you, write down what you drank and about how much. Include beverages consumed with meals and snacks. Remember to include water you drank from a water fountain, tap, or dispenser on the refrigerator.

	Water	Other Beverages	How much?
MORNING			
AFTERNOON			
EVENING			

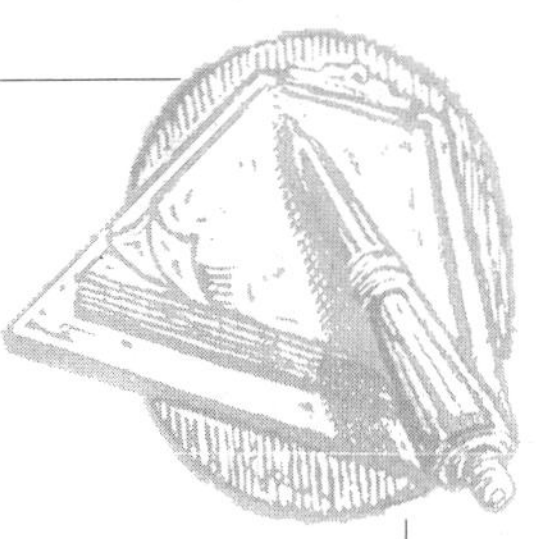

your nutrition check-up (continued)

About how many cups of fluids did you drink? _____

For your good health, drink at least 8 cups of fluid daily—more if you've been exercising or if it's a hot day. The rest of the water you consume comes from the food you eat. If you came up short, jot down ways you might drink a little more!

Remember, caffeinated drinks and alcoholic beverages may not provide as complete a fluid-replacement benefit as noncaffeinated or nonalcoholic beverages because of their diuretic effect.

real life nutrition

Eight Glasses a Day?

When it comes to beverages, Phil works in an office building that doesn't offer him many options. There's no cafeteria, just a pot of caffeinated coffee, microwave oven in the stock room, and a vending machine with soft drinks. He keeps his brown bag lunch in the refrigerator, and plunks two quarters into the vending machine for a cola to go with it. There's a drinking fountain down the hall, but he forgets it's there.

As Phil figures it, he still gets enough water during the workday. He drinks an 8-ounce orange juice as well as coffee with breakfast, sips a mug of coffee at his desk, downs his lunch with a cola, relaxes with a 12-ounce beer when he gets home, drinks a 12-ounce glass of milk with dinner, and drinks a glass of water as he gets ready for bed. That all counts as eight glasses of water each a day. Or does it?

Every other day, Phil also works out after work, building up a real sweat. Should he drink more?

Advice for drinking fluids during the workday

Phil drinks eight glasses of fluids during the day. But his caffeinated beverages—regular coffee and cola—and beer don't offer a complete fluid replacement. So his beverage intake counts as less than what he thinks. These few changes would make a difference. He might:

➢ Bring juice, bottled water, or even a carton of milk to keep in the refrigerator at work. He can enjoy them with lunch or as a break.

➢ Switch to decaffeinated coffee to drink at work. He might bring instant "decaf" from home, and heat water in the microwave oven at work.

➢ Stop at the drinking fountain when he takes a restroom break or goes to and from the building.

➢ Fill his coffee mug with cold water from the drinking fountain to sip at his desk.

➢ Drink soft drinks and beer as extras—if he can handle the calories and if he has consumed enough other fluids.

➢ Make a point of drinking water when he gets home and perhaps sometime in the early evening.

➢ Since Phil is working out, he needs to drink extra fluids to replace what he loses. He might bring a water bottle to drink from as he works out. Or take breaks to the water fountain. After his workout he should replace what he loses: 2 cups of water for every pound of body weight lost.

CHAPTER NINE

SENSITIVE ABOUT FOOD

Sensitive to certain foods? Maybe and maybe not. A queasy stomach, itchy skin, or case of the "trots" might seem like a food sensitivity. But it may or may not be what you think. So avoid the urge to give foods a bum rap without exploring the cause!

Food sensitivities can't be overlooked as a health issue. However, the causes are more complex than you may think.

> ➢ Some people experience food intolerances. For metabolic reasons, their bodies can't digest part of certain foods or a food component. Food intolerances have other causes, too.
>
> ➢ Among certain people, food allergies create unpleasant and sometimes serious symptoms. A food allergy rallies the body's disease-fighting system to action. In other words, the immune system starts to work even though the person isn't sick. That's why symptoms appear.
>
> ➢ Adverse reactions also occur for other reasons: infectious organisms, such as bacteria, parasites, or viruses, which cause foodborne illness; or contaminants, such as chemicals in water where seafood is harvested.
>
> ➢ Feelings of discomfort after eating can also be psychological because food is wrapped up with so many emotions. Even though there's no physical reason, just thinking about a certain food that may be associated with an unpleasant experience can make some people feel sick!

Food Intolerances: Copycat Symptoms

If your body reacts to food or a food component, you may have a food intolerance—not an allergy. Unlike food allergies, food intolerances usually don't involve the immune system, at least not in the same way. However, because they prompt many of the same symptoms—nausea, diarrhea, and abdominal cramps—food intolerances are often mislabeled as "allergies."

With a food intolerance, physical reactions to a food often result from faulty metabolism. The body can't adequately digest a certain component of a particular food—perhaps because a digestive enzyme is deficient. Substances that are part of foods' natural chemistry—such as theobromine in coffee or tea, or serotinin in bananas or tomatoes—may cause reactions, too.

Depending on the type of food intolerance, most people can eat small servings of the problem food without unpleasant side effects. (People with gluten intolerance and those with sulfite-sensitivity are exceptions.) In contrast, people with food allergies usually need to eliminate the problem food from their diet altogether.

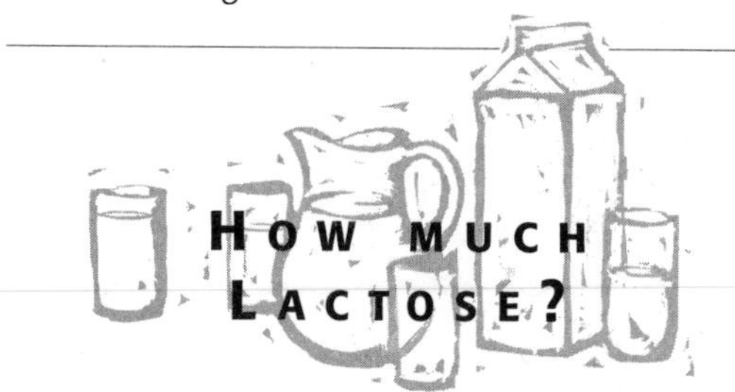

How Much Lactose?

Product	Serving Size	Approximate Lactose (gm)
Milk: whole, low-fat, skim, sweet acidophilus milk, or buttermilk	1 cup	10-12
Goat milk	1 cup	9
Lactose-reduced milk	1 cup	2-4
Nonfat dry milk	1/3 cup	12
Half-and-half	1/2 cup	5
Whipping cream	1/2 cup	3
Sour cream	1/2 cup	4
Sweetened condensed milk	1 cup	30
Evaporated milk	1 cup	24
Butter, margarine	1 teaspoon	trace
Cottage cheese	1/2 cup	2-3
Yogurt, low-fat	1 cup	5
Cheese: American, Swiss, blue, cheddar, Parmesan, or cream cheese	1 ounce	1-2
Ice cream, regular and low-fat	1/2 cup	6-9
Sherbet, orange	1/2 cup	2

Lactose-free foods include:

- Broth-based soups
- Plain meat, fish, and poultry
- Fruits and vegetables, plain
- Tofu and tofu products
- Breads, cereal, crackers, and desserts, made without milk, dry milk, or whey

Lactose Intolerance: A Matter of Degree

Do you like milk but think that milk doesn't like you? Then you may be lactose intolerant—and not allergic to milk. The good news is: A serving of milk may be "friendlier" than you think!

Lactose is a natural sugar in milk and milk products. During digestion, an intestinal enzyme called lactase breaks down lactose into smaller, more easily-digested sugars. *Refer to page 123, "Sugar: What Is It?" for more about sugars in food.*

People with lactose intolerance produce too little lactase to adequately digest the amount of lactose in foods and beverages containing milk. Left undigested, lactose is fermented by "healthy" bacteria in the small intestine. This fermentation produces uncomfortable symptoms, for example, nausea, cramping, bloating, abdominal pain, gas, and diarrhea.

For people with lactose intolerance, symptoms may begin anytime from 15 minutes up to several hours after consuming foods or drinks containing lactose. The severity of symptoms varies from person to person—and how much and when lactose is consumed in relation to other foods.

A milk allergy is quite different. It's an allergic reaction to the protein components, such as casein, in milk. People who have a milk allergy usually must avoid all milk products. People with lactose intolerance can eat dairy products in varying amounts. That's because lactose intolerance is a matter of degree. *Refer to "Lactose: Tips for Tolerance" on page 196.*

If you suspect lactose intolerance, avoid self-diagnosis. Instead, see your doctor for a medical diagnosis. The symptoms might be caused by another condition.

Who's Likely to Be Lactose Intolerant?

Anyone can be lactose intolerant. From birth, most infants produce the lactase enzyme. With age, however, the body may produce less lactase. Because this is an inherited condition, that doesn't happen to everybody.

In the United States, Asians and Native Americans (about 80 percent of them) tend to be the most lactose-intolerant group. An estimated 75 percent of African-Americans, 50 percent of Hispanic Americans, and 20 percent of Caucasian Americans have varying degrees of lactose intolerance. People whose ancestors come from northern and western Europe tend to maintain adequate lactase levels throughout their lives.

Lactose intolerance is sometimes linked to other issues. For example, some medications lower lactase production in the body. Lactose intolerance can be a side effect of certain medical conditions, such as intestinal disease or gastric (stomach) surgery. Depending on the cause, lactose intolerance may be just short term.

Lactose in Food: Which "Whey"?
Lactose usually comes from foods containing milk or milk solids. *The chart* "How Much Lactose?" *on page 194 suggests how much*. Prepared foods, even those labeled "non-dairy," may contain lactose, too. If you're *very* lactose intolerant, you may need to check labels carefully.

- ➢ Look for label ingredient terms that suggest lactose: milk, dry milk solids (including nonfat milk solids), buttermilk, lactose, malted milk, sour or sweet cream, margarine, whey, whey protein concentrate, and cheese.

- ➢ Recognize baked and processed foods that often contain small amounts of lactose: bread, candy and cookies, cold cuts and hot dogs, salad dressings, drink mixes, commercial sauces and gravies, cream soups, drink mixes, dry cereals, prepared foods (such as frozen pizza, lasagna, and waffles), salad dressings made with milk or cheese, and sugar substitutes.

Be aware that some medications also contain lactose. If you're lactose intolerant, consult with your physician about appropriate medications.

Dairy Foods: Don't Give 'Em Up!
So, you've been diagnosed as lactose intolerant. That's not a reason to give up dairy foods! Lactose intolerance isn't an "all-or-nothing" condition. Instead it's a matter of degree. Most people with difficulty digesting lactose can consume foods with lactose. It's just a matter of knowing which foods contain lactose—and knowing your personal tolerance level.

Needlessly eliminating milk and other dairy foods from the diet may pose nutritional risks! They're important sources calcium, protein, riboflavin, vitamins A and D, magnesium, phosphorus, and many other nutrients.

Calcium, for example, is especially important because of its role in growing and maintaining

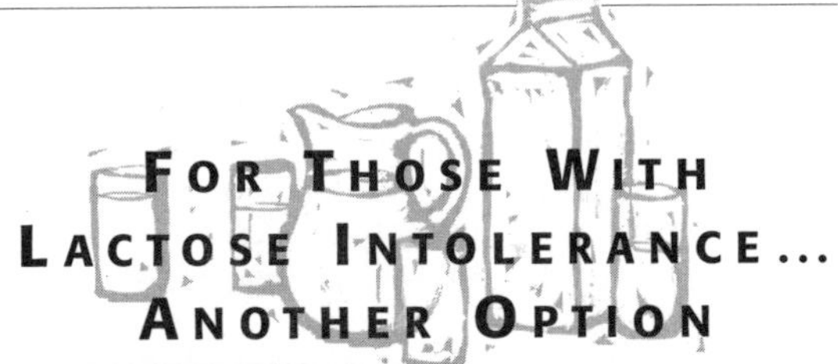

FOR THOSE WITH LACTOSE INTOLERANCE... ANOTHER OPTION

As another option, food products have been developed for people with lactose intolerance. Some products are lactose reduced. Others contain lactase, the enzyme that digests milk sugar and that's deficient to some degree in people with lactose intolerance. If you're lactose intolerant and if the "Tips for Tolerance" on page 196 aren't enough:

Look for lactose-reduced or lactose-free milk and other dairy foods at the supermarket. Lactose-reduced milk has 70 percent less lactose than regular milk, and lactose-free milk is virtually free of any lactose.

Add lactase enzyme, available in tablets or in drops, to fluid milk before drinking it. You'll find instructions on the package. Your milk will taste slightly sweeter because added lactase breaks down the lactose in milk into simpler, sweeter sugars.

As another option, look for a lactase supplement to chew or swallow before eating lactose-rich foods. With a supplemental supply of lactase, you can eat without discomfort. ✦

strong bones. An adequate amount of calcium helps children and teens grow strong, healthy bones and helps prevent the bone-thinning disease called osteoporosis. Milk and other dairy foods supply 75 percent of the calcium in the American food supply. Without these foods, meeting your calcium requirement can be difficult. *For more about calcium in a healthful diet, refer to "Calcium: A Closer Look" on page* 105.

If you're lactose intolerant, consult a registered dietitian (RD) for help with planning a diet that's adequate in calcium, while controlling the lactose in your meals and snacks. In extreme cases or for children or pregnant women with lactose intolerance, a registered dietitian also may recommend a calcium supplement.

Lactose: Tips for Tolerance

Lactose intolerance is easy to manage. Most people with difficulty digesting lactose can include dairy and other lactose-containing foods in their meals and snacks. In fact, 80 percent of people with lower levels of lactase can drink a cup of milk without discomfort.

If you—or someone in your family—has trouble digesting lactose, try these tips to comfortably include lactose-containing foods in meals and snacks:

Experiment! Start with small amounts of lactose-containing foods. Then gradually increase the portion size to determine your personal tolerance level.

Enjoy lactose-containing foods as part of a meal, rather than alone. The mix of foods slows release of lactose into the digestive system, making it easier to digest. Think of this as "diluting" the lactose!

Eat smaller, more frequent portions of lactose-rich foods. For example, drink 1/2- or 3/4-cup servings of milk several times throughout the day instead of 1-cup servings one, two, or three times daily.

Choose calcium-rich foods that are naturally lower in lactose, such as aged cheese. When cheese is made, curds (or solids) are separated from the whey (or watery liquid); most lactose is in the whey. Aged cheeses, such as Swiss, colby, Parmesan, and cheddar, lose most of their lactose during processing and aging. Much of the lactose is removed with the whey.

Try dairy foods (yogurt and buttermilk), made with active cultures. They're easier to digest because their "friendly" bacteria help digest the lactose. Not all cultured dairy foods contain live cultures. Look for the National Yogurt Association's seal "Live and Active Cultures" on the yogurt carton.

Opt for whole-milk dairy products. The higher fat content of whole-milk dairy products may help to slow the rate of digestion, allowing a gradual release of lactose. In your overall food choices, choose other foods with less fat. *See "Quick, Easy Trade-Offs" on page* 256.

Even if you're sensitive to lactose, include a variety of calcium-rich foods in your diet every day. In addition to dairy foods, enjoy these other calcium sources: dark-green leafy vegetables, such as broccoli and greens; calcium-fortified products, such as juice, bread, and cereal; and canned sardines and salmon with bones. For canned fish, you need to eat the bones to get the calcium!

Become a label sleuth. Check the ingredient list on the food label for words that may indicate lactose. *Refer to page* 195, *"Lactose in Food: Which 'Whey'?"*

have you ever wondered

...if goat's milk is a good substitute for cow's milk for someone with lactose intolerance? Goat's milk has slightly less lactose: 9 grams of lactose per cup, compared with 11 grams of lactose in one cup of cow's milk.

...if a nondairy creamer can replace milk for someone who's lactose intolerant? How about nonfat dry milk? No. Nondairy creamers may contain lactose. Check the label! The nutrient content of the creamer and the milk is different. In a nondairy creamer, the protein quality and the amounts of calcium and vitamins A and C are lower than in milk. Regarding nonfat dry milk, remember that fat, not lactose, has been removed from milk. ✦

Look for kosher foods that display the word "parev" or "parve" on the label. These foods are milk-free. *Refer to page 276 for kosher symbols.*

Don't be fooled by lactobacillus or sweet acidophilus milks. Most are no lower in lactose, and so may not be tolerated any better than other forms of milk.

Gluten Intolerance... Often a Lifelong Condition

Gluten intolerance is an intestinal disorder. For those who have it, the body can't tolerate gluten, which is the protein component of some grains, including wheat. In our bodies, gluten breaks down into two parts—gliadin and glutenin.

For people with gluten intolerance, consuming gliadin damages the lining of the small intestine. As a result, the damaged intestine cannot absorb essential nutrients, including carbohydrate, protein, fat, and fat-soluble vitamins. For someone with gluten intolerance, the risk for malnutrition is high. This condition also may be referred to as gluten-sensitive enteropathy, celiac disease, or nontropical sprue.

What are the symptoms? Weakness, appetite loss, weight loss, diarrhea, and abdominal cramps are common. Among women, gluten intolerance may interfere with the menstrual cycle. For children, gluten intolerance is especially risky. Unless the condition is well managed, a child may not grow properly. For growth and development, a child's high energy and nutrient needs require adequate nourishment.

Gluten intolerance can occur at any age. Symptoms may appear first during infancy when cereal is started. But most cases are diagnosed in the adult years. Temporary lactose intolerance may accompany gluten intolerance. That happens at least until the condition is under control, and the small intestine heals.

The primary treatment for gluten intolerance is to follow a strict eating regimen. A gluten-restricted, gliadin-free diet is a "must" for successfully managing this condition. Once gliadin is eliminated from the diet, the small intestine can heal itself. Nutrient absorption will then improve, and the symptoms will disappear. If you think you have gluten intolerance, consult your physician for a diagnosis.

Which Foods for Gluten Intolerance?
Four grains—wheat, rye, oats, and barley—contain gliadin. To manage gluten intolerance, these four grains, and any food or food component made from them, must be eliminated from the diet. Although not technically a grain, buckwheat should be avoided, too. Even trace amounts of gliadin in the diet can damage the small intestine.

Avoiding wheat is probably the biggest challenge for people with gluten intolerance. That's because wheat is the main ingredient in so many foods:

Words That May Indicate Gliadin

For people with gluten intolerance, label reading is very important! These are ingredients on the label that indicate the presence of gliadin:

flour, self-rising flour, enriched flour
modified food starch
monosodium glutamate (MSG)
hydrolyzed vegetable protein (HVP)
cereals
malt or cereal extracts
malt flavoring
distilled vinegar
emulsifiers
stabilizers
wheat starch

Source: Gluten Intolerance, by Merri Lou Dobler, Chicago, IL: The American Dietetic Association, 1996. ✦

baked foods, bread, breakfast cereal, breaded foods, crackers, pretzels, and pasta, among others.

Gliadin is also a common food additive and may appear under a different name as part of another ingredient. So even foods labeled "gluten-free" may not be "gliadin-free." *See page 197, "Label Lingo: Words That May Indicate Gliadin."*

Knowing the difference between gluten and gliadin is important when you're asking for ingredient information from food manufacturers. Technically, "gluten" is a generic term that describes the protein component of grain. Although rice and corn contain gluten, they don't have the gliadin found in barley, oats, rye, and wheat.

Eating Gliadin-Free!

Coping with gluten intolerance requires a strict eating regimen. While it's hard to follow at first, the results are well worth the effort! Without gliadin in the diet, the intestine heals and those with gluten intolerance can live a long, healthy life.

If you—or someone you know—deals with gluten intolerance, these are some guidelines to follow:

Consult a registered dietitian. He or she can help you learn how to live with gluten intolerance—and enjoy eating! *Refer to "How to Find Nutrition Help" on page 580 for tips on finding a qualified nutrition expert.*

Find gluten-free grains and food products in local food stores. Can't find them in your grocery store? Check specialty or health food stores. Mail-order outlets also can be a source of alternate flours for baking, as well as prepared foods, mixes, grains, and specialty ingredients.

Read food labels carefully! Many commercially-prepared foods—baked, frozen, and canned—contain gliadin. Spotting ingredients and additives with gliadin must become second nature. *Check the ingredient list for terms such as those on page 197, "Label Lingo: Words That May Indicate Gliadin."*

Get to know the origin and composition of ingredients. For example, the ingredient "vinegar" on a food label may appear harmless. However, vinegar is often distilled from a grain with gliadin; so it's inappropriate for someone with gluten intolerance. Avoid distilled vinegar and instead, look for the food labels that specifically state rice vinegar, wine vinegar, or pure cider vinegar; these products are gliadin-free and can be safely consumed. Be aware that ingredients used in prepared foods, such as marinades and barbecue sauce, may have vinegar, too.

Substitute gliadin-free flours for wheat flour in food preparation. Use corn, rice, soy, arrowroot, tapioca, and potato flours, or perhaps a mixture, instead of wheat flour in recipes. These flours are gliadin-free. Because they give a different flavor and texture to the baked foods, using these flours takes practice and experimentation.

This gliadin-free flour mixture is an excellent substitute for wheat flour.

2 cups white rice flour
2/3 cup potato starch flour
1/3 cup tapioca flour

Source: The Gluten-Free Gourmet, Living Well Without Wheat, by Bette Hagman. New York, NY: Henry Holt & Company, 1990. Reprinted with permission.

Keep up-to-date with food products so you can choose gluten-restricted, gliadin-free foods. Contact food manufacturers for their current ingredient lists. As you know, recipes for prepared foods change. You'll find the company name, address, and perhaps a toll-free consumer information service number on the food label.

Eating away from home? If you're on the road, pack along gluten-free foods. Order a gluten-free meal when you make your airline reservation. Read restaurant menus carefully, and ask questions. If you're a guest in someone's home, tell them about your special food needs ahead, and offer to bring food. *For more tips on ordering from a menu, refer to page 360, "Restaurant Eater's Tip List."*

Seek out local and national support groups. It's a great way to share information and recipes with others who have the same condition. Many support groups publish lists of acceptable food products by brand name. That makes shopping and following a gluten-restricted, gliadin-free diet easier. A registered dietitian can help you find a support group.

Sensitive to Additives? Maybe, Maybe Not

Do you wonder about the functions of those hard-to-pronounce ingredients listed on the label of your favorite foods? You probably know most are additives, but you may not know exactly why they are added to foods.

Additives serve a number of important functions in food. For instance, they may improve the nutritional value of food, just as B vitamins and iron are added to flour. Some additives, such as spices and colors, enhance the taste and appearance of food products. Others prevent spoilage or give foods the consistency you expect. Without them, our food supply likely would be far more limited. *Refer to "Additives: Safe at the Plate" on page 225 for more on food additives.*

Except on rare occasions, we consume many food additives without side effects. For those who do experience adverse reactions, the response is commonly an intolerance—not a true allergy—to the additive.

In the United States, the Food and Drug Administration (FDA) regulates food additives; food intolerances and allergies are considered as part of their approval process. *"Testing, Testing" on page 230 summarizes the approval process.* Certain food additives—preservatives, colors, and flavors—are linked more commonly to food sensitivities than others. But just how strong is the link? Read on...

For the Sulfite-Sensitive...

Have you ever wondered why dried apricots and dehydrated potatoes list "sulfites" on the ingredient list of a food label? Sulfites are used to prevent certain foods from browning, such as light-colored fruits, dried fruits, and vegetables. Added to beer, wine, and other fermented foods, sulfites slow the growth of bacteria.

The term sulfites is a catch-all, referring to a variety of additives commonly used in food. Usually they have "sulfite" in their names. Sulfites may be listed on food labels as sulfur dioxide, sodium sulfite, sodium or potassium bisulfite, and sodium or potassium metabisulfite.

Sulfites, as part of a varied diet, pose no risk of side effects for most of us. However, in 5 to 10 percent of the population, sulfites may provoke an adverse reaction. People with asthma more often react to sulfites than others do, and the reaction may be severe.

For those who are sulfite sensitive, reactions may include wheezing, diarrhea, stomachache, hives, or swelling. Fortunately, side effects are mild for most people. However, reactions may become life-threatening in hypersensitive individuals. In rare cases, these individuals may experience anaphylactic shock. As with other food intolerances and allergies, consult a doctor if you think you're sulfite sensitive. Don't self-diagnose.

Because sulfites can trigger intense reactions in sulfite-sensitive asthmatics, the Food and Drug

Where Might You Find Sulfites?

- Dried fruits, such as apricots
- Frozen or prepackaged avocado dip
- Instant and frozen potatoes, such as french fries, potato chips, dried potatoes, and potato flakes
- Wine, beer
- Cider
- Fruit juices
- Wine vinegar
- Gelatin
- Maraschino cherries
- Lemon juice
- Salad dressings and sauces from dry mixes
- Shrimp, canned seafood soups
- Pickled products
- Canned or dried soups ✦

Administration prohibits the use of sulfites on fruits and vegetables (except potatoes) intended to be served or sold raw. In the past, sulfites were sometimes used to keep fruits and vegetables fresh longer on restaurant salad bars, but that's no longer allowed.

Sulfites also can destroy the B vitamin called thiamin. For that reason, they're not allowed in foods such as enriched bread and flour. These foods are major sources of thiamin in the American diet.

If you're among those rare individuals who are sulfite-sensitive, follow these guidelines:

Check food labels, and choose foods without sulfite-containing additives. Be aware that they're used in varying amounts in many packaged foods—not just dried fruit, dehydrated potatoes, and fruit juices. By law, when sulfites are present in detectable amounts, the label must indicate it has sulfites. *Refer to "Where Might You Find Sulfites?" on page 199 for a list of foods that might contain sulfites.*

Be careful of alcoholic beverages. Since 1988, labels on beer and wine must state "Contains Sulfites" if applicable.

Ask questions in restaurants before you order. For example, ask if canned foods, vegetables, or potato products contain—or were treated with—sulfites.

MSG—Sensitive?

You probably know about monosodium glutamate, or more simply, MSG. Common in many types of ethnic cooking, MSG is a flavor enhancer. It blends well with salty or sour flavors...and brings out the taste of many prepared foods, such as "heat 'n eat" meals, sauces, and canned soups.

Besides accenting the natural flavor of foods, MSG adds a unique taste of its own. Called "umami," its taste is described as "meaty" or "broth-like." Studies show "umami" actually elicits a fifth taste sensation. Sweet, sour, salty, and bitter are the classic sensations. Just as oranges are sweet and lemons are sour, the umami taste may be distinctive in cheese, meat, and tomatoes.

As its name implies, monosodium glutamate contains sodium, and glutamate or glutamic acid. Glutamic acid is an amino acid found naturally in our body and in high-protein foods. Meat, fish, dairy foods, and some vegetables all contain glutamic acid.

Over the years, consumers have asked about the safety of MSG. The U.S. Food and Drug Administration considers MSG as "generally recog-

DOES FOOD CAUSE CHILDHOOD HYPERACTIVITY?

The commonly-held notion linking sugar, MSG, or other food additives to hyperactive behavior or attention deficit hyperactivity disorder (ADHD) in children has never been scientifically proven. Although the exact cause of ADHD isn't known, factors such as genetics and environmental influences have been suggested.

The Feingold diet, popularized for its claimed ability to manage ADHD, has been touted as an approach for treating hyperactive children. The eating plan restricts foods containing salicylates, which are present in almonds, certain fruits and vegetables, artificial flavors and colors, and preservatives. However, the reported success is based on anecdotal data, not scientifically-proven methods. The extra attention given to children on the Feingold diet may be the reason for the child's behavior change, not the change in food choices. Although many other studies have been conducted attempting to link eating with hyperactivity, the Feingold results haven't been replicated.

Until researchers learn more, the best management of ADHD includes behavioral modification and medication, if warranted by a doctor.

For more about the misconceptions between sugar and behavior, refer to page 129, "Sugar Myths." ✦

nized as safe" (GRAS) for consumption. Other GRAS substances include commonplace food "additives," such as sugar, salt, and baking soda. *Refer to "Testing, Testing" on page 230 for more about the GRAS list.*

Some people feel they are sensitive to MSG. They describe varying symptoms, including migraine headaches, body tingling or warmth, and chest pain after eating foods containing MSG. The symptoms, usually mild, often last less than one hour. Perhaps you've heard the symptoms collectively referred to as the "Chinese restaurant syndrome" because MSG is so common in Chinese cuisine. However, research hasn't found a definitive link between MSG or Chinese food and any adverse side effects. Other components in those foods, such as a common allergen or soy, could be the culprit.

If you want to moderate your MSG intake—or if you seem sensitive to it—you often can order food in Asian restaurants without added MSG. The menu might even identify foods made without it. Check food labels to guide your food selection, too. Glutamate that naturally occurs in food won't be on the ingredient list, so you may want to consult a registered dietitian for guidance.

MSG has nutrition-related benefits that may go unrecognized. Since a little goes a long way, MSG provides a bigger "bang" for the "shake." Because it contains only one-third as much sodium as salt, it may be an option for those controlling their sodium intake. *Refer to chapter 7 for more on sodium sensitivity.*

Adding MSG to foods such as soups and stews may make eating more enjoyable for older adults. As we grow older, our sense of smell may weaken and our taste buds decrease in number. As a result, foods lose some of their "taste appeal." The decline in smell and taste often causes seniors to lose interest in eating, putting them at nutritional risk. Adding MSG to certain foods can perk up the taste! *Refer to "Aging With 'Taste'" on page 518 for more about taste and older adults.*

Coloring...By Any Other Name!
Although the incidence is rare, a very small number of people are sensitive to a coloring added to food. FD&C Yellow No. 5, also called tartrazine, is a dye used to color foods, beverages, and medications.

Two to 20 percent of us suffer migraines. Migraine headaches can affect anyone, but women are three times more likely than men to suffer from them. Certain foods are often blamed, but there's little agreement about the link between foods and headaches.

A migraine is a disease characterized by severe head pain, plus one or more of a range of symptoms, such as nausea, vomiting, and increased sensitivity to light, sound, and smells. A migraine attack can last from 4 to 72 hours, often causing sufferers to virtually "put their lives on hold."

The causes of migraine headaches are complicated and not well understood. Certain components of food—natural or added—have been suspected, but not proven, to be causes of headaches in some people. Tyrosine (in cheese and chocolate), histamine (in red wine), caffeine (in coffee and cola), benzoic acid (a preservative), sodium nitrites (in smoked foods), monosodium glutamate, and alcohol may be food-related triggers. Susceptible individuals may be affected by a combination of factors, not just food.

If you experience chronic headaches, check with your physician for a medical diagnosis. That's the first step toward coping and overcoming headaches. To determine which foods, if any, trigger migraine attacks, keep a diary of what you eat. Depending on how often your attacks occur, you may need to keep the diary for several weeks.

If you're diagnosed with migraine and you're susceptible to food triggers, a registered dietitian can recommend appropriate substitutes for suspected food triggers. ✦

Research indicates FD&C Yellow No. 5 may trigger hives, itching, and nasal congestion. But the incidence is limited to just one or two out of every 10,000 people. Yellow No. 5 is the only food coloring known to cause problems.

Whenever added to a food or medication, FD&C Yellow No. 5 must be listed on the label or package insert. If you're sensitive to this coloring, read labels carefully. Foods and beverages likely to contain tartrazine include soft drinks, ice cream and sherbets, gelatins, salad dressings, cheese dishes, seasoned salts, candies, flavor extracts, and pudding, cake, and frosting mixes.

Intense Sweeteners: How Sweet It Is!
Intense sweeteners provide the sweet taste of sugar with just trivial amounts of calories. After years of testing their safety, the FDA approved three for use in the United States: aspartame, saccharin, and acesulfame K. *"Trio of Sweet Options" on page 136 takes a close look at these sweeteners.*

Since their discovery, these intense sweeteners have been thoroughly investigated by regulatory agencies around the globe, as well as by leading scientific organizations. Evidence indicates that their long-term intake is safe and not associated with adverse health effects.

To assure their safety, the FDA established an acceptable daily intake, or ADI. The ADI is the amount of any food additive that can be safely consumed every day—for a lifetime—without adverse effects. It's highly unlikely that anyone would consume any intense sweetener at the ADI level.

Intense sweeteners don't appear to cause symptoms of food sensitivity. However, people with the rare genetic disorder called phenylketonuria (PKU) should avoid foods sweetened with aspartame.

Aspartame is made from two amino acids: aspartic acid and phenylalanine. The same amino acids are found naturally in foods such as meat, milk, fruit, and vegetables. Regardless of the source, people with PKU cannot metabolize phenylalanine properly, so they can only consume limited amounts. Unmanaged, PKU can cause tissue damage, and in infants, brain damage. As a precaution, all babies are screened for PKU at birth.

For those who suffer from this disorder, foods and beverages containing aspartame carry a label warning stating "PHENYLKETONURICS: CONTAINS PHENYLALANINE." One of the most widely accepted food additives, aspartame is found in many products, including carbonated and powdered soft drinks, yogurt, pudding and gelatins, frozen desserts, hot beverage mixes, and candy. You'll find aspartame listed in the ingredient list of the food label—and the PKU warning also lets you know it's there.

Saccharin, the oldest and most intense non-nutritive sweetener, has never been shown to provoke any symptoms of allergies or food intolerance. In 1977, however, the FDA proposed a ban on saccharin because it was implicated as a weak carcinogen,

WARNING: FOODBORNE ILLNESS

Nausea, diarrhea, fatigue—many symptoms of foodborne illness mimic those of a food allergy or a food intolerance. In fact, the most common adverse reactions from food come from foodborne illness, caused by eating food contaminated with harmful bacteria. Bacteria multiply at a rapid rate in food that isn't handled properly.

Three food handling guidelines offer the best protection from foodborne illness:

- Keep cold food cold.
- Keep hot food hot.
- Keep all food clean!

Refer to chapter 13, "The Safe Kitchen," for a closer look at identifying and preventing foodborne illnesses. ✦

or cancer causing agent, when given to animals in very, very large amounts. No human studies ever confirmed the findings. Because of the strong public opposition to the ban, the FDA withdrew its proposal. But there's still a warning label on products containing saccharin.

Food Allergies: Commonly Uncommon

Have you ever heard parents say their child is allergic to milk, then remark that he or she has no adverse reactions to chocolate milk? Or maybe you avoid a particular food yourself, believing you have an allergy to it? Although nothing to be taken lightly, you may be surprised at just how infrequently true food allergies occur. Consider that:

> ➢ One in three adults believe they're allergic to milk. However, fewer than 2 percent of adults suffer from true food allergies of any kind!
>
> ➢ Although an estimated 5 percent of children are diagnosed with food allergies, they usually outgrow them by the time they become adults.

If food allergies are so uncommon, why do millions claim they're allergic? Because food allergies are often self-diagnosed and because the symptoms can mimic other food-induced ailments, such as foodborne illness and food intolerances. People often use the term "allergy" loosely to describe almost any physical reaction to food—even if it's psychological!

Who is likely to develop a food allergy? Anyone can. However, most occur among people with a family history of allergies. Nonfood allergies are more common than food allergies. Food allergies are often inherited, and almost all are identified early in life. Children are much more likely to have food allergies than adults, although many allergies are outgrown.

Food Allergies: What Are They?

True food allergies cause changes in the body's immune system even though the person isn't sick. An allergen, which is a protein in the troublesome food, actually sets off a chain of immune system reactions. When an allergy-prone person eats a food that causes an allergic reaction, his or her body scrambles to protect itself by making antibodies. These antibodies trigger the release of body chemicals, such as histamine. In turn, these body chemicals cause uncomfortable symptoms associated with food allergies, such as a runny nose, itchy skin, or even a rapid heartbeat.

Something You Ate?

It's lunchtime. You make your toddler his or her first peanut butter-and-jelly sandwich. An hour later you notice the child has broken out with an itchy rash. You've heard that peanuts commonly contain food allergens. Is your child allergic to the peanut butter on the sandwich? Maybe...or maybe not! In any case, a call to the child's doctor is certainly in order.

Actually, any food can cause an allergic reaction in a susceptible person. However, some foods, such as peanuts, are more likely than others to set off a reaction. Milk, eggs, and shellfish (especially shrimp), as well as soy, fish, wheat, legumes (dried beans and peas), and tree nuts (such as walnuts), also frequently contain allergens. An allergy to egg, milk, soy, or wheat often is outgrown.

Symptoms? Something to Sneeze About

What are the symptoms of a food allergy? Different people react to the same allergen in different ways. Even if a food contains a common allergen, you can't predict whether or not you may have an allergic reaction. Symptoms may appear within seconds or up to several hours after eating the food that triggers the reaction. In exceptionally sensitive people, just the touch or smell of the food can provoke a reaction!

What's the Sign?
The most common symptoms include swelling, sneezing, and nausea. Most symptoms affect the skin, respiratory system, stomach, or intestines:

➢ ***Skin Reactions***
Swelling of lips, mouth, tongue, face, or throat
Hives
Rash or redness
Itchy skin or eyes

➢ ***Nose, Throat, and Lung Reactions***
Sneezing
Nasal congestion or runny nose
Coughing or wheezing
Asthma
Breathing difficulty

➢ ***Stomach and Intestinal Reactions***
Nausea
Abdominal pain and bloating
Vomiting
Diarrhea
Cramping
Gas

Adapted from: Food Allergies, *by* Merri Lou Dobler, *Chicago*, IL: *The American* Dietetic *Association*, 1991

have you ever wondered

...if avoiding certain foods during pregnancy can prevent food allergies in the baby? There's no evidence that restricting foods during pregnancy makes any difference. In fact, it's not recommended. Babies born to mothers who have restricted their diets during pregnancy often have lower birthweights. *Refer to "Food Sensitivities and Your Baby" on page* 408 *for more guidance.*

...if breast-feeding can prevent food allergies in the baby? Perhaps so. For those with a family history of allergies, breast-fed babies are less likely to have food allergies—if breast-feeding continues for at least six months. ✦

Keep in mind these symptoms may be caused by other food- or nonfood-related conditions. For an accurate diagnosis, you need a complete medical evaluation.

Emotions associated with food experiences, and not the food itself, can even cause a reaction. Just the appearance, smell, or taste of food might trigger an emotional reaction, which results in symptoms that mimic a food allergy or food intolerance. Or someone might get these symptoms by believing the food is harmful. Even if you suspect that emotions are at the root of an adverse reaction to food, check with your physician. Symptoms may stem from a more serious physical condition.

To date, there's no scientific link between food allergies and arthritis, migraine headaches, behavioral problems, ear infections, and urinary tract infections, although research in these areas is underway.

Food Allergies: The Dangerous Side
For most people with food allergies, the reactions are more uncomfortable than dangerous. In rare cases, however, an anaphylactic reaction can occur. When many different body systems react at the same time, this allergic response to food can be severe and even life-threatening.

With an anaphylactic reaction, symptoms often develop quickly—often within a few seconds or minutes after eating. They may include extreme itching, a swelling of the throat that makes breathing difficult, sweating, rapid or irregular heartbeat, low blood pressure, nausea, diarrhea, and shock. Without immediate medical attention, the affected person may die. What foods may cause a severe reaction? Although the cases are rare, tree nuts, eggs, peanuts, and shellfish are most likely to cause such a severe reaction in allergy-prone individuals.

Warning! If you—or a family member—experience severe food reactions, plan in advance how you would handle accidental ingestion of the "trigger" allergen. The person should wear an identification bracelet or necklace to alert others. And he or she should carry epinephrine (adrenaline) that can be injected quickly to counter the allergen.

Itching for a Cause?

If you have symptoms, a doctor can help you "scratch" the surface to find the cause with a medical diagnosis. A board-certified allergist (certified by the American Board of Allergy and Immunology) is best equipped to diagnose food allergies. Never try to self-diagnose. Someone with a food allergy should be under a doctor's care.

True food allergies can be measured and evaluated clinically—with no need for "hunches." That way, unrelated medical conditions are eliminated. Typically, the diagnosis includes a medical history, a physical exam, and possibly a food diary, elimination diet, and laboratory tests.

Keeping track of how your body reacts to a specific food one time after another may help you detect a food allergy or intolerance on your own. But be careful about self-diagnosis. The cause may be a more serious medical problem. Eliminating groups of foods from your eating pattern because you suspect a food allergy is not a smart idea. Sweeping dietary changes, based only on a "hunch," actually may keep you from getting the nutrients needed for good health!

For the Record...
Suspect a food allergy? During a medical exam, you'll likely need to describe your symptoms and give some medical history to unravel the mystery. Be prepared to answer such questions as:

- What are your symptoms?
- How long does it take for symptoms to appear after eating the food in question?
- How much of the food must you eat before you get a reaction?
- Do the symptoms occur every time you eat the food?
- Does anyone in your family have allergies? Food allergies?

You may be asked to keep a food diary, too, with all the foods, beverages, and medications you consume over a determined period. You'll also keep track of your reactions and how soon after eating they appeared. By itself, the diary can't confirm a cause-and-effect relationship between a food and

Terms for Common Allergens

Allergen	Ingredient Terms
Milk	Casein Caseinate Casein hydrolysate DMS (dried milk solids) Lactolbumin Lactate solids Milk solid pastes Sweetened condensed milk Whey or whey solids
Egg	Albumin Dried egg solids Globulin Ovomucin Ovomucoid Ovoglobulin Livetin Vitellin
Corn	Corn solids Cornstarch Corn syrup Vegetable starch Dextrose Glucose Corn oil Corn alcohol Corn sugar Food starch—modified
Legume	Acacia gum Arabic gum Carob Haraya gum Locust bean gum Tragacanth
Soy	Hydrolyzed vegetable protein Soy concentrate Soy protein Soya flour TVP (textured vegetable protein) Vegetable protein concentrate

symptoms. But the information can suggest a connection to investigate further.

An elimination diet offers another way to uncover a cause. Your doctor may instruct you to eliminate the suspicious food from your diet for awhile. If the symptoms go away, then reappear when you eat the food again, you may be allergic to it.

Keeping a food diary or following an elimination diet on your own may seem easy. However, detecting ingredients in prepared foods that cause allergic reactions may not be so easy. A registered dietitian has the expertise to help you.

Pass the Test?

Various medical tests can help diagnose food allergies. With the results, a true food allergy may be confirmed or ruled out.

- The skin-prick test uses small amounts of diluted food extracts "pricked" into the skin. If the skin reacts to the extracts with a mosquito-like bump, you may have a food allergy.
- Blood tests are done by checking for antibodies. Remember, the presence of antibodies, released by your immune system, signals a reaction to an allergen. For example, a test called a radioallergosorbent test (RAST) uses a sample of blood to determine the presence of antibodies.
- In a challenge test, likely given in a doctor's office, the patient gets a sample that's either the suspected food allergen or a placebo. The placebo won't produce an allergic reaction. The response is watched carefully. If there are no symptoms, the challenge gets repeated with higher doses. This test must be done under the supervision of a physician—never on your own.
- Tests using a food extract are considered unreliable and quite costly.

have you ever *wondered*

...if chocolate really causes acne? No, chocolate doesn't cause or make acne worse. Hormones and hygiene, rather than an allergy to chocolate, are more likely the culprits. A true food allergy to chocolate is rare. Instead, a reaction to eating a chocolate bar may come from other ingredients mixed in, such as the nuts or milk.

...if foods modified by biotechnology contain allergens? It's possible. But scientists don't know yet what specific substances in any food cause an allergic reaction. Until more is known, the Food and Drug Administration policy states that any protein taken from a food causing a known allergic reaction should be considered allergenic, too. And it must be listed on the label of a food produced by biotechnology. *Refer to "Food Biotechnology: The Future Is Today!" on page 235.* ✦

"How-Tos" for Coping With Food Allergies

If you're diagnosed with a true food allergy, what's next? You'll likely need to avoid the troublesome food—and choose meals and snacks with care! If you must eliminate a food, or category of food, plan carefully to ensure that your eating plan is nutritionally adequate and fits your food preferences and lifestyle.

Here's how to keep tabs on a food allergy:

Start by seeking professional help. A registered dietitian can help you learn to manage a food allergy while eating a varied and balanced diet. For example, ask about making food substitutions, reading food labels, and dining away from home.

Read food labels for "undercover" allergens. If, for example, you're allergic to eggs, you'd need to know that eggs are common ingredients in mayonnaise, many salad dressings, and ice cream. Food labels list the ingredients in the food that is inside the package. *The chart, "Label Lingo: Terms for Common Allergens," on page 205 gives ingredients to watch for on ingredient lists of food labels if you have a food allergy. Refer to page 270, "Today's Food Labels" for more on reading food labels.*

Keep up-to-date on food products. Periodically, food manufacturers change the ingredients. So, even if you're a long-time customer of a certain food, check the label regularly.

Contact food manufacturers for their current ingredient lists or for answers to your questions. You'll find the company name, address, and perhaps a toll-free consumer information service number on the food label.

Practice new ways of cooking. In time, substituting one food for another in food preparation will become second nature.

Become "ingredient savvy" when you eat away from home. Keep copies of restaurant menus handy to review before going out. Ask about the ingredients and preparation of menu items before you order. Play safe by ordering plain foods, such as grilled meats, steamed vegetables, and fresh fruits. *For more tips on eating out, refer to page 360, "Restaurant Eater's Tip List."*

If you're not sure about the food when you eat out, brown-bag your own food. If you're a guest in someone's home, offer to bring your own food.

For more education about food allergies, and a cookbook, newsletters, and other support, contact the Food Allergy Network. Refer to page 597 for more information.

real life nutrition

Nathan Has a Food Allergy...or Does He?

Three-year-old Jackson and his mom, Earlene have invited his little friend Nathan and Nathan's mom, Pauline, to their home. After an active morning of playing in the backyard, it's time for the boys to come in and wash for lunch.

Earlene pours chocolate milk into cups and passes one to Nathan. "Oh, no thank you," Pauline says. "Nathan is allergic to milk...his stomach gets upset."

Knowing that true food allergies are uncommon, Earlene asks if Nathan's doctor has diagnosed a food allergy. "No," Pauline says, "We're handling it ourselves by avoiding milk and cheese until Nathan outgrows his allergy."

"Hmmm," Earlene thinks to herself, "Nathan might not have an allergy at all...and he might not be getting all the nutrients he needs to grow properly without any milk and other dairy foods." What suggestions might Earlene offer?

Suggestions about dairy foods in Nathan's diet:

➢ Earlene might encourage Pauline to have Nathan evaluated by his doctor to rule out a food allergy. If he doesn't have an allergy, Nathan may be lactose intolerant and still able to consume milk and other dairy foods. If he does have a food allergy, the physician and a registered dietitian could help make sure that Nathan gets the nutrients he needs.

➢ For growth and development, Nathan needs the nutrients in dairy foods. Milk group foods are important sources of calcium, needed for growing and maintaining strong bones. Unless under the careful supervision of a registered dietitian and physician, Pauline shouldn't eliminate an entire food group from Nathan's diet.

➢ If Nathan is lactose intolerant, he may be able to tolerate chocolate milk more easily than regular milk. A smaller portion, consumed with meals, may help, too. Or Pauline might try serving regular milk pretreated with the enzyme lactase. Cheese and crackers, and flavored yogurt layered with fruit and dry cereal are popular high-calcium, low-lactose snacks for toddlers. And lower-lactose foods such as aged cheese and yogurt with active cultures would help him get the recommended three or more daily milk group servings.

➢ Calcium-fortified products, such as juice, cereal, and bread, as well as dark-green, leafy vegetables or tofu processed with calcium, also would add calcium to Nathan's diet.

➢ Nathan's problem might not be a food allergy or a food intolerance at all. He just might need to relax after playing and before eating.

Chapter Ten

What's On Today's Table?

In the past decade or two, there's been a real "change of plate" on the family table. As a consumer, perhaps you've noticed a shift in food products, or in your own shopping and cooking patterns, lifestyles, and attitudes about food and health. You may be more aware of eating to promote health. Like many others, you may be more adventuresome with food and want more flavor. And in spite of ever-better kitchens and cooking equipment, convenience and speed may be more important to you than ever.

The diversity of foods in today's marketplace reflects the diversity of today's consumers. Rather than selling just to the mass market, food producers know the value of "different strokes for different folks." As a result, you'll find a variety of foods, produced and marketed to match different needs: age, health, lifestyle, ethnic or religious background, and economic resources, among others.

From all the foods available for today's table, why do consumers—why do you—choose one food over another? Consumer research says taste comes out on top—followed by nutrition, food safety, price, and convenience! What's on top for you?

Food: What's "In Store" for You?

Miniature vegetables, peanut-butter milk, ostrich tenderloin, blue potatoes, spinach-flavored pasta—you may find all these foods alongside your traditional favorites in today's supermarkets and on restaurant menus.

When it comes to food choices, consumers in the United States have more variety of food to choose from than ever before—and more ways to eat healthy. A single store stocks, on average, about 30,000 different items, mainly food. In a typical year, more than 17,000 new products may be introduced in the marketplace. Yet only about 2 percent of all new food products make it past the consumer cut.

Among the many foods in today's marketplace, you'll find: more nutrient-modified versions of traditional products; increased choices of ethnic foods; greater variety of fresh fruits, vegetables, and grain products; more foods packaged and processed for convenience; new types of packaging; and foods sold in more specialty areas, such as salad bars, sushi bars, bakeries, and take-out.

If you eat away from home, you know about other changes that have come to your plate. Quickservice menus offer more variety—often more grain, fruit, and vegetable choices, and more broiled, steamed, and stir-fried, not just fried, foods. And some supermarket foods seem almost like homemade. Traditional restaurant menus and recipes for at-home cooking reflect an interest in healthful eating, ethnic cuisine, and a blending (or fusion) of ingredients and cooking styles.

With more choices come more decisions for you, and with that, more for you to know about your food supply.

FUNCTIONAL FOODS: A NEW WAVE

There's a new wave of foods appearing on supermarket shelves. The term "functional foods" has been coined to describe foods promoted as having special health benefits.

Currently, there's no legal definition for a functional food. But the term generally refers to a broad category of foods formulated for special health benefits. A food, or its components, may promote health, prevent disease, or both.

Actually, functional foods have been around for a long time. For example, vitamin D added to milk has a functional quality. In fact, any nutrient-modified food might be termed a "functional" food, such as calcium-fortified orange juice or iron-fortified cereal.

Functional foods also include those touted for their ability—or the ability of their components—to reduce cancer risk, aid digestion, decrease the risk of tooth decay, or improve various other body functions or reduce disease risk. The United States currently has no regulations—nor standards—for functional claims. And research related to functional foods is still unfolding.

Until we learn more about functional qualities of food, choose foods for variety, moderation, balance, and taste. That way, you'll get their known benefits, as well as the benefits that science may reveal in the future! ✦

Nutrition Sells!

You can hardly walk through the supermarket without being exposed to nutrition messages. Almost every department carries products with packaging that promotes nutrition advantages. Signs in many produce departments remind you to eat at least five fruits and vegetables daily. Nutrition brochures appear in information racks. Some stores have shelf labels tagging products with nutrition benefits.

In today's supermarket, nutrition sells. And more and more new foods are being positioned for nutrition-conscious consumers. For example, you'll find plenty of "fat free," "more fiber," and "calcium added" foods. In many cases, these newer foods are modified versions of traditional foods...often produced with less fat, saturated fat, cholesterol, sugar, or sodium, or with more fiber or certain vitamins or minerals. Fat-free taco chips and fat-free refried beans, high-fiber cereal, and reduced-sodium soup are some examples.

To create these foods, the food industry adjusts the "recipes." By modifying the nutrients, qualities of food often change, too. For example, to cut back on fat, some foods may contain more carbohydrate. That may change the flavor and mouth feel of foods you're accustomed to. And formulating foods with less salt often makes them less flavorful, too—unless other flavor-intense ingredients are added.

How can you fit today's new nutrient-modified foods into a healthful eating plan?

Remember the big picture. Enjoy them as alternative choices in an overall way of eating that's varied, moderate, and balanced. For example, being "fat-free" doesn't mean calorie-free. And "calcium added" juice doesn't make it a substitute for all the nutrients in milk.

Check all the Nutrition Facts on food labels to see how foods with nutrition claims compare with traditional foods. For example, cutting back on fat won't necessarily make a food low in calories. *Refer to "Get All the Facts!" on page* 271.

Count nutrient-modified foods in your eating plan just as you'd count their traditional counterparts. Either way, 1 1/2 ounces of fat-free or of regular cheddar cheese count as one serving from the Milk, Yogurt, and Cheese Group of the Food Guide Pyramid. *Refer to "The Food Guide Pyramid: Your Healthful Eating Guide" on page* 243.

Savor new flavors in food. More spices, herbs, and other ingredients may be added to boost the flavor of some reduced-fat or sodium-reduced foods. For example, reduced- and low-fat breakfast sausages may have more seasonings.

On the Tip of Your Tongue... The Flavor Connection

Relax for a moment, and imagine...the aroma of homemade, whole-wheat bread baking in your oven...the sweet, juicy taste of a ripe peach or strawberry—just picked...the cool sensation of an ice cold glass of milk...the crispy crunch of a raw carrot, or the smooth, creamy texture of chocolate ice cream...the fiery feeling of a hot chile pepper...and the mouthwatering aroma of meatloaf or lasagna, just as mom made it!

There's no question: Foods that appeal to your senses are probably those you enjoy most. As consumer research tells us, taste ranks number one when choosing food, even before nutrition and price.

Just what is flavor? And how does it contribute to nutrition?

Flavor is actually several sensations closely linked together: taste plus smell, as well as touch (temperature and mouth feel). With one sensation diminished, your flavor experience is entirely different. As an experiment, hold your nose so you can't smell, then bite an onion. It may taste somewhat sweet, more like an apple. Or think about the taste of food when your nose is stuffed up—not much flavor and not much pleasure either.

As an average adult, you have about 10,000 taste buds, which respond to different tastes: sweet, sour, salty, bitter, and also "umami" (flavor of monosodium glutamate). You can sense these tastes on every part of your tongue. However, some parts of the tongue are especially sensitive to certain tastes: sweet on the tip, sour on the sides, bitter on the back, and salty mostly around the front. Even the lining of your mouth, the back of your throat, and your tonsils (if you still have them) have some taste buds.

Aromas that waft through the room get picked up by smell receptors high up in your nasal passage. Temperature, mouth feel, even the "irritation" from a jalapeño pepper or the "numbing" effect from a persimmon also affect your perceptions of food and its flavor—and what you may describe as its "taste."

Not surprisingly, we're born with a preference for sweet tastes. Other flavor preferences appear to be learned—starting from early childhood.

Have you ever wondered why the same food may

have you ever wondered?

...what makes chile peppers taste "hot"? A component of chile peppers, called capsaicin, actually stimulates pain receptors in your mouth. The irritation, or "heating" effect, of chiles depends on the amount of capsaicin. It can be measured in Scoville heat units... anywhere from 1 to 300,000 (mild to very hot). For the record, a sweet bell (pimento) pepper is rated at 0 to 5; an anaheim pepper, at 1,000; a jalapeño pepper, at 5,000 to 10,000; and a habanero (Scotch bonnet) pepper, from 80,000 to 300,000! ✦

be too spicy-hot for some, but not for others? People may sense the same foods very differently. Among the factors that make a difference: saliva (affected by diet, heredity, and other factors), the number of taste buds, medication, some illnesses, and smoking. The senses of taste and smell also diminish with age. That's why older people may say that foods just don't taste the way they remember. *For more about flavor in foods for older adults, refer to* "Less Sense-able" *on page* 518.

Today, taste and smell are getting more attention in the scientific world—in part because flavor is a priority for food choices. Since people eat for taste, then there's good reason to think of nutrition and taste together. That's why research is being done: for example, to make food more flavorful for older adults; to find ways to magnify salty tastes while lowering levels of salt in food; and to use biotechnology to develop more flavorful fruits and vegetables. *Refer to* "Food Biotechnology: The Future Is Now!" *on page* 235.

To get the most flavor from foods...

Eat foods when they're at their peak of freshness.

Include a variety of foods with different flavors at a single meal to continue to stimulate taste buds.

Prepare food to retain and enhance its flavor. *For tips, refer to* "Food 'Prep': The Nutrition-Flavor Connection" *on page* 328.

did you know

...of the 80,000 known edible plants, only 300 are cultivated for food? There's a lot more food variety for the marketplace to explore!

...that about 50 percent of foods eaten in the world today originated in the Americas?

...even with more nutrition awareness and so many nutritious foods available, most people still don't eat enough fruits, vegetables, and whole-grain products? In spite of all the fat-reduced and fat-free products, many continue to eat a diet that's higher in fat than current health recommendations. ✦

Take time to savor the flavor of food. Enjoy its aroma. Chew it well to release taste and aromas.

Serve food at the temperature that most enhances its flavor.

The Multicultural Palate

Not so long ago, bagels, pita bread, and tortillas were considered trendy, ethnic foods—and salsa was a new flavor experience for many! Today, these foods and many other ethnic foods have become part of the supermarket mainstream and our multicultural palate.

The idea of "ethnic food" isn't new. Throughout history, the foods of one culture have traveled to another, infusing cuisines with more variety and new flavors. Those foods also became new sources of nutrients and food energy.

The quest for flavor—exotic Eastern spices—launched the Age of Discovery and the exploration of the "New World." Among the discoveries: a vast array of food! Among other foods, the Americas contributed tomatoes to Italy, potatoes to Ireland, peanuts (or groundnuts) to West Africa, and hot chiles to Thailand. And foods unknown to the Americas 500 years ago came from all parts of the "Old World": for example, chickens, pigs, beef, wheat, oats, barley, okra, Asian rice, peaches, pears, watermelon, citrus fruit, bananas, and lettuce.

American cuisine has strong roots in its native foods: corn, legumes, pumpkin, peanuts, potato, tomato, peppers, pineapple, squash, wild rice, and turkey, among many others. In addition, as each wave of immigrants came to the colonies, and later the United States, they brought their ethnic cuisine. In time, many ethnic foods were adapted and eventually became "typically American": for example, pizza, tacos, and chop suey. That wave of "food immigration" continues today.

Regional specialties developed as people adapted their cooking style to foods that were available: for example, sweet potato pie, cooked collard greens, black-eyed peas and rice, and grits, created in the South by African-American cooks...crab cakes and clam chowder on the Atlantic coast...tamales, bean burritos, and cactus salad in the Southwest...and smoked salmon and berry cobblers in the Pacific Northwest.

Today, new waves of immigrants—for example, Latin Americans, Asians, and Middle Easterners—offer a new influence on foods Americans eat. Travel and the restaurant world have exposed Americans to different flavors and foods unknown to them. Supermarkets become teachers when they offer new food varieties to their customers. And as the world shrinks through global communications and transportation, the "world of food" gets bigger. As a result, there's a greater variety of food, food combinations, and flavor for you to choose from.

What has sparked the interest in ethnic food? Perhaps a sense of curiosity and adventure, a desire to learn—and more than ever, the search for nutritious and flavorful alternatives. Many ethnic cuisines offer health benefits, especially those that focus on grains, vegetables, legumes, and fruits. And consumers seeking vegetarian alternatives can find many nutritious, good-tasting dishes in ethnic cuisines from other places. *Refer to "Vegetarian Dishes in the Global Kitchen" on page 575.*

A Fusion of Flavor

"Fusion cuisine" may be described as a new cooking phenomenon. It combines the ingredients or cooking techniques of two or more cultures. The result: Unique new dishes, such as a Mexican pizza, or chili in a pita pocket, or perhaps couscous topped with Chinese stir-fried vegetables.

The fusion of ingredients and flavors isn't really new. It's been going on for centuries, as people gradually adapted their cuisines to available foods—sometimes by choice, often by necessity.

Today, fusion cooking has brought an explosion of new dishes to the American table—and added variety, adventure, and enjoyment to eating. In many cases, these new "fused" dishes uniquely combine grain products, fruits, and vegetables. Their combinations may offer nutritional benefits for you. *For ways to "fuse" ingredients in your meals and snacks, refer to "Kitchen Nutrition: For Variety, Health, and Eating Pleasure!" on page 216.*

Simply adding seasonings from an ethnic cuisine also creates fusion foods: perhaps a touch of curry powder from India blended into pumpkin soup...or basil and garlic, borrowed from Italian cooking, added to beef stew. *For more about seasoning combinations, refer to "Name That Cuisine!" on this page.*

Culture on Your Plate

Moroccan or Lebanese, Filipino or Thai, Indian or Ethiopian, ethnic fare has captured consumer inter-

NAME THAT CUISINE!

Would you combine tomato with basil, or with cinnamon, or with chile powder? Whatever you choose, the subtle blend of the two ingredients often defines the distinctive flavor of an ethnic cuisine...in this case, Italian, or Middle Eastern, or Mexican.

You may be able to identify many ethnic cuisines by their mix of seasonings. Just for fun...can you match these flavor blends with the ethnic cuisine they're noted for?

1. tomato, olive oil, garlic, and basil	a. India
2. tomato and chile	b. Greece
3. tomato, peanut, and chile	c. Mexico
4. lemon and parsley	d. West Africa
5. olive oil, lemon, and oregano	e. Hungary
6. curry, cumin, ginger, and garlic	f. Italy
7. onion and paprika	g. China
8. soy sauce, rice wine, and ginger	h. Morocco
9. cinnamon, cumin, coriander, ginger, and fruit	i. France
10. thyme, rosemary, sage, marjoram, and tomato	j. Middle East

ANSWERS
1. f 3. d 5. b 7. e 9. h
2. c 4. j 6. a 8. g 10. i

For more about these seasonings, refer to "Quick Reference: Herbs and Spices" on page 353.

est. And many people want to go beyond "ethnic" basics—Italian, Chinese, and Mexican. If you're among them...

TAKE YOUR TASTE BUDS TO THE MEDITERRANEAN

There's no single cuisine for regions that border the Mediterranean Sea. The dishes of Greece, Southern Italy, Spain, Southern France, Tunisia, Lebanon, and Morocco, for example, are all distinctive. Yet they typically contain plenty of grain products, vegetables, legumes, nuts, and fruits; less meat and poultry; and more fish. Their fat is mostly monounsaturated (from olive oil). And yogurt and cheese offer other sources of animal protein.

Traditional Mediterranean eating may have several health benefits—especially for reducing risks of heart disease, and perhaps for some cancers. Studies show that the death rate from heart disease and the incidence of cancer are lower among many Mediterranean populations. And the incidence of these health problems has gone up among people who no longer eat in their traditional way.

The reasons for this are not yet clear to scientists. In general, the total fat intake of the Mediterranean diet isn't lower than the typical American diet. It's just shifted to more monounsaturated fat. Other dietary factors, not fully understood, may offer some protection. But the research evidence isn't conclusive.

Before you switch your eating style, be aware that the benefits of the Mediterranean lifestyle may go well beyond food. Traditionally, the people studied in the region were also more physically active. Body weight and genetics are factors, too. And the overall lifestyle was more relaxed. ✦

Order food that's entirely new to you. *For restaurant tips, refer to "Eating Out Ethnic Style" on page 375.* Ethnic foods and other new food combinations often get introduced first in the restaurant world! If you feel a bit cautious, try an appetizer portion.

Check the ethnic food section of your supermarket, or visit a specialty store. Buy a food you've never had before. In an ethnic food store, you often can get advice on its preparation.

Give yourself an ethnic cookbook, or check one out from a library. Choose at least one new dish—perhaps one with more grains, vegetables, beans, or fruits—to serve to your whole family.

For quick preparation ideas, refer to "Kitchen Nutrition: For Variety, Health, and Eating Pleasure" on page 216.

What's "New"?

Besides more emphasis on nutrition and ethnic foods, other products have appeared on supermarket shelves that weren't there several years ago. All this variety can offer you more ways to eat for health and taste.

➢ ***More convenience.*** You'll find more prepackaged foods. Sometimes called meal kits, speed scratch, or component meals, they provide the ingredients or components that let you serve a "home-prepared" meal in record time. Most require a few food preparation steps or added ingredients on your part—assembly and perhaps heating. The cost? Usually it's higher than starting from scratch yourself. Supermarket take-out food of all kinds is a growing phenomenon, too.

Read the Nutrition Facts on food labels as you choose convenience foods. And choose those that match your nutrition needs.

➢ ***More variety of fruits and vegetables.*** As people have become more health-conscious, produce departments are stocking a greater variety of fruits and vegetables year-round, including more varieties of the same type. For example, an apple isn't just an apple anymore;

it may be a Granny Smith, a Rome Beauty, or a Gala! *For fruits and vegetables that may be new to you, refer to "Garden of Eatin': Uncommon Vegetables," which begins on this page, and "Fresh Ideas: Uncommon Fruit" on page 219.*

Consume your "Five a day" with new varieties of fruits and vegetables.

➢ ***More variety of grains.*** Interest in breads has shifted. You'll find more coarse-textured, denser, whole-grain breads. Breakfast cereals are made with more whole grains—and not just corn, oats, or wheat. And whole-grains of all kinds are used in salads, soups, and mixed dishes. *Refer to "Today's Grains" on page 221.*

Eat at least three servings of whole-grains a day—a choice made easier with so many new whole-grain products to select from.

➢ ***More "fresh."*** Even in ingredient mixes, you'll find more fresh foods—fresh salad mixes, stew and stir-fry mixes, vegetable snacks, and herbs. Mixes for bread-making machines enable consumers to enjoy fresh bread in the morning without any effort. Fresh pasta is sold in refrigerated displays. And the fresh seafood department has become more commonplace. Be aware that fresh foods aren't necessarily more nutritious. *Refer to "Fresh vs. Processed: Either Way to Health" on page 224.*

Enjoy the food variety that fresh products offer for meal and snack choices.

➢ ***More vegetarian entrées.*** With growing interest in vegetarian eating, you'll find more meatless, prepared entrées, such as bean burritos or vegetarian lasagna. There's a greater variety of pasta, vegetables, and legumes (dry, canned and fresh) for home-cooked vegetarian meals, too. *For ways to use legumes and more about vegetarian eating, refer to chapter 22, "The Vegetarian Way."*

Include legumes—perhaps in vegetarian entrées—in your overall eating plan several times a week.

➢ ***More specialty foods.*** As people are getting more sophisticated with food, you'll find more specialty foods, too. And so-called gourmet and unique foods are sold alongside traditional fare.

Enjoy specialty products. But remember, being "gourmet" doesn't make food any better than other foods—you need to read the Nutrition Facts on the food label to find out.

Environmental awareness—with "green" marketing—has come to the supermarket, too. For example, look for food packaging made from recycled materials. Or look for the recycling symbol on plastic containers. *Refer to "The 'Eco' Kitchen" on page 323.*

Garden of Eatin': Uncommon Vegetables

What's your vegetable quotient? Starting on page 217, identify all the vegetables that you've never tried before. Then make a point of buying and trying one or two of them the next time you're in the supermarket or restaurant.

have you ever wondered

...if foods sold in health food stores are more nutritious? The nutritional quality of "health foods" or foods sold in "health food stores" isn't necessarily any better than those sold in traditional supermarkets. In fact, the term "health food" is technically a misnomer. Both supermarkets and health food stores sell nutritious foods that can fit within an overall healthful eating plan.

What's the difference? Perhaps price. Specialty stores may charge more for similar foods. In most health food stores, the overall variety of foods is limited, too. But health food stores may carry foods you won't easily find elsewhere: perhaps amaranth, quinoa, millet, or a wide variety of legumes.

...if buying from bulk food bins offers any advantage? Foods sold in bulk food bins are usually the same foods you find on supermarket shelves...just sold without packaging and brand promotion. So the cost may be less. The ability to buy just the amount you need is often their best advantage. ✦

Kitchen Nutrition: For Variety, Health, and Eating Pleasure!

Look for this multicultural array of foods in your supermarket aisles. Then enjoy these quick-to-fix dishes at home.

Bread, Cereal, Rice, and Pasta	Cuisine*	Serving/ Preparation Ideas	Nutrition Contribution
Couscous (tiny, round pasta)	Moroccan	Serve hot with tomato sauce and Parmesan cheese, or serve cold as a salad with raisins, mandarin oranges, and spices.	Complex carbohydrate, B vitamins
Kasha (buckwheat kernels)	Eastern European	Serve as a hot side dish with chicken or beef. Mix with pasta shapes.	Complex carbohydrate, B vitamins, fiber
Pozole (soup made with fermented corn kernels)	Mexican	Serve warm with diced onion, shredded cabbage, and a lime wedge.	Complex carbohydrate, vitamin C, fiber
Wonton wrappers (thin wheat dough used to wrap spring rolls)	Chinese, Vietnamese	Wrap thin strips of cooked lean barbecued pork or chicken, and shredded cabbage and carrots inside, then steam.	Complex carbohydrate, B vitamins

Vegetable	Cuisine	Serving/ Preparation Ideas	Nutrition Contribution
Jicama	Mexican	Slice in thin strips, and dip into salsa or reduced-fat or fat-free ranch dressing. Use to replace water chestnuts in stir-fry dishes.	Negligible
Collard greens	African-American/ Southern	Boil greens with chopped, smoked turkey, vinegar, and seasonings.	Beta carotene, fiber
Tomatillos	Mexican	Dice, and boil with jalapeño peppers for salsa. Dice, and combine with onions for an omelet.	Vitamin C, beta carotene, potassium, fiber
Shiitake mushrooms	Japanese	Add raw to salads and sandwiches, or toss in stir-fry dishes.	Negligible

Fruit	Cuisine*	Serving/ Preparation Ideas	Nutrition Contribution
Lychee	Chinese	Serve on top of frozen yogurt.	Vitamin C, potassium
Kumquat	Chinese	Pack a few for snacking, or slice for fruit salad.	Vitamin C, beta carotene, folate
Papaya	Mexican, Central American	Blend with pineapple for tropical juices, dice and add to salsas, or simmer in a chutney recipe.	Vitamin C, beta carotene, potassium
Plantain	Puerto Rican, Central American	Cube, and add to stews and soups.	Potassium, complex carbohydrate
Mango	Caribbean	Slice for fruit salads, or simmer in a chutney recipe	Vitamin C, beta carotene, potassium

**Although these foods are identified with these cuisines, they may be used in the dishes of cuisines of other parts of the world, as well.*

➢ *Arugula* (*ah*-ROO-*gu-lah*) is a green, leafy vegetable with a distinctive flavor. It's often used in mixed garden salads. But it also may be cooked and tossed with pasta or risotto.

➢ *Bok choy* (BAHK *choy*) (*also called pak choi*) is one variety of Chinese cabbage. It doesn't form a head, but instead has a bunch of white, bunched stems with thick, green leaves. It can be eaten raw or cooked, and is used often in stir-fry dishes.

Bok Choy

➢ *Breadfruit* looks like a green, bumpy melon (brown when ripe) on the outside, and is creamy-white on the inside. Like other starchy vegetables, it's peeled and prepared in many ways: baked, boiled, fried, grilled, or cooked with stew and soup. Its flavor is somewhat sweet, yet mild. Some dishes from the Caribbean are made with breadfruit.

➢ *Cactus pads* (*nopales, or noh*-PAH-*lays*), which are cactus leaves, are used in a variety of Mexican and Southwest dishes. Their thorns are removed before cooking them. Then they're usually sliced, then simmered or cooked in a microwave oven. You can also buy canned nopales.

Nopales

Kitchen Nutrition (continued)

Meat, Poultry, Fish, Dry Beans, Eggs, and Nuts	Cuisine*	Serving/ Preparation Ideas	Nutrition Contribution
Squid	Mediterranean, Asian	Slice in rings, and broil. Serve with marinara sauce. Or cook in stir-fry dishes.	Protein, iron, B vitamins
Veal, lamb	Mediterranean	Marinate in Italian vinaigrette, then grill.	Protein, iron, B vitamins
Hummus (mashed chickpeas)	Middle Eastern	Serve as a dip for raw vegetables or pita triangles.	Protein, B vitamins, fiber
Chorizo (sausage)	Mexican	Slice in bite-size pieces, add to omelets or stews.	Protein, iron, B vitamins
Tofu	Japanese	Slice for stir-fry dishes, or dice for salads or soups.	Protein, calcium
Black beans	Latin American	Use in place of red beans in chili or soup, mash for homemade refried beans, or mix with rice.	Protein, B vitamins, fiber
Milk, Yogurt, and Cheese	**Cuisine***	**Serving/ Preparation Ideas**	**Nutrition Contribution**
Plain yogurt	Middle Eastern	Top falafel sandwiches (chickpea and vegetable-stuffed pita). Blend with mint as a dip or dressing for cucumbers.	Protein, calcium, riboflavin
Goat milk	Middle Eastern, African (some areas)	Drink goat milk plain. Make a thick drink by mixing with juice. Use it in place of cow milk in baking.	Protein, calcium, riboflavin
Ricotta cheese	Italian	Use in lasagna, or stuffed jumbo pasta shells.	Calcium, protein, riboflavin
Queso blanco (white cheese)	Mexican	Shred, and melt over enchiladas and quesadillas.	Calcium, protein, riboflavin

**Although these foods are identified with these cuisines, they may be used in the dishes of cuisines of other parts of the world, as well.*

Source: National Center for Nutrition and Dietetics/The American Dietetic Association, 1996

➢ *Cassava* (*kah-*SAH-*vah*) (*manioc, or* MA-*nee-ahk; yuca, or* YOO-*kah*), a starchy root vegetable, has a thick, brown peel, but inside it's white or yellow like a potato. It's often cooked in dishes similar to the way potatoes are used.

➢ *Celeriac* (*seh-*LER-*ee-ak*), a member of the celery family, is enjoyed for its root, not its stalks. It has a fibrous, brown, bumpy peel…and a sweet, celery flavor inside. Once peeled, it can be enjoyed raw, perhaps in salads, or cooked—boiled, steamed, or fried. Use it in soups or stews, too, perhaps in place of celery.

➢ *Chard*, actually a white-rooted beet, is grown for its leaves, and creamy-white or red stalks. With its mild yet distinctive flavor, it's used in food preparation much like spinach.

➢ *Chayote* (*cheye-*OH-*tay*) is a pale-green, pear-shaped vegetable with a mild flavor. Baked, boiled, braised, or stuffed, it complements the flavors of other ingredients and flavorings in mixed dishes. It can be used like squash.

➢ *Chicory* (*curly endive*) has a frizzy, green leaf in a loose head of greens. Its bitter flavor adds a nice touch to salads—in small amounts.

➢ *Daikon* (DEYE-*kuhn*) is a Japanese radish, which looks like a smooth, white parsnip. It has a stronger, more bitter flavor than a red radish. Often it's used to make sushi (fish rolled with rice in seaweed) and in vegetable carvings.

➢ *Dasheen* (*dah-*SHEEN) is a large, round root vegetable, with a coarse, brown peel, that's similar to taro. Usually prepared either boiled or baked, dasheen is starchy, somewhat like a potato.

➢ *Escarole* (EHS-*kah-role*) is a somewhat bitter-tasting salad green. Sometimes its green leaves have a reddish tinge. Unlike leaf lettuce, it forms a loose head.

➢ *Fennel* looks somewhat like a squat bunch of celery with feathery leaves. Its flavor is distinctive, like a sweet, delicate anise. The bulb and stalks are often braised, steamed, sautéed, or used in soups. The feathery leaves may be used in salads, as an herb, or as an attractive garnish.

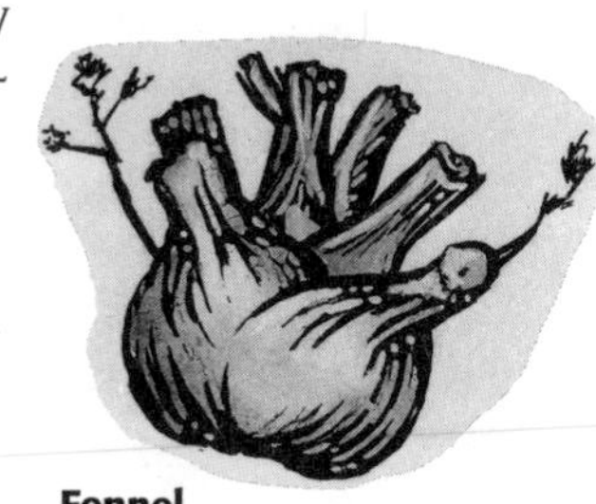
Fennel

➢ *Jerusalem artichoke*—native to North America—has nothing in common with a globe artichoke, except for its name. Like a potato, it's a tuber, grown under the ground. But it is knobby and irregularly shaped, with a sweet flavor and a light brown or purplish-red peel. It's often cooked in its peel, but a little lemon juice in the cooking water keeps peeled Jerusalem artichokes from browning. Use them in dishes that call for potatoes, or eat them raw.

➢ *Jicama* (HEE-*kah-mah*), another root vegetable, is crisp and slightly sweet. It's often peeled, sliced, and eaten raw, perhaps in salads. Or it's cooked in stews and stir-fried dishes.

➢ *Kale* is a leafy vegetable that belongs to the cabbage family, but it doesn't form a head. It has a curly, purple-tinged, green leaf. Use it in salads and in ways that you would cook spinach.

➢ *Kelp* is brown seaweed, often used in Japanese cooking and wrapped around sushi.

➢ *Kohlrabi* (KOLE-*rah-bee*), a member of the cabbage family, looks and tastes somewhat like a turnip. It's light green in color. It can be used in recipes that call for turnips, or sliced and used in stir-fry dishes, or peeled and eaten raw or in salads.

➢ *Leeks* are onions, and look like a bigger, sturdier, flat-leaved version of green onions. Both the bulbs

have you ever wondered

…if food grown in soil that's depleted of minerals or nitrogen is less nutritious? There's no scientific evidence suggesting that crops grown in depleted soil have fewer nutrients than those grown in fertilized soil. When soil lacks minerals or nitrogen, plants don't grow properly and may not produce their potential yield. If soil has the ability to grow crops, the food produced is nutritious. ✦

and leaves are eaten. Bulbs are usually sliced and steamed in soups or baked in casseroles. The leaves are often used in salads. They need to be cleaned well to remove soil that gets between the leaves.

➢ *Lotus root*, which is the root of the water lily, is often peeled, sliced, then cooked—stir fried, steamed, or braised, with mixed Chinese dishes. It has the texture of a potato and a flavor more similar to fresh coconut.

➢ *Plantain* actually belongs to the banana family. But it's longer and thicker, starchier and less sweet. For that reason, it's eaten as a vegetable—always cooked. It can be eaten at any of its three stages: green, yellow, or black, but it's sweetest when it's black. Plantains are cooked in or out of the peel. They may be baked, boiled, or fried, and often are mixed in stews.

➢ *Radicchio* (*rah*-DEE-*chee-oh*) is a small, purplish head of leaves with white ribs. It's somewhat bitter in flavor, and adds a nice touch to salads, or even to pasta and stir-fry dishes.

Radicchio

➢ *Rutabaga* (ROO-*tuh-bay-guh*) is another root vegetable, with a turnip-like flavor and appearance. Use it in any recipe that calls for turnips: stews, soups, and casseroles, for example.

➢ *Seaweed*, used most often in Asian dishes and some Irish, Welsh, and Scottish dishes, includes a variety of types. Kelp may be the most commonly used in the United States. Another seaweed used in many Japanese dishes is nori (NOH-ree).

➢ *Taro* (TAIR-*oh*) is a rough, brown or purplish tuber vegetable that looks much like a yam, although some varieties look different. It has edible leaves, which are called callaloo in the Caribbean. It isn't easily available in the United States. Taro is peeled and usually boiled, baked, or fried, much like potatoes. Hawaiian poi is made from taro.

➢ *Tomatillo* (*tohm-ah*-TEE-*oh*), a member of the tomato family, has a paper-like husk. Under the husk it looks like a small green tomato. It's often used in food like a green tomato, although the flavor is more citrus-like. It is used often in Southwest and Mexican dishes, including salsa and salads.

For more about the nutrients in these foods, refer to "Vegetables: From A to Z" on page 250.

Fresh Ideas: Uncommon Fruit

Rather than reaching for fruit you know already, try something new! Many of these fruits aren't well known in the United States because they grow in tropical or subtropical areas. Fortunately, today's transportation systems are increasing the variety of fruits available from near and far—at all times of the year. Look for these or other unusual fruits in the produce department of your store.

Take another look at common fruits, too, such as apples, plums, and pears. You'll probably find new-to-you varieties.

➢ *Asian pear* looks like a yellow apple—and has a similar firm, crunchy texture. It's sweet and juicy and nice to eat as a whole fruit or mixed in salads.

➢ *Charimoya* (*chair-ih*-MOY-*ah*) (custard apple) has a custard-like consistency and flavor. On the outside, it looks like a little green pineapple without the leaves. The inside has little black seeds. Its flavor can be compared to a mixture of other fruit flavors: strawberry, banana, pineapple, and mango. It's best to eat it as whole fruit; just cut in half, remove the seeds, and scoop out the fruit.

Charimoya

➢ *Fig* is a small, round or oval fruit, which may be yellow, green, or purple. The soft, mild-tasting fruit inside has many edible seeds. It can be enjoyed whole—dried or fresh—or stewed with meat.

➢ *Guava* (GWAH-*vah*) (*guayaba, or gwey*-AH-*bah*) is a sweet, fragrant fruit that's about the size of a lemon. Its peel varies in color, from yellow to purple, and the fruit inside may be yellow, pink, or red. Guavas are eaten as whole fruit, or used in sauces, salads, juices, frozen desserts, and jams.

➢ *Kumquat* (KUHM-*kwaht*), members of the citrus

family, look like small, olive-shaped oranges. Because the peels are very thin, kumquats are eaten with the peel on—either uncooked or cooked with meat, poultry, or fish. When sliced, they're nice as garnishes or in salads.

➢ *Loquat* (LOH-*kwaht*), a small, pear-shaped fruit, is light orange in color on the inside and outside. Somewhat tart, it has a pit which must be removed. Loquats are eaten whole, and often prepared in salads or in cooked poultry dishes.

➢ *Lychee* (LEE-*chee*) (*litchi*), a fruit that's just 1 or 2 inches in diameter, and has a pink to red shell. The inside fruit is white and sweet with a consistency like a grape. Its seed isn't edible. Lychees make a nice snack or dessert just as they are.

➢ *Mango*, a sweet-tart and juicy fruit, ranges in size and shape. It can be anywhere from about 6 ounces to 5 pounds, and it may be round or long. Its inedible peel is orange when ripe, with orange fruit inside and a large seed. The best way to eat a mango is to either peel back the skin and eat it with a spoon...or remove both peel and seed and cut into pieces. Mangos are eaten in fruit salads and may be prepared with cooked meat, poultry, rice, or grain dishes.

➢ *Mangosteen* (MAN-*goh-steen*), small in size, has leathery, brown skin that cannot be eaten. Inside, the soft, white, juicy fruit divides into segments. This fruit is often hard to find.

➢ *Papaya* (*pah*-PEYE-*ah*) (*pawpaw*) may weigh anywhere from 1 to 20 pounds in an elongated, oval shape. Its inedible peel is yellow or orange, with an orange fruit inside and many black seeds. It has a tart, sweet flavor that is delicious as is or mixed in salads.

➢ *Passion fruit* (*granadilla, or gra-nah*-DEE-*yah*) is a small, spherical fruit with a leathery peel, which may appear shriveled. It has a perfumy, sweet-tart flavor. The color varies from light yellow to reddish-purple. It may be eaten as a whole fruit, or added to salad, sauces, desserts, or beverages.

➢ *Persimmon* (*puhr*-SIHM-*uhn*) looks somewhat like an orange-red tomato with a pointy end. If it's ripe, it's sweet. If not, a persimmon is mouth-puckering, bitter, and sour. It may be eaten as whole fruit or used in desserts and baked foods.

➢ *Pomegranate* (PAH-*meh-gran-uht*) is unlike any other fruit. It has a red, leather-like peel; inside, membranes hold clusters of small, edible seeds with juicy, red fruit around the seeds. The flavor is both tart and sweet. Pomegranate seeds are often used in salads and in many cooked dishes.

Pomegranate

➢ *Pomelo* (*pom*-EH-*loh*), a huge citrus fruit, can be as big as a watermelon! But it's more commonly the size of a cantaloupe. In many ways, it looks and tastes like a grapefruit.

➢ *Prickly pear* (*cactus pear*), which is yellow-green to deep yellow, is the fruit of the cactus plant. It has a sweet, mild flavor. It should be peeled and seeded before eating. It may have small hairs or needles in the peel that can be uncomfortable if they get into your skin. The fruit itself is eaten fresh or used in salads, sauces, and other dishes.

➢ *Sapodilla* (*sah-poh*-DEE-*yah*) is a small, egg-shaped fruit that has a rough, brown peel. Only the creamy pulp inside is edible—when it's ripe. The flavor is mild, much like vanilla custard.

➢ *Starfruit* (*carambola, or kar-am*-BOH-*lah*), with its unique shape, form stars when the fruit is sliced. The flavor varies from sweet to tart. It can be eaten as fresh fruit, in salads, or as a garnish.

➢ *Tamarillo* (*tam-uh*-RIH-*yoh*), with its tough but thin peel, is about the size and shape of a small egg. Because it's so tart, it is often sweetened with sugar. Often it is used in baked or cooked foods.

➢ *Ugli* (UH-*glee*) *fruit* is a cross between a tangerine and a grapefruit. It's sectioned on the inside but looks like a small grapefruit on the outside.

Starfruit

➢ *Zapote* (*zah-POH-tay*) (*white sapote*) is a sweet, yellowish fruit, about the size of an orange.

For more about the nutrients in these foods, refer to "What's in the Fruit Bowl?" on page 250.

Today's Grains

Most of today's grains are as old as the hills. Although unfamiliar to many in the United States, some are staple foods that nourish millions of people around the world. Whole grains are good fiber sources, along with B vitamins, vitamin E, and trace minerals, such as copper and zinc. Refined grains are enriched with vitamins and minerals. What's more, all grains are rich in complex carbohydrates and low in fat. The fat they supply is mostly unsaturated. Seeds such as amaranth and wild rice are high in protein and often are used as grain substitutes.

Some grains and seeds are used mainly in distinctive ethnic dishes. And most also are used creatively in nutritious dishes that blend foods of two or more cultures.

➢ *Amaranth* (AM-*ah-ranth*), a seed rather than a true grain, is a protein-rich food. The seeds may be used as a cereal grain.

➢ *Arborio* (*ar-BOH-ree-oh*) *rice*, a plump medium- or long-grain rice, absorbs a lot of liquid. The result is a creamy-textured rice. Often, it's used to make Italian risotto, a rice-based dish; the rice usually is cooked in broth.

➢ *Basmati* (*bahz-MAH-tee*) *rice*, a long-grained rice, has a distinctive nutlike, fruity flavor. It's often used in Asian and Middle-Eastern recipes—and in salads—because it's light and fluffy. Basmati rice may be polished or brown (whole-grain) rice.

➢ *Brown rice* is the whole grain of rice with only the inedible outer husk removed. Any variety of rice—long-, medium-, or short-grain—can be brown rice.

Amaranth

➢ *Buckwheat*, which is a seed, not a grain, often is prepared like rice. The crushed, hulled kernels, called buckwheat groats, most commonly are used in dishes of Russian origin, such as kasha.

➢ *Bulgur*, wheat kernels that have been parboiled, dried, and crushed, has a variety of textures—from coarse to fine. It has a soft but chewy texture that's nice in many grain-based dishes, such as tabouli. Bulgur isn't the same as cracked wheat.

➢ *Glutinous rice*, either black or white, is very sticky because it's high in starch, making it easier to pick up with chopsticks. The grain is either short- or medium-grain. This is the type of rice typically served in Japanese and Chinese restaurants.

➢ *Hominy* (HAH-*mih-nee*) is the dried corn kernel with the hull removed. It's usually soaked in liquid to soften, then cooked, often in stews, casseroles, or other mixed dishes. Note: Although we eat corn as a vegetable, it's really a whole grain.

have you ever *wondered*

...if couscous is a grain? Actually, it's not. Instead couscous is a form of pasta. Traditionally, couscous (made from ground millet) has been the pasta of northern Africa. In the United States, it's made from ground semolina wheat, and often used in salads, mixed with fruit, and used in other grain dishes. Because it's made from wheat, it's a good source of B vitamins.

...what brown rice is? All rice starts as brown rice. Unlike refined white rice, brown rice is a whole grain that still contains the bran, germ, and endosperm parts of the grain. When whole grains of any kind are refined, the bran and germ are removed, taking away fiber and much of the iron, B vitamins, and other nutrients, too. The remaining endosperm has far fewer nutrients, unless it's enriched with B vitamins and iron. Fiber cannot be replaced. *For more about whole grains, refer to "What Is a Whole Grain?" on page* 140. ✦

➢ *Jasmine* (*JAZ-mihn*) *rice*, another fragrant rice, is used in many Asian dishes. But it's equally nice whenever a subtle "sweet" side dish is called for, perhaps with pork or fruit-glazed poultry. A polished rice, it's often sold in specialty stores.

➢ *Millet*, a small, round, yellow grain, is a staple grain in many parts of the world, including Europe, Asia, and northern Africa. It's less commonly used as food for humans in the United States. Bland in flavor, millet is used for mixed dishes, such as pilaf, for cooked cereal, and, when ground into flour, for bread, such as roti from India.

Millet

➢ *Pearl barley* is an ancient, hardy grain, used throughout the world. Pearl barley, with the bran removed, is the more polished and most common form of barley; the vitamins and minerals lost in processing are added back. Whole-grain barley is sold, too. Barley typically is served in soups.

➢ *Quinoa* (*KEEN-wah*), a grain native to South America, cooks much like rice, but faster. Nutritionally, it stands out because it's higher in protein than other grains, and it's a good source of iron and magnesium. The grain itself is small, ivory in color, and bead-shaped. With its bland flavor, quinoa can be used in any dishes that call for rice.

➢ *Triticale* (*trih-tih-KAY-lee*) is a modern grain, developed as a hybrid of both rye and wheat! The result: a nutty-flavored grain with more protein and less gluten than wheat alone. Cooked as a whole berry (not as flour), it is used in grain-based salads, casseroles, and other grain dishes.

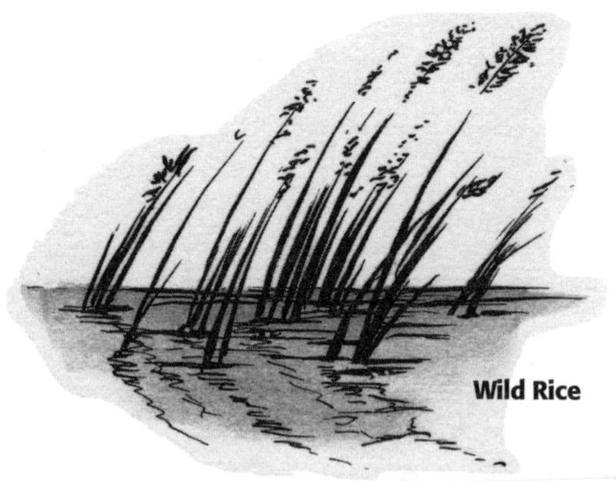

Wild Rice

➢ *Wheat berries* are whole grains that haven't been processed. They're often cooked and used in grain-based dishes. Cracked wheat isn't bulgur but instead is wheat berries that have been crushed. Also look for rye berries in specialty stores.

➢ *Wild rice* isn't a grain, but the seed of a water grass. With its nut-like flavor, often it's used in place of grains, or perhaps mixed with them. As a seed, it's higher in protein and a good fiber source.

To learn how to prepare these grains, refer to "Cooking Grain by Grain" on page 345.

Anytime, Anywhere... Enjoy Variety From the Marketplace

Today's marketplace—supermarkets, food stands, specialty stores, restaurants, delis—offers more food choices than ever before! The benefits are yours. With more food variety, it's easier to choose meals and snacks that match your needs and food preferences.

Anytime, anywhere... explore today's diverse food marketplace. Expand your meal and snack options:

Bring out the flavor, aroma, texture, and color of all kinds of food with seasonings. Try a variety of herbs, spices, flavored vinegars, fruit juices, and chile peppers. *For tips on using seasonings, check "Quick Reference: Herbs and Spices" on page* 353.

Bring out the natural qualities of food with low-fat cooking methods. Brush vegetables with garlic and lemon juice; then grill. Stir-fry lean meat with thinly-sliced vegetables. *For more on low-fat ways to cook, refer to "Fat and Cholesterol Trimmers" on page* 335.

Prepare familiar foods in different ways. For example, prepare rice as paella (cooked with poultry or seafood, vegetables, and saffron), Mexican rice (cooked with tomato, peppers, and onion), risotto (cooked in broth with vegetables), sushi (rolled with cooked fish in seaweed) or as your favorite mixture of rice and beans.

Prepare different foods in familiar ways. Perhaps switch the variety of beans in homemade chili.

Make lasagna with whole-wheat pasta. Prepare fruit salad with papaya, mango, or prickly pear. Try a new cheese variety in macaroni and cheese. And enjoy mashed sweet potatoes as a side dish.

Explore new varieties of fruits and vegetables. Strive for at least "five-a-day"—new types and all-time favorites. *Look for unfamiliar varieties in "Garden of Eatin': Uncommon Vegetables" on page 215 and "Fresh Ideas: Uncommon Fruits" on page 219.*

Build your personal Pyramid with more foods from grains, including multi-grains. Try pasta, risotto, polenta, gnocchi, basmati rice, and couscous. (Note: polenta is an Italian version of cornmeal mush, and gnocchi is an Italian dumpling.) Enjoy breads by other names: tortilla, bagel, pita, focaccia, naan from India, baguette, cornbread…to name a few. *For more about uncommon grains, refer to "Today's Grains" on page 221.*

Savor "ethnic" flavor: Mediterranean tabouli (bulgur salad) or cucumber-yogurt dip, Japanese sukiyaki (stir-fried meat and vegetables) with udon noodles, Brazilian black bean soup, or vegetarian curries from India.

Explore America's regional foods, too: perhaps Louisiana's Cajun-style chicken, Southern black-eyed peas and rice, Northwest fresh berry cobbler, or East Coast fish chowder.

Enjoy the growing array of today's new products, such as "fat-free," "fiber-rich," and "calcium-fortified" foods. Many are varieties of your all-time favorites. They simply have fewer calories…or less fat, saturated fat, cholesterol, sodium, or sugars…or perhaps more fiber, calcium, or other nutrients. *To learn what these nutrition descriptions mean, refer to "The Language of Labels" on page 271. You'll also find Label Lingo in chapters 2 through 7.*

For all kinds of foods, check the Nutrition Facts on food labels! You'll discover nutrition information to make wise choices throughout the store. *Refer to "Get All the Facts!" on page 271.* Food labels aren't the only place to find nutrition information. Check menus in quickservice restaurants. And look for recipes with nutrition facts in magazines, newspapers, and cookbooks.

Ensuring Your Food Supply

The United States' food supply offers a wide variety of food to a diverse population. With today's technology, food is safe and plentiful. Variety is no longer just for people who live in cities. "Fresh" is more than seasonal. Compared with other nations, food is often less expensive. Even though food safety remains a consumer concern, strict regulations safeguard the food supply and minimize potential health risks.

Modern methods of agriculture, food processing, biotechnology, and transportation systems work together to make food available for you. Hunger is still a serious problem in the United States. But an excess amount of food may be at the root of many nutrition-related health problems.

Processing—Making Food Available

Throughout much of recorded history, people have processed foods to make them edible and to preserve them for times of scarcity. At opposite sides of the world 10,000 years ago, both native Americans and ancient Egyptians ground grain into meal. In Europe and other parts of the world 8,000 years ago, foods were smoked and dried. In the Middle East, cheesemaking developed 4,500 years ago as a way to store milk. And about 2,500 years ago, Europeans mastered skills needed to salt foods for preservation.

Modern methods of processing began in the 1800s with canning. With canning, perishable food finally had a longer shelf life, so people could eat a variety of fruits and vegetables throughout the year. During the 19th century, pasteurization—a process of heating milk or other liquids to kill disease-causing bacteria—was developed. Today foods are still pasteurized, or perhaps ultra-pasteurized at higher temperatures, to keep food safe and extend shelf life. In the early 20th century, technology allowed for frozen foods. And in the 1960s, freeze-dried foods were developed as lightweight food for the space program. Today these foods are popular with backpackers and cyclists.

What are today's breakthroughs in food processing? Many relate to nutrition—for example, reducing or eliminating fat without losing flavor or texture...changing the ratio of saturated to unsaturated fats...or adding fiber to bread while keeping its texture light. *Refer to* "Nutrition Sells!" *on page* 210.

Food processing continues to provide more variety of foods—with more for you to choose from. Some have more nutrients than others. It's up to you to read food labels to choose what's right for you. *Refer to "Supermarket Smarts," chapter 12, for tips on reading food labels and choosing processed foods from every aisle in the supermarket.*

Fresh vs. Processed: Either Way to Health
The flavor of fresh produce is hard to beat. Freshly picked, handled properly, and eaten right away, it's certainly a nutritious part of any meal or snack. For consumers looking for convenience, the frozen and canned counterparts offer another option. And they're usually just as nutritious as fresh—sometimes even more so.

The moment you pick a fruit or vegetable, or catch a fish, or milk a cow, the food starts to change in texture, taste, perhaps color, and nutrient content. That's why food producers usually process food as quickly as possible, while nutrient content and overall quality are at their peak. By processing food immediately, these qualities are locked into food. For example, canneries on board many fishing vessels allow for the immediate processing of seafood. And tomatoes are processed and packed just yards away from the fields.

As long as processed foods are handled properly—from the food manufacturer to the supermarket to your home—there's little nutrient loss. Freezing, drying, and canning maintain the nutritional quality of foods.

The processing method called fortification increases the nutritional value of food by adding nutrients, such as vitamins or minerals, not present naturally. Milk, for example, is fortified with vitamin D.

The nutritional quality of fresh fruit and vegetables depends on the care they receive after harvest. Handled improperly or stored too long, they may not be quite as nutritious as their processed counterparts.

Whether food is fresh or processed, it's up to you to minimize nutrient loss in your kitchen. Store, prepare, and handle food with care. *Refer to* "Kitchen Nutrition: Simple Ways to Keep Vitamins in Food" *on page* 88.

Irradiated Foods: Safe to Eat?
Like canning and freezing, irradiation is a food processing method that enhances an already safe food supply. It extends the shelf life of food, helping to retain its quality and safety longer.

Because it destroys disease-causing bacteria, irradiation can be compared to pasteurization. Poultry is irradiated to control salmonella, a bacteria that can cause foodborne illness; pork, to control the trichina parasite. The process also slows ripening and retards sprouting, for example, in potatoes.

Irradiation destroys bacteria, mold, fungi, and insects by passing food through a field of radiant energy, much like sunlight passes through a window or like microwaves pass through food. It leaves no

have you ever *wondered*

...why boxed fluid milk is sold on the grocery shelf, not the dairy case? Aseptic packaging, a relatively new food processing method in the United States, allows fluid milk to be stored on the shelf at room temperature for up to a year without preservatives. Sterilization is the key to preventing spoilage. Food is first heated quickly (3 to 15 seconds) to ultra-high temperatures to kill bacteria. Then it's packaged in a sterilized container, such as a box, within a sterile surrounding. This process of flash heating minimizes loss of nutrients, texture, color, and flavor—and extends shelf life. Besides milk, look for many other grocery items sold in aseptic packaging: for example, soup, tofu, liquid eggs, tomatoes, soy drinks, juice and juice drinks, syrup, nondairy creamers, and wine. ✦

residue. A small number of new compounds are formed when food is irradiated, just as new compounds are formed when food is exposed to heat. These changes are the same as those caused by cooking, steaming, roasting, pasteurization, freezing, and other forms of food preparation.

Irradiated foods retain their nutrient value. Like freezing, canning, drying, and pasteurization, irradiation results in minimal nutrient loss. The amount lost is often too insignificant to measure.

Irradiation can't take the place of good food handling practices—nor improve the quality of food. As a consumer, you still need to store, prepare, and cook food in clean, safe ways to avoid foodborne illness.

What's the advantage of irradiation? Agricultural losses, caused by insects or spoilage, can be cut dramatically. A longer shelf life can mean less food waste in your kitchen. And irradiation is another way to control disease-causing parasites.

Like other processing methods, irradiation is regulated and approved by the Food and Drug Administration (FDA). The level of radiant energy used in the United States is the most restrictive in the world. By law, whole foods that have been irradiated must be labeled on the package. Look for the symbol and the phrase "Treated by Irradiation" or "Treated with Radiation." Irradiated ingredients in prepared, deli, or restaurant foods usually aren't labeled.

As a way to control foodborne illness, irradiation was approved in 1997 by the FDA for fresh and frozen meats, including beef, pork, and lamb. The process protects these foods from contamination by Escherichia coli 0157:H7 and salmonella, two disease-causing bacteria. Irradiation does not compromise the nutritional quality of meat. *For more about foodborne illness, refer to page* 303. Research continues to evaluate irradiation as part of the overall system of ensuring food safety.

Additives: Safe at the Plate

Do you ever consider that most peanut butters don't separate? That products made from prepared baking mixes rise in the oven? That ice cream is smooth and creamy? And that breakfast cereal has been fortified with many vitamins you need for health? Probably not. Most likely, you take many desirable qualities of food for granted. Even if you do, you may not attribute these qualities to food additives. Food additives are any substances added

CANNED FOOD: UNCANNY SAFETY IN THE PACKAGE

More than 1,500 varieties of canned foods are sold on today's supermarket shelves: traditional fare, along with a variety of nutritionally-positioned products, for example, sodium-free, low-fat, no-added-sugar, and others. Besides their nutritional contribution, what are some benefits of canned foods?

➢ ***Long shelf life.*** Canned food remains safe as long as the container remains intact. Although most canned foods are coded with "use-by" dates, you're wise to rotate them. Change your supply of canned products at least every other year.

➢ ***Tamper resistance.*** Cans are very tamper resistant. Any opening of the package is clearly evident. Rust spots on the outer surface or dents don't affect the contents of the can, as long as the can doesn't bulge or leak.

➢ ***Food safety.*** Food is heated to destroy bacteria and then sealed in cans within hours of harvesting. For maximum flavor and nutritional value from canned foods, use the product immediately after opening it. Handle any leftover as a perishable food—stored in the refrigerator to retain taste and nutritional quality. ✦

to food for specific purposes such as these.

Adding substances to food for preservation, flavor, or appearance isn't a modern invention, but instead a centuries-old practice. Before refrigeration, meat, fish, and poultry were preserved with salt; vegetables were pickled in vinegar; and sugar was added to cut fruit to prevent spoilage. Ancient Egyptians used food colorings, and Romans used sulfites to help preserve wine. The spice trade between Asia, the Middle East, and Europe flourished because the public demanded the flavors that spices added to food.

Today, about 2,800 substances are used as food additives. Sugar, salt, and corn syrup are among the most frequently used additives. Very small amounts of other substances also may pass unintentionally into food during production, processing, distribution, or storage. One example is the small amount of packaging material that may come from the food container. These are called incidental additives. Both intentional and incidental additives are subject to government safety regulations.

What do they do? Food additives serve a number of functions, giving you a wide variety of wholesome, convenient, and attractive foods to choose from. Many offer qualities that you've probably come to expect. Additives are used in food for these reasons: nutritional value, freshness and safety, food preparation and processing, and flavor and appeal. All additives are listed by name in the ingredient list on food labels.

For Nutritional Value...
Vitamins and minerals, as well as fiber, are added to many foods to make them more nutritious. Until the last 75 years or so, nutritional deficiency diseases, such as goiter, rickets, scurvy, and pellagra, were relatively common. Adding nutrients to food has almost eliminated many of these health problems in the United States. Today, nutrients and fiber often are added to help protect against health problems.

➢ Some foods are enriched with nutrients that are lost in processing. "Enriched" means that nutrients are added back to foods. Bread, flour, and rice, for example, are all enriched with B vitamins and iron.

➢ Some other foods are fortified with nutrients often lacking in a consumer's typical eating plan. "Fortified" means adding nutrients not present before processing: for example, iodine in salt, vitamin A and D in milk, folic acid in some grain products, and calcium in some orange juice. Since the 1920s, salt has been fortified with iodine in the United States, eliminating goiter as a public health problem.

What nutrients are added? Check the food label to find out. Any nutrient added to food shows up in two places on a food label: (1) ingredient list, where the additive (nutrient) itself is listed, and (2) nutrition information on the Nutrition Facts panel, telling the total amount of that nutrient in a single serving of that food. If it's a vitamin or mineral, it's listed as % Daily Value. *Refer to "Get All the Facts!" on page* 271.

What foods have additives to improve or maintain nutritional value? Nutrients as additives... in beverages, bread, cereal, flour, margarine, milk, pasta, rice, and salt, among others.

For Freshness and Safety...
Air, bacteria, fungi, mold, and yeast all promote food spoilage. Some additives, called preservatives, slow the process of spoilage and help maintain the appeal and wholesome qualities of food. For example:

➢ ***Tocopherols* (*vitamin* E), BHA, *and* BHT** help keep vegetable oils and salad dressing from becoming rancid. Working as antioxidants, they help protect nutrients that are naturally present in foods: essential fatty acids (linoleic

have you ever wondered

...if a breakfast cereal fortified with 100% *Daily Value for nutrients is always your best choice?* It's certainly one choice. But you may not need "100%" if you're already get enough variety and balance in your day's food choices. Breakfast cereals fortified at a lower level may offer enough nutrition for you. ✦

and linolenic acids) and fat-soluble vitamins (A, D, E, and K). Studies have verified the safety of BHA and BHT as food additives; they are GRAS substances, or "generally recognized as safe."

➢ ***Citric acid,*** a natural component of citrus fruits, also works as an antioxidant, helping food keep its color. When you sprinkle sliced apples with lemon juice, you're doing the same thing—keeping fruit from turning brown.

➢ ***Sulfites*** help prevent color and flavor changes in dried fruits and vegetables. They're used to inhibit bacterial growth in wine and other fermented products. Some baked foods, snack foods, and condiments also may contain sulfites. Most people have no adverse reactions to sulfites. But packaged and processed foods containing sulfites are labeled for the small percentage of the population that is sulfite-sensitive. *For more on sulfites, refer to* "For the Sulfite-Sensitive..." *on page* 199.

➢ ***Calcium propionate,*** produced naturally in Swiss cheese, is a preservative that keeps bread and other baked foods from getting moldy.

➢ ***Sodium nitrite,*** used as a preservative in processed meats, such as ham, hot dogs, and lunch meat, keeps the meat safe from botulism bacteria. It also adds to the flavor and pink color. *For more on botulism, refer to* "Bacteria: Hard Hitters" *on page* 305.

➢ ***Several food additives work as antioxidants to preserve food***—among them, ascorbic acid (vitamin C), citric acid, tocopherols (vitamin E), BHA and BHT, and sulfites. They protect food from chemical changes caused by contact with oxygen.

What foods have additives for freshness?

➢ ***Antimicrobials*** (to prevent spoilage)... in baked foods, beverages, bread, cheese, cured meats, fruit juice, fruit products, margarine, pie filling, table syrup, and wine, among others.

➢ ***Antioxidants*** (to prevent rancidity or discoloration)... in baked goods, cereals, fats, oils, processed foods, and salad dressings, among others.

For Food Preparation or Processing...
From helping bread rise...to keeping chocolate suspended in chocolate milk...to keeping seasoning blends from clumping, food additives fulfill a wide variety of tasks in food production. Without them, food manufacturers couldn't achieve many food qualities that consumers want.

➢ ***Emulsifiers*** are mixers that keep ingredients and flavorings blended. For example, they're used to keep the oil, vinegar, and seasonings in salad dressings from separating. In peanut butter, emulsifiers keep the peanuts and oil from separating. Even in baked foods, they help keep the dough uniform. Some emulsifiers come from food itself: for example, lecithin from milk and egg yolks, and mono- and diglycerides from vegetables and beef tallow.

➢ ***Anti-caking agents*** keep seasonings, baking powder, confectioners' sugar, table salt, and other powdered or granular products flowing freely. Because they keep food from absorbing moisture, it won't lump together. Calcium silicate and silicon dioxide are two anti-caking agents.

did you know

...it takes 4,400 *pounds of cocoa beans to get less than an ounce of cocoa oil?* It's no surprise, then, that synthetic flavors are more economical than natural flavors. And they can provide a stronger taste that many people prefer.

...bacon contains less nitrite today than it did a decade ago? Nitrite in some processed meats helps preserve color and prevent spoilage. Sodium nitrate, for example, inhibits the growth of *botulinum* bacteria that produce a potentially deadly poison. *For more about botulinum, refer to* "Bacteria: Hard Hitters" *on page* 301. ✦

➢ ***Humectants,*** such as glycerine or sorbitol, help foods keep their moisture and soft texture. Shredded coconut stays moist and marshmallows stay soft because a humectant is added.

➢ ***Leavening agents*** help create the light texture of waffles, bread, muffins, and other baked goods. Baking sodium (sodium bicarbonate) and baking powder (sodium bicarbonate and acid salts), as well as yeast, produce carbon dioxide that makes dough rise. Without them, the texture would be compact and heavy.

➢ ***pH control agents*** influence the texture, taste, and safety of foods by adjusting their acidity or alkalinity. Adding acids, such as lactic acid or citric acid, gives a tart taste to frozen desserts and beverages. It also inhibits the growth of bacteria in low-acid processed foods, such as beets, and helps prevent discoloration and rancidity. Alkalizers neutralize acids in foods such as chocolate so that the flavor is more mild.

➢ ***Thickeners and stabilizers*** give food a uniform texture. In ice cream, they keep the texture smooth without forming ice crystals. In chocolate milk, they allow the chocolate particles to stay in suspension. With stabilizers, oils that add flavor to food also stay in food. Carbohydrates in food—such as gelatin from animal bones and pectin from fruit—commonly are used as thickeners and stabilizers.

➢ ***Maturing and bleaching agents*** improve the baking qualities of foods made with wheat flour and improve the appearance of certain cheeses. When the yellow pigment of wheat flour is bleached, the dough becomes more elastic and the baking results, better. The white curd in some cheese, such as gorgonzola and blue cheese, is the result of adding a bleaching agent to milk.

What foods have additives to aid food processing or preparation?

➢ ***Emulsifiers*** (to distribute particles evenly)... in baked foods, bread, breakfast cereal, chocolate, chocolate milk, cocoa, frozen desserts, margarine, mayonnaise, nut butter, pie and pudding mixes, and salad dressings, among others.

➢ ***Stabilizers, thickeners, and texturizers*** (for smooth, thick, uniform texture)... in baked goods, beverages, candy, cream cheese, frozen desserts, jam, jelly, pie filling, pudding, salad dressings, sauces, soups, among others.

➢ ***Leaveners*** (to help food rise)... in baked goods, such as bread, cake, freezer waffles, and muffins, among others.

➢ ***pH control agents*** (to control pH levels)... in baked goods, candy, chocolate, gelatin desserts, processed cheese, salad dressings, sauces, soft drinks, and vegetable oils, among others.

➢ ***Humectants*** (to retain moisture)... in candy, shredded coconut, gum, and marshmallows, among others.

➢ ***Maturing and bleaching agents*** (to improve baking quality)... in bread, cereal, some cheese, flour, and instant potatoes, among others.

➢ ***Anti-caking agents*** (to prevent lumping)... in baking powder, powdered foods, and salt, among others.

For Flavor and Appeal...

Some additives add adventure to eating. They may add color, provide flavor or enhance it, or sweeten food.

➢ ***Colorings*** won't affect the nutrients, safety, or taste of food. But they make a nutritional contribution when they make food look more appealing to eat. Cheese and margarine often get their yellow coloring from annatto, which comes from the tropical annatto tree. Ice cream and many baked foods also are among the many foods with added coloring.

Food colors may be added to food for many reasons: to restore the original color; to ensure a uniform color; to help protect flavor and light-sensitive vitamins, which may be destroyed during storage; to give an attractive appearance to foods; to help you identify it; and to help you visually recognize food quality.

Thirty-three colors are approved for use in food, but only seven are synthetic. More and more natural pigments from vegetables are being used to color food. For example, look for foods colored with beet juice, paprika, carrot oil, or saffron. Only one food coloring is known to cause allergic reactions in rare cases: Yellow No. 5. *Refer to* "*Coloring by Any Other Name!*" *on page* 201 *for more about it.*

➢ ***Flavorings,*** which may be natural or synthetic, make up about 1,700 of the additives approved for use in food. They include spices, herbs, extracts, salt, caffeine, and other seasonings. To make artificial flavorings, food scientists carefully study the make-up of natural flavors, then approximate the complexity of the natural flavor. Natural flavors come from food itself after a minimum amount of processing. They're often taken from one food and added to another to enhance the flavors. The chemical structure of natural and artificial flavors is similar—although artificial flavors may not have all the complex elements that give a distinctive natural taste.

➢ ***Flavor enhancers*** don't add flavor of their own. Instead they heighten natural flavors already present in food. The best-known flavor enhancer is monosodium glutamate (MSG). MSG comes from a common amino acid, which is a protein called glutamic acid. MSG comes mostly from vegetable proteins. *For more about* MSG, *refer to* "MSG—*Sensitive?*" *on page* 200.

➢ ***Sweeteners*** are flavorings, but they're grouped separately from the others. Some, such as sucrose (table sugar), fructose, dextrose, and mannitol, are nutritive, which means they produce energy in your body. Besides adding a sweet flavor, these sugars add mouth feel and work as browning agents in food. And they may be used as a preservative. Intense, or non-nutritive, sweeteners such as saccharin and aspartame don't contribute energy. *For more about sugars and other sweeteners, refer to chapter* 5, "*Sweet Talk: Sugar and Other Sweeteners.*"

What foods have additives to increase food appeal?

➢ ***Colorings...***in baked goods, candy, cheese, gelatin mixes, ice cream, jam, jelly, margarine, pie and pudding fillings, among others.

➢ ***Flavorings...***in baked goods, candy, gelatin, pie filling, pudding, salad dressing mix, sauces, and soft drinks, among others.

No Surprises

Additives in food are no secret to consumers. Just by reading the ingredient lists on food labels, you can identify specific additives in any food.

Emulsifier to keep ingredients blended

Flavoring to add sweetness

INGREDIENTS: CRUST: WHEAT FLOUR WITH MALTED BARLEY FLOUR, WATER, PARTIALLY HYDROGENATED VEGETABLE OIL (SOYBEAN AND/OR COTTONSEED OIL) WITH SOY LECITHIN, ARTIFICIAL FLAVOR AND ARTIFICIAL COLOR (BETA CAROTENE), SOYBEAN OIL, YEAST, HIGH FRUCTOSE CORN SYRUP, SALT, CALCIUM PROPIONATE ADDED TO RETARD SPOILAGE OF CRUST, L-CYSTEINE MONOHYDROCHLORIDE; **SAUCE:** TOMATO PUREE (WATER, TOMATO PASTE), WATER, GREEN PEPPERS, SALT, LACTOSE AND FLAVORING, SPICES, FOOD STARCH - MODIFIED, SUGAR, CORN OIL, XANTHAN GUM, GARLIC POWDER. **TOPPING:** LOW MOISTURE PART SKIM MOZZARELLA CHEESE (PASTEURIZED MILK, CHEESE CULTURES, SALT, ENZYMES.)

Preservative to retard spoilage

Thickener to give a uniform texture

➢ ***Flavor enhancers...***in canned vegetables, gravy, processed meats, sauce mixes, and soups, among others.

➢ ***Sweeteners...***baked foods, canned and frozen fruit, frozen desserts, fruit yogurt, fruit-juice drinks, gelatin mixes, jam, jelly, pudding mixes, and soft drinks, among others.

As a reference for specific additives, refer to "A Close-Up Look at Additives" *on page* 611.

Testing, Testing

Did you know that new additives must pass rigid safety tests before they can be used? During the past 75 years, the use of food additives has allowed a more varied and plentiful food supply. And beginning in 1938, government regulations have helped guide and ensure the safety of their use in food.

Today food additives are regulated more tightly than at any other time in history—with safety as the primary goal. In 1958, the federal government passed the Food Additives Amendment. The amendment gave the Food and Drug Administration responsibility for approving additives used in food. The FDA sets safety standards, determining whether a substance is safe for its intended use. If it's found to be safe, the FDA decides what types of foods the additive may be used in, in what amounts, and how it must be indicated on a food label.

Federal food laws distinguish among additives: those generally recognized as safe (GRAS), prior-approved additives, regulated additives, and color additives.

***Generally recognized as safe* (GRAS).** In 1959, the FDA established a list of 700 additives that were exempted from the regulatory process. This list—called the GRAS list—recognized that many additives had an extensive history or existing scientific evidence of their safe use in food. Additives that appear on the list include salt, sugar, spices, and vitamins.

From time to time, GRAS substances may be reevaluated, and perhaps removed or reclassified. Sulfites are an example. In 1986 FDA revoked their GRAS status for use on raw fruits or vegetables, except for potatoes. That occurred because research showed that some people are sensitive to sulfites. *For more about sulfite sensitivity, refer to "For the Sulfite-Sensitive..." on page 199.*

Prior-approved substances. Before the 1958 Food Additives Amendment, some additives—such as nitrites used to preserve processed meat—had been approved by the FDA or the U.S. Department of Agriculture. If used as originally approved, these substances didn't need to go through the approval process again; the government already had judged them as safe.

As with the GRAS list, prior-approved substances are continually monitored. Current scientific evidence of their link to health is always reviewed, recognizing that the statutes of prior-approved substances can be changed.

Regulated additives. Any additive not considered as GRAS or prior-approved must be approved before it can be marketed and used in food. The burden of proof for additive safety falls on the manufacturer. These are the regulatory steps that the food industry follows:

have you ever *wondered*

...if food additives are OK *for everyone?* Except for a small number of reactions that occur in people with specific allergies, food additives are "safe at the plate." In fact, one of the primary uses of additives is protecting food quality and safety. For someone with a sensitivity to any additive, the reaction should be about the same whether the additive is natural or synthetic. The chemical make-up is quite similar. *For specifics on those rare cases of allergic responses, refer to "Sensitive to Additives? Maybe, Maybe Not" on page 199.*

...if people with gluten intolerance should avoid certain additives? Yes, they need to read food labels carefully. Some food additives contain gliadin, the substance that people with gluten intolerance cannot handle. *Refer to "Gluten Intolerance...Often a Lifelong Condition" on page 197.* ✦

➢ First, the additive manufacturer must prove that the additive is effective—that the additive does what it is supposed to do, and that it can be detected and measured when put into a food.

➢ Second, the manufacturer must prove that large amounts of the food additive, when given to two kinds of test animals over an extended period of time, won't cause cancer, birth defects, or other problems. Results of human studies also may be submitted.

➢ After testing, you can have your input. The FDA reviews the results, then invites public response to the manufacturer's petition for the new additive.

➢ If approval is given, the FDA establishes regulations for the types of food in which the additive can be used, the maximum amount, and how the substance must be described on the label.

When the food industry proposes an additive for use in meat or poultry products, another approval also is required—this time from the U.S. Department of Agriculture's Food Safety and Inspection Service (FSIS). FSIS applies different standards that consider the unique characteristics of meat and poultry. For example, FSIS doesn't allow the use of sorbic acid, which is an approved additive, in meat salads because it could mask spoilage.

Color additives. In 1960, the government passed another law—the Color Additive Amendments. The amendments required that dyes used in foods, drugs, cosmetics, and medical devices needed testing, similar to tests for regulated food additives. Before the law, nearly 200 colors were used in foods. After the required testing, only 33 of them are approved for use today. Many have been withdrawn from the market.

Safety Check

Approval of additives, including those on the GRAS and prior-sanctioned lists, doesn't guarantee that they'll be used in food forever. The FDA continues to review all categories of food additives. And it judges them by the latest scientific standards. Based on new evidence, approval is either maintained or withdrawn.

As another safety check, the Food Additive Amendment also has a section called the Delaney Clause. The clause states that no additive known to cause cancer in animals or humans can be put in food in any amount. One artificial sweetener called cyclamate was removed from the GRAS list for that reason. Tests showed that large amounts were linked to cancer in test animals. The safety of cyclamate is currently being re-evaluated; it is approved for use in some other countries.

In order to monitor and investigate complaints of adverse reactions to additives, the FDA also maintains the Adverse Reaction Monitoring System (ARMS). The computerized system records updated safety data. Incidences of allergic reactions to food and color additives and to dietary supplements, reported by individuals or their doctors, are recorded, too. These reports help determine whether further investigation is warranted—and if action is required to maintain public health. *For more about adverse reactions to food additives, refer to "Sensitive to Additives? Maybe, Maybe Not" on page* 199.

Additives—Your Choice

With such a wide variety of foods available, consumers have considerable choice about food additives. If you have a history of food-related allergies, you may choose to limit or avoid foods with ingredients that you're sensitive to. If you have a food reaction and think it may be additive-related, talk to your doctor. *If you choose or need to limit certain food additives, learn to read the ingredient lists on food labels.* *Refer to "A Word About Ingredients..." on page* 273.

Pesticides: Carefully Controlled

The vast array of safe, nutritious food available in your supermarket throughout the year doesn't happen by chance. Successful growers carefully manage their croplands and orchards, ensuring an ongoing supply of high-quality fruits and vegetables for you and your family.

In order to produce high-quality produce with adequate yields, most farmers use some pesticides—either in the field or grove, or just after harvest to prevent mold or insect damage during transport or storage.

Without prudent use of pesticides, many farmers couldn't control crop damage from disease, insects, molds and fungi, weeds, and other pests. And their crop yields would be much lower. In spite of pesticide use, U.S. farmers annually lose a significant amount of crops because of damage from pests. That number would be far higher without careful use of pesticides.

About Pesticides...

Pesticides include a broad range of chemicals—including herbicides, fungicides, insecticides, and disinfectants—that protect crops (plants, vegetables, and fruits). They're applied by dusting, fogging, spraying, or injecting them into the soil.

- Herbicides control weeds.
- Fungicides control mold and fungi that cause plant disease, and inhibit molds that may be harmful to consumers.
- Insecticides control harmful insects, often those that damage crops or carry plant disease.
- Disinfectants act against bacteria and other disease-carrying microorganisms.

When people think of pesticides, synthetic chemicals often come to mind. However, naturally-occurring chemicals in the environment, such as copper, nicotine, and sulfur, are also used to control pests. And many plants protect themselves by producing their own pesticides in low levels.

IPM—Best of Both Worlds

What does sex have to do with pest control? Interestingly, sex scents, called pheromones, can confuse pest mating patterns, allowing farmers to use less chemical pesticides. It's all part of a biological system of pest control.

IPM stands for integrated pest management—a new farming approach that uses pesticides, biological control, and biotechnology—to reduce crop damage. As farmers work in partnership with nature, they apply pesticides on crops selectively, ultimately using less.

IPM incorporates a variety of strategies—not just limited pesticide use—into pest management. For example:

- Crop rotation, for example, switching from soybeans to corn, helps limit pest buildup because insects lose their natural food source.
- Farmers may use living organisms to help control pest diseases, or use pest predators (when "good" bugs eat "bad" bugs).
- Growers may choose plant varieties that are more resistant to pests. Traditional plant breeding and genetic engineering can help crops develop their own natural resistance. *Refer to "Food Biotechnology: The Future Is Today!" on page 235.*
- Computers can help growers forecast disease and weather conditions. The more they know, the more prudent they can be with pesticides.

Safety: Whose Job?

Safety starts with growers; most are prudent with pesticides for many reasons. One is cost. Pesticides are expensive, so farmers use them judiciously to remain profitable. Second, successful growers project toward the future. By using too much pesticide with one year's crop, they may cause crop damage in the future. Some pesticide residues remain in the soil. And third, today's farmers are more aware than ever of the environment (wildlife, ground water, and soil quality)—their livelihood depends on it.

Several government agencies are responsible for regulating and monitoring pesticide safety in food:

- The Environmental Protection Agency (EPA) regulates the manufacture, labeling, and use of pesticides—and sets maximum levels, or tolerances, for pesticide residues. Before a pesticide can be used on crops, it must be thoroughly tested to assure that it's safe for the environment and for human health. If approved, the EPA may limit its use—amount, frequency, or crop—and require that these limitations be listed on the product label. Growers who misuse pesticides, even mistakenly, risk having their crop seized or destroyed. And the grower may be charged with a civil or a criminal lawsuit.

➢ The Food and Drug Administration monitors pesticide residues in most foods—both raw and processed—and enforces the tolerance levels set by the EPA. If residues exceed these levels, the food can be seized or destroyed—and a lawsuit may be filed. Any pesticide residues that remain on raw foods are usually removed during washing or peeling.

➢ Like the FDA, The Food Safety and Inspection Service (FSIS) monitors pesticide residues and enforces tolerance levels for meat, poultry, and eggs.

➢ Several states, including California, which grow many fruits and vegetables, have their own regulations, too.

Tolerances, or maximum levels, for pesticide residues are set in parts per million, parts per billion, and parts per trillion. For example, 1 part per million would mean 1 gram of residue is the maximum allowed in 1,000,000 grams of food. That equates to one cherry in about 20,000 1-pound cans.

Tolerances for pesticide residues are legal limits. Most foods have less. Tolerances are 100 to 1,000 times lower than the amount that might cause an adverse reaction. So there's a very wide margin of safety. FDA testing has shown that foods rarely exceed limits, and many samples are below the tolerance level or show no residues at all. In order to pass through customs, imported foods must meet the same stringent standards set for foods grown domestically. FDA tests show no difference in levels of pesticide residues.

Benefits Versus Risks
The presence of low levels of pesticide residues doesn't signal a risk. Tolerances are legal limits, not medical limits—set far below what is considered safe for the most sensitive part of the population. In fact, the use of pesticides may reduce other risks related to food. For example, fungicides help control aflatoxin B_2, a naturally-occurring toxin in grains and peanuts. Most important, the prudent use of pesticides helps ensure a wide variety of fruits and vegetables, which supply important vitamins, minerals, and dietary fiber for human health.

There's no such thing as a risk-free world. The real issue is weighing the benefits against the risks—then deciding what's right for you.

What You Can Do...
Any pesticide residues in foods you buy are present at minimal levels. It's safe to say that they probably won't pose any risk to your health. You can add more to your safety net by the way you handle food in your kitchen...or the way you grow fruits and vegetables in your own garden:

➢ Choose produce carefully. Avoid fruits and vegetables with cuts, insect holes, mold, or decay.

➢ Wash fresh fruits and vegetables with water to remove residues on the surface. For foods

have you ever *wondered*

...if wax on fruits and vegetables is safe to eat? Yes, it is. There's no need to peel waxed produce. Simply wash it with water. You might use a brush to remove any dirt, bacteria, and pesticide residues. The thin, waxy coating on foods such as cucumbers and apples is applied after picking to help produce maintain its quality. Wax helps by retaining moisture, protecting the food from bruising, and preventing spoilage.

...if you should avoid any specific fruit or vegetable to reduce your exposure to pesticides? No. For any crop, the use of pesticides varies with the time of year, the soil conditions, the climate, and the presence of pests. There's no way you can tell the difference. The best guideline is to wash produce thoroughly, and remove outer leaves on leafy greens—then enjoy the nutritional benefits that all fruits and vegetables provide. ✦

such as carrots, squash, apples, and pears, use a vegetable brush to clean them even more. Avoid soap, unless it's especially meant for produce, because it leaves its own residues.

➢ Remove outer leaves of lettuce, cabbage, and other leafy vegetables.

➢ Although you could peel some fruits and vegetables, recognize what you'd be giving up—the nutrients and fiber that the peel contains.

➢ Eat a variety of foods. Not only do you get the nutritional benefits of food variety, but you also minimize pesticide risks. Different crops require different pesticides, so variety limits exposure to any one type.

➢ If you're a home gardener, minimize your use of pesticides. And follow the directions for their safe use, storage, and disposal. Contact your county extension service if you need guidance. *Refer to "Resources You Can Use!" on page* 595 *to help locate your local extension service.*

Organically Grown

Organically-grown foods aren't sold just in health food stores anymore. You'll likely find them in your supermarket, too. But how do they compare to other foods?

The term "organic," used to describe a certain group of foods, is really a misnomer. All foods come from living organisms—plant and animal. Because they all contain carbon, they're all technically organic. The more accurate terms are "organically grown" or "organically produced." These terms describe how some fresh and processed foods are grown or produced, typically with little or no synthetic fertilizers or pesticides.

Perspective: Organically-Produced Foods
Organic farming offers an alternative to conventional agriculture. With organic methods, insects and crop rotation are often used to control pests that damage crops. Chemicals found naturally in the environment, such as sulfur, nicotine, copper, and pyrethrins, may be used as pesticides instead. Manure, compost, and other organic wastes are used for fertilizers. Livestock and poultry are raised without antibiotics or hormones.

Despite the claims, no scientific evidence shows that organically-produced foods are any healthier or safer for you. Either approach—organic or conventional farming—can supply nutritious foods. And while well intended, organic farming alone can't produce enough food for large populations.

From a nutrition standpoint, foods produced organically and conventionally are about the same. Plants, for example, can't distinguish synthetic from organic fertilizers. Both types of fertilizer break down in the soil to nurture growing plants. Climate and soil conditions, genetic differences, maturity at harvest, and the way food is handled—not the type of fertilizer—all can affect the nutrient content of raw foods.

Organically-grown foods may or may not be pesticide-free. Organic farmers may use both natural pesticides and insects to prevent crop damage. Certain insects, for example, might be used as natural predators for some insects that cause crop damage. On a large-scale basis, the food supply may be inadequate if only organic methods for pest control are used. With conventional farming, pesticide levels are set low, so they're not harmful to health. *Refer to "Pesticides: Carefully Controlled" on page* 231.

How does the taste compare? Studies don't show any significant flavor difference between

have you ever *wondered*?

...if antibiotics used in agriculture affect human health? Antibiotics are used in animal agriculture to prevent or cure diseases in animals. With 30 years of study, no link has been identified between antibiotics given to livestock or poultry and effects on human health. FDA regulations ensure that any residues are minimal and very safe—and research shows no special reaction among humans. Like other proteins, any residue is broken down during human digestion of the food. ✦

organically-grown and conventionally-grown foods. Instead, the variety of food, its growing conditions, and its maturity at harvest time may account for any taste differences that consumers perceive.

Organically-produced foods often cost more. That's usually due to higher production costs (more labor, transportation, processing, retailing), more crop losses, and smaller yields. In the future, costs may go down. Many farmers who choose organic farming methods now are developing techniques, yields, and systems that are more cost-efficient.

Coming to Terms

What do "organically-grown" or "organically-produced" mean? Effective in 1998 under the Organic Foods Production Act, federal regulations require consistent standards. Under the law, any food sold as "organically-grown" or "organically-produced"—produce, meat, dairy products, bakery, and processed foods—must be certified by the U.S. Department of Agriculture. The law requires that an organically-produced food must have a least 50 percent of its ingredients produced organically. Processed foods must be at least 95 percent organically produced. In addition, the food can't contain any nitrates, nitrites, or sulfites.

Food Biotechnology: The Future Is Today!

If you peek into a supermarket of the 21st century, you might find an intriguing array of products: foods that taste fresher and more flavorful, more nutritious varieties of foods you already eat, and a greater variety of produce all year long. All these products will result from today's food biotechnology.

Where did biotechnology begin? For centuries, farmers raised animals and grew plants to produce food with desirable traits: higher yields, new food varieties, better taste, faster ripening, and more resistance to drought. Five thousand years ago in Peru, potatoes were grown selectively. In ancient Egypt—4,500 years ago—domesticated geese were fed to make them bigger and tastier. About 2,300 years ago, Greeks grafted trees, a technique that led to orchards and a more abundant fruit supply. In fact, products as commonplace as grapefruit or wine could be described as coming from traditional biotechnology.

Over the years, farmers have replanted seeds or cross-pollinated from their best crops. And they've bred new livestock from their best animals. For example, within the past few decades, hogs have been bred to be leaner, in turn producing lean cuts of pork for today's consumers. *Refer to "Today's Meat" on page* 236.

With traditional breeding, farmers change the genetic makeup by selecting plants and animals with desirable traits. They then raise them and select again and again until a new, more desirable breed or food variety gets established. Even in the "old days," all of this breeding required genetic change.

Traditional breeding takes time. Often it's unpredictable. Each time one plant pollinates another, or one animal inseminates another, thousands of genes cross together. Along the way, less desirable traits—and the genes that cause them—may pass with desirable ones. Several generations of breeding, perhaps 10 to 12 years, may go by before desirable traits get established and less desirable qualities are bred away.

The "new" biotechnology offers a faster, more precise way to establish new traits in both plants and animals—and so provides foods for consumers that are safe, nutritious, healthful, abundant, and tasty.

"New Biotech": What's It All About?

In a nutshell, biotechnology refers to using living organisms—plants, animals, and bacteria—to develop new products, not just for food, but also for medical treatment, waste management, and alternative fuels, among others.

Food biotechnology started about 25 years ago, as more was learned about DNA (deoxyribonucleic acid), the genetic code in living organisms. It builds on traditional breeding methods, which change genetic makeup slowly and selectively.

Today, agricultural scientists can identify specific genes that carry traits they want, such as disease

TODAY'S MEAT

Through breeding, feeding, and management at the farm, hogs and beef cattle are leaner than ever. Processing methods, too, also help create leaner meat. The reason? The need to provide products for consumers with high nutrient content, yet lower levels of total fat and saturated fat. In fact, in 1995, pork cuts sold in the supermarket had an average of 43 percent less fat than they did in 1983.

One reason for leaner hogs is genetics. Of the eight major hog breeds in the United States, some carry genes that produce leaner, meatier hogs. With selective breeding, hog producers have genetically changed the fat and muscle composition of hogs, gradually producing leaner animals over the past few decades.

As with humans, a hog's food and "lifestyle" affect its body composition. With a scientifically-balanced diet matched to its age, current weight, and nutrient needs, a hog is fed what it needs without excess.

The next step in producing lean meat is with the meat packer or processor. They usually trim the fat surrounding cuts of meat to between 1/8- to 1/16-inch, rather than to 1/4-inch, as done in the past. There are often financial incentives offered by the packer to the farmer for producing lean animals. Even processed meat, such as ham and hot dogs, is being produced with less fat and cholesterol than ever before.

Finally, it's up to you to keep lean meat lean...by using low-fat cooking methods and avoiding high-fat sauces. *For more about preparing meat, refer to* "Fat and Cholesterol Trimmers" *on page* 335. *For tips on buying lean meat, refer to* "Meat and Deli Case" *on page* 282. ✦

resistance, better nutrient quality, or flavor. Then they can transfer just those genes to a plant or animal—leaving undesirable traits behind. Today's biotechnology is more efficient, more predictable, and less time-consuming than traditional breeding—an approach that wasn't possible when we knew less about the biological world around us.

Our "biotech" world has spawned a new vocabulary. Terms such as genetic engineering, gene splicing, cell culture, and recombinant DNA all refer to some methods of biotechnology. Recombinant DNA is the process of splicing genes from one organism into the genetic code, or DNA of another. That's how a trait is transferred.

The Benefit Package

The benefits of food biotechnology are just beginning. Already scientists know that foods can be produced more efficiently. They can be more nutritious and spoil less quickly. Fruits and vegetables can be tastier. And a greater variety of fresh food can be available year-round, not just seasonally.

Biotechnology offers an approach for protecting the environment—while still producing a high-quality, abundant, and inexpensive food supply.

- ➢ ***Disease resistance.*** Through genetic engineering, disease-resistant crops can be developed that need fewer chemical pesticides and herbicides—perhaps because plants can destroy pests themselves. Crop yields may increase while requiring less dependence on pesticides and herbicides.

- ➢ ***Weather resistance.*** Crops can be developed to withstand severe weather. They'll less likely be destroyed by early or late frost, heavy rainfall, drought, or a heat wave. And you'll have more fresh fruits, vegetables, and grains available throughout the year.

- ➢ ***Higher quality.*** Fruits and vegetables are being developed to ripen longer on the plant without being spoiled or damaged before they're eaten. This will mean fresher, better-tasting produce throughout the year. And those living in isolated places may be able to enjoy fresh produce more often.

➢ ***Nutrition advantages.*** Bioengineered foods can offer greater nutritional advantages that promote your long-term health: more nutrients, such as protein, vitamins, and minerals, or less fat and saturated fat. For example, fruits and vegetables may be produced with more antioxidant vitamins (vitamin C and E, and beta carotene); these nutrients may help reduce the risk of heart disease and certain cancers, although there's much more to learn. *Refer to "Antioxidant Vitamins: A Closer Look" on page* 90. And for regions of the world where protein malnutrition is a problem, crops can be grown with more protein.

➢ ***New food varieties.*** Foods can also be crossbred, creating new foods, identified by new names. Broccoflower, or green cauliflower, is an example, that you may already enjoy on your dinner plate.

Bioengineered tomatoes are already on the market. Their natural flavor develops more fully because they ripen on the vine. Since their "softening" gene is slowed down, they don't spoil during transport. These slow-ripening tomatoes taste more flavorful than commercial tomatoes that are picked and shipped green to protect them from bruising, then are ripened artificially.

Another product has been bioengineered for cheesemaking. Traditionally, rennet—an enzyme extracted from the lining of calves' stomachs—was used to form curds and whey from milk, a first step in making cheese. Through biotechnology, scientists have transferred the gene in rennet into bacteria, where it produces the same enzyme. Not only is the enzyme grown in bacteria more active, more pure, and consistently available to food manufacturers, but calves are no longer needed for their rennet.

Now About Food Safety...

With any new technology, consumer safety is one of the first questions people ask: "Are foods produced with biotechnology safe for me to eat?" The answer's "yes—just as safe as traditional foods."

Biotechnology doesn't change the composition or nutritional quality of food very much—unless that's a trait specifically desired. And any foods produced through bioengineering are regulated strictly, like other foods in the United States' marketplace.

Although the responsibility for proof falls with the food manufacturer, food safety—including potential allergic qualities and toxicity—is regulated by federal law. Regulations are similar to those required for new food additives. *Refer to "Testing, Testing" on page* 230 *and "Safety Check" on page* 231.

Among other issues, manufacturers of bioengineered foods or ingredients also must address: changes in nutrient levels, changes in allergens or natural toxins, scientific procedures for product development, environmental effects, and the history of safe use. For substances that differ significantly from existing foods and ingredients, special testing will be required. *Refer to "Natural Toxins" on page* 238.

have you ever *wondered*

...*what* BST *refers to*? BST, or bovine somatotropin, is a naturally-occurring protein hormone made by cows. When used as a supplement, it helps adult cows improve their efficiency in producing milk. Even without supplementation, BST is normally present in milk and meat from cows, in small quantities. It has no effect on humans. Like other proteins, it's broken down during digestion. With BST supplementation, a cow's milk production goes up, but the normal level of BST in milk itself doesn't change. The cow uses it up herself. There's no change in the flavor or nutritional qualities of milk either. As always, milk remains an excellent source of calcium, protein, vitamins, and other nutrients.

In 1990, the National Institutes of Health reinforced the safety of BST for humans. In 1993, the Food and Drug Administration approved BST supplementation, based on its safety for humans, cows, and the environment. And regulatory agencies in 20 countries have authorized milk and meat from cows receiving BST as safe for people of all ages. ✦

In all, 11 agencies of the U.S. Department of Agriculture (USDA) are involved in biotechnology. And three agencies share responsibility for the safety of your food. The Food and Drug Administration has the main responsibility for food safety. The Environmental Protection Agency regulates new chemicals, as well as genetically-modified bacteria, fungi, and viruses, and plants that can protect themselves from pests. And the Animal and Plant Health Inspection Service manages and enforces all the USDA regulations related to biotechnology.

With new technology comes some controversy. Some groups have expressed concern about genes being transferred from animals to plants or between plants that wouldn't breed normally. A gene from fish, for example, can be transferred to make freeze-resistant tomatoes. But this isn't being done in the United States.

Plants and animals are made of millions of genes. Many of the same genes are found naturally in both plants and animals. Whether an organism has characteristics of a plant or an animal isn't affected by the transfer of a single gene from an animal to a plant. So a bioengineered plant won't take on any animal characteristics.

NATURAL TOXINS

Many plants have their own built-in mechanism for pest control. Unlike animals, plants can't flee when they sense danger. So they produce natural compounds—actually low levels of pesticides—to protect against invading organisms.

Of interest, the level of these natural toxins, or poisons, in food may be higher than any level of pesticide residue or food additive.

Natural toxins are found in foods you eat every day: for example, oxalates in rhubarb, solanine in green potatoes, nitrates in broccoli, and cyanide in lima beans. At high levels, some might cause illness or may be carcinogenic, or cancer causing. However, in the amounts normally eaten, they rarely cause health problems.

Through advances in biotechnology, scientists now have the ability to identify genes that produce natural toxins, then either remove or suppress their action if there's any benefit to health. ✦

"Biotech" Labeling: When You Need to Know
For the most part, foods produced through biotechnology won't seem much different than foods you enjoy already. They may taste good, look fresh, and be available longer in the year. Most of these foods won't need any special food label—because they're not much different.

In fact, bioengineered foods are subject to the same labeling regulations as any other foods. In some cases, special food labeling will be required on "biotech" foods:

...if a food contains an allergen. Allergic reactions can come from proteins in foods. And genes are made of proteins. So when a gene is taken from a food known to cause allergic reactions (such as peanuts), then transferred to another food (such as potatoes), the new food must be labeled clearly. That label would indicate that an allergen may be present—information consumers with food allergies will rely on. (*An added note*: Research is underway to develop bioengineered foods from which proteins that cause allergic reactions are removed.)

...if the nutritional content changes. Foods that are bioengineered to change their nutritional content will be labeled, too—perhaps rice with more protein, or cooking oil with less saturated fat. That way you'll know how those foods fit nutritionally into your overall food choices for the day.

...if the food changes composition. Perhaps it would be labeled with a new varietal name. Or maybe, like broccoflower, it would carry a new identity altogether.

Growing Possibilities...
Food biotechnology holds great promise for feeding the world. It's being developed in the global marketplace, not just in the United States. These changes won't happen all at once. But gradually, you might find the following foods in your supermarket:

- low-caffeine coffee beans
- freeze-resistant tomatoes
- low-fat potato chips or french fries, made from higher-starch potatoes that absorb less fat
- vegetables and fruits with higher levels of vitamins C and E and beta carotene
- rice, corn, soybeans, and other vegetables that contain a higher-quality protein (more amino acids)
- insect- and virus-resistant fruits and vegetables, such as cantaloupe, cucumbers, tomatoes, corn, and squash, which require less pesticides for growing them
- vegetable oils—canola, corn, soybean, and others—that are lower in saturated fat
- drought-resistant corn for growing in regions with extreme heat and drought

FOOD: A NEW LOOK WITH DESIGNER GENES

You've heard of designer clothes, designer linens, designer furniture. The next wave of biotechnology may be designer foods. It's a new "look" in the world of nutrition, often—but not always—resulting from genetic engineering.

With genetic engineering, foods might be developed for specific health benefits. For example, a gene from the Brazil nut can be transferred to soybeans so that they contain more methionine, an essential amino acid. That would improve the protein quality of soybeans.

In the future, foods may be genetically altered for other functional reasons, perhaps to help reduce disease risk. Foods made with "designer genes" are often considered one type of functional food. *Refer to "Functional Foods: A New Wave" on page 210.* ✦

your nutrition check-up

Have a Flavor-able Reputation

This quiz can help you measure your willingness to try new foods from today's marketplace...and to add food variety, nutrition and flavor to your plate.

1. How would you describe yourself as a food tryer?

I don't experiment.	1
I'll try if offered.	2
I'm a willing adventurer.	3

2. When was the last time you bought an unfamiliar vegetable or fruit at the store?

last year or longer	1
last month	2
last week	3

3. When a new food product hits the market...

I'm rarely aware of it.	1
I give it a try after it's been on the market a while.	2
I try it right away—if it matches my needs.	3

4. I try to eat a wide variety of foods.

never	1
sometimes	2
almost always	3

5. I look for new ways to prepare familiar foods...perhaps from cookbooks, magazines, newspapers or from friends.

never	1
sometimes	2
all the time	3

6. The variety of foods becoming available due to biotechnology...

doesn't interest me	1
mildly interests me	2
intrigues me	3

7. When was the last time you ate at an ethnic restaurant (other than Italian, Chinese, or Mexican)?

last year or longer	1
within the last six months	2
within the last month	3

8. If preparing an Italian meal, I would make...

spaghetti noodles	1
spaghetti noodles or other types of pasta (whole wheat?)	2
any type of pasta, polenta, or risotto	3

Now, how did you fare? Add up your points.

Now Score Yourself

20 *to* 24: You're probably a "foodie" who enjoys the adventure and flavors of new foods. If you're meeting guidelines of the Pyramid, you also may reap the nutritional benefits of eating a greater variety of food.

13 *to* 19: You're open to experiencing new foods...a healthy attitude toward eating.

8 *to* 12: You're more comfortable with your "tried and true." Is your cautious approach to new foods causing you to miss out on a variety of nutritious foods?

real life nutrition

Debunking the Myths

"Pesticides, additives, organic foods, processed foods—and now there's biotechnology, functional foods, and designer foods!" sighed Shariffa, with newspaper and magazine articles about food strewn around her. "It's all just a bunch of words to me—confusing words!"

"I don't know if I need to avoid them or not. And I really don't know what foods I should buy—or if I should just grow my own." Shariffa pointed to an article she was reading about a pesticide study... another about processed foods...and another about bioengineered vegetables. "All I do know is that I really enjoy eating. And I plan to stay healthy in the process!"

Her friend Ann, a registered dietitian, smiled. "You and just about everybody else. Sometimes it seems like a real jungle out there for consumers, especially when one new study after another gets printed. It's easy to lose sight of the big picture."

Ann continued. "When you read about a single study—like that one on pesticides—it's easy to jump to conclusions. Federal regulations for pesticides and additives are really stringent. They can't be used in the food supply unless they've been tested for safety in animal studies. And the results of their safety tests need to be repeated in many tests. Even then, the amounts allowed in foods are far less than the amount that's been proven safe."

Shariffa nodded, "OK, that makes sense...but then, is there anything I should think about?"

More advice that Ann might offer Shariffa on today's food supply:

➢ Read the Nutrition Facts on food labels to find out the nutrition content of processed foods. Freezing and canning—two processing methods—help foods retain their nutritional value.

➢ Eat a wide variety of foods—even try some uncommon varieties. Besides getting more nutrient variety, you'll minimize your exposure to any substance used to produce or process food.

➢ To remove any potential pesticide residues, wash fresh fruits and vegetables. And remove outer leaves of leafy vegetables.

➢ If you grow your own food, minimize your use of pesticides, and follow directions for their safe use, storage, and disposal.

➢ Be aware that organically-grown foods aren't necessarily the answer to your concerns. They may be pesticide-free, or may not be. Likely, you'll pay more for them. Nutritionally speaking, foods produced organically and conventionally are about the same.

➢ Before making changes in your food choices from a single study, get the bigger picture. Find out what qualified food professionals, such as a registered dietitian, have to say. *Refer to "Read Between the Headlines" on page 584 for more about evaluating news reports on food and nutrition research.*

Chapter Eleven

Planning to Eat Smart

Food, glorious food! We've explored how nutrients function in human health. But it's the wide array of food, not nutrients, that entices most people to eat. The aromas, flavors, textures, and appearance of all kinds of food stimulate the appetite, satisfy tastebuds, and give the contented feeling that goes with a wonderful meal or a tasty snack.

The challenge of making healthful food choices involves satisfying your hunger and desire for certain foods, as well as ensuring that meals and snacks have the variety, balance, and moderation that help to maintain, and even enhance, health.

The Food Guide Pyramid: Your Healthful Eating Guide

Remember the four food groups that most of us grew up with? Since the 1950s, the "basic four" offered simple messages for a varied diet. But in the 1990s, we know there's more to healthful eating than variety alone. Balance and moderation in our overall diet now have greater emphasis as we strive to promote, even improve, our health.

No matter what eating style, the Food Guide Pyramid is your personal guide for making healthful food choices. It's flexible, practical, and visual. It shows how you—and your family—can put the Dietary Guidelines for Americans into action for good health. *Refer to "A Glimpse at the Dietary Guidelines" on page* 5.

The Pyramid is a guideline, not a rigid prescription. It's meant for all healthy people, male or female, young or old—aged two or more. It allows plenty of flexibility to enjoy foods that match your lifestyle and your food preferences.

Think of any food or beverage you've ever had. Whatever the food, it fits somewhere in the Food Guide Pyramid—either in one food group, or in more food groups if it's a mixed food, or in the Pyramid tip.

The Pyramid contains the building blocks of a healthful diet. Five food groups—in the three lower levels of the Pyramid—are filled with nutrient-rich foods. Each group supplies some, but not all, of the nutrients your body needs. Because their nutrients differ, foods in one food group can't replace those in another. In fact, no one food group is more important than another. For good health, you need them all!

The Pyramid also advises moderating the fats and added sugars in the diet. Symbols on the Food Guide Pyramid show the categories of foods with naturally-occurring and added fat (●) and added sugars (▽). Foods that are mainly fats, oils, and sugars are found in the Pyramid tip. Foods within the five food groups also may have varying amounts of fat and added sugars, too, as indicated by the symbols. When you're choosing foods, be aware that fats and added sugars are found in all food groups, not just those in the Pyramid tip.

Pyramid Power... For Variety, Balance, and Moderation

The Food Guide Pyramid conveys the three main messages about healthful eating: variety, balance, and moderation. Here's its overall advice for you and your family:

➢ ***For variety,*** eat different foods from the Pyramid's five food groups. No one food supplies all the nutrients the body needs. Eating a variety of foods—both within each food group and among the five food groups—ensures that you meet your nutritional requirements.

➢ ***For balance,*** eat appropriate amounts—enough, but not too much—from each food group every day. A balanced diet supplies the nutrients and calories the body needs. The range of servings for each group suggests how much you and your family need based on age, gender, and activity level. Making trade-offs is one way to balance your food choices. *Refer to page 256, "Quick, Easy Trade-Offs," for tips.*

➢ ***For moderation,*** choose foods and beverages to meet your energy needs and to control calories and the total amount of fat, cholesterol, sodium, sugars, and, if consumed, alcoholic beverages. For example, to moderate fat, opt mostly for lower-fat choices in your overall eating plan. A moderate diet helps you maintain a healthy weight and may help protect you from health problems such as heart disease and cancer later in life. More good news: With moderation, you have more flexibility to enjoy a variety of food, including your favorites!

Food Guide Pyramid: A Guide to Daily Food Choices

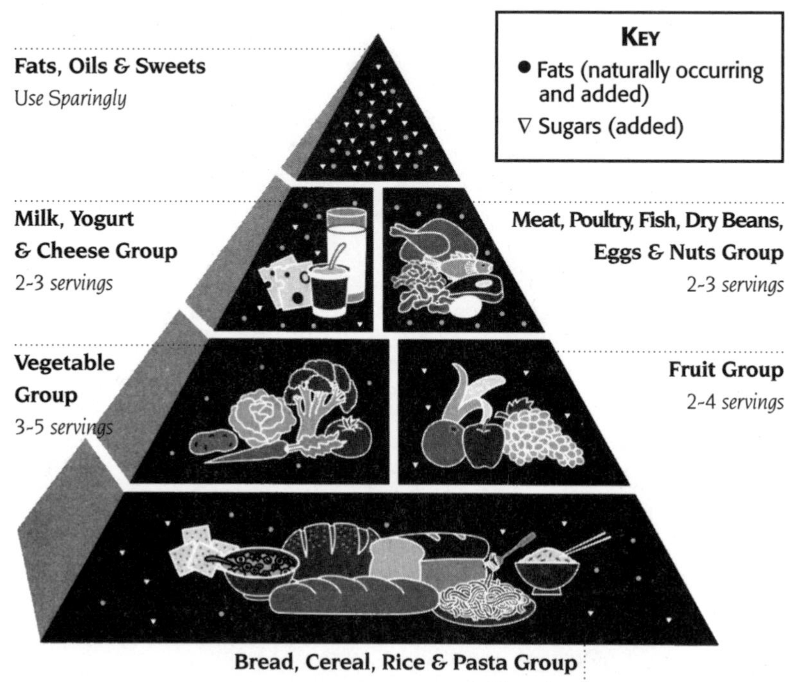

Sizing Up Healthful Servings

Variety is the first step toward eating smart. To follow Pyramid advice for balance and moderation, you need to know about servings: how many and what size.

Servings: Enough, But Not Too Much

The Food Guide Pyramid gives a range of servings, not a single amount. Being flexible, these guidelines help you choose enough servings to match your individual nutrient needs—without overdoing on calories, fat, and other food components.

Everyone aged two and over needs at least the minimum servings daily from all five food groups. However, the specific number of servings for you depends on the amount of energy you need each day. And your energy needs depend on your age, gender, health status, and level of physical activity.

Where do you fit within the serving ranges? The minimum servings from each food group supply about 1,600 calories. That's about right for many inactive women and some older adults. The midpoint in the serving ranges provides about 2,200 calories. That's an appropriate calorie target for many children, teenage girls, active women, and many inactive men; women who are pregnant or breast-feeding may need somewhat more. Teenage boys, active men, and many athletes may eat from the top of the serving ranges, or about 2,800 calories. *For specific calorie recommendations for children and teenagers age 11 to 18, refer to "The Pyramid for Teens" on page 446.*

Pyramid guidelines apply to young children (ages 2 and up), too. Like you, they need variety from all five food groups. But, because their stomachs are small, younger children may not be able to eat the same size servings as older children and adults. And preschoolers may need fewer than 1,600 calories daily. While smaller servings are appropriate to meet the energy needs of young children, the total number of servings for the day should add up the minimum Pyramid requirements. For normal growth, however, their Milk Group servings should add up to two cups (16 ounces) of milk each day. *Refer to "Feeding Guide for Young Children" on page 423 for serving sizes for young children*

The chart, "How Many Servings for You?" offers three plans—each at a different calorie level—for choosing a day's servings from the Pyramid. These plans are simply guidelines. Your own choices may differ somewhat. Just try to consume at least the minimum amount from each food group daily. *To estimate your energy needs, refer to "Your Weigh: Figuring Your Energy Needs" on page 28.*

Keep in mind that the Pyramid's recommendations do not change if you take a multivitamin supplement. Dietary supplements are just what their name implies—supplements intended to supplement the nutrients from the foods you eat. They don't take the place of food group servings. All healthy people need to follow food group guidelines first. Then, with the recommendation of a health professional, a supplement—not to exceed 100 percent of the Recommended Dietary Allowance for a nutrient—may be advised. *For more information, refer to "Dietary Supplements: Use and Abuse" on page 111.*

What Counts As One Serving?

To make the Pyramid work, you need to know not only *how many* servings you need daily, but also *how much* counts as a serving. That way, your day's food choices will supply enough of the nutrients your body needs.

How Many Servings for You?

These are the serving amounts if you choose mostly lowfat and lean foods with moderate amounts of fats, oils, and sweets.

	Less Active Women, Older Adults	Children, Teen Girls, Active Women, Less Active Men	Teen Boys, Active Men
Calories	about 1,600	about 2,200	about 2,800
Bread Group	6	9	11
Vegetable Group	3	4	5
Fruit Group	2	3	4
Milk Group	2-3*	2-3*	2-3*
Meat Group	2, for a total of 5 ounces	2, for a total of 6 ounces	3, for a total of 7 ounces

* *Women who are pregnant or breast-feeding, teenagers and young adults to age 24 need three servings.*

How much is one serving? It isn't a helping, a plate full, or a small garnish. It's not the flavoring added to fruit-flavored yogurt or vegetable-flavored pasta (such as spinach pasta) either. And it's not always the entire contents of one food package. Instead servings are specific, standardized amounts of food. They're meant as guides to help you plan and judge your own portions.

Serving sizes differ among food groups. Even among similar foods, serving sizes aren't always the same. *Refer to the serving sizes given on pages* 244 *to* 250 *in this chapter to see what counts as one serving.*

If your portion is bigger than one serving, it counts as more than one serving; smaller amounts are partial servings. For example, one serving of cooked vegetables measures as 1/2 cup. If you usually eat a 3/4 cup portion of green beans, this counts as 1 1/2 servings of vegetables, and a 1/4 cup portion counts as only 1/2 serving.

Not sure about your own portion sizes? To get an idea, take out measuring cups and a kitchen scale. Serve typical portions of food on your plate. Then measure or weigh them and compare your portions to the Food Guide Pyramid portions. You might be surprised to find your portions are bigger or smaller than you think!

For good health, you don't need to weigh or measure your meals and snacks. Serving sizes are meant as general guides. It's okay to eat smaller or larger serving sizes as long as you come close to the recommended totals on average over several days. To quickly estimate portion size, use these quick, visual comparisons:

- Three ounces of meat, poultry, or fish are about the size of one deck of playing cards or the palm of a woman's hand.
- One-half cup of fruit, vegetables, pasta, or rice is about the size of a small fist.
- One cup of milk, yogurt, or chopped, fresh greens is about the size of a small hand holding a tennis ball.
- One ounce of cheese is about the size of your thumb.

The Nutrition Facts panel on a food label offers a reference for serving sizes. However, serving sizes on food labels may differ slightly from serving sizes recommended by the Pyramid because labels list "typical" serving sizes. "*Get All the Facts!*" *on page* 271 *explains how serving sizes are used on food labels.*

have you ever wondered

...how a vegetarian can use the Food Guide *Pyramid?* A vegetarian who avoids meat, poultry, and/or fish can choose Meat Group servings from a list of alternate, protein-rich foods: dry beans and peas, eggs, nuts and seeds, peanut butter, and tofu. Foods from the Milk Group also supply the protein that vegetarians need. By combining these foods with enough servings from the other groups, a vegetarian can use the Food Guide Pyramid to choose a healthful diet. *For nutrition guidelines on vegetarian eating, refer to chapter* 22. ✦

What's Inside the Pyramid?

Local foods, ethnic foods, your favorites, quick-service foods, snack foods, foods you grow yourself, supermarket foods—foods of every kind fit somewhere within the Food Guide Pyramid!

Foods actually are grouped together because their nutrient content is similar. They promote health in comparable ways. In fact, each of the five food groups supplies your body with some, but not all, nutrients you need for health.

Bread, Cereal, Rice, and Pasta Group

The base of the Pyramid is filled with breads, cereals, rice, and pasta—all foods made from grains. Foods from the Bread Group are described as the foundation of the diet, perhaps because their complex carbohydrates are an excellent energy source. *Read more about complex carbohydrates, "From Complex to Simple..." on page* 125.

Good news for health-conscious consumers: as long as you keep within your calorie level, consuming more complex carbohydrates, perhaps in place of a higher-fat food, helps to lower the percent of fat calories in your overall diet. Consider the 2,200 calorie menu in "A Day's Menu for the Whole Family" on page 257. This menu gets 28 percent of its calories from fat. If 3/4 cup french fries were served in place of 3/4 cup brown rice, the total calories consumed would be similar, but then 31 percent of the calories would come from fat.

Many grain products also supply B vitamins and iron, especially if they're enriched or whole grain. Enriched means adding back nutrients that were lost in processing. Grain products are often enriched with B vitamins (thiamin, riboflavin, niacin) and iron and may be fortified with folic acid. *For more about food processing and additives, refer to "Additives: Safe at the Plate" on page* 225. The more whole grains or bran the foods contain, the higher the fiber content. Try to consume half your grain servings, or at least three servings daily, from whole-grain foods.

Being plant sources of food, most grain products are low in fat and cholesterol. Exceptions are those foods, such as croissants, pastries, some crackers, and many muffins, which are prepared with higher-fat and cholesterol-containing ingredients, as well as foods that are fried, such as doughnuts, hush puppies, and beignets. Remember, it's not bread, pasta, or rice that supplies fat, but instead what you serve with or put on them or how they're prepared!

The serving range—6 to 11 servings from the Bread Group—may seem like a lot. But servings add up easier than many people realize. Starting with breakfast, one medium bagel counts as two Bread Group servings (depending on the size; a premium or bakery bagel can count for up to 4 Bread Group servings). At lunchtime, a sandwich with two slices of whole-grain bread supplies two more servings. For dinner, 1/2 cup of rice pilaf and a dinner roll count as two servings. And for snacks, 1/2 cup of pretzels counts as one more serving. That's a total of seven Bread Group servings.

Pyramid Pointers

Boost "carbs" by putting pasta, rice, or other grain foods center stage at your meal or snack. Add flavor and interest with vegetables, small amounts of seafood, lean beef or skinless poultry, or fresh herbs.

For fiber, choose foods made with whole-grains (whole wheat, corn, multi-grain) and bran: perhaps whole-grain bread, whole-grain cereal, bran flakes, whole-wheat pasta, and brown rice. *Refer to "Whole Grains: For Goodness Sake" on page* 103.

Opt for breads made with less fat and sugars, such as bagels, bread sticks, English muffins, Italian bread, hamburger buns, pita bread, or corn and flour tortillas. Go easy on those with more fat or sugars, such as croissants, doughnuts, and sweet rolls.

Try Bread Group foods that may be new to you, such as quinoa, buckwheat, millet, amaranth, or couscous. Enjoy grain-based salads, perhaps pasta salad, rice pilaf salad, or tabouli (made with bulgur). Or take your tastebuds for northern Italian cuisine;

have you ever wondered

...where potato chips and corn chips fit in the Pyramid? Potato chips fit within the Vegetable Group, and corn chips fit within the Bread Group. Yet they're among those foods in the Pyramid Groups that supply more fat and more calories per serving. Eating these foods occasionally is OK, but other foods in each foods group supply more nutrients and less fat.

...if potatoes can substitute for bread since they're both high in complex carbohydrates? Potatoes are among the starchy vegetables that belong in the Vegetable Group. Breadfruit, cassava, corn, green peas, hominy, lima beans, rutabaga, taro, and yautia are some other starchy vegetables. Although high in complex carbohydrate, vegetables have a different nutrient profile than foods in the Bread Group. Potatoes, for example, supply vitamin C, while Bread Group foods supply some B vitamins and iron. ✦

enjoy risotto, made with arborio rice, or polenta, made with cornmeal. *Refer to "Today's Grains" on page 221 for descriptions of various grains and "Cooking Grain by Grain" on page 345 for tips on cooking various grains.*

Look for crackers and crunchy snacks with less fat: air-popped popcorn, graham crackers, matzos, pretzels, rice cakes, saltines, bread sticks, zweiback, baked tortilla chips, and lower-fat crackers and cookies.

Make ready-to-eat cereal or instant oatmeal a quick breakfast choice. Top with fresh fruit, yogurt, or milk for extra flavor and more nutrients.

As sweet desserts from the Bread Group, choose angel food cake, gingersnaps, and low-fat cookies and cakes, which have less fat and sugar. Go easy on frosted cake, brownies, and pie.

Reach for breadsticks, whole-wheat crackers, toasted pita bread points, or a bagel half as snacks. They're all good with vegetable dips or fruit spreads!

Add cooked barley, rice, or pasta to soup or stir-fry dishes.

A Bread Group Serving Is...

- 1 slice enriched or whole-grain bread (1 ounce)
- 1/2 hamburger roll, bagel, pita bread, or English muffin
- 1 (6-inch) tortilla
- 1/2 cup cooked rice or pasta
- 1/2 cup cooked oatmeal, grits, or cream of wheat cereal
- 1/2 cup cooked barley
- 1/2 cup quinoa, bulgur, millet, or other whole grains
- 1 ounce ready-to-eat cereal
- 3-4 small crackers
- 1 (4-inch) diameter pancake or waffle
- 3 tablespoons wheat germ
- 2 medium cookies

Vegetable Group

How many Vegetable Group servings do you eat daily? And how many different vegetables do you eat on a regular basis? The Food Guide Pyramid is filled with all kinds of varieties to choose from—*as you can see in the chart, "Vegetables: From A to Z" on page 250.*

The nutrients in vegetables vary a lot. Deep yellow and dark green leafy vegetables, such as carrots, sweet potatoes, kale, and spinach are great sources of beta carotene, which forms vitamin A. Others, such as brussels sprouts, bell pepper, and tomato, have more vitamin C. Some others, such as green peas, have less of these vitamins, but are still good sources of complex carbohydrates. Most, including dry beans and peas, supply fiber. And many supply folic acid, too. *For more about vitamins A and C, refer to "Antioxidant Vitamins: A Closer Look" on page 90.*

Unless it's added during food preparation, vegetables have little or no fat, and they're cholesterol free. In cases like the ever-popular french fries and fried onion rings, or salads with heavy dressing, it's the preparation method or toppings that increase the fat content.

Vegetables are far more than a pretty garnish on a plate. For your good health, eat three to five servings from the Vegetable Group daily. If you're looking for nutritious, low-fat snacks, go ahead and enjoy even more!

Pyramid Pointers

Eat many different types of vegetables. Because vegetables supply varying amounts and types of nutrients, variety makes good health sense.

Eat a variety of dark green leafy and deep yellow vegetables (red, orange, and yellow), which supply carotenoids, such as beta carotene, which form vitamin A in your body. For example, make salads more interesting and more nutritious with a greater variety of darker greens: arugula, bibb lettuce, chicory, kale, leaf lettuce, romaine lettuce, spinach, and watercress. *Refer to "Carotenoids: 'Color' Your Food Healthy" on page 90.*

For fiber, keep the edible peels on vegetables such as potatoes, cucumber, and summer squash.

Enjoy the vegetables you've always eaten—just more of them! Broaden your personal vegetable menu beyond favorite standbys. Also try brussels sprouts, Swiss chard, kale, parsnips, beets, bok choy, okra, and various squashes, such as spaghetti, butternut, acorn, and dumpling squashes.

Look for ways to add more vegetables to everyday meals. "Fortify" pasta dishes with steamed, sliced vegetables: zucchini, carrots, broccoli, and bell peppers. Add tomato or cucumber slices and sprouts to sandwiches. Tuck a can of tomato juice into your lunch or snack bag. Top a baked potato with vegetable salsa or stir-fried vegetables. Keep a bowl of cleaned, raw veggies in the refrigerator, ready for a quick nibble.

If you want more legumes, enjoy some for Vegetable Group servings and others for Meat Group servings. They have a "split personality." You can count them in either group—but the same bowl of beans can't count for two different food-group servings.

For more about the vitamins and minerals supplied by vegetables in a healthful eating plan, refer to "Fruits and Vegetables: Count Five a Day!" on page 96.

A Vegetable Group Serving Is...

- 1/2 cup chopped raw, nonleafy vegetables
- 1 cup of leafy, raw vegetables (lettuce, spinach, watercress, or cabbage)
- 1/2 cup cooked vegetables
- 1/2 cup cooked legumes (beans, peas, or lentils)
- 1 small baked potato (3 ounces)
- 3/4 cup vegetable juice

Fruit Group

What's in the fruit bowl? You'll find all of America's favorites: apples, oranges, and bananas. Some we enjoy, yet eat less often: cherries, nectarines, pineapple, and honeydew melon. For more variety, the bowl has others you may never hear about, such as cherimoya, lychee, loquat, and mangosteen!

Like vegetables, foods in the Fruit Group supply varying amounts of vitamins A and C. Citrus fruits (orange, grapefruit, tangerine), melons, and berries

What are Cruciferous Vegetables... and What Do They Do?

A potential cancer-fighting connection has focused attention on cruciferous vegetables. These members of the cabbage family derive their name from their four-petaled flowers, which look like a crucifer, or cross. They include a diverse selection of vegetables: arugula, bok choy, broccoli, brussels sprouts, cabbage, cauliflower, collards, kale, kohlrabi, mustard greens, radishes, rutabaga, turnip, turnip greens, and watercress.

Although inconclusive, studies suggest that vegetables from the cabbage family may help protect against colon and rectal cancer. While the reasons are unclear, experts believe that they contain nutrients, compounds, and phytochemicals that seem to have a cancer-fighting component: beta carotene, fiber, and vitamin C, among others. Cruciferous vegetables are also fat-free. As an added bonus, cruciferous vegetables supply varying amounts of calcium, iron, and folic acid, too.

The cabbage family of vegetables has something else in common: a strong cooking aroma. Proper food handling enhances the flavor of these vegetables without intensifying the aroma:

- Eat cruciferous vegetables soon after you buy them—raw or cooked.
- Cook them quickly, just until tender-crisp.
- Don't keep leftovers more than a day. ✦

Vegetables: From A to Z

From A to Z—alfalfa sprouts to zucchini—foods in the Vegetable Group offer more variety and more nutrients than most people realize! Some also make good raw, finger foods. Cut them in interesting shapes. Pack them in lunches. Eat them as snacks. Perhaps serve them with dips. Look for these and other vegetables in stores and restaurants. *Refer to "'Garden of Eatin': Uncommon Vegetables" on page 215 for a description of the more unusual types.*

➢ Dark green leafy vegetables supply vitamin A, in the form of carotenes, and vitamin C… as well as riboflavin, folate, iron, calcium, magnesium, and potassium.

arugula	**beet greens**	**broccoli**	**chard**
chicory (curly endive)	**collard greens**	**dandelion greens**	**escarole**
kale	**mustard greens**	**romaine lettuce**	**spinach**
turnip greens	**watercress**		

➢ Deep yellow vegetables supply vitamin A in the form of carotenes.

acorn squash	**butternut squash**	**carrots**	**plantain**
pumpkin	**sweet potatoes**	**yams**	

➢ Starchy vegetables supply varying amounts of vitamins and minerals, such as niacin, vitamin B_6, zinc, and potassium.

breadfruit	**cassava (yuca, manioc)**	**corn**	**dasheen**
green peas	**lima beans**	**potatoes**	**rutabaga**
taro (malanga)			

➢ Legumes provide protein, as well as thiamin, folate, iron, magnesium, phosphorus, zinc, and potassium.

black beans	**black-eyed peas**	**chickpeas (garbanzos)**	**kidney beans**
lentils	**lima beans (mature)**	**mung beans**	**navy beans**
pinto beans	**split peas**		

➢ Other vegetables provide varying amounts of vitamins and minerals, such as vitamin C, vitamin A, and potassium.

artichokes	**asparagus**	**bamboo shoots**	**bean and alfalfa sprouts**
beets	**bok choy (pak choi)**	**brussels sprouts**	**cabbage**
cactus pads (nopales)	**cauliflower**	**celeriac**	**celery**
chayote	**cherry tomatoes**	**Chinese cabbage**	**cucumbers**
daikon (Japanese radish)	**eggplant**	**fennel bulb**	**green beans**
green pepper	**Jerusalem artichoke**	**jicama**	**kelp**
kohlrabi	**lettuce**	**lotus root**	**mushrooms**
okra	**onions**	**parsnips**	**radicchio**
radishes	**rutabaga**	**seaweed**	**snow peas**
sugar snap peas	**summer squash**	**tomatillos**	**tomatoes**
turnips	**vegetable juice**	**water chestnuts**	**wax beans**
zucchini			

Refer to "Kitchen Nutrition: Cooking a Pot o' Beans" and "Bean Bag" on pages 151 and page 154 for more about types of legumes and cooking methods. "A Word About Legumes…" on page 346 provides ideas for adding more legumes to your meals.

(*Adapted from*: Dietary Guidelines for Americans: Eat a Variety of Foods, *Home and Garden Bulletin Number* 253-2, USDA/*Human Nutrition Information Service, July,* 1993.)

are excellent sources of vitamin C. Many deep yellow fruits, such as cantaloupe, apricots, mangos, and peaches, are rich in vitamin A. Fruits, especially edible peels on apples, pears, peaches, other fruits, and dry fruits provide fiber, too. Many fruits also supply potassium and folic acid.

Fruit's sweet flavor comes from its natural sugar, a simple carbohydrate called fructose. *Refer to chapter 5 for more information about sugars.* Sometimes sugars are added to canned and frozen fruits and fruit juice as flavor enhancers or to help maintain quality. Since fruits are plant sources of food, most are low fat and all are cholesterol free. Not always thought of as fruits, avocados and olives contain fat—a monounsaturated fat. Avocados also supply vitamin A.

How many Fruit Group servings do you need? The Pyramid recommends two to four servings daily. A versatile and "fast" food, whole fruits can be snacks, side dishes, or desserts. They may be sliced in a main-dish salad, or in a meat, poultry, or seafood dish. Get your fruit servings from a variety of fruits and their juices.

Pyramid Pointers

Every day, include vitamin-C rich fruit or fruit juice among your food choices: citrus fruit, berries, or melon.

Go beyond the basics. Paint your plate with less common fruits: prickly pear, papaya, mango, starfruit, figs, kiwi, or guava. Try new-to-you varieties of apples, pears, plums, or melons.

Keep dried fruits—raisins, prunes, dried apricots, dried apple slices, dried cranberries—handy for healthful nibbling and pack-and-carry meals. Be aware: serving sizes of dried fruits are smaller than for fresh fruit because they don't have water; drying concentrates the calories and nutrient content.

Drink fruit juice as a snack beverage. Mix with sparkling water for a refreshing fizz.

Add fruits to all kinds of dishes. Toss orange slices, tangerine segments, grape halves, and other fresh fruits with garden salads. Add crushed pineapple, raisins, or chopped apple to coleslaw. Sprinkle dried fruits of all kinds on breakfast cereal, pudding, or frozen yogurt. Blend them with stuffing and rice dishes. Or mix them in dough for homemade muffins.

For more about the vitamins and minerals supplied by fruits in a healthful eating plan, refer to "Fruits and Vegetables: Count Five a Day!" *on page* 96.

A Fruit Group Serving Is...

- 1 medium fruit (apple, orange, banana, or peach)
- 1/2 grapefruit, mango, or papaya
- 3/4 cup juice
- 1/2 cup berries or cut-up fruit
- 1/2 cup canned, frozen, or cooked fruit
- 1/4 cup dried fruit

Milk, Yogurt, and Cheese Group

Besides milk, foods made from milk—yogurt, cheese, cottage cheese, buttermilk, frozen yogurt, and ice cream—as well as pudding and milk shakes, all belong in the Milk Group.

Milk, yogurt, and cheese are our body's best sources of calcium and riboflavin. Without dairy foods, getting enough calcium for bone health can be difficult. Many dairy foods are also good sources of protein, phosphorus, potassium, vitamin A, and vitamin D.

The amount of fat and cholesterol in dairy foods varies. Skim milk, or fat-free milk, contains 0.5 percent fat or less. One percent (1%) milk, labeled lowfat or light milk, has 50 percent less fat than whole

have you ever wondered

...where calcium-fortified fruit juice fits on the Food Guide Pyramid? Since calcium is just one nutrient in milk, calcium-fortified fruit juice can't replace one Milk Group serving. As with any juice, 3/4 cup counts as one serving from the Fruit Group—with an added calcium bonus. ✦

What's in the Fruit Bowl?

Apples, bananas, and oranges: they're America's favorites! But there's lots more in our fruit bowl. Depending on the season, sweeten your palate—and nourish your body—with a variety of fruit and juices made from them. Look for these and other fruits in stores and restaurant menus.

	Good Sources of:		
	Vitamin A	Vitamin C	Potassium
acerola		X	
apple		X	
apricot	X	X	X
Asian pear			
avocado	X		X
banana		X	X
blueberries		X	
cantaloupe	X	X	X
cherimoya		X	
cherries, sweet			X
cranberries		X	
dates		X	
figs			X
grapefruit		X	
grapes		X	
guava (guabaya)	X	X	X
honeydew melon		X	X
kiwi		X	X
kumquat	X	X	
loquat	X		X
lychee (litchi)		X	
mango	X	X	
mangosteen			
nectarine	X	X	X
orange		X	X
papaya	X	X	X
peach	X	X	
pear		X	
persimmon	X	X	
pineapple		X	
plum		X	
pomegranate		X	X
pomelo		X	
prickly pear		X	
prune			X
raspberries		X	
sopadilla		X	X
starfruit (carambola)	X	X	
strawberries		X	
tamarillo	X		X
tamarind			X
tangerine	X	X	
ugli fruit		X	
watermelon	X	X	

Refer to "Fresh Ideas: Uncommon Fruits" on page 219 for descriptions.

"Good source" means it contributes at least 10 percent of the % Daily Value, based on 1 medium fruit, 1/2 cup canned or chopped fruit or 1 cup melon.

milk. Two percent (2%) milk is now called reduced-fat milk and has 25 percent less fat than whole milk. And whole milk contains 3.25 percent fat. These percentages refer to the amount of fat by weight, not calories. *For the fat and cholesterol content of various types of milk, refer to "Milk: A Good Calcium Source" on page 180.* The many varieties of cheese vary slightly in fat content, although reduced-fat and fat-free varieties contain considerably less fat. Dairy foods with less fat usually have less cholesterol, too. Regardless of the fat content, the amount of other nutrients—calcium, protein, phosphorus, and vitamin D—remain about the same.

Dairy foods may contain two types of sugars: naturally-occurring sugar called lactose and added sugars. *Refer to "Sugar: What Is It?" on page 123 for more about the various types of sugars, including lactose; "Lactose Intolerance: A Matter of Degree" on page 194 addresses lactose intolerance, or the sensitivity to the naturally-occurring sugar in dairy foods.* Any added sugars in dairy foods come from flavorings, such as those added to ice cream, flavored yogurt, and milk.

A few dairy foods don't belong in this Pyramid group: butter, cream, cream cheese, and sour cream. These are made from the cream that naturally separates from unhomogenized milk. Unlike Milk Group foods, these foods contribute only small amounts of minerals, vitamins, and protein to the diet. Because they're high in fat, though, they belong with fats, oils, and sweets in the Pyramid tip.

Many people—teens and adult women especially—neglect the Milk Group. The Food Guide Pyramid advises two to three Milk Group servings daily. However, nutrition experts suggest more to meet the calcium needs of teens, young adults to age 24, pregnant and breast-feeding women, and menopausal women.

Pyramid Pointers

For the calcium you need, look for ways to include Milk Group foods in meals and snacks: milk on breakfast cereal, cheese on a sandwich, yogurt dips with veggies, coffee au lait (with milk), shredded cheese on soups and salads, or cottage cheese as a side dish.

Include calcium-rich dairy foods at snacktime. Yogurt, milk, and cheese cubes are three good choices! Dessert gives another chance; try frozen yogurt or pudding.

Use evaporated skim milk instead of cream in coffee, on cereals, whipped as a topping and in recipes calling for cream. Evaporated skim milk has a creamy texture, and it counts as a Milk Group food!

Add Milk Group servings by using plain, lowfat yogurt or cottage cheese (processed in a blender) in recipes as a substitute for sour cream.

As a beverage alternative, drink thick and creamy buttermilk. Even with its "buttery" name, it's low in fat. Usually it's made from skim or lowfat milk.

Start your day with dairy: a carton of yogurt or cup of yogurt-fruit smoothie with breakfast.

Buy a carton of milk with food from a supermarket deli or quickservice restaurant.

A Milk, Yogurt, and Cheese Group Serving Is...

- 1 cup of milk or buttermilk
- 1 cup yogurt
- 1/2 cup evaporated milk
- 1/3 cup dry milk
- 1 1/2 ounces natural cheese (cheddar, mozzarella, Swiss, Monterey Jack)
- 1/2 cup ricotta cheese
- 2 ounces processed cheese (American)
- Count 1/2 cup frozen yogurt or 1 cup cottage cheese as 1/2 serving. Count 1/2 cup ice cream as 1/3 serving.

Meat, Poultry, Fish, Dry Beans, Eggs, and Nuts Group

Even though we use its shortcut name, the Meat Group is much more than meat! It's filled with a variety of foods, all excellent sources of protein: beef, pork, chicken, turkey, finfish, shellfish, game, eggs, dry beans (legumes, lentils, and peas), tofu (made from soybeans), nuts, and peanut butter.

Besides protein, Meat Group foods supply varying amounts of iron, zinc, and B vitamins (thiamin, niacin, vitamin B_6, and B_{12}). In fact, meat, poultry, and fish are one of the body's best sources of iron. The iron, called heme iron, in these foods is better absorbed than iron from plant sources of food. *Refer to "Iron in Foods: Heme vs. Non-Heme" on page 110.*

Looking at the symbols on the Food Guide Pyramid, you see that the Meat Group is also a source of dietary fat. Lean meat and skinless (not fried) poultry are lower-fat choices. But because they're animal products, meat and poultry also have varying amounts of cholesterol. Finfish—for example, flounder, cod, haddock, and catfish—have less saturated fatty acids and cholesterol than meat and poultry do, while shellfish tends to be very low in saturated fat and somewhat higher in cholesterol than finfish. Some types of fish are fairly high in fat: salmon, mackerel, and herring. *Refer to chapter 3 for more about fat and cholesterol.*

Even though they're plant sources of food, dry beans—legumes and lentils—are part of the Meat Group because they're excellent sources of protein. Combined with grains, their protein is complete and can substitute for meat, poultry, or fish. *For more*

have you ever wondered

...if fertilized eggs are more nutritious than unfertilized eggs? No, the difference in nutrient content is too small to make a difference.

...if brown eggs are more nutritious than white eggs? Shell color doesn't affect nutrition quality. The color of the egg shell varies with the breed of hen. ✦

about protein, refer to "Protein Power" on page 561. Legumes also are a great source of complex carbohydrate and fiber, and they're cholesterol free and virtually fat free! While nuts and nut butters supply protein and some vitamins, they're higher in fat (mostly unsaturated) and calories. Legumes actually lead a double life. One-half cup of dry beans can count toward the Vegetable Group or the Meat Group. *Refer to chapter 21 for more on including legumes in your meals.*

How much do you need from the Meat Group? Two to three servings per day, equivalent to about 5 to 7 ounces, is enough to get the protein most people need. This is often a surprise to people, who sometimes eat much more.

Pyramid Pointers

Include a variety of Meat Group foods—lean meat, skinless poultry, fish, and legumes—as one-fourth of your plate. Enjoy fish and poultry several times a week. *Refer to "Meat, Poultry, and Fish: Lean Cuts and Cooking Methods" on page 336 for preparation tips.*

Consider the size of meat and poultry portions. Remember, you need only a total of 5 to 7 ounces a day. While it's okay to occasionally eat large portions of meat or poultry, an 8- or 12-ounce steak is probably more than you need at one sitting.

Make legumes—dry beans, peas, lentils—or tofu the focus of your meals several times a week. Try vegetarian chili or lasagna, vegetable tofu stir-fry, or a bowl of bean soup—or mix canned legumes with a vegetable salad. *Refer to "A Word About Legumes..." on page 346 for ideas on adding legumes to your meals.*

Enjoy eggs as a meat alternate. To control cholesterol, limit egg yolks to four per week. That includes eggs used in prepared and baked foods. If you prefer more, use egg substitutes or egg whites in recipes that ask for whole eggs. *For fat and cholesterol trimming ideas for egg dishes, refer to page 339.*

Eat nuts and nut butters in moderate amounts. Although higher in fat than many other Meat Group foods, they're good protein sources and add variety to meals. For example, toss chopped nuts in a vegetarian main dish salad or casserole.

have you ever wondered

...where venison, rattlesnake, and buffalo fit within the Pyramid? How about ostrich? Because their nutrient content is similar to other meats, these foods count toward servings from the Meat Group. Their fat content varies. However, many types of game—venison, bison, elk, moose, squirrel—are quite lean.

Ostrich, a relatively new food in the United States, has the flavor of red meat, even though it's poultry. Standing seven to eight feet high, it's the biggest bird in the world. From a nutritional standpoint, it's quite lean—fewer than 3 grams of fat in 3 ounces, which is less than chicken and beef round. It's also a good source of protein and iron. ✦

A Meat, Poultry, Fish, Dry Beans, Eggs, and Nuts Group Serving Is...

- 2 to 3 ounces cooked lean meat, poultry or fish (*4 ounces raw meat, poultry, or fish equal 3 ounces when it's cooked*)
- 2 to 3 ounces lean sliced deli meat (turkey, ham, beef, or bologna)
- 2 to 3 ounces canned tuna or salmon, packed in water

...for a total of 5 to 7 ounces each day.

Count as 1 ounce meat:

- 1/2 cup cooked lentils, peas, or dry beans
- 1 egg
- 1/4 cup egg substitute
- 2 tablespoons peanut butter
- 1/3 cup nuts
- 4 ounces tofu

Count as 2 ounces meat:

- 1/2 cup tuna or ground beef
- 1 small chicken leg or thigh
- 2 slices sandwich-size meat

Count as 3 ounces meat:

- 1 medium pork chop
- 1/4-pound hamburger patty
- 1/2 chicken breast

- ➢ 1 unbreaded 3-ounce fish filet
- ➢ cooked meat the size of a deck of cards

Fats, Oils, and Sweets

What's in the tip of the Pyramid? Salad dressings, oils, cream, butter, gravy, margarine, cream cheese, sugars, soft drinks, fruit drinks, jams and jellies, candies, sherbet, and gelatin desserts. In small amounts, they add flavor and pleasure to meals and snacks.

As the symbols on the Pyramid show, foods with high proportions of naturally occurring or added fats, such as bacon and pork rinds, and those with added sugars come mostly from the Pyramid tip. Because they supply mostly calories and few nutrients, the guideline is: use fats, oils, and sweets sparingly.

Fats, oils, and sweets aren't designated as part of a food group because there are no minimum requirements for these foods. For this reason, no recommended serving ranges or serving sizes are given either.

Pyramid Pointers

Limit dressing on salads to 1 or 2 tablespoons, or switch to low-fat and fat-free varieties.

Go easy on spreads, toppings, gravies, and sauces that add fat or sugars to foods from all five food groups.

Go easy on cream cheese, sour cream, and margarine—or try low-fat varieties. Cream cheese and sour cream are also sold in fat-free versions.

Enjoy soft drinks and candies in moderation.

Build Your Personal Pyramid

Eating smart isn't just for today! To keep fit, you need to make balanced food choices for a lifetime. Start building your personal Pyramid now.

1. *Modify your food choices gradually.* That may be easier than overhauling your whole diet at one time. Perhaps start with one meal of the day or snack...or try working with just one food group for a few months. Then move on gradually from there.

2. *Choose foods each day from the five major food groups.* Build your Pyramid from the bottom up—with plenty of grains, fruits, and vegetables. How might your dinner plate look? Divide your plate into four sections. Fill three sections with vegetables and grains and the fourth with a serving from the Meat Group. Then add a glass of low-fat milk.

3. *Make moderation, not elimination, your goal.* Eat foods lower in fat more often than those that

PIZZA: WHAT FOOD GROUP?

Pizza, fajitas, lasagna, and cioppino (fish stew)...many foods don't fit neatly into a single food group. Prepared with ingredients from several food groups, mixed foods count as partial servings from two or more food groups. Use your best "guess-timate" to determine how many servings they represent.

Pizza, topped with ground beef, cheese, tomato sauce, and green peppers, offers a good example. The crust counts toward the Bread Group, and the toppings add partial servings to the Meat, Milk, and Vegetable Groups. If you change the toppings—perhaps switch to a Hawaiian pizza with ham (Meat Group) and pineapple (Fruit Group)—food group servings change.

For fajitas, chicken or beef (Meat Group) are stir-fried with peppers and onions (Vegetable Group) and served inside a soft tortilla (Bread Group). The cioppino with its seafood and vegetables counts toward the Meat and Vegetable Groups.

Now it's your turn. What partial food-group servings might one portion of your favorite lasagna recipe supply? ✦

have more. Make trade-offs to keep your meals and snacks in balance.

4. *Go for variety within the food groups.* Take your taste buds on an adventure by trying new foods. Besides the nutritional benefits, variety adds interest to meals and snacks.

5. *Consider your lifestyle...* and how many calories you need daily. Then, from each food group, eat enough servings—at least the minimum daily—to maintain a healthy weight.

The beauty of the Food Guide Pyramid is its flexibility. As you get older or your lifestyle, health condition, or activity level changes, simply adjust how many servings you eat.

Source: The Food Guide Pyramid: Your Personal Guide to Healthful Living, International Food Information Council Foundation, U.S. Department of Agriculture/Center for Nutrition Policy and Promotion, and Food Marketing Institute, 1995.

With the Pyramid's flexibility, the variety of foods from ethnic cuisines can fit within its many food groups. *In chapter 15, you'll find Pyramids showing Chinese, Italian and Mexican fare.*

Health-Wise Eating Strategies

Do you prefer a hearty breakfast or a light morning bite? A big meal at lunchtime or at dinner? Snacks or no snacks? Three meals a day or several mini-meals? There's no one pattern for smart eating. However, several strategies can make a difference as you and your family develop an eating style to match Pyramid guidelines.

Quick, Easy Trade-Offs

Are some foods you enjoy higher in fat, sugars, or salt? You don't need to give these foods up—just trade them off! If variety, balance, and moderation are already hallmarks of your eating style, you can use trade-offs to eat any food you like—at least in small amounts.

What is a trade-off? It's simply balancing food choices over the course of the day. Foods with less fat, sugars, or salt are balanced with foods in meals and snacks that have more, while keeping within nutrient and Pyramid guidelines for good health.

With trade-offs, any foods can fit in a healthful eating plan, including those from the five food groups and those from the Pyramid tip with more fat, sugars, or salt. You simply need to balance how much and how often you consume these foods. Remember, your goal isn't to eliminate foods, but to moderate and balance your day's meal and snack choices.

Trading Off...

Consider these easy trade-offs, then apply the strategies to your own eating style. Remember, when you trade off for fat, you're trading off for calories, too.

...for fat.

Enjoy a baked potato (without a high-fat topping) for supper rather than french fries to save on fat. Spend some of the savings on a small dish of ice cream for dessert.

Top homemade pizza with reduced-fat, rather than regular, mozzarella. Then spend some of the savings on cookies and milk later in the day.

...for sugars.

Top French toast with sliced fresh peaches, rather than syrup. Fruit contains natural sugars along with vitamins A and C; the syrup likely has sugars only.

Enjoy fruit canned in natural juices as a snack, rather than fruit packed in syrup, to save on calories. Then spend those calories on jam or honey on your biscuit for dinner.

To make trading off easier, use the nutrition information on food labels. *Read about how to use the Nutrition Facts panel to identify the amounts of fat, sugars, and sodium in "Get All the Facts!" on page 271.*

Meal Skipping: Poor Option!

People give all kinds of excuses for skipping meals: "no time," "nothing to eat," "tied up in meetings," "had to work out instead," "didn't bring any cash," "woke up too late," "eating alone is no fun," "on a diet," and "not hungry," among others.

As a regular habit, skipping or skimping on meals usually catches up with you, however. For one, meal skipping usually affects productivity: less concentration, more difficulty with problem solving, and increased fatigue—serious problems for children and adolescents. Often, meal skipping leads to missed food-group servings and nutrients during the day, too. If you have to skip a meal, try to make up for what you missed during other meals or with snacks. Moreover, skipped meals often lead to overeating at snacktime or the next meal. The bottom line is this: skipping meals doesn't make good nutrition sense!

Quick-to-Fix Meal Tips

When time is short, don't give up on healthful eating. Just take some short cuts to save on time and energy!

When you have time to cook, make a double or triple batch. For example, simmer enough pasta for two days. Serve it hot on one night with meat sauce, then chilled as a salad with tuna, parsley, and low-fat salad dressing the next.

Buy prepared foods: for example, grated cheese; precut stir-fry vegetables; shredded cabbage; skinless chicken strips; mixed salad greens; prewashed spinach; and chopped onion. Even thin-sliced, lean deli meat is quick for stir-fried recipes.

Plan ahead: prepare ingredients ahead of

A Day's Menu for the Whole Family

Food Choices	1,600 Calories (Child 4-6 yrs)	2,200 Calories (Active Mom)	2,800 Calories (Active Dad)
Breakfast			
bran flakes topped with			
low-fat fruit yogurt	1 ounce	1 ounce	1 ounce
or 1% milk	1/2 cup	1/2 cup	1/2 cup
whole-wheat toast	1/2 slice	1 slice	2 slices
with jam	2 teaspoons	1 tablespoon	1 tablespoon
orange juice	3/4 cup	3/4 cup	3/4 cup
coffee	0	6 ounces	6 ounces
Lunch			
sandwich with			
rye bread	1 slice	2 slices	2 slices
lean beef	1 ounce	2 ounces	2 1/2 ounces
Colby cheese	0	1 ounce	1 ounce
alfalfa sprouts	1/4 cup	1/4 cup	1/4 cup
tomato	1 slice	1 slice	1 slice
mustard	1 teaspoon	1 teaspoon	1 teaspoon
broccoli florets	1/2 cup	1/2 cup	1 cup
banana	1/2	1	1
milk, 1 percent	1 cup	1 cup	1 cup
Snack			
grapes	1/2 cup	1/2 cup	1 cup
peanuts	1/3 cup	1/3 cup	1/3 cup
Dinner			
broiled chicken (skin removed)	3 ounces	3 ounces	4 ounces
herbed brown rice	1/2 cup	1 cup	1 cup
carrot coins	1/2 cup	3/4 cup	3/4 cup
tossed green salad	1 cup	1 cup	1 cup
with low-fat dressing	1 Tbsp.	1 Tbsp.	1 Tbsp.
whole-wheat roll with	1	1	2
margarine or butter	1 tsp.	1 tsp.	2 tsp.
angel food cake	1 slice	1 slice	1 slice
milk, 1%	1 cup	1 cup	1 cup
Snack			
oatmeal cookies	2	2	2
Food Group Servings			
Bread	6	9	11
Vegetable	3 1/2	4	5
Fruit	2 1/2	3	4
Milk	2 1/2	3	3
Meat	5 ounces	6 ounces	7 ounces
Fat Grams	47 grams	74 grams	93 grams

Give the Gift of Health

From your kitchen to theirs, give the gift of good nutrition—a variety of healthful foods—as a hospitality, holiday, birthday, or anytime gift.

Drop off "breakfast in a basket": homemade quick bread or bagels, jar of fruit spread, fresh fruit, and Spiced Mocha-Cocoa Mix. (For spiced mocha-cocoa mix, combine 1 3/4 cups nonfat dry milk powder, 1/4 cup cocoa powder, 1 to 2 tablespoons instant coffee granules, 1/4 cup sugar, and 1 teaspoon cinnamon. Put it in a pretty container with instructions to combine 1/3 cup mix with 6 ounces hot water.

Create an Italian gift basket with fancy-shaped, flavored pasta, sun-dried tomatoes, tomato sauce, a wedge of Parmesan cheese, an Italian cookbook, and a red-and-white checkered tablecloth.

Take a fruit-picking outing to a local orchard, vineyard, or berry farm. Pick enough for yourself—and enough to fill a decorative basket to give as a gift along with a favorite recipe.

Give bean bags! Buy bags of different dry legumes: navy beans, lentils, black kidney beans, and more. Mix them up, then repackage them in special containers or cloth bags. Attach a recipe for homemade chili or bean soup.

Find a recipe for a grain that's new to you: perhaps quinoa, jasmine rice, or barley. Prepare it for a potluck meal; bring a gift package of the grain with the recipe for the host or hostess.

Create a crudité (raw veggie) basket. Tuck an herb blend and reduced-fat cream cheese in the basket for making a dip. *For an easy herb blend recipe, refer to page* 164. (*Hint*: Keep your basket cool while it's transported.) ✦

time yourself. For example, wash and trim broccoli florets. Skewer kebobs with vegetable and meat pieces the night before. Cook lean ground meat ahead for soft tacos.

Stock your pantry with quick-to-fix foods: pasta, rice, frozen and canned vegetables, canned fruits, bread, lean deli meats, salad ingredients, salsa, canned beans, milk, yogurt, and cheese, among others.

Cook on weekends; save food "prep" time on weekdays. Freeze leftovers in individual meal containers for quick thawing mid-week.

Use quick cooking methods. Stir-frying, broiling, and microwaving usually are faster than baking or roasting. Slice meat and poultry in thinner slices for faster cooking.

Prepare meals that pack variety in just one dish. Try chicken fajitas in a soft taco. Stuff tuna and vegetable salad into a pita pocket. Prepare a ham and spinach quiche. Make a chef's salad, requiring no cooking at all. Or prepare risotto with seafood, Swiss chard, and shredded cheese.

Keep a variety of prepared foods on hand. Check the Nutrition Facts panel on the food label to choose those that match your family's nutrition needs. Prepare them along with fresh foods: for example, prepared pasta sauce heated with cooked ground meat, then served over pasta or a microwave-baked potato.

Serve assemble-your-own menus: perhaps deli sandwiches, mini-pizzas on English muffins, or burgers with veggies and cheese toppings.

Breakfast: Off to a Healthy Start!

You've heard it many times before: breakfast is the healthful way to start the day. Thirty years of breakfast-related studies show that jump starting the day with breakfast benefits everyone—children, teens, and adults.

However, despite its benefits, breakfast may be the

meal most often neglected and skipped. Some people blame their body clock for not feeling hungry when they wake up. With the hectic lifestyles of the '90s, others come up short on time and energy first thing in the morning. And some falsely believe that skipping breakfast offers an effective strategy for weight control.

Why Breakfast?

Breakfast is your body's early morning refueling stop. After 8 to 12 hours without a meal or snack, your body needs to replenish its glucose, also called blood sugar. A new supply of food produces more glucose. The brain needs a fresh supply of glucose, its main energy source, because it has no stored reserves. Sustained mental work—in school or in the workplace—requires a large turnover of glucose in the brain. Your muscles also need a replenished blood glucose supply for physical activity throughout the day.

Actually, you may not feel hungry by mid-morning if you skip breakfast. Conversely, you may feel hunger pangs even if you do eat early in the day. That's because your body reverts back to its normal metabolic response. Hunger pangs are a healthy signal. You need to respond to, not deny, them. Denying often leads to bingeing.

Are you a breakfast skipper, skimper, or eater? According to research, breakfast skippers often feel tired, irritable, or restless in the morning. On the flip side, breakfast eating is associated with better attitudes toward work or school and higher productivity in the late morning. Breakfast eaters tend to have more strength and endurance, and better concentration and problem-solving ability. What about breakfast skimpers? Eating even small amounts of food helps restore glucose stores.

The nutrient connection. Breakfast contributes Pyramid servings and nutrients. The good news: Total nutrient intake for the day is usually higher for those who eat a morning meal, especially for children and women. A whole-grain cereal, milk, and citrus juice can provide 100 percent of the vitamin C, 33 percent of the calcium, thiamin, and riboflavin, and a good supply of fiber, iron, and other nutrients for a day. Breakfast skippers may never make up the nutrients they miss without a morning meal.

Breakfast and learning. For children and teens, a morning meal is especially important. Breakfast prepares children to meet the challenges of learning. Those who regularly eat a morning meal tend to perform better in school, often scoring higher on tests. While adults may condition themselves to overcome symptoms caused by breakfast skipping, children cannot. They experience the very real effects of transient, or short-term, hunger.

Nutrition experts note that morning hunger has a significant effect on learning since it reduces concentration, problem-solving, and muscle coordination. That's especially hard on young children because basic skills—reading, writing, and arithmetic—are often taught first thing in the morning. Consider the long-term effect of transient hunger on learning. When children can't reach their learning potential day after day, then can get further and further behind.

Skipping breakfast often results in missed class time, too. Stomachaches or hunger pangs, caused by breakfast skipping or skimping, are the main rea-

KITCHEN NUTRITION

"jazz up" cooked cereal

For a "great grain" breakfast, add flavor and nutrition to cooked cereals (instant or not), like oatmeal, cream of wheat, grits, or couscous:

➢ Use fruit juice—apple, orange, or any other juice—for some or all of the cooking liquid.

➢ To cooked cereal, blend in grated cheese, chopped fruit (apple, peach, banana, kiwi), dried fruit (chopped apricots, papaya, dates, raisins), or nuts.

➢ Liven it up with spices: cinnamon, nutmeg, allspice, or cloves.

➢ Top it with fresh fruit of any kind! ✦

son for morning visits to the school nurse. And breakfast skippers tend be tardy or absent from school more often.

Breakfast for better health. Studies suggest two other reasons for being a breakfast convert: weight control and reduced risk for heart disease. Breakfast eaters are less likely to be ravenously hungry for mid-morning snacks or lunch; overall they tend to eat less fat during the day, too. Compared to breakfast eaters, studies show that those who skipped breakfast tend to have higher blood cholesterol levels, which is a risk factor for heart disease. Further research is needed to explore this link.

An Energizing Start

Once you're committed to eating breakfast, also consider that what you choose for breakfast can make a difference in your energy level for the morning. When a breakfast consists mostly of sugary foods, such as fruit, fruit juice, candy, or soda pop, a quick rise in your blood sugar occurs, causing a surge in energy. After about an hour, blood sugar and energy decline, bringing on symptoms of hunger. This scenario is depicted below at left.

When a balanced breakfast, consisting of foods containing carbohydrate, sugar, protein, and fat, is consumed, a sustained release of energy occurs. This delays symptoms of hunger for several hours and maintains blood sugar levels. This scenario is depicted below at right.

Beating Breakfast Barriers

Every excuse or apparent barrier to breakfast actually has an easy solution!

Not hungry in the early morning? Start with a light bite, perhaps juice or toast. Later when you are hungry, have a nutritious mid-morning snack: a hard-cooked egg, milk, yogurt, cheese, or a bagel.

Short on time? Keep quick-to-fix foods on hand: breakfast cereal, instant breakfast mix, bagels, toaster waffles, bread for toast, yogurt, canned and fresh fruit, juice, milk, cheese, and cottage cheese. Get breakfast foods ready the night before, such as mixing a pitcher of juice. Or plan on a breakfast that goes with you: a carton of yogurt; a bagel spread with peanut butter; or grapes, crackers and cheese. If all else fails, set your alarm clock a few minutes earlier.

Try these one-minute breakfasts:

- ready-to-eat cereal topped with sliced banana and yogurt
- bran muffin and yogurt topped with berries
- peanut butter on whole-wheat toast and milk
- pizza slice and orange juice
- instant oatmeal topped with raisins and grated cheese
- breakfast shake (milk, fruit, and a teaspoon of bran, whirled in a blender)
- toasted whole-wheat waffle, topped with fruit and yogurt or light whipped cream

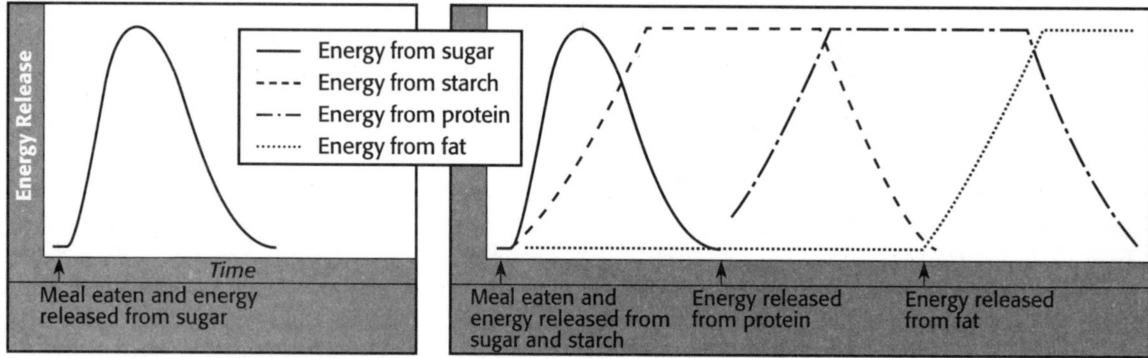

Sugary foods, such as fruit, fruit juice, candy, or soda pop, eaten in place of a meal cause a quick rise in blood sugar and energy. About an hour later blood sugar and energy decline rapidly, bringing on symptoms of hunger.

Balanced breakfast containing sugar, starch, protein, and fat (like a typical school breakfast containing fruit or juice, toast or cereal and 2 percent or whole milk) gives a sustained release of energy in children, delaying symptoms of hunger for several hours.

- ➢ bagel topped with fruit chutney, milk
- ➢ lean ham on a toasted English muffin, vegetable juice

Think you'll gain weight? There's no evidence to support this belief. To be on the lean side, choose grain products, fruits, juice, lean meat, and lower-fat dairy foods. Go easy on higher-fat breakfast foods, such as bacon, breakfast sausage, hash browns, and biscuits with gravy.

Don't like traditional breakfast foods? That's okay. Breakfast can be any food you like, even a slice of pizza, chicken sandwich, or soup. Leftover macaroni and cheese, heated in the microwave oven, makes a fine breakfast. Or try something new to make breakfast more interesting, perhaps a new yogurt flavor or an exotic fruit on cereal. Just make your meal count toward food-group servings.

Doesn't fit your travel schedule? If you're on the road, breakfast can be easy to manage—even without going to a restaurant. Room service is often faster than eating in a crowded coffee shop or dining room. Place your order the evening before to ensure on-time delivery. If you're on the road for long trips, balance low-fat breakfast options—fresh or stewed fruits, cereal with milk, for example—with omelet-and-sausage breakfasts. *For more choices, refer to "Breakfast on the Road" on page 387.*

That Snack Attack!

At the office, in the car, by the television set, at a sports event, in the movie theater—snacking is part of the American lifestyle. We often chide ourselves for between-meal nibbling, sometimes with good reason. Too often, people snack mainly on high-calorie, high-fat foods, then skimp on meals. Then they come up short on overall nutrition for the day—and perhaps overdo on calories.

Calcium is a case in point. Compared with moderate snackers, research suggests that people who frequently consume a lot of soft drinks and sugary snacks take in less calcium. Likely, they're substituting these foods for servings from the Milk Group, the best sources of calcium.

Carefully chosen, snacks promote good health and add pleasure to life. They can supply needed nutrients, such as vitamins A and C, calcium, and fiber, without adding too much fat or too many calories.

For children, snacks supplement meals. Because

Two Food-Group Snacks

- ➢ whole-grain cereal and milk
- ➢ fruit smoothie (fruit or juice, blended with milk or yogurt)
- ➢ yogurt and fresh fruit
- ➢ peanut butter on whole-wheat crackers
- ➢ pita bread and hummus (chickpea dip)
- ➢ apple or pear slices topped with cheese
- ➢ bagel chips (oven baked) and salsa
- ➢ dried cranberry and peanut mix
- ➢ pita bread stuffed with lettuce, tomato, cucumber, and low-fat salad dressing
- ➢ raw veggies with a cottage cheese or yogurt dip
- ➢ light microwave popcorn and fruit juice
- ➢ quesadilla (soft tortilla and cheese, folded and heated)
- ➢ flaked tuna and chopped celery, tossed with low-fat mayonnaise
- ➢ microwave-baked potato topped with salsa and cheese shreds ✦

their stomachs are small, kids may need to eat more often than adults do, perhaps every three to four hours. Teenagers, who are active and growing rapidly, need the calories that snacks supply. *For more about snacking for kids and teens, refer to "Snacks Equal Good Nutrition" on page 426 and "Great Snacking!" on page 448.* Adults may enjoy a snack as a break in the day and as a way to satisfy mid-day hunger. Older adults with small appetites or limited energy may find several small meals easier to handle. And almost everyone enjoys the social value of snacking with others.

When you think about snacking, remember this simple axiom. When you eat is far less important than what and how much you eat throughout the day. For good health, make the Food Guide Pyramid your anytime, anywhere guide to healthful eating.

Myths About Snacking

Despite what they know about nutrition, many people feel guilty about snacking. To them, snacks seem like a questionable extra, rather than a part of healthful eating. Good nutrition sense, however, challenges the popular myths about snacking:

Myth: *Snacking makes you fat!*
Fact: There's no direct link between snacking and body weight. The issue is total calories, not how often you eat. Your calorie, or energy, balance at the end of the day—based on the number of calories you ate and the number you burned—determines whether you gain, lose, or maintain weight.

did you know

...munching on a handful of baby carrots will meet your vitamin A needs for the entire day?

...preschoolers get nearly one-third of their energy from snacks?

...snacking is on the rise: 75 percent of men and women eat at least one snack a day?

...a planned snack can help prevent overeating?

...watching television tends to increase snacking—particularly on high-fat, high-calorie "goodies"? ✦

Snacking, in fact, may have weight-control advantages. Eaten well before mealtime, snacks help take the edge off hunger, helping you avoid overeating at meals. Smart snackers choose foods carefully to match their calorie target—without going over.

Myth: *Snacking causes cavities.*
Fact: Frequent snacking can promote cavities. The longer teeth come in contact with food, particularly carbohydrate foods, the more time bacteria in plaque has to produce acids that damage tooth enamel.

However, you can control a plaque attack. Consume the whole snack at one time rather than nibbling. Then brush when you finish snacking to remove food that sticks to and in between teeth—or rinse your mouth with water. Enjoy snacks, such as cheddar cheese, with properties that protect teeth from cavity formation. *For more information, refer to "A Sticky Issue" and "Snack for a Healthy Smile" on pages 127 and 129.*

Myth: *Snacking gets in the way of good nutrition.*
Fact: Snacks can contribute to a healthful eating style. Snack foods include any variety of foods and beverages from all five food groups. Food-group snacks help fill in the nutrition gaps from meals, helping to balance food choices for the day.

Myth: *Snacks spoil your appetite.*
Fact: Eaten two to three hours before mealtime, a small amount of food won't ruin your appetite. In fact, snacks quell hunger pangs so you're less likely to overeat at the next meal.

Myth: *Healthful snacking means giving up some fun foods.*
Fact: Any food can be eaten as a snack. You can eat foods such as chips and soft drinks in moderation and still consume a nutritious diet. Just plan snacks into your food choices for the day. Balance higher-fat or higher-calorie snack foods with lower-fat choices at meals. For example, if you snack on two chocolate chip cookies, enjoy chicken-vegetable stir-fry for dinner, rather than fried chicken and creamy slaw.

Remember, one snack, one meal, or one day of high-fat eating won't make or break your health. It's your food choices and eating style over the long term that counts!

Snacking Smart

Chosen wisely, snacks can work for you! As with other food choices, you need to snack with variety, balance, and moderation in mind. These 10 smart-snack tips can make between-meal eating a valuable part of your eating style!

1. *Make snacks part of your personal Pyramid for the whole day.* Rather than thinking of them as "extras," choose snacks to contribute food-group servings for your personal Pyramid. It's a great way to add fruits, vegetables, milk, and grains.

2. *Choose snacks for variety.* Add to the enjoyment and nutritional quality of your diet; consume a variety of snack foods within each food group. Even try snacks with an international flavor: spring rolls, bean burrito, or foccacia bread.

3. *Snack when you're hungry.* Skip the urge to nibble when you're bored, frustrated, or stressed. "Feed" that urge to munch by walking around the block or doing another activity instead.

4. *Make snacking a conscious activity.* Without realizing it, you can overeat easily when you absentmindedly snack while doing something else, such as watching television.

5. *Eat snacks well ahead of mealtime.* A light bite, eaten two to three hours before meals, probably won't interfere with your appetite.

6. *Eat snack-size portions.* Snacks aren't meal replacers. Smaller portions usually are enough to take away between-meal hunger pangs without interfering with your mealtime appetite.

7. *Match snack calories to your activity level.* A physically-active person or growing teenager can consume more substantial snacks—with more calories—than an armchair athlete can. Whether from snacks or meals, calories can add up unless you watch what you eat and maintain physical activity.

8. *Consider snacks in your fat budget.* Balance snacks with mealtime foods to keep the total amount of fat in your diet to no more than 30 percent of your day's energy intake. If you're not certain of the fat content of snacks, read the Nutrition Facts panel on the food label.

9. *Go easy on snacks from the Pyramid tip.* Enjoy them in small amounts, but snack mostly on nutrient-dense foods from the five food groups.

10. *Plan ahead for smart snacking.* Keep a variety of tasty, nutritious, ready-to-eat snacks on hand at home, at work, or wherever you need a light bite to take the edge off hunger. That way, you won't be limited to snacks from vending machines, quickservice restaurants, convenience stores, or your own randomly-stocked kitchen.

Healthy Bites

Take some healthy bites! When snacks contribute food group servings, they also make a sizable contribution to your nutrition needs for the day.

Each snack listed provides several nutrients for your good health. Take a peek at just one nutrient or compound in each food to see how snacks, wisely chosen, can add to the nutritional quality of your day's intake.

THIS SNACK...	SUPPLIES...
1/2 bagel	15% of thiamin
1 homemade bran muffin	10% of fiber
1 slice whole-wheat bread	5% of iron
1 medium carrot	> 100% of vitamin A
1/2 cup broccoli florets	66% of vitamin C
6 ounces tomato juice	50% of vitamin C
3/4 cup orange juice	> 100% of vitamin C
1/2 cup cantaloupe	50% of vitamin A
1 banana	33% of vitamin B_6
1 cup yogurt	30% of calcium
1 1/2 ounces low-fat string cheese	25% of calcium
1 cup cottage cheese	50% of protein
1 (3-ounce can) tuna	50% of niacin
2 ounces lean ham	22% of protein
1/2 cup vegetarian refried beans	15% of iron

Percentages based on Daily Values for a 2,000-calorie a day diet. See Chapter 12 for an explanation of Daily Values.

Go Anywhere Snacks

Satisfy your snack tooth anytime, anywhere with these fun, healthful snacks. Remember: perishable foods, such as dairy foods and meats, need to be refrigerated or stored on ice.

Refrigerator Snacks. Stock your refrigerator with ready-to-go snack fixings: yogurt; cottage cheese; traditional, reduced-fat, or fat-free cheese; lean deli meats, such as lean ham and smoked turkey; fruit juice; milk; and washed, ready-to-eat fruits and vegetables.

Office Snacks. Prepare for unscheduled meetings and deadlines by stashing nutritious snacks in your office or workplace: instant vegetable or bean soup; pretzels; snack-size, whole-grain cereal; mini-cans of water-packed tuna; boxes of raisins; instant oatmeal or couscous; dried fruit or single serve fruit cups; or whole-wheat crackers. Keep boxed dry milk on hand; add cold water and refrigerate before you drink it for best taste.

Microwave Snacks. Heat single-serving soups. Make an instant pizza by topping pocket bread or English muffins with tomato sauce, Italian herbs, and mozzarella cheese. Make a hot bean dip with vegetarian refried beans, salsa, and mild green chiles, and serve with tortillas. Melt cheddar cheese on a microwave-baked potato.

Snack Sacks. Pack a mini-cooler or sack of snacks so they're on hand for car trips, outdoor events, or wherever you are. Take along canned or boxed juice, crackers and cheese, pretzels, air-popped or light microwave popcorn, fresh fruit, dried fruit, or raisin-nut mixes.

Vending Machine Snacks. Drop in your coins, then select pretzels, yogurt, fruit juice, peanuts, raisins, fresh fruit, or milk.

Convenience Store or Mall Snacks. Try soft pretzels, frozen yogurt, raisins, or juice.

Thirst-Quenching Snacks. Start with water; it's an essential nutrient! Try milk, fruit juice, and vegetable juice. Or opt for other flavorful fluids: juice spritzers (juice and mineral water), flavored mineral water, and fruit smoothies (fruit or juice, blended with milk or yogurt).

Fiber-Filling Snacks. For a "fiber favor," snack on air-popped or light microwave popcorn, bran muffins, whole-grain crackers, whole-wheat toast, fresh fruit kebobs, vegetable kebobs, three-bean salad, or lentil or bean soup.

Sweet Tooth Snacks. Try these goodies: pudding, oatmeal-raisin cookies, fig bars, graham crackers, hot chocolate, frozen yogurt, dried fruit, raisin toast, vanilla wafers, gingersnaps, frozen juice bars, sorbet, or fruit-flavored bagel.

Try...	Go easy on...
baked tortilla chips	corn chips
pretzels or saltines	potato chips
bagel with fat-free ricotta cheese or fruit preserves	doughnut
spiced applesauce	apple pie
frozen yogurt	ice cream
soft pretzel	croissant
fruit-yogurt shake	milk shake
salsa	sour cream dip
gingersnaps or vanilla wafer	butter cookie
angel food cake	pound cake

Grazing for Good Health

Many Americans have moved away from the pattern of "three square meals" a day. They've discovered that eating several mini-meals, sometimes called "grazing," matches an active, on-the-go lifestyle. As with traditional meal patterns, the goals for this alternative eating style remain the same: variety, balance, and moderation throughout the day.

Little meals aren't snacks eaten between larger meals; instead they're a variety of small portions throughout the day. As long as food choices add up to the Pyramid recommendations, eating five or six mini meals can be as nutritious as a three-meal-a-day eating style.

Little meals are nothing new. Instead, they're part of the traditional eating style in many places outside the United States. A variety of small portions of traditional Spanish dishes are served as "tapas." In Greece, Turkey, and Egypt they're called "mezze." A little meal, or "spuntino," in Italy might be a mini-pizza, grilled bread with tomatoes and cheese, or small skewers of meat and vegetables. And "dim sum," which means "to do (or touch) the heart" in Chinese, is a savory snack of spring rolls, pot stickers, and steamed dumplings, to name a few.

Eating a series of mini-meals may have several benefits. Like traditional eating styles, mini-meals contribute full or partial food-group servings. For some people, especially those with small appetites, a series of little meals matches their personal needs and lifestyles. Eating fewer calories more frequently may burn a few extra calories; eating and digesting food has a thermogenic, or calorie-burning, effect for a short time. Some researchers also say that spreading the same number of calories in four to six meals throughout the day, rather than at three meals, may relate to somewhat lower blood cholesterol levels, too. But these findings aren't conclusive.

For healthful "grazing"...

Balance the amount of food. To avoid overeating, yet still satisfy your appetite, each mini-meal should be about the same size.

Choose appetizer-size portions in restaurants and at home. That's about right for mini-meals.

Use the power of the Food Guide Pyramid. The real challenge with this eating style is keeping within Pyramid guidelines—eating enough servings yet not too much.

your nutrition check-up

How Did You Build Your Pyramid?

Step One: Jot down all the foods and beverages you consumed yesterday for meals and snacks. Include the portion size and where it fits on the Pyramid.

Foods and Beverages	Portion Size	Food Group(s) or Pyramid Tip
Breakfast		
Lunch		
Dinner		
Snacks		

Step Two: Approximate your calorie level on the chart, "How Many Servings for You?" on page 241.

I need about ________ calories a day.

Step Three: Total the number of servings you consumed from each food group. Then compare the number of servings you consumed with the serving amounts on page 257. Remember, if your portion is bigger than one Pyramid serving, it counts as more than one serving; smaller servings count as partial servings. Pyramid serving sizes are listed on pages 248 to 254.

	How many servings are right for you?	How many servings did you consume?
Bread Group	6 7 8 9 10 11	_____
Vegetable Group	3 4 5	_____
Fruit Group	2 3 4	_____
Milk Group	2 3	_____
Meat Group (ounces)	5 6 7	_____

Step Four: Take a few moments to look at your food record. Write down some changes you could make for a healthier eating style. You might start with small changes, such as adding an extra serving of vegetables or using less dressing on your salad, then make more changes gradually until healthful eating becomes your habit. Or if you do best by making major changes, it's OK to do them all at once...as long as you succeed over time.

(*Adapted from* The Food Guide Pyramid, *Home and Garden Bulletin Number* 252, U.S. *Department of Agriculture/ Human Nutrition Information Service,* 1992.)

real life nutrition

The Pyramid for Families

Julie is a single mom raising Tad, her teenage son, and Trish, her grade-school daughter. Like many working parents, she needs to provide meals and snacks with efficiency. Julie has limited time and energy to prepare food—including breakfast and dinner. The kids help, but homework and after-school activities put demands on them, too.

Julie knows that she cannot be a short-order cook, trying to satisfy the very different food needs of her two children and herself. "The stomach of a growing boy really seems to be a bottomless pit, especially after basketball practice," she sighs. "And Trish is such a picky eater!" Trish is active enough but hasn't started her next growth spurt yet.

Julie is very committed to the health of her family. The Food Guide Pyramid on her refrigerator magnet constantly reminds her of what it takes to eat smart. But sometimes the challenge seems too big.

Suggestions for meeting the Pyramid guidelines:

➢ The day's calorie needs for each member of Julie's family are quite different: about 1,600 for Trish, about 2,800 for Tad, and about 2,200 for herself. Since they all need the same nutrients, just in somewhat different amounts, they could enjoy many of the same foods…for Tad, just more Pyramid servings, and as a result, more calories. Trish needs fewer Pyramid servings—less than Julie does.

➢ Julie can keep a variety of food-group snacks on hand for the kids. Tad probably needs snacks to meet the Pyramid advice for his age and activity level. With her smaller appetite, Trish may not eat enough at meals to get the servings she needs from each food group; food-group snacks are equally important for her. Even Julie would benefit from easy snacks such as fresh fruit, a carton of yogurt, or a bagel to take for a midafternoon work break.

➢ On weekdays when time is short, Julie can short cut her food preparation and still provide her family with nutritious meals. Among her other "kitchen tricks," she can prepare foods ahead, use pre-prepped ingredients, and let the kids help assemble the meals.

A spaghetti dinner is a great example. For one, she can prepare the meat sauce ahead or use a prepared sauce. Secondly, she could add some frozen vegetables (cooked in the microwave oven) to the spaghetti for a Vegetable Group serving. And third, Tad can get the extra Bread Group servings he needs by eating more pasta and enjoying another slice of Italian bread.

CHAPTER TWELVE

SUPERMARKET SMARTS

With about 30,000 items available in today's supermarket, it's no wonder you have so many decisions to make! From food labels, to brochures and posters, to "in-store" consumer affairs professionals, you have more food facts at your fingertips than ever before. You can shop for taste, nutrition, safety, price, and convenience, all at the same time.

Self-service grocery stores began springing up around the nation in the late 1930s. As recently as the 1920s, consumers made their purchases from a butcher, bakery, fish market, corner fruit store, small stores selling canned and bulk foods, milk wagon, and even a horse-and-wagon peddler. Shopping was time-consuming and tiring. Canned foods were the only true convenience foods. Frozen foods were just making an appearance. Although food safety was important, standards weren't as high as they are today. The variety of food and information about food was limited, and not until the mid 1970s did nutrition labeling appear on package labels.

Both supermarkets and the food supply are quite different today. And food labels with Nutrition Facts appear on virtually all food products.

While supermarkets comprise 75 percent of the retail food business, that's not the only place you can buy food to prepare and eat at home. Consider all the other retail food outlets: specialty stores, warehouse and bulk food stores, health food stores, restaurants, convenience stores, farm stands, mail-order, and even on-line computer services.

No matter where you shop, look for these basic qualities of excellence in a food store:

- The store should be clean—display cases, grocery shelves, and the floor. And it should have a pleasing smell.
- Produce, meat, poultry, fish, and dairy foods should show qualities of freshness.
- Refrigerated cases should be cold. Freezer compartments should keep food solidly frozen.
- Bulk bins, salad bars, and other self-serve areas should be clean and properly covered.

Beyond these minimum standards, today's supermarkets may offer other useful services: credit-card shopping, home delivery, electric carts, cooking schools, consumer newsletters, electronic scanning for quick checkout, video rental, banking and postal facilities, pharmacies, florists, and recycling programs, to name just a few.

Today's Food Labels

At the store, food labels are your best sources of consumer information. Food labels tell the basics. They identify the food, the amount inside the package, and the manufacturer.

If you need to eat less fat, more calcium, or more fiber, Nutrition Facts labels can help you. Nutrition information on labels helps you choose foods in your overall diet to meet recommendations of the Dietary Guidelines for Americans and the Food Guide Pyramid. *As a quick refresher on the Dietary Guidelines, refer to page 5. Review the Food Guide Pyramid on page 6.*

The ingredient list, safety guidelines, preparation tips, and freshness dating—food labels tell still more about food inside the package. *"More Reading on the Food Label" on page 270 identifies additional information you may find on labels.*

What's on the Label?

Wrapped around almost every packaged food in the supermarket you'll find nutrition information. Today's food labels may carry up to four different types of nutrition and health information, all designed to help you make choices and fit foods into your overall eating style.

- The *Nutrition Facts* panel gives specific information about the calories and nutrients, such as fat, cholesterol, sodium, fiber, and certain vitamins and minerals, in a single serving of the food. This information must appear on virtually all food labels.
- The *ingredient list* on packaged food gives an overview of the "recipe," with the ingredients listed from most to least.
- A *nutrition description,* such as "low fat" or "high fiber," helps you easily find foods that meet specific nutrition goals.
- A *health claim* describes the potential health benefits of a food or nutrient, such as consuming calcium as a benefit for reducing the risk for osteoporosis.

The Nutrition Facts panel and the ingredient list appear on almost every packaged food in the supermarket. Today, many fresh fruits and vegetables, as well as meat, poultry, and seafood, may be labeled voluntarily with nutrition information, too, either on the package or on a poster or pamphlet displayed nearby. If you don't find this information in your supermarket, ask the supermarket manager to start providing it.

With food labels, you can make nutrition-related decisions as you shop. And it's information you can take home.

- Use labels to compare the nutrition of similar foods and to choose foods for an overall diet that's varied, moderate, and balanced.
- Use Nutrition Facts to make trade-offs and include all kinds of foods in your healthful diet. *Refer to "Quick, Easy Trade-Offs" on page 256.*

The Language of Labels

Imagine rolling your shopping cart through the supermarket. Your eyes dart from one food product to another. Some canned peaches say "no added sugar." Certain breakfast cereals are "high in fiber"; others are "fortified." On packages of luncheon meat you see the term "lean." The words "high in calcium" on a milk carton catch your eye. You can choose "lite" salad dressing. And a box of cookies says "fewer calories." What does all this label language mean?

These terms describe the amount of nutrients, cholesterol, fiber, or calories in food. But they don't give exact amounts. Usually, they appear on the front of food labels where you can use them for quick comparisons.

For example, suppose you're comparing fat in Italian salad dressing. Terms such as "reduced fat" and "fat free" offer a general idea of the fat content. To find the exact amount in one serving, check the Nutrition Facts panel, usually found on the package's side or back.

Keep in mind that these nutrition descriptions mean the same thing for all foods, no matter what food or manufacturer. That's because nutrition descriptions are defined strictly by regulation. Like Nutrition Facts, nutrition descriptions are defined for a single serving. That's a standard serving size set by the government—not necessarily what you consider one helping.

Nutrition descriptions are optional, however. Many foods that meet the criteria don't carry these terms on the label. It's up to the food manufacturer. So if you need—or want—to know about the food—read the Nutrition Facts panel! *For definitions of nutrition descriptions, refer to the "Label Lingo" on this page. You'll find more specific definitions of label lingo throughout the book.*

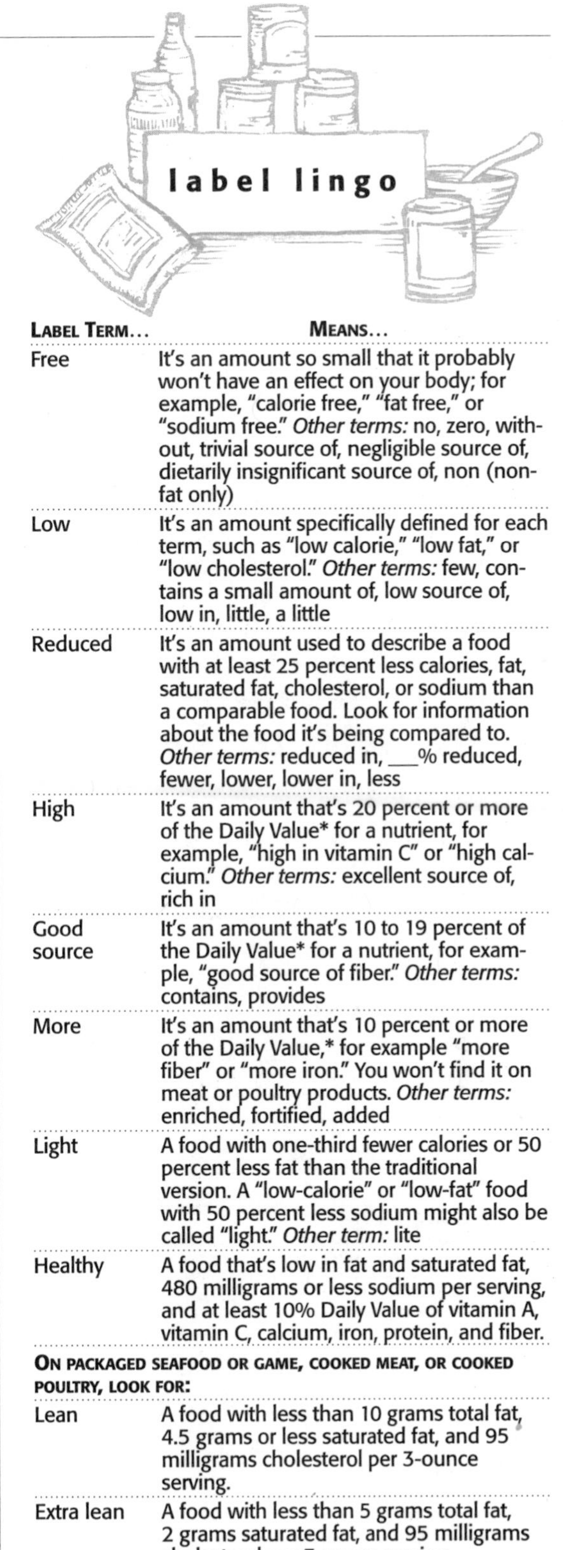

LABEL TERM...	MEANS...
Free	It's an amount so small that it probably won't have an effect on your body; for example, "calorie free," "fat free," or "sodium free." *Other terms:* no, zero, without, trivial source of, negligible source of, dietarily insignificant source of, non (nonfat only)
Low	It's an amount specifically defined for each term, such as "low calorie," "low fat," or "low cholesterol." *Other terms:* few, contains a small amount of, low source of, low in, little, a little
Reduced	It's an amount used to describe a food with at least 25 percent less calories, fat, saturated fat, cholesterol, or sodium than a comparable food. Look for information about the food it's being compared to. *Other terms:* reduced in, ___% reduced, fewer, lower, lower in, less
High	It's an amount that's 20 percent or more of the Daily Value* for a nutrient, for example, "high in vitamin C" or "high calcium." *Other terms:* excellent source of, rich in
Good source	It's an amount that's 10 to 19 percent of the Daily Value* for a nutrient, for example, "good source of fiber." *Other terms:* contains, provides
More	It's an amount that's 10 percent or more of the Daily Value,* for example "more fiber" or "more iron." You won't find it on meat or poultry products. *Other terms:* enriched, fortified, added
Light	A food with one-third fewer calories or 50 percent less fat than the traditional version. A "low-calorie" or "low-fat" food with 50 percent less sodium might also be called "light." *Other term:* lite
Healthy	A food that's low in fat and saturated fat, 480 milligrams or less sodium per serving, and at least 10% Daily Value of vitamin A, vitamin C, calcium, iron, protein, and fiber.
ON PACKAGED SEAFOOD OR GAME, COOKED MEAT, OR COOKED POULTRY, LOOK FOR:	
Lean	A food with less than 10 grams total fat, 4.5 grams or less saturated fat, and 95 milligrams cholesterol per 3-ounce serving.
Extra lean	A food with less than 5 grams total fat, 2 grams saturated fat, and 95 milligrams cholesterol per 3-ounce serving.

*when compared with a standard serving size of the traditional food.

Get All the Facts!

Let's get specific. Nutrition Facts differ from nutrition descriptions. The Nutrition Facts panel specifically states the amount of nutrients and calories in food...while terms such as "low in fat" or "more fiber" help you quickly spot foods with nutritional qualities that match your needs.

Check these features on the Nutrition Facts panel:

Serving size. Serving size is based on how much people actually eat—not necessarily the amount recommended or the amount you eat. It's important because nutrition information applies to one serving. So, if a serving is one cup and you ate two, you consumed twice the amount of calories and other nutrients given on the label.

Calories. You'll find the number of calories in a single serving and how many of these calories come from fat. *Tip*: Avoid confusing "calories from fat" with the dietary advice, "Eat no more than 30 percent of total calories from fat." Percent of calories from fat does not appear on the label and applies only to your overall intake, not a single food or meal.

Nutrition Facts

Serving Size 1 cup (248g)
Servings Per Container 4

Amount Per Serving	
Calories 150	Calories from Fat 35
	% Daily Value*
Total Fat 4g	**6%**
Saturated Fat 2.5g	**12%**
Cholesterol 20mg	**7%**
Sodium 170mg	**7%**
Total Carbohydrate 17g	**6%**
Dietary Fiber 0g	**0%**
Sugars 17g	
Protein 13g	
Vitamin A 4% •	Vitamin C 6%
Calcium 40% •	Iron 0%

* Percent Daily Values are based on a 2,000 calorie diet. Your daily values may be higher or lower depending on your calorie needs:

		2,000	2,500
	Calories:	2,000	2,500
Total Fat	Less than	65g	80g
Sat Fat	Less than	20g	25g
Cholesterol	Less than	300mg	300mg
Sodium	Less than	2,400mg	2,400mg
Total Carbohydrate		300g	375g
Dietary Fiber		25g	30g

Calories per gram:
Fat 9 • Carbohydrate 4 • Protein 4

% Daily Values. These percentages give you a general idea of how one serving contributes nutritionally to a 2,000-calorie diet. Use them to see if the food has a little or a lot of a nutrient.

Depending on your age, gender, and activity level, you may need more or less than 2,000 calories. So for some nutrients, you may need more or less than 100% Daily Value. *To estimate how much energy, or calories, you need daily, refer to page* 22.

Nutrient amounts. Of all the nutrients in food, only a few are listed on the Nutrition Facts panel—those that relate to today's most important health issues. Numbers on the label are rounded. If the math seems slightly off, you probably don't need to send a letter to the manufacturer! Food companies follow government rules for rounding.

Fat, saturated fat, cholesterol, and sodium are listed because many people consume too much. Your goal is no more than 100 percent of your Daily Value for the day. Be aware that total fat includes all types of fat—saturated fat as well as polyunsaturated and monounsaturated fat. Labels show the various types of fat because diets low in saturated fat and cholesterol may decrease the risk of heart disease.

Fiber, vitamins A and C, calcium, and iron are listed because they often come up short. For these, your goal is to consume a variety of foods that add up to at least 100 percent per day. But be aware that consuming 100% DV for some nutrients may, or may not, be the optimal amount recommended for you. For example, for food labels, the DV for calcium is 1,000 milligrams and the specific Dietary Reference Intake (DRI) recommendation for adults through age 50 is also 1,000 milligrams daily. However, teens through age 18 are urged to consume 1,300 milligrams calcium daily, and for adults over age 50, the advice is 1,200 milligrams calcium daily. *For more about* DRIs, *refer to page* 4.

Fat, saturated fat, cholesterol, total carbohydrate, fiber, sugars, protein, vitamins A and C, calcium, and iron are required on the label—unless their amounts are insignificant. Other nutrients may be listed voluntarily.

If you see a nutrition description, perhaps for milk, "fortified with vitamin D," you'll find that nutrient on the Nutrition Facts panel. Nutrients added to a food, such as fortified breakfast cereal, also are listed.

Daily Values footnote. This reference chart shows some Daily Values. For two calorie levels (2,000 calories and 2,500 calories), it shows the maximum amounts recommended for total fat, saturated fat, cholesterol, and sodium—and the target amounts for total carbohydrate and fiber. Depending on your calorie needs, you may need less or more. This footnote is the same on every food label.

Calories-per-gram conversion. You may see the number of calories in 1 gram of fat, carbohydrate, and protein. Notice that fat supplies more than twice the calories per gram (9 calories) than carbohydrate and protein (4 calories).

Metric Conversion Key

28 grams (g) = 1 ounce
1,000 milligrams (mg) = 1 gram

A Word About Ingredients...

Imagine that you're reaching for a can of chunky beef stew. What's the stew like inside? The Nutrition Facts panel gives the scoop on calories and nutrients. The ingredient list, like a recipe, tells you what's in the food container.

By regulation, any food made with more than one ingredient must carry an ingredient list on the label. Food manufacturers must list all ingredients in descending order by weight. Those in the largest amounts are given first. For example, canned tomato soup that lists tomatoes first contains more tomatoes by weight than anything else. Next time you reach for canned stew, check what ingredients are listed first, second, and third.

The ingredient list offers useful information—especially for people with special food needs, perhaps for health or religious reasons, for example:

- People with a food allergy or food sensitivity, perhaps to peanuts, eggs, milk sugar, or wheat. If you're sensitive to artificial color, the colors are named individually, not just listed as "coloring." If the ingredient list isn't clear to you, write or call the food manufacturer. *Refer to chapter 9, "Sensitive About Food," for more information on food sensitivities.*

- People who avoid pork, shellfish, or other meat for religious or other reasons.

In some cases, the ingredient list gives the source of the ingredients. For example, on the label for Mark's Cheese Pizza (see below), you'll see that "partially hydrogenated vegetable oil" is followed by "soybean and/or cottonseed oil" and that "tomato puree" is water and tomato paste. What is the part-skim mozzarella cheese made from? The ingredient list says pasteurized milk, cheese cultures, salt, and enzymes. *For more about hydrogenated vegetable oil, refer to "Hydrogenated: Firmer at Room Temperature" on page 58.*

Nutrition Facts

Serving Size 1 pizza (184g)
Servings Per Container 1

Amount Per Serving	
Calories 560 Calories from Fat 230	
	% Daily Value*
Total Fat 25g	**38%**
Saturated Fat 13g	**65%**
Cholesterol 45mg	**16%**
Sodium 1,090mg	**45%**
Total Carbohydrate 60g	**20%**
Dietary Fiber 4g	**16%**
Sugars 7g	
Protein 23g	

Vitamin A 45% • Vitamin C 0%
Calcium 50% • Iron 8%

* Percent Daily Values are based on a 2,000 calorie diet. Your daily values may be higher or lower depending on your calorie needs:

	Calories:	2,000	2,500
Total Fat	Less than	65 g	80g
Sat Fat	Less than	20g	25g
Cholesterol	Less than	300mg	300mg
Sodium	Less than	2,400mg	2,400mg
Total Carbohydrate		300g	375g
Dietary Fiber		25g	30g

Calories per gram:
Fat 9 • Carbohydrate 4 • Protein 4

MARK'S Cheese Pizza

MICROWAVE OVEN DIRECTIONS

1. Open pizza carton carefully. Remove frozen pizza and microwave disk; unwrap pizza. For best results, do not add additional toppings.
2. Reclose carton by inserting tab into slot. Place carton in center of microwave oven. Place disk silver side up on carton.
3. Center frozen pizza on top of disk. **Microwave at HIGH 3 to 4½ minutes,** or until most of cheese is melted, rotating carton ½ turn after 2 minutes.
4. Remove pizza from oven by holding sides of carton. Loosen pizza from disk with spatula.
CAUTION: Disk and pizza will be very hot.
NOTE: Microwave directions were developed using 600 to 700 watt ovens.

INGREDIENTS: CRUST: WHEAT FLOUR WITH MALTED BARLEY FLOUR, WATER, PARTIALLY HYDROGENATED VEGETABLE OIL (SOYBEAN AND/OR COTTONSEED OIL) WITH SOY LECITHIN, ARTIFICIAL FLAVOR AND ARTIFICIAL COLOR (BETA CAROTENE), SOYBEAN OIL, YEAST, HIGH FRUCTOSE CORN SYRUP, SALT, CALCIUM PROPIONATE ADDED TO RETARD SPOILAGE OF CRUST, L-CYSTEINE MONOHYDROCHLORIDE; **SAUCE:** TOMATO PUREE (WATER, TOMATO PASTE), WATER, GREEN PEPPERS, SALT, LACTOSE AND FLAVORING, SPICES, FOOD STARCH - MODIFIED, SUGAR, CORN OIL, XANTHAN GUM, GARLIC POWDER. **TOPPING:** LOW MOISTURE PART SKIM MOZZARELLA CHEESE (PASTEURIZED MILK, CHEESE CULTURES, SALT, ENZYMES.)

Manufactured by Mark's Pizza, Silver Spring, MD 20000

Health Claims on the Label

Another bit of nutrition information might appear on food labels: a health claim. Health claims link food—or food components—in your overall diet with a lowered risk for some chronic diseases. Since this information is optional, many foods that meet the criteria don't carry any health claim on their label.

Strictly regulated by the Food and Drug Administration, only health claims supported by scientific evidence are allowed on food labels. So far, eight health claims have been approved.

1. *Calcium and osteoporosis.* A calcium-rich diet may help prevent osteoporosis, a condition in which bones become thin and brittle.

2. *Fat and cancer.* Limiting the amount of total fat you eat may help reduce your risk for some cancers.

3. *Saturated fat and cholesterol and heart disease.* Limiting the amount of saturated fat and cholesterol you eat may help prevent heart disease.

4. *Fiber-containing grain products, fruits, vegetables, and cancer.* Eating high-fiber grain products, fruits, and vegetables may help prevent some cancers.

5. *Fruits, vegetables, and grain products that contain fiber and heart disease.* Eating fruits, vegetables, and grain products that contain fiber may help prevent heart disease.

6. *Sodium and high blood pressure.* Limiting the amount of sodium you eat may help prevent hypertension, or high blood pressure. Hypertension is a risk factor for heart attacks and strokes.

7. *Fruits and vegetables and some cancers.* Eating fruits and vegetables that are low in fat and good sources of dietary fiber, vitamin A, or vitamin C may help prevent some cancers.

8. *Folate and neural tube birth defects.* Women who consume 400 micrograms of folate daily reduce their risk of giving birth to a child afflicted with a neural tube defect. *Refer to "Pregnancy: Before You Begin" on page 457 to learn more about nutrition during pregnancy.*

When you read health claims, remember: Diet is just one factor that can reduce your risk for certain health problems. Heredity, physical activity, and smoking are among other factors that affect your health and risk for disease.

A Little "TLC" on Food Labels

For your good health, some food labels offer guidance for "tender, loving care": food safety and handling tips. To reduce the risk of foodborne illness, raw and partially-cooked meat and poultry products must be labeled with guidelines for safe handling. *"Safe Handling Instructions" on this page shows a sample food safety label.* The simple graphics—a refrigerator, bar of soap, fry pan, and clock—each represent a safe handling tip.

Following these guidelines not only helps keep food safe to eat. They also help food retain its appealing flavor, texture, and appearance. *For in-depth information on food safety and handling, refer to chapter 13, "The Safe Kitchen."*

Safe Handling Instructions

This product was prepared from inspected and passed meat and/or poultry. Some food products may contain bacteria that could cause illness if the product is mishandled or cooked improperly. For your protection, follow these safe handling instructions.

Keep refrigerated or frozen. Thaw in refrigerator or microwave.

Keep raw meat and poultry separate from other foods. Wash working surfaces (including cutting boards), utensils, and hands after touching raw meat or poultry.

Cook thoroughly.

Keep hot foods hot. Refrigerate leftovers immediately or discard.

More Reading on the Food Label

If you take a few more moments with food labels, you'll learn even more about the food inside the package!

Type of food. The product name lets you know exactly what's in the container. Besides naming the specific food, it tells the form it's in, perhaps smooth or chunky, sliced or whole, or miniature size—important information when you're following a recipe.

Quantity. Food labels tell you the total amount in the container, either in volume, count, or net weight. Net weight refers to the amount of food inside the container, including any liquid. But it doesn't include the weight of the container.

For juice products, total percent juice content. This tells you how much juice and how much water the beverage contains. But keep on reading. You'll want to read the Nutrition Facts panel to compare nutrients, like vitamin C along with sugars and calories, before making selections.

A "100 percent" juice may—or may not—supply 100 percent of the Daily Value for vitamin C. For example, a 6-ounce serving of orange or grapefruit juice provides more than 100 percent of the Daily Value for vitamin C, while the same amount of 100 percent grape juice supplies about 50 percent, and apple juice, much less. A juice "drink", "beverage," or "cocktail" may be fortified with vitamin C to 100 percent of the Daily Value for vitamin C, but may contain more calories from added sugars. To the body, the sugar in fruit, called fructose, and added sugars in juice drinks can't be distinguished. They're used in the body in the same way. *For more on the differences between juice and juice drinks, refer to "Juicy Story: Fruit Juice or Juice Drink?" on page 179.*

Name and address of the manufacturer, packer, or distributor. With this information, you can contact a food company with your consumer questions and concerns. On many labels you may find an "800-" phone number, too.

Food product dating. You can't see inside the food package, so how do you know if it's fresh? Many foods, such as dairy products, have a date on the product. It may be given as numbers, such as "12-15" or "1215", or as "Dec. 15" to mean December 15. Food manufacturers and retailers use three types of dates you can read:

- "Sell by" or pull date: That's the last day a food should be sold if the food is to remain fresh for home storage.
- Pack date: That's when the food was manufactured, processed, or packaged.
- "Best if used by" date: For optimal quality, it's recommended that a food be used by this date. It's not a safety date. For example, the label may indicate, "Best if used by 4-17-97." Depending on the food and if it has been stored properly, it will likely be safe beyond this date. (*As a quick tip*: The term "fresh" on some food labels is different from the freshness date.)

For guidelines on home storage, refer to "The Cold Truth: How Cold, How Long?" on page 313.

Grading and inspection symbols on some products. These symbols indicate that foods have met certain standards set by the government:

- Inspection stamps on meat, poultry, and packaged meats mean the food is wholesome and was slaughtered, packed, or processed under sanitary conditions.

- Food grades, for example on some types of meat, poultry, eggs, dairy foods, and produce, suggest standards of appearance, texture, uniformity, and perhaps taste. With the exception of marbling fat in meat, food grading does not suggest nutrient value. *Refer to pages 282 to 286 and page 289 for specific information on grading for meat, poultry, and eggs.*

Preparation instructions. Some products suggest oven or microwave times and temperatures, or perhaps other preparation or serving tips. Some even include recipes.

Universal Product Code (UPC). This series of black bars identifies the manufacturer and the food, and is used by the food industry for inventory control and price scanning.

Star-K

OU

OK

KOF-K

Kosher symbols. The term "kosher" means "proper" or "fit" in Hebrew. Kosher symbols indicate that the food has met the standards of a Jewish food inspector, done in addition to government safety inspection. The kosher code, which may appear on foods throughout the store, doesn't imply any nutritional qualities.

Often the word "Parev" is written next to these symbols, meaning the food has neither meat nor dairy ingredients. During March and April, a large "P" next to the symbols means it's kosher for Passover.

Health warnings for special conditions. A few foods carry health warnings for people with special needs. For example:

- Foods and beverages made with aspartame (a non-nutritive sweetener) offer a warning for people with phenylketonuria (PKU). Aspartame contains the amino acid phenylalanine, which people with PKU cannot metabolize.
- You'll find "Contains Sulfites" on labels for beer and wine for those who are sulfite sensitive.
- Alcoholic beverages also carry warnings for pregnant women.

Refer to chapter 9 for more information on PKU and other food sensitivities.

Besides nutrition and health claims, some labels carry other label terms.

LABEL TERM...	REFERS TO...
Fresh	food in its raw state. The term can't be used on food that has been frozen or heated, or on food that contains preservatives.
Fresh frozen	food that is quickly frozen while very fresh.
Homogenized	process of breaking up and separating milk fat. This makes the texture of milk smooth and uniform.
Pasteurized	process of heating foods, such as raw milk and raw eggs, to a temperature high enough to destroy bacteria and inactivate most enzymes that cause spoilage.
Ultra pasteurized	process of heating food to a temperature higher than pasteurization. This extends the time it can be stored in the refrigerator or on the shelf.
UHT	(Ultra High Temperature) process similar to ultra pasteurization. With high heat and sterilized containers, food can be stored unopened without refrigeration for up to three months. Once opened, it needs refrigeration.

Labels—and You

What nutrition information do you use to make food selections—food labels or the Food Guide Pyramid? Use both!

The Food Guide Pyramid helps you choose a variety of foods in amounts you need. *Tip*: Serving sizes on the Pyramid may differ from those on food labels. Servings on food labels are based on how much most people typically eat. Serving sizes on the Pyramid are recommended amounts for good health. Use serving sizes from the Pyramid as your guide to healthful eating. *For Pyramid serving sizes, refer to chapter 11.*

Food labels offer Nutrition Facts for choosing foods within each food group and the Pyramid tip. Suppose you're shopping for dinner. You want a vitamin A-rich vegetable or fruit. Using food labels, you see that frozen broccoli fits the bill. And it can supply one serving from the Vegetable Group of the Food Guide Pyramid. But which package of frozen broccoli? Again read the label. Broccoli with sauce has more calories and fat than plain broccoli. You pick the one that you prefer and that fits within your day's energy needs and fat budget.

Or suppose you're buying spaghetti sauce. Made with tomatoes, it counts toward the Vegetable Group. If you need to control your sodium intake, check the Nutrition Facts panel for the exact sodium content per serving. The label also may offer other information, such as "reduced sodium" or "low sodium." And if you're curious, the ingredient list tells what ingredients contribute sodium.

Nutrition Facts help you make trade-offs, too. For example, a switch from regular to lean hot dogs likely saves both fat grams and calories without giving up protein. The label tells how much. You might "spend" some of the savings on some ice cream for dessert. *See "Quick, Easy Trade-offs" on page* 257.

Supermarket Psychology

Understanding food labels can help you make nutrition-wise purchases. But that's just part of your overall shopping strategy. Following a few practical tips can make your grocery trips more time efficient, economical, and hassle free.

Nutrition $ense

With thousands of foods to choose from, how can you get the most nutrition for your food dollar? Be an educated consumer and plan ahead. Know exactly what you need. And be aware of marketing ploys that may encourage you to buy beyond your shopping list.

Keep a shopping list—and stick to it! A list jogs your memory and saves time as you walk the supermarket aisles. And with a list, you're less likely to spend money on items you really don't need.

For time management, keep a running list in your kitchen of items you need to replace. Organize your list by category to match the store layout, for example, produce department, dairy case, meat counter, deli, bakery, and grocery shelves.

Avoid extra shopping trips. If possible, shop just once or twice a week. You'll spend less on impulse items—and save time, too.

Check supermarket specials printed in newspaper inserts. Then plan menus around them. If the store runs out of an item on special, ask for a rain check.

Clip coupons for items you really need. Don't assume that items with coupons are always the best buy. Another brand or similar food might be cheaper even without a coupon.

Try not to shop when you're hungry. You'll less likely succumb to impulse items, including more expensive, less nutritious snack and dessert foods.

Buy fresh produce—fruit and vegetables—in season. Most are available year-round. In season, however, the price may be lower, and the produce, more flavorful.

have you ever wondered

...why a food label that says "no sugar added" shows some grams of sugars on the Nutrition Facts panel? Many foods—fruits, vegetables, milk, cereals, grains, and legumes—have naturally-occurring sugars. The "sugars" category on the food label includes both added and naturally occurring sugars.

...why the label doesn't give a % Daily Value for sugars? Since there's no recommended amount for sugars, the label cannot list a percentage. Showing the grams of carbohydrates, including sugars, shows where some calories in the food come from. Scientific evidence shows that dental caries is the only health problem directly linked to eating sugars. Complex carbohydrates and poor oral hygiene also are linked to dental caries. *Refer to "Your Smile: Sugar and Oral Health," on page* 126. ✦

Use food labels as you shop. Remember that information on food labels can help you find foods that match your needs, provide the facts for comparison shopping, and help you get the most nutrition for your food dollar.

Decide what quality food you need. For example, if you're making a casserole, chunky tuna may be fine. But more expensive solid-pack tuna has more eye appeal in a tuna-vegetable salad.

Buy the economy size or family packs only if you can use that much. There's no savings if food spoils and must be discarded. For foods that freeze, take time to repackage food into smaller amounts in freezer bags, then freeze for later use.

Compare prices using unit pricing on supermarket shelves. To make comparisons easier, especially for similar foods in different size containers, prices are given as cost per unit, rather than price per package or container. The unit might be an ounce, a quart, or some other measurement. If the foods themselves and the units being compared are the same, the best value is the lowest price per unit.

Compare the prices of national brands, store brands, and generic brands. Store brands and generic products may cost less than national brands, since they don't have the same promotional costs. But the quality may not be as consistent as a national brand. If you watch store specials, prices may be comparable.

If available, and if you qualify, take advantage of senior citizen discount days.

Stock up on canned and other nonperishable foods when they're on sale. At home, rotate your food supply, so that the "first in" is the "first out."

Buy perishable foods in amounts that will be consumed during peak quality. An extra bunch of broccoli that spoils in the refrigerator is no savings.

Consider buying foods sold in bulk bins. Because you're not paying for packaging or branding, bulk foods often cost less. And you can buy just the amount you need. Foods such as dry fruits, rice, pasta, other grains, snack mixes, and spices are among those sold in bulk.

Consider the cost for convenience. Prepared, presliced, and precooked foods usually cost more. Depending on your schedule, the time savings may be worth the price.

Remain flexible as you shop. If you see a better bargain or a new food (perhaps a vegetable or fruit) to try, adjust your menu.

Shop during off hours. If time is at a premium, shop when stores aren't crowded—often early in the morning, late in the evening, or midweek rather than on weekends. You may feel more relaxed as you make shopping decisions.

Pay attention at checkout. See that prices ring up as advertised or as indicated on the shelf label, especially for sale items.

"Small-Scale" Shopping

How do small households maximize their food dollars? Besides general cost-saving tips, consider these suggestions if you're a household of one or two people:

Buy frozen vegetables and fruit in bags, not boxes. As long as they aren't thawed, you can pour out as much as you need, then reseal and return the package to the freezer.

Look for foods sold in single servings: including juice, yogurt, frozen meals, soup, and pudding. That way you can have a greater variety of food on hand.

Today's stores know that small households are a big segment of the consumer market, so more and more products are available in single-size servings.

Share with a friend. To take advantage of the savings of economy-size packages, share your food purchases with someone else.

Shop from bulk bins. That way, you can buy only what you need.

Repackage meat, poultry, and fish into single portions in freezer wrap. Freeze these portions to use later.

Talk to the butcher and produce manager if you want a smaller amount of prepackaged fresh meat or produce. Usually they can repackage the food so you buy just what you need.

Buy produce that keeps longer in the refrigerator: broccoli, brussels sprouts, cabbage, carrots, parsnips, potatoes, sweet potatoes, and apples, grapefruit, melons, oranges, pears, and tangerines.

Shop for convenience. Often mixed salad greens (perhaps from the salad bar) or raw vegetables, already cut and mixed for stir-fry dishes or salads, cost less than buying individual foods in quantity.

Buy small loaves of bread. Or wrap and freeze what you won't use right away.

Your Shopping Guide

Filling your shopping cart? Choose plenty of foods from the five food groups, and then add a few extras. Overall, the foods you buy should allow you to make meals and snacks with variety, moderation, and balance.

Now, let's tour the supermarket, department by department, focusing on tips for buying high-quality, nutritious, and safe foods that match your needs.

Produce Department

In many stores, the produce department, with its appealing array of fresh fruits and vegetables, is the first stop on a shopping trip. Today's supermarkets offer a great variety to choose from—about 300 different types of produce in the average store. Because fruit and vegetables are most nutritious and best-tasting at their peak quality, you need to be savvy with your selections.

Check the produce department. Besides being clean, organized, and appealing, fresh fruits and vegetables should be held at a proper temperature. Most are kept chilled; lettuce and other greens are often sprayed with a fine mist of water to keep them crisp.

For fresh fruit and vegetables, consider ripeness. If you're buying produce to eat today, buy ripe. For tomorrow or the next day, look for produce that needs just a little ripening. And if you don't plan to eat produce until later in the week, buy fruit and vegetables that aren't yet ripe. *Tip*: To hasten the ripening of some fruits, such as pears and peaches, put them in a loosely closed paper bag at room temperature.

Buy the amount you need. Even when properly stored, produce is perishable. The freshest produce contains the most nutrients.

Look for Nutrition Facts. If packaged, the label on produce may carry nutrition information. If not, check for a poster or pamphlet with these facts nearby. Ask the store manager to provide this information if it's not available. *For fruits and vegetables which are good sources of vitamins A and C, refer to "Vegetables: From A to Z" on page 250 and "What's in the Fruit Bowl?" on page 252.*

Go for variety! That includes fruits and vegetables rich in vitamin A or C, or both. Rather than just the old standbys, add a new fruit and vegetable to your shopping cart each week, too. The store may have preparation and handling tips for unfamiliar produce.

Explore different varieties of a familiar food. For example, try different apples: perhaps Cortland, Granny Smith, Newtown Pippin, and Rome Beauty.

Shopping for Freshness!

FOR FRUIT…

***apples*:** firm with smooth, clean skin and good color. Avoid fruit with bruises or decay spots.

***apricots*:** plump with as much golden orange color as possible. Blemishes, unless they break the skin, will not affect flavor. Avoid fruit that is pale-yellow, greenish yellow, very firm, shriveled, or bruised.

***bananas*:** plump with uniform shape at desired ripeness level. Avoid produce with blemished or bruised skins.

***blueberries*:** plump, firm berries with a light-grayish bloom. The bloom is the thin coating on the surface.

***cantaloupe*:** slightly oval fruit, five inches or more in diameter, with yellow or golden (not green) background color. Signs of sweetness include pronounced netting on the rind and a few tiny cracks near the stem end. Smell the melon, it should be noticeably strong and sweet. At home, check for ripeness before you eat it; the stem area will be slightly soft when ripe.

***cherries*:** plump, bright colored sweet or sour cherries. Sweet cherries with reddish-brown skin promise flavor. Avoid overly soft or shriveled cherries or those with dark stems.

***grapefruit*:** firm, thin-skinned fruit, full colored, and heavy for its size. The best grapefruit are smooth, thin-skinned, and flat at both ends. Avoid fruit with a pointed end or thick, deeply-pored skin.

***grapes*:** plump grapes firmly attached to pliable green stems. Color is the best indication of ripeness and flavor. Avoid soft or wrinkled fruits and those with bleached-looking areas at the stem end.

***honeydew melon*:** melons weighing at least five pounds, with waxy white rind, barely tinged with green. Fully ripe fruit has a cream-colored rind. When ripe, the blossom end should give to gentle pressure.

***kiwifruit*:** softness similar to a ripe peach. Choose evenly firm fruit.

***lemons*:** firm, heavy fruit. Generally, rough-textured lemons have thicker skins and less juice than fine-skinned varieties.

***mangoes*:** usually quite firm when sold and need to be ripened further at home before eating. Avoid those with shriveled or bruised skin. Once ripened, they will give to gentle pressure.

***nectarines*:** orange-yellow (not green) background color between areas of red. Ripe nectarines feel slightly soft with gentle handling, but not as soft as ripe peaches.

***oranges*:** thin-skinned, firm, bright-colored fruit. Avoid oranges with any hint of softness or whitish mold at the ends.

***papayas*:** fruit with the softness of peaches and more yellow than green in the skin. Most papayas need to be ripened further after purchase in a loosely closed paper bag at room temperature. Avoid bruised or shriveled fruit showing any signs of mold or deterioration.

***peaches*:** creamy or yellow background color. Ripe peaches feel slightly soft with gentle handling. Avoid green, extra-hard, or bruised fruit.

***pears*:** fruit with firm skin. Pears gradually ripen after picking.

***pineapple*:** large, plump, fresh looking fruit with green leaves and a sweet smell. Avoid fruit with soft spots, areas of decay, or fermented odor.

***plums*:** fruit that is full colored. Ripe plums are slightly soft at the tip end and feel somewhat soft when handled gently. Avoid fruit with broken or shriveled skin.

***raspberries*:** firm, plump, well shaped berries. If soft or discolored, they are overripe. Avoid baskets that look stained from overripe berries.

***strawberries*:** firm, plump berries that are full colored.

***watermelon*:** fruit heavy for its size, well-shaped, with rind and flesh colors characteristic of the variety. Ripe melons are fragrant and slightly soft at the blossom end. A melon that sloshes when shaken is probably overripe. The stem should be dry and brown, not green. When thumped, you should hear a low-pitched sound, indicating a full, juicy interior.

Source: Smith, M.J. The Miracle Foods Cookbook. *Minneapolis: Chronimed Publishing,* 1995. ✦

Shopping for Freshness! (continued)

FOR VEGETABLES...

***artichokes*:** tight, compact heads that feel heavy for their size. Surface brown spots don't affect quality.

***asparagus*:** firm, brittle spears that are bright green almost their entire length, with tightly closed tips.

***beans (green or waxed)*:** slender, crisp beans that are bright and blemish-free. Avoid mature beans with large seeds and swollen pods.

***beets*:** firm, smooth-skinned, small to medium beets. Leaves should be deep green and fresh looking.

***bok choy*:** heads with bright white stalks and glossy dark leaves. Avoid heads with slippery brown spots on the leaves.

***broccoli*:** compact clusters of tightly closed, dark green florets. Avoid heads with yellow florets or thick, woody stems.

***brussels sprouts*:** firm, compact, fresh looking sprouts that are bright green. They should be heavy for their size.

***cabbage*:** firm heads that feel heavy for their size. Outer leaves should have good color and be free of blemishes.

***carrots*:** firm, clean, well shaped carrots with bright, orange-gold color. Carrots with their tops still attached are likely to be freshest.

***cauliflower*:** firm, compact, creamy-white heads with florets pressed tightly together. A yellow tinge and spreading florets indicate over-maturity. Leaves should be crisp and bright green.

***celery*:** crisp, rigid, green stalks with fresh looking leaves. Avoid celery with limp stalks.

***corn*:** fresh looking ears with green husks, moist stems, and silk ends free of decay or worm injury. When pierced with thumbnail, kernels should give a squirt of juice. Tough skins indicate over-maturity.

***cucumbers*:** firm, dark green cucumbers that are slender but well shaped. Soft or yellow cukes are over-mature.

***eggplants*:** firm, heavy for their size, with taut, glassy, deeply colored skin. Stems should be bright green.

***greens*:** fresh, tender leaves that are free of blemishes. Avoid bunches with thick, coarse-veined leaves.

***jicama*:** firm, well formed tubers, free of blemishes. Size does not affect flavor, but larger roots do tend to have a coarse texture.

***kohlrabi*:** young, tender bulbs with fresh, green leaves. Avoid those with scars and blemishes. The smaller the bulb, the more delicate the flavor and texture.

***leeks*:** clean, white bottoms and crisp, fresh looking green tops.

***mushrooms*:** blemish-free mushrooms without slimy spots or signs of decay.

***okra*:** small to medium pods that are deep green and free of blemishes. Pods should snap or puncture easily with slight pressure.

***onions*:** green onions with crisp, bright green tops and clean, white bottoms. Choose firm, dry onions with brittle outer skin, avoiding those with sprouting green shoots or dark spots.

***parsnips*:** small to medium, smooth, firm, and well shaped. Avoid large roots because they may have a woody core.

***peas*:** small, plump, bright green pods that are firm, crisp, and well filled.

***peppers*:** bright, glossy, firm, and well shaped. Avoid those with soft spots or gashes.

***potatoes*:** firm, smooth with no wrinkles, sprouts, cracks, bruises, decay, or bitter green areas (caused by exposure to light).

***rutabagas*:** small to medium, smooth, firm, and heavy for their size.

***salad greens*:** crisp, deeply colored leaves, free of brown spots, yellowed leaves, and decay.

***summer squash*:** yellow squash and zucchini of medium size with firm, smooth, glossy, tender skin. Squash should be heavy for their size.

***sweet potatoes and yams*:** firm, well shaped, with bright, uniformly colored skin.

***tomatoes*:** smooth, well formed, firm, not hard.

***turnips*:** firm, smooth, small to medium size, that are heavy for their size.

***winter squash*:** hard, thick-shelled. ✦

Or choose one of each variety of plums: perhaps Laroda, Queen Ann, Santa Rosa, and Wickson.

Look for signs of quality. Bruised or wilted produce suggests that it hasn't been handled properly or that it's past its peak. Some nutrients may be lost as a result. *Refer to the chart, "Shopping for Freshness," on page* 280 *and* 281 *for signs of quality in commonly-eaten fruits and vegetables.*

For flavor, buy small. Small fruit is often sweeter than larger pieces of the same fruit.

Handle fresh fruits and vegetables gently. Damage and bruising hastens spoilage. Place produce in the shopping cart where it won't get bruised. At the checkout, make sure produce is packed on top or in separate bags.

For juice oranges, other citrus fruits, and melons, "weigh" the fruit by palming it in your hand. The fruit should feel heavier than its size indicates.

Consider choosing your own produce, rather than buying it prepackaged. That way you can examine and pick out items at their peak of quality.

Besides fruit and vegetables, look for other items in the produce department: fresh herbs, herbs in jars, and sun-dried tomatoes, among others. Fresh herbs are often prepackaged; choose those that look fresh, not wilted.

Look for dried fruits, which may be in the produce department, too. They're a nonperishable option from the Fruit Group of the Food Guide Pyramid, and they supply the same nutrients as fresh fruit. If you're sensitive to sulfites, check the label; sulfites are used to prevent browning in many dried fruits.

Shopping at a farm stand? Be aware that the produce sold may not be fresh from the field. Ask around. Sometimes produce is brought in from the same commercial markets used by supermarkets, then sold as "farm fresh."

Meat and Deli Case

Through advanced breeding and feeding practices, today's animals are leaner than ever. Leaner cuts are available also because of closer trimming of beef, veal, pork, and lamb cuts. The average thickness of fat around the edge of steaks and roasts has trimmed down from 1/2- to 3/4-inch in the past to less than 1/8-inch today.

For the "lean advantage"—and the other nutrients that meat supplies (especially protein, B vitamins, iron, and zinc)—consider these shopping tips:

Shop for meat's "skinny" cuts. Certain cuts of meat are leaner than others. Use this rule of thumb in selecting lower fat cuts of fresh meats: Look for the words "round" or "loin" in the name when shopping for beef, and the words "loin" or "leg" when buying pork or lamb. Here are some examples of lean cuts.

Beef: eye of round, top round steak, top round roast, sirloin steak, top loin steak, tenderloin steak, and chuck arm pot roast

Veal: cutlet, blade or arm steak, rib roast, and rib or loin chop

Pork: tenderloin, top loin roast, top loin chop, center loin chop, sirloin roast, loin rib chop, and shoulder blade steak

Lamb: leg, loin chop, arm chop, and foreshanks

If you're not sure of the cut, check the meat label. It identifies the kind and cut, along with the net weight, unit price, and cost per package.

Choose leaner grades of meat. "Select" grades of beef have the least marbled fat (or thin streaks of fat between the muscle) followed by "choice" cuts, then "prime" beef cuts. Veal and lamb use the same grading system; however, the term "good" is used instead of "select." Grading, which is determined by the U.S. Department of Agriculture, is based on fat content, appearance, texture, and the age of the animal. Pork is not graded.

The more costly "prime" grade of beef has more marbled fat, which helps make the meat juicy and flavorful. However, with moist methods of cooking and proper carving, the leaner "select" and "choice" meats can be tender, juicy, and flavorful, too.

Nutritionally speaking, nutrients in meat—protein, thiamin, niacin, iron, and zinc, among others—are the same, regardless of grade.

Buy well-trimmed meat: 1/8-inch fat trim or less. "Trim" refers to the fat layer surrounding a steak or other cut of meat. *Note*: Marbled fat cannot be trimmed away. Only cooking methods can remove some, but not all, marbled fat.

Check the "numbers" for ground meat. For ground meats, look for packages that have the greatest percent lean to percent fat ratio. Ground beef labeled as 95 percent lean may also include the nutrition description "Lean" because it meets the definition of a lean product. Note: "Percent lean" refers to the weight of the meat, not the calories it contains.

On ground meats, you may also see other names. Ground round is the leanest, followed by ground sirloin, ground chuck, then regular ground meat. If you don't see ground round, the butcher can grind meat for you from a round cut of meat.

Buy enough meat, without overdoing on portion size. For moderate-size portions (2 to 3 ounces cooked), figure 3 to 4 ounces of uncooked, boneless meat per person. *Refer to the chart, "Meat Buying Guide," on page 284 to help you decide how much meat to buy.*

Use nutrition labeling to find lean packaged meats. By regulation, packaged deli meats must carry nutrition labeling. That helps you find today's leaner hot dogs, luncheon meats, and sausage patties.

Check out the lean options from the deli case. When buying ready-to-slice luncheon meats from a deli, ask for nutrition information if you're unsure of a product's leanness. Some lean products will be identified with a nutrition description term such as lowfat, __% fat-free, or lean.

Look for nutrition information for fresh meat, poultry, and seafood. Single-ingredient, raw meat, poultry, and seafood may be labeled under the Nutri-Facts name. Look for this information on materials (poster or pamphlet) near the meat or seafood counter for 45 commonly-consumed meat and poultry cuts, and 20 seafood items. For meat, you'll see nutrition information for meat with and without trimmable fat. The Nutri-Facts program is voluntary, so it may not appear in all supermarkets.

When shopping for bacon, try Canadian bacon. Canadian bacon is lean, much like ham, and fits in the Meat Group of the Food Guide Pyramid. In contrast, traditional bacon is mainly fat and fits in the Pyramid tip, not the Meat Group. If you're watching your sodium intake, check the label.

Occasionally choose organ meats, also called variety meats. Brain, chitterlings (pig intestines), heart, kidney, liver, sweetbreads (thymus gland), tongue, and tripe (stomach lining of cattle) are all organ meats. Organ meats are good sources of many nutrients; liver, in particular, is high in iron. However, most are higher in cholesterol than lean meat. And some, such as chitterlings, sweetbreads, and tongue, have more fat than others, such as liver and heart.

Recognize the qualities of fresh meat. The color of meat indicates its freshness. Beef is typically a bright red color. Both young veal and pork are grayish pink.

Reading Meat Labels

1. The kind of meat—It is listed first on every label.
2. The primal (wholesale) cut—Tells where the meat came from on the animal.
3. The retail cut—Tells from what part of the primal cut the meat comes.

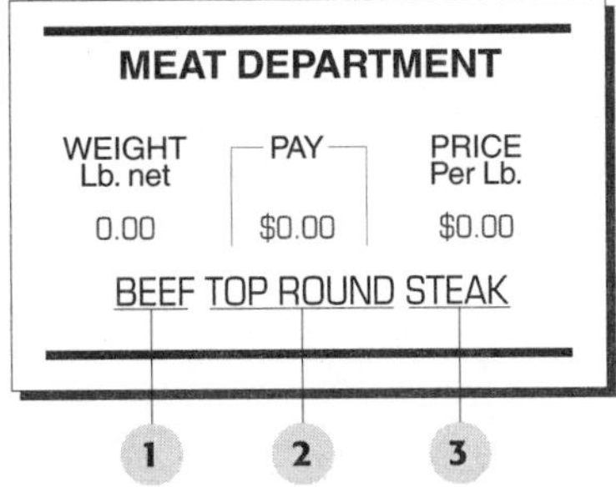

Older veal is a darker pink. And lamb can be light to darker pink, depending on how it was fed.

Check food product dating on meat. Only buy fresh and processed meats that will still be fresh when you're ready to eat them. Or plan to freeze immediately for later use.

Notice the safe food handling label. *A sample label is shown on page 274. For more about the safe handling of meat, refer to chapter 13, "The Safe Kitchen."*

Meat Buying Guide

How much raw meat should you buy? If you figure about 3 ounces of cooked, lean meat per person, that's about 4 ounces of raw meat per person. For some meats, you'll need to take the amount of bone and fat into account.

FORM OF MEAT	SERVINGS PER POUND*
Boneless or ground meat	4 servings
Meat with a minimum amount of bone (steaks, roasts, chops, etc.)	2 to 3 servings
Meat with a large amount of bone (shoulder cuts, short ribs, neck, etc.)	1 to 2 servings

**Three ounces of cooked trimmed meat equals one serving.*

Adapted from: Food and Nutrition Section, American Home Economics Association, Handbook of Food Preparation, *Dubuque, Iowa:* Kendall/Hunt *Publishing Company,* 1993.

Poultry Buying Guide

How much poultry? Here's how many servings come from one pound of chicken, duck, goose, game hens, or turkey.

POULTRY	SERVINGS PER POUND*
Whole chicken (broiler-fryer or roaster)	2 servings
Boneless chicken breast	4 servings
Duck, whole	1 serving
Goose, whole	1 1/2 to 2 servings
Rock Cornish game hen, whole	1 serving
Whole turkey, bone in	2 servings
Boneless turkey roast	3 servings
Ground turkey	4 servings

**Amounts are based on 3 ounces of cooked poultry without bone per serving.*

Adapted from: Food and Nutrition Section, American Home Economics Association, Handbook of Food Preparation, *Dubuque, Iowa:* Kendall/Hunt *Publishing Company,* 1993.

Poultry Counter

Besides being economical, chicken and turkey offer high-quality protein, and they're usually very lean. Consider these tips as you choose poultry for your shopping cart:

Choose mostly lean varieties of poultry—turkey and chicken. Domesticated duck and goose are higher in fat. A 3 1/2-ounce cooked portion of roasted, skinless chicken (light and dark meat) has about 7 fat grams compared with 11 fat grams in the same portion of roasted, skinless duck. Pheasant and quail, especially without the skin, are lean, too.

To trim fat, shop for skinless poultry—chicken and turkey. You'll cut the grams of total fat and saturated fat in half. Or buy poultry with the skin on because it costs less, then take the skin off at home.

For less fat, choose light meat, such as the turkey or chicken breast. Compare the difference: Three and one half ounces of roasted, skinless, dark-meat chicken has about 10 fat grams and 3 grams of saturated fat; the same amount of roasted, skinless, light-meat chicken has about 3 fat grams and 1 gram of saturated fat. The cholesterol content is about the same.

When you buy whole turkey, know that self-basting varieties are higher in fat. Self-basting turkeys are moist because they're injected with fat—fat that may be high in saturated fatty acids. Instead, you can baste turkey regularly with broth, juice, or juices from the poultry. H*int*: Roasting any whole bird with the breast side up makes it more moist.

Is ground meat on your shopping list? Look for lean ground turkey breast, too. Ground turkey breast can be as lean as 99 percent fat free. The fat content is higher if it's ground with dark meat and skin.

Recognize the qualities of fresh poultry. Look for meaty birds with skin that's creamy-white to yellow and that are free of bruises, tiny feathers, and torn or dry skin. Check for food product dating on food labels, too.

Read the Nutrition Facts before you buy turkey dogs, turkey ham, or turkey bologna. They may—or may not—be low in fat. Compare the sodium content with traditional processed meats; processing typically adds sodium. For fresh cuts of poultry, look for Nutri-Facts posted in the retail case.

For cost savings, buy a whole bird. You'll usually save money if you carve a chicken in parts yourself.

Buy enough poultry for moderate portions. *The chart, "Poultry Buying Guide," on page 284 shows how much to buy per person when you serve 3-ounce cooked portions.*

Fish Counter

There's increased attention to seafood these days, often for its nutritional benefits. Besides being a good protein source, seafood is low in fat, especially saturated fats. And fish offers potential health benefits from omega-3 fatty acids. That's why health experts recommend eating seafood several times a week. *Refer to page 56 for a discussion of omega-3 fatty acids.*

The many varieties of fish on the market today can offer great taste and versatility in menu planning. So learn to shop for seafood confidently; choose high-quality, safe seafood that also matches your personal needs and preferences.

A few definitions before you start shopping: seafood includes both finfish and shellfish. Catfish, cod, haddock, flounder, mahi mahi, snapper, tuna, and trout are among the many types of finfish. Shellfish are both crustaceans (crab, crayfish, lobster, and shrimp) and mollusks (clam, mussel, oyster, scallop, octopus, squid, abalone, conch, and snail).

Check the fish counter before you buy. Always buy seafood from a reputable source, not a pickup truck. Seafood should be displayed with food safety in mind: properly iced, well refrigerated, and in clean display cases. Be sure that the seafood is wrapped separately in a leak-proof package.

Recognize the different fat contents of various fish. In general, most fish has less fat than other protein-rich foods, including meat and poultry with skin. And most fat in seafood is polyunsaturated.

Fish that's white or light in color, such as orange roughy, perch, snapper, and sole has less fat than fish that is firm and darker in color, such as mackerel, salmon, and blue fin tuna. Fattier fish tend to have more omega-3 fatty acids than lean fish or shellfish; "omega-3s" may offer heart-healthy benefits.

Choose fish that's best for the recipe. Lean fish is great for baking, microwaving, and poaching. Fish with more fat tends to be better for grilling and roasting because it doesn't dry out as quickly and

have you ever wondered

...if free-range chickens have less fat? It's a common misperception that free-range chickens—those that "roam the barnyard and forage for food"—are always leaner than chickens raised in coops. Whether they're raised in a coop or a barnyard, their exercise level often is about the same. Genetic stock, age, and growth rate have greater influence on fat levels. Older, larger chickens and those that grow faster tend to have more fat. That's true of all chickens, no matter how they're raised. There's no legal definition for free-range chicken. Some people are willing to spend more for free-range chickens because they prefer the taste.

...if the tiny red spots on finfish are safe to eat? These spots are bruise marks, not contamination. They occur when fish is not handled gently, either when it's caught or in the supermarket. It's safe to eat. But be aware that bruised areas often deteriorate faster.

...how the fat and cholesterol in surimi (imitation crabmeat) compare with crabmeat? Surimi is imitation crabmeat, made from pollock or another mild-flavored fish. The fish is processed by rolling "sheets" of fish and adding color so it looks like crab legs. The nutrient content reflects the fish it's made from. Surimi is comparable in fat content but lower in cholesterol than crabmeat. ✦

because it holds its shape better. For example, salmon and tuna are better for kebobs. Mild-flavored fish tends to be the lowest in fat, while fish with more fat usually has a fuller flavor.

Learn to recognize the qualities of fresh seafood.

Finfish. At peak quality, whole finfish have a fresh ocean-breeze scent. They're naturally firm to the touch, with stiff fins and scales that cling tightly to the skin. Skin is shiny and "metallic." Gills are pink or bright red and free from mucous or slime. If undamaged, their eyes are clear, bright, and protruding. Fish fillets or steaks also have a mild scent, firm and moist flesh, a translucent appearance, and no browning around the edges. If wrapped, the packaging should be tight.

Shellfish. Crustaceans and some mollusks are sold live. In fact, unless frozen, canned, or cooked, crab, crayfish, and lobster should be alive when sold. They'll move slightly if they're alive, and live lobsters curl their tails a bit when handled.

If their shells are still on, clams, mussels, and oysters must be alive, too; shells shouldn't be damaged. When these mollusks are alive, their shells are slightly open, but they close tightly when tapped. As another easy test, hold the shell between your thumb and forefinger and press so that one part of the shell slides across the other. If the shells move, it isn't fresh.

Freshly-shucked mollusks (shells removed) have a mild, fresh scent. A somewhat clear liquid—not too milky or cloudy—should cover the shucked "meat."

Scallops are removed from their shells at sea. They vary in size and color—from creamy white to light orange, tan, or somewhat pinkish. When fresh, they're not dry or darkened around the edges.

Regardless of size and color, fresh raw shrimp will have a mild odor. For all fish—finfish and shellfish—use your nose. A strong, "fishy" odor is a sign that fish is no longer fresh.

Know the qualities of frozen fish, too. Frozen seafood should be solidly frozen, mild in odor, and free of ice crystals and freezer burn. Freezer burn is indicated by drying and discoloration. The package shouldn't be damaged or water stained. And it should be stored below the frost line in the store's display freezer. These qualities apply to both frozen fish and frozen prepared items, such as crab cakes and breaded shrimp.

Seafood Buying Guide

Type of Seafood	Approximate Amount of Raw Seafood Needed per Adult Serving
Whole fish	3/4 pound
Dressed or pan-dressed fish	1/2 pound
Fish fillets	1/4 to 1/3 pound
Fish steaks with bone	1/2 pound
Fish steaks without bone	1/3 pound
Live clams and oysters	6 to 8
Shucked clams and oysters	1/3 to 1/2 pint
Live lobsters and crabs	1 to 1 1/2 pounds
Cooked lobster or crabmeat	1/4 to 1/3 pound
Scallops	1/4 to 1/3 pound
Shrimp, headless and unpeeled	1/3 to 1/2 pound
Shrimp, peeled and deveined	1/4 to 1/3 pound

Note: The smaller amounts in the ranges shown provide a cooked portion that is approximately 3 ounces when prepared by most common cooking methods.

Source: Gall, Ken. "Seafood Savvy." Information Bulletin 1041B226, *A Cornell Cooperative Extension Publication, Cornell University,* 1992.

Check the food product dating on the label of fresh, frozen fish. Choose packaged seafood that doesn't show signs of thawing, then refreezing. Check the "sell by" date, if it has one, for a quality product. *Review information about food product dating on page* 275.

Choose cooked shrimp, lobster, crab, and crayfish that's moist with a mild odor and a characteristic color. The shells of cooked shrimp should be pink to reddish. For other crustaceans, the shells should be bright red.

For safety, don't buy cooked seafood that's displayed alongside raw seafood. Bacteria from raw fish can contaminate cooked fish, creating a potential for foodborne illness. *To learn more about cross-contamination and food safety, refer to "Checklist for a Clean Kitchen" on page* 308.

Choose smoked fish, such as smoked salmon or smoked trout, that is bright, glossy, and free of mold. Since it may not be cooked before serving, smoked fish should be wrapped and kept away from raw fish to avoid cross contamination.

Substitute one fish for another. When the store doesn't have the seafood you want or it costs more than you anticipate, don't despair. Just make a switch. For example, when a recipe calls for flounder, almost any mild finfish (probably one that's low in fat, such as haddock, halibut, or perch) can take its place.

Be aware of differences in nutritional content when you make substitutions. Squid, shrimp, and lobster, for example, have more cholesterol than clams, crab, mussels, and scallops do. Three ounces of boiled shrimp supply about 165 milligrams of cholesterol, while the same amount of scallops has about 55 milligrams of cholesterol.

Whether it's sold in the seafood counter or freezer section, go easy on breaded items, such as shrimp and fish sticks, which often contain more fat.

For nutrition information, check the* Nutrition Facts *panel on packaged seafood products. For fresh seafood, you'll find this information displayed nearby.

Buy the amount of seafood you need. Because of waste, you need more when preparing whole or dressed fish. A dressed fish has the head, tail, and fins removed. Usually fish steaks, fillets, and shellfish, which have less waste, cost more per pound. *The chart on page 286, "Seafood Buying Guide," helps you estimate how much you need for a cooked 3-ounce portion.*

Refrigerated Case

Although you'll find tortillas, refrigerator rolls, and yeast among the many products in the refrigerated case, dairy foods and eggs take the most prominent spots. For both, you have many decisions to make.

Dairy Foods

Choose milk that matches your needs. No matter what type, milk is an excellent source of calcium, with one cup supplying 30 percent of the Daily Value. Milk also provides protein, riboflavin, vitamins A and D, phosphorus, and other vitamins and minerals. How do the various forms of milk differ? Fat content is the main difference. *The chart, "Milk: A Good Calcium Source" on page 180 makes some nutrition comparisons. See "Which Milk for You?" on page 288 for the definitions for different types of milk.*

Look for different types of yogurt—fruit-flavored or plain, and whole, low-fat, or nonfat. Yogurt is another high-calcium, high-protein dairy food. In fact, 8 ounces of either yogurt or milk supply about 300 milligrams of calcium. If you don't drink much milk, you might buy more yogurt.

Like milk, yogurt comes in whole, low-fat, and nonfat varieties. The fat and calorie content reflect the milk it's made from. Yogurt may also be flavored with fruit, fruit preserves, or extracts such as vanilla or coffee. If you're watching calories, reach for yogurt flavored with a low-calorie sweetener, such as aspartame.

Yogurt is made with a "friendly" bacteria, which gives a distinctive taste and consistency. As an added benefit, active live cultures may offer health benefits, perhaps in boosting immunity or helping the body digest milk's sugar. However, the research on active, live cultures in yogurt isn't conclusive.

Yogurt with labels that state "made with active cultures" may not contain *live* cultures because it has been heat treated. Frozen yogurt may or may not contain live and active cultures. If you want the potential benefit of active live cultures, look for this statement on regular and frozen yogurt containers: "contains live and active yogurt cultures."

Next to the cartons of juice, you also may find yogurt-juice beverages—another source of calcium. Or look for the yogurt drink called kefir.

If you're sensitive to lactose, or milk sugar, look for low-lactose milk. By adding the enzyme lactase, manufacturers can produce dairy foods with much less lactose. *Refer to page 194 for more information on lactose intolerance.*

Check out the wide variety of cheese sold today. Cheese is milk in concentrated form; about 10 pounds (5 quarts) of milk are used to make every pound of cheddar cheese. That's why cheese is a great source of milk's nutrients: calcium, protein, and riboflavin. Cheese also has considerably more fat per serving than milk does. Its fat is highly saturated.

To cut back on fat and still get plenty of nutrients, you might look for lower-fat cheeses, such as low-fat ricotta, part-skim mozzarella, string cheese, or varieties of reduced-fat cheese. As a rule of thumb—any cheese made with skim milk will likely have less fat. Lower-fat cheese has anywhere from 50 to 75 percent of the fat in whole milk cheese. You'll also find fat-free cheese in today's supermarkets. Cheese with less fat usually has less cholesterol, too, but you need to check the label to be sure.

Consider buying shredded cheese and sharp-flavored cheese. For cheese shreds, you may pay a little more per ounce for the convenience of "pre-prep." When it's grated you may use a little less cheese in recipes than if you had used sliced or chunk cheese. That's another way to savor the flavor, yet control fat. *Tip*: using stronger flavored cheese, such as Parmesan and sharp cheddar, delivers more flavor with less cheese than mild cheese does.

Look for reduced-sodium cheeses if you're watching your sodium intake. Traditional cheese has sodium because it's a key ingredient in cheese making.

Cream and sour cream? Buy them—just go easy on how much you use. Both are high in fat and deliver very little calcium. For less fat and fewer calories, try lower-fat and nonfat varieties. Try half-and-half rather than cream. Choose sour half-and-half or fat-free sour cream. Read the labels since the fat content among products varies.

Look for spreads—butter, margarine, and cream cheese—in the dairy case. From a fat and calorie standpoint, butter and margarine are the same with about 35 calories and 4 grams of fat per teaspoon. Both are primarily fat; only the source differs. Butter contains more saturated fats than most margarines. Because margarine is made from vegetable oil, it has no cholesterol.

For a spread with less saturated fat, buy soft tub margarine, rather than stick. Whipped versions of butter or margarine have less fat per tablespoon, too; air adds to the volume. Reduced- and low-fat margarines are sold, too, but they aren't suitable for some recipes.

Enjoy small amounts of cream cheese. But don't confuse its nutrient content with other forms of cheese. Cream cheese is mainly milk fat, with very little milk solids. If you want the creamy texture with less fat, look for reduced-fat or fat-free cream cheese. Or buy regular cream cheese, then spread a little less on your morning bagel. Whipped cream cheese is often easier to spread, so you use less.

Buy fluid milk and other dairy foods that are properly refrigerated in the store. They won't spoil as quickly. Check the "sell-by" date on the carton, too.

Which Milk for You?

From a nutritional standpoint, the difference among whole, 2 percent, 1 percent, and skim milk is the fat and calorie content. Because milk solids make up at least 8.25 percent for each of these

have you ever wondered

...how cow's milk and soy milk compare? People with a milk allergy, as well as strict vegetarians, might choose soy milk. However, the nutrient content isn't the same as cow's milk. Unless fortified, soy milk, made by pressing ground, cooked soybeans, is low in calcium. Soy milk is lower in protein and riboflavin, too, and it has little vitamin A. The fat content of soy milk is comparable to 2 percent cow's milk, but soy milk is cholesterol free.

If you use soy milk as a substitute for cow's milk, make sure it's calcium fortified. And choose other foods that contribute protein, riboflavin, and vitamin A. ✦

types of milks, their nutrient content is about the same. (Milk solids are the part of milk that's neither milkfat nor water.) Keep in mind that the percentages of milkfat used to distinguish different types of milk refer to the percent milkfat by weight and not by calories.

In the Refrigerator Case...

Whole milk contains not less than 3.25 percent milkfat.

Reduced-fat milk contains 25 percent less fat than whole milk. Milk with 2 percent milkfat is labeled "reduced-fat."

Low-fat or light milk has 3 grams or less fat per 8 ounce serving. Milk with 1 percent milkfat is considered "low-fat." When fat is removed to make milk lower in fat, some of the vitamin A is lost, too. For this reason, it must be fortified with vitamin A.

Skim milk has less than 0.5 percent milkfat. Like low-fat milk, skim milk must be fortified with vitamin A, too. Skim milk may also be labeled as "fat-free" or "nonfat."

Chocolate milk can be whole, 2 percent, 1 percent, or skim milk with added chocolate or cocoa, and sweetener. Fruit-flavored milk is available in some stores, too.

Cultured buttermilk is made by adding "friendly" bacteria cultures to milk, usually skim or low-fat milk. The bacteria culture produces its unique flavor, aroma, acidity, and thick texture. Salt is often added for more flavor. Despite its name, butter isn't added.

Eggnog, sold around certain holidays, is a blend of milk, eggs, sugar, cream, and flavors. Because eggnog is higher in calories and fat, some people prefer eggnog-flavored milk, made with skim or 2 percent milk.

Acidophilus milk, usually made from low-fat or skim milk, is processed with a "friendly" bacteria, which gives it a distinctive flavor.

Lactose-free and lactose-reduced milks (whole, low-fat, and skim) are treated with the lactase enzyme. Because lactose, the sugar in milk, converts to glucose and galactose, people with lactose intolerance can drink it. To be considered "lactose-reduced," the lactose level must be reduced by 70 percent.

Protein-fortified milk is milk that has nonfat milk solids added so that the milk solids level reaches 10 percent. It's often added to skim or low-fat milk for a fuller flavor.

Low-sodium milk has most of the sodium removed. Per 8-ounce serving, it has 25 milligrams of sodium, which is 80 percent less than nonflavored milk. This is an option for those on a sodium-restricted diet.

On the Grocery Shelf...

Nonfat dry milk is milk with the fat and water removed. It has the same nutrients as skim milk.

Shelf-stable milk has been processed quickly by very high heat to destroy bacteria. That allows it to be aseptically packaged and stored on a shelf until it's opened. Once opened, it needs refrigeration.

Condensed milk has been concentrated. It has at least 8 percent milkfat and at least 28 percent milk solids. It may have other ingredients, including sweeteners.

Evaporated milk has been concentrated. It's sold as both skim and whole evaporated milk, and has no less than 20 percent milk solids. Evaporated milk is fortified with vitamins A and D. Once it's opened, it needs refrigeration.

(*Source*: *National Dairy Council*)

Eggs

If you're looking for an economical, convenient, and easy-to-prepare source of high-quality protein, buy eggs. A single egg supplies about 10 percent of the protein you need in a day, along with good amounts of vitamins A, D, and B_{12}. Although eggs are high in cholesterol, 213 milligrams per large egg, they have 5 grams of fat—no more than an ounce of cheese. Shell color—brown or white—doesn't affect the nutritional quality of eggs; the color varies with the breed of hen.

From jumbo to small eggs: what size should you buy? Size is determined by minimum weight per dozen eggs. The nutrient content of an egg will depend on its size.

The size is different from the grade printed on the label. Eggs are graded AA, A, and B. Grading refers to the interior and exterior quality of eggs when they're packed. Most eggs sold in supermarkets are Grade A; they're almost the same as Grade AA eggs, which are considered slightly higher in quality.

Open cartons of eggs before you buy. Are the eggs clean and whole? Avoid cartons with cracked eggs. They may be contaminated with salmonella.

Buy eggs that are refrigerated, not kept at room temperature in the aisle. Even though eggs are stored in their own natural package, they spoil quickly when they're not refrigerated.

Need to limit egg yolks because of their cholesterol content? Try cholesterol-free or reduced-cholesterol egg substitutes. You'll find them either in the freezer or refrigerated section of the store. Since cholesterol is in the yolk and not the white, you can also buy eggs and use just the whites to replace some or all of the whole eggs.

Freezer Case

Bagels and bread dough, waffles and cookies, fruit and fruit juice, pizza and burritos, vegetables and full dinners, fish and poultry, ice cream and frozen yogurt—the freezer case is stocked with every kind of convenience food. Many of these foods are preportioned, or partly or fully cooked, so you can serve these foods with little or no work.

To control fat, choose frozen plain vegetables or those made with low-fat sauces. Some sauces mixed with frozen vegetables add fat, saturated fat, and calories; check the Nutrition Facts panel on the label.

Look for frozen fruits as an option when berries and other fruits are out of season. They're sold in both sweetened and unsweetened varieties. To help frozen fruit keep its shape, serve while it's still somewhat frozen.

Buy fruit and vegetables in loose-pack plastic bags. You'll only need to pour out what you need, then immediately return what you don't use to the freezer.

Choosing frozen juice concentrate? *The tips in "More Reading on the Food Label" on page 275 apply.* Read the label to compare products. Bear in mind, juice concentrates often cost a bit less that juice sold in cartons—and you can store them longer.

Use nutrition labeling to compare frozen prepared meals and entrées. Along with traditional foods, you'll find many products with fewer calories and with less fat, cholesterol, and sodium—even pizza, lasagna, enchiladas, and burritos! When you're comparing the nutrients in one frozen dinner with another, check the serving size. For example, some may be 7 ounces; others, 11 ounces.

Whether vegetables, fish, or poultry, go easy on breaded and fried frozen foods. They supply more fat. When you buy them, check the package directions for oven heating rather than deep-fat frying, to control calories and fat.

For frozen desserts, compare frozen yogurt, various ice cream, and sherbet. Most frozen yogurt has less fat than ice cream—although you'll also find lower-fat brands of ice cream in today's freezer section, too. You may prefer the creamy texture and rich flavor of premium ice cream, which contains more fat and so, more calories. If so, cut back on fat somewhere else so you can enjoy premium ice cream.

What about ice milk? It has a new name: "reduced-fat ice cream" or "low-fat ice cream." Not every brand is the same, however. Some are reduced-fat versions of premium ice cream, and they still may have as much fat as regular ice cream. To get the whole story, check out the Nutrition Facts panel for the calories and fat grams in one serving.

Sold alongside ice cream and frozen yogurt, sherbet is sweetened fruit juice and water, and it may contain milk, egg white, and gelatin. While it has less fat, it contains more sugar than ice cream and belongs in the Pyramid tip. Fruit sorbet—whipped and frozen fruit juice—is sold commercially, or you can make at home; it may be counted as a Fruit Group serving.

Buying a whipped topping? Frozen whipped toppings are convenient to keep in the freezer. Many have the same calorie and content as real whipped cream. If they're made with palm and coconut oils, frozen whipped toppings are high in saturated fat. If you enjoy the taste of the real thing, buy it—then use just a dollop, not a heaping spoonful. Or look for light or low-calorie versions of whipped toppings.

Grocery Aisles

By going up and down the inside aisles of the supermarket, you'll find an immense variety—foods from all five food groups and the Pyramid tip, convenience foods, ethnic foods, baking ingredients, snack foods, seasonings, and beverages.

Canned Fruit and Vegetables

For a nonperishable supply of fruit and vegetables, buy canned varieties. They're convenient to keep on your kitchen shelves—especially when their fresh counterparts are not in season.

For canned fruit, examine the label. You'll find descriptions like "packed in its own juices," "packed in fruit juice," "unsweetened," "in light syrup," or "in heavy syrup." Fruits packed in juices have less sugar than fruits packed in syrup and so fewer calories. If you prefer the flavor of fruit packed in syrup, just be sure the extra calories match your own calorie target.

Canned juice, juice cocktail, or juice drinks—which should you buy? *For tips, refer to* "More Reading on the Food Label" *on page* 275. As a quick tip, juices may cost less per serving than soft drinks—and juice is more nutritious.

Canned vegetables: if you're cutting back on sodium, which should you buy? Read the Nutrition Facts panel for sodium content, or look for descriptions such as "no salt added."

For less fat, look for vegetarian or fat-free baked beans and refried beans. Compared with traditional products, you may cut the fat by 50 percent or more. Some canned beans are reduced in sodium, too. *Note*: Refried beans may be made with lard, which contains saturated fat and cholesterol.

Canned Fish

Be aware that tuna, salmon, sardines, crab, clams, mackerel, and other fish are canned in water or oil. Even when the oil is drained away, fish packed in oil has significantly more fat than water-packed varieties—and less omega-3 fatty acids. With oil-packed canned fish, some of the omega-3 fatty acids transfer to the oil, which may be discarded. Besides the fat and calorie difference, fish packed in spring water has a milder flavor.

Compare the fat and calories in 3 ounces of water-packed and oil-packed tuna. *For more about omega-3 fatty acids, refer to* "Eat your Omega-3s" *on page* 56.

	Calories	Fat Grams (for 3 ounces)
water-packed tuna	115	2
oil-packed tuna, drained	160	7
oil-packed tuna	210	15

For more calcium, buy canned fish (salmon and sardines) with edible bones. Three ounces of salmon eaten with the bones has about 200 milligrams of calcium, almost as much as 6 ounces of milk. (Not all canned salmon has edible bones—check the ingredient list.) The canning process softens bones, making them edible. Canned tuna and crabmeat don't have edible bones.

Although tuna outsells other canned fish, give yourself a change in flavor with canned salmon. Besides adding variety to your eating pattern, salmon is higher in omega-3 fatty acids.

Soups, Stews, and Convenience Foods

As a main dish, choose stews and hearty soups. Because chunky soups are full of nutritious foods, they usually provide more nutrients. Use the Nutrition Facts panel and the ingredient list to find out.

If you're heating a quick meal at the office, look for ready-to-eat soup or dehydrated soup. Unlike condensed soup, ready-to-eat soup doesn't require added liquid. Just open the can, heat, then serve. For dehydrated soup, just add hot water.

For quick meals on your cupboard shelf, buy canned and shelf-stable microwaveable entrées: perhaps pasta with meat or cheese, or chili con carne. If you eat them on a regular basis, you might look for varieties with less fat and, depending on your needs, less sodium.

If you're watching how much sodium you eat, read the* Nutrition Facts *panel for sodium content. Many canned and instant soups, as well as canned stews, tend to be high in sodium. Check the grocery shelves, though; you'll see many that are prepared with less sodium.

For instant noodles (Oriental noodles) and entrée mixes (macaroni and cheese), consider using half of the seasoning packet to cut back on sodium. Depending on your overall food choices for the day, you might toss in some chopped vegetables for more vitamins and fiber, too. Or if you need to reduce fat, use a little less butter or margarine than the directions call for.

To cut back on fat, look for defatted broth. Or put a canned soup or stew in the refrigerator prior to use. The fat will congeal so you can skim it off.

How Much Pasta? How Much Rice?

Because dry pasta and rice cook to a larger volume, use these general guidelines when deciding how much to buy.

	UNCOOKED	EQUALS… COOKED
egg noodles	8 ounces (2 cups)	4 cups
spaghetti, fettuccine, other long shapes	8 ounces (1 1/2-inch diameter bunch)	4 cups
macaroni, shells, bow ties, penne, other small to medium shapes	8 ounces (2 cups)	4 cups
brown rice	1/2 pound (1 1/4 cups)	4 1/3 cups
polished, long-grain white rice	1/2 pound (1 1/4 cups)	3 3/4 cups
converted white rice	7 ounces (1 cup)	3 1/2 cups
instant white rice	8 ounces (2 cups)	4 cups

Pasta, Rice, and Other Grains

To make meals more appealing, buy a variety of pasta shapes. For thick sauces, use thicker pastas: fettuccine, lasagna, and tagliatelle. Chunky sauces are best with sturdy pasta shapes: fusilli (twists), farfalle (bow ties), macaroni, rigatoni, and ziti. With smooth, thin sauces, use thinner strands of pasta: cappellini (angel hair), vermicelli, and spaghetti.

Look for whole-grain pasta: spaghetti, lasagna, macaroni, and fettuccine. Like traditional pasta, whole-wheat pasta is high in complex carbohydrate. But the fiber content is almost three times higher; a half-cup of whole-wheat pasta has about 3 grams of fiber, compared with about 1 gram of fiber in traditional pasta.

For more variety, savor the appeal of vegetable and herbed pasta. The addition of tomato, beet, carrot, spinach, and other vegetables adds a variety of colors and flavors to pasta dishes. And herbs add a delicate flavor. What about the nutrients? Tomato pasta and spinach pasta don't count toward servings from the Vegetable Group. The nutritional contribution of vegetable purées used to make commercially-flavored pasta usually is quite small. It's the vegetables tossed with pasta that carry the extra nutrients.

Wonder about the fat content of egg noodles? While pasta is made from flour and water, noodles also contain eggs, egg yolks, or egg whites. Non-egg pasta contains no cholesterol and very little fat. Egg noodles may have small amounts of cholesterol and a little more fat; still egg noodles are considered low in fat and cholesterol.

Try different forms of rice. Use the label to compare their nutrients. Brown rice contains slightly more nutrients, followed by polished white rice, then instant white rice. Because it's a whole grain, brown rice—with 1.5 grams of fiber per half cup—has about three times the fiber of white rice. When you read the label, check for uncooked and cooked rice; it may give the nutritional content for prepared rice with added butter or salt.

Despite its name, wild rice is actually a long-grain marsh grass. From a nutritional standpoint, wild rice has a little more protein, riboflavin, and zinc, and a little less carbohydrate than brown rice. The fiber content is about 0.5 grams per half cup. For its nutty flavor, serve wild rice in salads, stir-fries, soups, stuffing, and side dishes. Or mix it 50-50 with regular or brown rice.

What about rice mixes? If you need to watch sodium, consider using just half the dry seasoning mix.

Browse the grocery shelves for other grain products: barley, bulgur, couscous, kasha, and quinoa, to name a few. *"Today's Grains" on page 221 lists grains to look for. On page 345, "Cooking Grain by Grain," you'll find guidelines for cooking with other grains.*

How much should you buy? Base the amount of dry pasta and rice on their cooked volume. And remember, you may eat more than one serving, so figure the nutritional contribution based on the amount you really eat.

Breakfast Cereals

Stocking up for quick breakfasts? Choose from the huge variety of ready-to-eat breakfast cereals. Besides being fortified with vitamins and minerals, you'll also find many high-fiber cereals. Because cereals use different parts of the grain—bran, germ, and endosperm—in differing amounts, their nutritional content varies. Use the Nutrition Facts panel to compare. *Refer to "What Is a Whole Grain?" on page 144 to see the three parts of a whole grain.*

Most people don't eat cereal dry. Instead they add milk or yogurt, making cereal a great "vehicle" for calcium and other nutrients in milk. For this reason, cereal labels often give the Nutrition Facts both for cereal only and for cereal with added milk.

When buying sweetened cereals, use the same criteria for choosing any cereal—sweetened or unsweetened. Read the Nutrition Facts for the nutrient and fiber content in one serving, then make your choice. Sweetened cereals are no more cavity-causing than unsweetened cereals; both complex carbohydrates in all kinds of cereal, and sugars that linger on tooth surfaces can promote cavities. Choose the cereal that matches your child's preferences and needs, and encourage good oral hygiene.

Look for clues to breakfast cereals with more fiber. They may carry label terms such as "high fiber," "whole grain," and "bran." If the label gives a nutrition description, check the Nutrition Facts panel for specific nutrient information. Cereals that are good fiber sources supply at least 2.5 grams of fiber per serving; whole-grain cereals typically have more. The ingredient list reveals the whole grains and bran in the cereal's "recipe."

Check the nutrients in "fortified" cereals. Most supply about 25 percent of the Daily Value for vitamins and minerals. And some have much more—100 percent—making these cereals comparable to a nutrient supplement. Being super fortified won't necessarily make this cereal better for you. If you're eating a varied diet, other foods supply these nutrients, too. Like any food, consider fortified cereal within the context of your whole day's eating plan.

Like many other breakfast cereals, bran cereals usually are fortified. Although high in fiber, bran lacks the vitamins and minerals supplied by the germ portion of grain.

Tip: Because many of the vitamins and minerals may be sprayed onto cereals, they can be lost if all the milk in the bottom of a cereal bowl isn't eaten along with the cereal.

Check the variety of cooked cereals, too: cream of rice, grits, rolled oats, and toasted wheat. Many are low in fat and sodium.

Think cooked cereals take too long to prepare? With today's packaging, you'll find microwave instructions for quick preparation. And many to-be-cooked cereals—oatmeal, grits, cream of wheat—are sold in instant varieties, too. The nutritional content is comparable to their traditional counterpart, although sodium may be higher in instant cereals. Read the label to compare.

Check the Nutrition Facts on cereal labels. The nutritional content varies from product to product, brand to brand. "Natural" cereals or granola may have more fat, sugars, or sodium than you'd think; many are made with more saturated fats, such as palm and coconut oils. For something new, you might try muesli, made with grains, nuts, and dried fruit.

Beans, Nuts, and Peanut Butter

Add a variety of legumes (beans and lentils) to your shopping list: adzuki, cannellini, garbanzos, navy, and pinto beans, to name a few. With the demand for low-fat, high-fiber recipes and the interest in ethnic cooking, today's supermarkets stock a greater variety of beans and lentils—both dry and canned. You may even find fresh legumes in the produce department.

If the store doesn't carry the type you're looking for, you usually can substitute another. For example, pinto, adzuki, and black beans can substitute for kidney beans, giving a dish a slightly different look. Cannellini, lima, and navy are the same color, just a different size. Nutritionally, most legumes are about the same, even though their appearance, texture, and flavor may differ somewhat. *To explore the nutrients in and varieties of legumes, refer to "Bean Bag" on page 154.*

For freshness, look for these qualities in dry beans: no pinhole marks or discoloration, beans with a bright color, and bags that aren't torn.

When food preparation time is short, opt for canned, rather than dry, beans. Unlike canned varieties, dry beans require cooking and perhaps soaking time. If your blood pressure is sodium sensitive, be aware that salt is added to canned beans; check the Nutrition Facts panel and ingredient list to compare similar products. *Tip:* Rinse canned beans under cold running water to reduce sodium.

have you ever *wondered*

...if dry-roasted nuts are lower in fat than oil-roasted nuts? An ounce of dry- or oil-roasted nuts has about the same amount of fat and calories—almost 14 fat grams per ounce. Nuts don't absorb much oil when they're roasted. The fat comes from the nuts themselves. Nuts are also a good protein source. ✦

Read labels on peanut butter. Peanut butter is simply peanuts that are roasted and ground into a paste. The style—smooth, chunky, or crunchy—doesn't affect the nutritional content. All are good sources of protein, but the ingredients added may have an impact. To the ground peanuts, salt or small amounts of sugar may be added for flavor; unsalted and sugar-free varieties are also sold. You'll also see reduced-fat varieties, which may not be lower in calories because sugar and other ingredients may be added to enhance flavor and texture. Naturally-occurring oils in peanut butter may be hydrogenated for spreadability, making them somewhat more saturated. *For a discussion of hydrogenated fats, see page 58 in chapter 3.*

To keep oil and solids from separating, stabilizers usually are added to peanut butter. However, in "natural" peanut butter, the oil separates out. At home, avoid the urge to make peanut butter lower in fat by pouring that fat away. Your peanut butter will become too stiff to spread. Instead mix it well, or turn the jar upside down to let the oil run through.

Be aware that nuts are often sold in salted and unsalted varieties. Unsalted nuts are typically found in the baking aisle; salted nuts, with snack foods. Try ground or chopped nuts; you can use less—but still get the nutty flavor.

Beverages

Enjoy flavored waters, and know their nutrition content. Peach, lemon, mango, and other fruit-flavored waters are refreshing. For the "fizz," some are made of sparkling water and juice. Others are flavored with sweeteners but contain little juice. Unlike plain water, they may not be calorie-free. *Refer to "What About Bottled Water?" on page 176.*

For a no-calorie beverage, look for club soda, mineral water, and plain seltzer. Don't confuse these beverages with tonic or quinine water, which has 125 calories per 12 ounces.

For carried meals, camping, and emergencies, stock up on boxed, or* UHT, *milk. Because boxed milk is ultra pasteurized, or heated to an ultra high temperature (UHT), then sealed in a sterile container, it can be stored unopened at room temperature for about three months without spoiling or nutrient loss. For added appeal, simply chill it before drinking. Once opened, UHT milk is as perishable as milk sold in the refrigerated dairy case.

For more convenience, try nonfat dry milk or evaporated, canned milk. They're both shelf stable. Nonfat dry milk powder has the same amount of nutrients as skim milk—without the water. When reconstituted and chilled, it's a nutritious beverage. *Tip*: For one cup fluid milk, combine 3/4 cup water with 1/3 cup dry milk powder. Dry milk powder also can be used to fortify casseroles and other mixed dishes with calcium and other nutrients from milk. It costs less than skim milk, too.

Evaporated milk has about 60 percent of the water removed, so its nutrients are more concentrated than regular fluid milk. If reconstituted, the nutrients are equivalent for the same-size serving. Evaporated milk may be whole or skim. Sweetened condensed milk—whole or skim—is concentrated, too, but because sugars are added, it's higher in calories. *Refer to the chart,* "Milk: A Good Calcium Source," *on page* 180 *to compare the calories, fat, cholesterol, and calcium in evaporated milks.*

Tip: Once evaporated milk is opened and dry milk is reconstituted, both should be refrigerated for safety.

Either dry or liquid—don't assume nondairy creamers are low in saturated fat. Although nondairy creamers are made with vegetable oil, the fats—often coconut or palm oil—are highly saturated. To lighten your coffee or tea, nonfat dry milk or evaporated skim milk are both good substitutes from the grocery aisle—or use fluid milk instead.

Sensitive to caffeine? Then look for decaffeinated coffee and tea, and caffeine-free soft drinks. Flavored varieties of coffee and tea are sold as both caffeinated and "decaf" varieties. Being flavored doesn't mean it's caffeine free. "Decaf" often costs slightly more. *Refer to* "Drinks: With or Without Caffeine?" *on page* 181.

As a tip, you won't find caffeine-free for all types of soft drinks. Seltzer, sparkling water, and most fruit-flavored soft drinks don't have caffeine. And know that flavored coffee mixes typically contain sugars and coconut oil, a saturated fat.

For soft drinks, know the calorie differences as you shop. A regular soda has 150 to 200 calories per 12-ounce can—with carbohydrates and water as the only significant nutrients. Diet sodas may quench thirst, too, and they're essentially calorie-free. *For more about including soft drinks in your overall eating plan, refer to* "Soft Drinks: OK?" *on page* 184.

Soft drinks and other beverages with non-nutritive, or intense sweeteners, carry nutrition labeling. If you're sensitive to their non-nutritive sweetener, avoid these products. In moderation, non-nutritive sweeteners are fine. *Refer to* "Aspartame" *on page* 136.

Buy single-serving containers of juice and boxed milk. They're handy for packing along to lunch, meetings, or a spectator sport. Rather than rely on a vending machine, you'll have a nutritious option on hand to go with you.

If you enjoy the taste of alcoholic drinks, but choose to cut back, look for nonalcoholic versions of beer and wine. The taste compares favorably. Regarding calories, you'll need to check the label. *For more about alcoholic beverages, refer to* "Alcoholic Beverages: In Moderation" *on page* 184.

Crackers and Snack Foods

For meals or snacks, consider the growing array of crackers, including those with "less fat" or "less sodium." A few popular crackers are typically low in fat, or even fat free: packaged bread sticks, graham crackers, melba toast, rice crackers, matzos, rusk, saltines, and zwieback. For more fiber, look for whole-wheat crackers, too!

have you ever wondered

...if a beverage is made with corn syrup or high-fructose sweetener, does it have fewer calories? Not necessarily. Used in the same amount, these sweeteners are equal in calories to table sugar, or sucrose. They are slightly sweeter than sucrose, however, so a little less might be used. ✦

Many snack foods are made with oil—but what kind of oil? Check the ingredient list and the Nutrition Facts panel. Those made with partially hydrogenated vegetable oils may have more saturated fats. If you snack on these foods in moderation, they fit into an overall healthful diet.

For a low-fat, crunchy snack food, buy pretzels or plain popcorn. They have less fat than potato chips, corn chips, bagel chips, or buttered popcorn. If your blood pressure is sodium sensitive, look for unsalted snack foods, such as unsalted pretzels. For a lower-fat option, look for oven-baked tortilla and potato chips; 1 ounce of baked tortilla chips has about 1 fat gram compared with about 7 fat grams in the same amount of regular tortilla chips. And check the label on microwave popcorn. Some contain high-fat flavorings.

When it comes to cookies, explore the growing variety of reduced-fat and fat-free varieties. If calories are your challenge, read the label for calorie content, too. Although the calorie and fat savings are fairly small, they can be significant if you eat these cookies frequently. Some types of commercial cookies are typically lower in fat: animal crackers, fig bars, gingersnaps, and vanilla wafers.

If you buy candy, look for small, portion-controlled packs. That way, it's not as easy to overindulge. To check the calories, read the Nutrition Facts panel. Some sugar-free candies have calories. And remember, candy bars may have fat, too.

have you ever wondered

...if virgin olive oil has fewer calories than pure olive oil? No matter what the type, olive oil is high in monounsaturated fatty acids and the calories are the same. Terms that may confuse consumers, such as "virgin" and "extra virgin" olive oil, refer to the acid content—not the nutrient content. Extra virgin olive oil has less acid and a fruitier flavor than "pure" or "virgin" olive oil. ✦

Dressings, Sauces, Oils, and Condiments

Mayonnaise or salad dressing? For less fat, choose "light," "reduced-fat," "low-calorie," or "fat-free" varieties. Fat-free dressings typically have 5 to 20 calories per tablespoon, compared with 75 calories and 6 to 8 fat grams in 1 tablespoon of regular salad dressing. Typically vinegar and water are the first two ingredients in fat-free dressing.

Buy dry blends for mixing your own salad dressing. Then you can control the amount of oil and vinegar you add. Often you can use less oil and more vinegar, water, or other flavorful liquid than the package directions call for.

Shopping for a prepared pasta sauce? Alfredo, clam, and meat sauces—marinara and primavera—you'll find sauces of all kinds. The type of sauce doesn't indicate nutrient content (although creamy sauces such as alfredo and clam usually have more fat). You'll need to read the Nutrition Facts panel.

If you're trying to cut back on sodium, look for soy sauce, teriyaki sauce, chile sauce, and marinades that are "reduced sodium." Their traditional counterparts may be quite high in sodium.

Look for nonstick cooking sprays. These sprays allow you to use less oil in a fry pan or casserole dish, or on a baking pan.

When you buy vegetable oil, remember that oils all contain the same amount of calories: about 120 calories per tablespoon. And, while the amount of saturated, monounsaturated, and polyunsaturated fatty acids differs, all vegetable oils are cholesterol free. "Light" oil refers to the color or mild flavor, not the fat content.

Oils high in polyunsaturated fatty acids include corn, safflower, and sunflower oils. And those high in monounsaturates include olive and canola (rapeseed) oils. *Refer to "Fats and Oils: How Do They Compare?" on page 57 for a comparison of various vegetable oils.*

Experiment with stronger-flavored oils: for example, sesame, walnut, or chile-flavored oils. Just a splash adds a distinct flavor to salads, stir-fries, pasta, rice, and other dishes.

Buy ketchup, mustard, and pickle relish as tasty spreads, with just 2 fat grams or less per tablespoon. Check the label for sodium content if you're watching your sodium intake. Unless prepared with less salt or sodium, most of these condiments provide 150 to 200 milligrams of sodium per tablespoon. For more flavor with fewer calories, buy prepared horseradish. And look for chutney—a condiment made with fruit or vegetables, vinegar, spices, and sugar that's low in sodium and fat.

Don't overlook the salsas. They're fat-free and bursting with flavor. Experiment with the different levels of spiciness—usually labeled as mild, medium, or hot—to see which you like best.

Fruit jams and jellies—from a nutritional standpoint they're much the same. Check the label. You'll see that both have relatively small amounts of nutrients. H*int*: Fruit jams and jellies belong in the Pyramid tip, not the Fruit Group. Fruit spreads—sweetened with juice—can have the same number of calories as jam or jelly, or they may have less sugar. And they provide some nutrients. Check the Nutrition Facts panel on the label.

Baking Aisle

Recognize different types and qualities of wheat flour before you buy. Whole-grain flour contains more fiber than refined wheat flour because the bran layer of the grain is still intact. That's where most of the fiber comes from. Unlike refined flour, whole-grain flour also contains the germ layer, which provides many vitamins and minerals. *For more on the different parts of a whole grain, refer to* "What Is a Whole Grain?" *on page* 144.

Refined flour, used in about 80 percent of baked goods, including white bread, is made only from the endosperm of the grain. While the flour has a snowy-white appearance, almost all the fiber and many of the vitamins and minerals are lost. Refined flour may be bleached or unbleached. Bleaching simply whitens the somewhat yellowish unbleached flour. From a nutritional standpoint, bleached and unbleached flours are almost the same.

When flour is enriched, four nutrients that were lost in processing—thiamin, riboflavin, niacin, and iron—are added back. The amounts of these four nutrients compare to those of whole-grain flour.

The label also may describe the flour as "all-purpose," "bread," "cake," or "self-rising."

- *All-purpose flour* is a mixture of high-gluten hard wheat and low-gluten soft wheat.
- *Bread flour* is mainly high-gluten hard wheat, suitable for yeast bread.
- *Cake, or pastry, flour* made from low-gluten soft wheat has a finer texture that makes tender pastry and cake.
- *Self-rising flour* is all-purpose flour with baking powder and salt already added for making quick breads.

Although bread can be made with only 100 percent whole-wheat flour, the result will be a dense, heavy loaf. For a lighter texture, use a combination of whole-wheat and white flour.

Look for other types of whole-grain flour in the supermarket and specialty stores: barley, buckwheat, corn, oats, brown rice, rye, and triticale. Triticale flour, which is a blend of wheat and rye flour, has less gluten than all-purpose wheat flour, making bread very dense. To lighten up your baked goods, go "50-50" with triticale and bread flour. Corn flour, made from the whole kernel, is finely-ground cornmeal; masa harina is a specialty corn flour used to make tortillas. Yellow corn flour—and other yellow cornmeal—has more vitamin A than white.

Other types of flour, such as corn and rice flours, are useful for people who have a wheat allergy or are sensitive to gluten. *Refer to* "Gluten Intolerance... Often a Lifelong Condition" *on page* 197.

Choose baking mixes—cakes, breads, waffles, muffins, etc.—that allow you to add ingredients. When you add the fat, eggs, and liquid, you can control the type you use. If you need to watch cholesterol carefully, you might add an egg substitute rather than an egg. Or to cut back on saturated fats, you could use margarine rather than butter. Check the label; some manufacturers provide tips for preparing mixes with less fat and less cholesterol.

Breads and Bakery Items

Breads help to form the foundation of the Food Guide Pyramid. They provide carbohydrates, fiber, and other nutrients, and many are low in fat. Choose products that add to the variety, balance, and moderation of your eating plan.

Look for "whole-grain" and "whole-wheat" bakery products. Other label terms may suggest whole grain—for example, oatmeal and multi-grain—but check the label to be sure. Whole-wheat flour must be first on the ingredient list.

Just because it's called "wheat bread" doesn't mean it's whole grain. Instead it may be made mostly from refined wheat flour. Terms such as "stone ground" don't mean whole wheat either. And most store-bought rye and pumpernickel breads are made mostly from white flour, too. For more fiber, check the Nutrition Facts panel and the ingredient list for those made with mainly whole-wheat flour.

On the Nutrition Facts panel, you'll see that a 1-ounce slice of whole-wheat bread has about 1.6 fiber grams compared to 0.5 to 1 gram of fiber in the same-size slice of enriched white bread. Bakery products that supply 2.5 or more grams of fiber per serving are a good fiber source.

For white bread and rolls, look for "enriched" products. Like whole-grain breads, white bread made from enriched flour is another good source of complex carbohydrates, B vitamins, and iron. Whole-wheat products still have a nutrition advantage.

have you ever wondered

...if all brown bread is whole wheat? Whole-wheat bread is always brown, but brown bread may not be whole wheat. Instead, the color may come from molasses or caramel coloring, and the flour may be mostly white flour. To be labeled "whole wheat," bread must be made from 100 percent whole-wheat flour. ✦

When flour for white bread is enriched, B vitamins and iron are added back—but not fiber or other vitamins and minerals. Many grain products are also fortified with folic acid.

Choose mostly bread and other bakery products with less fat. Most Italian bread, French bread, bagels, pita bread, kaiser rolls, English muffins, rye bread, corn tortillas, and pumpernickel bread have 2 grams of fat or less per serving. Check the Nutrition Facts panel for serving size and nutrient content.

Go easy on bakery products with more fat: croissants, many muffins, doughnuts, sweet rolls, and many cookies and cakes. Although croissants make a tasty sandwich bread, half of a croissant has 5 fat grams compared with 1 fat gram in half of an Italian roll. And a doughnut has about 10 fat grams compared to 2 grams in a cinnamon raisin bagel.

Check the product date on the package label for freshness. Packaged bakery products may have a longer shelf life than those baked in the in-store bakery.

Seasonings: Dry or Fresh

Herbs and spices enhance the flavor of food without sodium. Dry or fresh, add them to your list.

Buy herbs and spices in the amounts you need. Fresh herbs last in the refrigerator for only a short time. Dry herbs can be stored much longer—up to a year. *Tip*: Ethnic food stores often sell herbs and spices in bulk at lower prices.

Know that seasoned salts are high in sodium. This includes garlic salt and onion salt. As an alternate choice, look for garlic powder and onion powder. To check the sodium content, read the ingredient list.

Look for salt-free herb blends. Different combinations of herbs, such as Italian herb blend, or herbs de Provence (typical in French cooking), take the guessing out of seasoning.

Be adventuresome—try seasonings that may be new to you: perhaps sage in chicken soup, tarragon with peas, fresh ginger for sweet potatoes, or cumin in chili.

Try liquid smoke. It adds the smoky flavor of cured meat without the salt that's added during the curing process.

For tips on using herbs and spices in food preparation, refer to page 348, *"Add Life to Your Spices—and Herbs, Too!"*

Carry-Out Foods

Consumers increasingly shop at supermarkets for the most convenient home-served meals of all: salad bars, rotisserie chicken, steamed shrimp, deli sandwiches, as well as a variety of heat-only main dishes, appetizers, and side dishes. If you're short on time, buy your main dish—or a whole meal—already prepared. Then just heat and serve.

Guidelines for supermarket take-out foods are similar to buying and handling foods from a carry-out restaurant. *Refer to "Safe Take-Out" on page* 366.

Food Safety: Start at the Store

While the safety of the food supply has been monitored and regulated all along the food chain, it's your responsibility to select foods carefully at the store, then keep them safe until they're eaten. These shopping tips help you set a safe and healthful table.

Check the package. Frozen foods should be solid, and refrigerated foods should feel cold. Frozen foods shouldn't show signs of thawing. The packaging shouldn't have holes, tears, or open corners.

Check safety seals and buttons. Safety seals often appear on milk, yogurt, and cottage cheese. Jars of foods are often vacuum sealed for safety. Check their safety seals with your finger. If the indented safety button on the cap pulls down, it's still in place; if it's up, don't buy or use the food.

Reject cans that are swollen, damaged, rusted, or dented. These are warning signs for the bacteria that causes botulism. *Refer to "Bacteria: Hard Hitters" on page* 305 *for information on botulism.*

When possible, put raw poultry, meat, and fish in separate plastic bags before placing them in your cart. Occasionally their packaging may leak and drip onto unprotected foods.

Pay attention to "sell by" and "use by" dates on perishable foods. If the "sell by" date has passed, don't buy the product. The "use by" date applies to its use at home. Purchase only those that will be fresh when you're ready to eat them. *Refer to "More Reading on the Food Label" on page* 275 *for more about food product dating.*

Select perishable foods, such as meat, poultry, and seafood, last before check out.

In the check-out line, pack cold foods together. They'll stay chilled longer for the trip home.

Take groceries home immediately, and store them right away. If you must run a few quick errands, bring a cooler with chill packs for perishable foods if you'll be longer than 30 minutes. *For guidelines on keeping food safe once you get home, refer to chapter* 13, *"The Safe Kitchen."*

your nutrition check-up

What's in Your Shopping Cart?

According to annual supermarket surveys done by the Food Marketing Institute, consumers rank taste, nutrition, safety, price, and convenience as important reasons for making decisions in the store. If that's true for you, just how do your supermarket smarts stack up?

Do You...	**Always (3 pts)**	**Usually (2 pts)**	**Sometimes (1 pt)**	**Never (0 pt)**
For nutrition...				
Read the Nutrition Facts panel on a food label?	___	___	___	___
Use nutrition descriptions to quickly spot foods you want?	___	___	___	___
Check the % Daily Values to get specific information after you read a nutrition description?	___	___	___	___
Use food labels to compare the nutrients and ingredients in similar foods?	___	___	___	___
Look for nutrition information for fresh foods: produce, meat, poultry, and fish?	___	___	___	___
Buy foods to match your needs using nutrition information on food labels?	___	___	___	___
Use Nutrition Facts on food labels to plan healthful meals and snacks?	___	___	___	___
Subtotal for nutrition	___	___	___	___
For safety...				
Look for dates printed on packages to buy foods at their peak?	___	___	___	___
Check packaging and cans to be sure they're clean and not damaged?	___	___	___	___
Shop in a store that's clean and free of unpleasant odors?	___	___	___	___
Check to be sure that frozen foods are solid and that refrigerated foods are cold?	___	___	___	___
Choose produce and raw meat, poultry, and fish with qualities of freshness?	___	___	___	___
Put fresh meat, poultry, and fish in separate bags when you can so they don't drip on other foods in your cart?	___	___	___	___

your nutrition check-up (continued)

Do You...	Always (3 pts)	Usually (2 pts)	Sometimes (1 pt)	Never (0 pt)
Put foods that need to be refrigerated in separate bags to help maintain a cooler temperature when they're bagged?	___	___	___	___
Subtotal for safety	___	___	___	___
For cost savings...				
Use unit price codes on shelves to compare the cost of similar products?	___	___	___	___
Take advantage of cents-off coupons and in-store specials?	___	___	___	___
Buy only the amount you'll use to avoid waste?	___	___	___	___
Shop for seasonal produce?	___	___	___	___
Pay attention to the price as the cashier scans each item?	___	___	___	___
Consider carefully before buying a new food after you sample it or see an attractive display?	___	___	___	___
Subtotal for cost savings	___	___	___	___
For convenience...				
Keep a shopping list to use as you shop?	___	___	___	___
Shop during off hours to save time and avoid crowds?	___	___	___	___
Buy foods that are partly or fully prepared?	___	___	___	___
Buy single-portion or small-sized packages when you're feeding one or two?	___	___	___	___
Keep shopping trips to a minimum— no more than once or twice a week?	___	___	___	___
Subtotal for convenience	___	___	___	___

Now Score Yourself

Count up your "supermarket smarts" category by category, then add up the total.

Total Score ___

For nutrition and safety, a perfect score is 21 for each. For cost savings, it's 18; for convenience, 15. That adds up to 75 points.

If you come close to a perfect score in any category, count yourself as "supermarket smart" in that area. And make it your goal to be a well-rounded shopper—with top scores in every category!

real life nutrition

To market, to market

Anxious to stay fit, Dot decided to attend a series of brown bag seminars about eating for health offered during her lunch hour. Today's topic: "Food Shopping: For the Health of It!"

After the seminar, Dot paused to talk further with Lana, the registered dietitian who'd given today's presentation. "From what you said, I think my shopping habits need a makeover. My family has a history of heart disease…although we're all healthy. We pretty much buy what we like—what we've always eaten. And we are eating more vegetables than we used to. But perhaps we're eating more fat than we think."

They talked further and discussed what changes Dot and her husband Dwight could make at the supermarket—and talked about fat trade-offs so they could enjoy moderate amounts of some higher-fat foods.

Once home, Dot and Dwight decided that the whole family could benefit by cutting back on fat. So with shopping list in hand, they began their shopping cart makeover. How could they shop to cut back on fat in foods they buy?

Advice for buying foods with less fat:

- Use nutrition descriptions, such as "reduced fat," "low-fat," "less saturated fat," and "lean," on food labels to spot foods with less fat.
- Check the Nutrition Facts panel on food labels to compare the fat and saturated fats in similar foods at the supermarket.
- Using information on food labels, choose packaged foods—including deli meat, canned foods, frozen entrées, dairy foods, bakery goods, frozen desserts, breakfast cereals, salad dressing, and snack foods—with less fat.
- Buy lean meat, including "select" grades, lean cuts, and processed meats that are at least 90 percent fat free.
- Buy skinless chicken breast and lean seafood.
- Buy more fruits, vegetables, and grains, and fewer higher-fat foods in order to eat more carbohydrate and less fat in their overall diet.

CHAPTER THIRTEEN

THE SAFE KITCHEN

America's food supply is one of the safest in the world. All along the food chain—farmers, food manufacturers, supermarkets, and restaurants—are required by law to follow strict food safety regulations, which are carefully monitored. However, once food leaves the grocery store, the responsibility for food safety is up to you.

We've all heard the most important rules for handling food safely: keep all food clean, keep hot foods hot, and keep cold foods cold. But just what is the temperature connection? What are the best ways to keep foods clean and safe...for "goodness sake"? And, most important, how does food safety affect your health?

Foodborne Illness: More Common Than You Think!

Imagine...your muscles ache, you feel dizzy, you're tired, or perhaps your stomach just doesn't feel right. Do you have the flu or a bad cold?

Disguised as flu, your illness actually may be foodborne illness. Foodborne illness, sometimes called food poisoning, comes from eating contaminated food. But the symptoms can easily be mistaken for other health problems.

Food safety and health experts estimate that between 6.5 and 33 million cases of foodborne illness occur in the United States each year. The estimates vary because many cases go unreported. Because symptoms vary from fatigue, chills, a mild fever, dizziness, headaches, an upset stomach, and diarrhea to dehydration, severe cramps, vision problems, and even death, diagnosing foodborne illness is difficult. Although actual incidence is unknown, foodborne illness may lead to a small percentage of some long-term health problems, too. While many reported cases are caused by food prepared outside the home, small outbreaks in home settings are considered to be far more common.

Also, people are different. After eating the same contaminated food, you may react differently from someone else. One person may show no symptoms. Another may get very ill. The reaction depends on the type of bacteria or toxin, how extensively the food was contaminated, how much food was eaten, and the person's susceptibility to the bacteria.

Anyone can be a victim of foodborne illness. But some people are at increased risk: infants, young children, pregnant women, older people, and those with a weakened immune system, such as those with HIV or cancer.

Bacteria cause most cases of foodborne illnesses, usually due to improper food handling. But foods can also be contaminated by viruses, parasites, and household chemicals, too. With proper food handling and sanitation, most foodborne illness can be prevented.

Bacteria Basics

Life begins at 40! Between 40° and 140° F, a single bacterium can multiply to become trillions in just 24 hours! Why the exponential leap? Under the right conditions, bacteria double in number every 20 to 30 minutes.

Even with so many, you can't see bacteria without a microscope. Unlike microorganisms that cause food to spoil, you can't taste or smell most bacteria. Yet they live everywhere—in many foods, on your skin, under your fingernails, on all kinds of other surfaces, and on pets and other live animals. Foods of animal origin—raw meat, poultry, fish, eggs, raw (unpasteurized) milk—are the most common food sources of bacteria.

Although far less common, harmful bacteria also can be transferred to fresh produce, perhaps through contaminated irrigation water. For foods grown in the United States, irrigation water is closely monitored for safety.

Because they're everywhere, you can't avoid harmful bacteria completely. Fortunately, from a food safety standpoint, most adults don't need to worry about harmful bacteria—at least not in small numbers. Your body can handle small amounts with no threat to your health. However, you are at risk for foodborne illness when bacteria multiply to very large numbers. Caution: Young children, the very old, and people whose immune systems don't function normally are at greater risk, even for small amounts of harmful bacteria.

To survive and multiply, bacteria need time and the right conditions: food, moisture, and warm temperature. Many need oxygen, too. Bacteria thrive on protein. Foods with protein—meat, poultry, fish, eggs, milk—offer the medium for bacteria to grow. The ideal temperature for bacterial growth is between 40° and 140° F. Above 160° F, heat destroys bacteria. Refrigerating foods below 40° F slows their growth. And freezing stops but doesn't kill bacteria. *Check the thermometer for "The Danger Zone" on page* 305.

Mishandled food—improper preparation, cooking, or storage—is the culprit that allows bacteria to grow and multiply in your kitchen. With its rich supply of nutrients and often moist quality, food offers the perfect medium for bacteria to grow in.

Most bacteria won't harm you. Some, such as the

have you ever wondered

...how much you need to worry about mayonnaise in picnic foods and brown-bag lunches? Mayonnaise is a perishable spread, so it does need to be keep chilled. And homemade mayonnaise is more perishable than its commercial counterpart. Commercial mayonnaise and salad dressings are made with salt and with vinegar or lemon juice, which actually slow bacteria growth. In unrefrigerated mayonnaise-based salads such as chicken, tuna, or egg salad, it's not the mayonnaise that poses the risk but rather the chicken, tuna, or eggs.

...if fish you catch are safe to eat? About 20 percent of fish eaten in the United States are caught by people for personal use. There's no safety problem if you catch fish in familiar and safe waters. However, seafood toxins, which occur naturally in some waters, and fish contaminated by chemicals in the water pose health risks. If you're unsure about the safety of fish, contact your local and state health department, state fishery agency, or Sea Grant office. ✦

ones used to make yogurt, some cheeses, and vinegar, are actually helpful. Yet bacteria are the main source of foodborne illness in the United States. That's why keeping bacteria under control is so vital to your health.

If you suspect food is contaminated, don't even taste it! You can't see, smell, or taste bacteria that cause foodborne illness. Securely wrap the suspected food, and discard it where neither humans nor animals can get at it.

Bacteria: Hard Hitters

Although as many as 100 bacteria cause foodborne illness, these are among the worst troublemakers: *salmonella, staphylococcus aureus, campylobacter, clostridium perfringens, clostridium botulinum, escherichia coli* 0157:H7, and *listeria monocytogenes*. You also may hear about *shigella* and *vibrio vulnificus*, two other bacteria that cause foodborne illness.

Salmonella is found mostly in raw or undercooked poultry, meat, eggs, fish, and unpasteurized milk. Control is simple enough—proper cooking kills *salmonella*. Combat this bacteria by cooking foods thoroughly, by keeping foods clean, and by consuming only pasteurized milk.

Raw milk, even if it's certified, may not be a wise choice to drink because it isn't pasteurized. Pasteurized milk is quickly heated to a temperature high enough to kill harmful bacteria, such as salmonella. Raw milk isn't widely available to consumers.

Staphylococcus aureus (staph) spreads from someone handling food. It's carried on the skin, nose, and throat and in skin infections, then it spreads to food. Toxins, or poisons, produced by staph aren't killed by ordinary cooking. That's why personal hygiene and cleanliness in the kitchen are so important!

Campylobacter jejuni is a major bacterial cause of foodborne illness in the United States. Like salmonella, campylobacter can be transferred to raw and undercooked poultry and meat, unpasteurized milk, and untreated water.

The Danger Zone

Effects of temperature (°F) on growth of bacteria in food. The most dangerous zone of temperatures is between 40° and 140° F.

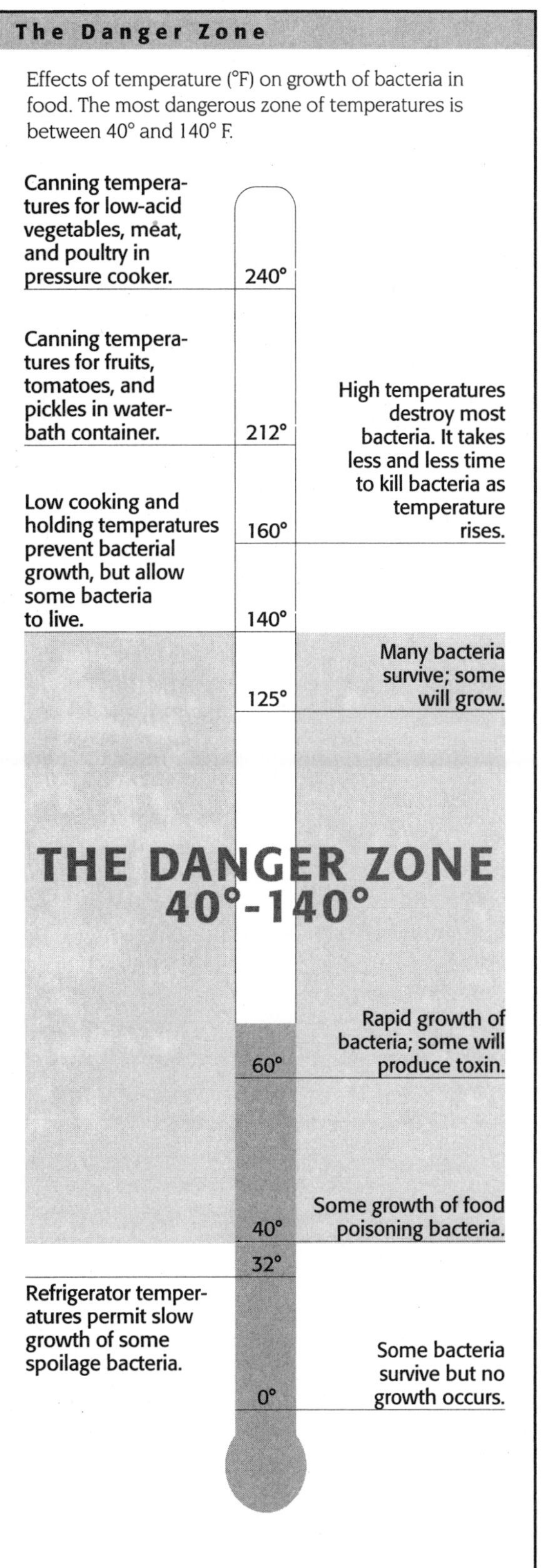

The good news is, campylobacter can be easily destroyed through safe food handling and water treatment systems. To protect yourself, always cook food thoroughly and avoid cross-contamination by washing utensils, cutting boards and hands after handling raw poultry or meat. Avoid raw, unpasteurized milk. And, if you're camping, always treat water from streams or lakes.

Clostridium perfringens is present everywhere, growing where there's little or no oxygen. Sometimes called the "buffet germ," it grows fastest in large portions—such as casseroles, stews, and gravies—held at low or room temperatures in "the danger zone." Chafing dishes that aren't hot enough and large portions that don't cool quickly in the refrigerator are breeding grounds. To slow this bacteria, replenish buffet table servings often, rather than putting out large portions for an extended time, and refrigerate leftovers quickly.

Clostridium botulinum is rarely found. But left untreated, botulism is often fatal! Botulism-causing bacteria can come from home-canned or commercially-canned foods. Usually these are low-acid canned foods, such as meats and vegetables, that haven't been processed or stored properly. Foods improperly canned at home pose a higher risk. For home canning, always use approved methods. And heat home-canned meats and vegetables thoroughly, about 15 to 20 minutes, before serving.

FOR THE MILE-HIGH COOK

If you live at an altitude of 1,000 feet or more, you may need to cook food longer to kill bacteria. At higher altitudes, water boils at a lower temperature, which makes it less effective for killing bacteria. Most cooking and canning temperatures are based on food preparation at sea level. ✦

To combat this bacteria, look for warning signs: swollen or dented cans or lids, cracked jars, loose lids, and clear liquids turned milky. Beware of cans or jars that spurt when they're opened. Never eat—or even taste—these foods!

***Escherichia coli* (E. *coli*),** a common bacteria, exists in your intestinal tract. For the most part, it's harmless. However, some strains are associated with traveler's diarrhea, caused by contaminated drinking water, as well as diarrhea among infants.

One strain—E. *coli* 0157:H7—has received much attention because its effects can be so severe. This strain, associated with eating raw or undercooked ground beef, or unpasteurized milk, can result in life-threatening health problems: hemorrhagic colitis with severe abdominal cramps, bloody diarrhea, nausea, and vomiting and perhaps hemolytic uremic syndrome (HUS), which may cause kidney failure, brain damage, strokes, seizures, and death, especially in young children and the elderly.

To combat all strains of E. *coli*, cook and reheat meat thoroughly. Be especially careful of ground meat—for example, hamburgers—because bacteria on the surface of the meat get mixed into the center, which takes longer to cook. Keep cutting surfaces clean. Avoid cross contamination of raw food, or transferring bacteria from one food to another with dirty utensils, cutting boards, plates, and hands.

Listeria monocytogenes can cause a less common, but potentially fatal, foodborne illness called listeriosis. Pregnant women, infants, and those with weakened immune systems are more susceptible. Listeria are part of your everyday surroundings, including places where food is processed.

Because *listeria* is commonly found in milk and cheese made from unpasteurized milk, it's wise to avoid unpasteurized milk products. *Listeria* can also be found in raw meat, poultry, seafood, and eggs. As with any packaged food product, follow the "keep refrigerated" advice on the label, the "use by" date on the package, and the reheating instructions.

From Parasites and Viruses, Too...

Bacteria are responsible for most cases of foodborne illness. However, parasites and viruses—other tiny organisms that contaminate food—are culprits, too. Parasites, such as *trichinella spiralis* and *toxoplasnosa gondii*, survive by drawing on the nutrients of a living host. Viruses, such as hepatitis A, act like parasites. Through the food chain, both can infect humans.

Trichinosis is contracted by consuming undercooked pork or game that has been infested with trichina larvae. With careful controls in the food industry, trichinosis is less common today than it was in the past. However, you're still wise to cook pork, game, and other meat to the recommended internal temperature to destroy any live trichina larvae. *Refer to "Meat, Fish, and Poultry: Target Temperatures" on page 316.*

Toxoplasmosis is caused by a parasite indirectly linked to undercooked meat or poultry. It's also directly transferred to humans from cat feces. Pregnant women are at special risk because they can pass the parasite to their unborn baby. To combat this parasite, cook meat, especially pork, lamb, and poultry thoroughly. And for pregnant women, limit exposure to cats and cat litter boxes; if you do handle cats, wash your hands well with soap and water.

Hepatitis A virus comes from food that's been contaminated by feces. The conditions caused by hepatitis, such as jaundice and liver problems, can be severe. Sometimes hepatitis A comes through the food chain from shellfish that's been harvested from contaminated waters—perhaps where raw sewage is dumped. More commonly, an infected person who handles food without properly washing his or her hands can transmit the disease—often from a restaurant or other foodservice operation. As a precaution, always choose a restaurant that appears clean. And eat only well-cooked seafood. *Refer to "Eating Out Safely!" on page 362 for guidelines.*

Basic "Safe Food" Rules

To prevent foodborne illness, keep these rules in mind:

Keep food clean. Keep everything that comes in contact with food clean. Wash your hands frequently while you prepare food. Use clean towels, sponges, cooking dishes, and utensils. Scrub counters and sanitize cutting boards between food preparation steps. Let cleaned utensils and cutting boards air dry. *Refer to the "Checklist*

SHOULD YOU CALL YOUR DOCTOR?

Suppose you suspect foodborne illness. You or a family member has an upset stomach, diarrhea, vomiting, fatigue, abdominal discomfort, or a fever. Symptoms of foodborne illness can appear anywhere from 30 minutes to 2 weeks after eating contaminated food. Most often though, symptoms appear within 4 to 48 hours after eating. Symptoms usually pass within 24 to 48 hours—rest and plenty of fluids are the best ways to treat foodborne illness. There are circumstances, however, when it's important that you receive care from a doctor.

- When diarrhea is bloody. This may be a symptom of E. *Coli* 0157:H7.
- When diarrhea or vomiting is excessive. This may lead to dehydration if fluids aren't replaced.
- When these three symptoms all appear: stiff neck, severe headache, and fever. The victim may have listeria, which can be life-threatening.
- When the victim is at high risk—perhaps a young child, elderly person, or someone whose immune system is compromised due to illness.
- When symptoms persist longer than 3 days. ✦

for a Clean Kitchen" on this page for how to sanitize cutting boards and more about cross contamination.

Keep hot food hot. Cook and hold cooked foods at temperatures higher than 140° F. High temperatures (160° to 212° F) kill most bacteria. Temperatures between 140° and 159° F prevent their growth but may let bacteria survive. Cooked foods containing meat, poultry, fish, eggs, and milk products should never be allowed to sit at room temperature for longer than two hours.

Keep cold food cold. Rapidly cool any cooked foods that are to be served cold or refrigerated to 40° F or below. At this temperature, bacteria that spoil food grow slowly. Below 32° F, which is freezing, bacteria survive but won't grow.

Follow safe handling instructions on food packages and labels. *For an example of a safe food handling label found on fresh meat and poultry items, see page 274.*

WHAT DO YOU DO IF YOU SUSPECT FOODBORNE ILLNESS?

➢ Call or see a medical professional. Physicians and laboratories are responsible for contacting the health department to report diagnosis of foodborne illness. However, most cases of foodborne illness aren't diagnosed; the symptoms simply are treated to relieve discomfort.

➢ Report the incident to the local health department if the suspected food came from a public place or large gathering—a restaurant, sidewalk vendor, employee cafeteria, company picnic, or grocery store, among others.

➢ If you are reporting the incident, try to preserve the suspected food. If you can, keep the packaging, too, because it identifies where the product was produced. Mark it with a warning label so no one else consumes it.

If you suspected that a food has been contaminated by a household chemical...

➢ Check the label for an antidote or remedy. Likely you'll find an "800-" number for first-aid advice, too. Follow the advice.

➢ Contact the local Poison Control Center or health department. As a safety precaution, post their phone numbers by your telephone. You'll have them handy if household chemicals do contaminate food or are misused in any way. ✦

Checklist for a Clean Kitchen

From top to bottom, a clean kitchen offers a main line of defense against the spread of colds, flu, and other foodborne illness. Before you work with food, eliminate the breeding grounds for harmful bacteria:

➢ ***Hands.*** Wash your hands—front and back, between your fingers, under your fingernails—in warm, soapy water for at least 20 seconds before and after every step in preparing foods. Be sure your kitchen helpers—especially children—do, too!

Remember to wash your hands if you've switched tasks, especially if you put a load of dirty clothes in the washer, diapered a baby, petted an animal or touched its feeding bowl, or used the bathroom. Bandage cuts and sores on your hands, too.

Why is hand-washing so important? Bacteria live and multiply on warm, moist hands. Hands pick up germs, spreading them from surface to surface, food to food, and person to person. One of the best ways to control the spread of illness is thorough hand-washing.

➢ ***Work surfaces.*** Clean them often to remove food particles and spills. Use a multi-purpose cleaner for everyday spills and a disinfectant, such as a chlorine-beach solution or a disinfectant cleaner, to kill bacteria.

To avoid cross contamination, sanitize cutting boards after each use with a chlorine bleach-water solution. To make the solution, mix 2 teaspoons of bleach in a quart of water. Let the cutting boards air-dry. Use a brush to reach grooves and other hard-to-reach places.

Cross contamination happens when bacteria in one food spread to another, often from a cutting board, knife, plate, spoon, or your hands. For example, drippings from raw meat left on a cutting board can transfer bacteria to vegetables, which are being sliced next.

➢ ***Utensils.*** Avoid cross-contamination with utensils, too. Unless it's cleaned well in between, avoid using the same knife to slice meat and chop vegetables.

Although hard to resist, remind everyone who ventures in the kitchen—never taste with the stirring spoon! If children reach for a finger-licking taste, be sure they wash their hands before continuing to help in the kitchen.

Wash dishes and cookware carefully, too—in the dishwasher or in hot (at least 140° F), soapy water. Then rinse well. Be aware that chipped crockery and china can collect bacteria.

➢ ***Towels and dishcloths.*** Change and wash them often. And allow them to dry out between each use. Being damp, they're the perfect breeding ground for bacteria. Throw out dirty sponges, or wash them in a bleach-water solution.

➢ ***Appliances.*** On any appliance, clean up spills right away. Wash appliance surfaces with hot, soapy water. Pay special attention to the refrigerator and freezer—shelves, sides, and door—where foods are stored. (Pack perishables in coolers while you clean or defrost your refrigerator and freezer.) Splatters inside your microwave oven can harbor bacteria, too. Keep it clean!

Safe Keeping

Store food in the right container, in the right place, at the right temperature, for the right length of time. Foods maintain their quality, safety, and nutrients when they're stored properly and used within a certain time. Besides, you stretch your food dollar when you don't need to discard spoiled food. *To determine the freshness of a packaged food product, refer to page* 275, "*More Reading on the Food Label.*"

In the Cupboard...

How long do nonrefrigerated foods keep their quality? That depends on how carefully you store them. For safe dry storage, here's how you store food for keeps!

- ➢ Countertop thawing
- ➢ Leftovers left out of the refrigerator
- ➢ Unclean cutting board
- ➢ Room-temperature marinating
- ➢ Store-to-refrigerator lag time
- ➢ BBQ blunder: same platter for raw and grilled meats
- ➢ Restaurant "doggie bag" delay
- ➢ Stirring-and-tasting spoon
- ➢ Shared knife for trimming raw meat and chopping vegetables
- ➢ Hide-and-eat Easter eggs
- ➢ Undercooked high-risk foods, such as eggs, meat, poultry, and fish

(Adapted from: Plating It Safe: A Market-to-Mealtime Checklist to Help Keep Food Safe, National Association of County Health Officials and Beef Board and the Beef Industry Council of the Meat Board, 1994. ✦

Keep your cupboards and pantries clean, dry, dark, and cool—preferably away from heat-producing appliances. Ideally 50° to 70° F is the best storage temperature. High temperatures (over 100° F) lower the quality of canned foods.

Organize your cupboards with older cans up front for first use. The good news is: canned foods do have a long shelf life. Stored properly, most canned foods keep for at least one year.

Be alert for signs of food spoilage. Never use food from cans that are cracked, bulging, or leaking or that spurt liquid when opened. The food may be contaminated with the deadly botulism organism. Toss—don't taste!

Store opened food in dry airtight containers. That keeps out insects and rodents. Well-sealed containers also keep one food from absorbing the odors of others.

Store foods away from kitchen chemicals and refuse. As important, keep chemicals and refuse away from places where food is prepared and eaten, too.

In the Fridge...

Do "science experiments" ever grow in your refrigerator? Is yesterday's meatloaf hiding behind tomorrow's juice carton? Has that special cheese become as dry as old leather? With the hustle and bustle of today's living, these things happen, even in the best kitchens. To keep perishable food safe and out of the "danger zone," you need to wrap it and store it right.

Keep your refrigerator cold—between 34° and 40° F. Temperatures fluctuate, especially from season to season. Use an inexpensive refrigerator thermometer to check; buy one at the supermarket. Remind your family to make their refrigerator raids quick so the door doesn't stay open too long.

Store all foods wrapped or in covered containers. Seal storage containers well to prevent moisture loss and absorption of off-odors. Unless the package is torn, leave food in its store wrapping. The less you handle food, the better. And it's okay to store food in cans after opening them. Just cover the can with plastic wrap or foil, then store it in the refrigerator. You may notice a slight change in flavor, however.

Keep packages of raw meat, poultry, and fish in separate plastic bags, in a bowl or pan, on the lowest refrigerator shelf. That keeps the juices from dripping onto other foods. The lowest refrigerator shelf is usually the coldest, too.

Store food quickly. Avoid keeping perishable foods at room temperature for long. That includes foods from the supermarket, as well as leftovers. Cool leftovers and food cooked for later use in the refrigerator or freezer, not on the counter. Leftovers shouldn't be left at room temperature for longer than two hours.

For faster cooling, store cooked food in small portions and in shallow containers. Large portions can take a long time to drop below 40° F.

Keep leftovers where you'll see them. Then use them up within three or four days at the most. Toss them out if you can't remember when you stored them.

Avoid overloading your refrigerator. Cold air needs room to circulate.

have you ever wondered

...if molds on cheese are dangerous? Not usually. Few molds on cheese produce toxins, or poisons. But just to be on the safe side, discard one inch of the cheese on all sides where mold is visible. Recover the food with fresh, clean wrap. Soft cheeses, such as cream cheese, brie, and cottage cheese, and other foods with mold on them should be discarded. The exceptions are mold-ripened cheeses, such as blue, gorgonzola, Roquefort, and Stilton. Check the color and the pattern of the mold. If it's different from the usual blue or green veins and you see furry spots or white, pink, blue, green, gray, or black flecks, discard the cheese. Mold spores may have spread throughout the cheese. ✦

Use special compartments in your refrigerator. The meat keeper keeps meat extra cold so it stays fresher longer. And crisper bins help produce retain its moisture. Keep eggs, however, in their carton, not the egg tray, to keep them fresher longer. And use them within three weeks.

Eat perishable foods while they remain at peak quality. Discard foods, rather than risk foodborne illness, after they've passed their prime. Use beef steaks, roasts, deli meats, and poultry within three to four days. Use ground meat, ground poultry, and fish within one to two days. You may notice that the interior of ground beef often is purplish red in color. The color doesn't mean the meat is spoiled. Instead, it hasn't been in direct contact with oxygen. As it's exposed to air, meat will turn the familiar bright red. *Check the chart, "The Cold Truth: How Cold, How Long?" on page 313.*

If you're not sure about a food's safety, toss it out! Never trust the odor or appearance. Food may look, taste, and smell OK—even when it's no longer safe to eat. When in doubt, throw it out!

Discard moldy foods "under wraps." Put them in a bag or wrap so mold spores don't spread. Check other foods for mold. Then clean the container and the refrigerator well.

In the Freezer...

In freezer storage, the colder, the better. Freezing extends the shelf life of all kinds of foods.

Keep your freezer "iceberg" cold! For long-term storage, maintain a freezer temperature of 0° F or less. A free-standing freezer can stay that cold. However, the freezer compartment of most refrigerators usually won't; plan to use foods stored there more quickly. To check the temperature, install a freezer thermometer, available at many kitchen stores or supermarkets.

Store foods purchased frozen in their original packaging. Commercial packaging is usually airtight.

Freezing home-prepared foods? Take time to properly package them for the freezer. Use freezer

CAUTION—DECORATIVE DISHES

For years lead has been an ingredient in the glaze, or coating, on ceramic bowls, dishes, and pitchers. With proper firing, or heating in a kiln, glazes with lead are safe. However, when dishes are fired incorrectly or copper is added to the glaze, hazardous amounts of lead can leach from dishes into food. Lead is harmful to health, collecting in bones and some soft tissues. Among other problems, lead poisoning can cause learning disabilities, organ damage, and even death. Children and pregnant women are particularly sensitive to the toxic effects of lead.

To be sure your dishes are safe enough for food, follow these guidelines:

Inspect the surface of ceramic dishes. The surface that contacts food should be smooth and shiny, not rough or painted on top of the glaze.

Check both sides of dishes, bowls, and pitchers. If it says "Not for Food Use" or "For Decorative Purposes Only," don't use it for food!

Don't store food in ceramic dishes or leaded crystal. Lead can leach out when acidic foods and beverages, such as coffee, tomato juice, fruit, or wine, come in contact with glaze or leaded crystal over time.

Beware of ceramic ware made by untrained potters. For the most part, today's hobbyists are well aware of the problems of lead glazes.

Beware of ceramic ware brought back from foreign travel and older dishes, imported before government monitoring.

To check your own dishes, purchase a lead-test kit. Hardware or hobby stores are the best places to find one. ✦

containers, foils, and moisture-proof paper, plastic bags, or other wraps. Traditional plastic wraps aren't suitable. Use freezer tape to help keep the package airtight and free of freezer burn. For storage that's longer than a few days, fresh meat retains its quality best when it's rewrapped or overwrapped.

Before freezing, label each package with the food, date, and the number of servings. When you open your freezer, you'll be able to identify the foods on hand and their freshness.

Organize your freezer. Rotate foods, keeping the oldest foods in front so they're used first. Stack similar foods together. They'll be easier to find.

Remember some foods don't freeze well: bananas, fresh tomatoes, lettuce, celery, gelatin salads, custard, mayonnaise, hard-cooked eggs, sour cream, cream (unless it's whipped), raw potatoes, unblanched vegetables, and foods made with these ingredients. For these foods, freezing affects the quality, not the safety.

Blanch vegetables to lengthen their freezer life. Blanching is immersing foods in boiling water for one to three minutes, then plunging them in cold water to stop the cooking. Freeze in airtight plastic bags after draining well.

Thaw foods in the refrigerator, not on the counter. Bacteria thrive at room temperature. Put thawing food in a plastic bag or on a plate to collect any juices. If you need a fast thaw, remove the store wrap first, put meat, poultry, or fish in a microwave-safe container, and defrost on "low" or "defrost" settings in your microwave oven. Then cook it right away!

have you ever wondered

...if freezer burn on food is harmful? Freezer burn, which is the white, dried-out patches on improperly wrapped frozen food, won't make you sick. But it will make food tough and tasteless. To prevent freezer burn, wrap food that hasn't been previously frozen in proper freezer wrap (aluminum foil, heavy freezer paper, or plastic freezer bags), push the air out, then seal with freezer tape. Well-sealed freezer containers work, too; before putting on the lid, cover food with plastic wrap to avoid freezer burn from air inside the container.

...if partially thawed food can be refrozen? Yes, with caution—if it still has ice crystals and has been kept in the refrigerator for one day or less. Be aware that quality may be lost with refreezing. Try cooking the food first, then refreezing it. ✦

When Your Power Goes Out...

Suppose a storm, an accident, or another event shuts off power to your home—along with your refrigerator and freezer. You may not need to toss out food if you take a few precautions.

Keep the refrigerator and freezer doors closed so heat stays out and cold stays in. Unopened, most refrigerators stay chilled for at least four to six hours, depending on the warmth of your kitchen. If the power is out longer, you might buy a block of ice to keep the refrigerator cool.

Frozen foods can hold for about two days in a full, free-standing freezer—if it stays closed. Half full, a freezer remains cold for about one day. Freezers are well insulated; each package of frozen food is a block of ice, protecting foods around it.

Once the Power's Back On...

Avoid using appearance or odor as your guide to food safety. Instead follow these guidelines:

If foods in the freezer still have ice crystals, refreeze them right away. Then use them as soon as you can.

Discard perishable foods held at room temperature for more than two hours: meat, poultry, and fish; milk, soft cheese, and yogurt; soups; leftover prepared foods; cooked pasta; mayonnaise; and many refrigerated desserts. In that time, bacteria can multiply enough to cause illness. Dispose of these foods safely—where animals can't eat them.

If the power's been out for only a few hours, keep less perishable foods. Fresh fruits and vegetables, peanut butter, nuts, hard and process cheeses,

The Cold Truth: How Cold, How Long?

How long can refrigerated food keep safely and remain at top quality? Freezer and refrigerator times vary. As long as the food is properly packaged, these are basic guidelines:

Food	Refrigerator (40° F)	Freezer (0° F)
Eggs		
Fresh eggs, in shell	3 weeks	Don't freeze
Raw egg yolks, whites	2 to 4 days	1 year
Hard-cooked eggs	1 week	Don't freeze well
Liquid pasteurized eggs or egg substitutes,		
opened	3 days	Don't freeze
unopened	10 days	1 year
Commercial Mayonnaise		
Refrigerate after opening	2 months	Don't freeze
Frozen Dinners and Casseroles		
Keep frozen until ready to serve		3 to 4 months
Deli & Self-Serve Foods		
Store-prepared (or homemade) egg, ham, chicken, tuna, macaroni salads	3 to 5 days	Don't freeze
Prestuffed pork and lamb chops, chicken breasts stuffed with dressing	1 day	Don't freeze
Store-cooked convenience meats	1 to 2 days	Don't freeze
Vacuum-Packed Products		
Commercial-brand, vacuum-packed dinners with USDA seal	2 weeks, unopened	These products don't freeze well.
Soups & Stews		
Vegetable or meat-added soups and stews	3 to 4 days	2 to 3 months
Hamburger, Ground, & Stew Meats		
Hamburger and stew meats	1 to 2 days	3 to 4 months
Ground turkey, veal, pork, lamb, and mixtures	1 to 2 days	3 to 4 months
Hot Dogs & Lunch Meats		
Hot dogs,		
opened package	1 week	
unopened package	2 weeks	in freezer wrap, 1 to 2 months
Lunch meats,		
opened	3 to 5 days	
unopened	2 weeks	
Bacon & Sausage		
Bacon	7 days	1 month
Sausage, raw, from pork, beef, turkey	1 to 2 days	1 to 2 months
Smoked breakfast links, patties	7 days	1 to 2 months
Hard sausage—pepperoni, jerky sticks	2 to 3 weeks	1 to 2 months
Corned Beef & Ham		
Corned beef, in pouch with pickling juices	5 to 7 days	Drained, wrapped, 1 month
Ham, canned (label says keep refrigerated)	6 to 9 months	Don't freeze
Ham, fully cooked,		
whole	7 days	1 to 2 months
half	3 to 5 days	1 to 2 months
slices	3 to 4 days	1 to 2 months
Fresh Meat		
Steaks, beef	3 to 5 days	6 to 12 months
Chops, pork	3 to 5 days	4 to 6 months
Chops, lamb	3 to 5 days	6 to 9 months
Roasts, beef	3 to 5 days	6 to 12 months
Roasts, lamb	3 to 5 days	6 to 9 months
Roasts, pork and veal	3 to 5 days	4 to 6 months
Variety meats—tongue, brain, kidneys, liver, heart, chitterlings	1 to 2 days	3 to 4 months
Meat Leftovers		
Cooked meat and meat dishes	3 to 4 days	2 to 3 months
Gravy and meat broth	1 to 2 days	2 to 3 months
Fresh Poultry		
Chicken or turkey,		
whole	1 to 2 days	1 year
pieces	1 to 2 days	9 months
Giblets	1 to 2 days	3 to 4 months
Cooked Poultry, Leftover		
Fried chicken	3 to 4 days	4 months
Cooked poultry dishes	3 to 4 days	4 to 6 months
Cooked chicken pieces, plain	3 to 4 days	4 months
Cooked chicken pieces covered with broth, gravy	1 to 2 days	6 months
Cooked chicken nuggets, patties	1 to 2 days	1 to 3 months

Source: "A Quick Consumer Guide to Safe Food Handling," *House and Garden Bulletin* 248, August 1995.

condiments, butter, and margarine often keep for several days at room temperature. Toss food out, however, if it turns moldy or smells bad.

Plan for Unexpected Emergencies.
No matter where you live, experts advise a three-day supply of food and water for you, your family—and your pets.

Stock up on nonperishable foods: ready-to-eat canned meat, fruits, juices, milk, soups, and vegetables. Canned foods are better than foods in glass bottles or jars because they won't break in a disaster. Choose single-serving portions, too; you may have no way to keep leftovers cold. Keep some high-energy foods on hand, too, such as peanut butter, nuts, and trail mix.

Rotate your emergency food supply every year or so. That way, it's fresh when you need it.

Fill plastic containers with enough water for your family: one gallon of water per person per day. *Refer to page 178 for advice on making contaminated water safe to drink.*

Keep manual can openers on your emergency shelf.

have you ever *wondered*

...if it's better to use a plastic or a wooden cutting board? There was debate about cutting surfaces. Studies suggesting that bacteria don't thrive on wooden boards did receive considerable attention—but have not been repeated with the same results. Instead newer research from the Food and Drug Administration indicates that plastic cutting boards have the edge in the "safe kitchen." Bacteria in raw meat doesn't stay on plastic as it does on wood, and plastic boards are cleaned more easily.

Whether you choose wood or plastic, keep them clean. Wash them in hot soapy water, rinse, and dry well, perhaps in the dishwasher. Clean the cutting board after using it to cut raw meat. If you prefer a wooden cutting board, keep one for raw meat only. Discard wooden boards with deep grooves that can't be cleaned easily. ✦

A well-stocked emergency shelf with no way to open food cans doubles any disaster!

For more advice about handling food in disasters (fires, floods, hurricanes), contact experts: The American Dietetic Association's Consumer Nutrition Hot Line (1-800-366-1655), the U.S. Department of Agriculture's Meat and Poultry Hotline (1-800-535-4555), your local American Red Cross chapter, Cooperative Extension Service, Civil Defense, or emergency management office.

Safe Preparation and Service

Preparing, cooking, and serving can't make your food safe—if it hasn't been handled properly from the very start. But, assuming food's been cared for safely all along, you can ensure its quality as you prepare and serve it.

"Prep" It Safe

Wash all fresh fruits and vegetables—even if rinds or peels will be discarded—with clean running water, but not soap. Porous surfaces of produce can absorb ingredients in soap products. If necessary, use a brush. Remove soft spots and wilted leaves. They're signs of spoilage, but not a food safety issue.

Check canned and jar foods before opening them. Make sure that safety buttons on jar lids are depressed and that canned goods are still safe: not bulging or leaking. Wipe the tops of canned goods.

Rinse poultry and seafood in cold water; check for off-odors, too. Deveining shrimp is up to you. Cooking destroys any bacteria in shrimp, including in the intestinal vein. However, for cosmetic purposes, you may want to remove it. In large shrimp, the vein may contain a lot of grit.

Keep juices from raw meat, poultry, or fish from coming in contact with other foods—cooked or raw.

Use separate cutting boards, plates, trays, and utensils for cooked and uncooked meat, poultry, and fish.

Marinate meat, poultry, and seafood in covered, nonmetallic containers—in the refrigerator! Many marinades have acid-containing ingredients—wine, vinegar, and citrus juice—which react with metals. These metals can then leach into the food.

If marinades have been in contact with raw meat, poultry, or seafood, boil them for at least one minute. Then they're safe to use as a sauce for cooked food. Better yet, make a double batch of marinade. Use half to marinate, then discard it after marinating. Reserve the other half to use as a sauce at serving time.

Avoid mixing dark-colored sauces into ground meat or poultry. Dark-colored sauces, such as teriyaki sauce, soy sauce, and Worcestershire sauce, make it hard to judge the doneness of ground meat. Instead brush the sauces on cooked patties when they're almost through cooking. Ground meat is cooked through when the juices run clear.

Avoid eating raw seafood, meat, poultry, and eggs, or foods containing these foods. Foods with raw eggs include some recipes for homemade mayonnaise, homemade eggnog, homemade ice cream, Hollandaise sauce, and Caesar salad dressing. For people with a compromised immune system, even lightly-cooked egg dishes, such as soft custards and French toast, can be risky.

If you stuff the poultry, do so just before roasting, and stuff loosely. Be sure that the temperature of the meat reaches 180° F and the center of the stuffing reaches 165° F before removing from the oven. As an option, cook stuffing separately from chicken or turkey. Never cook stuffed poultry in a microwave oven. Always refrigerate leftover poultry and stuffing separately.

If you infuse oil with herbs or garlic, use it right away. Avoid storing it to use later. Cases of botulism have been linked with some home-prepared herb and garlic oils. Commercially-prepared herb- and garlic-oils are required to contain protective additives to prevent possible foodborne illness. As an added precaution, always store commercial herb and garlic oil products in the refrigerator.

Direct your coughs and sneezes away from food. Coughs and sneezes spread germs. Cover your mouth and nose with a tissue when you sneeze or cough. Then wash your hands.

Is Raw Seafood Safe to Eat?

With sushi bars and seviche (a popular Mexican and Caribbean appetizer), many people have come to enjoy raw and uncooked marinated seafood. With careful control, they can be safe. A few precautions reduce the risk of eating raw seafood:

➢ Shellfish, especially mollusks (oysters, clams, mussels, and scallops), may carry a bacterium called *vibrio vulnificus*, which multiplies even during refrigeration. While this bacterium is destroyed in the intestinal tract or by the immune system of most healthy people, this form of food poisoning can be very serious, and even fatal for high risk individuals. Other viruses in uncooked or partly cooked mollusks can also cause severe diarrhea.

➢ High-risk individuals—those with HIV, impaired immune systems, chronic alcohol problems, liver and gastrointestinal disorders, kidney disease, inflammatory bowel disease, cancer, diabetes, and steroid dependency—should avoid eating any raw or partly-cooked fish.

➢ If you prepare raw fish at home, start with high-quality seafood—very, very fresh. Buy from a reputable dealer. For mollusks (clam, mussel, oyster), you can ask to see the certified shipper's tag. If you harvest your own, make sure the waters are certified for safety. Follow the rules for safe food handling described in this chapter. Even at that, eating raw fish at home isn't advised. You're wiser to cook fish to an internal temperature of 145° F to destroy parasites.

➢ If fish is sushi grade or high quality, sushi, sashimi, seviche, and oyster bars are generally safe. Reputable restaurants have highly-trained chefs who not only know how to buy fish that meets safety and sanitation standards, but also know how to handle fish safely. *Refer to page 383 for tips on Japanese cuisine.*

Cook It Safe

Get the right tools for the job: a meat or "quick-read" thermometer to see when foods are thoroughly cooked; an oven thermometer to check your oven heat; and a timer to accurately time the cooking.

Check the internal temperature of food, especially roasts, thick steaks (over 2-inches thick), large cuts of meat, whole chicken or turkey, and large casseroles. Put the thermometer or oven temperature probe into the center of the thickest part of the food, but not near the bone or fat. *Refer to the chart, "Meat, Fish, and Poultry: Target Temperatures" on this page for recommended internal temperatures, and "Using a Meat Thermometer" on page 319 for guidelines on inserting and reading a meat thermometer.*

Meat, Fish, and Poultry: Target Temperatures

For food safety—and the best flavor—cook meat and poultry to the right internal temperature. To check, use a meat or "instant-read" thermometer.

MEAT, FISH, OR POULTRY	INTERNAL, COOKED TEMPERATURE (° F)
FRESH BEEF, VEAL, LAMB	
Ground products, such as hamburger (prepared as patties, meatloaf, meatballs, etc.)	160, or cook until no longer pink and juices run clear
Non-ground products, such as roasts and steaks	
Medium rare	145
Medium	160
Well done	170
FRESH PORK	
All cuts including ground products	
Medium	160
Well done	170
HAM	
Fresh, raw	160
Fully cooked, to reheat	140
FISH	145
POULTRY	
Ground chicken, turkey	165
Whole chicken, turkey	180
Stuffing (cooked alone or in bird)	165
Poultry breasts, roasts, thighs, wings	170, or cook until juices run clear
Duck, goose	180

Source: A Quick Consumer Guide to Safe Food Handling, Home and Garden Bulletin No. 248, August 1995.

Cook ground meat and poultry thoroughly—until no longer pink inside, juices run clear, and the internal temperature reaches 160° F. Thorough cooking is especially important with ground meat; bacteria on the outside get mixed inside as meat and poultry are ground and mixed.

Instead of "rare," cook beef until "medium rare" (to an internal temperature of 145° F) for safety. Steaks, roasts, and other cuts of beef cooked to a "rare" doneness increase your risk for foodborne illness.

When in doubt, cook ham. If the label says "cooked ham," it's okay to eat without cooking or heating. If not, don't take chances. Cook it before eating it. Words such as "smoked," "aged," or "dried" are no guarantee of safety without cooking.

Follow the "10-minute" rule for cooking finfish—whole fish, steaks, and fillets. For every inch of thickness, cook fish for 10 minutes at a temperature of 425° to 450° F. The internal temperature should reach 145° F. If one end is thinner than another, fold it underneath so the thickness is uniform. This rule applies to broiling, grilling, steaming, baking, and poaching. Cooking times for frying and microwaving are generally faster ways to cook. If fish is cooked from a frozen state, double the cooking time. Cooked fish is opaque and flaky.

Know that shellfish cook faster than finfish. Scallops and shrimp take 3 to 5 minutes, depending on size. Scallops turn white and firm; shrimp turn pink. Live clams, mussels, and oysters should cook for 3 to 5 more minutes after the shells open. When they're shucked, bake them for about 10 minutes, or boil them for 3 minutes. Boiling lobster takes 5 to 6 minutes per pound after the water comes back to a boil; when fully cooked, they'll turn bright red.

Know the visual signs of doneness: eggs that aren't runny; fish that is opaque and flakes easily; juices from meat and poultry that aren't pink; and poultry joints that move easily.

If you've been basting, or brushing sauces on food, as you cook, switch to a clean brush and fresh sauce for cooked foods. That way, you won't transfer bacteria from raw to cooked foods. Discard the marinade used for raw meat, poultry, or fish, or boil it for at least one minute before using on cooked food.

Avoid very low oven temperatures (below 325° F) for roasting meat, or long or overnight cooking for meat. With oven cooking, these low temperatures encourage bacterial growth before the meat is cooked.

If using a slow cooker, know how to use it safely. Even though the food is cooked at a lower temperature, a slow cooker is safe because the moist heat used to cook foods in a crockpot is more lethal to bacteria than dry heat, such as oven cooking. Set the cooker on high until the food begins to bubble, then turn to a simmer or "low" setting to continue cooking. Use the lid, and check the internal temperature, which should be at least 160° F. Always choose a recipe that contains a liquid. When including meat, use small pieces of thawed meat. Avoid filling the cooker to more than two-thirds of its capacity.

Cook food through at one time. Don't cook it partially, then finish later. Partially-cooked food may not get hot enough inside to destroy bacteria, which may encourage bacteria to grow.

Heat leftovers to 165° F or until steaming hot. Reheat sauces and gravies to a rolling boil for at least one minute.

Play It Microwave Safe

Today, a microwave oven is almost as common as a television set in our homes, workplaces, schools, and even recreational vehicles! For most people, the main reason is cooking speed. However, microwaving also has nutrition benefits. Faster cooking helps retain nutrients and allows food to be cooked without added fat.

General cooking guidelines apply to microwave cooking. Since foods cook differently in a microwave oven, follow these special precautions:

Use only microwave-safe containers. To see if your glass bowls, dishes, or cups are safe, place each one empty in the microwave oven with a separate cup of tap water. Microwave it on high for one minute. If the empty container stays cool, it's microwave-safe; slightly warm, use it for reheating only. Any bowls, dishes, or cups that get hot shouldn't be used in a microwave oven. Unless approved for microwave use, avoid using these containers: margarine or butter tubs, other plastic tubs, foam trays, plastic bags, brown paper bags, paper towels, paper plates, and paper napkins. Chemicals from these products may transfer to food.

Cut food so the pieces are the same size. This helps ensure even cooking.

Keep food well covered while cooking. Use waxed paper, microwave-safe plastic wrap, or a lid that fits. This keeps food from drying out and helps ensure even cooking. For safety, allow a little space for some steam to escape.

Rotate food for even cooking. Halfway through cooking, do one of the following: turn the dish; stir or reposition the food on the plate or bowl; turn large foods over; or reposition the dish on the turntable.

Allow for standing time. Food keeps cooking after the microwave oven turns off, spreading the heat more evenly. In fact, the internal temperature can go up several degrees as food stands.

Check for doneness—after the standing time. Then, as with food cooked in the oven, check the internal temperature and the visual signs of doneness. Check in several places, but not near the bone.

Be aware of differences in the power, or wattage, of microwave ovens. The cooking times may differ. Use a thermometer to check for doneness.

Follow microwave instructions on food packaging. By law, package directions are approved by the Food and Drug Administration.

Avoid using your microwave oven for canning. The pressure that builds up inside the jar may cause it to explode.

For more on microwave safety, refer to "Play It Safe: Warming Baby's Bottle and Food" on page 411 and "Microwave Safety for Kids" on page 444.

Safe Grilling Tips

Before you put another burger on the grill, you're smart to take some precautions.

Adjust the grill so the food cooks evenly—inside and outside. When meat or poultry are too close to the heat, the outside surfaces cook quickly and may appear to be done, but the inside may not be cooked well enough to destroy bacteria.

Transfer food to a clean plate once it's cooked—with a clean utensil! Don't use your fingers. To avoid cross contamination, carry cooked meat to the table on a clean dish—not the same dish you used to bring raw meat to the grill.

Where to Place a Meat Thermometer?

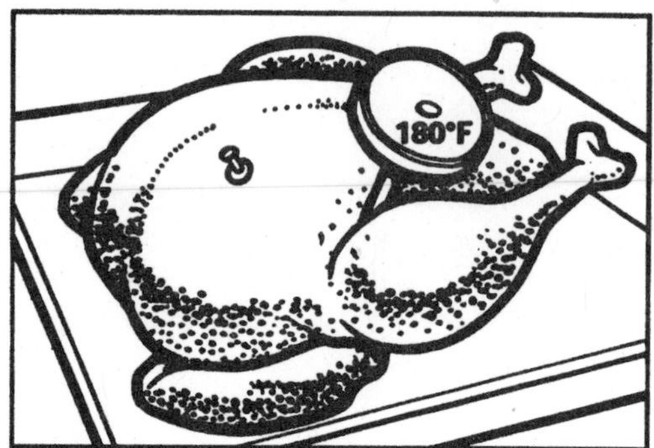

Poultry

Insert the meat thermometer into the inner thigh area near the breast of the chicken or turkey but not touching bone.

If stuffed, stuffing temperature must reach 165° F. Do this near *and* at the end of the stand time.

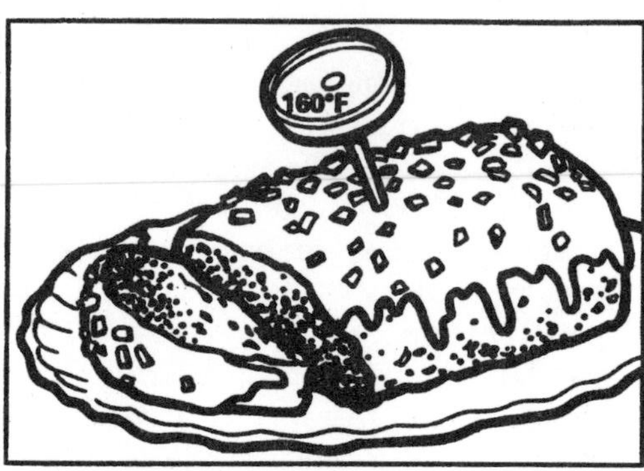

Ground Meat & Poultry

The thermometer should also be placed in the thickest area of ground meat or poultry dishes like meatloaf. The thermometer may be inserted sideways in thin items such as patties.

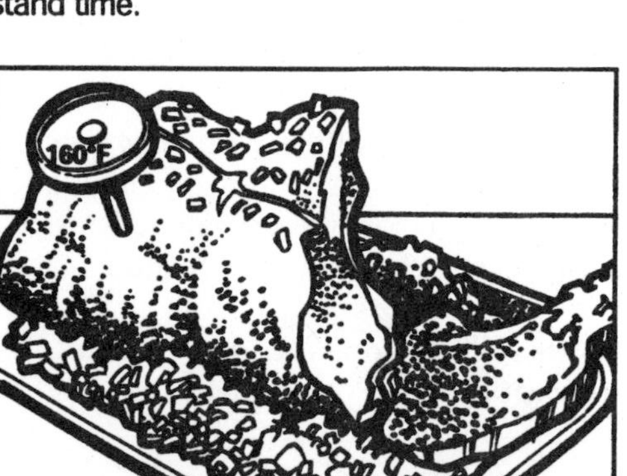

Beef, Pork, Lamb, Veal, Ham—Roasts, Steaks or Chops

The thermometer should be inserted into the center of the thickest part, away from bone, fat and gristle.

Casseroles and Egg dishes

The thermometer should be inserted into the thickest portion.

Clean the grill between each use. Removing the charred food debris from the grill reduces exposure to bacteria and possible cancer-causing substances.

If you're grilling at a picnic site, do all the cooking there—from start to finish. Partial cooking at home encourages bacteria to grow.

Grill meat, poultry, and fish until it's cooked through, but not charred. The charring, for example on a well-done steak, is a possible cancer-causing compound, called heterocyclic aromatic amines, or HAAs. While the research is inconclusive, you're smart to avoid the "black stuff"! Instead cook meat to medium, rather than well done. Grill poultry and fish until the internal temperature reaches its target, but the surface isn't blackened. Scrape off any charred areas before you eat.

Control hot coals to avoid flame flare-ups. The smoke caused by fat dripping on hot coals contains another possible cancer-causing compound called polyaromatic hydrocarbons. Again, the research isn't conclusive. This may not pose a cancer risk, but you're still wise to trim visible fat from meat before cooking, catch additional fat in a drip pan, drain any high-fat marinades, and have a spray bottle with water for flare-ups.

Using a Meat Thermometer

Using a meat thermometer takes the guesswork out of cooking. Besides helping to prevent foodborne illness, a meat thermometer helps to prevent over-cooking and can be used to hold foods at a safe temperature. Use a meat thermometer every time you prepare poultry, roasts, ham, casseroles, meat loaves, and egg dishes.

Types of Meat Thermometers

➢ ***Regular, oven proof:*** inserted into food at the beginning of cooking and remains there throughout cooking. Easy to read; placement is important.

➢ ***Instant-read and digital:*** not intended to stay in food while cooking; gives a quick reading when the stem is inserted into food about 2 inches.

➢ ***Pop-up:*** often found already inserted into poultry; also may be purchased for other types of meat. Verify that meat is done by checking the temperature with a conventional thermometer as well.

➢ ***Microwave-safe:*** designed for use in microwave ovens only.

Note: When buying a meat thermometer, read the package label carefully to be sure you are buying the type designed for use with meat, and not other food items such as candy. Look for a thermometer made from stainless steel, with an easy-to-read dial and shatterproof clear lens.

"Egg-Stra" Cooking Tips for Food Safety

If they're not handled properly, eggs and egg-rich foods are a perfect medium for salmonella to grow. To enjoy all the benefits that eggs provide, take these precautions:

How Do You Know When Cooked Eggs Are Done?

Cooking eggs? Look for these signs of doneness to ensure than any salmonella are destroyed.

Cooking Method	Signs of Doneness
Scrambled, omelet, frittata	No visible liquid egg remains
Poached, fried over easy, sunny-side up	White completely set; yolk starting to thicken but not hard (Hint: For sunny-side up eggs, cover with lid to ensure adequate cooking.)
Soft-cooked	White should be completely set; yolk is starting to thicken but not hard (Bring to a boil; turn off heat. Let eggs stand in water for 4-5 minutes.)
Hard-cooked	White and yolk are completely set. (Bring to a boil; turn off heat. Let eggs stand in water for 15 minutes.)
Stirred custard, including ice cream and eggnog	Mixture coats the spoon; temperature reaches 160° F
Baked custard, including quiche	Knife placed off center comes out clean (Note: cheese in a properly-cooked quiche will leave particles on the knife, too.)

Cook eggs until they're done. *Refer to "How Do You Know When Cooked Eggs Are Done?" below for visual signs of doneness.*

Prepare soft meringues and mousse made with slightly-cooked eggs to destroy any salmonella. To prepare, put the egg whites in a double boiler or heavy pan. Add 2 tablespoons of sugar for each egg white. Cook over low heat, beating as you cook until soft peaks appear. Then proceed with the recipe as directed.

Avoid foods with raw eggs, such as Caesar salad or homemade ice cream, mayonnaise, or eggnog— unless they're made with an unopened carton of pasteurized eggs. However, once pasteurized eggs are open, they must be treated like any other eggs because they can be contaminated by bacteria. How about homemade cookie dough? If it contains raw eggs, there can be risk. Commercially prepared dressing, mayonnaise, cookie dough, and cookie dough ice cream, all use pasteurized eggs.

As another option, use cooked yolks in recipes that call for raw eggs. Cook the yolks in a double boiler or heavy skillet with liquid from the recipe: 2 tablespoons liquid for each yolk. Beat it while it cooks until the yolk coats a spoon, or bubbles form around the edges, or the temperature reaches 160° F.

Keep eggs and egg-rich foods at 40° to 140° F for no longer than two hours, including serving time. Otherwise, keep them refrigerated. Use leftovers made with eggs within a week.

Store Easter eggs in the fridge. Hard-cooked eggs don't keep as well as raw shell eggs; use them within a week. Like other high-protein foods, hard-cooked eggs shouldn't sit out at temperatures of 40° F or higher for longer than two hours.

Plate It Safe

Use clean dishes and utensils for serving—use nothing that touched raw meat, fish, or poultry, unless it was cleaned in hot, soapy water first.

Avoid keeping perishable foods on a serving table for longer than two hours. That includes cooked meat, poultry, fish, eggs, and dishes made with these ingredients.

For buffet-type service, keep cold foods cold and hot foods hot. Serve cold foods on ice, at a temperature of 40° F or below. Use heated servers, such as a chafing dish, to keep hot foods hot. After two hours, even these foods should be discarded.

When replenishing serving dishes, don't mix fresh food with food that's been sitting out already.

Carry It Safe

Picnic Foods...

It's summertime. The season's "ripe" for picnics—and foodborne illness. Keep food fit to eat in your fresh-air kitchen with the three basic food-safe rules: keep food clean, keep hot food hot, and keep cold food cold.

For perishables, use clean, insulated coolers chilled with ice or chemical cold packs. As a rule of thumb, pack your cooler with 75 percent food and 25 percent ice or frozen cold packs. Freeze cold packs at least 24 hours ahead so they stay cold as long as possible. Chill the cooler ahead, too. Secure the lid. Then keep the cooler closed—no peeking!

Store nonperishable foods in a clean picnic or laundry basket—with the heaviest foods on the bottom.

Seal all foods tightly in bags, jars, or plastic containers. That keeps out moisture and bugs.

Pack foods that are cold or frozen already. Don't assume your cooler can cool foods adequately if they're packed at room temperature. Pack perishable foods between ice or cold packs; they'll stay cold longer.

Pack uncooked meat, poultry, or fish carefully—in well-sealed containers—for grilling at the picnic spot. Make sure the juices don't leak.

Keep your cooler in a cool place—not in the hot trunk or in the sun. Instead, place it under a tree or picnic table.

Return perishable foods to the cooler immediately when you're done serving. And only serve the amount of food you'll eat right away. Keep the rest in the cooler until it's needed.

For picnics nearby that will be eaten right away, consider a hot dish—covered and wrapped well. Wrap the dish in several layers of newspaper, then in an insulated container. Baked beans are a popular choice.

Bring premoistened towelettes to wash up after handling meat, poultry, or chicken—or any food, for that matter. Or bring soap and a bottle filled with clean water to wash your hands and cooking surfaces.

Be prepared to clean the grill at the picnic site—unless you bring your own grill. Pack a brush, soap, and perhaps water.

After the picnic, toss perishable leftovers. Or repack them in a cold cooler.

Carried Meals and Snacks...

Anytime a bag lunch with perishable food is left at room temperature for two hours or more, there's risk for foodborne illness. That's especially true when it's stuffed in a school locker with a dirty gym bag or left on a warm window sill at the office!

Use a clean insulated bag or lunch box. Tuck in a small refreezable ice pack to keep food cold. Or freeze a juice box or small plastic container of water to keep the lunch box and food cold.

Refrigerate an insulated vacuum bottle ahead. Then fill it with milk or juice to carry with you. If your meal goes to work, keep a carton of juice or milk in the fridge at work.

Assemble your meal the night before, and chill it well. You'll "buy" a little more time in the morning!

Keep carried, perishable food in a clean, cool place—away from sunlit window sills, radiators, or warm vehicles. If a refrigerator is available, use it.

Pack nonperishable foods: canned soup or stew to heat up in the microwave at work, dried raisins or

HOW TO AVOID CHOKING

You can save a life by knowing the Heimlich Maneuver, or abdominal thrusts. Respond quickly to the signs of choking: squealed breathing sounds, violent coughing, a victim who can't talk or who clutches his or her throat, bluish color in the face and throat, or perhaps, unconsciousness.

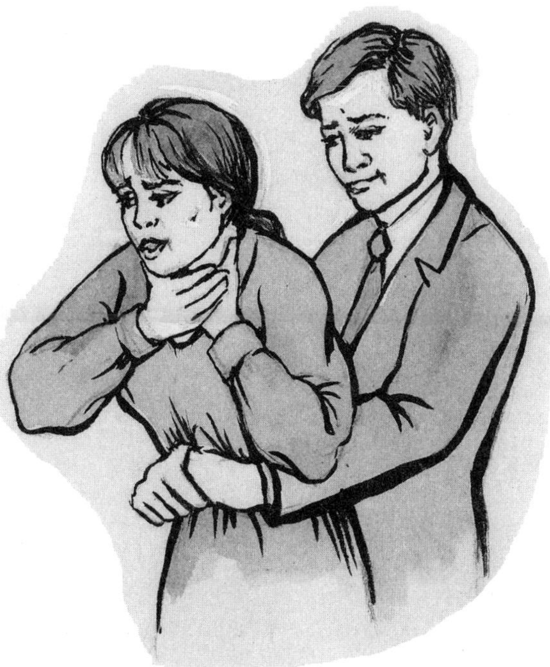

What if you're the choking victim—and you're alone? Immediately lean forward over the back of a chair. Press your abdomen against the chair. Air released from your lungs should force food loose.

For infant and child safety, refer to "For Babies, Toddlers, and Preschoolers: How to Avoid Choking" on page 414.

apple slices, crackers and peanut butter, boxed juice or milk, beef jerky, to name a few. For canned foods, remember to tuck in a can opener! Fresh fruit doesn't require refrigeration either.

Launder your lunch bag or wash lunch box with soapy water after every use.

Quick Tips for Injury Prevention

Kitchen safety is more than preventing foodborne illness. Keep your kitchen safe from hazards that cause injury:

Wipe up spills immediately. Someone who enters the kitchen may not notice water or grease on the floor before he or she slips.

Avoid teetering on a chair or bar stool to reach a high cabinet. Invest in a stable stool.

have you ever wondered

...if liquid smoke is safe to eat? Bottled liquid smoke is sold alongside herbs and sauces in many supermarkets. It gives a smoky flavor without grilling. The flavoring is created by burning wood, then trapping the smoke; most potential carcinogens are removed. About 60 percent of processed meats sold in supermarkets are "smoked" with liquid smoke.

...if mail-order foods are safe to eat? Yes, if handled properly. Before you order, ask how and when perishable foods will be sent, and if a cold source, such as dry ice or cold packs, will be shipped with food. Some mail-order foods, such as dry-cured ham and hard salami, don't require refrigeration. Other meat, poultry, fish, and perishable foods should arrive just as cold as they would be in your refrigerator. If not, contact the mail-order company for a replacement or refund. ✦

Keep cabinets, drawers, and doors closed so you don't bump into them. And put safety catches on drawers so they won't fall out when they're opened too far.

Keep pot holders handy—and use them. Be careful if they get wet; water conducts heat.

Turn the handles on pots and pans inward and away from the edge of the stove where they may be knocked...or where children can grab them.

Avoid overfilling pots and pans. Too much hot soup, stew, or pasta can quickly burn if it spills on you.

Be careful with the hot water tap—especially if you have small children around.

Allow enough time for the pressure to release if you use a pressure cooker.

Avoid dropping water into hot oil. The splatters may burn you. Remember, water and oil don't mix!

Douse grease fires with baking soda—not water! Or "put a lid on it" to control the flame.

Avoid electrical fires. Keep electrical cords away from the burners on your stove.

Use a safety latch on cabinets with household chemicals, alcoholic beverages, matches, plastic bags, and sharp utensils (knives, toothpicks) so they're out of reach of children.

Handle knives for safety. Store them carefully, perhaps in a knife holder. Avoid leaving them in the dishpan where you can't see them. Use sharp knives; dull knives are harder to use and promote injury. Always cut away from you, using a cutting board.

Watch out for broken glass. Remove it immediately. If glass breaks in the sink, empty the water so you find all the pieces before you cut yourself.

Watch your fingers near your garbage disposal! And teach children how to use it safely.

The "Eco Kitchen"

Along with food safety, you and your family are wise to follow practices for kitchen ecology—conserving energy and water—and minimizing and properly disposing of waste.

Water in the "Eco Kitchen"...

➢ Choose the proper-size pots and pans for cooking. Utensils that are too big use more cooking water.

➢ Cook in a microwave oven or a pressure cooker to conserve water—and time.

➢ Cut down on evaporation of liquid—and nutrient loss—by covering pots with tight-fitting lids during cooking.

➢ Prepare vegetables in just a small amount of water. This saves both water and nutrients!

➢ To heat water for cooking or beverages, use a tea kettle or covered pot. You'll lose less water through evaporation.

➢ Time foods that need to boil or simmer so you don't lose too much water through evaporation.

➢ Washing dishes? Turn the faucet on and off as you rinse, rather than allowing the water to run continually.

➢ Wait until your dishwasher is full before running a full cycle.

➢ Repair your faucet if it leaks.

Energy Savers...

➢ If you preheat your oven, do so right before you use it.

➢ To make your freezer more energy efficient, defrost it regularly.

➢ Turn off your kitchen lights when you leave the kitchen.

➢ Avoid the habit of leaving the coffee pot on all day. Turn if off when it's no longer needed.

Resource Conservation...

➢ Resist the urge to buy food you don't need. To avoid excessive food waste, buy only the amount of food your family will eat.

➢ When shopping, look for products in packaging that can be recycled, such as aluminum cans, steel cans, glass containers, recycled plastic, and paperboard cartons that are gray on the inside. On plastic containers, look for the recycling symbol with a number in the center. Lower numbers are recycled more easily.

➢ Recycle. Keep a recycling bin for food containers. Dispose of recyclables according to the regulations and services of your municipality.

➢ Reuse glass or plastic food packages. Clean them well with hot, soapy water if they're used for food storage.

➢ If you grow your own vegetables, make a compost heap. Use it for some kitchen waste, as well as garden waste: for example, corn husks and melon rinds.

➢ Keep your refrigerator in check. Use perishable foods before they spoil and need to be discarded.

your nutrition check-up

Kitchen Safety

How's your food safety savvy? Are you clean and careful enough to keep foodborne illness out of your kitchen? Take this "kitchen safety check-up" to find out.

Do You...	**Always**	**Usually**	**Sometimes**	**Never**
Wash your hands with warm, soapy water before handling food?	___	___	___	___
Change your dish towels and dish cloths every few days?	___	___	___	___
Clean up splatters in your microwave oven immediately?	___	___	___	___
Sanitize cutting boards after each use with a chlorine-bleach solution?	___	___	___	___
Clean your refrigerator each week, discarding foods that are too old?	___	___	___	___
Put dates on frozen foods?	___	___	___	___
Thaw foods in the refrigerator, not on the counter?	___	___	___	___
Rotate foods in your freezer and cupboards, with the oldest foods in front?	___	___	___	___
Check foods in cans and jars for bulging or leaking before opening?	___	___	___	___
Marinate meat, poultry, and seafood in the refrigerator?	___	___	___	___
Grill food so it cooks evenly—inside and outside?	___	___	___	___
Use a clean plate and fork to take cooked food from the grill to the table?	___	___	___	___
Clean your picnic cooler before you use it?	___	___	___	___
Use leftovers within three or four days?	___	___	___	___
Remove stuffing from chicken and turkey before refrigerating leftovers?	___	___	___	___

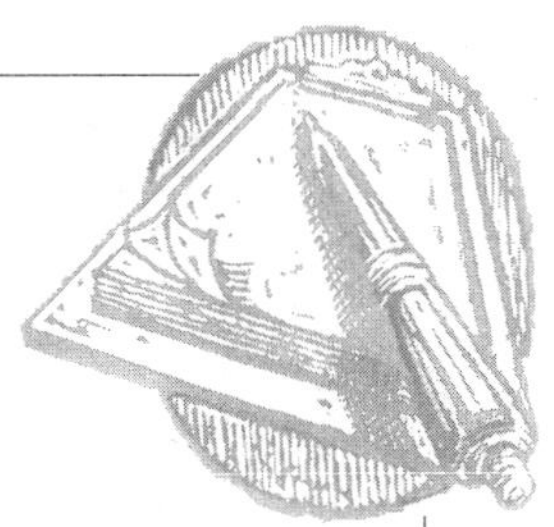

your nutrition check-up (continued)

Avoid the urge to use the stirring spoon for a quick taste?	___	___	___	___
Use a clean knife and cutting board for vegetables after cutting meat or poultry?	___	___	___	___
Cook meat and poultry to a safe internal temperature?	___	___	___	___
Use pasteurized eggs in recipes calling for eggs that won't be cooked?	___	___	___	___
Put leftovers in the refrigerator within two hours of cooking?	___	___	___	___
Cook hamburger patties until they're no longer pink inside?	___	___	___	___
Heat leftovers until they're steaming hot?	___	___	___	___
Clean the outdoor grill after every use?	___	___	___	___
Remove perishable foods from a buffet after two hours?	___	___	___	___
Store meat, poultry, and fish in containers that won't leak?	___	___	___	___
Subtotal	___	___	___	___

Now Score Yourself

"Always"	4 points
"Usually"	3 points
"Sometimes"	2 points
"Never"	1 point

Your Total Score ______

When it comes to food safety, you need a perfect score—100 points! Anything less and you're putting yourself—and anyone who eats with you—at risk for foodborne illness. It's safe to assume that the higher your score, the lower the risk.

For any item that scored "3" or less, make a conscious effort to make a change to "always"!

real life nutrition

What do you eat when the power's out?

The Pauley family had enjoyed a wonderful weekend camping trip. Now it was 6 p.m. on a summer evening. All were pleased to be home—including Lady, their springer spaniel.

Weary and hungry from the outdoor recreation, they had little energy for what they faced. An electrical storm had downed a tree and knocked out the power to their home for the past two hours! Neither the refrigerator, nor the freezer, nor the air conditioner were running. A quick call to the electric company confirmed that they wouldn't have power for at least four more hours—and maybe not until morning.

With two hungry kids, Sarah checked the camping cooler. "Hmmm…some leftover chicken breasts, grilled over last night's campfire," she sighed, as she felt the lukewarm chill packs.

With an impish smile, little Jason had the perfect supper solution, "Mom, how 'bout eating up all the ice cream? Then we won't need to worry about the freezer!" Lauren was ready to check out the refrigerator. And John, their dad, just opened the cupboard, looking from can to box to can to box. "There's got to be something to eat before we confront this problem," he groaned. What should they do?

Advice for food safety in an emergency:

➢ Food in the freezer would stay cold enough until the power goes on—if no one opened the freezer door. That would disappoint Jason, who'd love ice cream.

➢ Unfortunately, the leftover chicken wasn't an option. Since the chill packs had lost their "chill," the chicken hadn't been kept at a safe temperature. Sarah needed to toss it out safely so that even Lady couldn't eat it.

➢ Someone should head to the convenience store for ice to put in the refrigerator. And Lauren—in fact, no one—should open the refrigerator door unnecessarily, even to find something to eat.

➢ Although Jason, Lauren, John, Sarah, and Lady were "starved," they wouldn't go hungry. Canned fruit, peanut butter, crackers, and canned tomato juice may not be the most exciting meal. But, as Sarah had planned, they sure came in handy in an emergency! And there was plenty of dry dog food for Lady.

CHAPTER FOURTEEN

KITCHEN NUTRITION

Kitchen nutrition—the concept isn't new. Almost 150 years ago, *The Book of Household Management* described the kitchen as "the great laboratory of the household...much of the 'weal and woe' as far as regards bodily health, depends on the nature of the preparations concocted within its walls."

Now, as consumers prepare for the next century, no place in today's home shows technological progress more than the kitchen. Equipment, as well as foods themselves, food preparation methods, recipes, even lifestyles have changed dramatically. Yet we still identify the kitchen as the place where foodstuffs are transformed into nourishment for the body.

"Resetting" Your Table...For Taste and Health

What are your favorite foods? And why do you like them so much? Taste is likely a major reason!

Taste actually is a bigger nutrition issue than many of us realize. According to consumer research, taste tops nutrition as the number one reason why consumers buy one food over another. There's a lot wrapped up in why you prefer certain foods, including a multitude of social, emotional, and physical reasons. In any case, the foods you enjoy are likely the ones you eat most. And the more often you eat them, the more important their nutritional impact on your overall health. *For more on the impact of flavor in foods, refer to "On the Tip of Your Tongue...The Flavor Connection" on page 211.*

For most Americans, enjoyment, along with nutrition, is an important reason for eating. So if you're nutrition savvy, you'll make the appeal of food—its appearance and flavor—a major priority in your kitchen. As an easy rule of thumb, remember this: when it comes to nutrition, think about taste...and when it comes to taste, think about nutrition!

Variety: A Meal With Appeal

Like a well-decorated room or a beautifully-landscaped garden, an appealing meal follows basic principles of design. Different foods add a variety of color, flavor, texture, shape, and temperature to meals or snacks. At the same time, a variety of foods supplies different nutrients to your eating style. After all, variety is one of the main messages of the Food Guide Pyramid! *For more about the Food Guide Pyramid, refer to page 243.*

Vary the color. Contrast the visual differences: meatloaf, mashed potatoes with gravy, corn, and applesauce...compared with meatloaf, baked potato with chopped chives, asparagus, and sliced tomatoes. Which one has more interest? The meal with an artist's palette of color has far more appeal!

Add color to your meals and snacks with an array of fruits and vegetables. What foods can you add to this rainbow of colors? Green (broccoli, spinach, snow peas, salad greens, brussels sprouts, grapes, kiwi, honeydew melon), orange (carrots, acorn squash, sweet potatoes, apricots, cantaloupe, papaya), and red (beets, red cabbage, plums, berries). As a nutrition reminder, most dark green and deep yellow fruits and vegetables are good sources of vitamin A. *For more about vitamin A, refer to page 81.*

Vary the flavor. From a physiological standpoint, flavor blends these sensations: taste and smell, as well as touch. Within a meal, offer foods with different flavors: sour, sweet, bitter, and salty. All of these flavors come naturally in food, including sweet and salty tastes. Instead of serving orange-glazed chicken with candied sweet potatoes and fruit compote, complement chicken with wild rice pilaf and a fresh garden salad.

Vary the texture. Crunchy foods offer a nice contrast when served with soft foods, for example, chopped nuts in brown rice, or raw veggies with herbed cottage cheese dip. Think about the two meatloaf dinners described earlier. Variety of texture is as important as variety of color!

Vary the shape. Round meatballs, round peas, round new potatoes, and round grapes look somewhat boring if they're all plated together. Perhaps add variety to the plate with finger carrots instead of peas, pasta spirals instead of potatoes, or sliced apple wedges instead of grapes.

Vary the temperature. Meals don't require foods with different temperatures. For example, a cold summer supper or a picnic from the cooler can be refreshing. However, a warm whole-wheat roll offers a nice contrast to a chef's salad. And frozen yogurt makes a nice ending to a hot dinner.

FOR A TASTE LIFT...

Spark up sauces, soups, and salads with a splash of flavored, balsamic, or rice vinegar. *See "Herbed Vinegars" on page 350 for ways to make your own herb and fruit vinegars.* Balsamic vinegar gets its sweet, pungent flavor when grape juice is aged in special wooden barrels. Rice vinegar, often used in Asian dishes, comes from fermented rice.

Add a tangy taste with citrus juice or grated citrus peel: lemon, lime, or orange.

Pep it up with peppers! Use red, green, and yellow peppers of all varieties—sweet, hot, and dried. Or add a dash of hot pepper sauce.

Give a flavor burst with good-quality condiments, such as horseradish, flavored mustard, chutney, and salsa of all kinds! *See "Give It a Little Salsa" on page 330for unique salsa combos.*

Concentrate the flavors of meat, poultry, and fish stocks. Reduce the juices by heating them—don't boil! Then use them as a glaze. ✦

Food "Prep": The Nutrition-Flavor Connection

Nutrition and flavor go hand-in-hand. You don't need to sacrifice one for the other. Proper food storage and handling enhance the naturally-good flavor of food and keep nutrient loss to a minimum.

Start with high-quality ingredients. These don't need to be the most expensive foods in the store. But they do need to be handled properly all along the food chain—right to your kitchen.

Store foods properly until they're prepared. Cooking can't improve food. It only can enhance the flavors of already high-quality foods. *Chapter 13, "The Safe Kitchen," offers many tips for keeping food fresh and safe in your kitchen.*

Cook to retain nutrients, flavor, color, and texture. High temperatures and long cooking times can destroy heat-sensitive nutrients, such as B vitamins, vitamin C, and folate. Some minerals and water-soluble vitamins dissolve in cooking water; they're lost when cooking water is discarded. And light destroys riboflavin (vitamin B_2) and vitamin A. However, proper cooking techniques keep nutrient loss to a minimum and food quality at its peak. *For more about vitamins and minerals, refer to chapter 4, "Vitamins and Minerals: Enough, But Not Too Much."*

Every food deserves careful preparation. The following techniques apply especially to fruits and vegetables:

➢ **Clean vegetables and fruits well with a brush.** But don't peel away edible skins, for example on carrots and potatoes. You'll throw away valuable nutrients and fiber. Peels are also natural barriers that help protect nutrient loss. *For more about waxed vegetables, refer to page 231.*

➢ **Cook vegetables in a very small amount of water—or better yet, steam them.** Steaming retains most of the nutrients because vegetables never come in contact with cooking liquids. *Refer to "Well Equipped" on page 342 for a brief description of a vegetable steamer.*

➢ **For longer cooking times, cut vegetables into larger pieces so less surface area is exposed.** The more surface is exposed, the more nutrients are lost in cooking water.

➢ **Cover vegetables while you cook them.** This speeds cooking time and helps retain nutrients that might be lost through steam.

➢ **Cook many vegetables—such as asparagus, green beans, broccoli, and snow peas—only until they are tender-crisp.** Or eat them raw. The shorter the time that vegetables are cooked, the more nutrients are retained. Short cooking times help vegetables keep their bright color and flavor, too. The flavors of strong-flavored vegetables, such as brussels sprouts and turnips, can get even stronger when they're overcooked. For beets and red cabbage, add a little lemon juice or vinegar to the cooking water. This helps retain their bright-red color. Don't add baking soda! It increases the loss of thiamin, also known as vitamin B_1.

MORE TASTE LIFTERS

For grains that absorb fluid (rice, couscous, and barley), cook them in defatted chicken or beef broth. Risotto, an Italian rice specialty, typically is prepared by cooking arborio or white short-grain rice in broth, along with herbs and other ingredients.

Blend herbs, spices, sun-dried tomatoes, and shredded cheese into bread dough before baking it.

Experiment with herbs and spices. Add flavor with basil, chives, cilantro, rosemary, savory, garlic, ginger, caraway, and cumin.

Sharpen up the flavor with cheese. Even a little sharp cheddar, Romano, feta, Asiago, or blue cheese—sprinkled on vegetables, rice, or pasta—goes a long way in adding a distinctive flavor.

Add intense flavors with dried ingredients: sun-dried tomatoes, dried mushrooms, dried cranberries, dried apricots, prunes, and red pepper flakes. Plump up sun-dried tomatoes and dried mushrooms in broth or cooking wine. ✦

➢ ***Save cooking water from vegetables for soups, stews, and sauces.*** That's one way to "recycle" vitamins and minerals that otherwise would be tossed with the cooking water.

Microwaving is a healthful way to cook for two main reasons. First, foods retain more nutrients. Because microwaving is so fast, heat-sensitive nutrients aren't subjected to heat for long. Second, microwaving doesn't require added fat. There's a flavor advantage, too; unless overcooked, vegetables retain the color and tender-crisp qualities that make them appealing.

As an added note, rinsing grains, such as rice, before cooking doesn't make nutrition sense. That practice just washes nutrients down the drain.

"Salsa" is simply the Spanish word for "sauce." With today's cuisine, salsa has become a lot more sexy! By combining a variety of chopped vegetables, fruits, herbs, and even hot sauce, there's a salsa for every flavor mood.

Tomato Salsa: Combine chopped plum tomatoes, onion, and cilantro with a touch of cider vinegar and sugar. Add red pepper flakes for some zip. Chill. *Tip*: plum tomatoes, especially when they're in season, often have more flavor than salad tomatoes.

Pineapple Salsa: Combine chopped, fresh pineapple with chopped cilantro, fresh lime juice, and a touch of sugar and minced garlic. Chill.

Black Bean Salsa: Combine canned, drained black beans with chopped tomato, chopped onion, chopped cilantro, and a little jalapeño and red wine vinegar. ✦

Besides retaining nutrients, the way you prepare food adds to its overall taste appeal. *For quick flavor enhancers, refer to "For a Taste Lift..." and "More Taste Lifters" on page 328 and page 329.*

Beyond Parsley... Quick, Easy Garnishes

Garnishes do more than add eye appeal to food. They offer flavor, color, and texture contrasts and, if eaten, some nutritional value. Garnish food with edibles that complement the ingredients in the food. For example, a sprig of basil goes with many Italian dishes; a slice of lemon or lime complements many seafood dishes. Arrange the garnish artistically around, under, or on top of the food.

Parsley, which may be the most common garnish, dresses up a plate and serves as a natural breath freshener. While having less flavor than flat-leafed varieties, curly parsley adds texture to the plate, too, and both varieties have some vitamins A and C! *Refer to pages 81 and 89 for more about these vitamins.*

When it comes to garnishing, go beyond parsley and "paint your plate" with other foods, too:

On Salads... alfalfa or sunflower sprouts; capers; fennel slices; pomegranate seeds; red onion slices; red, green, and yellow pepper strips; toasted, chopped walnuts or pecans; shredded apple (tossed with lemon juice to prevent browning); watercress; mandarin orange sections; blueberries or raspberries; grated cheese; snow peas; shredded jicama; or marigold petals. *For edible flowers that may be used as garnishes, see "Please Don't Eat the Daffodils" on page 331.*

On Soups... alfalfa sprouts; an avocado slice dipped in lemon; shredded carrot; minced chives; sprigs of fresh herbs; minced fresh herbs; snow peas; a dollop of plain yogurt; orange peel strips; a thin slice of lemon; croutons; pesto sauce; edible flowers; shredded green, yellow, and red pepper; grated cheese; or plain, air-popped popcorn.

On Cooked Vegetables... toasted, sliced almonds; toasted pine nuts; grated Parmesan cheese; stir-fried onion slices; stir-fried mushroom slices; chopped lean ham; or chopped fresh herbs.

In Beverages... a mint sprig; scented geranium leaves; orange, lime, or lemon slices; fresh, whole berries; sliced starfruit (carambola) or kiwi; or a cinnamon stick.

With Meat, Poultry, or Fish... tomato slices; a small bunch of grapes; lemon and lime wedges; crab apple slices; a grilled peach or pear half; baby corn, squash, and carrots; or chutney or salsa in endive or a lettuce cup.

Recipes: Judge for Yourself!

According to culinary historians, an ancient Greek philosopher named Archestratus may have written the first known "cookbook" about 2,300 years ago! Interestingly, the herbed vinegar and oil seasonings he described are similar to our own today.

Each year, seemingly hundreds of new cookbooks appear on bookstore shelves. Many focus on healthful eating! Besides cookbooks, you find recipes of all kinds in magazines, newspapers, supermarket racks, package labels, and even computer software and online services.

To find a cookbook or food magazine that matches your needs, read the introduction or editorial page. Today's magazines and cookbooks are sold for every market niche: health conditions (such as diabetes and gluten intolerance), large-type print, vegetarians, children, and healthful eating, to name just a few. How can you sort through their recipes and endless combinations of ingredients?

Look at the main ingredients and the portions. You'll get an idea of how just one recipe portion fits within your personal Pyramid for the day. *See page* 243 *for more about the* Food Guide Pyramid.

Check the nutrient analysis of the recipe—if it's provided. Unlike food labels, nutrition information for recipes isn't standardized. Recipes may list some, but not all, the nutrients you find on a label. Usually the nutrient analysis in a recipe is provided for a single portion, but not always. And serving sizes aren't standardized. So a portion of lasagna in one recipe might be bigger or smaller than a serving of lasagna in another recipe. And neither one might equal one serving of frozen lasagna on the Nutrition Facts panel of a food label. *For more about nutrition information on food labels, refer to page* 270.

Computerized cookbooks offer the advantage of technology. Using many of them, you can plan meals for the whole day—with recipes from the cookbook—then total up the calories and nutrients. Changing the menu for nutrient and calorie needs is as easy as a few computer keystrokes!

Choose recipes to complement the whole meal—in fact, the whole day! For one meal, choose recipes

Edible flowers add a distinctive flavor and a unique splash of color to all kinds of foods. But you can't eat just any flower!

Some are poisonous; even edible flowers may be contaminated by chemicals if they weren't grown for eating. Don't eat flowers you buy from a florist or a greenhouse—or that you pick along the road. There's a long list of flowers that aren't edible: buttercup, lily of the valley, foxglove, periwinkle, oleander, delphinium—and daffodils, to name just a few!

For edible flowers, you need to either grow your own or buy them in the produce section of your supermarket. They should be labeled as "edible flowers." Only eat flowers if you're absolutely sure of their safety!

You might grow these edible flowers in the kitchen garden outside your back door: marigolds, nasturtiums (enjoy the leaves and the blossoms), borage, pansies, violets, and roses. Fertilize your flowers as you would a vegetable garden. Then, when harvesting, wash them well, and gently pat them dry. Bon appetit! ✦

for variety of color, flavor, texture, taste—and nutrition. Nutrients and calories in any one recipe aren't the real issue. If the recipe you choose has more fat or sodium, then choose others that have less. How you balance recipes and meals and snack choices for the whole day makes the difference.

Most important, choose recipes that appeal to you. No matter how nutritious a recipe sounds, the end result should be something you enjoy—or a food you're willing to experience, perhaps for the first time.

Recipe Makeovers

Ready to make changes in your eating style—perhaps to reduce calories, fat, or sodium or to boost calcium, fiber, or complex carbohydrates? You can transform almost any recipe, even Mom's specialties. A few subtle modifications may improve their nutrition content without much change in flavor.

There's nothing sacred about most recipes (except perhaps Mom's). Chefs and test-kitchen food experts change recipes all the time, for all kinds of reasons. Nutrition and health are big factors. Recipes get altered when new ingredients come on the market, when cooking equipment changes, when consumers want recipe shortcuts, when ingredients are in or out of season or become more or less costly, and when consumers shift their food preferences.

In your own "test kitchen," you can modify recipes in several ways, too: change the ingredients, modify the way the recipes are prepared, cut portion sizes, or do all three. Even one or two small recipe changes can net a significant difference in the nutrition content. *"Simply Nutritious, Simply Delicious" on page 335 gives specific ways to modify recipes for nutrition-conscious cooking.*

1. *Change the ingredients.* There's no single way to change a recipe. You might use less of one or more ingredients...or substitute one ingredient for another...or take an ingredient out entirely...or add something new. The end result of each change may be just a bit different. And that's OK.

➢ ***Start by analyzing the ingredient list.*** Decide what ingredients could be changed to achieve your goals: perhaps less fat, sugar, or sodium...or more calcium or fiber. If they have a functional purpose, some ingredients may not be changed easily. *Refer to page 54, "Why Foods Contain Fat," for the functions of fat and to page 132, "Sugars: More Than Sweeteners," for the functions of sugars in recipes.*

➢ ***Pick the ingredients you might reduce.*** For example, in many baked foods, you may be able to cut back on sugar by one-third and still enjoy good results. And with sautéed foods, or foods cooked in oil, you may be able to cut way back on cooking oil.

➢ ***As easy substitutions, try modified foods available in today's supermarkets.*** For example, use cholesterol-free egg products, reduced-fat cheese, or sodium-reduced chicken broth.

➢ ***Think about why ingredients are used in the recipe.*** Then make suitable substitutions. For example, in meat, poultry, fish, and vegetable dishes, salt enhances taste; herbs make flavorful substitutes. Regular ground beef is a key ingredient in hot chili, but lean ground turkey works just as well. And low-fat yogurt can take the place of sour cream in dips, potato toppers, and some creamy sauces.

➢ ***Decide which ingredients you can eliminate.*** Optional ingredients are easy to take out. But others may alter the appearance or flavor.

➢ ***To boost nutrients, decide what ingredients you might add.*** For example, fortifying casseroles with wheat germ or dry milk powder may go unnoticed. But adding shredded carrots to mashed potatoes or adding dried cranberries to muesli gives extra flavor and color, along with nutrients.

➢ ***Make changes gradually, perhaps one ingredient at a time.*** That's especially important when the ingredient has a functional purpose, such as eggs or sugar in baked foods.

➢ ***Consider taste, texture, and appearance.*** Adjust the flavor. For example, season with extra herbs if you cut back on salt. And if ingredient modifications don't work, make a different change!

An Easy Makeover: Tuna-Noodle Bake

Compare these two recipes for Tuna-Noodle Bake. How has the traditional recipe been changed to make it lower in fat, cholesterol, and sodium, yet higher in vitamins A and C and fiber?

Original Recipe

8 ounces egg noodles
2 tablespoons butter
2 cans (7 ounces each) tuna,
packed in oil
1 cup sour cream
3/4 cup whole milk
1 can (3 ounces) sliced mushrooms
1 teaspoon onion salt
1/2 teaspoon salt
1/4 teaspoon pepper
1/4 cup plain bread crumbs
1/3 cup grated Parmesan cheese
2 tablespoons butter, melted

Preheat oven to 350° F. Cook noodles in salted water as directed on package. When cooked, drain and rinse. Return noodles to pot; add butter or margarine. Stir in tuna, sour cream, milk, mushrooms, onion salt, salt, and pepper. Pour into a greased 2-quart casserole. Combine bread crumbs, Parmesan cheese, and melted butter. Sprinkle over casserole. Bake uncovered for 35 minutes. Makes 6 servings.

Nutrition information per serving

480 Calories (235 Calories from Fat)

	% Daily Value
Total Fat: 26 g	39%
Saturated Fat: 13 g	64%
Cholesterol: 102 mg	34%
Sodium: 1,100 mg	46%
Total Carbohydrate: 34g	11%
Dietary Fiber: 0 g	1%
Sugars: 3 g	
Protein: 28 g	
Vitamin A	21%
Vitamin C	1%
Calcium	19%
Iron	15%

Makeover Recipe

8 ounces whole-wheat noodles
2 cans (7 ounces each) tuna,*
packed in spring water, drained
1/2 can (10 1/2-ounce) cream of mushroom soup
1/2 cup puréed low-fat (1%) cottage cheese
3/4 cup skim milk
1/2 cup chopped celery
1/2 cup shredded carrot
1/4 cup chopped green pepper
1 teaspoon onion flakes
1/4 teaspoon each: paprika and tarragon
1/4 teaspoon pepper
1/3 cup grated Parmesan cheese

Preheat oven to 350° F. Cook noodles in unsalted water as directed on package. When cooked, drain. Return noodles to pot; add tuna, soup, cottage cheese, milk, celery, carrot, green pepper, onion flakes, paprika, tarragon, and pepper. Pour into a nonstick 2-quart casserole. Sprinkle with Parmesan cheese. Bake uncovered for 35 minutes. Makes 6 servings.

Nutrition information per serving

295 Calories (45 Calories from Fat)

	% Daily Value
Total Fat: 5 g	8%
Saturated Fat: 2 g	10%
Cholesterol: 25 mg	8%
Sodium: 640 mg	27%
Total Carbohydrate: 35 g	12%
Dietary Fiber: 2 g	8%
Sugars: 3 g	
Protein: 29 g	
Vitamin A	32%
Vitamin C	19%
Calcium*	17%
Iron	16%

* Use canned salmon in place of canned tuna to increase calcium to 32% Daily Value.

Daily values are used with food labeling. To help you compare these two recipes, they're used with this nutritional analysis. *To learn about* Daily Values on the Nutrition Facts of food labels, *refer to page* 272.

2. *Modify the way food is prepared.* Simple changes in cooking techniques may require little or no extra investment in time—just some know-how. For example, skim the fat that collects on stews, scrub rather than peel fiber-rich potato skins, skip the salt in cooking water, or oven-bake frozen french fries, rather than fry them.

3. *Reduce portion sizes.* If a recipe is high in fat or sugars, try serving less. For example, instead of 1/4 cup of cheese sauce on a baked potato, use just two tablespoons—and add some steamed, chopped vegetables for flavor.

Stocking the Kitchen...With Easy Nutrition

Stock your kitchen with the basics. This list may get you started. With a variety of foods on hand, nutritious meals and snacks are always quick and easy to prepare. Just buy fresh ingredients as you need them!

Many of these foods are sold with reduced amounts of fat or sodium—or they're fat- or sodium-free. Decide which form of the food to buy within the context of your overall meal and snack choices.

On the Kitchen Shelf...
whole- or mixed-grain breakfast cereal
rice (white and brown)
brown and wild rice pilaf mix
pasta (spaghetti, macaroni, others)
couscous
bulgur or barley
gingersnaps or vanilla wafers
whole-wheat or mixed grain bread and rolls
beans (dry and canned)
peanut butter
tuna or salmon (canned, packed in spring water)
fat-free refried beans
fruit (canned)
vegetables (canned)
fruit (dried)
vegetable soup
nonfat dry milk powder
evaporated skim milk
salsa or picante sauce
pasta sauce
chicken or beef broth
fruit spread
mustard
ketchup
vinegar
vegetable oil (olive and others)
salad dressing
vegetable oil cooking spray
herbs and spices
flour (whole-wheat, bleached, and white)
sugar
brown sugar
cornstarch
baking powder
baking soda

In Your Refrigerator...
baking potatoes
onions
apples
oranges
tortillas
milk
yogurt
Parmesan cheese
cheese
sliced smoked turkey breast, deli meat
eggs (or in your freezer, egg substitute)
bottled lemon juice
bottled garlic (minced)

In Your Freezer...
fruit juice concentrate (or fresh juice in your refrigerator, or juice boxes on the shelf)
frozen vegetables
frozen green pepper (chopped)
frozen onion (chopped)
frozen waffles or whole-wheat bagels
frozen fish fillets
lean ground beef
pork loin chops
chicken breast
frozen yogurt or fruit sorbet

Simply Nutritious, Simply Delicious

Modifying recipes without compromising taste doesn't require extra time—just quick and easy know-how in food preparation. *The tips on pages 336 through 348 offer many options for moderating fat, cholesterol, sugars, and sodium in your food preparation.* You'll also find ways to add fiber and calcium. Now cook for the health of it!

Fat and Cholesterol Trimmers

Hardly a day goes by without a new magazine or newspaper article giving tips for trimming fat, saturated fat, and cholesterol in foods prepared at home. And with good reason—many people consume much more fat than their bodies need.

We know that many health conditions—heart disease, cancer, and obesity, among others—are linked to high-fat diets. Instead, moderate amounts of fat, providing no more than 30 percent of total calories for the day, are recommended for healthy Americans. *For more information on fat and cholesterol, refer to chapter 3, "Fat Facts."*

Fats have many roles in traditional recipes. For one, they carry flavor and nutrients. In baked foods, fat also tenderizes, adds moisture, holds air in baked goods so they're light, and affects the shape, for example, in cookies. In sauces, fat keeps foods from curdling and forms part of an emulsion, so that water and fats don't separate. Fat in recipes also conducts heat, for example when sautéeing and frying; it seals in moisture when foods are basted; and it lubricates so food doesn't stick to the pan.

Although it doesn't make cooking sense or health sense to cut all the fat, preparing food with less fat does make sense. With simple changes, you can cook "leaner"—and still prepare great-tasting food. Food preparation can make a big difference in reducing the total fat, saturated fat, and cholesterol in your meals and snacks!

Braise: to simmer over low heat in liquid—water, broth, or even fruit juice—in a covered pot

Broil: to cook with direct heat, usually under a heating element in the oven

Grill: to cook with direct heat directly over hot coals

Panbroil: to cook uncovered in a preheated, nonstick skillet without added oil or water

Poach: to cook gently in liquid, just below boiling

Roast: to cook with dry heat in the oven

Sauté: to cook quickly in a small amount of fat, stirring so the food browns evenly

Simmer: to cook slowly in liquid, just below the boiling point

Steam: to cook with steam heat over (not in) boiling water, or wrapped in foil or leaves over boiling water or on a grill

Stew: to cook in liquid, such as water, juice, wine, broth, or stock, in a tightly-covered pot over low heat

Stir-fry: to cook small pieces of meat, poultry, fish, and/or vegetables in a very small amount of oil over very high heat, stirring as you cook ✦

Lean Tips... for a Variety of Foods

Broil or grill, roast, braise, or stew foods, rather than fry them, most of the time. Or steam, poach, stir-fry, or microwave foods, too. That way, you won't add fat during cooking. *For a definition of these cooking techniques, refer to "Culinary Lingo" on page 335. You'll also find the techniques explained in detail: "Meat Cookery: Dry Heat Methods" on page 338 and "Meat Cookery: Moist Heat Methods" on page 339.*

Stretch higher-fat ingredients. For example, grate cheese so less looks like more. Or spread 1 tablespoon peanut butter on toast rather than 2 tablespoons.

Substitute reduced fat and fat-free products in all kinds of recipes. *Refer to chapter 12, "Supermarket Smarts," for suggestions throughout the supermarket.*

Coat cooking pans with a thin layer of oil, then wipe with a paper towel. Two tablespoons of oil add up

Meat, Poultry, and Fish: Lean Cuts and Cooking Methods

	Dry Heat					Moist Heat			
	Roast	Broil	Grill	Panbroil	Stir-fry	Braise	Stew	Steam	Poach
Beef									
Eye Round*						X	X		X
Top Round*						X	X		
Round Tip*						X	X		
Bottom Round*						X	X		
Sirloin	X	X	X	X	X				
Top Loin	X	X	X	X	X				
Tenderloin	X	X	X	X	X				X
Flank		X	X		X				
Ground Round	X	X	X	X					
Pork									
Tenderloin	X	X	X	X	X				
Boneless Top Loin Roast	X	X	X						
Loin Chop		X	X	X		X			
Loin Strips					X				
Boneless Sirloin Chop		X	X	X		X			
Boneless Rib Roast	X		X			X	X		
Rib Chop		X	X	X		X			
Boneless Ham	X	X	X	X	X				
Poultry**									
Whole Chicken	X		X			X	X		X
Whole Turkey	X		X			X			
Cornish Game Hens	X		X			X	X		X
Breast	X	X	X	X	X				X
Drumstick	X	X	X						
Fish									
Cod	X	X	X	X	X		X	X	X
Flounder	X	X	X	X				X	X
Halibut	X	X	X	X	X		X	X	X
Orange Roughy		X	X	X	X		X	X	X
Shrimp		X	X	X	X		X	X	X

Source: Lean 'N Easy: Preparing Meat with Less Fat and More Taste, *Chicago*: National Cattlemen's Beef Association, 1994.
**May be cooked by dry heat methods if they are tenderized first by pounding or marinating.*
***White meat has less fat than dark meat. Skin should be removed before eating.*

to 28 fat grams (240 calories); a thin coating of vegetable oil spray has just 1 fat gram (10 calories).

Prepare yogurt cheese as a substitute for higher-fat spreads. *To learn how to make it, refer to page 70.*

Drain pan-fried foods on a paper towel to absorb extra grease. Go easy on the oil.

When adding ingredients to packaged mixes (such as macaroni and cheese, scalloped potatoes, or brownies), try low-fat options. Use extra-lean ground beef in casserole mixes, skim milk in instant pudding, or just half the margarine or butter in packaged macaroni and cheese.

Lean Tips... for Meat, Poultry, and Fish

Cook with lean meats (round, sirloin, and loin cuts), lean poultry, and lean fish. *Refer to page 282 for tips on buying lean meat. To decide how to cook them, refer to "Meat, Poultry, and Fish: Lean Cuts and Cooking Methods" on page 336.*

Use smaller amounts of processed meats that tend to have more fat: bacon, hot dogs, and luncheon meats. Or use leaner versions, such as 95% fat-free.

When recipes call for bacon, use lean ham or Canadian bacon. You'll still get the smoky flavor.

Trim away any visible fat on meat and poultry. Even on lean meat, you'll find some fat. Trimming the fat removes some, but not all the cholesterol because cholesterol is in both the lean tissue and the fat in meat, poultry, and fish. On whole birds, find fat near the opening of the cavity.

Go "skinless" on poultry before or after cooking it. Under the skin, there's a layer of fat. By removing the skin, you can cut the fat content in half! As a tip, cook poultry with the skin on to keep it tender and moist.

Drain off fat from ground meat just after it's cooked. Or microwave ground beef in a microwave-safe strainer so fat drains as meat cooks. You can also pour hot water over cooked ground meat in a strainer to rinse away between 2 and 5 grams of fat per 3-ounce serving.

Brown meat, poultry, and seafood in a nonstick skillet with little or no added fat, except for vegetable oil spray. Compare the difference: 2 tablespoons of oil, used to brown meat, carries an extra 240 calories from fat, compared with less than 10 from vegetable oil spray.

Grill, broil, or roast meat and poultry on a rack so fat drips through. In that way, fat drippings aren't reabsorbed.

Marinate meat, poultry, and fish in marinades with little or no fat: orange, lime, or lemon juice; defatted broth; wine; tomato juice; plain, low-fat yogurt; or buttermilk. Add fresh herbs to the marinade.

To keep fish or chicken moist, poach fillets in heavy aluminum foil with fruit, herbs, onions, vegetables,

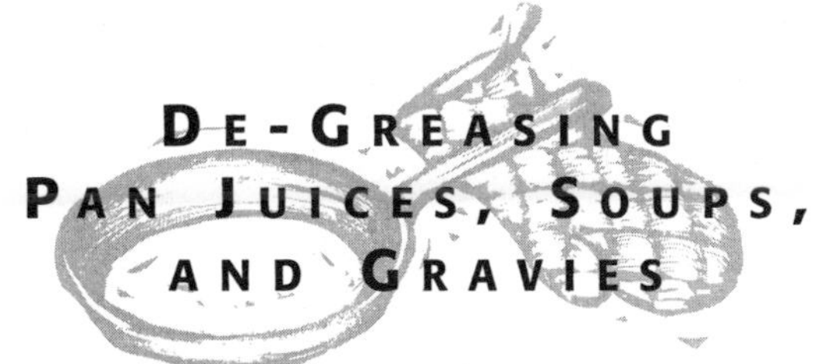

DE-GREASING PAN JUICES, SOUPS, AND GRAVIES

Remember your science lessons? Fat rises to the top because it's lighter than water. The same thing happens in cooking. Fat in pan juices, soups, gravies, and canned broth collects on top, making it easy to skim off. Every tablespoon of fat you discard removes about 13 fat grams and 120 calories from the dish you're preparing.

Remove fat from meat and poultry juices with a wide-mouthed spoon or a fat separating pitcher. *See "Well Equipped" on page 342 for a description.*

Refrigerate soups and stews before they're served. Do the same with homemade and canned broth, soups, and chili. Fat, which hardens when chilled, is easy to remove with a spoon.

When time is short, add a few ice cubes to the broth. Fat will rise and congeal around the ice, but may dilute the broth slightly. ✦

Meat Cookery: Dry Heat Methods	
ROASTING	• Place roast (from refrigerator) on rack in shallow roasting pan. • Season meat before or after cooking. • Insert thermometer into thickest part of roast, not touching bone or fat. • Do not add water and do not cover. • Roast to 5 to 10 degrees below desired doneness. • Allow roast to stand 15 to 20 minutes before serving. Temperature of the roast will continue to rise to desired doneness during standing to 145° F (medium rare) or 160° F (medium). Roast will also be easier to carve.
BROILING	• Set oven for broiling. Preheating is not essential. • Place meat on rack in broiler pan. • Position thinner cuts (3/4- to 1-inch thick) so surface of meat is 2 to 3 inches from the heat; thicker cuts 3 to 6 inches from the heat. • Broil for half the recommended time. • Season if desired. • Turn and continue cooking to the desired degree of doneness. • Season second side if desired, and serve.
GRILLING	*Direct:* • For quick cooking meat and poultry items such as chops, steaks, burgers, breasts, or kebobs. Place meat on grid directly over the coals. *Indirect:* • For cuts that require longer cooking at lower temperatures, such as roasts, thick steaks, or chops, whole chicken or turkey. The meat is placed over a drip pan on the grid with coals on each side. Cover and open vents on grill. • To check temperature for either grilling method, carefully hold your hand, palm side down, at cooking height (just above the grid). Count the number of seconds you can hold your hand in that position before the heat is uncomfortable and you have to pull it away; four seconds for medium coals, five seconds for low.
PANBROILING	• Place meat in preheated, heavy nonstick skillet. • Do not add oil or water. • Do not cover. • For cuts thicker than 1/2-inch thick, use medium or medium-low heat and turn occasionally. Cook thinner cuts over medium-high heat, turning once. Do not overcook. • Remove fat as it accumulates. • Season, if desired, and serve. *To reduce fat from ground meat crumbles:* • After browning ground meat crumbles, transfer crumbles with slotted spoon to plate lined with white, nonrecycled paper towels. • Transfer to colander and rinse with 4 cups of hot (but not boiling) water. Do not use hot water directly from the tap; the pressure from the faucet can change the texture of the meat. • The crumbles may be browned with onion and garlic for added flavor and then rinsed. Add dry seasonings after the rinsing process has been completed.
STIR-FRYING	• Partially freeze meat for easy slicing. • Cut into thin, uniform slices, strips, or pieces. • Marinate in refrigerator to add flavor while preparing other ingredients, if desired. • Cook meat and vegetables separately and then combine. • Stir-fry meat (half at a time) in a small amount (about 1 tablespoon or less) of hot oil or use a vegetable cooking spray in a nonstick skillet or wok. • Cook at medium-high temperature. • Continuously turn meat pieces with a scooping motion. • Combine meat with cooked vegetables and serve.

Source: Lean 'N Easy: Preparing Meat with Less Fat and More Taste, *Chicago*: *National Cattlemen's Beef Association*, 1994.

and other flavorings. Secure the "package" and then bake it in the oven or on the grill. For the oven, you can also wrap and bake meat, fish, or poultry in parchment paper; chefs call this "en papillote," or paper package.

Oven-fry fish or chicken. Dip the meat first in egg whites, then coat with seasoned bread crumbs. Bake on a nonstick pan that has been coated with vegetable oil spray.

As a quick, low-fat main dish, bake fish with a splash of white wine or catawba juice, chopped tomatoes, and fresh basil or oregano.

Lean Tips... for Egg Dishes

Eggs, which supply protein and iron to the diet, contribute toward your servings from the Meat Group on the Food Guide Pyramid. While nutritious, health experts advise healthy Americans to eat no more than four egg yolks a week as a way to control dietary cholesterol.

Egg yolks, not whites, contain fat and cholesterol. That's why you can use egg whites liberally in place of egg yolks in many foods.

Use two egg whites in place of one whole egg in breads, pancakes, casseroles, French toast, cookies, cheesecake, pudding, and other recipes that call for whole eggs. Recipes that require egg yolks, such as puff pastry, are best made with whole eggs.

As another option, use a cholesterol-free liquid egg product in place of whole eggs. Usually 1/4 cup egg

Meat Cookery: Moist Heat Methods	
Braising	• Slowly brown meat or poultry on all sides, using small amount of oil, if necessary, in a heavy pan. • Pour off drippings. • Season with salt, herbs or spices, as desired. • Add a small amount of liquid (as little as 2 tablespoons may be used, however, 1/4 to 1/2 cup is recommended), such as water, juice, wine, broth, or stock. • Cover tightly to provide a moist atmosphere for cooking. Simmer on low heat on top of the range or in oven (300-325° F) until fork tender. • Vegetables should be added toward the end of cooking to prevent overcooking. • The cooking liquid may be reduced or thickened after removing fat to make a sauce.
Stewing	• Coat meat or poultry lightly with seasoned flour, if desired. • Slowly brown on all sides using a small amount of oil, if necessary, in heavy pan. • Pour off drippings. • Cover meat or poultry with liquid, such as water, juice, wine, broth, or stock. • Season as desired. • Cover tightly and simmer on top of the range until fork tender. • Vegetables should be added toward the end of cooking time to prevent overcooking. • Reduce or thicken cooking liquid after removing fat, if desired.
Poaching	• Season meat, poultry, or fish as desired. • For roasts, tie with heavy string at 2-inch intervals, if needed. Brown on all sides in nonstick pan. Pour off excess drippings. • Cover meat, poultry, or fish with liquid. Season with additional ingredients, if desired. • Bring to a boil. Reduce heat, cover, and simmer until done.
Steaming	*Stovetop:* • Place fish on a steamer pan or perforated tray. • Set into pan, above simmering liquid. • Cover pan, and continue simmering at a low heat until fish flakes. *Microwave:* • Place fish in microwave-safe dish in spoke fashion for even cooking. • Add a small amount of liquid or seasoned vegetables, if desired. • Cover with microwave-safe plastic wrap, venting on one corner. • Following manufacturer's directions, microwave on high until fish flakes.

Source: Lean 'N Easy: Preparing Meat with Less Fat and More Taste, *Chicago:* National Cattlemen's Beef Association, 1994.

product equals one whole egg; check the package label to be sure. *To learn more about this product, refer to page* 290.

In recipes that call for two or more eggs, substitute just some of the whole eggs with egg whites. For example, for two whole eggs, instead use two egg whites and one whole egg. That way you'll get the color and flavor of the yolk, but less cholesterol. This ideas works well for scrambled eggs, quiche, and omelets.

Lean Tips… for Vegetables

For vegetables, sauté with liquid, not oil. Cook them in a little liquid—defatted broth, juice, wine, or water—in a covered, nonstick pan. It's great for onions and mushrooms, which are sautéed for many recipes!

Cook vegetables by steaming, stir-frying, simmering, or microwaving. If you really enjoy the crispiness of french fries and fried onion rings, oven bake them instead of frying them.

Purée or mash potatoes, sweet potatoes, and other vegetables with milk or liquid left from cooking them. Go easy on the butter or margarine. Boost the flavor and the nutrients by blending in some shredded carrots or zucchini, too!

For the flavor of butter on vegetables, add a smaller amount—but just before serving. Cooking dilutes the flavor. You need less if you add it last. As another just-before-serving option, try a butter-flavored spray.

Sprinkle some Parmesan or Romano cheese on vegetables. It adds a lot of flavor but not much fat.

Easy Substitutions to Cut Fat and/or Cholesterol

When cooking calls for…	Use…
Sour cream	Plain low-fat yogurt, or 1/2 cup cottage cheese blended with 1 1/2 tsp. lemon juice, or light or fat-free sour cream
Whipped cream	Chilled, whipped evaporated skim milk, or a nondairy whipped topping made from polyunsaturated fat
Cream	Evaporated skim milk
Whole milk	Skim, 1 percent, or 2 percent milk as a beverage or in recipes
Full-fat cheese	Low-fat, skim-milk cheese, cheese with less than 5 grams of fat per ounce, or fat-free cheese
Ricotta cheese	Low-fat or fat-free cottage cheese or nonfat or low-fat ricotta cheese
Ice cream	Low-fat or nonfat ice cream, or frozen low-fat or nonfat yogurt, frozen fruit juice products, or sorbet
Ground beef	Extra lean ground beef, or lean ground turkey or chicken
Bacon	Canadian bacon or lean ham
Sausage	Lean ground turkey, or 95% fat-free sausage
Whole egg	Two egg whites, or 1/4 cup cholesterol-free liquid egg product, or 1 egg white plus 2 tsp. oil
One egg yolk	One egg white
One egg (as thickener)	1 tablespoon flour
Mayonnaise	Low-fat or fat-free mayonnaise or whipped salad dressing, or plain low-fat yogurt combined with low-fat cottage cheese
Salad dressings	Low-calorie commercial dressings, or homemade dressing made with unsaturated oils, water, and vinegar or lemon juice
Cream soups	Defatted broths, or broth-based or skim milk-based soups
Nuts	Dried fruit, such as raisins, chopped dried apricots, or dried cranberries
1 ounce baking chocolate	3 tablespoons cocoa powder and 1 tablespoon oil
Butter, lard, and other saturated fats (coconut oil, palm oil)	Soft, tub margarine (first ingredient on food label as liquid vegetable oil); corn, cottonseed, olive, rapeseed (canola), safflower, sesame, soybean, or sunflower oil

Roast or grill vegetables (sliced eggplant, bell pepper chunks, sliced zucchini) as a low-fat way to bring out the flavor. Coat them lightly with vegetable oil spray. Then roast in the oven at 400° F or grill for about 15 minutes until tender-crisp.

Lean Tips... for Salads

Flavor salads with lower-fat, commercial dressings. Or make your own with less oil and more vinegar.

On taco salads, use lots of salsa, made with tomato, chiles, onion, herbs, and lime juice. Use a lighter touch with sour cream, by going "50-50": 50 percent sour cream and 50 percent plain, low-fat yogurt. Or use reduced-fat or nonfat sour cream.

Instead of creamy coleslaw made with regular mayonnaise, moisten cabbage and other shredded vegetables with vinaigrette dressing. Or use low-fat or nonfat yogurt or mayonnaise with seasonings as a dressing.

Adjust the proportions in homemade vinaigrette. Make it with three parts vinegar to one part oil, instead of the other way around. Experiment with different types of vinegars! *Refer to "Herbed Vinegars" on page 350 for varieties you can make in your kitchen.*

Lean Tips... for Grain Dishes and Breads

Skip the oil in pasta cooking water—add fresh herbs for flavor instead. Toss with sauce immediately so pasta won't stick together; use a lower fat sauce, such as a tomato-based or other vegetable sauces.

Cook couscous, rice, and other grains with herbs, defatted broth, or juice instead of adding fat. And don't rinse rice; you'll wash away some of vitamins, especially B vitamins which are added to enrich grains.

Serve breads, rolls, muffins, bagels, and biscuits with low-fat spreads: fruit butter, chutney, jam, mustard, reduced-fat margarine spread, nonfat mayonnaise, and reduced-fat or nonfat cream cheese. *For a list of condiments with less than 1 gram of fat per tablespoon, refer to "Lighter Condiments" on page 343.*

Lean Tips... for Soups, Stews, and Sauces

Instead of gravy and rich sauces, enhance the flavors of foods with fat-free ingredients: garlic, ginger, lemon juice, onion, tomato, herbs, and spices, among others. Before cooking, use an herb rub on meat, poultry, or fish; for a spicy taste, rub cumin, chili powder, coriander, red and black pepper, and cinnamon on a pork roast. Or glaze meat, poultry, or fish with salsas or chutneys. *Refer to pages 330 and 351 for herb rubs and salsa ideas.*

Cut back on or eliminate oil in homemade marinades. Or marinate with fat-free salad dressing.

"Sauce" up the flavor of vegetables, poultry, fish, and pasta with puréed vegetables rather than cream-based sauces. To give a creamy texture, add milk, plain yogurt, or low-fat cottage cheese to vegetables as you process them in the blender or food processor.

Try these "creamy" sauces. Blend fresh dill into nonfat, plain yogurt as a sauce for seafood or chicken. Blend horseradish with plain yogurt to serve with lean beef. For an easy sauce, braise poultry, fish, and meat in low-fat canned soups.

Skim fat from pan juices, soups, and stews. *For quick techniques, see "De-Greasing Pan Juices, Soups, and Gravies" on page 337.*

Thicken soups with puréed vegetables and nonfat dry milk. Vegetables can boost the vitamin A and C content; milk "ups" the calcium. Neither adds fat. For another "creamy" ingredient, try buttermilk or evaporated skim milk.

If the recipe calls for a rich sauce, go easy. You want to add flavor, not overwhelm the food, with sauce.

Lean Tips... for Baked Goods

Experiment a little. In baked breads, cakes, muffins, and brownies, try substituting an equal amount of applesauce, mashed bananas, other puréed fruit, or cottage cheese for at least half the oil, margarine, or butter in recipes. Try buttermilk or nonfat or low-fat yogurt in place of sour cream, butter, and margarine in biscuits, muffins, and other breads.

Enjoy the flavor of nuts? Use less, but toast them so you get the most flavor. For even more flavor, yet less fat, mix in chopped dried fruits, too: dried apricots, dried apples, raisins, dried cranberries, or prunes.

Coat baking pans very lightly with nonstick spray, rather than margarine, butter, or oil.

Instead of whipped cream toppings, whip chilled evaporated skim milk—with just a touch of sugar—for a creamy topping. Serve it right away since it's less stable! Evaporated skim milk can be used as a substitute in many recipes that call for heavy cream.

Frosting on a cake can add a great deal of fat. Instead, dust it with powdered sugar, or top with fresh fruit or fruit purée.

Instead of flaky pastry shells with their high-fat content, make desserts with graham cracker crumb crusts. Prepare crumb crusts with half the margarine or butter called for in the recipe. If more is needed, add just enough to moisten the crumbs.

As another pastry option, prepare single-crust pies. Either make an open-face pie, or arrange the fruit in the pie pan first, then put the crust on top.

As an easy substitution, use low-fat, skim, and nonfat dairy products. Although they have less fat than whole-milk products, they still supply all the calcium!

To cut down on saturated fat, you might experiment with cooking oil instead of margarine, butter, or lard. Be aware, however, that the texture will differ, being coarser, mealier, and perhaps more oily. In fact, this substitution isn't suggested for quick breads, pastry, or sweet baked goods that are higher in fat to begin with.

If you do make the switch, use less oil than solid fat. Oil has more shortening power, but doesn't have the small amount of water that most solid fats contain. Use this substitution:

For Solid Fat...	Try Liquid Oil...
1 tablespoon	3/4 tablespoon
1/3 cup	4 tablespoons (1/4 cup)
1/2 cup	6 tablespoons
3/4 cup	9 tablespoons
1 cup	12 tablespoons (3/4 cup)

Well Equipped!

To cook the "lean" way, equip your kitchen with a few simple utensils!

Cheese Grater—With a grater, a little cheese goes a longer way. When cheese is grated, a smaller cheese portion still adds plenty of flavor. It's also a "grate" idea for shredding vegetables, such as carrots and squash, or for grating lemon, lime, and orange rinds for flavor.

Egg Separator—An egg separator helps you easily separate the yolks from the whites. That's important when you're cutting back on dietary cholesterol.

Fat Separating Pitcher—With the position of the spout, a fat separating pitcher lets you pour out the liquid from the bottom, leaving the fat behind.

Food Processor or Blender—With this countertop appliance, you can purée low-fat cottage cheese to the consistency of thick cream; chop, grate, or purée vegetables for use in soups, sauces, salads, and side dishes; or purée fruit, yogurt, and milk for a thick, yet low-fat milk shake.

Hot-Air Popcorn Popper—This type of popcorn popper requires no oil or butter. So popcorn can be a quick, low-fat, low-calorie snack.

Kitchen Scale—A scale that measures in ounces helps you figure portion sizes. If you have a hard time determining the size of your meat, poultry, fish, or cheese servings, a kitchen scale is helpful.

Indoor Grill—Indoor grills either fit over the burners on your stove or they may be free-standing appliances. Either way, you can easily discard the excess fat, which drips through the grates into a drip pan.

Kitchen Scissors—Along with knives, kitchen scissors come in handy for trimming visible fat from meat and poultry.

Microwave Oven—A microwave oven cooks food fast, without the need for added fat. The fast cooking time also helps food retain vitamins and minerals.

Nonstick Pots and Pans—Some cookware is specially coated, allowing you to cook with little or no added fat. Although today's nonstick finishes last a long time, you need to care for them properly. Use nonmetal utensils to prevent scratching, and avoid abrasive cleaners that strip away coatings. Most nonstick finishes are dishwasher safe.

Pastry Brush—A small pastry brush lets you just lightly coat meat, poultry, and fish with fats or oils.

Roasting Pan with a Grate—With a grate, roasted and broiled meat or poultry can't absorb fat drippings. They collect in the pan below.

Slotted Spoon—A slotted spoon allows you to lift food out of the pan, leaving any fat drippings behind.

Steamer—Rather than fry foods, steam them! Actually there are several kinds of steamers to choose from: an electric steamer for vegetables, rice, fish, or chicken; a stackable bamboo steamer set that fits in a wok or stockpot; or a small aluminum vegetable steamer that fits in a saucepan.

Strainer—With a microwave-safe plastic strainer, you can cook ground meat in the microwave oven, collecting fat drippings in a container underneath.

Wok—A wok's sloped sides allow food to cook fast without much oil. Unless it has a nonstick surface, season a new stainless-steel wok to keep food from sticking. Here's how. First coat the cooking surface with vegetable oil, then heat the pan in a 350° F oven for about one hour. The oil will work its way into the porous surface of the wok.

Salt "Shakers"

Cooking with salt may seem so natural that it goes unnoticed. If you're an average American, about 25 percent of your sodium comes from food preparation or salt you add at the table. A preference for salt—and the habit of cooking with salt—is learned. You can unlearn it, too.

You don't need to eliminate sodium from your cooking. In fact you probably can't—and you shouldn't! Sodium occurs naturally in many foods. And it's a nutrient your body needs in limited amounts. *For a quick review of sodium, refer to chapter 7, "Sodium: A Salty Subject."*

Especially if your blood pressure is sodium-sensitive, learn to cut back and use salt in modera-

Consider adding chutneys and sauces, made with little or no fat, to the kitchen cupboard. Most of these colorful, but lean, ingredients spice up the looks and flavor of light menus. The following all have less than 1 gram of fat per tablespoon:

barbeque sauce	chili sauce
cranberry-orange chutney	horseradish
ketchup	Dijon mustard
pickle relish	seafood cocktail sauce
soy sauce	
Worcestershire sauce	teriyaki sauce

tion. Do so gradually...especially if you're a salt lover. After a while, your taste for salt will change. You might even be surprised when some foods seem too salty!

Taste before you reach for the salt shaker. Food may taste great just as it is!

Shake the habit! Remove the salt shaker from the kitchen counter and the table. A 1/8-teaspoon "salt shake" adds more than 200 milligrams of sodium to your dish. Health experts suggest that healthy adults consume moderate amounts of salt and sodium: about 2,300 to 2,400 milligrams a day.

Instead of added salt, spark up the flavor with herbs and spices, garlic, onions, and citrus juice. *For food preparation tips, refer to "A Pinch of Flavor: How to Cook With Herbs and Spices" on page 349.*

Make a little salt go a longer way. Salt your food lightly just before serving. When it's on the surface of food, the salty taste seems more intense. Instead of salt, add a touch of flavor with foods that contain some salt and a little fat, such as olives, Parmesan or Romano cheese, and salted nuts. The fat helps keep the salty taste in your mouth longer.

Except for recipes with yeast, you can cut back on salt, perhaps by 50 percent—or even eliminate it altogether. Baked goods made with yeast need salt to control the rising of the dough.

Drain liquid from some salty canned foods, such as canned beans or vegetables. Rinse and cook in tap water, defatted broth, or juice.

Be aware that baking powder and baking soda—used in some recipes—contain sodium. Because these ingredients give baked goods a quick rise, you can't eliminate them. Just make trade-offs elsewhere to keep your whole day's diet within your sodium range.

Reduce or skip the salt in cooking water...even if a package label says to add salt. Salt won't make water boil any faster. Instead season pasta, rice, vegetables, and cereals with spices and herbs after they're cooked.

Substitute prepared ingredients that have less sodium—perhaps low-sodium broth, no-salt-added canned vegetables, light soy sauce, and salt-free seasoning mixes. *Refer to Chapter 12, "Supermarket Smarts," for more tips on sodium-savvy shopping.*

Read the label. If foods have ingredients with salt or sodium already, you don't need to add more.

Fiber Boosters

Does your plate lack fiber? You're not alone. With so many refined ingredients in breads, pasta, and other grain products and too few fruits and vegetables, many people come up short. Yet, with a few easy changes in your cooking style, you can boost your fiber factor—and add interest and flavor, too!

Why boost the fiber in your eating plan? Although it's not a nutrient, fiber promotes your health in many ways—by aiding digestion and by reducing the risks for intestinal problems, some types of cancer, and heart disease. In food, fiber is often bundled with essential nutrients, too. *To brush up on fiber, refer to chapter 6 "Fiber: Your Body's Broom." On the chart "Counting Up Fiber" on page 150, you'll also find a list of high-fiber ingredients.*

Keep peels on fruits and vegetables. A medium baked potato with the skin on has about twice the fiber of a "naked" potato!

Add legumes and lentils to all kinds of dishes. *Check "A Word About Legumes..." on page 346 for ideas!*

Substitute whole-grain pasta—lasagna noodles, macaroni, spaghetti, and other whole-grain pastas—in all kinds of dishes. Use brown or wild rice in place of white rice, too—or use a combination.

Experiment with unfamiliar whole grains: barley, buckwheat, bulgur, millet, quinoa, rye berries, and wheat berries. *To learn about these grains, refer to "Today's Grains" on page 221. The chart "Cooking Grain by Grain" on page 345 shows how to prepare them.*

Add bran to casseroles, meatloaf, and cooked cereal. Sprinkle a little bran or wheat germ on breakfast cereal, or blend some with yogurt for a little crunch.

Each tablespoon of bran adds a little more than 1 gram of fiber.

When making breads, muffins, pancakes, waffles, and other grain products, substitute whole-wheat flour for half of the white flour. Don't go 100 percent, though; the texture will be too dense.

Add extra vegetables to casseroles, soups, salads, sandwiches, and pasta and rice dishes. For example, adding 1/2 cup of broccoli to a pasta dish adds 2 grams of fiber. A quarter cup of cooked spinach, mixed in soup or risotto, adds 2 grams of fiber. And half a medium-size carrot, shredded as a salad topper, adds 1 gram of fiber.

Get whole-grain goodness on sandwiches. Use whole-grain breads, whole-grain bagels, and whole-grain pita pockets.

Enjoy the fiber factor of fruits. Use all kinds of fruit in salads, cooked cereals, and as toppers on frozen desserts and angel food cake. For example, try berries, pears, or peaches. A half cup of strawberries and a half of a pear (skin on) each add 2 grams of fiber!

Mix dry fruit—raisins, dry cranberries, and prunes—into breads, cookies, salads, and other dishes. One-quarter cup of raisins adds 2 grams of fiber; three prunes have almost as much!

Cooking Grain by Grain

Wonder how to cook whole grains? You can use the same simple steps for all these whole grains.

Bring the cooking water to a boil; stir in the grain. Cover, reduce heat, and simmer. Let stand, covered, if indicated below. Then use these wonderful cooked grains in salads; as side dishes flavored with sauces or seasonings; or in soups.

1 CUP UNCOOKED GRAIN	COOKING WATER (CUPS)	COOKING TIME (MINUTES)	STANDING TIME (MINUTES)	YIELD (CUPS)	COMMON USES
amaranth	3	25	-	3 1/2	cereal, side dish
buckwheat (kasha)	2	20	10	3	side dish (buckwheat groats flour also used in baked foods)
bulgur	1 1/2	*	30	2 1/2	side dish, stew, salad (tabbouleh)
hominy (corn) (soak 8 hours)	4	30	5	3 1/2	side dish, stew, soup, cereal
millet	2 3/4	30	15	3	side dish, bread
pearl barley	3	40	5	3 1/2	side dish, cereal, soup
quinoa (rinsed)	2	15	-	3	side dish, stuffing, soup, salad, stew
rice, brown	2 1/2	45	5	3	wherever rice is used
rice, wild **	3	55	-	3 1/2	side dish, stuffing, soup, salad
rye berries	2	60	-	2 3/4	side dish, bread
triticale (wheat and rye) (soak overnight)	2 1/2	40	-	4	side dish, soup, cereal, bread
wheat berries (soak overnight)	2	45	-	2 1/2	side dish, bread

**Bulgur isn't cooked. Put bulgur in a bowl, pour boiling water over it. And let it stand until the water is absorbed.*

***Wild rice is actually a seed, and not rice.*

Sources: Peterson, LC. "The ABC's of Whole Grains." Food Management. March 1993:108. Brody, JE. Jane Brody's Good Food Book. New York: Bantam Books, 1987.

Choose whole-grain breakfast cereals. Look for the words "whole-grain" on the package. Other label clues are a "good source of fiber" or "rich in fiber." *Refer to page* 270 *for more on label reading.*

A Word About Legumes...
Legumes—dried beans, peas, and lentils—are packed with fiber! A half-cup serving of cooked legumes supplies 4 to 10 grams of fiber. (As a healthy adult, you need 20 to 35 grams of fiber a day.) Legumes are such a valuable food that it's well worth the effort to learn how to add them to meals and snacks—several times each week.

Have you heard this complaint in your family? "I don't like beans!" When boiled and served plain, they don't have much flavor. But when combined with other foods, they're versatile, taking on many flavor dimensions.

Make minestrone soup with kidney or garbanzo beans and vegetables. Flavor the soup with beef or chicken broth or canned tomatoes and their juice.

Fill tacos or burritos with drained, cooked, or canned pinto beans. Accent the flavor with a little grated cheese and lots of salsa, tomatoes, and chopped lettuce or cabbage.

Top green salads with drained, canned, or cooked beans. Or mix up a three-, four-, or five-bean salad!

For an easy lunch, open a can of split pea, navy bean, or lentil soup. Some shredded carrot or apple tastes great on top!

As an easy side dish, baked potato topper, or pasta sauce, simply heat up canned beans, prepared in tasty sauces: tomato, molasses, or jalapeño pepper.

have you ever wondered

...where buttermilk got its name? The term "buttermilk" sounds like a misnomer. Its name refers to the way buttermilk was first made—from the whey, or liquid, left after butter was churned from cream. Today, most buttermilk actually is made from skim or low-fat milk.✦

Use legumes as a meat substitute in many mixed dishes: kidney beans in chili, lentils in meatloaf, pinto beans in enchiladas, black beans in chunky soups, mashed kidney or pinto beans in meatballs, lentils in curry, and white beans in stews.

Create a high-fiber pasta sauce that's low in fat, too! In a blender or food processor, purée drained, canned beans with beef or chicken stock. White cannellini beans make a creamy, white sauce, but any variety of beans will do. Add a blend of fresh herbs: basil, chives, garlic, marjoram, and oregano, among others. Fresh tomatoes or tomato sauce add a nice flavor and color, too. Heat and toss with your favorite pasta!

Refer to page 151, *"Kitchen Nutrition: Cooking a Pot o' Beans," and page* 570, *"Vegetarian Way: Legumes and Other Meat Alternates" for more tips on cooking with beans.*

Calcium Boosters

If you're like many Americans, the calcium in your diet needs a boost! People of all ages need calcium for healthy bones and teeth, and for other body functions. Yet, too many of us just don't consume enough servings from the Milk, Yogurt, and Cheese Group in the Food Guide Pyramid.

Like younger children, the Recommended Daily Allowance (RDA) for adults (ages 25 and over) is about 800 milligrams of calcium daily. And for children ages 11 and over, teens, and young adults it's 1,200 milligrams of calcium daily. Dairy foods are the best source of calcium; in fact, they supply about 75 percent of the calcium in the United States' food supply. But small amounts come from other food groups too. *Refer to "Calcium: A Closer Look" on page* 105 *for more information. See page* 606 *for more about the* RDA.

To boost the calcium in your diet, consume two to three Milk Group servings daily. Skim and lower-fat varieties are good choices for fat-conscious individuals. Use these food preparation tips to add a little more calcium here and there. You'll help ensure your bones—in fact, your whole body—get the calcium needed:

Fortify mashed potatoes, casseroles, vegetable purées, and thick soups with nonfat dry milk, evaporated skim milk, or plain yogurt. Dry milk added to meatloaf won't even be noticed! One-quarter cup of nonfat dry milk adds 375 milligrams of calcium to a whole recipe for meatloaf.

Sprinkle shredded cheese on salads, soups, stews, baked potatoes, and vegetables. One ounce of cheddar cheese (1/4 cup) has 200 milligrams of calcium.

Make cooked cereal and hot cocoa with milk instead of water. One-half cup of milk adds 150 milligrams of calcium to your day's food choices. You might fortify them with extra nonfat dry milk, too.

Purée cottage cheese in a food processor or blender. Add herbs, then use it as a dip or bagel spread.

Instead of black coffee (regular or decaffeinated) in the morning, buy coffee latte (with milk, preferably skim) at the coffee shop. It's made with steamed milk. One-half cup of milk added to coffee adds 150 milligrams of calcium.

Use plain yogurt for some of the mayonnaise in salad dressings, sandwich spreads, and dips.

For something different, try goat cheese. It has a strong and unique flavor. A half-ounce portion of semi-soft goat cheese has about 42 milligrams of calcium. Serve it on crackers, on salads, or as a vegetable garnish. A half ounce of hard goat cheese has 127 milligrams of calcium. *Hint*: you might find herb-flavored goat cheese in your supermarket.

Add vegetables that have more calcium to many dishes: soups, salads, and stews, for example. One serving of broccoli, collard greens, kale, mustard greens, okra, and turnip greens all provide calcium, although not as much as a serving of milk.

For main dish salads and sandwich spreads, use canned salmon with bones as an occasional change from tuna. Fish with edible bones—salmon, sardines, perch—all supply calcium to the diet.

If you boost calcium with reduced-fat or fat-free cheese, recognize that it doesn't blend or melt as well as whole-milk cheese. For best results, shred lower-fat cheeses finely or use them in a mixture with whole-milk cheese. Blend them with other ingredients, rather than just sprinkling them on top.

Boost calcium, not fat, with yogurt cheese. Made by draining the whey from the solids in plain yogurt, it makes a great substitute for cream cheese or sour cream. *Refer to page* 70, "*Kitchen* Nutrition: *Yogurt Cheese.*"

Make stir-fried dishes with tofu, preferably made with calcium sulfate. One-quarter cup of tofu with calcium sulfate has about 130 milligrams of calcium. The same amount of tofu without calcium sulfate has 65 milligrams of calcium.

Sugar Savers

"Just a spoonful of sugar...," as Mary Poppins knew, adds flavor! Besides the taste, sugar adds to the aroma, texture, color, and body of a variety of foods. Sugar is the "food" for yeast that helps bread rise. In baked foods, it contributes to the light brown color and crisp texture. In canned jams and jellies, sugar helps inhibit the growth of molds and yeasts. In many baked foods and other products, sugar contributes to a food's bulk and texture.

Like other ingredients in food, eating added sugars in moderation is part of a healthy diet. Sugars are one source of food energy. For some people, mod-

Baking With Sugar

To ensure good results when reducing sugar in baked foods, use this guideline.

	For each cup of flour use:
Cakes and cake-like cookies (cookies made with juice, milk, water)	1/2 cup sugar
Muffins and quick breads	1 tablespoon sugar
Yeast breads	1 teaspoon sugar

(*Source*: "*Dietary Guidelines for Americans*: *Use Sugars Only in Moderation*," Home and Garden Bulletin *Number* 253-6, *Human Nutrition Information Service*/U.S. *Department of Agriculture*, *July*, 1993.)

eration means controlling sugar they add to foods, perhaps to cut back on calories. *For a quick review of sugars, refer to* Chapter 5, *"Sweet Talk: Sugar and Other Sweeteners."*

Before you change the sugar in a food you're preparing, think about its function and whether reducing or eliminating sugars will give the cooking result you want. Then if you need to cut calories, use sugars in moderation in your cooking:

In cakes, cookies, breads, and other baked goods, try using less sugar. Often you can reduce sugar by one-fourth to one-third, yet hardly notice the difference. Be aware, however, that many recipes have already done this for you. *Check the chart, "Baking With Sugar," on page 347 as your guide.*

"Sweeten" recipes with extracts, such as vanilla or peppermint, or so-called sweet spices, such as cinnamon or allspice. This enhances the sweetness of food. Warm these spicy foods; they'll taste sweeter! Other spices that give the perception of sweetness include cardamom, coriander, ginger, mace, and nutmeg. *For more tips, refer to "Kitchen Nutrition: Sweet Seasons" on page 135.*

Briefly broil or microwave peach, pear, or grapefruit halves. Sprinkle with a small amount of sweetener...or just enjoy the natural flavor. The warm temperature enhances their sweet flavors!

Sweeten with fruit puréed in a blender or food processor. Too thick? Add a little fruit juice. Fruit purées are great on pancakes, waffles, French toast, fruit salads, angel food cake, and frozen desserts. They're also a tasty glaze for chicken and poultry!

Instead of fruit-flavored yogurt, add your own fruit flavoring to plain yogurt with fresh, canned, or frozen fruit. Blend in chopped fruit, berries, or fruit purée.

As a way to get your "five-a-day" (fruits and vegetables), enjoy a baked apple or pear for dessert. Poach it in fruit juice and any "sweet" spice.

Substitute prepared foods from the supermarket, processed with less added sugars: canned fruits in natural juices and unsweetened cereals.

In some foods, you can use intense sweeteners, such as aspartame or saccharin. They're almost calorie free! However, because they don't function in food like sugars do, their use is limited. *Refer to page 136, "Intense Sweeteners: Flavor Without Calories," for more about these sweeteners.*

Making a gelatin salad or dessert? Rather than using flavored gelatin, dissolve unflavored gelatin in fruit juice. Then sweeten with an intense sweetener.

Add Life to Your Spices—And Herbs, Too!

With today's cuisine, we've discovered a new world of taste. Innovative uses of herbs and spices offer a flavor advantage as we trim fat and sodium from cooking. And the result is a new fusion of flavors!

Herbs and spices have a long culinary tradition. If you're a history buff, you know that spices have been traded throughout the Mediterranean and Middle East for more than 2,000 years. In the first century, Apicus, who was a Roman epicure, described herb combinations to enhance the flavor of food. Spices were the motive for Christopher Columbus' forays across the ocean. Now, with our nutrition interest and a world that's smaller than ever, we have more herbs and spices...in new combinations...than we've known before.

Many people confuse the terms "spice" and "herb." There is a difference. Spices, which grow in tropical areas, come from the bark, buds, fruit, roots, seeds, or stems of plants and trees. Usually, they're dried; garlic and gingerroot are two common exceptions. Herbs, which grow in temperate climates, are the fragrant leaves of plants. The same plant may supply both. For example, the seeds of coriander are used in curry powder, while the leaves of the same plant are called cilantro, a favorite seasoning in Mexican dishes.

Locking In Flavor: How to Store Herbs and Spices

Your herbs and spices won't keep indefinitely—even dried! To lock in the aromatic flavors of fresh and dry herbs, you need to store them carefully.

Store dry herbs and spices in tightly-covered containers—in a cool, dry, dark place (not the refrigerator). Avoid placing your spice rack near a window or above the stove. Heat, bright light, and air destroy flavor. Moisture can cause herbs and spices to mold.

Date dry herbs and spices when you buy them. Then use them as you need them, but preferably within a year. After a while, even properly stored seasonings lose their full "bouquet."

To check the freshness, rub seasonings between your fingers, and smell the aroma. If there's not much, get a new supply.

One way to keep fresh herbs longer: treat them like a bouquet of flowers! Snip the stem ends, then stand them in a glass of water. Cover them with a plastic bag, and store in the refrigerator. Change the water every couple of days.

Growing your own herbs? Preserve them for those long, cold weather months. Either freeze, dry, or add fresh herbs to oils and vinegars. Be aware that some herbs are better dried, for example bay leaves, marjoram, oregano, and summer savory.

➢ *To freeze them...* Wash and dry them well; then seal them in plastic freezer bags. Or snip herbs, then freeze them with water in ice cube trays. Adding an "herb ice cube" to soups and stews is easy! Basil, chives, dill, fennel, parsley, rosemary, and tarragon are among the herbs that freeze well.

➢ *To dry them in the oven...* Wash the herbs first, blot them dry, and remove the leaves from the stems. Place the herbs on baking trays in a single layer. Heat them in the oven at 100° F for several hours with the door slightly open. Remove the leaves before they get browned. Cool, then store in tightly-covered containers.

➢ *To dry them in the microwave oven...*Wash the leaves first, then place them between paper towels. Then dry the herbs on the lowest setting for two or three minutes.

A Pinch of Flavor: How to Cook With Herbs and Spices

Add a pinch of this and a pinch of that. Used carefully, herbs and spices make many foods distinctive and "simply flavorful"!

Dry or fresh—which herbs should you use? Nothing beats the delicate flavor of fresh herbs. But they're not always available. And unless you have your own herb garden in your backyard or on your windowsill, fresh herbs can be expensive. Whether you use fresh or dry seasonings, use them carefully to gain their best flavor advantage:

have you ever wondered

...how to reduce the "fire" caused by eating hot chile peppers? Try dairy foods! Caesin, the main protein in milk, washes away the substance in hot chiles that makes your mouth and throat "burn." Hot chile peppers do "fire up" the flavors of Thai dishes, Mexican salsas, and Cajun foods, among others. To tone down the heat, remove the seeds and inner membranes of hot chiles. To avoid a burning sensation on sensitive skin as you handle hot chiles, use rubber gloves. Never touch or rub your eyes—or any other sensitive areas—when you're handling them.

...what a flavor extract really is? Extracts are concentrated flavorings that come from different foods and plants. Some are made by distilling fruits, seeds, or leaves; anise, vanilla, peppermint, and almond extracts are made this way. Because they are so concentrated, use just a few drops. Meat, poultry, and vegetable extracts are made by concentrating the stock, or cooking juices. ✦

Before using fresh herbs, wash them! Then pat them dry with paper towels.

If fresh herbs have woody stems, strip off the leaves before using them. Discard damaged leaves. If the stems are soft and pliable, use them, too. Stems often carry a lot of flavor and aroma.

HERBED VINEGARS

Although today's supermarket shelves are stocked with herbed vinegars, why not make your own? They're less costly—and very satisfying to make. They also make great gifts from your kitchen!

Sterilize the bottle. Wash the cap, or obtain a clean cork.

Insert a combination of fresh herbs (stems and leaves) and spices into the bottle.

Fill the bottle with vinegar. You can use any vinegar as a base: white, red wine, cider, or rice vinegar. Herbs and spices may go better with some vinegars than others.

Put on the cap, or insert the cork. Store the bottle in a cool, dark place. Allow the flavor to develop for two to three weeks.

Try these flavorful combinations: fresh tarragon in cider vinegar; garlic cloves, fresh rosemary or sage, and lemon peel in white wine vinegar; and fresh mint and orange peel in cider vinegar. For fun, make herbed vinegar with edible flowers: for example, nasturtiums with peppercorns, garlic cloves, whole cloves, and cider vinegar.

Note: Homemade herbed oils and garlic oils may pose a food safety risk. *Refer to page* 315. ✦

To harvest herbs, pick them at their peak of flavor. That's just before they bloom. Remember, the flowers on many herb plants are very flavorful, too.

To release more flavor and aroma, crumble dry, leaf herbs—basil, oregano, savory, and tarragon, among others—between your fingers. Or use a mortar and pestle. Finely chop fresh herbs.

In dishes that require a long cooking time, such as soups, stews, and braised dishes, add herbs and spices toward the end of cooking. That way, their flavor won't cook out.

For chilled foods, such as salads and dips, add seasonings several hours ahead. That allows time for their flavors to blend.

When substituting fresh for dry herbs, use this equivalent: 1 tablespoon of fresh herb equals 1 teaspoon of dried herb. Dry herbs are stronger than fresh; powdered herbs are stronger than crumbled herbs.

Add dry herbs and spices to liquid ingredients. They need moisture to bring out their flavors.

Chop fresh herbs very fine. Kitchen shears are great for mincing and snipping. With more cut surfaces, more flavor and aroma are released.

Use seasonings with care—especially if you're not familiar with their flavor. They should enhance, not disguise, the aroma and taste of food. Start with 1/4 teaspoon of dry herbs for 1 pound of meat or 1 pint of sauce. You can always add more herbs and spices, but you can't take them away!

Avoid overwhelming a dish with seasonings. A few simple herbs and spices bring out the flavor of food without confusing your tastebuds.

If you're doubling a recipe, you may not need to double the herbs. Use just 50 percent more. If you triple the recipe, double the seasonings.

Vary herbs and spices in your meal. Variety is the spice of a pleasing meal!

Use seasoning blends, including curry, fine herbes, and bouquet garni. Each one is really a blend of herbs—and maybe spices, too. Curry powder is a pulverized mixture of as many as 20 different spices, herbs, and seeds. The spice turmeric is the ingredient that makes curried dishes so yellow. *For a recipe to make your own curry, refer to* "Kitchen Nutrition: Salt-Free Herb Blends" *on page* 164. Fine herbes usually refers to a mixture of chopped herbs, such as chervil, chives, parsley, and tarragon. Bouquet garni is a bundle of herbs, often parsley, bay leaf, and thyme, that's added to soups, stews, and braised meat or poultry. Usually they're tied up in cheesecloth or placed in a metal tea ball. That way, bouquet garni is easy to remove later.

If you grow an herb garden, experiment with less common varieties: pineapple sage, orange mint, burnet, lemon basil, and coriander, among others.

Grow scented geraniums, too: apple-, lemon-, peppermint-, and rose-scented geraniums, to name a few. Their aromatic leaves and flowers offer a nice garnish and flavor to sauces, salads, vinegars, and baked foods. Besides, they'll give your garden a wonderful scent!

The chart on page 353, "Quick Reference: Herbs and Spices," *suggests the herbs and spices that complement a variety of foods. Refer to the chart* "Name That Cuisine!" *on page* 213 *for the unique seasonings that define various ethnic cuisines. Refer to* "Kitchen Nutrition: Salt-Free Herb Blends" *on page* 164.

Foods for All "Seasons"!

For a few easy ideas to use herbs and spices in food preparation, start with these tips:

For baked chicken, fill the cavity with herbs and citrus peel—perhaps rosemary and sliced lemon—then roast it in the oven.

Cook strong-flavored vegetables, such as cabbage, with savory to cut down on the strong aroma, yet enhance the flavor.

Add flavor with herb and spice rubs. Rub an herb mixture onto the surfaces of tender cuts of meat, poultry, and fish before cooking. Flavors usually develop more when the rub is on the food longer. To intensify the flavor, use more herb rub. For a simple rub, just combine garlic and lemon pepper. *For more ideas, refer to the chart, "Rub Combos," below.*

Use herbed yogurt as a flavorful dip or vegetable topping. To get you started, blend dill, parsley, chives, and garlic into low-fat yogurt.

Make no-fat marinades with an acid ingredient—vinegar or fruit juice—and herbs or spices. For

RUB COMBOS

Experiment with your own favorite blend of herbs and spices for all sorts of great rubs. You don't need a recipe. Just combine flavors that taste good together. Use rubs on tender cuts of meat, poultry, and fish. To apply the rub, gently press the mixture onto the surface of the meat prior to cooking. Flavors usually become more pronounced the longer the seasoning mixture is on the meat. Try these for starters:

Citrus Rub: Combine grated lemon, orange, or lime peel (or a combination) with minced garlic and cracked black pepper.

Pepper-Garlic Rub: Combine garlic powder, cracked black pepper, and cayenne pepper.

Italian Rub. Combine fresh or dried oregano, basil, and rosemary with minced Italian parsley and garlic.

Herb Rub. Combine fresh or dried marjoram, thyme, and basil.

Source: Lean 'N Easy: Preparing Meat with Less Fat and More Taste, *Chicago:* National Cattlemen's *Beef Association,* 1994. ✦

example, orange juice and nutmeg make a nice combination. A splash of herbed vinegar adds a flavor spark to salads and soups.

Flavor mineral water, iced tea, lemonade, and spritzers with the leaves of scented geraniums, sprigs of fresh herbs, and edible flowers. Allow enough time for the infusion of their flavors and aromas.

Quick Reference: Herbs and Spices

Not sure what herbs and spices to use? Use this quick reference to enhance the flavor of foods in every part of your meal. This is just a partial list—add your flavor creativity to this list, too.

CHEESE AND OTHER DAIRY FOODS	
Cheddar and American cheese	chile powder, chives, mustard seed, paprika, turmeric
Cottage cheese	chives, paprika, parsley
Yogurt	cinnamon, chives, dill
EGGS	
scrambled eggs, omelets, quiche	basil, chives, marjoram, oregano, tarragon, thyme
FISH	
finfish (mild)	basil, bay leaf, chile powder, dill, fennel, ginger, oregano, paprika, sage, tarragon, thyme
lobster	garlic, tarragon
shrimp	basil, dill, ginger
FRUIT	
All kinds of fruit	cinnamon, cloves, ginger, mint, nutmeg, rosemary
MEAT	
Beef	basil, rosemary, savory
Ham	cloves, mustard seed, tarragon
Hamburger, meatballs, meatloaf	basil, celery seeds, marjoram, oregano, onion
Lamb	garlic, mint, oregano, rosemary
Liver	basil, onion
Pork	cayenne pepper, chile powder, cinnamon, cloves, rosemary, sage, thyme
Pot roast	bay leaf, black pepper, thyme
Stew (beef)	basil, bay leaf, black pepper, celery seed, cinnamon, garlic, marjoram, oregano, thyme
Veal	basil, curry powder, oregano, rosemary, sage, thyme
POULTRY	
Chicken	ginger, marjoram, sage, tarragon
Stuffing	basil, marjoram, onion, parsley, sage, savory
POTATOES, PASTA, RICE	
Potatoes	basil, caraway, chives, dill, marjoram, parsley, savory
Pasta and couscous	basil, chives, marjoram, oregano, saffron
Rice	cumin, fennel, saffron, turmeric
SALADS	
Chicken	chives, celery seed, oregano, tarragon
Egg	marjoram, tarragon
Fish	chives, marjoram, oregano, tarragon
Garden greens	basil, black pepper, chives, garlic, marjoram, mint, onion, tarragon, thyme
Vegetables	oregano
SAUCES	
General	parsley
Cheese	chives, paprika, red pepper
Tomato	basil, fennel seed, oregano, paprika, red pepper, sage, thyme
Creamy	basil, curry powder, marjoram, tarragon, thyme
SOUPS	
Chicken	bay leaf, mace, marjoram, paprika, parsley, sage, thyme
Clear broth	basil, paprika, parsley
Creamy	chives, rosemary, sage, tarragon
Fish	bay leaf, celery seed, saffron, tarragon, thyme
Legumes	basil, coriander, oregano, rosemary, savory, thyme
Mushroom	tarragon
Potato	chives, curry powder, dill
Tomato	allspice, basil, cloves, garlic, sage
Vegetable	allspice, basil, bay leaf, marjoram, black pepper
VEGETABLES	
General	basil, parsley
Baked beans	allspice, chile powder, cloves, mace, red pepper
Broccoli	caraway, oregano
Brussels sprouts	marjoram, sage
Cabbage	caraway, celery seed, mint, tarragon
Carrots	basil, bay leaf, ginger, marjoram, mint, oregano, thyme
Cauliflower	marjoram, nutmeg
Green beans	basil, cloves, marjoram, sage, savory
Lima beans	sage, savory
Mushrooms	marjoram, oregano, tarragon, thyme
Onions	basil, oregano, thyme
Peas	basil, marjoram, mint, oregano, sage, tarragon, thyme
Potatoes	garlic, parsley
Spinach	marjoram, nutmeg, rosemary
Squash and sweet potatoes	allspice, cinnamon, cloves, ginger, thyme
Tomatoes	basil, bay leaf, cloves, marjoram, nutmeg, oregano

Adapted from Gilliard, Judy with Joy Kirkpatrick. The Flavor Secret, *Minneapolis: Chronimed Publishing,* 1994.

your nutrition check-up

Kitchen Nutrition IQ

Do you cook with nutrition in mind? Test your kitchen nutrition IQ to see if what you know shows up in how you cook!

Do You…	**Always**	**Usually**	**Sometimes**	**Never**
Trim visible fat from meat and poultry?	___	___	___	___
Keep edible peels on fruits and vegetables—just wash them, not peel?	___	___	___	___
Remove the skin from poultry before eating it?	___	___	___	___
Use garnishes to make food look more appealing?	___	___	___	___
Cook vegetables just until they're tender-crisp?	___	___	___	___
Skip the salt in cooking water for pasta, rice, other grains, and vegetables?	___	___	___	___
Cook with whole-grains?	___	___	___	___
Try to include foods with different colors and tastes in a meal?	___	___	___	___
Add legumes to salads, soups, or other foods?	___	___	___	___
Sprinkle cheese on salads, soups, and vegetables for more calcium?	___	___	___	___
Cook vegetables with the lid on the pot—in just a small amount of liquid?	___	___	___	___
Sweeten foods with fruit, fruit juice, or fruit purées?	___	___	___	___
Use ingredients with less fat, such as low-fat yogurt, lean ground meat, and defatted broth?	___	___	___	___
Boost calcium in soups, cooked cereals, and casseroles with dry milk?	___	___	___	___
Drain fat off meat when it's cooked?	___	___	___	___
Use herbs, spices, or lemon juice, rather than salt, to flavor food?	___	___	___	___

your nutrition check-up (continued)

Do You...	Always	Usually	Sometimes	Never
Prepare foods with vegetables that have more calcium, such as broccoli and greens?	___	___	___	___
Use lower-fat cooking methods: broil, grill, roast, stir-fry, steam, microwave, and braise?	___	___	___	___
Taste before adding salt to foods?	___	___	___	___
Use cooking water from vegetables for soups, stews, or sauces?	___	___	___	___
Subtotal	___	___	___	___

Now Score Yourself

"Always" 3 points
"Usually" 2 points
"Sometimes" 1 point
"Never" 0 point

Your Total Score ____

With 50 to 60 points, you're "kitchen nutrition savvy."

With 40 to 49 points, improving your food preparation skills would make a nutrition difference!

With 21 to 39 points, you've got the hang of it. Now turn those "sometimes" answers to "usually" and "always."

With 20 points or less, read the chapter again. There's lots to learn!

real life nutrition

What's for Dinner?

Darren's in charge of dinner on Saturday night. And he's got a good lasagna recipe. "This is great," he thought, "and we've got all the ingredients in the kitchen." But as he checked the recipe, he realized it could use some changes. "Hmmm...just like the car. It needs a major overhaul!"

Look at Darren's recipe for lasagna. What 10 ways might he change the recipe for taste, nutrition, and overall appeal?

Lasagna

8 ounces lasagna noodles
2 tablespoons cooking oil
1/4 cup chopped onion
1/2 pound ground beef
1 1/2 cups water
1 can (8-ounce) tomato sauce
1 can (6-ounce) tomato paste
1/2 cup canned mushrooms, drained
1/2 teaspoon garlic salt
1 teaspoon dried basil
1 teaspoon dried parsley
1/2 teaspoon dried oregano
2 cups creamed cottage cheese
1 egg
1 teaspoon salt
1/4 teaspoon pepper
4 ounces mozzarella cheese, shredded (1 cup)
1 cup grated Parmesan cheese

Preheat oven to 350° F. Cook lasagna noodles in salted water according to package directions. Drain and rinse. Heat oil in a medium-size skillet; add onions and sauté until translucent. Remove from pan and set aside. Brown beef in the skillet. Add water, tomato sauce, tomato paste, mushrooms, garlic salt, basil, parsley, and oregano. Simmer for 1 hour.

In a separate bowl, combine cottage cheese, egg, salt, and pepper. In another bowl, combine mozzarella cheese and Parmesan cheese.

In a greased 12- x 8-inch baking dish, alternate layers of lasagna noodles, ground beef sauce, mozzarella-Parmesan mixture, and cottage cheese mixture, ending with mozzarella-Parmesan cheese mixture. Bake for 40 minutes. Remove from oven; let stand for 15 minutes before serving. Makes 6 servings.

Nutrition information per serving

490 Calories   260 Calories from Fat

	% Daily Value*		% Daily Value*
Total Fat: 29 g	45%	Protein: 31 g	
Saturated Fat: 10 g	50%	Vitamin A	26%
Cholesterol: 72 mg	24%	Vitamin C	30%
Sodium: 1,790 mg	75%	Calcium	51%
Total Carbohydrate: 27 g	9%	Iron	20%
Dietary Fiber: 4 g	16%		
Sugars: 1 g			

**Daily values are used with food labeling.*

real life nutrition (continued)

To change the recipe for taste and nutrition, Darren might:

For less fat and/or cholesterol:

➢ Use extra lean ground beef, not regular ground beef.

➢ Cook ground beef in a strainer in the microwave oven; drain off fat.

➢ Cook and stir onion in a nonstick pan coated with nonstick vegetable oil spray; skip the cooking oil.

➢ Use low-fat or reduced-fat cottage cheese, perhaps combined with plain low-fat yogurt.

➢ Use part-skim mozzarella cheese.

➢ Cut back on the Parmesan cheese.

➢ Use two egg whites instead of one whole egg.

➢ Use a nonstick baking pan; avoid greasing the pan.

➢ Change the recipe yield to 8 servings.

For less sodium:

➢ Skip the salt in the cooking water for pasta.

➢ Use no-salt-added tomato sauce and tomato paste.

➢ Switch from garlic salt to minced garlic cloves.

➢ Substitute herbs for the salt in the cottage cheese mixture.

For more fiber and other nutrients:

➢ Switch to whole-wheat lasagna noodles.

➢ Add shredded carrots, chopped bell peppers, or chopped spinach to the sauce mixture.

For taste and appeal:

➢ Use fresh rather than dry herbs.

➢ Use defatted, low-sodium beef broth instead of water.

➢ Sprinkle with chopped parsley or another garnish just before serving.

Now give yourself a taste treat. Make Darren's version of lasagna with at least five recipe modifications.

Chapter Fifteen

Your Food Away From Home

Whether a rushed, fast-food meal, lunch in the company cafeteria, a pizza delivered from a fax order, or an elegant evening of fine dining in a relaxing atmosphere, eating out is no longer just for special occasions. Instead, it's become part of our everyday lifestyle!

According to the National Restaurant Association, Americans (age eight and over) eat out four times a week on average—or about 200 meals a year. We eat lunch out almost twice as often as dinner. Even breakfast is gaining a growing market share of the foodservice dollar. Overall, foodservice currently receives about 44 percent of every dollar consumers spend on food.

Foodservice is any food that's not prepared in the kitchen at home. So who's cooking for us?

In growing numbers, we're looking for speed! Starting in 1994, fast-foodservice, more recently referred to as quickservice, slightly edged out table-service restaurants in the amount of revenue they took in.

Table-service restaurants remain popular. Yet more and more, they're adding services, such as selling their own baked bread or bottled salad dressings. Menus feature traditional dishes prepared in traditional ways. In addition, many restaurant kitchens are reducing fat and sodium in their food preparation, while enhancing taste with a fusion of new food and seasoning combinations. The result: a new style of American dining.

Supermarkets also have gotten into the foodservice business, allowing consumers to "take out" in order to "eat in." The foodservice industry feeds us in many other places, too: airlines, convenience stores, recreational facilities, institutions (schools, hospitals, businesses, others), sports and cultural events, home-delivered meals, and vending machines, among others.

Where do you typically eat out—and how often? Whatever the answer, the more you eat away from home, the greater the impact foodservice meals and snacks make on your overall daily food intake.

Dining Out the Healthy Way

Eating out? When you pick up an item here and there, it's easy to lose sight of your overall eating pattern. And there's always the urge to splurge when away from home. Too many calories, too much fat and sodium, too few vitamins and minerals, and too little fiber—these can be typical nutritional challenges of any eating style, home or away. It takes a little more thought when you eat a significant number of meals away from home.

With a little forethought and planning, eating out can be as nutritious as it is great tasting. Just follow a few smart-eating strategies, and enjoy a variety of healthful and flavorful foods in moderate amounts.

did you know

...a do-it-yourself salad, chosen from the salad bar, often has more calories than a deluxe burger, fries, and a shake?

...a quickservice chicken or fish sandwich may be higher in fat than a hamburger?

...pasta with a tomato-based sauce usually has fewer calories than pasta with a creamy white sauce?

...without charge, most airlines will substitute a fruit or seafood platter, or a low-fat, low-sodium, or other special meal for the regular in-flight menu?

...at your request, many restaurants will adjust the seasoning and sauces on menu items?

...drinking a glass of water or juice per hour of airline flight prevents dehydration and minimizes jet lag? Alcoholic beverages can promote dehydration and may increase jet lag.

...during a long car trip, a stop every hour or two for a brisk walk and drink of water helps prevent constipation—a frequent complaint of long-distance automobile travelers? ✦

Restaurant Eater's Tip List

An occasional meal with elegant, creamy sauces or a rich dessert pastry needn't upset your balanced, moderate eating plan. So enjoy! There's no reason to feel guilty about your meal.

If you do eat out regularly, though, don't throw caution to the wind. Whether you choose a full-service restaurant, cafeteria, or quickservice chain, you can follow the same smart-eating habits that you practice at home. Plan your meal out ahead, ask about the menu, and order carefully to match your needs.

Plan Ahead

Before you get to the restaurant, plan. That way, you can fit the meals you eat away from home into your whole day's eating plan—without overdoing on calories and fat.

Map out your restaurant plan of action—perhaps planning a light dinner if you just ate a big lunch, or deciding ahead to skip a rich dessert (order fresh fruit instead). Stick to your plan when you order. Select the kinds and amounts of food that best fit your plan rather than succumb to temptations on the menu.

Think about your food choices over the whole day. If you know that your restaurant meal will have more calories or fat, eat foods with less calories or fat during other meals that day. Just make trade-offs so you stick to your fat budget. *Refer to "Quick, Easy Trade-Offs," on page 256 for more about making trade-offs.*

Avoid skipping breakfast or lunch to "save up" for a fancy restaurant dinner. This strategy often backfires! It's easy to overindulge at the restaurant when you're over-hungry. Eating small meals earlier in the day is a better approach.

Pick Your Restaurant Wisely

Your choice of restaurants can affect your ability to order healthfully.

Patronize restaurants with a variety of menu alternatives. That gives you more to choose from. Selecting restaurants that prepare food to order allows more control over the calories, fat, or sodium if you can make special requests.

To save a little money, look for restaurants with "early bird" specials. They may offer smaller portions for a lower price. A small portion may be enough.

For variety, try "ethnic" food. Chinese, Italian, and Mexican foods are the most popular ethnic cuisines in the United States. If you have the choice, stretch your food experience further with other ethnic restaurants, perhaps Indian, Thai, Mid-Eastern, or Caribbean. *Refer to "Eating Out Ethnic Style" on page 375 for tips on food selection.*

Get to Know Menu Language

Primavera, bearnaise, scalloped. What do all these menu terms mean? Knowing menu terms and cooking basics makes ordering easier, especially if you need to control calories, fat, and other nutrients in your menu choices.

Learn to speak the language! *Check the chart "Menu Language" on page 362 for terms that alert you to foods with more or less fat, and with more sodium.*

Look for foods with simple preparation, such as steamed vegetables or broiled chicken. Often, foods that are prepared simply are lower in fat and calories. For instance, the term "al dente" is used to describe how pasta and vegetables are cooked—only until firm when bitten, not soft or overdone. Literally translated, it means "to the tooth." Vegetables cooked "al dente" retain more nutrients than those that are overcooked.

To "lighten" up, look for menu items typically prepared with less fat. *"May I Take Your Order?" on page 363 shows healthy choices that tend to be lower in fat and calories, alongside menu items that probably have more.*

Check the menu language even further! With new government regulations, terms like "lean" and "light" on restaurant menus are defined consistently effective May 1997. This means that menu terms will have roughly the same meaning as terms used on food labels. *For more on label terms, refer to "Label Lingo" on page 271.*

Have It Your Way!

Be assertive about menu questions and special requests—and realistic, too. Service-oriented restaurants want to please customers so they'll come back. In fact, many will change the way food is prepared or served if you request changes in advance.

Not sure what to order? For leaner cuisine, you can order these foods with confidence. Even if they don't appear on the menu, restaurants that prepare food to order may serve these items to you. Just ask.

Appetizers fresh fruit cup, broth, bouillon, or consommé, fruit or vegetable juice, marinated vegetables, crudités, or raw vegetables, with a yogurt or salsa dip, seafood cocktail

Breads hard rolls or whole-wheat buns, French or Italian bread, bread sticks, melba toast, or saltine crackers

Salads salads with dressing on the side, vegetables, steamed vegetables, plain or with a lemon wedge, grilled or roasted vegetables

Entrées lean meat, fish, and poultry that are broiled, grilled, or roasted, with any sauces served on the side (remove visible fat and poultry skin); vegetarian dishes that go easy on cheese or cheese sauces

Desserts fruit ice or sorbet, fresh fruit, angel food cake with fruit, low-fat frozen yogurt, cappuccino ✦

Ask how the food is prepared, especially if the description isn't clear or the food is unfamiliar. And find out what ingredients are used and if substitutions can be made. These are the type of questions you might ask:

➢ How are the vegetables seasoned? Are they salted? Is butter or margarine added?

➢ Is the fish broiled or fried? Is it cooked with butter, margarine, or some other fat?

➢ How is the sauce prepared?

➢ Can I have the sauce (or salad dressing or whipped topping) on the side?

➢ Is the soup clear or cream-based?

➢ Can I substitute a baked potato or a salad for the fries?

Ingredients in sauces stump many restaurant goers. What, for example, is the difference between a bearnaise sauce and a bolognese sauce? Which one is apt to be lower in fat? *For a quick description of sauces you may see on restaurant menus, refer to page 364, "Gourmet's Guide to Sauces."*

Find out about portion sizes. Big portions tend to be the hallmark of restaurant service. For example, a 4- to 6-ounce portion of meat, poultry, or fish probably is enough, especially if you've eaten another Meat Group serving during the day. (*Refer to chapter 11, "Planning to Eat Smart," for more about the five food groups.*) If the menu offers a choice—a 12-ounce steak or a 6-ounce filet mignon—go for the smaller portion to save on calories, fat, and money.

If a portion seems bigger than you need, ask for a half portion, choose an appetizer portion, take part of it home, or share with your meal companion.

Don't see anything on the menu that matches your needs? Ask if you can order "off the menu." If you're watching your fat intake, you might request broiled fish or chicken breast with just a little herb and lemon juice, or fresh fruit for dessert, or low-fat milk if it's not on the menu. *See "On the 'Leaner' Side" on page 361 as a quick reference for nutritious menu items with less fat.*

Choose a varied meal when you eat out, as you would at home. If you can order à la carte, make sure you choose from a variety of food groups in the Food Guide Pyramid. À la carte means that each item is separately ordered and priced. *Refer to chapter 11 for a review of the Food Guide Pyramid.* À la carte ordering offers an advantage. You can get just what you want without the extras you won't eat.

Take your palate on a taste adventure. When you eat out, order something you've never tried before—or that you usually don't eat at home. Feeling a little cautious about something new? Try an appetizer portion. Restaurants are a great place to try new foods—and add variety to your eating!

Menu Language

Looking for foods with less fat or sodium? Check the language on the menu. Although they offer no guarantee, terms used to describe menu items often give clues to more sodium, or more or less fat.

MENU CLUES: LESS FAT

baked	poached
braised	roasted
broiled	steamed
cooked in its own juices	stir-fried
grilled	

MENU CLUES: MORE FAT

au gratin or in cheese sauce	french fried
batter fried	hollandaise
bearnaise	pan fried
breaded	pastry
beurre blanc	prime
buttered	rich
creamed	sautéed
crispy	scalloped (escalloped)
deep fried	with gravy
double crust	with mayonnaise
en croute	with thick sauce

MENU CLUES: MORE SODIUM

barbecued	smoked
cured	teriyaki
in broth	with creole sauce
marinated	with cocktail sauce
pickled	with soy sauce

Be specific and direct when you make a special menu request or ask the kitchen to alter the preparation. For example, politely ask the wait staff to "hold the mayonnaise," "broil fish without butter," "bring dry toast," or "serve dressing on the side." (Often a hefty amount of dressing is served on salads.) Or ask "can you omit the salt?"

If you don't plan to eat a side dish or sauce that's served with your order, ask to have it left off your plate—perhaps skip tartar sauce served with fish, or chips served with a sandwich.

Pass on all-you-can-eat specials, buffets, and unlimited salad bars if you tend to eat too much. Unless you pay attention to feelings of fullness, these food bars easily add up to too many calories.

For a lighter meal, choose an appetizer as a main course. Along with a side salad, bread, and a beverage, that may be all you need.

If you choose a higher-fat entrée, balance it with lower-fat choices for the rest of the meal. Perhaps balance fettuccine alfredo, which is higher in fat, with fresh fruit for dessert. Remember no food is off limits. Just make trade-offs to trim fat or sodium when you dine out, as you do at home. *To learn how to make trade-offs, refer to "Quick, Easy Trade-Offs" on page* 256.

Order what you want, despite what others choose. For example, you don't need to order an appetizer just because your companions do.

If the food isn't prepared as you ordered, send it right back. Ask for something else if necessary.

Help Yourself

Practice the art of balance and moderation as you help yourself to a variety of food and beverage choices.

Can't resist the urge to overindulge on tortilla chips or the basket of bread served when you're seated? Do you nibble mindlessly on snacks, such as pretzels, nuts, and chips, brought to the table with a beverage order? Take a few and then move them, or ask to have them removed from the table.

If you need help in curbing a big appetite, enjoy plenty of lower-calorie foods, such as a salad or appetizer crudités (raw vegetables). And go easy on dressing and dip.

Variety on the menu? The choices on the left have fewer fat and calories than their counterparts on the right.

ENJOY MORE OFTEN...	ENJOY SOMETIMES...
Consommé, gazpacho	Cream soups, soups topped with cheese
Vegetable plate with salsa, steamed vegetables	Pâté, quiche lorraine, stuffed appetizers
Garden, tossed, or spinach salad with dressing on the side, crisp and crunchy vegetables	Salads with large amounts of dressing, bacon, avocado, cheese, croutons, and mayonnaise-laden salads such as potato, macaroni, and tuna
Grilled meats, broiled or flame cooked	Breaded or batter-dipped meat or extra gravy
Broiled, steamed, poached, roasted, baked, Cajun, or blackened	Breaded, fried, sautéed, au gratin, escalloped, en croute, creamed, en casserole, or Kiev entrées
4- to 8-ounce steak	More than 8-ounce steak
Au jus, provençal, or fruit sauces	Gravy, bearnaise, hollandaise, or bechamel sauces
Baked potatoes (plain or with a small amount of of margarine or sour cream), red skin potatoes	Home-fried and deep-fried potatoes, twice-baked potatoes, croquettes, buttered noodles
Sandwiches on whole-wheat, pita, or rye with mustard or low-fat mayonnaise	Sandwiches on croissants or biscuits
Plain whole-wheat or multi-grain rolls or bread sticks	Garlic bread, cheese spreads, flavored butters
Fruit fruit or sorbet	Cheesecake, French pastries

Gourmet's Guide to Sauces

What's in the sauce? Use this list as a quick reference to make you a savvy restaurant patron.

Alfredo: creamy Italian sauce, typically prepared with butter, heavy cream, and Parmesan cheese

Bechamel: basic white sauce, made with flour, milk, and butter, and flavored with onion

Bearnaise: thick French sauce made with white wine, tarragon, vinegar, shallots (onion), egg yolks, and butter

*Bourguignonne**: French sauce made with red wine, carrot, onion, flour, and a little bacon

Bolognese: Italian meat sauce, made with ground beef and sometimes pork and ham and sautéed in a small amount of butter and/or olive oil with tomatoes, other vegetables, herbs, and sometimes wine. Also referred to as a ragu bolognese sauce.

Hollandaise: thick sauce, made with vinegar, egg yolks, melted butter, and lemon juice

*Marinara**: Italian tomato sauce, made with tomato and basil, and perhaps other seasonings, such as onions, garlic, and oregano

*Neapolitan**: Italian tomato sauce with garlic, onion, olive oil, and no meat

*Sweet-and-Sour**: sugar and vinegar added to a variety of sauces, typically to Chinese and German sauces

*Velouté**: light, stock-based sauce. Stock is the broth left from cooking meat, poultry, fish, or vegetables. Velouté is like a bechamel sauce, but stock is used instead of milk.

*Vinaigrette**: oil-and-vinegar combination ✦

**These sauces tend to be lower in fat. But the ingredients vary and so does the fat content.*

Eat slowly, and stop eating before you feel too full. Eating slowly gives your body time to feel full. Ask the wait staff to remove your plate when you're done, even if a little food is left. You also might ask for a carry-home container.

Limit alcoholic beverages. Healthy eating guidelines advise no more than one (if you're a woman) or two (if you're a man) alcoholic drinks per day. That includes wine and beer. Alcohol provides calories with no nutrients, and it tends to increase the appetite, resulting in overeating. Try mineral water or club soda with a twist of lemon or lime as another option.

Trying to control calories? If you choose to resist rich desserts, don't even peek at the dessert tray when the wait staff brings it by. If you really want a rich dessert, share with someone else.

Enjoy, Enjoy, Enjoy!
Eating is an occasion that can "nourish" the soul as well as the body. Food, including meals eaten away from home, can be one of life's true pleasures.

Savor each bite, and enjoy food at a leisurely pace. After all, you won't need to spend time afterward washing dishes!

If you're eating with others, enjoy the social time, the ambiance of the restaurant, and all the other pleasures that go with a meal "on the town."

Sizing Up Salad Bars

A salad bar can serve up a healthful meal all by itself—or as a great side dish. The variety of vegetables and fruits is often loaded with vitamins A and C, folic acid, and fiber. A trip to the salad bar may also surprise you! It can supply more calories than a burger and fries, or a steak-and-potato dinner. An average plate from the salad bar can top out at more than 1,000 calories, depending on the choices and portions selected. Not so surprisingly then, salads are reported to be a main source of dietary fat for many women.

Where do excessive amounts of calories, fat, even sodium come from on a salad? Not from the lettuce, tomatoes, cucumbers, and other fresh vegetables. Depending on the amount, regular salad dressings, along with many higher-fat toppers such as cheese, croutons, bacon bits, nuts, chow mein noodles, and olives, can heap calories on a bed of raw vegetables. "Dressed" side dishes (potato salad, pasta salad, and macaroni salad), creamy soups, cheese and crackers, even desserts—all with more calories—line up on the salad bar, too.

The calories and fat in salads that fill your plate depend on the items you choose. To control calories and fat in your salad concoctions:

Build a Healthful Salad

Imagine a salad bar with bowls and bowls of ingredients. Your plate is empty. How would you build your salad? Choose the ingredients from the list below—and decide how much you'd take of each one. When your salad plate is "full," add up the calories and fat. You may be surprised.

	Amount	Calories	Fat (g)
GREENS			
bean sprouts	1/4 cup	8	trace *
lettuce	1 cup	10	trace
spinach	1 cup	10	trace
OTHER VEGGIES			
artichoke hearts	1/4 cup	20	trace
beets	1/4 cup	15	0
bell pepper	2 Tbsp	3	trace
broccoli	1/4 cup	6	trace
carrot, shredded	1/4 cup	15	trace
cauliflower	1/4 cup	6	trace
cucumber	1/4 cup	4	trace
green peas	2 Tbsp	30	trace
mushrooms	1/4 cup	5	trace
olives, ripe	2 Tbsp	30	4
onion	1 Tbsp	8	0
radishes	2 Tbsp	2	trace
tomato	1/4 cup	15	trace
FRUIT			
avocado	1/4 cup	75	8
canned peaches, in juices	1/4 cup	25	0
fresh melon	1/4 cup	15	trace
fresh strawberries	1/4 cup	10	trace
mandarin orange segments in juice	1/4 cup	25	0
raisins	2 Tbsp	60	0
BEANS, NUTS, AND SEEDS			
chickpeas	1/4 cup	40	<1
kidney beans	1/4 cup	55	trace
sunflower seeds	1 Tbsp	80	7

* *"Trace" on all the vegetables and fruits is about .05 to 0.2 grams of fat.*
** *Nutrient values have been rounded.*

	Amount	Calories	Fat (g)
MEAT, POULTRY, FISH, AND EGGS			
eggs, chopped	2 Tbsp	25	2
ham, chopped	1 oz	35	1
popcorn shrimp	1 oz	30	<1
turkey in strips	1 oz	35	<1
tuna in spring water	1 oz	35	<1
surimi	1 oz	30	<1
CHEESE			
cottage cheese, creamed	1/4 cup	60	3
cottage cheese, 1% lowfat	1/4 cup	40	<1
Cheddar cheese, grated	2 Tbsp	55	5
Parmesan cheese	2 Tbsp	45	3
OTHERS			
chow mein noodles	1 Tbsp	50	2
bacon bits	1 Tbsp	25	2
MIXED SALADS			
potato salad, made with mayonnaise	1/4 cup	110	9
tuna salad, made with mayonnaise	1/4 cup	190	10
three-bean salad in vinaigrette	1/4 cup	60	0
DRESSINGS			
blue cheese, reg.	2 Tbsp	155	15
Italian, reg.	2 Tbsp	160	15
French, reg.	2 Tbsp	135	15
Italian, low cal.	2 Tbsp	15	0
lemon juice	2 Tbsp	8	0
oil and vinegar	2 Tbsp	100	8
1000 Island, reg.	2 Tbsp	120	10
vinegar	2 Tbsp	4	0

SAFE TAKE-OUT

Whether from restaurants, supermarkets, or quickservice establishments, take-out foods have become part of our way of life. Many of these foods are perishable, so they need to be handled with care to avoid foodborne illness.

For Hot Foods...

Hot foods need to be held above 140° F, and cold foods, at 40° F or below. Make sure the food is hot when it's picked up or received. Then eat it within two hours.

If the food won't be eaten for more than two hours, you might refrigerate it in shallow, covered containers. Then reheat it to a temperature of 165° F, or until it's hot and steaming. You might check the temperature with a meat thermometer. *Refer to "Using a Meat Thermometer" on page* 319. Or reheat it in a microwave oven—covered and rotated for even heating. Then let it stand for two minutes for more thorough heating.

As another option, you might keep hot take-out food in the oven or in a crockpot at 140° F or above—but not if you'll hold it much longer than two hours. Food will lose its appeal if it's held longer. Cover it with foil to keep it moist. And check the temperature with a meat thermometer.

For Cold Foods...

Cold foods need to be held at 40° F or below. If you don't eat cold take-out foods right away, refrigerate them. Discard any foods kept at room temperature for more than two hours. If the heat tops 90° F, toss it after one hour.

For deli platters that stay on the buffet, keep the platters on bowls of ice. And for take-out foods, store them in chilled, insulated coolers. ✦

Enjoy plenty of vegetables, legumes (such as kidney and garbanzo beans), and fresh fruit. Dark green leafy vegetables, such as spinach and romaine, supply more vitamins than iceberg lettuce does.

For protein, add legumes, lean meat, turkey, crabmeat or surimi, and cheese. Cottage cheese, cheese, and yogurt on the salad bar add calcium to your salad.

Go easy on higher-fat toppers and mayonnaise-based side salads.

If you're tempted to overdo, use a small salad plate, not a dinner plate, at the salad bar.

Dress your salad for success! A 2-tablespoon ladle of French, Italian, blue cheese, or Thousand Island dressing adds about 150 calories to an otherwise low-calorie salad. Too often, people spoon on double that amount or more! Go easy on how much you add, and occasionally try a low-fat or fat-free dressing—or just a splash of flavored vinegar.

Eating Out Safely!

Almost nothing can ruin a trip or a pleasant meal out more than foodborne illness. Although restaurants in the United States, Canada, and many other developed nations must pass strict public health regulations, you're still wise to double check for cleanliness. Any restaurant can have an occasional lapse in sanitation procedure, and in some parts of the world, these regulations may not exist. For help in finding a restaurant with high standards, ask for recommendations from hotel staff or other knowledgeable people, if possible.

These tips can help ensure that the meal you eat away from home won't come back to "bite you":

Check for cleanliness. Although you probably can't see into the kitchen, you can learn a lot about a restaurant by looking at the public areas. Look for:

- tables that are wiped clean—using clean cloths

- well-groomed waiters and waitresses
- clean silverware, tablecloths, glasses, and dishes
- adequate screening over windows and doors to keep out insects
- an absence of flies, which can spread disease
- clean restrooms with soap, hot water, and towels or air dryers
- a clean exterior with no uncovered garbage outside

Before you eat from a food bar, check the temperature. A hot buffet should be piping hot. And a cold salad bar should be well chilled or placed on ice.

Order food from food bars and displays only if the food is properly covered with a sneeze guard or hood. This includes desserts and appetizers.

Avoid eating raw meat, which may carry bacteria and parasites. These menu items are served raw: steak tartare (raw ground beef and raw eggs) and carpaccio (thin-sliced raw beef). Sashimi, or raw fish, is popular among many restaurant goers. *Refer to page 315, "Is Raw Seafood Safe to Eat?" for specific guidance on sashimi.*

Check your burgers. They should be cooked until the center is no longer pink and the juices run clear, usually "medium" or "medium-well." If it's not cooked thoroughly, send it back!

For more information on foodborne illness—and how to prevent it—refer to chapter 13, "The Safe Kitchen."

Fast Food, Healthful Food

Fast food: it's been part of the American food culture for many more years that most people realize! If your great-grandparents traveled by train in the early 1900s, they likely devoured "fast-food," or quick meals, from the dining car. When the automobile took over, the dining car concept was transformed and reinvented as fast-food restaurants dotting the roadside.

As we know it today, the so-called "fast-food chain," or quickservice restaurant, is a phenomenon that's only about 45 years old. Quickservice food for a fast-oriented society was launched in the 1950s. Changing lifestyles and family mobility after World War II gave birth to this huge segment of the foodservice industry. That's when eating out became a necessity, rather than an occasional treat. By 1978, fast-food sales amounted to about $9 billion annually in the United States. And that figure multiplied to a projection of almost $106 billion for 1998, almost equalling the projected $110 billion for table-service restaurants.

At the start, quickservice was limited to mainly fried chicken, hamburgers, french fries, ice cream, and soft drinks. While these items still dominate, today's quickservice menus offer far more options. From grilled chicken sandwiches and broiled fish, to salads, to low-fat milk, most major chains now also feature lower-calorie, lower-fat menu items. Besides hamburger and fried chicken outlets, quickservice restaurants feature pizza, seafood, pasta, Tex-Mex food, stuffed baked potatoes, and deli items, along with every type of quick ethnic cuisine. The food court in shopping malls has fast foods to please every palate. Breakfast has become a big quickservice food business. And more entrepre-

have you ever wondered

...if Caesar salad on the menu is safe to eat? Probably so, but ask how it's prepared. In the past, a Caesar salad, made with a raw egg, was often prepared right at your table. Today, most Caesar salads are made in the kitchen with a pasteurized egg product or cooked salad dressing, following safe food handling techniques. Some Caesar salads are eggless.

...what a reduction sauce is? A reduction sauce is usually broth or pan juices boiled down to concentrate the flavor and thicken the consistency. Unlike many other sauces, flour or others starches aren't used as thickeners. ✦

DINING SOLO

Whether on a business trip, a lunch hour break, or a dinner in town, eating out can feel lonely, boring, even uncomfortable when you're alone. Some "singles" have the urge to skip meals; some, to order more. However, your body's nutrition needs don't change just because you're by yourself. With a few strategies, dining solo offers a different set of pleasures:

Take an avid interest in the dining experience. Talk with the waiter or waitress, and study the menu and the decor.

While waiting for your food, make your time productive. Read a book, write a letter, jot down your "to do" list, do a little work from the office, or simply reflect on your day.

Once your meal is served, put down the book or office work, and savor the flavors of the food. Eat slowly and pay attention to your feeling of fullness; you'll be less apt to overeat.

Give yourself variety! Rather than always heading for a quickservice meal when you eat out alone, try restaurants with a wider range of menu items. Perhaps an ethnic restaurant is nearby.

If you feel conspicuous by yourself, ask for a table off to the side. The reality is, however, you may be the only one who notices that you're a single diner.

When you're traveling and truly need to let down and be alone, choose a hotel with room service! ✦

neurs attract customers with fresh- and nutrition-positioned menus.

Other segments of the food industry are getting into the quickservice restaurant business, too. For example, your supermarket may sell quickservice foods for take-out: deli sandwiches, a salad bar, rotisserie chicken, hot soups, chili, and tacos, among other foods. Even convenience stores where you gas up your automobile sell fast-food—truly the "dining car" of the highway!

"Fast," "convenient," "reasonably priced," and "predictable" describe the collective identity for today's quickservice foods. Because menus are so varied, no overall comment can describe the nutritional value of fast foods.

Many ask: Are quickservice foods healthful? Overall, yes. They can supply the variety of nutrients the body needs if you choose wisely. In response to consumer demand, quickservice restaurant chains are offering more varied menus—and lower-fat options, too. Traditional meals—such as a burger, fries, a fried fruit turnover, and a soft drink, or fried chicken, biscuit, creamy slaw, and mashed potatoes with gravy—remain high in fat, saturated fat, sodium, and calories, yet low in vitamins A and C or calcium.

If you're a regular at the quickservice restaurant counter, keep these pointers in mind. And make your fast foods fit into an eating style that's varied, moderate, and balanced for your good health.

Be aware of the trend toward "big," "deluxe," or "super" size. Whether it's a sandwich, an order of fries, a milk shake, or another menu option, bigger portions mean more calories, and likely more fat, cholesterol, and sodium. For most people, the regular size is enough.

Go easy on snacks. A large order of fries and a large soft drink can add a hefty 500 or so calories to your day's intake!

Balance quickservice meals with other food choices during the day. As you order, consider the other foods you have eaten—or will eat—during the day.

As with any foods, look for variety in your order. Select a side order of salad, raw vegetables, or coleslaw for vitamins A and C, and fiber. Boost the calcium in your diet with a carton of 1 percent or skim milk.

Remember moderation and variety. Enjoy quickservice foods as part of your eating style, but not the same foods every day.

For more variety, enjoy quickservice food outlets with an ethnic theme: perhaps Chinese stir-fry dishes, a Mexican burrito, Japanese domburi, or a vegetable-stuffed pita with cucumber-yogurt dressing. Often food courts in shopping malls allow you to travel the world of flavor without leaving home.

On sandwiches and salads, go easy on condiments and dressings. Just one packet of mayonnaise (about 1 tablespoon) adds about 60 calories and 5 fat grams. The same size packet of tartar sauce has about 70 calories and 8 fat grams. And a 1 1/2-ounce packet of French dressing contains about 185 calories and 17 fat grams. Ask if low-fat or fat-free condiments, spreads, and dressings (mayonnaise, sour cream, or cream cheese) are available.

For fried foods, pay attention to the oil used for frying if you need to watch saturated fats. Most quickservice restaurant chains use 100 percent vegetable oil, which is cholesterol free and may be high in polyunsaturated fats. And they may say so on the menu. When french fries and other foods are fried in fat that's partly beef tallow, these foods contain more cholesterol and saturated fats.

Better yet, choose fried foods only as "sometimes" foods. Rely mostly on grilled, broiled, steamed, and microwaved fast foods instead.

Split your order. Halve the calories, and double the pleasure by sharing your fries or snack sandwich with a friend!

For some general nutrition facts, check "Quickservice Food Facts" on page 373, or at quickservice restaurants, look for nutrition information on posters or printed in brochures.

Break-FAST

Breakfast out—with the more hectic pace today, it's not surprising that more and more consumers, particularly those heading to work, buy breakfast on the run. It may be a quick breakfast sandwich from the drive-up window, a sit-down meal of eggs and hash browns or pancakes from the quickservice counter, or coffee and a deli muffin or bagel to eat at the desk. When these quick breakfasts become a regular eating pattern, it's time to take stock of their nutritional impact!

The quickservice menu usually offers fewer options for breakfast than for lunch and dinner. Many choices are high in calories, fat, cholesterol, and sodium. Follow these tips to fit quickservice breakfasts into your own healthful diet.

EATING AND DRIVING: A SAFETY ISSUE?

With Americans' hectic lifestyles, about 8 percent of all meals are eaten in the car. However, eating and driving can pose a risk to your personal safety!

When time is short, many people assume that the fastest food comes from the drive-up window. Not so. Many times the drive-in line is longer than that for counter service. Beyond that, eating or drinking while driving not only can be messy, it's also dangerous when one hand is on the wheel and the other is holding a burger or steaming hot beverage. And if the car phone rings at the same time, you may really be in trouble!

If you do eat in the car, pull over first—in a parking lot, city park, or by the curb. Then enjoy those few minutes of eating without thinking about driving, too. Better yet, relax with your food in the mall or on a bench in the park. ✦

Order dry cereal and milk. Cereal offers a serving from the Bread Group, along with complex carbohydrates and B vitamins and almost no fat. If you choose a whole-grain or bran cereal, you get more fiber, too. A carton of milk, which equals one Milk Group serving, supplies about 300 milligrams of calcium; that's about 25 to 30 percent of the calcium you need daily. Pour some on your cereal, perhaps some in your coffee—and drink the rest!

Start your day with pancakes! For less fat, top with syrup rather than margarine or butter. Enjoy a half serving of bacon, or ask for Canadian bacon, which is leaner.

Order juice as your breakfast beverage. With just one cup or carton of orange juice, you'll get 100 percent of the vitamin C your body needs in a day.

At a deli? Ask for yogurt to go with your bagel and juice. An 8-ounce carton of low-fat fruit yogurt supplies about 315 milligrams of calcium, 225 calories, and just 2 to 3 fat grams.

Go easy on breakfast sandwiches. They're usually high in calories, fat, cholesterol, and sodium. A typical bacon,egg, and cheese biscuit sandwich, for example, has about 475 calories, 30 fat grams, and 1,260 milligrams of sodium.

To cut down on fat and sodium, ask to skip the bacon or sausage on your breakfast sandwich. Or substitute ham or Canadian bacon for less fat. Order a breakfast sandwich on a bread that's very low in fat: an English muffin, bagel, or even a hamburger bun. To compare, a typical quickservice breakfast biscuit can have about 18 fat grams, and a croissant, about 10 fat grams, compared to 1 fat gram in an English muffin.

Instead of a breakfast sandwich, order an English muffin, bagel, or toast. To save on fat grams, spread cream cheese, margarine, or butter on bread lightly, or use jam or jelly. Round out your meal with fruit juice and milk or yogurt.

If you're a quickservice regular, go easy on egg entrées. One egg every other day is probably enough. The reason? A large egg has 213 milligrams of dietary cholesterol. Health experts advise that healthy people consume 300 milligrams of cholesterol or less per day, and no more than four egg yolks a week in their overall diet.

Choose breakfast muffins wisely. Even muffins such as "bran" or "oat bran" muffins can be higher in fat than you'd think. A typical muffin has about 5 fat grams—more if it's jumbo size!

Burgers, Chicken, or Fish?

A burger, chicken, or fish—any one might be the centerpiece of your quickservice meal. Hamburgers may be America's all-time favorite fast food. But chicken and fish have gained a significant market share, in part because consumers perceive them as lower in fat. It's true that chicken and fish sometimes have a lean advantage. However, quickservice food preparation—breading, battering, and frying—bump up the calorie and fat content significantly. As a result, a fried fish or chicken sandwich may supply more calories and fat than a hamburger.

To keep the lean advantage of hot sandwiches and boost the contribution of other nutrients, consider these guidelines:

Order leaner varieties of traditional sandwiches. For example, some restaurant chains sell burgers made with lean ground beef.

Boost the nutrients in all kinds of hot sandwiches—burgers, chicken, or fish—by adding tomato slices and other vegetables. If you're coming up short on calcium during the day, add cheese. For a fiber boost, ask for a whole-wheat bun.

Cut calories by ordering sandwiches without higher-fat condiments and special sauces, such as mayonnaise-based spreads and tartar sauce. Instead use mustard, relish, or ketchup. As a rule of thumb: calories go up with the number of "extras."

Skip the super-size sandwich; go for the regular size instead. The bigger size can about double everything, including the calorie, fat, and sodium content. A large hamburger, for example, supplies about 510 calories and 28 fat grams compared with

275 calories and 12 fat grams in a regular hamburger. A regular burger has about 2 ounces of cooked meat, compared with 3 to 4 ounces in a larger sandwich.

To lower the calories and fat, remove the crispy crust from fried chicken and the skin from rotisserie chicken. If you prefer fried chicken, order the regular variety rather than "extra-crispy," which soaks up more oil when cooked. The batter or breading may have a high-sodium seasoning, too, so you lower the sodium by removing the crust. And eat just one piece, rather than a two- or three-piece order. Chicken nuggets are usually fried and may contain skin and meat (white and dark). Poultry skin is high in fat.

Choose broiled or baked fish if you have a choice. But be aware, the fillets on most fish sandwiches are battered and fried. Go easy on tartar sauce; ask for tomato-based cocktail sauce instead.

On the Side...

Whether a quickservice meal or any other meal, variety adds nutrients. So round out your meal with other menu items—perhaps a salad, potato, fruit, juice, milk, or frozen yogurt. In most quickservice restaurants, your options may be limited. But you still can get maximal nutrition mileage from the choices available to you.

Spuds...

Order a baked potato either as a side dish or an entrée. Served plain, a baked potato is fat-free and cholesterol-free with almost no sodium. It also supplies complex carbohydrate, fiber, vitamin C, and other vitamins and minerals. Go easy on higher-fat toppings: bacon, sour cream, and butter. For less calories and fat, top with broccoli, salsa, chili, or cottage cheese—and boost the nutrient content, too. Along with a salad and milk, a broccoli-cheese spud or a chili spud makes a nutritious meal!

Go easy on fries when you're watching calories and fat grams. Or ask for the small order, then share with someone. French fries themselves offer some vitamin C; however, they also add fat to an already higher-fat meal. If you have the option, consider a plain, baked potato or mashed potatoes to control fat—and go easy on the gravy! Find out how mashed potatoes with gravy are prepared; check the nutrition information if it's posted.

As another alternative to fries or fried onion rings, order corn on the cob.

Salads...

Order a garden salad with dressing on the side. Use a reduced-fat dressing, and cut the calories in half. *For tips on eating from the salad bar, refer to* "Sizing Up Salad Bars" *on page* 364.

Go easy on prepared salads made with a lot of mayonnaise or salad dressing, such as creamy coleslaw, potato salad, and macaroni salad. They have more fat than salads prepared with a vinaigrette, such as coleslaw or three-bean salad in an oil-and-vinegar dressing.

Beverages...

Make beverages count! For both the flavor and the nutrients they supply, round out your meal with milk or juice. Many quickservice restaurant chains offer low-fat and skim milk. For a flavor switch, try chocolate or other flavored milk.

An 8-ounce carton of milk supplies about 300 milligrams of calcium, as well as protein, riboflavin, vitamin D, and other nutrients. And an 8-ounce carton of orange juice supplies 75 milligrams of vitamin C, which more than meets your daily need.

have you ever wondered

...why you might see a sign on a salad bar that says "sulfite-free?" A small percentage of the population is sensitive to sulfites, often used in the past to keep raw fruits and vegetables fresh. However, in 1986 the Food and Drug Administration banned their use on salad bars. Some restaurants still post the sign to reassure customers. *For more information on food sensitivities, refer to chapter* 9. ✦

Recognize the nutritional differences in quickservice beverages. Soft drinks are okay to drink sometimes, too. They provide fluids, a source of energy, and enjoyment. They don't, however, contribute the other nutrients supplied by milk or fruit or vegetable juice.

If the added calories match your eating plan, enjoy a milk shake as part of your quickservice meal or snack. A shake of any flavor is a good calcium source—if it's made from milk. A 10-ounce strawberry shake contains about 320 calories. It can serve double duty—as both your beverage and dessert. Super-size shakes, with their 18 ounces, may supply a hefty 575 calories.

For an ideal thirst quencher, choose water. Unless bottled, it's usually offered free as a customer service!

Desserts...

Go easy on fried fruit fritters or turnovers—eat them only if they fit within your daily calorie and fat budget.

Check to see if fresh fruit is available. You may be pleasantly surprised. As another option, bring fresh fruit from home, perhaps an apple, banana, pear, or grapes.

For a refreshing dessert, enjoy frozen yogurt—or a scoop of ice cream. For fewer calories, go easy on fudge sauce or syrup toppings.

Pizza—As You Like It!

Pizza is nutritious fast food because you can reap the nutritional benefits of three or more food groups from pizza. The crust supplies complex carbohydrates and B vitamins, the cheese is a good source of calcium and protein, and the tomato sauce and vegetable toppings add vitamins A and C. Meat or seafood toppers add protein, iron, and some vitamins, too. *Also refer to "Pizza: What Food Group?" on page 255.*

The actual nutrient content depends on what you put on top. Crust piled high with veggies has more fiber and vitamins A and C. Sausage and pepperoni up the protein as well as the fat and sodium content. The good news is: You can be the architect of your pizza, controlling the toppings along with the nutrient and calorie content and the flavor.

Consider the crust. For more fiber, build your pizza on a whole-wheat crust. To trim the calories, order a thin-crust pizza, rather than a thick crust or deep-dish pizza.

Load up on vegetable and fruit toppings for less fat, more fiber, and more vitamins A and C. *Check the "Pizza Toppers" on this page for low-fat choices.*

Go easy on higher-fat toppings: bacon, pepperoni, prosciutto, sausage, olives, anchovies, and extra cheese. If you like higher-fat toppings, one is likely enough! If your blood pressure is sodium-sensitive, know that these foods add sodium, too.

Choose lean toppers from the Meat Group, such as lean ham, Canadian bacon, or shrimp.

Enjoy the variety of toppings and new combinations available in some pizza parlors. Many "new toppers" are vegetables—artichoke hearts, broccoli florets, and asparagus spears!

Pizza Toppers

ENJOY MORE OFTEN...	ENJOY SOMETIMES...
artichoke hearts	anchovies
bell peppers	bacon
broccoli florets	extra cheese
Canadian bacon or lean ham	pepperoni
crabmeat	prosciutto
eggplant slices	sausage
green onion, chopped	
jalapeño peppers	
lean ground meat	
mushroom slices	
onion slices	
pineapple chunks	
shrimp	
spinach	
tomato slices	
tuna	
zucchini slices	

QFF – Quickservice Food Facts

MENU ITEM	PORTION SIZE	CALORIES	FAT (G)	SATURATED FAT (G)	CHOLESTEROL (MG)	SODIUM (MG)
BREAKFAST						
Egg and sausage biscuit	1 (180g)	580	39	15	300	1,140
Egg and cheese croissant	1 (127g)	370	25	14	215	550
Danish, cheese	1 (91g)	355	25	5	20	320
Danish, fruit	1 (94g)	335	16	3	20	330
English muffin with butter	1 (63g)	190	6	2	15	390
English muffin with egg, cheese, and Canadian bacon	1 (146g)	385	20	9	235	790
French toast sticks	5 (141g)	355	19	8	115	510
Hash brown potatoes	1/2 cup	150	9	4	10	290
Pancakes with butter and syrup	3 (232g)	520	14	6	55	1,100
CHICKEN						
Chicken nuggets	6 pieces (102g)	290	18	6	60	540
Fried chicken, dark meat	drumstick & thigh	430	27	7	165	760
Fried chicken, white meat	side breast & wing	495	30	8	150	980
Chicken fillet sandwich	1 (182g)	515	30	9	60	960
Rotisserie chicken white meat, quarter with skin	5 oz	330	18	5	150	530
Rotisserie chicken dark meat, quarter with skin	5 oz	330	22	7	150	450
Grilled chicken breast sandwich	1	310	9	1	60	890
FISH						
Fish fillet, fried	3 oz (91g)	210	11	3	30	480
Fish sandwich with tartar sauce	1 (158g)	430	23	5	55	620
SANDWICHES						
Bacon cheeseburger, double patty	1 (150g)	470	28	13	100	800
Cheeseburger, regular	1 (113g)	295	14	6	40	610
Hamburger, regular	1 (90g)	275	12	4	35	390
Hamburger, large, with lettuce and tomato	1 (218g)	510	28	10	85	830
Hamburger, double meat patty	1 (226g)	540	27	10	120	790
Submarine sandwich	1 (228g)	455	19	7	35	1,650
Roast beef sandwich	1 (139g)	345	14	4	50	790
Hot dog	1 (3.5 oz)	240	15	5	45	670
Chili dog	1 (4.5 oz)	295	13	5	50	480
MEXICAN						
Taco, small	1 (171g)	370	21	11	55	800
Taco salad, large with shell	21 oz	905	61	19	80	910
Burrito, bean and cheese	2 (93g)	375	12	7	25	1,170
Burrito, beans and meat	2 (110g)	510	18	8	50	1,340
Enchilada, beef and cheese	1 (192g)	325	18	9	40	1,320
Frijoles (refried beans) with cheese	1 cup (167g)	225	8	4	35	880
Nachos with cheese	6-8 nachos (113g)	345	19	8	20	820
Nachos with cheese, beans, beef, and peppers	6-8 nachos (255g)	570	31	13	20	1,800

Continued on next page…

QFF – Quickservice Food Facts (continued)

Menu Item	Portion Size	Calories	Fat (g)	Saturated Fat (g)	Cholesterol (mg)	Sodium (mg)
OTHER						
Pizza, cheese	1/8 of 12-inch pie (63g)	140	3	2	10	340
Pizza, meat and vegetables	1/8 of 12-inch pie (79g)	185	5	2	20	380
Pizza, pepperoni	1/8 of 12-inch pie (71g)	180	7	2	15	270
Chili con carne	1 cup (253g)	255	8	3	135	1,010
SIDES						
Coleslaw	3/4 cup (99g)	145	11	2	5	270
French fries, fried in vegetable oil	30-40 fries (115g) 20-25 fries	355 235	19 12	6 4	0 0	190 120
Onion rings	8-9 rings (83g)	275	16	7	15	430
Potatoes, mashed, with gravy	1/2 cup (80g)	100	10	6	25	510
Potato, large, baked, plain	1 (8.8 oz)	270	<1	trace	0	20
Potato, large, baked, with cheese and broccoli	1 (339g)	400	21	9	20	480
Potato, large, baked, with cheese and chili	1 (339g)	480	22	13	30	700
New potatoes	1 cup (4.6 oz)	130	4	<1	0	20
Salad, vegetables without dressing*	1 1/2 cups (207g)	30	<1	0	0	50
Salad with egg and cheese, without dressing *	1 1/2 cups (217g)	100	6	3	100	120
Salad with chicken without dressing *	1 1/2 cups (217g)	105	2	<1	70	210
Vegetables, steamed	1 cup (3.7 oz)	30	<1	trace	0	10
BBQ baked beans	1/2 cup	130	2	1	5	540
Pasta salad, tortellini	1 cup	430	25	5	55	660
DESSERTS						
Cookies, animal crackers	1 box	300	9	4	10	270
Cookies, chocolate chip	1 box	235	12	5	10	190
Sundae, hot fudge	1 (158g)	285	9	5	20	180
Ice milk, soft serve	1 cone (103g)	165	6	4	30	90
Fruit pie, fried	1 pie (85g)	265	14	6	15	330
BEVERAGES						
Milk, whole	8 oz	150	8	5	35	120
Milk, 2% low-fat	8 oz	120	5	3	20	120
Milk, skim	8 oz	85	<1	<1	5	130
Milk, chocolate, 2% low-fat	8 oz	180	5	3	15	150
Soft drink, cola, regular	12 oz	150	0	0	0	10
Soft drink, cola, calorie-free	12 oz	1	0	0	0	10
Iced tea, sweetened	12 oz		0	0	0	10
Iced tea, unsweetened	12 oz	5	0	0	0	<10
Orange juice	8 oz	105	<1	0	0	6
Shake, chocolate	10 oz	360	11	7	35	270
Shake, low-fat, chocolate	10 oz	320	2	<1	10	240
Coffee, black	6 oz	5	0	0	0	<10
Coffee with 1 Tbsp half-and-half cream	6 oz	25	2	1	5	10

**Refer to page 365, "Build a Healthful Salad," for nutrition information about salad dressings.*

Order a salad to complement your pizza. Salad not only adds nutrients and fiber, but also helps you fill up. You may be less likely to eat another pizza slice.

Order a reasonable-size pizza. Limit yourself to two or three slices—or one slice if you're really watching calories. Calories from any pizza, even a veggie pizza, add up when you overeat. A typical slice—one-eighth of a 12-inch meat and cheese pizza—supplies about 185 calories.

Deli Sandwiches

Sandwiches, as well as yogurt, fruit, salads, soups, bagels and muffins, milk, flavored waters, coffee, and tea—the deli bar sells an array of foods and beverages.

Of the many foods at the deli bar, the sandwich takes center stage. It's true that some sandwiches have more calories, fat, and perhaps sodium than others. The great thing is that you often can order a deli sandwich just as you want it!

Just start with bread. Choose a whole-grain bread, roll, or pita pocket for more fiber.

Next, the filling—2 to 3 ounces of lean meat or poultry contribute protein, iron, and nutrients. Add a slice of cheese to boost the calcium content. For fillings with less fat, order lean roast beef, ham, or turkey. Some delis use meats that are 90 percent or more fat-free—just ask. Request tuna, ham, or egg salad made with less mayonnaise or with reduced-fat dressing, if available.

Have your sandwich made to order with a spread that adds flavor, such as mustard. To control fat and calories, ask the server to go easy on higher-fat spreads.

Layer on vegetables: perhaps red or green pepper, jalapeño, tomato, sprouts, cucumber, carrot shreds, or onion. They're low in fat, yet they supply vitamins A and C, fiber, and other nutrients.

Choose sandwich accompaniments to fit your healthful eating style. To cut down on fat, ask for carrot or green pepper sticks, rather than chips or creamy slaw. For less sodium, enjoy a cucumber spear instead of a pickle.

Eating Out Ethnic Style

As a nation of immigrants, the United States has always been home to ethnic cuisine. The real interest in "foreign-theme" restaurants grew in the 1960s with pizza parlors and Japanese table-top cooking. From there, our exposure to ethnic foods became more sophisticated. We added Mexican and more Asian flavors to our restaurant repertoire. Today, ethnic restaurants of one kind or another appear in almost every city and town. And according to the National Restaurant Association, 98 percent of all restaurants offer ethnic menu items.

What cuisines are most popular? Italian, Mexican, and Chinese (Cantonese), say trend-trackers. And French cuisine has been an upscale restaurant cuisine for years. But, according to the National Restaurant Association, our appreciation for ethnic flavors is growing with more and more restaurants featuring German, Greek, Japanese, and other Chinese cuisines, too. Others, including Caribbean, Mid Eastern, Korean, Thai, and Vietnamese, with their emphasis on grains and vegetables, likely will become more common as the decade wears on.

For fun, find the restaurant pages of your phone book. Now count—how many different ethnic cuisines are represented? To expand the variety in your eating style, try a new cuisine the next time you eat out!

Italian...Not Just Pizza and Pasta!

Italian cuisine is the most popular restaurant food in the United States. Two-thirds of all restaurants feature Italian dishes—and not just pizza and pasta! With the broad range of foods from every region, Italian foods are simple, flavorful, and nourishing.

Italian food is one of several Mediterranean cuisines receiving attention from both food and nutrition experts. Featuring pasta, risotto (rice dish), and polenta (cornmeal dish), Italian food is high in complex carbohydrates. The cuisine relies on smaller meat portions, and cheese is used to flavor many dishes.

Particularly with the foods of Southern Italy, olive oil is the primary cooking fat, in contrast to butter used in many northern Italian dishes. High in monounsaturated fatty acids, olive oil has some nutritional benefits. Regardless, go easy; any oil is still fat with the same number of calories per ounce as margarine and butter. *Refer to page* 56 *for more on monounsaturated fatty acids. For more about Mediterranean cuisine, refer to page* 214.

Consider these tips the next time you order Italian foods in any restaurant:

Enjoy crusty Italian bread—a slice or two, but not the whole basket! For less fat, go easy on butter or on olive oil for dipping, or enjoy the flavor of fresh bread as it is, without a spread. H*int*: Garlic bread is usually lathered in high-fat spreads, Parmesan cheese, and garlic before it arrives at your table. Plain bread is a lower-calorie, lower-fat choice.

Go easy on antipasto. "Antipasto" means "before the pasta," and it usually refers to a variety of hot or cold appetizers. In the Mediterranean tradition, they include cheese, olives, smoked meats, and marinated vegetables and fish. While they're nutritious, some may be high in fat and sodium. And nibbling appetizers, followed by a heavy meal, may add up to more calories than you expect.

have you ever wondered

...what "primavera" and "fresco" on menus mean? Translated from Italian, "primavera" means "spring style." In cooking terms, it refers to dishes garnished with raw or lightly-cooked fresh vegetables. "Fresco" means fresh. ✦

Order a fresh garden salad, or "insalata," to round out your meal, with salad dressing, perhaps herbed vinegar and olive oil, served on the side. Salads in Italian restaurants often are tossed with a variety of raw vegetables and mixed greens, including arugula, radicchio, bell peppers, tomatoes, and onion. As an entrée, salad with bread makes a nice, light meal.

Look for traditional bean and vegetable dishes on many Italian menus. Minestrone is a hearty, tomato-based soup with beans, vegetables, and pasta. White beans, called "fagioli," are featured in soups and risotto (rice dishes). "Florentine" dishes may be prepared with spinach.

Know menu lingo. For example, dishes described as "fritto" (fried) or "crema" (creamed) are higher in fat. "Primavera" refers to dishes prepared with fresh vegetables and herbs and varying amounts of olive oil. Sometimes primavera dishes are served with a creamy sauce; ask your waiter or waitress.

For enjoyment, order different types of pasta dishes—in shapes and sizes you may not find on supermarket shelves. Made of flour and water, pasta is a carbohydrate-rich food. Fat comes from the sauces and other ingredients tossed with pasta. Look for tomato-based sauces, such as marinara, that usually have more vegetables and less fat than creamy, white sauces, such as alfredo.

As a change of pace, order polenta, gnocchi, or risotto instead of pasta. Ask how these are made before ordering.

➢ Polenta, similar to a cornmeal mush, typically is served with sauce, vegetables, and meat; some ingredients may have more fat.

➢ Gnocchi, usually made from potatoes or flour, means dumplings; sometimes eggs, cheese, or chopped vegetables are mixed into the dough. After they're cooked in boiling water they may be baked or fried, then served with a flavorful sauce.

➢ Risotto, typically made from arborio rice, usually is cooked in broth and perhaps butter, often with meat, seafood, cheese, and vegetables. If your blood pressure is sodium sensitive, be aware that the broth may be salty.

➢ As another option, order ravioli, which are square "pillows" of pasta, filled with meat, cheese, or vegetables. Usually they're served with a sauce. Ask about preparation before you order; as appetizers, they may be fried.

Watch portion size. If you know the restaurant serves generous servings, order an appetizer portion, or share with someone else.

If you need to watch fat carefully, go easy on veal scaloppini, and chicken or veal parmigiana, which are sautéed or panfried. Parmigiana entrées also are breaded so they absorb more fat. As an alternative and a lower-fat option, order chicken or veal cacciatore or marsala. Cacciatore is a tomato-based sauce, and marsala is broth-based and cooked with wine.

For tips on ordering pizza, refer to page 372 of this chapter.

From the Italian Menu...

Enjoy More Often...

- ➢ Minestrone soup
- ➢ Garden salad
- ➢ Bread sticks
- ➢ Vinegar and oil dressing
- ➢ Pasta with red sauce, such as marinara
- ➢ Chicken cacciatore
- ➢ Cappuccino
- ➢ Italian fruit ice or fruit

Food Guide Pyramid with Popular Italian Fare

Fats, Oils, and Sweets—Use sparingly
Olives, olive oil, chocolate, pine nuts, Italian ice, whipping cream

Milk, Yogurt, and Cheese Group—2-3 servings daily:
gelato, mozzarella cheese, ricotta cheese, milk

Meat, Poultry, Fish, Dry Beans, Eggs, and Nuts Group—2-3 servings daily
beef, veal, sausage, squid, beans, lentils

Vegetable Group—3-5 servings daily
eggplant, mushrooms, peppers, artichoke, marinara sauce, spinach

Fruit Group—2-4 servings daily: blueberries, raspberries, dried figs,

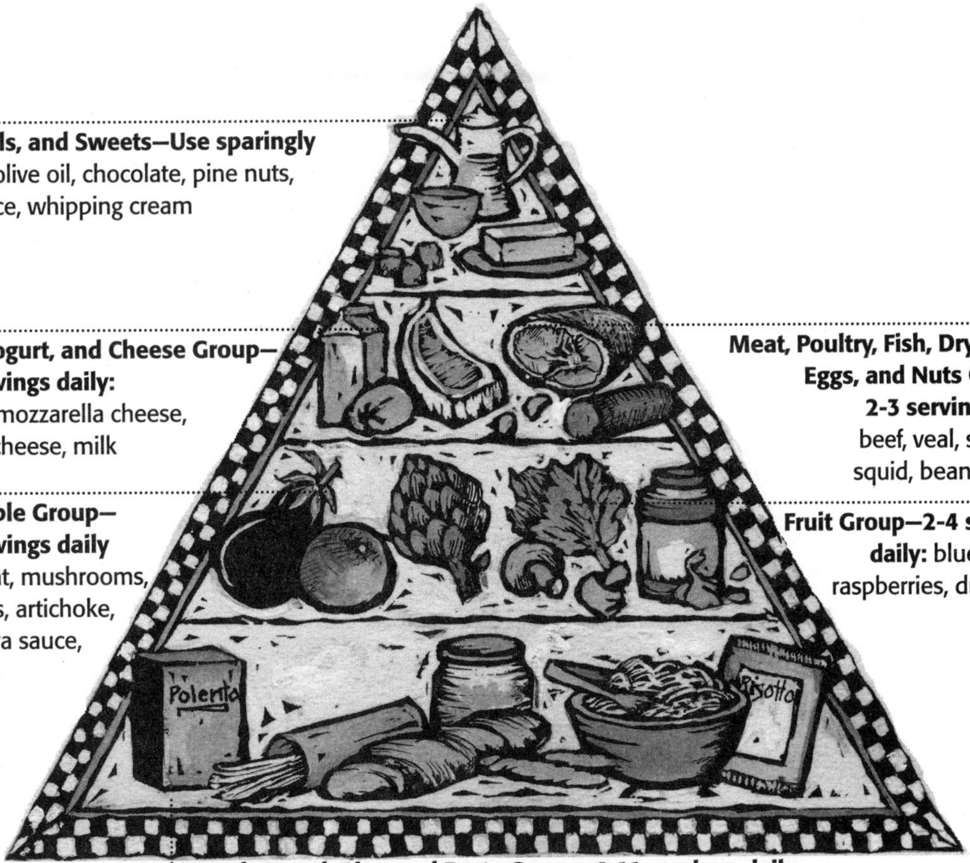

Bread, Cereal, Rice, and Pasta Group—6-11 servings daily
spaghetti, linguine, polenta, gnocchi, risotto

Eat Right America ® 1996

Enjoy Sometimes…

- Antipasto plates
- Buttered garlic bread
- Creamy Italian dressing
- Pasta with white sauce, such as alfredo
- Italian sausage and prosciutto
- Fried dishes such as eggplant Parmesan
- Cannoli (*Cannoli, cannelloni, and cannellini often get mixed up. Cannoli are deep-fried pastry shells, filled with ricotta cheese or whipped cream, and perhaps chocolate bits, nuts, and candied fruit. Cannelloni are pasta tubes filled with meat and cheese, and topped with sauce. And cannellini are white kidney beans.*)

It's Greek Food to Me!

According to reports from the National Restaurant Association, another Mediterranean cuisine is rising in popularity—Greek food. For many consumers, experience with Greek restaurants comes from fast-food courts in shopping malls. The popular gyro sandwich, souvlaki, Greek salad, rice pilaf, moussaka, and baklava are best known. But like other cuisines, full-service restaurants offer far more variety. To be a bit smarter with your order in Greek restaurants, consider these menu tips:

For a creamy dressing on salads, or a sauce on pita sandwiches, enjoy tzatziki. It's made with yogurt, garlic, and cucumbers. Sometimes tzatziki is listed on the menu as a salad.

Try tzatziki as an appetizer dip with pita bread, too. Enjoy smaller amounts of baba ghanoush, a higher-fat dip made with eggplant and olive oil, and of hummus, made with mashed chickpeas and sesame seed paste. Flavorful olive oil for dipping is often served with a basket of pita bread. Again go easy. Although low in saturated fat and cholesterol free, olive oil contains just as much fat as butter or margarine.

Ordering saganaki as an appetizer? Saganaki is thick kasseri cheese that's fried and sometimes flamed in brandy. To trim the fat, share with someone else.

For nutritious fast food, order pita bread, stuffed with Greek salad, lean meat, tabouli, or other ingredients. Tabouli is bulgur, mixed with chopped tomatoes, parsley, mint, olive oil, and lemon juice. For more fiber, ask for whole-wheat pita. Another popular use of the pita is the gyro, which is minced lamb, molded and roasted vertically. When cooked, the lamb is sliced and tucked into pita bread with grilled onion, bell peppers, and tzatziki sauce.

As a main dish, look for broiled and grilled meat, poultry, and seafood. The menu might have shish kebob, which is skewered and broiled meat and vegetables; souvlaki, which is lamb, marinated in lemon juice, olive oil, and herbs, then skewered and grilled; or plaki, which is fish broiled with tomato sauce and garlic.

As another menu option, try dolmas, or stuffed vegetables. Grape leaves are most commonly stuffed with ground meat; other vegetables, such as bell peppers, cabbage leaves, eggplant, and squash, are stuffed with mixtures of ground meat, rice, dried fruit, and pine nuts, too. Because they're steamed or baked, fat usually isn't added with cooking.

To boost fiber, order dishes made with legumes. In a full-service restaurant, you'll likely find mixed dishes and soups made with fava beans and other legumes.

Order a Greek salad to go with meals. Ask for dressing on the side. And go easy on the higher-fat, higher-sodium ingredients: anchovies, kalamata olives, and feta cheese.

Go easy also on rich Greek desserts, such as baklava. Made with phyllo and plenty of butter, sugar, and nuts, this sweet, compact pastry is very high in calories. It's wonderful, but a small serving is enough to satisfy an appetite!

From the Greek Menu…

Enjoy More Often…

- Broiled, grilled, simmered, and stewed dishes
- Greek salad
- Tabouli
- Dolmas
- Tzatziki
- Fresh fruit
- Pita bread

Enjoy Sometimes…

- Pan-fried dishes
- Vegetable pies such as spanakopita and tyropita
- Baba ghanoush
- Baklava
- Deep-fried falafal

Mexican Food: Tacos, Tamales, and More

From quickservice establishments to full-service restaurants, Mexican food and its Tex-Mex offspring are among America's favorite ethnic foods. One-fourth of all restaurants today feature foods with a Mexican flavor. The staples—tortillas, beans, and rice—are great sources of complex carbohydrates, and beans supply fiber, as well. Moderate portions of meat and poultry contribute adequate, but not lavish, amounts of protein. And beans and rice, or beans and tortillas when eaten together, also supply high-quality protein.

Depending on the choices, Mexican or Tex-Mex cuisine can be high in fat—and sodium, too. As with foods of every culture, you need to keep variety, moderation, and balance in mind:

For less fat and calories in Tex-Mex foods, order guacamole and sour cream on the side so you control the amount. For more vitamin A and C, use a heavy hand with tomato-based salsa. Because it's made with tomato, onion, chiles, and herbs, it's virtually fat-free, yet bursting with flavor!

Ask for soft tacos. Crispy tacos and tostadas are fried.

Ordering a taco salad? Enjoy, but go easy on the big tortilla shell it's served in or the taco chips on top—if you need to trim fat and calories. Enjoy warmed, soft tortillas on the side.

Go easy on nachos and cheese, or chile con queso, especially if it's just the appetizer before the meal. To cut in half the fat and calories from cheese, ask for half a ladle of cheese sauce, or half as much cheese shreds.

Order a low-fat appetizer: gazpacho (cold tomato soup), jicama and salsa, tortilla soup, or black bean soup.

Since portions for Mexican meals tend to be large, choose the regular plate, not the "deluxe combo" plate. For most people, that's plenty!

Choose mostly baked or stir-fried entrées, such as enchiladas or fajitas. Go easy on fried entrées, such as chile relleños, chimichangas, or flautas.

Although tacos, tamales, enchiladas, and burritos are among the most popular items, especially in

Menu Language

Learn to speak Mexican menu talk. Look for descriptions that offer clues to the fat content.

MENU CLUES: LESS FAT

- asada (grilled)
- mole sauce (chile-chocolate sauce)
- served with salsa verde (green chile sauce)
- simmered
- tomato sauce, picante
- topped with lettuce and tomato
- Veracruz-style (tomato sauce)
- with chiles
- wrapped in a soft tortilla

MENU CLUES: MORE FAT

- crispy
- fried
- layered with refried beans
- mixed with chorizo (Mexican sausage)
- served in a crisp tortilla basket
- smothered in cheese sauce
- topped with guacamole and sour cream
- chile con queso

Tex-Mex restaurants, Mexican and Southwestern restaurants offer a far broader menu. Next time, check the menu further. You may find salads with nopales, or cactus pads; chayote and jicama, which are starchy vegetables; and tomatillos, or green tomatoes. For prepared foods, look for Veracruz-style seafood dishes, which are cooked in an herbed tomato sauce; or chile verde, which is pork simmered with vegetables and green chiles.

From the Mexican Menu...

Enjoy More Often...

- Jicama with fresh lime juice
- Salsa
- Soft tacos
- Burritos, enchiladas, tamales, fajitas
- Red beans and rice*
- Spanish rice*
- Refried beans (no lard)
- Steamed vegetables
- Black bean soup, menudo, gazpacho
- Arroz con pollo (chicken with rice)
- Fruit for dessert, such as guava, papaya, or mango
- Flan or pudding

Enjoy Sometimes...

- Guacomole dip with taco chips
- Sour cream and extra cheese
- Crispy, fried tortillas
- Crispy tacos, taco salad
- Tostadas, chile relleños, quesadillas, chimichangas
- Refried beans (in lard)
- Honey-sweetened pastry and sopapillas
- Fried ice cream

* *The fat content varies depending on the ingredients and preparation method..*

Food Guide Pyramid with Popular Mexican Fare

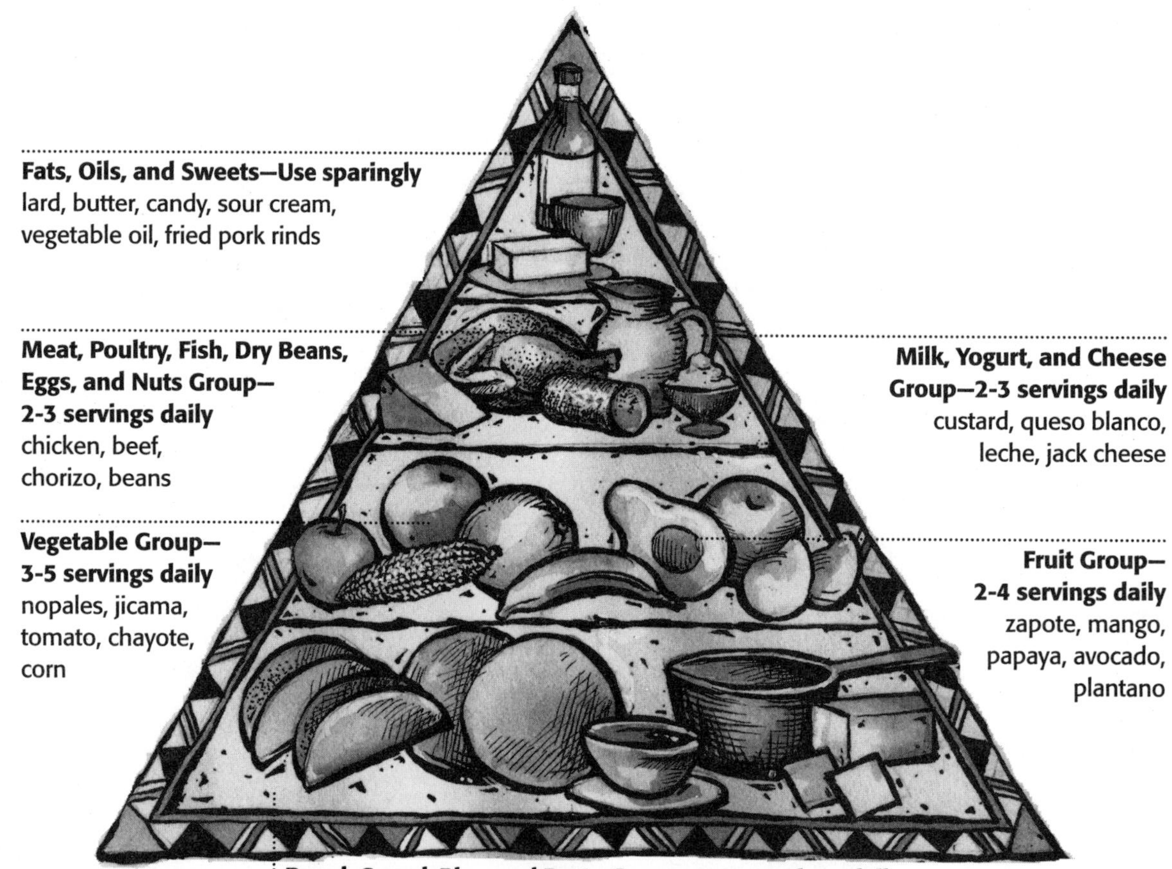

Eat Right America ® 1996

Chinese Fare

Most of us have said, "I know a great Chinese restaurant!" Chinese restaurants—full service or take-out—are among the three most popular for ethnic dining. From a culinary standpoint, Chinese cuisine is among those that have made significant contributions to the world's food choices. With its focus on vegetables, rice, and noodles, Asian-style cooking also has earned its place as a nutritious option in a healthful diet.

Chinese cuisine reflects the different cooking styles, ingredients, and flavorings of China's many regions. Restaurants may specialize in foods from Canton, Hunan, Peking (Beijing), or Szechuan, for example. Cantonese-style cooking is the most popular in the United States, largely due to the number of Cantonese immigrants in the mid-1800s who brought their cooking styles with them. Cantonese cuisine of southeastern China features roasted and grilled meat, steamed dishes, stir-fried dishes, and mild flavors. Szechuan and Hunan foods tend to be hot and spicy, and perhaps higher in fat. Peking cuisine of northeastern China is noted for skillful, subtle uses of seasonings. The term "Mandarin" on menus usually refers to aristocratic cuisine, featuring the finest aspects of all regional cuisines.

Unlike meals in the United States, Chinese meals emphasize rice or noodles and vegetables, with their contribution of complex carbohydrates. Vegetables are a good source of fiber and vitamins A and C, too. Meat, poultry, and seafood are served in small portions, often sliced and cooked with vegetables. Tofu, or soybean curd, is a common, high-protein, low-fat, cholesterol-free ingredient, too. Many Chinese dishes are roasted, simmered, steamed, or stir-fried, so they're likely low in fat.

The areas to watch in Chinese dining are fat and sodium. Deep-fat frying is a common cooking technique for many menu items. And sometimes, foods are stir-fried in large amounts of oil. For those who are sodium sensitive, know that two ingredients with more sodium—monosodium glutamate (MSG) and soy sauce—are often used to flavor foods. Even MSG, however, has one-third the sodium of table salt. *For more information, refer to "MSG—Sensitive?" on page 200.*

Calcium-rich foods are limited on Chinese menus since milk, cheese, and yogurt aren't part of the traditional cuisine. Most calcium comes from fish with edible bones and vegetables, such as broccoli and greens, although the amount per serving is much lower than a serving of milk.

Whether you eat in or carry out, keep these ordering tips in mind at a Chinese restaurant:

Enjoy the flavorful soups as a starter or main dish. Many are clear broth, made with small amounts of meat and vegetables. Made by cooking eggs in the broth, egg drop soup and hot-and-sour soup are higher in cholesterol; the amount, however, is small since there's not much egg in a single serving.

Go easy on fried appetizers at the start of your meal. Fried wontons, crab rangoon, and many egg rolls are deep-fat fried. As an option, order steamed spring rolls or egg rolls. Interesting tidbit: The term "egg roll" is an American term for what the Chinese call a "spring roll"; you'll find spring rolls on Vietnamese and Thai menus, too.

Enjoy the variety of vegetables in Chinese dishes! Besides the familiar bell peppers, broccoli, cabbage, carrots, chile peppers, green onion, mushrooms, and sprouts, Chinese dishes are prepared with bamboo shoots, bean sprouts, bok choy, lily pods, napa, snow peas, and other vegetables. For more choices, flip to the vegetarian section of the menu, where you'll find dishes featuring tofu and legumes, too.

For less fat, look for dishes that are braised, roasted, simmered, steamed, and stir-fried (with little or no oil). Ask that stir-fried dishes be cooked in just a small amount of oil.

Order plain rice and noodles, rather than fried versions. Plain rice and noodles are usually lower in sodium, too, than fried versions, which are flavored with soy sauce. Crispy skin on poultry dishes, such as Peking duck, is high in fat.

Be aware that the meat, poultry, or fish in sweet-and-sour dishes is typically breaded and deep-fat fried. Instead, ask for roasted or grilled meat with sweet-and-sour sauce to cut down on fat.

If you're watching your sodium intake, go easy on foods prepared with MSG, soy sauce, or high-sodium sauces, such as black bean, hoisin, and oyster sauce. Ask the server to have your dish prepared to order without high-sodium seasonings or sauces. You might ask for light or reduced-sodium soy sauce that you can add yourself. Or instead choose dishes prepared with hot mustard, sweet-and-sour, plum, or "duck" sauce that have less sodium.

For a small bite, enjoy dim sum. Translated as "little heart," these small portions include steamed dumplings and steamed spring rolls. Go easy on fried dim sum dishes. To order dim sum, you choose your dishes from a server who passes your table with one dish after another. As a result, you can easily overeat!

Enjoy your fortune cookie—and the fortune inside! A single cookie has just 15 calories and 0 fat grams. Typically, Chinese meals don't give much attention to sweet desserts. Usually, you'll have ice cream, fresh fruit, or almond cookies as options.

Control the urge to overeat. In Chinese restaurants portions are often quite ample. Take leftovers home with you, or plan to share a dish. Perhaps order two or three dishes to serve four people.

From the Chinese Menu...

Enjoy More Often...

- ➢ Wonton soup
- ➢ Hot-and-sour soup
- ➢ Steamed spring rolls
- ➢ Chicken, scallops, or shrimp with vegetables
- ➢ Whole steamed fish

Food Guide Pyramid with Popular Chinese Fare

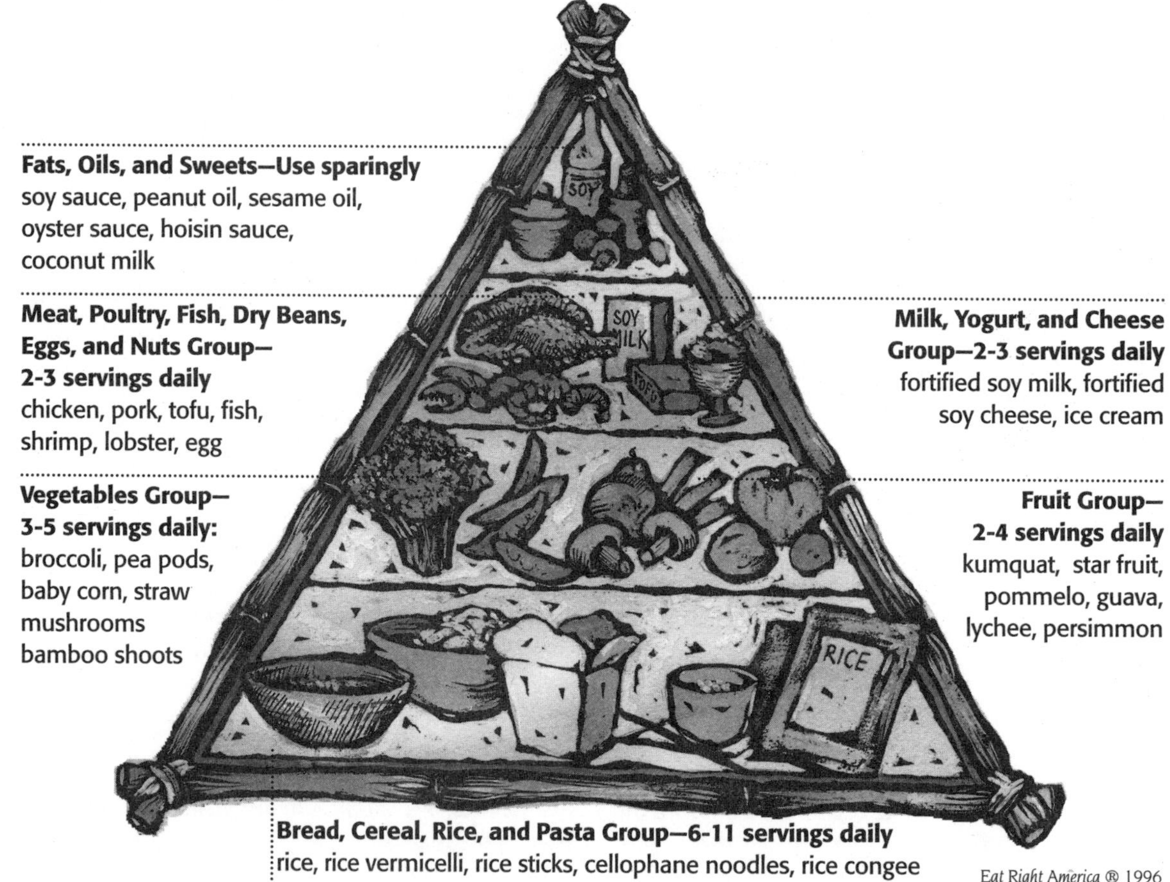

Eat Right America ® 1996

- Steamed rice
- Steamed dumplings and other dim sum
- Soft noodles
- Stir-fried dishes,* steamed and simmered dishes
- Tofu
- Fortune cookies

Enjoy Sometimes...

- Fried wontons
- Fried egg rolls or spring rolls
- Peking duck
- Fried fish with lobster sauce
- Fried rice
- Fried dim sum
- Fried noodles
- Fried "crispy" dishes, sweet-and sour dishes with breaded, fried ingredients

**If cooked in just small amounts of oil, they can be quite low in fat. Stir-fry dishes, however, can be quite oily (for example, lo mein).*

Japanese Cuisine

Although Chinese restaurants have a long history in the United States, interest in Japanese-style restaurants is much newer, starting with the Japanese steak house. There, Americans experienced the flair of table-top, stir-fry cooking, seated around the grill. In either full-service or quickservice restaurants, today's Japanese menu offers far more variety.

With its heavy use of rice, noodles, tofu, vegetables, and seafood, small meat portions, and limited use of oils, Japanese cooking is noted for being low in fat. Glazes and sauces are typically made with ingredients that are low in fat: broth, soy sauce, rice wine, and sake (rice wine). While some foods are fried, the more common cooking methods include braising, broiling, grilling, simmering, and steaming. Rice, noodles, and vegetables contribute complex carbohydrates, and vegetables supply fiber and vitamins A and C. Meat, poultry, seafood, and tofu are high-protein ingredients, usually served in moderate-size portions. Calcium-rich foods are limited. For those whose blood pressure is sodium-sensitive, the use of high-sodium flavoring is a nutrition caution.

To the Japanese cook, artistry ranks as important as nourishment. Edible garnishes of ginger or vegetables, or seaweed carefully wrapped around raw fish and rice, or an artful food arrangement on a plate are among the aesthetic touches that make Japanese food beautiful. Enjoyment of food has always been an important dietary guideline for the Japanese diet!

The language of a Japanese menu might be new to you. Use these guidelines to sharpen your menu savvy:

Know that tempura, for example, is a popular battered, fried dish. Agemono and katsu dishes are also breaded and fried. To control fat and calories, go easy on fried dishes, but don't avoid them altogether or you'll miss some outstanding taste treats! Just balance these foods with other lower-fat choices.

Look for menu terms that suggest less fat, such as "nimono" (simmered), "yaki" (broiled), and "yaki-mono" (grilled). These are two examples for meat, poultry, or fish: yakitori, which is skewered then grilled or broiled; and teriyaki, which is marinated in soy sauce and mirin (rice wine), then grilled.

Looking for another low-fat choice? Try sashimi (raw fish) or sushi (vinegared rice, prepared with seaweed, raw fish and/or vegetables). Go easy on the soy sauce for dipping. *Refer to page 315, "Is Raw Seafood Safe to Eat?" for tips on choosing a sushi restaurant.*

As another meal in a bowl, try domburi, or rice covered with vegetables, meat, or poultry, and perhaps egg. To cut back on cholesterol, ask for this dish without the egg.

If you're watching your sodium intake, go easy on high-sodium sauces, such as soy sauce, miso sauce, or teriyaki sauce, as well as broth and pickled vegetables. Many dishes, such as soup, noodle dishes, and stir-fried dishes, are flavored with soy sauce. As an alternative, ask for dishes prepared without soy sauce, such as shabu shabu, foods that are not marinated, or steamed seafood; then dip them in a low-sodium soy sauce. For flavor without sodium, use a bit of the shredded wasabi, which is a very strong and hot horseradish. Beware—a very little wasabi goes a long way!

For more vegetables, order a salad as a side dish. For less sodium, ask for a lemon slice to squeeze on your salad, rather than miso dressing. Miso, a common flavoring in Japanese cooking, is derived from fermented soybean paste.

As a switch from rice, enjoy Japanese noodles—udon (wheat noodles) or soba (buckwheat noodles). Noodles are often served under cooked dishes such as sukiyaki or in soups.

Enjoy fresh fruit for dessert. You won't find rich pastries on Japanese menus.

Take time to enjoy the aesthetics of a Japanese meal in a full-service restaurant. It's part of the dining experience!

From the Japanese Menu...

Enjoy More Often...

- Stir-fried dishes such as sukiyaki
- Simmered dishes such as shabu shabu
- Grilled dishes such as yakitori
- Stir-fried tofu
- Clear soups such as miso and suimono
- Steamed rice
- Sashimi and sushi

Enjoy Sometimes...

- Deep-fried dishes such as tempura
- Breaded and fried dishes such as tonkatsu
- Fried tofu

Eating on the Road

Eating as you travel can challenge a trim waistline and good nutrition sense. Often meals on the road require special attention. Overdoing is all too easy—especially when portions are big, the desserts are rich, and the menus, tantalizing. Other considerations, such as dehydration and food safety, also are issues that demand consideration and action for travelers.

Dining at 35,000 Feet!

What's to eat at 35,000 feet? Foodservice depends on the carrier, where you sit on the plane, and the length and time of your flight. Usually the meal is lighter in coach than in business or first class. As airlines have cut back to control costs, foodservice has changed. Portions have become smaller on many carriers, and meal service may be just a light snack. For a short, mid-day trip, flight attendants may serve only a small snack sandwich or packet of pretzels or peanuts, and your choice of beverage.

Whether you're a frequent flyer or an occasional passenger, plan ahead so the plane "fare" fits into your eating style:

Don't count on an airline meal. Instead, check with your travel agent or the airline before the flight to verify the type of foodservice. But check the envelope with your ticket first; this information may be tucked inside if your ticket came from a travel agent. If there's no meal served and you know you'll be hungry, eat before you board the plane—either at home or at the airport—or pack and bring your own.

Want a special meal? It's only a phone call away—for no extra cost for any traveler! If you or your travel agent call at least 24 hours before your flight, you can arrange for special meals on major carriers: vegetarian, kosher, low-calorie, low-fat, low-sodium, diabetic, and fruit plate, among others. Often special meals are available for infants and children—if you request ahead. On some carriers you can even order a Hindu, Muslim, or Oriental meal.

Standard airline fare is prepared to match the tastes of most travelers; for that reason, many people find them mundane. However, a special meal, ordered ahead, can match your eating style and nutrition needs—and offer variety if you're a frequent flyer.

For frequent flyers, your travel agent can keep your meal request in your client profile, along with your seating preference. That way, your request is automatic. In fact, the most efficient time to place your request is when you make your reservation.

Bring your own food in your carry-on bag or briefcase. You don't need to feel uncomfortable. It's OK with the airlines—and may be the best "survival" technique if you're traveling with small children. Dry fruit, such as raisins or apricots; whole fruit, such as an apple or banana; raw vegetables; crackers and sliced cheese; a muffin; a bagel; and pretzels are among portable foods that travel well.

You might also bring a sandwich from home or buy one in the airport. For safety's sake, don't keep a sandwich with meat or other perishable food for too long at cabin temperature—no more than two hours.

Say "no." You don't need to eat an airline meal just because it's offered. If you just ate lunch or plan a nice meal on the ground at the end of the flight, let the serving cart roll right on by.

Drink lots of water—even if you're not thirsty! With the low humidity and recirculating air within the pressurized cabin, airline travel is dehydrating, meaning that you lose body fluids through evaporation on your skin. Rushing to catch a plane may work up a sweat that already puts you in a "fluid deficit." Dehydration only aggravates symptoms of jet lag.

To avoid dehydration, drink plenty of fluids—8 ounces of fluids for every hour of your flight. Drink juice, water, and milk. You might pack some bottled water in your carry-on luggage as an extra supply. Especially on a long trip, drink plenty of liquids before, during, and after flying to avoid dehydration and minimize the effects of jet lag. Dehydration causes fatigue.

Want to relax or sleep on the flight? If you're sensitive to caffeine, avoid caffeinated beverages: coffee, tea, and colas. For some people, too much caffeine can promote sleeplessness, anxiety, and overstimulation...especially if you're anxious about flying anyway.

If you drink alcoholic beverages, go easy—even if you're in first class where they're free! Just one or two is enough. On a long flight, wine or cocktails may not help you to sleep—and may not relax you either. Instead, larger amounts may have the opposite effect, making you more restless.

When the beverage cart rolls by, make your choice count as one serving from the Food Guide Pyramid—especially if you may come up short during the day. Ask for fruit juice from the Fruit

Organize yourself so you're well rested and relaxed before you travel. Avoid skipping meals as you rush to prepare for your trip; stick to a healthful meal pattern. Drink extra fluids before and during your flight—but not too many alcoholic beverages. And during long flights, get up, stretch and walk around the cabin.

Once you're on the ground, keep on drinking fluids. After a long flight, drink extra fluids for several days. Immediately adjust your meals and sleep to the new time if you've traveled over several time zones. If your body clock skips from late afternoon to early morning and you lose the night (as you often do with a flight from Chicago to London), take a short nap when you arrive if you need to, then continue with a normal day—lunch, dinner, and an early evening. If, instead, you leave in the morning and arrive at night, have dinner and go to bed—even if your body clock says it's just mid-day.

Be aware that no evidence shows anti-jet lag formulas or diets to be effective. You may have heard anti-jet lag claims about a dietary supplement called melatonin. While this claim may be partially true, the amount of melatonin that promotes sleep is far less than the amount in over-the-counter products. *For more information on melatonin and other questionable supplements, refer to "Beyond Vitamins and Minerals: What's Known About Supplements" on page 588.* ✦

ON THE MOVE...

Planes, trains, and automobiles get you where you're going. But as a passenger, you burn little of your own fuel along the way. When traveling, build physical activity into your daily plans:

Pack comfortable clothes and footwear, including workout clothes or a bathing suit. Take a jump rope, running or walking shoes, or plastic dumbbells you can fill with water. That way, you won't need special facilities to work out.

On a long train or plane trip, walk up and down the aisle several times each hour. Ask for an aisle seat so you won't have to climb over your fellow passengers. Do simple stretching exercises to avoid feeling stiff.

If you're driving, take regular breaks. Your passengers—including kids—will ride more comfortably after some physical activity.

Choose a hotel with exercise equipment—and make time to use it. Ask about the facilities—an indoor or outdoor pool, tennis courts, bicycle rentals, and gym equipment.

Ask for an early wake-up call so you can get a jump start on your day with a 30-minute walk or jog. Get a guidebook to map out your way—or the hotel's front desk may have a walking map.

Check the local television guide for a televised workout or yoga stretching class. Or take along a tape player and exercise tape.

Skip the taxi cab. If it's a safe, reasonable distance, walk to your business meeting, museums, shops, or restaurants—in comfortable walking shoes.

For more about physical activity and health, refer to "Ready? Set...Go For It!" on page 30. ✦

Group, tomato juice from the Vegetable Group, or milk from the Milk, Yogurt, and Cheese Group.

Especially on a long flight, get out of your seat and move around. Even a little exercise, such as walking the aisles, will help you feel better than just sinking into the seat with your headset on.

Travel Fare—On the Ground

For the business person, eating on the road can be an "occupational hazard." For the leisure traveler, calories add up, too, especially when food is the main event. Eating just 500 extra calories a day can add up to 3,500 extra calories in a week. Unless you compensate with more physical activity, those 3,500 extra calories can turn into a pound of body fat!

Whether traveling on business or leisure, be a wise restaurant consumer. *As with any meal out, the "Restaurant Eater's Tip List" on page 360 and the suggestions in "Fast Food, Healthful Food" on page 367 apply to eating on the road.*

On an expense account? Avoid the urge to overeat just because you aren't paying the bill. Promising to "cut down when I get back home" may not be enough to keep trim, especially if you're a frequent traveler.

Schedule your wake-up call to allow time for breakfast. An early morning meal is, after all, a smart way to start a business or travel day. If you're in a hotel with room service, order breakfast the night before, perhaps by hanging your order on the tag outside of your door. *For some quick and nutritious breakfast menus, check on page 387, "Breakfast on the Road."*

When you're working during a meal or cocktail hour, be as attuned to your food and drink as you are to business issues. Over-ordering is easy when you're not paying attention to your body's signals. A second round of drinks or another basket of chips can arrive without much notice.

If you drink alcoholic beverages, go easy. Drinking is often part of the social side of business travel, or viewed by the traveler as a way to relax. However, calories in a cocktail or two, and perhaps wine with dinner, add up faster than people think. Depending on the size, a single drink can supply 10 percent of your day's calorie needs. (*Refer to page* 188 *for calories in alcoholic drinks.*) Moreover, be careful that cocktails and salty snacks don't replace a nutritious meal. And for those doing business on the road, drinking and driving is hazardous!

As a leisure traveler, balance the activities on your trip. To keep from overdoing on meals, avoid making food the centerpiece of every day. Take time for sight-seeing, physical activity, and perhaps time visiting friends or relatives, too.

As the fitness counterpoint to healthful eating, take time to exercise when you're on the road. All too often people complain that travel upsets their exercise routine. Yet, with a little planning, physical activity can dovetail with a busy travel schedule—and add pleasure and stress-relief to any trip. *For tips on fitting physical activity into your travel schedule, refer to page* 386, "On the Move..."

Breakfast on the Road

A 2-egg omelet, 3 strips of bacon, 1/2 cup hash browns, 1 slice of toast with 2 teaspoons of butter or margarine, 3/4 cup of fruit juice, and coffee: this hearty restaurant breakfast can total up to 685 calories and 40 fat grams. For a quick, nutritious start on your day, order one of the following breakfasts instead for 400 calories or less:

➢ Fresh fruit, bagel with jam, low-fat milk

➢ Cereal (hot or cold) with low-fat milk, fresh berries or banana

➢ Low-fat yogurt, whole-wheat English muffin with spread served on the side, fruit juice or fresh fruit

➢ Whole-wheat pancakes topped with fruit, hot cocoa made with milk

➢ One poached egg, whole-wheat toast with jam, 1/2 grapefruit, skim milk

CRUISING: A FLOATING FEAST

Sampling all kinds of food is one delight of cruising! Plan ahead so you don't feel guilty about enjoying the tempting variety of foods.

Use the ship's upper deck as a running or walking track. With more physical activity, your body needs more energy from food—so you can indulge a little more. Take time every day to do a few laps to keep fit and burn off the extra calories you eat. Or take advantage of the ship's fitness center or workout classes.

Check the menu. Many of today's cruise ships offer lighter fare that's clearly indicated. In fact, as you order, use all the tips you already read about for menu reading and ordering in a restaurant.

Take advantage of built-in variety on cruise ship menus. For example, enjoy all kinds of fruits and vegetables—perhaps some that are new to you!

If you can't resist the urge to order another course, ask the wait staff to bring a small portion. And remember, just because your meals are prepaid and you may order anything on the menu, doesn't mean you must!

If you stay up to enjoy the midnight buffet, go easy at other meals.

Be aware that cocktail beverages, poolside drinks, and wine with dinner can add up to a lot of calories—and a big bill at check-out! And don't feel forced to order a beverage when you sit down to an evening show.

Have a problem with sea sickness? Skipping food entirely isn't the answer. Instead ask the passenger services desk for motion sickness medication, and eat something light, perhaps crackers, to keep something in your stomach. ✦

Ordering just a continental breakfast (bread, juice and coffee)? For breads with less fat, ask for a bagel, toast (perhaps whole-wheat or rye), or an English muffin with jam or with butter or margarine served on the side. Skip doughnuts, sweet rolls, croissants, and other pastries to cut down on fat.

Have Food, Will Travel

If your job, vacation, or weekend outings take you on the road, brown bag it—or fill a cooler—to eat as you go. By taking nutritious meals and snacks along, you don't need to rely on vending machines, convenience stores, quickservice establishments, or snack bars.

Take foods from all five food groups of the Food Guide Pyramid when you travel in the car. *Refer to chapter 11, "Planning to Eat Smart," for a discussion of the food groups.*

Fill sealable plastic bags with vegetable finger foods: raw vegetables (broccoli and cauliflower florets, jicama and carrot sticks, zucchini and bell pepper circles, snow peas, among others). Vegetables are good sources of complex carbohydrates, fiber, and vitamins A and C.

Take all kinds of fresh fruit. Besides taking the edge off hunger, fruit can be a thirst quencher. Fruit is low in fat, yet a good source of vitamins A and C.

Tuck in single-portion beverages: canned or boxed fruit juice, canned tomato juice, and boxed milk. Keep it cool in a small, insulated container with a chill pack. Or an insulated vacuum bottle works well, too.

Take other portable, nonperishable foods: for example, crackers, peanut butter, raisins, small boxes of ready-to-eat cereal, and other dried fruit, pretzels, and plain popcorn. Tuck in packages of instant oatmeal for a quick, easy, hot breakfast.

Stock an insulated cooler with perishable foods: deli sandwiches, yogurt, and cheese, among others. Keep your raw vegetables in the cooler, too, to keep them crisp. *For more tips on pack-and-carry food, refer to page 317.*

When you're hungry, stop to eat your lunch or dinner. Get out of the car. Stretch. Take a short walk. You'll enjoy your meal more—and feel more relaxed as you continue driving.

Food in Faraway Places

From cozy cafes, small food stores, and open-air markets...to rice paddies, hillsides with tropical fruit trees, and fishermen hauling in their nets, food offers a unique cultural experience for the curious traveler. Many experts say that Americans' growing enjoyment of ethnic foods comes from their travel experiences. Savvy travelers take the opportunity to acquaint themselves with new foods, rather than eat at a familiar quickservice restaurant chain when they travel abroad.

As the world continues to grow smaller, more business and pleasure travelers are venturing beyond the United States, Canada, Europe, Australia, and parts of Asia...to places where sanitation standards are not as high. In certain environments, bacteria, parasites, and viruses can transfer to food either from poor sanitation or agricultural practices.

No matter what you call it, Montezuma's Revenge, "turista," or something else, travelers' diarrhea most often is caused by contaminated food and water. Typically, it lasts no more than three to four days, but that's enough to slow down an otherwise wonderful vacation—and certainly puts a business trip into a tail spin. The first bout won't "immunize" you from the next. But the good news is: you can reduce your risk by being cautious and careful. Pay attention to everything you eat and drink.

Food Safety: An Ounce of Precaution

Like other types of foodborne illness, travelers' diarrhea is most commonly caused by bacteria—probably 80 percent of the cases. *To avoid foodborne illness, the guidelines in "Eating Out Safely!" on page 366 apply no matter where you eat away from home.* But in less developed areas, you need to take added precautions: "boil it, cook it, peel it, or forget it."

Be cautious with produce. Eat only raw, peeled fruit or cooked fruit, and skip salads and other raw vegetables. Instead choose vegetable dishes that are cooked.

Eat well-cooked meat, poultry, or fish. Avoid these foods if they're raw, rare, or partly cooked or just re-warmed after sitting for a while.

Avoid food sold by street vendors unless you know it's hot and well-cooked—best if cooked while you watch. Buy only commercially-bottled drinks from vendors. The food preparation area and the dish and utensils should be clean. Perishable foods should be held at safe temperatures. And the cook should be well-groomed.

Order well-cooked scrambled eggs or hard-cooked eggs, rather than those prepared sunny-side up (unless the egg is well cooked) or just softly scrambled.

Unless milk comes from a large, commercial dairy, drink canned or ultra-pasteurized (UHT) boxed milk. Before drinking milk, find out if it's pasteurized.

Always wash your hands before eating! This should be your habit back home, too. It's just as important when you travel since your hands can transfer diarrhea-causing bacteria to your mouth.

When you aren't sure what you may encounter, carry some favorite packable foods. Single-serve foods, sold for lunch boxes, are great for travelers.

Check travel guides and talk to staff in the better hotels, or to your tour guide, to find restaurants with high sanitation standards. Restaurants in the better hotels usually have a high standard.

What's Safe to Drink?

You're always smart to play it safe. In developed countries, the tap water should be fine. Better hotels in lesser developed areas may also filter and chlorinate their tap water to make it safe. Before you use water from the faucet, find out if the hotel has a water purification system. When you're not sure, don't drink or brush your teeth with tap water. Instead, use commercially-bottled or canned water with the seal or cap intact. Keep a bottle in the carry bag that travels with you.

Soft drinks, canned or bottled juices, beer, and wine are safe to drink. Coffee, tea, and other hot beverages are usually safe because the long heating time destroys most and perhaps all of the bacteria, viruses, and parasites that might be present in water. You can also boil or chemically treat water you drink. *For guidelines on treating water to make it safe for drinking, refer "Safe Enough to Drink" on page 178.*

In less-developed areas, avoid beverages made with water or ice cubes—unless you know that commercially-bottled water was used. Also avoid bottled water served to you without an intact seal or cap; it may have been refilled with local tap water. Be cautious of locally-bottled water because the standards may not be high for bottling. Even crystal-clear water in wilderness areas anywhere, including the United States and Canada, should be treated before drinking it.

If You Do Get Sick...

For most cases of travelers' diarrhea, dehydration is the biggest concern. If it strikes you, increase your fluid intake—with plenty of safe water, canned juice, and soup. Canned soft drinks are okay, too.

If the problem persists (more than three or four days) or if your symptoms are severe, seek qualified medical care. Your hotel or tour guide should be able to suggest a physician. Be prepared before you travel, too. Talk with your physician at home about your trip, and take along any medication he or she recommends.

your nutrition check-up

How Do Your Quickservice Meals Measure Up?

Reflect back on your last quickservice meal or snack. What did you order? Did you consider how your menu choices fit within your overall diet? Take a moment to rate your food choices.

➢ On the chart below, write in the last quickservice meal or snack that you ordered and the portion size for each menu item.

➢ Using the chart on page 373, "QFF—Quickservice Food Facts," find out how your food choices measured up. Write in the amount of calories, fat, saturated fat, cholesterol, and sodium for each menu item you ordered. Then total the amounts at the bottom of the chart.

➢ Go a little further. Using information from the Food Guide Pyramid in chapter 11, write the food group and the serving(s) contributed by each menu item.

➢ Surprised by the results? What did you learn about your quickservice food choices? What might you change if you order this meal or snack again?

There's no right or wrong answer to quickservice eating. The best meal or snack for you depends on you—your needs, your health, and the overall food choices you make every day!

Write It Down

MENU ITEM	SERVING SIZE	CALORIES	FAT (G)	SATURATED FAT (G)	CHOLESTEROL (MG)	SODIUM (G)	FOOD GROUP/SERVING
TOTALS:							

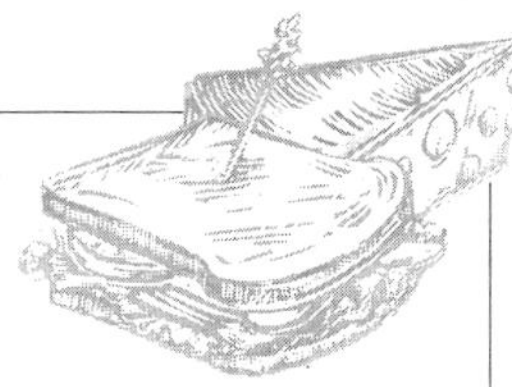

real life nutrition

Dining out!

After a long, arduous work day, Mary and Al had little energy for preparing dinner. The idea of eating out was a relief—a chance to relax and talk about the day. Deciding where to eat and what to order, then enjoying a meal together was the perfect agenda for the evening.

They wanted a convenient restaurant with plenty of choices. Mary wanted a restaurant with lower-calorie choices. Because she'd enjoyed a big lunch with clients, she wasn't too hungry anyway—certainly not as hungry as Al, who'd eaten just a light lunch in between customers. He was starved!

They settled on a new Chinese restaurant, featuring Cantonese-Szechuan cuisine. They noted that some items on the menu were familiar; others, unfamiliar.

As they studied the menu, they wondered: How do we know what's in these unfamiliar dishes? Can we be adventurous, order something new, and still satisfy our individual needs? What questions do we need to ask? What could each of us order?

Advice for ordering restaurant food:

➢ Mary and Al should order foods that fit their whole day's eating plans. A full-service restaurant offers enough choices to meet their differing needs.

➢ Since some items on this menu are unfamiliar, Mary and Al may ask the server questions about the dishes: for example, do you prepare each dish to order? Is the shrimp fried or steamed? What are these unfamiliar vegetables? Can we order individual dishes? Can we substitute hot-and-sour soup for the fried egg roll? How large is the portion?

➢ Since Mary's watching calories, she should pay careful attention to menu language. She'd note words that suggest more calories, such as "crispy," "fried," and "breaded," and terms that suggest less calories, such as "braised," "steamed," and "stir-fried."

➢ Since Mary wants a smaller meal with fewer calories, she might enjoy a bowl of soup and a half portion of her favorite dish, or share a dish with Al, or plan to take part of her meal home.

➢ Al might need the extra nourishment from an appetizer, perhaps potstickers; Mary doesn't need to order an appetizer just because Al orders one.

➢ To control the urge to nibble, they don't need the temptation of crispy, fried wontons brought to the table with the menu. They could enjoy a few and then ask the server to have them removed.

➢ They might order a dish that's new to them. So they know how it fits within their eating plan, the server can describe the ingredients and preparation.

➢ Together they're both wise to choose menu items that offer balance and moderation to their diet, and to order foods that help them meet the guidelines of the Food Guide Pyramid.

Chapter Sixteen

Off to a Healthy Start

"Should our baby be breast-fed or bottle fed?" "Can solid foods be given too soon?" "How do I know if the baby has eaten enough?" "Is it OK to put juice in a bottle?" "Should solid foods be warmed?"

New *and* experienced parents ask a myriad of questions. Unfortunately for parents and other caregivers, newborns aren't delivered into their parents' arms with a "how-to" manual filled with feeding instructions. However, knowing what, how much, and when to feed baby is easier than many people think. Parents and other caregivers need to focus on the main goals for infant feeding: providing enough food energy (or calories) and nutrients to support a baby's optimal growth and development… and nourishing the emotional bonds between parent and child.

Sound nutrition information takes the guesswork out of infant feeding. Patience, time—and a bit of creativity—build warm, memorable feeding experiences for tiny tots and for their parents and caregivers.

Breast-Feeding Your Baby

Nature provides ideal nourishment for babies: breast milk. Medical and nutrition experts highly recommend breast-feeding for an infant's first year of life, especially during the first few weeks after birth. Breast milk alone can provide enough nourishment to support a baby's optimal growth and development during the first four to six months of life. Even when solid foods are introduced, breast milk can continue to be an important part of a baby's diet until his or her first birthday—and even longer.

The decision to breast-feed is a personal one. It takes into account the mother's lifestyle, economic situation, and cultural beliefs, along with her own physical ability to do so. Know that breast size—small or large—makes no difference in the success of breast-feeding or the volume of milk production. Breast size depends on the amount of fat and fibrous tissue, not glandular tissue.

Done properly, either method—breast- or bottle-feeding—can provide the adequate nourishment and strong emotional bond that growing babies need. Women who aren't sure which approach to use might start with breast-feeding. If it isn't right for them, they can switch to bottle-feeding. Starting with a bottle, then trying later to breast-feed is difficult.

For Good Reasons...

Breast-feeding offers a host of physical, emotional, and practical benefits for both baby and mother. The benefits of breast-feeding are greatest when mother's milk is baby's exclusive source of nourishment for a least 4 months. However, the baby benefits even when breast-feeding lasts only for a short time. Let's start with the advantages for baby.

Breast milk is a specialized liquid food designed to meet the growth, development, and energy needs of infants. And as a baby matures and grows, the composition and amount of breast milk from a healthy mother automatically changes.

For most nutrients, a mother's diet has little, if any, affect on the nutritional content of breast milk. Selenium and some vitamins are exceptions. But if the mother's nutrient intake is low, her own stores may be used for breast milk, putting her at potential nutritional risk. That's especially true for calcium and the B vitamin, folate. For overall health, a nutritious diet during breast-feeding is important, as it was during pregnancy. *For more information, refer to "For Those Who Breast-Feed" on page 469.*

Breast-fed babies receive protection from both allergies and common illnesses through breast milk. Breast milk is rich in antibodies and other protective factors passed on from the mother to help protect an infant from illnesses such as middle ear infections, pneumonia, intestinal infections, and sudden infant death (SIDS). In fact, human milk contains at least 100 ingredients that infant formula doesn't have!

Colostrum, which is the clear or yellow fluid secreted for two to four days after delivery, has higher levels of antibodies than the mature milk which follows. It helps protect a newborn's intestines from infection. Think of colostrum as a newborn's first immunization. Colostrum also helps a baby pass his or her first stool.

Breast milk is easy for babies to digest. It's clean and safe. Babies may react to something their mothers eat, but they're rarely allergic to their mother's milk.

Breast-feeding requires more sucking than bottle feeding. This helps strengthen and develop the baby's jaw.

Breast-feeding helps develop a strong, nurturing relationship between a mother and her baby.

An older child who was breast-fed may be less likely to develop certain chronic diseases, including diabetes, some types of cancer, and certain stomach and intestinal diseases. Research in this area is not conclusive, but is promising.

did you know

...babies usually double their birthweight by four to six months? They triple their birthweight during the first year. And by their first birthday, they're also likely to be 50 percent longer.

...feeding cereal to a very young baby won't make the baby sleep through the night?

...a very young infant who only knows how to suck can choke on solid food?

...experts recommend breast milk or iron-fortified infant formula—not cow's milk—until the first birthday? After that, it's OK to start cow's milk. ✦

How About Mom?

Besides knowing that her baby is well-fed, a nursing mom receives many benefits from breast-feeding, too.

Many moms quickly identify the close bond with their infant as an important "plus" to breast-feeding. It's often a gratifying, emotionally-fulfilling extension of pregnancy.

Both parents note the convenience. Always ready-to-feed, breast milk doesn't need measuring, mixing, or warming. So it's easy, especially in the wee hours of the night. With no bottles to prepare or wash and no infant formula to shop for, there's more time to relax with the baby, or to catch a nap as baby sleeps.

Breast-feeding also may help a new mother regain her pre-pregnancy figure. Because nursing stimulates the uterus to contract and become smaller, a mother's abdomen trims down more quickly. Her body also uses the fat pad that was deposited on her hips and thighs during pregnancy as some of the fuel for milk production during the period of breast-feeding. Gradual weight loss during a period of breast-feeding doesn't affect milk production.

Breast-feeding is economical, too—even when you account for the extra food a mother should eat. The average cost of infant formula is about $100 per month. Women who breast-feed do need to add about 500 calories a day to their normal diet to cover the energy costs of milk production. These calories are best added with extra servings from the five food groups of the Food Guide Pyramid. *For more about the Pyramid, refer to "The Food Guide Pyramid: Your Healthful Eating Guide" on page 243.*

There's less odor involved with breast-feeding. Diaper changing is easier because the odor is less offensive, and if a breast-fed infant spits up, there's very little smell and it doesn't stain clothing.

An added benefit...with nursing, mother takes time to relax every few hours. That's often a welcome and needed change of pace from the added demands of being a parent.

What about long-term benefits? Women who have breast-fed may have a lower risk of developing premenopausal breast cancer, ovarian cancer, and osteoporosis.

To learn more about eating while breast-feeding, refer to "For Those Who Breast-Feed" on page 469.

Perfecting the Breast-Feeding Technique

While breast-feeding is nature's way of providing ideal nutrition for infants, the "art" of breast-feeding might not come as naturally! Like learning any

Do Babies Need Extra Water?

Newborns need little or no extra water. Breast milk or infant formula usually supply enough fluid. The exceptions are during periods of hot weather when your baby loses body fluids by perspiring. Then offer 1 to 2 ounces of plain water after a feeding; water shouldn't take the place of breast milk or formula. To ensure its safety for babies under four months of age, boil water first, then chill it, or offer sterilized bottled water. When babies begin eating solid food, offer plain water.

Your child needs water to replace fluids lost through diarrhea or vomiting. Diarrhea and vomiting can lead to dehydration—and its complications—if fluids aren't replaced. Rather than water or juice, your doctor or pediatric nurse may recommend an oral electrolyte maintenance solution, sold near baby foods in your grocery store, to prevent dehydration. Besides fluid, the solution contains glucose (a form of sugar) and minerals (sodium, chloride, and potassium) called electrolytes. Electrolytes help maintain fluid balance in your baby's body cells. These minerals are lost through body fluids.

Important: Consult your doctor or pediatric nurse before feeding an oral electrolyte maintenance solution to children under two years of age. Besides the risk of dehydration, diarrhea and vomiting signal possible illness that may require medical attention! This solution can be given to children age two and older, too. But if diarrhea, vomiting, or fever persists longer than 24 hours, consult your doctor or pediatric nurse.

An electrolyte maintenance solution won't stop diarrhea or vomiting, but it does prevent dehydration. *For more about fluids and the risks of dehydration, refer to "Water: An Essential Nutrient" on page 171.* ✦

new skill, the keys to success are knowledge, practice, and the support of family and friends.

Many hospitals have certified lactation consultants to help teach the techniques and answer questions. Some may visit a mother and baby later at home to help them perfect their skill. Women who have been successful at breast-feeding, such as La Leche League volunteers, can also help a new mother learn the techniques and offer support. You can also look to a registered dietitian (RD) and nurse midwife for support and guidance. *To find people who can offer sound, reliable advice on breast-feeding, refer to page* 580, "*How to Find Nutrition Help.*"

Within the first 1 to 2 weeks, nursing mothers and their newborns should see their pediatrician or health-care professional. For those discharged from the hospital less than 48 hours after delivery, the first check-up should take place within two to four days after birth.

To build confidence and help ensure an adequate milk supply, start nursing as soon after delivery as possible.

Relax and make yourself comfortable. These are important prerequisites. Find a comfortable chair with good arm and back support. Or lie down with pillows strategically positioned to help you support the baby. If you are comfortable and well-supported, extra energy will not be needed to hold the baby, and tension in the neck, back, and shoulders will be minimized.

Plan to nurse on demand—that is, whenever your baby says it's time to eat. Increased alertness or activity, rooting toward your breast, or mouthing are all signs that your baby is hungry. Typically, crying is a late signal of hunger. Trying to establish a schedule early on may frustrate you both. As reassurance, you can't "spoil" your baby by feeding him or her on demand. Most babies fall into their own schedule with time.

Be prepared to nurse very frequently during the first months—about 8 to 12 times every 24 hours. That's not only because a newborn's stomach is small, but also because nutrient needs are exceptional during this period of rapid growth and development. Frequent nursing helps establish the milk supply, too, and keeps breasts from becoming hard and swollen. Breasts that feel full and heavy are a mom's signal that it's time to nurse. Then as the milk "lets down," or moves from the inner breast to the nipple, there may be a tingling sensation.

Try to offer both breasts at each feeding, and let your baby nurse as long as he or she wants. The last portion of milk your baby drinks from each breast is called "hind milk." This milk is higher in fat and helps the baby feel full and satisfied after feeding.

Release your baby from the breast by gently putting your finger into the corner of his or her mouth. This will ease the baby's grip and break the suction without discomfort. Wait until you feel the suction release before removing your baby.

Because babies nurse more vigorously at the start of a feeding, alternate the breast you offer first. Clip a safety pin to your bra as a reminder. Alternating the breast has several benefits. It ensures that both breasts are emptied regularly. And it helps prevent breast tenderness. Other tips for curbing breast tenderness: Vary the nursing position and allow your nipples to "air dry" after feedings.

Burp the baby when you change breasts and at the end of the feeding. This relieves any discomfort from air swallowed while nursing. To burp a baby, hold him or her upright on your shoulder, or lay the baby "tummy-side down" across your lap. Then gently rub or pat the baby's back. It's normal for a baby to spit up a bit of milk.

Trust baby to let you know when he or she has had enough to eat. When babies feel full, they may close their lips, turn away, or even fall asleep. Sometimes they take a rest during a feeding, too, making it hard to know when one feeding stops and the next begins! Is your baby getting enough? *Refer to "Nursing: Reassuring Signs of Success" on page* 398.

Don't worry about your baby's loose stools. It's normal for a breast-fed baby to have loose, yellowish stools, which may resemble watery "mustard seeds."

If your breasts are tender or reddened, or if you feel achy and feverish, contact your doctor. You may have a plugged duct or breast infection (mastitis). An antibiotic might be prescribed. Usually you can continue to nurse while an infection clears up.

If your breasts feel tight and full, soften them with a warm shower, or express a small amount of milk. To express milk means to stimulate milk flow by hand or with a breast pump. Fullness and discomfort are signs of engorgement and may happen when your milk supply first comes in or if you've gone too long between feedings. Wearing undergarments with proper support helps, too. When breasts become too full, your baby won't be able to latch on correctly, which can cause nipple soreness.

Don't be surprised if your milk "lets down" and leaks a bit when you hear your baby cry, or even when you think about him or her. It's natural. You might wear pads (without plastic liners) to protect from any leaking.

Use caution if smoking, drinking alcoholic beverages, or taking medication. These substances may affect milk production and the let-down reflex. But some pass into the mother's milk, too, at the same levels as in her bloodstream. Nursing mothers are wise to avoid smoking and to drink alcoholic beverages in moderation—and not right before breast-feeding. When mothers smoke, babies are more likely to get sinus infections, colic, or become fussy. Talk to your physician about taking medication during breast-feeding.

Seek help if you think it's needed, perhaps from a lactation consultant, La Leche League leader, or other health professional with experience in lactation counseling. Remember, you and your baby are learning about breast-feeding together. *Refer to page* 580, *"How to Find Nutrition Help."*

Some Steps in Breast-Feeding

1. Snuggle Tummy to Tummy

Cradle baby in your arms with his tummy against your tummy. His head should rest in the bend of your elbow. Your forearm should support the baby's back, with your hand on his bottom.

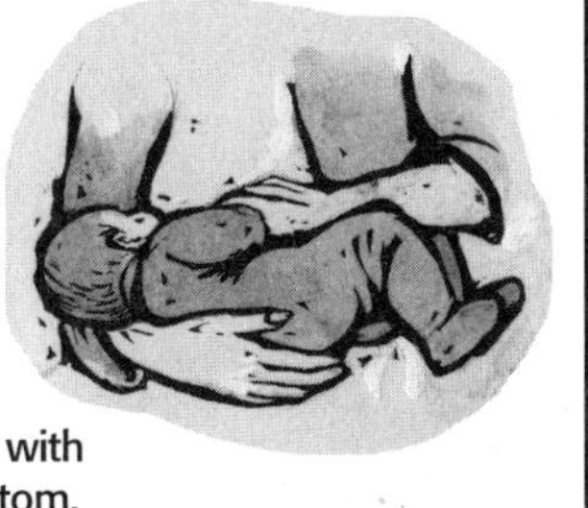

2. Place Nipple Directly in Front of Baby's Mouth

Baby's head should be in a straight line with his body. If his head is tilted back or he has to turn to reach your nipple he is in the wrong position.

3. Keep a Good Position

Keep the baby well supported. Make sure he is facing straight on to the nipple and does not have his head back or his neck turned. Make sure your back is straight and you are not leaning over him.

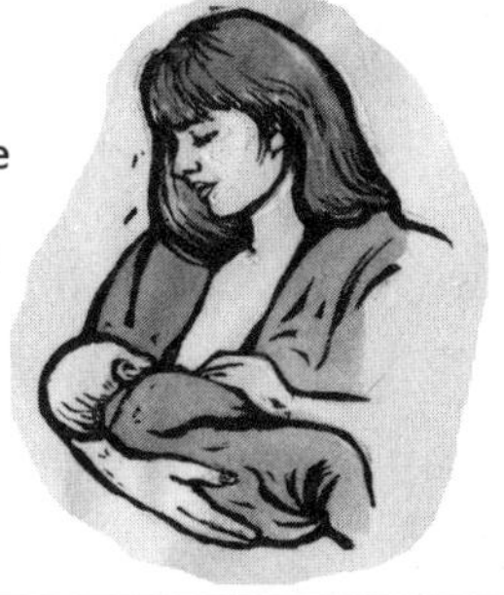

4. Nurse as Long as Your Baby Wants

Try to use both breasts at each feeding. To take him off the breast, release the suction by putting your little finger in the corner of his mouth. Wait until you feel the suction release before removing him.

Nursing: Reassuring Signs of Success

Not knowing how much milk their infant consumes, some parents feel uncomfortable about breast-feeding. Most women don't need to worry about having enough milk for their baby. The human body is miraculous. If a baby needs and demands more, a woman's body usually makes more milk to satisfy the demands of nursing—even when mom's working to lose extra pounds gained during pregnancy. Even mothers of twins and triplets can nurse their babies successfully.

Look for these signs that nursing is going well:

Following the third or fourth day after birth, your baby has six or more wet diapers, soiled with light-colored urine, every 24 hours. Most newborns will wet fewer diapers while receiving only colostrum.

Breast-Feeding Positions

If you're a nursing mom, you may want to experiment with these positions as you feed your baby:

Cradle Position: Sit up straight with your baby cradled in your arm. His or her head should be slightly elevated and resting in the crux of your elbow. You and your baby should be comfortably positioned "tummy-to-tummy" with baby's mouth level with your nipple. Be sure that your baby is facing straight towards you, without having his or her head, back, or neck turned.

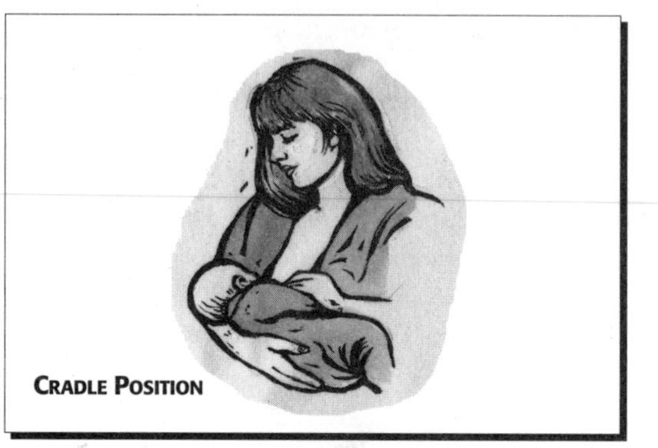

CRADLE POSITION

Lying Down: Lie on your side with the baby on his or her side, too. Place pillows under your head and behind your back for comfort. Position your baby "tummy-to-tummy" so his or her mouth is next to your nipple. Use a folded towel or a pillow to elevate your baby to the correct height. This position is especially comfortable for women who've had a cesarean delivery. You can feed your baby from both breasts on one side or turn onto your other side to nurse from your second breast.

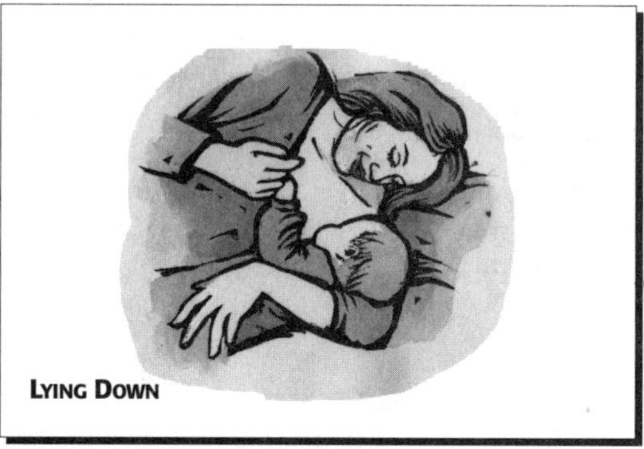

LYING DOWN

"Football" Position: Hold your baby with the head facing your breast and body tucked under your arm at your side. Your forearm supports the baby's back and his or her legs and feet should point towards your back. Rest the baby on a pillow near your elbow to give support and slightly raise his or her head.

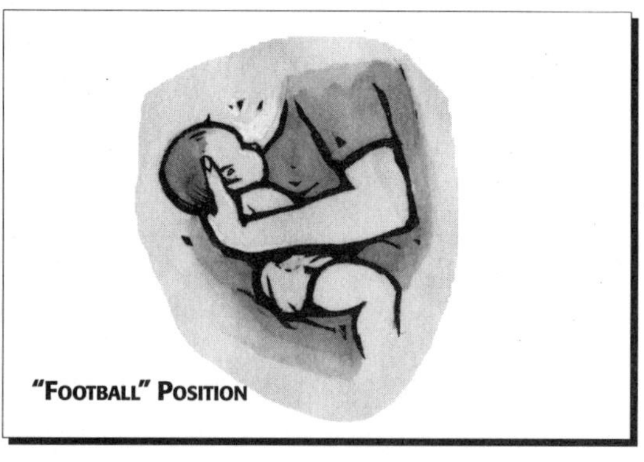

"FOOTBALL" POSITION

Whatever position, enjoy the eye contact with your baby. This helps build the mother-baby bond and helps your baby feel secure. ✦

Your baby nurses at least 8 times every 24 hours, and maybe up to 12 times, in the first month. If your baby sleeps longer than a four-hour stretch, you may need to awaken baby for a feeding. While nursing, the mother should feel sucking and hear the infant swallowing.

The baby's weight steadily increases. Make certain your baby is weighed at the doctor's office within a week or two after delivery to monitor weight gain, and regularly thereafter. During check-ups, your baby's weight and length will be measured and assessed. Doctors check a baby's measurements against reference growth curves. If your child doesn't gain weight properly, there may be a feeding problem or a medical problem.

Initially babies may lose a little weight right after their birth. That's normal. However, if your baby doesn't regain his or her birthweight by three weeks of age, your doctor or pediatric nurse will need to monitor your baby frequently to rule out any problems. From birth to six months, the typical weight gain is 4 to 8 ounces per week.

A Few Words for Dad...

A father can play a very important role in the success of breast-feeding. He can offer support, encouragement, and confidence to a new mother. Ways that fathers can get involved include attending prenatal breast-feeding classes with an expectant mother, reading a book on breast-feeding, arranging pillows and bringing a snack or beverage for mom when breast-feeding, burping and changing baby's diaper, and massaging mom's neck and shoulders to encourage relaxation. By sharing household responsibilities, caring for other children, shopping, and doing other tasks, he takes other pressures and interruptions away from mom.

What About Supplemental Bottles?

Breast-feeding abides by the law of supply-and-demand. Nursing stimulates the flow of milk—and increases its production as baby demands more to meet his or her needs. So supplemental bottles are not needed.

Although nursing may temporarily limit a woman's independence, offering a supplemental bottle too soon may discourage a baby from nursing. Until her milk supply is established, a new mother wisely stays close at hand for feeding.

If you choose to offer a supplemental bottle or pacifier, wait about four weeks after birth, or until breast-feeding is well established. Because the nipple on a bottle or pacifier is different from the breast, it can confuse a baby who is just learning to breast-feed.

Once the milk supply is constant—and both mother and baby are comfortable with nursing—dad, siblings, and other caregivers may share in feeding. Expressed breast milk or commercially-prepared infant formula may be used for supplemental bottles. Note: When nursing sessions are replaced regularly with supplemental bottles—without expressing milk—a mother's breasts will compensate by producing less milk.

For guidance on storing breast milk, refer to "Breast Milk: Safe Handling" on page 400. For more about infant formula and bottle feeding, refer to "Another Healthful Option: Bottle Feeding" on page 402.

Breast-Feeding for a Back-to-Work Schedule

The change from maternity leave to a back-to-work schedule takes adjustment for new moms. Some moms express milk during their workday so baby receives bottles of expressed breast milk when mom is away. Other moms decide to continue breast-feeding when they can be with their baby and have caregivers offer bottles of infant formula when they're away. And some babies may receive both bottles of expressed breast milk and formula. Choose the option that works best for you and your baby.

If you're a back-to-work nursing mom, consider these guidelines for breast-feeding success:

Select a caregiver for your baby who is supportive of breast-feeding.

BREAST MILK: SAFE HANDLING

➢ Wash your hands before expressing milk.

➢ If you use a breast pump, review the operation and cleaning instructions.

➢ Use plastic storage bags (made specifically for storing breast milk) or clean collection bottles. Glass or plastic? For breast milk that will be refrigerated, store in plastic containers. The protective properties of refrigerated breast milk are better retained in plastic. Breast milk can be frozen in either plastic or glass containers.

➢ Use expressed breast milk stored in the refrigerator within 8 days. *Exceptions*: Use milk kept at room temperature within 6 to 10 hours; colostrum within 12 hours.

➢ If you're a working mom, consider stocking a supply of milk in your freezer during maternity leave for use after you return to work. Breast milk can be frozen:

in a freezer compartment inside the refrigerator for up to two weeks,
in a refrigerator-freezer with a separate freezer door, for three to four months,
in a separate freezer at temperatures below 0° F for six months or longer.

Date expressed milk kept in the refrigerator or freezer. Then rotate the milk—first in, first out.

➢ Store expressed milk in 2- to 4-ounce portions to avoid wasting unused milk after a feeding. Because bacteria from the baby's mouth can contaminate milk in the bottle, always discard milk that's left over after feeding.

➢ Thaw breast milk in the refrigerator, under warm, running water, or in a pan of water on the stove. Do not thaw or heat breast milk in the microwave. Before feeding thawed breast milk, gently shake the container to mix layers that may have become separated. Use thawed breast milk within 24 hours and avoid refreezing it. ✦

Plan to nurse before work, soon after work, and during the evening to keep your milk supply strong. A routine helps working mothers continue breast-feeding successfully.

If you choose to express milk during the workday, make your plans even before you take maternity leave. If necessary, arrange for a private area where you can relax and stay free from interruptions. Unoccupied offices or women's lounges may be options. *For tips on safe handing of expressed milk, refer to "Breast Milk: Safe Handling" on page 400.*

Before you start working, help your baby learn to take expressed breast milk or infant formula from a bottle. Wait at least four weeks after delivery so your own milk supply is well established. But don't wait too long, or your baby may be less willing to feed from a bottle. You may need to experiment with different types of bottle nipples to find one that your baby prefers. This may be the perfect opportunity to get dad involved in feeding! *For more about the different types of bottle nipples, see "Bottles and Nipples: Baby Feeding Supplies" on page 404.*

If the schedule and travel distance from work permit, schedule feeding visits with your baby during workday breaks. Alert the caregiver to your arrival time. That way, your baby won't be fed too soon before your visits. To make it easier for you, choose a caregiver near your workplace.

For the same reason, let the caregiver know when you'll pick up your baby after work. Together, schedule feedings so your baby won't eat too close to the end of your workday.

Vitamin & Mineral Supplements for Breast-Fed Babies

Until solid foods are introduced—around four- to six-months of age—breast milk can be a complete source of nutrition for infants. However, three nutrients may warrant additional consideration. Ask your doctor for advice.

Iron. Iron is important for the manufacture of hemoglobin, which is the part of red blood cells that carry oxygen throughout the body. Iron is also critical for a baby's brain development.

In the last trimester before birth, babies accumulate enough iron stores to last through their first four to six months of life. Breast milk also contains easily-absorbed iron. After four to six months, however, baby's need for iron increases, and breast-fed babies may risk becoming iron deficient if another source of iron—usually iron-fortified cereal—isn't introduced. Talk to your dietitian or health professional about what is best for your baby. Premature babies may need additional iron sooner than full-term babies do.

Premature infants being breast-fed may need iron supplementation earlier since they had less time to build adequate iron reserves from birth.

Fluoride. A baby's teeth are developing even though you can't see them. Fluoride, a mineral often found in tap water, is important for the development of strong teeth and the prevention of cavities later on.

Breast milk contains little fluoride—even if the mother's drinking water is fluoridated. If your breast-fed infant is receiving supplemental formula made with fluoridated water—at least 0.3 ppm (parts per million) of fluoride, intake of fluoride may be adequate. If your child is breast-fed only or drinks formula made from well water, distilled water, unfluoridated bottled water, or city unfluoridated water, fluoride supplements are advisable. Breast-fed infants receiving supplemental ready-to-use formula may also need fluoride supplements since these formulas are usually prepared with water low in fluoride.

If fluoride supplementation is needed, it should not begin until about six months of age. At your baby's six month check-up, ask your doctor about fluoride supplements, available only by prescription.

***Vitamin* D.** This vitamin helps the baby use calcium from mother's milk (and infant formula) for growing and developing strong bones. The body can make vitamin D when skin is exposed to sunlight—but a little sunshine goes a long way! A baby doesn't need much sunlight to produce enough vitamin D. Unlike infant formula and fortified cow's milk, breast milk doesn't contain much vitamin D. If the baby stays indoors (perhaps in winter) or if a mother's diet is low in vitamin D, a supplement for baby might be advised. Breast-feeding moms who are strict vegetarians (no animal foods) may need to give their babies a vitamin D supplement because their own diet likely has very little.

Other vitamins. Vitamin B_{12} may also need to be supplemented for breast-fed babies of strict vegetarian mothers. *Refer to "The Vegetarian 'Mom'" on page 566 for more advice for vegetarian moms who breast-feed.*

Always get the advice of your baby's health care provider or a registered dietitian before giving nutrient supplements to a baby or child of any age!

Weaning...When and What?

The time for weaning is an individual matter for mother and baby. Experts encourage moms to breast feed for at least 12 months. Regardless, babies benefit from breast-feeding for as long as it's mutually desirable to both mother and baby. When you choose to wean your baby, either infant formula or cow's milk should be introduced, depending on baby's age. If you're weaning a baby under 12 months of age, breast milk should be replaced with iron-fortified infant formula. If 12 months or older, whole cow's milk is an appropriate substitute.

Should a baby be weaned to a bottle or a cup? That depends on age, too. Between 4 and 6 months, most infants will drink or suck small amounts of liquid from a cup or glass when held by another person. Older babies and toddlers usually have the coordination to handle fluids given by cup or straw. However, for infants under 6 months of age, a bottle is probably the best choice to ensure adequate fluid intake.

Another Healthful Option: Bottle Feeding

Breast-feeding may not be right for every woman. In rare cases, a woman may not be able to breast-feed for physical reasons. Some may feel uncomfortable about breast-feeding. Others may take medications that wouldn't be safe if passed through their breast milk to the baby. Still others have cultural reasons. In all of these cases, bottle feeding can be a healthful option.

Infant formula may also be a good supplement for other reasons: when a mother chooses to skip a breast-feeding, or when the mother doesn't supply enough breast milk for her baby.

Women who choose bottle feeding can feel assured that commercially-prepared infant formulas are a healthful alternative. Although they don't contain factors that protect babies from allergies and other illness, infant formulas are nutritionally similar to breast milk. In fact, they can provide all the nutrients and food energy that babies need until solid foods are introduced—usually around four to six months of age. Even after babies take solids, infant formula should continue until baby's first birthday.

Similar to breast-feeding, cuddling a baby while he or she takes a bottle also builds a close, nurturing relationship with those who share the responsibility of feeding.

KNOWING WHEN BABY'S HAD ENOUGH

There's no exact science to bottle feeding. But these are some signs that suggest that your baby's had enough:

- The baby may close his or her mouth or turn away from the bottle.
- The baby may fall asleep.
- The baby may get fussy with your repeated attempts to offer the bottle.
- The baby may bite or play with the bottle nipple. ✦

Formula: What Type?

Commercially-prepared infant formulas are sold in powdered, liquid concentrate, or ready-to-feed forms. Before feeding, you need to dilute powdered and liquid-concentrate formulas with water. Ready-to-feed formulas don't need to be diluted. Instead they're ready "as is" to feed your baby—packaged in cans or in a bottle.

What's in a name? Regardless of the form of formula you use, commercially-prepared infant formulas are usually cow's milk-based or soy-based. Formulas based on modified cow's milk are appropriate for most babies. However, some babies are sensitive to the protein in cow's milk. Others may have trouble digesting lactose, which is the sugar in milk. For them, a soy-based or specialty formula might be best.

Old-fashioned homemade formulas made from canned milk and corn syrup may have nourished you or your mother, but they're nutritionally inferior to today's commercial formulas. In addition, the corn syrup may contribute botulinum spores. Your baby's better off with a commercially-prepared, iron-fortified infant formula.

Iron. Many infant formulas are fortified with iron, which is a key mineral in forming hemoglobin, the part of red blood cells that carries oxygen throughout the body. Iron also is important for brain development. Full-term babies are born with enough iron stores to last four to six months. An iron-fortified formula right from the start helps keep a baby's iron stores adequate.

Choose an iron-fortified formula for your baby, or ask your baby's doctor, pediatric nurse, or a registered dietitian to recommend one. If your baby starts on a formula without iron, switch to an iron-fortified formula by four months. To clear up a common misperception, iron added to infant formula won't cause constipation or other feeding problems.

Fluoride. Fluoride is a mineral, important for the development of strong teeth and for cavity prevention. When you mix powdered or liquid concentrate formulas with water, you add fluoride, too—if your water supply is fluoridated. Be aware that ready-to-feed formulas aren't prepared with fluoridated water. If you regularly offer ready-to-feed formula or if your water supply isn't fluoridated to a level of 0.3 ppm (parts per million) of fluoride, ask your baby's doctor about fluoride supplementation.

Recipe for Success

Careful measuring, cleanliness, and refrigeration is the "recipe for success" when it comes to mixing powdered or concentrated infant formula. When properly mixed, powdered, concentrated, and ready-to-feed infant formulas are identical in their nutritional composition. The primary differences are in the time required to prepare the formula for feeding and in price.

No matter what type of formula you choose, follow these guidelines:

Pay careful attention to the mixing instructions on the infant formula label. Adding too much water during preparation dilutes the formula, meaning that baby may not get an adequate supply of nutrients or energy. Conversely, adding too little water concentrates the formula too much. Then it's hard for a baby to digest, and it supplies too much food energy at one feeding and not enough fluids to prevent dehydration.

Powdered and concentrated formulas are best mixed with water that has been boiled and then allowed to cool. Bottled water that's labeled as "sterile" is also an option, unless otherwise advised by your baby's doctor. *For more on bottled waters, refer to "What About Bottled Water?" on page 172.*

If your baby does well with one type and brand of infant formula, stick with it unless your baby's doctor advises otherwise. If you do change, check the label on the new formula. Its "recipe" for mixing may be different from the brand you've been using.

Always use clean bottles and baby-bottle nipples. *Refer to "Bottles and Nipples: Baby Feeding Supplies" on page 404 for tips on cleaning them.*

For convenience, prepare a supply of bottles ahead. Mix the amount your baby will eat within 24 to 48 hours. Date and store the prepared infant formula in the refrigerator. Once opened, ready-to-feed formula and liquid concentrates must be refrigerated and used within 48 hours.

Infant formula can be fed to a baby at cold, room temperature, or slightly warm temperatures. Always

COW'S MILK: WHEN? WHAT TYPE?

As a great source of calcium and other nutrients, cow's milk is an ideal food for toddlers, children, and adults—and for calves! However, it isn't appropriate for infants younger than 12 months of age. While some infant formulas are made from cow's milk, it's been modified to meet an infant's special needs.

There are several reasons why unmodified cow's milk isn't the best food for young infants. Its high-protein content is hard for baby's immature system to digest and process. The potassium and sodium content are also higher than recommended for babies. Cow's milk is low in iron, and the iron it does contain isn't absorbed well. And it doesn't provide enough zinc, vitamins C and E, copper, and essential fatty acids—nutrients that babies need to grow and develop.

Goat's milk isn't a suitable alternative either for many of the same reasons as cow's milk. ✦

test the temperature of the formula to avoid burning the baby. *To bring chilled bottles to room temperature or to slightly warm, refer to "Play It Safe: Warming Baby's Bottle and Food" on page* 411.

Discard formula left in the bottle after feeding. Bacteria from your baby's mouth can contaminate and cause formula to spoil. To avoid too much leftover, fill the bottle with smaller amounts of formula. Then add more as your baby's appetite dictates.

Bottles and Nipples: Baby Feeding Supplies

Baby bottles: Plastic or glass bottles, or disposable bottle bags? The type you choose is up to you. Some parents keep a variety of baby-bottle sizes and styles on hand for different purposes. For example, disposable bottle bags are handy when you're on the go and when washing facilities are limited. Small-sized bottles are perfect for holding 2- or 3-ounce feedings during the first weeks after delivery. Be cautious of bottles with cute shapes; they're often hard to clean.

Baby-bottle nipples come in a variety of shapes and sizes, too. Choose nipples that correspond to your baby's mouth size and developmental needs. A baby's comfort and ease of sucking are the criteria to use when choosing a nipple.

There are four basic baby-bottle nipple types: a regular nipple with slow, medium, or fast flow (the number and size of the holes will determine flow); a premature nipple for very small or premature babies; an orthodontic nipple, which imitates the shape of a human nipple during breast-feeding; and a cleft-palate nipple. A cleft-palate nipple is meant for babies who have a lip or palate problem that keeps them from sucking properly.

Keep bottle-feeding equipment in good working order:

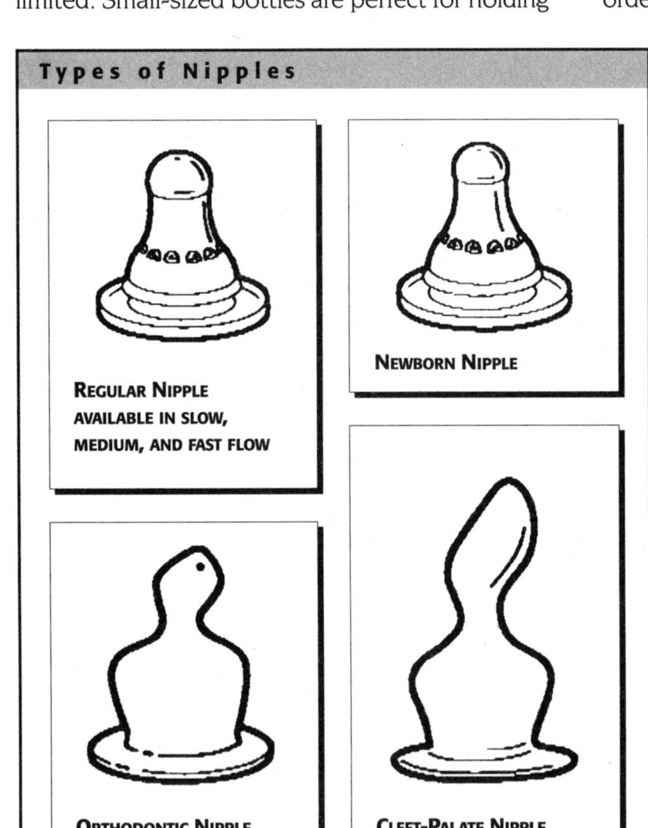

- Discard cracked or chipped bottles that could break and spill formula onto your baby.
- Replace nipples regularly as they can become "gummy" or cracked with age. Check them by pulling the tip before each use.
- Check the size of the opening on new nipples and then periodically as you use them. Formula should flow from the nipple in even drops—not a steady stream. If the milk flows too quickly, your baby could choke. Discard the nipple. If the milk flows too slowly for your baby, consider trying a nipple designed for older babies with more holes.

When it comes to preparing infant formula and washing bottles, cleanliness is essential! Their immune systems aren't fully developed, so infants are very susceptible to foodborne illness caused by bacteria in improperly cleaned feeding equipment.

Use plenty of hot, soapy water to wash your hands, work area, measuring utensils, bottles, and nipples. If possible, wash bottles right away when they're easier to clean.

Thoroughly clean bottles and nipples by washing with hot, soapy water and rinsing well. Nipples and bottles can be sanitized by placing them in boiling water for 2 minutes. Then let them air dry. Or wash bottles, rings, and caps in the top rack of the dishwasher. Look for special baskets designed for the dishwasher to secure bottle pieces and keep them from falling to the bottom of the dishwasher.

Remember that the outer "shell" of bottles with disposable bottle bags needs regular washing to keep bacteria away from your baby, too.

Bottle-Feeding Techniques: All in the Family!

Bottle feeding allows warm, cozy moments the whole family can share. Nestled in the arms of a parent, sibling, grandparent, or other caregiver, babies feel safe and comfortable. Consider these suggestions as you all refine your bottle-feeding techniques:

Find a comfortable place, perhaps a chair with an arm rest. Hold your baby with his or her head slightly raised, resting on your elbow. That allows a baby to suck from the bottle and to swallow easily.

Avoid propping your baby in bed or in an infant seat with a bottle. Babies can choke! And when they fall asleep with a bottle in their mouth, formula that bathes the teeth can promote baby-bottle tooth decay.

Keep the bottle angled during feeding to help prevent your baby from swallowing too much air. The nipple should stay full with formula when your baby nurses.

To ease discomfort from air bubbles, burp your baby in the middle and at the end of feedings. Hold him or her upright at your shoulder, or lie your baby "tummy down" across your lap. Then gently pat or rub your baby's back.

Keep a clean, damp washcloth handy. It's normal for babies to spit up some formula during burping.

When your baby's done, take the nipple out of his or her mouth. Sucking on an empty bottle causes air bubbles.

Baby's Bottle-Feeding Routine

Newborns eat frequently in the first months after birth—perhaps every two hours! They need nutrients and food energy to fuel their rapid growth. Since their stomachs are small, just 2 ounces, or as much as 4 ounces of infant formula, may be enough for the early feedings. *Refer to "How Much Formula?" for guidelines during the first 12 months.*

Formula-fed babies usually take 20 to 30 minutes to finish a bottle. If it takes less than 15 minutes for a newborn to finish a bottle, use a nipple with smaller holes. If it takes a long time and if the baby is sucking actively, make sure the holes aren't clogged. Or try a nipple with more holes.

As with a breast-fed baby, plan to bottle feed on demand—when a baby signals that it's time to eat. Trying to impose a feeding routine will only frustrate you both. And don't worry—you can't spoil baby by feeding on demand.

Should formula be warm, cool, or room temperature? That's up to you. Your baby will

How Much Formula?

The amount of infant formula babies need—and how often they eat—relates, in part, to their stage of development. In addition, some babies drink a little more or less depending on when solid food is introduced. Use this chart only as a guide.

Age	Number of Feedings per Day	Total Amount of Formula per Day (oz)
Birth to 4 months	6–8	18–32
4 to 6 months	4–6	28–45
6 to 9 months	3–5	24–32
9 to 12 months	2–4	24–32

become accustomed to whatever temperature you usually provide. If you warm it, just be careful so your baby doesn't get burned. *For tips, refer to* "*Play It Safe: Warming Baby's Bottle and Food*" *on page* 411.

Let the baby decide how much to drink. It's OK not to finish a bottle. If your baby has six or more wet diapers a day, seems content between feedings, and his or her weight increases steadily, the baby's probably getting enough. If not, check with your doctor or pediatric nurse. *For more signs that baby has had enough to eat, refer to* "*Knowing When Baby's Had Enough*" *on page* 402.

Solid Advice on Solid Foods

Just when parents master breast-feeding routines or formula mixing, babies show that they're ready to join the high-chair crowd! Starting solid foods is just one more adventure in the journey of child feeding. Throughout the first year, breast milk or iron-fortified infant formula continues to be your baby's most important source of nutrients and energy. At four to six months, most infants are physically ready to begin solids. Typically they're added in this order:

- Iron-fortified, single-grain infant cereal (mixed with breast milk or formula), single strained fruits and vegetables—*4 to 6 months*
- Strained meats/poultry, unsweetened fruit juices (vitamin-C fortified), plain toast, and teething biscuits—*7 to 9 months*
- Chopped soft fruits and vegetables; meats; unsweetened dry cereals; plain, soft bread; and pasta—*10 to 12 months*

For more detailed guidelines for introducing foods during the first year, refer to "*Infant Feeding Plan: A Basic Guideline*" *on page* 410.

Ready, Willing, and Able

Although most babies are ready to start solid foods between four to six months of age, don't rely solely on the calendar! Babies must be physically and developmentally ready for solid foods. Remember, each baby is different. Age is just a point of reference. If babies aren't ready to eat solid foods, most of it will end up on their lap—not in the tummy. Offering solids too soon only frustrates baby, parents, and other caregivers.

Until about four months, babies are unable to effectively coordinate their tongue to push food to the back of their mouth for swallowing. Well-meaning friends and family may advise starting solid foods earlier to help babies sleep through the night. However, they sleep through the night only after their nervous system develops more fully. In fact, offering solids too soon stresses a baby's immature digestive system. Much of what is given passes right through to the diaper.

Caution: Giving solids from a bottle could delay the development of feeding skills. This feeding method also could cause choking and perhaps the ingestion of too much food energy. Cereal in a bottle may also take the place of breast milk or formula, along with the nutrients they supply. To clarify a misconception, offering cereal in a bottle won't help baby sleep through the night either.

When is the right time to start solid foods? For most babies, no earlier than four months of age. After that, let your baby be the judge. Watch for these milestones that suggest that he or she may be ready to join the leagues of solid-food eaters:

Baby can sit with little support. Your baby can control his or her head and may even be able to lift up his or her chest, shoulders, and head when lying "tummy down." By this time, your baby can also turn away to signal "enough."

Baby shows interest in foods you're eating. As the baby watches, he or she leans forward and may even open his or her mouth in anticipation. Take a trial run with solid foods. If your baby doesn't seem interested, wait a few weeks, then try again. Avoid forcing a child to eat solid foods.

Baby can move foods from the front to back of the mouth. Up to about four months of age, babies will try to push food out with the tongue. As they develop, the tongue becomes more coordinated and moves back and forth. This allows your baby to swallow foods from a spoon.

Something New: Eating from a Spoon!

Learning to eat the first solid food—iron-fortified cereal—from a spoon is a big transition in infant feeding. It's a step towards independence and learning to eat on one's own. And it encourages chewing and swallowing skills.

Spoon feeding has its own challenges. It's messier. Initially more food may end up on the bib than in the mouth. But these tips might help make the transition pleasant:

Relax, and make this new eating adventure a good experience for both of you. Pick a time when your baby is relaxed and not ravenously hungry. Smile, and talk as you feed your baby. Your soothing voice will make new food experiences more pleasant—and talking helps with language development, too.

Use a small spoon with a long handle—and just a little bit of food on the tip of the spoon.

Start with a teaspoon or two of food. Then work up to one to two tablespoons, two to three times a day.

Let your baby set the pace for feeding. Don't try to go faster or slower.

Have your baby sit up straight or propped upright and face forward while eating. This makes swallowing easier and helps avoid choking.

As new foods are introduced, offer them at the start of the meal. Once satisfied, your baby may be less willing to try a new taste. If he or she refuses a new food, that's OK; try it again in a few days or weeks.

Infant Cereal: Timing Is Everything

A baby's first solid food should be iron-fortified infant cereal. Opt for cereals developed just for babies. They're easier to digest than varieties for

Caring for Baby Teeth

Good dental care begins at birth—even before baby teeth appear!

The American Dental Association advises parents to wipe their baby's gums with a clean, wet washcloth or gauze pad after every feeding. When the first of the 20 baby teeth appears, usually at about six months of age, begin using a soft toothbrush. Toothpaste isn't needed. Some parents make cleaning baby's teeth part of the bathtub routine.

Fluoride is a mineral that helps teeth develop and resist decay. In many places, fluoride is naturally present in local water supplies at various levels. If you live in an area that doesn't have fluoridated water, ask your baby's doctor if your baby or child needs a fluoride supplement. *Refer to "Vitamin and Mineral Supplements for Breast-Fed Babies" on page 400 and "Formula: What Type?" on page 402. For more about fluoridated water, refer to "The Fluoride Connection" on page 175.*

To avoid tooth decay, infants, toddlers, and young children shouldn't be put to bed with a bottle of juice, formula, or milk. The liquid that bathes the teeth and gums as they suck on the bottle stays on their teeth and can cause tooth decay, even if the teeth haven't yet erupted through the gums. If your child won't nap or go to bed at night without a bottle, fill it with plain water instead.

For more about dental care, refer to "Your Smile: Sugar and Oral Health" on page 126. ✦

Food Sensitivities and Your Baby

Some babies are sensitive to certain foods. You know by their reaction, perhaps a rash, wheezing, diarrhea, or vomiting. Most babies outgrow these reactions once their digestive and immune systems mature. (*To reassure you*...a baby's stool often changes color and consistency when new foods are eaten. These changes don't necessarily indicate a food sensitivity.) To best monitor your baby for food-induced reactions:

Keep tabs on the foods your baby eats. Choose single-grain infant cereals and plain fruits, vegetables, and meats instead of mixed varieties or "dinners" until you know what foods your baby can handle. If your baby has a reaction, stop that food for a while.

As you introduce new foods, offer one new food at a time. Wait three to five days before offering the next new food. If your baby has trouble with a certain food, you'll more likely know what food causes the reaction.

Save egg whites until after your baby's first birthday. Young babies may be sensitive to the protein in egg whites. Cooked egg yolks are okay—although the iron they contain isn't well absorbed.

Be watchful of foods considered to be common allergens including peanuts, tree nuts, soy, eggs, fish, shellfish, wheat, and milk.

If any food causes a significant and ongoing reaction, talk to your baby's doctor, pediatric nurse, or registered dietitian about it. Together, you can establish an eating plan that's best for your baby.

For more about food intolerances and allergies, refer to chapter 9, *"Sensitive About Food."* ✦

older children and adults. Iron-fortified cereals help babies maintain their iron stores, too.

Start with rice. It's often best as the first cereal because it's least likely to cause allergic reactions.

When it comes to your baby's first cereal feedings, keep the cereal mixture thin. Start with just one part cereal to four parts of breast milk or infant formula. Once your baby develops eating skills—and a taste for cereal—mix in less liquid so it's thicker. Don't mix in honey or corn syrup, which may contain small amounts bacteria (botulism) spores that can be harmful to infants.

Be prepared if your baby refuses it at first. Just try again in a few days. Infant cereal tastes different than the familiar breast milk or formula. The texture is different, too—not to mention the difference between a nipple and a spoon!

Once your baby has eaten rice cereal for several days with no signs of intolerance or allergy, expand his or her tastes by offering barley or oat cereal. *To determine if a food may be causing a reaction, refer to "Food Sensitivities and Your Baby" on this page.* Hold off on wheat cereal until after your baby's first birthday. Some infants are sensitive to wheat before one year of age.

Once your baby starts eating more cereal, he or she will take less breast milk or infant formula. Breast milk or iron-fortified formula still should be the "main stay" of the diet during the first year.

Solid Foods: What Comes Next?

Once your baby accepts cereal, it's time to try strained vegetables and fruits, then meats and breads. It doesn't matter which you offer first: vegetables or fruits. Some parents opt for vegetables first. But it doesn't make any difference.

One by one, offer a variety of foods to your baby. This lays the groundwork for a healthful diet throughout life. *For more about the importance of eating many different foods, refer to "Variety: Good for You, Good for Baby!" on page* 409.

Try single foods first: for example, fruits—applesauce, pears, peaches, prunes, bananas; vegetables—sweet potato, carrots, squash, peas, green beans; juice—apple, pear; meat—chicken, turkey, ham; and egg yolks. Juice fortified with vitamin C helps your baby absorb iron from food.

Start with smooth foods that are easy to swallow. Babies can eat mashed or finely-chopped foods when their teeth start to appear and when they start to make chewing motions. Foods with a bit of texture help with teething.

Offer juice in a cup, not a bottle. Sucking juice too long from a bottle exposes a baby's teeth to natural sugars in fruit juice. Prolonged contact with sugars can promote tooth decay.

Around six to nine months of age, most babies enjoy drinking from a cup—or at least trying to use this new "tool"! Offer juice, water, or formula in a child-sized, unbreakable cup. A cup without handles may be easier for a young child to hold. Covered cups with a spout are also helpful at this stage. Babies are clumsy with a cup at first, but usually catch on quickly.

As your baby gets more teeth and becomes interested in self-feeding—around 9 to 12 months of age—introduce finger foods. Soft ripe fruit without peels or seeds and cooked vegetables are good for tiny fingers. Avoid foods a baby can choke on. *Refer to "For Babies, Toddlers, and Preschoolers: How to Avoid Choking" on page* 414.

Teething biscuits, bread sticks, and rice cakes are good natural "teethers" for your baby, too. Chewing on these foods eases a baby's sore gums while offering a chance to eat a healthful snack—"all by myself"! *For more on self-feeding, refer to "'Feeding Myself'" on page* 412.

Remember, plain tastes best. Babies need the opportunity to develop a taste for the natural flavor of foods, without added sugar, salt, or other flavorings. Seasonings are not added to many varieties of commercially-prepared baby foods. Read the product label to find out.

As you choose foods for your baby, don't restrict fat. Growing babies need the energy and essential fatty acids that fat provides. *Refer to "Fat Facts for Tots" on page* 425.

As your baby grows and develops a bigger appetite, increase the amount of solid foods. *The chart, "Infant Feeding Plan: A Basic Guideline" on page 410 gives some general amounts.*

Variety: Good for You, Good for Baby!

Variety certainly is the spice of life—especially when it comes to forming good eating habits for your baby. Offering your baby a wide variety of foods with different flavors, colors, shapes, and textures

have you ever wondered

...if it's OK to sweeten baby foods with honey or to dip a pacifier in honey? No. Until after a baby's first birthday, avoid giving honey or corn syrup to your baby in any form. Very occasionally, honey can harbor the spores of a toxic bacteria called *clostridium botulinum*. For adults and older children, these spores in honey are harmless. But for babies younger than 12 months, they can cause botulism, a severe foodborne illness that can be fatal. *Note*: Sucking on a sweetened pacifier promotes cavities, too.

...what you can do to relieve the discomfort of teething? You might rub your baby's tender gums gently with your clean finger. A chilled teething ring—kept in the refrigerator, not in the freezer can also help. Chewing on textured solid foods helps teething, too.

...if a chubby baby is more likely to become an overweight adult? Relax if you're concerned. Chubbiness during infancy generally isn't an indicator of adult overweight. Restricting your baby's food intake may keep him or her from getting nutrients and energy needed for development and health and cause a failure to thrive. ✦

Infant Feeding Plan: A Basic Guideline

Babies differ in their size, appetite, and readiness for solid food. This guide offers a general time frame for introducing baby foods and table foods into an infant's eating pattern.

However, some babies may be ready for certain foods a little sooner; others, somewhat later. Your baby's doctor, pediatric nurse, or a registered dietitian will recommend an eating pattern to meet your baby's individual needs.

AGE AND DEVELOPMENT	WHAT TO FEED
BIRTH TO 4 MONTHS Baby can suck, swallow, and stick out tongue.	Breast milk or formula
4 TO 6 MONTHS Baby stops pushing food out of mouth with tongue and can support head and sit up with help.	Breast milk or formula. Add iron-fortified rice cereal (oat and barley cereals can be introduced next). Mix 1 tablespoon of cereal with breast milk or formula and offer two to three times daily with a spoon.
5 TO 6 MONTHS Baby can learn to eat from spoon. Lip closure is present.	Breast milk or formula; iron-fortified cereal. Add plain, strained baby vegetables (such as peas, carrots, squash, and green beans) and strained baby fruits (such as bananas, applesauce, peaches, pears, and apricots). Offer 1 to 2 tablespoons of strained vegetables or fruit 2 to 3 times daily. Offer one new food every 3 to 4 days and watch for signs of intolerance (rash, spitting up, or diarrhea).
6 TO 8 MONTHS Chewing motion is present.	Breast milk or formula; iron-fortified cereal—increase to 4 tablespoons or more daily. Add plain, strained baby meats (such as beef, veal, lamb, turkey, chicken, or egg yolk). Offer 1/2 to 1 tablespoon one to two times daily. Try one new meat every 3 to 4 days and watch for signs of intolerance. Increase strained vegetables to 2 tablespoons or more per day. Increase strained fruits to 2 tablespoons or more per day. Offer 2 to 4 ounces of fruit juice, either plain or fortified with vitamin C, in a bottle or cup. Begin trying unsweetened dry cereals, crackers, and soft breads or buns as finger foods.
8 TO 9 MONTHS Teeth are present. Chewing improves. Baby can grasp food with hands.	Breast milk or formula; iron-fortified cereal. Begin trying junior foods (half jar) or mashed and chopped table foods (4 tablespoons or more per day), such as meat, poultry, potato, and well-cooked pieces of vegetable. Chopped canned fruit may replace strained fruit. Offer 1 to 2 small servings of bread, crackers, toast, or zwieback. Small servings of cottage cheese, plain yogurt, and soft cheeses can be offered. Increase amounts of foods according to baby's hunger.
10 TO 12 MONTHS Baby has more ability to chew and swallow foods. Better grasping.	Breast milk or formula; continue iron-fortified cereals (4 tablespoons or more per day). Add cooked, cut-up pieces of vegetables and soft fruits (4 tablespoons or more per day), and tender meats. Casseroles with pasta or rice may be offered. Increase amounts according to baby's hunger.

Adapted from: Edelstein, Sari. Nutrition and Meal Planning in Child Care Programs: A Practical Guide. *Chicago*: The American Dietetic Association, 1992.

helps ensure that your baby's nutrition needs are met. Variety makes mealtime more fun, too!

Like you, your baby or toddler may like some foods better than others. That's normal. A baby may like a food one week, then decide otherwise the next week. Continue to offer food variety. You may offer a new food or flavor several times before a child accepts it—so keep trying. Don't let your own food biases limit your baby's preferences. Offer foods you may not like. Your baby or toddler just may like them! If not, try again in a few days.

Eating a variety of solid foods gradually helps establish a lifetime of good eating habits. This is why variety is so important, even in the early years:

Fruits and Vegetables
They're good sources of vitamin C and beta carotene. Frequent feeding of these foods at mealtime helps children become familiar with the flavors of fruits and vegetables, setting the stage for lifetime acceptance and enjoyment.

Breads, Cereals, and Other Grain Foods
Offer iron-fortified cereal to babies and toddlers. To enhance iron absorption, serve those that contain iron along with foods that contain vitamin C, such as fortified infant juices. Other grain products include soft, cooked pasta or rice, soft breads, dry cereals, crackers, and teething biscuits.

A word of caution with high-fiber foods: Some high-fiber cereals, such as bran, and raw vegetables are low in calories yet high in "bulk." Avoid offering large amounts of these foods to infants; they fill an infant's small stomach without providing many nutrients or calories. Infants and young children get enough fiber by eating a variety of foods.

Meats and Milk Products
These foods are valuable sources of protein and minerals needed for developing bones and muscles. Offer a variety of soft, puréed or finely chopped meats, such as chicken, turkey, or beef. After 12 months, when children no longer take breast milk or infant formula, whole milk is an important source of energy, calcium, protein, essential fatty acids, and some other nutrients. Growing bones need an adequate supply of calcium from food. Good sources include cheese, yogurt, milk, and cottage cheese. Health experts don't advise feeding lower-fat dairy foods, such as 2 percent or skim milk, to children under two years of age.

Play It Safe: Warming Baby's Bottle and Food

Babies enjoy breast milk, infant formula, and baby foods either warm or cool. Unlike most adults, they have no physical or emotional need for warmed liquids and infant foods. However, they often develop preferences to what they become accustomed to.

If you opt for warm temperatures, play it safe so your baby won't get burned. Warm bottles of formula or breast milk in a pan of warm water or under a stream of warm tap water. You can do the same with frozen breast milk, or defrost it overnight in the refrigerator.

Avoid heating milk to a boiling temperature. Boiling temperatures destroy some nutrients and for breast milk, some protective properties.

Shake the bottle during and after warming to evenly distribute the heat. And always test a few drops on the back of your hand, not your wrist. The back of your hand is more sensitive. The formula or milk should be tepid, or just slightly warm to the touch.

Microwave Warming: Be Very Cautious
Be very cautious if you heat formula or baby food in a microwave oven. Microwaving creates uneven heating, or "hot spots," that can burn a baby's mouth and skin. A bottle or food may feel cool on the outside while the inner contents reach scorching temperatures. And since food doesn't heat evenly, bacteria that cause foodborne illness may not be killed. Avoid using the microwave oven to warm breast milk.

Sometimes plastic bottle liners explode if their contents become too hot. And because microwave heating produces high temperatures quickly, some vitamins and protective factors in breast milk may be destroyed.

For warmed bottles...heat them only until the formula or milk is tepid.

➢ Warm only chilled formula (portions of 4 ounces or more) in the microwave.

➢ Use clear, microwave-safe, plastic baby bottles. Avoid glass and colored plastic bottles, and plastic liners, which may crack, melt, or burst.

➢ Remove the bottle top (cap and ring) and nipple before warming the bottle in the microwave oven. The bottle shouldn't be covered when warming it.

➢ Warm a 4-ounce bottle on high power (100 percent) for no more than 30 seconds; 45 seconds is tops for an 8-ounce bottle. Remember, you're only warming the bottle—not making it hot.

➢ After warming, replace the nipple and bottle top (ring and cap). Invert the bottle 10 times to distribute the heat.

➢ Test the temperature of the formula or milk on the back of your hand. If it feels barely warm, offer it right away. Don't allow the warmed bottle to sit out at room temperature. If the bottle was overheated, place in the refrigerator until cool enough to feed to baby.

For solid foods...warm foods in the microwave oven just until lukewarm.

➢ Place food in a microwave-safe dish, rather than leaving it in the jar. As in baby bottles, food in jars can develop hot spots.

➢ Heat only the amount you'll need. Less food heats faster than more food. And some ovens heat faster than others. Fifteen seconds on high (100 percent power) for 4 ounces of baby food is enough. Remember that higher-fat foods, such as meat and eggs, often heat faster, too.

➢ Read warming guidelines on baby food labels. And remember baby foods can be served cold, at room temperature, or slightly warm.

➢ After microwaving, allow food to "rest"; food will continue to heat through. Stir the food to distribute the heat.

➢ Test the temperature of the food before feeding it to baby. It should be just lukewarm. Use a clean spoon to feed your baby.

For more about the safe use of a microwave oven, refer to *"Play It Microwave Safe" on page 317.*

FEEDING MYSELF

As babies master spoon feeding, they're gradually ready to start feeding themselves. Watch for signals that suggest your baby is ready for self-feeding: perhaps trying to help you, or taking a cup away, or putting his or her hand on yours.

Start with finger foods. It's easy because eating by hand is utensil free.

Give your baby a spoon to hold in one hand while you use another for feeding. This gives your baby practice grasping a utensil.

Offer baby-friendly utensils: a small, rounded spoon with a straight, wide handle and a dish with high straight sides.

Use the two-spoon approach. Give an empty one to your baby. And fill the other with baby food. Then switch so baby has a filled spoon for self-feeding.

Be patient—and relaxed. Food will end up on the floor. Your baby will need lots of practice before being able to eat a whole meal without your help.

Always stay with your baby when he or she is self-feeding. That way, you'll be around if he or she starts to choke. ✦

Baby Food—Make It Yourself?

In spite of the added work, some parents get satisfaction from preparing baby food themselves. However, making baby food requires extra care to keep it safe and to retain nutrients in fresh foods.

Commercial baby foods are nutritious options for feeding baby, too. Today's commercial baby foods provide balance and variety with carefully controlled and consistent nutrient content.

Follow these guidelines if you choose to prepare homemade baby food:

Wash your hands before preparing baby food.

Always use clean cutting boards, utensils, and containers to cook, purée, and store homemade baby food.

Wash, peel, and remove seeds or pits from produce. Take special care with fruits and vegetables that come into contact with the ground. They may contain spores for clostridium botulinum that can cause food poisoning.

Start with fresh or frozen vegetables. Cook them until tender by steaming or in the microwave, then purée or mash. There's no need to add salt, other seasonings, or sweeteners. Remember, a baby's tastes aren't the same as yours.

Purée or mash fresh fruit or fruit canned in its own juice. Never add honey or corn syrup.

Avoid putting egg whites in homemade baby food until the baby's first birthday. Egg whites, more likely than egg yolks, may cause an allergic reaction. Cook any egg whites you feed your toddler.

Cook meats, poultry, and egg yolks until well done. Babies are especially susceptible to foodborne illnesses caused by eating undercooked meats, poultry, and eggs. Again, there's no need for added flavorings.

Prepare foods with a texture appropriate for the baby's feeding stage. Purée foods in a food processor, blender, or baby food grinder. Or mash them with a fork. Or chop them well, so your baby won't choke.

Cover, and refrigerate or freeze homemade baby food immediately after it's prepared. If refrigerated, keep homemade baby food in a covered container for no more than three days.

For convenience, freeze prepared baby food for later use. Freeze it in small portions in a clean ice cube tray. Once frozen, put the cubes into clean, air tight, plastic bags for single-serve portions. As another method, use the "plop and freeze" technique: Plop meal-size spoonfuls of puréed food onto a cookie

Avoid Feeding from the Baby Food Jar

Feeding directly from the jar introduces bacteria from your baby's mouth to the spoon and into the food. If the uneaten food is saved, bacteria in the leftovers can grow and may cause diarrhea, vomiting, and other symptoms of foodborne illness, if used at a later feeding.

Instead, spoon small amounts of baby food from the jar into a feeding dish, and feed from there. If your baby needs a second helping, just take more from the jar with a clean spoon.

As soon as you finish feeding your baby, cap opened jars of baby food that haven't come in contact with your baby's saliva. You may then safely refrigerate them for up to three days.

Unopened jars of baby food have the same shelf-life as other canned foods. Check the product dating on the label or lid, then use the baby food while it's still at its peak quality. *To learn how to read product dating, refer to* "More Reading on the Food Label" *on page* 275. Most jars of baby food have a safety button on top. If the button's indented, the food should be safe. As the vacuum is released on the seal, you'll hear a "pop" when you open the jar. ✦

sheet. Freeze, then transfer the frozen baby food to clean plastic bags for continued freezing.

Label and date homemade baby food. Fruit and vegetable purées may be kept frozen for six to eight months; frozen, puréed cooked meat, poultry, and fish, for 10 weeks.

For Babies, Toddlers, and Preschoolers: How to Avoid Choking

Having teeth doesn't mean children can handle all foods. Small, hard foods…slippery foods…and sticky foods can block the air passage, cutting off a child's supply of oxygen.

Food Labels: For Infants Under Two Years

The Dietary Guidelines for Americans don't apply to children under age two—and neither do the Nutrition Facts on the labels of foods for adults.

Although they use the Nutrition Facts format, infant food labels look different from adult food labels—and they supply different information, too. The illustration below shows a typical infant food label. The label gives information that helps parents choose food with the kinds and amounts of nutrients their youngsters need.

Serving Size. For infant foods, serving sizes are based on average amounts that infants under two years of age usually eat at one time. For oatmeal, that's 1/4 cup. On adult food labels, serving sizes are based on average amounts adults typically eat at one time; again for oatmeal, that may be given as 1/2 cup or 1 ounce uncooked oatmeal.

Total Fat. Infant food labels list the total fat content in a single serving of food. But unlike adult food labels, they don't give the calories from fat, saturated fat, nor cholesterol content. These details aren't included because babies under two years of age need fat as a concentrated energy source to fuel their rapid growth. Parents and other caregivers shouldn't try to limit an infant's fat intake.

Daily Values. Daily values for protein and some vitamins and minerals are listed on food labels for infants and children under four years of age. However, fat, cholesterol, sodium, potassium, carbohydrate, and fiber have no Daily Values because they haven't been set for children under age four.

For more about food labels in general, refer to "Today's Food Labels" on page 270. "Get All the Facts" on page 271 gives more detail on the Nutrition Facts panel on adult food labels. ✦

Nutrition Facts

Serving Size 1/4 cup (15g)
Servings Per Container About 30

Amount Per Serving	
Calories 60	
Total Fat	1g
Sodium	0mg
Potassium	50mg
Total Carbohydrate	10g
Fiber	1g
Sugars	0g
Protein	2g

	Infants	Children
% Daily Value*	**0-1**	**1-4**
Protein	7%	6%
Vitamin A	0%	0%
Vitamin C	0%	0%
Calcium	15%	10%
Iron	45%	60%
Vitamin E	15%	8%
Thiamin	45%	30%
Riboflavin	45%	30%
Niacin	25%	20%
Phosphorus	15%	10%

Don't offer these foods to children younger than three or four years of age:

- *small, hard foods*—nuts, seeds, popcorn, snack chips, pretzels, raw carrots, snack puffs, raisins. Instead offer foods cut into larger pieces, allowing kids to bite and chew, but not put a whole piece into their mouths.

- *slippery foods*—whole grapes; large pieces of meats, poultry, and frankfurter; and candy and cough drops, which may be swallowed before they're adequately chewed. Make sure grapes, meat, poultry, frankfurters, and other foods are chopped into small pieces. Avoid offering chewing gum.

Offer appropriate foods. Finger foods for older babies and toddlers are pieces of banana, graham crackers, strips of cheese, or bagels.

Always watch young children while they eat. That includes watching older brothers and sisters who may offer foods that younger children can't handle yet.

Insist that children sit down to eat or drink. They shouldn't eat when they're lying down or running around. As children develop eating skills, encourage them to take enough time to chew well.

Tips for Travel, Tips for Daycare

Pack unopened jars of commercial baby food. All kinds of foods come in jars, including cereals. Ready-to-feed formula in a prepackaged bottle is handy, too, especially as it doesn't require refrigeration. Or use powdered formula. Just premeasure water and powder into separate containers, then mix when it's needed.

Keep perishable food, such as bottles of prepared infant formula or breast milk, well chilled. Pack them in an insulated container with frozen cold packs. When you arrive at your destination, refrigerate them.

Have everything handy: food, utensils, bib, and baby wipes or a clean, damp washcloth. If someone else is feeding your baby, provide feeding instructions, too, including the time and approximate amount to feed.

Keep food separate from soiled diapers. And don't put food and bottles in a diaper bag that's frequently exposed to fecal and urine particles. ✦

When an Infant Is Choking

IF CONSCIOUS BUT CHOKING...

Give five back blows and five chest thrusts. Repeat blows and thrusts until object comes out.

IF UNCONSCIOUS...

Look for and clear any object from the mouth. Give two slow breaths. Give five back blows and five chest thrusts. Repeat until breaths go in or help arrives.

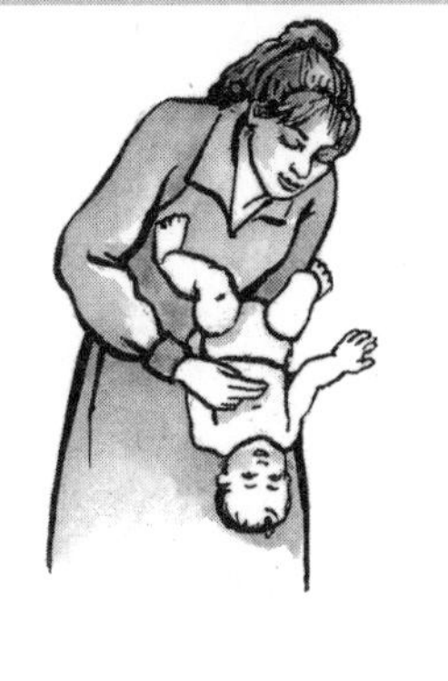

Be prepared to use the Heimlich Maneuver quickly to dislodge solid foods that obstruct the air passage. Do this when a child is choking and can't breathe, cough, talk, or cry. The technique for infants and toddlers differs somewhat from that for adults. *For an illustrated description, see below. For a description of the Heimlich Maneuver for older children, teens, and adults, refer to page* 321.

Always have the child seen by a doctor after a serious choking incident to be sure that the lungs and airway are clear.

your nutrition check-up

Do You Baby Your Baby?

There's a lot to know about feeding an infant and toddler—and about ensuring a positive eating experience from day one.

Check yourself out on these baby-feeding basics. Which infant-feeding practices do you follow (have you followed) when feeding your baby—or perhaps when helping out a new parent?

Yes No

❒ ❒ 1. Monitor the number of wet diapers (six or more every 24 hours), to make sure your breast- or formula-fed baby is getting enough to eat.

❒ ❒ 2. Offer breast milk or formula, not cow's milk, to your baby up to 12 months of age.

❒ ❒ 3. If your baby is bottle fed, choose an iron-fortified formula—unless your baby's doctor advises otherwise.

❒ ❒ 4. Discard leftover expressed breast milk or infant formula after a feeding.

❒ ❒ 5. Wait until at least four months of age before starting solid foods.

❒ ❒ 6. Always wash your hands before feeding your baby.

❒ ❒ 7. Clean all baby-feeding equipment with hot, soapy water—then rinse well.

❒ ❒ 8. Avoid putting your baby to bed with a bottle.

❒ ❒ 9. Offer infant cereal that's iron-fortified.

❒ ❒ 10. Start with single foods—one new food at a time.

❒ ❒ 11. Monitor your baby's reaction to a new food, just in case he or she has a reaction.

❒ ❒ 12. Give your baby enough to eat, rather than trying to restrict calories or fat.

❒ ❒ 13. Check the temperature of food or bottles to be sure they're evenly warmed, not hot!

❒ ❒ 14. Try new foods several times, rather than giving up after one or two rejections.

❒ ❒ 15. Let your baby—not you—set the feeding pace.

❒ ❒ 16. Remain patient as your baby learns to feed himself or herself.

❒ ❒ 17. Offer smooth foods until your baby is ready for mashed or finely-chopped foods.

❒ ❒ 18. Always stay with your baby while he or she is eating.

❒ ❒ 19. Discard leftover formula or food after a feeding.

❒ ❒ 20. Make infant feeding a special time to nurture and enjoy your baby—these days don't last!

Now Score Yourself

Give yourself—and your baby—a big hug if you said "yes" to all 20 items.

If you said "no" to any item, go back and read that part of the chapter again. Practice what you learn. Your baby's health depends on it!

real life nutrition

Parent-to-Parent Feeding Advice

"Maddie, you're a beautiful baby! Dark hair just like your mommy and daddy." Judy and Mike glowed as they introduced their tiny girl to the family.

"I've loved being home with Maddie these first few months," Judy remarked to her cousins, Bill and Fran, wishing she could stretch out the last few weeks before going back to work.

"And we're all doing great learning how to be a family of three." Mike was a terrific dad, doing household tasks so that Judy could relax and nurse Maddie ... even taking his turn with a supplemental bottle in the wee hours of the night or when Judy headed out on errands.

From the start, they'd planned for Judy's return to work, offering a supplemental bottle of breast milk after Maddie was two weeks old. Now, Maddie took a bottle without fussing just as naturally as she nursed.

"Judy, do you think Maddie will be ready for solid foods soon? She's sitting up—and moving her head to watch us. And look how she's watching my spoon," smiled Fran, an experienced mom with a 12-month-old self-feeder, who delights in painting her face with applesauce.

Judy nodded. Maddie was showing signs of being ready for solid foods. They didn't want to rush her. But now that Maddie was almost five months old, they wanted to try solid foods—their goal before starting Maddie with daycare.

"Fran, Bill—how do you work out a feeding schedule with your daycare center? You must have some advice to pass along to us less experienced parents," Mike said with a wink.

Advice on infant feeding when both parents work:

➢ Judy and Mike were wise to start planning ahead for Judy's return to work. That way, bottle feeding won't be an issue. She can express her breast milk, so Maddie can take it from a bottle. Or they can wean her to iron-fortified infant formula.

➢ If they switch to formula, they might try a prepackaged bottle of formula that doesn't need mixing.

➢ They should take prepared bottles of formula or breast milk to Maddie's daycare in

real life nutrition (continued)

an insulated container with cold packs—then refrigerate them on arrival.

➢ If Judy is able to nurse Maddie during the day, they might find daycare near her job. Then Judy can visit and nurse during her work breaks and lunch hour. If not, Judy can express milk during her breaks for later feedings. She's wise to check ahead before starting back on the job to know how she can mesh breast-feeding with her work situation.

➢ As Maddie learns to eat new foods at home, they can send unopened jars of those baby foods with her. That includes iron-fortified cereal, which should be her first solid food.

➢ Judy and Mike would be wise to provide feeding instructions for the caregiver—including when and how much to feed Maddie. And from the start, their caregiver should tell them how Maddie eats each day since they're all part of the "feeding team."

➢ Most important, they should make eating a relaxed time, both at home and at daycare. As with Fran and Bill's daughter, they're wise to enjoy and remain patient with each step as Maddie learns to eat—even when she starts to paint her face with applesauce!

CHAPTER SEVENTEEN

FOOD TO GROW ON

Food nourishes at every age and stage in a child's life: infancy, the toddler and preschool years, school-age years, and adolescence. Through carefully-made food choices, parents and caregivers help ensure the physical nourishment of growing bodies. However, children's experiences with food nourish even more—the social, emotional, and psychological aspects of their lives.

No matter what their age, youngsters need the same nutrients as adults. Only the amounts change. Like you, they need energy from food — but more relative to their body weight. They enjoy many of the same foods you like, but the form and combinations may differ.

The challenge for parents and caregivers is to recognize and respect the differences, to make foods available that are appropriate for children, and to set the time and place for eating. Children need to learn how to make food choices and decide how much food they need to consume.

Toddlers and Preschoolers: Food for the Early Years

Do young children seem like sponges, absorbing all the sights, sounds, and tastes of the world around them?

Children in these early years truly are impressionable. The preschool years are a great time to help children form positive attitudes toward food and to develop sound eating habits—attitudes and lifestyles to last a lifetime!

While toddlers and preschoolers grow at a slower rate than infants, they need enough energy and nutrients from food to fuel their active play and the next stages of growth. For young children, healthful eating helps to establish a foundation of good nutrition and healthful lifestyle habits that can reduce the risks for obesity, heart disease, cancer, and other chronic diseases later in life.

Food for Hungry Tummies

Young children need specific nutrients, such as calcium, protein, vitamin A, and iron, rather than specific foods. Eating a variety of foods—in adequate amounts—is the key to getting the nutrients they need to thrive.

For every nutrient, children have many choices. If children won't touch sweet potatoes, try a wedge of cantaloupe; they're both good sources of vitamin A. Is milk rejected? Offer other calcium-rich foods—like cheese and yogurt. If you offer different kinds of healthful foods, your child will learn to enjoy many of them—and reap their benefits. *For a general meal and snack guideline, refer to the "Feeding Guide for Young Children" on page 423.*

Whole milk, rather than low-fat varieties, is recommended for children 12 to 24 months of age. Whole milk supplies more fat and calories than 2 percent, 1 percent, or skim milk. As a concentrated source of energy, fat helps fuel this period of fairly rapid growth. And the extra cholesterol in whole milk helps a young child's brain develop properly. After the second birthday, any type of milk is okay to drink. Choose the type that matches your child's energy needs.

have you ever wondered

...what to do about a preschooler who seems overweight? First discuss your concerns with your child's doctor before taking any action. Restricting calories can be harmful for young children. Low-calorie diets often don't supply the energy and essential nutrients they need to grow, develop, and learn properly. In most cases, healthful eating habits, combined with plenty of active play, allow most overweight kids to grow into their weight—without the need for a special diet. *For more about children and overweight, refer to "Weighty Problems for Children" on page 438.*

...if a vegetarian diet is OK for kids? A well-planned vegetarian diet can supply all the nutrients that children need for their growth and energy needs. However, those who exclude all meats, poultry, fish, eggs, and dairy foods need to be especially cautious about consuming good sources of vitamin B_{12} and vitamin D. Eating foods with enough calcium, iron, and zinc also needs special attention. *For more guidance, refer to chapter 22, "The Vegetarian Way."* ✦

How Much? How Often?

You can lead a young child to the table. But you can't make that child eat—nor should you!

How much do toddlers and preschoolers typically eat? Although they're no longer babies, young children aren't ready for adult-sized portions. Adult servings can overwhelm small appetites and children's stomachs aren't big enough to handle such large portions.

Serve toddlers or preschoolers servings that are one-fourth to one-third the size of adult portions. As a guide to portion size, some experts advise one tablespoon of every food served for every year age. *As another guideline, refer to child-sized servings in "Feeding Guide for Young Children" on page 422.*

Offer children less than you think they'll eat. Then, let them ask for more.

Listen to children's hunger cues. Respect your child when he or she says "enough." Children only need to eat enough to satisfy their hunger. When they start to play with food, become restless, or send signals of "no more," remove the food. Or let children leave the table.

Avoid forcing membership in the "clean-plate" club. This practice may encourage overeating or a food aversion—habits that could cause weight or nutritional problems later.

From day to day and meal to meal, appetite fluctuations are normal. Children's appetites often decrease after their first birthday as their growth slows. In fact, expect a child to "pick at" meals on occasion. Chances are, he or she will make up for it later.

A child's food intake usually increases just before a growth spurt. During childhood, growth is gradual, accelerating most just prior to and during early adolescence: for girls, between ages 10 through 14, and for boys, between the ages of 12 through 16. As long as a child is growing normally, he or she is getting enough calories.

How often should young children eat? Try to keep to a eating schedule. Children seem to do best with a routine—when meals and snacks are served at about the same time each day. "Pacifier snacks" eaten while standing in line at the supermarket…or snacks just one-half hour before a meal may interfere with a child's eating routine.

Younger children may need to eat five to six times a day because their stomachs have limited capacity. Plan nutritious snacks as part of the day's meal schedule, and space them between meals. *Refer to "Snacks Equal Good Nutrition" on page* 426.

For sample menus that meet the nutrient and energy needs of most young children, refer to "To Get Started: Sample Menus for Toddlers and Preschoolers" on page 424.

Mealtime Tactics

Parents and caregivers supply the three "Ws" of meals and snacks: **W**hat foods are offered, and **W**hen and **W**here they're eaten. The child fills in the other "W" and "H": **W**hich offered foods to eat and **H**ow much.

While activity helps to build a child's appetite, plan a quiet time before meals and snacks. Kids eat best when they're more relaxed.

Remember your child learns by watching you. Eat with your kids. Set a good example by eating a variety of foods yourself. Older siblings can have a similar effect. So make healthful eating a family affair. Eating together is also a good chance to demonstrate appropriate table manners.

Feeding Guide for Young Children

Foods	Serving Size: 1-3 years old	Serving Size: 4-5 years old
BREADS, CEREALS, RICE, AND PASTA: ≥ 6 servings daily		
Bread	1/4-1/2 slice	1 slice
Buns, bagels, muffins	1/4-1/2	1/2
Plain crackers	2-3	4-6
Dry cereal (whole grain or enriched)	1/4-1/3 cup	1/2 cup
Cooked cereal, rice, pasta	1/4-1/3 cup	1/2 cup
FRUITS AND VEGETABLES RICH IN VITAMIN C**: ≥ 1 serving daily		
Chopped, cooked, or canned	1/3 cup	1/2 cup
Juice	1/3 cup	1/2 cup
DARK GREEN/ORANGE FRUITS AND VEGETABLES RICH IN VITAMIN A**: ≥ 1 serving daily		
Cooked or chopped raw	1/4 cup	1/4-1/3 cup
Juice	1/4-1/3 cup	1/2 cup
OTHER FRUITS AND VEGETABLES (INCLUDING POTATO)**: ≥ 3 servings daily		
Cooked, canned, or chopped raw	1/4 cup	1/4-1/2 cup
Whole	1/4-1/2 piece	1/4-1/2 cup
Juice	1/4 cup	1/2 cup
MILK, YOGURT AND CHEESE*: 3 servings daily		
Milk, yogurt	1/2 cup	3/4 cup
Cheese	1/2 oz	3/4 oz
MEATS, POULTRY, FISH, DRY BEANS AND PEAS, EGGS, AND NUTS: 2 servings daily		
Lean meat, fish, and poultry	1-3 Tbsp chopped or 1-2 oz	4-5 Tbsp chopped or 2-3 oz
Eggs	1	1
Dried peas and beans	1-3 Tbsp	2-4 Tbsp
Peanut butter	1 Tbsp	2 Tbsp
FATS AND OILS*: 3-4 servings daily		
Margarine, butter, or oil	1 tsp	1 tsp

**Children under two years should not be placed on fat/cholesterol-restricted diets and should consume whole milk and whole milk products. Children older than two should gradually make a transition to a lower fat intake to meet health promotion guidelines.*

***The goals for "five-a-day" include good sources of vitamin C and vitamin A.*

Source: Manual for Clinical Dietetics, Fifth Edition. *Chicago: The American Dietetic Association,* 1996.

Even if you can't eat together, be there! Young children need supervision in case they start to choke. Someone who's choking may not be able to make sounds you can hear easily. *For more about avoiding or handling a choking incident, refer to "For Babies, Toddlers, and Preschoolers: How to Avoid Choking" on page 414.*

Encourage kids to sit while they eat. Give youngsters a "boost" so they can reach their food easily. Discourage eating while standing, walking, or lying down.

Reward children with affection and attention—not food. Using food as a reward or punishment only promotes unhealthy attitudes about food.

Give young children the freedom to choose foods, just as older children and adults do. Respect their food preferences, and allow them to reject certain foods. Just encourage them to politely say "no, thank you." Making food choices is a competency children need to master.

Avoid the notion of "forbidden" foods. That may cause your child to want them more. All foods can be part of your child's healthful eating plan.

Serve "designer dinners," featuring a variety of colors and textures. Cut food in interesting shapes, and arrange it attractively on the plate. Kids react to inviting foods just like you do!

To Get Started: Sample Menus for Toddlers and Preschoolers

SAMPLE MENU FOR THE 1- TO 3-YEAR-OLD PRESCHOOL CHILD	SAMPLE MENU FOR THE 4- TO 5-YEAR-OLD PRESCHOOL CHILD
BREAKFAST Whole milk* (1/2 cup) Cream of wheat (1/4 cup) Banana (1/2) Margarine (1/2 tsp)	BREAKFAST 1% Milk (3/4 cup) Cream of wheat (1/2 cup) Banana (1/2)
MIDMORNING SNACK Vanilla wafers (2) Orange juice (1/2 cup)	MIDMORNING SNACK Vanilla wafers (3) Orange juice (1/2 cup)
LUNCH Whole milk* (1/2 cup) Chicken strips (1 1/2 oz) Whole-wheat bread (1 slice) Cooked carrots (2 Tbsp) Margarine (1 tsp) Canned peaches (1/4 cup)	LUNCH 1% milk (3/4 cup) Chicken strips (2 oz) Whole-wheat bread (1 slice) Cooked carrots (3 Tbsp) Margarine (1 tsp) Canned peaches (1/4 cup)
MID-AFTERNOON SNACK Cheese (1/2 oz) Crackers (3)	MID-AFTERNOON SNACK Cheese (3/4 oz) Crackers (5)
DINNER Whole milk* (1/2 cup) Spaghetti (1/4 cup) with meat sauce (2 Tbsp) Broccoli (2 Tbsp) Margarine (1 tsp) Dinner roll (1/2) Applesauce (1/4 cup)	DINNER 1% milk (3/4 cup) Spaghetti (1/2 cup) with meat sauce (1/4 cup) Broccoli (3 Tbsp) Margarine (1 tsp) Dinner roll (1 medium) Applesauce (1/3 cup)
EVENING SNACK Whole milk* (1/2 cup) Graham crackers (2)	EVENING SNACK 1% milk (3/4 cup) Graham crackers (2)

**Children older than 2 years can be given lower-fat milk.*

Offer foods with kid appeal. Many younger children prefer plain, unmixed foods. Foods with funny names—such as monster-mash potatoes (mashed sweet potatoes) or bugs on a log (raisins and peanut butter on celery)—may help kids to try new foods. Kids often like finger foods, too. Offer raw vegetables so they can be easily nibbled in hand. *For vegetables that taste good raw, refer to "Vegetables: From A to Z" on page 250.*

Encourage children to practice serving themselves: for example, pouring milk from a pitcher, spreading peanut butter on bread, or spooning food from a serving bowl to their plate. Even though spills are messy, they're a necessary part of developing a sense of independence.

Make eating and family time the focus of meal and snacktime—not TV watching. This is a good opportunity to focus on the social aspects of food and to reinforce positive eating behaviors.

Avoid undue focus on desserts. Serve them with meals, rather than after the main course, and never as a reward.

Stock your kitchen with child-size dishes and utensils children can use with ease: cups they can get their hands around; broad, straight, short-handled utensils;

spoons with a wide mouth; forks with blunt tines; and plates with a curved lip.

Even in this fast-paced world, give kids enough time to eat. Remember, they're less skilled at self-feeding. Time pressure puts stress on eating, and takes the pleasure away.

Toddlers and preschoolers live to play! Encourage that same sense of fun and adventure at mealtime. Make meals a pleasant family gathering. Recall the day's events, share each other's company, and enjoy the food. This approach does a lot to develop positive attitudes about food.

Feeding "Finicky" Eaters

Does your child refuse to eat green foods? Does he or she suddenly react to an all-time favorite food with an "I don't like this," or simply "no"? Are you concerned because your youngster won't eat vegetables? Toddler-hood and the preschool years are characterized by bouts of independence. What appears to be "finicky" eating instead may be your child's early attempts to be assertive—a natural part of growing up.

Arm yourself with these tips for handling what may appear to be the "downs and ups" of child feeding:

Avoid the "short-order-cook" routine. At mealtime, serve at least one food you know your child likes. But expect your tot to eat the same foods as the rest of the family.

Know that young children often prefer plain foods that they can easily recognize. So "unmix" the food if it's a problem. Put aside a portion of the ingredients for mixed dishes before assembling the recipe. That even works for a salad or a sandwich. Then let children put food together in any way that suits them. *Tip*: Sometimes they don't like different foods to "touch" each other.

Get kids involved. Even finicky eaters will more likely eat foods they help make. Small children can wash fresh fruit or put meat between bread slices for a sandwich.

Remember meal planning and grocery shopping. Let your child help plan a meal around favorite foods. Or, let children select a new food for the family on trips to the store. Even encourage children to try ethnic foods when shopping for a new taste sensation.

Fat Facts for Tots

Put away your adult notions about fat where a young child's diet is concerned. A low-fat eating plan is not advised for children under two years of age. Fat is an excellent source of the energy, or calories, that supports a young child's rapid growth and active lifestyle. Some fatty acids—linoleic and linolenic acid—are essential for growth. They must be supplied by food because the body can't make them.

Between age two and five, it's OK to gradually reduce fat. As they consume less calories, or energy, from fat, children can get more energy from nutrient-rich foods that have less fat: grain products, fruits, vegetables, low-fat dairy foods, and other protein-rich foods.

By age five, a child's eating style should conform to the same Dietary Guidelines as older children and adults—limiting fat to no more than 30 percent of total calories, and saturated fat to no more than 10 percent of total calories. Remember that this guideline refers to your child's overall diet—not to one food, meal, or even one day's intake. This guideline is meant for the total fat in food choices over several days.

Higher-fat foods—in moderate amounts—can fit in a child's healthful eating plan. They're a concentrated energy source that fuels growth, development, and active play. These foods also add taste and variety to a balanced diet.

For more about fat in a healthful diet, refer to chapter 3, "Fat Facts." ✦

Children often dislike extreme temperatures. Allow hot food to cool down and cold food to warm up a little before serving.

If your child won't eat certain foods, perhaps spinach, don't worry—just offer other foods from the same food group, maybe broccoli or carrots. Foods from the same food group supply similar nutrients.

Moisten dry foods, such as meat, if they're hard to chew. Perhaps add a little cheese sauce, or fruit or vegetable juices. Serve drier foods alongside "naturally" moist foods, such as mashed potatoes or cottage cheese. Or offer "dipping" sauces with finger foods—kids love to dip!

Most of all, relax. Focus your attention on the positive aspects of your child's eating behavior, not on your child's food.

What do you do when youngsters get "stuck" on a food? If he or she keeps asking for the same food meal after meal, the child is experiencing a "food jag." Food jags are common in the toddler years.

More frustrating for you than harmful for kids, you're smart to remain low key about food jags. The more you focus on them, the longer they may last.

Actually, it's OK to offer the food they want again and again and again! Just include other foods alongside to encourage variety. Your "monotonous diner" will soon tire of eating the same food so often.

If whole categories of food are rejected for more than two weeks, talk to your child's doctor or a registered dietitian. ✦

Tasting Something New!

Babies try one new food after another as they start solids, each time adding more food variety to their diet. The tasting adventure continues throughout the childhood years—and on into adulthood. More variety increases the opportunity for good nutrition and adds to the pleasure of eating.

Helping young children be willing food "experimenters" is part of the challenge and pleasure of feeding them:

Offer new foods at the start of meals. That's when children are the most hungry. But make the rest of the meal familiar.

Encourage children to taste at least one bite of a new food—or a food prepared in a different way. Don't force them. Just be matter-of-fact.

Keep your thoughts to yourself if there are foods you don't like. Try not to let your food dislikes hinder your child from trying new foods.

Before offering the new food, talk about it. Let kids help you prepare it. They'll be more willing to taste!

Serve the same food in different forms: for example, raw carrot sticks and cooked carrot coins. That way, they'll learn to enjoy a more varied eating style—the same food prepared in different ways.

Keep trying! Kids may need to taste a food 5 to 10 times before they learn to like it.

Remember, whenever you expose children to some foods, but limit others, you also limit the variety of foods they learn to eat and enjoy. That has an impact on the overall nutritional quality of their food pattern for life!

Snacks Equal Good Nutrition

Toddlers and preschoolers like to snack. And that's good news! Because their stomachs are small, they may not be able to meet their nutrition needs with just three meals a day. Snacks can provide nutrients and food energy that are missing from their meals.

If snacks conjure up images of high-calorie, low-nutrient foods—think again! Wise snack foods for people of all ages, including young children, come mostly from the five food groups of the Food Guide Pyramid. Make snacks a healthful part of your child's diet:

Keep snacks as supplements to regular meals, not replacements.

As with meals, schedule snacks as planned eating events. By serving snacks no less than two hours before meals, youngsters come to meals with their appetites intact—ready for good food and good company.

Offer two to three nutritious snacks plus three meals a day. That should keep the "munchies" under control—and supply the nutrients and energy children need to grow and play. Children aged two to five usually need to eat every two to three hours. Younger children may need to eat more often.

Choose snack foods that complement the child's meals. If his or her meals come up short on servings of vegetables or grain products, snack time is a good time to enjoy more. Vary snack foods as you do foods offered at mealtime.

Check the chart "Child-Friendly Snacks," at right, for snack ideas from each food group of the Food Guide Pyramid. Be cautious of foods that may cause choking. Refer to "For Babies, Toddlers, and Preschoolers: How to Avoid Choking" on page 414.

Think "fun-time" at snack time, too. Children especially enjoy foods with plenty of sensory appeal. Brightly-colored fruits and vegetables entice children to try a bite. Use your nose! Point out the aroma of baking bread or freshly-cut watermelon; then enjoy a slice as a snack. For fun with textures, combine soft, creamy cheese with crisp, crunchy crackers.

Exploring More About Food

Food offers a world of experiences, well suited to the learning styles of children. Because food can be a "hands-on" activity, everyday tasks can get kids involved in food—and so promote positive attitudes about eating. Try these simple ways to explore food with young children:

As you walk the aisles of the supermarket, encourage children to name the foods. For example, list the fruits and vegetables in the produce aisle, or say the colors of foods they know. Find foods that are new to them, and talk about their color, shape, size, and feel.

At home, as you take vegetables out of grocery bags, talk about the part of the plant each one grows on: leaf (cabbage, lettuce, greens), roots (carrot, potato), stalk (celery, asparagus), flower (broccoli, cauliflower, artichoke), and seed (peas, corn).

Grow foods from seed in your backyard garden. Perhaps start the seeds in paper cups on your windowsill. Kids enjoy eating foods they grow themselves—and it's a great science lesson!

Have children help decide what foods to serve. Perhaps show them pictures of vegetables and

Child-Friendly Snacks

BREADS, CEREALS, RICE, AND PASTA
Animal crackers; cereal (dry or with milk); bagel; English muffin; graham cracker; pita (pocket) bread; rice cake; toast; tortilla; air-popped popcorn; pretzels
MILK, YOGURT, CHEESE
Cheese; cottage cheese; pudding; milk; string cheese; yogurt
VEGETABLES
Any raw vegetable (in strips); vegetable soup
FRUITS
Any fresh fruit; canned or frozen fruit; fruit juice; fruit leather; dried fruit
MEAT, POULTRY, FISH, BEANS, EGGS, AND NUTS
Bean soup; peanut butter; yogurt; hard-cooked eggs; turkey or meat cubes; tuna salad

See "Vegetables: From A to Z" on page 250. ✦

fruits. Have them pick out the ones to make for family meals.

As preschoolers are ready, give them simple tasks to help with family meals. They might wash fruit, arrange bread in a basket, put ready-to-eat cereal in the bowls, or help set the table. Most children like to help. They feel good about themselves when they can say, for example, "I poured it!" And working together in the kitchen offers many opportunities to nurture children.

Expand their world by reading books about food to children. Ask a librarian, preschool teacher, or head of the children's book department in a store to suggest titles. Prepare some of the foods in the stories.

For more about cooking with kids, including kitchen safety tips, refer to "Kids' Kitchen" *on page* 443.

Food in Child Care: Check It Out!

Warm and caring staff, a safe environment, opportunities for development and self expression—most parents look for these important qualities when they choose child care. Good nutrition and food-safety standards also should rank high on your child-care check list.

have you ever wondered

...what to do if you think your child can't drink milk? Before you say "can't," know that milk sensitivity is often a matter of degree. Lactose intolerance, or difficulty digesting the sugar in milk, is more common than a milk allergy. And it's easy to manage—often by giving the child smaller, more frequent portions of milk. If you suspect a sensitivity to milk, seek advice from your child's doctor, pediatric nurse, or a registered dietitian. Don't simply give up milk! Children need calcium and other nutrients from milk for proper growth. *For tips on handling a child's sensitivity to milk, refer to* "Lactose Intolerance: A Matter of Degree" *on page* 194. ✦

Consider the importance of food. A child may eat two or more meals and snacks in a child-care facility, so the nutritional quality must be high. Since a young child is developing eating skills and food attitudes that will affect long-term health, the overall eating environment is important.

A child-care setting offers many opportunities for spreading illness: food service, diapering, toileting, and close contact with others. For this reason, cleanliness and safe food handling are "musts." Infants and young children have immature immune systems; they're more vulnerable to catching a cold, flu, or other illness from others.

As you look for child care, these factors suggest high standards of cleanliness and nutrition:

Food preparation and storage areas...

- neat and very clean
- properly labeled and well-covered foods
- adequate refrigeration and heating equipment
- perishable foods stored in the refrigerator

Hand-washing area...

- child-sized sinks, or safe stepping stools for adult-sized sinks
- soap and paper towels

Meal and snacktime...

- meals and snacks with a variety of foods—from the various groups of the Food Guide Pyramid
- tables and chairs appropriately sized for children's comfort, or high chairs, or booster seats
- child-sized utensils and covered cups with spouts to help young children master their feeding skills

➢ adult supervision at snack and mealtimes

Diaper-changing and toilet areas…

➢ very clean

➢ located away from food, eating, and play areas

➢ closed containers for soiled diapers, tissues, and wipes

➢ daily removal of soiled items

Other areas…

➢ separate storage for each child's toothbrush, comb, and clothing

➢ ample space between cots, nap rugs, or cribs.

Observe what goes on in the child-care setting, too. You should be able to answer "yes" to these questions:

➢ Do both children and staff wash their hands before eating or participating in food activities?

➢ Do children wash their hands after outdoor play, toileting, touching animals, sneezing, or wiping their nose?

➢ Does each child have his or her own washcloth?

➢ Are child-care providers practicing appropriate sanitation and food-handling techniques?

➢ Are bottles and foods brought from home refrigerated, and if necessary, heated safely? (*Hint*: When you send food, always label it with your child's name. Transport perishable foods in an insulated sack with a cold pack.)

➢ Is food that's left on a child's plate discarded properly?

➢ Do children each have their own dish, cup, and utensils, rather than share?

➢ Does an adult eat with the children, serving as a good role model?

➢ Are menus posted, or are they sent home with the children?

➢ Are the foods appropriate for the age of the children (e.g. no foods that may be choking hazards)?

➢ Are plates, cups, and utensils washed and sanitized after each use?

➢ Are toys that go into a child's mouth sanitized regularly?

➢ Do child-care providers and parents wash their hands thoroughly after every diaper check and change?

➢ Are food activities—such as tasting parties, food preparation, growing food from seed, and circle time activities—part of the child-care program?

For more about protecting children from foodborne illness, refer to chapter 13, "The Safe Kitchen."

have you ever wondered

…about iron poisoning—how does it happen? Iron poisoning from iron capsules or tablets—or from vitamin pills with iron—occurs when children accidentally swallow them. This can happen, too, if iron tablets meant for children aren't taken as directed, but instead at a higher dosage in a short period. If your doctor prescribes extra iron for your child, give it only as directed.

Iron poisoning can cause serious injury, even death. Call your doctor or poison control center immediately if your child accidentally swallows a supplement with iron. Keep iron pills and all other pills in child-safe containers where they cannot be reached. *Note*: Iron poisoning won't result from eating a healthful diet with iron-fortified foods! ✦

Parents as Partners

For the many children in child care, feeding is a shared responsibility. Together parents and child-care providers offer foods that nourish kids. And together they help children develop skills and a positive attitude about eating. When kids have a feeding problem—perhaps a food sensitivity—they need to address it together.

Child-care providers might record menus and snacks served and share them with parents. That way, parents can encourage and reinforce these foods at home.

At home, parents can teach about handwashing before kids start child care. They can reinforce food tasting by serving foods their children first try at the center. They can talk positively about food on the child-care menu, and even try new foods ahead as a family.

If schedules allow, parents who are able to volunteer in a child-care setting can add to the center's nutrition program. Preparing a family food as a group activity offers a chance for their child to share with classmates. Occasionally parents might eat with children or help chaperone a food-related field trip. Or they might help in gathering empty food packages and other kitchen supplies for play areas or for food activities. This type of help is always received well!

Eating ABCs for School-Age Children

School-age youngsters—no longer toddlers, not yet teens—are establishing habits that last a lifetime. For their good health, both good nutrition and physical activity habits should rank high on their list of priorities.

During these years, children gain control of the world around them. They push for independence, associate more with their peers, and make more choices of their own. Because they're away from home more often, other people have a growing role in shaping their food decisions. A recent study showed that school-age children acknowledge teachers and schools, then parents as their main sources of nutrition information; television, books, then health professionals were ranked next.

Keep these thoughts in mind as you help school-age children develop healthful eating and physical activity habits:

Nutrients. Many different foods can provide the nutrients essential for growth, energy, and health—and to prepare for the growth demands of adolescence. By eating at least the minimum number of servings recommended by the Food Guide Pyramid, most children can consume the nutrients their bodies need. *Refer to "Pyramid Power for Kids" on page* 431.

Growth. Children aged 6- to 12 years old grow an average of two inches per year. This represents a weight gain of about five pounds a year. To look at it another way, they grow one to two feet and almost double their weight during these years. During this period, children's body sizes and shapes vary a great deal from one child to the other.

Preferences. Children's appetites and food preferences may change quickly. Eating small amounts or not eating certain foods may simply mean that they are testing their own tastes.

Habits. Children learn by watching others. Parents, friends, teachers, and television all may influence what and how children eat. Eating nutritious meals and snacks yourself provides a good example, as one of the many influences that affect their food decisions.

Nutrition Knowledge. The nutrition message is getting through to children. Depending on their age, many know the basics of healthful eating. And most know that a balanced diet and physical activity are important for their health. The challenge for parents, teachers, and other adults is to help them make the link between what they're learning and the food choices they make.

Physical Activity. For good health, children need to balance their lifestyles with physical activity. Many of today's children aren't getting enough exercise. In fact, studies estimate that 20 to 40 percent of American children are not physically fit!

For simple, easy-to-remember steps for fitness that you can share with children, refer to "Ten Tips to Healthy Eating and Physical Activity" on this page.

Nutrition for Growing Up

School-age children love to measure their progress from year to year on a growth chart. They want energy to run and play—and the energy to do well in school. Parents, teachers, and other caregivers have the same priorities. How can children eat to grow up healthy... and have energy to learn and play?

Pyramid Power for Kids

Meant for children aged two or more, as well as for teens and adults, the Food Guide Pyramid is a guideline for healthful eating. The Pyramid is flexible enough for everyone—even the food preferences of youngsters.

Children don't need any specific foods for their growth and health, just specific nutrients. In fact, they need the same nutrients as their parents do, only in different amounts. *Check the information in "Pyramid Servings for Children" on page* 432.

Eating many different foods provides energy and a variety of nutrients children need—protein, carbohydrates, fat, and different vitamins and minerals. These are just some reasons why food variety, both among and within the five food groups, is so important for growing children:

- ***Milk, cheese, and yogurt provide protein, calcium, and vitamin D for their strong bones, teeth, and muscles.*** *For more on the role of vitamins and minerals in health, refer to chapter 4, "Vitamins and Minerals: Enough, But Not Too Much." And for more about growing healthy bones, refer to "Calcium: A Growing Issue" on page 447.*
- ***Meat, poultry, fish, eggs, beans, nuts, and seeds supply protein, iron, B vitamins, and some minerals for strong muscles and healthy blood.***

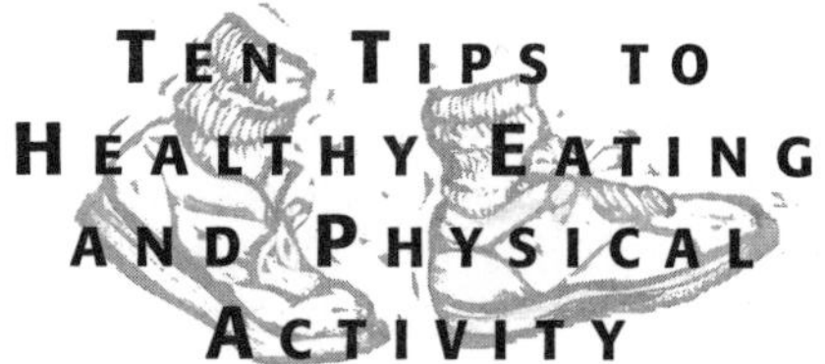

Ten Tips to Healthy Eating and Physical Activity

Are you helping children learn about healthful eating and physical activity? Then these are 10 tips—in kid-friendly language—that they're wise to know and to put into practice. (Hang them on your refrigerator door.)

- Eat lots of different kinds of food.
- Eat more whole-grain breads and cereals, fruits, and vegetables.
- Keep moving to stay in shape.
- Start your day with breakfast.
- Snack smart.
- Balance your food choices so you don't eat too much of any one thing.
- Be adventurous.
- Set healthy eating goals.
- Remember, all foods can be part of a healthful diet.
- Make healthy eating and physical activities fun!

Adapted from: 10 Tips to Healthy Eating for Kids. *International Food Information Council, National Center for Nutrition and Dietetics/The American Dietetic Association,* 1994. ✦

PYRAMID SERVINGS FOR CHILDREN

The energy needs of school-age children vary, largely due to growth rate, activity level, and body size. All children need at least the lowest number of servings from each of the five food groups. Most school-age children need about 1,800 to 2,200 calories a day, which fits within this range:

Food Group	Number of Servings
Bread, Cereal, Rice, and Pasta	6 to 9
Vegetable	3 to 4
Fruit	2 to 3
Milk, Yogurt, and Cheese	2 to 3
Meat, Poultry, Fish, Dry Beans, Eggs, and Nuts	2 to 3 (about 5 to 6 ounces)

For specific serving sizes for each group, refer to "What's Inside the Pyramid?" on page 246. Children may prefer smaller servings than those indicated. Several smaller servings can still add up to the total recommendation for the day.

For the "Fats, Oils, and Sweets" on the Pyramid tip, go easy—using small amounts to add flavor and enjoyment to your child's meals. ✦

➢ ***Breads, cereals, pasta, and other grain products provide B vitamins, iron, other minerals, and fiber.*** They also are a good source of complex carbohydrate—great for the energy kids need to fuel active lifestyles.

➢ ***Vegetables provide vitamins A (beta carotene) and C, complex carbohydrates, and fiber.*** They also supply significant amounts of some B vitamins, potassium, calcium, and other minerals. *For ways to encourage children to eat more vegetables, refer to "Five-a-Day for Kids: The Vegetable Challenge" on page 433.*

➢ ***Fruit supplies vitamins A (beta carotene) and C, potassium, and some other minerals to keep their skin, eyes, and gums healthy.*** Fruit also supplies carbohydrate and fiber. Kids like fruit—a nutritious sweet snack with a natural supply of sugar! *For more about sugars, refer to chapter 5, "Sweet Talk: Sugar and Other Sweeteners."*

As for adults, a healthful eating plan for children is balanced—enough, but not too much, of any one food or food group. Children can enjoy the foods they like: typically hamburgers, fries, and ice cream. They just need to be smart about balancing these foods with others, and not eating too much, too often. Conversely, missing out on a food group for a period of time may deprive their bodies of nutrients essential for growth.

For growing children, moderation also promotes health in the short- and long-run. As for their parents' diets, a healthful eating plan for children controls fat: no more than 30 percent of calories from fat. For children who need about 1,600 calories a day, that's no more than 53 fat grams, or 480 calories from fat per day on average. Children who need more food energy may also consume more energy from fat, still averaging no more than 30 percent of total calories from fat and no more than 10 percent of total calories from saturated fat. *For more about "The 30% Guideline," refer to page 68.*

What about the "fun" foods—candy and soft drinks—that children may like to eat? If they eat enough food-group servings, children can enjoy moderate amounts of foods from the Pyramid tip...and some food-group foods that have more fat. What they eat overall is what counts, not just one food or one meal.

For teaching about healthful eating, primary-grade children are ready to learn the basic messages of the Food Guide Pyramid: for example, where foods fit in the food groups, understanding how to choose foods for variety, and how many food group servings they need each day. Older children are better able to learn about moderation and balance.

To help children judge the "Pyramid Power" of their own meals and snacks, suggest this simple finger game. Have them name each finger and the thumb on one hand for one of the five food groups. Then have them count the food groups they ate. Eating three or four at a meal is healthful. For snacks strive for one or two food groups.

To learn more, refer to "The Food Guide Pyramid: Your Healthful Eating Guide" on page 243.

Five-a-Day for Kids: The Vegetable Challenge
Over the years, parents have encouraged kids to eat vegetables and fruits—with good reason! As good sources of fiber, and vitamins A and C, they promote health, growth, and development. They add color and texture to the plate, and flavor to a meal. That's why kids—and adults, too—are urged to eat "five a day": three vegetable and two fruit servings. What's a parent to do when vegetables are greeted with a chorus of "yuck"?

Add veggies to kid-favorites. Mix peas into macaroni and cheese. Add carrot shreds to spaghetti sauce, chili, lasagna, even peanut butter. Put zucchini shreds into burgers or mashed potatoes.

"Fortify" ready-to-eat soup with extra vegetables or canned beans.

Offer raw finger-food veggies. Kids may prefer uncooked vegetables. They like to "dip," too. So offer salsa, bean dip, or herb-flavored, plain yogurt.

Kids like the bright color and crisp texture of vegetables. To keep them appealing, steam or microwave veggies in small amounts of water, or stir-fry.

Start a "veggie club." Try to taste vegetables from A to Z, and check off letters of the alphabet as you go! As you shop, let kids pick a new vegetable as a family "adventure." Post a tasting chart on the fridge to recognize your family tasters.

Grow veggies together. If you don't have a garden, plant a container garden. Most kids eat vegetables they grow!

From your library, check out children's books about vegetables. Read the story, then taste the veggie together!

Nothing works? Offer more fruit, which is another source of vitamins A and C!

You've heard about your own need for fiber. But kids need fiber, too. From childhood on, following an eating pattern that's low in fat and cholesterol and high in fiber-containing foods, such as whole grains, legumes, vegetables, and fruits, helps reduce the risk of heart disease and some types of cancer later in life.

How much fiber do kids need? That depends on their age. As they grow and develop, they need more and more.

Adding five to your child's age is an easy-to-remember formula. And it applies to healthy kids from age 3 to 18:

child's age + 5 = the grams of dietary fiber daily

For example, a 6-year-old child would need about 11 grams of fiber daily, 6 + 5 = 11. And a 12 year old would be smart to eat about 17 fiber grams daily, 12 + 5 = 17.

Remember: Just add five! ✦

Source: "*Healthy Start: Food to Grow On,*" *Volume IV, Food Marketing Institute, The American Dietetic Association, and American Academy of Pediatrics*, 1995.

What About Nutrient Supplements?
Your child probably doesn't need a supplement if he or she eats a variety of foods and follows the guidelines of the Food Guide Pyramid. Your child's meals and snacks will supply all the vitamins and other nutrients that active, growing children need.

If feeding problems persist over several weeks, or if you think you're child isn't getting enough vitamins, talk to your child's doctor or a registered dietitian. A supplement may be recommended if your child avoids an entire food group due to a food dislike, allergy, or food intolerance. Children who follow a vegetarian diet also may be advised to take a nutrient supplement. If your water supply isn't fluoridated, a fluoride supplement may be advisable.

If a nutrient supplement is recommended, buy one that has no more than 100 percent of the Daily Values (DV). Unless stated otherwise, the % Daily Values stated on the Supplement Facts panel are meant for children age 4 or older, as well as adults. On supplements meant for younger children, look for the % DV for children under age 4. Choose a supplement that has a child-proof cap, and store it out of children's reach. Remind children that even those in fun colors and shapes aren't candy. *For more about nutritional supplements, refer to* "Dietary Supplements: Use and Abuse" *on page* 111.

Chances are, many of your child's favorite foods are higher in fat and food energy, compared to the amount of nutrients they provide. Any food can be part of a nutritious diet. "Chews-ing" foods that offer balance over time is what counts.

To get the most nutrition and trim the fat, these are foods that youngsters can choose:

MORE OFTEN...	SOMETIMES...
baked potato	french fries
baked or grilled chicken	fried chicken
bagels or English muffins	doughnuts and breakfast pastries
graham crackers, animal crackers, fig bars	chocolate-chip cookies, cupcakes, vanilla wafers, ladyfingers
pretzels, plain popcorn	potato chips
milk, fruit juice	soft drinks
raw vegetable snacks, fruit	candy
yogurt	ice cream

Eating Strategies for Children

Most children do best when they eat on a regular schedule. Children continue to need a routine, just as they did as preschoolers. They can't compensate for hunger as adults can. When meals aren't regular, children tend to snack more heavily throughout the day, so they're less hungry at mealtime.

For the same reasons, frequent meal skipping isn't a good idea. Kids also need breakfast to get a healthful start on their day. *Refer to* "Nutrition and Learning" *on page* 435.

Mealtime can be a good family time. Telling kids to eat nutritious foods is one thing; showing them is another. When children eat with their families, they often eat more varied, more nutritious meals. At the same time, they develop social skills. Whether breakfast, lunch, or dinner, regular family meals set the stage for children to build good eating habits.

➢ Eat as a family—if possible, at least once a day. If it's breakfast, set the table the night before to make it easier.

➢ If your family is always "on the go," you might designate some nights as family dinner nights. By planning ahead, it may be easier to stick to a schedule. *To make preparing family meals faster and easier so you can spend more time together, refer to* "Quick-to-Fix Meal Tips" *on page* 257.

Children need to make their own food decisions. They usually eat better when they have a sense of control and the chance to make food choices. The job of adults and other caregivers is to provide a variety of nutritious foods—new and familiar—from which children can choose.

➢ Give children chances to make food choices—what to eat and how much. Respect their personal food preferences and appetite. Give them the freedom to politely refuse foods they don't want.

➢ Involve kids in planning meals and snacks, too. It's another chance to help them learn to make food decisions. They often eat foods that they help plan and prepare.

➢ Encourage them to try new foods—without forcing or bribing them. Trying new foods is like trying a new hobby; it expands their world of knowledge, experience, and skill. Include foods from cultures other than your own. If they try it, they may like it!

Kids learn to like mostly those foods they have more often. If you offer them fruits and vegetables regularly—and if you eat them, too—chances are, kids will learn to like them.

Snacks contribute to a child's healthful eating plan. Chosen carefully, they supply food group servings—and nutrients—that may be missing from children's meals during the day. And they can supply food energy that growing, active children need. *For snacks kids can make, refer to "Kitchen Nutrition: Healthful, No-Cook Snacks for Kids" on page 443. For more about snacking, refer to "That Snack Attack!" on page 261.*

What children eat over several days counts—not what they eat for one meal or one day. There's no need for concern if children occasionally skip certain foods or don't eat much at a meal.

Children develop the best eating habits when meal and snacktimes are pleasant. Stress at mealtime can become associated with food.

➢ Enjoy pleasant conversation at mealtime—no fussing, arguing, or complaining.

➢ Serve foods that appeal to children. Like you, they prefer foods they like and foods that are tasty and look inviting.

In addition to these eating strategies, many approaches to feeding preschoolers apply to school-age children. Refer to "Mealtime Tactics" on page 423.

Nutrition and Learning

A well-nourished child is ready to learn. Kids who are fit are more likely to have the energy, stamina, and self-esteem that enhance their ability to learn. Healthful eating, along with regular physical activity, helps kids get fit.

Nutrition experts, other health professionals, and educators have long recognized the negative effects on learning of severe nutrient deficiencies: improper growth, retarded mental development, and very low energy levels. Studies show that iron deficiency among children leads to poor behavior, difficulty concentrating, and poor performance.

Mild undernutrition isn't as easily recognized. But it too may have a lasting effect on learning. Mild undernutrition may not be an economic issue, but instead be a matter of poor food choices or meal skipping.

Why do kids need breakfast? On a regular basis, meal skipping—perhaps breakfast skipping—can have a negative effect on a child's achievement and performance in school. Conversely, a morning meal helps children succeed with learning. They have energy to learn. Studies show that breakfast eaters tend to have higher school attendance, less tardiness, and fewer hunger-induced stomachaches in the morning. And their overall test scores are better. They concentrate better, solve problems more easily, and have better muscle coordination. Kids who eat breakfast are less likely to be overweight, too. *For more about the importance of breakfast to learning, refer to "Why Breakfast?" on page 259.*

For Kids Only—Today's School Meals

What's for school lunch? What's for school breakfast? For children and teens, meals served at school contribute significantly to their overall nutrient and energy needs. For more than 50 years, school lunch has provided nourishment to

America's children. Recently, more and more schools are offering nutritious breakfasts to students, too—a valued service that many working parents appreciate.

In most school districts, school meals are regulated through the U.S. Department of Agriculture (USDA). The meal pattern is designed carefully to supply about one-third of the nutrition needs for young people at five different age or grade groups.

EASY BREAKFASTS FOR KIDS TO MAKE

Breakfast—with food from the milk, bread, fruit, and/or meat groups—can set children in a healthful nutrition direction for the day. What's for breakfast? Even if kids are on their own in the morning, most can make these easy breakfast foods. They go down even "healthier" with juice or milk!

- cheese slices served with—or melted on—toast
- iron-fortified cereal with banana slices
- peanut butter spread on toasted whole grain bread or a waffle, or rolled inside a wheat tortilla
- fruit—bananas, strawberries, raisins—and milk on instant oatmeal
- cold pizza
- leftover spaghetti or macaroni and cheese
- apple and cheese slices between whole-wheat or graham crackers
- breakfast cereal topped with fresh fruit and a scoop of frozen yogurt ✦

Through guidance from the USDA, many schools are improving the nutritional quality of breakfast and lunch. Meals are planned to moderate the fat content. For example, schools serve leaner beef and offer 2 percent and skim milk along with whole milk. More high-fiber and whole-grain foods are served, and both dried and fresh fruits often appear on school menus. Student appeal remains a high priority.

Because of federal financial support for school meals, children and teens of all income levels have access to nutritious meals. Some qualify for free or reduced-price meals.

The National School Food Service Program has taken a lead in a national effort to help children make food choices for a healthy diet. To support the messages of the Food Guide Pyramid and the Dietary Guidelines, menus in more and more schools throughout the country are planned and served to help children:

- expand the variety of foods in their diet,
- add more fruits, vegetables, and grains, preferably whole-grains, to the foods they already eat, and
- construct a diet lower in fat.

Many schools give students choices on the cafeteria line. Perhaps they have more than one vegetable or several types of milk to choose from. In many schools, students can select anywhere from three to five items from the school lunch menu—for the same price. Other schools have expanded this option, allowing up to seven items, including more fruits and vegetables. Having choices helps students build nutrition skills—and it helps ensure than children eat healthful meals. It's part of "eating right" education!

Parents can also play a role in meals served to children and teens at school. These are some ways you can help children and teens choose healthful meals at school:

Get familiar with the menu. Keep a current school lunch and perhaps a breakfast menu in your kitchen. Typically they're sent home in school mailings or printed in the local newspaper. You can ask for nutrition information from the school food service director.

Go over the menu with your kids—especially if there's a new food. Talk with your children about making choices on the cafeteria line, and practice at home.

Get involved. Join the parent advisory committee for the school food service program. If none exists, take the lead and work with the school staff to set one up.

Have lunch—or breakfast—with kids. Parents are usually welcome to eat a meal at school. And you have a chance to become more familiar with the school food program, the types of foods children are served, and the overall atmosphere.

Get to know the school food service staff. Let them know that you appreciate their commitment to feeding children. As you build relationships, you can also pass along positive suggestions. Volunteer to help with special meal events, tastings to introduce new foods, or at regular meal hours.

Support the nutrition education efforts at school. Find out what your children are learning, and help them apply it at home.

Brown Bagging It!

Often, the older the children are, the more they want to join classmates in the cafeteria line. But some children prefer to carry a bag lunch to school from home. If that's so with your child, pack meals that please—foods that are easy to prepare and fun to eat, as well as healthful, safe, and nutritious.

What tote will you choose: brown bag, insulated bag, or lunch box? Ask what your child prefers. A lunch box is easier to clean, and it may keep food cool longer. Just be sure to wash it after every use! If a brown bag is preferred, always use a new one.

If you send perishable foods, such as a sandwich with meat, include a small, frozen cold pack. And remind the child to bring it back home! A frozen can or box of juice also keeps food cool.

Plan easy-to-eat foods: for example, sandwiches, raw vegetable pieces (carrots, red or green bell peppers, cucumbers, cherry tomatoes), crackers, cheese slices or cubes, string cheese, whole fruit, individual containers of pudding, or oatmeal cookie. *Refer to "Vegetables: From A to Z" on page 250 for easy-to-pack raw veggies.* If you pack an orange, score the rind so it's easy to peel—or tuck in a tangerine instead! It's OK to pack a brownie or chips as part of a healthful bag lunch. Kids may need the extra energy they supply.

Remember the milk money. Kids need the calcium in dairy foods for their growing bones!

Expect children to help plan and prepare their school lunches. When they're involved, they'll probably eat every morsel—rather than trade their raw veggies for someone else's cookie.

Remind kids to store their carried meals at school in a clean, safe place: away from sunlight and the heat vent in the classroom and not in a dirty gym bag!

Hint: Add extra pleasure to a carried meal with an occasional surprise tucked inside—a riddle, a comic, or a note that says, "You're somebody special!" Knowing that someone cares is "nourishing" in its own way.

have you ever wondered

...how I know if my child is eating right? One way to determine is to ask yourself another question: Is your child growing well? If so, he or she probably is eating enough. Your child's doctor, pediatric nurse, or a registered dietitian can help you monitor your child's growth and development by plotting his or her progress on a growth chart. The other question to ask: Is your child eating a variety of foods and enough servings from the Food Guide Pyramid. If so, he or she probably is getting enough nutrients to grow well.

...if sugar causes kids to be hyperactive? No. There's no scientific evidence linking sugar to behavior. *For more about hyperactivity and eating, refer to "Does Food Cause Childhood Hyperactivity" on page 200.* ✦

For more about carried meals and food safety, refer to "Carry It Safe" *on page* 320.

Weighty Problems for Children—Overweight

Within the past decade, the number of overweight children ages 6 to 17 has doubled—from 5 to 11 percent! Children may not be eating any more calories than earlier generations did, but they are less physically active.

Excess weight during these early years can have long-term consequences—both physically and psychologically. Excessive weight gain during the childhood years can increase the risk later for certain diseases, among them diabetes, heart disease, high blood pressure, stroke, and some forms of cancer. The psychological price can be high, too, if children lose self-esteem and perhaps isolate themselves from their peers. Overweight children also may become overweight adults.

Why do children become overweight? There's no one reason. Family history, inactivity, and poor food habits can all contribute to childhood weight problems. Children who snack heavily, eat irregular meals, lead a sedentary life, and eat a lot of high-fat foods are at greater risk for weight problems. In fact, children often mimic the food behavior they observe at home; it's important for parents to be role models for their children when it comes to healthful eating habits.

A family history doesn't destine children to being overweight adults. Often they shed extra "kid" fat during the rapid growth spurt of puberty. Increased physical activity and balanced, healthful eating are key to preventing a child from becoming overweight.

How do you know if your child is overweight? Kids aren't shaped like little adults. Adults should never assess a child's body weight by their own standards. At each stage of development, they have different amounts of body fat. Your child's doctor should make the assessment.

How can adults help overweight children achieve a healthy weight—without giving up good nutrition? Because their bodies are growing and developing, weight loss isn't the best approach for most children. Instead, for most kids, it's best to slow weight gain so they grow into their weight. In other words, let their height catch up with their weight. A diet that's too restrictive—with too few calories—may not supply the food energy and nutrients that children need for normal growth and development.

Weight problems aren't just about food. Many other factors, such as emotions, family problems, lifestyle, and self-image intertwine with eating behavior. Address the whole child—emotionally, socially, mentally, and physically—as you seek approaches to weight management.

In many cases, lifestyle changes—often for the whole family—offer the best approach for helping overweight children manage their weight. *The* "Eating Strategies for Children" *on page* 434 *also apply to every child—overweight, normal weight, or underweight.*

If your child has a weight problem…

Seek professional advice. A registered dietitian or your doctor can offer support on an approach that's right for the nutrition and development needs of your child. Keep in mind that weight loss approaches for adults are not right for children. *Refer to page* 580, "How to Find Nutrition Help."

Encourage kids to participate in physical activities that they enjoy. Besides burning calories, physical activity has many indirect links to eating: for example, appetite control, stress release, and mental diversion from eating. As with mealtime, physical activity should be a family affair. Be a role model yourself. When parents are physically active, their kids are more likely to be active, too.

Be aware that overweight children are often self-conscious in organized or competitive games; instead encourage activities such as walking the dog or biking where skill is less important. *For more about physical activity, refer to* "Get Up and Move, Turn Off the Tube!" *on page* 441.

Avoid severe food restriction in an effort to manage your child's energy intake. An overly restricted diet may keep children from getting nutrients they need and may lead to sneaking food and binge eating.

Offer kids a variety of foods from the five food groups of the Food Guide Pyramid: especially lower-fat, lower-calorie foods: grains, vegetables, and fruits, as well as low-fat dairy and other protein-rich foods. Go easy on foods with more calories and fewer nutrients.

Tailor portion sizes for the child's, not an adult's, needs. Too-large portions may encourage children to overeat. Use smaller plates so their portions don't appear to be skimpy to them. If they're still hungry, they can ask for more.

Make meals and snacks enjoyable. Encourage overweight children to follow their own internal cues to eating, rather than regulating the amount of food they eat. And avoid putting undue attention on eating. For example, avoid rewarding or punishing a child with food. That way, you won't reinforce an emotional link to eating.

Since snacking goes along with childhood, stock your kitchen with lower-calorie choices: for example, raw vegetables, fruit, juice, milk, and vanilla wafers. Instead of heavy snacking, count on meals to provide most of the nutrients and food energy your child needs.

Avoid labeling food choices as "good" or "bad." Instead help your child see how any food can fit in an eating pattern that's healthful. Even kids who need to trim extra pounds of body fat can have a cookie or piece of candy. In fact, they probably need a high-calorie snack from time to time to meet their energy needs. Labeling food as "good" or "bad" puts inappropriate significance on food. Anyway, the body doesn't see food in black-and-white terms. It's the whole diet that counts.

Store food so it's not in sight, and be careful about bringing a lot of higher-calorie foods into the house. When food sits on the kitchen counter, grabbing a cookie or a handful of chips may be more habit than hunger. For many people—kids too—just seeing food stimulates the appetite.

Set time limits on watching television—no more than one or two hours daily. Inactivity often leads to weight problems. Children who watch four or more hours of television a day are twice as likely to be overweight as youngsters who don't. *Remember:* Computer and video games can develop mental skills, but they require little physical exercise.

Make a house rule: Eat only in the kitchen or dining room. Kids probably won't eat as much—and they'll be more conscious about eating. High-calorie snacks that may go along with TV watching can add to any problem.

Take time to talk to the child about his or her feelings. Observe emotions and subsequent behavior. Together look for ways other than eating to address emotions. Even though eating may feel good for a while, food can't solve problems!

Be aware that sometimes kids say they're hungry when they're really bored or when they're looking for attention. Probe a little. Offer a snack, perhaps a cracker or an apple. If neither one sounds right to the child, he or she is probably bored, not hungry.

have you ever wondered ?

...if foods grown with pesticides are safe for kids? With over 100 required tests directly relevant to children and infants, there's no evidence that children are being harmed from pesticide residues in food, water, or the environment. Any residue is hundreds to thousands of times lower than what might potentially pose a health risk. The safety evaluation takes children's diets, body weight, and rapid growth into account. And the recent Food Quality Assurance Act of 1996 includes additional provisions aimed at protecting children from pesticides. The health benefits of eating fruits and vegetables far outweigh any potential risk. *For more answers to questions about foods grown with pesticides, refer to* "Pesticides: Carefully Controlled" *on page* 231.

...if lead in drinking water is harmful to children? Infants and children are at higher risk for lead poisoning than others. Among other problems, lead that builds up in the body over time can cause brain damage. *To learn how to detect and deal with lead in drinking water, refer to* "Get the Lead Out!" *on page* 178. ✦

SHOULD YOU HAVE YOUR CHILD'S CHOLESTEROL LEVEL CHECKED?

Perhaps. But it's not routinely recommended for all children. Do so if… your own total count is 240 mg/dL (milligrams per deciliter of blood) or higher, or if you or your spouse has suffered a heart attack before age 55, or if you have a family history of heart disease before age 55. Then your child may be at risk for high blood cholesterol levels.

If your child has a higher than normal blood cholesterol level, don't panic. High cholesterol levels among children don't necessarily predict high levels in adulthood. But when children come from high-risk families, you're prudent to check with your doctor and work with a registered dietitian to bring the level down. It may be good advice for the whole family!

For young people ages 2 through 19 years with a parent with high blood cholesterol or a family history of early heart disease, these blood cholesterol levels should be noted:

➢ Total blood cholesterol level for children and teens of high-risk families:

High: 200 mg/dL or higher
Borderline: 170 to 199 mg/dL
Acceptable: less than 170 mg/dL

➢ LDL (low-density lipoprotein), or "bad" cholesterol, levels for children and teens of high-risk families:

High: 130 mg/dL or higher
Borderline: 110 to 129 mg/dL
Acceptable: less than 110 mg/dL

For more about blood cholesterol levels, refer to "Heart Disease: The Blood Cholesterol Connection" *on page* 487. ✦

For more on childhood obesity, refer to "Obesity and Kids: A Heavy Burden" *on page* 28.

Weighty Problems for Children—Fear of Weight Gain

Children as young as age six or seven may be concerned about their body image and afraid of gaining weight. A desire to be overly thin, which is so common today, is reaching down to children who are very young. Among other things, inappropriate weight loss at this age can interfere with a child's growth—and may lead to eating disorders down the road.

Parents need to strive for a positive eating relationship with their children. Avoid pressuring them to conform to any particular body size or shape. Instead, teach healthful eating habits. Set a good example. Encourage physical activity to build muscle and coordination. And work to develop your child's social skills, self-confidence, and self-esteem.

Refer to "Eating Disorders: Problems, Signs, and Help" *on page* 42 *and* "Mainly for Girls: Pressure to Be Thin" *on page* 450.

Eating Out With Kids

Eating out occasionally is a necessity for some busy families and a special treat for others. To make restaurant meals a healthful, pleasant experience for the whole family…

Choose a restaurant that caters to children. If you have toddlers and preschoolers, ask for a high chair. Save upscale table service for older children and adults.

Match your eating-out schedule to a child's needs. When meals are delayed, kids can't compensate for hunger pangs as adults can. You'll only end up with a cranky meal companion!

Ask for a children's menu or look for simply prepared foods on the regular menu. Even when there's nothing suitable, most restaurants can prepare kid foods, such as a hamburger or a grilled cheese sandwich.

Before ordering from the regular menu, ask about the preparation. Most young and school-age children like plain foods with the sauce or dressing on the side. That way, they have a choice.

Let children choose what they want to eat—and even place their own order. Making choices encourages independence and gives kids control over their eating.

Instead of trying a new food when they eat out, let kids order a familiar favorite. For a new taste, offer a bite or two from your order.

If regular portions are too big for a young child's appetite, ask for appetizer portions. Or share an order...perhaps between two kids or with you. Kids shouldn't be expected to "polish" their plate.

Curb your child's appetite while you wait for the order. Ask for a small portion of raw vegetables or bread—just enough to take the edge off hunger, but not enough to interfere with a meal. You might ask that water be served with the meal, rather than before, so your child doesn't fill up on liquids.

For more about ordering in a restaurant, refer to "Have It Your Way!" *on page* 361.

Get Up and Move, Turn Off the Tube!

Smart eating is just part of a healthy start on life. Kids need to be physically active, too!

Today's children often watch TV during their "prime time" for play. In fact, by first grade, many kids have watched 5,000 hours of TV. According to health experts, children who watch too much TV may not get enough physical exercise or creative activity. That's why health experts recommend limiting TV time—no more than one to two hours per day. So prevent your "tater tots" from becoming the next generation of "couch potatoes." Make physical activity fun and part of your family's routine.

Ten Things for Kids to Do Instead of Watching TV

1. ***Encourage kids to set up a jump rope contest.*** If they're older, go "double dutch" with two ropes. (A hula-hoop contest is fun, too.)

2. ***Take the dog for a brisk walk together.*** Don't have a dog? Have kids take their teddy bears for a stroll instead. Walking as a family is good talking time!

3. ***Give kids colored chalk to create a sidewalk mural.*** Or draw a hopscotch game—fun to play alone or with friends.

4. ***Don't let rainy days put a damper on fun!*** Turn up the radio and dance inside.

5. ***Start a "100" walking club.*** Who's first in your family to walk 100 times up and down the sidewalk or the stairs in your house?

6. ***Play a game of tag or kick ball in the playground, park, or backyard.***

7. ***If there's snow, make a snowman or go sledding.*** Or take the family ice skating any time of year at an ice rink—even in July!

8. ***On warm days, go in-line skating or ride bikes (remember the helmet and pads), or run through sprinkler "rain."***

9. ***Enjoy a hike together in a nearby park or forest preserve.*** Have kids find 10 points of natural interest to enjoy as you hike.

10. ***Host a neighborhood bicycle wash outside—or a dog wash instead!***

Adapted from: "Healthy Start: Food to Grow On," Volume IV, Food Marketing Institute, The American Dietetic Association, and the American Academy of Pediatrics, 1995. ✦

Active Play: Good Moves for Children

Just what makes physical activity so important for kids? Good physical health and fitness are obvious reasons. Through active play, children also can develop social skills, build a positive self-image, enhance their ability to learn, and even help protect themselves from danger. An active child is also more likely be an active adult!

Regular physical activity helps with a child's physical development. It builds muscular strength, including a strong heart muscle. Strong muscles promote good posture, which in turn, affects a child's health and self-image. Weight-bearing activities, such as running and skating, help strengthen growing bones. Being active also helps build stamina, a quality that promotes learning and play.

Can children quickly run in case of danger? Although each circumstance requires different physical demands, strong, physically fit children deal better with many emergencies. Regular physical activity offers better protection from danger!

Active kids are more likely to keep their bodies lean. Obesity is a growing problem among children. A main reason is their lack of exercise. Conversely, health experts recommend increased physical activity as one of the best ways for kids to trim extra body fat.

Regular physical activity supports the learning process in other ways. Many activities develop a child's coordination. Playing catch, for example, develops eye-hand coordination. Jumping rope or hopscotch helps teach spatial relationships, while soccer helps develop manipulative skills.

As children play actively with others, they also develop and practice social skills. With games of all kinds, they can share, cooperate, communicate, support each other, and act as a team.

Being on a winning team isn't the only way to build self-esteem. Succeeding at any physical activity—riding a bike, swimming a lap, or catching a ball—helps build self-confidence and a positive self-image.

Active play can be part of the joy of childhood! When physical activity is pleasant, it more likely becomes a lifelong habit. In the long run, a lifestyle that includes regular physical activity lowers the risk of many chronic diseases.

Kids, Go for It!

For a child's good health, the Centers for Disease Control and American College of Sports Medicine advise 20 to 25 minutes of continuous activity three or more times a week for children ages 6 to 16 . Kids don't need a structured activity program to meet this goal. And competitive sports may not be appropriate for some kids; they can create unnecessary pressure and take the fun away.

Active play—biking, in-line skating, playing tag, jump-roping, swimming, tossing a frisbee, among others—can offer enough exercise for most children. Besides, it can be fun! (*Hint*: Be sure that children have appropriate safety gear, such as helmets, knee pads, or life jackets.)

Are you a parent? Next time your kids say they don't know what to do besides watch TV, you might suggest something active. *Refer to "Ten Things for Kids to Do Instead of Watching TV" on the previous page.*

To promote an active lifestyle, you need to make your moves, too. As role models, you might join kids in active play—perhaps hike together as a weekend outing, ride bikes after dinner, play a quick game of catch after work, or take an active vacation (perhaps with hiking, swimming, or skiing). Plan for family activities, perhaps after dinner or every Saturday morning so that exercise happens!

Until the teen years, avoid the urge to compete with your kids in organized games such as tennis; usually a child is no match for adult strength and skill. Physical activity needs to feel good to the body and mind!

Do you need after-school care for your kids? Look for programs that include physical activity: perhaps in scout groups, outdoor centers, recreational centers, or your child's school. Or sign them up for gymnastics, dance, or swim classes.

For more ideas on putting physical activity into your whole family's lifestyle, refer to "20 Everyday Ways to Get Moving!" on page 32.

Kids' Kitchen

Your kitchen can be a laboratory for learning! Just like learning to read and write, becoming self-sufficient with eating is a life skill for children. The kitchen is one place where they learn about food and become health-wise consumers of food.

With single-parent and dual-career households, today's children also may share responsibility for family nutrition. They may be expected to feed themselves sometimes. Depending on their age, they may need to help with family food shopping, preparation, and cleanup. Becoming skilled in the kitchen is more than fun. Often it's a necessity!

Let's Cook!

Preparing food with children offers an ideal opportunity to help them explore a wide variety of foods. At the same time, they learn how to handle and prepare foods in a healthy and safe way.

When kids cook, they practice all kinds of other skills—besides how to handle and prepare foods to nourish themselves and keep food safe to eat. By reading a recipe, children learn new words and practice reading. They identify foods and learn their qualities as they gather ingredients. By preparing a recipe, they practice measuring, counting, timing, sequencing, and following directions. Slicing, pouring, rolling dough, and shaping meat patties are among the food preparation activities that develop small-muscle movement and eye-hand coordination. Food preparation is practical science, too. Children might watch dough rise, see eggs coagulate, or observe how sugar dissolves in water.

Preparing food also promotes a child's social and emotional development. Children feel good about themselves when they successfully create foods they can eat—and share with others. And it's an opportunity to explore foods of other cultures and respect the similarities and differences. Most important, preparing food together can be a nice time for a child to spend with you.

KITCHEN NUTRITION

healthful, no-cook snacks for kids

Kids have a case of the after-school munchies? Try these healthful, no-cook snacks. They're easy and fun to make—and depending on your child's age, require little or no adult supervision.

Snack Kebobs. Cut raw vegetables or fruit into chunks. Skewer them onto thin pretzel sticks. (*Note*: To prevent discoloration, dip cut apples, bananas, or pears in orange juice.)

Veggies with Dip. Cut celery, zucchini, cucumbers, or carrots into sticks or coins. Then dip them into prepared salsa or low-fat dip.

Banana Pops. Peel a banana. Dip it in yogurt, then roll in crushed breakfast cereal; freeze.

Fruit Shake-Ups. Put 1/2 cup low-fat fruit yogurt and 1/2 cup cold fruit juice in a non-breakable, covered container. Make sure the lid is tight. Then shake it up, and pour into a cup.

Pudding Shakes. Use the same technique for making fruit shake-ups, but instead mix 1/2 cup milk with 3 tablespoons of instant pudding.

Sandwich Cut-Outs. Using cookie cutters with fun shapes like dinosaurs, stars, and hearts, cut slices of cheese, meat, and whole-grain bread. Then put them together to make fun sandwiches. Eat the edges, too.

Peanut Butter Balls. Mix peanut butter and bran or cornflakes in a bowl. Shape the mixture into balls with clean hands. Then roll them in crushed graham crackers.

Ice Cream-Wiches. Put a small scoop of ice cream or frozen yogurt between two oatmeal cookies or frozen waffles. Make a batch of these sandwiches ahead, and freeze them.

Ants on a Log. Fill celery with peanut butter or cream cheese. Arrange raisins along the top. ✦

MICROWAVE SAFETY FOR KIDS

Because burns are a common hazard related to their use, make sure children know how to use a microwave oven safely.

- Make sure the microwave oven is on a sturdy stand—one that's low enough for kids. If children need to reach too high, they may pull a hot dish down on them.
- Teach children to read the controls on the microwave oven—the time, the power level, and the "start" and "stop" controls. If kids can't read them, they're too young to operate a microwave oven alone.
- Keep microwave-safe containers in one place—within a child's reach. Have them use only these containers.
- Always have a child use potholders to remove heated food from the microwave oven—whether the food is hot or not. That way, it becomes a habit. Keep potholders handy for kids.
- Teach children to stir heated food before tasting. That distributes the heat and avoids hot spots that can cause burns.
- Show them how to open containers so that steam escapes away from their face. That includes packages of microwave popcorn.
- Until you're sure that children have mastered the art of microwaving, provide supervision.

For more tips on using a microwave oven safely, refer to "Play It Microwave Safe" on page 317. ✦

To get started, consider these guidelines for success in the kitchen with kids:

Choose foods and recipes that match the abilities of your child. With foods a child might prepare alone, prepare them together once first.

For young cooks, choose illustrated children's cookbooks that show the foods, measurements, and steps along the way. Go over the safety and sanitation tips that usually appear at the front of a child's cookbook.

Ask children to suggest foods they'd like to make. Turn the event into a total experience by shopping for the ingredients together, too.

Before you start working together in the kitchen, review the safety precautions. Supervise children as they learn to work with knives, the stove, and other potentially dangerous equipment. Follow good cleanliness habits, too. *Refer to "Kitchen Safety Alert," below.*

Besides cooking together, have children help you store food. Use this chance to show how to handle food to avoid spoilage and foodborne illness.

For easy recipes that children can prepare for snacks—or any meal of the day—refer to "Kitchen Nutrition: Healthful, No-Cook Snacks for Kids" on page 443.

Kitchen Safety Alert

With all that goes on in a kitchen, food preparation can send up some "red flags" when it comes to kids' safety. But it doesn't need to be dangerous—not if they learn how to be careful. Make the kitchen a fun, rewarding place for kids by teaching them the basics of kitchen safety.

Remind children to always wash their hands with soap and water before and after they handle food. Because children practice what they see, you'll probably get the message across easily—by always washing your own hands.

Always provide age-appropriate supervision to children as they're preparing food... especially when they handle hot liquids, knives, appliances, and other potentially dangerous equipment.

As they are ready, teach them kitchen safety tips: to use potholders when handling hot pans, pots, and dishes... to handle knives safely... to be very careful with hot liquids... and to use any age-appropriate appliances safely. *Refer to* "Microwave Safety for Kids" *on page* 444.

Set limits on what kids can—and can't do—without proper supervision. For example, they can't use the oven if they're home alone.

Remind children to be aware of their hair and what they're wearing before they use the stove. Large, loose-fitting garments and long hair can catch fire.

Practice what you preach. Children will take their kitchen-safety cues from you.

Practice what to do in case of fire. That includes "drop and roll" to smother the flames in case their clothes catch fire. Keep a fire extinguisher in view and teach them how to use it.

Try to keep food and utensils they'll use within easy reach. Keep a sturdy stool handy if they do need to reach higher. Remind them not to climb on the counters or a wobbling stool!

Teach kids—even preschoolers—to call 911 (or emergency numbers, such as the fire department, poison control center, or police, in your area). Post the phone numbers in your kitchen where children can see them easily. Include the phone numbers of your doctor, a neighbor, and a relative.

Practice the Heimlich Maneuver with children. Like you, they can save the life of someone who's choking—if they know how. *Refer to "How to Avoid Choking" on page 321. For infants, refer to "For Babies, Toddlers, and Preschoolers: How to Avoid Choking" on page 414.*

Keep a first-aid kit handy and well stocked. Teach children how to use it in case of a minor injury while they cook.

For more on preventing injuries, refer to "Quick Tips for Injury Prevention" on page 322.

Feeding the Teen Machine

By adolescence, many teenagers are major decision makers in their food choices. Other than filling the refrigerator and having meals and snacks available, parents have far less control over what their adolescent child eats. Teenagers themselves exert stronger influence over family eating, perhaps sharing in food shopping and food preparation. Compared with their childhood years, they probably eat more food and beverages away from home.

Chances are, teenagers know the basics of nutrition and healthful eating. However, peer pressure, school and work schedules, a sense of independence, lack of personal discipline, and unrealistic notions about body weight can get in the way of their own healthful eating. In other words, foods choices may not reflect what teens

teens, did you *know*

...dieting can stop you from growing to your full height? Your body needs calories and other nutrients to grow and develop fully.

...your bones take in the most calcium during your teen years and early twenties? Calcium gives your bones strength. The best sources are milk, yogurt, and cheese.

...if you don't eat breakfast, your body is like a computer without power?

...eating cookies, candy, or other sweet foods before an athletic event won't give you an energy boost?

...for girls, when you have a period you lose iron? If you don't eat iron-rich foods to replace this loss, you may feel weak and tired.

...pizza and hamburgers are healthful food choices, especially if you know which toppings to choose?

...good nutrition makes you feel good and look good! ✦

know about eating for long-term fitness—much to the dismay of many parents!

The same holds true for physical activity. They know the benefits of exercise, but may not follow through by living an active lifestyle.

In a nutshell, adolescents often don't connect their immediate food and exercise patterns to their long-term health.

Food, Nutrients, and the Teen Years

Second only to infancy, adolescence is the fastest growth stage in life! Even when teens reach their adult height (for girls sooner than for boys), their bodies are still growing and developing.

How much teenagers grow has more to do with genes than food choices. However, eating a healthful diet does help determine if a person grows to his or her maximum height potential. Nutrients, not specific foods, affect how a person grows. For example, everyone needs calcium for bone growth, protein for muscles, carbohydrates and fats for energy, and vitamins and minerals for the "spark" that makes it all happen.

Puberty marks the start of the teenage growth spurt. That time differs for each child. For girls, it typically comes at about age 12 or 13, about two years younger than for boys.

Energy and nutrient needs increase to meet the growth demands of adolescence and set the stage for lifelong health.

The Pyramid for Teens

The Food Guide Pyramid truly is a family guideline—meant for teens, as well as their younger siblings, their parents, and their grandparents. It's key messages of variety, balance, and moderation apply to adolescence, too. The only difference is the amount of food-group servings they may eat.

Teenage boys have high energy needs: about 2,500 calories a day if they're 11 to 14 years old, and 2,800 calories a day if they're 15 to 18 years of age. That's up from 2,000 calories a day as a 7- to 10-year-old child. Teenage girls need more, too: about 2,200 calories a day if they're 11 to 18 years old, compared to 2,000 calories a day when they were a bit younger. These are average amounts. Some may need less, others more if they're involved in strenuous physical activity, such as soccer, basketball, football, or other sports.

Since teens need more energy than they did as children, they probably need more food-group servings. The extra energy should come mainly from foods high in complex carbohydrates—and not from a high-fat food pattern. *For more about fat in a healthful eating plan, refer to chapter 3, "Fat Facts."*

Many nutrient recommendations go up during adolescence. *Check the Recommended Dietary Allowances on page 606 as a quick reference.* As teens consume more food-group foods, they also get a nutrient boost to meet the demands of growth. Teenage boys, for example, can eat from the top of the serving range—11 servings from the Bread Group—to partly meet their high energy demands. *As a guide to serving amounts for teens, refer to "How Many Servings for You?" on page 245.*

Two nutrients are typically short in a teenager's food choices: calcium and iron. That's usually because of poor food choices or simply not eating enough. *Both of these minerals are explored here: "Calcium: A Growing Issue" and "Iron: The Fatigue Connection" on page 447.*

Typically, teens need to eat more fiber-rich foods, too. *For advice about fiber in a teenage eating pattern, refer to "How Much Fiber? Just Add Five!" on page 433.*

Many nutrition issues that concern adults, such as fat in a healthful diet, quickservice foods, meal skipping, weight control, and eating more fruits and vegetables, also apply to teenagers. You'll find a discussion of these concerns in chapters throughout this book. *For more about school meals, refer to "For Kids Only—Today's School Meals" on page 435.*

Pregnancy will also affect a teenage girl's nutrition needs. Like any pregnancy, the need for nutrients and energy go up. For teens, the recommendations are higher than those for adult women. Teenage girls still need to meet their body's nutrition needs for their own growth spurt and provide for those of a developing fetus. *For more on the nutrition needs of a teenage pregnancy, refer to* "For Pregnant Teens: Good Nutrition" *on page* 465.

Calcium: A Growing Issue

"I'm 16, and I've stopped growing. So why do I need milk?" Actually, bones keep on growing into the adult years. Even when teenagers reach their adult height, bones continue to grow stronger and more dense. In fact, almost half of an adult's bone mass was formed during the teen years. By about age 30 to 35, bones are as strong as they're ever going to get. Calcium-rich foods, such as milk, supply the nourishment that healthy, developing bones need.

For children and teens, ages 9 through 18, three to four servings of calcium-rich foods each day help provide the calcium needed for growing bones. According to 1997 Daily Reference Intakes, 1,300 milligrams of calcium daily is considered an Adequate Intake (AI). An 8-ounce glass of milk has about 300 milligrams of calcium. *For more about* AIs, *refer to* "Nutrients: How Much?" *on page* 4.

What foods are the best sources of calcium for young people? Milk group foods—including milk, yogurt, and cheese—are the most calcium-rich sources, although smaller amounts of calcium are found in a variety of foods. Canned salmon and sardines with bones, as well as some vegetables (such as mustard greens, okra, broccoli, and bok choy), supply calcium. And some prepared foods are calcium fortified, including some orange juice and other beverages, breads, and breakfast cereal. *For more on calcium and a list of calcium-rich foods, refer to* "Calcium: A Closer Look" *on page* 105.

Teenagers—children, too—who don't consume enough calcium put their bones at risk for the long term. Many teenage girls especially don't consume enough because they fear getting fat. They may start their adult years with a calcium deficit in their bones. With bone loss that comes as a natural part of aging, they have less to draw on, and their risk for osteoporosis, or brittle bone disease, goes up.

Instead, teens are advised to consume enough calcium so their bones become as strong as they can be. Teens who watch calories can consume low-fat dairy foods. One 8-ounce serving of skim milk supplies only 86 calories and almost no fat, yet it has as much calcium as whole milk!

For more about bone health during adulthood, refer to "Osteoporosis: Reduce the Risks" *on page* 496.

Iron: The Fatigue Connection

Does your teenager seem chronically tired? Fatigue has many reasons: too little sleep, an exhausting schedule, strenuous activity (a good kind of fatigue), or the emotional ups-and-downs of adolescence. But feeling tired also may be caused by low iron levels in the blood.

Iron is part of the hemoglobin in blood, which carries oxygen to body cells. Once there, oxygen helps cells produce energy. When iron is in short supply, there's less oxygen available to produce energy—hence, a feeling of fatigue.

Iron needs go up dramatically in the teen years. During childhood (ages 7 to 10) both boys and girls need about 10 milligrams of iron daily, according to current recommendations. That amount jumps to 15 milligrams of iron daily for girls, and 12 milligrams daily for boys during adolescence. Girls need more to replace iron losses from menstrual blood flow. *Refer to* "Nutrition and Menstruation" *on page* 458. For boys and girls, more muscle mass and a greater blood supply also demand more iron.

Many teens—girls especially—don't get enough iron. Poor food choices or restricting food to lose weight are two common reasons. Unlike calcium,

have you ever wondered

...besides drinking milk, what else might teens do to keep their bones healthy? Enjoy a variety of calcium-rich foods, including milk. Get involved in regular weight-bearing activities, such as dancing, soccer, running, weight lifting, and volleyball. These activities trigger bone tissue to form. Go easy on soft drinks if they edge out calcium-rich milk. Smoking also may have a negative effect on bone formation. ✦

the effects of low in iron intake can be apparent during the teenage years.

Iron comes from a variety of foods: meat, poultry, and seafood, as well as legumes, enriched grains, and some vegetables. For example, the iron in some common foods is:

- 3-ounce hamburger—2 milligrams
- 1/2 cup of baked beans or refried beans—2 milligrams
- 1 slice of enriched bread—1 milligram
- 1 cup of iron-fortified breakfast cereal—4 milligrams (more or less). For cereal, you need to check the Nutrition Facts on food labels for the specific amount. *For information on reading labels, refer to "What's on the Label?" on page* 270.

Teens who drink orange juice with their morning toast or cereal get an iron boost, too. Its vitamin C content makes iron from plant sources more available to the body. Those who just grab toast to eat at the bus stop, but skip the juice, don't get the full benefit of the iron in bread. For some teens, vitamin C is a problem nutrient, too.

For more on iron in a healthful diet, refer to "Iron: A Closer Look" on page 109.

have you ever wondered

...if you should be concerned if your teenager skips meals? An occasional skipped meal is no cause for concern. But when teens skip meals on a regular basis, they may be missing out on essential nutrients. Teenage girls often skip breakfast or lunch as a way to save on calories. In so doing, they often miss out on foods needed for health: high-calcium foods, such as milk; iron-fortified cereals; and vitamin C-rich fruits and juices. Often they satisfy their hunger later with high-calorie, high-fat snack foods. The net result: they may consume more calories and come up short on nutrients. *For more on meal skipping, refer to "Meal Skipping: Poor Option!" on page* 257. ✦

Great Snacking!

Teenagers are well known for their snack attacks—and for good reason. With their high energy and nutrient needs, they often need snacks as a "refueling stop." Boys especially may need snacks to fill their bottomless pit. For some, snacks help to fill in nutrient gaps that meal choices miss. Snacking is also part of a teenager's social pattern. Typically teenagers eat when they're together, as do adults!

Because snacking often defines teenagers' eating styles, they need to learn how to choose snacks with nutrition in mind. Food-group snacks can help fuel their growth and supply nutrients they need for growth, energy, and health.

The real issue with snacking isn't whether they do or don't. Instead, displacing nutritious food and perhaps meals with low-nutrient, high-calorie, high-fat snacks is the issue. Snacks from the Pyramid tip and foods high in fat are best enjoyed occasionally.

For more nutritious snacks, teenagers might select juice or milk at a vending machine, a small burger with milk at a quickservice restaurant, or fruit, raw vegetables, yogurt, or cereal with milk from the kitchen at home. *For more about healthful snacking—and easy, nutritious snack ideas—refer to "That Snack Attack!" on page* 261.

Your Teen's Food Choices: What You Can Do

While it can be a challenge to feed a teenager, it's well worth the effort. There are ways to influence the eating habits of a teenager—subtly, of course! You can:

Provide lower-fat foods at home to help balance higher-fat foods eaten away from home.

Build skills. Let your teenager plan, shop for, and then cook meals.

Talk to your teen about lower-fat food choices at restaurants and how they can help in weight control.

Discuss wellness and lifestyle, such as regular exercise, lower-fat eating, and not smoking. Set a good example yourself. Kids are the first to notice when adults "walk their talk." And talk to your teenager about nutrition in terms of what matters to them—feeling good, looking good, and performing well. Even when teens seem to disregard what you suggest, the information, encouragement, and example you provide may become the basis for their lifestyle decisions that promote life-long good health.

If your teen decides to become a vegetarian, support the decision by helping him or her make food choices that continue to promote growth and health. It's not uncommon for teenagers to opt for an eating style that reflects their independence and emerging beliefs. Regardless, a vegetarian eating style can supply all the nutrients and energy teenagers need if they know how to do so. A strict vegetarian diet with no animal foods, if not planned properly, may not supply all the nutrients an adolescent needs to grow. It's easiest to meet nutrient needs of growing teens with an eating plan that includes dairy foods and eggs, plenty of legumes, and small amounts of meat, seafood, and chicken. *For more about a healthful vegetarian eating style, refer to chapter 22, "The Vegetarian Way."*

If your teenager is overweight, the best approach is positive—no nagging, forbidden foods, or criticism. Instead be a partner in supporting your teenager as he or she makes lifestyle changes to control weight. Help eliminate factors that trigger eating, such as high-calorie snacks on the kitchen counter. Enjoy physical activities together. Communicate and offer support for the emotional problems of adolescence that trigger eating. Keep nutritious, lower-calorie foods on hand. Most of all, be accepting. That goes a long way in promoting a positive self-image, which helps promote a healthy weight.

Move Your "Bod"

Teenagers move in high gear—going from school to after-school activities and perhaps to a job. They also fit in homework, time with friends, and seemingly hours on the phone. However, a busy schedule may not mean an active lifestyle!

Physical activity is important for all the reasons that are near and dear to the teenage heart: looking good, being in shape, being strong, feeling energetic, being self-confident, doing well in school, and having an overall good outlook on life. So why are more and more teenagers less and less active?

There's no one reason. Teenagers watch on average 20 hours of television a week, which doesn't burn much energy. They ride in or drive in cars, rather than bike or walk. Video games and computer time are sedentary activities, too. For some, leisure time for physical activity is limited. And many don't take physical education at high school!

If you have a teenager in your life, offer these suggestions for ways to be more active—and have fun at the same time.

Make a date to do something active: play tennis, go hiking, or enjoy dancing at a school function. H*int*: You don't need a date to go line dancing.

Instead of talking on the phone with your best friend, go for a walk together and talk.

Join an aerobic class with someone else.

Sign up for a school or community sports team. It doesn't need to be the varsity team to offer good health benefits.

Join the marching band if you play a musical instrument. Try out for cheerleading, majorettes, or the pom-pom squad.

Volunteer as a stage hand for school plays. You'll get plenty of activity doing stage chores.

Walk to or from school with a neighbor; skip the school bus, if you can.

For more ideas to put physical activity in a teen's life, refer to "20 Everyday Ways to Get Moving!" on page 32. ✦

Establishing a lifelong habit of physical activity is a smart goal for adolescents. Besides the benefits just indicated, being active now helps reduce the risk for some chronic health problems later, including heart disease, obesity, and osteoporosis.

To live a physically active lifestyle, encourage teens to follow the "Activity Pyramid" as carefully as they do the Food Guide Pyramid. For fitness, adolescents up to age 16 are advised to get 20 to 25 minutes of continuous activity three or more times a week. At age 16 and over, like adults, they need 30 minutes of moderate physical activity most, if not all, days of the week; for heart health, aerobic exercise (continuous activity) three to five times a week for 30 to 60 minutes is advised. *For more about guidelines and benefits of physical activity, refer to "Get Physical!" on page* 31.

have you ever wondered

...what to eat to control acne? Although all kinds of foods get blamed, teenage acne is linked to hormonal changes, rarely to food choices. The best approach to healthy skin is to eat an overall varied and balanced diet, keep skin clean, get enough rest—and wait. After the body matures, most acne clears up. If problems are severe or persist, talk to a dermatologist. Sometimes a skin application which contains a derivative of vitamin A is prescribed; simply taking a vitamin A tablet won't clear the skin.

...if kids who wear braces should avoid eating raw vegetables and fruit? No! It's true that hard, crunchy, or sticky foods can damage braces. But kids don't need to give up vegetables or fruits. Instead they might choose softer types: perhaps a ripe peach or banana rather than a crisp apple, or cucumber sticks rather than a whole, raw carrot. Or they might cut these foods into bite-size pieces, instead of eating them whole. Consult your child's orthodontist for a list of foods that might damage braces. ✦

Mainly for Girls: Pressure to Be Thin

To many teens, looks are almost everything! As their bodies develop and take on adult curves, it's normal to focus on body image. Often, however, teens have unrealistic notions about the best weight for their height. Girls especially—about 50 percent of 9- to 15-year-olds—see themselves as overweight. And about 23 percent of boys in the same age group do, too. In reality, about 12 percent of 12- to 17-year-olds are overweight.

Pressure to be thin is closely linked to pressure to fit in and be accepted by peers. Thin people are viewed as successful, popular, and attractive. This message gets reinforced by the images in magazines, advertisements, movies, and television shows.

Teenage girls tend to diet as their main approach to an attractive body, while boys often put more emphasis on exercise. For girls, the pursuit of thinness often leads to fad diet approaches—usually ineffective, often dangerous. These diets are especially risky during adolescence when teenagers need a varied and balanced diet for growth and energy. *For more on fad diets, refer to "'Diets' That Don't Work" on page* 43.

Teens who truly are overweight need a sensible long-term approach to weight management. That includes both physical activity and an eating plan that promotes health. Trying to lose five pounds to look good in a bathing suit in one week is neither realistic or healthful. *Refer to "Weight Management: Strategies That Work!" on page* 29.

Sometimes the pursuit of thinness leads to obsession—which is a more serious health concern. Even though the scale doesn't reveal a weight problem, and even when they're underweight, some teenagers have a distorted body image. They see themselves as fat. Typically this perception begins as teens develop sexual characteristics.

The result may be an eating disorder. Teens may starve by eating very little, or purge themselves of food by self-induced vomiting or the use of laxatives. The result may be extreme undernourishment—even death. Because eating disorders are linked to psychological problems, anyone with an eating disorder needs professional attention.

Most victims of eating disorders are teenage girls and young women. Although much less common, some teenage boys have eating disorders, too. *To learn more, refer to* "*Eating Disorders: Problems, Signs, and Help" on page* 42.

Mostly for Boys: Body Building

Most teenage boys want to build muscle, not lose weight, to look good. Many know the value of weight training for body building. But some have the misguided notion that eating more protein builds muscle mass, too. Some opt for more meat portions, perhaps at the expense of foods high in complex carbohydrates; others take protein supplements.

Although the need for protein goes up from childhood, an extra amount has no body-building benefits. Following the recommendations of the Food Guide Pyramid supplies all the protein that teenage boys need—whether they're involved in weight training or not. Like extra carbohydrate or dietary fat, extra protein is deposited in the body as fat, not muscle.

A high-protein diet also can have a high percentage of calories from fat. That's especially true when teenage boys opt for fewer foods high in complex carbohydrates, such as bread, pasta, rice, and cereal. The best advice for teenage body builders? Follow guidelines of the Food Guide Pyramid and be sensible with a weight-training program.

Activity Pyramid

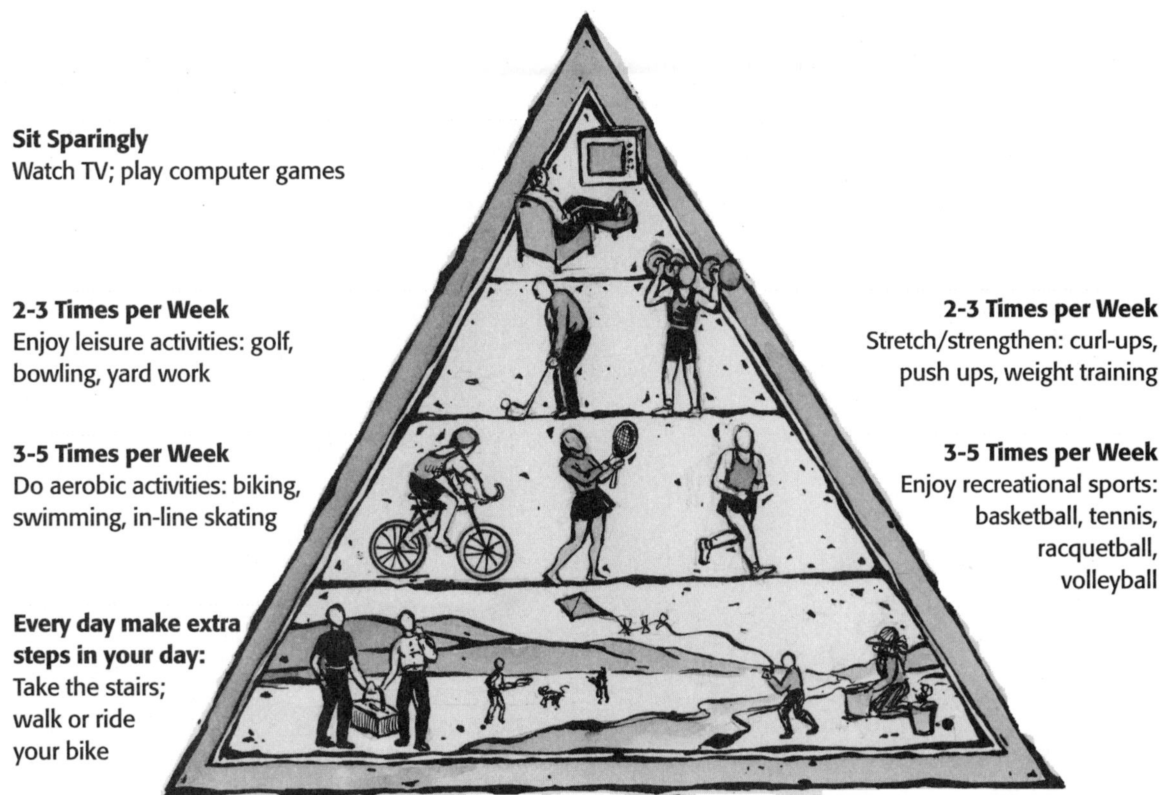

Adapted from: Activity Pyramid *by Jane Norstrom. Park* Nicollet *Medical Foundation*

The key to building muscle is an overall good exercise program and plenty of carbohydrates to fuel longer workouts. Through exercise, protein enters the muscles and makes them larger. *Refer to "Muscle Myths" on page* 539.

What about making weight for wrestling or football? Offer this advice to teenage boys: Cutting down on food or beverages to "make weight" won't promote physical performance. Instead, muscles may get weaker and smaller, even if you consume protein. If you don't eat enough calories, your body burns some protein in your muscles for energy. And drinking too little water can make you dehydrated, which may hinder physical performance, too.

For more on food for sports and making weight, refer to "Making Weight" on page 547.

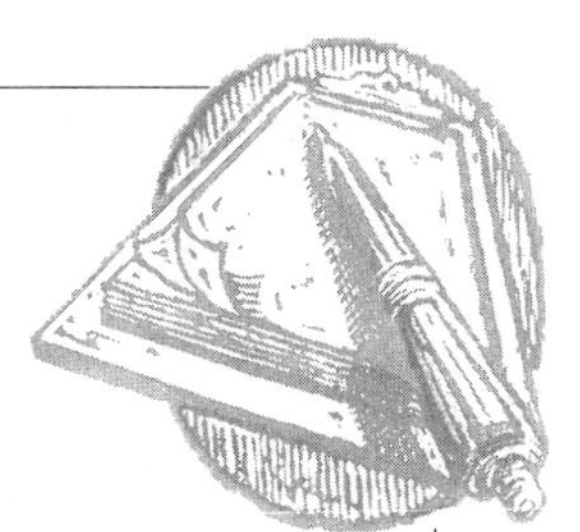

your nutrition check-up

Eating and Activity: Family Matters

You know that family styles influence a child's eating and physical activity patterns and attitudes—for life. What children do and how they feel about food has implications for nutrition and overall health. Take a moment to assess your own family's eating and physical activity practices.

As a parent, family member, or caregiver, do you...

	Always	Usually	Sometimes	Never
Eat your meals as a family?	___	___	___	___
Serve meals and snacks on a regular schedule?	___	___	___	___
Give your youngster freedom to choose the foods he or she eats?	___	___	___	___
Respect a child's appetite when he or she has had enough?	___	___	___	___
Involve children in planning and preparing family food?	___	___	___	___
Make an effort to keep mealtimes pleasant?	___	___	___	___
Include snacks as part of the day's eating plan?	___	___	___	___
Attempt to keep eating to the kitchen, dining room, or another designated place?	___	___	___	___
Set a good role model with your food decisions?	___	___	___	___
Avoid rewarding or punishing a child with food?	___	___	___	___
Give kids enough time to eat?	___	___	___	___
Turn off the TV while you eat together?	___	___	___	___
Offer foods that appeal to children?	___	___	___	___
Serve a variety of foods for meals and snacks?	___	___	___	___

your nutrition check-up (continued)

Offer new foods and new food combinations?	___	___	___	___
Avoid forcing a child to eat?	___	___	___	___
Set a good role model by being physically active?	___	___	___	___
Limit TV time to one to two hours daily?	___	___	___	___
Encourage children to play actively?	___	___	___	___
Enjoy physical activity regularly as a family?	___	___	___	___
Subtotal	___	___	___	___

Now Score Yourself

Count the number of check marks in each column. Then multiply by these scores. What's your total?

"Always": 3 points
"Usually": 2 points
"Sometimes": 1 point
"Never": 0 point

Your Total Score ____

What does your score suggest?

➢ If you scored 40 to 60 points, you apply what you know about nurturing positive eating and physical activity patterns.

➢ A score of 20 to 39 suggests you're on the right track for feeding and exercising with kids, but there's still room to make positive changes in your family's lifestyle.

➢ Less than 20, you'd be wise to make significant changes in your family's approach to food and physical activity.

real life nutrition

Feeding the Family, Feeding the Kids!

"The challenges of feeding youngsters," sighed Betsy to herself as she wiped up the milk that P.J., her preschooler, spilled all over the table. "Just hold onto the pitcher with both hands." P.J. is four, and he's helping by pouring milk for supper. "Should I just do it myself?" Betsy asked herself.

After picking P.J. up from preschool, Betsy was trying to put the last touches on supper for their family of five. Her husband, Paul, had gotten home earlier and put the meatloaf and potatoes in the oven, then headed out to do some yardwork. "Mommy, I don't like that!" P.J. said as he watched his mother stir-fry broccoli in a wok. She still had a salad to make.

Their teenage daughter, Cam, breezed in after soccer practice. "Hi, Mom, Dad, I'm not hungry. I had fries and a soda right before soccer practice. Besides, I'm on a diet, remember? I'm heading up to do my homework. I'll have an apple later if I'm hungry." Betsy had planned meatloaf tonight because she knew that Cam liked it—and she wanted the family to eat together. "Fries, an apple, and soda—what kind of supper is that for a growing teenager?" she remarked.

Their nine-year-old son, Ian—a little overweight—finally extracted himself from the TV set to help set the table and put the bread in a basket, but first he reached for an oatmeal cookie on the counter. "Mom, I'm not big on meatloaf, you know that. And broccoli—yuck!"

Just then the phone rang. It was the single mother next door, "Can Angie eat dinner with you tonight? I've got to work late tonight. Oh, and please remind her to feed the dog."

"Why me?" Betsy asked herself.

To get the family meals to run more smoothly... and ensure everyone is well-nourished, Betsy might take these approaches...

➢ Betsy wisely encouraged P.J. to help with the family meal. She knows that spills are part of learning and that children should be given the chance to learn.

➢ Instead of offering P.J. stir-fried broccoli, Betsy might cut a few florets into finger foods that he could eat raw. Preschoolers like finger foods and raw vegetables better than cooked.

real life nutrition (continued)

➢ Betsy might also involve her kids in planning the foods for meals—rather than always deciding on the menu herself. That way, she'll offer foods they enjoy.

➢ Betsy and Paul might establish regular family dinner times with the understanding that everyone eats and spends time together—including Cam.

➢ Cam has one side of the weight-control program in place—regular physical activity. But she needs to change her eating habits. A healthful dinner is a better weight-control strategy than snacking on whatever's around. She missed out on some nutritious foods by skipping dinner.

➢ Ian should be encouraged to be more active after school—perhaps help his dad in the yard. He'd probably lose his extra body fat just by moving more.

➢ Betsy and Paul might encourage son Ian to refuse food with a polite, "No, thank you," rather than with "yuck."

➢ Betsy might store food, such as the oatmeal cookies, out of sight so her family can't nibble before meals, or put out raw vegetables.

➢ It's nice for Betsy to be supportive to another parent, such as Angie's mom. Betsy may need the same help sometime.

CHAPTER EIGHTEEN

FOR WOMEN ONLY

If you're female and of child-bearing age, this chapter is meant especially for you. Or if menopause is fast approaching, the end of this chapter offers guidance for your continued health and well-being.

As a woman, your nutrition needs change at different stages of adulthood to meet the physical demands of child-bearing. Pregnancy, breast-feeding, and menstruation all affect your nutrient and calorie intake.

In general, most women don't need as much energy, or calories, as men do. But because their need for some nutrients is higher, women have a greater chance for nutrient deficiencies. In contrast, the nutrition needs of healthy males don't change much throughout life, unless they increase or decrease their level of physical activity.

For other nutrition issues related to women's health (including heart disease, cancer, anemia, and osteoporosis), refer to "Prevention: Nutrition and Health Problems" on page 484.

Pregnancy: Before You Begin

Thinking about pregnancy? If so, now is the time to inventory your health and nutrition habits. Your baby develops rapidly during the first weeks of pregnancy, perhaps before you even know you're expecting! So, initiating good health and nutrition habits now—or simply nudging them back into practice—promotes good health for you and a healthy environment for your developing baby.

Start your "health inventory" with a look at your nutrition habits. Are you eating a balanced and varied diet that provides the 40 or so nutrients essential to your good health—and your baby's health, too? Do you drink milk? Or do you skip meals or avoid whole categories of food, such as breads or vegetables? *The Food Guide Pyramid, explained on page 243, is your "before, during, and after" pregnancy guide to healthful eating.*

All nutrients are important to a healthy pregnancy. But there's one worth special consideration: folate, or folic acid (a B vitamin). Essential to good health, your body needs folate to manufacture new cells and genetic material. During pregnancy, folate helps develop the neural tube, which becomes your baby's spine. The neural tube starts to form soon after conception.

Women who consume enough folate, particularly in the weeks prior to conception and during the first three months of pregnancy, may reduce the risk of neural tube birth defects, such as spina bifida. Neural tube defects involve incomplete closure of the spinal column. Nearly 2,500 newborns in the United States are born each year with neural tube defects. Diet is one cause.

Women in their childbearing years are encouraged to consume 400 micrograms of folic acid daily from fortified foods, vitamin supplements, or a combination of the two, in addition to foods with naturally-occuring folate. Folic acid is the form of folate used in fortified foods and supplements. *For more on folate, refer to pages* 86-87.

Eat a variety of folate-rich foods. Good sources of naturally-occuring folate include citrus fruits and juices; dark green, leafy vegetables; nuts; legumes; and liver. Foods fortified with folic acid include enriched grain products such as most breads, flour, crackers, cornmeal, farina, pasta, and rice. *Refer to page* 86 *for food sources of folate.*

Read the Nutrition Facts panel on food labels to identify foods rich in folate. If folic acid is added, it must be on the food label. On packages of foods with a significant amount of folate, the label also might advise that adequate folate intake may decrease the risk for neural tube defects.

Consult your doctor or a registered dietitian (RD) about vitamin supplements with folic acid. Taking in too much folate, more than 1,000 micrograms a day, can mask the symptoms of pernicious anemia, a condition that can cause nerve damage. (Pernicious anemia may result from a vitamin B_{12} deficiency.) Consuming too much folate usually comes from taking large doses from vitamin pills, not from food sources.

Even before you get pregnant, refrain from any other practices that may harm your developing baby: cigarette smoking, drinking alcoholic beverages, and inappropriate use of drugs. Important stages in your baby's development start right after conception. Before you know you're pregnant, they already may have harmful effects.

Now's the time to discuss any over-the-counter and prescription medications you take with your doctor, too. Some may be harmful to your developing baby. If necessary, other medications may be substituted.

have you ever wondered

...if women who use oral contraceptives need extra vitamins? No. An overall eating plan that's varied and balanced can supply nutrients in amounts you need for good health.

...if eating yogurt every day prevents vaginal yeast infections? There's no conclusive evidence that eating a cup of yogurt with active cultures each day will protect women from vaginal yeast infections. However that same cup of yogurt does supply 300 to 450 milligrams of calcium, which is good for bone health!

...if there's a link between fibrocystic breast disease and caffeine? Between 10 and 20 percent of women experience fibrocystic breast disease, benign but often painful breast lumps. However, no conclusive evidence links these noncancerous breast lumps to caffeine intake. Because fibrocystic breast disease is linked to hormone levels, it usually subsides with menopause—unless a woman receives hormone replacement therapy. Above all, examine your breasts carefully each month. Get regular mammograms. And consult your doctor about any breast lumps that appear. ✦

Nutrition and Menstruation

For women of child-bearing age, overall nutrition is important. But the monthly menstrual cycle offers other nutrition issues for women only.

Iron—More for Women

During the years of menstruation, increased need for iron is a nutrition concern. On average, women lose about 1/4 cup of blood with each menstrual period. Women with a heavy flow may lose more. Some nutrients, especially iron, leave the body with menstrual blood loss.

To meet their iron needs during the child-bearing years, women are urged to consume 15 milligrams of iron daily. The amount doubles during pregnancy. To compare, men need only 10 milligrams of iron daily. With menopause, a woman's need for iron drops and equals that of men.

Iron deficiency is common among women. When food doesn't replace iron losses, a woman may feel weak and tired, and may develop anemia. Menstrual losses, combined with low iron intake, frequent dieting, and a low intake of vitamin C, all contribute to the problem.

Include good sources of iron, such as meat, poultry, fortified cereal, enriched rice, and legumes, in your overall eating plan. To help your body absorb iron from plant sources, consume vitamin C-rich foods, such as citrus fruit. And consult your doctor about an iron supplement. *For more about iron and a list of food sources, refer to* "Iron: A Closer Look" *on page* 109. *For more about anemia, refer to* "Anemia: That Run-Down Feeling" *on page* 484.

Can Diet Control PMS?

Premenstrual syndrome, or PMS, is a condition described with many symptoms and varying severity. It starts as much as 14 days before a period, then stops when your period starts. There's not much consensus on its treatment. And there's little conclusive research on the connection between nutrition and PMS symptoms. But shifts in hormone levels are likely the cause.

Some women experience bloating, tender breasts, and headaches prior to their period. That's usually because body water fluctuates during the menstrual cycle. Prior to your period, your body may retain fluids, which disappear soon after it's over.

If you suffer from these problems, you might cut down on salt for a week to 10 days before your period. Sodium, a component of salt, holds water in your body and can cause tissues to swell. That includes tissues in your abdomen, breasts, and the blood vessels in your head.

What about claims for vitamin B_6 and other dietary supplements? Except for the psychological effect, no evidence shows that taking nutrient supplements can alleviate the symptoms of PMS. And no studies show that PMS is caused by nutritional deficiencies or caffeine. *For more about supplements, refer to* "Dietary Supplements: Use and Abuse" *on page* 111.

Until more is known, general guidelines for good health may help you cope with PMS. Eat an overall healthful diet. Live an active lifestyle. And relax and get plenty of rest. Consult your doctor if needed.

Congratulations! You're Expecting a Baby!

Take good care of yourself and your developing baby during the next nine months. By eating wisely, being physically active, and getting plenty of rest, you'll help maintain your good health—and your baby's too!

Many things influence the birth of a healthy baby. Some you can't control, such as your age and inherited family traits. But others are up to you—seeing the doctor regularly, stopping smoking, avoiding alcohol and inappropriate drugs, and eating healthful foods.

Women who eat well and avoid known risks tend to have fewer complications during their pregnancy and labor. And they deliver larger, healthier babies. A nutritious diet is one of the most important elements for ensuring the future well-being of you and your unborn child.

"Weighting" for Your New Arrival

Did you count calories before pregnancy to keep tabs on your figure? If so, put dieting aside for the next nine months. Pregnancy isn't the time to skimp on calories, follow a weight-loss diet, or restrict weight gain. For most pregnant women, the extra pounds of pregnancy are healthful "additions" for you and baby!

Why is appropriate weight gain so important during pregnancy? Your baby's birthweight is related to the weight you gain over the next nine months. Restricting weight gain can increase your chance for delivering a low-birthweight infant. Babies who tip the scales at less than 5 1/2 pounds at birth are at greater risk for developmental difficulties and illnesses than babies who weigh more than that.

Weight gain is important to provide for maternal body changes, too. Besides the weight of the fetus, increased blood volume, enlarged breasts, placenta, and amniotic fluid all add up to increase mom's weight. *Refer to "Where Does Weight Gain Go?" on page 461 to see how weight gain for a full-term pregnancy is distributed.* Women with normal weight gain generally have fewer problems than those who gain more or less.

Extra body fat, naturally deposited during pregnancy, benefits mom if she opts to breast-feed, too. These fat stores are used after delivery to provide the extra energy nursing moms need for milk production.

How much should you expect to gain during pregnancy? That depends on several factors:

Your weight before pregnancy. Woman at their healthy weight for their height can expect to gain 25 to 35 pounds during pregnancy. Underweight women are advised to gain a little more, 28 to 40 pounds. Overweight women may be advised to gain less, 15 to 25 pounds. *For more about healthy, pre-pregnancy weight, refer to "Body Basics: What's Your Healthy Weight?" on page 17.*

Your height. Because all women are different, a range of weight gain is recommended—not just one targeted weight. For instance, most shorter women (five feet two inches or shorter) should aim for the lower end of the range for weight gain.

Your age. Young teens (until age 18) are encouraged to gain at the higher end of their weight-gain range. Because teens are still growing, the extra provides for mom's growth and development and promotes a healthy pregnancy. *For more on teenage pregnancy, refer to "For Pregnant Teens: Good Nutrition" on page 465.*

Your race. Black women are encouraged to gain at the higher end of their weight-gain range. That's because African-American women are at greater risk for delivering low-birthweight infants.

Expecting twins? If so, your doctor may recommend a 35- to 45-pound weight gain.

Because every woman is unique, talk to your doctor about the weight-gain range that's right for you.

did you know?

...it takes more than 85,000 calories over the course of nine months, in addition to the ones needed for your own energy needs, to build a healthy baby?

...during pregnancy, blood volume increases about 50 percent and accounts for 3 to 4 pounds of your total weight gain?

...skipping meals and dieting are serious threats to a developing baby?

...pregnant women should not restrict salt or use diuretics to control swelling?

...full-term babies that weigh 7 pounds or more tend to have higher IQs and fewer physical problems than full-term babies weighing less than 5 1/2 pounds?

...if you don't gain enough weight during pregnancy, you may have a smaller baby?

...pregnant teens need to gain more weight than other pregnant women? ✦

Weight Gain and Loss: Slow and Steady

Just as the amount of weight gain is important to a healthy pregnancy, so is the *rate* you gain. Expect 2 to 4 pounds of weight gain during your first three months of pregnancy; for teens, 4 to 6 pounds. After that, expect to gain about 1 pound per week. You may gain a little more or a little less depending on your overall expected weight gain.

If you gain weight at a faster rate, these steps can help you cut calories without depriving you or your baby of nutrients:

- Substitute skim or lower-fat milk, yogurt, and cheese for whole-milk products. And choose leaner meats, poultry, and fish.
- Broil, bake, grill, or stir-fry foods instead of frying them.
- Cut down on foods high in fat and calories and low in nutrients, such as candy, cake, pastries, and rich desserts.
- Increase your physical activity within the guidelines advised by your doctor.

Delivering your baby may be the fastest weight you ever lose! Between the baby and fluid loss, some new moms lose up to 10 pounds right after delivery, and another 5 pounds within the first month or so. For others, weight may come off more gradually over a longer time period. Most women will find that weight will continue to drop slowly and steadily over 6 to 12 months following delivery. How fast you shed "baby weight" depends on how physically active you are, your calorie intake, and whether you breast-feed. *For guidance on healthy weight loss, refer to "Weight Management: Strategies That Work!" on page 29.*

Nutrients: For You and Baby, Too!

During pregnancy, the need for most nutrients increases to ensure the development of a healthy baby. If your overall diet is inadequate, your baby's development may be impaired. And he or she may be underweight at birth.

Eating a variety of foods from all five food groups is the best way to provide for these increased nutrient needs. Keep in mind that just because you're eating for two (or more!), your need for calories does not double. In reality, to ensure you get the energy you and baby need—an additional 300 calories of extra energy each day are all that are needed! *For more help, refer to "The Food Guide Pyramid: Your Healthful Eating Guide" on page 243.*

Caution: If you've recently carried another baby, or if you've breast-fed within the past year, your nutritional reserves may be low. And if you've had problems during a previous pregnancy, make a special effort to make food choices now to help promote a healthy pregnancy.

For specific nutrient recommendations during pregnancy, refer to the appendix on pages 606-607. If you're a vegetarian, refer to "The Vegetarian 'Mom'" on page 566.

Where Does Weight Gain Go?

Suppose your baby weighs about 7 pounds at birth. So why did you gain so much more? Because many parts of your body support the development of your baby. For example, your blood volume expands about 50 percent. Your breasts increase in size. Your body also builds reserves to sustain the baby's rapid growth and provide energy for labor, delivery, and breast-feeding. This is where weight gained during pregnancy typically goes:

	APPROXIMATE WEIGHT GAIN (IN POUNDS)
BABY	7-8
PLACENTA	1-2
AMNIOTIC FLUID	2
MOTHER	
Breasts	1
Uterus	2
Increase in blood volume	3
Body fat	5 or more
Increased muscle tissue and fluid	4-7
TOTAL	MINIMUM 25 POUNDS

Baby-Building Protein

Body cells of a developing baby are made largely of protein. Changes in your own body, particularly the placenta, also require protein. An eating plan that matches the Food Guide Pyramid provides enough protein for a healthy pregnancy.

PREGNANCY: A MEAL TICKET FOR TWO

An additional 300 calories a day to support the energy needs for you and baby doesn't sound like much. And it really isn't! You'll see that eating for two really is quite easy. The key is to "choose your calories by the company they keep"—in other words, choose foods that supply needed nutrients, such as calcium and iron, as well as calories.

Following guidelines from the Food Guide Pyramid provides the nutrients and energy for your "meal ticket for two." Compared with your needs before pregnancy, the Pyramid advises an increase to three servings from the Milk Group daily. *Refer to page 243 for more about the Pyramid.*

How do 300 calories translate in "real food"? Some nutrient-rich food choices that supply about 300 calories include:

➢ 1 ounce cold cereal, a banana, and one cup of skim milk, or

➢ one baked potato with skin topped with one-half cup each of broccoli and cauliflower, and 1 ounce of low-fat cheese, or

➢ 2 ounces of turkey on two slices of whole grain or enriched bread, topped with lettuce, tomato, and sprouts.

These three food combinations each supply more than 10 grams of protein—the extra amount needed during pregnancy. ✦

When you're pregnant, you need only 10 extra grams of protein a day. That's 60 grams of protein, compared with 50 grams recommended for nonpregnant women. To put 10 grams of protein into perspective, a 3-ounce meat patty has about 20 grams of protein, and 8 ounces of milk supplies about 8 grams of protein. Most nonpregnant women easily consume more than 60 grams of protein daily.

If you're a vegetarian, and you consume a variety of legumes, grain products, vegetables, and fruits, obtaining enough protein should not be a problem. *If you're concerned, consult a registered dietitian to make sure you're getting enough.* *Refer to "Protein Power" on page 561.*

Fuel for the Fetus

For protein to do its job, you need an adequate supply of energy. If you don't consume enough, your body uses protein for energy instead of cell building. After the first trimester, it takes about 300 extra calories a day for the development of a healthy baby. So if you needed about 2,200 calories daily to maintain your weight before pregnancy, you need about 2,500 calories a day now.

Carbohydrates should be your main source of energy. They're quickly and efficiently converted to energy. Because your baby grows every minute for 280 days, he or she needs a constant supply of energy. Carbohydrate-rich foods, such as fruit, bread, cereal, pasta, rice, potatoes, corn, and legumes, are the fuel of human life. Fats in food can be used for energy, too. But most energy should come from carbohydrates.

To fuel a healthy pregnancy, "spend" your extra energy allowance wisely on nutrient-rich foods that provide you and your baby with energy and a healthful dose of nutrients. Go easy on foods that supply calories but few nutrients. *For ways to "spend" 300 extra calories, refer to "Pregnancy: A Meal Ticket for Two" on this page.*

Vital Vitamins

If carbohydrates are the fuel of human life, vitamins are the spark plugs! They're a necessary part of most body functions. All vitamins affect the many processes that occur in the body. And the need for certain vitamins goes up during pregnancy. Certain ones are especially important for cell division, which is part of the formation of a new life.

Vitamin A, for example, promotes the growth and health of cells and tissues throughout the body—yours and your baby's. Your normal diet can provide enough vitamin A during pregnancy—no need for any extra from a supplement. In fact, new research suggests that consuming 10,000 IU of vitamin A (two times the Recommended Dietary Allowance, or RDA) may increase the risk of birth defects. Some dietary supplements contain this much; some have a potency of 25,000 IU. (*Note*: The recommended level for vitamin A is 5,000 IU daily). Only take supplements in amounts recommended by your doctor. Check the Supplement Facts panel on the label, and choose one with no more than 100 percent of the Daily Value for vitamin A. Eating fruits and vegetables high in beta carotene isn't a problem because beta carotene does not convert to vitamin A when blood levels of vitamin A are normal. *Refer to* "Nutrients: How Much?" *on page* 4.

By consuming an extra 300 calories a day, you'll likely consume enough extra of most B vitamins. During pregnancy, you need more thiamin, riboflavin, and niacin to use the energy from food for a healthy pregnancy. And you need more vitamin B_6 to help protein make new body cells.

The need for vitamin B_{12} goes up during pregnancy. This vitamin is found in foods of animal origin, such as milk, eggs, cheese, and meats. Vegetarian women who don't consume any foods of animal origin need a reliable source of vitamin B_{12}—perhaps fortified breakfast cereal or a vitamin B_{12} supplement.

The need for another B vitamin, called folate, increases during pregnancy from 400 micrograms daily before pregnancy to 600 micrograms daily. Getting enough during the first three months is especially important. The risk for neural tube, or spinal cord, damage goes down when women consume enough folate. *For more about folate prior to and during pregnancy, refer to* "Pregnancy: Before You Begin" *on page* 457.

The need for vitamin C goes up a bit, too. But a 3/4-cup serving of orange juice supplies enough for a day! Besides its other functions, vitamin C helps your body absorb iron from plant sources of food. That's important because your iron needs almost double during pregnancy.

To help your body absorb the calcium needed for pregnancy, you need enough vitamin D. Drinking vitamin D-fortified milk supplies enough. For vegetarians who don't consume dairy foods, you may need a vitamin D supplement—especially if you aren't exposed to direct sunlight. Your body produces vitamin D when your skin comes in contact with sunlight.

Following an eating plan that's varied and balanced is the best way to get vitamins for you and your baby. In addition, many doctors prescribe a special prenatal vitamin/mineral supplement. *For more about obtaining vitamins in a healthy diet, refer to* "Vitamins: The Basics" *on page* 80.

have you ever *wondered*

...if non-nutritive sweeteners are safe to consume during pregnancy? To help control calories during pregnancy, it's OK for most women to include moderate amounts of foods and beverages sweetened with intense sweeteners. Because they supply flavor with fewer calories, they leave room for other, more nutritious foods. The Food and Drug Administration has approved three for use in the United States: aspartame, saccharin, and acesulfame K. All are considered safe for most moms-to-be. Although saccharin can pass through the placenta, there's no evidence that it's harmful to baby. Like anything, consuming just moderate amounts of saccharin during pregnancy and breast-feeding is wise.

Exception: Pregnant women with the rare genetic disorder called phenylketonuria (PKU) should avoid foods sweetened with aspartame. People with PKU cannot break down phenylalanine, which is an amino acid in aspartame. Then phenylalanine can reach high levels in the mother's blood and may affect the developing baby. *For more about aspartame and* PKU, *refer to* "Intense Sweeteners: How Sweet It Is!" *on page* 202. ✦

Minerals—Giving Body Structure

Minerals are used to develop the body's structure—the bones and teeth. Along with protein and vitamins, minerals make blood cells and other body tissues. And they take part in many body processes that support a healthy pregnancy.

Two minerals require special attention during pregnancy: calcium and iron. If you don't consume enough, your growing baby will use the calcium in your bones and the iron in your blood. You can't afford these losses! You need to be at your full strength to give birth and to care for your baby afterward.

An adequate intake of bone-building calcium during pregnancy helps ensure that the mother's bone mass is preserved while the baby's skeleton develops. Consuming enough calcium during pregnancy helps protect you from osteoporosis later on—as long as there's enough calcium coming in. *Refer to* "Osteoporosis: Reduce the Risks" *on page* 496.

Pregnant women need 1,000 milligrams of calcium daily; pregnant teens need more—1,300 milligrams calcium daily. An 8-ounce serving of milk or yogurt provides about 300 milligrams of calcium daily. Leafy, green vegetables, canned fish (with bones), tofu processed with calcium, and calcium-fortified foods like juice, cereal, and bread also are good dietary sources of calcium. *For more about calcium and ways to include calcium-rich foods in your meals and snacks, refer to* "Calcium: A Closer Look" *on page* 105. A calcium supplement may be recommended for women under age 25 whose dietary calcium is low.

have you ever *wondered*

...if you need a multi-vitamin/mineral supplement during pregnancy? Except for iron, most healthy women can meet the nutrient demands of pregnancy by consuming a balanced diet with a variety of foods. Your doctor or registered dietitian may recommend a prenatal multi-vitamin and mineral supplement to help ensure that you meet your needs for iron, folic acid, and other important nutrients.

Other reasons your doctor may prescribe a supplement during pregnancy include—if you follow a strict vegetarian diet (no foods of animal origin), if you're pregnant with more than one baby, or if your diet lacks critical nutrients. *Refer to* "Dietary Supplements: Use and Abuse" *on page* 111. ✦

Why do you need more iron? A mother's blood volume increases by about 50 percent during pregnancy. Iron is essential for making hemoglobin, a component of blood. Hemoglobin carries oxygen throughout the body, including through the placenta to the developing baby. Several foods supply iron—meat, poultry, fish, legumes, and whole-grain and enriched grain products.

Getting enough iron to meet the demands of pregnancy can be difficult. Even though it's widely available in food, iron isn't necessarily well absorbed. And many women have marginal iron stores in their body before pregnancy. For that reason, your doctor may prescribe an iron supplement, in addition to an iron-rich diet. Most prenatal vitamin supplements also contain iron.

For optimal absorption of iron from a supplement, take it on an empty stomach or with juice, rather than with meals. For some women, iron supplements cause side effects such as nausea, constipation, and appetite loss. If so, taking it with meals helps, although the iron may not be absorbed as well. Talk to your doctor about a lower dosage, if necessary, and take special care to include more food sources of iron.

Eating a good source of vitamin C, such as citrus fruits and juices, broccoli, tomatoes, and kiwi, with meals, helps the body absorb the iron in foods. Absorption of iron supplements is best when taken on an empty stomach or with a vitamin C-containing juice to enhance absorption. Be aware that taking an iron supplement with coffee or tea may decrease its absorption. *For more about iron in a healthful diet, refer to* "Iron: A Closer Look" *on page* 109.

Zinc, another mineral, is essential for making new body proteins. That includes cell growth and brain development in your baby. Zinc comes in a variety of foods. But it's most available from foods of animal origin, such as meat, seafood, and poultry. Whole-grain products have zinc, too, but it's not absorbed as well. Most women, except perhaps some vegetarian women, get enough zinc during pregnancy from their everyday food choices, especially from protein-rich foods. *Caution*: Take an iron supplement according to the recommended dosage; too much iron can interfere with zinc absorption.

Restricting sodium during pregnancy was once thought to reduce fluid retention and protect against high blood pressure. Now that's believed unnecessary. Whether you're pregnant or not, consuming salt and sodium in moderation is still good advice. The slight increase in sodium needs during pregnancy are supplied by the typical American diet, which can be quite high in sodium. If you limited your sodium intake before pregnancy, continue to do so as your doctor recommends. *Refer to chapter* 7, *"Sodium: A Salty Subject."*

For more about minerals in a healthy diet, refer to "Minerals—Not 'Heavy Metal'" on page 94.

And Water, Too

Remember, water is a nutrient. As part of your body's transportation system, it carries other nutrients to body cells and carries water products away. That includes nourishment that passes through the placenta to your baby. You need fluids—at least 8 to 12 cups daily—for your own and your baby's increased blood volume. When you feel thirsty, drink more!

For Pregnant Teens: Good Nutrition

School, activities, and frantic social schedules may keep good nutrition off the "top ten" list of many teens. But for a pregnant teen, what she eats today can affect her health and that of her baby in the future. Her food habits help determine if her baby is born at a normal birthweight.

Adolescent pregnancy is considered high risk. A teenager's body is still growing, perhaps competing with the baby for nutrients. For this reason, a pregnant teenager needs more calories, protein, calcium, and vitamins than other pregnant women.

Many teenage girls are conscious of their figure. However, pregnancy isn't the time for a weight-control diet! Weight-conscious teens need to know that extra pounds aren't just body fat. Pregnancy temporarily changes her body. And these changes add up to weight gain. *Refer to "Where Does Weight Gain Go?" on page* 461. Until age 18, teens need to gain more weight during pregnancy than adult women do. Most healthy young mothers gain about 35 pounds by the end of their pregnancy. The extra pounds for the mother add up to a healthier, stronger baby.

Eating a varied and balanced diet is the only way to fuel weight gain during pregnancy and "feed" a developing baby! Although doctors often prescribe a multi-vitamin/mineral supplement for pregnant teens, these nutrients are meant as a supplement to a healthful diet—not as a replacement for meals or snacks.

Because a baby grows "around the clock," pregnant teens need to follow a regular eating schedule, and eat a varied, balanced, and moderate diet from the five food groups. A pattern of three meals and three nutritious snacks daily can provide the nourishment needed for a teenage pregnancy. *Use the Food Guide Pyramid, explained on page* 243, *as a guide.*

Teenagers are at special risk for problems related to pregnancy. Prenatal care that includes nutrition counseling is important for a healthy teenage pregnancy. The nutritional demands of pregnancy and a teen's own growth, along with typically poor eating habits, increase the chances of anemia, pre-eclampsia (or toxemia), and a low birthweight baby. Untreated pre-eclampsia is dangerous and potentially life-threatening for the mother and baby. Symptoms include sudden weight gain, abdominal pain, and high blood pressure. *Refer to page* 468 *for more about pre-eclampsia.*

For more about nutrition during adolescence, refer to "Feeding the Teen Machine" on page 445.

Discomforts of Pregnancy

There's nothing very fulfilling about the discomforts that often go with pregnancy: morning sickness, constipation, heartburn, and swelling. But considering all the changes taking place in your body, it's no wonder you feel occasional discomforts. Fortunately, some problems can be relieved—sometimes by what and how you eat.

Beyond Morning Sickness

Fifty to 90 percent of moms-to-be suffer morning sickness. Somewhat of a misnomer, "morning sickness" may occur at any time—day or night. And it may continue past the first three months of pregnancy.

For some, morning sickness is just minor queasiness. For others, it may be persistent, severe nausea with spells of vomiting that can leave pregnant women at risk for dehydration and weight loss. Nausea and vomiting during pregnancy isn't a psychological ailment as people once explained. Today health experts think that hormonal changes, particularly rising estrogen levels, may be responsible.

If you're pregnant, try these ways to keep nausea at bay:

Avoid strong food flavors (perhaps spicy foods), cooking smells, or other scents that trigger your nausea. Pregnant women often have an exaggerated sense of smell, making an unassuming odor seem unappealing.

have you ever wondered

...if vegetarian eating can promote a healthy pregnancy? Like any pregnant woman, vegetarians also need to plan their food choices carefully. Women who've already mastered the skills of vegetarian eating should have no trouble getting the nutrients and energy they need for a healthy pregnancy. If you decide to begin following a vegetarian eating plan during pregnancy, consult a registered dietitian for guidance. *For specific guidance, refer to "The Vegetarian 'Mom'" on page 566.* ✦

Eat starchy foods, such as crackers, plain toast, or dry cereal, before getting out of bed in the morning. That starts the digestive processes and removes acid from your stomach.

Get out of bed slowly.

Try to eat small, frequent meals during the day to prevent an empty stomach. And drink beverages between, not with, meals.

Eat easy-to-digest carbohydrates, such as plain pasta, crackers, potatoes, rice, fruit, and vegetables. And limit fried and other high-fat foods.

Savor every bite! Eat meals slowly.

Eat a snack, such as peanut butter on crackers and a glass of milk, or cereal and milk, before going to bed.

Let taste and tolerance be the deciding factors! Within the context of a healthful diet, choose those foods that appeal and "stay down"!

Consult your doctor if you vomit more than twice daily.

Constipation During Pregnancy

Have you noticed occasional bouts of constipation since you've become pregnant? Many women do. Hormonal changes of pregnancy relax muscles to accommodate your expanding uterus. This relaxation also causes the action in your intestine to slow down, possibly making you feel constipated. If you take an iron supplement, that too can aggravate constipation.

For some women, constipation, along with pressure from the baby, leads to hemorrhoids. Hemorrhoids are large, swollen veins in the rectum.

These are ways you might ease constipation and the discomfort of hemorrhoids:

Eat high-fiber foods. Choose at least five daily servings of fruits and vegetables. Enjoy whole-grain foods from the Bread, Cereal, Rice, and Pasta Group of the Pyramid. Try bran, and include legumes regularly in your food choices.

Drink at least eight cups of fluid daily. Besides water, include milk, fruit juice, and perhaps broth in your fluid allowance. *For more about fluids in a healthful eating plan, refer to* "A Fluid Asset" *on page* 171.

Enjoy the natural laxative effect of prunes, prune juice, and figs to help prevent constipation.

Be physically active. Walking is good exercise during pregnancy, as are swimming and prenatal exercise classes. Regular activity stimulates normal bowel function. Talk to your doctor about a safe level of activity for you during pregnancy.

Unless your doctor prescribes them, don't take laxatives. For hemorrhoids, ask your doctor to recommend a safe suppository or ointment.

Just Heartburn

Especially during the last three months of pregnancy, many women complain about heartburn. That may happen as the baby puts pressure on the digestive organs. Try these ways to relieve your discomfort:

Eat small meals, frequently—every few hours.

Go easy on highly-seasoned, rich, and fatty foods.

Cut down on caffeinated beverages. For some pregnant women, caffeine can cause nausea and heartburn. While there's no conclusive evidence about the effects of caffeine on the fetus, limiting caffeine intake to less than 300 milligrams per day is generally considered safe if you're expecting. *For the caffeine content of various beverages, refer to* "Caffeine: What Sources, How Much?" *on page* 182.

Walk after you eat to encourage gastric, or stomach, juices to go down, not up. If you don't take a walk, at least remain seated after eating, rather than lying down.

Sleep with your head elevated.

Wear comfortable clothes.

Consult your doctor about antacids. Some contain sodium bicarbonate (baking soda) that can interfere with the absorption of vitamins and minerals.

Your blood passes through every organ in your body. And it goes through the placenta and into the circulatory system of your unborn baby. If alcohol or other drugs are in your blood, your baby is exposed to them, too.

The harmful effects of excessive alcohol are well known. Women who regularly consume alcohol during pregnancy, even at moderate levels (one to two drinks a day), may miscarry or deliver low birthweight babies. Excessive alcohol intake throughout pregnancy is associated with a condition called fetal alcohol syndrome (FAS). Infants with FAS may be born with birth defects: retarded growth, mental impairment, and physical malformations.

There's no proof that an occasional drink is harmful, but a safe level for alcohol intake during pregnancy is unknown. And health experts don't know if babies differ in their sensitivity to alcohol. So women trying to conceive and those already pregnant are wise to avoid beer, wine, or other alcoholic beverages and foods made with them.

As a reminder, alcoholic beverages carry a warning on the label. It advises women of the dangers of drinking during pregnancy and its relation to birth defects. ✦

GOVERNMENT WARNING:

(1) ACCORDING TO THE SURGEON GENERAL, WOMEN SHOULD NOT DRINK ALCOHOLIC BEVERAGES DURING PREGNANCY BECAUSE OF THE RISK OF BIRTH DEFECTS. (2) CONSUMPTION OF ALCOHOLIC BEVERAGES IMPAIRS YOUR ABILITY TO DRIVE A CAR OR OPERATE MACHINERY, AND MAY CAUSE HEALTH PROBLEMS.

Swelling—Part of Pregnancy
Swelling is natural, especially in the last three months of pregnancy. Your body retains water in the ankles, hands, and wrists as a reservoir for your expanded blood volume. This water offsets losses during delivery. And it's used later to produce breast milk.

Unless your doctor advises otherwise, avoid diuretics, or medications that increase water loss through urination. And do drink more, rather than less, water. There's no need to limit salt to prevent swelling, either; use iodized salt—just enough to match your taste. Iodine is a mineral, essential for you and your baby.

To relieve the discomfort of moderate swelling, use these techniques:

Put your feet up. And when you sit, get up to stretch to improve your circulation. Try not to stand for a long period of time.

Rest on your left side to aid circulation.

Wear comfortable shoes, perhaps a larger size.

Avoid tight clothes, tight stockings, tight-fitting rings, and anything else that restricts circulation.

If swelling is excessive, this may be a sign of pre-eclampsia, or toxemia. Other signs include high blood pressure, a sudden weight gain, headaches, and abdominal pain. Advise your doctor of these symptoms right away. Untreated, pre-eclampsia can be dangerous later in pregnancy, even life threatening for both mother and baby. *Note*: Pre-eclampsia has been linked to low calcium and low protein intake during pregnancy.

Pass the Pickles: Cravings!

For many women, cravings and food aversions are common during pregnancy. Taste changes probably result from hormonal changes, although the exact cause is unknown. Usually tastes realign themselves after your first three months of pregnancy or, in some cases, after the baby's birth.

Unless you avoid an entire food group, food aversions are harmless. You can substitute foods that are nutritionally similar. For instance, if broccoli loses its appeal when you're pregnant, substitute another vegetable that you enjoy and tolerate.

Whether it's pickles and ice cream or other foods, many women have cravings during pregnancy. Most cravings are harmless unless these foods take the place of other more nutritious foods. Then nutrient deficiencies may occur.

Caution: Cravings for nonfood substances, a condition called pica, can be dangerous. The practice of craving cornstarch, ashes, laundry starch, clay, and other odd substances comes from folklore that started hundreds of years ago. It was believed that eating a particular substance may decrease nausea, promote a healthy baby, or ease delivery. There's no evidence that this practice works—and it can be harmful for you and your baby. ✦

Pregnancy and Diabetes

Among some women, blood sugar levels go up toward the middle of pregnancy. The risk is higher for women with a family history of diabetes, women who are overweight, and those who've had problem pregnancies. As a safeguard, most women are routinely tested for gestational diabetes. Diabetes during pregnancy can increase the risk for high blood pressure, and for babies with birthweight over 10 pounds (who may be difficult to deliver), or with breathing problems.

Doctors monitor gestational diabetes carefully and prescribe treatment. Typically a registered dietitian helps develop an eating plan to control blood sugar levels. Gestational diabetes usually goes away after delivery. *Refer to "Diabetes: A Major Health Concern" on page* 499.

Stay Active!

For most pregnancies, physical activity is important. Besides helping you feel fit and energetic, exercise helps improve muscle tone and circulation. Moderate activity can relieve leg and back pain, help your posture, help you sleep better, prepare you for labor—and help you look and feel your best. It may also help prevent varicose veins. (*Caution*: Pregnancy isn't the time to exercise to lose or keep from gaining weight.)

For most women, some form of moderate activity is suggested, perhaps walking, swimming, modified low-impact aerobics, or stationary cycling. Your level of physical activity during pregnancy depends on your health and how active you've always been.

With minor changes, you may be able to continue your regular routine. Just remember, as your body shape changes, your center of gravity shifts, too. Some activities won't be as easy to do. Injury is more likely, too, as changes in hormones cause the ligaments in your joints to stretch. So exercise with care—and don't overdo.

Keep these pointers in mind:

Always talk to your doctor about your exercise regimen during pregnancy—including any new activities you plan to do. Women with high-risk pregnancies may need to limit physical activity.

With your doctor, choose an activity plan that keeps you fit, matches your health needs and lifestyle, and prepares you for delivery. Your hospital, clinic, or health club might offer an exercise program designed for pregnant women. It usually includes exercises to help with labor, including deep breathing and stretching.

Start slowly. If you haven't been active, start with low-intensity activity—according to your doctor's advice.

Stick with your routine. This isn't the time to stop and start with spurts of heavy exercise. Get physically active at least three times a week.

Keep some variety in your activity plan. Include activities that build strength and condition your heart and lungs.

If you experience any problems, stop your activity, and consult your doctor right away. These are symptoms for concern: pain (in general, or in your back or pubic area), dizziness, vaginal bleeding, shortness of breath, rapid or irregular heart beat, or discomfort when you walk.

For Those Who Breast-Feed...

Your decision to breast-feed is a personal one, dependent on many factors. If you decide breast-feeding is for you, keep good nutrition on the top of your "to do" list. In fact, your needs for energy and some nutrients are higher during breast-feeding than while you were pregnant!

For the benefits of breast-feeding for you and your baby, and for guidance on breast-feeding techniques, refer to "Breast-Feeding Your Baby" on page 393.

Your Energy Sources

Your fuel supply for milk production comes from two sources: energy stored as body fat during pregnancy and extra energy from food choices. To produce breast milk, your body uses up about 100 to 150 calories a day from its own energy stores. That's why breast-feeding helps many new mothers lose the weight gained during pregnancy—often without trying!

After the first three months of pregnancy, you needed 300 extra calories each day from food. Now while breast-feeding, you may need more. An extra 500 calories a day, beyond your nonpregnancy intake, is recommended to fuel milk production. If you needed 2,200 calories to maintain your weight before you became pregnant, you may need about 2,700 calories a day now.

For added energy, stock up on nutrient-rich foods from the five food groups. Adding an extra serving or so from each food group during the day provides the extra energy and nutrient needs you need. How many food group servings do you need as you breast-feed? *Refer to "How Many Servings for You?" on page* 245.

After you've been breast-feeding a while, evaluate your energy intake. Consider your activity level, weight gain during pregnancy, and weight loss since delivery. You may need more than 500 extra calories a day—or you may need less. Talk to your lactation counselor or a registered dietitian for guidance.

A strict weight-loss regimen isn't recommended when you're nursing. If your intake dips below 1,800 calories daily, you probably won't get enough of the nutrients your body needs. And, especially early on in nursing, a diet with too few calories may reduce your milk supply. Losing two to four pounds a month probably won't affect your milk supply. But more than four to five pounds a month, after the first month, isn't advised.

Now About Nutrients...

The need for most nutrients increases during breast-feeding. A few nutrients may need special attention while you're breast-feeding, especially if you breast-feed for more than two or three months:

Protein. While breast-feeding, you can get enough protein from your normal diet. For example, the protein from an extra serving or two of milk can supply the extra amount needed, along with more calcium.

Calcium. As during pregnancy, pay close attention to your calcium intake. If you don't consume enough, your body may draw from its calcium reserves in your bones. That's your body's way of keeping the calcium content of your breast milk adequate. The calcium losses in your bones may put you at greater risk for osteoporosis when you're older.

Keep your bones strong by choosing three to four calcium-rich dairy foods daily—more if you're a teenager. And eat vegetables and fish with edible bones; they're both good calcium sources, too. *Refer to "Calcium: A Closer Look" on page* 105 *and to "Osteoporosis: Reduce the Risks" on page* 496.

Magnesium and Zinc. Pay special attention to these two minerals, too, since many women don't consume enough. Magnesium comes from legumes, nuts, and whole grains, as well as green vegetables. Nursing increases the need for zinc. Zinc that's most easily used by your body comes from foods of animal origin. *Pages* 98 *and* 104 *explain their role in health and their food sources.*

Vitamin B_{12} and Vitamin D. These two vitamins may require special attention to ensure an optimal quantity in breast milk. Because vitamin B_{12} is found only in foods from animals, some vegetarians may need a vitamin B_{12} supplement. If you eat meat, poultry, fish, eggs, and dairy products, you're likely getting enough.

Breast milk doesn't have much vitamin D. And if your diet is low in vitamin D or if you don't get enough sunlight, your breast milk may have even less. Sunlight helps your body produce vitamin D. Some vegetarians may need a vitamin D supplement.

have you ever wondered

...if a mother's food choices affect the flavor of breast milk? Eating strongly-flavored foods, such as onions, garlic, broccoli, cabbage, cauliflower, garlic, "hot" spicy food, or beans, may give breast milk an off-flavor. This can make some babies fussy; other babies won't even notice. If certain foods seem to upset your baby, just decrease the amount or frequency that you eat them. Your breast milk, usually white or bluish-white, may take on a different hue, too, depending on the food you eat. Certain fruits, vegetables, or food dyes may cause a harmless color change. ✦

Folate. Getting enough folate can be difficult if you don't eat many leafy vegetables and fruits. Especially if you're considering another pregnancy in the near future, make sure you get the recommended amount of 500 micrograms daily of folate while breast-feeding. *For more about folate, refer to "Pregnancy: Before You Begin" on page 457.*

Vitamin B_6. This vitamin often comes up short with breast-feeding, too, since a woman's food choices may not supply enough. Chicken, fish, and pork are the best sources, followed by whole grains and legumes. *Refer to "Vitamins: The Basics" on page 80 for more information.*

Multi-Vitamin/Mineral Supplement. If you took a prenatal vitamin/mineral supplement, your doctor may recommend that you continue. If your diet lacks energy or nutrients, in most cases, your breast milk still will be sufficient to support your baby's growth and development. But it'll be at the expense of your nutrient reserves!

For specific Recommended Dietary Allowances for breast-feeding, refer to the appendix on pages 606-607.

Remember Fluids!

To ensure an adequate milk supply, drink enough fluids to satisfy your thirst and prevent dehydration. That should supply enough for milk production. As before, you need at least 8 to 12 cups of fluids daily—and more if you feel thirsty.

You might keep water, milk, or fruit juice handy to sip as you nurse. *Tip*: Milk and juice also supply other nutrients you need in extra amounts for breast-feeding. For example, you get calcium from milk, and vitamin C from most fruit juices.

Nonfoods: Effect on Breast Milk?

While you breast-feed, take the same precautions you did during pregnancy. Whether it's food, beverages, or other substances, what you consume may be passed to your baby through breast milk.

Alcoholic Beverages

The alcohol you drink passes into breast milk. So a glass of wine or beer to relax you isn't the best advice. An occasional alcoholic drink probably won't affect your baby or interfere with nursing. But heavy drinking may affect your "let-down" reflex. Alcohol in breast milk may cause your baby to be less alert, and even affect brain development.

Because there's no guideline on how much is safe, you're wise to avoid alcoholic beverages when you're nursing. Or if you want to sip an occasional drink, do so after breast-feeding. That way, your body has time to break down the alcohol before you nurse again.

Smoking

If you're a smoker and quit during pregnancy, breast-feeding isn't the time to take up the habit again. Nicotine does pass into breast milk. It can reduce your milk supply, and your baby may be more likely to develop colic or a sinus infection, or just be fussy. Smoking near your baby can expose him or her to second-hand smoke, and possibly to

have you ever wondered

...if you can drink caffeinated beverages while you're nursing? Yes, you can enjoy your morning coffee... or a soft drink for a snack... in moderation. Caffeine does pass into breast milk. If you drink just one or two cups a day, the caffeine probably won't bother your baby.

...if vegetarian eating affects breast-feeding? A vegetarian mom who consumes dairy products and perhaps eggs, can easily get the nutrients she needs. Vegans, who avoid all foods of animal origin, need to pay special attention to obtaining adequate amounts of these nutrients: calcium, vitamin D, iron, and vitamin B_{12}. *For more on vegetarian eating, refer to "The Vegetarian 'Mom'" on page 566.*

...if breast-feeding reduces the risk for breast cancer later on? That's been speculated, but the evidence isn't conclusive yet. Still, the other benefits of breast-feeding are well worth the effort! ✦

burns. Too close to a nursing session, smoking may even inhibit your "let down" reflex.

Advice for those who choose to smoke: Don't smoke near your baby—not even in the same room. Try to avoid smoking for 2 1/2 hours before nursing, and never smoke as you nurse your baby!

Medications

Consult your doctor about medications—just so he or she knows what you're taking. That includes both prescription and over-the-counter medication. Most pass into breast milk in concentrations that pose no harm to your infant. However, there are exceptions. So talk to your doctor or pharmacist before taking any medication, even an aspirin!

Recreational drugs are never considered safe for you or your baby. These substances pass into breast milk, potentially being dangerous for your baby!

Now for Menopause...

Menopause, when monthly periods stop, is a natural part of a woman's life cycle. Once symptoms such as hot flashes, mood swings, and sleeplessness disappear, post-menopausal women are free of the discomforts that came with their monthly menstrual cycle.

As always, an overall healthful diet—with enough servings from the Food Guide Pyramid—is important advice for menopause. Healthful eating promotes good health. And good health minimizes the discomforts of menopause. *Refer to "The Food Guide Pyramid: Your Healthful Eating Guide" on page* 243.

have you ever wondered

...if extra magnesium will ward off hot flashes? There's no evidence that dietary supplements—including extra magnesium—effectively treat the discomforts of menopause. However, adequate magnesium from food does help promote bone health after menopause by helping the body use calcium properly. *Refer to page* 98. ✦

At this stage of life, physical activity remains a priority. Besides the benefits to weight management and heart and bone health, an active lifestyle also can reduce the discomforts of menopause. *For ways to add physical activity to your lifestyle, refer to "Get Physical!" on page* 31.

Read on for more about the nutrition and lifestyle issues that accompany menopause.

Iron Needs Drop

On the "up" side, your need for iron drops with menopause. So the risk for iron deficiency also goes down. Unless your doctor advises otherwise, now's the time to stop taking iron supplements. Taking in too much iron, typically in the form of a supplement, can be harmful—especially if you have a genetic disorder called hemochromatosis.

Weight Gain: A New Problem?

On the "down" side, some women gain weight, even though they never had weight problems before. Metabolic rate, or the speed at which the body uses energy, often slows down as hormone levels change. A shift in midlife activity level may be partly responsible, too. Many people live a more sedentary lifestyle and use less energy as they get older.

Adjust your food choices and lifestyle to maintain your weight. Even drop a few pounds if you need to anyway. Being overweight is a risk factor for many health problems that start to appear after menopause. *Refer to chapter* 2, *"Your Healthy Weight."*

Calcium Needs Go Up

Bone loss is part of aging. With a drop in estrogen levels during menopause, women lose bone faster. So calcium needs increase. Boosting your calcium intake helps slow bone loss.

The National Institutes of Health advises 1,500 milligrams of calcium a day after menopause for women who don't take estrogen, and 1,000 milligrams of calcium for those who do. After age 50, 1,200 milligrams calcium daily is considered an Adequate Intake, according to 1997 Daily Reference Intakes. As a reference, one 8-ounce glass of milk supplies about 300 milligrams of calcium. *For more about Adequate Intake levels, refer to* "Nutrients: How Much?" *on page* 4.

For more about calcium and bone health, refer to "Calcium: A Closer Look" *on page* 105 *and* "Osteoporosis: Reducing the Risks" *on page* 496.

Heart Disease: A Woman's Issue, Too!

As estrogen levels drop with menopause, women no longer have protection from heart disease and high blood pressure. That's true whether menopause is natural or surgical. As a result, women's risks for heart disease parallel those of men—but 7 to 10 years later in life! And their death rate is higher, perhaps due to increased age or more risk factors.

The signs of heart disease for women may differ from those of men. Women often have angina first, rather than a heart attack. Using exercise tests for diagnosis is less reliable for women than men, too.

Women...if you haven't done so already, make heart-healthy choices. Start with small steps, then work up:

Eat a diet that's low in fat, saturated fat, and cholesterol. *Refer to chapter* 3, "Fat Facts."

Enjoy plenty of grain products, vegetables, and fruits. *Refer to* "Fruits and Vegetables: Count Five a Day!" *on page* 96 *and* "Whole Grains: For Goodness Sake" *on page* 103.

Stay physically active (or get started). *Refer to* "20 Everyday Ways to Get Moving!" *on page* 32.

Keep a healthy weight. *Refer to chapter* 2, "Your Healthy Weight" *for guidance.*

Go easy on salt and sodium, in case your blood pressure is sodium-sensitive. *Refer to* "Link to High Blood Pressure" *on page* 159.

Consult with your doctor about hormone replacement therapy once you reach menopause. It may offer some protection. *Refer to* "HRT: For Some Women" *below.*

Control stress in your daily life.

If you smoke, quit.

For more on preventing heart disease, refer to "Keeping a Healthy Heart" *on page* 486.

HRT: For Some Women

Hormone replacement therapy (HRT), also referred to as estrogen replacement therapy (ERT), may ease hot flashes and other discomforts of menopause. New studies also suggest that HRT after menopause may help reduce the risk for heart disease, as well as osteoporosis and stroke. That may be especially important for women with premature menopause. Along with other heart-healthy benefits, the combination of two hormones—estrogen and progestin (a form of progesterone)—may help raise HDL-blood cholesterol. *For more about hormone replacement therapy and bone health, refer to* "Protect Your 'Support System'" *on page* 498.

HRT isn't right for every woman, for example, those with a greater risk for breast cancer. Women with a history of migraine headaches, diabetes, and some other health problems may be advised against it, too. If you're approaching or experiencing menopause, talk to your doctor about HRT. It may offer benefits for you.

Researchers are now looking at the potential benefits of foods that contain phytoestrogens (also called isoflavones). It's thought that these substances, found in soy products, may help offset the effects of reduced estrogen production by the ovaries, helping to decrease the symptoms of menopause. They also may play a role in reducing the risk for breast cancer, heart disease, and osteoporosis.

your nutrition check-up

Ironing Out the Differences, For Calcium, Too!

Three nutrients are of special concern to women: folic acid, calcium, and iron.

Fruits and vegetables are among the best sources of folic acid. *If you haven't done so already, assess your fruit and vegetable intake using "Fruits and Vegetables: Count Five a Day!" on page* 96. Whole-grains, nuts, legumes, and liver are good sources, too.

Now, see how your meal and snack choices stack up for calcium and iron. In each pair, which food would you choose…

For more calcium…

Column A	*or*	*Column B*
___ 1/2 cup frozen yogurt		___ 1/2 cup ice cream
___ 1/2 cup carrots		___ 1/2 cup broccoli
___ 1 oz. cheddar cheese		___ 1/2 cup cottage cheese
___ 3 oz. canned salmon with bones		___ 3 oz. canned tuna
___ 1 cup milk		___ 1 cup apple juice
___ 1 slice cheesecake		___ 1/2 cup pudding
___ 2 Tbsp. yogurt cheese		___ 2 Tbsp. cream cheese
___ 1/2 cup turnip greens		___ 1/2 cup lettuce
___ 1/2 cup tofu (made with calcium sulfate)		___ 1/2 cup pinto beans
___ 1 cup chocolate milk		___ 1 oz. milk chocolate bar

For more iron…

Column A	*or*	*Column B*
___ 1 cup fortified breakfast cereal		___ 1 slice whole-wheat toast
___ 1/2 cup unenriched rice		___ 1/2 cup enriched rice
___ 3/4 cup prune juice		___ 3/4 cup cranberry juice
___ 3 oz. broiled sirloin steak		___ 3 oz. broiled cod
___ 1/2 cup cooked kidney beans		___ 1/2 cup cooked green beans
___ 1/2 cup cooked zucchini		___ 1/2 cup boiled spinach
___ 1 egg yolk		___ 1 egg white
___ 1/3 cup grapes		___ 1/3 cup raisins
___ 2 Tbsp. peanut butter		___ 3 oz. broiled chicken breast
___ 1 oz. pumpkin seeds		___ 1 oz. pretzels

Now Score Yourself

For each pair, these foods contain more calcium: yogurt, broccoli, cheddar cheese, canned salmon with bones, milk, pudding, yogurt cheese, turnip greens, tofu (made with calcium sulfate), chocolate milk.

To check the specific amounts of calcium in these pairs of foods, see the chart, "Counting Up Calcium" on page 107.

For each pair, these foods contain more iron: fortified breakfast cereal, enriched rice, prune juice, sirloin steak, kidney beans, spinach, egg yolk, raisins, chicken breast, pumpkin seeds.

To check the specific amounts of iron in these pairs of foods, see the chart, "Counting Up Iron" on page 110.

Give yourself 5 points for each pair you got right—perfect score, 50 points for calcium and 50 points for iron. The higher your scores, the more calcium and iron in your food choices—if these foods really are your "picks" for the day. *Tip*: For plant sources of iron, partner them with meat or a vitamin C-rich food for more iron benefits.

real life nutrition

Baby Your Baby

Tonight would be a special celebration. Sonja tied a big bow around the neck of a brand new teddy bear, attaching a note for her husband that said: "We're having a baby!"

All along, Sonja has tried to eat in a healthful way and to stay physically active. So she's rather confident about being ready for a healthy pregnancy. But she knows her food choices still may have some shortcomings.

She nestled the bear into one corner of the couch. Then before making dinner, she snuggled into the other corner—with a plate of cookies and a soft drink—to study the eating guidelines she'd just received. She was hungry now. Earlier in the day she had felt too nauseated to eat.

"I need enough folic acid—thank goodness I've always been fond of vegetables and fruits," she mused, rubbing her stomach. "Hmmm…and I need three servings of milk, yogurt, or cheese every day. I've only been eating one serving! I wonder how much more food I get to eat now that I can finally eat for two? In fact, what are we going to eat for dinner tonight?"

Sonja put the pamphlet down and headed to the kitchen. She thought through the meal—broiled flounder, broccoli, herbed rice, papaya-mango salad, bakery-fresh bread sticks, strawberry cheesecake…and what to drink? "Wine to celebrate? I'm not sure."

Nutrition advice for Sonja throughout her pregnancy might include:

➢ Sonja is wise to save the wine for later celebrations. Pregnancy and breast-feeding aren't the times for drinking alcoholic beverages. In fact, toasting with milk would get her pregnancy off to a terrific start. Both dinner and snacks are good times to consume at least one Milk Group serving.

➢ If Sonja feels nauseated in the morning, she might eat a starchy food, such as crackers, before getting out of bed. Easy-to-digest foods, such as those she's planned for dinner, are better tolerated, too.

➢ Eating a variety of foods—from all five food groups—is important for Sonja during her pregnancy. (Hint: The cheesecake doesn't count as a serving from the Milk Group.)

➢ Sonja should keep up her consumption of fruits and vegetables, and take a folic acid supplement if her doctor advises. Getting enough folic acid helps avoid spinal cord damage to her developing baby.

➢ Eating for two doesn't mean Sonja can eat twice as much. She only needs 300 extra calories a day to support her pregnancy. Her snack and dessert are fine to enjoy if she doesn't overdo on overall calories, or energy, for the day. And she's wise to go easy on foods that supply calories but few nutrients.

➢ She'll need plenty of iron-rich foods, including meat, legumes, enriched rice, and fortified breakfast cereal, among others. Because it's iron-enriched, the herbed rice is a good place to start.

➢ Her doctor also may advise Sonja to take an iron supplement. For the best absorption, she should take it between meals.

➢ Getting enough fluids are important! Sonja might drink water, as well as milk, with her dinner.

➢ Sonja should keep up her regular routine of physical activity, making adjustments as needed during her pregnancy as her body changes. Talking with her doctor about her activity level should be part of her prenatal counseling.

CHAPTER NINETEEN

SMART EATING *for* HEALTHY ADULTS

Let's give a toast! Raise a vegetable or a fruit or a slice of toast to your good health! The ages and stages of your young and middle adult years depend on healthful eating and smart living. Living a healthful lifestyle from the start is the best approach for promoting health and preventing health problems—or a least slowing their course! Most health problems don't start with a single event in your life. Instead they're a combination of factors. Some you can't control, such as your family history, gender, or age. In the long run, though, your food choices and lifestyle set you up for healthy aging.

Nutrition... Your Health Investment

A long and healthy life—that's what most people wish for. You may not realize it, but more than two-thirds of all the illnesses and mishaps likely to injure or kill you are linked directly to choices you make. That also means most illnesses and mishaps are preventable—or at least can be postponed.

Two types of factors, or "assets," affect your health and well-being:

- fixed assets, or those factors that you can't change, such as family history, your age, and your gender
- variable, interest-bearing assets, or those factors that are under your direct control, such as your lifestyle, surroundings, and self-care choices

Your variable assets play a large role in your health status, both today—and 10 to 20, perhaps even 30 to 40, years from now. Your lifestyle choices—what you eat, how active you are, whether you smoke or abuse alcoholic drinks or drugs—are especially critical. Your long-term investment in healthful living can generate valuable health dividends. Added bonuses: Slowing the decline associated with aging, and living a more pleasant life!

Whether you're 25, 40, or 55 years old, consider your lifestyle. And invest in your own good health now. The sooner your start, the healthier you may be in the long-run. After all, waiting to make changes is like buying life insurance at an older age—the cost rises with time. *For nutrition issues related especially to women, refer to* "For Women Only," *chapter* 18.

Staying Fit: The Bottom Line

Adults of all ages: The secret to feeling your best is keeping fit. Throughout adulthood, several physical factors affect your overall health as you get older.

Muscle Strength

As you get older, the size and strength of your muscles decrease naturally. For each decade of adult life, the average person loses six to seven pounds of muscle. And the rate often gets faster after age 45. Many qualities of youth depend on muscle strength and flexibility: for example, stamina, ease of movement, ability to handle heavy objects, feeling energetic, and even physical appearance.

Maintaining muscle size and strength—along with other qualities of youth—takes regular physical activity. That includes physical activities that build strength. So the bottom line for fitness is: When you stay physically active, you feel and look younger and healthier!

Body Fat

Especially if you're less active as you age, body fat gradually replaces muscle. Besides losing that firm, muscular shape of youth, extra body fat increases the risk for some health problems. And "midriff bulge" is a sure sign that you're probably not 25 anymore! The bottom line: Try to avoid extra body fat, and instead keep lean.

Again the guideline for fitness: Avoid excess body fat through regular physical activity. Manage your overall energy intake. Over time, consume no more calories than your body uses. And eat an overall healthful diet that's varied, balanced, and moderate. What does that mean? *Refer to "The Bottom Line: Variety, Balance, Moderation" on page* 8.

The Rate Your Body Uses Energy

Again, the rate your body uses energy declines with age. With every decade you need about 2 percent less energy, or calories, a day. For example, if you need 2,200 calories a day at age 25, you may need 2 percent less, or 2,154 calories per day, at age 35. Body composition, along with hormone changes, is part of the reason.

You can't fool mother nature entirely. But if you're physically active and keep your muscle mass, your body will burn energy a little faster because muscle burns more energy than body fat. Physical activity also gives a short-term boost to the rate your body uses energy.

Bone Strength

You can't see how strong your bones are. But healthy bones are important to active aging, because they allow you to enjoy physical activity with less risk of fractures. And you may avoid the "dowager's hump," which often appears with osteoporosis as people age.

Through food choices and weight-bearing activity, you can build bone mass while you're still young, up to age 30 to 35. After that, make choices to keep bones strong and slow the rate of bone loss. *Refer to "Osteoporosis: Reduce the Risks" on page* 496.

Your "Thermostat"

Fluids are your body's natural cooling system. But as you get older, your sense of thirst may diminish. Even though you may not feel thirsty, your body needs at least eight cups of fluid daily from water, juice, milk, other beverages, and food.

A fitness routine—healthful eating and physical activity—shouldn't wait until you notice signs of aging. If you're in your early adult years, get fit, and stay fit now. If you already have a few more years under your belt, you can still slow or reverse some physical signs of aging with the food and lifestyle choices you make.

did you know

...a man in his 50s who exercises regularly has more energy and a better sex life and can work longer hours than someone who doesn't?

...four of the 10 leading causes of death and disease in the United States are associated directly with diet?

...women are at high risk for heart disease, just 7 to 10 years later than men? ✦

Your Nutrition Needs

As an adult, you need the same 40 or more nutrients you needed as a child and teenager. Only some of the amounts have changed. Since no single food supplies all the vitamins you need, eat moderate amounts of a variety of foods. *The Food Guide Pyramid, described on page 243, offers an eating guideline for all healthy adults to follow.*

Choose your calories wisely. Since you may need fewer calories as you get older, go easy on foods that offer few nutrients for a large calorie investment. Enjoy mostly nutrient-packed foods from the five food groups.

Just about everyone can benefit from an eating plan that's low in fat. High-fat diets are linked to heart disease, obesity, certain cancers (prostrate, rectum, and colon), high blood pressure, and gallbladder disease. Diversify your food choices and focus on lower-fat foods. *For tips on controlling the fat in your overall eating plan, refer to "Moderation: Key to a Healthful Diet" on page 67.*

Invest in your health with plenty of grain products, vegetables, and fruit, too. These foods supply complex carbohydrates, which is your body's best energy source, and dietary fiber, which comes up short in the diets of most American adults. Vegetables, fruits, and whole-grain products are also good sources of vitamins A, C, and E, which may offer protection from heart disease, some forms of cancer, cataracts, and other problems of aging. *Refer to "Antioxidant Vitamins: A Closer Look" on page 90. For more about complex carbohydrates, refer to "From Complex to Simple..." on page 125.*

For most adults, it's sensible to eat a moderate amount of sodium and salt, especially for those whose blood pressure is sensitive to sodium. For some, that may mean cutting back. Consuming less sodium may reduce chances for high blood pressure and may help to lower blood pressure that's already elevated. *For more about sodium in a healthful eating plan, refer to chapter 7, "Sodium: A Salty Subject."*

Eat Healthy, Work Smart

In spite of technology that makes life easier, today's world seems to put more demands on us, with a need to be increasingly more productive. One way to get the most out of your day: Eat for success!

Start your workday with breakfast. You'll replenish your body's blood sugar stores, needed for sustained mental work and physical activity throughout the day. You'll also stave off midmorning hunger that may reduce your concentration. *Refer to "Breakfast: Off to a Healthy Start!" on page 258.*

For Healthy Adults: The Nutrition Bottom Line

What's the best nutrition advice for a healthy adulthood? It's all summed up in the seven Dietary Guidelines for Americans. The same nutrition advice applies to preventing many health problems that start to crop up with age.

- Eat a variety of foods.
- Balance the food you eat with physical activity. Maintain or improve your weight.
- Choose a diet with plenty of grain products, vegetables, and fruits.
- Choose a diet low in fat, saturated fat, and cholesterol.
- Choose a diet moderate in sugars.
- Choose a diet moderate in salt and sodium.
- If you drink alcoholic beverages, do so in moderation.

For more about the Dietary Guidelines for Americans, refer to page 5. ✦

Take short breaks to relieve work stress. Take a brisk, five-minute walk. Stretch your muscles, and hold for 30 seconds. Relieve tension in your shoulders and neck by tilting your head from side to side, and front to back. Or switch tasks for a while. Avoid the urge to nibble for stress relief.

Work from an office at home? If you're accustomed to a company cafeteria or a convenient deli, you may need to devise a new eating pattern than promotes good health:

Keep routine in your life. Instead of rolling out of bed right into your office, start your day with breakfast. You'll be more productive! And try to set a regular time for lunch.

Need a break from work? Opt for a walk outside, rather than make an automatic trip to the refrigerator every time you need to stretch.

Keep food on hand for quick workday meals and snacks. With a kitchen handy, you have more options.

Occasionally give yourself a treat. Go out to eat with someone else who works at home or who works in a traditional setting. The social contact that goes with eating out is "good for your head."

Take advantage of working at home for other food preparation. As a work break, start making after-work meals. Perhaps simmer bean soup, or put a turkey breast in the oven.

Make time for physical activity. When you work at home, you may have less opportunity for routine activity, for example, no need to walk from the parking lot, bus, or train. ✦

Take time for a lunch break—even when you're under pressure. You may avoid a dip in your afternoon energy level. *Refer to "Meal Skipping: Poor Option!" on page* 257. And no, eating a big lunch does not make you sleepy in the afternoon. Instead, your overall sleep habits, age, and body cycle may cause your drowsiness. New research also suggests that a mid-afternoon slump may be normal and induced by hormones. To stay alert all day, regularly rest well at night. If you feel sleepy in the afternoon, try a 10- to 20-minute nap to renew your energy (if your workplace allows).

When you go out for lunch, order a nonalcoholic beverage. For a business lunch, sparkling water with a lemon twist is a great "cocktail." Alcoholic drinks can make you feel drowsy—a problem when you need to feel alert at work. The effects of just one beer or glass of wine can last about an hour. Blood-alcohol levels from two drinks may stay with you the better part of the afternoon. When you handle potentially dangerous equipment or drive as part of your job, drinking and working is risky.

Need a snack break? Keep nutritious foods on hand. *For easy ideas, refer to "Go Anywhere Snacks" on page* 264.

If you're caffeine-sensitive, limit coffee, tea, and soft drinks with caffeine. Enjoy a cup if that helps wake you up in the morning. But switch to "decaf," milk, water, or juice if caffeine bothers you. *Refer to "Drinks: With or Without Caffeine?" on page* 181.

Inactivity: Hazardous to Your Health

Tackle the pressures of living by staying fit! Regular physical activity can make a big difference in your outlook on life. Natural tranquilizers secreted during exercise promote a sense of well-being. And they help drain away stress and tension in a natural, positive way. If you're physically active, you may feel more in control of your life, your appetite, and your body weight. And you just may feel better overall!

Conversely, inactivity can be hazardous to your health. It's associated with many health problems that start to appear in the middle years: for example, heart disease, stroke, some cancers, weight problems, osteoporosis, and diabetes. Not surprisingly, the death rate of sedentary men is more than three times higher than that of fit men!

Have you ever thought, "I just don't have time to exercise?" In fact, you can't afford to be inactive. Many successful people have learned to make physical activity a natural, enjoyable part of life. You're wise to do that, too!

Think of physical activity as your body's preventive maintenance plan. You probably do that for your car—so why not for your body?

Start with a physical exam, especially if you're over age 40, overweight, or have heart, circulation, joint, or bone problems. Talk to your doctor before you begin a physical activity program.

Find a variety of activities you enjoy. They don't need to be elaborate or expensive.

Start slowly. Begin with moderate physical activity, such as walking or working in your yard. Every bit helps! Don't expect to shape up or trim down in a single weekend. Overdoing it may cause injuries and discourage you from continuing.

Build up over a month or two to more intense activity. For overall fitness, you need a total of 30 minutes of moderate activity most, if not all, days of the week. Adjust your schedule until you find the best time of day for physical activity.

If you lack motivation, find a partner. Or join a group, perhaps for tennis or volleyball, that meets regularly. As activity becomes routine, you'll find that your motivation to exercise comes from within—that's when you know you're succeeding!

Take time to see how far you've come. It's easy to notice sore muscles. But also think about the good things. Do you feel more energetic? And do you feel less stressed? Are you in a better mood?

For more about the benefits and approach to active living, refer to "Get Physical!" on page 31. You'll find "20 Everyday Ways to Get Moving!" on page 32. And for tips on eating for more strenuous physical activity, refer to chapter 21, "Athlete's Guide: Winning Nutrition."

Get Your Zzzzzzzs!

Do you wake up with a sleep deficit? Many Americans are short on sleep. Yet, adequate rest, along with good nutrition and regular physical activity, is part of the good health equation.

On average, adults need about 7 1/2 hours of sleep daily. Research shows that people who rest enough accomplish more. The quality of their work is better. And their chances for accidents and absenteeism at

have you ever wondered

...if extra vitamin E will keep you young? We all dream of the fountain of youth. But there's no evidence that taking nutrient supplements, including vitamin E, will stop or reverse the aging process. And it won't cure other problems: sterility, premenstrual syndrome, and ulcers, to name a few. Many claims made for vitamin E are really distortions of research done with animals, that shouldn't be applied to humans. As more research is done, we'll know more about vitamin E's potential role in health promotion.

...if you can treat chronic fatigue with a special diet? Maybe. New research has suggested that chronic fatigue syndrome may be linked with a disorder called neurally mediated hypotension, or low blood pressure. Treatment for this condition involves boosting salt and fluid intake to help regulate blood pressure, combined with medication. While this treatment holds promise for some, additional studies are underway to determine the best treatment regimen for most sufferers. Of course, an overall healthful eating pattern that provides nutrients and calories you need to feel energetic, combined with adequate rest and physical activity, also can make a difference. And for most people, moderate intakes of sodium are still advised. ✦

work go down. Besides, being rested feels good—physically and emotionally. And it may help you better handle the everyday stress.

Consider these tips for getting the rest you need:

Do you ever feel too tense to sleep well? Learn to relax as a way to break the cycle of sleeplessness. Stress leads to sleeplessness. And sleeplessness often leads to more stress.

If you're sensitive to caffeine, avoid caffeinated drinks six to eight hours before sleep time. Opt for decaffeinated beverages—or enjoy milk, juice, or water—with meals and snacks later in the day.

Don't expect a glass of wine or other alcoholic beverage to help you sleep well. Initially, you may feel drowsy. But even if you sip a drink two to three hours before bedtime, your sleep might be light, not the deep, most restful kind of sleep pattern.

Make your surroundings "sleep-friendly"—a darkened, quiet room, comfortable surface and pillow to lie on, and temperature on the cool side. And try to stick to a regular sleep schedule.

Promote rest through regular physical activity. Being active actually helps your body relax and sleep soundly. Just refrain from exercise too close to bedtime. Exercise speeds up your metabolism for a while, perhaps keeping you "pumped up" and unable to sleep right away.

If you need to "energize" yourself during the day, take a 10- to 20-minute nap. That's all you may need to renew yourself after a mid-day slump.

Damage Control

Of the 10 leading causes of death and disease in the United States, 4 are associated directly with diet, and 3 with excessive intake of alcoholic beverages. Paying attention to what you eat and drink can pay off in good health and longevity.

10 Leading Causes of Illness and Death

Rank and Cause	Diet-Related	Alcohol-Related
1. Heart Disease	X	
2. Cancers	X	
3. Strokes	X	
4. Respiratory Diseases		
5. Accidents and Injuries		X
6. Pneumonia and Influenza		
7. Diabetes	X	
8. HIV Infection		
9. Suicide		X
10. Homicide		X

Source: *National Center for Health Statistics, U.S. Department of Health and Human Services*, 1995

Prevention: Nutrition and Health Problems

Throughout your adult life, you can control many risk factors that contribute to health problems later. Those factors include your overall eating plan and how actively you live your life.

Anemia: That Run-Down Feeling

Have that "run-down" feeling? Perhaps you're overworked and under-rested. More sleep and relaxation may be what you need to feel energetic again. Or perhaps your fatigue is a symptom of anemia.

Actually, anemia isn't a disease, but instead a symptom of other health problems. Often there's a nutrition connection.

With anemia, there aren't enough red blood cells, or enough hemoglobin in red blood cells, to transport oxygen to body cells. Hemoglobin is the part of red blood cells that carries oxygen. When that happens, cells can't produce enough energy. Then fatigue, pale skin, headache, weakness, lack of concentration, or irritability, among other symptoms, sets in. To produce enough red blood cells, you need enough iron in your diet, as well as enough folic acid and vitamin B_{12}.

Is It Iron Deficiency?

Anemia isn't a symptom of just one health problem. A form often described as "iron poor blood" might come to mind first. In fact, iron-deficiency is the most common form of anemia, often affecting adult women of child-bearing age, children, and teens.

Women need more iron than men do. So they're more at risk for anemia. Why?

- Monthly blood loss from menstruation is one reason women need more.
- Pregnancy doubles iron need. That's attributed to increased blood volume—at least three more pints of blood! Often a woman's iron stores get used up to meet the demands of pregnancy.
- Women often don't consume enough iron-rich foods in their everyday diet. That may be because they've restricted their food intake to control weight.
- Vegetarian women may come up short on iron. Plant sources of iron aren't absorbed as well as iron from meat, poultry, and fish.

An iron-rich diet can prevent this most common type of anemia. For some, especially pregnant women, iron supplements might be recommended, too. *For more about iron and ways to boost the iron content of your eating plan, refer to "Iron—More for Women" on page 459, and "Iron: A Closer Look" on page 109. "Iron: The Fatigue Connection" on page 447 addresses iron needs for adolescent girls.*

Anemia: More Than One Cause

Although the most common, iron deficiency isn't the only nutrition-related cause of anemia. Other nutritional deficiencies may be the reason. And sometimes other physical disorders, perhaps in body cells, may be the reason. The treatment differs for various types of anemia.

Deficiencies in vitamin B_{12} or in folate also cause anemia. It's hard to discern the difference between the anemias caused by these two vitamins. In both, red blood cells get bigger. The right treatment is important because their harmful effects differ. Taking large doses of folate may seem to cure the anemia caused by vitamin B_{12} deficiency. However, taking too much folate can mask the symptoms of pernicious anemia, caused by vitamin B_{12} deficiency, which may cause nerve damage.

Because vitamin B_{12} comes only from animal sources of food (meat, fish, poultry, eggs, milk, and milk products), strict vegetarians can be at particular risk. They need a reliable source of vitamin B_{12}, perhaps a fortified breakfast cereal or supplement, to protect against anemia. *Refer to "Vitamin B_{12} : A Challenge for Vegans" on page 563.*

Besides poor diet, a vitamin B_{12} deficiency may have other causes. Stomach juices may lack a body chemical called intrinsic factor, which helps the body absorb vitamin B_{12}. Or secretion of stomach juices may be impaired. Or with age, the acid content of stomach juice may decrease, affecting vitamin B_{12} absorption. If you have any of these problems, your doctor will diagnose it.

Folate, or folic acid, comes from a variety of foods, including leafy vegetables, some fruits, legumes, liver, yeast breads, and some fortified cereals. A

---

have you ever wondered

...if eating spicy foods causes ulcers? No. Your food choices neither cause nor cure ulcers. Most ulcers are caused by bacteria, called *Heliobactor pylori*, and are treated with antibiotics.

...if you should heed the advice: "Starve a cold, and feed a fever"? Illness is no time to "starve" your body of nutrients. To fight infection, your body needs a supply of nutrients to build and maintain your natural defenses. So you still need balance and variety in your food choices. Extra rest helps, too. With a fever, drink plenty of fluids: juice, milk, soup, or water. If you don't have much appetite, eat bland, simple foods, perhaps more often. How about vitamin C? Well, it won't cure the common cold. No scientific evidence proves that a large dose, perhaps from a vitamin supplement, boosts immunity. ✦

deficiency may show later in pregnancy when folate needs are high. Whether you're at risk for folate anemia or not, consume enough, especially if you're planning to get pregnant—or if you already are pregnant. A folate deficiency also leads to birth defects of the spinal cord. *For more about folate and pregnancy, refer to "Pregnancy: Before You Begin" on page* 457.

Other types of anemia, including sickle cell anemia, are caused by defects in blood cells or in body processes that use iron. Proper diagnosis is important for getting the right treatment for anemia. Consult your doctor about any symptoms you experience.

A Weighty Issue

Are extra inches creeping onto your hips, thighs, and waistline during your adult years? With each decade of adulthood, your need for calories drops by about 2 percent. So even if you keep your diet and activity pattern at an equilibrium, you may gain weight, along with extra body fat!

The risks related to excess body fat are certainly clear. High blood pressure, heart disease, stroke, some cancers, diabetes, arthritis, breathing problems, and other types of illness are all linked to being overweight.

On the flip side, the benefits are well worth the effort of keeping trim. If you have a weight problem, losing just 5 to 10 percent of body weight may reduce your risk for some health problems associated with being overweight.

As a heart-healthy strategy, losing weight—if you have excess body fat—helps bring down your total and your LDL-blood cholesterol levels. If you're physically active, your "good" HDL-blood cholesterol levels likely go up, too. What's more, trimming off a few excess pounds reduces stress on your heart because there's less of you to pump blood to. The benefits of sticking to your healthy weight certainly go beyond disease prevention—to overall health promotion!

Issues related to body weight are complex—among them, their connection to a high-calorie, high-fat diet and a lack of physical activity. *Chapter 2, "Your Healthy Weight," addresses the "ups and downs" of weight control: the causes, the risks, and the strategies for keeping your own healthy weight. "Your Basic Energy Needs" on page 23 addresses the impact of age on energy needs.*

CONTROL YOUR RISK FOR HEART DISEASE

Several factors contribute to heart disease. Which ones apply to you?

- cigarette smoking
- high blood pressure
- high blood cholesterol levels (over 200 milligrams per deciliter)
- lack of exercise
- overweight
- diabetes
- inability to handle stress
- too much alcohol
- taking birth control pills (if you smoke)
- family history of heart disease
- getting older (over age 55)
- black race
- menopause

Source: *American Heart Association* ✦

Keeping a Healthy Heart

We've all heard the statistic. Heart disease is America's number one killer. Although slightly postponed for women, it's a disease that affects both sexes. About 25 percent of the nation's almost 300 million people have some form of cardiovascular disease. And it accounts for about 960,000, or more than 42 percent, of deaths annually in the United States. The truth is, many deaths from either heart attacks or strokes are preventable.

The term "heart disease" describes several conditions that relate to the heart and blood vessels. Heart attacks and strokes may come to your mind first. However, high blood pressure, angina (chest pain), poor circulation, and abnormal heartbeats are heart disease, too. *High blood pressure is addressed separately on page 492, "High Blood Pressure: Under Control?"*

A genetic tendency is one cause of heart disease. But for most of us, other risk factors play a role. *Refer to "Control Your Risk for Heart Disease" on page 486 to see if you're at risk.*

Heart Disease:
The Blood Cholesterol Connection

For years we've known that heart disease is linked to high total blood cholesterol levels. But only recently have we learned that lowering blood cholesterol levels reduces the risk.

Like everyone, you have blood cholesterol in your bloodstream. That's normal. It only becomes a problem when your level gets too high. *The chart on page 488, "Strive for Desirable Blood Lipid Levels," shows normal levels for healthy adults.*

If elevated, blood cholesterol is more likely to collect on the walls of your arteries and other blood vessels. When these fatty plaques build up on artery walls, arteries gradually become more narrow and block the flow of oxygen-rich blood. This condition is called atherosclerosis.

All this happens silently, usually without symptoms. Warnings in the form of chest pains may not occur until the vessels are about 75 percent blocked. But often heart attacks strike with no warning at all. A heart attack occurs when a clot in a narrowed artery blocks blood flow to the heart. When blood can't flow to the brain, a stroke occurs.

The higher the blood cholesterol level, the greater the chance of developing heart disease. When abnormally high blood cholesterol levels go down, so does the risk for a heart attack. A blood cholesterol level in the normal range is healthy. Your blood cholesterol goals shouldn't be zero!

Remember: High blood cholesterol isn't the only risk factor for heart disease.

Why Do Blood Cholesterol Levels Rise?

That's a complex question. Usually there's no single reason. Some people inherit the tendency. But families with heart disease share more than their genetic makeup. People also grow up with similar lifestyle habits—eating, physical activity, drinking, and smoking. All these lifestyle factors play a role.

From a nutrition standpoint, a diet high in fat and cholesterol are factors. So is obesity. Some people are cholesterol-sensitive. That is, a high-cholesterol diet significantly boosts their total blood cholesterol level and LDL-blood cholesterol level. But total fat, especially saturated fats, has the most significant cholesterol-raising effect for most of us.

As an aside, fiber helps lower blood cholesterol, offering some protection. Not all fiber—just soluble fiber—has this effect, however. In the intestine, soluble fiber binds to bile acids, which are produced from cholesterol, and so helps remove some cholesterol. Oatmeal, oat bran, rice, wheat bran, barley, dry and canned beans (such as kidney and pinto beans), and some fruits and vegetables all contain soluble fiber. *For more on soluble fiber, refer to "Soluble Fiber: Protective Benefits," on page 144.*

HDLs and LDLs: The Ups and Downs

Lipoproteins work like the post office, transporting "packages" of cholesterol through your blood. Here's how they work:

➢ High-density lipoproteins (HDLs), or "good" blood cholesterol, act like waste removal vehicles. They take cholesterol from blood and artery walls to your liver, so it can be excreted.

Clogged Arteries

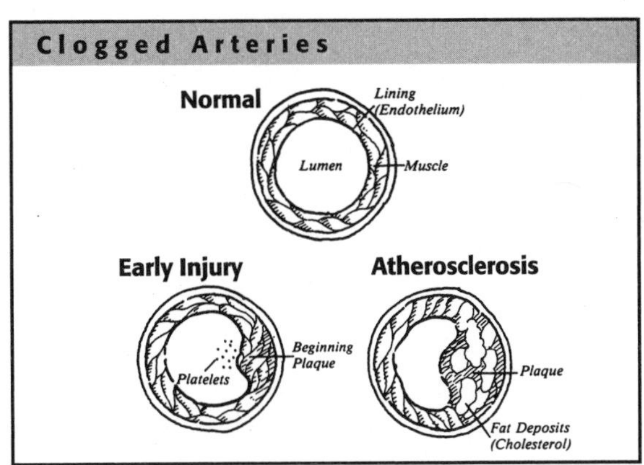

➢ Low-density lipoproteins (LDLs), or "bad" blood cholesterol, work like delivery vehicles. They keep blood cholesterol circulating in your bloodstream, allowing plaque to attach to artery walls. As plaque builds up, the risk for atherosclerosis goes up, too.

Next time your blood cholesterol level is checked, find out what your HDL- and LDL-blood levels are, too. The heart-smart goal is this: high levels of HDLs and low levels of LDLs (both within normal limits). The obvious next question is: How do you boost your HDLs and lower your LDLs?

***To increase your* HDL-*blood cholesterol*:** The best way is to stay physically active. In addition, trim your extra pounds of body fat...if you're not at your healthy weight. Reduce fat intake to no more than 30 percent calories from fat. Replace some saturated fats with monounsaturates. And if you smoke, quit.

***To decrease your* LDL-*blood cholesterol*:** Substitute unsaturated fats for saturated fats, while keeping total fat low. Consume an overall diet that's high in fiber with just moderate amounts of fat and cholesterol. And trim excess body fat through regular physical activity.

The chart on this page, "Strive for Desirable Blood Lipid Levels," shows target levels for HDLs *and* LDLs. *For more about* HDLs *and* LDLs, *refer to "The 'Good' and the 'Bad'" on page* 65.

Beat the Odds—Know Your Numbers!
Concerns about blood cholesterol are part of everyday life. But many people don't know if high blood cholesterol levels are an issue for them. Their blood cholesterol levels have never been tested. Knowing your blood cholesterol level may help you lower your risk for heart disease!

Unless your blood is screened regularly, high blood cholesterol levels usually go unnoticed because symptoms aren't obvious. If you're age 20 or more, have your cholesterol level checked at least every five years—and more often if you're considerably older or at risk for heart disease. If your first results are high, your doctor may advise another test soon.

What's considered a high blood cholesterol level? The National Heart, Lung, and Blood Institute sets the following total blood cholesterol risk level guidelines for adults age 20 and older.

➢ *Desirable*: Less than 200 milligrams per dL

➢ *Borderline High*: 200-239 milligrams per dL

➢ *High*: 240 or more milligrams per dL

Blood cholesterol levels are measured through a blood sample, taken from either your finger or a vein. As an initial screening, a finger stick test in a shopping mall or health fair may be reliable. Depending on the techniques and equipment, however, this screening may not be as accurate as the tests done in your doctor's office or health center. If your number comes up on the borderline-high or high side—or if you have other risk factors for heart disease—have it checked again with your health care provider to verify the results.

As part of your physical check-up, your doctor may want a more complete picture of your blood. Besides total blood cholesterol, HDL- and LDL-

Strive for Desirable Blood Lipid Levels

Your risk of heart disease stays lower when your blood lipid levels remain at desirable levels for life.

Total blood cholesterol	**< 200 milligrams per dL**
LDL cholesterol	**< 130 milligrams per dL**
HDL cholesterol	**> 35 milligrams per dL**
Blood triglycerides	**< 250 milligrams per dL**

have you ever wondered

...if adding more olive oil to your diet will help prevent heart disease? Perhaps, but not if you end up eating a diet that's high in total fat. A low-fat diet, especially one low in saturated fat, is still recommended for heart health. In your quest for a heart-healthy eating plan, you might substitute some monounsaturated fats for some saturated fats in your food choices. Olive, canola, and peanut oils are all high in monounsaturated fats. ✦

blood cholesterol levels, as well as blood triglycerides might be checked.

What about over-the-counter cholesterol tests? If properly done according to package instructions, they can be relatively accurate. However, home tests only measure total blood cholesterol levels, not HDLs and LDLs. Like any finger stick test, results are best verified by health professionals—especially if the level measures 200 mg/dL or more and if you have other risk factors, such as a family history of heart disease.

If you don't know your blood cholesterol "number," have it checked soon, and keep on reading. If you do know your cholesterol level, congratulations. But keep reading anyway!

Knowing your "number" is just your first step. Next, you need to act on the results. Your doctor or registered dietitian (RD) can interpret the numbers—and guide you to achieve and maintain your cholesterol numbers at healthy levels. *Refer to page* 580, "*How to Find Nutrition Help*" *to locate a registered dietitian.*

Blood Cholesterol Countdown

If you're among the 50 percent of Americans with high or borderline high total blood cholesterol levels, a few changes in your food choices and lifestyle may bring your total blood cholesterol and LDL-blood cholesterol numbers down....and your HDL-cholesterol numbers up. At the same time, your risk for heart disease goes down, too.

Remember: Heart disease is an issue for both men and women. *Refer to* "*Heart Disease*: *A Women's Issue, Too!*" *on page* 473.

A heart-healthy eating pattern—a diet low in saturated fatty acids and dietary cholesterol and more foods high in complex carbohydrates—helps reduce blood cholesterol levels. Or at least it'll keep total blood cholesterol levels from increasing. *For more about fat and cholesterol in a healthful eating plan, refer to* "*Fat Facts,*" *chapter* 3.

As preventive maintenance...

Eat a diet low in fat. Reduce your daily fat intake to no more than 30 percent of your total calories a day. Don't attempt to cut fat out of your diet entirely—you shouldn't and you can't. Just cut back. You need some fat to keep you healthy. And many foods with fat also contain other nutrients your body needs.

If you're already at your healthy weight, you'll want to boost the starches, or complex "carbs," in your

A Toast to Heart Health

Does moderate drinking reduce the risk for heart disease? Maybe. Although people who don't drink aren't advised to start, moderate drinking may offer heart-health benefits for some people. But there's a fine line between how much is beneficial and how much actually may promote heart disease, high blood pressure, and strokes.

There's reason for caution. Research linking alcoholic beverages and heart health isn't conclusive. And we don't yet know who may benefit. Even if a minor benefit exists, moderate drinking is only one factor related to heart health. *Refer to* "*Red Wine*: *Heart-Healthy?*" *on page* 185.

Until we know more, moderation is advised. No more than one drink a day for women, or no more than two drinks a day for men may lower the risk for heart disease. A drink is 12 ounces of regular beer, or 5 ounces of wine, or 1.5 ounces of distilled spirits.

Alcoholic beverages also supply extra calories. So if you're trying to control weight for heart health, control calories from alcoholic beverages, too.

For more about alcoholic beverages in a healthful eating plan, refer to "*Alcoholic Beverages*: *In Moderation*" *on page* 184. ✦

diet as you cut back on fat. Otherwise, you'll lose weight. Grain products, beans, and vegetables all contain complex carbohydrates. *Refer to "From Complex to Simple" on page 125. Refer to "Moderation: Key to a Healthful Diet" on page 67 for more guidance on the fat and cholesterol in your diet.*

Follow an eating pattern with less saturated fat. Reduce the saturated fatty acids in your diet to less than 10 percent of your total daily calories. That's about one-third of your total fat intake. "Sat fats" boost blood cholesterol levels more than anything else you consume.

You probably won't need to track "sat fats." As you cut down on total fat, you'll likely consume less saturated fat at the same time.

Substitute unsaturated fat for saturated fat. Don't increase your total fat intake beyond 30 percent of daily calories. But do shift the proportions of saturated and unsaturated fats.

Polyunsaturates should contribute no more than 10 percent of your total daily calories, and monounsaturates, 10 percent or more of your total daily calories. You can do that by replacing fats of animal origin and solid margarine with more vegetable oils. Remember that olive oil is high in monounsaturated fatty acids.

have you ever wondered

...if eating garlic is good for your heart? The effect is likely insignificant in the amounts used. The benefits of large amounts are untested and may have negative side effects. Although you can buy garlic extracts, they may lack the chemicals that impart potential benefits. And garlic supplements may cause stomach irritation and nausea. *Best advice:* Enjoy the flavor of garlic, but don't count on it for heart-healthy benefits.

...if taking medications has an effect on what you eat? It may, so talk to your doctor or pharmacist about the possibility of any drug and nutrient interactions. *Refer to "Food and Medicine" on page 526 for more information.* ✦

Follow an eating plan that's low in cholesterol. You don't need to eliminate foods with cholesterol. These same foods—milk, cheese, poultry, fish, and meat—supply plenty of nutrients your body needs. Just limit your cholesterol intake to less than 300 milligrams a day. Although not as significant as cutting back on saturated fat, reducing your dietary cholesterol may help lower your blood cholesterol.

Eat more fiber. Eating more fiber-rich foods may help lower blood cholesterol levels. That's because soluble fiber, for example in oats, may help take cholesterol away before it can be absorbed into your bloodstream. *Refer to page 146, "Fiber—Heart Healthy, Too!" "Ten Great Ways to 'Fiber Up'" on page 152 gives ideas for boosting your fiber intake.*

Eat more fruits and vegetables. Eating a low-fat diet is well accepted as a strategy to promote heart health. But emerging research also suggests a link to high intakes of antioxidant vitamins: beta carotene, and vitamins A and C. There's no clear-cut advice yet—but eat your fruits and veggies, just in case! *Refer to "Antioxidant Vitamins: A Closer Look" on page 90.*

Diet alone isn't the only way to lower blood cholesterol levels. A few other lifestyle changes also can reduce your risk for heart disease.

➢ ***Maintain or improve your weight.*** You're wise to keep lean. The more excess body fat you have, the greater your risk for heart disease. *Refer to "A Weighty Issue" on page 486 for more about the link between body weight and heart disease.* Where your body stores extra body fat also makes a difference to heart health. Those who carry a spare tire around their abdomen have a higher cardiac risk than those with extra padding in their hips and thighs. *Refer to chapter 2, "Your Healthy Weight," for guidelines on maintaining or improving your healthy weight.*

➢ ***Keep moving!*** Get the heart-healthy benefits of regular, moderate activity. Active living helps keep your blood cholesterol and triglyceride levels normal, may boost your HDLs, reduces blood pressure, helps your body control stress, and helps control body weight as you burn energy. More vigorous aerobic activity gives your heart muscle a good workout, too, and ultimately helps your whole cardiovascular system work more efficiently. *For more about physical activity and health, refer to chapter 21, "Athlete's Guide: Winning Nutrition." "Get Physical!" on page 31 offers reasons and ways to be more active.*

➢ ***If you have high blood pressure, get it under control.*** High blood pressure, or hypertension, is a key risk factor for heart attack and stroke. Those factors that "up" the chances for high blood pressure include a family history of high blood pressure, excess body weight, a high-fat diet, a high-sodium diet (for people whose blood pressure is sodium sensitive), and high alcohol consumption. *Refer to "High Blood Pressure: Under Control?" on page 492 for more on high blood pressure.*

➢ ***If you smoke, give up the habit.*** It's a key factor in sudden death from cardiovascular disease. Smoking seems to raise blood pressure levels and heart rate. It may lower HDL-cholesterol levels. And smoking may increase the tendency of blood to clot and so lead to a heart attack.

The good news is: For those who stop smoking, the risk for heart disease goes down over the years, even for long-time smokers.

➢ ***Reduce stress.*** Although the evidence linking stress and cardiovascular disease is weak, you're still wise to learn how to control stress... especially if you eat or smoke to relieve stress.

➢ ***If you have diabetes, keep it under control.*** Diabetes is a risk factor, too. African-Americans have a greater risk, mainly because they have a higher risk for high blood pressure and diabetes.

➢ ***A few other factors that you can't control also increase your risk for heart disease:*** gender, age, and family history of early heart disease. For women, hormone replacement therapy may offer some protection after menopause; talk to your doctor about it. *Refer to "HRT: For Some Women" on page 473.*

Triglycerides: Another Way to Look at Fat

High blood triglycerides get much less attention than cholesterol. But they're linked to heart disease, too. Having high blood triglyceride levels doesn't mean you'll develop heart disease. But the chance goes up if you have other risk factors.

Triglycerides are the main form of fat in foods. Whether they're saturated, polyunsaturated, or monounsaturated, most fats you consume are in the form of triglycerides. Once consumed, your liver processes them. If you eat excess calories from any source—carbohydrates, protein, or fat—your body produces triglycerides and stores the extra as body fat. Drinking alcohol also can boost the liver's production of triglycerides.

When blood cholesterol levels are checked, your doctor may measure your blood triglyceride levels. Usually that's done for people who have other risk factors. Those factors might be high total blood cholesterol; two or more risk factors for heart disease, such as smoking and obesity; or health problems related to triglycerides, such as diabetes, high blood pressure, obesity, chronic kidney disease, and circulatory disease.

For triglycerides, the normal level is 250 mg/dL (milligrams per deciliter of blood); 250 to 500 mg/dL is borderline high, and over 500 mg/dL is high. *Note*: For older adults, desirable levels may be different.

Blood triglyceride levels normally increase after you eat. And measurements also are affected by alcohol intake, medication, hormones, diet, menstrual cycle, time of day, and recent exercise. For an accurate triglyceride assessment, you need to give two or three blood samples after you've fasted (no food or drink except water for 12 hours)—at least one week apart.

If your blood triglyceride level exceeds "normal," a few changes in your food choices and your lifestyle may bring that level down. In fact, much of the same advice for lowering blood cholesterol levels also applies to reducing triglyceride levels:

Choose a diet that provides no more than 30 percent calories from fat and less than 10 percent from saturated fat. And limit cholesterol to 300 milligrams daily, and include plenty of complex carbohydrates and fiber.

Maintain or improve your weight. Frequently, weight loss alone can significantly lower triglyceride levels.

Live an active lifestyle. Along with regular exercise, maintaining a healthy weight can lower triglyceride levels. It also raises HDL-blood cholesterol.

If you're a smoker, stop.

If you drink alcoholic beverages, drink just moderate amounts or none at all. In some people, alcohol increases triglyceride levels. Check with your doctor and registered dietitian.

High Blood Pressure: Under Control?

Do you know your blood pressure reading? High blood pressure often creeps up slowly and quietly. Until it's advanced, there usually are no symptoms. But if it's not detected and controlled, high blood pressure may cause damage to the heart, brain, and kidney for years without anyone knowing.

have you ever wondered

...what causes heartburn? The discomfort of heartburn, or indigestion, occurs when digestive juices and food from your stomach back up into your esophagus. Your stomach lining protects against acids that form during digestion. But the lining of your esophagus is sensitive to the burning sensation of stomach acids. That's why you feel discomfort or pain.

Foods themselves don't cause heartburn, but they may aggravate the condition by stimulating acid production. Those foods high in acids, such as citrus fruit, as well as fatty or highly-seasoned foods, may also cause problems for some people. Heartburn isn't dangerous—just uncomfortable. And it can be treated with antacids. Consult your doctor about the best type for you. The danger can come if you ignore a heart attack, thinking it's simply heartburn. If the pain continues or if it happens an hour or more after eating, call your doctor immediately! ✦

Sometimes the first sign of high blood pressure is a heart attack or stroke!

High blood pressure is both a health concern and a health risk. Untreated over time, it's a main risk factor for heart attacks and strokes. About 50 million Americans (one in four adults) have high blood pressure. Fortunately, it can be treated.

What Is High Blood Pressure?
You've heard the term "high blood pressure" many times. But do you know what it really is?

High blood pressure, or hypertension, means higher-than-normal pressure on blood vessel walls. It occurs as blood gets pushed through arterioles, which are small blood vessels, that have become stiff and restricted. The passage for blood is narrowed. High blood pressure causes the heart to work harder, and over time may damage artery walls. Damage to blood vessels in the brain may cause a stroke.

To correct a common misconception, hypertension is not the same as emotional tension or stress...although stress may temporarily raise blood pressure levels. Even people who are calm and relaxed can have high blood pressure.

High Blood Pressure: A Risk?
High blood pressure appears to be a complex problem. And in most cases, its causes are still unknown. Only about 5 to 10 percent of cases can be attributed to known health problems, such as kidney disease. Yet, health experts can identify people with increased risk. Check to see if you're at risk.

Family history of high blood pressure? People appear to have a genetic tendency for high blood pressure. Among African-Americans, average blood pressure levels are higher, and they tend to be more sodium sensitive than Euro-Americans. Typically African-Americans develop hypertension earlier in life. As a result, they're at significantly greater risk for kidney disease as hypertension progresses and for death from strokes and heart disease. Some Asians are also at greater risk.

Overweight? Extra body fat, especially around the waist and midriff, increases the risk for high blood pressure. If you have a few pounds to shed, do so. Bringing your weight down to normal may be all you need to do to keep your blood pressure under control. *Refer to chapter 2, "Your Healthy Weight."*

Your age? For many people, blood pressure goes up as they get older. For men it's sooner, perhaps starting by age 45 to 50. Women often are protected through menopause; for them, high blood pressure often starts about 7 to 10 years later. Just because you're older doesn't mean you'll develop high blood pressure, however.

Inactive lifestyle? Sedentary living doesn't cause high blood pressure, and physical activity alone won't bring it down. But it has some effect as part of an overall lifestyle that protects against high blood pressure and heart disease. For example, physical activity can help you maintain a healthy weight. As always, you're wise to "get moving."

Sodium-sensitive? For up to 30 percent of the American population, a diet high in sodium may contribute to high blood pressure. And cutting back on sodium may help lower blood pressure. There's no way to predict whose blood pressure may be sodium-sensitive. Just in case, healthy normal adults are advised to choose a diet moderate in salt and sodium, no more than 2,400 milligrams sodium daily.

For more about sodium, refer to "Link to High Blood Pressure" on page 159. "Flavor...With Less Salt and Sodium" on page 162 offers specific tips for lowering your sodium intake.

Stressed? For some people, stress may be a factor, although the evidence isn't clear-cut. Just in case—and for the overall quality of your life—learn how to relieve stress.

Smoker? If you smoke, your chance of heart disease goes up.

Too much drinking? Heavy drinking may increase the risk for blood pressure, too. Health experts advise no more than one drink a day for women, and two for men.

Diabetes? People with diabetes may develop high blood pressure if their condition isn't managed carefully. That's another reason to keep diabetes under control from the time it's first diagnosed. *Refer to "Diabetes: A Major Health Concern" on page 499.*

Know Your Blood Pressure Reading

Blood pressure is really two readings that look like a fraction. For example, an optimal reading is 120/80, or 120 over 80.

- The number on top, which is higher, is called the systolic pressure. That's the pressure when your heart (actually the ventricle) contracts, pumping blood out to your arteries.

- The number on the bottom is called diastolic pressure, which is the pressure on your arteries between heart beats, when your heart is at rest.

To find out if you have high blood pressure, have it checked at least every two years. If it's high normal (130-139 over 85-89) or high, have it checked more often. Even children should be checked as part of their regular physical exams.

Blood pressure may fluctuate a bit during the day. And often the doctor's visit itself makes the number rise slightly. To diagnose high blood pressure, you need two higher than normal readings, which are taken one to several weeks apart.

Whether you suspect high blood pressure or not, have your blood pressure checked regularly. If either your systolic or diastolic number, or both are consistently above 140/90, there's cause for concern. Take steps to bring your blood pressure down. Usually high blood pressure is managed by a combination of medication, diet, and lifestyle changes.

Note: Your local pharmacist may offer blood pressure readings as a free service.

Not Too "Pressured"

Just because you have a family history of high blood pressure doesn't mean you'll get it, too. You can take some preventive steps to lower the odds.

You've already been advised to maintain a healthy weight; to live a physically active lifestyle; to quit if you're a smoker; and to go easy on alcoholic drinks. For prevention sake, choose a diet moderate in salt and sodium. Other nutrition factors may offer added protection, too.

Eat plenty of fruits and vegetables: at least five servings a day. Potassium, a mineral found in many fruits and vegetables, may help control blood pressure. Oranges, bananas, okra, potatoes, and tomatoes are among those foods that supply potassium. *For more about potassium, refer to page* 99 *and to "Potassium: Another Reason for Five a Day" on page* 159.

There's another reason to drink milk. Three of its minerals—calcium and magnesium, as well as potassium—help regulate blood pressure. And they may have a protective effect. But no research suggests that taking high doses in dietary supplements offer any extra benefits. Until science learns more, consume calcium-rich foods: at least two servings from the Milk, Yogurt, and Cheese Group of the Food Guide Pyramid, along with other good sources of calcium. *Refer to "Counting Up Calcium" on page* 107.

Cancer Connection

After heart disease, cancer is the second leading cause of illness and death in the United States. It will strike almost one in three adults. Among men, the incidence of prostate cancer is highest, followed by lung, then colerectal cancer. And for women, the prevalence of breast cancer is highest, followed by lung, then colerectal cancer.

Overall, the death rate is highest for lung cancer, then colorectal cancer. Yet, almost half of all cancer deaths can be prevented with early detection and treatment.

have you ever wondered

...if diet can protect you from breast cancer? Scientists don't yet know the answer, but the question is under investigation. Until we learn more, women are advised to eat a low-fat diet, eat plenty of fruits and vegetables, maintain a healthy weight, and get regular physical activity. ✦

What Is Cancer?

Cancer is more than one disease. But they all have characteristics in common: abnormal cell growth that spreads and destroys other organs and body tissue. Cancers are classified by the body tissues where the cancer starts, such as the colon, breast, or skin.

Cancer starts with a single cell that gets out of control. An altered body cell multiplies at an abnormally fast rate. Because they're abnormal, they no longer function normally. Yet, they use the body's resources, including nutrients, to multiply. In the process, they disrupt and eventually destroy the normal function of the tissue or organ where they grow. Gradually, these cancerous cells spread to other parts of the body, invading and destroying healthy body tissues and organs.

The causes of cancer aren't clear. However, cancer-promoters, called carcinogens, include viruses and chemicals, as well as lifestyle and environmental factors. Some cancers appear to run in families, but not always. The link may be genetic, but also may be a similarity in lifestyle.

Since some risk factors are controllable, the best prevention is to keep cancer from starting in the first place. The best cure: Stop it as soon as possible. That's why early detection is so important!

Nutritious Ways to Reduce Your Cancer Risk

The relationship between nutrition and cancer isn't as clear as nutrition's link to heart disease. However, one-third of cancer deaths in the United States may relate to how people eat. And diet is a factor you can control.

Until health experts learn more about cancer and diet, guidelines for cancer prevention remain similar to those for heart health. Keep in mind, no single food or nutrient causes or prevents cancer.

Eat your veggies—and fruits! Vegetables and fruits have a complex composition with more than 100 vitamin, mineral, fiber, and other substances which may offer protection from cancer. Because science doesn't know which ones offer protection or how, you're wise to eat at least 5 servings of fruits and vegetables daily. Vegetables and fruits contain beta carotene (which turns into vitamin A in the body) and vitamin C. Along with vitamin E and selenium, these nutrients are called antioxidants because they protect body cells from damage caused by oxygen by-products. Antioxidants seem to work by rounding up free radicals, which are formed when body cells burn oxygen for energy. They also may keep your immune system healthy and reduce your risk for cancer and other diseases. Each antioxidant appears to protect different parts of the body.

Vegetables and fruits also have other cancer-fighting properties. They supply fiber and phyto-chemicals, or plant chemicals—and they're low in fat. Besides beta carotene, other carotenoids, such as lutein (in broccoli and dark, leafy greens) and lycopene (the red pigment in tomatoes), may be among the phytochemicals that play a role.

Phytochemicals work in different ways. For example, some may spark enzymes that neutralize cancer-causing substances; others may degrade these substances. *Refer to "Phytochemicals—What Role in Health?" on page 92.*

Could dietary supplements with beta carotene, vitamin C, vitamin E, selenium, or phytochemicals offer these benefits, too? That's an answer that science doesn't yet have. But currently there's no scientific evidence that shows benefits for taking supplements to reduce the risk. In fact, selenium supplements are not advised because grain products can supply enough. It may be the combination of nutrients and plant chemicals that offer the full benefits. Fruits, vegetables, beans, and grains are still the best sources. *Refer to "Antioxidant Vitamins: A Closer Look" on page 90.*

Vegetables from the cabbage family (cruciferous) have many properties that fight cancer, including fiber, antioxidant vitamins (beta carotene and vitamin C), and phytochemicals. Broccoli, cauliflower, brussels sprouts, collards, bok choy, and kale all belong in the cabbage family. *Refer to "What Are Cruciferous Vegetables...And What Do They Do?" on page 249.*

Go for legumes and whole grains. A diet that's high in fiber, and low in fat, may protect you from colon and rectal cancer. The reasons? Fiber helps move waste through your digestive tract faster, so harmful substances don't have much contact time with your intestinal walls. And because fiber makes stools bulkier, potentially harmful substances get diluted.

Consume more carbohydrate-rich, fiber-rich foods, including fruits with edible skins, legumes, vegetables, and whole-grain foods. To get enough fiber each day, try to consume at least two fruit servings, three vegetable servings, and three servings of whole-grain breads and cereals. *Bonus:* A high-fiber diet is often low in fat, too! *For tips on boosting your fiber intake, refer to "For Fiber—Variety!" on page 148.*

Limit the fat. When it comes to health risks related to a high-fat diet, heart disease is "top of mind" for many people. Yet, a high-fat diet, especially animal fat, also is linked to some types of cancer, including breast, colon, and prostate cancers. Excess body weight, which itself can be linked to a high-fat diet, may play a role, too. But the issues are still under debate.

Although some cancers are more common in countries with a high-fat diet, the nutrition connection is probably more complex. Diets high in animal fats usually are high in saturated fat, cholesterol, protein, and calories, too, and often lower in high-fiber foods of plant origin.

The bottom line: Choose foods low in fat, especially saturated fat! *For tips on moderation, refer to "Moderation: Key to a Healthful Diet" on page 67.*

Stay physically active and keep trim. Maintain your own healthy weight by keeping calories under control. Obesity is linked to cancers of the breast, colon, gallbladder, and uterus. The best approach to weight management is two-fold: Stay physically

have you ever wondered

...how you can relieve hemorrhoids or constipation? A high-fiber diet, enough fluids, and a physically active lifestyle all help prevent constipation and hemorrhoids. *Refer to "Avoiding the Trio: Constipation, Hemorrhoids, and Diverticulosis" on page 145. For tips for easing the problems, refer to "Constipation During Pregnancy" on page 466.* ✦

active with 30 minutes or more of moderate activity on most, if not all days of the week and control your energy intake. *Refer to chapter 2, "Your Healthy Weight."* Physical activity may offer other cancer protection, too—with effects on hormone levels and by helping to stimulate your colon to eliminate waste.

Go easy on alcoholic beverages, if you drink at all. Excessive drinking increases your chances for liver cancer. And if you drink and smoke, the chances for cancers of the mouth, throat, larynx, and esophagus are higher. As with other health problems, moderation is the key—no more than one drink daily for women, and two for men. For women, more than moderate drinking also may increase the chances of breast cancer.

Nonfood Tips

Make your life a "nonsmoking" zone. Smoking is responsible for a major number of cancer deaths in the United States—and it's a major cause of heart disease. Although women fear breast cancer, more die annually of lung cancer, linked to cigarette smoking. Smoking also lowers blood levels of some protective nutrients.

And limit your exposure to sun. Too much increases the risk for skin cancer. As part of your daily routine if you'll be outside, use sun block protection on your skin with an SPF of at least 15. Many moisturizing creams have a built-in sun screen.

Which Bone Is Healthy?

The dense structure of healthy bone depends largely on its calcium stores. As your body withdraws calcium, bone dissolves, leaving a void where calcium was once deposited. Gradually bones become more porous and fragile. Once the structure of bone disappears, there's no place to redeposit calcium and new bone tissue.

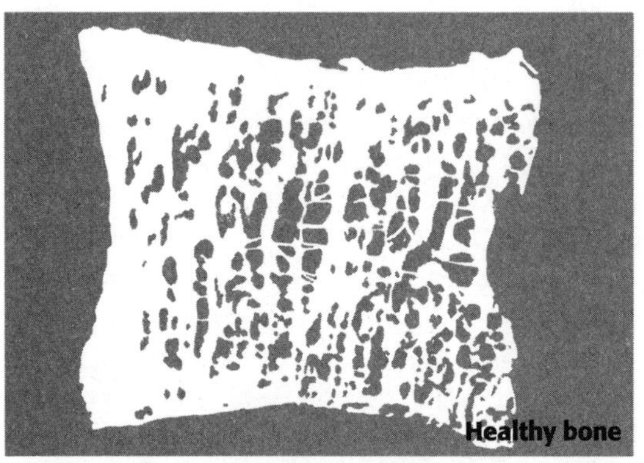

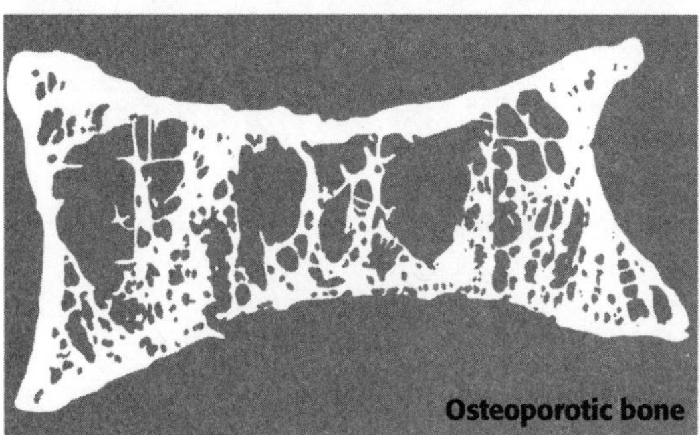

Source: National Dairy Council

Osteoporosis: Reduce the Risks

Care for your bones—no matter what your age! Although the signs of osteoporosis don't show up until later (usually age 60 or older), keeping your bones healthy is a lifelong process. From adolescence on, your eating and lifestyle habits can protect you from this debilitating disease later in life. But no matter what your age now, it's not too late to start caring for your bones!

Osteoporosis Is...

Osteoporosis is a condition of gradually weakening, brittle bones. As bones lose calcium and other minerals, they become more fragile and porous. And they may break under normal use or from just a minor fall. Because it progresses slowly and silently, people often don't realize they have osteoporosis until they fracture a bone. The spine, hip, and wrist are the most common places for fractures.

Among older adults, a "dowager's hump" is an obvious sign of osteoporosis. Vertebrae in the spine compress as a result of bone loss. As people with osteoporosis of the spine become more and more hunched over, they gradually lose height and may develop back pain and disabilities.

Osteoporosis: Are You at Risk?

While bone loss is a natural part of aging, osteoporosis and fractures don't need to be, according to the National Osteoporosis Foundation.

Yet osteoporosis affects most Americans over the age of 70. In fact, by the time women go through menopause, nearly one in three have developed osteoporosis! As with any health problem, some people, both women and men, are at greater risk than others.

What's your risk? Check (✓) all those that apply to you. Are you...

___ 1. Female?

___ 2. Caucasian or Asian?

___ 3. Underweight for your height? Or small boned, with a slight body frame?

___ 4. Physically inactive?

___ 5. Over age 55?

___ 6. From a family with osteoporosis?

___ 7. Consuming an overall diet that's low in calcium?

___ 8. A smoker?

___ 9. A heavy drinker of alcoholic beverages?

Now, how bone-healthy are you? For every check-mark, your risk for osteoporosis goes up. Let's explore the reasons.

Gender. If you're female, you're about four times more likely than males to develop osteoporosis for three reasons. (1) On average, most women have less bone mass to start with—and they lose it faster as they get older. (2) In young women, the hormone estrogen helps deposit calcium in bones. But as estrogen levels drop with menopause, bones are no longer protected. For the first five years after menopause, usually starting at age 50, they lose bone faster. (3) From the teen years on, women typically eat fewer calcium-rich foods than men do.

Race. Because Caucasians and Asians usually are smaller-boned, they have a higher risk. African-Americans develop osteoporosis, too, but their risk is lower. Their bones are usually stronger and more dense throughout their lives.

Low body weight or small body frame. If you're underweight, you likely have less bone mass than people with a healthy weight. Bone health is one of the benefits of keeping your weight within a healthy range for your height.

Women with eating disorders and those who exercise very strenuously increase their risk, too, because they may stop menstruating. Changes in their hormone levels may speed bone loss. Women with eating disorders may not consume enough calcium-rich foods either. *Refer to "Eating Disorders: Problems, Signs, and Help" on page 42.*

Physical activity. Being inactive for a long time weakens bones. On the other hand, regular weight-bearing activities, such as walking, strength-training, and dancing, trigger your body to deposit calcium in your bones. That makes them stronger and more dense.

Age. Bone is dynamic. Until age 30 to 35, more bone tissue is reformed than lost. After that, more bone is lost than reformed. People may lose up to 1 percent of bone each year; however, each person is different. For women, menopause starts a period of rapid bone loss.

Family history. Osteoporosis runs in families. Not only do people inherit a genetic tendency toward bone disease, but families often live similar lifestyles that may "up" their risk.

Smoking. For both men and women, smoking promotes bone loss. Among women, smoking lowers estrogen levels in the blood, which, in turn, further contributes to bone loss. If you're a smoker, that's another good reason to quit.

Calcium intake. Throughout life, calcium is a bone builder. If your calcium supply consistently has come up short before age 30 to 35, your bones may not be as dense as they could be. Lower calcium intake means that less bone was built. After age 35 or so, adults may lose bone faster when their food choices don't supply enough calcium.

Heavy drinking. Heavy drinking is linked to weaker bones. But reasons aren't clear—perhaps because heavy drinkers also have poor diets. ✦

Osteoporosis affects many older people, especially women. But men get it, too. In fact, even if you add up all the cases of heart disease, stroke, and diabetes in a year, osteoporosis is more common! In the United States alone, 1.5 million bone fractures annually are attributed to this bone disease, costing about $10 billion in annual medical expenses. Each year, 20 million American women are affected.

Many hip fractures, common among older adults, are linked to bone disease. Besides pain, fractures cause changes in lifestyle and a loss of independence. A person may no longer be able to dress alone or walk across a room. Hip fractures also can be fatal. An estimated 12 to 20 percent of people with hip fractures die from complications within a year after their fracture.

To keep your bones healthy, help them become strong and dense while you can (until age 30 to 35). After that, help keep them strong by slowing the natural loss that comes with age. *For more about building bones, refer to* "Bone Up on Calcium" *on page* 105.

Protect Your "Support System"
Good health is more than skin deep. Moisturizers and sun screens may help keep your skin looking young. But to truly prolong the qualities of youth, bones also need your loving care!

You can't control all factors that keep your "support system," or your skeleton, healthful. But regardless of age, gender, or body build, you can help reduce your risk. Your food choices and your lifestyle make a difference.

Never Too Young—or Too Old—To Start! Ideally, your osteoporosis prevention strategies started in childhood and continued throughout your young adult years. By age 30 to 35, bones likely are—or were—as dense as they'll ever be. The denser your bones are before middle age, the better able they'll withstand the bone loss that goes with aging.

No matter what your age, however, you're still young enough to make a difference. At any age, your food choices and lifestyle patterns can slow the natural process of bone loss. *For more about caring for bones on the older adult years, refer to* "Calcium: As Important As Ever" *on page* 509.

The Calcium Gap. By now, you're well aware of the connection between calcium and bone health. So if your food choices are coming up short, now's the time to close the calcium gap.

Keep Smiling: Prevent Gum Disease

From an oral health standpoint, a cavity-free mouth doesn't get you home free! Gum, or periodontal, disease, which affects about three-quarters of American adults, is the main cause of tooth loss. As with tooth decay, bacteria in plaque—that gummy film that forms on teeth—and calculus are at the root of the problem. In fact, right along the gumline.

Throughout your adult years, help prevent tooth loss by protecting your teeth from gum disease:

Brush your teeth twice a day, and floss daily. By removing plaque along the gum line, bacteria in plaque are less able to irritate your gums. Plaque that isn't removed turns into calculus, or hard deposits, which you can't remove with brushing or flossing.

Choose an overall eating plan that's balanced and varied. Good nutrition makes your gums more resistant to infections caused by bacteria in your mouth. Your gums need nutrients to stay healthy. *The Food Guide Pyramid, described on page* 243*, is the eating guideline to follow.*

Have your teeth checked regularly by your dentist. Besides checking for gum problems, the dentist or dental hygienist will remove calculus build-up between teeth and along the gumline. Calculus promotes gum disease.

For more on oral health, refer to "Your Smile: Sugar and Oral Health" *on page* 126 *and to* "Chewing Problems?" *on page* 521. ✦

As an adult you still need plenty of calcium; 1,000 to 1,200 milligrams daily is considered an Adequate Intake (AI). Remember, an 8-ounce glass of milk supplies about 300 milligrams of calcium. To protect against osteoporosis, the National Institutes of Health advises more—1,500 milligrams of calcium daily—for post-menopausal women not on estrogen and for adults over age 65 *Refer to "Calcium: Enough vs. Optimal Amounts" on page 106. On page 105 you'll find "Calcium: A Closer Look," a list of calcium-rich foods.*

The Vitamin D Connection. Vitamin D helps deposit calcium in bones. If you drink milk, you're likely getting enough to protect against bone disease. But if you get your calcium from other sources, try to get a little sunshine. Your body makes vitamin D when ultraviolet light touches your skin. If you can't go outdoors or if you need to cover up, you might need a vitamin D supplement. *Refer to "Vitamin D: The Sunshine Vitamin" on page 510.*

Move Those Bones! Weight-bearing activity helps maintain bone density—if you consume enough calcium. If you're swimming, bicycling, or riding a stationary bike regularly, that's great. But these activities don't promote bone health because they aren't weight-bearing.

Add activities such as these to your "activity repertoire": walking, jogging, aerobic dancing, volleyball, tennis, dancing, or weight-lifting—even mowing the grass or shoveling snow. You don't need expensive equipment or a fitness club to lift weights. To build arm and shoulder strength, use things you have around your house, such as canned goods.

***Hormone Replacement Therapy* (HRT).** Going through menopause? Consult your doctor about hormone replacement therapy. A low dose of estrogen, typically given with progestin (a form of progesterone), helps slow bone loss and may protect you from other side effects of menopause, including hot flashes.

If you decide to take estrogen, remember that it's just one strategy for your continuing bone health. Consuming enough calcium and regular weight-bearing activity continue to be very important! *Refer to "HRT: For Some Women," on page 473.*

The National Institutes of Health advise post-menopausal women to consume 1,500 milligrams of calcium if they aren't taking estrogen.

Calcium Supplements. For many woman, supplements help ensure an adequate calcium intake and offer protection from osteoporosis. However, the main nourishment for healthy bones should come from food, not pills. Food supplies other nutrients that your bones (and your whole body) need.

If you take calcium pills, use them as a supplement, not a replacement for food. *For more about taking calcium supplements, refer to "Calcium Supplements: A Bone Builder?" on page 106.*

Bone Density Screening. For high-risk women, bone-density screening may be recommended. But it's not necessary for everyone. Consult your doctor. *Refer to "Osteoporosis: Are You at Risk?" on page 497.*

Caffeine. While caffeine can reduce your absorption of calcium, the effect is quite small. Each cup of regular coffee prevents the absorption of the amount of calcium found in one teaspoon of milk. If your caffeine intake is high, however, you may want to cut back because this effect can add up.

Consider Other Lifestyle Changes. If you smoke, consider the bone-healthy benefits of quitting. And if you drink alcoholic beverages, drink only in moderation: for women, no more than one drink a day.

Diabetes: A Major Health Concern

Diabetes affects more than 14 million Americans. Yet many don't even know they have it.

On its own, diabetes can have serious, even life-threatening, effects on health, if it isn't managed properly. It's also a risk factor for other health problems. Heart disease, eye problems (blindness if untreated), circulatory problems, foot problems, and kidney disease are among the many health conditions related to diabetes.

What Is Diabetes?
Simply defined, diabetes is a condition that affects the way the body uses energy in food.

During digestion, glucose, a form of sugar, is released from carbohydrates in food. Once absorbed into the blood, it's referred to as blood glucose, or blood sugar. Among healthy people, insulin (made in the pancreas) regulates blood sugar levels. It allows glucose to pass into your body cells where it's changed to energy. And it helps your body use amino acids and fatty acids from food.

People with diabetes have trouble controlling their blood sugar, or blood glucose, levels. With diabetes, the body doesn't produce enough insulin or can't use it properly. As a result, the body cannot use energy nutrients—carbohydrates, protein, and fat—in their normal way. Glucose accumulates in blood, causing blood sugar levels to rise. Rather than being used for energy, blood sugar passes out of the body through urine. That makes extra work for the kidneys, causing frequent urination and excessive thirst.

Actually, there are three types of diabetes:

- Type 1 (Insulin-dependent) diabetes is less common. It happens when the pancreas can't make insulin, or at least not enough. Often this form of diabetes begins in childhood or the young adult years, but people of any age can get it. Insulin shots are required daily.

- Type 2 (Non-insulin-dependent) diabetes is more common. Typically it runs in families. And people of African-American, Hispanic, and Native American descent have a higher risk. It's a disease that develops slowly and usually becomes evident after age 40. Being overweight is a common risk factor for this type of diabetes. Often it can be controlled through diet, weight control, and exercise.

- Gestational diabetes may occur during pregnancy, as a result of changes in hormone levels. Although it usually disappears when the baby is born, it still needs careful control during pregnancy. Women with gestational diabetes often develop diabetes later in life, and usually in later pregnancies. *Refer to "Pregnancy and Diabetes" on page 468 for more information on gestational diabetes.*

Early Detection
How do you know if you have diabetes? According to the American Diabetes Association, many people don't. And that can have harmful consequences, especially if diabetes goes undetected for several years. Some people experience these symptoms: fatigue, increased thirst, increased urination, infections and cuts that don't heal, blurred vision, hunger, and weight loss. Others have no outward signs associated with high blood sugar levels.

Diabetes often is detected by a urine test, given as a routine part of most physical exams. If positive, blood glucose readings are taken to measure blood sugar levels. However, everyone age 45 and over should have a blood glucose test every three years. If you're at high risk, glucose testing should begin sooner and be done more often.

A blood glucose reading is done after an eight-hour fast. Two readings over 125, taken on different days, are criteria for a diabetes diagnosis. Even if your reading is slightly lower, there's need for careful monitoring. A level of 110 to 125 is considered impaired fasting glucose, indicating a high risk for Type 2 diabetes.

What else puts you at risk for Type 2, or non-insulin-dependent, diabetes? If you have two or more of these risk factors, your chances are higher:

- over age 40
- close family member with diabetes
- more than 20 percent over the weight that's healthy for you
- have high blood pressure, or high blood cholesterol or triglyceride levels
- have had gestational diabetes, or delivered a baby weighing over nine pounds
- have had a previous blood sugar problem

Even if you're at risk for Type 2 diabetes, there's good news. If you're inactive or overweight, you can reduce your risk. Just follow a plan of action for regular exercise and weight management.

The following is an overview of diabetes, but not specific advice on managing individual cases of diabetes. Consult your doctor and a registered dietitian if you—or anyone in your family—has diabetes or its symptoms.

If You Have Diabetes...
Everyone who has diabetes needs to follow an eating plan. And most should follow a physical activity plan, too. For some people, weight loss and active living are enough to control their blood sugar levels and maintain good health. For others, pills or injections also may be needed to keep blood sugar levels under control.

If you've just found out that you have diabetes, you may feel quite healthy. This makes it harder to remember to stick with your eating and physical activity program.

In the early years of diabetes, you can do the most to protect your body from the long-term hazards of this disease. If your blood sugar level is high for long periods of time over many years, diabetes may cause major damage to your nervous system and to the blood vessels in your eyes, kidneys, heart, and feet. *The good news is*: You can prevent or reduce this damage. In turn, you may live a longer life with fewer problems.

Manage how you eat. If you have diabetes, there's no single way to eat. The proportions of carbohydrates, protein, and fat in your eating plan depend on you, including your weight, blood cholesterol level, and medical needs. What you eat also depends on what foods you enjoy. Your doctor, along with a registered dietitian, can help you plan what's right for you—portion sizes, types of food, and overall timing.

In the past, a strictly-planned diet for diabetes prescribed specific ratios for energy nutrients: carbohydrates, protein, and fat. Recently, the guidelines became more flexible to meet individual needs. Actually, a diabetic diet isn't too different from any healthy eating pattern. That's especially true for people with non-insulin-dependent diabetes.

It's long been known that sugar doesn't cause diabetes. But experts now know that starches (from pasta, rice, bread, fruits and vegetables, and other starchy foods) and sugars have a similar effect on blood sugar levels. Sugar doesn't cause blood sugar levels to rise any more rapidly than starches do. So people with diabetes can have sugary foods in moderation. The total amount of carbohydrate consumed is the issue, not just how much sugar.

How about fiber? Follow the same guidelines as others: 20 to 35 grams of fiber a day. Extra amounts, perhaps from fiber supplements, won't offer significant added benefits. *Refer to chapter 6, "Fiber: Your Body's Broom."*

Whether you have weight to lose or not, you'll need to follow fairly simple guidelines to control your weight and your blood sugar level. If you're overweight, dropping just 10 to 20 pounds can help to maintain blood sugar at a safe level. A registered dietitian will help you plan an eating pattern that's typically low in fat and high in complex carbohydrates. The wide variety of foods may offer a healthy way of eating that's good for your whole family.

People with diabetes often have high blood pressure. Or they may get it down the line. So if you have diabetes, you're wise to control your sodium intake, too. *Refer to "Flavor...With Less Salt and Sodium" on page 162.*

Check your clock. Keeping your blood sugar at a steady level means you need to make regular "refueling" stops. Skipping meals or eating at different times each day can make it difficult to keep your blood sugar level under control. People who skip meals often get too hungry. Then they overeat or follow a pattern that doesn't match their plan for managing diabetes. *Advice*: Try to eat on a regular meal schedule. And stick to it. Consult a registered dietitian about snacking—whether it's a good idea for you and what foods are the best choices.

Get moving! Regular physical activity is an important part of managing diabetes. For one, physical activity helps your body transport glucose to body cells. You also burn energy, making weight-management easier. Physical activity also can help lower your blood sugar level; that's because your muscles use glucose for energy. An added benefit: Regular physical activity helps reduce your risk for heart disease, which is linked to diabetes.

Before you start a physical activity program, talk to your doctor, along with a registered dietitian. You'll need to balance your exercise with your eating plan. For those who take insulin, planning for exercise is a little more tricky.

Walking, swimming, and bicycling are often recommended. But whatever activities you choose, make them a regular part of your lifestyle.

Control your weight. If you're overweight, try to lose. Being overweight is one risk factor for diabetes. If you trim even a few pounds, your blood sugar levels may be easier to control. If you achieve and maintain your healthy weight, non-insulin-dependent diabetes might stay under control.

Consult a registered dietitian about weight loss: how much you need to lose, and the rate at which you need to lose it. *Refer to chapter 2, "Your Healthy Weight," for more guidance on weight management.*

Are alcoholic drinks allowed? That's a question you need to discuss with your doctor. Do so before you drink any alcoholic beverages. Some people are advised to avoid alcoholic beverages. Drinking may interfere with their medical condition or with some medications. If your doctor indicates you can enjoy an occasional alcoholic beverage, talk to a registered dietitian to find out how you can work it into your meal plan. Keep these guidelines in mind:

➢ At most, have one or two servings of alcoholic drinks once or twice a week. A serving of alcohol is 5 ounces of wine, 12 ounces of beer, or 1 1/2 ounces of liquor. Again, discuss the exact amounts with your doctor and registered dietitian.

➢ If possible, choose "light" beer and dry wine. They have fewer calories than regular beer or sweet wine, respectively.

➢ Recognize that some wine coolers and mixed drinks (made with regular soda and juice) contain sugars. Count them as part of your diabetic eating plan.

Be a team player. If you have diabetes, you may get advice from many people: a registered dietitian, doctor, nurse practitioner, physician's assistant, nurse, podiatrist, and pharmacist. This is your health-care team. And you're the most important member! For the team to work well, you need to do your part:

➢ Keep all appointments for check-ups, counseling, and laboratory tests. Call ahead, and change your appointment if you can't make it.

➢ Take any diabetes medications as directed. Tell your doctor or pharmacist about all other medicine you take, both prescriptions and over-the-counter medications. Also tell your team about any side effects or problems you have with any medicine. Remember to plan ahead, and call for new prescriptions or refills well before old ones run out.

➢ Check your own blood sugar level at home, if you're advised to do so. Self-monitoring is especially important when you're diagnosed with diabetes. That's when your eating plan and medications are being adjusted. Your doctor will explain how.

➢ Consult a registered dietitian about the best eating plan for you, including an approach to managing weight. The dietitian also can offer specific advice on shopping, label reading, eating out, and using alcoholic beverages.

➢ Know that you don't need to struggle with diabetes alone. If your medications, eating plan, or physical activity program cause problems or concerns, make an appointment, and talk to your health team members. Managing diabetes can be complicated at times. Know that your questions are welcome.

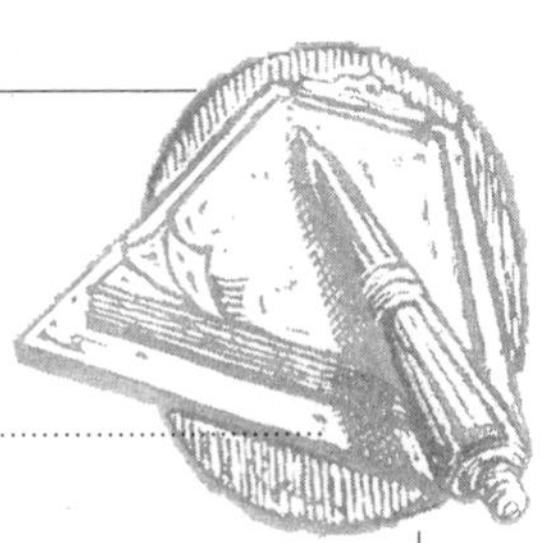

your nutrition check-up

Do It for You!

Take care of you for you—and all those in your life! It's true that you can't control your age, gender, or family history. But there's plenty you can do to stay fit. For many health problems, the risk factors are the same. So the same smart living patterns may protect you from several chronic diseases. How well are you protecting your health? If you can answer yes to the following questions, check the box.

Your Body's "Maintenance" Program

❐ Do you keep your body weight within a range that's healthy for you?

❐ Have you had a recent physical exam?

If you know your "numbers," are they within a healthy range?

- ❐ total blood cholesterol (less than 200 mg/dL): _____
- ❐ HDL-blood cholesterol (more than 35 mg/dL): _____
- ❐ LDL-blood cholesterol (less than 130 mg/dL): _____
- ❐ blood pressure (below 140 over 90): _____
- ❐ fasting blood sugar (below 110): _____

Eat—For the Health of It!

❐ Do you try to consume at least six servings of breads, cereals, rice, pasta, and other grains daily?

❐ Of these grain products, do you eat at least three whole-grain products each day?

❐ Do you try to eat at least five servings of fruits and vegetables, including some from the cabbage family, each day?

❐ Do you consume enough calcium-rich dairy foods daily: at least two servings and perhaps more if you're a woman going through menopause?

❐ Do you try to eat protein-rich foods that add up to 5 to 7 ounces daily (for example, meat, poultry, fish, eggs, beans, and nuts)?

❐ Do you choose foods with less fat, especially saturated fat, and cholesterol most of the time (for example, lean meat, skinless poultry, fish, low-fat dairy foods and no more than four egg yolks a week)?

❐ Do you try to eat legumes several times a week? (Besides being low in fat, they're high in protein, iron, and fiber.)

❐ Do you go easy on foods that deliver energy, or calories, but few nutrients (for example, fats and sweets)?

❐ Do you make food choices to moderate your sodium and salt intake?

Now...Your Lifestyle

❐ Do you get at least 30 minutes of moderate physical activity most days of the week?

❐ Are some of your activities weight-bearing? (for example, walking, dancing, tennis)

❐ If you drink, do you do so in moderation? (no more than one drink daily for women, or two for men)

❐ Do you avoid smoking?

your nutrition check-up (continued)

Now, count up all your "yes" answers.

For each check mark, give yourself five points. What's your total score? _______

Of course, these 20 factors aren't the only ways to promote your health. But the more often you said "yes," the better your chances are for a long, healthy life.

What does your score suggest? It only indicates how many different ways you're already protecting yourself from health problems. And it shows where you might improve.

Having a score of 50 compared with a perfect 100 doesn't mean you're twice as likely to develop heart disease, cancer, diabetes, or some other problem. And this quick "check-up" isn't meant to diagnose any health problem. That's the role of your doctor. Be sure you have regular physical check-ups!

real life nutrition

The Sandwich Generation

Jeannette and Richard belong to the "sandwich generation." They're among the many age 40-something couples with increasing demands from their jobs, teenage children, and aging parents. Both Jeannette and Richard work long, often stressful, hours. Even though they know the value of good nutrition and physical activity, their lack of time and energy often interferes.

"Let's just get past this month. Then we'll make time for exercise and pay more attention to what we eat. We've put on a few extra pounds—but not much. Fortunately, we're healthy." Jeannette and Richard wearily voice their good intentions month after month after month, as they spend their few leisure moments relaxing in their family room with a bottle of wine.

Most days, they charge out the door in the morning with just a cup of coffee and toast to eat during drive time. The kitchen is stocked with cereal, milk, and juice for their teenage kids—if they get up in time for breakfast. For lunch, Jeannette often eats an apple and cottage cheese at her desk and eats a few higher-calorie, higher-fat snacks during the day. Richard, who's on the road for his job, often gets a quick super burger and fries from the drive-through window.

With late work hours, community activities, checking on aging parents, and after-school activities for the kids, the whole family eats at different times. In spite of the fact that they both love to cook, meals often end up being what's on hand, perhaps a frozen pizza that any family member can bake.

"You know, Richard," remarked Jeannette, as she opened the refrigerator, looking for something for dinner, "One of these days this is going to catch up with us. Remember, both of us have a family history of early heart disease!"

What might Richard and Jeannette do now to live and eat healthy—and protect themselves from health problems that may start to appear in midlife?

real life nutrition (continued)

Suggestions for healthier living and eating

To reduce their risk for a variety of age-related health problems:

➢ For both Richard and Jeannette, regular physical activity and healthful food choices can help keep them healthy and able to cope with the increasing demands of work, raising teenagers, and caring for older parents. A healthy lifestyle also reduces their chances of developing health problems that may begin to appear in their midlife. With a family history of heart disease, they're wise to make some changes now!

➢ For a healthful lifestyle, they need regular physical activity, perhaps a brisk walk in the morning before work or as a lunch break. An accumulated 30 minutes of moderate activity most days of the week would promote their heart health, bone health (with weight-bearing activity), healthy weight, stamina, strength, and endurance.

➢ Eating healthy doesn't need to be time demanding. By getting up five minutes earlier, they could enjoy bran or whole-grain cereal, milk, and juice for breakfast—and still take their coffee to go. That's a low-fat breakfast that also supplies calcium from milk, fiber from cereal, and vitamin C from juice. (They'd also set a good example for their kids.)

➢ If Richard eats super burgers and fries as a regular lunch, he needs to balance this with lower-fat food choices at other meals to keep his overall fat intake low. Jeannette's lunch has less fat, but not much variety. Both could benefit from nutritious pack-and-go meals, which offer more variety, and as a result, more nutrients. A lean meat or chicken sandwich on whole-wheat bread, along with fruit, raw vegetables, and yogurt would be a healthful lunch. (Yogurt has much more calcium than cottage cheese does; Jeannette needs plenty of calcium to keep her bones healthy.) And perishable foods such as yogurt travel safely in insulated containers.

➢ Jeannette might bring some lower-fat, nutritious foods to snack on during the day: perhaps fruit or canned juice, pretzels, whole-wheat crackers, or carrot sticks.

➢ By planning ahead, they can keep the kitchen stocked with foods that offer convenience, as well as variety. Along with frozen pizzas and other prepared entrées, they might have chicken breasts, frozen vegetables (including broccoli, cauliflower, brussels sprouts, and others from the cabbage family), canned or frozen legumes, fruit, pasta, rice, bread, and milk.

➢ They can continue to enjoy wine—but in moderation. Daily no more than one (5-ounce) glass for Jeannette, and two for Richard.

➢ If they've gained a few pounds recently, they may be wise to trim down through their food choices and regular physical activity.

CHAPTER TWENTY

NUTRITION *for* OLDER ADULTS

Are you catching the age wave—or how about your parents? As baby boomers enter the 21st century, the number of older American adults will grow steadily. By 2030, people aged 65 and older are expected to make up 20 percent of the U.S. population, with the 85-plus group projected to grow the fastest. That compares to 12 percent in the mid-1990s. This age wave is happening in many other Western nations as post-World War II babies everywhere enter into that "golden age."

What does it mean to be an older adult? Older adults don't fit into one neat category, especially not today. Their ages span a half century—from their 50s into their 100s. Some live a full, active lifestyle, while others are sedentary or bedridden. Calendar age has less to do with the definition and needs of aging, however, than overall health and attitude does.

You can't stop the clock. But you can feel good longer. Your choices now can affect your overall health in the years to come.

Aged to Perfection!

With what you know now, don't you wish you were age 16 again? Well, how about 25? That's probably true of what you know about many things in life, including nutrition and physical activity. The sooner you start living a healthy life, the longer, healthier, and perhaps more enjoyable your life may be. Sound good? It isn't too late to start—no matter what your age now!

Anyone who's lived awhile already knows something about staying healthy. But the effort to stay healthy shouldn't stop. Eating wisely and staying physically active are life-long goals.

How you eat has a lot to do with how you age. The three guideposts—variety, balance, and moderation—remain as important as ever. *The Food Guide Pyramid, described on page 243, continues to be an eating guideline for healthy older adults. And the Dietary Guidelines for Americans, described on page 5 also offer sound advice.*

There's a lot yet to learn about nutrition and aging. The older years themselves differ for each individual—and for you as your health and activity level changes.

Eating for Healthy Aging

As an older adult, you need the same nutrients—protein, carbohydrate, fat, vitamins, minerals, and water—as younger folks, but perhaps in slightly different amounts. Getting enough may be challenging if health problems limit what you eat, or if you're trying to coordinate meals and medications.

A few nutrients may require special attention: protein, calcium, vitamin D, vitamin C, iron, vitamin A, folic acid, vitamin B_{12}, zinc, and water. Eating enough fiber-rich foods aids digestion and helps to prevent the discomfort of constipation. *Refer to "A Few Words About Constipation..." on page* 520.

Recently-updated nutrient recommendations reflect increased understanding of nutrient needs for older adults. In 1997, Dietary Reference Intakes (DRIs), which include Recommended Dietary Allowances, were released with specific calcium, phosphorus, magnesium, vitamin D, and fluoride recommendations for adults age 51 to 69 and for adults over age 70. Refer to the chart on page 601. When DRIs for other nutrients are updated in the future, look for specific guidelines for older adults.

Refer back to "Prevention: Nutrition and Health Problems" on page 484, *too*. You might be able to prevent, or at least delay, some health problems—especially if you're within the "active-aging" crowd.

Energy: Spending Calories Wisely

As people get older, most use less energy, or calories, than they did in younger years. That's because basic body processes use energy at a slower rate, and many older adults live a less active lifestyle. Yet, people still need plenty of nutrients to stay healthy.

So here's the challenge for older adults: Get about the same amount of nutrients, but with fewer calories! That means choosing mostly nutrient-dense foods from the five food groups on the three lower levels of the Food Guide Pyramid. These foods supply the protein, vitamins, and minerals you need for health.

Although calorie needs vary depending on activity level and age, many older adults need about 1,600 calories daily. Doesn't seem like much? Chosen carefully, those 1,600 calories can be nutrient-packed and can supply the minimum recommendations from the Pyramid. Foods from the Pyramid tip

DETERMINE THE WARNING SIGNS OF POOR NUTRITION

If you're an older adult, or if you care for someone older, look for these warning signs of poor nutrition. They spell the word "determine." Anyone with three or more of these risk factors should consult a doctor, registered dietitian (RD), or other health-care professional:

Disease
Eating poorly
Tooth loss or mouth pain
Economic hardship
Reduced social contact
Many medicines
Involuntary weight loss or gain
Needs assistance in self care
Elder years above age 80

Source: Nutritional Screening Initiative, a project of the American Academy of Family Physicians, The American Dietetic Association, and the National Council on Aging. ✦

can be included sparingly. The following daily servings, with a few additions from the Pyramid tip, add up to about 1,600 calories.

Bread Group	6 servings
Vegetable Group	3 servings
Fruit Group	2 servings
Milk Group	2 servings
Meat Group	2 servings (or a total of 5 oz.)

To learn about serving sizes and food in each food group, refer to "The Food Guide Pyramid: Your Healthful Eating Guide" on page 243.

If you're an older adult, it's still wise to keep fat intake moderate, with no more than 30 percent of your calories from fat. A gram of fat supplies more than twice the energy that a gram of either carbohydrate or protein do. So watching your fat intake can help keep you from consuming too many calories.

As when you were younger, get most of your energy from carbohydrates. Foods with complex carbohydrates, such as bread, cereal, pasta, rice, vegetables, and beans, supply many nutrients and fiber, too. Fruit supplies vitamin A and C, and fiber.

Protein: An Issue for Some

You don't need any more protein as you reach the older years than you did when you were younger. And if you're eating two servings, or a total of 5 ounces, from the Meat Group of the Food Guide Pyramid, you're likely consuming enough. So what's the issue?

For some elderly people, protein-rich foods, such as meat or poultry, may be hard to chew. Unless these foods are cut well, they may be left on the plate. Others have trouble digesting them. Those with limited finances might avoid meat, poultry, or fish because they often cost more than many other foods.

How can you be sure to get enough protein?

- If you're on a budget, keep meat, poultry, and fish portions small or stretch meat, poultry, and fish in casserole dishes. Consider other, less expensive protein sources, too, such as eggs, legumes, and peanut butter. Remember, you need a total of about 5 ounces a day.
- Chop your meat or poultry well if you need to.
- If you have trouble chewing, have your teeth and gums (and perhaps dentures) checked. *Refer to "Chewing Problems?" on page 521.*
- Include dairy products. Milk, cheese, and yogurt—and foods made with these ingredients—supply protein, too.
- Consult a registered dietitian for other ways to ensure enough protein in your day's food choices.

For more about protein, refer to "Protein Power" on page 561.

Calcium: As Important As Ever

You're not growing, so why is calcium still so important? Calcium plays a primary role in keeping your bones healthy, and so helps reduce the risks of osteoporosis, or brittle bone disease. That's true for both men and women!

have you ever wondered

...why milk doesn't seem to agree with you anymore? Some older people have trouble digesting milk, even though this was never a problem in younger years. That may happen if your small intestine no longer produces as much lactase. Lactase is an enzyme that digests the natural sugar, called lactose, in milk.

You might try several things. Drink milk in small amounts; usually, your body can handle a little at a time. Try buttermilk, yogurt, cheese, or a special lactose-reduced milk. Custard, pudding, and cream soup are often better tolerated, too. To get enough calcium, try other foods that supply calcium, including some dark green leafy vegetables and canned fish (sardines and salmon) with bones. *For more tips, refer to "Lactose Intolerance: A Matter of Degree" on page 194.* ✦

As adults get older, calcium needs go up. To help maintain bone mass, calcium recommendations increase by 20 percent. For both men and women over age 50, the Adequate Intake level has been set at 1,200 milligrams calcium daily, according to the 1997 Dietary Reference Intakes. That's almost as much as growing children and teens need daily. *For more about Dietary Reference Intakes, refer to "Nutrients: How Much?" on page 4.*

The risk for osteoporosis goes up with age. By age 70, between 30 and 40 percent of all women have had at least one fracture linked to osteoporosis. The percent continues to climb, even for men who develop bone disease later in life. *Refer to "Osteoporosis: Reduce the Risks" on page 496.*

Age is only one reason why older adults have a higher risk for bone disease. Many don't consume enough calcium-rich foods, especially if dairy foods aren't a regular part of their meals or snacks. With age, the body doesn't absorb calcium from food as well either. In addition, many older adults don't get enough weight-bearing exercise, which keeps bones stronger. Vitamin D, which helps the body use calcium, may be limited, too. *Refer to "Vitamin D: The Sunshine Vitamin," on this page.*

There's good news if you're an older adult: Even if you haven't been consuming enough calcium all along, it's not too late to consume more. You still can reduce your risk of bone fractures as you get older. At the same time, consume enough vitamin D and do some weight-bearing exercise, such as walking. Aim for a total of 30 minutes of activity each day, taken all at once or split into shorter segments throughout the day.

Which foods supply calcium? Milk, cheese, and yogurt are the best sources. For example, an 8-ounce glass of milk supplies about 300 milligrams of calcium. So two or three servings put you well on your way. Milk is a good source of vitamin D and potassium, too, which might come up short for many older adults. In addition, some dark green leafy vegetables, fish with edible bones (such as canned salmon), and tofu made with calcium sulfate also have significant amounts of calcium. *For more about calcium and foods that provide calcium, refer to "Calcium: A Closer Look" on page 105.*

Hint: If you take a calcium supplement, do so between meals. Calcium can hinder the absorption of iron from your meals. *Refer to "Calcium Supplements: A Bone Builder?" on page 106.*

Vitamin D: The Sunshine Vitamin

To keep bones strong, you need calcium—along with its partner, vitamin D. Vitamin D helps deposit calcium in your bones and helps protect you from bone disease by keeping them stronger.

Vitamin D is unique. It's known as the "sunshine vitamin" because your body makes it after sunlight, or ultraviolet light, hits your skin. For adequate vitamin D production, you need about 20 to 30 minutes of sun on your hands and face two to three times per week. If you stay indoors, your body may lack vitamin D, especially if you don't drink milk fortified with vitamin D. This is often a problem when people are housebound or dark-skinned, or live in northern climates where exposure to sunshine is limited. With age, the body doesn't seem to make vitamin D from sunlight as easily either.

Like calcium, the need for vitamin D goes up after age 50. In fact, it doubles to 400 International Units (IUs), or 10 micrograms, daily. And after age 70, the recommended level for Adequate Intake goes up again to 600 IUs daily for both men and women.

Vitamin D is added to most fluid milk, and it may be added to other foods such as cereals. You'll find vitamin D listed on the Nutrition Facts panel if it has been added. If you drink milk regularly, though, you probably consume enough—even if you can't get outdoors.

Otherwise you may need a vitamin D supplement, but consult your doctor or registered dietitian first. Taking high doses from a dietary supplement can be harmful. Kidney damage, weak bones or muscles, and excessive bleeding are all associated with taking too much over time.

For more about vitamin D, refer to "Vitamin D" on page 82.

The Iron-Vitamin C Connection

Most people who follow guidelines of the Food Guide Pyramid consume enough iron and vitamin C. Yet, for older adults, a poor diet may lead to a deficiency in one or both of these nutrients. Iron deficiency causes anemia, which can make you feel weak, tired, and irritable, or lose concentration. *Refer to "Anemia: That Run-Down Feeling" on page* 484.

Iron deficiency may have other causes, too: reduced iron absorption as the body secretes less digestive juices or when antacids interfere; blood loss from ulcers, hemorrhoids, or other health problems; and medications, perhaps taking too many aspirins, that cause blood loss.

Although iron and vitamin C come from very different foods, their role in health is quite connected. Vitamin C helps your body absorb iron from plant sources of food. It's especially important if you rely heavily on beans, whole-grains, and iron-enriched cereals as iron sources.

A few tips to avoid iron-deficiency:

- Choose economical sources of iron, including iron-enriched cereals, beans, whole-grains, lean ground meat, and liver.
- Enjoy a vitamin-C rich fruit or fruit juice, such as citrus fruit, melon, or berries, with your meal to boost your absorption of iron. It's easy to get enough vitamin C if fruits are a regular part of your meals and snacks.
- Add a little meat, poultry, or fish to grain-based meals. Their iron content will help your body absorb the iron in the grains.

For more about these nutrients, refer to "Vitamin C: More Jobs Than You Think!" on page 91 *and "Iron: A Closer Look" on page* 109. Consult with your doctor before taking an iron supplement. For some people with a genetic illness called hemachromatosis, iron is absorbed more readily and can build up in various body organs, causing irreparable damage.

Other Nutrients...
Besides those just mentioned, a few others may come up short in the diets of older Americans.

- Vitamin A (and beta carotene which turns into vitamin A), found in deep green leafy and yellow vegetables, helps eyes adjust to dim light and protects skin and other body tissues. Eating more vitamin A won't cure poor eyesight, but not having enough could make it worse.
- Folate is a B vitamin that helps your body make red blood cells. If you don't get enough over a period of time, you may develop anemia. Good sources include leafy, green vegetables, some fruits, legumes, liver, enriched grain products, wheat germ, and some fortified cereals.

Eat Your Fruits and Vegetables

Compared to other foods, fruits and vegetables are the best sources of many important vitamins, such as beta carotene, vitamin C, and folate. They also can be a good source of fiber, which is important in the battle against constipation.

Have chewing problems? You don't need to give up fruits or vegetables. Just make softer choices: ripe bananas, baked or steamed winter squash, cooked peas, sliced peaches, baked sweet or baking potatoes, and steamed cauliflower.

Concerned that fresh produce might take a bite out of your pocketbook? Look for seasonal fruits and vegetables. At certain times of the year, fresh produce may cost less. And stock up on canned and frozen fruits and vegetables when they're specially priced.

Many frozen and canned fruits and vegetables are excellent choices. If you're following a special diet, talk to a registered dietitian about shopping for these foods. Some canned and frozen vegetables with sauces contain added salt. So plain, frozen vegetables may be a better choice if you're on a low-sodium diet. ✦

➢ Vitamin B_{12}, or cobalamin, works with folate to make red blood cells. Not getting enough can also lead to anemia, and in some older adults, is linked to neurological problems. Meat, poultry, fish, eggs, and dairy foods are all good sources. To avoid deficiency, older adults are urged to eat vitamin B_{12}-fortified foods and perhaps a supplement.

A Day of Good Nutrition

Here's an easy menu for a whole day of good nutrition. If you count up the servings, you'll see it supplies enough from all five food groups of the Food Guide Pyramid.

***Breakfast*:**
1/2 grapefruit or 3/4 cup orange juice
3/4 cup bran flakes with 1/2 cup 1% or skim milk
1 slice toast with margarine or jam
Coffee, tea, or water

***Snack*:**
3 graham crackers
1 cup fruit yogurt

***Lunch*:**
1 cup lentil or split-pea soup
1/2 cup cole slaw
1 corn muffin
1/2 cup canned, juice-packed fruit
Coffee, tea, or water

***Dinner*:**
1 chicken breast or thigh baked with Italian seasoning
1 baked sweet potato with margarine
1/2 cup creamed spinach
1 dinner roll
1/2 cup low-fat ice cream
Coffee, tea, or water

***Snack*:**
1/2 whole-wheat English muffin with apple butter
1 cup 1% or skim milk ✦

➢ Zinc, from foods such as beef, whole-grains, and milk, helps your body fight infections and repair body tissue.

Not getting enough of any single nutrient on one day or even for several days should not be a cause for concern. But for those who don't consume a balanced diet with enough nutrients over a longer period, such as several weeks or months, a dietary supplement may be prescribed. *To learn more about vitamins and minerals, refer to chapter 4, "Vitamins and Minerals: Enough, But Not Too Much."*

Thirst-Quenchers: Drink Fluids

Thirsty? The average healthy adult uses up about 2 1/2 quarts of fluid daily by urinating, perspiring, breathing, and eliminating other body wastes. To keep from getting dehydrated, fluids need to be replaced. Thirst is the body's signal to drink more. With age, the sense of thirst diminishes, however. Older adults may not be able to count on thirst as their primary reminder to drink fluids. Kidneys may not conserve fluids as they once did, so the body holds on to less water. And those who have trouble getting around may deliberately limit fluids to avoid trips to the bathroom.

Besides keeping kidneys healthy, drinking enough water has many health connections:

➢ For those who don't drink enough fluids, dehydration and its effects are common problems among older people, especially in warmer weather. Dehydration can cause kidney problems.

➢ Everyone needs enough water to help rid the body of wastes. With less fluids, the chances of constipation rise.

➢ Drinking water or other liquids at meals also makes eating easier. Many older adults have less saliva to help with chewing and swallowing.

➢ For those taking medications, drinking enough water has another important role. Some medications need to be taken with water. And some, such as diuretics, cause the body to lose water.

Older adults need plenty of fluids: 8 to 12 cups a day. Food provides some water, but drinking at least 8 cups daily is advised. Water can come from all kinds of beverages, including juice, milk, soup, tea, coffee, and soft drinks. Plain water is great, too! Remember that juice, milk, and soup offer other nutrients, too.

Caffeinated beverages, such as regular coffee, tea, and colas, should be consumed in moderation. Caffeine often causes you to urinate more and may prevent you from meeting your fluid needs.

Tip: If you have trouble remembering how much water you drank during the day, try this. Fill a jug or jar with 8 cups (64 ounces) of water each morning. Place it in your refrigerator. Use that water to drink, and to make juice, lemonade, soup, tea, and coffee. When the water is gone, you likely have met your fluid goal for the day.

For more about water as an essential nutrient and the risks of dehydration, refer to "A Fluid Asset" on page 171.

Never Too Late for Exercise

No matter what your age, it's never too late to get moving. Whether you're pushing 70, 80, or 90, you can strengthen your muscles and benefit from exercise, even if you haven't been active for a long time. Regardless of overall health, most people can participate in some form of enjoyable physical activity.

The Reasons Are Many

What are the benefits of physical activity for older adults? For the most part, they're the same as for anyone else. Among them...

Moving your body burns energy. That's an aid to keeping a healthy weight.

Activities that put weight on your bones, such as walking, help keep your bones stronger. The benefit? Helping to reduce your risk for bone disease.

Regular physical activity of all kinds helps keep your heart and lungs healthier. Aim for a total of 30 minutes of moderate activity on most days of the week.

Health Alert: Foodborne Illness

Keep food safe! Older adults are at greater risk for foodborne illness than many others. The reason? The immune system can't always fight back as easily with age, especially for those battling other health problems. Even mild food poisoning can have a serious health effect.

Even when the kitchen seems clean, poor eyesight or inadequate lighting may keep people from noticing food spills or visual signs of food spoilage. And for those with less energy, proper cleaning may be hard to do. The following tips apply to people of any age, and especially to older adults.

If you need glasses, wear them as you cook.

Turn up the lights. Get better kitchen lighting if needed. Evenly distributed light is better; older adults have more trouble with glare from one light source.

Label perishable food with a date. Use a dark marker that's easy to read. Don't count on memory alone to know your own "use by" date.

Don't rely on your senses of smell or taste to determine if food is safe to eat. Contaminated food may not have an off-flavor or smell.

Keep cooking simple so you have energy for cleanup, too. Frozen and canned foods are quick and safe, too.

Feeling short on energy? Feel comfortable about asking a younger family member or friend to help occasionally with kitchen tasks.

Follow the general steps for food safety described in chapter 13, "The Safe Kitchen." ✦

Being active helps keep your blood pressure, blood cholesterol, and blood sugar normal. That reduces the risks related to several health problems, such as high blood pressure, heart disease, and diabetes.

Many activities help your muscles stay strong. When you stay stronger, you often have better balance and may be able to remain more independent. And you're less likely to fall and fracture your bones.

Being active often helps your digestion and appetite—a benefit if food seems to be losing its appeal.

For those with trouble sleeping, an annoying problem that often comes with getting older, physical activity helps promote sleep.

If you're feeling depressed, being active—especially if you enjoy group activities—can be just the antidote!

Being active has a way of boosting your feeling of overall well-being.

You Can Do It!

For healthy older adults, like their younger counterparts, health experts advise a total of 30 minutes of moderate activity on most, if not all, days. If you walk, that's about two miles. You don't need to do all your activity at one time, however. Instead try three 10-minute spurts of activities that you enjoy.

The key to fitting physical activity into your everyday routine is to make it fun! Here are some ideas:

Try walking—around the block or around the mall. Walk a dog or invite a friend if you'd like companionship.

Do some gardening without electric tools.

Go swimming. That's a great activity, especially if you're not steady on your feet. It may help relieve some of the joint pain that accompanies arthritis.

If you golf, "go the course"—without the golf cart.

Sign up for an exercise class especially designed for older adults. If needed, check with your community center or area hospital for special classes meant for people with special needs. You can "sit and be fit," even if you're confined to a wheelchair or need a walker.

Go dancing. Even a moderate two-step is good exercise—and a great way to be with other people.

To keep your arms strong, lift "weights." Use canned foods from your kitchen shelves.

For more ideas, refer to "20 *Everyday Ways to Get Moving" on page* 32.

If you haven't been physically active, talk to your doctor before getting started. Together plan activities and a sensible approach that's right for you. Most important, start slowly, work toward your goal gradually, and enjoy!

Tip: No matter what activity you're involved in, drink plenty of water before and afterwards.

When Lifestyles Change...

Lifestyle changes accompany each stage in life. Think about the independence that came with becoming an adult, the responsibility that comes with parenthood, or the freedom of having kids finally leave the "nest." The older years may bring new lifestyles and health conditions that impact what, where, and when you eat.

Eating Alone—Special, Too!

For many people, eating is a time to enjoy the company of others, especially for those who cook for a family or share meals with someone else.

When older adults lose a spouse or living companion, eating alone can feel boring or depressing. And some people don't feel much like preparing food, or even eating. If you're in that position, or know someone who is, you can help spark a tired appetite.

You don't need to dine alone all the time. Eat with friends occasionally:

Get together with other seniors for weekly or monthly potluck suppers. Cut down on the work by taking turns acting as host. Encourage everyone to bring a favorite dish.

Visit the local senior citizens' center. They typically serve a full midday meal on weekdays. Usually the price is right. In some communities, meals for seniors are served in other local buildings, including churches or schools.

Added benefits: Senior citizen meals offer a place to meet old and new friends. And you can enjoy a meal that takes more work to prepare than you'd likely do for yourself.

When eating out, take advantage of early bird specials when the portions are usually smaller and the prices are right. Consider splitting an order or take home half for another meal if restaurant portions seem too large. Some restaurants also have senior citizen prices—be sure to ask. *For tips on ordering healthful restaurant food, refer to chapter 15, "Your Food Away From Home."*

Have a standing date with a friend or relative for lunch or dinner at your home.

If you're still "into cooking," but need someone to cook for, organize a gourmet club of like-minded friends.

When you do dine solo, make eating a special event. Looking forward to mealtime can offer a boost to both your appetite and your morale!

Set your place at the table, perhaps with a placemat, napkin, candles, and centerpiece. You'll feel more like you've had a meal—and with more enjoyment—than if you had eaten right from the cooking pot!

For a change of pace, enjoy eating in different places: the kitchen, patio or deck, dining room, or perhaps on a tray by the fireplace.

Create some atmosphere or interest. Turn on the radio. Play a favorite music tape or CD. Or watch your favorite television show as you eat.

Make food preparation easy, especially when you cook for one. *Refer to "Quick-to-Fix Meal Tips" on page 257 for some hints. For tips on eating alone in a restaurant, refer to "Dining Solo" on page 368.*

Meals—Fast, Simple, Nutritious

Some older folks say they have no time to cook. They're too busy living life to its fullest. For others, lack of inclination or energy, or perhaps a little less mobility, is the reason for quick and easy solutions to nutritious eating.

Try these tasty meals in minutes for starters:

For a quick breakfast, add hot water or hot milk to instant hot cereal. It's just as fast as many ready-to-eat cereals. *For other ideas, refer to "One-Minute Breakfasts" on page 260.*

Keep a few frozen dinners and entrées on hand for quick cooking and easy cleanup. For the most nutrition, look for frozen meals with meat, poultry, or fish; a starchy food (such as rice, pasta, or potato); and a vegetable. Team them up with a salad, roll, piece of fruit, and milk for a hearty meal that takes little effort.

Trying to lose weight? Then choose from one of the many lower-calorie frozen dinners available.

If you're watching your salt intake, check the sodium on frozen meals and canned ones (stews, soups, and chili). Many have more sodium; look for those with less.

Prepare food ahead for later in the week, or to freeze as leftovers. For instance, make lower fat meatballs with lean ground turkey or beef. Brown the meatballs, drain any grease, then combine with tomato sauce. Serve over pasta on one day, over rice the next, and freeze the rest for later.

Freeze homemade soups, stews, lasagna, and other casserole dishes in small containers. Then thaw enough for one or two meals at a time. Label and date your packages to keep track of what you have in the freezer.

For easy-to-prepare salads, wash, tear, and dry salad greens. Then store them in a plastic container for three or four days. Or, you can even purchase washed, cut salad greens in a bag. So when you want a salad, put a handful of greens in a bowl, and add your favorite toppings, perhaps sliced tomatoes, grated carrots, or canned kidney beans.

KITCHEN NUTRITION

meals in minutes

Check the clock. You can prepare this nutritious, flavorful supper in minutes!

➢ Place a sliced red or white potato into a baking dish sprayed with vegetable oil spray. Toss with 2 teaspoons of olive oil and 1/2 teaspoon of crushed rosemary or basil, or your favorite herbs. Bake at 400° F for about 40 minutes, until they're tender.

➢ In another baking dish, bake a chicken breast or two smaller pieces of chicken. Sprinkle the chicken with lemon juice or Italian salad dressing before popping it into the oven.

➢ Set the table. Relax with a book or television for about 35 minutes.

➢ Spoon canned apricot halves into a dish.

➢ Take out a dinner roll. And pour a tall glass of refreshing milk.

➢ Enjoy your dinner! ✦

For more tips for kitchen convenience, refer to "Quick-to-Fix Meal Tips" on page 257.

"Maxing Out" Your Food Dollar

There's another adjustment that may affect food decisions: learning to live and eat on a fixed income. If medical and prescription costs go up at the same time, there may not be as much money to spare. For many older adults, economic challenges can get in the way of healthy eating.

If you shop wisely, you can maximize your food dollar and get the most nutrition for your money. *For tips on stretching your food dollar, refer to "Nutrition $ense" on page 277. "'Small-Scale' Shopping" on page 278 offers cost-saving tips especially for the smaller household.*

Depending on income, many older adults qualify for food stamps, a program of the U.S. government. Food stamps are used like cash in food stores, giving people access to a healthful diet. Usually, food stamps aren't meant for dining out. Although for older adults, some restaurants are authorized to accept them in exchange for low-cost meals; you need to check before you order. To find out if you—or someone you know—qualifies for food stamps, talk to a registered dietitian social worker, or your local senior center. Or check the government pages in your phone book for your local food stamp office.

Hassle-Free Shopping

As people get a little older, popping in and out of the supermarket may take a little more effort. But there's no reason to let your kitchen shelves get bare. Learn to shop without the hassles:

➢ Start your shopping trip before you get to the store. Plan ahead. Make a grocery list. That way, you won't need to repeat your steps through the store.

➢ Shop at quiet times, such as weekday mornings, when stores aren't crowded.

➢ Ask for help with carrying your groceries.

Besides the assistance, it's extra security for you in the parking lot.

➢ Feeling less stable on your feet? Use the shopping cart for balance—even if you have just a few items to buy.

➢ If you're less mobile, shop in stores with a battery-powered, sit-down grocery cart. It's a courtesy service that your supermarket may offer.

➢ If you have trouble with night vision, shop during the daylight hours.

➢ Don't drive? Check with the Area Agency on Aging for shopping assistance. Your community may offer shopping transportation for senior citizens.

➢ Keep an emergency supply of nonperishable foods on the shelf: nonfat dry milk, dried fruit, canned foods (fruit, vegetables, juice, tuna, soup, stew, beans), peanut butter, and cereal. That way, you won't need to head to the store when it's raining or snowing outside.

➢ If you have ideas that could make shopping more convenient for older shoppers, talk with the store manager. With the growing numbers of senior citizens as customers, they'll likely listen to your thoughts.

➢ Ask about special services from your supermarket: home delivery or telephone ordering.

When Cooking Is Too Much

Can't cook anymore? That doesn't necessarily mean giving up living on your own. Many communities offer services for older adults to assure access to nutritious meals. Look for these services where you live:

➢ Meals-on-Wheels brings food to people who are housebound.

➢ Home health care aides help by shopping and preparing meals for older disabled people.

➢ Community centers offer hot meals. Some are part of adult day-care programs. Mini-vans may be available to transfer people to the center. *Refer to "Food in Adult Day and Nursing Care: Questions to Ask!" below.*

➢ Many churches, synagogues, and other community groups provide volunteers who help older adults with shopping and food preparation.

For assistance, talk to a registered dietitian or social worker. Or call your local Area Agency on Aging. Or *refer to "How to Find Nutrition Help" on page* 580.

Food in Adult Day and Nursing Care: Questions to Ask!

Besides nourishment, meals are important events in daily life. That's especially true for many older adults, who look forward to meals as a time to be with others and as "mileposts" in their day.

As you look for adult day or nursing care for yourself, or for any older friend or family member, find out about the food service. Look for "yes" answers to these questions:

Facilities...

➢ Is the dining area clean and attractive?

➢ Are menus printed with lettering that's big enough for older people to read?

➢ Is the dining area well-lighted throughout, not just with "mood" lighting?

➢ Does the dining area encourage socializing?

Food...

➢ Are people given choices from a variety of foods?

➢ Are plenty of beverages available throughout the day?

➢ Is the menu changed often, so the menu cycle doesn't get monotonous?

➢ Are fresh fruits and vegetables served often?

➢ Is food served attractively?

➢ Are religious and cultural food restrictions honored and respected? How about special food preferences?

➢ Are holidays and special events celebrated with special menus?

➢ Are special meals, such as low-sodium or soft meals, provided to those who need them?

➢ Are people offered a chance to make food requests that aren't on the menu?

Staff...

➢ Is mealtime considered to be an important part of daily life at the facility?

➢ Is a full- or part-time registered dietitian on staff?

➢ Are people encouraged to eat in a common dining room? Are they assisted to get there if needed?

➢ Do staff or volunteers help those with any eating difficulties, perhaps cutting food or helping them eat?

➢ Do staff or volunteers wear sanitary gloves when they're helping people eat so they don't spread infection?

➢ Are people given time to eat, and not rushed?

➢ For those who can't leave their rooms, is food brought to them on attractive trays?

➢ If they need help, is it given promptly so food doesn't get cold? Are trays also removed promptly?

➢ For a nursing home, does the staff keep track of each person's weight?

➢ Are people given individual attention for their food and nutrition needs?

Changes That Challenge

What's changed? That depends. If you've inherited a great set of genes, and taken care of yourself throughout life, you have a better chance of living a long, vital life. You may feel "fit as a fiddle" without many apparent physical signs of age. Those wrinkles and gray hairs hardly seem to count. In fact, they make you look wise and distinguished.

With age, some physical changes are inevitable in the long run. The reasons that the human body ages—and the rate of change—are still scientific speculation. But genetics, nutrition, lifestyle, disease, and environment are among the reasons. For some people, those changes come sooner than for others. And many changes influence food choices you have yet to make.

Aging With "Taste"

"That recipe just doesn't have the flavor that I always remembered!" You might hear that comment from an older adult. Maybe you've said it yourself!

The truth is that the senses of smell, taste, and touch may decline gradually with age. And medications or health conditions might alter your flavor perceptions. Fortunately, there are ways to boost the flavor and appeal of food.

Less Sense-Able

Throughout life, smell and taste affect the quality of life, overall health, and even personal safety. We all recognize such simple pleasures: the variety of flavors in a holiday meal, the aromas of bread baking or turkey roasting in the oven, and the sounds of popping popcorn or the sizzle of food on the grill.

Food's wonderful flavors encourage a healthy appetite and help stimulate digestion. And senses also may give clues to off-flavors of deteriorating food or to a gas leak in the kitchen stove.

With age, the senses change and perhaps decline. That happens for some people more than others. Fortunately, you can overcome, or at least accommodate, many body changes. For example, older adults may need glasses for the first time or change their eyeglass prescription. Some older adults need hearing aids. Many feel more sensitive to changes in temperature, perhaps wanting a sweater in summer months. By comparison, however, there's less attention to losses of smell and taste—and their effects on older adults.

At about age 60 or so, smell and taste gradually may start to wane. About a decade later, these sensory changes may be noticed. As with changes in sight and hearing, everyone isn't noticeably affected.

As the senses of smell and taste get duller, food may lose some of its flavor, appeal, and pleasure. Some older adults lose interest in eating. Poor nutrition can result when food "just doesn't taste as good as it used to."

Flavor is really several perceptions: the senses of smell and taste, as well as touch (temperature and mouth feel). With aging, tastebuds and smell receptors may not be quite as sensitive or numerous. The ability to sense sweet and salty tastes may wane sooner than bitter and sour tastes. That's why many foods may seem bitter, and why some older people reach for the salt shaker or sugar bowl. Differences in saliva—composition and amount—may affect flavor, too.

Age isn't the only reason for changes in taste and smell. Two other issues that face older adults—medications and health problems—may interfere, too. Some medicines leave a bitter flavor, which affects saliva, and as a result, the flavor of food. Some cause nausea, resulting in a loss of appetite. Medicines also may suppress taste and smell. Health problems, such as diabetes, high blood pressure, cancer, and liver disease, all common among older people, may alter taste and smell, too.

For more about food and flavor, refer to "On the Tip of Your Tongue...The Flavor Connection" *on page* 211.

"Sage" Advice for a Flavor Boost

Compensating for diminished taste or smell is within your control. Create meals that appeal to all your senses. When food seems to lose its appeal, give it a flavor boost. Learn to intensify the taste and aroma of food—and vary the temperature and texture, too.

Perk up flavors by using more herbs, spices, and lemon juice. For example, accent roasted poultry, poultry stew, or stuffing with sage. Carrots, acorn squash, and creamed spinach taste good with a dash of nutmeg. Simmer a bay leaf in soups and stews. Add a pinch of thyme or cumin to peas, lima beans, and other legumes. Or try dill weed or seed in potato soup, cooked cabbage, or cole slaw. *For more tips, refer to* "A Pinch of Flavor: How to Cook with Herbs and Spices" *on page* 349. *Hint*: If any spices cause stomach irritation, stick with herbs.

Add a little crunch to lunch—and dinner, too! Texture adds to the mouth feel and flavor of food. And a variety of textures helps make up for a loss of taste and smell. What's easy? Crushed crackers on soup, chopped nuts on vegetables or in rice dishes, or crushed cornflakes on ice cream or pudding.

Enjoy food variety. Different foods with different flavors add to the enjoyment of your meal.

Include foods of different temperatures at each meal to perk up your sensations of flavor. Extreme hot or cold temperatures, however, tend to lessen flavors.

Serve yourself colorful, attractive food. A simple sprig of parsley or tomato slice on the plate can

have you ever wondered

...if taking lecithin can help prevent memory loss? No, but it's a common wish, especially for those who constantly misplace eyeglasses or shoes! In fact, there's no evidence that shows that taking lecithin, a type of fat, or any other food substance or nutrient, can help prevent memory loss. ✦

add to its appeal. *For quick tips, refer to "Beyond Parsley...Quick, Easy Garnishes" on page* 330.

Take time to enjoy the full flavors of food by chewing food well.

If you smoke, stop. Smoking reduces the ability to perceive flavors.

Avoid overexposing your taste buds to strong or bitter flavors, such as coffee, which can temporarily deaden sensitivity to other flavors.

If you've lost interest in eating, talk to your doctor, and consult a registered dietitian about other ways to make food more appealing.

A Few Words About Constipation...

Constipation is a stubborn problem for many people as they get older. The reason? The digestive system may get a little sluggish. Not getting enough fluid or fiber, and being inactive may compound the problem. With constipation, stools get hard and can't be passed out of the body without straining. And your normal schedule may change.

Being physically active, drinking enough fluids, and eating enough fiber are ways you can stay regular—and avoid constipation. If these remedies don't work, ask a registered dietitian or your doctor about other steps.

- ➢ Drink at least eight cups of water or other fluids daily. Fluids help your stools stay softer, bulkier, and easier to eliminate.

- ➢ Consume plenty of fiber-rich foods: legumes, whole-grain breads and cereals, vegetables, and fruits. Fiber gives bulk to stools, making them easier to pass through the colon. *For more about fiber for health, refer to chapter* 6, *"Fiber: Your Body's Broom."*

- ➢ Listen to nature's call! The longer waste remains in your large intestine, the more difficult it is to eliminate. The body continues to draw out water, so stools get harder.

- ➢ Keep physically active. And get enough rest. Both help keep your body regular.

- ➢ Avoid taking laxatives, as well as fiber pills and powders, unless your doctor recommends them. Food may pass through your intestinal tract faster than the vitamins and minerals can be absorbed. And some may cause your body to lose fluids and potassium. A cup of tea or warm water with lemon, taken first thing in the morning can act as a gentle, natural laxative.

Refer to "About Fiber Pills and Powders..." on page 151.

have you ever wondered

...if taking mineral oil helps keep you regular? Taking mineral oil isn't recommended. It can promote the loss of the fat-soluble vitamins (A, D, E, and K). ✦

Not Hungry?

While many older adults say they just don't have an appetite, there's no single cause for that complaint. Some have digestive problems that cause appetite loss. And medication or health problems may also be a cause. For some, the problem is psychological: loneliness, depression, or anxiety, among others. Regardless, people who don't eat adequately increase their chances for poor nutrition and its negative consequences. Try these tips to perk up a tired appetite:

Try to identify the problem. If certain foods cause discomfort, such as heartburn or gas, find alternatives. Talk to your doctor about your medication; if it's causing a problem, something else might be prescribed.

Eat four to six smaller meals. And keep portions small. You may always take seconds if you're hungry for more. And smaller meals may be easier to digest.

Give yourself enough time to eat. Rushing through a meal can cause discomfort.

To get your digestive juices flowing, serve foods hot. Heat brings out the aroma of food, usually making it more enticing.

Make your overall meal look appealing. When food is attractively arranged and served, you may get your appetite back!

If possible, increase your activity. This often helps to perk up a tired appetite.

If you're confined to bed, ask someone to help keep your room appealing. Remove bedpans and other unpleasant things. And turn on some music!

Refer to "No Appetite?" *on page* 41 *for other ideas that might apply.*

Chewing Problems?

For many older adults, poor appetite isn't much of a nutrition problem. Instead, tooth loss or mouth pain is. An astounding number of people lose all their teeth by age 65. And many have poorly-fitting dentures that cause chewing problems and mouth sores.

What's at the root of oral health problems? Cavities may come to mind first. Yet, gum, or periodontal, disease is the most common cause of tooth loss among older adults. As a result, many have missing, loose, or diseased teeth and sore, diseased gums. People with dentures may be able to eat all the foods they've always enjoyed if dentures fit right. If not, the resulting discomfort and mouth pain may keep them from eating a well-balanced diet.

Having a dry mouth is another problem that may cause chewing and swallowing difficulties, especially if food is dry and hard to chew. As people get older, they may not have as much saliva flow to help soften food and wash it down. Medicine also may decrease saliva flow.

If you have chewing problems, make sure oral problems don't become a barrier to good nutrition.

Take a trip to your dentist, or to a dentist who specializes in care for older adults. Many oral health problems can be treated. And dentures that don't fit properly should be adjusted.

Choose softer foods that are easier to chew. Chop foods well to reduce your risk of choking. Within each of the five food groups of the Food Guide Pyramid, you'll find foods that are easier to eat:

- *Bread, Cereal, Rice, Pasta*: cooked cereal, cooked rice, cooked pasta, soft bread or rolls, softer crackers
- *Fruit*: fruit juice, cooked or canned fruit, avocado, banana, grapefruit and orange sections, soft fruit
- *Vegetable*: vegetable juice, cooked vegetables, salads with soft vegetables, chopped lettuce
- *Milk, Yogurt, Cheese*: milk, cheese, yogurt, pudding, ice cream, milk shakes
- *Meat, Poultry, Fish, Beans, Eggs, Nuts*: chopped, lean meat, chopped chicken or turkey, canned fish, tender cooked fish, eggs, creamy peanut butter

Refer to "The Food Guide Pyramid: Your Healthful Eating Guide" *on page* 243.

Drink water or other fluids with meals and snacks to make swallowing easier.

Consult with a registered dietitian. Together you can plan for foods that you can eat with comfort, without compromising your nutritional needs. *Refer to page* 580, "How to Find Nutrition Help."

There's good news: Tooth loss isn't an inevitable part of aging. Good oral care—starting now, whatever your age—can help you keep the teeth you were born with! *Refer to* "Keep Teeth and Gums Healthy!" *on page* 128.

Gum disease itself is highly preventable. Proper brushing, daily flossing, and regular cleaning by a dentist or hygienist can keep gum disease at bay. If you can, have your teeth cleaned twice a year, and perhaps more often if you have gum disease. *For more about gum disease, refer to* "Keep Smiling: Prevent Gum Disease!" *on page* 498.

Weight Loss—Or Gain?

Have you lost weight as a result of a poor appetite or health problems? Or have extra pounds crept on over the years? Maintaining or improving your weight may be good for your health! You need to talk to your doctor or a registered dietitian about the weight that's healthy for you.

Whether you need to keep weight on, or take if off, eat in a healthful way and remain physically active. *Refer to* "Never Too Late for Exercise" *on page* 513.

How to Gain—Or Maintain

Weight loss can be a problem, especially if you haven't been trying to lose. If you're not physically active, much of the weight you lose may be muscle; the more you lose, the weaker you'll get. If you're underweight, you're at greater risk for falls and bone fractures. And you may not recover from sickness or surgery as quickly either.

To gain or maintain weight...

- Make your day's food choices balanced and varied, with enough servings from all five food groups of the Food Guide Pyramid.
- Eat five or six small meals a day if you fill up quickly at meals.
- Stick to a regular meal schedule so you don't forget about eating.
- Keep healthful foods handy for snacking: milk, yogurt, fruit, vegetables, crackers, whole-wheat bread, cereal, and peanut butter.
- Eat with someone else to spark your appetite.
- Instead of coffee or tea, which supplies few calories, drink cocoa, milk, soup, or juice.
- Make casseroles, soups, stews, and side dishes hearty by adding milk, cheese, rice, or pasta.
- Talk to a registered dietitian or your doctor about ways to boost your diet with calories and nutrients. An RD can provide you with ideas for high-calorie meals and drinks and, if necessary, can help you select a canned nutrition supplement drink or a dietary supplement.

For more tips on gaining weight, refer to "When You Want to Gain" *on page* 40.

How to Lose

As you get older, you need fewer calories to maintain your weight. It's not surprising, then, if you've gained a few pounds—especially if you're less active and you haven't changed the way you eat.

Carrying extra weight may not be healthy for you. It's well known that being overweight increases the risks for high blood pressure, heart disease, diabetes, and certain cancers. If you have one of these problems already, dropping just a few pounds may lower your blood pressure, total blood cholesterol level, or blood sugar level.

To lose weight...

- Make your day's food choices balanced and varied, with enough servings from all five food groups of the Food Guide Pyramid.
- Eat regular meals. Meal skipping often leads to snacking and possibly, overeating.
- Choose snacks carefully. Fruit, vegetables, low-fat yogurt, skim milk, breakfast cereal, and frozen yogurt are all good choices.
- Trim fat from your food choices. Remove skin from turkey and chicken before eating. Choose lean meats, and trim visible fat. Bake, broil, microwave, or steam foods instead of frying them. Use 1 percent or nonfat milk, yogurt, and cheese. Switch to low-calorie salad dressings. *For more ways to trim fat, refer to* "Fat and Cholesterol Trimmers" *on page* 335.
- Eat smaller portions.

➢ If you drink alcoholic beverages, do so in moderation. That's no more than one drink a day for women, and two for men. If you're taking medication, you might need to avoid alcoholic drinks altogether.

➢ Keep active and busy to prevent eating from boredom or loneliness. And learn to recognize the signs of hunger before eating.

➢ Beware of weight-loss plans with unrealistic promises. *Refer to "'Diets' That Don't Work!" on page* 43.

For more tips on losing weight, refer to "When You Want to Lose..." on page 34.

"Moving Ideas" for Physical Limitations

Some older adults move with the same grace, stamina, and dexterity of their earlier years. For others, health problems limit physical abilities: for example, arthritis, diabetes, osteoporosis, Parkinson's disease, respiratory diseases, and strokes. Even healthy seniors may become gradually less active, so they have less strength and stamina for everyday tasks.

For those who enjoy the freedom of independent living, some general tips can make food preparation and eating easier.

Does your tile or wooden floor seem slippery? Wear flat, rubber-soled shoes in the kitchen. And wipe up spills immediately so you don't slip!

Be careful of loose rugs by the sink or other places in your kitchen. They may feel good under foot, but they're easy to trip or slip on.

If you're unsteady or need a cane, use a rolling tea cart to move food, dishes, and kitchen equipment from place to place. A wheelchair or walker with a flat seat can be used to move things, too; check with a medical supply store to find them.

Sit while you work. Use the kitchen table for food preparation, or get a stable chair or stool that's high enough for working at the counter or stove.

Give yourself time. Things may take a little longer to do as you get older.

Get yourself a loud kitchen timer if you have trouble hearing. Especially if you're forgetful, using a timer whenever you cook can avoid burned food and kitchen fires.

Cooking for just one? Use a microwave or toaster oven, rather than the oven.

Organize your kitchen for efficiency—everything within easy reach. Keep mixers, blenders, and other heavy small appliances on the counter. Keep heavy pots and pans on lower shelves, too.

If you have vision problems, keep a magnifying glass handy. That makes it easier to read expiration dates and small type on food labels.

Have trouble with manual tasks, such as opening jars and cans, or perhaps cutting? Kitchen devices are sold to make food preparation easier for people with arthritis or other problems, and for those partly paralyzed by a stroke. Again check a medical supply store to find these devices.

have you ever wondered

...*if you can eat anything to relieve arthritis?* To date, medical experts haven't found any food or nutrient that can relieve the pain that comes with arthritis. So beware of lures for products, including vitamin supplements, that claim to help. Be cautious of taking too many aspirins, too, to relieve pain. Over time, they can irritate your stomach, causing bleeding you may not be aware of. That can lead to an iron deficiency. Talk to your doctor about a safe dosage.

The best nutritional advice for arthritis is: Follow a healthful eating plan. And maintain a healthy weight. That way, you won't put too much strain on arthritic joints. ✦

Get a cordless phone. You won't need to dash to the phone while you're cooking. Just keep it near you. It's a good safety measure, too, in case you fall.

If you use a walker or wheelchair, talk to a registered dietitian or physical therapist about changes you might make in your kitchen. There's a lot that can be done to continue your freedom and independence in the kitchen.

Another kitchen safety tip: Avoid using your oven as a room heater. It can be dangerous! If heating is a problem where you live, let someone know: a relative, landlord, building manager, or social worker, among others.

For other kitchen safety tips, refer to "Quick Tips for Injury Prevention" on page 322.

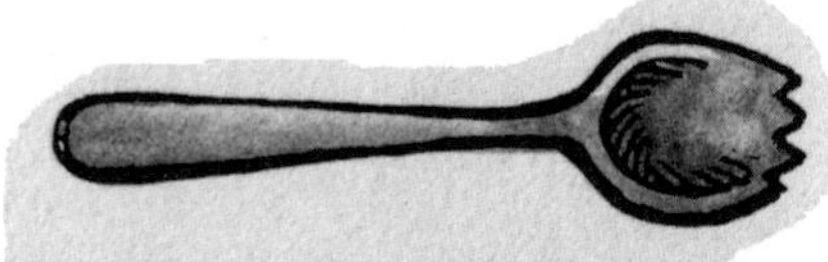

Use an all-in-one fork and spoon if you have trouble with one hand. Check with a medical supply store or catalog to find one.

Drink soup from a mug. It's easier than using a soup spoon—and there's one less utensil to wash.

Get dishes with a higher rim. The rim helps you push food onto your spoon or fork.

Set your table with plastic placemats. They're easy to clean. And dishes won't slide on them, as they might on the table surface.

Shaky with a cup? Get a covered cup with a drinking spout or place for a straw.

Rather than avoid certain foods, accept help if you need it. You need the nourishment that a variety of food provides for all the special moments of life still to come.

have you ever wondered

...if you need more potassium if you're taking a diuretic medication? That depends on the diuretic that's been prescribed for you. You need to talk to your doctor or a registered dietitian for advice. You probably don't need to take a potassium supplement, however. Many foods are great sources, including many fruits and vegetables, and milk. *For a list of foods high in potassium, refer to "Potassium: Another Reason for 'Five a Day'" on page* 159. ✦

When Health Problems Arise...

Health problems—physical and emotional—may arise as people get older. Many of these problems require changes in what and how people eat. Dietary modifications need as much attention as following directions for medications.

There's no one diet for a specific health condition because people's individual needs differ so much. And sometimes more than one health problem needs to be treated at the same time. That's why each person should be advised as an individual.

Make sure you have regular check-ups to monitor your health—annually or more often as your doctor advises. Never self-diagnose an ongoing disease, or prescribe your own special diet or dietary supplement to treat it! And be careful of miracle cures. *Refer to "Miracles? Dream On!" on page* 525.

If a special diet is prescribed for you, consult your doctor or registered dietitian for guidance. And have your progress monitored as they advise. It's all for your good health! *To find a registered dietitian, ask your doctor. Or refer to page* 580, *"How to Find Nutrition Help."*

Give a Helping Hand!

To people who are sick or injured, good nutrition is often the best medicine! Yet, they may be weak or unable to feed themselves. Regardless of age, they need your caring, helping hand. If you're offering help to those who are sick or injured, help make the meal pleasant by following these suggestions:

Help them wash their hands before and after eating. Use a wet, soapy washcloth or premoistened towels if they can't get to the sink.

Make sure that the food is the right consistency. You might need to chop or purée it if they have trouble chewing.

Let them decide what foods to eat first, next, and so on. Even when they can't feed themselves, most people want to feel in control of their lives.

For dignity's sake, provide a napkin or apron to help them keep clean.

Offer some finger foods to eat on their own. For example, try banana slices, orange sections, bread (cut in quarters), soft roll, cheese sticks, or meat (sliced in strips).

Offer a sip to drink between bites to help with chewing and swallowing. Provide a straw and a cup that's not too big. You can always pour more.

Relax together as you eat. The meal shouldn't feel rushed, especially if they have trouble chewing or swallowing.

Offer small bites. And use a spoon, rather than a fork. It's easier for holding food and less likely to jab their mouth.

Sit together as you offer food. The time together will feel more relaxed.

Clean up any spills right away. You might keep a clean cloth handy.

Most important, respect their needs and desires. It can be emotionally hard for them to count on others when they'd prefer to feed themselves.

Let the nurse or any other caregivers know what and how they've eaten. That way, other meals and snacks can be adjusted to meet their needs.

MIRACLES? DREAM ON!

All too often, charlatans prey on older adults with promises of easy cures or ways to stay young! Many of the products they peddle are foods, substances from food, or nutrition supplements. And there's no evidence that they do any good in treating arthritis, heart disease, cancer, Alzheimer's disease, or other maladies—or helping people live longer.

Many of these products are costly. It's money that is better spent on healthful, delicious foods.

And the harm may go further than the pocketbook! These remedies may mask symptoms, offer false hope, or worse yet, keep people from seeking reliable health care that can make a difference. They might interfere with the action of medications already being taken—or perhaps the absorption of nutrients in the food.

Always be cautious of promises that seem too good to be true! *To learn how to judge what you read and hear about nutrition and health, refer to* "Be Your Own Judge!" *on page* 583. And always consult your doctor or a registered dietitian before trying these products.

Be aware that many people claim to be experts in nutrition. But some aren't qualified. *To find a registered dietitian or other qualified expert, refer to page* 580, "How to Find Nutrition Help" *for resources in your community. For more information, refer to* "Case Against Health Fraud" *on page* 586. ✦

Food and Medicine

People of all ages take over-the-counter medications, prescription drugs, or both. Especially among many older adults, regular medications are common. Knowing how to use them safely and effectively is ultimately your responsibility. Your doctor, pharmacist, and perhaps a registered dietitian should provide the guidance you need.

Some Don't Mix

Taking medication may not seem like a nutrition issue. Yet, when food and medicines are taken together, they often interact. That's not surprising since the chemistry of the stomach and intestine differs before and several hours after eating. Food and the substances released in your body during digestion may either enhance or hinder the effectiveness of some medication. And medication can improve or interfere with the way nutrients are absorbed or used.

Your goal? To get the full benefits of both food and medicine. To do that, all medications, even aspirin, should be taken as directed:

- Some should be taken with meals. With food, they're less likely to irritate the stomach. Aspirin and ibuprofen are two examples.
- Some should be taken on an empty stomach, perhaps an hour before or three hours after eating. Food may slow their absorption and action. That's true of some antibiotics, for example.
- Some food and medications shouldn't be consumed within several hours of each other. For example, fruit juice and other high-acid foods can destroy one type of penicillin. And calcium in dairy foods and calcium supplements binds with tetracycline, so it passes through the body without being absorbed.
- Some medications should be taken with plenty of water. That's true of most cholesterol-lowering drugs.
- Medication shouldn't be taken with alcoholic beverages. Alcohol can block the effects of some drugs, and amplify the effects of others to potentially harmful levels. Medication can also intensify the effects of alcohol on your body.

How do you know to take medicine with a meal or on an empty stomach? Read the directions printed on the container. You'll find information about when, how much per dose, and how long to take the medication. The directions also may state what to do if you miss a dose. Ask the doctor or pharmacist if you don't fully understand. You can ask that directions be printed in large type. *Note*: With the long-term use of some medications, your doctor also may prescribe a nutrition supplement.

You can't know about the potential interactions between all medicines and food. That's where the advice of your doctor, pharmacist, or a registered dietitian comes in. *For a quick reference, refer to "Common Interactions Between Food and Medications" on page* 527.

have you ever wondered

...if antacids are OK for ongoing indigestion? Although the body may produce less stomach acid with age, many older adults still suffer from indigestion. Antacids, taken as directed, can help. But excess amounts can deplete your body's phosphorus reserves, which may lead to soft bones, or osteomalacia.

Another caution: Taking antacids with calcium at mealtime may also prevent your body from fully absorbing iron in food. Talk to your doctor about taking antacids. Symptoms that seem like indigestion could be something more serious! ✦

Medicine: For Safety's Sake

Talk to your doctor or pharmacist about all medications you're taking, including over-the-counter drugs and nutrition supplements. Some medications have harmful effects when they're taken at the same time.

Always take the medication as prescribed in the directions. If you don't take enough, or stop too soon, the medication may not work. And taking too much, too often can be dangerous. Depending on the medication, excessive amounts also may keep your body from absorbing essential nutrients or deplete your supply.

Always take medicine in a well-lighted place. And put on your glasses if you wear them! Otherwise you might take the wrong medication amount.

Keep medicines in their original containers with the directions intact.

Only take medicines prescribed for you, even if your symptoms seem similar to someone else's.

Flush unused or expired medicines down the toilet.

With each check-up, review your medication plan with your doctor to make sure it's still right for you.

Common Interactions Between Food and Medications

MEDICINE CABINET: PRESCRIPTION DRUGS AND OVER-THE-COUNTER PRODUCTS	KITCHEN CABINET: COMMON FOOD AND DRUG INTERACTIONS (FOR SPECIFIC INFORMATION ON YOUR MEDICATIONS, ASK YOUR DOCTOR OR PHARMACIST.)
PAIN RELIEVERS: Aspirin (Example: Anacin, Bayer) Ibuprofen (Example: Advil, Motrin, Nuprin)	Take these with food to avoid irritating your stomach. Also limit other stomach irritants, such as alcohol and caffeine.
ANTIBIOTICS: Tetracycline (Example: Achromycin, Sumycin) Penicillin (Example: Pen-Vee K)	The calcium in dairy foods and calcium supplements can block the absorption of tetracycline-based products. Take these drugs one hour or more before or after having dairy products or calcium supplements. When taken together, citrus fruits and fruit juices can destroy a type of penicillin.
BLOOD-THINNING DRUGS/ANTICOAGULANTS: Warfarin (Example: Coumadin, Dicoumerol)	Eat in moderation foods with vitamin K, such as dark leafy greens, spinach, kale, turnip greens, green tea, and cauliflower. Too much vitamin K can make your blood clot faster.
ANTIDEPRESSANTS: MAO inhibitors (Example: Marplan, Parnate)	When taken with foods high in tyramine (an amino acid found in protein foods), these medications can cause an increase in blood pressure. Ask your doctor or a registered dietitian for a list of foods to avoid, such as beer, cheese, red wine, and cured meats.
ANTACIDS containing: Aluminum (Examples: Maalox, Amphojel) Calcium (Example: Tums) Sodium (Example: Alka Seltzer)	Wait two to three hours after taking an aluminum-containing antacid before you drink or eat citrus fruits. Citrus fruits can increase the amount of aluminum your body absorbs. Antacids with aluminum also can cause a loss of bone-building calcium. Some antacids can weaken the absorption of heart regulating drugs such as digoxin (Lanoxin, for example). Some antacids can weaken the effect of antiulcer drugs (Tagamet, for example) or drugs that treat high blood pressure (such as Inderal). Be sure to read all the alerts on the labels. If you have high blood pressure, read the label of antacids for the amount of sodium present.
GARLIC PILLS	It is important for your blood to clot if you suffer a cut or undergo surgery. Substances in garlic appear to thin the blood. If you are already taking aspirin or other blood-thinning medications, taking garlic supplements may thin the blood too much.

Source: To Your Health! Food & Activity Tips for Older Adults, *the National Council on Aging, the National Institute on Aging, the President's Council on Physical Fitness and Sports, and the Food Marketing Institute,* 1995. *Used with permission.*

your nutrition check-up

Older Adults: Nutritionally Healthy?

Read each statement. If the statement applies, give yourself the number of points in the "Yes" column. Then tally up your score.

If you care for an older adult...or look in on an older parent...this checklist can offer insight on his or her nutritional health, too.

	Yes
I have an illness or condition that made me change the kind and/or amount of food I eat.	2
I eat fewer than two meals per day.	3
I eat few fruits or vegetables, or milk products.	2
I have three or more drinks of beer, liquor, or wine almost every day.	2
I have dental or mouth problems that make it hard for me to eat.	2
I don't always have enough money to buy the food I need.	4
I eat alone most of the time.	1
I take three or more different prescribed or over-the-counter drugs a day.	1
Without wanting to, I have lost or gained 10 pounds in the last six months.	2
I am not always physically able to shop, cook, and/or feed myself.	2
Total	_____

What's the nutritional score?

If it's...

0-2... Good! But check again in six months.

3-5... You're at moderate nutritional risk. Try to make some changes that improve your eating habits and lifestyle. Get advice from your senior citizens center, Office on Aging, health department, or senior nutrition program. And check again in three months.

6 or more... You're at high nutritional risk. Bring this checklist with you the next time you see your doctor, registered dietitian, or other qualified health or social service professional. Talk about any problems, and ask for assistance.

Source: Nutritional Screening Initiative, a project of the American Academy of Family Physicians, The American Dietetic Association, and the National Council on Aging.

real life nutrition

Aging with Grace

Seventy-plus years! In many ways, Jeane feels as good as she always has. Her important numbers score perfect: blood pressure—120/80; total blood cholesterol—under 200 mg/dL; and normal blood sugar. All those years of healthy eating and remaining physically active have paid off!

Yet other annoying problems that come with age are slowing her body down, but fortunately not her spirit nor her ability to find creative solutions for independent living. Being a widow, she lives on her own but enjoys the companionship of friends. And her adult children reside nearby.

For years, Jeane has overcome the problems of childhood polio. Throughout adulthood, she's been agile and active. But recently, she's less stable and gets tired standing too long. She needs a cane to walk, so carrying things is harder. She has some problems with osteoporosis, so knows she needs to be careful. Although she drives, shopping is more difficult than it used to be—a challenge for her as an avid shopper!

Jeane enjoys cooking and baking. But she acknowledges that eating alone isn't the same as being with others. How does food taste? OK—but not the same as she remembered. And sometimes food upsets her stomach a bit.

As she continues to cope with the annoyances of age, what might Jeane do to keep physically active and eat well—and remain independent and healthy?

Advice for keeping active and eating healthy during the older years:

➢ Swimming several times a week (not just paddling in the water) would be good exercise since Jeane wouldn't need to be on her feet. Swimming with a friend would make the activity more fun—and she'd more likely stick with the routine. She might also check within her community for exercise classes for older adults; she could learn more activities to do on her own.

➢ To keep her bones and muscles strong, Jeane's wise to keep mobile and use her cane to walk when she can. In addition, she might build arm strength while she's sitting; even canned goods from her kitchen make good "weights." Kneading bread, since she likes to bake, would build arm strength, too; she could do that sitting down.

➢ To make shopping easier, she might patronize a store with a battery-powered, seated shopping cart. And the bagger should carry her groceries to her car. When the weather is bad,

real life nutrition (continued)

she should ask her children to get her groceries, or check for home-delivery.

➢ In the kitchen, she should get a stable stool so she could sit by the counter or stove. A rolling tea cart could help her carry food, dishes, and other things from place to place. And for convenience she might cook in batches and freeze the extra, so cooking is less work.

➢ When she eats alone, she might make the event special—serving food on a pretty plate, or enjoying music or a television show with her meal.

➢ She might invite her friend to her home to eat. She could make the soup; her friend, the salad. Occasionally they might eat out together. Or she could join her kids for meals sometimes.

➢ Jeane needs to continue to drink plenty of calcium-rich foods, such as milk, cheese, and yogurt, to slow the progress of bone loss. And eating meals and snacks with enough variety of foods continues to be important for overall good nutrition. That includes plenty of fruits and vegetables; their fiber will help keep her system regular.

➢ To make food more flavorful, she might experiment with herbs—especially since she enjoys cooking.

➢ If her stomach feels upset occasionally, that's part of aging. She might find out what bothers her and find a nutritious substitute, try smaller meals, or eat more slowly.

➢ And she needs to remember to drink plenty of fluids all day long to avoid dehydration.

CHAPTER TWENTY-ONE

ATHLETE'S GUIDE

winning nutrition

On your mark...get set...go! Whether you train for competitive sports work out for your own good health, or just for fun, what you eat and drink—and when—is part of the formula for athletic success. Good nutrition can't replace training, effort, talent, and personal drive. But there's no question that it makes a difference when your goal is peak performance.

Whether competitive or recreational, physical activity puts extra demands on your body. As an athlete, you use more energy, lose more body fluids, and put extra stress on your muscles, joints, and bones. Fortunately, your "training table" can increase your endurance and help prevent dehydration and injury. And healthful eating helps you feel good and stay fit overall!

Ten Reasons To Make the "Right Moves"

Whether you're involved in sports or simply live an active lifestyle, physical activity pays big dividends. Physical activity is the "right move" for fitness—for almost everyone, not just for athletes. Here are a few reasons why:

Trimmer body. If you're physically active, you'll have an easier time losing weight and keeping it off. Many experts believe physical activity is the key to a healthy weight. *For the benefits of activity for weight management, refer to "The Exercise Edge" on page 32.*

Less risk for health problems. An active lifestyle—or a sports regimen—can help protect you from many ongoing health problems. Your risks for heart disease, diabetes, high blood pressure, high blood cholesterol levels, and some cancers are reduced when you get at least 30 minutes of physical activity most, if not all, days of the week. *For more about these health problems, refer to "Prevention: Nutrition and Health Problems" on page 484.*

Stronger bones. Regular, weight-bearing activities—such as walking, running, weight-lifting, cross-country skiing, and soccer—help make your bones stronger. If you're past age 35, weight-bearing exercise helps maintain your bone strength and reduce your chance of fractures. *Refer to "Osteoporosis: Reduce the Risks" on page 496 for more about bone health.*

Stronger muscles. Strength-training activities, such as lifting weights, at least two times a week, keep your body strong for sports and everyday living. When you're strong, it's easier to move, carry, and lift things. When you exercise your muscles, you also give your heart a workout. It's a muscle, too. A strong heart pumps blood and nutrients more easily through your 60,000 miles of blood vessels.

More endurance. You won't tire as easily when you're physically active. And you may have more stamina during the rest of the day, too.

Better mental outlook. Many athletes describe feelings of exhilaration and well-being when they work out regularly. It's a great way to reinforce that "can do" attitude.

Stress relief, and better sleep. Physical activity actually helps your body relax and release emotional tension. And that helps you sleep better.

Better coordination and flexibility. Your body moves with greater ease and range of motion when you stay physically active.

Injury protection. When you're in shape, you more easily can catch yourself if you slip or trip...and can move away from impending danger more quickly.

Feel younger longer. Research suggests that physical activity slows some effects of aging.

For the special benefits of physical activity for children, refer to "Active Play: Good Moves for Children" on page 442. And for older adults, refer to "The Reasons Are Many" on page 513.

did you know

...heat stroke, caused by severe dehydration, ranks second among the reported cases of death among high school athletes?

...taking extra vitamins or minerals (beyond the Recommended Dietary Allowances) offers no added advantage to athletic performance?

...a high-carbohydrate diet can boost your endurance? ✦

Nutrients for Active Living

For both world-class athletes and exercise enthusiasts, nutrition is fundamental to peak physical performance. To put in your best effort, you need the same nutrients as nonathletes: carbohydrates, protein, fat, vitamins, minerals, and water. As an athlete, however, you may need slightly more of some of these nutrients.

What are the major differences in your nutrient needs? To replace fluid losses, athletes need more fluids. And as fuel, working muscles need more energy-supplying nutrients, especially carbohydrates.

Thirst for Success!

Working toward top physical performance? Drink plenty of water. Fluids often are overlooked by athletes and nonathletes alike. Yet your physical endurance and strength depend on it.

When you're physically active, sweat evaporates from your skin. You need to replace the fluids lost. A 150-pound athlete can lose 1 1/2 quarts, or 3 pounds, of fluid in just one hour. That equals six 8-ounce glasses of water!

Fluids for Peak Performance

What's the risk if you lose too much fluid? Even small losses of 2 to 3 percent of your body weight can hinder your physical performance. (That's about 3 or 4 pounds for a 150-pound person.) Dehydration can hinder your strength, endurance, and aerobic capacity. Why do you need enough fluid?

For energy production. Fluids are important to the cycle of energy production. As part of blood, water helps carry oxygen and glucose to the cells in your muscles. There it's used to produce energy. Blood removes waste by-products as energy is generated by the muscles. Fluid losses decrease blood volume, so your heart must work harder to deliver enough oxygen to the cells.

For cooling down. Exercise generates heat. Fluids also help to reduce the heat and cool you down. As you move your muscles, your body's overall temperature goes up, and you sweat. And as sweat evaporates, your body cools and avoids overheating. If you don't replace these fluids, your body's fluid balance is thrown off. That's especially a problem as working muscles continue to generate more heat.

For transporting other nutrients. Water in your bloodstream carries other nutrients you need for fitness, including electrolytes. As part of urine, water also helps eliminate wastes.

As a cushion. The water around your body's tissues and organs offers protection from all the jostles and jolts that go along with exercise.

Besides reduced physical performance, dehydration has even greater risks. Continued fluid loss increases your chances of heat injury, such as heat cramps, heat exhaustion, and heat stroke. Severe dehydration can even be life threatening. *Refer to "Dehydration Alert!" on page* 535.

For more about water in a healthful eating plan, refer to "A Fluid Asset" on page 171.

Fluids: More Than Refreshing

No matter what your sport—running, bicycling, swimming, tennis, even walking and golfing—fluids are essential.

Drink plenty of fluids—before, during, and after physical activity. Be sure to carry a water bottle if you need to.

Drink fluids—even when you don't feel thirsty. Your thirst mechanism may not send thirst signals you need when you're exercising. In fact, thirst is a symptom of dehydration, so drink fluids before that happens. *Follow the schedule recommended on page* 534, *"For Sports: How Much Fluid?"*

Pick your fluid. Water, fruit juices, sports drinks, and other beverages all contribute fluid, too. For workouts of less than 60 minutes of continuous activity, sports drinks and juices are good choices, but tap water is cheaper.

Play it cool. Cool water is preferred by most exercisers. And it helps lower and normalize your body's core temperature when you're hot. Cold water is fine too. Contrary to popular myth, drinking cold water during exercise doesn't cause stomach cramps for most athletes. If you're dehydrated, you might get stomach cramps if you don't drink enough.

Do not have any alcoholic drinks before or during a heavy workout. Alcohol promotes dehydration. And it may impair your coordination, balance, muscle reflexes, and visual perception. Alcohol works as a depressant, affecting your brain's ability to reason and make judgments. And your reaction time may slow down. For the endurance athlete it has another effect, too. When you drink a beer, wine, or

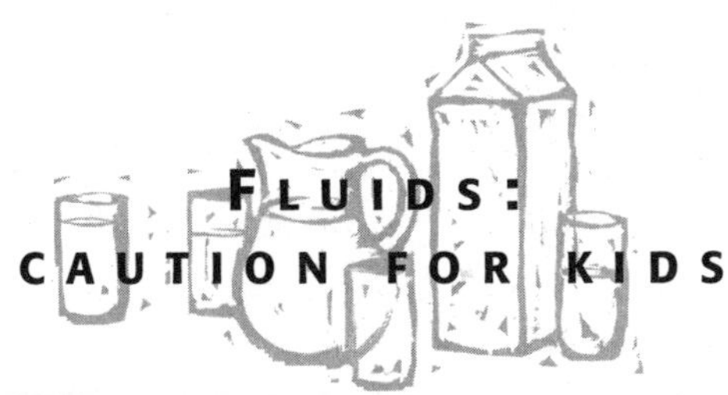

FLUIDS: CAUTION FOR KIDS

Children are more likely to get overheated from strenuous activity. As a result, they're at greater risk for dehydration.

➢ They don't perspire as much as teens and adults, so their body's "air-conditioning" system is less effective.

➢ They generate more body heat with exercise, too.

➢ Children don't adjust as quickly when they exercise in hot weather.

➢ Protective gear used in many sports, such as hockey and football, hinders their bodies' ability to cool off, too.

To protect children from becoming dehydrated, encourage them to drink enough fluids before, during, and after physical activities. Offer regular fluid breaks and ensure that fluids are readily available. Supervise them carefully when they're active, especially on hot days when fluid needs are even greater. ✦

mixed drink, your liver works to detoxify the alcohol. This can interfere with the liver's job of forming extra blood glucose for prolonged physical activity. The possible result? Early fatigue.

Replace water weight. Weigh yourself before and after a heavy workout. Your nude weight is best, or make sure you're wearing the same clothing when you weigh yourself. Replace each pound of weight you lose with two cups of water, high-carbohydrate drink, or other fluid to bring your fluid balance back to normal.

Check the color of your urine. Dark-colored urine indicates that you're short on water. You need to increase your fluid intake so your urine is light and clear before you start exercising again.

Be especially careful if you exercise intensely in hot, humid weather. Consider how much hotter you feel on humid days. Sweat doesn't evaporate from your skin as quickly, so you don't get the cooling benefits. That's why on humid days, it's easier to get overheated as you exercise.

Know the signs of dehydration. Some of the early signs are flushed skin, fatigue, increased body temperature, and increased breathing and pulse rate, followed by dizziness, increased weakness, and labored breathing with exercise. Replace fluids before the symptoms get too serious. *Refer to "Dehydration: Look for Body Signals!" on page 172.*

Sports Drinks?

Sports drinks—they're not necessary for all athletes. But they're recommended for activities lasting longer than one hour. So if you're a long-distance runner, or bicyclist, or if you're involved in other endurance events, a sports drink may offer some performance benefits.

Besides water, sports drinks contain carbohydrate, which supplies energy, or fuel, to working muscles. That's important for endurance. With sports drinks, continued exercise won't deplete muscle glycogen as fast. And performance time may be lengthened. (Muscle glycogen is carbohydrate that's stored in your muscle.)

Most sports drinks contain 5 to 8 percent carbohydrate, or simple sugars. They're absorbed quickly into the body. Sugars in soft drinks and fruit juice are more concentrated: 10 to 15 percent carbohydrate. They aren't recommended during exercise because of their high sugar content and, for soft drinks, their carbonation. Drinks with a lot of sugar or carbonation take longer to be absorbed. And they may cause cramps, diarrhea, or nausea. Dilute soft drinks and fruit juices to half-strength if you drink them during prolonged workouts and competition.

For Sports: How Much Fluid?

If you're involved in a rigorous activity, you need to make a conscious effort to drink fluids at all times during the day—not just after your workout or competition. How much fluid should you drink? Here's a schedule that can keep you from becoming dehydrated:

WHEN...	HOW MUCH...
2 to 2 1/2 hours before activity	at least 2 cups of nonalcoholic fluids (water, juice, milk, others)
just prior to or up to 15 minutes before activity	2 cups of water or sports drink
every 15 minutes during activity	1/2 cup of water or sports drink
after activity	2 cups of water or preferably a high-carbohydrate drink, such as fruit juice, for every pound lost during your activity; continue to drink fluids throughout the day, until you return to your pre-exercise weight

have you ever wondered

...if swimmers need to worry about dehydration? Like any athlete, swimmers perspire. Their bodies sweat to keep from overheating. However, swimmers probably don't notice their sweat—not while they're in the water. Like other athletes, they need to drink plenty of fluids before, during, and after their workout session. ✦

If you'd like to determine if a drink falls in the 5 to 8 percent carbohydrate range, use this formula:

- Find the grams of carbohydrate and serving size (in milliliters—mL) on the label (8 ounces is about 240 mL).

- Divide the grams of carbohydrate by the serving size (mL) and multiply by 100 to determine percent of carbohydrate.

- Example:

$$\frac{14 \text{ grams carbohydrate}}{240 \text{ mL}} \times 100 = 6\%$$

Besides fluid and energy, sports drinks supply electrolytes. As you perspire, your body loses very small amounts of sodium and other electrolytes. For most athletes, a normal diet replaces what's lost. But endurance athletes perspire more. So they're at greater risk for sodium depletion. They might benefit from the added sodium and other electrolytes in sports drinks. During exercise that's longer than 60 minutes—or for exercise performed in high heat or humidity—drinks with electrolytes help to enhance fluid absorption. *For more about electrolytes, refer to "Electrolytes: Sweat 'Em!" on page* 540.

There's no need to buy sports drinks with extra vitamins. You don't lose vitamins when you sweat! And the vitamins you need are supplied easily by a varied, moderate eating plan. *Refer to "The Athlete's Pyramid" on page* 542.

If you're an endurance athlete, experiment with various fluids and sports drinks during practices and low-key competition. For some athletes, their carbohydrate content causes cramping or an upset stomach. That's usually only a problem when athletes don't drink them early enough and they become dehydrated. Then any fluid may upset the stomach.

Energy to Burn

Athletes: How much energy, or calories, should you consume per day? Actually, that's a very individual matter. A 200-pound body builder has very different needs than an 80-pound gymnast. A vigorous physical training program may use anywhere from 2,000 to 6,000 or more calories daily—a huge range.

The amount of energy you need for sports depends on your body composition, body weight, and level of fitness, as well as the intensity, duration, and frequency of your physical activity. In other words, the harder, the longer, and the more often you work out, the more energy you require for your muscles.

Not surprisingly, some sports burn more energy than others. That's simply because they're more intense or the duration is longer. For example:

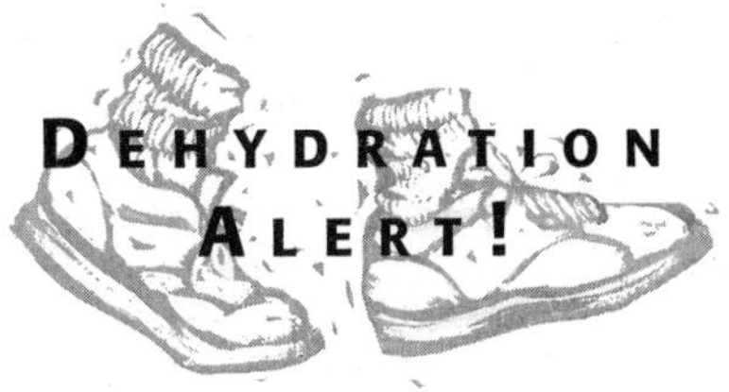

As you exercise, be alert for these conditions. They'll increase your loss of fluid through sweat, which could make your body become dehydrated faster.

- *Temperature*: The higher the temperature, the greater your sweat losses.

- *Intensity*: The harder you work out, the greater your sweat losses.

- *Body size*: The larger the athlete, the greater the sweat losses. Males generally sweat more than females.

- *Duration*: The longer the workout, the greater your fluid losses.

- *Fitness*: Well-trained athletes sweat more. And they start sweating at a lower body temperature. Why? The function of sweating is to cool the body. The well-trained athlete cools his or her body more efficiently than an untrained person.

Source: Jennings, Debbi Sowell and Steen, Suzanne Nelson. Play Hard, Eat Right, *The American Dietetic Association. Minneapolis: Chronimed Publishing,* 1995. ✦

➢ Both a golf game and downhill skiing may last several hours. But skiing uses more energy since it's more physically demanding for larger muscle groups.

➢ Any activity, such as cycling, power walking, or swimming, is a bigger energy burner if done more vigorously.

➢ When two people ski together at the same intensity, the person weighing more likely would burn more calories.

For the energy costs of several sports, refer to "Burning Calories with Activity" *on page* 26.

have you ever *wondered*

...if beer is a good fluid replacement after a workout? No. Water, fruit juice, or a sports drink are better choices for fluid replacement. The alcohol in beer has a dehydrating effect, just when you're trying to replace fluid loss.

...if caffeine can boost your physical performance? Maybe—and maybe not. People react to caffeine in different ways. Caffeine does stimulate the central nervous system, so it may help you feel more alert and attentive. Some say it enhances their energy level, too. Emerging research suggests some benefits, at least for some people.

For caffeine-sensitive athletes, caffeine may exacerbate pre-event anxiety. And it may promote headaches, stomach upset, or diarrhea, too. Be aware that caffeine is a diuretic, so it stimulates water loss.

If you enjoy coffee, tea, or soft drinks with caffeine, experiment during training, not competition. A single cup may help—or at least not hinder—your performance. But avoid caffeine tablets or several cups of caffeinated drinks. Drink plenty of other fluids to replace fluids lost through sweat and the diuretic effects of caffeine. *For more about caffeine, refer to* "Drinks: With or Without Caffeine?" *on page* 177. ✦

To estimate your own energy needs, refer to "Your 'Weigh': Figuring Your Energy Needs" *on page* 28. *Or have a registered dietitian* (RD) *or exercise physiologist help you.*

Carbohydrate Power

For sports and everyday living, carbohydrates are your body's foremost energy source: for sports, supplying 60 to 65 percent of your total energy needs. They're the main fuel for working muscles.

High-carbohydrate eating promotes overall fitness. Along with training, it offers a competitive edge. With "carbs" (not fat or protein) as the main fuel, most athletes can maintain rigorous activity for a longer period. Training helps the body use carbohydrates efficiently and store more as muscle glycogen. Stored in muscles, it's fuel ready for physical activity.

For Working Muscles...

To power working muscles, energy comes mostly from muscle or liver glycogen, which converts to glucose, and from blood sugar (also known as blood glucose). Glycogen is your body's storage form of carbohydrate. Depending on the intensity and duration of exercise, fat and, for endurance athletes, even a small amount of protein supply energy, too.

Carbohydrates are broken down during digestion and changed to blood sugar. Some blood sugar, which is circulated in your bloodstream, is used immediately for energy. The rest is stored as muscle and liver glycogen, or it's converted to fat if excess calories are consumed.

When you need energy, your body uses a mix of both carbohydrate (glycogen) and fat to fuel muscles. The higher the intensity of an activity, the greater the use of glycogen. Lower intensity and longer activities use more fat and less glycogen.

➢ For sports that require short, intense energy spurts, muscle glycogen is the main energy source used. That includes tennis, volleyball, baseball, weight lifting, sprinting, and even bowling.

➢ Sports that required both intensity and endurance use mostly muscle glycogen. Basketball and football are two examples.

➢ For endurance activities, such as long-distance running or bicycling, your body first uses some glycogen, then relies mostly on its fat stores for fuel.

Refer to "Carbohydrates: Your 'Power' Source" on page 125.

Fuel Up!
Carbohydrates from food include both complex carbohydrates (starches) and sugars (including sucrose, lactose, fructose, and glucose). Both supply energy and are used also to replenish muscle glycogen. The main difference is that sugars are digested and absorbed into your bloodstream more quickly.

What foods contain carbohydrates? Typically "carbs" are classified into two groups: foods that contain mostly complex carbohydrates and those with mostly sugars. Complex carbohydrates, also known as starches, are found in vegetables, cereals, breads, rice, pasta, vegetables, and legumes (beans and peas). Sugars (both naturally-occurring and added) are found in fruit, fruit juices, milk, cookies, cakes, candy, and soft drinks, among other foods.

Try these carbohydrate-rich foods and dishes:

➢ Made with breads, grains, cereals, and pastas: wild rice pilaf; salads made with different types of pasta, such as spinach pasta; whole-wheat or buckwheat pancakes; sandwiches made with every kind of bread, including a bagel or pita bread; animal crackers, gingersnaps, graham crackers, or oatmeal-raisin cookies; homemade fruit and nut breads.

➢ Made with fruits and vegetables: dried fruit mixes; stuffed spuds such as a baked potato stuffed with broccoli; fresh fruit salad; and raw vegetables with yogurt dip.

➢ Made with legumes (chickpeas, kidney beans, split peas, pinto beans, black beans, lentils, and other dried peas and beans): bean enchiladas; black bean and split pea soups; vegetarian baked beans; and chili.

For the carbohydrate content of many foods, refer to "'Carbo' Foods" on page 609.

Carbohydrate Loading
Muscles and liver store glycogen—but only a limited amount. It must be replaced after each bout of exercise. That's why endurance athletes worry that they may "hit the wall," or feel extremely fatigued, before finishing. What's happened is they've run out of glycogen.

With carbohydrate loading, you may "stockpile" two to three times more glycogen in your muscles. That way, you'll have "extra" stored glycogen on hand to use during extended activities.

With carbohydrate loading, a combination of rest and extra carbohydrate helps your muscles store more glycogen.

➢ For several days before an endurance event, gradually decrease your training. By tapering off on your exercise, your muscles get a rest. And they can "stock up" on glycogen.

➢ And for three days before the event, gradually increase your carbohydrate calories, in the form of complex carbohydrates, to 65 to 70 percent of your energy intake. But don't increase the number of total calories you consume.

Reminders: In your normal training diet, 60 to 65 percent of your energy should come from carbohydrates. Whole grains, cereal, legumes, and starchy vegetables are good sources of complex carbohydrates.

have you ever *wondered*

...if a seven-day regimen of carbohydrate loading is better? No. Until recently, some endurance athletes followed a week-long regimen of carbohydrate loading. But according to research, this practice of first depleting glycogen stores and then carbohydrate loading before an endurance event offers no additional benefits. Three days of rest and extra carbohydrate is simpler and just as effective. ✦

Carbohydrate loading won't make you pedal harder or run faster. But it may help you perform longer before getting tired. For endurance events such as marathons and triathlons that last longer than 90 minutes, carbohydrate loading may help trained athletes perform longer without fatiguing, and it may enhance performance. For all-day events, such as swim meets, a series of tennis matches, distance bicycling, or soccer games, carbohydrate loading may increase your endurance and performance.

Carbohydrate loading is most effective with trained athletes. Their bodies have a greater capacity to store extra glycogen because they generally have more muscle. "Occasional" athletes shouldn't expect the same results.

Caution: Carbohydrate loading is not advised for school-age children or teens. If you have diabetes or high blood triglycerides, you should talk to your doctor and a registered dietitian before trying this regimen.

Myth-ing the "Carb" Story

If carbohydrates supply energy, will eating a candy bar right before rigorous activity super-charge your body? No, that's a common myth. You won't get extra energy right away. Your energy supply is enhanced by eating a high-carbohydrate diet for several days before physical activity.

For endurance activities of 90 minutes or longer, a sugary snack or beverage before exercise may enhance your stamina. But too much sugar may slow the time it takes for water to leave your stomach, so your body won't replace fluids as quickly. Your best approach? Enjoy diluted fruit juice or a sports drink. You'll consume a little sugar to fuel your muscles—but not too much to impair rehydration.

Low-Fat Eating, Still Best!

Besides carbohydrate, fat provides fuel for working muscles. In fact, fat is a more concentrated energy source. And it performs other body functions, too, such as transporting fat-soluble vitamins. So don't try to cut fat out—just eat it in moderation—as one source of fuel. A low-fat diet is healthful for everyone—athlete and nonathlete alike.

Fat as Fuel

As an energy source, fat helps power activities of longer duration. It can't be converted to energy as fast as carbohydrate can. So it's not used for quick energy spurts, such as returning a tennis serve or running a 100-yard dash. Instead, fat helps power activities that last longer, such as hiking or marathon running.

Unlike glycogen, fat uses oxygen as it's converted to energy. That's why endurance sports, fueled in part by fat, are called aerobic activities. "Aerobic" means with oxygen, and aerobic activities require a continuous intake of oxygen.

Your body's fat stores supply energy for aerobic activity, so you don't need to eat more fat to power aerobic sports. No matter where it comes from—carbohydrate, protein, or fat, your body stores extra energy as body fat. Even if you're lean, you likely have enough fat stores to fuel prolonged or endurance activity.

For Athletes: How Much Fat?

The advice for athletes is the same as that for all healthy people: no more than 30 percent of your total calories should be from fat, and less than 10 percent of total calories from saturated fat. Carbohydrates should supply much more—60 to 65 percent of your energy needs. If your eating plan is too high in fat, you may not consume enough carbohydrate or protein.

If you're using a lot of energy, your calorie needs are higher. So your total fat intake may be higher, too, than it would be for moderate activity. That's often true for football linemen and weight lifters. Still, fats shouldn't contribute more than 30 percent of the total energy...even though you'll consume more total fat as you consume more calories.

Action plan: If you consume more than 30 percent of your calories from fat, cut back. Get more food energy from carbohydrates. If you don't replace energy from fat with energy from carbohydrate, you may have an energy shortfall when you're physically active. Then you won't have the calories needed to maintain your weight or keep your energy level high.

As one strategy, for example, you might trim fat by eating a baked potato more often than fries. With the energy you save from the fat in fries, add a slice of bread, which gets most of its calories from carbohydrates.

For more about fat in a healthful eating plan, and ways to moderate fat in your food choices, refer to chapter 3, "Fat Facts."

Protein—More Is Not Necessarily Better

Whether you're an athlete or not, you need protein. But it's not a nutrient that usually requires special attention just because you're physically active or building muscle.

Your body uses protein for a wide range of purposes: to build and repair body tissues; to make enzymes, hormones, and other body chemicals; to transport nutrients; to make your muscles contract; and to regulate body processes, such as water balance.

Protein also supplies energy. However, extra protein isn't your best source of extra energy for activity. Protein should supply only a small amount—12 to 15 percent of your overall energy.

When it comes to overall fitness, you need enough protein. But extra amounts offer no added benefits for athletes. Most athletes need just slightly more protein than nonathletes do. Because energy needs vary widely among athletes, it's best to base your protein needs on your body weight, rather than your energy need.

- Nonathletes need slightly less than 1/2 gram per pound of body weight.

- For most athletes (even weight lifters), 1/2 to 3/4 grams of protein per pound of body weight is typically enough. For a 150-pound athlete, that adds up to 75 to 115 grams of protein each day. And that's just 2 to 4 ounces more meat, chicken, or fish a day than the recommendation for nonathletes. As a point of reference, 3 ounces of lean beef supply about 30 grams of protein. (*Note*: More than 1 gram of protein per pound of body weight isn't advised.)

Muscle Myths

You've likely heard the long-held myth that extra protein builds more muscle. In truth, only athletic training builds muscle strength and size. Consuming more protein—from food or dietary supplements—won't make any difference. You've got to work your muscles!

Can amino acid supplements build muscle? In spite of the claims, amino acid supplements won't increase your muscle size or strength. By definition, amino acids are the building blocks of protein. Twenty different amino acids are linked together to make the proteins in food and in your body tissue. Food supplies amino acids in proportions your body needs. To your body, amino acids in foods are no different than those in supplements. And in food, they likely cost much less.

Most athletes get enough protein—and enough amino acids—from the food they eat. Protein-rich foods supply other nutrients, too, while amino acid supplements only supply amino acids.

Caution about excess protein: Extra protein isn't stored in your body for future use as protein. Instead, it's either used as energy or stored as body fat. A high-protein diet also may be high in fat.

Too much protein or amino acids actually can be harmful. Side effects include nutrient imbalance, kidney strain, and dehydration. When you consume excess protein, you need more water to excrete the urea, a waste product formed when protein turns to body fat. So, excess protein increases the chances of dehydration—and increases the need to urinate. That's an inconvenience during a workout.

*For more about substances touted for sports nutrition, refer to "*Ergogenic Aids: No Substitute for Training*" on page 553.*

Protein-Rich Foods: How Much?

The average American diet supplies more than enough protein. Two or three servings (just 6 to 7 ounces total) of lean meat, poultry, fish, eggs, beans, nuts, or seeds daily should supply enough to meet the needs of most athletes. Athletes involved in endurance sports and weight lifters need somewhat more: three to four servings of lean meat or alternatives daily.

Good sources of protein include lean meat, poultry, and fish; milk, cheese, and yogurt; eggs; beans and tofu; and nuts, seeds, and peanut butter. Cereal, breads, and vegetables also contain some protein —about 2 to 3 grams of protein per serving.

Chosen wisely, a vegetarian eating style can supply enough protein to support the nutritional needs of athletes. *Refer to chapter* 22, "*The Vegetarian Way.*"

For more about protein and amino acids, refer to "Protein Power" *on page* 561.

Vitamins and Minerals: Sense and Nonsense

Vitamins and minerals are the "spark plugs" of physical activity. Among their many functions, some help your body use energy from carbohydrate, fat, and protein. (But they don't supply energy themselves.) And others help your muscles relax and contract. *For more about their role in health, refer to chapter* 4, "Vitamins and Minerals: *Enough, But Not Too Much.*"

have you ever wondered

...if athletes benefit from extra chromium? No, but misleading claims about chromium picolinate, which is a dietary supplement, have raised the question. No scientific evidence shows that taking a chromium supplement improves physical performance, builds muscle, or aids weight loss. For that matter, the role of chromium in your overall health isn't well understood.

Whole-grain foods, apples, and peanuts are some food sources of chromium. Supplements aren't advised since taking too much of one nutrient may interfere with the work of another. And large doses of chromium may be toxic, or poisonous. ✦

If you're more active, you need more of some vitamins and minerals. But if you're eating more food, you're probably taking in these extra amounts. In fact, an athlete with a hearty appetite has a better chance of consuming enough vitamins and minerals than someone who's less active and so eats less. However, some athletes are at greater risk for nutrient deficiencies: especially those trying to lose weight by consuming too few calories or eliminating whole food groups.

For enough vitamins and minerals, eat a wide variety of foods from all five food groups of the Food Guide Pyramid. *Refer to "The Athlete's Pyramid" on page* 542.

Electrolytes? Sweat 'Em!

Your sweat is made of water, along with three minerals known as electrolytes: sodium, chloride, and potassium. Among their many functions, electrolytes help maintain the water balance in your body. They also help your muscles, including your heart muscle, contract and relax. And they help transmit nerve impulses.

As you perspire during a physical workout, your body loses small amounts of electrolytes, mostly sodium. Just by tasting the sweat on your upper lip, you know how salty it can be.

Like most athletes, you probably can replace sodium and other electrolytes just through foods you normally eat. Be assured: the average American consumes more than enough sodium to replace losses from perspiration. There's no need for extra sodium nor salt tablets. When you perspire heavily, focus your attention on extra fluids instead.

Endurance athletes, who sweat heavily for long periods, may need to replace sodium and other electrolytes. Again, salt tablets aren't advised; they may cause stomach irritation. Instead a sports drink with electrolytes, or a salty food, such as crackers and cheese, probably offers enough. *Refer to "Sports Drinks?" on page* 534.

For more about electrolytes, refer to "Sodium: *You Need Some!" on page* 158.

About Iron...
Because athletes rely on muscle cells to produce energy, having enough iron is essential. Iron is part of hemoglobin, that part of red blood cells that carries oxygen to your body cells. In your muscle cells, oxygen is essential for creating energy. An iron shortfall, even if it's small, can affect your physical performance.

Getting enough iron may be an issue. That's especially true when most of your iron comes from foods of plant origin, such as legumes and grains—or if you consume less than the Recommended Dietary Allowance (RDA)—or if you're a woman. Iron from plant sources isn't absorbed as efficiently as iron from animal sources. But eating a vitamin C-rich food, such as citrus fruit, with it improves its absorption.

The RDA for iron is 15 milligrams daily for premenopausal women and 10 milligrams daily for men. Premenopausal women have a higher need for iron than men because of iron losses in monthly menstrual periods. Teens need 18 milligrams of iron a day since they're growing.

Despite consuming enough iron, you may be iron depleted if you're involved in endurance sports. Prolonged exercise from endurance activities, such as marathon running and bicycling, promotes iron loss. With more exercise, you sweat more, losing iron through perspiration. Endurance athletes may lose iron through urine, feces, and intestinal bleeding, too. If you're an endurance athlete, have your iron status checked periodically.

"Sports anemia" is another issue related to iron. It's not really anemia. Instead it's caused by an increased blood volume, so iron is diluted slightly. This is the body's way of adapting to more physical activity at the start of an extended period of training. Typically sports anemia disappears once a training program is off and running. It doesn't seem to affect performance. And being tired may be caused by other aspects of training. If feelings of fatigue persist, or if you think you're at risk for anemia, you're smart to check with your doctor. *Refer to "Anemia: That Rundown Feeling" on page* 484.

All experts agree that athletes should consume plenty of iron-containing foods. Good sources include lean red meat, dark turkey meat, clams and oysters, iron-fortified cereals, legumes, and dried apricots.

Before you take an iron supplement, talk to your doctor or registered dietitian, especially if you're involved in rigorous, prolonged activity. Some recommend that endurance athletes, especially women, take iron supplements. Others recommend supplements only if an athlete is iron deficient. Be aware that taking large doses of an iron supplement can be harmful.

For more about iron and its food sources, refer to "Iron: A Closer Look" on page 109 *and "Iron—More for Women" on page* 459.

Calcium and Exercise: Bone-Building Duo
Calcium and weight-bearing exercise provide a winning combination. Together they help build and maintain strong, healthy bones. Your goal? To maximize your calcium stores early in life, then maintain that level, and later minimize the loss that comes with age.

Consuming enough calcium, at least 1,000 to 1,300 milligrams a day depending on your age, offers protection against bone loss. Weight-bearing activity, such as running, cross-country skiing, and soccer, promotes the deposit of calcium in the matrix, or structure, of bones. While swimming and cycling offer many benefits of physical activity, they aren't weight-bearing, so they don't build bone.

For young and female athletes, calcium is an issue. Young people may not consume enough calcium while bones are still growing. (*Tip*: Bones grow in strength until age 30 to 35.) Women can be at greater risk for osteoporosis, or bone disease, for many reasons: low calcium intake, family history, smaller body frame, and reduced estrogen levels with menopause. *Refer to "Osteoporosis: Reduce the Risks" on page* 496.

For female athletes who've stopped menstruating: High levels of physical activity, along with low levels of body fat and perhaps eating disorders, may cause periods to stop. For teen and young adult athletes, this hinders the deposit of calcium in bones at a time when bones should be developing at their maximum rate. Female athletes (typically teens and young adults) who've stopped menstruating are at special risk for bone problems later in life.

For your bones' sake, pay attention if periods stop. Talk to your doctor. This is not a normal outcome of physical activity. Stress fractures, caused by weakened bones, may seriously affect your physical performance. And the long-range impact on bone health can be damaging. For bone health, your doctor may recommend higher calcium intake, or perhaps a calcium supplement.

Supplements: Not "Energy Charged"
Contrary to some claims, there's no need for vitamin or mineral supplements for sports. They won't offer you an energy boost. No vitamin supplies energy, although some help your body use energy from foods. Your food choices can supply enough of the vitamins you need for physical activity. Extra nutrients from dietary supplements won't improve your physical performance either or provide any other added benefit.

If you decide to take a supplement, choose a multivitamin/mineral supplement with no more than 100 percent of the Daily Values (DVs) for vitamins and minerals—unless your doctor prescribes more for special health reasons. *Refer to "Dietary Supplements: Use and Abuse" on page 111.*

have you ever wondered

...how you eat after you're no longer in training? That's a question that many athletes never address. Whether you're a college athlete who stops training or an elite athlete who retires, you need to "retrain" for healthy eating. Less physical activity, loss of muscle mass, and for some, increased food intake can contribute to weight gain. You'll likely need fewer calories, even though your nutrient needs remain about the same. *For guidance, refer to chapter 11, "Planning to Eat Smart." A registered dietitian can help you, too.* *Refer to "How to Find Nutrition Help," on page 580.* ✦

A High-Performance Diet

The best training diet is a varied, moderate, and balanced eating plan. It supplies the right amount of nutrients and energy to help you achieve and maintain your strength, flexibility, and endurance.

The Athlete's Pyramid

What's a healthful eating plan for athletes? It doesn't differ much from recommendations for nonathletes.

For training both on- and off-season, the Food Guide Pyramid offers the best eating advice. Because it's flexible, it works, no matter how much energy you need or what sport you choose.

The Pyramid categorizes foods into five groups, with a serving range for each one. Fats, oils, and sweets fit in the Pyramid tip, with the advice: eat sparingly. From the bottom to the top of the serving ranges, food choices from the Pyramid can supply 1,600 to 2,800 calories, depending on your energy need.

For some athletes, energy needs are much higher—as much as 6,000 calories a day, for example, for some football players. To meet these energy demands, choose more nutrient-dense, carbohydrate-rich foods. That means eat extra servings mostly from the Bread, Vegetable, and Fruit Groups of the Food Guide Pyramid. *To see what a high-energy, high-carbohydrate menu includes, refer to "High-Energy Menu" on page 543.*

For more about the Pyramid, serving amounts, and serving sizes, refer to "The Food Guide Pyramid: Your Healthful Eating Guide" on page 243.

For Children...
In spite of the overall inactivity of today's kids, many are physically active, even involved in competitive sports. Their food and beverage choices are extremely important: first, for their

growth and development, and second, for the added demands of physical activity.

With the exception of calories and fluids, the nutrition needs for a child athlete don't differ much from nonathletes. So the Food Guide Pyramid can apply to all kids—athletes and nonathletes alike.

Energy needs depend on the child's age, body size, and sport. Estimated energy needs for children age 7 to 10 are 2,000 calories a day. For kids age 11 to 14, it's more: 2,500 calories a day for boys, and 2,200 calories a day for girls. Active kids may need even more to fuel activity.

How do you know if your child is obtaining enough energy from food? One clue is watching his or her performance. If children tire easily, they may not be eating enough. Talk to your doctor or registered dietitian about an eating plan that matches your child's energy needs.

Children are more susceptible to dehydration than teens and adults. Even when they're playing actively in the backyard, they need plenty of fluids. *To explore the reasons and ways to help them avoid dehydration, refer to "Fluids: Caution for Kids" on page* 533.

Remember, child athletes aren't the same as teens and adults. Because they're growing and their growth spurts aren't always predictable, you can't judge body composition in the same way. At certain times, for example before puberty, the body naturally stores more body fat to prepare for their growth spurt. And each child matures at his or her own time and rate. *For more about healthy eating during the childhood years, refer to "Eating ABCs for School-Age Children" on page* 430.

For Teenagers...

For many, going out for sports is part of teenage life. Because teens are still growing, their nutritional demands are especially high. Many teens need 2,500 to 3,000 calories daily for growth, health, and energy demands of sports. Some may need more, depending on their sport. The Food Guide Pyramid is an overall guideline for making choices; extra servings from the Bread, Vegetable, and Fruit Groups can supply the added energy they need.

High-Energy Menu

This high-carbohydrate menu follows guidelines of the Food Guide Pyramid. To help fuel an active athlete, extra servings of foods from each food group, with emphasis on high-carbohydrate food choices, are included to supply about 60-65% of calories from carbohydrate. About 25-30% of calories are supplied from fat and about 15% from protein.

Breakfast	
Orange juice	3/4 cup
Oatmeal	1 cup
Whole-wheat toast	2 slices
Margarine	2 teaspoons
Skim milk	1 cup
Snack	
Bagel	1 medium
Peanut butter	2 tablespoons
Grape juice	3/4 cup
Lunch	
Tuna salad	1/2 cup
Kaiser roll	1
Lettuce	2 leaves
Tomato	1 slice
Three bean salad	1 cup
Italian dressing	1 tablespoon
Fresh peach	1
Granola bars	2
Skim milk	1 cup
Snack	
Low-fat frozen yogurt	1 cup
Apricot nectar	3/4 cup
Dinner	
Vegetable soup	1 cup
Baked chicken breast, skinless	4 ounces
Brown rice	1 cup
Steamed broccoli	1 cup
Tossed green salad	1 cup
French dressing	2 tablespoons
Dinner roll	1
Margarine	1 teaspoon
Mixed fruit salad	1 cup
Skim milk	1 cup
Snack	
Apple juice	3/4 cup
Fig bars	3

Adapted from: Benardot, D., *ed.*, Sports Nutrition. *Chicago*: The American Dietetic Association, 1992.

Too often, however, the sport, social pressure, or both drive teenagers toward very low body-fat levels. That's especially true for dancers, gymnasts, rowers, swimmers, wrestlers, and others who make weight for sports. Those who exercise hard and have an eating plan that's low in energy and nutrients risk nutrient deficiencies, fatigue, reduced performance, and other health problems. *Refer to "Compete in a Weight Category?" on page* 548.

If you're a teenage athlete…

Make sure you consume the minimum servings from all five food groups of the Pyramid during the day. That includes at least two to three servings from the Milk Group; you need calcium for growing bones.

Choose snacks that count—nutritious and high in carbohydrates. Help your family keep nutritious snacks on hand. And keep some healthful snacks with you to eat after class or after practice: perhaps an apple, banana, dry fruit, juice, pretzels, bagels, or crackers. *For more ideas, refer to "'Carbo' Foods" on page* 609.

In spite of the time demands of practice, competition, and school, set time aside for meals. Don't count on constant snacking. You'll likely come up short on nutrients.

For all children, normal growth and development should be the top priority. Their weight should never be manipulated to meet goals required for sports!

Always talk to your doctor about the best weight for your child. An inaccurate assessment may result in a weight goal that isn't healthy.

For more information, refer to "Compete in a Weight Category?" on page 548. ✦

Establish realistic goals for your weight and body-fat levels. Get help from a registered dietitian to determine what's best for you.

For more about healthy eating during the teen years, refer to "Feeding the Teen Machine" on page 445.

During Pregnancy and Breast-Feeding…

Pregnancy. Being physically active during pregnancy has many benefits: among them, a psychological lift, optimal weight gain, better aerobic fitness, and an easier labor and delivery.

With their doctors' approval, active women may continue their sport. Others may initiate low-level activities gradually—again with their doctors' approval.

If you're pregnant, consult your doctor before continuing or starting a program of physical activity. Ask about precautions you need to take as you work out. Women with anemia, hypertension, diabetes, obesity, and other health problems may be advised to avoid an exercise program during pregnancy.

All the nutritional issues that relate to a healthy pregnancy apply to female athletes, too. If you fit this category, you need to eat a varied and balanced diet—with enough energy to support your pregnancy, your own needs, and the demands of physical activity. If your energy intake is too low, you may not gain enough weight and your baby may not grow adequately,

Fluid replacement is especially important. During pregnancy, you need more fluids as your own and your baby's blood volume increases. If you don't drink enough, you're at greater risk for dehydration.

Breast-feeding. The Food Guide Pyramid offers guidance for planning a varied, balanced, and moderate eating plan during breast-feeding—whether you're an athlete or not.

If you're not an athlete, breast-feeding requires an additional 500 calories more to produce breast milk for your energy and nutrient needs. With exercise, you need more; the actual amount depends on how active you are.

Your needs for fluids increase during breast-feeding, too. Without exercise, you need about 3 cups more, or about 11 cups daily. Drink even more fluids when you work out to avoid dehydration.

For more about healthy eating during pregnancy and breast-feeding, refer to "Congratulations! You're Expecting a Baby!" on page 459 and "For Those Who Breast-Feed..." on page 469. Talk to a registered dietitian, too, about any special needs for your active lifestyle and sports.

For Vegetarians...
Some athletes choose a vegetarian eating style. As with any approach, vegetarian eating can provide the fuel and nutrients needed for turning in a peak athletic performance. Meals and snacks need to be chosen with variety, balance, and moderation in mind. The focus should be on carbohydrate-rich foods in a varied and balanced diet, and not on avoiding fat.

For vegetarians who consume dairy foods and perhaps eggs, getting enough of most nutrients poses little challenge. The Food Guide Pyramid highlights many nutritious options. For vegans, who eat no foods of animal origin, more careful food choices are required to ensure adequate amounts of protein, vitamin B_{12}, iron, zinc, calcium, and perhaps energy (for muscular athletes, who use more energy).

If you're a vegetarian athlete, make sure you consume the variety of foods that provides enough nutrients for health and sports. *For guidance on healthy vegetarian eating, refer to chapter 22, "The Vegetarian Way."*

Different Sports, Different Diets?

No matter what sport you choose, the basics of high-performance eating are the same: variety, balance, and moderation. For every sport, you can use the Food Guide Pyramid as your eating guide. Only the serving amounts from each food group change—and perhaps the foods you choose often within each group.

Every sport demands adequate fluids to replace perspiration losses. In sports with prolonged, intense activity, athletes may perspire more. And with outdoor sports—especially during hot weather—fluid losses may increase, too.

Besides fluids, energy need is the most significant nutrition difference from sport to sport. Consider these differences among athletes and their sports—and how their energy, or calories, needs may be affected:

If you don't choose a rigorous physical activity regimen, try to get 30 minutes of moderate activity most, if not all, days of the week! That's all it takes for plenty of health benefits.

To get your body moving, refer to the following sections of this book. You'll find ways to fit activity into your daily life no matter what your age:

➢ *For most healthy people...* "20 Everyday Ways to Get Moving!" *on page* 32.

➢ *For children...* "Get Up and Move, Turn Off the Tube" *on page* 441.

➢ *For teens...* "Move Your 'Bod'" *on page* 449.

➢ *For travelers...* "When You're on the Road" *on page* 552.

➢ *For older adults...* "Never Too Late for Exercise" *on page* 513.

➢ *For some guidance on starting your plan for physical activity, refer to* "Inactivity: Hazardous to Your Health" *on page* 482. ✦

KITCHEN NUTRITION

food for your training table

For training meals that are high in carbohydrates, rich in protein, and lower in fat, try these combination foods or meal ideas:

➢ Chili made with kidney beans and lean beef.

➢ Vegetable stir-fry with lean pork cubes, chicken, shrimp, or tofu served over rice (go easy on the added oil).

➢ Soft corn tortillas, filled with vegetarian refried beans and topped with tomato sauce or salsa, and cheese. (On a can of refried beans, check the fat content on the Nutrition Facts label.)

➢ Grilled fish kebobs (chunks of fresh fish alternating with cherry tomatoes, green pepper, and pineapple on a skewer) served on brown rice.

➢ Lentils (alone or mixed with lean ground beef) in spaghetti sauce on whole-wheat pasta.

➢ Green peppers stuffed with a mixture of lean ground turkey and brown rice. Add a mixed green salad and finish the meal with angel food cake topped with strawberries.

➢ Strips of lean roast sirloin served with a baked potato, steamed carrots and cauliflower, and whole-wheat rolls.

➢ Chicken salad (made with reduced-calorie mayonnaise, grated lemon peel, and tarragon) on rye bread with tomato slices and sprouts. Serve with vegetable soup, whole-wheat crackers, and cantaloupe slices. ✦

➢ A 200-pound football player probably uses more energy than an 80-pound gymnast because of the difference in body size.

➢ A runner generally prefers a leaner body than someone who plays ice hockey.

➢ A baseball player probably uses less energy than a soccer player. Soccer requires almost constant physical activity.

➢ A tennis player uses intense spurts of energy; a long-distance runner, continuous energy.

➢ A cross-country skier probably needs more glycogen stores than a golfer, who uses spurts of energy.

Endurance Sports

Endurance sports generally require continuous activity for more than one hour and include sports such as cross-country running, cross-country skiing, distance bicycling, field hockey, long-distance swimming, and soccer.

Because endurance athletes spend so much time in training and competition, they use more energy than other athletes. Typically they train or compete at least one hour a day. The energy demands of training deplete glycogen stores. Fortunately, the well-trained athlete uses body fat for energy more efficiently. In addition, endurance athletes may use some protein for energy, which explains why these athletes require slightly more protein per pound than other nonendurance athletes, such as weight lifters or sprinters.

The number of calories used for endurance sports depends on several factors: body size, duration of activity, and overall effort. For the elite athlete, energy needs may be as high as 4,000 to 6,000 calories daily. A high-carbohydrate diet, with 60 to 65 percent energy from carbohydrate, provides the fuel that endurance athletes need. Most energy should come from foods in the Bread, Vegetable, and Fruit Groups of the Food Guide Pyramid.

Nonendurance Sports

Nonendurance sports typically use short bursts of energy—perhaps just for two or three minutes. While they take an all-out effort, they don't use as much energy overall. For example, a sprint swimmer is only racing for a few minutes.

Examples of sports using short spurts of energy include baseball, bowling, golf, softball, speed skating, swimming, tennis, track and field, volleyball, and weight lifting.

Nonendurance sports might be of high- or moderate-intensity. In either case, they require less energy intake than endurance sports, simply because their duration is shorter. The overall energy need depends on the length and intensity of the workout, and the athlete's body size.

Except for calories, nutrient needs are about the same. Again, the Food Guide Pyramid offers a healthful eating guideline. And 60 to 65 percent of overall energy should come from carbohydrate-rich foods.

If you need more information on nutrition and athletic performance—or if you wonder whether your food choices help or hinder your training program for a specific sport—talk to a registered dietitian or exercise physiologist. They can help you determine your energy needs, evaluate your eating plan, and suggest ways to eat for peak performance.

To find an expert specializing in sports nutrition, contact a sports medicine clinic, health club, or the national, state, or local dietetic association. *Refer to page* 580, "How to Find Nutrition Help."

Making Weight

For your peak performance, enter the competitive season at your best weight for your sport. Unless you train and compete year-round, this isn't the time to start to "make weight." Instead, being at your best weight all year should be your goal.

For some athletes, weight cycling is an issue. Those who weigh more during their off-season may want to drop a few pounds for training and competition. Others need to "bulk up," perhaps to train and compete in contact sports. If either one is true for you, what's the healthy, most effective approach to your best competitive weight?

Lose Fat, Not Muscle

Lose any extra body fat well before training and competition start. Achieve and maintain your healthy weight. That way you'll have energy and strength when you need it most.

Getting the Lean Advantage

Most important, start with a weight goal that's realistic and healthy for you. That's the weight that offers your best competitive edge.

The notion that you can never be too thin or too lean isn't true—and being so may compromise your physical performance. Body fat levels vary from athlete to athlete, sport to sport, and even for specific positions or events on a team. *The chart, "Body Fat Varies By Sport!" below shows percent body fat ranges for common sports.*

Body composition is best determined by experts with professional methods for measurement. For the sport of your choice, talk to a registered dietitian or exercise physiologist to target your healthy weight and percent body fat. *Refer to page* 580, "How to Find Nutrition Help."

If you need to drop a few pounds, make weight loss

Body Fat Varies By Sport!

	% Body Fat	
	Male	Female
Runners	4-9	6-15
Wrestlers	4-10	—
Gymnasts	4-10	10-17
Body builders	6-10	10-17
Swimmers	5-11	14-24
Basketball	7-11	18-27
Tennis	14-17	19-22

gradual: 1/2 to 1 pound a week. Cut back on your overall energy intake by about 250 to 500 calories a day, and exercise to step up your calorie expenditure. (*Hint*: 1 pound of body fat equals 3,500 calories.)

Lose weight on an eating plan that's varied, balanced, and moderate—following guidelines of the Food Guide Pyramid. *Refer to "The Athlete's Pyramid" on page* 542. Get most of your energy from complex carbohydrates; cut back on fatty foods. Besides having less energy, or calories, per gram than fat, carbohydrates are the fuel that working muscles need for peak performance.

Dieting alone isn't a good way for anyone to lose weight—especially an athlete. Unless you're physically active, you'll lose muscle along with body fat. Consider the ways that exercise aids weight loss. Besides using energy, exercise boosts your metabolic rate, or the rate your body uses energy. And the muscles you build by being more active use more energy than body fat does.

Be aware: A quick weight-loss regimen that's low in calories may interfere with your physical performance. You'll likely lose muscle, along with body fat, and you may deplete your stores of muscle glycogen. And depending on your approach, your weight loss may be partly water loss—a problem for athletes who need to be cautious of dehydration. *Refer to "'Diets' That Don't Work!" on page* 43.

For athletes whose weight continually cycles, there may be added risks. The "yo-yo" cycle of repeated weight gain and loss often results in muscle loss and more difficulty losing weight the next time around. Often a feeling of failure comes with the need to lose weight again and again; that may take away your "mental edge" for sports. As part of your off-season training program, learn how to maintain weight so you'll stay at the best weight for your sport. *Refer to "Weight Cycling: The 'Yo-Yo' Problem" on page* 30.

For guidelines to help you lose weight in a healthful way, refer to "Weight Management: Strategies That Work!" on page 29.

"Leanest" Isn't Always Better!

Athletes obsessed with a lean, thin body are at risk for eating disorders and all the dangers that accompany severe weight loss or compulsive eating and bingeing. For athletes, eating disorders may result in special health problems. The body may not sweat and cool down properly. The chance for dehydration goes up. And physical endurance is reduced. Most important, eating disorders can become life-threatening!

If you, someone you train with, or your child shows signs of an eating disorder, seek help. Talk to the person about your concern, as well as the family, friends, or the coach. A registered dietitian can also offer an expert perspective on eating disorders. *For more insight and guidance, refer to "Eating Disorders: Problems, Signs, and Help" on page* 42.

Compete in a Weight Category?

Wrestlers, weight lifters, boxers, body builders, and oarsmen know the importance of body weight. They compete in specific weight categories. And most want to be the largest competitor in a lower weight class. An extra pound or two may change their competition!

For good health and best performance, they need to maintain their optimal weight throughout the competitive season. That can be accomplished with a healthful eating plan and training.

The practice of sweating off pounds to make weight for wrestling—or any other sport—hinders performance. Because it leads to dehydration, losing as little as three or four pounds of "sweat" weight (6 to 8 cups of fluid) can be very dangerous to a 150-pound athlete.

Making weight by fasting, or drastically cutting back on food, isn't healthy either. And it keeps the athlete from storing muscle glycogen, needed to fuel training and competition.

Fasting keeps growing athletes from getting nutrients they need. Without sensible weight loss and management, an athlete might be in the same weight dilemma for the next competition—and the next and the next!

Gain Muscle, Not Fat

Hockey and football players are among those athletes whose physical performance benefits from extra body weight. Trying to "bulk up" too fast, however, may put more fat on your body than muscle—especially if you add calories without exercise. For athletes already involved in strenuous training, gaining weight may not be as easy at it sounds. They may use energy faster than they consume it!

To build muscle, you need strength-building activity, along with extra energy from food. Contrary to popular myth, you don't need more protein, just more energy from a variety of nutritious foods. *Refer to "Muscle Myths" on page* 539.

As with weight loss, the key to weight gain is "gradual and steady": perhaps one pound or so a week. To get the extra energy you need to support exercise and muscle building:

- Eat frequent, mini-meals.
- Increase portions at mealtime.
- Snack between meals.
- Get most of your extra energy from nutrient-dense, high-carbohydrate foods.
- As an extra meal or snack, try liquid meal supplements for convenient, high-carbohydrate nourishment.

For guidance on healthy weight gain, refer to "When You Want to Gain" on page 40.

Body Composition: Fit not Fat

For athletic performance, your body composition may be more important than your weight—unless you compete in a weight category. That's true even if you're not an athlete. Health risks go up as the proportion of body fat increases. A lean, muscular body has benefits beyond athletics and good looks—it's a quality of overall fitness.

For nonathletes, body fat levels of 15 to 18 percent for men, and 20 to 25 percent for women are considered acceptable. Body fat levels below 4 percent for men and 10 percent for women suggest an eating disorder. According to the Institute of Medicine, obesity is defined as more than 25 percent body fat for men and more than 30 percent for women.

What's healthy for athletes? Male athletes typically have body fat values of 5 to 12 percent; female athletes, 10 to 20 percent. The difference depends on the sport and it differs within a specific sport. *Refer to "Body Fat Varies By Sport!" on page* 547.

If you want to know your body composition, check with a trained health professional. Health professionals use specialized techniques, such as skinfold measurements, underwater weighing, and bioelectrical impedance (done with a computer). You can't get an accurate body fat measurement on your own.

For more about body composition, refer to "Body Weight Versus Body Fat" on page 19. ✦

The Game Plan

It's the day of the big event. You're excited—perhaps a bit anxious. You've trained hard. What should you eat to maximize your performance? Your "game plan" now—before, during, and after competition or a heavy workout—makes a difference.

For endurance events, think further ahead—before your pre-event meal. Several days beforehand, you might eat more carbohydrates and gradually rest your muscles. That way, you'll store extra muscle glycogen and won't tire as quickly during the event. *Refer to "Carbohydrate Loading" on page* 537.

In fact for any sport, eat for peak performance well ahead. Most energy for competition comes from foods you ate earlier in the week, not from your pre-event meal. For training, eat plenty of carbohydrates, moderate amounts of protein, and not much fat.

Remember: On competition day, even carefully-planned meals can't make up for a poor training diet. You need to eat with fitness in mind all along the way.

have you ever *wondered*

...if it's OK *to compete on an empty stomach?* You're better off eating. Research shows that food consumed within four hours of physical activity is used as fuel for working muscles. For morning events, eating is especially important for endurance. It replenishes liver glycogen and helps maintain your blood sugar level. So don't skip breakfast!

...what to eat before competition if you feel too nervous to eat? If you get pre-event jitters, a liquid meal supplement might help. It provides the nutrients and fluids needed for competition. And it might be more easily digested and absorbed than a full meal. Liquid meals also contribute fluids. ✦

Before You Compete...

Hungry before competition? Choose a pre-event meal that matches your physical performance goals. Your food choices should supply sufficient energy for your muscles. That way, you can perform to your ability without tiring too soon. Your meal should prevent the distraction of hunger pangs. And fluids should be enough to fully hydrate your body before strenuous exercise.

What you eat before competition is too important to leave to chance. So the pre-event meal that's best differs from athlete to athlete, and event to event.

Experiment ahead with different foods, food combinations, amounts, and timing. Remember, every athlete is different. Every sport is different. And the time of day you compete changes, too.

For your pre-event eating, keep these guidelines in mind:

Timing. Eat one to six hours before your workout or competition. The timing depends on your own preference. By eating ahead, food has time to digest, so you won't feel full. That helps avoid stomach discomfort, too.

What about a morning competition? Eat a hearty, high-carbohydrate dinner and bedtime snack. Then in the morning, eat a light, high-carbohydrate meal or snack to replenish your liver glycogen and satisfy any feelings of hunger.

Small meals. If you'll be eating between one and four hours before an event, choose a smaller meal. The amount depends on what makes you feel comfortable.

High "carbs." Enjoy a meal high in complex carbohydrates and fluids—and moderate in protein and low in fat. This type of meal (perhaps focusing on pasta, rice, potatoes, or bread) gets digested and absorbed faster than a meal that's high in protein and fat. The latter doesn't leave your stomach as quickly. So it may cause indigestion or nausea with heavy exercise. *Refer to "Pre-Event Meals—For Starters" on page* 551 *and "Carbo Foods" on page* 609.

There's no need to avoid all fat before competition, however. Just a little may make your meal taste better. Contrary to common belief, small amounts of fat in your food choices won't keep your body from storing muscle glycogen.

No discomfort. Skip foods that may cause intestinal discomfort. That includes high-fiber foods: raw fruits and vegetable with seeds and tough skin, bran, nuts, and seeds. Although very nutritious for other meals, gas-causing foods may cause discomfort during competition: for example, dried beans, cabbage, onions, cauliflower, and turnips.

Familiar foods. Enjoy familiar foods and beverages. This isn't the time to try something new. It just may disagree with you!

Enough fluids. Between 2 and 2 1/2 hours ahead, drink at least 2 cups of fluid. Then at about 15 minutes ahead, drink another 2 cups of fluids. And no, drinking milk before strenuous exercise does not cause "cotton mouth." Instead, stress and loss of body fluids often slow saliva flow, causing a dry mouth.

"Feel-good" foods. Food offers psychological benefits, too. If a certain food or meal seems to enhance your performance, enjoy it! Just be sure it doesn't detract from the overall nutritional quality of your pre-event meal.

During Competition...

Nourishment during physical activity depends on your sport.

During most activities, drinking plenty of fluids is the only real issue. Every 15 or so minutes, you're wise to drink 1/2 cup of fluids.

During endurance sports of 60 minutes or more, a high-carbohydrate drink or snack may help maintain blood sugar levels, and so may boost your stamina and enhance your performance. Often sports drinks are easier to digest, especially if you're involved in intense activity. And they count as fluids. Their flavor may encourage their consumption, too, especially among children. Whether you choose a sports drink or solid snack, perhaps orange slices, remember to drink 1/2 cup of fluid every 15 or so minutes!

During day-long events or regional tournaments, snack on high-carbohydrate, low-fat foods. Between matches, sets, or other competitive events, these foods are among the many good choices: crackers, bagels, rice cakes, orange slices, apples, bananas, and fruit bars. Bring snacks along so you don't need to rely on a concession stand. Consuming fluids all day long remain important.

After You Compete...

From an exercise standpoint, your cool-down routine is just as important as your warm-up. And what

Pre-event Meals—For Starters

There's no single menu prescribed for pre-event eating. But these three high-carbohydrate menus show what you might eat before you compete:

Meal #1	Meal #2	Meal #3
• 1 cup cereal • 1 banana • 8 oz. skim milk • 1 bagel with 1 tablespoon jelly • 3/4 cup cranberry juice	• 2 cups beef noodle soup • 6 crackers • 1 medium baked potato • 1 cup vegetable juice	• 2 pancakes with 2 tablespoons syrup • 1 cup nonfat yogurt • 1/2 cup strawberries • 1 cup apple juice
Calories		
630	620	625
Carbohydrate		
136 *grams*	116 *grams*	110 *grams*

you eat and drink after a workout is as important as your pre-event eating routine. Protect your health—and build your endurance for next time.

Make fluids your first priority! After competition or a heavy workout, you need to replace fluids lost through sweat. The amount depends on the weight you lose through exercise. That's easy to determine simply by weighing yourself before and after the event. The difference is your water weight. For every pound you lose, drink two cups of fluid. And continue to drink fluids throughout the day until you return to your pre-exercise weight.

What fluids are best? Drink fluids with carbohydrates, such as juice or sports drinks. They replace fluids and help your body replenish muscle glycogen. You might try plain water, milk, and watery foods, such a soup or watermelon, too. *Refer to "Food: A Water Source" on page 173.*

Refuel your muscles with carbohydrates. Within the first several hours after competition or a heavy workout, eat foods high in carbohydrate. For muscle glycogen recovery, the sooner you eat, the better.

For every pound of body weight, eat 1/2 gram of carbohydrate. For example, if you weigh 150 pounds, eat at least 75 grams of carbohydrate. That's easy to do with a high-carbohydrate meal. *For some high-carbohydrate foods, refer to "'Carbo' Foods" on page 609.*

If you don't feel hungry after heavy exercise, drink juice or a sports drink. They supply carbohydrates and fluids. But they shouldn't replace food; you still need the vitamins and minerals that carbohydrate-rich foods supply.

How about electrolytes? Through perspiration, you lose electrolytes, such as sodium. Because the average American diet supplies more than enough, enjoy your meal—and perhaps a sports drink after endurance sports. You'll get enough sodium and other electrolytes to replace your losses.

You don't need a salt tablet! It may cause cramping, dehydration, and stomach irritation. Concentrated amounts of salt cause the stomach to draw fluids from other parts of the body as they dilute the salt.

When You're on the Road

How do you keep physically active—or perhaps keep up a training regimen—when you travel? Plan ahead!

Pack comfortable clothes and footwear. Include any special equipment you need, such as workout clothes, a bathing suit, running shoes, or racquetball racket.

Choose a hotel with exercise equipment. Then make time to use it. Before you make your reservation, ask about the facilities: an indoor or outdoor pool, tennis courts, bicycle rentals, and gym equipment, such as a treadmill, step machine, or rowing machine.

If you belong to a health club at home, check ahead for membership benefits elsewhere.

Ask for an earlier wake-up call. That way, you can get a jump start on your day with a 30-minute walk or jog. Or instead, walk or jog at the end of the day. Get a local guidebook to map out your way.

Skip the taxicab. Walk to your business meeting in comfortable walking shoes. Use the stairs, rather than the elevator, at the hotel or workplace you visit.

Now, how do you eat for health on the road? *Refer to "Eating on the Road" on page 384.* ✦

Ergogenic Aids: No Substitute for Training

"Blast your body with energy!"..."Best muscle cell volumizers!"..."Guaranteed for fresh new muscle growth"..."Nutrition for faster muscle recovery and longer endurance!" You want to make the most of every workout and increase your competitive edge. But don't be lured by claims that ergogenic aids make a difference. "Ergogenic" means the potential to increase work output. Only proper training and all-out effort can do that!

Hundreds of ergogenic aids, often costly, are touted for their ability to improve strength, endurance, or recovery time. For example, amino acid supplements, bee pollen, brewer's yeast, carnitine, chromium picolinate, co-enzyme Q-10, creatine, kelp, lecithin, and wheat germ oil, as well as many herbs, have all been promoted for sports nutrition. Yet, their proclaimed benefits aren't backed by scientific evidence.

Perceived benefits of ergogenic aids are typically individual reports, not valid research. Or they simply may provide a placebo effect. A placebo may have a psychological, but not a physical, benefit. It's well documented that the side effects of many of these aids may be harmful or may interfere with performance.

Steroids are one type of ergogenic aid. Why is taking steroids for muscle building a concern? Muscle-building (or anabolic) steroids aren't nutrients or dietary supplements. Instead, they're powerful drugs. Steroids are synthesized to act like testosterone, which is a male sex hormone. While steroids can help build bigger muscles, physical performance won't necessarily improve. Their use also has dangerous side effects, which may be permanent. In men, steroids may cause acne, damage to the testes, enlarged breasts, and a lower sperm count. Used by women, steroids may cause masculine qualities: a lower voice, facial hair, smaller breasts, and loss of (or irregular) menstrual cycle. The use of steroids is banned by the International Olympic Committee.

Building muscle gradually through physical activity is still the healthy, time-honored approach! *For more information, refer to "Muscle Myths" on page 539. To learn about many specific ergogenic aids, refer to "Beyond Vitamins and Minerals: What's Known About Supplements?" on page 588.*

your nutrition check-up

Eat to Compete

Sports nutrition is filled with misconceptions—all based on the drive for top performance. As an athlete, are you tuned into the facts, or the myths?

True or False?

T F

❒ ❒ 1. If you train properly for sports, you don't need to worry as much about fluid replacements.

❒ ❒ 2. Vitamin supplements supply extra energy for heavy workouts.

❒ ❒ 3. A steak dinner is a great precompetition meal.

❒ ❒ 4. Fasting is a good approach for "making weight."

❒ ❒ 5. Except for football and other contact sports, the leaner you are, the better.

❒ ❒ 6. Drinking milk before a heavy workout causes stomach cramps.

❒ ❒ 7. Salt tablets prevent muscle cramps.

❒ ❒ 8. If you eat a lot of protein, you'll build a lot of muscle.

❒ ❒ 9. Bee pollen boosts your energy level and enhances physical performance.

Now Score Yourself

Do you eat smart to compete? Be aware that every statement above is false. For each true-false statement, these are the facts.

1. Fact: To avoid dehydration, everyone—even well-trained athletes—needs to drink plenty of water before, during, and after physical activity. Training does not protect you from dehydration!

2. Fact: Vitamins don't supply energy; carbohydrate, fat, and protein do. If you're already following the advice of the Food Guide Pyramid and eating enough servings to meet your energy needs, there's no reason for vitamin supplements. The small amount of extra vitamins—for example, B vitamins—you need to produce extra energy from carbohydrate, fat and protein comes from extra servings of food-group foods.

3. Fact: A high-carbohydrate meal is the best precompetition meal. It supplies the best fuel for working muscles. A steak dinner may taste great, but it's typically high in protein instead.

If steak gives you a "mental edge," enjoy a small portion. And eat plenty of carbohydrate-rich foods with it: baked potato, pasta, or rice; carrots; dinner roll; fruit salad; and frozen yogurt for dessert. *Refer to "Before You Compete..." on page* 550.

4. Fact: Fasting is never advised for athletes! It often causes fatigue, reduced glycogen stores, the potential for muscle loss, dehydration, and decreased performance. For athletes who are still growing, fasting keeps them from consuming nutrients essential to their development. *For more on healthful weight loss, refer to "Getting the Lean Advantage" on page* 547.

5. Fact: Yes, a lean, muscular body performs better. And being lean is healthier, too. But you can be too lean. *For the typical body composition, refer to "Body Fat Varies By Sport!" on page* 547.

Among its many functions, fat cushions body organs, providing protection from injury. For endurance sports, fat is converted to energy after glycogen stores are used. Being too lean may cause you to tire too quickly. And restricting energy intake too much to avoid body fat may create a deficiency of important nutrients.

6. Fact: Contrary to popular myth, drinking milk before physical exertion doesn't cause stomach discomfort or digestive problems. Over time, not consuming enough calcium—a key nutrient in milk—may contribute to muscle cramps instead. Whether or not you choose to drink milk before a heavy workout is a personal matter.

If you have trouble digesting milk, the problem might be lactose intolerance. If so, you can still drink milk as part of your training diet. *For guidance, see "Lactose Intolerance: A Matter of Degree" on page* 194.

7. Fact: It's not sodium loss, but instead severe water loss, that causes muscle cramps. Muscle cramps are a symptom of dehydration. You don't need salt tablets to replace the small amount of sodium you lose when you sweat. Your normal diet supplies enough.

8. Fact: Exercise, not a lot of extra protein, builds muscle mass. To build muscles, you need to work them more and gradually increase their work load. You may think of muscles as all protein. But actually 20 percent is protein, 70 percent is water, and 8 percent is fat.

Most athletes—even weight lifters—need about 1/2 to 3/4 gram of protein each day for every pound of body weight. That adds up to just 2 to 4 ounces more meat, chicken, or fish a day than the recommendation for nonathletes.

9. Fact: Like most other ergogenic aids, bee pollen appears to offer no benefit to athletic performance. Positive reports are individual reports. As sold, bee pollen is actually a mixture of bee saliva, plant nectar, and pollen. *Refer to "Ergogenic Aids: No Substitute for Training" on page* 553.

Although uncommon, some people may have a severe, or anaphylactic, reaction from taking bee pollen. *Refer to "Food Allergies: The Dangerous Side" on page* 204.

real life nutrition

Performance Counts

For Ursula, keeping in shape is a passion. And she loves the exhilaration of running a good race! Just about every workday, she fits in a long, strenuous workout, either running about eight miles at the nearby school track or working out at her health club. On weekends, she runs trails or goes bicycling. When she travels, her running shoes and workout clothes get packed right along with her briefcase.

Ursula gives plenty of attention to her workout—but less attention to the food that fuels her sports. "There's just no time. Besides, I'm too tired to cook after a busy workday and a strenuous workout. I just eat what's quick and easy—without too many calories, I think. I don't want to get fat."

But Ursula does want to make her performance count. Here's a typical day, with what she eats and how she works out.

6:45 am	1 bagel with 2 tablespoons cream cheese, 3/4 cup orange juice, 1 cup coffee
9:00 am	10-ounce coffee latte with whole milk
12:30 pm	*lunch from the deli*: turkey (3 ounces)-cheese (1 ounce) sandwich with sprouts, tomato, and mayonnaise (1 tablespoon) on whole-wheat bread; apple; 8 ounces seltzer water, 3 fig bars
2:45 pm	8 ounces seltzer water, 1 ounce peanuts
5:00 pm	granola bar
5:30-7:30 pm	*workout time*: 16 ounces water (She brings a water bottle.)
7:45 pm	16 ounces sports drink
9:00 pm	Commercially-frozen spaghetti and meatball dinner (12.5 ounces), 2 cups salad greens with 2 tablespoons salad dressing and 2 tablespoons Parmesan cheese, 2 slices garlic bread (flavored with 2 teaspoons olive oil and garlic powder), 8 ounces lemonade

	Her intake	**Target intake**
calories	2,800	2,800
% from carbs	51%	60 to 65%
% from protein	14%	10 to 15%
% from fat	35%	no more than 30%

Suggestions for a high-performance eating plan:

Although Ursula tries to follow a high-carbohydrate eating plan, she actually consumes more fat and less carbohydrate than she thinks. To hit her target intake, she might:

➢ Put jam on her breakfast bagel. Or perhaps choose a reduced fat or fat-free cream cheese.

➢ As an afternoon snack, she might nibble on pretzels rather than peanuts.

➢ As a Milk Group food, she might eat fat-free

or low-fat yogurt with lunch, and save the cheese for another day. At the deli, she likely doesn't have a choice of lower-fat cheese.

➢ Add more vegetables to her day's menu: perhaps carrot sticks for lunch and broccoli with dinner.

➢ Her salad dressing might be low-fat or fat-free, rather than regular, dressing.

So she doesn't tire as easily—and won't risk becoming dehydrated, Ursula might:

➢ Eat her granola bar two hours before her workout so it has time to digest and be absorbed before exercising. The carbohydrates can help keep her blood sugar level normal for her workout.

➢ Drink more fluids during the day, and especially right before, during, and after her workout. She might weigh herself before and after a workout to see how much fluid she needs to replace.

➢ Consider fruit juice as another option for fluid replacement after her workout when her body needs lots of glucose to replace what she's used during exercise.

➢ Adjust her workout schedule so she's not doing heavy physical activity every day. Her muscles need time to recover and replace muscle glycogen for endurance activity.

With a few changes, here's what her day's menu and workout schedule might look like instead:

6:45 am	1 bagel with 2 tablespoons jam, 3/4 cup orange juice, 1 cup coffee
9:00 am	10-ounce coffee latte with whole milk (She might choose low-fat or skim milk.)
12:30 pm	*lunch from the deli*: turkey (3 ounces) sandwich with sprouts, tomato, and mayonnaise (1 tablespoon) on whole-wheat bread; 1/2 cup raw carrot sticks; 1 ounce pretzels; apple; 8 ounces seltzer water, 3 fig bars
3:30 pm	granola bar, 8 ounces seltzer water
5:15 pm	8 ounces water
5:30-7:30 pm	*workout time, alternating hard days, easier days, and days off*: 24 ounces water (She brings a water bottle.)
7:45 pm	16 ounces sports drink or fruit juice
9:00 pm	Frozen spaghetti and meatballs (12.5 ounces), 2 cups salad greens with 2 table-spoons fat-free salad dressing and 2 tablespoons Parmesan cheese, 1 cup broccoli, 2 slices garlic bread (flavored with 2 teaspoons olive oil and garlic powder), 16 ounces lemonade

	Her intake	Target intake
calories	2,800	2,800
% from carbs	65%	60 to 65%
% from protein	14%	10 to 15%
% from fat	21%	no more than 30%

CHAPTER TWENTY-TWO

THE VEGETARIAN WAY

Vegetable-pasta salad. Polenta topped with homemade tomato sauce and freshly-grated Parmesan cheese. Bean burritos. Portobello mushroom sandwich, layered with stir-fried onions and peppers. Split-pea soup with rye bread. Veggie-cheese pizza. Barley-cheese stuffed peppers.

Today's cookbooks, magazines, and restaurant menus are full of vegetarian dishes created with nutritious and flavorful food combinations.

Whether you choose a vegetarian eating style or not, these dishes can offer food variety, interest, and perhaps a brand new taste experience.

Although vegetarian eating has been around throughout recorded history, in recent years, interest in this eating style has gone up dramatically. According to surveys, almost 7 percent of adult Americans called themselves vegetarians in the 1990s. That compares to about 4 percent in the 1960s.

Being Vegetarian

To some, being a vegetarian is a way of eating. For others, it's a whole lifestyle. And some simply enjoy the flavors and food variety in vegetarian meals—on a regular basis or as an occasional switch from their everyday fare. So just what does it mean to be a vegetarian?

What Type?

In its broadest definition, being "vegetarian" means eating no meat, poultry, and fish. Instead, plant sources of food—grains, legumes, nuts, vegetables, and fruits—form the basis of the diet.

As a matter of choice, many vegetarians also eat dairy products, and perhaps eggs. Others avoid meat, but eat fish or poultry—at least occasionally. Among today's "new vegetarians," only a small percent completely avoid foods of animal origin.

If you're a vegetarian, you may describe yourself in one of these ways:

Lacto-ovo-vegetarian, who chooses a diet with eggs and dairy products, but no meat, poultry, and fish. Most vegetarians in the United States fit within this group. The prefix "lacto" refers to milk; "ovo" refers to eggs.

Lacto-vegetarian, who avoids meat, poultry, fish, and eggs, but eats dairy products.

Strict vegetarian, or vegan (VEE-*gahn or* VEHJ-*ahn*), who follows an eating plan with no animal products: no meat, poultry, fish, eggs, milk, cheese, and other dairy products.

Vegans avoid foods with animal products as ingredients, too: for example, refried beans made with lard, baked goods made with butter or eggs, or perhaps margarine made with whey or milk solids. Vegans also may avoid honey, which is made by bees.

Semi-vegetarian, who mostly follows a vegetarian eating pattern and only occasionally eats meat, poultry, or fish.

Why Vegetarian?

There are many ways to eat vegetarian style. And there are many reasons cited for doing so.

With today's focus on fitness, many people follow a vegetarian eating style for health reasons. Others cite concerns about the environment, compassion for animals, or their belief in nonviolence. Religious, spiritual, or ethical reasons make vegetarianism a lifestyle for some. Still others simply prefer the flavors and food mixtures of vegetarian dishes. Or perhaps they recognize that a plant-based diet can cost less.

The reasons people become vegetarians influence their food choices. For example, people who become vegetarians for philosophical or religious reasons may be very strict about avoiding foods of animal origin. While those seeking health benefits or cost savings may eat meat, poultry, or fish occasionally—in small amounts.

have you ever wondered

...if "vegetarian" on a food label means "low-fat," too? No, it doesn't. Foods labeled as "vegetarian" on their package labeling—and on restaurant menus—may contain high-fat ingredients. Foods that can be higher in fat include textured soy patties and hot dogs, soy cheese, refried beans, and snack bars. You'll want to read the Nutrition Facts panel on food labels to find out.

...if a macrobiotic diet is healthful? No. A macrobiotic diet doesn't follow two basic principles of healthy eating: food variety and balance. It gradually eliminates food categories and restricts fluids. Ultimately a macrobiotic diet supplies only certain grains and small amounts of fluid. As a result, this eating style is deficient in many essential nutrients and can lead to dehydration, which may be life-threatening. To dispel a myth, a macrobiotic diet won't cure cancer. ✦

Health Benefits?

Both vegetarian and nonvegetarian eating styles can be healthful—or detrimental to your health. The nutrition bottom line depends on your food choices over time.

With the focus on grain products, legumes, vegetables, and fruits, vegetarian diets typically are low in fat and high in fiber. That's a goal consistent with the Dietary Guidelines for Americans. In fact, eating a vegetarian diet can be an easy way to follow the advice for healthful eating. *Refer to "A Glimpse at the Dietary Guidelines" on page 5.*

Studies show a positive link between vegetarian eating and health. In general, heart disease, high blood pressure, adult-onset diabetes, obesity, and some forms of cancer tend to develop less often among vegetarians than nonvegetarians. Vegetarians also appear to be at lower risk for osteoporosis, kidney stones, gallstones, and breast cancer.

Food choices may not be the only reason for these health benefits, however. Vegetarians often make other lifestyle choices that promote health: for example, regular physical exercise and not smoking.

Being vegetarian doesn't necessarily ensure a healthful eating style. Poorly planned, the chance for some nutritional deficiencies goes up. And like any way of eating, a vegetarian eating style also can be high in fat and cholesterol, low in fiber, or both.

The nutritional content of a vegetarian diet depends on overall food choices over several days.

For more about fat and fiber, refer to chapter 3, "Fat Facts," and chapter 6, "Fiber: Your Body's Broom."

Vegetarian Diets: Nutritionally Speaking

Can vegetarian eating supply your body with enough nutrients? Yes. As with any eating style, you need to choose foods carefully—and consume enough food energy, or calories.

If you're a vegetarian who consumes dairy products and perhaps eggs, the nutrition issues you need to address don't differ much from those of nonvegetarians. You still need to be cautious of too much fat, saturated fat, and cholesterol—even too many calories—and you're wise to consume moderate amounts of sugars, sodium, and salt. If you choose mostly lower-fat dairy products, along with plenty of grains, vegetables, and fruits, a typical lacto-ovo-vegetarian diet can be high in fiber and low in total fat, saturated fat, and cholesterol. That's a nutrition goal for all healthy people!

Vegans need to address somewhat different nutrition issues. Without any foods of animal origin, getting enough calories to maintain a healthy weight can be a challenge, especially for growing children and teens. And nutrients that may come up short need special attention: vitamin B_{12}, vitamin D, calcium, iron, and zinc. Nonetheless, planned wisely, a vegan diet can provide enough nutrients for overall good health, too.

Protein Power

For most vegetarians, adequate protein is not an issue. Except for fruit, almost every food of plant origin contains protein—at least a small amount. Concerns about protein arise because vegetarians usually don't eat meat, poultry, or fish—and perhaps no eggs or dairy foods. Foods of animal origin are concentrated protein sources. But legumes, nuts, seeds, grain products, and vegetables all contain protein, too.

Because protein is abundant in plant foods, vegetarian meals and snacks usually can supply enough proteins—and their building blocks, called amino acids. Just eat many different foods with protein throughout the day to get the full variety of amino acids.

More About Protein...
Protein is often referred to as a single nutrient. Yet, proteins in food and in your body cells are made up of 20 different amino acids. Like carbohydrate and fat, amino acids are composed of carbon, hydrogen, and oxygen. But proteins have nitrogen, too, which makes their structure and role in health unique.

How proteins are made. Nine amino acids are con-

Not Just for Vegetarians... Quick and Healthful Snacks

popcorn	dairy or soy yogurt
pretzels	cottage cheese
crackers	muffins
oatmeal cookies	sunflower and pumpkin seeds
fresh fruit	dried fruit
peanuts	fruit shakes
fruit juice	raw vegetables*
fruit leather	tomato juice
crackers and cheese	trail mix
bean tacos or burritos	cheese and veggie pizza
bagels and peanut butter	focaccia bread (with or without cheese)
hummus (mashed chickpea dip) with pita points	milk or soy milk (calcium-fortified)

*See "Vegetables: From A to Z" on page 250.

sidered essential. Because your body can't make them, your food choices must supply them. Their names may sound familiar: histidine, isoleucine, leucine, lysine, methionine, phenylalanine, threonine, tryptophan, and valine. You might see some—perhaps phenylalanine and tryptophan—on food labels.

Other amino acids are nonessential. Your body makes them—if you consume enough essential amino acids and enough calories during the day.

Amino acids are described as protein's "building blocks." Like notes in a music scale or letters of the alphabet, they're arranged in countless ways. The same music notes create symphonies, jazz, and pop hits. And the same 26 alphabet letters form thousands of words in many languages, each word with its own meaning. It's the same for amino acids. In a single cell of your body, 10,000 different proteins may exist—each with a different arrangement of amino acids.

To get their meaning, words must be spelled correctly. And amino acids in proteins must be arranged in a precise order to function normally. The genetic code in every cell—called DNA, or deoxyribonucleic acid—carries the instructions for "spelling" each protein.

What protein does. As a nutrient, protein performs many functions. For one, protein is part of every body cell. Your body's different tissues—skin, muscles, bone, and organs, for example—are unique because the amino acid patterns in their proteins differ. Your body needs a constant supply of protein to repair body cells as they wear out. During times of growth—infancy, childhood, adolescence, and pregnancy—the body needs protein to make new body tissues.

Beyond that, proteins help regulate body processes. For example, as enzymes and hormones, they make various chemical reactions happen. As antibodies, they protect you from disease-carrying bacteria and viruses.

Proteins also supply your body with energy if you don't consume enough from carbohydrate and fat. Otherwise, protein can be saved for its unique function: to build and repair body tissue. When you consume more protein than you need, it's broken down and stored as body fat, not as a reserve supply of protein.

Where protein comes from. Meat, poultry, fish, eggs, milk, cheese, yogurt, and soy provide all nine essential amino acids. For that reason, they're often referred to as "complete" proteins.

Legumes (beans and peas), seeds, and nuts supply plenty of protein, too. In smaller amounts, so do grain products and many vegetables.

Completing the Equation

For the body to make its many proteins, your food choices must supply essential amino acids—in sufficient amounts. Animal proteins supply them all, in proportions needed to make new body proteins. Except for soybeans, plant proteins lack one or more essential amino acids. That's why their protein is often called "incomplete." When your meals and snacks provide a variety of foods, you get all the amino acids your body needs.

To obtain complete protein, there's no need for combining specific foods at each meal, as once thought. Your body makes its own complete proteins if you eat a variety of plant foods—legumes, nuts, seeds, grains, vegetables, and fruits—and enough calories throughout the day. Whatever amino acid one food lacks can come from other foods you eat during the day. *The general guideline: Follow the advice of the "Vegetarian Food Guide" on page 572.*

have you ever wondered

...what wheat gluten is, and how it's used in cooking? Wheat gluten, also known as seitan, is wheat protein. It has a chewy, meaty texture, making it a good, protein-rich ingredient in casseroles, soups, pasta sauces, and other recipes calling for chopped or ground meat or poultry. Look for wheat gluten in specialty stores. *Caution*: People with gluten intolerance should avoid wheat gluten. *Refer to "Gluten Intolerance...Often a Lifelong Condition" on page 197.* ✦

Vitamin B_{12}: A Challenge for Vegans

Like other B vitamins, vitamin B_{12}, also called cobalamin, has a host of jobs in your body. For example, it helps your body make red blood cells and use fats and amino acids, and serves as part of every body cell! Over time, a deficiency of vitamin B_{12} can cause anemia and severe, irreversible nerve damage.

Unlike some nutrients, vitamin B_{12} doesn't make much health news, perhaps because it's so widely available in foods of animal origin. With few exceptions, it's not a concern for most vegetarians who consume dairy products or eggs.

For vegans, however, vitamin B_{12} is a nutrition concern. Plants only supply this nutrient when soil with vitamin B_{12}- producing microorganisms clings to fruits and vegetables and isn't removed completely before eating. In the United States, fruits and vegetables are scrubbed clean; they usually have no soil with these microorganisms on them. Most vegans need to look elsewhere for a reliable source of vitamin B_{12} :

- ➢ Look for breakfast cereals, soy milk products, or vegetarian burger patties that are fortified with vitamin B_{12}. Or consider a vitamin B_{12} supplement. Read the Nutrition Facts panel on food and supplement labels to check the vitamin B_{12} content. And know that "cyanocobalamin" is its most bioavailable form. In other words, it's the form the body absorbs easily.

- ➢ If you choose a supplement, don't take more than 100 percent of the Recommended Dietary Allowance (RDA) for vitamin B_{12}. *For more about the* RDAs, *refer to* "Nutrients: How Much?" *on page* 4.

- ➢ Be aware that seaweed, algae, spirulina, and fermented plant foods such as tempeh and miso aren't good sources of vitamin B_{12}—even if the package says so. The vitamin $B_{12}$is not in a form that the human body can use. Vitamin B_{12} in beer and other fermented foods isn't reliable either.

- ➢ Know that nutritional yeast can be a source of vitamin B_{12}—if it's grown on a medium that's enriched with vitamin B_{12}. However, the yeast typically used in baking doesn't supply any. Check the label to find out. Don't count on yeast to supply any vitamin B_{12} unless you've checked it out.

For more about vitamin B_{12}, *refer to page* 87.

People around the world have lots in common, including a high-protein food combination: rice and beans. For fun, can you match the vegetarian dish with the place where it's most popular?

1. tomato and herb-seasoned rice with refried beans	**a. Cuba**
2. pigeon peas and rice (gunga)	**b. Italy**
3. rice with black beans	**c. Saudi Arabia**
4. black-eyed peas and rice	**d. China**
5. herbed arborio rice with peas (risotto)	**e. Mexico**
6. curried lentils and basmati rice	**f. Bahamas**
7. stir-fried tofu (soybean cakes) over steamed rice	**g. India**
8. lentils and rice, seasoned with cumin, onion, and lemon (mujadarah)	**h. West Africa, Caribbean, southern U.S.**
9. kidney beans and rice, flavored with smoked meat and seasonings (pois et ris)	**i. Colombia**
10. kidney beans and rice, flavored with shredded coconut (ochos rios)	**j. Haiti**

Answers:
1-e; 2-f; 3-a; 4-h; 5-b; 6-g; 7-d; 8-c; 9-j; 10-i

Vitamin D: Not Just From Sunshine!

Vitamin D works as a nutrient partner, helping your body absorb calcium and phosphorus, then deposit them in bones and teeth. Few foods are naturally high in vitamin D. So, in the United States, milk is vitamin D-fortified to help people get enough. Egg yolks also supply smaller amounts. And your body also makes its own vitamin D when your skin is exposed to sunlight.

Vitamin D isn't an issue if you drink milk—or for you're regularly exposed to sunlight. Vegans, however, need to be careful to get enough vitamin D, especially during the winter in northern climates and if housebound. Infants who breast-feed longer than six months without consuming a vitamin D supplement or who aren't exposed to sunlight are at risk, too.

> If you're a vegan, check the Nutrition Facts on food labels for sources: some breakfast cereals and soy beverages are fortified with vitamin D.

> If you're in doubt, talk to your doctor or a registered dietitian (RD) about taking a vitamin D supplement. Be sure that the supplement supplies no more than 100 percent of the Recommended Dietary Allowance (RDA) per day. Larger doses can be dangerous and should be avoided.

For more about vitamin D, refer to page 82. For more about vitamin D and older adults, refer to "Vitamin D: The Sunshine Vitamin" on page 510.

Calcium: Getting Enough

Calcium—you know it best as a bone builder. But calcium also helps your muscles contract, transfers nerve impulses, helps your blood clot, helps your heart beat, and for kids, builds healthy teeth. If you're a vegetarian, how can you consume enough?

Vegetarians who consume dairy products have excellent calcium sources built into their daily intake: milk, cheese, and yogurt. Eating two to three servings from the Milk, Yogurt, and Cheese Group daily contributes much of the calcium advised by the Dietary Reference Intakes—at least for many adults.

Vegans, too, can get enough calcium from plant foods alone. But it may take more planning. Perhaps, as some studies suggest, vegans may not need as much either. This may be because vegetarians seem to absorb and retain more calcium from food. The typically high-protein diet of nonvegetarians may actually decrease calcium absorption and increase its excretion through urine. Vegetarians also have lower rates of osteoporosis, or brittle bone disease. Factors besides calcium in their food choices may play a part. *Refer to "Osteoporosis: Reduce the Risks" on page 496.*

Which foods of plant origin supply calcium?

> Try tofu processed with calcium, calcium-fortified soy beverages, broccoli, seeds (sunflower seeds), nuts, legumes, some greens (kale, collards, mustard greens), okra, rutabaga, bok choy, dried figs, tortillas (made from lime-processed corn), and calcium-fortified orange juice and breakfast cereal. *For specific amounts, refer to "Counting Up Calcium" on page 107.*

> Beet greens, rhubarb, spinach, Swiss chard, and a grain called amaranth supply calcium, too—but your body cannot use it. These foods also contain oxalates that bind calcium, blocking its absorption. Some grain products also contain small amounts of calcium, but they

have you ever wondered

...if you need nutrient supplements when you eat vegetarian-style? Maybe and maybe not—if you choose your foods carefully. Lacto-ovo-vegetarians probably don't, as long as they consume enough iron from plant sources of food. Vegans, however, may need extra calcium, iron, zinc, and vitamins B_{12} and D, depending on their overall food choices. Consult a registered dietitian and doctor if you think you might need a nutrient supplement. *Refer to "Multi-Vitamin/Mineral Supplements: Who Benefits?" on page 112.* ✦

may contain phytates that block calcium absorption.

For more about calcium for health, refer to "Calcium: A Closer Look" *on page* 105. *And for food preparation tips, refer to* "Calcium Boosters" *on page* 346.

Iron—Make the Most of It!

Because it often comes up short, iron needs special attention, especially by growing children and women of child-bearing age. That's true whether you're a vegetarian or not. Among other reasons, your body needs iron as part of the complex process of energy production. If you don't get enough, you'll likely feel fatigued, and you may develop iron-deficiency anemia.

What are the iron-related issues for vegetarians? Foods of plant origin certainly contain iron, called non-heme iron. But it's not absorbed as well as heme iron in meat and other foods of animal origin. So the challenge for vegetarians is this: Improve the absorption of non-heme iron from food—easy, if you know how.

➢ Start by consuming plant sources of food that contain iron: legumes; iron-fortified cereals and breads, especially whole-wheat breads; whole-grain products; tofu; some dark-green leafy vegetables (such as spinach and beet greens); seeds; prune juice; dried fruit; as well as blackstrap molasses. *For specific amounts of iron, refer to* "Counting Up Iron" *on page* 110.

➢ Include a vitamin C-rich food at every meal. Vitamin C-rich foods, such as citrus fruits or juices, broccoli, tomatoes, and green pepper, help your body absorb iron from plant sources of food. *For a list of vitamin C-rich fruits and vegetables, refer to* "Produce 'Package'" *on page* 97.

➢ If you're a semi-vegetarian, eating a little meat, poultry, and fish helps your body absorb non-heme iron from plant sources of food.

➢ If you cook foods in iron pots and skillets, some iron from the pot may pass into food. That's especially true when ingredients are high in acid, such as tomatoes, and when you simmer foods (such as soups and stew) for a while.

For more about iron, refer to "Iron: A Closer Look" *on page* 109.

Zinc: Not to Overlook

Zinc, a mineral, is essential for growth, repairing body cells, and energy production. And it's part of more than 70 enzymes that control your body processes. Without meat, poultry, and seafood, zinc may come up short in a vegetarian diet.

For lacto-ovo-vegetarians, milk, cheese, yogurt, and eggs all supply zinc. In addition, many foods of plant origin contain zinc—but less than animal foods. Most vegetarian diets supply enough zinc. But follow these tips to be sure:

➢ Eat a variety of foods with zinc: whole-wheat bread; whole grains, especially the germ and bran; legumes; tofu; seeds; and nuts in amounts recommended for health. Be aware that grains lose zinc when they're processed to make refined flour. And substances in plant sources, such as fiber and phytates, can inhibit zinc absorption.

➢ Be cautious of zinc supplements, which can have harmful side effects in high dosages. If your doctor or registered dietitian recommends a supplement, stick with a vitamin-mineral combination with 100 percent or less of the Recommended Dietary Allowance (RDA) for zinc.

For more about zinc, refer to page 104.

Throughout the Life Cycle...

People of any age might choose a vegetarian way of eating. Depending on the stage of life, the nutrition issues differ.

For help in planning for nutritious vegetarian eating, consult a registered dietitian. Some specialize in vegetarian nutrition. Getting sound nutrition advice is especially important during pregnancy, breast-feeding, or recovery from illness, and for times of growth (infancy, childhood, and adolescence). *Refer to "How to Find Nutrition Help" on page 580.*

The Vegetarian "Mom"

Pregnancy and breast-feeding require more nutrients and calories to support the increased needs of both mother and baby. Whether you're a vegetarian or not, plan your food choices carefully if you're a mom-to-be.

If you've already mastered the skills, vegetarian eating—including a vegan diet—can provide the nourishment you need for a healthy, full-term pregnancy. But if vegetarian eating is new to you, seek nutrition advice from a registered dietitian.

Reminder: Good nutrition during pregnancy and breast-feeding is important for mother and baby. When a mother puts herself at nutritional risk, her baby's development may be affected, too.

Follow these nutrition tips for a healthy pregnancy and nursing...the vegetarian way:

Keep tabs on weight gain during your pregnancy. For vegetarian and nonvegetarian women, pregnancy requires about 300 extra calories a day; breast-feeding, about 500 calories more. If you don't consume enough energy during pregnancy, you may not gain enough weight to sustain the development of the fetus. As a result, your baby may be born with a low birthweight. Healthy weight gain for a full-term pregnancy is 25 to 35 pounds. If you don't consume enough calories while nursing, your body may not produce enough breast milk.

For enough calcium, eat at least four servings of calcium-rich foods daily. If you consume dairy products, getting enough calcium for pregnancy and breast-feeding is easy. Just add one or two more Milk Group servings to an already healthful diet. *If you're a vegan, refer to "Calcium: Getting Enough" on page 564 for more about plant sources of calcium.* A calcium supplement may be advised for you, too.

Babies need calcium for developing bones and teeth. If you don't consume enough calcium during pregnancy and breast-feeding, you'll give up some calcium stores in your bones. In the long run, you may be at greater risk for bone disease as you get older.

During pregnancy and breast-feeding, you need more vitamin D, too, to help absorb calcium. Milk is fortified with vitamin D. If you're a vegan, you may need a vitamin D supplement. Or about 20 to 30 minutes of direct sunlight on your hands and face two to three times weekly may be enough for your body to produce an adequate amount of vitamin D.

Consult your doctor or a registered dietitian about an iron supplement. Most pregnant women—vegetarians and nonvegetarians—are advised to take an iron supplement. If you take a supplement, follow the recommended dosage. Too much iron can interfere with zinc absorption, putting your newborn at risk for a zinc deficiency.

For vegans, consume a reliable source of vitamin B_{12}—perhaps fortified breakfast cereals or a vitamin B_{12} supplement. You need more during pregnancy for the developing fetus and your own increased blood supply. If your diet doesn't supply enough vitamin B_{12} during pregnancy and nursing, your baby may be at greater risk for anemia and nerve damage.

As a precaution, make sure you get enough folic acid prior to and during pregnancy to avoid neural tube (spinal cord) defects in the fetus. Many plant sources of food are good sources of folic acid: leafy vegetables, legumes, some fruits, wheat germ, yeast breads, and some fortified cereals. Although vegetarians usually consume more folic acid than non-vegetarians, a folate (folic acid) supplement still may be advised. Consult your doctor or registered dietitian.

For more about nutrition during pregnancy and breast-feeding, refer to "Congratulations! You're Expecting a Baby!" *on page* 459 *and* "For Those Who Breast-Feed..." *on page* 469.

Feeding Vegetarian Kids

Are your kids vegetarians? Like all children and teens, they need enough food variety and energy, or calories, for their growth, energy, and health. Chosen carefully, a vegetarian eating style can fuel their rapid growth and provide for their relatively high nutrient needs.

For the voracious appetites of many children and teens, getting enough calories may seem easy enough. Yet, many vegetarian meals are low in fat and high in fiber. So they fill kids up without supplying enough calories. Vegan diets can be especially "bulky," yet be low in energy.

What happens when children and teens don't consume enough energy from food? Their bodies use protein from food for energy, not for growing new body cells. An energy deficiency can retard their growth and impair their brain function.

To meet the demands of growth, include higher-calorie foods in your child's or teen's vegetarian meals and snacks. Provide some foods with more fat, such as nuts, peanut butter, and cheese. And encourage frequent snacks that provide nutrients, as well as food energy. A peanut butter sandwich and milk, for example, makes a healthful snack. *For other snack ideas, refer to* "Not Just for Vegetarians...Quick and Healthful Snacks" *on page* 561.

Lacto-ovo-vegetarians generally can get enough nutrients from their food choices alone. But for vegan infants, children, and teens, some nutrients may need special attention: calcium, iron, zinc, vitamin B_{12}, and vitamin D. If your child is a vegan, make sure you offer a variety of foods with adequate amounts of these nutrients. *For guidance, refer to* "Vegetarian Diets: Nutritionally Speaking" *on page* 561.

Infants who are breast-fed for longer than six months are at risk for iron and vitamin D deficiencies. That's true whether mom is a vegetarian or not. For a baby's increased needs at this time, iron-fortified cereal or iron supplements, and perhaps a vitamin D supplement may be recommended.

Health advice: If your infant, child, or teen follows a vegetarian eating style, consult a registered dietitian, your doctor, or a pediatric nurse for support and nutrition counseling. For vegans, ask about the need for nutrient supplements.

For more about feeding infants, children, and teens, refer to chapter 16, "Off to a Healthy Start," *and chapter* 17, "Food to Grow On."

Vegetarian Fare for Older Adults

Does grandpa or great-grandma prefer a vegetarian eating style? If so, his or her nutrition concerns are

have you ever wondered

...*if soy milk is a good substitute for cow's milk for children?* You need to check the Nutrition Facts on the food label. The calcium content of soy milk varies. Some are calcium-fortified, but not all. Cow's milk also supplies other nutrients that growing children need, including riboflavin (vitamin B_2) and vitamin D. Make sure their food choices supply enough of these nutrients, too.

...*if it's OK for your teenager to control weight with a vegetarian diet?* Yes, if his or her food choices are varied and balanced—and if he or she achieves and maintains a healthy weight. However, when vegetarian eating results in too much weight loss, it may be a symptom of an eating disorder. Eating disorders can be harmful to health—even life threatening. If that happens, seek professional help. *Refer to* "Eating Disorders: Problems, Signs, and Help" *on page* 42. ✦

similar to those of other older adults and vegetarians overall.

Vegetarian menus can be easy to prepare—with foods that also match the food preferences of nonvegetarians around your dinner table.

BREAKFAST

- 1 cup oatmeal with 2 tablespoons sliced almonds, 2 tablespoons raisins, and 2 tablespoons wheat germ
- 1 cup skim milk or calcium-fortified soy milk
- 2 slices whole-wheat toast with jelly
- 3/4 cup orange juice

LUNCH

- 1 cup lentil soup
- mixed green salad with tomatoes and low-fat dressing
- carrot and green pepper sticks with salsa
- 1 whole-grain muffin
- water with fresh lemon

SNACK

- 1 medium apple
- 2 graham crackers

DINNER

- 1/2 cup marinated bean salad (kidney, garbanzo, and green beans)
- 1 cup cooked pasta tossed with 1 teaspoon each olive oil, garlic, and basil, with a sprinkling of Parmesan cheese
- 1/2 cup stewed okra with tomatoes
- 3/4 cup steamed broccoli with lemon juice
- 1 slice Italian bread
- 1/2 cup fresh fruit salad
- flavored sparkling water

SNACK

- bagel with jam or peanut butter

Two nutrients need special attention for older adults on vegetarian diets: vitamin D and vitamin B_{12}. Those confined to the house without exposure to sunlight may be deficient in vitamin D, unless they drink milk. With age, the body may not absorb vitamin B_{12} efficiently either. That's especially a concern for vegetarians who don't have a reliable source of vitamin B_{12}. Eating foods fortified with vitamin B_{12} or taking a supplement can prevent vitamin B_{12} deficiency.

In later years, people are at greater risk for some health problems if they don't get the variety of nutrients they need. *Use the "Vegetarian Food Guide" on page 572 as a guideline for variety, balance, and moderation.*

Elderly people, especially those recovering from illness, need to be cautious if they choose a vegan diet. *Refer to chapter 20, "Nutrition for Older Adults."*

"Vegging Out" the Healthful Way!

Planned carefully, a vegetarian eating style can promote good health. For healthful vegetarian eating...

- ➢ Get enough calories to meet energy needs. That's especially important during childhood, the teen years, pregnancy, and breast-feeding.
- ➢ Consume a variety of foods from the five food groups of the Food Guide Pyramid: plant-based foods (legumes, nuts, seeds, grains, fruits, and vegetables) and unless you're a vegan, dairy foods and eggs.
- ➢ Go easy on high-fat foods and those from the Pyramid tip (fats, oils, and sweets), even if they do come from plant sources.
- ➢ For vegans, consume a reliable source of vitamin B_{12}, such as fortified breakfast cereal or soy milk.

Follow the Food Guide

For your good health, take the advice of the Dietary Guidelines for Americans. It's meant for vegetarians and nonvegetarians alike.

To put the Dietary Guidelines into a plan of action, the Food Guide Pyramid can be adapted for vegetarian eating. *The "Vegetarian Food Guide" on page 572 shows how to get the variety of nutrients your body needs for your overall health and energy.* As an adult, try to consume at least the minimum number of food group servings that are recommended for a day.

For an explanation of the Dietary Guidelines for Americans, refer to "A Glimpse at the Dietary Guidelines" on page 5.

Vegetarian Way: Bread, Cereal, Rice, and Pasta

As for nonvegetarians, eat at least six servings of breads, cereals, rice, or pasta each day. *For tips, refer to "Pyramid Pointers" on page 247.*

Choose whole-grain products whenever you can—at least three servings per day. That includes whole-wheat bread, breakfast cereal, and pasta; brown rice; and other whole-grain products. *Refer to "What Is a Whole Grain?" on page 144.* Besides the complex carbohydrate and fiber they provide, whole-grains supply iron and zinc, too.

Make grain dishes the centerpiece of your menu, perhaps tabouli, barley, rice pilaf, risotto, rice or noodle dishes, gnocchi, and polenta. Add interest to vegetarian meals with a greater variety of breads, including focaccia, bagels, tortillas, pita bread, chapatis, and naan. And try breads made with a variety of grains: oats, rye, and cornmeal, to name a few. *Tip:* Because of their processing method, some corn tortillas supply calcium. Check the label.

Add cooked grains to all kinds of foods. For example, stuff vegetables (eggplant, bell peppers, cabbage, and zucchini) with cooked grain mixtures: rice, oats, and barley, among others. Blend cooked grains with shredded vegetables and perhaps tofu for vegetable patties or croquettes. Toss cooked grains (not just rice or noodles) with stir-fried vegetables. And add bulgur, barley, and other cooked grains to soups, stews, and chili.

Choose fortified breakfast cereals. Read the Nutrition Facts panel on food labels for added nutrients, including iron, vitamin B_{12}, and zinc.

Vegetarian Way: Vegetables

Aim for at least four daily servings of vegetables. To compare, nonvegetarians are urged to consume three to five Vegetable Group servings daily from the Food Guide Pyramid.

For everyone—especially vegans—choose vegetables that are good sources of calcium: dark green leafy vegetables (such as kale, mustard, collard, or turnip greens), bok choy, and broccoli. Dark green leafy vegetables also supply iron.

Choose vegetables that are high in vitamin C, for example, broccoli, tomatoes, and green pepper. Vitamin C helps your body absorb iron in plant sources of food. *For the vitamin C content of some vegetables, refer to "Vitamin C: More Than Citrus" on page 90.*

Plan meals with several different vegetables. That way, you get the nutritional benefits of variety.

For ways to include more vegetables in your eating plan, refer to "Fruits and Vegetables: Count Five a Day!" on page 96 and "Pyramid Pointers" on page 247.

Vegetarian Way: Fruits

Include at least three servings of fruit each day. To compare, nonvegetarians are urged to consume two to four Fruit Group servings daily from the Food Guide Pyramid.

Enjoy a variety of fruits, including a good food source of vitamin C, such as citrus fruits, melons, and berries. *For the amount of vitamin C in various fruits, refer to "Vitamin C: More Than Citrus" on page 90.*

To get enough fruit, serve it for dessert and snacks—either as fresh, whole, or sliced fruit, or prepared in cobblers, as ice-cream toppers, or in thick, fruity shakes.

Look for calcium-fortified juice as an added source of calcium—especially for vegans.

For ways to include more fruits in your eating plan, refer to

"Fruits and Vegetables: Count Five a Day!" on page 96 and "Pyramid Pointers" on page 251.

Vegetarian Way: Legumes and Other Meat Alternates

Include two to three servings of legumes and other meat alternates every day. These foods supply protein and iron, as meat, poultry, and fish do for non-vegetarians. Except for eggs, meat alternates are low in total fat and saturated fat, and they have no cholesterol.

Make legumes a mealtime regular—eat them most days of the week. Besides their contribution of protein, legumes are good sources of complex carbohydrates and fiber. *For a description of the variety of legumes, refer to "Bean Bag" on page 154.*

For tips on cooking dry beans, refer to "Kitchen Nutrition: Cooking a Pot o' Beans" on page 151.

Learn to use soybean products—tofu, tempeh, textured soy protein, and soy milk—in your food preparation. Try them in stir-fry dishes, casseroles, lasagna, soups, and burger patties. *Refer to "What's 'Soy' Good?" on this page.*

If you eat eggs, limit your intake to four yolks per week. That way, you'll moderate your cholesterol intake, too. Make egg-based dishes lower in fat by substituting egg whites for some of the whole eggs. Examples of egg-based dishes include: quiche, omelet, frittata, scrambled eggs, French toast, egg salad, or egg foo yung.

Include nuts, nut butters (cashew butter, peanut butter), seeds, and seed spread (tahini, or sesame seed spread). They, too, supply protein, but are fairly high in fat. So go easy.

Vegetarian Way: Milk, Yogurt, and Cheese

For lacto-vegetarians, eat two to three servings of milk, yogurt, or cheese daily. Choose lower-fat and skim milk products for less fat. *For ways to include more dairy products in your day's food choices, refer to "Pyramid Pointers" on page 253.*

As an alternative, choose calcium-fortified, soy-based milk, yogurt, and cheese. Read the Nutrition Facts panel on food labels to determine the calcium content per serving. If soy-based products are not calcium fortified, they cannot count as a serving from this food group. Plan other foods with calcium in your daily diet if you don't consume dairy products.

Vegetarian Way: Fats, Oils, and Sweets

Go easy on high-fat foods, such as salad dressings, cooking oils, and spreads. Being derived from plants doesn't make them low in fat.

For ways to moderate fats, oils, and sweets in your day's food choices, refer to "Pyramid Pointers" on page 255.

What's "Soy" Good?

Soybeans! Made into many food products, they're very versatile and nutritious. Compared with many other legumes, soybeans have more protein and calcium, yet they're lower in complex carbohydrate. Whole soybeans also contain polyunsaturated fats, which often are extracted as soybean oil.

Soybean products can be good sources of nutrients in any eating style—vegetarian or not.

miso (MEE-soh): fermented soybean paste, most commonly used as a flavoring in Japanese cooking. With a consistency like peanut butter, miso can be used as a condiment. But it's also prepared in dips, marinades, sauces, and soups. Depending on the amount used, miso adds protein, calcium, and some B vitamins to dishes. Unless it's a low-salt variety, miso tends to be high in sodium.

soy milk: nondairy beverage made from crushed, cooked soybeans. Soy cheese is made from soy milk. Soy milk is a good source of protein. Unless it's calcium-fortified, it provides much less calcium than cow's milk does. Like cow's milk, soy milk may be fortified with vitamins A and D. Check the Nutrition Facts panel on the carton to find out the calcium and vitamin content per serving. *For more about food labels, refer to "Today's Food Labels" on page 270.*

soy flour: flour that's much higher in protein but lower in carbohydrate than wheat flour. In baking, it's usually mixed with other types of flour.

tempeh (TEHM-peh): soybeans, mixed with rice, millet, or other grain, then fermented into a rich soybean cake. Tempeh has a smoky or nutty taste that adds hearty flavor to soups, casseroles, chili, or spaghetti. It can be grilled or marinated. Like tofu, tempeh is a good protein source, but it has somewhat less calcium.

***textured soy protein, or* TSP:** soy flour that's high in protein and often sold as granules. You can use TSP to replace or extend meat or poultry. Vegetable burgers and sausages often are made with TSP, too.

tofu (TOH-foo), or soybean curd: a cheese-like curd, made from curdled soybean milk and pressed into soft cakes. Tofu easily takes up the flavor of other ingredients in a dish. You can also buy seasoned tofu, such as smoked or teriyaki tofu.

Tofu is quite versatile and is sold in several forms:

Stocking the Vegetarian Kitchen

Your local supermarket sells all the foods you need for a healthful, vegetarian diet. Specialty food stores carry less common items (such as soy milk, textured soy protein, and wheat gluten). There, you also may find vegetarian convenience foods. No matter where you shop, plan ahead. Shop with a list. And read food labels to find foods with ingredients that match your needs.

For a vegetarian kitchen, stock up on some of these foods for your cupboard, refrigerator, or freezer.

BREADS, CEREALS, RICE, AND PASTA

- ready-to-eat, enriched, and whole-grain breakfast cereals
- quick-cooking whole-grain and enriched cereals, such as oatmeal and muesli
- whole-grain and enriched breads, bagels, rolls, and crackers, such as rye, whole-wheat, and mixed grain
- rice, such as brown, wild, white, and others
- pastas, such as macaroni, spaghetti, fettuccini, and couscous
- corn or flour tortillas
- popcorn
- wheat germ and bran
- other grains, such as barley, bulgur, and quinoa*

LEGUMES AND MEAT SUBSTITUTES

- canned legumes, such as pintos, black beans, split peas, and garbanzos **
- dried legumes **
- vegetarian refried beans
- dried legume mixes, such as refried beans, falafel, and hummus (mashed chickpeas)
- tofu and tempeh
- soy-protein patties and sausages
- soy milk
- textured soy protein
- nut or seed spreads, such as peanut or almond butter, and tahini (sesame seed spread)
- nuts, such as pecans, almonds, walnuts, and cashews
- seeds, such as sesame, pumpkin, and sunflower seeds
- eggs or egg substitute (optional)

FRUITS AND VEGETABLES

- plain frozen and canned vegetables
- fresh fruits and vegetables
- tomato sauce
- canned and frozen fruit and fruit juice
- frozen fruit juice concentrate
- dried fruits, such as raisins, prunes, and dried apricots

DAIRY AND NONDAIRY FOODS

- milk (dairy or nondairy)
- cheese (dairy or nondairy)
- yogurt (dairy or nondairy)

COMBINATION FOODS

- vegetarian soups
- frozen vegetarian entrées, such as bean burritos
- canned vegetarian dishes, such as chili without meat

FATS AND SUGARS

- vegetable oil, plain and flavor-infused
- margarine or butter (optional)
- salad dressing (perhaps made without eggs)
- vegetarian gravy and sauce mixes
- syrup, jam, jelly, and molasses
- sugar and other sweeteners

CONDIMENTS, SEASONINGS, AND OTHER FLAVORINGS

- herbs and spices
- vinegar, plain and flavored
- sauces, such as chutney, salsa, soy sauce, teriyaki sauce
- canned vegetable broth and broth mix

**For more about grains, refer to "Today's Grains" on page 221.*

***For more about legumes, refer to "Bean Bag" on page 154.*

soft or silken for dressings, dips, shakes, and sauces; medium-soft for puddings, cheesecakes, pie fillings, and salads; and firm or extra firm for grilling, marinating, slicing, and stir-frying and in casseroles, soups, and sandwiches. Tofu sold in bulk (not packaged) or in water needs to be refrigerated and used within a week because it's very perishable. It should be kept in water that's changed daily. Bought in an aseptic package, tofu doesn't need refrigeration until it's opened. You also can freeze tofu for up to three months for a chewier texture. Tofu is a good source of protein—and calcium—especially when it's calcium fortified.

***whole soybeans*:** purchased dry or fresh, soybeans can be cooked for soups, stews, and casseroles. For a snack, fresh soybeans can be roasted.

***soy sauce*:** a condiment used in many Asian dishes, is made from fermented soybeans. Although it adds flavor, soy sauce is not a significant protein source.

Vegetarian Food Guide

Eating the vegetarian way follows similar guidelines as the Food Guide Pyramid. For each food group, only the suggested amounts and variety of choices differ slightly.

Food Group	Suggested Daily Servings	Serving Sizes
Breads, cereals, rice, and pasta	6 to 11	1 slice whole-grain or enriched bread 1/2 bun, bagel, or English muffin 1 tortilla 1/2 cup cooked cereal, such as oatmeal, bulgur, barley, quinoa, or millet 1/2 cup cooked rice or pasta 1 ounce dry cereal
Vegetables	3 to 5	1/2 cup cooked vegetables 1 cup raw vegetables 3/4 cup vegetable juice
Fruit	2 to 4	1 whole apple, peach, orange, banana, or other similar-sized fruit 1/2 cup chopped fruit or berries 1/2 cup canned, frozen, or cooked fruit 3/4 cup fruit juice 1/4 cup dried fruit
Legumes and other meat alternates	2 to 3	1/2 cup cooked beans or peas 1/4 cup tofu or tempeh 1 cup soy milk 3 ounces soy-protein patties 2 tablespoons peanut butter 2 tablespoons nuts or seeds 1 egg or 2 egg whites or 1/4 cup egg substitute
Milk, cheese, and yogurt	0 to 3 servings*	1 cup milk or yogurt 1 1/2 ounces natural cheese or 2 ounces processed cheese
Fats, oils, and sweets	Eat sparingly.	Oil, margarine, mayonnaise, salad dressings Candy and sugars

**Vegetarians who choose not to use milk, yogurt, or cheese need to select other foods rich in calcium.*

Adapting Your Recipes

Looking for vegetarian recipes? Check the bookstore for many flavor-filled dishes from vegetarian cookbooks. Some magazines devote their pages to vegetarian-style eating. With just a few changes, you also can adapt recipes in almost any cookbook or magazine for vegetarian-style meals—even if you choose to avoid eggs and dairy products.

A few recipe hints when you adjust recipes…

***In casseroles, stews, soups, and chili, substitute cooked legumes for meat*:** perhaps kidney beans in chili or stew, or red lentils in spaghetti sauce or stuffed cabbage rolls, or refried beans in burritos, tacos, and enchiladas. *For more cooking tips, refer to "A Word About Legumes…" on page* 346.

***Eggs offer functional qualities to recipes*:** for example, thickening, binding ingredients together, clarifying stock, coating breaded foods, and leavening. A leavener lightens the texture and increases the volume of baked goods. Without eggs, the qualities of food often change. If you're a vegan or lacto-vegetarian, experiment with recipes by replacing one egg with one of these ingredients—but know that the results may differ:

- 1 mashed banana (in breads, muffins, or pancakes)
- 2 tablespoons of cornstarch or arrowroot
- 1/4 cup tofu (Blend it with liquid ingredients until smooth; then add to dry ingredients.)
- vegetarian egg replacement (often sold in specialty stores)

In stir-fry dishes, use firm tofu, tempeh, cooked beans, nuts, and sesame seeds in place of meat, poultry, or seafood. Firm tofu and tempeh can even be cubed and skewered as kebobs for grilling. Try scrambled tofu for breakfast! *Hint*: For more flavor, marinate tofu before adding it to dishes.

Prepare pasta sauces, pizza toppings, soups, stews, and other mixed dishes as you always do—but skip the meat and add more chopped vegetables. If you eat dairy products, sprinkle cheese on top for more protein and calcium.

Use soy-protein patties, bacon, and sausages on pizza, hot sandwiches, sloppy joes, and other dishes that typically call for meat. Textured soy protein, often sold in granular form, also may be used in casseroles, soups, stews, lasagna, chili, enchiladas, and other mixed dishes.

For vegans, you might use a soy margarine in place of butter. Be aware that cookies, pastries, and other baked goods may have a different texture, however. *Remember*: Lard is another fat of animal origin.

Enjoy thick, creamy shakes? If you're a lacto-vegetarian, enjoy the traditional recipe. If you're a vegan, blend fruit instead with soft tofu and soy milk or juice.

Again for vegans, try tofu, soy milk, soy cheese, and soy yogurt in recipes that call for dairy products. Crumbled tofu, for example, can take the place of ricotta cheese in lasagna. And in baked foods, 1 cup of soy milk plus 1 tablespoon of vinegar can be used in place of 1 cup of buttermilk.

Now for Eating Out...

More and more traditional restaurants and cafeterias cater to "all-the-time" or "sometimes" vegetarians. Quickservice restaurants offer meatless salads that are big enough to enjoy as an entrée—as well as vegetarian deli sandwiches, pita pockets, pizzas, and tacos.

Whether you're a vegetarian—or simply enjoy an occasional vegetarian meal—consider these tips when you eat out:

Before you order, talk to your server about ingredients in the dish. Feel comfortable about asking for vegetarian dishes—prepared without eggs or dairy products if that's your choice. *For tips on ordering, refer to "Restaurant Eater's Tip List" on page 360.*

If the menu doesn't carry a vegetarian entrée, order a salad with vegetable soup and bread, or several vegetable appetizers. A fruit plate—with or without cheese or yogurt—can make a very appealing entrée, too.

If you choose the salad bar, "toss" your salad with kidney beans, chickpeas, and a few sunflower seeds...as well as vegetables that have more vitamin C. (*Remember*: Vitamin C helps your body absorb iron from plant sources of food.) If you're a lacto-ovo-vegetarian, you might spoon on some cottage cheese, shredded cheese, and chopped or sliced hard-cooked eggs. (*Hint*: Go easy on high-fat salad dressing or choose a low-fat dressing.)

Choose an ethnic restaurant that's likely to have vegetarian options. You might try those with traditional menus that include vegetarian dishes. Perhaps try the cuisines of the Middle East, Greece, India, China, Mexico, and parts of Africa. (*Tip for vegans*: Ghee, used in many dishes from India, is melted, clarified butter.) *Also refer to "Vegetarian Dishes in the Global Kitchen" on page 575.*

For airline meals, ask for a vegetarian meal when you book your flight. If you need to, find out ahead if the meal is egg- and dairy-free. For airlines that don't offer vegetarian meals, request a fruit plate or pack your own snacks. *Refer to* "*Dining at* 35,000 *Feet!" on page* 384.

School Meals for Vegetarian Kids

Review school menus with your child. And discuss ahead what might be ordered. If the school doesn't provide menus to parents, ask the school staff to provide them.

Suggest the salad bar as a nutritious option—if it's available. A salad bar can be a good place to go for fresh vegetables and possibly for other nutrient-packed choices including fruits, beans, sunflower seeds, cheese, or hard-cooked eggs.

When the menu doesn't offer an option for your child, pack a lunch. A peanut butter sandwich is always popular. For the child who doesn't want to appear different, it's the food that almost all kids eat—vegetarian or not!

Vegetarian Dishes in the Global Kitchen

Delicious and nutritious—vegetarian dishes are typical fare in many parts of the world. As you flip the pages of ethnic cookbooks or glance through the menu of an ethnic restaurant, try to build your meal around dishes like these. They're typically made without meat, poultry, or fish—but check to be sure.

Caribbean	CALLALOO: one-pot meal (stew) made with dark green leafy vegetables, a variety of other vegetables, peppers, and seasonings BLACK-EYED PEA PATTIES: black-eyed peas mashed with eggs and seasonings, then quickly pan-fried in a small amount of oil
China	VEGETABLE-TOFU STIR-FRY: variety of thinly-sliced vegetables and cubed bean curd, stir-fried with soy sauce and perhaps vegetable broth EGG FOO YUNG: frittata-like dish, made by combining slightly-whipped eggs with sliced vegetables, then frying in a skillet until browned; also may be prepared with meat or poultry
France	VEGETABLE QUICHE: pie made with a custard of egg and cheese, mixed with chopped vegetables such as leeks, spinach, asparagus, and mushrooms RATATOUILLE: soup or stew made of eggplant, tomatoes, onion, green pepper, and other vegetables. Enjoy with crusty French bread.
India	DOHKLA: steamed cakes made of rice and beans
	VEGETABLE CURRY DISHES: combination of chopped vegetables and lentils, flavored with a curry mix
Italy	PASTA PRIMAVERA: cooked pasta tossed with steamed fresh vegetables, with or without Parmesan cheese VEGETABLE RISOTTO: arborio rice, cooked in vegetable broth and combined with cooked vegetables and perhaps cooked beans or nuts, with or without grated cheese EGGPLANT PARMESAN: sliced eggplant, prepared by dipping it into a mixture of eggs and milk, coating it with bread crumbs and Parmesan cheese, and sautéeing it. To serve, it's topped with tomato sauce.
	PASTA E FAGIOLI: pasta and white bean "stew," seasoned with herbs, usually prepared without meat
Greece	TZATZIKI (CUCUMBER-YOGURT SALAD): plain yogurt, mixed with shredded cucumber, garlic, and perhaps black olives, served with crusty bread VEGETABLE-STUFFED EGGPLANT: eggplants hollowed and filled with chopped vegetables and cooked grain, and sometimes nuts SPANAKOPITA (SPINACH PIE): pita made with a phyllo-dough crust, and filled with a mixture of spinach, feta cheese, and eggs
Indonesia	GADO-GADO: cooked vegetable salad with a peanut sauce, often seasoned with chiles
Native American (Southwest)	MARICOPA BEAN STEW: stew made of corn, beans, and cholla buds
Mexico	BEAN BURRITO: vegetarian refried beans wrapped in a soft tortilla, with or without cheese topping CHILES RELLENOS: poblano peppers stuffed with cheese, dipped in an egg batter, and baked or fried (If they're fried, they're high in fat.) HUEVOS RANCHEROS (MEXICAN EGGS): scrambled eggs, prepared with onion, and served with tomato salsa, vegetarian refried beans, and tortilla
Middle East	FALAFEL SANDWICH: ground chickpea patties (fried), tucked in pita bread with lettuce shreds and chopped tomato, topped with tahini (sesame seed spread) TABOULI: salad made with bulgur, tomatoes, parsley, mint or chives, lemon juice, and perhaps cooked white beans FUL: brown bean casserole, made with tomatoes, lemons, parsley, and eggs
Spain	SPANISH OMELET (TORTILLA À LA ESPAÑOLA): egg omelet, made with potatoes, onions, and other vegetables
Switzerland	CHEESE FONDUE: cheese melted with wine and served with chunks of crusty bread RACLETTE: cheese, "scraped" from a melted piece of hard cheese, then spread on a boiled potato or dark bread
East Africa	BEAN AND GROUNDNUT STEW (KUNDE): stew made of black-eyed beans, peanuts (groundnuts), tomato, and onion (A similar stew is made in West Africa, often without peanuts.) INJERA AND LENTIL STEW: flat bread served with cooked lentils. (This is an Ethiopian dish.)

your nutrition check-up

For Vegetarians...

You've chosen to follow a vegetarian diet—perhaps with your own good health in mind. But are you making choices that help you achieve that goal? Take this 10-question survey as a quick check.

Do You Eat...

Yes No

❒ ❒ 1. A wide variety of grain products (including whole-grains), legumes, nuts, vegetables, and fruits?

❒ ❒ 2. At least six servings of bread, rice, pasta, and other grain products daily?

❒ ❒ 3. At least four vegetable servings daily?

❒ ❒ 4. At least three fruit servings daily?

❒ ❒ 5. A vitamin-C rich food with meals whenever you can?

❒ ❒ 6. Enough calories to maintain a healthy weight?

❒ ❒ 7. Mostly nutrient-dense foods, and go easy on fats, oils, and sugars?

❒ ❒ 8. Two to three servings of legumes and other meat alternates each day?

Just for lacto- and lacto-ovo-vegetarians: (If you're a vegan, skip ahead.)

❒ ❒ 9. Two to three servings of milk, yogurt, or cheese daily?

❒ ❒ 10. Eggs occasionally—no more than four yolks a week?

Just for vegans: (If you're a lacto- or lacto-ovo-vegetarian, skip these two questions.)

❒ ❒ 9. Foods of plant origin that are high in calcium?

❒ ❒ 10. Foods that are fortified with vitamins B_{12} and D (or take a supplement that provides no more than 100 percent of their Daily Value)?

Now score yourself

Give yourself a point for every "yes."

If you scored a perfect "10," your food choices do promote your good health. They probably supply enough nutrients, and perhaps have other low-fat benefits.

If you said "no" to any item, check back through the chapter, and make changes you need to eat healthy—the vegetarian way!

real life nutrition

My Choice

After trying occasional meatless meals, Winona, a 17-year-old, made a decision. "I've decided to become a vegetarian," she confided to her friend Eddie as they headed out to join their friends at a restaurant. "I'll be the only vegetarian in my family. It may not be easy."

"What are you going to eat? Just vegetables?" asked Eddie. "Like tonight, what are you going to order after the game—fries, a salad, and a soft drink?"

Feeling only a bit confident, Winona answered, "For one, I could order a cheese pizza...and enjoy a salad along with it. I'm not a strict vegetarian, you know. I can eat dairy foods—and maybe eggs, too!"

Tonight's meal was her first step...after that, she knew she needed some guidance. But who should she ask? And what does she need to know?

To eat a healthful lacto-ovo-vegetarian diet, Winona might follow this advice:

- Consult a registered dietitian or other qualified nutrition expert for guidance on choosing a healthful vegetarian diet for her teen years.

- Involve her family, so foods appropriate for her are available at home. She might help with cooking to make meals easier for her family to prepare since some of her food choices are different. Continue to respect the food choices of her family—even though not all will be the same as hers.

- Eat a wide variety of foods: Those made with whole-grain products, legumes, nuts, vegetables, and fruit—not just teenage favorites, such as pizza and salads.

- Since she consumes dairy foods, continue to enjoy milk, cheese, yogurt, and other calcium-rich dairy foods: for example, milk with meals, yogurt for breakfast or snacks, and cheese on sandwiches and other foods. She needs enough Milk Group servings for the increased calcium needs of adolescence.

- To avoid too much fat in her meal tonight, order a regular—not a double—cheese pizza. And go easy on salad dressing.

- Eat mostly nutrient-dense foods that are lower in fat. Even a vegetarian diet—with too many fried foods, high-fat salad dressings, and rich desserts and snacks—can be high in fat.

- Enjoy vitamin-C fruit or juice with meals and snacks to help her body absorb iron. (Soft drinks usually don't supply vitamin C.)

- Check the school lunch menu ahead. If there is nothing appropriate for her, she'll need to bring her own lunch.

CHAPTER TWENTY-THREE

WELL INFORMED?

Are you well informed? That is, do you have sound nutrition information at your fingertips when you make eating decisions? For that matter, how do you stay up to date?

Magazines, newspapers, and television reports may be your main sources of nutrition information. That's true for most consumers. For your own good health, your sources need to be credible, and you need the ability to judge what you hear and read.

For teens and children, the picture is a little different—school and family rank as their top nutrition information sources. You—as a parent, caregiver, or teacher—may convey nutrition information to kids. Your challenge? It's knowing enough so you provide accurate information... and it's knowing where to direct them for other sources of sound nutrition advice, too!

Need Nutrition Advice?

When do you need nutrition advice? Every day! And at certain times, you may need to know a little more...

- ➢ if you're pregnant or trying to get pregnant
- ➢ if you're breast-feeding
- ➢ if you're feeding an infant
- ➢ if you're serving meals for a child or teen
- ➢ if you're involved in sports or fitness activities
- ➢ if you're trying to lose, maintain, or gain weight
- ➢ if you're modifying your eating habits to prevent or control a health problem
- ➢ if you're caring for an aging parent or friend
- ➢ if you want to change your food choices and lifestyle to stay fit!

When you need nutrition advice, seek a qualified expert. Your health—and that of your family—depends on it!

The Real Expert... Please Stand Up

Just who is a qualified nutrition expert? Sometimes it's hard to tell. Qualified nutrition experts have specific academic and training credentials. They know the science of nutrition. Their degrees in nutrition, dietetics, public health, or related fields (such as biochemistry, medicine, or a nutrition specialty in family and consumer sciences) come from well-respected colleges and universities. They may use the title "dietitian" or "nutritionist" to describe what they do.

Who Is a Registered Dietitian?

The initials "RD" after someone's name mean "registered dietitian." An RD is an authority on the role of food and nutrition in health. He or she is a reliable source of nutrition information and advice on eating and health. An RD plays an important role on the health care team by providing specific food and nutrition expertise.

To earn the RD credential, an individual must complete at least four years of education in nutrition or a related field from a regionally accredited college or university program that's approved by The American Dietetic Association. He or she is also required to complete a supervised internship program. Many dietetics professionals earn graduate degrees, as well.

To become registered, candidates must demonstrate their knowledge by passing an extensive examination. The exam is administered by the Commission on Dietetic Registration, the credentialing agency of The American Dietetic Association. All RDs are required to stay current by completing at least 75 hours of continuing education every five years. Only dietitians who have passed the exam and maintain their continuing education are considered "registered." ✦

The initials RD for "registered dietitian" or DTR for "dietetic technician, registered" mean the person has met specific educational requirements for the field of nutrition and health. *Refer to "Who Is a Registered Dietitian?" on this page and "Who Is a Dietetic Technician, Registered?" on page* 582. In some states, dietitians also may be licensed. Some qualified nutrition experts may have advanced degrees, such as MS, MEd, ScD, MD, or PhD.

Having letters after his or her name doesn't necessarily qualify someone to provide nutrition services. Even when that person holds other academic degrees, nutrition may not be his or her specialty. You may need to probe further.

In many states, the title "nutritionist" isn't regulated. Neither is the title "diet counselor." For this reason, either one may be used by anyone—including people who aren't properly qualified to give you accurate nutrition information or advice.

Salespeople for dietary supplements, so-called health advisors, and some authors, for example, may call themselves "nutritionists." In reality, they may only be self-proclaimed experts. Some may have just a little nutrition training. Others may have only mail-order credentials.

Mail-order credentials from a diploma mill may appear impressive—but don't be fooled. The U.S. Department of Education defines a "diploma mill" as an organization awarding degrees without requiring its students to meet educational standards that are established and followed by reputable institutions. Through diploma mills, even pets have been awarded nutrition degrees! Some states are addressing these problems by licensing qualified nutrition experts. But these laws aren't in place everywhere, and qualifications differ from state to state.

How to Find Nutrition Help...

Nutrition services are provided throughout the community by health, education, and social service organizations, as well as by individuals in private practice. To find a qualified nutrition expert or to get answers to your nutrition questions, contact:

➢ your doctor, health maintenance organization (HMO), or local hospital for a referral.

➢ your local dietetic association, public health department, extension service, or the nutrition department of an area college or university.

➢ the Consumer Nutrition Hot Line of The American Dietetic Association's National Center for Nutrition and Dietetics (800/366-1655). Ask to be referred to a registered dietitian (RD) in your area.

Refer to "The Real Expert... Please Stand Up" on page 580 to help you choose a qualified nutrition expert.

Community agencies and institutions also may provide food or nutrition services for specific groups of citizens. Many are staffed with qualified nutrition experts. Be aware of these services so you can suggest them to someone who needs them.

Food stamps program. The food stamp program, administered by state agencies and funded by the U.S. Department of Agriculture (USDA), is meant to provide food assistance to needy families and individuals.

Women, Infants, and Children (WIC) program. This federal government program offers food assistance and nutrition education to pregnant women, infants, and preschoolers.

Child nutrition programs. Schools, as well as early childhood centers, provide nutritious breakfasts and lunches for children. Often these programs are supported partly through the USDA's Child Nutrition Program. By regulation, school meals must meet strict nutrition guidelines. The program also provides nutrition education for children. *Refer to "For Kids Only—Today's School Meals" on page 435.*

Extension Service. The Extension Service provides consumer information on a variety of topics, including food, nutrition, and food safety. Nutrition experts are staff members of your state's land-grant university.

Senior citizens' meal programs. Community agencies may serve low-cost meals to senior citizens. These programs offer social contact, along with nutritious meals. Check with a social worker, health department, religious group, or the Office on Aging to find services for senior citizens.

Home-delivered meals. People who can't leave their homes or who aren't able to prepare food on their own may seek services for home-delivered meals. Through government or community agencies, meals are provided at a low cost for those who qualify. Check with a social worker, religious group, or Office on Aging to find these services.

Local soup kitchens and food pantries. Private groups may provide food at no cost to those who are homeless or without resources for food. Often social workers, social agencies, and religious groups know about these programs.

Food industry groups. Many food industry groups provide nutrition information about their products, as well as general nutrition information. A registered dietitian or other qualified nutrition professional may be on staff to answer consumer questions.

When You Consult an Expert...

Whether you seek nutrition counseling on your own or follow up from a doctor's referral, make the most of your time with a qualified nutrition professional. For an office visit...

Have a medical check-up first. A qualified nutrition professional will want to know your health status before making dietary recommendations. Your health care provider can share your blood pressure and information from a blood analysis, such as level of blood cholesterol level, triglycerides, blood glucose (sugar), hemoglobin, and hematocrit, among others. Your doctor may then consult with a dietitian to determine the appropriate diet therapy.

Share your goals. If you seek nutrition advice on your own, be prepared to share your health goals. Know what you want to accomplish. Do you want to lose weight? Gain weight? Have more energy for sports? Lower your blood cholesterol level? Live a healthier lifestyle? Think about your goals in advance... and make them realistic.

Forget miracles and magic bullets. A qualified nutrition professional will focus on changes in lifestyle and food choices, not on quick results, miracle cures, or costly dietary supplements.

Tell about dietary supplements you're taking. That includes herbal remedies. Some interact with medications (even over-the-counter types), rendering them ineffective. Some nutrient-drug interactions have harmful side effects, too. *Refer to "Food and Medicine" on page* 526. Dietary supplements, taken in very large doses, also may cause adverse reactions and serious health problems. *Refer to "Dietary Supplements: Use and Abuse" on page* 111.

WHO IS A DIETETIC TECHNICIAN, REGISTERED?

The initials "DTR" after a person's name stand for "Dietetic Technician, Registered." It signifies that the individual is qualified to be part of the nutrition care or food service management team. That may include teaching nutrition classes, offering diet counseling, performing diet histories, assessing a person's nutritional status, or managing aspects of a foodservice operation.

A DTR has at least an associate degree from a regionally accredited college or university and has completed a dietetics practice program approved by The American Dietetic Association. That includes 450 hours of supervised practice experience in health care, foodservice facilities, and community programs. The DTR also has successfully completed a registration exam administered by the Commission on Dietetic Registration, the credentialing agency of The American Dietetic Association.

Once they earn their credential, Dietetic Technicians, Registered, must keep current by completing at least 50 hours of continuing education every five years. ✦

Be prepared to answer questions. Expect to talk about your eating habits, any adverse reactions to food, dietary supplements, your weight history, food preferences, general medical history, family history of health problems, medications, special diets, and any nutrition instruction you've had. That way, the nutrition advice you receive will match your lifestyle and health needs.

For weight counseling or sports nutrition, expect to have your weight and body composition checked. Usually that's just simple measuring and a skinfold measurement in several spots on your body.

Ask for clarification. If you don't understand the terms used in the counseling session, ask! Terms such as "blood glucose level," "HDLs," "triglycerides," "anaphylactic reaction," "enriched" or "fortified" bread and cereal products, "saturated fat," "sodium," and "Nutrition Facts panel" are nutrition-related lingo. If they come up, you need to know what they mean.

Be specific with your questions. You're the most important person on your health care team. You can only comply with dietary recommendations if you have a clear understanding of the advice that's offered.

Keep careful eating records—if you're asked. You may be asked to keep a record of everything you eat and drink for several days. That includes snacks. You'll be asked for amounts and a record of how the foods were prepared, such as "fried" or "baked." *For a few other tips, refer to "Dear Diary…" on page* 37.

Involve your family. If you take a nutrition class or seminar or have a one-on-one appointment with a nutrition professional, bring your support along. Having family support is important to your success.

Follow up as advised. Continue with follow-up visits so your progress can be monitored and so your questions can be answered along the way. It's great moral support if you need it, too.

Stick with it! Positive changes in body weight, blood cholesterol levels, and other physical conditions may take time. Plan together for gradual results.

Be Your Own Judge!

Do you rely on popular media for nutrition updates? Fortunately, there's more reliable nutrition information for the public than ever before. And much of it makes good sense! Still, be a cautious consumer of nutrition information. Just being in print, on TV and radio, or in "cyberspace" doesn't make information reliable.

You Can't Judge a Book by Its Cover

Magazine racks, bookstore shelves, newspaper columns, and regular newsletters provide plenty of nutrition advice. Some sources are reliable. Others are completely inaccurate. Still others have many threads of truth, but still may contain some misinformation too. How do you sort fact from fiction? Before you accept nutrition information in print, give it a reliability check.

Who Wrote It?
Check the author's qualifications. A reputable nutrition author usually is educated in the field of nutrition, medicine, or a related specialty. His or her degree(s) comes from an accredited college or university, not a diploma mill. A reputable author may be affiliated with an accredited university or medical center with nutrition or related health programs or courses, too. And he or she may be a member of a credible nutrition organization. *Refer to "The Real Expert... Please Stand Up" on page* 580.

An "accredited" institution generally is certified by an agency that's recognized by the U.S. Department of Education. By contacting the reference department of your local library, you can check an institution's accreditation.

Today, more and more consumer books, magazine articles, and newspaper columns are written by qualified nutrition experts, such as registered dietitians.

Why Was It Published?
Look for books, magazines, and newsletters with a balanced nutrition message. Some publications are

Food and nutrition information is proliferating in cyberspace. Your computer can direct you to breaking nutrition news, dietary guidelines, healthful recipes, nutrition resources, labeling information, government agencies, and even the chance to "chat" with a registered dietitian. Like other media, the "information highway" also is littered with misinformation. Use the same healthy skepticism with on-line information that you use to evaluate other nutrition information.

Look for these signs to determine if the web site provides information you can trust. Does it...

➢ Identify the sponsor or owner of the site? (That's your clue to the site's perspective and potential bias.)

➢ Name contributors with their credentials, and perhaps an affiliation? (No matter what the media, credible information comes from qualified nutrition experts, such as registered dietitians.)

➢ Provide facts with cited sources, not just opinions? (Look for information supported by established scientific findings.)

➢ Link to credible on-line sites? (Other sites may have supporting data or guidelines.)

➢ Indicate regular updates and postings? (Credible web sites are updated often to offer the most current advice. Caution: being current doesn't make it accurate. The site needs to pass other tests of credibility.)

To check for reliable on-line information, refer to "News You Can Use!"—you'll find the on-line addresses for many computerized nutrition resources. ✦

meant mostly to advertise, not to inform. As a consumer, try to analyze what's being said or implied. If it's not clear, ask a qualified nutrition expert.

How Are Nutrition Claims Supported?

Nutrition advice in any publication should be backed up by credible sources. Guidelines often come from government agencies, such as the U.S. Department of Health and Human Services (DHHS) or the U.S. Department of Agriculture (USDA). Government agencies depend on experts to establish nutrition advice. Credible professional and health organizations in nutrition and medicine often are cited; they base their advice on established scientific findings.

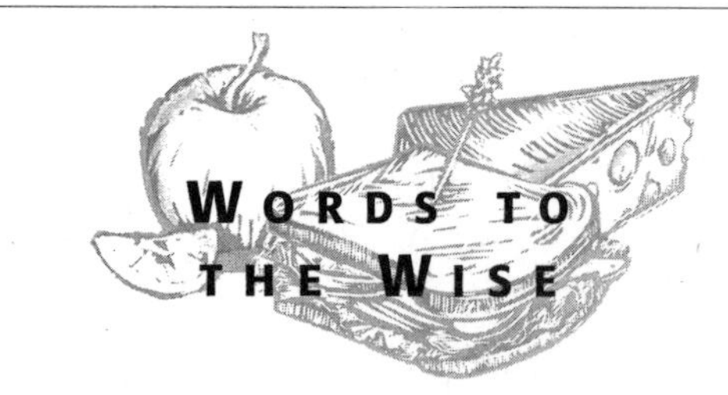

"May"	Does not mean "will"
"Contributes to," "is linked to," or "is associated with"	Does not mean "causes"
"Proves"	Scientific studies gather evidence in a systematic way, but one study, taken alone, seldom proves anything.
"Breakthrough"	This happens only now and then—for example, the discovery of penicillin or polio vaccine. But today the word is so overworked as to be meaningless.
"Doubles the risk," "triples the risk"	May or may not be meaningful. Do you know what the risk was in the first place? If the risk was one in a million, and you double it, that's still only 1 in 500,000. If the risk was 1 in 100 and doubles, that's a big increase.
"Significant"	A result is "statistically significant" when the association between two factors has been found to be greater than might occur at random (this is worked out by a mathematical formula). But people often take "significant" to mean "major" or "important."

Source: "Why do those #&?@! 'experts' keep changing their minds?" Reprinted with permission from the* University of California at Berkeley Wellness Letter, *© Health Letter Associates,* 1996.

Check "Resources You Can Use!" on page 595. It lists many—but not all—government and health agencies, professional organizations, and food industry groups that provide credible information.

For emerging science, writers should cite evidence from peer-reviewed scientific journals. That way, you can read the original research if you choose to. Reliable nutrition experts don't claim to have all the answers. If scientific evidence isn't conclusive or if the issues are controversial, they say so.

What Do Other Experts Say?

Look for reviews by reliable experts. Start by checking inside the book itself. You may find a list of reviewers. Like those of the author, reviewers' credentials or affiliations help you judge the reliability of nutrition information in the book.

For an expert judgment, contact a registered dietitian or other qualified nutritionist connected with a local college, university, hospital, extension service, public health department, or in private practice.

Read Between the Headlines

Practically every week, nutrition and health news make the headlines. However, in this age of instant communication, research often hits the media before nutrition experts can review and interpret the findings. Today's report may appear to contradict what you heard last week. The result? You may feel confused.

Legitimate scientists aren't out to mislead you. Uncovering the mysteries of nutrition and the human body is a complex process. As new factors emerge, research may seem to contradict itself. But the differences in results may be a factor of how scientists continue to learn—questioning each step along the way. Scientific debate leads to more studies. Eventually recommendations based on sound science are shared with the public. But the process often takes years.

As science unravels more about the links among nutrition, health, and chronic disease, you'll read and hear a lot—reports that will eventually prove to be both true and false. You can't expect to dissect every research report. But you can use caution and common sense before jumping to conclusions:

Go beyond headlines. An attention-grabbing headline may leave a different impression than the full newspaper article or news brief itself. Read or listen to the whole story. Often response from other experts or bottom-line recommendations appear at the end of the story.

Remember—once isn't enough! The results of one study aren't enough to change your food choices. They're just one piece of a bigger scientific puzzle. True nutrition breakthroughs take years of study and the support of repeated findings from many scientific studies.

Check the report. Do other studies support the evidence? And does it build on what scientists know already? Responsible scientists and careful journalists report research within the context of other studies. And one study rarely changes their nutrition advice.

Recognize preliminary findings for what they are—preliminary! Read them with interest. But wait for more evidence before you make major changes.

Look for the human dimension. Animal studies may be among the first steps in researching a hypothesis. But the results don't always apply to humans.

Learn to be research-savvy. Read more about the study itself before applying its conclusions to you. Ask yourself: Are the people studied like you—perhaps in age, gender, health, and lifestyle? Did the study include a large group of people? Was the study long-range? Longer studies, with more people, more likely produce valid results. Even by asking these questions, it may be hard for consumers to assess research methods.

Consider its context in the real world of healthy eating. Does the study tell how the findings relate to overall food choices, lifestyle, and other research? A responsible report tells how research fits with the broader context of what is already known.

Know what the words mean. Credible nutrition reports are careful with what they say so they won't mislead you. Research results may "suggest," but that isn't the same as "prove." And "linked to" doesn't mean "causes." *Don't jump to conclusions—get to know the "Words to the Wise" on page 584.*

Check out the source—ask a qualified nutrition expert to help. Credible research comes from credible institutions and credible scientists... and it's reported in credible scientific and professional journals. Before nutrition research is published in reputable journals, it must be reviewed by peers. They determine whether it meets well-established standards of nutrition research. If research is attributed simply to "they" or to some other elusive source, be wary of its results.

Watch for follow-up reports. Breaking scientific news is often followed up by review and advice from nutrition experts. For example, registered dietitians often appear in media, helping to interpret news reports on nutrition issues.

Even when the research has been well conducted, different scientists may view the results differently. And it may take time for nutrition experts to study the research methods and findings. So don't always expect an immediate response.

Keep a healthy skepticism. That's especially true when evaluating news about fantastic nutrition "discoveries." *Refer to "Case Against Health Fraud" on page 586.*

Watch out for absolutes! Responsible scientists don't claim "proof" or "cause" until repeated studies show that the findings are conclusive.

Seek a qualified opinion. Before you change your eating style, consult a registered dietitian, other qualified nutrition expert, or doctor. Even reliable research advice may not apply to you.

Case Against Health Fraud

Can you "lose weight while you sleep"? Can a dietary supplement assure "no more arthritic pain" or "no more baldness"? Can a device guarantee "a bigger bustline" or "spot reduction"?

Americans spend billions of dollars annually on products and services that make such claims. Health quackery is the most common type of fraud aimed at the elderly and others. Easy remedies are hard to resist! Yet many are simply useless; others, potentially harmful. Either way, it's health fraud.

Health fraud means promoting, for financial gain, a health remedy that doesn't work—or hasn't yet been proven to work. The remedy may be a device, treatment, service, plan, or product. Although fraud is rampant in many areas of health, often it's linked to nutrition—perhaps a dietary supplement, weight-loss device, or a new diet program.

So what is quackery? The term comes from the term "quacksalver." The word refers to medieval peddlers of salves, who sounded like quacking ducks when they used their voices to promote their wares. That's why they were called "quacks."

Quacks promote health fraud. Their motivation may be strictly financial gain. But often, quacks sincerely believe in the value of their product, treatment, or service. They don't mean to deceive you. Instead, they either lack scientific understanding or don't believe that they're distorting the truth.

Health fraud and quackery have grown dramatically in the past several decades. Why such growth? Among the reasons, there's an unprecedented interest in personal health care. In general, people today take more personal responsibility for staying healthy. That interest has created a huge demand for products and services that promote health. Legitimate business uses this opportunity to provide products, treatments, and services that have scientifically-proven benefits. But this same wave of interest also has spawned a fanfare of health fraud and quackery.

There's another common reason for the growth of health fraud. Some people expect a quick or easy "health fix." They may count on today's "medicine" to undo the results of an unhealthy lifestyle. It's not that simple—even if quacks lead you to believe otherwise.

What Are the Consequences?

Nutrition quackery exploits consumers. And it carries significant health and economic risks along the way. Among them:

False hopes. Dream on! Quacks may promise—but unsound nutrition advice, products, or services won't prevent or cure disease.

A *substitute for reliable health care.* False hopes, created through quackery, may delay proper health promotion or medical care. If you follow the advice of quackery, you may lose something you can't retrieve—time for effective treatment!

Unneeded expense. In the best-case scenario, some products and services touted by quacks simply don't work—and cause no harm either. Why waste your hard-earned money on devices, products, and services that have no effect?

Potential harm. Nutrition quackery also can put your health at risk. Taking very large doses of some vitamins and minerals, in the form of dietary supplements, can have very harmful side effects. For example, excessive vitamin K is risky if you take blood-thinning drugs. And excessive amounts of vitamin A during pregnancy increase the chances of birth defects. *For more about specific vitamins and minerals, refer to chapter 4, "Vitamins and Minerals: Enough, But Not Too Much."* Over-the-counter herbal products are sources of potent drugs. They, too, are marketed as dietary supplements. Yet, unlike medications, herbal products aren't well regulated. *Refer to "Herbals—Help or Harm?" on page 587.*

Quackery: What You Can Do

No one has to be the victim of nutrition fraud. To protect yourself, you just need to know how to identify fraud and quackery, and where to find sound nutrition information.

Retain a healthy skepticism. Find out more before you invest in a nutrition product, treatment, or service. *Give it the "10-question" test from page 591 before you buy.*

Seek advice from reliable sources. It's not always easy to discern nutrition facts from misinformation. Even if you try to stay informed, it's a challenge to keep up on all the products and services—reliable or not—that hit the market.

If you're suspicious about a statement, product, or service, contact a credible nutrition source: for example, a registered dietitian, your public health department, the medical or nutrition department of a nearby college or university, or your county Extension office. *Refer to "Need Nutrition Advice?" on page 579.*

Report nutrition fraud. If you suspect that a statement, product, or service is fraudulent or false, inquire with the appropriate government agency or file a complaint.

To the Postal Service... Contact your postmaster or Postal Service if you've been the victim—or target—of nutrition fraud through the mail. It's illegal to use the Postal Service to make false claims about or to sell fraudulent products or services.

To the FDA... Make inquiries or file complaints about false claims for dietary supplements with the Food and Drug Administration (FDA). That includes concerns about inadequate information on package labels.

To the FTC... For questions or concerns about false or misleading claims in advertising, contact the Federal Trade Commission (FTC).

Herbals—Help or Harm?

Herbal remedies may seem safe enough. After all, they're made from herbs! Indeed many are known to have medicinal qualities. And like medicines, they may offer either positive health benefits or harmful side effects. The problem is—there's little known about most herbal remedies.

Unlike medicines, herbal remedies aren't well regulated. And other dietary supplements aren't, either. So you are not as protected from fraudulent dietary supplement claims as you might think.

According to current regulation, herbal remedies, along with other dietary supplements, can enter the

TEN RED FLAGS OF JUNK SCIENCE

A new health or nutrition report? Before you jump to conclusions, check it out. Any combination of these signs should send up a red flag of suspicion.

1. Recommendations that promise a quick fix
2. Dire warnings of danger from a single product or regimen
3. Claims that sound too good to be true
4. Simplistic conclusions drawn from a complex study
5. Recommendations based on a single study
6. Dramatic statements that are refuted by reputable scientific organizations
7. Lists of "good" and "bad" foods
8. Recommendations made to help sell a product
9. Recommendations based on studies published without peer review
10. Recommendations from studies that ignore differences among individuals or groups

Source: Food and Nutrition Science Alliance (FANSA) ✦

marketplace without approval by the Food and Drug Administration (FDA)—and without years of safety testing. Only those known to be truly dangerous are forbidden. Currently the dosages of herbal remedies aren't standardized, so dosages vary.

You may find claims on packaging for herbal products, too, although they can't say that the product cures or prevents disease. Claims may have only scant evidence to back them up. And they don't require FDA approval.

Protect yourself by following these guidelines:

Go with the tried-and-true. There's plenty of scientific evidence supporting the benefits of physical activity, healthful eating, and a healthful lifestyle. That's the wise approach to fitness.

Before taking any herbal remedy or other dietary supplement, check with your doctor, a registered dietitian, or other qualified nutrition expert. Decide together if it's safe and appropriate or if other known treatments would yield safe, effective results.

Always consult a qualified health professional. Be cautious of those who call themselves an "herbalist," "herb doctor," "health counselor," or "master herbalist." These job titles aren't regulated.

Skip herbal remedies if you're taking medication—either prescription drugs or over-the-counter medications. These products may interfere with your medications. The combination could make your medication ineffective, or together they may create a harmful side effect.

If you're pregnant (or trying to get pregnant) or breast-feeding, avoid herbal remedies unless your doctor gives them an OK. Substances in these remedies may pass to your baby. These products aren't meant for children either.

If you get a doctor's OK, use herbal products only in small amounts—and not for very long. Take single-herb products, not those with many ingredients. Then if you have an adverse effect, you more easily can identify the source.

If an herbal product seems to cause any negative side effects, stop taking it. And contact your doctor right away. Your doctor should contact FDA's MedWatch hotline. This professional service helps experts monitor adverse reactions.

Be aware that many of these products are quackery. *Refer to "Play '10 Questions'" on page 591 to help you evaluate their claims.*

Refer to "Herbal Teas: Health Benefits?" on page 183.

Beyond Vitamins and Minerals: What's Known About Supplements

Dietary supplements cover a broad range of products. Although multi-vitamin/mineral supplements have the biggest share of the market, other products also belong in the broad category of dietary supplements, as defined by the Dietary Supplement and Health Education Act of 1994. That includes herbal remedies, amino acids, enzymes, plant extracts, other botanicals, and concentrates.

Even though these products are sold over the counter, talk to your doctor, a registered dietitian or another qualified nutrition expert about them. Many of these products don't provide the benefits they claim. Others may have harmful side effects. Some may be more fraud than fact.

These are just a few products you might encounter:

➢ *Amino acids.* Amino acid supplements, such as arginine and ornithine, are often promoted to build muscle and increase fat loss among athletes. But most athletes consume more than enough amino acids from food. So these products are an unnecessary expense. *Refer to "Muscle Myths" on page 539.*

➢ *Bee pollen.* Bee pollen is promoted to cure many ailments—and improve physical performance. But it has no magical quality. It's composed of the same nutrients found naturally in food: starch, sugars, protein, and a small amount of fat. For some people, taking bee pollen results in an allergic reaction. Anyone with kidney disease or a predisposition for gout should avoid it.

➢ *Brewer's yeast.* Also called "nutritional yeast," brewer's yeast is a rich source of many B vitamins—but not necessarily vitamin B_{12}. It also may have protein and some trace minerals. Claims for using brewer's yeast say that it can decrease constipation, treat diabetes, lower blood cholesterol, and improve athletic performance. However, no scientific evidence supports these claims. In fact, its possible side effects include diarrhea and nausea.

➢ *Carnitine.* Carnitine is a body chemical, composed of two essential amino acids (lysine and methionine). As an ergogenic aid, it's been promoted for more energy, aerobic power, and body fat reduction. The human body produces adequate amounts. And foods of animal origin are good sources. There's no need to take extra. *For more on amino acids, refer to* "Protein Power" *on page* 561.

➢ *Chromium picolinate.* Chromium picolinate is promoted as an ergogenic aid for athletes, as well as an aid to weight loss. Because chromium is part of insulin, it plays a role in energy production. Deficiencies of chromium from food choices are rare, however. When chromium levels are normal, there doesn't appear to be any benefit to taking a supplement. In supplements, chromium levels are significantly higher than the Recommended Dietary Allowance (RDA). Excess levels may have adverse effects—and offer no benefits.

➢ *Co-enzyme* Q10 *(also known as ubiquinone).* This body chemical, produced in body cells, aids in energy production and works as an antioxidant. In spite of the claims, there's no agreement that ingesting additional co-enzyme Q10 offers extra benefits.

➢ *Creatine phosphate.* This ergogenic aid is promoted to enhance energy and delay fatigue. However, creatine is an amino acid that's made in the liver from other amino acids. Because the body makes an adequate supply, taking creatine as a supplement isn't warranted. There's no adequate research on its effectiveness as a supplement. Researchers are currently studying creatinine's role in building muscle mass.

➢ *Fish oil supplements.* Fish oil supplements are promoted for their omega-3 fatty acids and their potential for lowering the risk for blocked blood vessels and heart attacks. However, their safety, effectiveness, and proper dosage haven't been determined. And they can't make up for a high-fat diet. You're better off to enjoy seafood instead and follow an overall low-fat eating plan. *Refer to* "Eat Your Omega-3s" *on page* 56.

➢ *Garlic supplements.* Garlic supplements, sold as pills and extracts, are promoted for lowering blood cholesterol levels. Although some studies suggest that consuming garlic cloves (5 or more cloves a day) may offer benefits, there's no conclusive evidence. Garlic supplements don't appear to have the same benefits. Until more is known, follow accepted methods to keep your blood cholesterol under control: stay physically active and eat a diet that's low in fat, saturated fat, and cholesterol.

➢ *Ginseng.* Ginseng, which is a plant root, is promoted as an aphrodisiac and a cure-all for almost everything from memory loss to menopause to stress to chronic ailments. Although it's been used in Asia for hundreds of years, few human studies show true benefits. And high intakes of ginseng taken over time may have harmful side effects, including dangerous changes in blood pressure,

have you ever wondered

... *if extra protein makes nails stronger?* Appearance-conscious teens often hear that taking gelatin strengthens nails. But there's no magic nutritional cure for nails that break and split.

... *if ma huang is a dietary supplement?* Being a medicinal herb, ma huang (also called ephedra) is touted as an energy enhancer. Classified as a dietary supplement, it's also a component of many weight-loss teas and other aids. Ma huang contains a stimulant called ephedrine. Used improperly or taken too long, it can have harmful side effects: high blood pressure, rapid heart beat, muscle injury, and nerve damage, among others. People with health problems already, such as high blood pressure, heart disease, and diabetes, are at special risk. Always talk to your doctor before using this product. Better yet, avoid it. ✦

sleep loss, anxiety, tranquilizing effects, breast pain, and vaginal bleeding.

➢ *Laetrile.* Promoted as vitamin B_{17}, laetrile isn't a vitamin. Instead it's a substance derived from the pits of apricots and other fruits with stones. It contains cyanide, which can be lethal.

➢ *Lecithin.* Lecithin is a phospholipid, or a type of fat. Promoters make many claims for lecithin, for example, as a cure or prevention for arthritis, skin problems, gallstones, and nervous disorders. Others claim it dissolves cholesterol that's deposited in arteries. Because your body makes lecithin, taking it as a supplement doesn't appear to have added benefits. Synthetic lecithin isn't well absorbed.

➢ *Medicinal herbs.* Herbal products have different plant chemicals. So they have different effects on the body. Some, such as chamomile, echinacea, feverfew, ginger, garlic, and valerian, may have physical benefits, Another herb, St. John's wort, is promoted to alleviate some symptoms of depression; however, its use makes skin more sensitive to sunlight. Ginkgo biloba, which has received attention for treating circulatory-related symptoms, has had limited study; in large amounts, it can cause digestive problems. For these herbs and others, further study is needed. Until more is known, there's no recommendation or safe dosage for ingesting them. And they should never replace proven medical treatment; your doctor should always be informed if they're used.

According to the Food and Drug Administration, other medicinal herbs may have serious side effects. At least five herbal remedies have been linked to health problems or death:

- *Chaparral*—liver damage
- *Comfrey*—liver damage
- *Ephedra*—high blood pressure, rapid heart beat, muscle injury, and nerve damage, among others
- *Lobelia*—breathing problems, rapid heart beat, sweating, coma, and death
- *Yohimbe*—nervous disorders, paralysis, fatigue, stomach problems, and death

Refer to "Herbals—Help or Harm?" on page 587.

➢ *Melatonin.* This hormone is classified as a dietary supplement, too. It's been promoted to aid sleep and jet lag, prevent disease, slow aging, slow some cancers, or enhance sexual performance. However, there's little evidence for these claims. And melatonin's long-term effects, safe dosage, and interactions with food and medicine aren't known. Moreover, there's no control over its purity. Until more is known, caution is advised.

➢ *Pangamic acid.* Touted as vitamin B_{15}, it's not a vitamin at all. Instead it's an inconsistent mixture of substances, including some that are potentially hazardous. Although extolled as an energy enhancer for athletes, it has no proven benefits.

➢ *Royal jelly.* Royal jelly is touted as a supplement for many health conditions, including menopause for women and sexual performance for men. Royal jelly itself is produced by worker bees to nourish future queen bees. But no evidence shows physical benefits to humans. It's an exotic and expensive product that may offer psychological value to some.

➢ *Shark cartilage.* Touted as an anti-cancer agent, shark cartilage is actually gristle. It provides calcium; however, scientific findings don't support its use in blocking tumor formation. Because it can effect the development of blood vessels, taking shark cartilage could be risky for pregnant women, and those recovering from wounds, surgery, and heart ailments. Beyond that, shark cartilage taken as an oral supplement may not be absorbed by the body—and it may not be pure shark cartilage.

➢ *Spirulina.* Spirulina, a blue-green algae, is often touted as a high-energy food. It can offer nutrients to the diet. But it has no energy-producing qualities. Although it's often promoted as a source of vitamin B_{12}, it contains a form of the vitamin that is not reliably absorbed by humans.

➢ *Wheat germ and wheat germ oil.* Both products are promoted as ergogenic aids. Although no proven benefits exist, there aren't any known side effects or adverse reactions from ingesting them. In fact, wheat germ, often an ingredient in food, supplies nutrients such as protein, B vitamins, and vitamin E.

Refer to "Dietary Supplements: Use and Abuse" on page 111 *and "Ergogenic Aids: No Substitute for Training" on page* 553.

your nutrition check-up

Play "10 Questions"

Suspicious when something sounds too good to be true? Your best defense against a "quack attack" is healthy skepticism and taking time to be well informed.

Nutrition quackery thrives among people who are uninformed or already misinformed or misled. And quacks can more easily manipulate those people who are already leaning in their direction.

So avoid their lure. Arm yourself with these questions—even when you aren't suspicious!

Does the promotion of a nutrition product, regimen, service, treatment, or device...

Yes No

- ❒ ❒ 1. Try to lure you with scare tactics, emotional appeals, or perhaps with a "money-back guarantee" rather than proven results?
- ❒ ❒ 2. Promise to "revitalize," "detoxify," or "balance your body with nature"? Or does it claim to increase your strength, stamina, or energy level?
- ❒ ❒ 3. Offer "proof" based on personal anecdotes or testimonials, rather than sound science?
- ❒ ❒ 4. Advise supplements for everyone? Or recommend very large doses of nutrients? "Very large" means significantly more than 100 percent of the Recommended Dietary Allowances (RDAs). *Refer to page* 606 *for* RDA *levels*.
- ❒ ❒ 5. Claim it can "treat," "cure," or "prevent" diverse health problems... from arthritis to cancer to sexual impotence?
- ❒ ❒ 6. Make unrealistic claims, such as "reversing the aging process" or "curing disease" or "quick, easy approach"?
- ❒ ❒ 7. Blame the food supply as the source of health problems? Belittle government regulation? Or question the advice of recognized medical authorities?
- ❒ ❒ 8. Claim that its "natural" benefits surpass those of "synthetic" products?
- ❒ ❒ 9. Mention a "secret formula"? Or fail to list ingredients on its product label or to state any possible side effects?
- ❒ ❒ 10. Come from a so-called "nutrition expert" without accepted credentials? Does that person also sell the product?

your nutrition check-up (continued)

Now Score Yourself

In this game of "10 questions," you might spot quackery with just one "yes" answer! Here's why.

1. *Fact.* Playing on emotion, misinformation, or even fear is common among nonscientific pseudo-experts. Emotional words used to promote a product can be an instant tip-off to quackery: "guaranteed," "breakthrough," and "miraculous" are used for emotional appeal. *For a list of commonly-used terms, refer to "Spotting a Fraud" on page 47.*

2. *Fact.* Pseudo-medical jargon, such as "detoxify," "rejuvenate," or "balance your body chemistry," suggest misinformation. They have no meaning in physiology. To sort valid medical terms from hype, ask a credible expert to decipher any confusing terms or phrases. A supplement can't increase your strength, stamina, or energy level, either. *For more about dietary supplements promoted to athletes, refer to "Ergogenic Aids—No Substitute for Training" on page 553.* "Ergogenic" means the potential to increase work output; a supplement can't do that!

3. *Fact.* Be skeptical of case histories and testimonials from satisfied users—if that's the only proof that a product works. Instead look for medical evidence from a reputable institution or qualified health expert. Without scientific evidence, a reported "cure" may have other causes. Sometimes the ailment disappears on its own. The "cure" actually may have a placebo effect; its benefit may be psychological, not physical. The person may have been misdiagnosed in the first place. And even chronic ailments don't always have symptoms all the time.

4. *Fact.* For the record: Everyone doesn't need a vitamin supplement! A varied, balanced eating plan with enough servings from the Food Guide Pyramid provides the nutrients most healthy people need. *Refer to "The Food Guide Pyramid: Your Healthful Eating Guide" on page 243.*

For most people, there's no added benefit to taking more than 100 percent of the RDAs for vitamins and minerals. Except for a nutrition deficiency, there's no proof that nutrients alone prevent or cure anything. So ignore the hype! To the contrary, taking too much may be harmful. *Refer to "Dietary Supplements: Use and Abuse" on page 111.*

5. *Fact.* No nutrition regimen, device, or product can treat all that ails you. And they can't cure many health conditions, including arthritis, cancer, and sexual impotence. Even when they're part of credible treatment or prevention strategies, nutrition factors are typically just one part of overall health care.

6. *Fact.* Claims that sound too good to be true probably are. But that's what people want to hear. Quackery thrives because people want simple cures and magic ways to change what's imperfect.

7. *Fact.* Quacks often belittle the regular food supply, government regulation, and the established medical community. Instead they call for "freedom of choice"... and describe unproved methods as alternatives to current proven methods. However, alternatives promoted through quackery may be unsafe, ineffective, or untested. Among proven methods, you'll find choices.

your nutrition check-up (continued)

8. *Fact.* There's nothing magical about products promoted as "natural." From the standpoint of science, the chemical structure of natural and synthetic dietary supplements is essentially the same. And the body uses them in the same manner. Herbal products aren't necessarily safe just because they're "natural." Some substances found in nature can have potent, drug-like effects.

9. *Fact.* By law, a medication must carry product information on its packaging. That includes the product's ingredients, use, dosage, warnings and precautions, and what to do if adverse reactions occur. However, products or regimens sold through quackery seldom report all this information, including potential side effects or dangers.

10. *Fact.* Quacks are typically salespeople. Rather than offering accurate advice, their bottom line is to sell you something. Be wary when someone tries to diagnose your health status, then offers to sell you a remedy. Be wary of the methods used to assess your health, too. Many invalid tests may be hard to distinguish from the legitimate clinical assessments. Those often used by quacks include hair analysis, iridology, and herbal crystallization analysis, among others. Get an opinion from a qualified health professional before getting these assessments or making changes based on the results.

Quackery underlies many regimens focused on weight loss or gain, too. *To judge programs for their effectiveness and safety, refer to* "Questions to Ask… About Diet Programs" *on page* 46.

real life nutrition

Jumping to the Cure!

Robert switched on the car radio—just in time for some breaking health news. He listened: "In a new study, scientists report that garlic may be linked to lowering blood cholesterol...."

His mind wandered to his dinner, not listening to the whole report. Robert pondered, "That's just the cure I need—and with no pain! Tonight it's garlic bread, then a trip to the store for some of those garlic supplements I've heard advertised."

After shopping, he nestled into his easy chair with the newspaper and his remote control for the television. That was his daily ritual for several hours after an intense day at his desk job.

As he glanced through the headlines, Robert noticed the garlic study again. He read a couple of paragraphs and felt good that he was already on a garlic regimen. The 10 o'clock news led off with the same story. He shook his head, "I just hope those scientists don't change their minds about this garlic cure!"

What might you say to Robert about this approach to nutrition news?

Before Robert leaps to conclusions about a news report on nutrition, he might consider these points:

➢ The news report never suggested that garlic was a "cure" for high blood cholesterol—as Robert perceived. It only indicated a "link."

➢ Robert should listen to and read the full report, not just count on headline news. The newspaper report might tell more about the study: who conducted it, how many subjects there were, if the subjects were animals or humans, and if the results applied to him. He didn't read enough to see if qualified nutrition experts provided advice!

➢ Robert might contact a local nutrition expert, such as a registered dietitian, to get a qualified opinion on the study. He needs to take time to learn more.

➢ If Robert hears a conflicting report later, he shouldn't conclude that scientists are just changing their minds. Scientific study is a process of research, debate, and more research and debate. What sounds like conflicting findings is really the process of learning more.

➢ Robert shouldn't count on a dietary supplement—or any seemingly easy approach—to treat his health problem. Instead he would be wiser to follow accepted forms of treatments: for example, increase his physical activity and make changes in his food choices, as needed.

RESOURCES

Resources You Can Use!

Looking for sound nutrition information? You have many reliable resources: professional associations, health agencies, government agencies, and credible nutrition newsletters. Besides brochures, booklets, and consumer hotlines, many provide reliable on-line nutrition information. Your local hospital, public health, extension service, and many food industry groups are other reliable resources you might tap.

General Nutrition

The American Dietetic Association
National Center for Nutrition and Dietetics
216 West Jackson Boulevard
Chicago, IL 60606-6995
On-line: http://www.eatright.org

Consumer Nutrition Hot Line:
900/CALL-AN-RD (900/225-5267); to speak to a registered dietitian (RD)
800/366-1655; to listen to recorded messages in English or Spanish, or to obtain a referral to an RD in your area

Center for Nutrition Policy and Promotion
U.S. Department of Agriculture
1120 20th Street, NW, North Lobby
Suite 200
Washington, DC 20036
202/418-2312

Cooperative Extension Service
(Contact your state's land-grant university.)

Food and Nutrition Information Center
National Agricultural Library
U.S. Department of Agriculture
Room 304
10301 Baltimore Avenue
Beltsville, MD 20705-2351
301/504-5719
Online : http://www.usda.gov/fnic

International Food Information Council (IFIC)
1100 Connecticut Avenue, NW
Suite 430
Washington, DC 20036
202/296-6540
On-line: http://ificinfo.health.org

National Academy of Sciences/Food and Nutrition Board
2101 Constitution Avenue, NW
Washington, DC 20418
202/334-1732

Nutrition, Health, and Food Management Division
American Association of Family and Consumer Sciences
1555 King Street
Alexandria, VA 22314
On-line: http://www.aafcs.org

Society for Nutrition Education
7107 Wisconsin Ave NW, Suite 901
Bethesda, MD 20814
301/656-4938

Food Safety, Labeling, and Advertising

U.S. Environmental Protection Agency
Drinking Water Hotline
800/426-4791

Federal Trade Commission (FTC)
(Contact your regional FTC office.)

Food and Drug Administration (FDA)
Consumer Information Office
5600 Fishers Lane, HFE 88
Rockville, MD 20857
301/443-3170
(Or contact your regional FDA office.)
On-line: http://www.fda.gov

FDA's AIDS/Nutrition Information
P.O. Box 6003
Rockville, MD 20849-6003
800/458-5231

FDA's Food Information and Seafood Hotline
800/332-4010

FDA's MEDWatch Program
800/FDA-1088

FDA's Center for Food Safety and Applied Nutrition
800/FDA-4010
On-line: http://www.vm.cfsan.fda.gov

Food Safety and Inspection Service
U.S. Department of Agriculture
14th St. and Independence Avenue SW
Washington, D.C. 20250
202/720-2791

National Lead Information Center
1019 19th Street NW
Suite 401
Washington, DC 20036
800/532-3394

USDA's Meat & Poultry Hotline
800/535-4555

Food Sensitivities

American Academy of Allergy, Asthma, and Immunology
611 East Wells Street
Milwaukee, WI 53202
414/272-6071
On-line: http://www.aaaai.org

American Allergy Association
P.O. Box 7273
Menlo Park, CA 94026-7273

American Celiac Society
58 Musano Court
West Orange, NJ 07052-4103
201/762-4401

Celiac Sprue Association/USA
P.O. Box 31700
Omaha, NE 68131-0700
402/558-0600

Children's P.K.U. Network
San Diego, CA
619/233-3202

Food Allergy Network
10400 Eaton Place
Suite 107
Fairfax, VA 22030
703/691-3179
On-line: http://www.foodallergy.org

Gluten Intolerance Group of North America
P.O. Box 23053
Seattle, WA 98102-0353
206/325-6980

P.K.U. Parents
8 Myrtle Lane
San Anselmo, CA 94960
415/457-4632

Maternal, Infant, Child, and Adolescent Nutrition

American Academy of Pediatrics
141 Northwest Point Boulevard
P.O. Box 927
Elk Grove Village, IL 60009-0927
847/228-5005
On-line: http://www.aap.org

American Foundation for Maternal and Child Health
439 East 51st Street
New York, NY 10022
212/759-5510

American School Food Service Association
1600 Duke Street
7th Floor
Alexandria, VA 22314
703/739-3900
On-line: http://www.asfsa.org

La Leche League International
1400 North Meacham Road
Schaumburg, IL 60173
800/LALECHE (800/525-3243)
847/519-7730
On-line: http://www.lalacheleague.org

Nutrition and Aging

American Association of Retired Persons
1900 K Street NW
Washington, DC 20049
202/434-2277
On-line: http://www.aarp.org

Center for the Study of Aging
706 Madison Avenue
Albany, NY 12208
518/465-6927

Elder Care Locater
1112 16th Street, NW
Suite 100
Washington, DC 20036
800/677-1116

National Association of Nutrition and Aging Services
Programs/National Meals on Wheels
2675 44th Street, SW
Suite 305
Grand Rapids, MI 49509
800/999-6262
616/531-5555

National Institute on Aging Information Office
Building 31
Room 5C-27
31 Center Drive, MSC 2292
Bethesda, MD 20892
301/496-1752
On-line: http://www.nih.gov/nia

General Health and Disease Prevention/ Treatment

General

American Academy of Family Physicians
8880 Ward Parkway
Kansas City, MO 64114
816/333-9700

American Health Foundation
320 East 43rd Street
New York, NY 10017
212/953-1900

American Medical Association
515 North State Street
Chicago, IL 60610-4377
312/464-5000
On-line: http://www.ama-assn.org

American Public Health Association
1015 15th Street, NW
Washington, DC 20005
202/789-5600
On-line: http://www.apha.org

Center for Disease Control and Prevention
1600 Clifton Road Northeast
Atlanta, GA 30333
404/639-3311
On-line: http://www.cdc.gov

Congress for National Health
National Wellness Institute
P.O. Box 827
1319 Freemont Street, South Hall
Stevens Point, WI 54481-0827

Minority Health Resource Center
P.O. Box 37337
Washington, DC 20013-7337
800/444-6472

National Center for Health Statistics
U.S. Department of Health & Human Services
Presidential Building
6525 Belcrest Road
Hyattsville, MD 20782
301/436-8500
On-line: http://www.fedstats.gov

National Health Information Center
P.O. Box 1133
Washington, DC 20013-1133
301/565-4167
800/336-4797
On-line: http://nhic-nt.health.org

National Institutes of Health
9000 Rockville Pike
Bethesda, MD 20892
301/496-4000
On-line:http://www.nih.gov/health

U.S. Department of Health and Human Services
On-line: http://www.healthfinder.gov

Alcoholism

National Clearinghouse for Alcohol Information
P.O. Box 2345
Rockville, MD 20852
301/468-2600

National Council on Alcoholism
12 W. 21st Street
New York, NY 10010

Anorexia Nervosa and Bulimia

Anorexia Nervosa and Associated Disorders, Inc.
P.O. Box 7
Highland Park, IL 60035
847/831-3438

National Anorexic Aid Society, Inc.
6655 South Yale Avenue
Tulsa, OK 64137
918/481-4044

Cancer

American Cancer Society
1599 Clifton Road NE
Atlanta, GA 30329
404/320-3333
800/227-2345
On-line: http://www.cancer.org

American Institute for Cancer Research
1759 R. Street, NW
Washington, DC 20009
202/328-7744
On-line: http://www.aicr.org

Disease Prevention and Health Promotion (ODPHP)
National Health Information Resources
P.O. Box 1133
Washington, DC 20013-1133
800/336-4797
301/565-4167

National Cancer Institute
National Institutes of Health
31 Center Drive, Building 31, Room 10A07
Bethesda, MD 20892
800/4-CANCER (800/422-6237)
On-line: http://www.cancernet.nci.nih.gov

Cardiovascular (Heart) Disease

American Heart Association
7272 Greenville Avenue
Dallas, TX 75231
214/373-6300
800/AHA-USA1 (800/242-8721)
On-line: http://www.amhrt.org

National Cholesterol Education Program and National Heart, Lung, and Blood Institute
P.O. Box 30105
Bethesda, MD 20824
301/251-1222
On-line: http://www.nhlbi.nih.gov/nhlbi/nhlbi.htm

Diabetes

American Diabetes Association
1660 Duke Street
Alexandria, VA 22314
800/232-3472
On-line: http://www.diabetes.org

Juvenile Diabetes Foundation International
120 Wall Street, 19th Floor
New York, NY 10005
212/785-9500
800/JDF-CURE (800/533-2873)

Joslin Diabetes Center
Nutrition Services
Joslin Clinic
1 Joslin Place
Boston, MA 02215
617/732-2571

National Diabetes Information Clearinghouse
1 Information Way
Bethesda, MD 20892-3560
301/654-3327

Digestive Disease

National Digestive Diseases Information Clearinghouse
2 Information Way
Bethesda, MD 20892-3570
301/654-3810

Digestive Disease National Coalition
507 Capitol Court NE, Suite 200
Washington, DC 20002
202/544-7497

Obesity

Overeaters Anonymous
World Service Office
P.O. Box 44020
Rio Rancho, NM 87174-4020
515/891-2664

Shape Up America
P.O. Box 1995
Monroe, CT 06468-1995
On-line: http://www2.shapeup.org/sua

Oral Health

American Dental Association
211 East Chicago Avenue
Chicago, IL 60611
312/440-2500

Osteoporosis

National Osteoporosis Foundation
1150 17th Street, NW
Suite 500
Washington, DC 20036-4603
202/223-2226
800/223-9994
On-line: http://www.nof.org

Sports Nutrition and Physical Activity

American College of Sports Medicine
P.O. Box 1440
Indianapolis, IN 46206-1440
317/637-9200

American Council on Exercise
Consumer Fitness Hot Line
800/529-8227

American Alliance for Health, Physical Education, Recreation and Dance
1900 Association Drive
Reston, VA 20191
703/476-3400

American Running and Fitness Association
4405 East-West Highway
Suite 405
Bethesda, MD 20814
301/913-9517
800/776-ARFA (-2732)

Fifty-Plus Fitness Association
P.O. Box D
Stanford, CA 94309
415/323-6160

International Center for Sports Nutrition
502 South 44th Street
Suite 3012
Omaha, NE 68105-1065
402/559-5505

National Fitness and Wellness Coalition
1800 Silas Deane Highway
Rocky Hill, CT 06067
203/721-1055

President's Council on Physical Fitness and Sports
701 Pennsylvania Avenue, NW
Suite 250
Washington, DC 20004
202/272-3421

YMCA of the USA
101 North Wacker Drive
Chicago, IL 60606
800/USA-YMCA (800/872-9622)

Women's Sports Foundation
Eisenhower Park
East Meadow, NY 11554
800/227-3988
516/542-4700

Vegetarian Eating

North American Vegetarian Society
P.O. Box 72
Dolgeville, NY 13329
518/568-7970

Vegetarian Resource Group
P.O. Box 1463
Baltimore, MD 21203
410/366-VEGE
On-line: http://www.vrg.org

Food Technology/ Biotechnology

Functional Foods for Health
University of Illinois at Urbana-Champaign, Chicago
On-line: http://www.ag.uiuc.edu/~ffh/ffh.html

International Food Additives Council
5775 Peachtree-Dunwoody Road
Suite 500-G
Atlanta, GA 30342
404/252-3663

International Food Biotechnology Council
1126 16th Street NW
Washington, DC 20036
202/659-0789

Office of Biotechnology
Food and Drug Administration
200 C Street SW
Washington, DC 20204
202/205-4144

Health Fraud

Consumer Health Research Institute
300 East Pink Hill Road
Independence, MO 64057
816/228-4595
On-line: http://www.ncahf.org

National Council Against Health Fraud, Inc.
P.O. Box 1276
Loma Linda, CA 92354-1276
909/824-4690
On-line: http://wwwncahf.org

Quackwatch, Inc.
On-line: http://www.quackwatch.com

Food Industry Associations

American Dry Bean Board
115 Railway Street
Scottsbluff, NE 69361
308/632-8239

American Egg Board
1460 Renaissance Drive
Suite 301
Park Ridge, IL 60068
847/296-7043
On-line: http://www.aeb.org

American Seafood Institute
212 Maine Street
Suite 3
Wakefield, RI 02879
800/EAT-FISH (800/328-3474)

American Soybean Association
540 Maryville Center Drive
St. Louis, MO 63141
314/576-1770

Calorie Control Council
5775 Peachtree-Dunwoody Road
Suite 500-G
Atlanta, GA 30342
404/252-3663
On-line: http://www.caloriecontrol.org

Food Marketing Institute
800 Connecticut Avenue, NW
Washington, DC 20006-2701
202/452-8444
On-line: http://www.fmi.org

Glutamate Association
5775 Peachtree-Dunwoody Road
Suite 500-G
Atlanta, GA 30342
404/252-3663

Infant Formula Council
5775 Peachtree-Dunwoody Road
Suite 500-G
Atlanta, GA 30342
404/252-3663

International Bottled Water Association
113 North Henry Street
Alexandria, VA 22314
703/683-5213

National Coffee Association
110 Wall Street
New York, NY 10005
212/344-5596

National Dairy Council
O'Hare International Center
10255 West Higgins Road
Suite 900
Rosemont, IL 60018-5616
847/803-2000

National Broiler Council
Madison Building, No. 614
1155 15th Street, NW
Washington, DC 20005
202/296-2622

National Fisheries Institute, Inc.
200 M Street NW
Suite 580
Washington, D.C. 20036
202/296-3428

National Cattlemen's Beef Association
444 North Michigan Avenue
Chicago, IL 60611
312/467-5520
On-line: http://www.cowtown.org

National Pasta Association
2102 Wilson Blvd., Suite 920
Arlington, VA 22201
703/841-0818
On-line: http://ilovepasta.org

National Pork Producer's Council
P.O. Box 10383
Des Moines, IA 50306
515/223-2629
On-line: http://www.nppc.org

National Restaurant Association
1200 17th Street NW
Washington, DC 20036-3097
202/331-5960
On-line: http://www.restaurant.org

National Turkey Federation
1225 New York Ave., NW
Suite 400
Washington, DC 20002
202/898-0100

Produce for a Better Health Foundation
5 A Day Program
P.O. Box 6036
Newark, DE 19714
302/738-7100

Produce Marketing Association
1500 Casho Mill Road
P.O. Box 6036
Newark, DE 19714-6036
302/738-7100

Snack Food Association
1711 King Street
Suite One
Alexandria, VA 22314
703/836-8262

The Sugar Association, Inc.
1101 15th Street, NW
Suite 600
Washington, DC 20005
202/785-1122

The Tea Council of the U.S.A.
230 Park Avenue
New York, NY 10169
212/986-6998

United Fresh Fruit & Vegetable Association
727 North Washington Street
Alexandria, VA 22314
703/836-3410

U.S.A. Rice Council
P.O. Box 740121
Houston, TX 77274
713/270-6699

Wheat Foods Council
5500 South Quebec
Suite 111
Englewood, CO 80111
303/694-5828
On-line: http://www.wheatfoods.org

Nutrition Newsletters

Environmental Nutrition
52 Riverside Drive
Suite 15-A
New York, NY 10024-6599
On-line: 76521.2250@compuserve.com

Tufts University Diet and Nutrition Letter
P.O. Box 57857
Boulder, CO 80322-3889
800/274-7581

Consumer Reports on Health
Box 52148
Boulder, CO 80322-2148
800/234-2188

FDA *Consumer*
Superintendent of Documents
Government Printing Office
Washington, DC 20401
202/512-1800

Mayo Clinic Health Letter
Subscription Services
P.O. Box 53889
Boulder, CO 80322-3889
800/333-9037

University of California at Berkeley Wellness Letter
Health Letter Associates
P.O. Box 420148
Palm Coast, FL 32142
800/829-9080

APPENDICES

Recommended Dietary Allowances (Abridged)

The following Recommended Dietary Allowances, expressed as average daily intakes over time, were established by the Food and Nutrition Board, National Academy of Sciences. The recommendations are designed for the maintenance of good nutrition for practically all healthy people in the United States. As always, the best eating style is based on a balanced diet of a variety of foods. That way, you'll be sure to get the required nutrients, even those for which requirements have been less well defined. Refer to the Dietary Reference Intakes on page 607 for calcium, phosphorus, magnesium, vitamin D, fluoride, the B-vitamins, and choline.

			Vitamins				Minerals			
	Age	Protein (g)	A (mcg RE)	E (mg)	K (mcg)	C (mg)	Iron (mg)	Zinc (mg)	Iodine (mcg)	Selenium (mcg)
Infants	0-6 mos	13	375	3	5	30	6	5	40	10
	6-12 mos	14	375	4	10	35	10	5	50	15
Children	1-3 yrs	16	400	6	15	40	10	10	70	20
	4-6	24	500	7	20	45	10	10	90	20
	7-10	28	700	7	30	45	10	10	120	30
Males	11-14 yrs	45	1000	10	45	50	12	15	150	40
	15-18	59	1000	10	65	60	12	15	150	50
	19-24	58	1000	10	70	60	10	15	150	70
	25-50	63	1000	10	80	60	10	15	150	70
	51+	63	1000	10	80	60	10	15	150	70
Females	11-14 yrs	46	800	8	45	50	15	12	150	45
	15-18	44	800	8	55	60	15	12	150	50
	19-24	46	800	8	60	60	15	12	150	55
	25-50	50	800	8	65	60	15	12	150	55
	51+	50	800	8	65	60	10	12	150	55
Pregnant		60	800	10	65	70	30	15	175	65
Lactating	1st 6 mos	65	1300	12	65	95	15	19	200	75
	2nd 6 mos	62	1200	11	65	90	15	16	200	75

Adapted with permission from Recommended Dietary Allowances, 10th Edition. © 1989 *by the* National Academy of Sciences. *Published by* National Academy Press, *Washington,* DC.

mcg RE = *microgram Retinol Equivalents* **mcg** = *micrograms* **mg** = *milligrams* **g** = *grams*

Dietary Reference Intakes (DRIs), Recommended Levels for Individual Intake

Food and Nutrition Board, National Academy of Sciences–Institute of Medicine (1997–98)

Age/Life-Stage	Calcium (mg)	Phosphorus (mg)	Magnesium (mg)	Vitamin D[a,b] (mcg)	Flouride (mg)	Thiamin (mg)	Riboflavin (mg)	Niacin[c] (mg)	Vitamin B_6 (mg)	Folate[d] (mcg)	Vitamin B_{12} (mcg)	Pantothenic Acid (mg)	Biotin (mcg)	Choline[e] (mg)
Infants														
0–5 months	210*	100*	30*	5*	0.01*	0.2*	0.3*	2*	0.1*	65*	0.4*	1.7*	5*	125*
6–11 months	270*	275*	75*	5*	0.5*	0.3*	0.4*	3*	0.3*	80*	0.5*	1.8*	6*	150*
Children														
1–3 yrs.	500*	460	80	5*	0.7*	0.5	0.5	6	0.5	150	0.9	2*	8*	200*
4–8 yrs.	800*	500	130	5*	1*	0.6	0.6	8	0.6	200	1.2	3*	12*	250*
Males														
9–13 yrs.	1300*	1250	240	5*	2*	0.9	0.9	12	1.0	300	1.8	4*	20*	375*
14–18 yrs.	1300*	1250	410	5*	3*	1.2	1.3	16	1.3	400	2.4	5*	25*	550*
19–30 yrs.	1000*	700	400	5*	4*	1.2	1.3	16	1.3	400	2.4	5*	30*	550*
31–50 yrs.	1000*	700	420	5*	4*	1.2	1.3	16	1.3	400	2.4	5*	30*	550*
51–70 yrs.	1200*	700	420	10*	4*	1.2	1.3	16	1.7	400	2.4[f]	5*	30*	550*
>70 yrs.	1200*	700	420	15*	4*	1.2	1.3	16	1.7	400	2.4[f]	5*	30*	550*
Females														
9–13 yrs.	1300*	1250	240	5*	2*	0.9	0.9	12	1.0	300	1.8	4*	20*	375*
14–18 yrs.	1300*	1250	360	5*	3*	1.0	1.0	14	1.2	400[g]	2.4	5*	25*	400*
19–30 yrs.	1000*	700	310	5*	3*	1.1	1.1	14	1.3	400[g]	2.4	5*	30*	425*
31–50 yrs.	1000*	700	320	5*	3*	1.1	1.1	14	1.3	400[g]	2.4	5*	30*	425*
51–70 yrs.	1200*	700	320	10*	3*	1.1	1.1	14	1.5	400[g]	2.4[f]	5*	30*	425*
>70 yrs.	1200*	700	320	15*	3*	1.1	1.1	14	1.5	400	2.4[f]	5*	30*	425*
Pregnancy														
≤ 18 yrs.	1300*	1250	400	5*	3*	1.4	1.4	18	1.9	600[h]	2.6	6*	30*	450*
19–30 yrs.	1000*	700	350	5*	3*	1.4	1.4	18	1.9	600[h]	2.6	6*	30*	450*
31–50 yrs.	1000*	700	360	5*	3*	1.4	1.4	18	1.9	600[h]	2.6	6*	30*	450*
Lactation														
≤ 18 yrs.	1300*	1250	360	5*	3*	1.5	1.6	17	2.0	500	2.8	7*	35*	550*
19–30 yrs.	1000*	700	310	5*	3*	1.5	1.6	17	2.0	500	2.8	7*	35*	550*
31–50 yrs.	1000*	700	320	5*	3*	1.5	1.6	17	2.0	500	2.8	7*	35*	550*

mg = milligrams mcg = micrograms

*Note: This table presents Recommended Dietary Allowances (RDAs) and Adequate Intakes (AIs). (AI values are followed by an asterisk.) RDAs and AIs may both be used as goals for individual intake. RDAs are set to meet the average daily needs of almost all (97 to 98 percent) healthy individuals in a life-stage group. The AIs are believed to cover the daily needs of most healthy people, but lack of data or uncertainty in the data prevent clear specification of an RDA.

See additional notes on page 608.

Notes to "Dietary Reference Intakes (DRIs), Recommended Levels for Individual Intake" (page 607)

[a] As cholecalciferol (1 mcg cholecalciferol = 40 IU vitamin D)

[b] In the absence of adequate exposure to sunlight.

[c] As niacin equivalents. 1 mg of niacin = 60 mg of tryptophan

[d] As dietary folate equivalents (DFE). 1 DFE = 1 mcg food folate = 0.6 mcg of folic acid (from fortified food or supplement) consumed with food = 0.5 mcg of supplemental folic acid taken on an empty stomach.

[e] Although AIs have been set for choline, there are few data to assess whether a dietary supply of choline is needed at all stages of the life cycle.

[f] Since 10 to 30 percent of older people may malabsorb food–bound B_{12}, it is advisable for those older than 50 yrs. to meet their RDA mainly by taking foods fortified with B_{12} or a B_{12} containing supplement.

[g] It is recommended that all women capable of becoming pregnant consume 400 mcg of folic acid from fortified foods and/or supplements in addition to intake of food folate from a varied diet.

[h] Women should continue taking 400 mcg of folic acid until their pregnancy is confirmed, at which time the recommended daily intake increases.

Chart adapted with permisssion from the National Academy of Sciences. Copyright 1997 and 1998.

Estimated Safe and Adequate Daily Dietary Intakes of Selected Trace Elements

Since the toxic levels for many trace elements may be only several times usual intakes, the upper levels for the trace elements in this table should not be regularly exceeded.

	Age	Copper (mg)	Manganese (mg)	Chromium (mcg)	Molybdenum (mcg)
Infants	0-6 mos	0.4-0.6	0.3-0.6	10-40	15-30
	6-12 mos	0.6-0.7	0.6-1.0	20-60	20-40
Children and adolescents	1-3	0.7-1.0	1.0-1.5	20-80	25-50
	4-6	1.0-1.5	1.5-2.0	30-120	30-75
	7-10	1.0-2.0	2.0-3.0	50-200	50-150
	11+	1.5-2.5	2.0-5.0	50-200	75-250
Adults		1.5-3.0	2.0-5.0	50-200	75-250

Adapted with permission from Recommended Dietary Allowances, 1*0th edition.* © 1989 *by the* National Academy of Sciences. *Published by* National Academy Press, *Washington,* DC.

"Carbo" Foods

	Serving	Energy (calories)	Carbohydrates (grams)
BREAD, CEREAL, RICE, AND PASTA These foods provide a higher percentage of complex carbohydrate.			
Bagel	1/2	85	15
Biscuit (2" across)	1	105	15
Blueberry muffin	1	110	15
Bread (white, whole-wheat)	1 slice	60	10
Bread sticks	2 sticks	75	15
Bun (hot dog, hamburger)	1/2	60	10
Cereal	1 oz. (1 cup)	110	25
Cereal (cooked Cream of Wheat)	1/2 cup	65	15
Corn bread (2" square)	1/2 piece	90	15
English muffin	1/2	75	15
Graham crackers	2 squares	60	10
Noodles (spaghetti)	1/2 cup cooked	80	15
Oatmeal (cooked)	1/2 cup	75	15
Oatmeal (flav. instant)	1 packet	110	25
Pancakes (4" across)	1	55	10
Popcorn (plain)	1 cup popped	25	5
Pretzels	1 oz.	105	20
Rice (brown)	1/2 cup cooked	115	25
Rice (white)	1/2 cup cooked	110	25
Saltines	5 crackers	60	10
Tortilla (flour)	1	85	15
Waffles (3 1/2" across)	1	60	10
OTHER BAKED GOODS These foods provide both complex and simple carbohydrate.			
Angel food cake	1 piece	140	30
Animal crackers	5	55	10
Chocolate cake	1 piece	235	40
Fig bar	1	50	10
Granola bar	1	110	15
Oatmeal raisin cookie	1	60	10
COMBINATION FOODS These foods provide a higher percentage of complex carbohydrate.			
Bean burrito	1	395	30
Pizza (cheese)	1 slice	290	40

For the carbohydrate content of specific foods, check the Nutrition Facts *panel on food labels. To learn more about label reading, refer to "Get All the Facts!" on page 271.*

"Carbo" Foods (continued)

	Serving	Energy (calories)	Carbohydrates (grams)
FRUITS These foods provide a higher percentage of simple carbohydrate.			
Apple	1 medium	80	20
Apple juice	3/4 cup	85	20
Applesauce	1/2 cup	115	30
Banana	1	105	25
Cantaloupe	1/2 cup	30	5
Cherries (raw)	10	50	10
Dates (dried)	5	115	30
Fruit cocktail (packed in own juice)	1/2 cup	55	15
Grape juice	3/4 cup	70	15
Grapes	1/2 cup	75	20
Orange	1 med.	65	15
Orange juice	3/4 cup	85	20
Pear	1	75	20
Pineapple	1/2 cup	40	10
Prunes (dried)	5	100	25
Raisins (seedless)	1/3 cup	150	40
Raspberries	1/2 cup	30	5
Strawberries	1/2 cup	25	5
Watermelon	1/2 cup	25	5
VEGETABLES These foods provide a higher percentage of complex carbohydrate.			
Carrot	1 med.	30	10
Corn	1/2 cup	90	20
Lima beans	1/2 cup cooked	110	20
Peas (green)	1/2 cup	65	10
Potato (baked, plain)	1 large	220	50
Sweet potato	1 large	120	30
MILK, YOGURT, AND CHEESE These foods provide a higher percentage of simple carbohydrate.			
Frozen yogurt (low-fat)	1 cup	220	35
Fruit flavored yogurt	1 cup	225	40
Milk (1%)	1 cup	120	10
Milk (skim)	1 cup	85	10
Pudding	1/2 cup	160	30

Source: Jennings, *Debbi Sowell and Steen, Suzanne Nelson.* Play Hard, Eat Right, *The American Dietetic Association. Minneapolis: Chronimed Publishing,* 1995.

A Close-Up Look at Additives

	Improves or Maintains Nutritional Value	Prevents Spoilage	Prevents Rancidity and Discoloration	Distributes Particles Evenly	Prevents Lumping	Retains Moisture	Makes Food Rise	Controls pH	Gives Smooth, Thick, or Uniform Texture	Improves Baking Quality	Gives Color	Gives or Enhances Flavor	Sweetens
Acetic acid								X					
Acidulants or acidifiers			X					X				X	
Agar									X				
Alginate									X				
Annatto											X		
Aspartame													X
Baking powder (sodium bicarbonate and acid salts)							X						
Baking soda (sodium bicarbonate)							X						
BHA/BHT			X										
B vitamins	X												
Caffeine												X	
Calcium	X												
Calcium bromate	X									X			
Calcium proprionate	X	X											
Calcium silicate	X				X								
Calcium sulfate	X								X				
Caramel color											X		
Carob gum				X					X				
Carotene	X										X		
Carrageenan				X					X				
Cellulose						X			X				
Citric acid			X					X				X	
Corn syrup												X	X
Dextrin						X			X				
Disodium gyanylate or inosinate												X	
EDTA			X										
Gelatin									X				
Glycerine						X							
Glycerol monostearate						X							
Guar gum									X				
Herbs												X	
Hydrolyzed vegetable protein												X	
Iodine	X												

A Close-Up Look at Additives (continued)

	Improves or Maintains Nutritional Value	Prevents Spoilage	Prevents Rancidity and Discoloration	Distributes Particles Evenly	Prevents Lumping	Retains Moisture	Makes Food Rise	Controls pH	Gives Smooth, Thick, or Uniform Texture	Improves Baking Quality	Gives Color	Gives or Enhances Flavor	Sweetens
Iron	X												
Iron ammonium					X								
Lactic acid		X						X					
Lecithin			X	X									
Modified food starch				X	X				X				
Mono- and diglycerides				X									
Monosodium glutamate (MSG)												X	
Paprika											X		
Pectin				X					X				
Phosphoric acid								X					
Polysorbate				X									
Potassium sorbate		X											
Proprionic acid		X											
Propyl gallate			X										
Saffron											X	X	
Salt												X	
Silicon dioxide					X								
Sodium benzoate		X											
Sodium citrate				X									
Sodium nitrate/nitrite		X											
Sorbitan monostearate				X									
Sorbitol						X						X	X
Spices												X	
Sugar		X										X	X
Turmeric											X	X	
Vanilla												X	
Vitamin A	X												
Vitamin C	X		X										
Vitamin D	X												
Vitamin E (tocopherols)	X		X										
Xanthan gum									X				
Yeast							X						

Body Mass Index (BMI)

This table allows you to determine your body mass index without having to perform calculations. Locate your height in the left-hand column. Scanning across that row, find the number closest to your weight. At the top of that column is your BMI. If your height or weight isn't listed in the table, here's a shortcut method for calculating BMI: multiply your weight (in pounds) by 703 and then divide this number by your height (in inches) squared (i.e., height x height). *For more information on what your* BMI *number means, refer to page* 20.

BODY MASS INDEX / **WEIGHT (LBS)**

HEIGHT	19	20	21	22	23	24	25	26	27	28	29	30	35	40
4'10"	91	96	100	105	110	115	119	124	129	134	138	143	167	191
4'11"	94	99	104	109	114	119	124	128	133	138	143	148	173	198
5'0"	97	102	107	112	118	123	128	133	138	143	148	153	179	204
5'1"	100	106	111	116	122	127	132	137	143	148	153	158	185	211
5'2"	104	109	115	120	126	131	136	142	147	153	158	164	191	218
5'3"	107	113	118	124	130	135	141	146	152	158	163	169	197	225
5'4"	110	116	122	128	134	140	145	151	157	163	169	174	204	232
5'5"	114	120	126	132	138	144	150	156	162	168	174	180	210	240
5'6"	118	124	130	136	142	148	155	161	167	173	179	186	216	247
5'7"	121	127	134	140	146	153	159	166	172	178	185	191	223	255
5'8"	125	131	138	144	151	158	164	171	177	184	190	197	230	262
5'9"	128	135	142	149	155	162	169	176	182	189	196	203	236	270
5'10"	132	139	146	153	160	167	174	181	188	195	202	207	243	278
5'11"	136	143	150	157	165	172	179	186	193	200	208	215	250	286
6'0"	140	147	154	162	169	177	184	191	199	206	213	221	258	294
6'1"	144	151	159	166	174	182	189	197	204	212	219	227	265	302
6'2"	148	155	163	171	179	186	194	202	210	218	225	233	272	311
6'3"	152	160	168	176	184	192	200	208	216	224	232	240	279	319
6'4"	156	164	172	180	189	197	205	213	221	230	238	246	287	328
									OVERWEIGHT				**OBESE**	

Source: World Health Organization

INDEX

Charts, tables, and diagrams are in italics.

B

E

G

N

P